Philosophy in the Islamic World

Handbook of Oriental Studies

Handbuch der Orientalistik

SECTION ONE

The Near and Middle East

Edited by

VOLUME 115/1

The titles published in this series are listed at *brill.com/ho1*

Philosophy in the Islamic World

Volume 1: 8th–10th Centuries

Edited by

Ulrich Rudolph, Rotraud Hansberger, and Peter Adamson

English translation by

Rotraud Hansberger

BRILL

LEIDEN | BOSTON

This volume is an English version of *Philosophie in der islamischen Welt. Band 1: 8.–10. Jahrhundert* (ed. by Ulrich Rudolph with the assistance of Renate Würsch, Schwabe, Basel, 2012), which is part of the series *Grundriss der Geschichte der Philosophie* founded by Friedrich Ueberweg.

Cover illustration: Abbasid Caliph al-Ma'mūn sends an envoy to Byzantine Emperor Theophilus. Source: History of John Skylitzes (*Skyllitzes Matritensis*, Biblioteca Nacional de España).

Library of Congress Cataloging-in-Publication Data

Names: Rudolph, Ulrich, editor.
Title: Philosophy in the Islamic world / edited by Ulrich Rudolph, Rotraud Hansberger, and Peter Adamson ; English translation by Rotraud Hansberger.
Other titles: Philosophie in der Islamischen Welt. English
Description: Leiden : Boston : Brill, 2017– | Series: Handbook of oriental studies = Handbuch der Orientalistik. Section 1, The Near and Middle East, ISSN 0169-9423 ; Volume 115/1 Contents: Volume 1. 8th–10th centuries. | Includes bibliographical references and index.
Identifiers: LCCN 2016046750 | ISBN 9789004323162 (volume 1 : hardback : alk. paper)
Subjects: LCSH: Islamic philosophy.
Classification: LCC B741 .P4413 2017 | DDC 181/.07—DC23
LC record available at https://lccn.loc.gov/2016046750

Typeface for the Latin, Greek, and Cyrillic scripts: "Brill". See and download: brill.com/brill-typeface.

ISSN 0169-9423
ISBN 978-90-04-32316-2 (hardback)

This book is printed on acid-free paper and produced in a sustainable manner.

Contents

Preface to the English Edition IX
Preface to the German Edition XI

Introduction 1
Ulrich Rudolph
1 Stages of the History of Research 1
2 Principles of Presentation 11
3 Characteristics of the First Volume: Philosophy from the 8th to the 10th Century 16
4 Secondary Literature 21

1 **The Late Ancient Background** 29
Ulrich Rudolph
1 Principal Features of Late Ancient Philosophy 29
2 The School of Athens 36
3 The School of Alexandria 40
4 Philosophy and the Sciences 48
5 Channels of Transmission 51
6 Secondary Literature 64

2 **The Syriac Tradition in the Early Islamic Era** 74
Hans Daiber
1 Primary Sources 74
2 Introduction 77
3 Jacobite Authors 78
4 Nestorian Authors 83
5 A Maronite Author: Theophilus of Edessa 87
6 Secondary Literature 88

3 **The Rebirth of Philosophy and the Translations into Arabic** 95
Dimitri Gutas
1 Primary Sources 95
2 The Historical Causes of the Graeco-Arabic Translation Movement 97
3 Method, Phases, and Significance of the Translations 104

4 The Beginnings of Philosophical Literature in Arabic and the Rebirth of Philosophy 108
5 Greek Philosophical Texts in Arabic Translation 121
6 Secondary Literature 135

4 Abū Yūsuf al-Kindī 143
Gerhard Endress and Peter Adamson
1 Primary Sources 143
2 Life and Influence 152
3 Translations Available in al-Kindī's Time 155
4 Works 158
5 Doctrine 189
6 Secondary Literature 202

5 The Beginnings of Islamic Philosophy in the Tradition of al-Kindī 221
Hans Hinrich Biesterfeldt, Elvira Wakelnig, Gerhard Endress, and Cleophea Ferrari
1 Al-Kindī's School: From Baghdad to Transoxania 221
2 Neoplatonic Developments 250
3 The Integration of Philosophical Traditions in Islamic Society in the 4th/10th Century: al-Tawḥīdī and al-Siǧistānī 272
4 Ancient Ethical Traditions for Islamic Society: Abū ʿAlī Miskawayh 304
5 Bridging the Gap between the Kindian Tradition and the Baghdad School: Ibn Hindū 344
6 Secondary Literature 350

6 Abū Bakr al-Rāzī 381
Hans Daiber
1 Primary Sources 381
2 Translations Available in al-Rāzī's Time 384
3 Life 386
4 Works 389
5 Doctrine 401
6 Secondary Literature 413

7 **The Baghdad Aristotelians** 421
Gerhard Endress and Cleophea Ferrari
1 The Arabic Aristotle and the Transmission of Aristotelian Philosophy in Baghdad: Abū Bišr Mattā b. Yūnus 421
2 Yaḥyā Ibn ʿAdī 434
3 ʿĪsā Ibn Zurʿa 468
4 Ibn al-Ḫammār 480
5 Ibn al-Samḥ 490
6 Abū l-Farağ Ibn al-Ṭayyib 496
7 Secondary Literature 506

8 **Abū Naṣr al-Fārābī** 526
Ulrich Rudolph
1 Primary Sources 526
2 Life and Influence 536
3 Works 545
4 Doctrine 594
5 Secondary Literature 636

9 **The Dissemination of Philosophical Thought** 655
Dimitri Gutas, Paraskevi Kotzia †, Eva Orthmann, and Daniel De Smet
1 Popular Ethics, Practical Politics 655
2 Scholars as Transmitters of Philosophical Thought 680
3 Philosophy and Natural Science 727
4 The Religious Application of Philosophical Ideas 733
5 Secondary Literature 759

Index of Arabic Words 787
Index of Subjects 796
Index of Names 834

Preface to the English Edition

This volume is an English version of a book that originally appeared as *Philosophie in der islamischen Welt. Band 1: 8.–10. Jahrhundert* (ed. by Ulrich Rudolph with assistance from Renate Würsch, Basel 2012). Both versions contribute to a wider project whose goal is to chart the history of philosophy in the Islamic world from its beginnings to the present day. This endeavour is described in detail in the original preface (see below, pp. xi–xiii). As explained there, four volumes are envisioned, which will follow one another in chronological sequence, stretching from the 8th to the 20th century, offering extensive information on authors from all periods, divided into biography, descriptions of individual works, doctrines, and influence.

It is planned that all four volumes should appear in both German and English. The German version forms part of a series of comprehensive reference works, the *Grundriss der Geschichte der Philosophie* (Ueberweg); the English version is intended to reach a wider audience in Europe and beyond, including especially the Islamic world itself. While the German volumes are appearing with the publisher Schwabe, the English series will be published by E. J. Brill, whose series 'Handbuch der Orientalistik' ('Handbook of Oriental Studies') offers an appropriate forum for a project of this all-embracing nature. We are grateful to both publishers for agreeing to this arrangement and for their readiness to cooperate with one another.

The publication of this English translation was made possible by the personal dedication of several people. Rotraud Hansberger expended considerable personal effort to translate the entire book—except where the German version was based on an English original—combining linguistic fluency with a keen sense of judgement and enormous knowledge of the thematic field. Peter Adamson edited and proofread the translation with care and expertise. Peter Tarras and Hanif Amin Beidokhti contributed greatly to the production of the manuscript, tracking down additional information and helping with crucial aspects of the copy-editing process. All three editors have gone through the entire manuscript and are responsible for the final redaction. The authors of the original German chapters have also been involved in the production of this new version, and have helped with the addition of new references to literature that appeared since 2012. In this respect, the English version actually adds new information and offers an updated picture of the state of research. One section, however, could not be revised by its author, since our cherished colleague Paraskevi Kotzia sadly passed away since the appearance of the German version.

The translation has been funded by Brill, the Ludwig-Maximilians-Universität in Munich, and the Leverhulme Foundation. We are especially grateful to Joed Elich and Kathy van Vliet, who have overseen our project at Brill since its inception. Their engagement and enthusiasm have been essential to the production of the volume in its final form.

Ulrich Rudolph
Zurich, June 2016

Preface to the German Edition

This volume opens the series on philosophy in the Islamic world that is part of the *Grundriss der Geschichte der Philosophie*. It will consist of four volumes dedicated to presenting the development of philosophical thought in the Islamic realm from its beginnings up to the present (I: 8th–10th cent.; II: 11th–12th cent.; III: 13th–18th cent.; IV: 19th–20th cent.). No previous compendium or general work on this topic has adopted such an ambitious goal. On the one hand, this concerns the temporal and geographical scope of the work: it is not restricted to one specific epoch (e.g. the early period up to Ibn Rušd); nor to a single later school tradition (e.g. the Iranian thinkers of the 16th and 17th centuries). Instead, this series attempts to do justice to the subject matter in its entirety, temporally as well as regionally. On the other hand, the individual chapters strive to present their contents in a rather dense manner. This results from the rules that govern the volumes of the *Grundriss* in general and therefore also apply to the present series. They dictate that attention should be given to lesser-known thinkers as well as to the prominent ones. Moreover, each author is supposed to be introduced with as detailed information as possible, comprising primary and secondary literature, a biography (including references to the author's influence), a systematic account of doctrine and – particularly important – detailed descriptions of individual works.

This way of proceeding is not only new, but also extremely laborious. To this date, research into the philosophy of the Islamic world has only provided a limited amount of the material required for such an undertaking. Numerous authors and topics that are presented here have never been discussed in monograph studies. This even applies to some of the thinkers covered in volume 1 (e.g. ʿĪsā Ibn Zurʿa and Ibn al-Samḥ), but will become the rule rather than the exception in later volumes (particularly 3 and 4). Moreover, the primary sources are fraught with a number of problems. Even in the case of better-known authors like al-Kindī (§ 4) or al-Fārābī (§ 8), few works are available in critical editions. This means that unreliable prints or even manuscripts had to be consulted, something that can turn the composition of work descriptions, normally a routine task for historians of philosophy, into a time-consuming and adventurous act.

Given these circumstances it is not surprising that the series on the Islamic world should differ from other series of the *Grundriss* in various respects. Like them, it attempts to trace the current state of research and the topical scholarly debates as objectively as possible. However, this procedure has its natural limitations where there is barely any secondary literature on a particular author or topic. Therefore the reader will often find entirely new material and original contributions to research in this volume, as well as in those that will follow. They are apt to widen our knowledge of the history of philosophy, or at least to outline more clearly the tasks awaiting the research community. At the same time the reader should bear in mind that such contributions, which are only just opening up the investigation of a particular topic, cannot claim to provide secure knowledge or to represent an advanced state of a scholarly debate.

The basic theoretical assumptions adopted as guidelines for the presentation of the material are explained in the introductory chapter below (p. 1ff). It describes in detail the concept of philosophy that underlies the *Grundriss* volumes on the Islamic world, and how the series wants to position itself within the history of research. Here it only remains to address a few practical aspects of the work that has gone into this project. On the one hand, they concern the genesis of the present volume (and, in a broader sense, all four volumes), on the other hand the manifold support that our project has received.

It was clear from the outset that a project of this order of magnitude would have to rely on the expertise of a large number of scholars. This applies not only to the actual writing of the individual chapters, but also to arranging the material and designing the structure that underlies the entire series. It was devised in close consultation with a circle of authors, which from the start included Gerhard Endress, Dimitri Gutas, Anke von Kügelgen, Sabine Schmidtke, and Renate Würsch. The basic concept of the series was formed in discussion with them; it has, since then, been reviewed and refined time and again in meetings of the collaborators of the individual volumes.

For this cooperation I am very grateful. The same goes for the close collaboration with the authors of volume 1, which was ready to go to press in autumn 2011. The editorial process was overseen by Renate Würsch; thanks to her diligence and circumspection the volume could be made to correspond to the specific formal characteristics of the *Grundriss* series, despite manifold linguistic and contextual peculiarities. In addition, we have been able to count on valuable support from many other quarters. Wolfgang Rother from Schwabe publishers has been looking after our project expertly, subjecting all our typescripts to his subtle and perceptive editorial examination, in scholarly as well as linguistic respects. Sibylle Herkert did the proofreading for the volume; Giuseppe Tamburello took care of the rather complicated font. Sarah Farag, Tobias Heinzelmann, Roman Seidel and Deniz Yüksel from the Oriental Faculty of the University of Zurich undertook another round of proofreading, while Johannes Thomann could be relied on to procure primary and secondary literature that was difficult to obtain. In this context I would furthermore like to mention the 'University Research Priority Program Asia and Europe' at Zurich University. It repeatedly presented me with the opportunity to discuss fundamental questions about (non-European) philosophy in comparative perspective with interested colleagues from other disciplines: Robert H. Gassmann (Chinese Studies), Angelika Malinar (Indian Studies), Raji C. Steineck (Japanese Studies), and Ralph Weber (Chinese Studies).

In addition, several colleagues from the fields of Islamic Studies, Classics and Philosophy were so kind as to read and comment on my own draft contributions to volume 1: Jean Grondin, Wilfried Kühn, Anke von Kügelgen and Dominik Perler read the introductory chapter; Richard Goulet (who also kindly provided me with a pre-publication version of volume 5 of *Dictionnaire des philosophes antiques*), and Christoph Riedweg read § 1, and Dimitri Gutas § 8. I am indebted to all of them for their valuable comments and suggestions.

Finally, I would like to thank several institutions for their generous financial support of our work: the Swiss National Fund for endowing, over several years, an editorial position for the project and for taking over part of the printing costs; the Freiwillige Akademische Gesellschaft Basel for their contribution to the printing costs; the Swiss Academy for Humanities and Social Studies for funding the collaborators' meetings; and the Dean's Office of the Faculty of Philosophy at the University of Zurich for additional staff funding.

Ulrich Rudolph
Zurich, June 2012

Introduction

Ulrich Rudolph

1 Stages of the History of Research – 2 Principles of Presentation – 3 Characteristics of the First Volume: Philosophy from the 8th to the 10th Century 4 – Secondary Literature

1 Stages of the History of Research

When Friedrich Ueberweg wrote the chapter on 'Arabic philosophers of the Middle Ages' for his *Grundriss der Geschichte der Philosophie* (Ueberweg 1864 [*4: 49–62]), there was not much for him to go on in terms of previous work done in the field. This applies to primary texts, of which only a few had been printed, let alone translated into European languages, and to secondary literature alike. Nevertheless the subject matter he was writing about was not new. Shortly before he began his work on the *Grundriss*, Arabic philosophy, which had not received much scholarly attention up to the middle of the 19th century (Daiber 1999 [*68: xvi–xx]), had begun to attract discussion. The reason was Ernest Renan's epochal work *Averroès et l'averroïsme* (Renan 1852 [*2]), which for the first time had directed attention to this subject, and at the same time had led to a certain image of philosophy in the Islamic world being spread universally amongst European scholars and interested readers.

Renan's study discussed Ibn Rušd's life and thought as well as the vast influence he exerted on many Jewish thinkers and the Latin Middle Ages. It led Renan to a series of ground-breaking results which not only moved Latin Averroism into the centre of interest, but attracted attention also to its Arabic-Islamic cultural context. Yet he undermined his own project of casting light on the Arabic tradition. His book contained a number of (prejudiced) verdicts which were able to exert all the more influence as they were brilliantly formulated, and pronounced with the apodeictic gesture of the expert. This included his convictions (1) that the Arabs, or rather the Semites in general, had no natural aptitude for philosophy; (2) that their historic 'task' had merely consisted in preserving Greek philosophy and transmitting it to the Latin Middle Ages; and (3) that only 'pure, classical' Greece had been able to create philosophy; this was also why philosophy had never been properly understood or further developed before the advent of the Renaissance, which was closely related to antiquity in spirit; by contrast, the Latin and especially the Arabic authors of

 | DOI 10.1163/9789004323162_002

the Middle Ages had merely 'imitated' it and passed it on (Renan 1852 [*2: VII–IX]; on all this, but in particular on the second point cf. also Renan 1883 [*5]).

Renan's judgements in many respects corresponded to certain expectations current in his day and age; apart from other ideological entanglements they reflected a certain aspect of the 'orientalism' that loomed large in Europe (not only) in the 19th century. One should furthermore grant that his study, despite arguing in a conventional way, also broached unexpected viewpoints which in fact called Renan's own stance into question. Thus we find buried in his book the proclamation that 'the true philosophical movement' of Islam was to be found in its theological schools (Renan 1852 [*2: 89]; cf. von Kügelgen 1994 [*59: 102]). Nevertheless Renan limited scholarship even as he was stimulating it. His pointed rhetorical formulations were essential in the establishment of a one-sided perspective on the philosophy of the Islamic world as the first paradigm of scholarly engagement with the field. According to him, the achievements of the 'Arabic philosophers' were confined to adopting the Greek heritage and passing it on to Latin Europe, leading naturally to the often-quoted conclusion that 'with Averroes' death in 1198, Arabic philosophy lost its last representative, and the Quran was to triumph over independent thought for at least six centuries' (Renan 1852 [*2: 2]).

The basic elements of this paradigm can be traced in numerous accounts published after the middle of the 19th century. To begin with, this applies to Salomon Munk's *Mélanges de philosophie juive et arabe*, which appeared only a few years after *Averroès et l'averroïsme* (Munk 1859 [*3]). Munk went far beyond Renan in his engagement with the subject matter, unlocking extensive new source material, and for the first time sketching detailed portraits of individual Jewish and Islamic authors. Nevertheless he, too, took it for granted that 'the last great philosophers flourished in the 12th century' (Munk 1859 [*3: 333]). Resorting to a thesis he had advanced earlier (Munk 1845 [*1: 512]), he suggested as an explanation that philosophy in the Orient had never managed to recover from the blow dealt to it by the fierce critique of al-Ġazālī (d. 505/1111; on him cf. vol. 2, § 3) (Munk 1859 [*3: 382; cf. 334]).

Ueberweg, who followed Munk's account in many points, arrived at a similar assessment. He, too, had 'Arabic philosophy' ending in the 12th century, again stating the very same reasons: in the East of the Islamic world, its demise was the result of al-Ġazālī's attacks; in the West, it was the outcome of Ibn Rušd's death and the subsequent Spanish Reconquista (Ueberweg 1864 [*4: 58–59]).

The same temporal boundaries can be found in numerous 19th century publications in the field of Islamic Studies, at times explicitly, at others mentioned only in passing. However, and this would prove to be of much greater importance for further developments, we also encounter it in the scholarly literature of the early 20th century – despite being, by then, based on much broader textual foundations. Again the year 1200 is on principle accepted as an endpoint. In the first instance, this concerns Tjitze de Boer's *Geschichte der Philosophie im Islam* (de Boer 1901 [*6]), which was widely read, in its German original as well as in an English translation (*The History of Philosophy in Islam*) released only two years later, in 1903. In the second instance, it applies to Max Horten's account of 'Syriac and Arabic philosophy' (*Die syrische und arabische Philosophie*), which was published in the eleventh edition of Ueberweg's *Grundriss der Geschichte der Philosophie*, revised by Bernhard Geyer (Horten 1927 [*11]).

Remarkably, though, it was not just Renan's pointed claim that lived on in these works, but also his doubts concerning it. This emerges in de Boer as well as in Horten: both clearly articulate their misgivings about the very scientific paradigm they follow. At some point, de Boer comments on it in the following words: 'That Gazali has annihilated philosophy in the East, for all time to come, is an assertion frequently repeated but wholly erroneous, and one which evidences neither historical knowledge nor understanding. Philosophy in the East has since his day numbered its teachers and students by hundreds and by thousands' (de Boer 1901 [*6: 150, Engl. transl. 169]). Horten expressed his doubts in an even more emphatic manner. Before taking up his work on the new edition of the *Grundriss*, he had published several studies on Islamic authors after al-Ġazālī and Ibn Rušd, for instance on Faḫr al-Dīn al-Rāzī (d. 607/1210), Naṣīr al-Dīn al-Ṭūsī (d. 672/1274) (Horten 1910 [*7], 1912 [*8]) and Mullā Ṣadrā (d. 1050/1640) (Horten 1912 [*9], 1913 [*10]). This may have been the reason why he felt compelled to add the following declaration to his contribution to the *Grundriss*: 'It is a consequence of the tradition of this *Grundriss* (lit., 'outline'), that from among the vast abundance of philosophies, i.e. world views, only those are included that are dependent on the Greeks, and that became known to the Latin schoolmen – i.e. only the Greek strand, which to the Orient itself was and remained a foreign body, and as an entire system was rejected, even if its individual concepts were put to use as building blocks within originally Oriental systems. This means that the real essence, and the main component of Oriental philosophy is excluded from this account, while only a comparatively minor, marginal strand within this entire complex is given attention [...] Due to prejudice and lack of comprehension, the old Orientalist school had grown used to the phrase: "after al-Ġazālī or after Averroes no philosophy can be found in Islam." They had not the least idea that the true philosophy internal to Islam begins only after 1100!' (Horten 1927 [*11: 298]).

The persuasiveness of Horten's own ideas concerning the history of philosophy is not at issue here; his diffuse concepts and his sweeping comparisons were at any rate repeatedly criticized in scholarly literature (a summary is provided by Daiber 1999 [*68: xxiii–xxv]). What is important in the present context is simply that both he and de Boer early on expressed concerns regarding the prevalent labelling and periodization of philosophy in the Islamic world. Yet the uneasiness manifest in their remarks was to remain without consequence. As mentioned already, neither of the two authors ventured past the magical line apparently drawn by Ibn Rušd's death (if we disregard a brief section on Ibn Ḫaldūn [d. 808/1406] in de Boer 1901 [*6: 177–184, Engl. transl. 200–208]). Thus de Boer and Horten contributed to disseminating the paradigm they themselves had called into question, and to its treatment as a 'fait accompli'.

It was, therefore, not easy for alternative approaches to gain recognition. This first affected an interpretative model which had been developed in Egypt since the 1930s. An independent branch of research into the history of philosophy had established itself there, whose most important and influential representative was – alongside Aḥmad Amīn (d. 1954), Yūsuf Karam (d. 1959) and Maḥmūd al-Ḫuḍayrī (d. 1960) – Muṣṭafā ʿAbd al-Rāziq (d. 1947). Following various preparatory studies, he drew up a new conspectus of philosophy within Islamic culture, which he laid out in a widely read study entitled *Prolegomena to a History of Islamic Philosophy* (*Tamhīd li-taʾrīḫ al-falsafa al-islāmiyya*) (ʿAbd al-Rāziq 1944 [*13]).

At the core of this account stood the thesis that the concept of philosophy ought to be understood differently in the Islamic world and in Europe: in the Islamic context, it could not be reduced to the tradition that followed Greek role models, but would have to include all forms of reflection that were in any way responsible for laying the foundations of Islamic religion and culture. As a central point in this context, ʿAbd al-Rāziq considered Islamic law. It had its theoretical foundation in the science of 'principles of law' (*uṣūl al-fiqh*), which he regarded as basis of Islamic philosophy, or rather Islamic thought; this is also why in his account of philosophy, the development of *uṣūl al-fiqh* was accorded the largest space by far. Only Islamic theology (*ʿilm al-kalām*) was able to claim a similarly prominent position in his presentation. To all other traditions, including Greek inspired philosophy (*falsafa*) and Sufism (*taṣawwuf*), ʿAbd l-Rāziq by contrast assigned subsidiary roles: they might have shaped or passed on certain elements of Islamic philosophical thought, but were never constitutive for its development as such (von Kügelgen 1994 [*59: 103–105], 2008 [*94: 13–14]).

The suggestion to broaden the concept of 'philosophy' in the Islamic context in the direction of 'Islamic thought', or 'pensée islamique' (thus the term later used by Arkoun 1973 [*33] and other authors arguing in a similar vein) constituted a challenge for European scholarship. It contested the identification of 'philosophy' with 'Greek philosophy', which in older scholarship had been taken for granted. Moreover, shortly after 'Abd al-Rāziq's publications, a further concept of (history of Islamic) philosophy emerged, which again vehemently questioned Renan's old paradigm. It did not come from the pen of an Arabic scholar, but from that of a European author, whose perspective was influenced by a strong affinity with Iran.

This was Henry Corbin, who in 1946 became the director of the Département d'iranologie at the Institut franco-iranien in Tehran. In his early work he had concerned himself mainly with Šihāb al-Dīn al-Suhrawardī (d. 587/1191) (Corbin 1939 [*12], 1945 [*14]). Now, in Tehran, he began to research the later Persian thinkers (13th-19th centuries) on this basis. This was first reflected in a large number of individual studies, many of which made previously unknown authors and texts accessible for the first time, through editions, translations and introductory commentaries. From the very beginning, however, these publications were based on a new overall concept of 'Islamic philosophy'. This concept was presented to a larger audience when Corbin set out his ideas in two detailed and comprehensive works. One of them is the four-volume work *En islam iranien*, which follows a thread from the beginnings of the Twelver Shia up to the Persian authors of the 19th century (Corbin 1971–1972 [*31]); the other work is the shorter, but even more influential *Histoire de la philosophie islamique*, which was published in several stages, beginning in 1964 (Corbin 1964 [*21], 1974 [*34], 1986 [*42]).

Corbin aimed to provide an entirely new interpretation of philosophy and its history within Islamic culture. In his opinion, the early authors (up to Ibn Rušd), who previously had drawn all scholarly attention to themselves, were merely 'philosophes hellénisants', that is, thinkers that had been completely under the spell of the Greek heritage (with the exception of Ibn Sīnā; on this cf. p. 9 below). Real 'Islamic philosophy', by contrast, developed its own, unmistakable character, and began to flourish only in the 12th century. The location of this blossoming is, for Corbin, Iran. The distinguishing mark of 'Islamic philosophy' is supposed to consist in its having linked rational cognition, spiritual experience, gnostic insight, and prophetic knowledge to one another. This had been done particularly impressively and successfully by Mullā Ṣadrā (d. 1050/1640; on him cf. vol. 3), who accordingly was regarded by Corbin as the pinnacle of Islamic philosophy as a whole, or, as he puts it, of 'theosophy' ('theosophy' here rendering the Arabic term *ḥikma ilāhiyya*; cf. Landolt 1999 [*70: 486]). Even Mullā Ṣadrā, however, is but one link in a long tradition of philosophico-mystical speculation and 'Oriental wisdom' for Corbin. He lastly describes it as eternal wisdom (*sophia perennis*), which supposedly harks back to early Islam and even beyond that, to pre-Islamic Iran, with a correspondingly lengthy list of characteristic features. These features in fact have no real historical connection, but Corbin puts them together on the basis that they form a unified intellectual structure. Amongst other things, they comprise (Twelver) Shiite thought, including the deeper knowledge it attributes to the Imams, al-Suhrawardī's metaphysics of light, which supposedly combined Platonism and old Iranian as well as gnostic wisdom, and the mystical speculations advanced by Ibn ʿArabī (Shayegan 2011 [*108: 116–166. 187–194. 338–365]).

It is Corbin's great merit to have read the history of philosophy against the grain, moving entire epochs that had long since suffered neglect into the centre of attention. He thus opened up new horizons for scholarship, something that has been duly acknowledged by scholars reacting to his writings (Vajda 1964 [*23: 275], Rosenthal 1965 [*24]; for a summary see Landolt 1999 [*70: 484–485. 489–490]). At the same time, however, his outline also posed new problems. First of all, he intentionally applied the concept of 'philosophy' in a rather diffuse manner, distinguishing it neither clearly from theology, nor from mysticism or spirituality, but understanding it instead in the sense of a higher, spiritual-metaphysical wisdom, whose blurry outlines were supposedly characteristic of 'Islamic philosophy' (Vajda 1964 [*23: 273], Rosenthal 1965 [*24: 504], Wernst 1967 [*26: 355], Adams 1985 [*40: 141–145]). In addition, he explicitly subscribed to the concept of *métahistoire*, which allowed him to dissociate ideas from their historical context and to interpret them as archetypal phenomena of the soul. Thus he developed a vision of 'Islam' with highly subjective and selective features (Vajda 1964 [*23: 276–278]). Examples include his ahistorical interpretation of the Shia; its pointed prioritization over the Sunna (Adams 1985 [*40: 137–141]); the biased assessment of Sunni Sufism, which he regards as an extension of the Shia or as Proto-Shiism (Adams 1985 [*40: 136], Landolt 1999 [*70: 489]); and – more than anything else – the spiritual elevation of Iran (Adams 1985 [*40: 134–137]). The latter marks Corbin's account as a kind of Orientalism in reverse: whereas Renan and other earlier authors had usually construed a defective 'Orient', inferior and lastly subservient to Europe, in Corbin's works the 'Orient' is hypostasized as an ideal and the true home of the soul (Adams 1985 [*40: 147–148], Landolt 1999 [*70: 485]).

Notwithstanding such objections, Corbin's approach was fascinating, and it is not surprising that he acquired numerous followers. Among the first was Seyyed Hossein Nasr, who had already had a hand in the genesis of the *Histoire de la philosophie islamique* (Corbin 1964 [*21]), and later on contributed significantly to the promulgation of its aims in the English-speaking world. Nasr studied natural sciences and the history of science in the USA (Boroujerdi 1996

[*61: 120]), which had a pronounced influence on his early works. In them he attempts to interpret Ibn Sīnā, al-Suhrawardī and Ibn ʿArabī as three types of Islamic thinkers that he characterized as 'philosopher-scientist', 'illuminationist', and 'mystic' (Nasr 1964 [*22]; for a critical review see Wernst 1967 [*26]). In all fundamental questions, however, Nasr acknowledged that he was following Corbin. For him, too, 'Islamic philosophy' is a quest for truth under the guidance of God, uniting rationality, spiritual illumination, and prophetic knowledge in the sense of an 'eternal wisdom' (Nasr 1983 [*39: 59–63], 1995 [*60: 328]; cf. Boroujerdi 1996 [*61: 122–123.125]). This quest for truth supposedly developed first and foremost in Iran, finding its ultimate expression in Mullā Ṣadrā's 'theosophy' (Nasr 1983 [*39: 66–68. 77–79], 1995 [*60: 331–332], 2006 [*90: 223–234], 2010 [*100: 156–161]). Thus Nasr stressed time and again that this 'theosophy' preserved a form of wisdom which had been lost in Western thought since the Renaissance – delivering what we need to understand as a decided plea for traditional Islamic metaphysics, and against modern, 'Western' civilization (Nasr 1983 [*39: 80], 2010 [*100: 193–201. 224–225]; cf. Boroujerdi 1996 [*61: 123–124. 128–130]).

Besides the paradigm that was developed by Corbin and disseminated by his students (including Nasr), there also have been other new trends of research since the 1950s. Leo Strauss' theoretical approach, for instance, was based on the assumption that within Islamic culture, philosophers were constantly exposed to suspicion and repression on the part of religious orthodoxy; from this he inferred that they had developed a certain literary strategy (or rather a 'political philosophy') in order to hide their true opinions from hostile readers and thus to avoid possible sanctions (Strauss 1952 [*15]). Several scholars applied this approach to their interpretations of individual texts; but ultimately it was not able to yield a new overall perspective on the history of philosophy. Therefore we can, at this point, dispense with a more detailed account and evaluation of Strauss' arguments (for a critical discussion see Tamer 2001 [*74], Gutas 2002 [*76: 19–24]). Here we are primarily interested in the question as to which general framework – if any – should be used in the study of philosophy in the Islamic world. As we have seen, by the 1950s this question had been given three basic answers. One of them took Arabic philosophy to be a continuation of Greek philosophy, up to Ibn Rušd. The second postulated the concept of an 'Islamic thought' ('pensée islamique') that would encompass law, theology, philosophy (in the narrow sense) and mysticism. The third one, linked to Corbin's name, formulated the idea of an 'Islamic philosophy' that was rooted in perennial Oriental wisdom, that united rational speculation with spirituality and prophetic insight, and had found its completion in 16th and 17th century Iran.

This state of the discussion has been reflected in several surveys published since the 1960s. They are too numerous to be listed and introduced individually (cf. the bibliographical information in Daiber (1999 [*68: xxvi–xxix]; for a detailed account of the development of research during this period see Endress 1989 [*49]). However, a number of frequently quoted and widely read publications may nevertheless be mentioned briefly here, in order to indicate how they position themselves in the face of the three historiographical models described above.

The two-volume survey *A History of Muslim Philosophy* edited by M. M. Sharif in 1963 and 1966 [*20] mainly follows the idea of an 'Islamic thought': its aim is to include multiple intellectual traditions within its presentation. For Sharif, these comprise, apart from the 'philosophers' proper, the Quran, the theologians, the Sufis and the political thinkers. Majid Fakhry's *A History of Islamic Philosophy* (Fakhry 1970 [*28]; cf. also 1997 [*63]), by contrast, distances itself from any integrative historiographical conception. Though containing two brief chapters on Mullā Ṣadrā, several theologians and Sufis (insofar as they came into immediate contact with philosophical thought) and some more recent intellectual trends (19th and 20th centuries), the focus of Fakhry's work lies entirely on those topics which have traditionally formed the centre of attention, i.e. the string of early philosophers up to and including Ibn Rušd. The short contribution Shlomo Pines wrote for *The Cambridge History of Iran* (Pines 1970 [*29]) steers a middle course: under the title 'philosophy' he deals with Islamic theology as well as with philosophy up to 1200 (with a brief glance at later authors). ʿAbd al-Raḥmān Badawī's two-volume *Histoire de la philosophie en islam* (Badawī 1972 [*32]) is similar in this respect: its first part introduces the most important theological schools, the second the philosophers up to Ibn Rušd. Michael Marmura's explications concerning 'Islamic philosophy of the Middle Ages' (*Die islamische Philosophie des Mittelalters*, Marmura 1985 [*41]) again focus only on the well-known philosophical tradition from al-Kindī to Ibn Rušd. Marmura emphasizes, however, that there did exist philosophers after 1200 (basing themselves on the doctrines of the aforementioned authors), and that one ought to separate philosophy from the tradition of 'Islamic religious and theological thought' (Marmura 1985 [*41: 323]). By contrast, the two-volume *History of Islamic Philosophy* edited by Seyyed Hossein Nasr and Oliver Leaman in the mid-1990s renews the integrative approach, being indebted both to the idea of a 'pensée islamique' (reminiscent of Sharif 1963–1966 [*20]) and to Corbin's conception. The former is evidenced by the extensive chapters on Quran, *ḥadīṯ*, theology, mysticism, and law (Nasr, Leaman 1996 [*62: I 27–40. 71–89. 105–119; II 947–959. 979–1000]); the latter by the great weight placed on the topics central to Corbin (Shiism, mysticism, Illuminationism, Iranian tradition), and on the explication of Corbin's hermeneutics (Nasr, Leaman 1996 [*62: I 119–155. 367–663; II 1037–1051. 1149–1156]).

By the time Nasr's and Leaman's work was published, however, scholarship had already taken a new turn. Since the 1980s, several corrections had been made to Corbin's model as well as to the other, older conceptions, eventually ushering in a new paradigm of the historiography of philosophy in the Islamic world. The starting point for this turn was a reappraisal of Ibn Sīnā's thought. Ibn Sīnā held a special place within the debate, insofar as the question how to position his philosophy in historical as well as conceptual terms was a key element in Corbin's scheme. According to his view, Ibn Sīnā performed a remarkable U-turn in the course of his life. It supposedly induced him to distance himself from Aristotelian philosophy, and instead to design a mystical-visionary, 'Oriental philosophy', thus becoming the pioneer for all further significant developments within 'Islamic philosophy' – by which Corbin meant al-Suhrawardī's illuminationism and the 'theosophy' of the later Iranian authors (Corbin 1954 [*16]; cf. Landolt 1999 [*70: 486–487], Shayegan 2011 [*18: 243–259]). These assumptions, however, were met by increasing criticism in the 1980s. As a precise analysis of Ibn Sīnā's œuvre was able to show, it is impossible to diagnose a break with the philosophical heritage. Instead it was demonstrated that Ibn Sīnā mastered the philosophical tradition systematically, and modified it with new ideas (Gutas 1988 [*48]; cf. Wisnovsky 2003 [*78]), though always – against the assumptions of Corbin and certain medieval authors (e.g. Ibn Ṭufayl) – holding on to a rational understanding of philosophy that was ultimately based on Aristotle (Gutas 1994 [*58], 2000 [*71]).

These important findings were complemented by a second epochal development in recent scholarship. It consisted in the realization that Ibn Sīnā's very same rational philosophy, with its re-interpretation of the philosophical heritage, was of paramount historical significance, having been studied over centuries by a large number of authors in the Islamic world who had taken it as starting point for their own philosophical reflections. This insight rendered the earlier question, whether Ibn Rušd had found any readers after 1200, obsolete (even though his writings indeed continued to be read for some time; cf. Endress 2001 [*73: 24. 55]). As it now emerged, engagement with Ibn Rušd was not, after all, the decisive criterion for answering the question whether philosophy continued to exist beyond the 12th century. Instead it was Ibn Sīnā whose writings on logic, metaphysics and physics constituted the focus of interest from this time onwards. This insight was bound to lead to a new paradigm of research. It ties in with Corbin's ideas insofar as it shares his conviction that philosophy continued to prosper in the Islamic world after 1200. At the same time, however, it distances itself from his conceptual approach, as it does not buy into the idea of limiting philosophy from this point forward to mystical-intuitive speculations on metaphysical topics, but conceives of it, even after 1200, as a rationally-based, argumentative science comprising logic, metaphysics and physics as well as ethics.

This new historiographical approach was evident in Gerhard Endress' section on 'philosophy' within the *Grundriss der arabischen Philologie* ('outline of Arabic philology') (Endress 1992 [*53: 25–61]). It includes chapters on topics like 'the development of philosophy as a discipline' ('Die Entwicklung einer philosophischen Disziplin'), 'hermeneutics and logic' ('Hermeneutik und Logik') and 'encyclopedia' ('Enzyklopädie'). Endress' observations do not end with the 12th century, but continue with references to important later authors, up to the 16th or 17th century (Endress 1992 [*53: 36–37. 56–57. 60–61]). The new historiographical paradigm was then presented in an explicitly programmatic fashion by Dimitri Gutas. In a 2002 article, he advocated calling the time from ca. 1000 to 1350 (not, that is, 1200!) the 'golden age of Arabic philosophy', producing at the same time a preliminary outline showing that in Iran, India, and parts of the Ottoman Empire, Ibn Sīnā's works and ideas were likely to have remained influential far into the 18th century (Gutas 2002 [*75]; cf. 2002 [*76: 7]). In parallel to these general surveys, new individual studies confirmed the continuation of philosophical activity in the 13th century and later. Noteworthy in particular are a number of publications produced by Sabine Schmidtke (2000 [*72]), Gerhard Endress (2006 [*89]), Heidrun Eichner (2007 [*91], 2011 [*102]), Sajjad Rizvi (2009 [*97]), Khaled El-Rouayheb (2010 [*98]), Reza Pourjavady (2011 [*105]), and Firouzeh Saatchian (2011 [*107]). The overwhelming majority of later authors, however, yet remain to be studied. According to careful estimates, not even 10% of the Arabic texts that were composed between the 13th and the 18th centuries on philosophical topics, and are extant in manuscripts, are available in print (Wisnovsky 2004 [*83: 160]). Hence one may well say that the new historiographical paradigm has opened up unexpected and promising avenues for research, which, however, will need to be refined and realized by many further studies.

A similar situation presents itself with regard to philosophy of the Islamic world during the 19th and 20th centuries. It had long been ignored entirely by scholars and had no impact on the discussions of philosophy's possible demise or continuation after 1200. If individual aspects of these developments were taken up at all, this happened within studies that were dedicated not to the history of philosophy as such, but to the history of ideas and the religio-political developments of the last two centuries (most convincingly in Hourani 1962 [*19]). Initial changes in this respect have, however, already been visible since the 1960s. Chapters that discuss contemporary philosophical thought are found first and foremost in Sharif (1966 [*20: II 1446–1656]), but also in Fakhry (1970 [*28: 333–367]; cf. 1997 [*63: 120–131]). The same applies for the history of philosophy edited by Nasr and Leaman (Nasr, Leaman 1996 [*62: II 1037–1140], though the temporal definition of 'modernity' is not consistent across the individual subsections). A proper branch of research into 19th and 20th century philosophy, though, has only begun to establish itself in the 1990s. In many respects this research is still in its infancy. Nevertheless it has already shown a surprising vitality and yielded important results, as is documented for instance by studies published by Anke von Kügelgen (1994 [*59]), Reza Hajatpour (2002 [*77]), Ursula Günther (2004 [*79]), Geert Hendrich (2004 [*81]), Jan-Peter Hartung (2004 [*80], 2009 [*96]) and Sarhan Dhouib (2011 [*101]). In addition, there have been several recent publications that chart the history of philosophy in the Islamic world up to the present day (Rudolph 2004/2013 [*82], Adamson 2015 [*109], 2016 [*110], and El-Rouayheb, Schmidtke 2016 [*111]).

2 Principles of Presentation

The circumstances outlined above have several consequences for our series of four volumes which now will appear successively within the framework of this series. On the one hand, they concern temporal boundaries. After all that has been said, the presentation cannot possibly be restricted to only one epoch, and most certainly not to the period before 1200. It must be chosen in such a way as to do justice to the entire development of philosophy in the Islamic world. This does not mean to say that, given the current state of research, compendia that impose temporal limits on themselves are unjustifiable. Two more recent publications in fact prove the opposite: the *Storia della filosofia nell'Islam medievale* (D'Ancona 2005 [*85]), which paints a very broad and detailed picture of philosophy up to 1200 (including the lesser known authors), and the *Cambridge Companion to Arabic Philosophy* (Adamson, Taylor 2005 [*84]), which focuses mainly on the 'big names' up to 1200, but also contains chapters on Ibn ʿArabī and Mullā Ṣadrā as well as systematic accounts of the different sub-disciplines of philosophy (logic, ethics, politics, etc.). For the *Grundriss*, however, a restriction to certain epochs or thinkers is out of the question, given that it is its conceptual aspiration to impart an overview of the history of philosophy that is as extensive and detailed as possible. Applied to the Islamic world, this means that its presentation of the subject matter will need to stretch from the beginnings of philosophical activity up to the present time. As far as the current state of research allows, it moreover should include authors that are lesser known or that have not yet been dealt with in general surveys at all.

This objective is subject to one caveat, however. As our overview of the history of research has brought to light, in many areas our knowledge is still rather limited. First of all this applies at the level of philosophical topics, of individual texts and their interpretations, where there is a multitude of open questions to be dealt with (such as inadequate knowledge of the extant manuscripts, a lack of [reliable] editions, uncertain attributions to authors, the lack of proper analysis and contextualization of individual works, etc.). Therefore many results of the research presented here will be preliminary, and will require further verification on the basis of textual material which is not available as yet. With regard to the period beginning with the 13th century, however, our ignorance also applies at the level of authors, and even of entire authorial traditions. It would even be fair to say that the philosophy of the 13th century and later so far has yet to be situated historically, institutionally, or in the sense of a taxonomy of the sciences. Notwithstanding the by now established consensus regarding its continued existence, scholars have not yet been able to agree on how it should be described, or how it should be seen in its relation to other intellectual traditions. This is not only due to the still ongoing discussion about Corbin's approach (which recently has been brought into play again by Jambet 2011 [*104: 11–20. 62–114]). Even those scholars who subscribe to the new paradigm of a continuation of rational philosophy as described at the end of the previous section have not yet established a clear, common view on how autonomous this philosophy would have been, or of its place in the wider context. On such questions, we so far only have several divergent hypotheses, awaiting verification (or falsification) on the basis of the textual material. They stretch from the claim that even after the 13th century, large parts of philosophy can be described as 'mainstream Avicennism' (Gutas 2002 [*75: 92–94]), to the assumption that in the long run, philosophy was only able to gain universal acceptance 'at the price of subordinating itself' to other disciplines, to wit, theology (Endress 1992 [*53: 37; cf. 27]), to the thesis that for the period between the 11th and the 19th century, it is in any case not possible to separate philosophy (*falsafa*) from Islamic theology (*kalām*), as they are best understood as 'a single hybrid enterprise' (Wisnovsky 2004 [*83: 154–156]).

Given these circumstances, it is impossible at this point to attempt an overview or even a classification of the various forms and expressions of philosophy that developed in the Islamic world over a period of many centuries. What we are hoping is rather that the four volumes which will be published within the framework of this series will help to increase our knowledge of the subject matter to an extent that will finally allow us to undertake a first description and (historical, institutional, taxonomical, etc.) contextualization of philosophy in its *longue durée*. One thing to mention briefly at this point, however, is the theoretical approach on which these volumes on *Philosophy in the Islamic World* are based. It may already have emerged to some extent in our account of the history of research. Nevertheless its essential elements shall be made explicit here.

Two basic assumptions have been decisive for the conception of the series. One of them concerns the fact that philosophical thought may be articulated in various ways, and will change over time. Even the concept of philosophy itself has a history, in the course of which it has time and again been subject to modifications, if not to far-reaching alterations. For research in European philosophy, this is a commonplace assumption (cf. e.g. the varied points of view charted in Aertsen, Speer 1998 [*65]). Scholars are of course aware of the fact that even Plato and Aristotle understood φιλοσοφία in different ways, and since then the concept of philosophy has seen numerous further interpretations in Europe. At least since the 19th century, this has led to a plurality of competing notions (Elberfeld 2006 [*87], Schnädelbach 2007 [*93: 12–20]). Insights that are commonplace within the European framework, however, are not always transferred to other contexts. When studying non-European philosophical traditions, the scholarly community rather tends towards setting narrower criteria, and demanding a concept of philosophy that is fixed unequivocally, on the basis of almost ahistorical features. This postulate does not, however, correspond to reality. Varying ideas of philosophy can be observed in other regions too, and most certainly in the Islamic world. In order to prove this, one does not even have to point to the major ruptures associated with the 13th and the 19th century respectively; it suffices to read some of the authors introduced in the present first volume more carefully. For they already display considerable differences: Abū Naṣr al-Fārābī (§ 8), the 'Iḫwān al-Ṣafā'', i.e. the 'Brethren of Purity' of Basra (§ 9.4.2), Abū l-Ḥasan al-ʿĀmirī (§ 5.2.3) and Abū Sulaymān al-Siǧistānī (§ 5.3.4–6) were practicing philosophy at nearly the same time, yet careful scrutiny quickly reveals that they all worked with different concepts of philosophy.

A first basic assumption is therefore the plurality and the internal diversity of the philosophical field. This does not mean that this field lacks unity, or cannot be demarcated from other intellectual traditions. To the contrary, a recognition of this diversity immediately demands that we find a suitably comprehensive definition. Even if philosophy is multifaceted, and even if its concept changes over time, the historian needs to circumscribe the philosophical field as a whole. This brings us to the second leading premise underlying the conception of this series. Like the first, it can be described as a consequence of the history of research: philosophy in the Islamic world is not defined relative to any specific culture. Rather, the same criteria and demarcations used in other areas of the history of philosophy are to be applied here.

This assumption implies a departure from the three older paradigms described above. For neither is philosophy here identified with 'Greek philosophy', as advocated by Renan and many authors after him; nor is there an assumption of a specifically Islamic concept of philosophy, as demanded by adherents of the 'pensée islamique' as well as by Corbin and his successors. Within the framework of this series, philosophy is rather understood as a distinct form of rationality which appears everywhere, or may appear everywhere. If one wanted to define its peculiar characteristics, one could say that it consists in a fundamental reflection on the structures of thought and being (that is, of thought as considered in itself and in respect of its representations), as well as structures of action.

This definition in fact corresponds to contemporary conceptions of philosophy. Even though contemporary philosophy focuses mainly on analysing our thought, or rather the language in which our thoughts are expressed, it also recognizes other problems and paths to knowledge (Stegmüller 1989 [*50: XXXVIII–XLIV]). Moreover, even where it primarily aims at analysing our thought, it never shuts out the fact that our thoughts refer both to what is and what ought to be (Schnädelbach 2007 [*93: 22–25]). In addition, it cannot be denied that for many earlier authors, it was natural to search for the laws of thought as well as for the structures of reality, and of the good. This most certainly applies to large parts of the philosophy of the Islamic world. The definition mentioned here has therefore already been adduced more than once in this context, for instance by Paul Wernst, who as early as 1967, in a critical review of the theoretical approaches of Seyyed Hossein Nasr and Corbin, argued for describing philosophy as 'the quest for the general interrelations of thinking and being, whose results can neither be proven by sense perception, nor rely on postulates of a "higher" (e.g. religious or esoteric) kind as their formal presupposition' (Wernst 1967 [*26: 356]).

Thus defined, philosophy may, as mentioned before, appear in various forms. It may be expressed in technical terminology, allegories, or symbols; it may discuss individual questions or design entire systems; it may be taught in private settings or within institutional frameworks, and in general may be pursued in various scientific contexts. The only important thing is that it is aware of its premises, and that it always gives reasons for the way in which it proceeds. This, however, happens by way of reflecting on its own procedure, by way of 'thinking about our thoughts' (Schnädelbach 2007 [*93: 22])

– something we can assume to be a constitutive feature of philosophy, in the Islamic world just as anywhere else.

In order to describe the philosophical tradition in the Islamic world specifically, yet another conceptual clarification is needed. It is connected with a question that has been discussed several times in recent scholarship: whether the subject matter under investigation should be termed 'Arabic philosophy', 'Islamic philosophy', 'Arabic-Islamic philosophy', or something else (e.g. Gardet 1959 [*18], Anawati 1967 [*25], Panella 1975 [*35], Wernst 1988 [*47: 321–322], Vollmer 1989 [*51], Brague 1998 [*66], 2006 [*86], Ramón Guerrero 1998 [*67], Jambet 2011 [*104: 53–62]). These discussions have not yielded a consensus, in part because each of the solutions on offer adequately represents some of the aspects of the issue, while suppressing other aspects, or even putting a wrong complexion on them.

The expression 'Arabic philosophy' (Butterworth 1983 [*38], Gutas 2002 [*76], Adamson, Taylor 2005 [*84]) emphasizes the linguistic aspect. This is justified insofar as most of the texts under investigation were indeed written in Arabic (which has always retained its position as scientific language of the Islamic world). It furthermore avoids tying the concept of philosophy to any particular religion, thus capturing the fact that philosophical debates were not conducted by Muslims only, but also by Jews, Christians and, it stands to reason, authors of yet other convictions. At the same time, a focus on the Arabic language also presents certain problems. As the philosophical tradition in the Islamic world progressed, its protagonists were increasingly likely to use other languages (Persian, Ottoman, Turkish, Urdu, French, English, etc.) The expression 'Arabic philosophy' therefore also implies a certain conceptual restriction, and it is not surprising that it was frequently used by Renan and other early authors, who regarded the end of philosophy around 1200 as a matter of course (Vollmer 1989 [*51: 881]).

The term 'Islamic philosophy' avoids this problem, as it allows for all sorts of linguistic affiliations, and indicates that Muslims of any provenance and any era were able to practice philosophy. In turn, however, it generates other difficulties, as it ignores the contributions of Jewish and Christian authors and wrongly suggests that in the Islamic world, the study of philosophy was tied to Islamic religion. Those who had rather avoid such interpretations therefore can only use the term 'Islamic philosophy' in a pragmatic way, where the attribute 'Islamic' is understood as a general imputation which does not refer to a religion but – taken more broadly – to a certain culture or culturally defined geographic area (Daiber 1999 [*69], Rudolph 2004 [*82], Brague 2006 [*86: 178]). A parallel case could for instance be seen in the expression 'Islamic art', which usually subsumes all artistic and architectural artefacts which have been created in Islamic culture.

Such comparisons are not, however, without their own problems. Therefore it has been determined that within the framework of this series, expressions like 'Arabic philosophy' or 'Islamic philosophy' (or a combination of both) will be avoided from the outset. Instead, the series title avails itself of the expression 'philosophy in the Islamic world', ultimately taking up a suggestion by Louis Gardet and Georges C. Anawati, who long time ago were already advocating the use of the expression 'philosophie en terre d'Islam' (Gardet 1959 [*18], Anawati 1959 [*17], 1967 [*25], 1968–1970 [*27], 1987 [*43]). The decision has several conceptual advantages for the project. It allows for the inclusion of philosophical texts in all languages, and independently of the religious affiliation of their authors. Furthermore, it makes it possible to avoid tying philosophy itself to certain religious or cultural conditions. Instead, as described above, it may be understood as an independent reflection on fundamental principles, open to all interested parties. Nevertheless one should be aware of the fact that this appellation, too, has its limitations. This will emerge in particular in the fourth volume of the series, which is concerned with the developments in the 19th and 20th centuries. It will feature, among others, Muslim authors in India or in France, and Marxist authors in Iran or in Turkey. In this context it will become clear in various ways that even the expression 'philosophy in the Islamic world' is no unequivocal term, but always ought to be understood pragmatically, and in relation to its respective context.

3 Characteristics of the First Volume: Philosophy from the 8th to the 10th Century

Such deliberations largely concern the developments of recent centuries. In the early Islamic era, which forms the topic of the present volume, the situation of philosophy in the Islamic world was very different. As indicated above, we do need to expect various philosophical approaches, manifest on the one hand in the plurality of doctrines and methods which we encounter in the 9th and 10th century, and on the other hand in the fact that philosophy was already being conceptualized in various ways. Nevertheless the philosophical field as a whole was still quite consistent. In this era, it may be described as a 'distinct, continuous, and self-contained school tradition' (Endress 1992 [*53: 25]) or as a community with its own epistemic norms. It constituted itself, once the requisite preconditions were in place, in 9th century Iraq, thereafter continuing to spread geographically, gaining increasing influence on the courtly and educated circles of society.

The characteristic features of this school tradition have been outlined several times, and have received an authoritative description by Endress. As he explains in his contribution to the *Grundriss der arabischen Philologie* (Endress 1987 [*44]), they included a number of features which were characteristic not just for philosophy but for all sciences that were able to hark back to ancient traditions (like arithmetic, geometry, astronomy, medicine, etc.). Among them are the explicit reference to late ancient curricula and Greek models (in philosophy, first and foremost Aristotle), at times supplemented by related points from the Iranian tradition and Indian knowledge; the tremendous interest in translations from the Greek, which usually were produced by Syriac-speaking scholars (often from intermediary Syriac translations); the adoption and further development of certain literary forms and genres of antiquity, as e.g. commentary, treatise, textbook and didactic poem; financial and ideological support through the caliphal and other courts, including their viziers and notables (Endress 1987 [*44: 402–473]); and, finally, the development of an Arabic technical terminology. The latter quickly turned into a precise and malleable instrument, suitable not only for adequately rendering ancient texts, but also for formulating new concepts and theorems (Endress 1992 [*53: 3–23]).

Many of these topics have entered the present volume in one form or another. This in particular applies to the late ancient background (here in § 1), the philosophical tradition of the Syriac Christians (§ 2) and the Graeco-Arabic translation movement (§ 3; cf. also §§ 4.3 and 6.2). They all receive detailed discussion because they were indispensable preconditions for the development of philosophy in the Islamic world. Philosophy itself then comes to the fore, beginning with § 4, which is dedicated to Abū Yūsuf al-Kindī (d. after 247/861), who was the first significant philosopher (and polymath) of the Arabic language. Then follows, in § 5, a long line of authors (Aḥmad b. al-Ṭayyib al-Saraḫsī, Abū Zayd al-Balḫī, Ibn Farīġūn, Abū l-Ḥasan al-ʿĀmirī, Abū Ḥayyān al-Tawḥīdī, Abū Sulaymān al-Siǧistānī, Abū ʿAlī Miskawayh, and Ibn Hindū) who took over al-Kindī's ideas either entirely or in part, applying them to various scientific contexts, disseminating them as far as Iran. § 6 introduces Abū Bakr al-Rāzī (d. 313/925), an original thinker whose ideas, however, seem to have been too eccentric to attract a large following. § 7 again discusses a number of authors: the so-called Baghdad Aristotelians of the 10th century, whose studies and commentaries mainly focused on Aristotelian logic (Abū Bišr Mattā b. Yūnus, Yaḥyā Ibn ʿAdī, ʿĪsā Ibn Zurʿa, Ibn al-Ḫammār, Ibn al-Samḥ and Abū l-Faraǧ Ibn al-Ṭayyib). From their circle arose Abū Naṣr al-Fārābī

(d. 339/950–951), who used his studies of the *Organon* in order to safeguard philosophy methodically, and place it on new foundations (§ 8). Thus he contributed substantially to its emancipation from the applied sciences, while at the same time ensuring that it devloped in new directions, and established itself as the authoritative path to demonstrative knowledge. Another point to consider is that in the mid-10th century, philosophical thought had ceased to be a matter for experts only, but had spread to all sorts of other areas. This is documented by traces in literature, popular ethics, natural science, and in certain religious currents. They are discussed in § 9, marking the philosophy of that era as a broad intellectual tradition embracing various options and possible applications. This also corresponds to its state at the turn of the 11th century – immediately, that is, before the emergence of Ibn Sīnā (d. 428/1037; on him cf. § 1 of the second volume in this series), which would permanently change the practice of philosophy in the Islamic world.

The philosophy of the 9th and 10th centuries was already perceived as a distinct tradition sustained by its own scholarly community – by its own protagonists as well as by other contemporary observers. This is evident from the specific linguistic expressions used to refer to it: someone who had a share in it was a *faylasūf* (borrowed from Greek φιλόσοφος, via Syriac *pīlōsōpā*) and practiced *falsafa* (an Arabic derivative of *faylasūf*). Apart from that, one also spoke of *ḥikma* (σοφία), which al-Fārābī understood as the universally valid, demonstrative 'wisdom', and which later was to become the most prevalent name for 'philosophy'. The distinctive position of philosophy can moreover be gleaned from the texts of medieval Arabic historians and historians of science. They separated philosophy from the other disciplines, and described its history, as far as it was known to them, as a continuous journey from its beginnings in Greece up to their own day and age (Rudolph 2011 [*106]). This explains why certain Arabic authors – bio-bibliographers like Ibn al-Nadīm (d. 380/990) or historians of science like Ṣāʿid al-Andalusī (d. 462/1070), Ibn al-Qifṭī (d. 646/1248) and Ibn Abī Uṣaybiʿa (d. 668/1270) – dealt with the lives and works of the philosophers in works or chapters reserved to them exclusively; which, incidentally, also means that these works are repeatedly referred to in this volume as primary sources for information on the individual philosophers.

These circumstances allow even the present-day historian to separate philosophy in the 9th and 10th centuries clearly from other intellectual areas. This first concerns its demarcation from Sufism, i.e. Islamic mysticism. Not many difficulties are attached to this, insofar as it was only at a later date (approximately with Ibn ʿArabī [d. 638/1240]) that mysticism began to engage significantly with philosophical questions. However, even if some of its early representatives, like al-Ḥakīm al-Tirmiḏī (d. 285/898), already leaned towards conceiving of mysticism as 'wisdom' (*ḥikma*) or as 'theosophy', this 'wisdom' meant something entirely different from anything that could be found in the works of the philosophers (Radtke 1988 [*46: 167–170]).

Matters are much more complicated with regard to Islamic theology, which was called *'ilm al-kalām* (speculative science, or science of dialectical disputation) or *'ilm uṣūl al-dīn* (science of the principles of religion) (van Ess 1991 [*52: I 51–54], Frank 1992 [*54: 9–12]). It naturally converged with philosophy on many more topics, which has induced several modern scholars, like Pines and Badawī (cf. p. 8 above), to present it as a second, as it were 'inner-Islamic', form of philosophizing (on the various positions scholars have held with regard to this question, cf. von Kügelgen 1994 [*59: 105 n. 245]). Therefore its case needs more detailed discussion, to explain why the Islamic theology of the 8th to 10th centuries has not been included in the present volume.

Prima facie there are several strong arguments for the inclusion of *kalām*. This is connected to the fact that like philosophy, early Islamic theology also developed in an environment that presupposed ancient learning and concepts (Endress 1992 [*53: 25–26]). In addition, one may regard it as a striking characteristic of the first significant theological school – i.e. the Mu'tazila (van Ess 1987 [*45], Gimaret 1992 [*55]) – that it justified the decisive points of its teaching with sophisticated rational deliberations (Frank 1977 [*36: 124–129. 137], Gimaret 1992 [*55: 791]). In this way the Mu'tazilites designed an epistemology that was essentially based on rational arguments (van Ess 1987 [*45: 228], 1997 [*52: IV 660–672]). Similar considerations apply to their ideas concerning the physical structure of the world (Dhanani 1994 [*57], van Ess 1992 [*52: III 67–74. 224–244. 309–369]), which allowed them to present a proof of God's existence 'from the contingency of the world' (van Ess 1992 [*52: III 229–232], 1997 [*52: IV 362–363]). They furthermore designed a rationalist ethics, which declares good and bad to be objective standards that do not depend on God, and from this infers the necessity of human free will (Gimaret 1992 [*55: 792], Kühn 1992 [*56: 607–612]; on details of Mu'tazilite theory of action see Gimaret 1980 [*37: 3–60]). Doubtless these are all philosophically relevant reflections (Frank 1992 [*54: 12–15]). On the basis of the Stoic division of philosophy into logic, physics, and ethics, one could even claim that the Mu'tazilites had produced a complete philosophical system.

There are, however, weighty arguments that can be mounted against their inclusion. To begin with, the rational arguments of the Mu'tazila, however impressive, never formed the only basis of their teachings. They were always accompanied by justification with reference to the pronouncements of the revelation. The foundations for this were laid down in Mu'tazilite epistemology: it accepted revelation or religious tradition as an important source of knowledge. This meant that their theological explanations often contained references to the Quran, as emerges clearly in respect of their explications on human free will, which lend themselves nicely to being divided into rational arguments and arguments based on the Quran (Gimaret 1980 [*37: 241–304. 334–360]). Of course, such a procedure is only to be expected. It would have been much more surprising if Islamic theologians had developed their dogmatics without any reference to the Quran. Nevertheless this has an important implication: theological speculation – even that of the Muʿtazila – was never truly free from presuppositions. It always laid claim to formulating orthodox doctrine, and ultimately conceived of itself as interpretation of God's revealed message to those that believed in Him (Frank 1992 [*54: 21–22. 25–27. 30. 37], Gimaret 1992 [*55: 791]).

This impression is further confirmed by a look at the taxonomy of sciences as it was commonly accepted in the early Islamic era. It indicates very clearly that philosophy and theology were not regarded as related or comparable disciplines, but were assigned to opposite poles within the system. The usual classifications were based on a dichotomy: sciences like philosophy, arithmetic, geometry, astronomy, and medicine, which had an ancient background, were assigned to one side. Depending on the aspect the thinker wanted to emphasize, they were called 'the ancient sciences' (*al-ʿulūm al-qadīma*), 'the sciences of the foreigners' (*ʿulūm al-ʿağam*), or 'the rational sciences' (*al-ʿulūm al-ʿaqliyya*). On the other side we find e.g. Arabic grammar, theology, jurisprudence, and Quranic exegesis. Their common characteristic consisted in aiming at understanding revelation, and reflecting its consequences for Islamic society. Therefore they were also called 'the Islamic sciences' (*al-ʿulūm al-islāmiyya*) or 'the religious sciences' (*ʿulūm al-šarīʿa*), or, later, 'the sciences that are based on traditions and conventions' (*al-ʿulūm al-naqliyya al-waḍʿiyya*) (Endress 1987 [*44: 400–401], 1992 [*53: 50–51]; on classifications of the sciences in general see Endress 2006 [*88]). Philosophy and theology were thus strictly separated. One of them was assigned to reason, the other to revelation, or to the linguistic expression of revelation. This separation corresponded to a *communis opinio*, which was also shared by the philosophers, as can be observed in striking form in al-Fārābī, who did take theology quite seriously (Rudolph 2008 [*95]), but insisted that it (including its Muʿtazilite variant) was merely a discipline for Muslim believers, and could not lay claim to universally valid knowledge (Rudolph 2007 [*92]).

In addition, there is a third point, which carries particular weight insofar as it brings the 9th and 10th century theological protagonists themselves into play, i.e. the very scholars who are under discussion here. What emerges in this respect is that they did not even want to be associated with the philosophers. In their eyes, philosophy was not a path towards knowledge, but a collection of dubious and misleading claims which were on a par with the doctrines of heretics, if not infidels. The only possible reaction to philosophy that could be expected from a theologian was its refutation. This was undertaken either in polemical works dedicated specifically to the purpose, or within the framework of systematic theological treatises. In those latter works, the authors did not only broach their own positions, but also the opinions of people who did not share their beliefs. In this context they discussed all dubitable arguments (*šubah*) advanced by their opponents, be they Muslim heretics or simply infidels – who, apart from dualists, Jews and Christians, usually also included the philosophers (Frank 1977 [*36: 134–135]).

It ought to be added, however, that the sources do present us with a problem in this context: a small number of exceptions and some fragments aside, the theological works of the 9th century are lost to us. With regard to this period, one therefore cannot do much more than pointing out that the extant bibliographical lists of the Islamic theologians repeatedly mention refutations of philosophy, or of Aristotle specifically (van Ess 1993 [*52: v 70 no. 8; 229 no. 8; 285 no. 49]). From the 10th century, by contrast, we do possess numerous theological works, in which an acid criticism of philosophy can be easily detected, for instance in texts by Abū l-Ḥasan al-Ašʿarī (d. 324/935–936) (van Ess 2010 [*99: 460. 474; cf. 456–457]) and by Abū Manṣūr al-Māturīdī (d. 333/944), who in turn explicitly mentions Muḥammad b. Šabīb, a Muʿtazilite author of the 9th century, as his source (Rudolph 1997 [*64: 227–228; cf. 183–197; Engl. transl. 207; cf. 166–179]). In such cases, the chasm that must have existed between philosophy and theology in the 9th and 10th centuries becomes glaringly obvious. Good reason perhaps to refrain from obliging the theologians of that time to become part of a history of 'philosophy in the Islamic world'.

4 Secondary Literature

1 Munk, Salomon. "Gazali (Abou-Hamed-Mohammed-ibn-Mohammed)." In *Dictionnaire des sciences philosophiques, par une société de professeurs de philosophie*, vol. 2. Paris, 1845, 506–512.

2 Renan, Ernest. *Averroès et l'averroïsme: Essai historique*. Paris, 1852. – Second, expanded ed. Paris, 1861. – Third, expanded ed. Paris, 1866. – Repr. of the third ed. in Henriette Psichari (ed.), *Œuvres complètes de Ernest Renan*, vol. 3. Paris, 1949,

11–365. 1153–1238; [and] ed. by Fuat Sezgin. Frankfurt a.M., 1985; [and] ed. with an intro. by Alain de Libéra. Paris, 2002.

3 Munk, Salomon. *Mélanges de philosophie juive et arabe*. Paris, 1859. – Repr. Paris, 1927, 1955, 1988; New York, 1980.

4 Ueberweg, Friedrich. *Grundriss der Geschichte der Philosophie von Thales bis auf die Gegenwart. Zweiter Theil: Die christliche Zeit. Zweite Abtheilung: Die scholastische Periode*. Berlin, 1864.

5 Renan, Ernest. "L'islamisme et la science." In *Conférence faite à la Sorbonne, le 29 mars 1883*, Paris, 1883. – Repr. in *Discours et conferences*, Paris, 1928 (9th ed.), 375–409. – German transl.: *Der Islam und die Wissenschaft*. Basel, 1883.

6 de Boer, Tjitze J. *Geschichte der Philosophie im Islam*. Stuttgart, 1901. – Engl. transl. by Edward R. Jones, *The History of Philosophy in Islam*. London, 1903. – Repr. 1967. – Arab. transl. by Muḥammad ʿAbd al-Hādī Abū Rīda, *Taʾrīḫ al-falsafa fī l-islām*. Cairo, 1938. – Repr. Beirut, 1981.

7 Horten, Max. *Die philosophischen Ansichten von Rázi und Tusi* (1209† und 1273†), aus Originalquellen übersetzt und erläutert. Mit einem Anhang: Die griechischen Philosophen in der Vorstellungswelt von Rázi und Tusi. Bonn, 1910.

8 Horten, Max. *Die spekulative und positive Theologie des Islam nach Rázi* (1209†) *und ihre Kritik durch Tusi* (1273†), nach Originalquellen übersetzt und erläutert. Mit einem Anhang: Verzeichnis philosophischer Termini im Arabischen. Leipzig, 1912. – Repr. Hildesheim, 1967.

9 Horten, Max. *Die Gottesbeweise des Schirázi* (1640), aus dem Arabischen übersetzt und erläutert. Ein Beitrag zur Geschichte der Philosophie und Theologie im Islam. Bonn, 1912.

10 Horten, Max. *Das philosophische System von Schirázi*, übersetzt und erläutert. Straßburg, 1913.

11 Horten, Max. "Die syrische und die arabische Philosophie." In *Friedrich Ueberwegs Grundriss der Geschichte der Philosophie*, vol. 2: *Die patristische und die scholastische Philosophie*. Ed. by Bernhard Geyer. Basel, 1927, 287–325. – Repr. Basel 1951.

12 Corbin, Henry. *Suhrawardî d'Alep* (†1191), *fondateur de la doctrine illuminative* (*ishrâqî*). Paris, 1939.

13 ʿAbd al-Rāziq, Muṣṭafā. *Tamhīd li-Taʾrīḫ al-falsafa al-islāmiyya*. Cairo, 1944, 1959 (2nd ed.). – Repr. 1996.

14 Corbin, Henry (ed.). *Ṣihābaddīn Yaḥyā as-Suhrawardī. Opera metaphysica et mystica*, vol. 1. Istanbul, 1945.

15 Strauss, Leo. *Persecution and the Art of Writing*. Glencoe, 1952. – Repr. Westport, 1973; Chicago, 1980.

16 Corbin, Henry. *Avicenne et le récit visionnaire*, 2 vols. Tehran, 1954 (2nd ed.). – Engl. transl.: *Avicenna and the Visionary Recital*. London, 1960.

17 Anawati, Georges C. "La philosophie en Islam au moyen âge." In *La philosophie au milieu du vingtième siècle*, vol. 4. Ed. by Raymond Klibansky. Florence, 1959, 79–87.

18 Gardet, Louis. "Le problème de la 'philosophie musulmane'." In *Mélanges offerts à Étienne Gilson*. Toronto, 1959, 261–284.

19 Hourani, Albert. *Arabic Thought in the Liberal Age, 1798–1939*. London, 1962. – Repr. Cambridge, 1995.

20 Sharif, M. M. (ed.). *A History of Muslim Philosophy. With Short Accounts of Other Disciplines and the Modern Renaissance in Muslim Lands*, 2 vols. Wiesbaden, 1963–1966. – Persian transl.: *Tārīḫ-i falsafa dar islām*. Tehran, 1983.

21 Corbin, Henry. *Histoire de la philosophie islamique*, vol. 1: *Des origines jusqu'à la mort d'Averroës* (1198). Avec la collaboration de Seyyed Hossein Nasr et Osman Yahya. Paris, 1964.

22 Nasr, Seyyed Hossein. *Three Muslim Sages. Avicenna, Suhrawardī, Ibn ʿArabī*. Cambridge, 1964. – Repr. 1969, 1976.

23 Vajda, Georges. Review of [*21]. *Journal asiatique* 252 (1964): 273–278.

24 Rosenthal, Franz. Review of [*21]. *Speculum* 40 (1965): 504–505.

25 Anawati. Georges C. "Philosophie arabe ou philosophie musulmane? Plan pour une bibliographie de philosophie médiévale en terre d'islam." In *Mélanges offerts à M.-D. Chenu, maître en théologie*. Paris, 1967, 51–71.

26 Wernst, Paul. Review of [*22]. *Oriens* 18–19 (1967): 355–358.

27 Anawati, Georges C. "Bibliographie de la philosophie médiévale en terre d'islam pour les années 1959–1969." *Bulletin de philosophie médiévale* 10–12 (1968–1970): 316–369.

28 Fakhry, Majid. *A History of Islamic Philosophy*. New York, London, 1970, 1983 (2nd ed.; repr. 1987), 2004 (3rd ed.).

29 Pines, Shlomo. "Philosophy." In *The Cambridge History of Islam*, vol. 2: *The Further Islamic Lands, Islamic Society and Civilization*. Ed. by Peter Malcolm Holt, Ann K. S. Lambton, and Bernard Lewis. Cambridge, 1970, 780–823.

30 Hourani, George F. *Islamic Rationalism. The Ethics of ʿAbd al-Jabbār*. Oxford, 1971.

31 Corbin, Henry. *En islam iranien. Aspects spirituels et philosophiques*, 4 vols. Paris, 1971–1972. – Repr. Paris, 1991.

32 Badawī, ʿAbd al-Raḥmān. *Histoire de la philosophie en islam*, 2 vols. Paris, 1972.

33 Arkoun, Mohammed. *Essais sur la pensée islamique*. Paris, 1973, 1977 (2nd ed.), 1984 (3rd ed.).

34 Corbin, Henry. "La philosophie islamique depuis la mort d'Averroès jusqu'à nos jours." In *Histoire de la philosophie*, vol. 3. Ed. by François Châtelet. Paris, 1974, 1067–1188.

35 Panella, Emilio. "Esiste una 'filosofia araba'?" *Memorie domenicane. Rivista di religione, storia, arte* 6 (1975): 380–397.

36 Frank, Richard M. "Reason and Revealed Law. A Sample of Parallels and Divergences in Kalâm and Falsafa." In *Recherches d'islamologie. Recueil d'articles offert à Georges C. Anawati et Louis Gardet*. Leuven, 1977, 123–138.

37 Gimaret, Daniel. *Théories de l'acte humain en théologie musulmane*. Paris, 1980.

38 Butterworth, Charles E. "The Study of Arabic Philosophy Today." *Bulletin/Middle East Studies Association* 17 (1983): 8–24. 161–177.

39 Nasr, Seyyed Hossein. "The Meaning and Role of 'Philosophy' in Islam." *Studia Islamica* 37 (1983): 57–80.

40 Adams, Charles J. "The Hermeneutics of Henry Corbin." In *Approaches to Islam in Religious Studies*. Ed. by Richard C. Martin. Tucson, 1985, 129–150.

41 Marmura, Michael. "Die islamische Philosophie des Mittelalters." In *Der Islam*, vol. 2. Ed. by William Montgomery Watt and M. Marmura. Stuttgart, 1985, 320–392.

42 Corbin, Henry. *Histoire de la philosophie islamique*. Paris, 1986. [revised version of *21 and *34 in one volume]. – Engl. transl. by Liadain Sherrard with the assistance of Philip Sherrard, *History of Islamic Philosophy*. London, New York, 1993 [with supplemented bibliography].

43 Anawati, Georges C. "Bilan des études sur la philosophie médiévale en terre d'islam 1982–1987." *Bulletin de philosophie médiévale* 29 (1987): 24–47.

44 Endress, Gerhard. "Die wissenschaftliche Literatur." In *Grundriss der arabischen Philologie*, vol. 2: *Literaturwissenschaft*. Ed. by Helmut Gätje. Wiesbaden, 1987, 400–506.

45 van Ess, Josef. "Muʿtazilah." In *The Encyclopedia of Religion*. Ed. by Mircea Eliade, vol. 10. New York, London, 1987, 220–229.

46 Radtke, Bernd. "Theosophie (*ḥikma*) und Philosophie (*falsafa*). Ein Beitrag zur Frage der *ḥikmat al-mašriq/al-išrāq*." *Asiatische Studien* 42 (1988): 156–174.

47 Wernst, Paul. Review of: Richard Walzer: *Al-Farabi On the Perfect State. Abū Naṣr al-Fārābī's Mabādiʾ ārāʾ ahl al-madīna al-fāḍila. A Revised Text with Introduction, Translation, and Commentary*. Oxford, 1985. *Oriens* 31 (1988): 314–334.

48 Gutas, Dimitri. *Avicenna and the Aristotelian Tradition. Introduction to Reading Avicenna's Philosophical Works*. Leiden, 1988, 2014 (2nd, revised and enlarged ed.).

49 Endress, Gerhard. "Die arabisch-islamische Philosophie. Ein Forschungsbericht." *Zeitschrift für Geschichte der Arabisch-Islamischen Wissenschaften* 5 (1989): 1–47.

50 Stegmüller, Wolfgang. *Hauptströmungen der Gegenwartsphilosophie. Eine kritische Einführung*, vol. 1. Stuttgart, 1989 (7th ed.).

51 Vollmer, Martin. "Philosophie, arabische (bzw. islamische)." In *Historisches Wörterbuch der Philosophie*, vol. 7. Ed. by Joachim Ritter and Karlfried Gründer. Darmstadt, 1989, 881–886.

52 van Ess, Josef. *Theologie und Gesellschaft im 2. und 3. Jahrhundert Hidschra. Eine Geschichte des religiösen Denkens im frühen Islam*, 6 vols. Berlin, 1991–1997.

53 Endress, Gerhard. "Die wissenschaftliche Literatur." In *Grundriss der arabischen Philologie*, vol. 3: Supplement. Ed. by Wolfdietrich Fischer. Wiesbaden, 1992, 3–152.

54 Frank, Richard M. "The Science of Kalām." *Arabic Sciences and Philosophy* 2 (1992): 7–37.

55 Gimaret, Daniel. "Muʿtazila." In *The Encyclopaedia of Islam*. New edition. Ed. by Clifford Edmund Bosworth et al., vol. 7. Leiden, 1992, 783–793.

56 Kühn, Wilfried. "Quel éthique accepte Dieu? Anselme de Cantobéry, al-Achʿari, ʿAbd al-Djabbar, Thomas d'Aquin." In *ΣΟΦΙΗΣ ΜΑΙΗΤΟΡΕΣ. «Chercheurs de sagesse». Hommage à Jean Pépin*. Ed. by Marie-Odile Goulet-Cazé, Goulven Madec, and Denis O'Brien. Paris, 1992, 595–625.

57 Dhanani, Alnoor. *The Physical Theory of Kalām. Atoms, Space, and Void in Basrian Muʿtazilī Cosmology*. Leiden, 1994.

58 Gutas, Dimitri. "Ibn Ṭufayl on Ibn Sīnā's Eastern Philosophy." *Oriens* 34 (1994): 222–241.

59 von Kügelgen, Anke. *Averroes und die arabische Moderne. Ansätze zu einer Neubegründung des Rationalismus im Islam*. Leiden, 1994.

60 Nasr, Seyyed Hossein. "Philosophy." In *The Oxford Encyclopedia of the Modern Islamic World*, vol. 3. Ed. by John L. Esposito. Oxford, 1995, 328–333.

61 Boroujerdi, Mehrzad. *Iranian Intellectuals and the West. The Tormented Triumph of Nativism*. Syracuse, 1996, 120–130 [on Seyyed Hossein Nasr].

62 Nasr, Seyyed Hossein and Oliver Leaman, eds. *History of Islamic Philosophy*, 2 vols. London, 1996.

63 Fakhry, Majid. *A Short Introduction to Islamic Philosophy, Theology and Mysticism*. Oxford, 1997, 1998 (2nd ed.).

64 Rudolph, Ulrich. *Al-Māturīdī und die sunnitische Theologie in Samarkand*. Leiden, 1997. – Engl. transl. by Rodrigo Adem, *Al-Māturīdī and the Development of Sunnī Theology in Samarqand*. Leiden, 2015.

65 Aertsen, Jan A. and Andreas Speer, eds. "Was ist Philosophie im Mittelalter?" In *Akten des X. Internationalen Kongresses für mittelalterliche Philosophie der Société internationale pour l'étude de la philosophie médiévale, 25. bis 30. August 1997 in Erfurt*. Berlin, 1998.

66 Brague, Rémi. "Sens et valeur de la philosophie dans les trois cultures médiévales." In J. A. Aertsen, A. Speer 1998 [*65: 229–244].

67 Guerrero, Rafael Ramón. "¿Qué es la filosofía en la cultura árabe?" In J. A. Aertsen, A. Speer 1998 [*65: 257–270].

68 Daiber, Hans. "What is the Meaning of and to Which End do We Study the History of Islamic Philosophy? The History of a Neglected Discipline." In H. Daiber 1999 [*69: I xi–xxxiii].

69 Daiber, Hans. *Bibliography of Islamic Philosophy*, 2 vols. Leiden, 1999. – Supplement (2007).

70 Landolt, Hermann. "Henry Corbin, 1903–1978. Between Philosophy and Orientalism." *Journal of the American Oriental Society* 119 (1999): 484–490.

71 Gutas, Dimitri. "Avicenna's Eastern ("Oriental") Philosophy. Nature, Contents, Transmission." *Arabic Sciences and Philosophy* 10 (2000): 159–180.

72 Schmidtke, Sabine. *Theologie, Philosophie und Mystik im zwölferschiitischen Islam des 9./15. Jahrhunderts. Die Gedankenwelten des Ibn Abī Ǧumhūr al-Aḥsāʾī* (um 838/1434–35 – nach 906/1501). Leiden, 2000.

73 Endress, Gerhard. "Philosophische Ein-Band-Bibliotheken aus Isfahan." *Oriens* 36 (2001): 10–58.

74 Tamer, Georges. *Islamische Philosophie und die Krise der Moderne. Das Verhältnis von Leo Strauss zu Alfarabi, Avicenna und Averroes*. Leiden, 2001.

75 Gutas, Dimitri. "The Heritage of Avicenna. The Golden Age of Arabic Philosophy, 1000 – ca. 1350." In *Avicenna and his Heritage. Acts of the International Colloquium, Leuven – Louvain-la-Neuve September 8 – September 11, 1999*. Ed. by Jules L. Janssens and Daniel De Smet. Leuven, 2002, 81–97.

76 Gutas, Dimitri. "The Study of Arabic Philosophy in the Twentieth Century. An Essay on the Historiography of Arabic Philosophy." *British Journal of Middle Eastern Studies* 29 (2002): 5–25.

77 Hajatpour, Reza. *Iranische Geistlichkeit zwischen Utopie und Realismus. Zum Diskurs über Herrschafts- und Staatsdenken im 20. Jh.* Wiesbaden, 2002.

78 Wisnovsky, Robert. *Avicenna's Metaphysics in Context*. London, 2003.

79 Günther, Ursula. *Mohammed Arkoun. Ein moderner Kritiker der islamischen Vernunft*. Würzburg, 2004.

80 Hartung, Jan-Peter. *Viele Wege und ein Ziel. Leben und Wirken von Sayyid Abū l-Ḥasan ʿAlī al-Ḥasanī Nadwī* (1914–1999). Würzburg, 2004.

81 Hendrich, Geert. *Islam und Aufklärung. Der Modernediskurs in der arabischen Philosophie*. Darmstadt, 2004.

82 Rudolph, Ulrich. *Islamische Philosophie. Von den Anfängen bis zur Gegenwart*. Munich, 2004, 2008 (2nd ed.), 2013 (3rd, revised and expanded edition). – French transl. by Véronique Decaix, *La philosophie islamique: Des commencements à nos jours*. Paris, 2014, 2015 (2nd ed.).

83 Wisnovsky, Robert. "The Nature and Scope of Arabic Philosophical Commentary in Post-Classical (ca. 1100–1900 AD) Islamic Intellectual History. Some Preliminary Observations." In *Philosophy, Science and Exegesis in Greek, Arabic and Latin Commentaries*, vol. 2. Ed. by Peter Adamson, Han Baltussen and Martin W. F. Stone. London, 2004, 149–191.

84 Adamson, Peter and Richard Taylor, eds. *The Cambridge Companion to Arabic Philosophy*. Cambridge, 2005.

85 D'Ancona, Cristina, ed. *Storia della filosofia nell'Islam medievale*, 2 vols. Turin, 2005.

86 Brague, Rémi. "Wie islamisch ist die islamische Philosophie?" In *Wissen über Grenzen. Arabisches Wissen und lateinisches Mittelalter*. Ed. by Andreas Speer and Lydia Wegener. Berlin, 2006, 165–178.

87 Elberfeld, Rolf, ed. *Was ist Philosophie? Programmatische Texte von Platon bis Derrida*. Stuttgart, 2006.

88 Endress, Gerhard, ed. *Organizing Knowledge. Encyclopaedic Activities in the Pre-Eighteenth Century Islamic World*. Leiden, 2006.

89 Endress, Gerhard. "Reading Avicenna in the Madrasa. Intellectual Genealogies and Chains of Transmission of Philosophy and the Sciences in the Islamic East." In *Arabic Theology, Arabic Philosophy. From the Many to the One. Essays in Celebration of Richard M. Frank*. Ed. by James E. Montgomery. Leuven, 2006, 371–422.

90 Nasr, Seyyed Hossein. *Islamic Philosophy from its Origin to the Present. Philosophy in the Land of Prophecy*. Albany, 2006.

91 Eichner, Heidrun. "Dissolving the Unity of Metaphysics. From Fakhr al-Dīn al-Rāzī to Mullā Ṣadrā al-Shīrāzī." *Medioevo* 32 (2007): 139–197.

92 Rudolph, Ulrich. "Al-Fārābī und die Muʿtazila." In *A Common Rationality. Muʿtazilism in Islam and Judaism*. Ed. by Camilla Adang, Sabine Schmidtke and David Sklare. Würzburg, 2007, 59–80.

93 Schnädelbach, Herbert. "Was ist Philosophie?" In *Was ist Philosophie? Qu'est-ce que la philosophie?* Ed. by Anton Hügli and Curzio Chiesa. = *Studia philosophica* 66 (2007): 11–28.

94 von Kügelgen, Anke. "ʿAbd al-Rāziq, Muṣṭafā." In *Encyclopaedia of Islam*, THREE [EI Three]. Ed. by Gudrun Krämer et al. Leiden, 2008–11, 12–14.

95 Rudolph, Ulrich. "Reflections on al-Fārābī's *Mabādiʾ ārāʾ ahl al-madīna al-fāḍila*." In *In the Age of al-Fārābī. Arabic Philosophy in the Fourth/Tenth Century*." Ed. by Peter Adamson. London, 2008, 1–14.

96 Hartung, Jan-Peter. "Philosophie. III: Islam." In *Enzyklopädie der Neuzeit*. Ed. by Friedrich Jaeger et al. Stuttgart, 2009, 1121–1125.

97 Rizvi, Sajjad H. *Mullā Ṣadrā and Metaphysics. Modulation of Being*. London, 2009.

98 El-Rouayheb, Khaled. *Relational Syllogisms and the History of Arabic Logic 900–1900*. Leiden, 2010.

99 van Ess, Josef. *Der Eine und das Andere. Beobachtungen an islamischen häresiographischen Texten*, 2 vols. Berlin, 2010.

100 Nasr, Seyyed Hossein. *Islam in the Modern World. Challenged by the West, Threatened by Fundamentalism, Keeping Faith with Tradition*. New York, 2010. – Extended version of: *Traditional Islam in the Modern World*. London, 1987.

101 Dhouib, Sarhan, ed. *Arabisch-islamische Philosophie der Gegenwart* = *Concordia* 59 (2011).

102 Eichner, Heidrun. "Das avicennische Corpus Aristotelicum. Zur 'Virtualisierung' des Aristotelestextes in der postavicennischen Tradition." In R. Goulet, U. Rudolph 2011 [*103: 197–239].

103 Goulet, Richard and Ulrich Rudolph, eds. *Entre Orient et Occident. La philosophie et la science gréco-romaines dans le monde arabe*. Vandœuvres-Genève, 2011.

104 Jambet, Christian. *Qu'est-ce que la philosophie islamique*? Paris, 2011.

105 Pourjavady, Reza. *Philosophy in Early Safavid Iran. Najm al-Dīn Maḥmūd al-Nayrīzī and his Writings*. Leiden, 2011.

106 Rudolph, Ulrich. "Die Deutung des Erbes. Die Geschichte der antiken Philosophie und Wissenschaft aus der Sicht arabischer Autoren." In R. Goulet, U. Rudolph 2011 [*103: 279–321].

107 Saatchian, Firouzeh. *Gottes Wesen – Gottes Wirken. Ontologie und Kosmologie im Denken von Šams-al-Dīn Muḥammad al-Ḫafrī (gest. 942/1535). Eine philosophische Analyse nach seinen Schriften al-Risāla fī iṯbāt wāǧib al-wuǧūd bi-l-ḏāt wa-ṣifātihī und al-Risāla fī l-ilāhiyyāt*. Berlin, 2011.

108 Shayegan, Daryush. *Henry Corbin. Penseur de l'islam spiritual*. Paris, 2011. – Second, expanded ed. of: *Henry Corbin. La topographie spirituelle de l'islam iranien*. Paris, 1990.

109 Adamson, Peter. *Philosophy in the Islamic World: A Very Short Introduction*. Oxford, 2015.

110 Adamson, Peter. *A History of Philosophy Without Any Gaps: Philosophy in the Islamic World*. Oxford, 2016.

111 El-Rouayheb, Khaled and Sabine Schmidtke, eds. *The Oxford Handbook of Islamic Philosophy*. Oxford, 2016.

CHAPTER 1

The Late Ancient Background

Ulrich Rudolph

1 Principal Features of Late Ancient Philosophy – 2 The School of Athens – 3 The School of Alexandria – 4 Philosophy and the Sciences – 5 Channels of Transmission – 6 Secondary Literature

1 Principal Features of Late Ancient Philosophy

The Arabic authors of the 3rd/9th and 4th/10th centuries entered into a philosophical heritage that was at once vast and variegated. If it did not contain the full spectrum of all the different doctrines that had been maintained and taught throughout antiquity, this was not for any shortcomings of the Greek-Arabic transmission or a lack of interest on the part of the Arab readers; it was, rather, the result of certain developments that had already begun to emerge during late antiquity. By concentrating their attention on certain doctrines and textual canons, the Greek schools had already established one specific intellectual tradition as the 'mainstream' way of doing philosophy – appropriately tagged 'the philosophy of the commentators' in recent years (Sorabji 2004 [*105]). By no means uniform, it nevertheless exhibited a certain range of characteristics that were to remain constitutive for centuries and still resounded in early Arabic philosophy. To name but the most conspicuous examples (for details cf. Sorabji 2004 [*105: I 1–32]): a fundamental commitment to Plato and/or Aristotle as pre-eminent authorities (along with a rejection of the Stoics and Epicurus); a methodological decision on the part of the authors to present their own reflections in the form of paraphrases of, and commentaries on works by these two authorities; and a certain tendency to push particular topics to the forefront of the philosophical curriculum. This tendency was not a rigid one; it varied depending on the different thematic requirements connected with the various institutional contexts in which philosophy was taught. It is nevertheless worth bearing in mind that particular topics (e.g. soul and intellect), themes (e.g. the thesis of the 'harmony' between Plato and Aristotle) and areas of the philosophical curriculum (e.g. logic) which later were to be given prominent roles by the early Arabic authors were likewise attracting marked attention in late antiquity.

 | DOI 10.1163/9789004323162_003

Most of these characteristics are already apparent in Alexander of Aphrodisias (ca. AD 200). While he himself was still working in an environment where all four schools (i.e. Platonism, Aristotelianism, Stoicism and Epicureanism) enjoyed respect and were furnished with endowed chairs (Sorabji 1990 [*47: 16], Thiel 1999 [*81: 5]), his own activity as a teacher of Peripatetic philosophy in Athens contributed considerably to the changing of the situation – both in form and content, as it were. On the one hand, Alexander's arrival on the scene boosted the position of Aristotelianism with regard to its doctrinal positions, as he was able to influence central debates of his time – e.g. concerning the soul, or the role of fate – by coming up with convincing solutions from his own school's perspective, and arguing critically against the views of the Platonists and (even more so) of the Stoics. On the other hand, Alexander also introduced new methodological standards; this arose not so much from his treatises and *quaestiones* on individual philosophical issues as from his extensive corpus of commentaries. Composed of numerous scholia explicating the Aristotelian corpus in argumentative detail, it was to remain a literary model not only for Aristotelian exegesis at the end of antiquity, but also, later on, for many Arabic authors (for a detailed survey of Alexander's life and work see Richard Goulet, Maroun Aouad in: DPhA 1989 [*37: I 125–139] and Silvia Fazzo in: DPhA 2003 [*37: Suppl. 61–70]; on his significance for the commentary tradition cf. Hadot 1997 [*71: 170–171], D'Ancona 2000 [*82: 319–327]).

It fell to Plotinus (d. 270) to make a further, and ultimately even greater impact. Through his philosophical activity, Platonism was systematized and re-interpreted; it would become the formative philosophical current of late antiquity. Plotinus oriented the Platonic teachings strictly towards metaphysical questions, making several doctrinal decisions that were to have far-reaching effects on subsequent philosophy, including Arabic philosophy. One of those decisions concerned the human soul. Plotinus interpreted it as an incorporeal reality which, though joining itself to the body, nevertheless retains its home in the intelligible world, and hence is able to recognize the real structure of things. Another doctrine concerned the intelligible world, or rather the forms, which were understood as the intelligible principles of all existing things. For Plotinus they are identical with the divine Intellect, which he equates with Plato's demiurge as well as with Aristotle's *nous*. All the same, the divine Intellect is not, according to his view, the highest principle there is; rather, it again refers to a further highest and first principle. The latter is 'beyond being' and in the *Enneads* is identified with the 'One' of Plato's *Parmenides* as well as the 'Good' of the *Republic* (on these doctrinal decisions see D'Ancona 2005 [*107: 11–13], 2005 [*108: 5–10]; on Plotinus in general cf. the contributions in: Gerson 1996 [*69]).

All these doctrines may be regarded as a continuation of the Platonic tradition, and as the result of a subtle reading of Plato. However, they also show Plotinus' thorough engagement with other schools, notably the Stoics and the Aristotelians. The latter in particular presented a challenge for him, especially since their doctrines had just been re-launched by Alexander of Aphrodisias. Hence it is not surprising that Plotinus frequently responds to Peripatetic viewpoints in his writings. His tenor remains critical and reserved, but taken individually his pronouncements prove to be differentiated and nuanced. For instance, in his doctrine of intellect/*nous*, Plotinus was prepared to take over certain aspects from Aristotle (Szlezák 1979 [*15], Armstrong 1991 [*53: 117–127]). Other points he criticized heavily, as is demonstrated by his elaborate and often quoted rejection of the Aristotelian categories (Sorabji 1990 [*47: 2], 2004 [*105: I 7]).

His relationship to Aristotle thus remained a point to be discussed extensively among his successors. This already applies to Porphyry (d. ca. 305), who, despite being a devoted pupil of Plotinus, deviated markedly from his master in this respect. It is due to Porphyry's efforts that Aristotle's writings not only continued to receive attention, but were permanently integrated into the Neoplatonic curriculum. He himself must have discussed them regularly in his lectures, as can be seen from the long list of his exegetical works on Aristotle. First on this list is the famous *Isagoge* ('Introduction'), which was written as a prologue to the *Categories* and later on came to serve as standard introduction to the *Organon*. It is followed by a brief commentary on the *Categories*, likewise extant in Greek and now available in an English translation (Strange 1992 [*60]). In addition, however, Porphyry composed further exegetical works, many of which are extant in fragments only, or known to us only through questionable testimonies. Among them are an extensive commentary on the *Categories* as well as explications of Aristotle's *On Interpretation*, *Sophistical Refutations* (Ebbesen 1990 [*42: 141–142]), *Physics*, *On the Soul*, and the *Nicomachean Ethics*. It is furthermore likely that Porphyry commented on the *Prior Analytics* and the *Posterior Analytics*, as well as on *Metaphysics* XII (on Porphyry in general, see Richard Goulet et al. in: DPhA 2012 [*37: Vb 1289–1468], offering detailed information on his commentaries on Aristotle by Michael Chase; on his commentary on the *Metaphysics* in particular cf. also Hadot 1990 [*44: 276]).

Such exegetical activity naturally went along with a higher esteem for Aristotle. This emerges, for instance, from the extant commentary on the *Categories*, where Porphyry, despite a number of borrowings from Plotinus' interpretation of the text (Strange 1987 [*31]), confronted his teacher's criticism of the work (according to Saffrey 1992 [*59: 43–44] it was this disagreement which provoked Porphyry's departure for Sicily). The most important and best-known argument Porphyry made in this respect was that the *Categories* was commonly misunderstood and wrongly classified. The work did not deal with 'things', as many authors supposed, but merely investigated 'words' in so far as they signified things. Hence its topic was not true being or the intelligible world, but our language, which was first and foremost used for the phenomena of the sensible world (Sorabji 1990 [*47: 2]; in more detail Hadot 1990 [*45: 125–140], who mentions further considerations by Porphyry).

This heightened appreciation of Aristotle was not, however, confined to single arguments; it was programmatic. This is indicated by two further works by Porphyry, which unfortunately are lost to us, but which seem to have broached the intellectual proximity between Plato and Aristotle explicitly. One of them, entitled 'Περὶ τοῦ μίαν εἶναι τὴν Πλάτωνος καὶ Ἀριστοτέλους αἵρεσιν' (*That the Philosophical System of Plato and Aristotle is One*), reportedly comprised seven volumes. The other, much shorter one was probably called 'Περὶ διαστάσεως Πλάτωνος καὶ Ἀριστοτέλους' (*On the Difference between Plato and Aristotle*). While the title does not exactly suggest harmony, we may nevertheless assume that this work, too, was not conceived as a criticism of Aristotle. Its aim seems to have been to demonstrate that despite their different approaches to philosophy, Plato and Aristotle ultimately did not disagree in essentials (Ebbesen 1990 [*42: 145], Sorabji 1990 [*47: 2], Richard Goulet in: DPhA 2012 [*37: vb 1301. 1305, nos. 8 and 37 of the list of works], Hadot 2015 [*128: 54–65]).

With these two works Porphyry popularized a topic which was to exercise generations of authors (for its origins in Middle Platonism cf. Hadot 1997 [*71: 171], 2015 [*128: 51–53]). For centuries, the 'harmony' between Plato and Aristotle remained a recurrent theme that was adopted by many philosophers, albeit not always in the same sense and with equal emphasis. Syrianus (d. ca. 437) and Proclus (d. 485), for instance, subscribed to the 'harmony' thesis with some reservations (Saffrey 1990 [*46: 173–175], Sorabji 1990 [*47: 3], 2004 [*105: I 14], Hadot 2015 [*130: 103–115. 121–125]). Ammonius (d. after 517), on the other hand, bolstered it by writing a treatise specifically devoted to the point that Aristotle's god is not only the final cause of our world, but also its efficient cause or creator. This claim met with broad approval: it can be found in several authors of the 6th century, such as Asclepius, John Philoponus, Simplicius, Olympiodorus, and David (Hadot 2015 [*130: 126–143]; for reservations likewise voiced in Alexandria cf. below pp. 46–47). Moreover, it also found its way into the Arabic speaking world. There we encounter it, for instance, in al-Fārābī (d. 339/950–951), who adopted it, together with many other claims belonging to the same complex of problems, in *al-Ǧamʿ bayna raʾyay al-ḥakīmayn Aflāṭūn al-ilāhī wa-Arisṭūṭālīs* (*The Harmony Between the Opinions of the Two*

Sages, Plato and Aristotle), a work ascribed to him (Sorabji 1990 [*47: 3–4], 1990 [*49: 182–187]; for al-Fārābī's text, the authenticity of which is still a matter of debate, cf. below pp. 585–586).

Even though the hypothesis of the 'harmony' between Plato and Aristotle is not unknown to modern scholarship (cf. e.g. similar evaluations of the matter in Schmitt 2003 [*98: 52–65] and Gerson 2005 [*109a]), it is sometimes regarded as evidence for a lack of discrimination in late ancient and early Arabic philosophy. Critics assume that anybody who held this thesis must either have been deficient in his knowledge about the complex philosophical theories involved, or else have been prepared to curtail and simplify them for reasons unrelated to the subject matter. While the latter may occasionally be true, it certainly was not the starting point for such considerations. To assume this would do justice neither to the concerns that gave rise to the harmony thesis in the first place, nor to the sincerity of the discussions that sprang from it. First and foremost they sought to defend philosophy's claim to truth against the expanding claims of religion, and to exonerate it from the charge that the philosophers were split into different rivalling schools. This is manifest already in Porphyry, whose arguments exhibit defensive as well as affirmative tendencies. On the one hand he wrote polemical treatises against Christianity (*Against the Christians*) and against certain 'pagan' religious practices such as theurgy, which was widespread e.g. in Egypt (*Letter to Anebo*). On the other hand he propagated the 'harmony' between Plato and Aristotle as a testimony proving that philosophy was a true and unified science, as long as one followed its most eminent exponents (Sorabji 2004 [*105: 7. 14. 19–20]). The sincerity of the discussions that resulted from the harmony thesis should equally be regarded as beyond doubt. For the idea that Plato and Aristotle ultimately converged in their teachings did not mean that their works were ignored; on the contrary, it led to scholars studying them more thoroughly, hunting for what they supposedly had in common. This has only recently been demonstrated convincingly for a whole range of central philosophical issues which were vividly discussed in late antiquity (rationalism *versus* empiricism; the Platonic forms; the definition of the individual; mortality *versus* immortality of the individual; God's activity; the substance of the heavens) (Sorabji 2004 [*105: 1 15–19; cf. also the detailed discussions in Gerson 2005 [*109a]).

Nevertheless we also find late ancient authors who attempted to question Porphyry's positioning of philosophy (as characterized by the continuation of the Platonic-Plotinian tradition, the claim of a general 'harmony' between Plato and Aristotle, and a critical stance towards religion). This already applies to Iamblichus (d. ca. 325), who probably studied with Porphyry, but seems to have distanced himself from his teacher in many respects, focusing on rather different points when teaching in his own school in Apamea in Syria (for a detailed account of his life and work, see John Dillon in: DPhA 2000 [*37: III 824–836]). To begin with, Iamblichus opposed Porphyry's criticism of theurgy and other religious practices to be found in Egypt and elsewhere (*On the Mysteries of Egypt*). He regarded it as biased, since it interpreted these ideas in a naturalistic way, thus failing to develop a higher, spiritual understanding of religion. This, however, seemed crucial to Iamblichus, who took religion to be an indispensable part of the spiritual life: if the human soul was to be liberated from the fetters of the body, philosophical theology needed to be complemented, in his view, by religious practice, in particular by theurgic rituals (John Dillon in: DPhA 2000 [*37: III 831–832], Sorabji 2004 [*105: I 7]).

Secondly, Iamblichus thought he could establish an even closer proximity between Plato and Aristotle. To this effect he re-opened the question of the correct interpretation of the Aristotelian categories. Porphyry's answer had been to deny that the *Categories* dealt with beings, restricting its scope instead to logic and to our speaking about the sensible world. Iamblichus countered this by arguing that Aristotle's doctrine of the categories also allowed for a higher, 'intellective' interpretation (comparable to the higher interpretation of religion). Rightly understood, it therefore was applicable not only to the sensible, but also to the intelligible world (Sorabji 1990 [*47: 17], 2004 [*105: I 8]; for the significance of the *Categories* by Pseudo-Archytas in this context cf. Hadot 1997 [*71: 172]).

Thirdly, and most conspicuously, Iamblichus did not want to restrict the idea of a 'harmony' between the authoritative philosophers to Plato and Aristotle alone. According to his view, Pythagoras also belonged in this line; in his eyes, he represented the sage *par excellence*, if not the origin of philosophy itself and the guarantor of its truth (attributing Pythagoras' wisdom to divine revelation; see Hadot 1997 [*71: 171], 2015 [*130: 65–73]; for precursors of this view in Numenius cf. Riedweg 2007 [*120: 165–166]). This position had significant consequences. Even though Iamblichus based his teaching on a standardized curriculum beginning with Aristotle's writings and culminating in Plato's dialogues (which, he determined, were to be read in a fixed canon of twelve dialogues; see p. 37 below for more details), he also seems to have given ample space to the Pythagorean tradition in his lectures. His most important work, in ten volumes, was the treatise 'Περὶ τῆς Πυθαγορικῆς αἱρέσεως' (*On the Pythagorean School*); four parts of it are still extant today. Apart from an ethical propaedeutics based on Pythagoras as a role model (*On the Pythagorean Way of Life*; see Staab 2002 [*89]) it contained numerous explications of mathematical questions, including an (extant) commentary on the *Introduction to Arithmetic* by the Neopythagorean Nicomachus of Gerasa (2nd cent.) as well as the (likewise extant) treatise *On General Mathematical Science* (on his work generally see O'Meara 1989 [*39: 30–105], John Dillon in: DPhA 2000 [*37: III 830–831], Riedweg 2007 [*120: 167–168]; on Nicomachus' *Introduction* see Hadot 1998 [*75: 234], Radke 2003 [*97: 6–8]). In addition, however, Iamblichus used plenty of pseudo-Pythagorean material, one example being the so-called *Golden Verses* (Riedweg 2007 [*120: 159–161]), on which he also wrote a commentary. While its Greek original is lost, it may possibly be available to us in an Arabic version (Daiber 1995 [*67], John Dillon in: DPhA 2000 [*37: III 834], Wakelnig 2014 [*129: 37–39]; doubts concerning Iamblichus' authorship are voiced in O'Meara 1989 [*39: 230–231]; on this issue, and his work in general, see also D'Ancona 2005 [*108: 14. 21–24. 218–219]).

Iamblichus' positions met with great interest among his Greek successors. At any rate it would be true to say that seen from the perspective of the late ancient Neoplatonic schools, he was the most eminent author of the 4th century. From the point of view of the Arabic tradition, however, it is necessary to highlight yet another philosopher of the same period: Themistius (d. around 385). Whereas his writings were but little studied in the context of late antiquity, parts of his work met with a broad reception in the Islamic philosophical tradition.

In many respects Themistius cut an exceptional figure among philosophers of the 4th century. This was due to the fact that he did not work within the framework of a philosophical school like the others, but was an active politician and orator in Constantinople (for a detailed account of his person and work see now Jacques Schamp, Robert B. Todd, John Watt in: DPhA 2016 [*37: VI s.v. Thémistios]; see also Heather, Moncur 2001 [*85a]). Accordingly, he came up with some rather unorthodox positions. Even though they, like those of other thinkers, resulted from a thorough study of Plato and Aristotle, the ways in which Themistius understood the works of these two thinkers did not correspond to the established Neoplatonic interpretations of his time. When it came to Plato, Themistius was mainly interested in his views on politics and ethics; at least that is what most of his comments on the Platonic corpus concern, whereas he did not pay much heed to theological questions, which is what primarily commanded people's attention in general (Blumenthal 1990 [*41: 115]). His engagement with Aristotle, however, was all the more extensive. He even developed a new method of presenting his Aristotelian exegesis: the brief, summarizing paraphrase, which, together with the long, elaborate commentaries (modelled on Alexander of Aphrodisias) were later to become a popular literary genre (Brague 1999 [*76: 22–24], D'Ancona 2000 [*82: 326], Sorabji 2004 [*105: I 8. 17]). Themistius composed a long series of explications in this form. Three of them – the paraphrases of the *Posterior Analytics*, the *Physics* and

On the Soul – are extant in Greek. Other important writings, including his famous commentary on *Metaphysics* XII, are only available in Arabic or Hebrew versions (Brague 1999 [*76: 9–14]; a list of his works is also compiled in D'Ancona 2005 [*108: 40 n. 118]). This demonstrates the intense interest with which Themistius was read in the Islamic world; the selection of transmitted texts meanwhile indicates that his Arabic readership regarded him exclusively as a commentator on Aristotle and a member of the Peripatetic tradition. Whether this assessment does full justice to his philosophical inclinations is a different question. For Themistius did make use of Neoplatonic terminology that was common coinage in his time; moreover, depending on the topics concerned he occasionally took up certain tenets that had originated in the (Neo-) Platonic milieu (Sorabji 2004 [*105: 8]). For this reason his position is still a matter of controversy in modern scholarhip (cf. the detailed discussion in Hadot 2015 [*130: 74–97]). Some authors are inclined to put him down exclusively as a Neoplatonist (Ballériaux 1989 [*36], 1994 [*63]). Most scholars, however, regard him as a Peripatetic (most recently Jacques Schamp, Robert B. Todd, John Watt in: DPhA 2016 [*37: VI s.v. Thémistios]), thus following Blumenthal's verdict, who has characterized him as the last genuine Aristotelian of antiquity (1990 [*41: 123]).

2 The School of Athens

This orientation towards Aristotle, however, was to remain a solitary exception within late ancient philosophy. At the time when Themistius was active, (Neo-) Platonism had long since established itself as dominant doctrine, in the variants developed by Plotinus, Porphyry and especially Iamblichus. This tendency was reinforced in the 5th century, when Neoplatonist views came to dominate the philosophical discourse outright. The tone was set by two intellectual centres: Athens and Alexandria, each of them being home to an important school and philosophical tradition.

The school of Athens appears to go back to an initiative of Plutarch's (d. 432), who started teaching philosophy towards the end of the 4th century, using his own house for the purpose (on his life and work see Concetta Luna, Alain-Philippe Segonds in: DPhA 2012 [*37: Vb 1076–1096]; on the possibility that Platonic philosophy might have been taught in Athens even before Plutarch's time by some of Iamblichus' pupils, cf. Saffrey, Westerink 1968 [*9: I XXXIX–XLVIII]). Thus once again there arose an Academy in the city that was dedicated to the study of philosophy; and apparently, it quickly began to attract numerous students. It turned out to be a stable institution, both in respect of its finances and in the way in which it discharged its activities. This is evident from the fact that teaching continued for more than a century, and that there was a regular succession of scholarchs, despite the occasional row between internal factions (Vinzent 2000 [*83: 55–59], Watts 2006 [*111: 90–142]).

We also find remarkable continuity in terms of the philosophical contents taught at Athens. Even though the individual members of the school held different, and occasionally rather original, views, as recent research has shown (van Riel 2000 [*82a], Gertz 2011 [*127]; cf. also Philippe Hoffmann in: DPhA 1994 [*37: II 572–574] regarding Damascius), the curriculum on which they all based their deliberations seems to have remained the same throughout the life of the Academy, in essence following the guidelines specified by Iamblichus. This meant that – after an introduction to the mathematical sciences (Watts 2006 [*111: 99]) – students focused on reading the works of Aristotle and Plato. The former were known as the 'lesser', the latter as the 'greater mysteries'. In practice, people studied logic, physics and metaphysics according to the Aristotelian corpus, followed by the Platonic dialogues in the order established by Iamblichus on the basis of an older arrangement (in the *Prologos* by Albinus; see Nüsser 1991 [*56: 174 n. 17], Reis 1999 [*80: 122–124]). To begin with, students read a series of ten dialogues supposed to lead from self-awareness to the knowledge of the First Cause (*Alcibiades 1, Gorgias, Phaedo, Cratylus, Theaetetus, Sophist, Politicus, Phaedrus, Symposium, Philebus*). After that, the *Timaeus* was discussed, with a view to expounding the theoretical foundations of physics; the final climax was reached by studying the *Parmenides*, out of which the actual doctrine of theological principles was developed (John Dillon in: DPhA 2000 [*37: III 829]). Another point to be considered is that Platonic theology – again following Iamblichus – was not derived from the dialogues alone, but was traced back, via Pythagoras, to divine revelation. This meant that Orphic writings and the so-called *Chaldean Oracles* were also included within the corpus that was studied and commented on in class, and that the cultivation of religious practices and the performance of theurgic rituals – which in fact was carried out in the School of Athens well into the 6th century – were advocated (Watts 2006 [*111: 99–103]; cf. also D'Ancona 2005 [*107: 16], 2005 [*108: 25–27]).

Unfortunately we do not possess the complete body of writings composed on this curriculum by any of the philosophers who taught at the school. Aristotelian exegesis in particular is extremely badly attested. The person for whom we can get the clearest picture is Syrianus (d. 437) (on his life and work see Wear 2011 [*128]; Longo 2009 [*124] and Concetta Luna in: DPhA 2016 [*37: VI s.v. Syrianus d'Alexandrie]). In his case we know that he commented on the *Categories*, *On Interpretation*, the *Prior Analytics*, *On the Heavens*, *On the Soul*, and the *Physics*. In addition, he composed a commentary on parts of the *Metaphysics* which is extant in Greek. Here he praises Aristotle explicitly as a logician, moral philosopher, and philosopher of nature. At the same time it is obvious that Syrianus did not always agree with the metaphysical ideas of the Stagirite (Saffrey 1990 [*46: 173–175]). They were particularly irritating to him where they contained implicit or explicit criticisms of Pythagoras or Plato. This may explain why Syrianus did not comment in writing on the whole of the *Metaphysics*, but only on those four books (III, IV, XIII and XIV) which can be described as the most anti-Platonic parts of the work (Concetta Luna in: DPhA 2003 [*37: Suppl. 252–253]).

With Proclus (d. 485) the situation is different. We do know that he, too, was in the business of interpreting Aristotle, as is evident, on the one hand, from his commentaries on *On Interpretation*, the *Prior Analytics* and the *Posterior Analytics* (as well as on Porphyry's *Isagoge*), for each of which we possess brief textual witnesses; and, on the other hand, from the (completely extant) *Elements of Physics*, in which he discusses books VI and VIII of the *Physics* and book I of *On the Heavens* (detailed information is provided by Concetta Luna, Alain-Philippe Segonds in: DPhA 2012 [*37: Vb 1555–1563]). All the same, it is first and foremost the 'Platonic' parts of Proclus' extensive œuvre that have survived. They include several interpretations of dialogues that have been transmitted almost in their entirety. The most prominent among them are the commentaries on the *Parmenides* and the *Timaeus*, which are counted among the most outstanding documents of late ancient Platonic exegesis. Apart from those, Proclus authored two systematic introductions to Platonic theology: the more detailed *Platonic Theology*, and the small handbook called *Elements of Theology*, which was to play a prominent role in the Arabic tradition, since it served as textual basis not only for the so-called *Liber de Causis* but also for a further influential Proclean paraphrase, the 'Proclus Arabus' (on the Arabic paraphrases cf. below p. 63; for brief surveys of the work as a whole see D'Ancona 2005 [*107: 16–17], 2005 [*108: 28–30]; for detailed information on the works just mentioned see: DPhA 2012 [*37: Vb 1564–1589. 1610–1616. 1657–1674], where the Greek tradition is summarized by Concetta Luna and Alain-Philippe Segonds, and the Arabic tradition by Gerhard Endress).

After Proclus it was primarily Damascius (d. after 538) who further developed Plato's theory of first principles. He did so first in a number of detailed commentaries on Plato's dialogues (Philippe Hoffmann in: DPhA 1994 [*37: II 580–586]), but followed this up even more impressively in his *On First*

Principles, a work that is said to be his masterpiece and is considered by some as one of the most impenetrable texts of ancient philosophy (Hoffmann ibid. 586; on original approaches in Damascius' physics see further Sorabji 2004 [*105: I 10]).

Simplicius, who was active in the Academy at the same time as Damascius, followed a rather different philosophical approach. More than any of the other Athenians he emphasized the 'harmony' between Plato and Aristotle again. As he explains at some point, he literally took it to be the 'duty' of each and every commentator to establish the agreement between these two undisputed authorities 'in most things' (Sorabji 1990 [*47: 4]; cf. Hadot 2015 [*130: 140–143]) – a maxim that he himself followed conscientiously. This is borne out by his extensive commentaries on Aristotle's *Categories*, *On the Heavens*, *Physics*, and *On the Soul*, but also, it would appear, on the *Metaphysics* (see Hadot 1990 [*44: 289–292]). These commentaries often take a mediating stance on questions that were discussed controversially among the schools. Since they contain long doxographical passages and draw on otherwise lost original works (e.g. by Empedocles) they furthermore constitute an invaluable source for our knowledge of early Greek philosophy (Sorabji 2004 [*105: I 11. 14]).

At the time when these commentaries were written, the School of Athens had already ceased to exist. For Simplicius composed his exegetical works on Aristotle after 529, i.e. after teaching had been suspended at the Academy. Where he did this, we do not know exactly; but in fact few historical developments following the closure of the Academy can be regarded as historically certain. The only thing we know with certainty is that in 531, the last scholarch Damascius and his colleagues (Simplicius, Priscianus, and others) travelled to King Ḫusraw I in Mesopotamia, which was under Persian control at the time. However, they left the Sasanian Empire again in 532, and we do not know any particulars concerning their whereabouts after that.

The dramatic events of those years have been described by scholars many times, and have been the subject of avid discussion (for overviews of scholarly opinions see Blumenthal 1978 [*13], Watts 2006 [*111: 128–142]). In as much as these discussions concern events in Athens, they are not directly relevant for our topic. However, the questions that arise in the context of the Athenian philosophers' journey to the Orient are very much pertinent for us. They will, therefore, be aired again more extensively below (cf. pp. 53–54). For the moment, it will suffice to take note of the fact that Damascius, Simplicius and their colleagues had no successors at Athens; which means that no further stimuli for the development of philosophy could arise from that quarter any longer.

3 The School of Alexandria

This happened instead in Alexandria, where a tradition of philosophical study had likewise been flourishing for some time (Vinzent 2000 [*83: 67–74], Watts 2006 [*111: 187–209]). Since the middle of the 5th century it had closely been connected with the school of Athens (Westerink 1990 [*52: 325], Sorabji 2004 [*105: I 9]). Nevertheless the Alexandrians managed to continue with their lecture courses even when all teaching activities were stalled at Athens. They were thus able to offer a qualified philosophical education to several generations of students throughout the 6th century AD.

A central player in all this was Ammonius Hermeiou (d. after 517). Originally from Alexandria, he spent several years in Athens in order to study with Proclus. Having returned to his native city, in about AD 470 he took possession of a chair in philosophy which he held for several decades; his success as a chair-holder is documented by his impressive line of pupils, which includes such famous names as John Philoponus, Asclepius, Simplicius, and Olympiodorus (Sorabji 2004 [*105: I 9]; Damascius is mentioned as a further pupil by Henri Dominique Saffrey in: DPhA 1989 [*37: I 168] and Philippe Hoffmann in: DPhA 1994 [*37: II 544]).

Ammonius' lecture course was broad in scope. He taught geometry and astronomy, two fields in which he published his own ideas (Henri Dominique Saffrey in: DPhA 1989 [*37: I 168], Hadot 1998 [*75: 240]). This was in addition to his lectures on philosophy proper, for which he adhered to reading works by Aristotle and Plato. His wide-ranging interests, however, are but dimly reflected in his extant work. This applies in particular to his exegesis of Plato; here, only a single treatise on *Phaedo* 65d5–6 is on record (besides oral explications of the *Gorgias* and the *Theaetetus*; see Saffrey in: DPhA 1989 [*37: I 168], Verrycken 1990 [*51: 227–228], Westerink 1990 [*52: 326–327]). The 'Aristotelian' side of his teaching is much better documented, though not even that much can be said without reservation. For Ammonius himself only ever published one commentary on Aristotle (on *On Interpretation*). In twelve further cases the extant texts go back to versions which were written down by his students, 'from his voice' (ἀπὸ φωνῆς; see Richard 1950 [*5]); hence it is not inconceivable that ideas of his students may have left their mark on the wording of these texts as they were transmitted. Three of them, the commentaries on the *Isagoge*, the *Categories*, and the *Prior Analytics*, still bear Ammonius' name, at any rate. In the other cases, it is the recording scribes who sign the works themselves, Asclepius in one case (on the *Metaphysics*), and John Philoponus in no fewer than eight (on the *Categories*, the *Prior Analytics*, the *Posterior Analytics*, the *Physics*, *On Generation and Corruption*, the *Meteorology*, *On the Soul*, and *On* *the Generation of Animals*). Philoponus in particular indicates that his notes do not only reproduce the explanations of his teacher, but include his own observations as well (Henri Dominique Saffrey in: DPhA 1989 [*37: I 168], Westerink 1990 [*52: 326]).

As far as we can tell, Ammonius was followed on the Alexandrian chair by Eutocius (Westerink 1990 [*52: 328], Watts 2006 [*111: 233–234]; Richard Goulet, however, points out the hypothetical character of this assumption, in: DPhA 2000 [*37: III 395]). This may well indicate how highly mathematics was esteemed in Alexandria: even though Eutocius is said to have taught introductory courses on the *Organon*, he earned his fame through his achievements in the field of geometry, which are documented by a number of commentaries he wrote on Archimedes and Apollonius of Perga (Hadot 1998 [*75: 240–241], Goulet in: DPhA 2000 [*37: III 392–395], 2003 [*37: Suppl. 87]).

With the next scholarch, a *bona fide* philosopher returned to the chair once more. This was Olympiodorus (d. after 565), who appears to have remained at the helm of the school for several decades. He once again managed to assemble a large number of pupils, to be initiated into the canon of philosophical texts according to a minutely structured syllabus, which was divided into lectures of equal length (Westerink 1971 [*10: 6–8]). Olympiodorus' style of lecturing is very well documented, since it is reflected in all of his works that we have at our disposal. Amongst them are commentaries on the Aristotelian Corpus (*Categories*, *Meteorology*) as well as explanatory notes on Plato's dialogues (*Alcibiades 1*, *Gorgias*, *Phaedo*; see Westerink 1990 [*52: 328–329], Henri Dominique Saffrey in: DPhA 2005 [*37: IV 769–770]). He furthermore appears to be the author of an anonymously transmitted commentary on Paul of Alexandria, which would show that astrology was still being taught in Alexandria in his days (Westerink 1971 [*10], Saffrey in: DPhA 2005 [*37: IV 770]).

Olympiodorus' successors, all of whom were Christians, adopted his meticulous style of lecturing (Westerink 1971 [*10: 7]), but may have reduced the scope of the programme that was taught at the school. In any case the extant œuvre of the three last philosophers who taught after him in Alexandria is rather narrow in scope. Of the works of Elias, a direct pupil of Olympiodorus (Westerink 1990 [*52: 336–337]), we possess *Prolegomena* to philosophy, scholia on *On Interpretation*, as well as commentaries on the *Isagoge*, the *Categories*, and the beginning of the *Prior Analytics* (though the authorship of the commentary on the *Categories* [CAG XVIII 1] is disputed; Richard Goulet in: DPhA 2000 [*37: III 60–65], after a thorough discussion of all arguments, endorses the ascription to Elias). However, a few scattered remarks within these texts allow us to surmise that Elias also taught Plato, and that he wrote a commentary on Galen's

Sects for Beginners (Westerink 1990 [*52: 336], Goulet in: DPhA 2000 [*37: III 60]).

Whether similar assumptions may hold true for his presumed successor, the Armenian-born David, is much more questionable. He only left *Prolegomena* to philosophy, and commentaries on the *Isagoge* (Muradyan 2015 [*131]) and on the *Prior Analytics* (Topchyan 2010 [*125]; for David in general cf. Agnès Ouzounian in: DPhA 1994 [*37: II 614–615]; she, in contrast to Goulet, attributes the disputed commentary on the *Categories* to David rather than to Elias).

The last Alexandrian scholarch Stephanus, who was summoned to Constantinople in about 610, apparently returned to offering a broader programme of instruction. From his hand we possess extant commentaries on *On Interpretation* and *On the Soul* (book III). He is furthermore said to have taught arithmetic and astronomy, and, possibly, Plato's dialogues – all apart from his alleged preoccupation with alchemy, which is highly controversial (Westerink 1990 [*52: 340–341]; on his life and work, as well as on the difficulties surrounding the transmission of his works, cf. Denis Searby in: DPhA 2016 [*37: VI s.v. Stéphanos d'Alexandrie]).

All this means that it was possible to study philosophy at Alexandria up to the beginning of the 7th century. While the year 529 marked a definite break for Athens, philosophical instruction was continued in Alexandria without any discernible interruptions. This does not mean that there were no conflicts with the Christian authorities in the city. In the 480s, for instance, Alexandria witnessed riots and the persecution of 'pagan' philosophers (Sorabji 2004 [*105: I 9. 20]; for details on the background to these events see Watts 2006 [*111: 216–222]). In some respects this is reminiscent of the attacks Proclus had experienced a few years before in Athens (Sorabji 1990 [*47: 11], 2004 [*105: I 20], Watts 2006 [*111: 105–106]). In Alexandria, however, the two parties involved were able to reach a settlement in the long term. Its success seems to have been influenced decisively by the agreement Ammonius negotiated with the Patriarch of the city. Its exact content is unknown and was the subject of conjecture and, occasionally, of wild speculation even in antiquity itself. The latest research, however, tends towards the assumption that the agreement did not result in drastic changes, but pursued merely pragmatic aims and was rather limited in scope: presumably it stipulated that the philosophers were to abstain from practising the religious and cultic aspect of their activity, which means that in contrast to their colleagues at Athens they were to give up teaching the Orphic texts and the *Chaldean Oracles*, and to relinquish the performance of theurgic rites (Sorabji 2004 [*105: I 21–22], Watts 2006 [*111: 222–225], both including information on other hypotheses as well).

The core of the philosophical doctrine, on the other hand, does not seem to have been touched by the agreement. In fact, the instruction in the philosophical curriculum, including Plato's dialogues, continued to be maintained afterwards. This impression is confirmed by the introductory writings (*Prolegomena*) to philosophy which were composed in Alexandria in the course of the 6th century. Judging from them, even at this time the curriculum still comprised the following elements (*idealiter* at least): the *Isagoge*; Aristotelian philosophy, consisting in logic, ethics, physics, mathematics and metaphysics; and Platonic philosophy, taught according to the series of dialogues specified by Iamblichus (Westerink 1971 [*10: 20], Endress 1987 [*25: 405]; for details on the *Prolegomena* literature see Hadot 1987 [*28: 100–110. 120–122], Reis 1999 [*80: 131–144]). That is to say, it was still based on the assumption that the material taught in the programme represented something like a complete 'system' of philosophy (Hadot 1997 [*71: 173]).

As has been indicated earlier, actual practice may have differed slightly. We know, for instance, that the teaching of ethics was reduced to a brief propaedeutical study (usually of Epictetus' *Encheiridion*). In mathematics, it was not, of course, Aristotelian writings that were taught, but the classical authors of the *quadrivium* (arithmetic: Nicomachus and Diophantus; music: Aristoxenus; geometry: Euclid and Heron; astronomy combined with astrology: Ptolemy, Theodosius, and Paulus). Regarding the study of Plato, scholars assume that it did not include all twelve dialogues anymore at the end, and that the *Parmenides* in particular was struck from the list (Westerink 1971 [*10: 19–21], 1976 [*12: 25–26], Endress 1987 [*25: 405]).

Nonetheless, in its essential points the teaching conformed to the same curriculum that had already been followed in the school of Athens. At any event one should note that the Alexandrians were continuing numerous traditions they had borrowed from Athens. This also holds for their self-image and their philosophical outlook which – according to current knowledge – continued to be committed to an intricate Neoplatonic metaphysics. This last point used to be assessed differently, due to a very influential thesis by Praechter. In a frequently quoted article from 1910 [*3], he argued that the Alexandrians had opened themselves up to Christian influence early on, and in consequence had developed a simplified system of Neoplatonism, if not dispensed with reading Plato's dialogues altogether (an overview of the older scholarly literature can be found in Verrycken 1990 [*51: 199–202]). More recent scholarship takes a different view, emphasizing that at Alexandria, just as at Athens, the whole gamut of Neoplatonic teaching was cultivated and transmitted without major restrictions. This thesis was first developed by Ilsetraut Hadot in her works on Hierocles (1978 [*14]) and several other authors (e.g. 1990 [*44: 278], 1991 [*54:

175–176], 1992 [*58: 408], 1997 [*71: 171. 173]) and by now can be regarded as a new scholarly consensus (Vinzent 2000 [*83: 50–51. 79–80], Sorabji 2004 [*105: I 9. 23–25], Hadot 2015 [*130: 13–25]).

Despite the fundamental agreement between the two institutions there were differences, too. For while the Alexandrians followed the philosophical programme of the Athenians on many points, they nevertheless developed their own specific characteristics in their doctrine and in their works – be it as a result of their elaboration of the Athenian programme, or based on their own scholarly tradition. It is not possible to present them here in detail, but a few particularly conspicuous features should be mentioned, albeit briefly. They are of great interest to us not least because in some aspects, they exhibit an uncanny resemblance with certain tendencies we will encounter later on in the Islamic world.

(1) One of the characteristic features which stand out in the works of the late Alexandrian authors is their preference for *Prolegomena* literature, as mentioned above. It apparently began with Ammonius and is documented for all his successors, the only exception being the very last scholarch, Stephanus. There are three different types of *Prolegomena* texts that need to be distinguished from each other: (a) *Prolegomena* to philosophy in general – after Ammonius prefixed to every commentary on the *Isagoge* (for their structure and development see Hein 1985 [*20: 33], Hadot 1987 [*28: 100–102. 120], Westerink 1990 [*52: 344–347]); (b) *Prolegomena* to Aristotelian philosophy, prefixed to explications of the *Categories* (Hein 1985 [*20: 238], Hadot 1987 [*28: 102–106. 120–121], Westerink 1990 [*52: 342–344], Reis 1999 [*80: 134–138]); and (c) *Prolegomena* to Platonic philosophy. The latter are least documented in the tradition, but we do possess one complete, anonymously transmitted example, which has been edited by Westerink (1962 [*6]; cf. Hadot 1987 [*28: 106–110. 121–122], Nüsser 1991 [*56: 162–163], Reis 1999 [*80: 138–144]; for a summary account of the genre see Hadot 1997 [*71: 172–173]). All these texts shared the purpose of introducing their readers (or listeners) to the subject matter that was supposed to be communicated. This pertains in particular to the *Prolegomena* to the *Isagoge* and to the *Categories*, which were studied at the very beginning of the course of instruction that was to last for several years. Hence it is no wonder that this genre experienced another round of success when, later on, the ancient writings were absorbed into new languages and by new readers. This applies to the Syriac reception of Aristotle (for information on authors and works see Hein 1985 [*20: 34–40. 242–246]), but even more so to Arabic philosophy, which demonstrably produced works of that kind as late as the 5th/11th century (Hein 1985 [*20: 47–56. 247–251]).

(2) A second peculiarity consisted in the fact that problems of physics were much more fiercely discussed at Alexandria than at Athens, attacking Aristotle's very concept of the physical world. This phenomenon was of course related to the strong position which Christianity held in the city; but independently of the occasion from which it arose it had fundamental significance for the further development of philosophy and science. In this case a single protagonist would prove to be crucial: John Philoponus (d. 574; on his life, work and influence see: DPhA 2012 [*37: Va 455–563], where the Greek tradition is summarized by Giovanna R. Giardina et al., and the Arabic tradition by Emma Gannagé). Himself a pupil of Ammonius, whose Aristotelian exegesis he had noted down and thus preserved for posterity (cf. pp. 40–41 above), he wound up using his knowledge first and foremost in order to criticize Aristotle and Proclus, and to establish an alternative to Aristotelian science (cf. the contributions in Sorabji 1987 [*29]). This new approach was to leave significant marks on Islamic philosophy and science, and thus it was not only the Platonic-Aristotelian 'mainstream' of the school of Alexandria but also a dissident minority opinion which had an impact on Arabic philosophers. At all events, the fundamental criticism of the thesis of the eternity of the world which Philoponus voiced in his works *Against Proclus On the Eternity of the World* and *Against Aristotle On the Eternity of the World* was taken over – wholesale including his arguments – by al-Kindī (d. after 247/861; on him see § 4 below) and al-Ghazālī (d. 505/1111; on him see vol. 2, § 3). Furthermore, certain concepts which Philoponus had formulated as alternatives to Aristotelian physics even found their way to authors like Ibn Sīnā (see Zimmermann 1987 [*34] on the impetus theory).

(3) There is further the question of the status that was accorded to Aristotelian philosophy in Alexandria, a question we have already touched upon several times in the context of the philosophical profiles of individual scholarchs, and of the positioning of the school in comparison with the school of Athens more generally. What has emerged so far is, basically, that the Alexandrians held on to reading Aristotle as well as Plato. The verdict of recent research points in the same direction, asserting that the entire body of Neoplatonic doctrine, including its metaphysical ideas, was cultivated and proliferated without any major alterations (cf. pp. 43–44 above). This, however, does not yet tell us anything about Aristotle's standing. Hence it remains to be asked how highly he was valued in comparison with his teacher, and how much weight his works carried within the school's teaching practice. Here we can see a difference emerge between Alexandria and Athens once again, even though our sources do not always indicate very clearly how great this difference actually was. On

the one hand there are indications that Aristotle enjoyed an enhanced status at Alexandria; we can therefore assume that his philosophy was given more space within the curriculum than at Athens. The most important pieces of evidence pointing in this direction are: the large number of commentaries on the Aristotelian corpus which were composed and transmitted in Alexandria; the critical interest in his physical works, already mentioned above, which demonstrates that at least parts of Aristotelian philosophy served as a focal point for the contemporary discussion; the fact that some authors strove to protect Aristotle against objections coming from a Platonist perspective (Sorabji 2004 [*105: I 24] on Olympiodorus' defence of Aristotle's theory of relations); and lastly the fact that many Alexandrians named the 'ascent to God' as the ultimate goal of their Aristotelian studies (Sorabji 1990 [*47: 5–6], Hadot 1991 [*54: 181]).

This last point indicates how broadly the 'harmony' between Plato and Aristotle was now understood: it was evidently thought possible to find the path to the highest principle, the One, not just *via* the Platonic dialogues, but also *via* the Aristotelian corpus. That Ammonius wrote a treatise dedicated specifically to Aristotle's theological ideas fits in well with this. Here he argued, as mentioned before, that Aristotle's god was final cause as well as efficient cause, or in other words the creator, of our world (cf. p. 32 above). This claim has often been interpreted as a fall-back position and as a concession to the dominant Christian doctrine. Nowadays, however, scholars tend to assume that instead it represents a 'Neoplatonization' and hence revaluation of Peripatetic metaphysics (Verrycken 1990 [*51: 204–210. 226], Sorabji 2004 [*105: I 9–10. 24], providing evidence for Ammonius' interpretation of the Aristotelian Intellect as Platonic demiurge and bearer of eternal forms). Thus a whole new dignity was bestowed on Aristotle: his *Metaphysics* was no longer being criticized – a treatment it still had suffered not too long ago at the hands of the Athenian commentator Syrianus (cf. pp. 37–38 above) – but instead was now understood as a legitimate source of theological knowledge. This indicated a change of paradigm: it opened up a new perspective from which Aristotle could be seen as the perfect master of thought and theoretical philosophy *per se* (Verrycken 1990 [*51: 231], with emphasis on Neoplatonic tendencies in the interpretation of Ammonius; Endress 1999 [*77: 4–5], D'Ancona 2005 [*107: 16–18], 2005 [*108: 35. 37. 41], more generally on the revaluation of Aristotle).

This last step, however, was never taken at Alexandria itself. For however greatly Aristotle was appreciated there, the view that his philosophy was ultimately inferior to Plato's still remained the prevailing opinion (Hadot 2015 [*130: 143–146]. This, too, can be gleaned from various pieces of evidence. We know, for example, that the Alexandrians continued to regard the study of Aristotle as a preparation for reading Plato's dialogues; this applies even to as late an author as Elias. He did not place Aristotle above Plato, even though all extant works from his pen are commentaries on the Aristotelian corpus (Westerink 1990 [*52: 336], Hadot 1991 [*54: 181. 185], 1992 [*58: 414–415]). The anonymously transmitted *Prolegomena* to Platonic philosophy, which in all likelihood originated in Elias' circle (Westerink 1962 [*6: XLIX–L]), went even further in this respect, with an explicit declaration that Plato had been superior to all other thinkers – meaning the Ionian physicists, Parmenides, the Stoics, the Epicureans, and, of course, Aristotle (Westerink 1962 [*6: 16–19]).

One reason for this lasting preference for Plato will have been the suspicion with which Aristotelian metaphysics was still regarded by some authors. Not even Ammonius' Neoplatonizing interpretation could provide a remedy for this. Although it was very popular with his students (cf. p. 40 above), it does not seem to have convinced all of them. At any rate, the aforementioned *Prolegomena* to Plato's philosophy insist on diagnosing a considerable disagreement between Aristotle and Plato on questions of metaphysics (Westerink 1962 [*6: 18–19]). A similar view is put forward in the late Alexandrian commentary on the *Categories* which some scholars have ascribed to Elias, others to David (cf. pp. 41–42 above). It suggests that in his metaphysical explorations, Aristotle was too prone to be led by considerations of natural philosophy, since his *Metaphysics* followed right after his *Physics* and was essentially determined by it (Hadot 1991 [*54: 182–184], 1992 [*58: 416–418]).

Such reservations were not, however, restricted to metaphysics. Even Aristotle's achievements in the field of logic, for which he was celebrated enthusiastically in the Islamic world, received only limited recognition in Alexandria. This is evident from a passage which we find in Olympiodorus, Elias, and John Philoponus, in similar wording. According to this passage (which reproduces an older, 'Middle Platonic' argument), Plato, in his dialogues, used logical proofs without fixing the corresponding rules in writing. Aristotle, on the other hand, meticulously extracted all the rules and laid them down in his *Organon* in exemplary fashion. Nevertheless it would be wrong to rate his achievements in logic higher than Plato's. For while Plato was, obviously, able to dispense with the *Organon* in his philosophical reflections, Aristotle needed Plato's dialogues in order to identify the rules of demonstration in the first place. This could be compared to Aristotle's relationship to Homer, where a notable difference obtained likewise: Homer had been able to compose his works without any knowledge of Aristotle's *Poetics*, whereas Aristotle had to rely on Homer's epics when composing his *Poetics* (Hadot 1991 [*54: 187–188], 1992 [*58: 422–423], 2015 [*130: 143–144]).

4 Philosophy and the Sciences

The late Alexandrians thus adhered to the old, traditional view which placed Plato above Aristotle. In any case one has the impression that with the exception of Damascius and, in particular, John Philoponus, philosophy in late antiquity did not really explore new territory but on the whole remained confined to imparting time-tested doctrines to an ever diminishing clientele, while increasingly losing its institutional backing (Goulet 2007 [*116: 60–61]). However, this appraisal does not quite capture all the circumstances which were to prove significant for the development of philosophy in the Islamic world. For it was not only in the schools of Athens and Alexandria that philosophical knowledge was transmitted; it was passed on in other contexts as well. Of particular importance in this respect were the sciences, which also laid great store by a proper philosophical education, thus creating a further channel for the acquisition and transmission of philosophical knowledge. It proved to be a stable channel, which was to have momentous consequences for the later Arabic reception (on the topic in general see Dihle 1986 [*22], Hadot 1998 [*75]; on its significance for the Arabic speaking world see Endress 2003 [*95: 47–48], 2007 [*115: 320–322]).

Medicine played a rather conspicuous role in this context. Due to the medics' interest in physiology as well as in the ethical implications that presented themselves to the medical profession it seems to have been particularly apt to attach itself to philosophy (Dihle 1986 [*22: 209]). Apart from that it had long since had the reputation of being the only individual science which could equal philosophy in its claim to being an *ars vitae* (see Flashar's discussion of Dihle 1986 [*22: 230]). It was Galen (d. around 216; on his person and life see Véronique Boudon in: DPhA 2000 [*37: III 440–466]) who finally took the decisive step: he was convinced that every physician needed to possess profound philosophical knowledge. This conviction is not only reflected in his programmatic work *The Best Doctor is also a Philosopher*, but also in the very fact that Galen wrote numerous works on philosophy, in which he discussed the opinions of the four great schools which were still competing against each other in his day (Platonists, Aristotelians, Stoics, and Epicureans; cf. the respective titles in the list of works drawn up by Boudon in: DPhA 2005 [*37: III 463–465]). This can make Galen's exposition sometimes seem eclectic, especially since he never championed any particular school wholeheartedly (Frede 2003 [*96: 74]). Nonetheless he did follow authorities: Hippocrates in the field of medicine, Plato in philosophy. For this we have an eloquent witness in his nine volume work *The Doctrines of Hippocrates and Plato*. Moreover, it is possible to show that Galen aligned himself with Platonic positions on many important issues (Frede 2003 [*96: 75–81]; Tieleman 2003 [*101: 135–136. 160–161]).

The thoughts voiced by Galen found approval for centuries to come. Thus we still find John Philoponus praising him as a physician who also was a true philosopher (Strohmaier 2003 [*99: 310]); and in general the link between medicine and philosophy was never really broken. On the contrary: physicians in Alexandria were increasingly delving into philosophy (Westerink 1964 [*7]), intensifying in particular the study of logic (Gutas 1999 [*78: 172–174]). One visible indication of this is the professional profile of the physician-philosopher, which rose to increasing prominence. It had, of course, been moulded by Galen; but in its characteristic form it seems to have emerged only in late ancient Alexandria (Westerink 1964 [*7: 169. 175]).

Mathematics was another subject of eminent importance. It was already surrounded by a special aura, given that the philosophers themselves had elevated it to the rank of paradigmatic science. The reason Plato gave for doing so was that mathematics draws our attention away from sense perception and prepares us for the cognition of intelligibles. For him, mathematics constituted the first step of a dialectical ascent which rendered it indispensable as propaedeutics for Platonic philosophy (Dihle 1986 [*22: 193. 195. 213]). Pythagoras appears to have gone even further; at least that is what the Pythagoreans reported about him later. According to them, he declared mathematics itself to be the goal of contemplation, thus to all intents and purposes identifying it with philosophy (Dihle 1986 [*22: 213]). Both perspectives reappear in Neopythagoreanism (Dihle 1986 [*22: 213–214]; on individual representatives see Riedweg 2007 [*120: 163–166]). From there, the path leads on to Iamblichus, in whose *œuvre* mathematics occupies a particularly prominent place, as we have seen above (cf. pp. 34–35). Mathematics ranked highly with the Athenian philosophers as well (cf. Hadot 1998 [*75: 235–236] on Proclus' commentary on Euclid), and even more so with the late Alexandrians. They combined philosophy with mathematics – as *e.g.* Ammonius and Philoponus – or even were mathematicians with philosophical interests – as *e.g.* Eutocius (cf. p. 41 above; on Philoponus' commentary on Nicomachus cf. Giovanna R. Giardina in: DPhA 2012 [*37: Va 489–491]). Therefore it is not really surprising that the title of 'philosopher' was also used for mathematicians, well into the 6th century (Dihle 1986 [*22: 210]).

Obvious connections likewise existed between philosophy and astronomy, even if perhaps not quite so closely-knit. They went back first and foremost to Ptolemy (2nd cent.), who combined his astronomical calculations with Aristotelian methodology and cosmology (Endress 2007 [*115: 323]). And it was in an Aristotelian spirit when, in the preface to his *Almagest*, he counted mathematics among the disciplines of theoretical philosophy. In terms of its precision and the certainty of its findings he even regarded mathematics as theoretical philosophy's most reliable part: nothing but mathematics, Ptolemy claimed, could ever lead us to demonstrative knowledge – a feat that neither theology or physics were able to accomplish, since they both depended on numerous conjectures, the former because its subject matter was beyond comprehension, the latter because its subject matter was in constant flux (Dihle 1986 [*22: 214–215]). This was a view that the philosophers of late antiquity would no longer have shared. An interest in maintaining connections to the science of astronomy nevertheless is manifest in their work, too. Ammonius lectured about Ptolemy (Henri Dominique Saffrey in: DPhA 1989 [*37: I 168]); his brother Heliodorus was involved in producing an edition of the *Syntaxis*. The latter furthermore appears to have concerned himself with astrology as well (Hadot 1998 [*75: 240]), an occupation likewise documented for Theon, Hypatia, and the late Olympiodorus (Westerink 1971 [*10], Saffrey in: DPhA 2005 [*37: IV 770]).

The final factor to be mentioned in this context is Christian theology. It constitutes a particular case since its relationship to philosophy was not always conceived of in the same way, but was subject to fluctuations. All the same, theologians contributed significantly to the dissemination of philosophical doctrines. First of all this concerned Platonism, which early on gained the approval of the Church Fathers; it dominated their discussions in the 4th and 5th centuries, and later on kept exerting major influence on mystically inclined authors through writings such as those by Pseudo-Dionysius (Brock 2007 [*113: 305–306]). However, in the 4th century theology also began to open up towards Aristotle's philosophy. Examples for this move can be found in the Greek Patristic authors on the one hand (cf. e.g. Eunomius, who died around AD 394; on him, see Georges Matthieu de Durand in: DPhA 2000 [*37: III 332–333]), and in the Syriac-speaking milieu on the other (cf. below, § 2.2). Their main point of interest was the theory of categories, which they applied to questions of metaphysics and Christology. Apart from that, Christian scholars studied dialectics and syllogistics. These disciplines were to arm the Christian theologians for their disputes with internal as well as external adversaries, and to generate a more general scientific systematization of their subject (Bruns 2003 [*92: 31], Endress 2007 [*115: 323]).

This was another factor that contributed to the dissemination of elements of Platonic and Aristotelian doctrine. If we add rhetorics (and rhetorical training), so-called 'popular philosophy', and the occult sciences including Hermetism (Endress 2007 [*115: 323]; on the Hermetic tradition cf. van Bladel

2009 [*123]), we see that there were a number of ways to acquire, and to pass on philosophical knowledge. All of them had their effects within the Islamic world: each of the phenomena that have just been mentioned will be encountered again in that context. For one, this concerns the connections between philosophy and the various sciences: medicine (cf. Abū Bakr al-Rāzī following in Galen's footsteps [§ 6.2]), mathematics (e.g. in al-Kindī, who combined this discipline with other traditions; see Adamson 2007 [*112: 364–370], Endress 2007 [*115: 324–350] and § 4 below), astronomy (in Abū Maʿšar [§ 9.3], but also in al-Fārābī's cosmology [§ 8]), and theology (most prominently in al-Ghazālī, who strove to support Islamic dogma through Aristotelian logic [cf. vol. 2, § 3]). However, it also extends to the image of the professions and the typology of scholars that we have mentioned, i.e. the physician-philosopher – as e.g. Abū Bakr al-Rāzī or Ibn Sīnā – or the mathematician-philosopher – as e.g. Ṯābit b. Qurra and, later, Naṣīr al-Dīn al-Ṭūsī (d. 672/1274) – to mention but a few prominent examples.

5 Channels of Transmission

5.1 'From Alexandria to Baghdad' – 5.2 The 'Harran'-Hypothesis – 5.3 The Role of the Syriac Christians – 5.4 The Appropriation of the Heritage in the Arabic Speaking World

5.1 *'From Alexandria to Baghdad'*

In view of these findings it seems unlikely that the transmission of Greek philosophy to the Arabs should have been restricted to a single strand. Instead there will have been many channels, individuals, and institutions that contributed to philosophy's passage into the Islamic world, be it in the name of philosophy itself, or by virtue of its application within the special sciences. Modern scholarship has long striven to illuminate the complex field of transmission and to delineate it more precisely. This endeavour has seen several attempts to identify a primary route which could have served as the decisive medium of transmission, or at least as its main axis.

The first and perhaps still best-known attempt of this kind is found in an essay published by Meyerhof (1930 [*4]) under the title 'Von Alexandrien nach Bagdad' ('From Alexandria to Baghdad'), in which he presented a report on the history of science which, as we know now, is preserved in several different Arabic versions. One of these versions is found in the historian al-Masʿūdī (d. 345/956). Two more versions are extant in works of Ibn Riḍwān (d. 460/1068), a Muslim physician, and Ibn Ǧumayʿ (d. 594/1198), Saladin's Jewish court physician. Apart from those there is a further version, which has been known for some time. It is transmitted by Ibn Abī Uṣaybiʿa (d. 668/1270), who ascribes it to al-Fārābī (d. 339/950–951). Entitled *On the Emergence of Philosophy* (*Fī Ẓuhūr al-falsafa*), it focuses entirely on the very question at issue here: how the discipline of philosophy came into being, and how it was transported from its Greek origins to 4th/10th century Baghdad (for the different textual witnesses and the history of their discovery see Gutas 1999 [*78: 155–157]).

According to al-Fārābī's account, it is possible to discern a continuous teaching tradition, beginning with Aristotle and leading up to al-Fārābī himself. Its route is supposed to have led *via* various stages in antiquity (described in detail in the text), until, in the end, Alexandria was the only place left where philosophy was being taught. From there philosophy found its way to the Orient. Al-Fārābī makes out several different stages on this route: the recommendation of the Christian bishops (at the behest of their ruler) to read the books of the *Organon* only up to the treatment of the figures of the categorical syllogisms (*i.e.* up to *Prior Analytics* I 7); the relocation of teaching activity (with said restriction still obtaining in the curriculum) from Alexandria to Antioch in the early Islamic era; the impact of scholars from Harran and Marw, who supposedly had studied with the last philosopher left in Antioch; and, at last, the arrival of philosophy in Baghdad (in the form of students of the scholars from Harran and Marw), where, after centuries of restriction, logic was once again allowed to be studied in full (transl. in Gutas 1999 [*78: 158–167]). Al-Fārābī does not say anything more concrete in this context, but we can supplement his account with some remarks made by al-Masʿūdī. He claims to know when the teaching was transferred from one location to the next: to Antioch during the reign of Caliph ʿUmar b. ʿAbd al-ʿAzīz (regn. 99–101/717–720); to Harran during the caliphate of al-Mutawakkil (regn. 232–247/847–861), and to Baghdad within a period of time marked by the reigns of al-Muʿtaḍid (regn. 279–289/892–902) and al-Muqtadir (regn. 295–320/908–932) respectively (Lameer 1997 [*72: 183–184], Gutas 1999 [*78: 165]).

The remarks sketched here are rather striking; and for a long time modern scholars took them at face value, as a historiographical report. This applies in particular to Meyerhof (1930 [*4]), who was the first to investigate and publicize the topic in his seminal study. Since then, however, numerous objections have been brought against the historicity of the picture sketched above. Strohmaier (1987 [*32: 380]) was able to prove that many of its details do not accord with historic facts as they are known to us; which is why he called it 'eine fiktive Schultradition' ('a fictitious school tradition'). Endress (1990 [*43: 16 n. 4]) likewise emphasized the discrepancy between the rather simplistic picture and the complex historical reality, but argued that it would be more appropriate to use the term 'one-sided' rather than 'fictitious'. Lameer (1997 [*72: 184–191]) concentrated on the problem why, of all places, it should be Antioch and Harran that are explicitly mentioned as stages on the (in his words 'artificial') route of transmission. Gutas, finally, drew attention to the question of when the narrative complex 'from Alexandria to Baghdad' had emerged in the first place, and why it would have been used by such divergent authors as al-Fārābī, al-Masʿūdī, Ibn Riḍwān, and Ibn Ǧumayʿ – a philosopher, a historian, and two physicians (1999 [*78: 169–187]). He suggested that we should consider the various parts of the narrative separately and distinguish between a core motive present in all four authors (to wit, the justification of the late Alexandrian medico-philosophical curriculum) and various embellishments specific to the separate versions (e.g. the anti-Christian tendencies of the narrative; or its incorporation into the history of philosophy, or of medicine).

It emerges clearly from these considerations that the intellectual impact arising from Alexandria cannot be described in the manner suggested by our 'report'. For neither did it travel by a single route leading *via* Antioch and Harran (or Marw) to Baghdad, nor did it take the shape of a mere transfer and continuation of the Alexandrian institutions as such. It is, however, equally clear that the Arabic authors referred to Alexandria when giving a justification for their activities; and there was a good reason for this, as scholars unanimously agree (Strohmaier 1987 [*32: 387–388], Endress 1990 [*43: 16–17], Lameer 1997 [*72: 184], Gutas 1999 [*78: 169–174]). Despite our qualms concerning simplifications and reductionist interpretations, we therefore can retain the conclusion that the 'report' rightly points to the fact that the Alexandrian heritage played a decisive role in the transmission of Greek thought to the Arabs.

5.2 *The 'Harran' Hypothesis*

This is much less obvious in another case, which likewise has been the object of intense discussion in recent scholarship: the question whether or not the School of Athens also had a central role to play in the transmission process, and more specifically, whether the school found an immediate continuation in Harran in Northern Mesopotamia. No such thing is mentioned anywhere in Arabic sources, but there are numerous indications that in the early Islamic era, Harran was a centre for the sciences (mathematics, and more specifically astronomy and astrology, in parts associated with Hermetic tendencies) and for philosophy (apparently of Platonic orientation). Based on these indications as well as on a number of cues from ancient texts, Michel Tardieu formulated a much-quoted hypothesis, according to which the last representatives of the School of Athens, notably Simplicius, settled in Harran when they returned to the Byzantine Empire after the period they spent at the Sasanian court (in 531–532). This is where Simplicius would have written large parts of his extensive œuvre. Apart from that, he and his colleagues supposedly taught at a Platonist school in Harran (which either had already been in existence, or was newly established by him), which survived uninterrupted well into the 4th / 10th century (Tardieu 1986 [*24], 1987 [*33], 1990 [*50]; cf. also his contribution in: DPhA 1994 [*37: II 313–314]).

Tardieu's hypothesis met with favourable reception in parts of the scholarly community and was adopted by several authors, who confirmed and supplemented his considerations (Hadot 1990 [*44: 280–289], 1996 [*70: 28–50], 2007 [*117], Thiel 1999 [*81: 41–56]) and even suggested extending the chain of Platonic tradition up to al-Fārābī, the most important philosopher of the 4th / 10th century (Vallat 2004 [*106: 17–23]). Predominantly, however, reactions have been negative. Many critics expressed the view that the hypothesis was based on doubtful assumptions, which were interpreted and combined in a speculative manner. This became manifest in numerous critical objections against individual arguments put forward by Tardieu (Gutas 1988 [*35: 44], Lameer 1997 [*72: 186–189], Luna 2001 [*86], Watts 2005 [*110], Hoffmann 2007 [*118: 141–145]), but also in several overall evaluations which took stock of, and assessed the ongoing discussion at various points in time (Endress 1990 [*43: 10], 1992 [*57: 29], Sorabji 2004 [*105: 11], D'Ancona 2005 [*107: 20 n. 42], 2005 [*108: 46–47]).

It is neither possible, nor would it be helpful to reproduce every detail of the debate here. Given the overwhelming evidence at our disposal, however, we may safely say that judging from what we know today, we will have to give up on the idea that the School of Athens continued its life in Harran. In its specific form, this assumption cannot be substantiated from the evidence that has been adduced in its favour so far. Besides, it does not match the findings which we will encounter, in the course of this volume, in many Arabic authors of the 4th / 10th century – who, were the hypothesis true, should be expected to betray some influence of a specific Athenian-Harranian tradition (cf. esp. § 5, 7, and 8). This does not, however, diminish the general importance of Harran. Without a doubt the city belonged to the places in which Greek science was fostered and passed on to the Arabic speaking world. Nevertheless we will once again be well advised not to reduce this process to one single path of transmission, but to conceive of it as taking place within a wider field containing several centres, in which many protagonists act and interact in various ways.

5.3 *The Role of the Syriac Christians*

This warning note needs to be heeded all the more as there was yet another form of reception, which had started long before the rise of Islam, and which also played an important role in our context. This is the Hellenistic tradition that had established itself with the Syriac-speaking Christians in the Near East. It has long received much scholarly attention (see the fundamental study by Baumstark 1900 [*1], 1905 [*2]). As it has turned out, the topics that deserve our attention here are immensely varied and range over a long period of time (for detailed state-of-the-art reports see Daiber 1986 [*21: 298–303], 2001 [*84]; for a compilation of the most important items of older literature see also Henri Hugonnard-Roche in: DPhA 1989 [*37: I 502–507]).

Insofar as they fall into the period after the Islamic conquest, these topics will be discussed in more detail later in this (as well as the following) volume. This applies to philosophy written in Syriac from the 8th to the 13th century (cf. § 2 and volume 2, § 10); to the contribution Syriac scholars made to the Greek-Arabic translation movement (cf. § 3.2), as well as to the role they played in the shaping of the philosophical tradition which is called the 'School of Baghdad' (cf. § 7.1). Insofar as the Syrians' activity took place in pre-Islamic times, it is not really subject-matter of this series. Therefore only a few basic outlines of the early processes of translation and appropriation from Greek into Syriac will be sketched here, insofar as they are of particular importance for our understanding of the ensuing Arabic tradition.

Reception of Greek philosophy in the Syriac-speaking realm seems to have begun in the 3rd century. Striking testimonies to this fact are the *Book of the Laws of Countries* composed by a pupil of Bardaiṣān (154–222; see Hugonnard-Roche 2007 [*119: 280 n. 3]), as well as the somewhat later œuvre of Ephrem the Syrian (306–373; see Possekel 1999 [*79]). Both furthermore indicate that during this first phase of reception, interest in Stoic thought was paramount. In addition we possess a number of early, albeit not exactly datable, texts that may be subsumed under the label 'popular philosophy'. Among other things, they touch on questions of cosmology and natural philosophy. Their main focus, however, is ethical maxims, which often circulated under the names of Greek authorities like Pythagoras or Socrates (Brock 1982 [*17: 26–27], 2003 [*91: 10–16], Possekel 1999 [*79: 30–32]).

However, parts of the *Organon* were already read at this time as well. Again it was probably in the 3rd century that they began to be studied, apparently with the schools of Antioch and Nisibis in Northern Mesopotamia in a pioneering role (Henri Hugonnard-Roche in: DPhA 1989 [*37: III 502]). Nevertheless, the occupation with Aristotle was, at first, subject to a double qualification: On the one hand, his texts were still being read in Greek at the time (limiting their audience). On the other hand, there were numerous voices among the Syriac Christians who were warning against any closer engagement with Aristotle's thought and Greek science and philosophy in general (Brock 1982 [*17: 17–19], Hugonnard-Roche 2004 [*104: 143–146]). However, this attitude changed in the course of the following centuries, in a lengthy process which Sebastian Brock (1982 [*17]) has characterized using the frequently quoted formula 'from antagonism to assimilation', and which eventually led to Aristotle being read in many schools. Once the knowledge of Greek declined in the Near East, parts of the Aristotelian corpus were translated into Syriac. This may have happened already in the 5th century, but in any case it did so in the 6th century. The oldest Syriac versions of the *Organon* that are extant date from this period (Hugonnard-Roche in: DPhA 1989 [*37: I 502], 2004 [*104: 12–13], 2007 [*119: 282]). It was in connection with them and, apparently, at the time of their emergence, that the scientific engagement with Aristotle in the Syriac language seems to have had its beginning.

The most important witness to this development is Sergius of Rešʿaina (d. 536). Having himself studied in Alexandria (probably with Ammonius), he became one of the main contributors to the assimilation and dissemination of Greek learning among Syriac Christians. As indicated by Sergius' extensive list of works (for brief surveys see Endress 1987 [*25: 409] and Hugonnard-Roche 1989 [*38: 6–8]; for a more detailed account Hugonnard-Roche 2004 [*104: 125–132]), three subject areas received his attention: (1) The main focus of his work was medicine, where Sergius earned himself special merits through his translation activities. The Syriac versions he produced of numerous works by Galen, at all events, remained in use for centuries (Hugonnard-Roche 2004 [*104: 125–127]). (2) Another area he was interested in was theology. In this context it is noteworthy in particular that he was the first to translate the writings of Pseudo-Dionysius the Areopagite into Syriac [*104: 127–128]. (3) Sergius also produced a considerable œuvre in the field of philosophy. We are in possession of a whole range of philosophical writings authored by Sergius himself (for a list of his works, with information on manuscripts and editions, see [*104: 128–131]). They include two commentaries, or treatises, on the *Categories* ([*104: 136–142. 149–164]; cf. also Hugonnard-Roche 2007 [*119: 286], where the close parallels between these texts and the commentaries on the *Categories* by Ammonius and John Philoponus are pointed out once more); a treatise on genus, species, and individual; a list of philosophical definitions; an explication of the meaning of the word 'figure' in Aristotelian syllogistics; a (lost) treatise on the concept of time; a translation of the Pseudo-Aristotelian tract *On the Universe* (on this, see Wim Raven in: DPhA 2003 [*37: Suppl. 481]); as well as, finally, a cosmological work 'according to the doctrine of Aristotle', which ultimately goes back to a work by Alexander of Aphrodisias (see Genequand 2001 [*85: 34]).

Next to Sergius of Rešʿaina, the most important representative of the early Greek-Syriac scientific tradition to be mentioned here is Prōbā (see now Hugonnard-Roche in: DPhA 2012 [*37: Vb 1539–1542]). Earlier scholarship had placed him in the 5th century, but more recent studies of his texts, in respect of both language and content, have shown that he was in fact active in the 6th century, perhaps even after Sergius (this was first indicated in Brock 1983 [*18: 12]; for a more detailed account see Hugonnard-Roche 2004 [*104: 60–67. 86–91]). Of Prōbā's writings three works are available so far in (partly incomplete) editions (for a survey see Brock 1993 [*61: 7. 11. 13–14]): a commentary on the *Isagoge* (see the detailed account in Hugonnard-Roche 2004 [*104: 86–91]), a commentary on *On Interpretation* [*104: 60–67. 275–291], and an interpretation of the first part of the *Prior Analytics* (i.e. up to I 7). Like the works penned by Sergius, these writings exhibit close parallels to several Alexandrian authors of the 6th century (Ammonius, John Philoponus, Olympiodorus, and their pupils; see Hugonnard-Roche 2007 [*119: 286]).

These details immediately reveal that in terms of subject area, the early Syriac reception was centred all but exclusively on Aristotelian logic. This applies to translations from the Greek no less than to original works written in Syriac which served to analyse and explicate the translated texts (information on all translations and commentaries can be found in Brock 1993 [*61: 11–15], Hugonnard-Roche in: DPhA 1989 [*37: I 507–528], 2004 [*104: 12–16], 2007 [*119: 284–286]). In fact, the focus of philosophical interest can be narrowed down even further. For in the older Syriac tradition, the *Organon* was really only read up to *Prior Analytics* I 7, i.e. up to and including the figures of the categorical syllogisms (Hugonnard-Roche in: DPhA 1989 [*37: I 505], 2004 [*104: 16], 2007 [*119: 283]). Therefore al-Fārābī was not entirely wrong when, in *On the Appearance of Philosophy*, he pointed out this limitation of logical instruction as practiced by Christian scholars (cf. above p. 52). However, al-Fārābī's remark is far too general, for this restriction of the curriculum was not lifted only in Baghdad around his own time (4th/10th cent.); there are indications that the entire *Organon* was being studied in Syriac much earlier than that. We possess, for instance, an unabridged version of the *Prior Analytics* which is ascribed to George, Bishop of the Arabs (d. 724; see Hugonnard-Roche in: DPhA 1989 [*37: I 517], 2007 [*119: 286–287]). Moreover, there are reports claiming that as early as the 7th century, the scholar Athanasius of Balad (d. 686) translated the *Posterior Analytics*, the *Topics*, and the *Sophistical Refutations* into Syriac (Hugonnard-Roche 1991 [*55: 189], 2004 [*104: 19. 39–40], 2007 [*119: 283 n. 13]; cf. below § 2.3.2).

In comparison with logic, other areas of philosophy merely played a minor role. In so far as they did constitute a subject of study at all, this is documented by few and disparate witnesses only. It appears to be certain that metaphysics was discussed, at least in parts. This can be gleaned from Jacob of Edessa's (d. 708) *Handbook* (*Encheiridion*), within which individual passages from Aristotle's *Metaphysics* are quoted in Syriac (Hugonnard-Roche 2004 [*104: 13.

52–53]). We may further assume that Plotinus was not entirely unknown. The Syriac translation of the scholia which John of Scythopolis (1st half of the 6th cent.) composed on works by Pseudo-Dionysius the Areopagite contains several passages which are clearly identifiable as quotations from *Enneads* I, III, and V (on the significance of these quotations, see Beierwaltes, Kannicht 1968 [*8]; on the Syriac translation, Frank 1987 [*26]; for a summary account, Brock 2007 [*113: 296–297. 302]). Beyond this, the early Syriac tradition remains a matter for speculation and conjecture. For instance, the information that Sergius of Rešʿaina wrote a (lost) treatise on time (Hugonnard-Roche 2004 [*104: 128]) may well indicate that the *Physics* was read in the Syriac-speaking world, without, however, offering any real clarity on this point (Hugonnard-Roche 2007 [*119: 289–290], who furthermore draws attention to the dissemination of some Pseudo-Aristotelian works).

This is why a rather different point is of much more consequence; leaving behind individual philosophical topics and the corresponding Aristotelian works, we shall turn to the question how Aristotle was rated by Syriac scholars more fundamentally – after they had traversed the distance 'from antagonism to assimilation'. An illuminating piece of testimony in this respect is provided by Sergius of Rešʿaina, who, in the prologue to one of his commentaries on the *Categories*, makes the following declaration: 'Aristotle was the origin, the beginning, and the principle of all knowledge, not just for Galen and all other physicians like him, but also for all those authors called philosophers who came after him. Up to the time when this man [i.e. Aristotle] entered the world, all parts of philosophy and knowledge were actually separate, like simple drugs, and were scattered among the [different] authors without order or scientific system. He on his own then joined together the scattered parts like a learned physician, united them through his art and science, and composed from them the perfect elixir of his teaching, which will cure from the disease of ignorance all those who earnestly devote themselves to his books' (Hugonnard-Roche 1989 [*38: 9–10], 2004 [*104: 168]).

These few sentences reveal how highly Aristotle was esteemed by Sergius, and probably by the other Syriac authors of his day. Their understanding of philosophy was no longer based on the harmony of Plato and Aristotle, as it had been for the Alexandrians, but apparently was defined entirely by their respect for the Stagirite. In consequence the Aristotelian corpus was not read any more as preparation for the study of Plato's dialogues. It stood on its own, because Aristotle had become the wellspring and yardstick of all knowledge, and was now considered as the true authority independent of anyone else (Hugonnard-Roche 1991 [*55: 188], 2004 [*104: 180–181], D'Ancona 2005 [*107:

19–20]). This estimation may at first have been little more than a postulate; after all, the Syriac authors normally knew only a small number of texts. Their philosophical activity was more or less confined to commenting on the *Organon* (or parts of it), and to applying it to their own arguments. Nevertheless their unequivocal allegiance to Aristotle deserves our attention, as it indicates a further significant step within the process that saw Aristotle being reappraised and rising to new esteem. As we have seen already, this process had begun back in Alexandria, and was now carried on by the Christian theologians, in both Greek and Syriac.

Lastly, we ought to mention that the Syrians also played an important role in the transmission of other ancient traditions of knowledge. For the philosophy and science that developed within Islamic culture did not only rely on the heritage of Greek antiquity; the scholars in the Islamic world also drew on the Indian scientific tradition, especially in the fields of astronomy and medicine (Endress 1987 [*25: 413–416]). In addition, they could take recourse to a vast Iranian heritage, which comprised several fields of knowledge, though it came with a particular focus on ethico-political maxims (mirrors for princes) and wisdom literature (Endress 1987 [*25: 412]). However, the Iranian tradition was itself already hellenized, having long since been part of a Near-Eastern community habitually trading ideas as well as goods. This is how the Syriac-speaking Christians come into play here yet again, as they settled in Byzantine as well as Sasanian lands, and contributed materially to the transmission of knowledge between both areas.

The most notable example for this transmission process is a scholar who became known by the name of Paul the Persian (see now Hugonnard-Roche in: DPhA 2012 [*37: Va 183–187]). He lived in the 6th century in the Sasanian Empire, perhaps even in its capital, Seleucia-Ctesiphon (Teixidor 2003 [*100: 27]; more cautiously Hugonnard-Roche 2004 [*104: 233–234]). At any event he must have been in contact with the Sasanian court, since several of his works are dedicated to Ḫusraw Anūšīrvān (regn. 531–578/9; Michel Tardieu in: DPhA 1994 [*37: II 315–316]). Only two of Paul's works are preserved, interestingly in Syriac versions: (1) a treatise on logic, which has been available in print for a long time; it summarizes various elements of the first parts of the *Organon*, apparently with the intended purpose of introducing beginners to Aristotelian syllogistics (Hugonnard-Roche 2004 [*104: 236–254. 259–260]; cf. also Teixidor 2003 [*100]); (2) a commentary on *On Interpretation*, which is as yet unedited; nonetheless it is now possible to gain information on its salient points since a first analysis of its contents has been provided recently (Hugonnard-Roche 2004 [*104: 260–269]). Paul the Persian furthermore wrote (3) an introduction to Aristotle's philosophy, again with a special focus on logic. Even though the original appears to be lost, parts of the work have been reconstructed from a later textual witness in Arabic (Gutas 1983 [*19]).

It is not entirely clear which language these texts were composed in originally. Current scholarship inclines towards the assumption that they were written in Middle Persian (Pahlavi; Endress 1987 [*25: 408]; for individual arguments cf. § 2.3.1 below). Nevertheless there are several indications that Paul was proficient in Syriac and that he received his entire philosophical education in Syriac (Hugonnard-Roche 2004 [*104: 234], now also in: DPhA 2012 [*37: Va 184–185]). Independently of that, there is a good amount of evidence that places his œuvre in the proximity of works by Sergius of Reš'aina and Prōbā. For Paul, too, was at pains to establish Aristotelian logic as the foundation of scientific thought, and like them he went about this in a way that is reminiscent of the *Prolegomena* literature and the commentaries of the late Alexandrians (Gutas 1983 [*19: 238–250. 261–265], Hugonnard-Roche 2004 [*104: 239. 253–254. 270–273]). Therefore we are justified in placing him in one and the same line with the two other authors, despite the geographical distance between them: Sergius, Prōbā, and Paul appear to have been the most prominent Syriac-speaking scholars of the 6th century, and each of them in his own way contributed to the dissemination of Greek thought throughout the Near East, as far as Iran.

5.4 *The Appropriation of the Heritage in the Arabic Speaking World*

There seem to have been, then, many channels through which ancient philosophy and science was preserved and passed on. Its transmission to the Arabic speaking world neither took place along a specific route with a determined course (from Alexandria to Baghdad), nor was its course set in a single late ancient city (Harran), where it was decided which authors and texts were going to be transmitted, and at what scale (D'Ancona 2005 [*108: 41–47]). As far as we can tell, the transmission process is likely to have been much more complex (see most recently D'Ancona 2007 [*114: XXI–XXXIII], using data from Ibn al-Nadīm's *Fihrist* as examples). Spanning a vast geographic area, it comprised several cultures and languages (mainly Greek, Syriac, and Middle Persian). The schools and educational institutions which are mentioned time and again in this context are dispersed across Palestine, Syria, and Mesopotamia, as far as Southwest Iran. Among them are, to name but the most important: Caesarea, Antioch, Qenneshre (on the upper Euphrates), Edessa, Harran, Nisibis, Mar Mattai (near Mosul), Seleucia-Ctesiphon, and Gundishapur in the province of Khuzestan (Aubert Martin in: DPhA 1989 [*37: I 528–529], Hugonnard-Roche

2004 [*104: 6–9], D'Ancona 2005 [*107: 20]; further localities named in Yousif 2003 [*102: 91–98]).

Moreover, the listing of places where the ancient intellectual heritage was transmitted in pre-Islamic times has only limited heuristic benefits for our understanding of the Greek-Arabic translation movement. For the recourse that the new society took to Greek philosophy cannot be explained simply as a continuation of earlier efforts to appropriate the Greek heritage. Instead, it was an active process which developed its own access to ancient philosophy and science, and in its scope and quality went far beyond any previous transmission processes in the Near East for which we have evidence. This circumstance was recognized early on by modern scholarship. Thus it has long been known that eminent translators like Ḥunayn b. Isḥāq (d. ca. 260/873) did not simply work on texts they happened to come across, but expended great efforts in order to acquire profound knowledge of the Greek language, undertaking long journeys (to Alexandria as well as into Byzantine territory) in order to locate previously unknown works and manuscripts (cf. e.g. Strohmaier 1987 [*32: 388]). However, only in recent times has the Arabic appropriation of the ancient heritage been examined as a major historical phenomenon. The decisive impetus was provided by Gutas (1998 [*74]), who was able to demonstrate how the translation activity developed from its first, rather pragmatic beginnings in the 2nd/8th century into a broad movement which was supported politically and socially, and in the course of which Arabic-Islamic society consciously instated itself as the heir and new representative of erstwhile Greek philosophy and science (for details see § 3.1 below).

This furthermore explains why the body of writings translated into Arabic deviates significantly from the textual *corpora* maintained previously in other contexts. It is neither equivalent to the canon of texts read for philosophical instruction in late Alexandria, despite numerous overlaps; nor can it be compared to the rather short list of works which were studied and transmitted in Syriac (though Brock 2003 [*91: 18 n. 41] warns us not to underestimate the Syriac contribution at the beginning of the Greek-Arabic translation activities). This is not the place to give a detailed description of the composition of the corpus (for this, cf. § 3.5 below); but we shall briefly sketch its general outlook and main focal points, so as to give an idea how it was related to the major trends of late antique philosophy.

Fundamentally, the Arabic translations made most of the philosophical works that were read or composed in late antiquity accessible to a new readership. This point will be all the more valid if we do not restrict late ancient philosophy to Neoplatonism, but understand it in a broader sense, i.e. as a predominantly Neoplatonic critical engagement with Plato and Aristotle in the vein of the 'philosophy of the commentators' mentioned at the beginning of this chapter (cf. p. 29 above). At the same time, it means that schools and trends that already had taken a back seat within the Greek context did not play any role within the Arabic transmission, either. This applies to the Stoics, Epicureans, Presocratics and Socratics, as well as to any other philosophical currents which had all but vanished from the Greek textual tradition (Goulet 2007 [*116: 49–53]). In the corpus of Arabic translations they find themselves at the margins again: what little material needs to be mentioned here concerns the Stoics (Gutas 1994 [*65: 4959–4963], who, in addition, mentions a few reminiscences of Cynics and Sceptics) and the hellenistic-imperial doxography which is represented first and foremost by the translation of the *Placita Philosophorum* by Aetius (Pseudo-Plutarch; Daiber 1980 [*16], 1994 [*64]).

However, within the shared Platonic-Aristotelian framework positions were shifting considerably in comparison with the late Greek schools. The first and most noticable shift concerns Plato himself, whose dialogues are not extant in Arabic, and quite likely were never translated as such into Arabic. Whatever the Arabs knew about Plato they owed to quotations in works by other authors, and to various later summaries of his works. In this respect, the epitomes composed by Galen were of particular significance within the transmitted material (for details see Dimitri Gutas in: DPhA 2012 [*37: Va 845–863]; cf. also Arnzen 2011 [*126: 1–12]).

Galen's name also marks a second crucial difference. He made his impact not only through the transmission of Platonic texts, but also through his own philosophical works. They were much more influential in the Arabic speaking world – at least in the early period – than they ever had been in the philosophical instruction of late antiquity. The reason for this is linked to the transmission situation: as mentioned above (cf. pp. 48–51), philosophical ideas were passed on to the Arabs not just on their own, but more often than not in connection with the sciences. Among the sciences, however, medicine played a prominent role. This explains why Galen's works were translated in unusually large numbers, and why together with his medical works his philosophical writings were disseminated as well (on Galen's significance, see Endress 1992 [*57: 117–121], on the continual influence of his ethics Strohmaier 2003 [*99]; on his great impact on Abū Bakr al-Rāzī cf. § 6.2 below).

Neoplatonism was broadly received in Arabic. Again, though, one needs to be aware of a peculiarity here: the extant Arabic versions as a rule are no faithful translations of the Greek originals we know, but convey their contents with alterations and interpretative additions. This indicates that Neoplatonic thought was still very much alive and was transmitted not as a static body of doctrine but as a still developing philosophical tradition. The most famous example of this kind is the *Arabic Plotinus* paraphrase, an adaptation of *Enneads* IV–VI, including, among other texts, the so-called *Theology of Aristotle* (Adamson 2002 [*87], D'Ancona 2003 [*94: 72–91], 2004 [*103]; on the long-standing question whether there ever existed a Syriac version of this text, see most recently Brock 2007 [*113]). Proclus' *Elements of Theology* provided a further important source of inspiration. It forms the basis of the *Liber de Causis* (D'Ancona 1995 [*68]; for its multi-layered history of transmission see now Wakelnig 2007 [*121]), as well as of a further paraphrase, which has become known as *Proclus Arabus* (Endress 1973 [*11], Zimmermann 1994 [*66]; for the entire transmission complex cf. also the various contributions in Kraye, Ryan, Schmitt 1986 [*23]). However, Arabic readers had even more opportunities to be introduced to Neoplatonic (and Neo-Pythagorean) thought: works by Porphyry and further works by Proclus are attested, and in parts preserved in Arabic (for Porphyry see Henri Hugonnard-Roche in: DPhA 2012 [*37: Vb 1447–1468], for Proclus see Gerhard Endress in: DPhA 2012 [*37: Vb 1657–1674]), as are certain texts by Nicomachus (for information see Endress 2007 [*115: 341–342]) and Iamblichus (Daiber 1995 [*67], Wakelnig 2014 [*129: 37–39]). Iamblichus' agenda of fusing Neoplatonism and Neo-Pythagoreanism moreover found its own adherents and will have exerted considerable influence on writings like the *Rasā'il Iḫwān al-Ṣafā'* (*The Epistles of the Brethren of Purity*; Straface 1987 [*30], Baffioni 1994 [*62]; on the Iḫwān al-Ṣafā' cf. § 9.4.2 below). In addition there were influential pseudo-epigraphical works like the texts of Pseudo-Empedocles (De Smet 1998 [*73]) and Pseudo-Ammonius (Rudolph 1989 [*40]). Moreover, due to the many elements within Neoplatonic thought that allowed it to be connected to decidedly religious interests, it left its mark not only within the narrow framework of philosophy, but was also taken up by Christian as well as Muslim theologians (for Christianity see Bruns 2003 [*92: 31], Brock 2007 [*113: 305–306]; for Islam see van Ess 2005 [*109]).

Even so it was not Neoplatonism that became the determining element within the body of texts that was shaped by the Arabic translations; this role was to be reserved for the writings belonging to the Aristotelian tradition. At its centre, of course, stood the master himself. Almost his entire œuvre was translated into Arabic (D'Ancona 2008 [*122: 154. 156–158]). However, the Arabic reception did not confine itself to the Aristotelian corpus only, but also included the extensive commentary literature from late antiquity, which to a large extent was translated as well. Interestingly, it was not the 'Neoplatonic' commentators from Athens and Alexandria that occupied the most prominent positions in this process (even though authors like Ammonius or Olympiodorus were indeed known to the Arabs; see D'Ancona 2008 [*122: 163–164]). Instead, the greatest attention was directed towards exegetes of a somewhat different profile: Themistius (Brague 1999 [*76: 9–14], D'Ancona 2008 [*122: 163]), John Philoponus (D'Ancona 2008 [*122: 164]), and first and foremost Alexander of Aphrodisias (D'Ancona, Serra 2002 [*88], D'Ancona 2008 [*122: 161–162]). This resulted in the constitution of a comprehensive *Corpus Aristotelicum* or, rather, *Corpus Peripateticum*, which replaced the old canon of instruction and turned Aristotelian philosophy into a synonym for science. Thus another stage of the development was completed: following Porphyry's decision in favour of the 'harmony' between Plato and Aristotle, the late Alexandrians' growing interest in the Stagirite, and Sergius of Reš'aina's avowed commitment to his exceptional position, in the 4th/10th century, when the Greek-Arabic translation process was completed, Aristotle was finally elevated to the position of sole master of knowledge and demonstrative science. For it was the Arabic Aristotle who established philosophy as universal mode of demonstration and claimed comprehensive authority for it; and it was his Arabic followers at whose hands Plato, who in late ancient Hellenism still had been the one to provide guidance to the deepest secrets of speculative philosophy, was finally banished from the realm of the theoretical sciences, and demoted to a mere harbinger of absolute and comprehensive rationalism (Endress 1999 [*77: 7]).

6 Secondary Literature

1 Baumstark, Anton. *Aristoteles bei den Syrern vom V.–VIII. Jahrhundert.* Leipzig, 1900.

2 Baumstark, Anton. "Griechische Philosophen und ihre Lehren in syrischer Überlieferung." *Oriens Christianus* 5 (1905): 1–25.

3 Praechter, Karl. "Richtungen und Schulen im Neuplatonismus." In *Genethliakon. Carl Robert zum 8. März 2010.* Berlin, 1910, 105–156. – Repr. in Praechter, *Kleine Schriften*. Ed. by Heinrich Dörrie. Hildesheim, New York, 1973, 165–216.

4 Meyerhof, Max. "Von Alexandrien nach Bagdad. Ein Beitrag zur Geschichte des philosophischen und medizinischen Unterrichts bei den Arabern." *Sitzungsberichte der Preussischen Akademie der Wissenschaften. Philologisch-historische Klasse* 23 (1930): 389–429.

5 Richard, Marcel. "Ἀπὸ φωνῆς." *Byzantion* 20 (1950): 191–222. – Repr. in Richard, *Opera Minora*, vol. 3. Turnhout, Leiden, 1977, no. 60.

6 Westerink, Leendert G., ed. *Anonymous Prolegomena to Platonic Philosophy. Introduction, Text, Translation and Indices.* Amsterdam, 1962. – New edition with French transl.: *Prolégomènes à la philosophie de Platon.* Transl. by Jean Trouillard and Alain-Philippe Segonds. Paris, 1990.

7 Westerink, Leendert G. "Philosophy and Medicine in Late Antiquity." *Janus* 51 (1964): 169–177. – Repr. in Westerink, *Texts and Studies in Neoplatonism and Byzantine Literature. Collected Papers by L. G. Westerink*. Amsterdam, 1980, 83–91.

8 Beierwaltes, Werner and Richard Kannicht. "Plotin-Testimonia bei Johannes von Skythopolis." *Hermes* 96 (1968): 247–251.

9 Saffrey, Henri D. and Leendert G. Westerink, eds. *Proclus. Théologie platonicienne*, 6 vols. Paris, 1968–1997.

10 Westerink, Leendert G. "Ein astrologisches Kolleg aus dem Jahr 564." *Byzantinische Zeitschrift* 64 (1971): 6–21. – Repr. in L. G. Westerink 1980 [cf. *7], 279–294.

11 Endress, Gerhard. *Proclus Arabus. Zwanzig Abschnitte aus der* Institutio *theologica in arabischer Übersetzung*. Beirut, Wiesbaden, 1973.

12 Westerink, Leendert G. *The Greek Commentaries on Plato's Phaedo*, vol. 1: *Olympiodorus*. Amsterdam, Oxford, New York, 1976.

13 Blumenthal, Henry J. "529 and its Sequel. What Happened to the Academy?" *Byzantion* 48 (1978): 369–385.

14 Hadot, Ilsetraut. *Le problème du néoplatonisme alexandrin. Hiérocles et Simplicius*. Paris, 1978.

15 Szlezák, Thomas A. *Platon und Aristoteles in der Nuslehre Plotins*. Basel, Stuttgart, 1979.

16 Daiber, Hans. *Aetius Arabus. Die Vorsokratiker in arabischer Überlieferung*. Wiesbaden, 1980.

17 Brock, Sebastian. "From Antagonism to Assimilation. Syriac Attitudes to Greek Learning." In *East of Byzantium. Syria and Armenia in the Formative Period, Dumbarton Oaks Symposium 1980*. Ed. by Nina Garsoïan, Thomas Mathews, and Robert Thomson. Washington D.C., 1982, 17–34. – Repr. in Brock, *Syriac Perspectives on Late Antiquity*. London, 1984, no. V.

18 Brock, Sebastian. "Towards a History of Syriac Translation Technique." In *III Symposium Syriacum 1980. Les contacts du monde syriaque avec les autres cultures*. Ed. by René Lavenant. Rome, 1983, 1–14. – Repr. in Brock, *Studies in Syriac Christianity. History, Literature, Theology*. London, 1992, no. X.

19 Gutas, Dimitri. "Paul the Persian on the Classification of the Parts of Aristotle's Philosophy. A Milestone between Alexandria and Baġdād." *Der Islam* 60 (1983): 231–267.

20 Hein, Christel. *Definition und Einteilung der Philosophie. Von der spätantiken Einleitungsliteratur zur arabischen Enzyklopädie*. Frankfurt a.M., Bern, New York, 1985.

21 Daiber, Hans. "Semitische Sprachen als Kulturvermittler zwischen Antike und Mittelalter. Stand und Aufgaben der Forschung." *Zeitschrift der Deutschen Morgenländischen Gesellschaft* 136 (1986): 292–313.

22 Dihle, Albrecht. "Philosophie – Fachwissenschaft – Allgemeinbildung." In *Aspects de la philosophie hellénistique*. Ed. by Hellmut Flashar and Olof Gigon. Vandœuvres-Genève, 1986, 185–223.

23 Kraye, Jill, W. F. Ryan, and C. B. Schmitt, eds. *Pseudo-Aristotle in the Middle Ages. The Theology and Other Texts*. London, 1986.

24 Tardieu, Michel. "Ṣābiens coraniques et 'Ṣābiens' de Ḥarrān." *Journal asiatique* 174 (1986): 1–44.

25 Endress, Gerhard. "Die wissenschaftliche Literatur." In *Grundriss der arabischen Philologie*, vol. 2: *Literaturwissenschaft*. Ed. by Helmut Gätje. Wiesbaden, 1987, 400–506.

26 Frank, Richard M. "The Use of the Enneads by John of Scythopolis." *Le Muséon* 100 (1987): 101–108. – Repr. in Frank, *Philosophy, Theology and Mysticism in Medieval Islam*, vol. 1: *Texts and Studies on the Development and History of Kalām*. Ed. by Dimitri Gutas. Aldershot, 2005, no. V.

27 Hadot, Ilsetraut. "La division néoplatonicienne des écrits d'Aristote." In *Aristoteles. Werk und Wirkung*, vol. 2: *Kommentierung, Überlieferung, Nachleben*. Ed. by Jürgen Wiesner. Berlin, New York, 1987, 249–285.

28 Hadot, Ilsetraut. "Les introductions aux commentaires exégétiques chez les auteurs néoplatoniciens et les auteurs chrétiens." In *Les règles de l'interprétation*. Ed. by Michel Tardieu. Paris, 1987, 99–122.

29 Sorabji, Richard, ed. *Philoponus and the Rejection of Aristotelian Science*. London, 1987, 2010 (2nd ed.).

30 Straface, Antonella. "Testimonianze pitagoriche alla luce di una filosofia profetica. La numeralogia pitagorica negli Iḫwān al-Ṣafā'." *Annali dell'Istituto Orientale di Napoli* 47 (1987): 225–241.

31 Strange, Steven K. "Plotinus, Porphyry, and the Neoplatonic Interpretation of the Categories." In *Aufstieg und Niedergang der Römischen Welt*, part II, vol. 36,2. Ed. by Wolfgang Haase and Hildegard Temporini. Berlin, New York, 1987, 955–974.

32 Strohmaier, Gotthard. "'Von Alexandrien nach Bagdad' – eine fiktive Schultradition." In J. Wiesner 1987 [cf. *27], 380–389. – Repr. in Strohmaier, *Von Demokrit bis Dante. Die Bewahrung antiken Erbes in der arabischen Kultur*. Hildesheim, Zürich, New York, 1996, 313–322.

33 Tardieu, Michel. "Les calendriers en usage à Ḥarrān d'après les sources arabes et le commentaire de Simplicius à la Physique d'Aristote." In *Simplicius. Sa vie, son œuvre, sa survie. Actes du colloque international de Paris, 28 sept. – 1er oct. 1985*. Ed. by Ilsetraut Hadot. Berlin, 1987, 40–57.

34 Zimmermann, Fritz. "Philoponus' Impetus Theory in the Arabic Tradition." In R. Sorabji 1987 [*29], 121–129.

35 Gutas, Dimitri. "Plato's *Symposion* in the Arabic Tradition." *Oriens* 31 (1988): 36–60.

36 Ballériaux, Omer. “Thémistius et l’exégèse de la noétique aristotélicienne.” *Revue de philosophie ancienne* 7 (1989): 199–233.

37 DPhA = *Dictionnaire des philosophes antiques*. Ed. by Richard Goulet. Paris, vol. 1, 1989; vol. 2, 1994; vol. 3, 2000; Supplément 2003; vol. 4, 2005; vol. 5a, 2012; vol. 5b, 2012; vol. 6, 2016.

38 Hugonnard-Roche, Henri. “Aux origines de l’exégèse orientale de la logique d’Aristote. Sergius de Rešʿaina (†536), médecin et philosophe.” *Journal asiatique* 277 (1989): 1–17.

39 O’Meara, Dominic J. *Pythagoras Revived. Mathematics and Philosophy in Late Antiquity*. Oxford, 1989.

40 Rudolph, Ulrich. *Die Doxographie des Pseudo-Ammonios. Ein Beitrag zur neuplatonischen Überlieferung im Islam*. Stuttgart, 1989.

41 Blumenthal, Henry J. “Themistius. The Last Peripatetic Commentator on Aristotle?” In R. Sorabji 1990 [*48], 113–123. – First published in *Arktouros. Hellenic Studies presented to Bernard M. W. Knox on the Occasion of his 65th Birthday*. Ed. by Glen W. Bowersock, Walter Burkert and Michael C. J. Putnam. Berlin, New York, 1979, 391–400.

42 Ebbesen, Sten. “Porphyry’s Legacy to Logic. A Reconstruction.” In R. Sorabji 1990 [*48], 141–171. – First published in *Commentators on Aristotle’s Sophistici Elenchi*, vol. 1. Ed. by S. Ebbesen. Leiden, 1981, 133–170.

43 Endress, Gerhard. “The Defense of Reason. The Plea for Philosophy in the Religious Community.” *Zeitschrift für Geschichte der Arabisch-Islamischen Wissenschaften* 6 (1990): 1–49.

44 Hadot, Ilsetraut. “The Life and Work of Simplicius in Greek and Arabic Sources.” In R. Sorabji 1990 [*48], 275–303. – First published in French: “La vie et l’œuvre de Simplicius d’après des sources grecques et arabes.” In I. Hadot 1987 [cf. *33], 3–39.

45 Hadot, Pierre. “The Harmony of Plotinus and Aristotle According to Porphyry.” In R. Sorabji 1990 [*48], 125–140. – First published in French: “L’harmonie des philosophies de Plotin et d’Aristote selon Porphyre dans le commentaire de Dexippe sur les Catégories.” In *Plotino e il neoplatonismo in Oriente e in Occidente. Atti del convengo internazionale, Roma, 5–9 ottobre 1970*. Rome, 1974, 31–47.

46 Saffrey, Henri D. “How did Syrianus Regard Aristotle?” In R. Sorabji 1990 [*48], 173–179. – First published in French: “Comment Syrianus, le maître de l’école néoplatonicienne d’Athènes, considérait-il Aristote?” In J. Wiesner 1987 [cf. *27], 205–214.

47 Sorabji, Richard. “The Ancient Commentators on Aristotle.” In Sorabji 1990 [*48], 1–30.

48 Sorabji, Richard, ed. *Aristotle Transformed. The Ancient Commentators and Their Influence*. Ithaca, 1990; London, 2016 (2nd ed.).

49 Sorabji, Richard. “Infinite Power Impressed: The Transformation of Aristotle’s Physics and Theology.” In R. Sorabji 1990 [*48], 181–198.

50 Tardieu, Michel. *Les paysages reliques. Routes et haltes syriennes d'Isidore à Simplicius*. Louvain, Paris, 1990.

51 Verrycken, Koenraad. "The Metaphysics of Ammonios Son of Hermeias." In R. Sorabji 1990 [*48], 199–231.

52 Westerink, Leendert G. "The Alexandrian Commentators and the Introductions to Their Commentaries." In R. Sorabji 1990 [*48], 325–348. – Revised version of the introduction to Westerink 1962 [*6], X–XXXII.

53 Armstrong, Hilary. "Aristotle in Plotinus: The Continuity and Discontinuity of *psychê* and *nous*." In *Oxford Studies in Ancient Philosophy*. Supplementary Volume 1991: *Aristotle and the Later Tradition*. Ed. by Henry J. Blumenthal and Howard Robinson. Oxford, 1991, 117–127.

54 Hadot, Ilsetraut. "The Role of the Commentaries on Aristotle in the Teaching of Philosophy According to the Prefaces of the Neoplatonic Commentaries on the *Categories*." In H. J. Blumenthal, H. Robinson 1991 [cf. *53], 175–189.

55 Hugonnard-Roche, Henri. "L'intermédiaire syriaque dans la transmission de la philosophie grecque à l'arabe. Le cas de l'Organon d'Aristote." *Arabic Sciences and Philosophy* 1 (1991): 187–209.

56 Nüsser, Olaf. *Albins Prolog und die Dialogtheorie des Platonismus*. Stuttgart, 1991.

57 Endress, Gerhard. "Die wissenschaftliche Literatur." In *Grundriss der arabischen Philologie*, vol. 3: Supplement. Ed. by Wolfdietrich Fischer. Wiesbaden, 1992, 3–152.

58 Hadot, Ilsetraut. "Aristote dans l'enseignement philosophique néoplatonicien." *Revue de théologie et de philosophie* 124 (1992): 407–425.

59 Saffrey, Henri D. "Pourquoi Porphyre a-t-il édité Plotin? Réponse provisoire." In *Porphyre. La vie de Plotin*, vol. 2: *Etudes d'introduction, texte grec et traduction française, commentaire, notes complémentaires, bibliographie*. Ed. by Luc Brisson et al. Paris, 1992, 31–64.

60 Strange, Steven K. *Porphyry. On Aristotle's Categories*. Ithaca, 1992.

61 Brock, Sebastian. "The Syriac Commentary Tradition." In *Glosses and Commentaries on Aristotelian Logical Texts. The Syriac, Arabic and Medieval Latin Traditions*. Ed. by Charles Burnett. London, 1993, 3–18.

62 Baffioni, Carmela. *Frammenti e testimonianze di autori antichi nelle Rasāʾil degli Iḫwān al-Ṣafāʾ*. Rome, 1994.

63 Ballériaux, Omer. "Thémistius et le néoplatonisme. Le ΝΟΥΣ ΠΑΘΗΤΙΚΟΣ et l'immortalité de l'âme." *Revue de philosophie ancienne* 12 (1994): 171–200.

64 Daiber, Hans. "Hellenistisch-kaiserzeitliche Doxographie und philosophischer Synkretismus in islamischer Zeit." In *Aufstieg und Niedergang der römischen Welt*, part II, vol. 36,7. Ed. by Wolfgang Haase. Berlin, New York, 1994, 4974–4992.

65 Gutas, Dimitri. "Pre-Plotinian Philosophy in Arabic (Other than Platonism and Aristotelianism). A Review of the Sources." In W. Haase 1994 [cf. *64], 4939–4973.

66 Zimmermann, Fritz. "Proclus Arabus Rides Again." *Arabic Sciences and Philosophy* 4 (1994): 9–51.

67 Daiber, Hans. *Neuplatonische Pythagorica in arabischem Gewande. Der Kommentar des Iamblichus zu den Carmina Aurea*. Amsterdam, New York, Oxford, Tokyo, 1995.

68 D'Ancona, Cristina. *Recherches sur le Liber de Causis*. Paris, 1995.

69 Gerson, Lloyd P., ed. *The Cambridge Companion to Plotinus*. Cambridge, New York, 1996.

70 Hadot, Ilsetraut. *Simplicius, Commentaire sur le Manuel d'Épictète. Introduction et édition critique du texte grec*. Leiden, New York, Cologne, 1996.

71 Hadot, Ilsetraut. "Le commentaire philosophique continu dans l'antiquité." *Antiquité Tardive* 5 (1997): 169–176.

72 Lameer, Joep. "From Alexandria to Baghdad. Reflections on the Genesis of a Problematic Tradition." In *The Ancient Tradition in Christian and Islamic Hellenism. Studies on the Transmission of Greek Philosophy and Sciences dedicated to H. J. Drossaart Lulofs on his Ninetieth Birthday*. Ed. by Gerhard Endress and Remke Kruk. Leiden, 1997, 181–191.

73 De Smet, Daniel. *Empedocles Arabus. Une lecture néoplatonicienne tardive*. Brussels, 1998.

74 Gutas, Dimitri. *Greek Thought, Arabic Culture. The Graeco-Arabic Translation Movement in Baghdad and Early 'Abbāsid Society (2nd–4th/8th–10th centuries)*. London, 1998.

75 Hadot, Ilsetraut. "Les aspects sociaux et institutionnels des sciences et de la médecine dans l'antiquité tardive." *Antiquité Tardive* 6 (1998): 233–250.

76 Brague, Rémi. *Thémistius. Paraphrase de la Métaphysique d'Aristote (livre lambda). Traduit de l'hébreu et de l'arabe, introduction, notes et indices*. Paris, 1999.

77 Endress, Gerhard. "Le projet d'Averroès. Constitution, réception et édition du corpus des œuvres d'Ibn Rušd." In *Averroes and the Aristotelian Tradition. Sources, Constitution and Reception of the Philosophy of Ibn Rushd (1126–1198). Proceedings of the Fourth Symposium Averroicum, Cologne 1996*. Ed. by Gerhard Endress and Jan A. Aertsen. Leiden, Boston, Cologne, 1999, 3–31.

78 Gutas, Dimitri. "The 'Alexandria to Baghdad' Complex of Narratives. A Contribution to the Study of Philosophical and Medical Historiography Among the Arabs." *Documenti e studi sulla tradizione filosofica medievale* 10 (1999): 155–193.

79 Possekel, Ute. *Evidence of Greek Philosophical Concepts in the Writings of Ephrem the Syrian*. Leuven, 1999.

80 Reis, Burkhard. *Der Platoniker Albinos und sein sogenannter Prologos. Prolegomena, Überlieferungsgeschichte, kritische Edition und Übersetzung.* Wiesbaden, 1999.

81 Thiel, Rainer. *Simplikios und das Ende der neuplatonischen Schule in Athen.* Stuttgart, 1999.

82 D'Ancona, Cristina. "Syrianus dans la tradition exégétique de la Métaphysique d'Aristote, II: Antécédents et postérité." In *Le commentaire entre tradition et innovation. Actes du colloque international de l'institut des traditions textuelles, Paris et Villejuif, 22–25 septembre 1999.* Ed. by Marie-Odile Goulet-Cazé. Paris, 2000, 311–327.

82a van Riel, Gerd. *Pleasure and the Good Life. Plato, Aristotle, and the Neoplatonists.* Leiden, 2000.

83 Vinzent, Markus. "'Oxbridge' in der ausgehenden Spätantike oder: Ein Vergleich der Schulen von Athen und Alexandria." *Zeitschrift für Antikes Christentum* 4 (2000): 49–82.

84 Daiber, Hans. "Die Aristotelesrezeption in der syrischen Literatur." In *Die Gegenwart des Altertums. Formen und Funktionen des Altertumsbezugs in den Hochkulturen der Alten Welt.* Ed. by Dieter Kuhn and Helga Stahl. Heidelberg, 2001, 327–345.

85 Genequand, Charles. *Alexander of Aphrodisias on the Cosmos.* Leiden, Boston, Cologne, 2001.

85a Heather, Peter J. and David Moncur. *Politics, Philosophy and Empire in the Fourth Century: Select Orations of Themistius.* Liverpool, 2001.

86 Luna, Concetta. Review of R. Thiel [*81], *Mnemosyne* 54 (2001): 482–504.

87 Adamson, Peter. *The Arabic Plotinus. A Philosophical Study of the Theology of Aristotle.* London, 2002.

88 D'Ancona, Cristina and Giuseppe Serra, eds. *Aristotele e Alessandro di Afrodisia nella tradizione araba. Atti del colloquio La ricezione araba ed ebraica della filosofia e della scienza greche, Padova, 14–15 maggio 1999.* Padua, 2002.

89 Staab, Gregor. *Pythagoras in der Spätantike. Studien zu De Vita Pythagorica des Iamblichos von Chalkis.* Munich, Leipzig, 2002.

90 Barnes, Jonathan and Jacques Jouanna, eds. *Galien et la philosophie.* Vandœuvres-Genève, 2003.

91 Brock, Sebastian. "Syriac Translations of Greek Popular Philosophy." In P. Bruns 2003 [*93], 9–28.

92 Bruns, Peter. "Aristoteles-Rezeption und Entstehung einer syrischen Scholastik." In P. Bruns 2003 [*93], 29–41.

93 Bruns, Peter, ed. *Von Athen nach Bagdad. Zur Rezeption griechischer Philosophie von der Spätantike bis zum Islam.* Bonn, 2003.

94 D'Ancona, Cristina. *Plotino. La discesa dell'anima nei corpi* (*Enn. IV 8*[*6*]) – *Plotiniana Arabica* (*Pseudo-Teologia di Aristotele, Capitoli 1 e 7; "Detti del sapiente greco"*). Padua, 2003.

95 Endress, Gerhard. "Athen – Alexandria – Bagdad – Samarkand. Übersetzung, Überlieferung und Integration der griechischen Philosophie im Islam." In P. Bruns 2003 [*93], 42–62.

96 Frede, Michael. "Galen's Theology." In J. Barnes and J. Jouanna 2003 [*90], 73–129.

97 Radke, Gyburg. *Die Theorie der Zahl im Platonismus. Ein systematisches Lehrbuch*. Tübingen, Basel, 2003.

98 Schmitt, Arbogast. *Die Moderne und Platon*. Stuttgart, Weimar, 2003.

99 Strohmaier, Gotthard. "Die Ethik Galens und ihre Rezeption in der Welt des Islams." In J. Barnes and J. Jouanna 2003 [*90], 307–326.

100 Teixidor, Javier. *Aristote en syriaque. Paul le Perse, logicien du VIe siècle*. Paris, 2003.

101 Tieleman, Teun. "Galen's Psychology." In J. Barnes and J. Jouanna 2003 [*90], 131–161.

102 Yousif, Ephrem-Isa. *La floraison des philosophes syriaques*. Paris, Budapest, Turin, 2003.

103 D'Ancona, Cristina. "The Greek Sage, the Pseudo-*Theology of Aristotle* and the Arabic Plotinus." In *Words, Texts and Concepts Cruising the Mediterranean Sea. Studies on the Sources, Contents and Influences of Islamic Civilization and Arabic Philosophy and Science. Dedicated to Gerhard Endress on his Sixty-Fifth Birthday*. Ed. by Rüdiger Arnzen and Jörn Thielmann. Leuven, Paris, Dudley, 2004, 159–176.

104 Hugonnard-Roche, Henri. *La logique d'Aristote du grec au syriaque. Études sur la transmission des textes de l'Organon et leur interprétation philosophique*. Paris, 2004. – Contains original contributions as well as revised versions of several older articles.

105 Sorabji, Richard. *The Philosophy of the Commentators, 200–600 AD. A Sourcebook*, 3 vols. London, 2004.

106 Vallat, Philippe. *Farabi et l'école d'Alexandrie. Des prémisses de la connaissance à la philosophie politique*. Paris, 2004.

107 D'Ancona, Cristina. "Greek into Arabic. Neoplatonism in Translation." In *The Cambridge Companion to Arabic Philosophy*. Ed. by Peter Adamson and Richard C. Taylor. Cambridge, 2005, 10–31.

108 D'Ancona, Cristina. "La filosofia della tarda antichità e la formazione della falsafa" [and] "Le traduzioni di opere greche e la formazione del corpus filosofico arabo." In *Storia della filosofia nell'Islam medievale*, vol. 1. Ed. by Cristina D'Ancona. Turin, 2005, 5–47. 180–258.

109 van Ess, Josef. "Arabischer Neuplatonismus und islamische Theologie. Eine Skizze." In *Platonismus im Orient und Okzident. Neuplatonische Denkstrukturen im*

Judentum, Christentum und Islam. Ed. by Raif Georges Khoury and Jens Halfwassen. Heidelberg, 2005, 103–117.

109a Gerson, Lloyd P. *Aristotle and Other Platonists*. Ithaca, 2005.

110 Watts, Edward J. "Where to Live the Philosophical Life in the Sixth Century? Damascius, Simplicius, and the Return from Persia." *Greek, Roman, and Byzantine Studies* 45 (2005): 285–315.

111 Watts, Edward J. *City and School in Late Antique Athens and Alexandria*. Berkeley, Los Angeles, London, 2006.

112 Adamson, Peter. "The Kindian Tradition. The Structure of Philosophy in Arabic Neoplatonism." In C. D'Ancona 2007 [*114], 351–370.

113 Brock, Sebastian. "A Syriac Intermediary for the Arabic Theology of Aristotle? In Search of a Chimera." In C. D'Ancona 2007 [*114], 293–306.

114 D'Ancona, Cristina, ed. *The Libraries of the Neoplatonists. Proceedings of the Meeting of the European Science Foundation Network 'Late Antiquity and Arabic Thought. Patterns in the Constitution of European Culture' held in Strasbourg, March 12–14, 2004*. Leiden, Boston, 2007.

115 Endress, Gerhard. "Building the Library of Arabic Philosophy. Platonism and Aristotelianism in the Sources of al-Kindī." In C. D'Ancona 2007 [*114], 319–350.

116 Goulet, Richard. "La conservation et la transmission des textes philosophiques grecs." In C. D'Ancona 2007 [*114], 29–61.

117 Hadot, Ilsetraut. "Dans quel lieu le néoplatonicien Simplicius a-t-il fondé son école de mathématiques, et où a pu avoir lieu son entretien avec un manichéen" and "Remarque complémentaire." *The International Journal of the Platonic Tradition* 1 (2007): 42–107. 263–269.

118 Hoffmann, Philippe. "Les bibliothèques philosophiques d'après le témoignage de la littérature néoplatonicienne des Ve et VIe siècles." In C. D'Ancona 2007 [*114], 135–153.

119 Hugonnard-Roche, Henri. "Le Corpus philosophique syriaque aux VIe–VIIe siècles." In C. D'Ancona 2007 [*114], 279–291.

120 Riedweg, Christoph. *Pythagoras. Leben – Lehre – Nachwirkung*. Munich, 2007. – Revised version of the first edition from 2002.

121 Wakelnig, Elvira. "Al-ʿĀmirī's Paraphrase of the Proclean Elements of Theology. A Search for Possible Sources and Parallel Texts." In C. D'Ancona 2007 [*114], 457–469.

122 D'Ancona, Cristina. "Aristotle and Aristotelianism." In *Encyclopaedia of Islam*, THREE. Ed. by Gudrun Krämer et al. Leiden, Boston, 2008–11, 153–169.

123 van Bladel, Kevin. *The Arabic Hermes. From Pagan Sage to Prophet of Science*. Oxford, New York, 2009.

124 Longo, Angela, ed. *Syrianus et la métaphysique de l'antiquité tardive: Actes du colloque international, Université de Genève, 29 septembre-1er octobre 2006*. Naples, 2009.

125 Topchyan, Aram. *David the Invincible. Commentary on Aristotle's Prior Analytics. Old Armenian text with an English Translation, Introduction and Notes*. Leiden, Boston, 2010.

126 Arnzen, Rüdiger. *Platonische Ideen in der arabischen Philosophie. Texte und Materialien zur Begriffsgeschichte von ṣuwar aflāṭūniyya und muthul aflāṭūniyya*. Berlin, 2011.

127 Gertz, Sebastian Ramon Philipp. *Death and Immortality in Late Neoplatonism. Studies on the Ancient Commentaries on Plato's Phaedo*. Leiden, Boston, 2011.

128 Wear, Sarah Klitenic. *The Teachings of Syrianus on Plato's Timaeus and Parmenides*. Leiden, Boston, 2011.

129 Wakelnig, Elvira. *A Philosophy Reader from the Circle of Miskawayh*. Cambridge, New York, 2014.

130 Hadot, Ilsetraut. *Athenian and Alexandrian Neoplatonism and the Harmonization of Aristotle and Plato*. Leiden, Boston, 2015.

131 Muradyan, Gohar. *David the Invincible. Commentary on Porphyry's Isagoge. Old Armenian Text with the Greek Original, an English Translation, Introduction and Notes*. Leiden, Boston, 2015.

CHAPTER 2

The Syriac Tradition in the Early Islamic Era

Hans Daiber

1 Primary Sources – 2 Introduction – 3 Jacobite Authors – 4 Nestorian Authors – 5 A Maronite Author: Theophilus of Edessa – 6 Secondary Literature

1 Primary Sources

1 Aristotle. *Categories* [Syr. transl. by George, Bishop of the Arabs]. – Ed. by Richard James Horatio Gottheil, in "The Syriac Versions of the Categories of Aristotle." *Hebraica* 9 (1992–1993): 166–215. – Further edition (together with Aristotle's *On Interpretation*) by Giuseppe Furlani, in "Le Categorie e gli Ermeneutici di Aristotele nella versione siriaca di Giorgio delle Nazioni." *Atti dell'Accademia nazionale dei Lincei: Memorie: Classe di scienze morali, storiche e filologiche*, ser. VI, 5 (1933): 1–68.

2 Aristotle. *Categories* [anonymous Syr. transl., revised by Jacob of Edessa]. – Ed. by Khalil Georr, in *Les Catégories d'Aristote dans leurs versions syro-arabes*. Beirut, 1948, 253–305.

2a Aristotle. *Categories* [anonymous Syr. transl., attr. to Sergius of Rēšʿainā] – Ed. by Daniel King, in *The Earliest Syriac Translation of Aristotle's Categories. Text, Translation and Commentary*. Leiden, 2010.

3 Aristotle. *On Interpretation* [Syr. transl. by George, Bishop of the Arabs]. – Ed. by Giuseppe Furlani [cf. **1*]. – Partial ed. by Johann Georg Ernst Hoffmann, in *De Hermeneuticis apud Syros Aristoteleis*. Leipzig, 1869, 22–28.

4 Aristotle. *Prior Analytics* [Syr. transl. by George, Bishop of the Arabs]. – Ed. by Giuseppe Furlani, in "Il primo libro dei Primi Analitici di Aristotele nella versione siriaca di Giorgio delle Nazioni." *Atti dell'Accademia nazionale dei Lincei: Memorie: Classe di scienze morali, storiche e filologiche*, ser. VI, 5 (1935): 143–230 [and] "Il secondo libro dei Primi Analitici di Aristotele nella versione siriaca di Giorgio delle Nazioni." *Atti dell'Accademia nazionale dei Lincei: Memorie: Classe di scienze morali, storiche e filologiche*, ser. VI, 6 (1937): 233–287.

5 Aristotle. *Sophistical Refutations* [Arab. transl.]. – Ed. by ʿAbd al-Raḥmān Badawī, in *Manṭiq Arisṭū*, vol. 3. Cairo, 1952, 735–1018.

6 Porphyry. *Isagoge* [anonymous Syr. transl.]. – Ed. by Sebastian Brock, in "Aqdam tarǧama suryāniyya li-Īsāġūǧī Furfūriyūs." *Maǧallat al-maǧmaʿ al-ʿilmī al-ʿirāqī,*

 | DOI 10.1163/9789004323162_004

al-ʿadad al-ḫāṣṣ bi-hayʾat al-luġa al-suryāniyya 12 (1988): 315–366. – Revised transl. by Athanasius of Balad, partially ed. by Aron Freimann, in *Die Isagoge des Porphyrius in den syrischen Übersetzungen*. PhD diss., University of Berlin, 1897. – Cf. S. Brock 1989 [*61].

7 Ammonius. *In Aristotelis Analyticorum Priorum* I, *prooemium*. – Ed. by Max Wallies, in *Commentaria in Aristotelem Graeca*, IV/6. Berlin, 1899.

8 Aḥūḏemmeh of Nisibis. *On Man Being Composed of Body and Soul*. – Ed. and French transl. by François Nau, in *Patrologia orientalis*, III. Paris, 1909, 97–115. Repr., with introduction by Ephrem-Isa Yousif: *La vision de l'homme chez deux philosophes syriaques*. Paris, 2007, 57–68 (Syr. text 35–42). – Ital. transl. by Giuseppe Furlani, in "La psicologia di Aḥūdhemmēh." *Atti della Reale Accademia delle Scienze di Torino* 61 (1926): 807–845.

9 Paul the Persian. *Compendium of Aristotelian Logic*. – Ed. by Jan Pieter Nicolaas Land, in: *Anecdota Syriaca*, vol. 4. Leiden, 1875, 1–32. – Selected passages in Javier Teixidor, "Les textes syriaques de logique de Paul le Perse." *Semitica* 47 (1997): 117–138.

10 Severus Sebōḵt. *Chapter on the Syrians' Superiority over all other Nations with regard to Astronomical Knowledge*. – Ed. and French transl. by François Nau, "La cosmographie au VIIe siècle." *Revue de l'Orient chrétien*, 2e série 5 [15] (1910: 225–254): 248–252.

11 Severus Sebōḵt. *Treatise on the Astrolabe*. – Ed. by François Nau, in *Le traité de Sévère Sebokt sur l'astrolabe plan*. Paris, 1899. – A previously unpublished part now in Émilie Villey, "Ammonius d'Alexandrie et le Traité sur l'astrolabe de Sévère Sebokht." *Studia Graeco-Arabica* 5 (2015): 105–128.

12 Athanasius of Balad. *Introduction to Aristotelian Logic and Syllogistics* [Syr. text]. – Ed. by Giuseppe Furlani, in "Una introduzione alla logica aristotelica di Atanasio di Balad." *Rendiconti della Reale Accademia dei Lincei: Classe di scienze morali, storiche e filologiche*, ser. V, 25 (1916): 717–778. – Ital. transl. by Giuseppe Furlani, in "L'introduzione di Atanasio di Bālādh alla logica e sillogistica aristotelica, tradotta dal siriaco." *Atti del Reale Istituto Veneto di scienze, lettere ed arti* 85/2 (1925–1926): 319–344.

13 Silwānōs of Qardu. Collection of Excerpts. – Ed. and French transl. by Robert Hespel, in Théodore Bar Koni: *Livre des scolies (recension d'Urmiah): Les collections annexées par Sylvain de Qardu*. Louvain, 1984 [Corpus Scriptorum Christianorum Orientalium 464 = Scriptores Syri 197 (edition) and Corpus Scriptorum Christianorum Orientalium 465 = Scriptores Syri 198 (transl.)].

14 Jacob of Edessa. *Encheiridion*. – Ed. and Ital. transl. by Giuseppe Furlani, in "L'Encheiridion di Giacomo d'Edessa nel testo siriaco." *Rendiconti della Reale Accademia nazionale dei Lincei: Classe di scienze morali, storiche e filologiche*, ser. VI, 4 (1928): 222–249.

15 Jacob of Edessa. *Hexaemeron*. – Ed. by Jean-Baptiste Chabot. Louvain, 1928 [Corpus Scriptorum Christianorum Orientalium 92 = Scriptores Syri 44]. – Repr. 1953. – French transl. by Arthur Adolphe Vaschalde. Louvain, 1932 [Corpus Scriptorum Christianorum Orientalium 97 = Scriptores Syri 48]. – Repr. 1953.

16 George, Bishop of the Arabs. Poems and Letters, in Victor Ryssel, *Georgs des Araberbischofs Gedichte und Briefe, aus dem Syrischen übersetzt und erläutert*. Leipzig, 1891.

17 Theodore bar Konai. *Book of Scholia*. – Seert's recension. – Ed. by Addai Scher. Paris, 1910, 1912 [Corpus Scriptorum Christianorum Orientalium 55, 69 = Scriptores Syri 19, 26]. – French transl. by Robert Hespel, René Draguet. Louvain, 1981–1982 [Corpus Scriptorum Christianorum Orientalium 431, 432 = Scriptores Syri 187, 188]. – Urmia's recension. – Ed. and French transl. by Robert Hespel. Louvain, 1983 [Corpus Scriptorum Christianorum Orientalium 447 = Scriptores Syri 193 (edition) and Corpus Scriptorum Christianorum Orientalium 448 = Scriptores Syri 194 (transl.)]. – Ital. transl. of Mimrā I and II (selection focusing on philosophical topics) by Giuseppe Furlani, in "La filosofia nel Libro degli scoli di Teodoro bar Kēwānāy." *Giornale della Società Asiatica Italiana* n.s. 1 (1925–1928): 250–296. – Annotated German transl. of parts of Mimrā XI with Syr. text cf. [*10].

18 Baḏōqā Michael. *Book of Definitions*. – Ed. of the Syr. text, Ital. transl. and commentary by Giuseppe Furlani, in "Il libro delle definizioni e divisioni di Michele l'Interprete." *Atti della Reale Accademia dei Lincei: Memorie: Classe di scienze morali, storiche e filologiche*, ser. VI, 2 (1926): 3–194. – Partial ed. and German transl. cf. [*9: 219–222].

19 Antony of Tagrit. *Rhetoric*. – Partial ed. and Engl. transl. by John W. Watt, *The Fifth Book of the Rhetoric of Antony of Tagrit*. Louvain, 1986 [Corpus Scriptorum Christianorum Orientalium 480 = Scriptores Syri 203 (edition) and Corpus Scriptorum Christianorum Orientalium 481 = Scriptores Syri 204 (transl.)].

20 al-Masʿūdī, Abū l-Ḥasan ʿAlī b. al-Ḥusayn. *Kitāb al-Tanbīh wa-l-išrāf*. – Ed. by ʿAbd Allāh Ismāʿīl al-Ṣāwī. Cairo, 1357/1938.

21 Ibn al-Nadīm, Abū l-Farağ Muḥammad b. Isḥāq. *Kitāb al-Fihrist*. – Ed. by Gustav Flügel, August Müller and Johannes Roediger. Leipzig, 1871–1872. – Repr. Beirut, 1964, Frankfurt a.M., 2005. – Ed. by Ayman Fuʾād Sayyid, 2 vols. London, 1430/2009. – Engl. transl. by Bayard Dodge, *The Fihrist of al-Nadīm*, 2 vols. New York, 1970.

22 Barhebraeus. *Chronicon ecclesiasticum*. – Ed. and Lat. transl. by Jean Baptiste Abbeloos and Thomas Joseph Lamy, 3 vols. Leuven, 1872–1877.

23 Barhebraeus. *Taʾrīḫ muḫtaṣar al-duwal*. – Ed. by Anṭūn Ṣāliḥānī. Beirut, 1890, 1958 (2nd ed.).

24 ʿAḇdīšōʿ bar Berīḵā. *Carmen Ebedjesu Metropolitae Sobae et Armeniae continens catalogum librorum omnium Ecclesiasticorum*. In Assemanus, *Bibliotheca Orientalis*

(cf. *25: III/1 [1725/1975] 1–362). – Engl. transl. by George Percy Badger, in *The Nestorians and Their Rituals*, vol. 2. London, 1852, 361–379. – Repr. 1957.

25 Josephus Simonius Assemanus. *Bibliotheca Orientalis Clementino-Vaticana: Avec une postface par Joseph-Marie Sauget*, 3 vols (I, II, III/1). Hildesheim, New York, 1975. – Repr. of the edition Rome 1719, 1721, 1725.

2 Introduction

Syriac Aramaic began to develop as a literary language in the 2nd century AD; as a result of the Hellenization of the Near East it was subjected to the influence of Greek (Brock 1996 [*19]). As the language of Hellenized Christians, it became a vehicle for the assimilation of Greek concepts, which were transmitted orally, but increasingly also via Greek-Syriac translations of theological and philosophical treatises (Brock 1982 [*18]). An eloquent witness of the beginning Hellenization of Syriac Christian theology in Mesopotamia is Ephrem the Syrian (306–373). He was born in Nisibis and spent most of his life in Edessa, the present-day Urfa in Southeast Turkey (Possekel 1999 [*84]). From the 4th century onwards, Ephrem's often critical engagement with Greek Stoic thought (Possekel 1999 [*84: esp. ch. 2 and 3]) was replaced by a growing interest in Aristotelian Logic and its terminology; this interest was linked to Christological controversies and concerned in particular concepts like φύσις, ὑπόστασις and οὐσία (Daiber 2001 [*85: 328–329]).

The reception of Greek popular philosophy constituted a parallel development, which may already have begun in the 3rd century. Ethical maxims and ideas were passed on under the names of Pythagoras, Theano, Menander, Socrates, Isocrates, Plato, Theophrastus, Sextus, Plutarch, Themistius, and others (Possekel 1999 [*84: 30–32], Hugonnard-Roche 2007 [*21: 279–282], on Menander cf. Monaco 2011 [*22]). It has rightly been pointed out that Greek philosophical ideas were transmitted through textual collections and introductory handbooks written in Syriac; in this context, both Aristotle's logic and ontology seem to have played a significant role (Possekel 1999 [*84: 32 n. 154]). However, it is the interest in Aristotle's *Organon* and Porphyry's *Isagoge* (as fashioned in the School of Alexandria and especially by Ammonius) that reigned supreme (Daiber 2001 [*80: 336–343]). This is attested by the translations, commentaries and adaptations that were produced from the 6th century onwards (Brock 1993 [*62]), reaching a first climax in the person of Sergius of Rēšʿainā, who died in 536 (GSL [*27: 167–173], Ortiz de Urbina 1965 [*30: 110–111], Hugonnard-Roche 2004 [*86: 123–232], Watt 2014 [*70], Aydin 2016 [*74a]). The following paragraphs will outline these developments in the Syrian Christian community of the 7th and 8th centuries, beginning with the Jacobite authors (today also called Syrian Orthodox or West Syrian authors), i.e. the Miaphysites of the West Syrian church, who – in contrast to the Dyophysites – asserted that Jesus Christ had a single nature. Dissociating themselves from the Jacobites, the Nestorians (today also: East Syrians) of the Syriac Church of the East, on the other hand, put more emphasis on Christ's humanity, thus following the tradition of Alexandrian theology (Spuler 1961 [*29: 174–176], Peters 1968 [*31: 37], King 2015 [*41], 2014 [*40]).

3 Jacobite Authors

3.1 Severus Sebōkt – 3.2 Athanasius II of Balad – 3.3 Jacob of Edessa – 3.4 George, Bishop of the Arabs

3.1 *Severus Sebōk̲t*

Severus Sebōk̲t (d. 666/7; GSL [*27: 246–247], Nau 1929 [*28: 279–281], Ortiz de Urbina 1965 [*30: 175–176], Yousif 2003 [*38: 115–120]), bishop of the Monastery of Qenneshre from 638, was famous for his Greek learning; thus Barhebraeus praises him for his knowledge in logic, mathematics, and church matters (Barhebraeus [*22: I 276–277]).

He composed several works on astronomy based on Ptolemy. These included a treatise, written in 662, discussing the Syrians' superiority to the Greeks in this field (GSL [*27: 246 n. 12]), the astrolabe (Severus [*11]), the lunar eclipse (GSL [*27: 246 n. 13], Reich 2000 [*66]), and the shape of the various phases of the moon (GSL [*27: 247 n. 1]); as well as an astronomically orientated cosmography, comprising 18 chapters and entitled *Treatise on the Constellations*, which he wrote in 659/660, and which he supplemented in 665 with answers to a number of questions from a Cypriote priest called Basil (GSL [*27: 246 n. 3–4]).

In the treatise on the Syrians' superiority to the Greeks in astronomy, Severus adopts an argument which, in Plato's *Timaeus* (21e1–23c3), Socrates' interlocutor Critias attributes to an Egyptian priest (Nau 1910 [*10: 249–250]): he remonstrated with Solon because unlike the Egyptians, the Greeks and other nations had allowed their ancient traditions time and again to be lost to floods, leaving behind only 'illiterate and uncultured people' (τοὺς ἀγραμμάτους τε καὶ ἀμούσους; *Timaeus* 23a6–7), who 'for many generations… passed on without leaving a written record' (ἐπὶ πολλὰς γενεὰς γράμμασιν τελευτᾶν ἀφώνους, *Timaeus* 23c2–3; transl. Zeyl, in Cooper, pp. 1230–31). Severus does not reproduce the Greek passage exactly; he interprets 'speech' (φωνή) in the sense of λόγος, which, apart from 'language', can also mean 'reason' or 'reasoning'. Thus he is able to deny the Greeks their claim to be the inventors of mathematics and astronomy. Severus adds: 'for knowledge does not exist for the sake of speech, i.e. for the sake of speaking, but speaking for the sake of knowledge.'

The conception of speech as a tool for transmitting knowledge Severus links with those parts of philosophy of language which focus on questions of hermeneutics and demonstration (syllogistics). In 638 Severus Sebōḵt thus composed a treatise, extant in five manuscripts (GSL [*27: 246 n. 11], Georr 1948 [*11: 25 no. 3], Brock 1993 [*62: 14]), on the syllogisms in Aristotle's *Prior Analytics*; he treated the same topic again in a letter to the periodeutes Jonan (ed., transl. and analysed by Hugonnard-Roche 2015 [*73], cf. Reinink 1983 [*60]). In this letter, in which Severus also discusses Aristotle's *On Interpretation*, Severus confines himself to *Prior Analytics* I 1–7 – perhaps following the Nestorian theologian Paul the Persian (Gutas 1983 [*81: 246. 249]). He was able to consider this text a self-contained part because it describes the three syllogistic figures accepted by Aristotle (Daiber 2001 [*85: 334–335]). Severus furthermore discusses some questions from Aristotle's *On Interpretation*. His exposition betrays the influence of the Alexandrian commentator Ammonius Hermeiou. It is possible that he was also following his model Paul the Persian again, whose Persian commentary on Aristotle's *On Interpretation* he translated into Syriac (Brock 1982 [*18: 19]). Several concepts from *On Interpretation* he later explained again in a letter to the priest Aitallahā/Aitilaha (Hugonnard-Roche) in Ninive, preserved in four manuscripts (GSL [*27: 246 n. 9], Georr 1948 [*11: 25 no. 1]; the text is analysed in Hugonnard-Roche 2015 [*73], 98–104.). Severus furthermore acquainted his Syriac readership with Aristotle's logic, through a translation of Paul the Persian's *Compendium*, which was written in Pahlavi and dedicated to the Sasanian Ḫusraw I Anūširvān (regn. 531–578/9). It introduces the subject beginning with Porphyry's *Isagoge* (*Introduction*) and ending with Aristotle's *Prior Analytics* I 7. This text may well have been what inspired his pupil Athanasius II of Balad to further studies.

3.2 *Athanasius II of Balad*

Athanasius II of Balad (d. 686; GSL [*27: 256–257], Ortiz de Urbina 1965 [*30: 183], Yousif 2003 [*38: 121–123]) became Patriarch of Antioch three years before his death. He studied with Severus Sebōḵt, and is the author of a comprehensive introduction to Aristotelian logic and syllogistics (Athanasius [*12]; cf. Furlani 1921–1922 [*50]). *Pace* Brock (1993 [*62: 11]) it is not a commentary on Porphyry's *Isagoge*; it furthermore differs from the version of Porphyry's *Isagoge* which he revised, in 645, on the basis of an anonymous translation from the 6th century (ed. Brock 1988 [*6]), and which is extant in four manuscripts (GSL

[*27: 257 n. 1], Georr 1948 [*11: 26]; for a partial edition see: Freimann [*6]; cf. Hugonnard-Roche 2004 [*86: 82–91], Brock 1989 [*32]).

In a letter written by Patriarch Timothy I to Mar Sergius some time between 782 and 799 (Brock 1999 [*65: 238]), Athanasius is furthermore credited with translations of the *Posterior Analytics* and the *Topics*. Finally, in glosses to the Arabic *Organon* manuscript Paris 2346 (cf. below p. 88), the Nestorian scholar Abū l-Ḫayr al-Ḥasan b. Suwār Ibn al-Ḫammār (on him cf. § 7.4), born 942 in Baghdad, names Athanasius as the Syriac translator of the *Sophistical Refutations* (Georr 1948 [*11: 198–199], Haddad 1952 [*12: 68–71], Peters 1968 [*14: 23–24]). This manuscript contains several quotations from Porphyry's *Isagoge* under Athanasius' name, as well as quotations from Aristotle's *Prior Analytics*, *Topics* (Hugonnard-Roche 2004 [*86: 40 n. 1]) and *Sophistical Refutations*.

3.3 *Jacob of Edessa*

Jacob of Edessa (d. 708) may be said to be the most versatile pupil of Severus Sebōkt (Assemanus [*25: I: 468–494], GSL [*27: 248–256], Ortiz de Urbina 1965 [*30: 177–183], Yousif 2003 [*38: 334–351], Kruisheer 2008 [*5], Ibrahim, Kiraz 2010 [*69]). Born around 633, he studied philology, philosophy and theology with Severus, together with his older contemporary Athanasius of Balad, and applied himself to the study of Greek. He then continued his philosophical studies in Alexandria, and after his return to Edessa devoted himself to Hebrew. He revised the Syriac translation of the Old Testament and became a recognized expert in the field of biblical exegesis and theology. Of his numerous works only two small treatises are devoted to philosophy: a short handbook entitled *Encheiridion* (ed./transl. Furlani 1928 [*14]), which explains the concepts of φύσις (*kyānā*), οὐσία, ὑπόστασις (*qnōmā*), essence (*yāṯā*), person/individual (*parṣōpā* = πρόσωπον) and εἶδος (*adšā*), and a lost philosophical-theological tract on 'the first creative, eternal, almighty and uncreated cause, which is God, the Sustainer of all things' (GSL [*27: 255 n. 4]). This subject finds a continuation in Jacob's late work, the *Hexaemeron* [*15] (cf. Martin 1888 [*45], Hjelt 1892 [*46: 9–45], Schlimme 1977 [*58: II 678–684], Wilks 2008 [*68]). Here Jacob presents a cosmological argument based on the Platonic understanding of man's likeness to God, of man's being, thanks to his reason, a mirror image of his Creator (cf. esp. ch. 7). The work was echoed in the *Commentary on the Hexaemeron* by Mošeh bar Kepha (d. 903; cf. vol. 2, § 10.1.1). It combines knowledge of the Bible with the scientific knowledge of the Greeks. This is demonstrated by its second chapter, which presents meteorological information e.g. about the various winds. It shows that independently of Sergius of Rēšʿainā's Syriac translation of Pseudo-Aristotle's *De mundo* (Peters 1968 [*14: 61–62], ed./transl. Takahashi 2014 [*71]), Jacob follows the twelve sector windrose mentioned there (394b-395a) – a tradition which had become dominant in post-Aristotelian times beginning with Timosthenes (Daiber 1975 [*78: 79–80]).

Another point to note is that, in Neoplatonic fashion, Jacob refers to God as the 'First Cause' (*ʿelltā qaḏmāytā*), whose effect is a mere image of it (Hübner 2001 [*37: 381]). This use of terminology is evidenced in his *Hexaemeron* [*15: 4b, 1–2; transl. 3, 5–6]. In the definitions of φύσις which he presents in his above-mentioned *Encheiridion*, Jacob reveals that he was familiar with Aristotle's *Metaphysics* IV 4 (Furlani 1921 [*49], Daiber 2001 [*85: 330]). In all these cases Jacob obviously resorted directly to Greek sources. For the subsequent definitions, which were prompted by the christological debates of his day (Hugonnard-Roche 2004 [*86: 53–54]), he was able to rely on two previous translations. One of them is an extant anonymous Syriac translation of Aristotle's *Categories* (ed. Georr 1948 [*11: 253–305]), which Jacob is said to have revised (Brock 1993 [*62: 4. 12], Hugonnard-Roche 2004 [*86: 25–33. 39–55], 2008 [*67: 205–222]). He further used a 6th century anonymous Syriac translation of Porphyry's *Isagoge*, revised by Athanasius II of Balad in 645 (cf. § 2.3.2) – without, however, following it slavishly (Furlani 1942 [*1: 131–132]).

3.4 *George, Bishop of the Arabs*

George, Bishop of the Arabs (d. 724) studied in Qenneshre with Severus Sebōḵt shortly before the latter's death, and with Athanasius II of Balad. In 686, he was elected 'bishop of the Arabs' in the border region between Syria and Mesopotamia (Assemanus [*25: I 494–495], GSL [*27: 257–258], Ortiz de Urbina 1965 [*30: 183–184], Miller 1993 [*63: 303–304], Yousif 2003 [*38: 123–125], Tannous 2008 [*39: 671–716]). Apart from poems and letters he wrote exegetical and theological works, including a supplement to the *Hexaemeron* by his teacher Jacob of Edessa (Ryssel 1891 [*16: XV]; for a partial translation into German see Ryssel 1891 [*16: 130–132]). His philosophical works (Daiber 2001 [*85: 339–340]) are limited to translations, accompanied by introductions and commentaries, of Aristotle's *Organon*: *Categories* [*1], *On Interpretation* [*3], and *Prior Analytics* [*4].

George's introduction to Aristotle's *Organon* and his commentary on the *Categories* both exhibit parallels to John Philoponus (Furlani 1923 [*54: 310–326]) – who in fact presents nothing but a record of Ammonius' Neoplatonic commentary on Aristotle (Westerink 1962 [*76: XI]; cf. p. 40 above). In his commentary on *On Interpretation*, George evidently quotes a lost commentary by Olympiodorus (Furlani 1922 [*51], 1923 [*54: 327]); another commentator used by George in the *Prooemium* as well as in his commentary on the *Prior Analytics* has so far evaded identification (Furlani 1923 [*54: 328–333], 1939–1940 [*56],

1942 [*1]). The latter text is again evocative of Ammonius (Furlani 1939–1940 [*56: 129–130]).

George's occupation with logic was motivated by his Christian faith. According to him, Aristotle's logic confirmed what God had proclaimed through religion; the triad of the syllogistic figures, which enable man's intellect to discern God's truth, was a reflection of the Christian Trinity. George sees the three syllogistic figures symbolized in the tripartition he perceives in the Greek uncial Φ: in the two halves of the circle, and the diagonal. This Φ, George said, was at the same time an abbreviation for Φύλαξ (guardian); the circle signified God's infinity. Furthermore, the circle and its diagonal, which constitute the letter Φ, could also be represented by the Greek letter Θ, the abbreviation for θεός (God); or with the Greek letter X, which also symbolized the cross and stood for χορηγός (leader) (Furlani 1939–1940 [*56: 125. 130], for a divergent view see Miller 1993 [*63: 314–315]).

Noteworthy here is the assessment of logic as an instrument of theology; we have here an answer to the question about the role of logic which had already been posed by Sergius of Rēšʿainā, the first great Syriac translator who died in 536 AD. Like his younger contemporary Paul the Persian [*9: 6], Sergius had debated the question – ascribed to Plato, but in fact of Neoplatonic origin (Ammonius [*7: 8. 15–11. 21], Daiber 1980 [*59: 329–330]) – whether logic was an instrument or a part of philosophy. In his treatise *On the Aim of the Works of Aristotle*, a paraphrase commentary of Aristotle's *Categories* which is furnished with a long introduction addressed to a certain Theodore (Hugonnard-Roche 2004 [*86: 165–186]), Sergius emphasized the role of Aristotle's logic in medicine and philosophy: every insight required definition and demonstration. The contents of the as yet unpublished Syriac text can be gauged from an – albeit incomplete – synopsis (Furlani 1922 [*53: 139–172], cf. Hugonnard-Roche 1989 [*82: 8–16]).

This interest in definition and demonstration as the foundations of knowledge, which had its roots in Aristotle (i.e. the *Categories*, *On Interpretation*, and the *Prior Analytics*), was continued by George (Ryssel 1891 [*16: 65–67]). In a Neoplatonizing treatise entitled *On Souls, Spirits, and Intellects* (MS British Museum 14538; Ryssel 1891 [*16: 142–144]), which has been overlooked in Baumstark's history of Syriac literature (GSL [*27]), George explains that the perfection of the intellect, and hence of the soul, is reached through its ever increasing enlightenment in its return to its origin, i.e. God. Thus, George continues Jacob of Edessa's doctrine of the rational human soul, which undergoes a process of enlightenment and so partakes in God's wisdom, being ever more assimilated to him. Jacob of Edessa had expounded his view in the seventh chapter of his *Hexaemeron* [*15] (German transl. Miller 1993 [*63: 305–309], wrongly labelled as George's text), whose ending (Jacob of Edessa [*15: ed. Chabot 347a24; German transl. Vaschalde 296, 13]) had been supplemented by George (German transl. Ryssel 1891 [*16: 130–138]).

Apart from the four prominent figures presented here there are certainly further Jacobite authors of the 7th and 8th centuries who had a theological interest in philosophical argumentation based on Aristotle's *Organon*. David bar Paulus of Bēṯ Rabban (d. ca. AD 920), for instance, is said to have praised the Greek philosophers, and especially Aristotle, in a letter (Barsoum 2000 [*36: 374]), but there is no extant treatise to confirm this. A Berlin manuscript ascribes an enumeration of the Aristotelian categories to him, accompanied by a few examples (in Syriac, Karšūnī, and Arabic) (MS Berlin no. 88 = Petermann 9, fol. 180ª, 24–36, mentioned in GSL [*27: 272 n. 11]; Brock 1993 [*62: 12]); however, the ascription is dubious and probably originates in the fact that several other treatises in the manuscript are attributed to David bar Paulus (Sachau 1899 [*8: no. 88], Furlani 1914 [*47: esp. 157]).

4 Nestorian Authors

4.1 Theodore bar Konai – 4.2 Silwānōs of Qardu – 4.3 ʿEnānīšōʿ – 4.4 Ḥnānīšōʿ – 4.5 Īšōʿbōḵt – 4.6 Mar(y) Aḇā II, Īšōʿdnaḥ, Denḥā

4.1 *Theodore bar Konai*

Theodore bar Konai (GSL [*27: 218–219], Ortiz de Urbina 1965 [*30: 216–217], Yousif 2003 [*38: 133–138]) was probably active towards the end of the 8th century (Ortiz de Urbina 1965 [*30: 216]) rather than in the 7th century (Yousif 2003 [*38: 133–134]) or the 9th century (Vandenhoff 1916 [*48: 126–132]). The available data on his life are contradictory. He supposedly founded his own school in Kashkar in ancient Babylonia. His main work, the *Book of Annotations* [*17], shows that Theodore was familiar with Aristotle's *Categories* and *On Interpretation*, as well as with Porphyry's *Isagoge* (Mimrā VI 15–27. 76–82), though his understanding of these works is yet to be studied systematically and in detail. He further presents definitions of concepts that he to some extent shares with Jacob of Edessa's *Encheiridion*. The same goes for a classification of man as a composite of body and soul (Mimrā I 96G, recension Urmia ed./transl. Hespel [*17]), even though an even earlier work has been pointed out as a possible source for Theodore in this respect (Furlani 1926 [*8: 843–844]): a treatise by the Nestorian bishop Aḥūḏemmeh of Nisibis (active in the 6th century; GSL [*27: 178]), which in turn may have been inspired by Isaac of Antioch, who lived in the 4th/5th century (Furlani 1926 [*8: 835];

for Isaac, see GSL [*27: 63–64]). Aḥūḏemmeh's treatise *On the Composition of Man* (i.e. from body and soul) [*8] was written in a fundamentally Aristotelian vein. In the 9th century – i.e. after Theodore – it also served as a source for the psychological doctrines of the Jacobite author Iwannīs of Dārā, the ancient Anastasiapolis between Mardin and Nisibis (Furlani 1926 [*8: 819–820]); they, however, are extant only as fragments (transl. Furlani 1928 [*55]). Iwannīs of Dārā used a Pseudo-Platonic treatise *On the Subsistence of the Soul's Virtues*, which is preserved in Arabic translation as *Maqāla fī Iṯbāt faḍāʾil al-nafs* (ed. Daiber 1971 [*57a]; cf. Zonta 2015 [*74]). According to Zonta, the Pseudo-Platonic treatise appears to have been known in the 9th century to the Jewish Karaite Dāwūd al-Muqammiṣ (in his *ʿIšrūn maqāla*), in the 10th/11th century to the Islamic philosopher Miskawayh (*Tahḏīb al-Akhlāq*), and in the 13th century to the West Syriac scholar Severus bar Šakkō (in his *Book of Dialogues*) (cf. also Zonta 2014 [*72]).

Theodore ascribes an irascible, a concupiscible, and a rational faculty to the soul (Mimrā I 51). Whether this Platonic doctrine (*Rep.* IV 439d4–440b7) was transmitted to Theodore through the above-mentioned Aḥūḏemmeh and his source of inspiration, Isaac of Antioch, cannot be determined with certainty (Furlani 1926 [*9: 835–837]). Theodore further discusses the soul's afterlife (Mimrā II 91–92); Jacob of Edessa's concept of the cognitive soul that returns to God (cf. § 2.1.3) appears, in rudimentary fashion, in yet another passage (Mimrā II 1).

Theodore furthermore argues that it is necessary that there should be a prophet 'who teaches people what they need to know and reveals the abundance of (God's) mystery to all human beings endowed with reason' (Mimrā IV 4). He possesses doxographical knowledge of Greek philosophy, albeit often at second hand only (Mimrā XI 7–12; Baumstark 1905 [*10: 7–17]; cf. Klinge 1939 [*75: 360–363], Daiber 1980 [*59: index s.v. Theodor]). Just as in the field of logic, he follows Aristotle in the field of natural science, for instance meteorology (Mimrā I 110; cf. Arist. *Meteor.* II 9; Daiber 1975 [*78: 84–90]).

4.2 *Silwānōs of Qardu*

Silwānōs of Qardu, who lived in the 8th or 9th century (GSL [*27: 197], Ortiz de Urbina 1965 [*30: 143]), produced two compilations, in which he collected excerpts not only from Theodore bar Konai's *Book of Annotations* but also from Porphyry's *Isagoge* and Aristotle's *Categories* and *On Interpretation* [*13]. The excerpts of the second compilation present an overview of the principal points of Aristotelian logic, composed in a pattern of question and answer. It begins with Porphyry's *Isagoge*, proceeds with the *Categories*, and ends with *On Interpretation*. The introduction also includes the *Prior Analytics*, the *Posterior*

Analytics, the *Topics* and the *Sophistical Refutations* in its list of Aristotle's works (Silwānōs [*13: 2nd collection, no. 2]). This confirms once more that these parts of the *Organon*, too, were known in the Syriac milieu (cf. pp. 52 and 57 above). In his synopsis of Porphyry's *Isagoge*, Silwānōs inserts a list of five definitions of philosophy – following the example of the Alexandrians, who, however, offer one additional definition (Daiber 1990 [*83: 118–120]); this is succeeded by a section on the parts of philosophy (Silwānōs [*13: 2nd collection, no. 7]). This list and the ensuing passage on the parts of philosophy have a near-literal parallel in the *Book of Definitions* of Baḏōqā Michael (text and transl.: Baḏōqā [*18: 20,3–25,9; transl. 101–104]; Baumstark 1900 [*9: 219–222]; for Baḏōqā Michael see § 2.4.3 below). As Silwānōs omits Greek names and shortens the text somewhat, Baḏōqā Michael appears to be the older text, or to reflect an older source that would have been written before Silwānōs' time.

Silwānōs' collection of excerpts is devised as a textbook for teaching purposes, and is prefaced by a theological introduction. From the multiplicity of the world, which does not move on its own accord, but instead is being steered, Silwānōs infers the eternity and unicity of a being (*ītyā*) which is perfect, which has neither life nor death, is neither good nor bad, and has neither light nor darkness. This corresponds to the Aristotelian and medieval 'argument from degree' (*argumentum ex gradibus*) for the existence of God, albeit tinged with Neoplatonic colours. To what extent it also exhibits an Islamic colouring is yet to be clarified in detail. Thus the denial that there is good and bad in God is linked to Silwānōs' refutation of those 'who claim that fate and destiny (*gaḏā w-ḥelqā*) lead people towards the good or bad' (Silwānōs [*13: 1st collection, no. 8]). What Silwānōs is targeting here is Islamic determinism, i.e. the adherents of the doctrine of divine predestination (*al-qaḍāʾ wa-l-qadar*).

4.3 *ʿEnānīšōʿ*

ʿEnānīšōʿ/ʿAnānīšōʿ from Nisibis lived in the 2nd half of the 7th century (GSL [*27: 201–203], Ortiz de Urbina 1965 [*30: 149–150]). He did not only occupy himself with the traditions of the Church Fathers, but moreover cherished a pronounced lexicographical interest. Apart from a dictionary of words that assume different meanings depending on their various vocalizations, the so-called *aequilitterae* (GSL [*27: 202 n. 1]), he also composed an anthology of philosophical definitions according to the Alexandrian School of Ammonius. It has not survived, but due to its popularity it has left its mark on later works, in particular on the probably anonymous *Book of Definitions* (Baumstark 1900 [*9: 212–223]; for the anonymity question see Abramowski 1999 [*64: 1–10]) attributed to Baḏōqā Michael, also called Bāzūḏ and Abzūḏ (GSL [*27: 129]). In its current version ([*18]), this book was in all likelihood composed at the turn of the 8th/9th century (GSL [*27: 129 n. 11]). It is possible to detect the echo of an even older collection, preceding ʿEnānīšōʿ/ʿAnānīšōʿ, in this text (Furlani 1922 [*52: 143–148], 1942 [*1: 138–140]): that of the Nestorian Aḥūḏemmeh, who died in 575 (GSL [*27: 178]). It will only become possible to clarify the transmission history if and when ʿEnānīšōʿ/ʿAnānīšōʿ's work is found and we can establish his textual sources.

4.4 *Ḥnānīšōʿ*

Ḥnānīšōʿ, who died in 700, spent most of his life in a monastery near Mosul (Wright 1894 [*25: 181–182]), GSL [*27: 209], Ortiz de Urbina 1965 [*30: 150–151]). Apart from theological and juridical works (which are extant), he is said to have written a commentary on Aristotle's *Analytics*, as well as a treatise on the *Causes of Being* (GSL [*27: 209 n. 12. 14]).

4.5 *Īšōʿbōḵt*

The 8th century scholar Īšōʿbōḵt of Rēwardašīr (Aubert 1997 [*34: 175]) is mentioned as the author of a work *On the Cosmos* (extant in excerpts; GSL [*27: 215 n. 16]), as well as of writings on Aristotle's *Categories* (GSL [*27: 216 n. 2]) and on the concept of possibility (GSL [*27: 216 n. 3]). The latter brief treatise, which is available in print (Furlani 1914 [*47: 157–159]), takes its cue from Aristotle's *Prior Analytics* I 13, and, following on from there, explicates three modes of the contingent: what will happen easily, with difficulty, or indeterminately. In the introduction to a longer version of *Kitāb al-Dalāʾil wa-l-iʿtibār ʿalā l-ḫalq wa-l-tadbīr* (*Book of the Demonstrations and of the Contemplation of Creation and* [*Divine*] *Direction*), which is ascribed to al-Ǧāḥiẓ and extant in manuscript form (Daiber 1975 [*79: 159–160]), Īšōʿbōḵt, 'the Metropolitan of Persia', is mentioned as the author of a Persian book, which allegedly was written during the Umayyad period and served as a source for *Kitāb al-Dalāʾil* (transl. Plessner 1975 [*80: 104]). There are no further reports, but in view of the contents of *Kitāb al-Dalāʾil* one can imagine a book written in the style of the Hexaemeron literature (cf. § 2.3.3–4) which, in this particular case, presented a teleological argument for God's existence (cf. Daiber 2014 [*87], esp. 172–173).

4.6 *Mar(y) Aḇā II, Īšōʿdnaḥ, Denḥā*

Historians of Syriac literature mention the following 8th century Nestorian writers as the authors of logical treatises; however, no manuscript material survives.

Mar(y) Aḇā II, or Aḇā II (d. 751) of Kashkar is mentioned by Barhebraeus [*22: II 153–154] as someone familiar with church matters as well as with logic; he is said to have commented on several books of Aristotle's *Organon* (GSL [*27: 215], Wright 1894 [*25: 186–187]; ʿAḇdīšōʿ, transl. Badger [*24: 372]; Assemanus [*25: III/1 154. 157]).

Īšōʿdnaḥ of Basra (9th century – his exact dates are uncertain; Fiey 1996 [*33: 431–450], 1997 [*35: 176]) is said to have composed a commentary on, or an introduction to logic (GSL [*27: 234], Wright 1894 [*25: 195]).

Denḥā (8th cent.), also known as Īhīḇā or Hīḇā (Ibas), was a pupil of Īšōʿ bar Nūn, who in turn had studied with Theodore bar Konai. According to a bibliographical catalogue compiled by ʿAḇdīšōʿ bar Berīḵā in 1298, he wrote, among other things, a commentary on Aristotelian logic (ʿAḇdīšōʿ [*24: transl. Badger 373]; GSL [*27: 220], Wright 1894 [*25: 218–219]). It is possible that this scholar is identical with the priest and philosopher Abū Zakariyyāʾ Denḥā, whom the Muslim historian al-Masʿūdī mentions in his *Kitāb al-Tanbīh wa-l-išrāf* [*20: 132,20–22] as one of the opponents in a disputation that took place in 313/925, and as the author of a book *On the Lives and Exploits of the Byzantine and Greek Kings and Philosophers*. It is, however, also conceivable that he is identical with another Denḥā who, in a treatise by Ibn al-Ṣalāḥ (d. 548/1153) on the fourth figure of the syllogism, is mentioned as the author of a work (a commentary?) on *Galen's Fourth Figure* (Rescher 1966 [*77: 50–51]). According to Ibn al-Ṣalāḥ (Rescher 1966 [*77: 53]), Galen's treatise on the fourth figure was circulating in a Syriac translation already during the lifetime of the philosopher al-Kindī (3rd/9th cent.).

5 A Maronite Author: Theophilus of Edessa

Barhebraeus' dynastic history *Taʾrīḫ muḫtaṣar al-duwal* [*23: 127,6] tells us that Theophilus (GSL [*27: 341–342], Wright 1894 [*25: 163–164]) was head (*raʾīs*) astronomer at the court of the caliph al-Mahdī (reg. 158–169/775–785); he calls him 'Theophilus, son of the Christian Thomas, the astrologer from Edessa' and presents him as the man who translated the 'two books' of Homer from Greek into Syriac [*23: 24,20–21]. Given that the Syriac *Rhetoric*, which was composed in 825 by Antony of Tagrit (GSL [*27: 278]; partial edition [*19]), contains quotations from the *Iliad* and the *Odyssey* – presumably from Theophilus' translation (Raguse 1968 [*15: 445–447]) – this remark does not refer to the first two books of the *Iliad* only, as Kraemer suspected (1956–1957 [*13: 261]). To

Syriac posterity, Theophilus is familiar first and foremost on account of his historiographical work, whereas his preoccupation with Aristotle is documented merely by a few quotations from his Syriac translation of the *Sophistical Refutations*, which appear in the marginal comments on ʿĪsā Ibn Zurʿa's Arabic translation (Aristotle [*5: 767. 784–785]; for ʿĪsā Ibn Zurʿa cf. § 7.3). However, the *Fihrist* [*21: 249,27 Flügel; transl. 601] by Ibn al-Nadīm, who lived at the end of the 9th century, mentions Theophilus as the author of a Syriac version which was rendered into Arabic by Yaḥyā Ibn ʿAdī. This contradicts the probably more reliable information we get from al-Ḥasan b. Suwār (Ibn al-Ḫammār, § 7.4), who was in fact the editor of three translations of the *Sophistical Refutations*: those of Yaḥyā Ibn ʿAdī, of his pupil Ibn Zurʿa, and of an earlier translator, allegedly Ibn Nāʿima al-Ḥimṣī (cf. Peters 1968 [*14: 23–24]). According to Ibn al-Ḫammār, the versions by Ibn ʿAdī and by Ibn Zurʿa go back to a Syriac version by Athanasius of Balad; he quotes it in his comments on his edition of Ibn ʿAdī's translation (cf. Endress 1977 [*17: 26–27]). The quotations in the comments to Ibn Zurʿa's Arabic translation therefore remain the only evidence for the existence of a Syriac translation of the *Sophistical Refutations* from Theophilus' hand.

6 Secondary Literature

6.1 Bibliographies [*1–*5] – 6.2 Textual Transmission and Textual History [*8–*22] – 6.3 Biographies, Introductions, Surveys [*25–*41] – 6.4 Specific Groups of Works, Writings, Problems, Concepts [*45–*74a] – 6.5 Reception [*75–*87]

6.1 *Bibliographies*

1 Furlani, Giuseppe. "I miei lavori dal 1925 al 1940 sulla filosofia greca presso i Siri." *Rivista di filosofia e d'istruzione classica* 19 (1942): 121–149.

2 Moss, Cyril. *Catalogue of Syriac Printed Books and Related Literature in the British Museum*. London, 1962.

3 Brock, Sebastian. *Syriac Studies: A Classified Bibliography (1960–1990)*. Kaslik, Lebanon, 1996.

4 Brock, Sebastian. "Syriac Studies: A Classified Bibliography (1991–1995)." *Parole de l'Orient* 23 (1998): 241–350.

5 Kruisheer, Dirk: "A Bibliographical Clavis to the Works of Jacob of Edessa (revised and expanded)." In *Jacob of Edessa and the Syriac Culture of His Day*. Ed. by Bas ter Haar Romeny. Leiden, 2008, 265–293.

6.2 *Textual Transmission and Textual History*

8 Sachau, Eduard. *Verzeichnis der syrischen Handschriften der Königlichen Bibliothek zu Berlin*. Berlin, 1899. [Die Handschriften-Verzeichnisse der Königlichen Bibliothek zu Berlin, 23].

9 Baumstark, Anton. *Aristoteles bei den Syrern vom V.–VIII. Jahrhundert*. Leipzig, 1900.

10 Baumstark, Anton. "Griechische Philosophen und ihre Lehren in syrischer Überlieferung." *Oriens Christianus* 5 (1905): 1–25.

11 Georr, Khalil. *Les Catégories d'Aristote dans leurs versions syro-arabes*. Beirut, 1948.

12 Haddad, Cyrille. *Trois versions arabes inédites des Réfutations Sophistiques*. PhD diss., University of Paris, 1952.

13 Kraemer, Jörg. "Arabische Homerverse." *Zeitschrift der Deutschen Morgenländischen Gesellschaft* 106 (1956): 259–316; 107 (1957): 511–518.

14 Peters, Francis E. *Aristoteles Arabus: The Original Translation and Commentaries on the Aristotelian "Corpus"*. Leiden, 1968.

15 Raguse, Hartmut. "Syrische Homerzitate in der Rhetorik des Anton von Tagrit." In *Paul de Lagarde und die syrische Kirchengeschichte*. Ed. by Göttinger Arbeitskreis für syrische Kirchengeschichte. Göttingen, 1968, 162–175.

16 Köbert, Raimund. "Bemerkungen zu den syrischen Zitaten aus Homer und Platon im syrischen Buch der Rhetorik des Anton von Tagrit." *Orientalia* 40 (1971): 438–447.

17 Endress, Gerhard. *The Works of Yaḥyā Ibn ʿAdī: An Analytical Inventory*. Wiesbaden, 1977.

18 Brock, Sebastian. "From Antagonism to Assimilation: Syriac Attitudes to Greek Learning." In *East of Byzantium: Syria and Armenia in the Formative Period, Dumbarton Oaks Symposium, 1980*. – Ed. by Nina Garsoïan, Thomas Mathews and Robert Thomson. Washington D.C., 1982, 17–34. – Repr. in Brock, *Syriac Perspectives on Late Antiquity*. London, 1984, no. V.

19 Brock, Sebastian. "Greek Words in Syriac: Some General Features." *Studia classica Israelica* 15 [Studies in memory of Abraham Wasserstein] (1996): 251–263. – Repr. in Brock, *From Ephrem to Romanos: Interactions Between Syriac and Greek in Late Antiquity*. Aldershot, 1999, no. XV.

20 Brock, Sebastian. "Syriac Translations of Greek Popular Philosophy." In *Von Athen nach Bagdad: Zur Rezeption griechischer Philosophie von der Spätantike bis zum Islam*. Ed. by Peter Bruns. Bonn, 2003, 9–28.

21 Hugonnard-Roche, Henri. "Le corpus philosophique syriaque aux VIe–VIIe siècles." In *The Libraries of the Neoplatonists: Proceedings of the Meeting of the European Science Foundation Network 'Late Antiquity and Arabic Thought:*

Patterns in the Constitution of European Culture' held in Strasbourg, March 12–14, 2004. Ed. by Cristina D'Ancona. Leiden, 2007, 279–291.

22 Monaco, David Gregory. *The Sentences of the Syriac Menander: Introduction, Text, Translation, and Commentary*. PhD diss., University of Chicago, 2011.

6.3 *Biographies, Introductions, Surveys*

25 Wright, William. *A Short History of Syriac Literature*. London, 1894. – Repr. Amsterdam, 1966.

26 Duval, Rubens. *La littérature syriaque*. Paris, 1899.

27 GSL = Baumstark, Anton. *Geschichte der syrischen Literatur mit Ausschluss der christlich-palästinensischen Texte*. Bonn, 1922.

28 Nau, François. "L'araméen chrétien (syriaque): Les traductions faites du grec en syriaque au VIIe siècle." *Revue de l'histoire des religions* 99 (1929): 232–287.

29 Spuler, Bertold. "Die westsyrische (monophysitische/jakobitische) Kirche." In *Religionsgeschichte des Orients in der Zeit der Weltreligionen*. Ed. by Johannes Leipoldt and Bertold Spuler. Leiden, 1961, 170–216.

30 Ortiz de Urbina, Ignatius. *Patrologia Syriaca: Altera editio emendata et aucta*. Rome, 1965.

31 Peters, Francis E. *Aristotle and the Arabs: the Aristotelian Tradition in Islam*. New York, 1968.

32 Brock, Sebastian. "Syriac Culture in the Seventh Century." *Aram* 1, no. 2 (1989): 268–280.

33 Fiey, Jean-Maurice. "Īchōʿdnah, métropolite de Basra, et son œuvre." *L'Orient syrien* 11 (1996): 431–450.

34 Aubert, Roger. "Ishoʿbokht." In *Dictionnaire d'histoire et de géographie ecclésiastiques*, vol. 26. Ed. by Roger Aubert. Paris, 1997, 175.

35 Fiey, Jean-Maurice. "Ishoʿdnah de Basrah." In *Dictionnaire d'histoire et de géographie ecclésiastiques*, vol. 26. Ed. by Roger Aubert. Paris, 176.

36 Barsoum, Ignatius Aphram I. *The Scattered Pearls: A History of Syriac Literature and Sciences*. Transl. and ed. by Matti Moosa with a foreword by Cyril Aphrem Karim. 2nd, revised edition. Piscataway, N.J., 2000.

37 Hübner, Johannes. "Ursache/Wirkung (I. Antike)." In *Historisches Wörterbuch der Philosophie*, vol. 11. Ed. by Joachim Ritter, Karlfried Gründer and Gottfried Gabriel. Basel, 2001, 377–384.

38 Yousif, Ephrem-Isa. *La floraison des philosophes syriaques*. Paris, 2003.

39 Tannous, Jack. "Between Christology and Kalām? The Life and Letters of George, Bishop of the Arab Tribes." In *Malphono w-Rabo d-Malphone: Studies in Honor of S. P. Brock*. Ed. by George A. Kiraz. Piscataway, N.J., 2008, 671–716.

40 King, Daniel. "Continuities and Discontinuities in the History of Syriac Philosophy." In *De l'Antiquité tardive au Moyen Âge. Études de logique aristotélicienne et de philosophie grecque, syriaque, arabe et latine offertes à Henri Hugonnard-Roche*. Ed. by Elisa Coda and Cecilia Martini Bonadeo. Paris, 2014, 225–243.

41 King, Daniel. "Logic in the Service of Ancient Eastern Christianity: An Exploration of Motives." *Archiv für Geschichte der Philosophie* 97 (2015): 1–33.

6.4 *Specific Groups of Works, Writings, Problems, Concepts*

45 Martin, Jean Pierre Paul. "L'Hexaémeron de Jacques d'Edesse." *Journal asiatique*, sér. VIII, 11 (1888): 155–219. 401–440.

46 Hjelt, Arthur. *Etudes sur l'Hexaméron de Jacques d'Edesse, notamment sur ses notions géographiques contenues dans le 3ième traité: Texte syriaque publié et traduit*. PhD diss., University of Helsinki, 1892.

47 Furlani, Giuseppe. "Contributi alla storia della filosofia greca in oriente: Testi siriaci I." *Rendiconti della Reale Accademia dei Lincei: Classe di scienze morali, storiche e filologiche*, ser. V, 23 (1914): 154–175.

48 Vandenhoff, Bernhard. "Die Zeit des Syrers Theodor bar Konī." *Zeitschrift der Deutschen Morgenländischen Gesellschaft* 70 (1916): 126–132.

49 Furlani, Giuseppe. "Di alcuni passi della Metafisica di Aristotele presso Giacomo d'Edessa." *Rendiconti della Reale Accademia dei Lincei: Classe di scienze morali, storiche e filologiche*, ser. V, 30 (1921): 268–273.

50 Furlani, Giuseppe. "Sull' introduzione di Atanasio di Baladh alla logica e sillogistica aristotelica." *Atti del Reale Istituto Veneto di scienze, lettere ed arti* 81/2 (1921–1922): 635–644.

51 Furlani, Giuseppe. "Aristoteles, de interpretatione, 16a,6–7 nach einem syrisch erhaltenen Kommentar." *Zeitschrift für Semitistik* 1 (1922): 34–37.

52 Furlani, Giuseppe. "ʿEnānīšōʿ, Aḫūdhemmēh e il libro delle definizioni di Michele l'Interprete." *Rendiconti della Reale Accademia Nazionale dei Lincei: Classe di scienze morali, storiche e filologiche*, ser. V, 31 (1922): 143–148.

53 Furlani, Giuseppe. "Sul trattato di Sergio di Reshʿaynā circa le categorie." *Rivista trimestrale di studi filosofici e religiosi* 3 (1922): 135–172.

54 Furlani, Giuseppe. "La versione e il commento di Giorgio delle Nazioni all'Organo aristotelico." *Studi italiani di filologia classica*, n.s. 3 (1923): 305–333.

55 Furlani, Giuseppe. "La psicologia di Giovanni di Dārā." *Rivista degli studi orientali* 11 (1928): 254–279.

56 Furlani, Giuseppe. "Il proemio di Giorgio delle Nazioni al primo libro dei Primi Analitici di Aristotele." *Rivista degli studi orientali* 18 (1939/40): 116–130.

57 Furlani, Giuseppe. "Sul commento di Giorgio delle Nazioni al primo libro degli Analitici anteriori di Aristotele." *Rivista degli studi orientali* 20 (1942): 47–64. 229–238.

57a Daiber, Hans. "Ein bisher unbekannter pseudoplatonischer Text über die Tugenden der Seele." *Der Islam* 47 (1971): 25–42; 49 (1972): 122–123.

58 Schlimme, Lorenz. *Der Hexaemeronkommentar des Moses Bar Kepha: Einleitung, Übersetzung und Untersuchungen*, 2 vols. Wiesbaden, 1977.

59 Daiber, Hans. *Aetius Arabus: Die Vorsokratiker in arabischer Überlieferung*. Wiesbaden, 1980.

60 Reinink, Gerrit Jan. "Severus Sebokts Brief an den Periodeutes Jonan: Einige Fragen zur aristotelischen Logik." In *III Symposium Syriacum 1980: Les contacts du monde syriaque avec les autres cultures*. Ed. by René Lavenant. Rome, 1983, 97–107.

61 Brock, Sebastian. "Some notes on the Syriac translations of Porphyry's Eisagoge." In *Mélanges en hommage au professeur et au penseur libanais Farid Jabre*. Ed. by Université Libanaise. Beirut, 1989, 41–50.

62 Brock, Sebastian. "The Syriac commentary tradition." In *Glosses and commentaries on Aristotelian logical texts: The Syriac, Arabic and Medieval Latin traditions*. Ed. by Charles Burnett. London, 1993, 3–18. – Repr. in Brock 1999 [cf. *19] no. XIII.

63 Miller, Dana. "George, Bishop of the Arab Tribes on True Philosophy." *Aram* 5 (1993): 303–320.

64 Abramowski, Luise. "Zu den Schriften des Michael Malpana/Badoqa." In *After Bardaisan: Studies on Continuity and Change in Syriac Christianity in Honour of Professor Han J. W. Drijvers*. Ed. by Gerrit Jan Reinink and Alexander Cornelius Klugkist. Leuven, 1999, 1–10.

65 Brock, Sebastian. "Two letters of the Patriarch Timothy from the Late Eighth Century on Translations from Greek." *Arabic Sciences and Philosophy* 9 (1999): 233–246.

66 Reich, Edgar. "Ein Brief des Severus Sēbōḵt." In *Sic itur ad astra: Studien zur Geschichte der Mathematik und Wissenschaften: Festschrift für den Arabisten Paul Kunitzsch zum 70. Geburtstag*. Ed. by Menso Folkerts und Richard Lorch. Wiesbaden, 2000, 478–489.

67 Hugonnard-Roche, Henri: "Jacob of Edessa and the Reception of Aristotle." In B. ter Haar Romeney 2008 [cf. *5], 205–222.

68 Wilks, Marina. "Jacob of Edessa's Use of Greek Philosophy in His Hexaemeron." In B. ter Haar Romeney 2008 [cf. *5], 223–238.

69 Ibrahim, Gregorios and George A. Kiraz, eds. *Studies on Jacob of Edessa*. Piscataway, N.J., 2010.

70 Watt, John W. "Sergius of Reshaina on the Prolegomena to Aristotle's Logic: The Commentary [addressed to Theodore of Karkh] on the Categories, Chapter Two." In E. Coda, C. Martini Bonadeo 2014 [cf. *40], 31–57.

71 Takahashi, Hidemi. "Syriac and Arabic Transmission of *On the Cosmos*." In *Cosmic Order and Divine Power: Pseudo-Aristotle, On the Cosmos. Introduction, Text, Translation and Interpretative Essays*. Ed. by Johan C. Thom. Tübingen, 2014, 153–167.

72 Zonta, Mauro. "Iwānnīs of Dārā's *Treatise on the Soul* and its Sources. A New Contribution to the History of Syriac Psychology around 800 AD." In E. Coda and C. Martini Bonadeo 2014 [cf. *40], 113–122.

73 Hugonnard-Roche, Henri. "Questions de logique au VIIe siècle. Les épîtres syriaques de Sévère Sebokht et leurs sources grecques." *Studia Graeco-Arabica* 5 (2015): 53–104.

74 Zonta, Mauro. "Iwānnīs of Dārā on Soul's Virtues. About a Late-Antiquity Greek Philosophical Work among Syrians and Arabs." *Studia Graeco-Arabica* 5 (2015): 129–143.

74a Aydin, Sami. *Sergius of Reshaina. Introduction to Aristotle and his Categories, Addressed to Philotheos. Syriac Text, with Introd., Transl., and Commentary*. Leiden, 2016.

6.5 *Reception*

75 Klinge, Gerhard. "Die Bedeutung der syrischen Theologen als Vermittler der griechischen Philosophie an den Islam." *Zeitschrift für Kirchengeschichte*, 3. Folge, 9 [58] (1939): 346–386.

76 Westerink, Leendert Gerrit, ed. *Anonymous Prolegomena to Platonic Philosophy: Introduction, Text, Translation and Indices*. Amsterdam, 1962.

77 Rescher, Nicholas. *Galen and the Syllogism*. Pittsburgh, 1966.

78 Daiber, Hans. *Ein Kompendium der aristotelischen Meteorologie in der Fassung des Ḥunain Ibn Isḥāq*. Amsterdam, Oxford, 1975.

79 Daiber, Hans. *Das theologisch-philosophische System des Muʿammar Ibn ʿAbbād as-Sulamī (gest. 830 n. Chr.)*. Beirut, Wiesbaden, 1975.

80 Plessner, Martin. *Vorsokratische Philosophie und griechische Alchemie in arabisch-lateinischer Überlieferung: Studien zu Text und Inhalt der Turba Philosophorum: Nach dem Manuskript ediert von Felix Klein-Franke*. Wiesbaden, 1975.

81 Gutas, Dimitri. "Paul the Persian on the Classification of the Parts of Aristotle's Philosophy: A Milestone Between Alexandria and Baġdād." *Der Islam* 60 (1983): 231–267.

82 Hugonnard-Roche, Henri. "Aux origines de l'exégèse orientale de la logique d'Aristote: Sergius de Reš'aina († 536), médecin et philosophe." *Journal asiatique* 277 (1989): 1–17.

83 Daiber, Hans. "Qosṭā Ibn Lūqā (9. Jh.) über die Einteilung der Wissenschaften." *Zeitschrift für Geschichte der Arabisch-Islamischen Wissenschaften* 6 (1990): 93–129.

84 Possekel, Ute. *Evidence of Greek Philosophical Concepts in the Writings of Ephrem the Syrian*. Leuven, 1999.

85 Daiber, Hans. "Die Aristotelesrezeption in der syrischen Literatur." In *Die Gegenwart des Altertums: Formen und Funktionen des Altertumsbezugs in den Hochkulturen der Alten Welt*. Ed. by Dieter Kuhn and Helga Stahl. Heidelberg, 2001, 327–345.

86 Hugonnard-Roche, Henri. *La logique d'Aristote du grec au syriaque: Etudes sur la transmission des textes de l'Organon et leur interprétation philosophique*. Paris, 2004.

87 Daiber, Hans. "Possible Echoes of *De mundo* in the Arabic-Islamic World: Christian, Islamic and Jewish Thinkers." In J. C. Thom 2014 [cf. *71], 169–180.

CHAPTER 3

The Rebirth of Philosophy and the Translations into Arabic

Dimitri Gutas

1 Primary Sources – 2 The Historical Causes of the Graeco-Arabic Translation Movement – 3 Method, Phases, and Significance of the Translations – 4 The Beginnings of Philosophical Literature in Arabic and the Rebirth of Philosophy – 5 Greek Philosophical Texts in Arabic Translation – 6 Secondary Literature

1 Primary Sources

1.1 *The Historical Causes of the Graeco-Arabic Translation Movement*

1 al-Masʿūdī, Abū l-Ḥasan ʿAlī b. al-Ḥusayn. *Kitāb al-Tanbīh wa-l-išrāf* [composed 345/956]. – Ed. by Michael Jan de Goeje, *Kitâb al-tanbîh wa'l-ischrâf auctore al-Masʿūdī*. Leiden, 1894. – Ed. by ʿAbd Allāh Ismāʿīl al-Ṣāwī. Cairo, 1357/1938.

2 al-Masʿūdī. *Murūǧ al-ḏahab wa-maʿādin al-ǧawhar*. – Ed. by Charles Pellat, 7 vols. Beirut, 1966–1979.

3 Ibn al-Nadīm, Abū l-Faraǧ Muḥammad b. Isḥāq (d. 380/990). *Kitāb al-Fihrist* [composed 377/988]. – Ed. by Gustav Flügel, August Müller and Johannes Roediger, 2 vols. Leipzig, 1871–1872 (ed. quoted below). – Repr. Beirut 1964, Frankfurt a.M. 2005. – Ed. by Riḍā Taǧaddud. Tehran, 1350 h.š./1971. – Ed. by Ayman Fuʾād Sayyid, 2 vols. London, 1430/2009. – Engl. transl. by Bayard Dodge, *The Fihrist of al-Nadīm*, 2 vols. New York, 1970.

4 Ṣāʿid b. Aḥmad al-Andalusī, Abū l-Qāsim (d. 462/1070). *Ṭabaqāt al-umam*. – Ed. by Louis Šayḫū (Cheikho). Beirut, 1912. – Ed. by Ġulāmriḍā Ǧamšīdnižād-i Awwal, *al-Taʿrīf bi-Ṭabaqāt al-umam*. Tehran, 1997.

5 Ibn Abī Uṣaybiʿa, Muwaffaq al-Dīn Aḥmad b. al-Qāsim (d. 668/1270). *ʿUyūn al-anbāʾ fī ṭabaqāt al-aṭibbāʾ*. – Ed. by August Müller, 2 vols. Cairo 1299/1882, Königsberg 1884. – Repr. Westmead, 1972.

6 al-Ṣafadī, Ṣalāḥ al-Dīn Ḫalīl b. Aybak (d. 764/1363). *Al-Ġayṯ al-musaǧǧam fī šarḥ Lāmiyyat al-ʿaǧam*. Beirut, 1975.

7 Ibn Nubāta, Abū Bakr Ǧamāl al-Dīn Muḥammad b. Šams al-Dīn al-Miṣrī (d. 768/1366). *Sarḥ al-ʿuyūn fī šarḥ Risālat Ibn Zaydūn*. – Ed. by Muḥammad Abū l-Faḍl Ibrāhīm. Cairo, 1383/1964.

 | DOI 10.1163/9789004323162_005

8 Ibn Ḫaldūn, ʿAbd al-Raḥmān b. Muḥammad (d. 808/1406). *The Muqaddima: An introduction to history*, 3 vols, translated from the Arabic by Franz Rosenthal. New York 1958, Princeton, 1967 (2nd ed.).

1.2 *Method, Phases, and Significance of the Translations*

11 Bergsträsser, Gotthelf. *Ḥunain ibn Isḥāq über die syrischen und arabischen Galen-Übersetzungen*. Leipzig, 1925.

12 Bergsträsser, Gotthelf. *Neue Materialien zu Ḥunain ibn Isḥāq's Galen-Bibliographie*. Leipzig, 1932.

1.3 *The Beginnings of Philosophical Literature in Arabic and the Rebirth of Philosophy*

20 *Ptolemy's Almagest*. – Engl. transl. by Gerald J. Toomer. London, 1984.

21 *Plotini opera*. – Ed. by Paul Henry and Hans-Rudolf Schwyzer, 3 vols (editio maior). Brussels, 1951–1973.

22 Ibn al-Muqaffaʿ (Pseudo-?). *Al-Manṭiq* (also: *Ḥudūd al-manṭiq li-Ibn Bahrīz*). – Ed. by Muḥammad Taqī Dānišpažūh. Tehran, 1357/1978, 1–93.

23 Ibn Bahrīz. *Ḥudūd al-manṭiq*. – Ed. by M. T. Dānišpažūh [*22: 95–126].

24 al-Kindī. *Fī l-Ṣināʿa al-ʿuẓmā*. – Ed. by ʿAzmī Ṭāhā al-Sayyid Aḥmad. Cyprus, 1987.

1.4 *Greek Philosophical Texts in Arabic Translation*

31 *Galens Dialog über die Seele: Aus dem Arabischen übersetzt von Jehuda ben Salomo Alcharisi*. Ed. by Adolph Jellinek. Leipzig, 1852.

32 *The Story of Aḥikar*. Ed. by Frederick Cornwallis Conybeare, James Rendel Harris, and Agnes Smith Lewis. London, 1898.

33 *Galen über die medizinischen Namen*. Ed. and German transl. by Max Meyerhof and Joseph Schacht. Berlin, 1931.

34 *Galeni in Platonis Timaeum commentarii fragmenta*, collegit, disposuit, explicavit Henricus Otto Schröder; appendicem Arabicam addidit Paulus Kahle. Leipzig, 1934.

35 Galen. *On the Parts of Medicine. On Cohesive Causes. On Regimen in Acute Diseases in Accordance with the Theories of Hippocrates*. Ed. by Malcolm Cameron Lyons. Berlin, 1969.

36 Endress, Gerhard. *Proclus Arabus: Zwanzig Abschnitte aus der Institutio theologica in arabischer Übersetzung, eingeleitet, herausgegeben und erklärt*. Beirut, Wiesbaden, 1973.

37 *Kitāb Ǧālīnūs fī firaq al-ṭibb li-l-muta'allimīn*. – Ed. by Muḥammad Salīm Sālim. Cairo, 1977.

38 Galen. *Al-Usṭuquṣṣāt 'alā ra'y Buqrāṭ*. – Ed. by Muḥammad Salīm Sālim. Cairo, 1987.

39 Tardieu, Michel. "La récension arabe des Μαγικὰ λόγια." *In Oracles chaldaïques. Recension de Georges Gémiste Pléthon*. Ed. by Brigitte Tambrun-Krasker. Athens, Paris, Brussels, 1995, 157–171.

40 *Al-Naṣṣ al-kāmil li-manṭiq Arisṭū*. – Ed. by Farīd Ǧabr [Farid Jabre], 2 vols. Beirut, 1999.

41 Ghersetti, Antonella, ed. *Il Kitāb Arisṭāṭālīs al-faylasūf fī l-firāsa nella traduzione di Ḥunayn b. Isḥāq*. Venice, 1999.

42 Abattouy, Mohamed, ed. "*Nutaf min al-ḥiyal*: A partial Arabic version of Pseudo-Aristotle's *Problemata mechanica*." *Early Science and Medicine* 6 (2001): 96–122.

43 Alexandre d'Aphrodise. *Traité de la providence: Version arabe de Abū Bišr Mattā ibn Yūnus*. – Edition and French transl. by Pierre Thillet. Lagrasse, 2003.

44 Alexander of Aphrodisias. *On Aristotle On Coming-to-Be and Perishing 2. 2–5*. – Engl. transl. by Emma Gannagé. London, 2005.

45 Maróth, Miklós, ed. *The Correspondence between Aristotle and Alexander the Great: An Anonymous Greek Novel in Letters in Arabic Translation*. Piliscsaba, 2006.

46 Hansberger, Rotraud Elisabeth. *The Transmission of Aristotle's Parva naturalia in Arabic*. PhD Diss., Oxford, 2007.

47 Robert Hoyland. "A New Edition and Translation of the Leiden Polemon." In *Seeing the Face, Seeing the Soul: Polemon's Physiognomy from Classical Antiquity to Medieval Islam*. Ed. by Simon Swain. Oxford, 2007, 329–463.

48 Theophrastus. *On First Principles (transmitted as his Metaphysics). Greek Text and Medieval Arabic Translation*. Edited and translated with introduction, commentaries and glossaries, as well as the medieval Latin translation, and with an excursus on Graeco-Arabic editorial technique by Dimitri Gutas. Leiden, 2009.

49 Averroes (Ibn Rushd) of Cordoba. *Long Commentary on the De Anima of Aristotle*, translated with introduction and notes by Richard C. Taylor with Thérèse-Anne Druart. New Haven, 2009.

2 The Historical Causes of the Graeco-Arabic Translation Movement

Translation had played a crucial role in the cultural history of multilingual Near Eastern peoples ever since the beginning of the second millennium BC with the translations of Sumerian texts into Akkadian. The conquest of the Near East by Alexander the Great and the ensuing spread of Hellenism and the Greek language led to two significant developments, before the rise of Islam, in the two major indigenous linguistic and cultural groups, Aramaic and Persian. Among the former, who in the meantime had embraced Christianity, an initial attitude of antagonism against pagan Hellenism eventually gave way to assimilation just at the time when the Muslim Arabs were moving into Syria and Palestine in the first half of the 1st/7th century. Helped by their knowledge of Greek and their training in the study of the Greek Church Fathers, Syriac speaking scholars were at this time translating pagan Greek works, primarily in the fields of Aristotelian logic, popular ethics, and medicine (Brock 1982 [*42], Hugonnard-Roche 2007 [*108; cf. also § 1.5.3 and § 2 above)]. In the Persian Sasanian empire (224–651), the historical memory of the devastation of Alexander's conquests was incorporated into an imperial ideology that simultaneously glorified the Sasanian dynasty and promoted the assimilation of Hellenism through translations from Greek into Middle Persian, which appear to have reached their high point during the reign of Ḫusraw Anūširwān (531–579). As the Zoroastrian thesaurus of pre-Islamic lore, the *Dēnkard*, has it (book IV), Alexander's conquest caused the books containing the sacred texts of the Avesta and the Zand to be scattered throughout the world, but the Sasanians, starting with their founder, Ardašīr I, took it upon themselves to collect these texts as well as other non-religious writings on science and philosophy which were conformable to Zoroastrian teachings (Shaki 1981 [*40: 119]). In this fashion, philosophical and scientific writings of all cultures were seen as ultimately either derived from or compatible with the Avesta, and translation as the means to 'repatriate' them into Persian (Shaked 1987 [*52: 217], Gutas 1998 [*71: 34–45]). This culture of translation in late Sasanian times, officially sponsored by the state, continued even after the fall of the Persian empire in 651 AD, and during the Umayyad and early Abbasid periods gave rise to numerous translations from Middle Persian into Arabic in a translation movement, still not fully studied, that ran parallel to the initial stages of the Graeco-Arabic one (Bosworth 1983 [*45], Zakeri 1994 [*67], de Blois 2002 [*79: X 231–232], Zakeri 2004 [*89]).

With the advent of Islam and a new political order, yet another language with universalistic claims, the last in a long series, made its appearance in the Near East. The move of Arab rulers and tribesmen into areas whose populations did not speak Arabic made translation into Arabic inevitable both in government circles and in everyday life during the Umayyad period. Necessity dictated that, for reasons of continuity, the early Umayyads keep both the Greek-speaking functionaries and the Greek language in their imperial administration in Damascus. The *Fihrist* [*3: 242,25–30] mentions that Sarǧūn b. Manṣūr al-Rūmī (the 'Byzantine' or 'Melkite'), who served as secretary to the first Umayyad caliphs from Muʿāwiya (regn. 41–60 / 661–680) to ʿAbd al-Malik (regn. 65–86 / 685–705), was asked by the latter to translate the administrative apparatus (*dīwān*) into Arabic. Also related to the need for royal models felt by the ruling elite in Umayyad times was the translation, sponsored by Hišām's (regn. 105–125/724–743) secretary Abū l-ʿAlāʾ Sālim, of the Greek mirror-for-princes literature in the form of correspondence between Aristotle and Alexander the Great (Grignaschi 1967 [*27: 223] following the *Fihrist* [*3: 117,30]; Maróth 2006 [*99], Gutas 2009 [*112]), and the same caliph's commission of an Arabic translation of the lives of Sasanian kings, this time from Middle Persian (as reported by al-Masʿūdī, *Tanbīh* [*1: 106, 18–19]). Similar needs must have occasioned the translation of the Syriac medical compendium (*kunnāš*) of Ahrun by Māsarǧawayh, allegedly for Marwān I (regn. 64–65/684–685) or ʿUmar II (regn. 99–101/717–720), if indeed the sources suggesting this are to be relied upon (Dietrich 2007 [*105]).

In private life, social and commercial intercourse in Syro-Palestine and Egypt, heavily Greek-speaking until well after the end of the Umayyads, made translation a quotidian reality. Bilingual Greek and Arabic papyri of deeds and contracts attest to this fact for 1st–2nd/7th–8th century Egypt; the practice was doubtless ubiquitous. Due also to the existence of numerous Greek speakers in these areas, translation from the Greek must have been easily available on an individual basis to everybody, scholar or otherwise, who knew an educated Greek person or where to find one. All these activities of translation during the Umayyad period are instances of random and *ad hoc* accommodation to the needs of the times, generated by Arab rule over non-Arab peoples. Deliberate and planned scholarly interest in the translation of Greek works (and Syriac works inspired by Greek) into Arabic appears not to have been present in Umayyad times. The report that the Umayyad prince Ḫālid b. Yazīd had had Greek books on alchemy, astrology, and other sciences translated into Arabic has been demonstrated to be a later fabrication (Ullmann 1978 [*38]).

It was with the accession of the Abbasids to power (132/749) and the transfer of the seat of the caliphate to Baghdad under al-Manṣūr (from 145/762) that translation into Arabic from Greek (on occasion through Middle Persian or Syriac intermediaries) became a movement, a historically significant social phenomenon (Gutas 1998 [*71: Part 1]). What sets the translation movement in Baghdad apart from the incidental translation activities of Umayyad times and other periods of Islamic history is that it lasted uninterruptedly for well over two centuries, that it was commissioned by both the Abbasid aristocracy and members of all literate classes of Baghdad society, that it was financially supported with an enormous outlay of funds, both public and private, and that it eventually proceeded on the basis of a scholarly methodology and philological exactitude that spanned generations and reflected, in the final analysis, a social attitude; more than any other trait it characterizes the public culture of early Baghdad society. At the end of the Graeco-Arabic translation movement, the majority of pagan Greek books on science and philosophy (high literature and pagan history excluded) that were available in late antiquity throughout the eastern Byzantine empire and the Near East had been translated into Arabic. To these should be added a few other marginal genres of writings, such as Byzantine military manuals (*tactica*), popular collections of wisdom sayings (*gnomologia*), and even books on falconry. In sheer quantity of volumes translated, let alone in quality of translation, the achievement was stupendous.

Historical sources credit the second Abbasid caliph, al-Manṣūr (regn. 136–158/754–775), with having initiated the translation movement (al-Masʿūdī, *Murūǧ* [*2: VIII 286–287]; Ṣāʿid, *Ṭabaqāt* [*4: 48]; Ibn Ḫaldūn, *Muqaddima* [*8: III 115]). The Abbasids came into power as the result of a civil war, and al-Manṣūr addressed the task of reconciling the different interest groups that participated in the Abbasid cause and legitimizing the rule of his dynasty in their eyes by expanding his imperial ideology to include the concerns of factions that were carriers of Sasanian culture. These included, among others, Persianized Arabs and Aramaeans, Persian converts to Islam, and especially Zoroastrian Persians – at the time of al-Manṣūr still the majority of Persians – who, as a number of Persian revivalist insurrections of the time (like that of Sunbāḏ) indicate, had to be convinced that the Islamic conquests were irreversible. This was done by promulgating the view that the Abbasid dynasty, in addition to being the descendants of the Prophet, was at the same time the successor of the ancient imperial dynasties in Mesopotamia, culminating with the Sasanians. As the most effective means for the diffusion of this ideology al-Manṣūr incorporated the translation culture of the Sasanians as part of his overall imperial ideology and employed the same technique as the Zoroastrians did for spreading their millennarianism, astrological history (political astrology), i.e., accounts and predictions of dynastic reigns in terms of cyclical periods governed by the stars (see Pingree 1986 [*49: V 130]). His court astrologer, Abū Sahl b. Nawbaḫt (on him, see Pingree 1982 [*43]), composed a book in which he incorporated the account of the transmission and preservation of the sciences from *Dēnkard* IV (mentioned above, p. 98) and placed heavy emphasis on the role of translation in the renewal of knowledge as ordained by the stars for each people (fragment from the *Kitāb al-Tohmagān*, quoted in the *Fihrist* [*3: 238–239]; see Pingree 1968 [*29: 7–13] and van Bladel 2012 [*114]). Astrological history performed for al-Manṣūr and his immediate successors both a political function – in that it presented the political dominion of the Abbasid state, whose cycle was just beginning, as ordained by the stars and ultimately by God, and hence inevitable – and an ideological function, in that it inculcated the view of the Abbasids as the legitimate successors, in the grand astrological scheme of things, of the ancient Mesopotamian empires, something which entailed translation of ancient texts as part of the renewal of sciences incumbent upon each imperial dynasty. Al-Manṣūr's adoption of this aspect of Sasanian ideology and its culture of translation indirectly initiated the Graeco-Arabic translation movement and gave it official sanction (Gutas 1998 [*71: ch. 2]).

The initial translations of Greek works were made from Middle Persian intermediaries or compilations (Nallino 1922 [*17], Duneau 1966 [*26], Kunitzsch 1975 [*35]), and they were preponderantly of astrological character. However, the translation movement was further invigorated and its role enhanced also by other causes which uniquely combined to sustain it for well over two centuries. The exigencies of religio-political confrontation played a major role. Religious debate within Islam and polemics between Islam and other religions became particularly acute after the Abbasids came to power both because the revolution raised expectations that were bound to be thwarted and because of the universalistic claims of Islam as a religion put forth by the new imperial ideology. Whenever the confrontations were not seen as a threat to the established order, they were resolved, or at least accommodated, by means of disputations which often involved recourse to translated materials.

By the time of the civil war between al-Amīn and al-Ma'mūn (195–197/811–813), the ideological orientation given to the Abbasid state by al-Manṣūr had won wide acceptance and the translation movement was firmly entrenched in the cultural life of Baghdad. Al-Ma'mūn, back in Baghdad as both a fratricide and regicide (regn. 198–218/813–833), made use, among other things, also of the culture generated by the translation movement in order to re-establish and expand the centralized authority of the caliph. He engaged in an intensive propaganda campaign that aimed at portraying him as the champion of Islam abroad and as the final arbiter of the true interpretation of Islam at home. In order to achieve the first objective, he initiated an aggressive foreign policy against the Byzantines who were portrayed not merely as infidels but also as culturally benighted and inferior both to their own ancestors, the ancient Greeks, and to the Muslims, who appreciated and translated ancient Greek science. The cultural superiority of the Muslims was presented as being due to Islam itself as a religion: the Byzantines had turned their back on ancient science because of Christianity, while the Muslims had welcomed it because of Islam. Anti-Byzantinism thus went hand in hand with pro-Hellenism (cf. Miquel 1975 [*36: II, ch. 8, esp. 458–481]). The second objective could be achieved only by divesting the criteria for religious authority from the religious and *ḥadīṯ* scholars among the common people and concentrating them in the person of the caliph; this in turn could be effected only by making the caliph's personal judgement in interpreting the religious texts, based on reason, the ultimate criterion, not the dogmatic statements of religious leaders based on transmitted authority. One of the public relations campaigns through which these policies were pursued was the dissemination, by al-Ma'mūn's general and right-hand man, ʿAbd Allāh b. Ṭāhir, of the dream which al-Ma'mūn allegedly had about Aristotle; this version, earlier than the one transmitted in the *Fihrist* [*3: 243,3], survives in Ibn Nubāta's *Sarḥ* [*7: 213]. According to this original version, the philosopher states that personal judgement (*ra'y*) is the ultimate criterion for the best (political and religious) speech, thereby promoting both the rationalist Ḥanafī orientation of the *miḥna* as instituted by al-Ma'mūn and the philhellenism of his campaign against Byzantium. The effectiveness of the dream depended on the culture of Hellenism generated by the translation movement, which it presupposed; the fabrication of the dream was thus the consequence of the translation movement, not its originator, as the *Fihrist* would have it, while at the same time the dream provided further incentive for its more aggressive prosecution and, indeed, expansion.

The impetus given to the translation movement by Abbasid ideology was further sustained by secondary causes, themselves generated by it, which continued to be active even after the original ideologies ceased to be relevant. The ideological campaigns of al-Manṣūr and his immediate successors achieved what they were designed to accomplish; those of al-Ma'mūn, which aimed to re-establish the caliph's political and religious authority, suffered a setback with the termination of the *miḥna* under al-Mutawakkil (regn. 232–247/847–861) and were subsequently rendered irrelevant by the humiliation of the office of the caliph at the hands of the Turkish military. By that time however, the translation culture had become the fashion among the elite in Baghdad, who continued to support it well into the Buyid century (334–447/945–1055). Sponsorship was not restricted to any identifiable source; the sponsors came from all ethnic and religious groups that played politically and economically significant roles during the first two centuries of Baghdad: Muslim Arab aristocrats, foremost among whom were members of the extended Abbasid family; Nestorian Arabs who converted to Islam in office, like the Wahb family, who were secretaries, viziers, and scholars (Sourdel 1959–1960 [*22: 312]); Zoroastrian and Buddhist Persians who converted to Islam in office, like the Nawbaḫt, Munağğim, and Barmak families, who were astrologers, literati, theologians, secretaries and viziers; Arabized Persian Muslims, like the Ṭāhirids, who were generals and politicians (Bosworth 1969 [*31]), and like the Zayyāt family, who were manufacturers, merchants, and secretaries (Sourdel 1959–1960 [*22: 254]); and Arabized Persian Nestorians, subsequently converted to Islam, like the al-Ǧarrāḥ family, who were secretaries (Sourdel 1959–1960 [*22: 520–748]).

Just as significant as the support of the political and social elite was the active sponsorship of scientists and scholars of all groups who commissioned the translation of Greek texts for their practice and research. Noteworthy among them were Muslim Arab aristocrats like al-Kindī, scientist and philosopher (Endress 1987 [*50: II 428]); the Gundishapur medical bosses: the Persian Nestorian families of Baḫtīšūʿ, Māsawayh, and Ṭayfūrī (Sournia, Troupeau 1968 [*30]); and the upstart brothers, the Banū Mūsā, of questionable pedigree.

The translation movement was naturally transformed during the Buyid era into the Islamic scientific and philosophical tradition (Endress 1992 [*50: III 24–152]); by the end of the 4th/10th century, the work of scholars who wrote in Arabic far surpassed, from the point of view of the society that demanded it, the scientific and philosophical level of the translated works, and royal or wealthy sponsors commissioned original works in Arabic rather than translations of Greek works. Most of the seminal Greek works had been translated; for the little that was left untranslated there was no longer any social or scholarly need.

After the end of the translation movement there are only few recorded instances, before the 19th and 20th centuries, of Arabic translations from the Greek. On an individual level, it was always possible to find a Greek speaker in the Islamic world for oral translation; al-Ṣafadī's (d. 764/1363) informant on Greek matters, for example, the famous scholar Shams al-Dīn al-Dimašqī, would appear to have received his information from some such source in Damascus (cf. *Ġayṯ* [*6: 54]). During the Ottoman period, especially in times of political and economic strength, some further attempts at Graeco-Arabic translations were made. The Sultan Meḥmed II (the Conqueror, d. 886/1481) commissioned some Arabic translations from the Greek – notably Ptolemy's *Geography* but also including some works by the last surviving pagan, George Gemistus Plethon (ca. 1360–1452) – while the Ottoman scholar Esʿad al-Yanyawī who lived during the Tulip Period (1130–1143/1718–1730), not satisfied with the early Abbasid translations of Aristotle, learned Greek from certain Greek functionaries in the Ottoman administration and translated anew into Arabic some Aristotelian treatises. This effort, which appears to have been short-lived, is to be seen as part of the trend for modernization in 11th-12th/17th-18th century Ottoman culture through translations and compilations from European languages into Turkish, and, within that context, in relation to the resurgent Aristotelianism among Greek intellectuals (Gutas 1998 [*71: 173–175]).

3 Method, Phases, and Significance of the Translations

The translators from Greek and Syriac into Arabic (see the list given by Ibn Abī Uṣaybiʿa [*5: I 203–205]), with the exception of the pagan scholars from Harran, belonged to the Christian churches dominant in the Fertile Crescent: Melkites (the Biṭrīq father and son, Qusṭā b. Lūqā), Jacobites (ʿAbd al-Masīḥ b. Nāʿima al-Ḥimṣī, Yaḥyā Ibn ʿAdī), and Nestorians (the family of Ḥunayn b. Isḥāq, Abū Bišr Mattā b. Yūnus). Ethnically they were preponderantly Arameans, in some cases Arabs (Ḥunayn) or even Greeks (Qusṭā b. Lūqā). Called upon by their various sponsors to translate Greek works into Arabic, they had two sources of expertise to fall back on as models: the translations of Christian Greek theological literature into Arabic, and the pre- and early Islamic Graeco-Syriac translations (cf. Brock 1983 [*46]). The former would appear to be co-terminous with the pagan Graeco-Arabic translation movement proper and needs to be more fully studied, especially since the translators were active in both sorts of endeavour (Griffith 1999 [*73]; Treiger 2015 [*118]). The second proved of limited usefulness. The Graeco-Syriac translations of non-Christian texts did not cover the wide range of subjects in demand for translation into Arabic, and, having been made for scholarly purposes in completely different circumstances than those into Arabic, they were not subject to the same keen criticism and demand for precision.

The translators therefore on the one hand improved their knowledge of Greek beyond the level of Syriac scholarship, and on the other developed an Arabic vocabulary and style for scientific discourse that remained standard well into the 14th/20th century. Throughout the various stages of the movement, the translations themselves were repeatedly revised with three objectives in mind: greater fidelity to the original, a more natural Arabic style, and greater accuracy in the technical terminology (for details see Endress 1992 [*50: III 3–23]). The translators worked as private individuals unaffiliated with any institution; the *Bayt al-ḥikma*, the celebrated 'House of Wisdom' which has been fabricated by the excited romantic imaginations of scholars and laymen alike to resemble a modern academy and research institution, was nothing else but the Abbasid palace library whose chief function was to store Arabic translations of Sasanian and Arab literature and history (Gutas 1998 [*71: 53–60], Gutas, van Bladel 2009 [*113]).

The translators invested time and effort into their work because it was a lucrative profession. According to a report by Abū Sulaymān al-Siǧistānī preserved in the *Fihrist* [*3: 243,18–20], Ḥunayn b. Isḥāq, Ḥunayn's nephew Ḥubaysh, and Ṯābit b. Qurra were each in receipt of a monthly salary of 500 dinars from the Banū Mūsā, meant to cover their translation services as well as their living expenses; the Arabic text says *li-l-naql wa-l-mulāzama*, the second term denoting (according to a personal communication by M. Ullmann, 21/07/1998) 'the costs of residing' (in the city; cf. WKAS [*4: II 557a34–45]; cf. also Endress 1987 [*50: II 427 n. 82]). Qusṭā b. Lūqā, as a young man out to make his fortune, left his home town of Baalbek and went to Baghdad where he translated, for pay, some of the books he had taken with him (*Fihrist* [*3: 243,18]). The high level of translation technique and philological accuracy achieved by Ḥunayn's circle and other translators late in the 3rd/9th century was due to the incentive provided by the munificence of their sponsors, a munificence which in turn was due to the prestige that Baghdad society attached to the translated works and the knowledge of their contents.

By the same token, however, the very munificence of the sponsors also dictated the choice of books to be translated – that is, Greek books which were of no interest to the sponsors, even if written by otherwise famous and sought-after authors, were not translated because no one would have paid the translators for their work. An excellent case in point is Galen's book on solecisms (Bergsträsser 1925 [*11: 42 no. 129]), which the renowned Ḥunayn could easily have afforded to translate gratis, just for the sake of learning. But he worked on commission for patrons. On occasion he also translated for his son or perhaps his nephew Ḥubaysh (Bergsträsser 1925 [*11: 28,18. 34,6. 44,17. 47,1]), from whom presumably he did not take any money, but such translations for his relatives were as a rule into Syriac, which means that his son or his nephew then translated the work into Arabic for a Muslim sponsor.

The method and approach of the translations changed according to the context in which, and the purpose for which they were made. Although it can be observed that the competence in Greek of the translators improved over time due to the increased demand as just described, it is not true that the translations followed a linear course of development from literal to those according to sense, as first stated by al-Ṣafadī (*Ġayṯ* [*6: I 46]; Rosenthal 1975 [*25: 17–18]) and accepted by most modern scholars. All styles of translation, including the revision of earlier ones, were in use at all times. It is therefore more conducive to an accurate understanding of the whole translation movement to discuss it not in terms of successive stages or phases, but in terms of *complexes* of translations, such complexes being identified either by the circles in which they appeared or by successive translations of a work or related clusters of works (Gutas 1998 [*71: 141–150]). This area of research has yet to be mapped out completely and accurately, but for the moment the following noteworthy complexes can be mentioned. It has to be stressed that this brief list is by no means exhaustive.

(a) The earliest translations before the time of Ḥunayn, those which were seen to be old even by later scholars in Baghdad such as Ibn-al-Nadīm, who calls them 'ancient translations' (*naql qadīm,* [*3: ch. VII]; see also Gutas 1983 [*47: 252–253 and n. 52]). He has little information about them other than what he read in manuscripts of later translations of a given work, and accordingly this complex of translations, most important for the reconstruction of the earliest history of the translation movement, is difficult to recapture due to the disappearance of most of those translations and the insufficient amount of philological research on those that have survived. These translations consist of, among others, pre-philosophical translations of philosophical literature, works like Aristotle's *Physics, Topics, and Rhetoric*. In the case of the latter, the work by Vagelpohl (2008 [*110]) throws considerable light on the earliest practices and on the nature of their relative clumsiness.

(b) Contemporary with Ḥunayn but separate from his activity is the complex of translations that were made in the circle of al-Kindī in which the overriding interest is on the substance and not the philology of the texts translated. Their characteristics have been studied in detail by Endress (1997 [*68], 2007 [*106], and see below § 4).

(c) The Ḥunayn translations are noteworthy for their scientific accuracy. This complex has been studied much more extensively than the rest (cf. Bergsträsser 1913 [*16]), and we are even in possession of a Greek and Arabic lexicon of its vocabulary (Ullmann 2002–2007 [*80]).

We do not know where Ḥunayn went to improve his knowledge of Greek – whether to one of the former centres of Greek learning in the Near East that were now within the Islamic world (Antioch, Damascus, Jerusalem, Alexandria) or to the Byzantine Empire itself (cf. § 9.2.1). However, from what we can judge by his extant translations and his own admission, he gained expertise primarily in scientific – and especially medical – Greek; his knowledge of literary Greek was not, apparently, as good. In a translator's note to Galen's *De nominibus medicinalibus* he mentions that despite a rather defective Greek manuscript, understanding Galen's language and translating it into Syriac had not posed a problem for him. 'But', he continues, 'I am not familiar with the language of Aristophanes, nor am I accustomed to it. Hence, it was not easy for me to understand the quotation, and I have, therefore, omitted it' (Rosenthal 1975 [*25: 19]).

Similarly Ḥunayn was said to have studied Arabic grammar in Basra with a famous scholar. Unverifiable as these reports are, the fact remains that his extant Arabic translations evince an unparalleled expertise in the comprehension of scientific Greek and a masterly Arabic style that is distinctive for its clarity and precision. His Syriac must have been equally good – he made many more translations into Syriac than into Arabic, it seems, though for the most part his Syriac translations have not survived (Brock 1991 [*58]).

Ḥunayn's reputation rested in fact on his translations, and rightly so. In addition to their accuracy and readability, he also developed a philological method for establishing a critical text before translating it (Strohmaier 1974 [*34]). He describes it himself in an essay he wrote on his own translations of Galen. There he says about his translation of *De sectis* that he first collected several Greek manuscripts of the work, which he then collated in order to produce a correct text. This text he subsequently compared with the already existing Syriac version of *De sectis*, thus producing an improved and corrected Syriac translation; 'this is how I proceed with everything I translate' (Bergsträsser [*11: 4]).

The scrupulousness and philological exactitude with which Ḥunayn approached his work of translation enabled him, among other translators in his circle (cf. pp. 104–105 above), to create an Arabic scientific vocabulary and expository style that by and large has remained standard to this day (Ullmann in WKAS [*4: II ix, and references in n. 14]; Endress 1992 [*50: III 3–23]).

(d) The complex of translations of the Aristotelian *Organon* by the Baghdad Aristotelians of the early 4th/10th century represents yet a further approach to the work of translation, one that uses fully all the apparatus of scholarship and philological sophistication, but for the paramount purpose of doctrinal understanding of the works concerned, not necessarily philological accuracy as such (Hugonnard-Roche 1993 [*63], Gutas 1998 [*71: 147]). To their diligence we owe the survival of the most important (and, for some treatises, the only extant) manuscript of the Arabic *Organon* (MS Paris, Bibliothèque nationale 2356) and the *Physics* (MS Leiden, Warner 583).

(e) Certain individual Greek works, because of their importance for Arabic scholarship during the translation movement, by themselves constitute a complex of translations by dint of the fact that they were repeatedly translated, revised, and commented upon. As such, they generated a scholarly tradition of their own and accordingly they have to be studied in their own context and in view of their contributions to the scientific and philosophical discussions in Baghdad. A prime example is Euclid's *Elements*, one of the very first books to be translated into Arabic and always at the center of intellectual life in Baghdad and beyond (cf. Brentjes 1994 [*65], Gutas 1998 [*71: 147–148], Brentjes 2006 [*96]), and Aristotle's *Metaphysics*, whose manifold translations of the various books at different times and with different approaches over a century and a half virtually chart the development of early Arabic philosophical studies (Bertolacci 2005 [*90]).

The particular linguistic achievement of the early Abbasid Graeco-Arabic translation movement was that it produced a scientific literature with a technical vocabulary for its concepts, as well as a high *koine* language that made Classical Arabic a fit vehicle for the intellectual achievements of Islamic scholarship; its particular historical achievement was to preserve for posterity both lost Greek texts and more reliable manuscript traditions of those extant. On a broader and more fundamental level, the translation movement made Islamic civilization the successor to Hellenic civilization. As such, not only did it ensure the survival of Hellenism at a time when the Latin West was ignorant of it and the Byzantine East busy suppressing it, but proved that it can be expressed in languages and adopted in cultures other than Greek, and that it is international in scope and the common property of all mankind.

4 The Beginnings of Philosophical Literature in Arabic and the Rebirth of Philosophy

A slightly altered version of the following section has been published in: Robert Pasnau, ed. The *Cambridge History of Medieval Philosophy*. Cambridge, 2010, 11–25.

Philosophy died a lingering death long before Islam appeared. The long demise started apparently with the reign of Diocletian (284–305 AD), as the social, demographic, administrative and other changes that would eventually lead to the end of the ancient world first set in; in consequence of these changes, philosophy, as the living practice of rational thinking about man and the universe outside socially instilled and institutionally sanctioned mythologies and superstitions, was seen to represent attitudes and habits of mind little appreciated and even less tolerated (Haldon 1990 [*56], MacMullen 1997 [*69: 83–92], 2006 [*98: ch. 4]). Whatever was left of even the academic practice of philosophy after Justinian's 529 edict prohibiting pagans to teach (cf. p. 39 above) limped on for another two or three generations until, as the current interpretation of the evidence has it, the last philosopher in Alexandria, Stephanus, was invited by the Emperor Heraclius to Constantinople around 610 (cf. p. 42 above). And that is the last we hear for some time of philosophy *in Greek*, for in the ensuing two centuries – during, that is, the Iconoclastic controversy in Byzantium and the so-called 'Dark Ages', – philosophical treatises were not even copied, let alone composed (Gutas 2004 [*85: 195–196]). This situation continued until the 'Macedonian renaissance' of the second half of the 3rd/9th century when there is, not a resurrection of philosophy, but at least some scholia by men like Photius and Arethas, indicating a certain renewal of philosophical interest. I say 'in Greek' because it is important to note that throughout antiquity, philosophy was done in Greek. After Alexander the Great and the spread of Hellenism throughout the Near East, we witness the remarkable fact that although *participation* in philosophy becomes internationalized, its *expression* was not envisaged in anything but Greek. Even after the Hellenistic empire of Alexander's successors was supplanted by that of the Latin-speaking Romans, the usual linguistic development – the language of the empire imposing itself on cultural activities – did not take place. We thus face such noteworthy situations as that of philosophers whose mother tongue was not Greek doing philosophy in Greek. A very pertinent case in point is provided by Plotinus and Porphyry. Plotinus, who dominated ancient philosophical activity in Rome in the middle of the third century, was most probably a native speaker of Latin, while his most eminent student, Porphyry, was a native Aramaic speaker from Tyre on the eastern coast of the Mediterranean. They both wrote their philosophy, which was to be a dominant force in thinking for at least a millennium, in Greek, and, what is even more interesting, Porphyry even corrected the rather sloppy Greek style of his teacher (Longinus, the literary critic, called the style of Plotinus 'defective' [διημαρτημένα]; Porphyry, *Life of Plotinus* [*21: § 19–20]) in preparation for an edition of the latter's work. To be sure, there were attempts at translating philosophy in Greek into other languages, the presumed intention being to implant it in the cultures of these languages – but such attempts, in the end, did not produce the intended results. Two contemporary great scholars at the antipodes of the cultural spread of Hellenism, Boethius in Rome (d. 525) and Sergius of Rēšʿainā in northern Mesopotamia (d. 536), conceived of the grand idea of translating all of Aristotle into Latin and Syriac respectively (Hugonnard-Roche 1989 [*55: 12]; for Sergius cf. pp. 56 and 58 above). The conception is to their credit as individual thinkers, in that they were ahead of their time; their failure indicates that the receiving cultures in which they worked had not developed the need for this enterprise. Philosophy in Latin was to develop, even if on some of the foundations laid by Boethius, much later, while in Syriac it reached its highest point, with Barhebraeus (d. 1286), only after it had developed in Arabic and had been translated from it (Gutas 2004 [*85: 196]). The emergence of philosophy in Arabic has to be seen against this background in order to realize its revolutionary character.

If living philosophy was dead in Greek, and had failed to be transplanted and acquire an independent status in other languages, what survived were its physical remains in terms of manuscripts and libraries (D'Ancona 2007 [*104]), and certain – much reduced, enfeebled, and diluted – *philosophical curricula* and *theological applications*, primarily of logical studies, in various schools and communities throughout the area that was to come under Muslim rule and be politically reunited for the first time since Alexander the Great. These have been discussed in detail in chapters 1 and 2 above. Here I would like to point to some specific developments that were to provide the necessary, but clearly not sufficient, conditions within which a philosophical literature in Arabic could begin. The most significant area to which these curricula were reduced was the rudiments of Aristotelian logic. It is possible to discern a major structural change in the medical curriculum in Alexandria toward the end of the 6th century, possibly as a reaction to the decline of philosophical instruction in that last remaining centre of philosophical studies. Some medical professors, whose names are given in the Arabic sources as Gessius, Anqīlā'us (?), Marinus, and Stephanus of Alexandria (perhaps the same Stephanus who was summoned to Constantinople in 610), decided to organize and simplify the medical curriculum. They restricted the number of medical books for study, and they added logic to the curriculum in a formal way, bringing the total number of books a medical student had to study to 24. Logic may have been studied in association with medicine earlier: Galen's devotion to logic is well known and two at least of his most popular works which were included in this new curriculum, *Ars medica* and *Methodus medendi*, start with significant sections on logical procedures in therapeutic methods. This new Alexandrian curriculum appears to have formally included as part of medical studies specific books on logic, the first four in Aristotle's *Organon*: *Categories, On Interpretation, Prior* and *Posterior Analytics*. The medical books consisted of four books by Hippocrates (*Aphorisms, Prognosticon, Acute Diseases*, and *Airs, Waters, Places*), and abridged versions and summaries of sixteen Galenic books, collectively known as the *Summaria Alexandrinorum*. These accounts, like the texts of Galen's summaries, have not survived in Greek but are prominent in Arabic medical and bibliographic literature (Gutas 1999 [*74: 169–174]). How far beyond the Islamic conquest of Egypt this instruction continued in Greek is not known, nor is there any evidence that this curriculum was transplanted to another city within the new and much reduced borders of the Byzantine Empire. But this is the only indication we have of any kind of philosophical *instruction* in Greek; active philosophizing had ceased to exist.

The theological applications of philosophy in Greek patristic literature, by contrast, were many and long-lived, though clearly harnessed to their theological, apologetic, and polemical goals and not to any free philosophical discourse. To the extent, however, that the patristic authors had been exposed to Greek philosophy they could be expected to be knowledgeable about philosophers and the main philosophical currents, especially Aristotelianism and Platonism (including its 'new' variety in late antiquity). The 6th-century theologian John of Scythopolis in Palestine, for example, wrote the first known commentary on the writings of Pseudo-Dionysius, in which he incorporated apparently extensive quotations from, and paraphrases of, passages in the *Enneads*.

The Pseudo-Dionysian work, *On the Divine Names*, was translated again into Syriac by Phocas bar Sergius some time in the early eighth century (the first translation had been produced by Sergius of Rēšʿainā, cf. p. 56 above), this time together with scholia by John. In this way some Plotinian material became available in Syriac translation, for we have no information that the *Enneads* as such was ever translated into Syriac (Brock 2007 [*103]). This casts an interesting light on the selective Arabic translation of *Enneads* IV–VI a century later by Ibn Nāʿima al-Ḥimṣī, and even if none of the Plotinian texts known to have been quoted by John reappears in the extant Arabic Plotinus, it gives some indication of the intellectual milieu in which the Arabic Plotiniana may have their roots (Frank 1987 [*51]).

In Syriac Christianity, there is a similar development of a logical curriculum as in Greek, except that it was rather shorter: the books studied and commented upon were Porphyry's *Isagoge* and Aristotle's *Categories, On Interpretation*, and *Prior Analytics* but only as far as book I, chapter 7, omitting the section on modal logic and the rest of the treatise. The reasons why this was so are not yet clear; it has been suggested that in Syriac there developed – or was adapted – an understanding of modality based on logical matter (*de re*), and hence there was no interest in Aristotle's modal logic based on logical form (Hugonnard-Roche 2004 [*86: 273]). The rest of the Aristotelian *Organon* appears to have been hardly studied, if at all. There are references to Syriac translations of the *Posterior Analytics, Topics*, and *Sophistical Refutations* by Athanasius of Balad (d. 686, cf. p. 80 above), done before the Graeco-Arabic translation movement, but it seems hardly likely that they amounted to much or were conducive to further study; the Baghdad Aristotelians, who had access to these versions, uniformly condemned them as hopelessly inaccurate. Ibn al-Ḫammār, for example, writes in a note in the Paris MS of the Arabic *Organon* (Bibliothèque nationale ar. 2346) that Athanasius understood nothing of the *Sophistics* (see Georr 1948 [*21: 198–199]). Similarly there are no Syriac commentaries attested for these later treatises of the *Organon* before the beginnings of Arabic philosophy. Awareness among Syriac scholars of these works and their tradition certainly existed (for a list of Syriac translations and commentaries of the *Organon* see Brock 1993 [*61], and cf. the discussion above, § 1.5.3 and § 2), but their study, let alone creative thinking about the issues discussed in them, was not part of the procedures in the Syriac schools (Daiber 2001 [*76], Watt 2004 [*87], King 2013 [*116]). What was, was the application of certain logical categories and an occasional biblically relevant thesis (like the question of the creation of the universe) to theological training and analysis, and more importantly, to theological disputations and inter-faith debates. These debates provide concrete and welcome evidence for the structure of theological education and religious disputation in the Syriac schools just before and after the Islamic conquests (Becker 2006 [*95: esp. ch. 7], Walker 2006 [*100: Part II, ch. 3]).

Some of these debates took place within the borders of the Persian Sasanian empire (226–642 AD), between representatives of the Nestorian community and Zoroastrians. It is evident that classical learning had also permeated Middle Persian literature, though perhaps not to the same extent as Syriac literature, mainly through translations, but also through osmosis and interpersonal contact. As mentioned above (§ 3.2), the Sasanian rulers actively endorsed a translation culture which viewed the transfer of Greek texts and ideas into Middle Persian as the 'restitution' of an Iranian heritage that was pilfered by the Greeks after the campaigns of Alexander the Great (Shaked 1987 [*52: 217 and n. 2], Gutas 1998 [*71: 34–45]). It was this cultural context, and the atmosphere of open debate most energetically fostered by Ḫusraw I Anūširwān (regn. 531–78/9), that must have prompted the Greek philosophers to seek refuge in his court after Justinian's 529 edict prohibiting them to teach. And yet, though there is evidence for the translation of a number of non-philosophical Greek books into Middle Persian, and of the integration in its literature of a certain amount of knowledge and some use of philosophical material for distinctly non-philosophical purposes (Shaked 1987 [*52]), there are no indications that any philosophical literature as such developed in it. Most accounts of philosophical activity in Sasanian Iran concentrate on ruling personalities, first and foremost Ḫusraw (Tardieu in: DPhA 1994 [*7: II 309–318], Walker 2002 [*81]), though this culture of translation and openness to Greek learning was apparently characteristic, to a greater or lesser extent, of the entire Sasanian dynasty.

The most important philosopher of the pre-Islamic period known to have come from Sasanian Iran, Paul the Persian, wrote treatises on logic dedicated to Ḫusraw. Although there are some references to his having written in Middle Persian, the fact remains that his works are extant in Syriac and that he was widely familiar with Syriac logical literature (Gutas 1983 [*47], Teixidor 2003 [*83], Hugonnard-Roche 2004 [*86: 233–235]; cf. also pp. 59–60 and 79 above). In general, then, and given the extensive presence of Nestorian Christians in the Sasanian empire, there does not seem to have existed in it, as far as a philosophical curriculum and its application are concerned, anything drastically different from what is found among Syriac Christians.

Finally, in connection with the Greek philosophers at the court of Ḫusraw, it should also be mentioned that upon their return from Persia they did not move to Harran (Carrhae) in upper Mesopotamia. The Syriac-speaking population of that city remained obstinately pagan until the 5th/11th century, and apparently had knowledge of and access to philosophical material, which they happily shared with their Muslim overlords, but there is absolutely no evidence either that they developed a philosophical tradition among themselves or that they provided a philosophical academic environment (a Platonic 'Academy') to the disappointed Greek philosophers upon their return from Persia (for references to Tardieu's thesis see Endress 2003 [*82: 163 n. 27]; for its refutation see Luna 2001 [*77], Watts 2004 [*88], 2005 [*94]; for a divergent opinion see Hadot 2007 [*107]; cf. also pp. 53–54 above).

With regard to other languages that were culturally significant during the period in question and were influenced by Hellenism, there is the case of Armenian and Georgian. The latter may be discounted insofar as a philosophical literature in translation developed much later than the period from the 7th through 9th centuries, with which we are concerned (van Esbroeck 1990 [*57]). In the case of Armenian, it is true that there exist some few translations of Aristotle (*Categories* and *On Interpretation*), Plato (five dialogues) and Porphyry (*Isagoge*), but these translations, even if it is accepted that they were made in the course of the 1st/7th century (though this is disputed), did not give rise to what may be called a philosophical literature, much less a philosophical movement; it appears that they are to be classed along with the similar productions in Syriac of a philosophical curriculum (Terian 1982 [*44], Zuckerman 2001 [*78: esp. 428. 436–438].

After the advent of Islam, the resurrection of philosophy as Arabic philosophy is intimately connected with the Graeco-Arabic translation movement described above, but not in the reductionist sense that an initial and unexplained translation of Greek philosophical texts gave rise subsequently to Arabic philosophy. As discussed, social and scholarly needs generated by early Abbasid society were met also by the translation of Greek scientific texts into Arabic, and the process eventually culminated in the rise of philosophy. The dialectic between scientific thinking and research on the one hand and the translation activity on the other was responsible for the amazingly rapid development of the sciences in Arabic in the second half of the 2nd/8th century and their establishment as a major cultural force in early Abbasid society.

The beginnings of Arabic philosophical literature can be described as having developed in two stages. The first occurs from about the middle of the 2nd/8th century until the appearance of al-Kindī in the first third of the 3rd/9th, and it is characterized by the continuation, in Arabic this time, of the engagement with the remnants of philosophy in Greek, Syriac, and Middle Persian that have been just reviewed: by the study, that is, of the logical curriculum and the application of philosophical ideas to theological concerns of the time. This stage is represented by some philosophical texts that appeared in Arabic incidentally, in the course of the translation movement, to serve non-philosophical purposes. The second starts with al-Kindī and represents a resurrection of philosophy as a discipline in its own right, independent of theological or other concerns.

The first Arabic philosophical text that is extant from the preliminary stage is an abridged and interpolated paraphrase of the beginning of the logical curriculum, including Porphyry's *Isagoge*, the *Categories*, *On Interpretation*, and *Prior Analytics* up to I,7 (Dānišpažūh [*22]; Furlani 1926 [*18]). It is fortunate that the manuscripts, though all of them of relatively late date, have preserved an ancient colophon which provides precious information about the earliest stages of the translation of Greek books into Arabic. This colophon runs as follows: 'End of the three books on logic [i.e. *Categories*, *On Interpretation*, *Prior Analytics*] from the translation by Muḥammad b. 'Abd Allāh [Ibn] al-Muqaffaʿ. After Muḥammad, they were translated by Abū Nūḥ, the Christian secretary, and then they were translated after Abū Nūḥ by Salm from Harran, the director of the Bayt al-ḥikma, for Yaḥyā b. Ḫālid the Barmakid. Before these translators whom we named, all four books [i.e., Porphyry's *Isagoge* and the three Aristotelian works] were translated by the Christian Hīlyā the Melkite' (Dānišpažūh [*22: 93]).

The translators named are all well known from other contexts, and it is clear that they belong to different generations. Salm's 'translation' can be dated to the time when Yaḥyā b. Ḫālid was Hārūn al-Rašīd's vizier from 170/786 to 187/803. Abū Nūḥ, the Christian secretary of the governor of Mosul, had helped with the translation of Aristotle's *Topics* around 782, during al-Mahdī's caliphate (regn. 158–169/775–785). Muḥammad b. 'Abd Allāh, secretary to al-Manṣūr's governor in Egypt, died apparently a little before 142/760 (Kraus 1934 [*20: 11–13], van Ess 1991–1997 [*60: II 27]). Hīlyā the Melkite (i.e., the Orthodox Christian), finally, who has remained unidentified, is in all likelihood the father of Sirǧīs b. Hilīyā al-Rūmī ('the Byzantine'); Sirǧīs is known as the translator from the Greek of Cassianus' *Eklogai* and Ptolemy's *Almagest* (in 211/827; see Ullmann 1972 [*33: 435]), and thus his father could have been active around the middle of the 2nd/8th century. Since new and complete translations of all these works were done around the middle of the 3rd/9th century by Ḥunayn b. Isḥāq and his collaborators, and these are not mentioned in the colophon, it would be reasonable to date it before Ḥunayn's time, some time in the first half of the 3rd/9th century.

The manuscripts ascribe the work to Muḥammad b. 'Abd Allāh [Ibn] al-Muqaffaʿ, i.e. the son of the famous litterateur and translator from Middle Persian. Modern scholarship for the most part has doubted this ascription and would rather see the father as the author (a view forcefully defended by Dānišpažūh, in his introduction to the edition), but since it would seem rather far-fetched to expect such a work from either one of them, there is no good reason to doubt the manuscript readings. The ascription to the father or son Ibn al-Muqaffaʿ would indicate that the translation, if this is a translation (the manuscripts say that it is) and not an independent composition in Arabic on the basis of Greek (or Pahlavi?) material, was done from the Persian (Furlani [*18: 213]) rather than from Syriac (or Greek), but even if one were to assume that such works existed in Middle Persian – something for which we have no evidence, as the situation with Paul the Persian described above indicates (cf. p. 112) – the language employed in the text would argue against such an assumption, as pointed out by Kraus (Kraus 1934 [*20: 8–9. 13–14]). However, the problem of the language from which the translation or paraphrase was made is related to the four translators listed in the colophon. What does it mean, if the statement of the colophon is to be taken at its face value, to have the same work translated four times within a period of fifty years? It is unlikely that four different translations or paraphrases would have been made of the first three treatises of the *Organon* between 750 and 800 AD and that this would leave no echo in subsequent literature. In all likelihood the colophon is referring to this particular paraphrase of the four books. But even in this case it would seem excessive to have it produced four times within so short a period. The most likely interpretation of the colophon would be to assume that it essentially refers to successive re-workings of one or, at most, two 'translations.' This hypothesis looks more probable when it is noticed that of the four names listed, two were scholars of Greek (Hīlyā and Abū Nūḥ) and two were Persians (Muḥammad and Salm). One may conclude, then, that Hīlyā (Elias), being Greek, first produced the text from the Greek around the middle of the 2nd/8th century, which was subsequently polished by Ibn al-Muqaffaʿ or his son, given the father's fame as expert Arabic stylist. Unfortunately we are not told who commissioned this project or what the occasion for it was. A few decades later, this time Yaḥyā b. Ḫālid the Barmakid, well known for his patronage of the translation movement, commissioned from Salm either a new translation (?) of the same piece or a revision of the old one executed by Hīlyā/Ibn al-Muqaffaʿ. Salm enlisted the labours of Abū Nūḥ for this project, for Abū Nūḥ must have made a name for himself as translator of Aristotelian logic. Thus we have the second version by Abū Nūḥ, polished (or perhaps merely edited) by Salm. In the early translations, such a collaboration between two individuals, one of whom would translate and the other correct the style, is common and well attested (*Fihrist* [*3: 244,16]; Gutas 1998 [*71: 137–138]). Of the two versions, that by Hīlyā/Ibn al-Muqaffaʿ survived both the one by Abū Nūḥ/Salm and the much more accurate and reliable later translations of these books of the *Organon* by Ḥunayn and his son, no doubt on account of the fame associated with the name of Ibn al-Muqaffaʿ.

The connection of Ibn al-Muqaffaʿ with this project, if it is indeed historical, need not be surprising. Intellectual life in the caliphal courts just before and after the Abbasid revolution, during which time Ibn al-Muqaffaʿ was active, was revolving very much around questions of 'rationalism', or, rather questions of verifiability of information beyond the claims of revealed religions, which, after all, contradicted each other. This attitude may hearken back to Sasanian times and indeed to the court of Ḫusraw II Anūširwān, during whose reign such attitudes are attested both in the works of Paul the Persian dedicated to him and in the introduction to the Middle Persian version of *Kalīla wa-Dimna* (Kraus 1934 [*20], Gutas 1983 [*47: 247–249]). Ibn al-Muqaffaʿ, with his translation of *Kalīla wa-Dimna* into Arabic and hence of its introduction (cf. Gabrieli 1931–1932 [*19: 201–205]), and in view of the manifestly enthusiastic reception of the *Kalīla wa-Dimna* in early Abbasid society, may have been reflecting this rationalistic attitude in the wider intellectual circles. In this context, his possible affiliation with the project of producing these texts from the *Organon* in Arabic is well understandable (see in general van Ess 1991–1997 [*60: II 22–36], Latham 1998 [*72: VIII 39–43] – who, however, does not mention the logic – and Schöck 2005 [*93]).

As mentioned, the occasion which prompted the production of this work is not known. But this paraphrase, standing as it does at the very beginning of the translation movement, clearly must reflect some attempt to put into Arabic the main text of the logical curriculum then available, as described at the beginning of this section. For the Arabic text intends to present precisely what that curriculum studied: Porphyry's *Isagoge* and the first three treatises of the *Organon*. In this regard the text belongs to the Greek tradition of this curriculum, as described above, something that would fit in well with the fact that Hīlyā the Byzantine was its translator. However, despite the author's express statement in the text to present all four books, in effect the text breaks off after *Prior Analytics* I,7, thus following the Syriac practice (Gutas 1999 [*74: 183–184]). How the contamination of the two traditions came about in this case is not known.

The nature of the text selected for translation shows that there were no philosophical intentions behind the choice: texts of this nature were routinely read in schools as part of the curriculum, and had no aspirations to philosophical profundity. One may guess that the commissioning of the translation must have come from a wish to have in Arabic what students were reading in the Christian schools as part of their general education; the Muslims appear to have been very much aware of the existence and usefulness of this curriculum in Syriac among the Christians, as al-Kindī mentions in his polemic against the doctrine of the Trinity (Adamson 2007 [*101: 41]). This wish must have been somehow related to the social developments at the very beginning of the Abbasid dynasty – or perhaps, more specifically, to the increased interest in questions of grammar, the structure of language, and meaning, issues manifestly treated in the first works of the *Organon* (cf. Troupeau 1981 [*41], Talmon 1991 [*59]).

Other social, political, and ideological concerns, more easily identifiable, played a role during this first stage of the appearance of philosophical texts and arguments in Arabic. Certainly the most significant of them was the development of Islamic theology and the intense debate among the various schools and individual opinions about its eventual orientation. It is generally acknowledged that the first discussions among Muslims of a theological nature were the result of political and social developments during the first century of Islam, before the beginning of the translation movement. At the centre of discussion were the questions of legitimacy of succession to the caliphate, the relationship of leadership to faith, and the concomitant problem of unbelief when that relationship was considered by some factions as inadequate. Out of this background there arose a 'Kontroverstheologie' (as termed by van Ess 1991–1997 [*60: I 48]), which constituted part of the political discourse of the nascent Muslim society (Gutas 1998 [*71: 70]).

Within Islam, there was injected into theological discussion a cosmological element, and in particular atomism, apparently by the Manichean sects (the Bardesanites; cf. van Ess 1991–1997 [*60: I 418–443], Dhanani 1994 [*66: 182–187]). The need for an alternative cosmology occasioned the translation of Aristotle's *Physics*, a work which, like the *Topics*, was to be re-translated repeatedly. Also related to such theological disputes is the first appearance, in the first half of the 2nd/8th century and before the beginning of the translation movement, of certain Plotinian ideas in the theology of Ǧahm b. Ṣafwān (d. 128/746), ideas which, in this case, would appear to have travelled without written translations (Frank 1965 [*24]).

Another aspect of the theological discussions that also played a role in the use of philosophical arguments is apologetics, i.e., Muslim disputations with non-Muslims, a practice which is directly affiliated with the inter-faith debates in both Greek and Syriac in pre-Islamic times, as mentioned. The need for Muslims, as newcomers to the genre, to understand better the rules of dialectical argumentation prompted the caliph al-Mahdī (regn. 158–169/775–785) to commission from the Nestorian Patriarch Timothy I, with whom he debated, a translation of the best handbook on the subject, Aristotle's *Topics*. Timothy engaged the services of the same Abū Nūḥ whom we saw above in connection with the translation of the logic, and thus there appeared what was to be the first of three Arabic translations of the *Topics* (Gutas 1998 [*71: 61–69], Watt 2004 [*87: 17–19], with references to recent literature). These inter-faith debates continued after the appearance of philosophy, and there are numerous such reports. A particularly interesting one is the dialogue on the prophethood of Muḥammad among the Nestorian Christian Ḥunayn b. Isḥāq, his Muslim patron Ibn al-Munağğim, and the Melkite Christian scholar and translator Qusṭā b. Lūqā (cf. below, § 9.2.1).

Yet another aspect of discourse with philosophical implications in early Islamic society was the appearance in Arabic, apparently towards the end of the Umayyad dynasty in the middle of the 2nd/8th century, of the alleged correspondence between Aristotle and Alexander the Great (Maróth 2006 [*99], Gutas 2009 [*112]). As a genre, this belonged to literature and particularly to the mirror-for-princes genre (discussed below, § 9.1.5). It had hardly any philosophical content, but it helped familiarize people both with the preeminent philosophical personality of all time (Aristotle) and with the very idea that philosophy is of absolute value as a guide to political rule.

In all these discussions, the philosophical arguments and texts whose translation was sought were geared to the service of other concerns, primarily political and theological. There was no question of an interest in philosophy as such. With al-Kindī at the beginning of the 3rd/9th century there is a qualitative change in the approach to these subjects, and philosophy is introduced as an intellectual discipline independent of religion and other ideological currents.

Al-Kindī (d. between 247/861 and 252/866), the first scientist to develop philosophical thought as such in Arabic, was a polymath in the translated sciences and very much a product of his age (see below, § 4). Like other scientists of his time, he gathered around him a wide circle of individuals capable of advising him on these issues and translating the relevant texts. He commissioned translations of scientific subjects and himself wrote on all the sciences: astrology, astronomy, arithmetic, geometry, music, medicine – he even has a treatise on swords. This broad and synoptic view of the sciences, along with the spirit of encyclopedism fostered by the translation movement for the half century before his time, led him to an overarching vision of the unity and interrelatedness of all knowledge. At the same time, and as a result of this view, he developed a unitary epistemological approach, that of mathematics. His goal became to approach mathematical accuracy in his argumentation and he held mathematical or geometrical proof to be of the highest order. In this he was influenced, as a mathematician, both by Ptolemy and Euclid. In the introduction of the *Almagest*, Ptolemy allows both theology and physics to be nothing more than speculative 'guesswork': in the case of theology 'because of its completely invisible and ungraspable nature', in that of physics 'because of the unstable and unclear nature of the matter' – while mathematics alone 'can provide sure and unshakable knowledge', since 'its kind of proof proceeds by indisputable methods, namely arithmetic and geometry' (*Almagest* 6.11–21, transl. by Toomer [*20: 36]; cf. also p. 50 above).

Al-Kindī echoed this understanding in his paraphrase of the *Almagest* where he spoke about the 'true methods of mathematics that are manifested by geometrical and arithmetical proofs which contain no doubt at all' (*Ṣināʿa* [*24: 127]). In his philosophical writings he thus regularly employed certain proofs where his method was quite clearly derived from the *Elements* of Euclid (Rashed 1993 [*64], Endress 2003 [*82: 127–131], Adamson 2007 [*101: 36 and ch. 7]), and he maintained that a prerequisite for the study of Aristotle's philosophy, even of logic, was mathematics. In this he was clearly influenced by Proclus' *Elements of Theology*, the translation of parts of which he commissioned. Proclus thus appears to be the link which connected al-Kindī's mathematical (indeed, geometrical) epistemology with philosophy. Proclus' work, with its geometrical mode of argumentation, was concrete proof for al-Kindī that abstract problems, such as those debated by the theologians of his time – Muslims and non-Muslims alike – could be resolved through philosophical discourse which transcends religious sectarianism and proceeds on the basis of a geometrical methodology acceptable to all, just like the rest of the sciences. Al-Kindī's coming to philosophy was therefore secondary and the result of his earlier preoccupations with science and scientific method; it was not primary.

Once introduced to philosophy by Proclus in this fashion – and hence to the possibility that theological questions can be treated with an amount of certainty equal to that in the mathematical sciences – al-Kindī tried to gain access to this methodologically rigorous discipline, that is, to philosophy. Accordingly he commissioned, and then corrected and edited, translations of Greek metaphysical texts, foremost among which are the selections from Plotinus (*Enneads* IV–VI) and Proclus (*Elements of Theology*) in Arabic known respectively as the *Theology of Aristotle* and *The Pure Good* (known in the medieval Latin translation as *Liber de Causis*), and Aristotle's *Metaphysics*. Al-Kindī and the circle of scholars he gathered around him further commissioned translations of other Greek works, both philosophical and scientific; a full list of what is now known would include, in addition to the works already mentioned, Pseudo-Ammonius' *De placitis philosophorum*, Euclid's *Elements* and Proclus' commentary on it (at least the first book), Proclus' *Elements of Physics*, Nicomachus of Gerasa's *Introduction to Arithmetic* and *Great Book on Music*, Aristotle's *On the Heavens*, *Meteorology*, *De animalibus*, *On the Soul*, *Parva naturalia*, and *Prior Analytics*, Alexander of Aphrodisias' *Questions*, and possibly

Porphyry's *On the Soul* (Endress 2007 [*106: 335–350]). Al-Kindī appears to have paid significant attention also to Platonic texts, especially to the Socratic dialogues, echoes of which we can still find in some of the surviving titles and fragments of his works (Gutas 1988 [*54], Endress 2007 [*106: 332–333]). This is as it should be, given his encyclopedic interests; but the core of his philosophical enterprise was centred in the geometrical approach to the solution of all metaphysical and cosmological problems.

This explains the fragmentary nature of the translations from Proclus and Plotinus that he commissioned, just as it explains his philosophical eclecticism: he was interested primarily in the question of the One or the First and all the issues – methodological, metaphysical, cosmological – related to the concept, and he was accordingly fashioning his own approach from the *disiecta membra* of Greek philosophy available in the written, but not living, tradition. This is why his philosophical thinking does not belong to a school tradition, why it does not rest on pre-existing translations of Greek philosophical works, and why it is an original creation, in Arabic, of the intellectualism of early Abbasid society (Gutas 2004 [*85]).

In the context of the efforts of al-Kindī are to be placed certain other early philosophical writings, like those of Ḥabīb Ibn Bahrīz, a Nestorian scholar apparently slightly older than al-Kindī but who may have belonged to his circle of translators and associates, for he translated for him Nicomachus of Gerasa's *Introduction to Arithmetic* (Freudenthal, Levy 2004 [*84: esp. 483–484]). Ḥabīb wrote a short essay on definitions in logic, which is extant, and which harks back to the *prolegomena* to philosophy from the last stages of Alexandrian Aristotelianism, and in particular to the work attributed to David (Dānišpažūh [*23]; Gutas 1993 [*62: 44]; for David cf. p. 42 above). He also wrote epitomes on the *Categories* and *On Interpretation*, which have not survived, but they may well be related to similar works by al-Kindī or even have provided the basis upon which al-Kindī wrote his similar works on logic (Troupeau 1997 [*70]).

Al-Kindī's work revived philosophy as living practice and introduced it into the new social environment of Abbasid Baghdad by making it relevant to its intellectual concerns and by making it widely acceptable as the indispensable means for critical and rigorous thinking based on reason, not authority. The resurrection of philosophy in Arabic in the early 3rd/9th century was a revolutionary event. Anybody doing philosophy creatively, regardless of his linguistic or ethnic background in multicultural post-classical antiquity, did it in Greek, while all the other philosophical activities were derivative from, and dependent upon, the main philosophizing going on simultaneously in Greek. When Arabic philosophy emerged with al-Kindī, the situation was completely different: it was from the very beginning independent, chose its own paths, and had no contemporary and living Greek philosophy either to imitate or seek inspiration from. Arabic philosophy was the same enterprise as Greek philosophy before the beginning of its gradual demise, but this time in Arabic: Arabic philosophy internationalized Greek philosophy, and through its success demonstrated to world culture that philosophy is a supranational enterprise. This, it seems, is what makes the transplantation and development of philosophy in other languages throughout the Middle Ages historically possible and intelligible.

Arabic philosophy was revolutionary in another way. Although Greek philosophy in its declining stages in late antiquity may be thought to have yielded to religion, Christianity, and indeed in many ways imitated it, Arabic philosophy developed in a social context in which a dominant monotheistic religion was the ideology par excellence. Because of this, Arabic philosophy developed as an ideology not *in opposition to* religion, but *independently from* religion – indeed from all religions – and intellectually superior to all of them in its subject and method. Arabic philosophy developed not as an *ancilla theologiae* but as a system of thought and a theoretical discipline which transcends all others and rationally explains all reality, including religion.

5 Greek Philosophical Texts in Arabic Translation

The following list has previously been published in a slightly different version in Robert Pasnau, ed. *The Cambridge History of Medieval Philosophy*. Cambridge, 2010, 802–814. It lists all Greek philosophical works which, according to our present state of knowledge, were translated into Arabic. It hence defines the body of texts which became accessible in Arabic through the translation movement between the second half of the 2nd/8th century and the end of the 4th/10th century. What has not been included is information on the circumstances surrounding individual translations (date, name of translator, etc.), which in many cases would require further investigation at any event.

In order to avoid ambiguities, Greek authors and their works are generally listed according to the *Thesaurus Linguae Graecae. Canon of Greek Authors and Works* (TLG), by L. Berkowitz and K. A. Squitier (Oxford ³1990), and provided with the following information:

(a) If the Arabic translation of a work is extant and published, the edition is referenced by the number assigned to it in H. Daiber's bibliography (1999–2007 [*8]), put in round brackets. If there is more than one edition, reference is given only to the latest (as it would normally mention the older editions in its introduction), or to the critically most sound. If none of the editions is satisfactory, they are all listed chronologically.

(b) If the Arabic translation of a work is extant but not published reference is given to the bibliographical source providing information on manuscripts and other sources connected with its textual tradition.

(c) If the Arabic translation, to the best of our current knowledge, is not extant but mentioned in Arabic bibliographical sources (in particular the *Fihrist*) its title is put in square brackets [ ]. The information provided by such sources is still unprocessed by modern scholarship, so that its nature cannot be ascertained. Specifically, we cannot tell whether such a translation existed in Syriac or in Arabic, whether Ibn al-Nadīm and other bibliographers saw the actual translation or merely heard about it from their own sources, and finally whether the attribution of the work to the philosopher concerned is authentic or not.

In order to facilitate using the list, the following sigla precede authors' names and titles of works:

* before an author's name: some works by this author which are lost in Greek are preserved in Arabic;

\+ before the title of a work: work extant in Arabic only;

> before the title of a work: the Arabic translation contains more text than the extant Greek original;

[ ] titles in square brackets: the work is listed or mentioned in Arabic sources but no manuscript of it so far has been recovered; extant fragments are normally listed.

5.1 *Abbreviations*

D Daiber 1999–2007 [*8]
DPhA *Dictionnaire des philosophes antiques* 1989 ff. [*7]
F *Fihrist* [*3]
GALex Endress/Gutas 2002 ff. [*9]
GAS Sezgin 1967–2007 [*3]
GCAL Graf 1944–1953 [*1: 1]

5.2 *List of Authors*

5.2.1 Aetius [Pseudo-Plutarchus]

– >*De placitis reliquiae*; ed. and transl. Daiber (D 2130).

5.2.2 *Alexander of Aphrodisias

As listed in the entries in DPhA I 125–139 (Goulet, Aouad) and Suppl. 61–70 (Fazzo), which should be consulted in all instances; the numbers before the titles refer to their numbers.

(1) [*In Aristotelis Analyticorum Priorum librum I commentarium*]; F 249,7–8.
(2) [*In Aristotelis Topicorum libros octo commentaria*]; F 249,18–24.
(3) [*In Aristotelis Meteorologicorum libros commentaria*]; F 251,9.
(5) *In Aristotelis Metaphysica commentaria*; F 251,27–28; fragment ed. Freudenthal (D 3179); Endress 1992 [*50: 32 n. 49].
(6) + *Commentary on Categories*; F 248,25; fragment ed. Zonta (D 9497/1).
(7) [*Commentary on De Interpretatione*; F 249,2].
(9) [*In Analytica posteriora commentaria*; F 249,13. 252,27–28].
(10) [*In Aristotelis sophisticos elenchos commentarium*; F 249,29].
(11) + *Commentary on Physics*; F 250,7. 252,27; frg. ed. Badawī (D 795); frg. ed. and transl. Giannakis (D 3540).
(12) [*Commentary on De Caelo*; F 250,29].
(13) + *Commentary on De Generatione et Corruptione*; F 251,4; ed. and transl. Gannagé (D 3301/3*S*); transl. Gannagé [**44*].
(16) *On the Soul*; cf. Gätje (D 3400), 69–70; frg. ed. Günsz (D 3798).
(19a–p) Ἀπορίαι καὶ λύσεις; various *questions* extant in Arabic (some are by Philoponus); cf. the lists in DPhA I 132–133 (Goulet, Aouad) and Suppl. 64–66 (Fazzo).
(21) >*De anima libri mantissa*; various treatises extant in Arabic; see the list in DPhA I 134–135 and Suppl. 66–67.
(22) + *On Providence*; F 253,8; ed. and transl. Thillet [**43*].
(23) + *On Times* (= *Refutation of Galen's On Time and Place*, F 253,5–6 ?); ed. Badawī (D 385).
(24) + *On the Principles of the Universe*; F 253,7; ed. and transl. Genequand (D 3431/1*S*); ed. Endress (D 2641/1*S*).
(25) + *Refutation of Galen's Critique of Aristotle on the Theory of Motion*; ed. and transl. Rescher, Marmura (D 395).
(26) + *Refutation of Xenocrates on Form and Genus*; ed. Badawī (D 382); transl. Pines (D 7058).
(27) + *Refutation of Galen on the Possible* (?); frg. ed. and transl. Rescher, Marmura (D 7503).
(28) + *On the Conversion of Premises*; F 253,6–7; ed. Badawī (D 377).
(29) + *On the Specific Difference*; F 253,11; ed. and transl. Dietrich (D 2344).

(30) + *On the Governance of the Spheres* (= a parallel version of *On Providence*, no. 22 above); ed. and transl. Ruland (D 7695).
(31) + *On Sound*; ed. Badawī (D 383).
(32) *On Form*; ed. Badawī (D 384); transl. Badawī (D 1119).
(33) (Pseudo-Alexander = Philoponus) *That the Act is More General than Motion*; ed. and transl. Hasnawi (D 4019).
(34) + *On the Division of Genera*; ed. Badawī (D 379); transl. Badawī (D 1119).
(35) (Pseudo-Alexander = Philoponus) *On Creation ex nihilo*; F 254, 9; ed. and transl. Hasnawi (D 4019).
(36) (Pseudo-Alexander = Philoponus) *That Every Separate Cause is in All Things and in None*; ed. and transl. Zimmermann (D 9484).
(37) *On the Celestial Sphere*; MS Istanbul, Carullah 1279, fols 53^b–54^a; part of (24) above.
(38) Pseudo-Alexander (?), *Poetic Gleanings*, actually on topics; see Zimmermann (D 9486).
(39) + *On the Cause*; ed. and transl. Genequand (D 3431/1*S*); ed. Endress (D 2641/1*S*).
(43) [*On Melancholy*]; F 253,11.
(57) [*That Being Is Not of the Same Genus as the Categories*]; F 253,7–8.
(59) >*Problemata*; Endress 1992 [*50: 139 n. 3]; cf. Filius (D 3084*S*), xvi.

5.2.3 *Alexandri Magni *Epistulae*

see Aristotle, *Epistulae*.

5.2.4 *Alexandrini Philosophi

see Summaria Alexandrinorum.

5.2.5 *Allīnūs (?)

– [*Commentary on the Categories*]; F 248,21.
– + Frg. transl. Rosenthal (D 7618).

5.2.6 Ammonius (Phil.)

– [*On the Purposes of Aristotle's Books*]; F 253,22.
– [*In Aristotelis Categorias commentarium*]; F 248,21.
– [*Commentary on the Topics*]; F 249,19–24.
– [*Commentary on Aristotle on the Creator*]; F 253,22.
– [*Aristotle's Proof of the Oneness (of God)*]; F 253,22–23.

5.2.7 Anacharsis

– + *Sayings*; in Arabic gnomologia, cf. Gutas (D 3818).

5.2.8 Anonymi *De Anima Paraphrasis*

– + ed. and transl. Arnzen (D 879).

5.2.9 Aristotle and Corpus Aristotelicum

– *Analytica Priora*; ed. Badawī (D 757); ed. Ǧabr [*40: 169–416].
– *Analytica Posteriora*; ed. Badawī (D 758); ed. Ǧabr [*40: 417–620].
– *De anima*; ed. Badawī (D 762. 1088); medieval Hebrew transl. from the Arabic ed. Bos (D 763); medieval Latin transl. from the Arabic ed. Crawford (D 4522); transl. of the Latin by R. C. Taylor and Th.-A. Druart [*49]; cf. Endress 1992 [*50: 29 n. 27; 33 n. 57]; survey of the transmission in Arabic by Gätje (D 3400); see Anonymi, *De anima Paraphrasis*.
– *De caelo*; ed. Badawī (D 1089); survey of the transmission in Arabic by Endress (D 2643); cf. GALex I 17*.
– *Categoriae*; ed. Bouyges (D 4550); ed. Badawī (D 761); ed. Ǧabr [*40: 1–96].
– [*De coloribus*]; apparently not translated; cf. Gätje (D 3404), p. 285.
– *De divinatione per somnum*; see *Parva naturalia*.
– *Divisiones Aristoteleae*; ed. Kellermann (D 5005); GALex I 33*.
– + *Epistulae*; ed. Maróth [*45]; survey of the transmission in Arabic by Gutas 2009 [*112]; cf. Gutas 1998 [*71: 194–195].
– *Ethica Nicomachea*; unpublished ed. and transl. Dunlop; ed. Akasoy and Fidora (D 778. 778S); corrections in M. Ullmann 2012 [*115].
– *De generatione animalium*; ed. Brugman, Drossaart Lulofs (D 765).
– *De generatione et corruptione*; medieval Hebrew translation from the Arabic translation ed. Tessier (D 768); survey of the transmission in Arabic by Eichner (D 4537/1S), 291–332.
– *Historia animalium*; ed. Badawī (D 779).
– *De insomniis*; see *Parva naturalia*.
– *De interpretatione*; ed. Badawī (D 770); ed. Ǧabr [*40: 97–166].
– *De longitudine et brevitate vitae*; see *Parva naturalia*.
– *Magna moralia*; ed. Kellermann (D 5005); GALex I 20*.
– *Mechanica*; extant paraphrastic summary ed. and transl. Abattouy [*42].
– *De memoria et reminiscentia*; see *Parva naturalia*.
– *Metaphysica*; ed. Bouyges (D 1591); ed. Badawī (D 786); ed. Miškāt (D 787); survey of the transmission in Arabic by Bertolacci (D 1432/1S).
– *Meteorologica*; the Arabic and medieval Latin transl. from the Arabic ed. Schoonheim (D 7978S); cf. Endress 1992 [*50: 28 n. 22].
– [*Mirabilium auscultationes*]; no trace has so far been found in Arabic; the entry on it in Peters 1968 [*28: 61] is based on a mistaken reference by Walzer, corrected later in Walzer 1962 [*23: 140 n. 5–6].

- *De mundo*; ed. Brafman (D 1603); cf. Endress 1992 [*50: 30 n. 41].
- *Oeconomica*; ed. Ma'lūf (D 793); transl. Shunnar (D 9049); cf. Peters 1968 [*28: 62–63].
- *De partibus animalium*; ed. Kruk (D 773).
- *Parva naturalia*; ed. Hansberger [*46]; survey of the transmission in Arabic by Gätje (D 3400), pp. 81–92.
- *Physica*; ed. Badawī (D 795).
- *Physiognomica*; ed. and transl. Ghersetti [*41].
- *Poetica*; ed. and modern Latin transl. Margoliouth (D 5935), ed. and modern Latin transl. Tkatsch (D 8661); ed. Badawī (D 797); ed. ʿAyyād (D 798).
- *Politica*; transl. of parts only; cf. Pines (D 7037), Brague (D 1607).
- >*Problemata*; ed. Filius (D 3084S); cf. Endress 1992 [*50: 139 n. 3].
- [*Protrepticus*]; cf. Fakhry (D 2789).
- *Rhetorica*; ed. Lyons (D 801).
- *Sophistici elenchi*; ed. Badawī (D 803); ed. Ǧabr [*40: II 897–1203].
- *De sensu et sensibilibus*; see *Parva naturalia*.
- *De somno et vigilia*; see *Parva naturalia*.
- *Testamentum*; ed. and modern Latin transl., references in GALex I 23*.
- *Topica*; ed. Badawī (D 809); ed. Ǧabr [*40: II 627–896].
- *De virtutibus et vitiis*; ed. Kellermann (D 5005); cf. GALex I 34*.
- >Sayings, ed. Gutas (D 3809); cf. Gutas (D 3818).

5.2.10 + Pseudo-Aristotle

- + *De lapidibus*, ed. Ruska; see Peters 1968 [*28: 60].
- + *De pomo*, ed. Khayrallāh (D 775); see DPhA I 537–541 (Aouad); Kotzia 2007 [*109].
- + *Secretum secretorum*, ed. Badawī (D 780), ed. al-Aʿwar (D 802); cf. Forster 2006 [*97].
- + Pseudepigrapha; see Peters 1968 [*28: 55–75]; Endress 1992 [*50: 31 n. 42].

5.2.11 *Bryson

- + Οἰκονομικός; ed. Plessner (D 7146); ed. and transl. by S. Swain 2013 [*117: 425–519].

5.2.12 Cebes

- *Cebetis tabula*; see DPhA II 251 (Gutas); cf. Rosenthal (D 7647).

5.2.13 *Corpus Hermeticum

Numerous works ascribed to Hermes are preserved in Arabic. The degree to which these are actually translations from the Greek or correspond to surviving works and fragments in Greek has been little investigated; GAS IV 38–44; Ullmann 1972 [*33: 165–170]; Endress 1992 [*50: 144–145]; cf. DPhA III 649–650 (Goulet); van Bladel 2009 [*111].

5.2.14 *Diogenes (Phil. et Trag.)

– >Sayings; transl. Gutas (D 3820).

5.2.15 *Eudemus (Phil. Rhodius)

– + Sayings; ed. and transl. Gutas (D 3807/1S).

5.2.16 *Galen

Only philosophically relevant works are given, as listed in DPhA III 440–466 (Boudon), which should be consulted in all instances; the numbers before the titles refer to Boudon's numbers; for the Plato paraphrase cf. DPhA V s.v. Plato Arabus (Gutas).

(1) *Adhortatio ad artes addiscendas* (*Protrepticus*); extant Arabic epitome ed. Badawī (D 3283); GAS III, 138 (#151); Ullmann 1970 [*32: 53 (#73)].

(3) *Quod optimus medicus sit quoque philosophus*; ed. and transl. Bachmann (D 1065).

(4) *De sectis ad eos qui introducuntur*; ed. Sālim [*37].

(6) [*De placitis Hippocratis et Platonis*]; GAS III 105 (#37); Ullmann 1970 [*32: 40 (#12)].

(7) *Quod animi mores corporis temperamenta sequantur*; ed. and transl. Biesterfeldt (D 1457, D 1456).

(8a) [*De propriorum animi cuiuslibet affectuum dignotione et curatione*]; Ullmann 1970 [*32: 51 (#65)].

(9) *De consuetudinibus*; ed. and transl. Klein-Franke (D 5210).

(10) [*Institutio logica*]; Ullmann 1970 [*32: 51 (#63)].

(12) *De elementis secundum Hippocratem libri II*; ed. Sālim [*38]; cf. Endress 1992 [*50: 120 n. 25].

(14) [*On the Authentic and Inauthentic Books by Hippocrates*]; Ullmann 1970 [*32: 53 (#72)]; GAS III 137 (#146).

(15) + *On Cohesive Causes*; ed. and transl. Lyons [*35].

(16) [*On Antecedent Causes*]; Ullmann 1970 [*32: 57 (#91)]; GAS III 135 (#138).

(17) [*An Outline of Empiricism in Medicine*]; Ullmann 1970 [*32: 52 (#67)]; GAS III 131 (#118).

(18) + *On Affections and their Cure*, III; see Steinschneider 1893 [*15: § 415,13].

(19) + *De experientia medica*; ed. and transl. Walzer (D 3284).

(20) = (8).

(21) + *That Good Men Benefit from Their Enemies*; Ullmann 1970 [*32: 65 (#117)].

(22) >*De demonstratione*; for ed. frg. see DPhA III 458 (Boudon); Ullmann 1970 [*32: 62 (#12)]; Endress 1992 [*50: 31 and 53 n. 180].

(23) *De propriis placitis*; for the surviving parts see DPhA III 458–459 (Boudon); Ullmann 1970 [*32: 51 (#64)].

(24) + *De nominibus medicinalibus*; ed. and transl. Meyerhof, Schacht [*33].

(25) + *De moribus*; ed. Kraus (D 3286); transl. Mattock (D 6129).

(26) >*In Platonis Timaeum commentarium*; frg. ed. Kahle [*34]; GAS III 126 (#90); Ullmann 1970 [*32: 64 (#115)].

(27) + *Compendium Timaei*; ed. and transl. Kraus, Walzer (D 3279); ed. Badawī (D 3280).

(28) + *Compendium Rei publicae*; used by Averroes for his *Middle* Commentary, ed. and transl. E.I.J. Rosenthal (D 4558; cf. D 4559–4562); Ullmann 1970 [*32: 64 (#114b)].

(29) + *Compendium Legum*; epitomes by al-Fārābī and Ibn al-Ṭayyib (see Gutas D 3808), ed. and transl. Gabrieli (D 2965); ed. Druart (D 2510/1); Ullmann 1970 [*32: 64 (#114c)].

(30) + [*Compendium Phaedonis*]; Ullmann 1970 [*32: 64 (#114d)]; cf. Rowson (D 7660), 29–41; for this and the following compendia cf. DPhA V s.v. Plato Arabus (Gutas).

(30.1) + [*Compendium of Cratylus*].

(30.2) + [*Compendium of Sophist*].

(30.3) + [*Compendium of Politicus*].

(30.4) + [*Compendium of Parmenides*].

(30.5) + [*Compendium of Euthydemus*].

(32) [*De dolore evitando*]; for frg. see DPhA III 460 (Boudon); Ullmann 1970 [*32: 65 (#118)].

(33) + *In primum movens immotum*; Ullmann 1970 [*32: 65 (#116)]; see DPhA III 460 (Boudon).

(34) [*On the Providence of the Creator*]; see DPhA III 460 (Boudon).

(36) [Περὶ οὐσίας τῆς ψυχῆς κατ' Ἀσκληπιάδην]; Syriac transl. Degen 1981 [*39: no. 124].

(41) [Περὶ τοῦ τῶν συλλογισμῶν ἀριθμοῦ]; Syriac transl. Degen 1981 [*39: no. 115].

(48) [*On the Possible*]; see DPhA III 461 (Boudon).

(95) + *Platonicorum dialogorum compendia octo*; see Endress 1992 [*50: 31 n. 43; 43 n. 121]; Ullmann 1970 [*32: 63 (#114)].

(98) [*Commentary on De Interpretatione*]; F 249,2–3.

Ars medica (parva); GAS III 80 (#4); Ullmann 1970 [*32: 45 (#38)]; Endress 1992 [*50: 120 n. 25].

De usu partium; GAS III 106 (#40); Ullmann 1970 [*32: 41 (#15)].

In Hippocratis aphorismos commentaria; GAS III 123 (#71); Ullmann 1970 [*32: 50 (#58)].

[*De libris propriis*]; GAS III 78 (#1); Ullmann 1970 [*32: 35 (#1)].

[*De ordine librorum suorum ad Eugenianum*]; GAS III 79 (#2); Ullmann 1970 [*32: 35 (#2)].

+*In Hippocratis de aere aquis locis commentaria*; ed. Strohmaier in preparation; Endress 1992 [*50: 119 n. 24]; GAS III 123 (#81); Ullmann 1970 [*32: 61 (#107)].
+*De examinando medico*; ed. Iskandar; cf. Endress 1992 [*50: 120 n. 25; 127 n. 73]; Ullmann 1970 [*32: 52 (#70)].
+ *De partibus artis medicativae*; ed. Lyons [*35]; GAS III 112 (#49); Ullmann 1970 [*32: 52 (#69)].
+ *De somno et vigilia*; GAS III 126 (#92); Ullmann 1970 [*32: 55 (#84)].
+ [*De voce*]; GAS III 103 (#30); Ullmann 1970 [*32: 54 (#79)].

5.2.17 *Pseudo-Galen

- [*Definitiones medicae*]; GAS III 138 (#153); Ullmann 1970 [*32: 38 (#3)].
- + *De plantis*; GAS IV 314.
- + *Book of Poisons*; GAS III, 121 (#67); Ullmann 1970 [*32: 61 (#106)].
- + *On the Soul*; ed. Jellinek [*31].
- + *In Hippocratis legem commentarium*; ed. Rosenthal; GAS III 123 (#70); Ullmann 1970 [*32: 62 (#111)].
- + *Oeconomica*; see Plessner (D 7146), pp. 205–213.

5.2.18 Georgius Gemistus Plethon

Works preserved in Arabic translation in MS Istanbul, Ahmet III, 1896; cf. Tardieu in: Tambrun-Krasker [*39: 157–158].

5.2.19 *Hippocrates and Corpus Hippocraticum

Only the philosophically relevant works are listed, as discussed in DPhA III 786–790 (Jouanna, Magdelaine).

- [*De prisca medicina*]; GAS III 43 (#24); Ullmann 1970 [*32: 31 (#13)].
- *De aere aquis et locis*; ed. Mattock, Lyons; cf. GALex I 27*-28*; GAS III 36 (#8); Ullmann 1970 [*32: 27 (#3)].
- *Aphorismi*; ed. Tytler; cf. GALex I 28*; GAS III 28 (#2); Ullmann 1970 [*32: 28 (#4)].
- *Jusjurandum*; ed. and transl. see Ullmann 1970 [*32: 32 (#25)]; GAS III 28 (#1); Endress 1992 [*50: 119 n. 23].
- *Lex*; ed. and transl. see Ullmann 1970 [*32: 33 (#27)]; GAS III 38 (#11).
- *De humoribus*; ed. Mattock; cf. GALex I 29*; GAS III 35 (#6); Ullmann 1970 [*32: 30 (#9)].
- *De natura hominis*, ed. Mattock, Lyons; cf. GALex I 29*-30*; GAS III 37 (#9); Ullmann 1970 [*32: 27 (#2)].
- *De ventis*; cf. Ullmann 1970 [*32: 32 (#22)]; GAS III 46 (#8).
- [*De carnibus*]; cf. GAS III 46 (#11).
- *De alimento;* ed. and transl. Mattock; cf. GALex I 28*; Ullmann 1970 [*32: 30 (#10)]; GAS III 41 (#16).

– [*De medico*] (?); cf. Ullmann 1970 [*32: 33 (#28)].
– >*De septimanis*; cf. Ullmann 1970 [*32: 32 (#20)]; GAS III 40 (#14).

5.2.20 *Pseudo-Hippocrates

– >*Epistulae*; see GAS III 43 (#21); Ullmann 1970 [*32: 34 (#30)].
– *Testamentum*; transl. Rosenthal; cf. Ullmann 1970 [*32: 33, #26]; GAS III 39 (#12).
– +*Secreta Hippocratis / Capsula eburnea*; see GAS III 39 (#12b); Ullmann 1970 [*32: 33 (#29)].

5.2.21 Hippolytus

– *Refutatio omnium haeresium*; partially preserved in Pseudo-Ammonius, ed. Rudolph (D 7681); see Endress 1992 [*50: 30 n. 37; 146 n. 52].

5.2.22 Historia et sententiae de Ahiqar

– *The Story of Aḥiḳar*; ed. Conybeare, Harris, Lewis [*32].

5.2.23 *Iamblichus

– [*Commentary on the Categories*]; F 248,23.
– [*Commentary on De Interpretatione*]; F 249,2.
– + *Commentaria in Carmen aureum Pythagorae*; ed. Daiber (D 2158).

5.2.24 Isocrates (Orat.)

– + Sayings; ed. Alon (D 436).

5.2.25 *John Philoponus

– [*In Aristotelis meteorologicorum libros commentaria*]; GCAL 418 (#4).
– [*In Aristotelis libros de generatione et corruptione commentaria*]; GCAL 418 (#4).
– >*In Aristotelis Physicorum libros commentaria*; F 250,18; 255,2; ed. Badawī (D 795); transl. Giannakis (D 3541); transl. Lettinck (D 7012); ed. and transl. of the corollaries on place and void by Giannakis (D 3542/1).
– *De aeternitate mundi contra Proclum*; F 254, 25; frg. (from al-Bīrūnī) ed. and transl. Giannakis (D 3541/1S); see above, Alexander of Aphrodisias, nos (33) and (35), and Hasnawi (D 4019).
– + *Contra Aristotelem*; F 254, 27; frg. ed. and transl. Mahdi (D 5784, D 5773); frg. ed. and transl. Kraemer (D 5265); frg. transl. Wildberg (D 9267).
– + *De contingentia mundi*; GCAL 418 (#1); ed. and transl. Troupeau (D 8713); transl. Pines (D 7036).
– + *In Galeni libros commentaria*; F 255,1; GCAL 418 (#4).
– [*Every finite body has a finite power*]; F 254,25–26.
– [*Commentary on Aristotle's Problemata*]; F 254,26–27.

5.2.26 Nemesius (Theol.)

– *De natura hominis*; F 255,10; Samir (D 7873).

5.2.27 *Nicolaus Damascenus

– + *De plantis*; ed. and transl. Drossaart Lulofs (D 2491); GAS IV 312–313; Endress 1992 [*50: 30 n. 40].
– + *Epitome of Aristotle's Philosophy*; F 254,4; frg. ed. and transl. Drossaart Lulofs (D 2489); frg. ed. and transl. Takahashi (D 8501/6S)
– [*Summary of Aristotle's De anima*, one book]; F 254,3.
– [*Summary of Aristotle's Zoology*]; F 251, 23; Ullmann 1972 [*33: 9].
– [*Refutation of those who make the act and what is acted upon identical*]; F 254,4.

5.2.28 Nicomachus Gerasenus

– *Introductio arithmetica*; ed. Kutsch; cf. Endress 1992 [*50: 65 n. 20].

5.2.29 Olympiodorus (The Alchemist)

– Εἰς τὸ κατ' ἐνέργειαν Ζοσίμου; see Endress in: D'Ancona 2007 [*104: 327 n. 18].

5.2.30 *Olympiodorus (The Philosopher)

– [*Commentary on Plato's Sophist*]; F 246,12.
– [*Commentary on De Generatione et Corruptione*]; F 251,5.
– + *In Aristotelis Meteora paraphrasis*; F 251, 8; ed. Badawī (D 6911).
– [*Commentary on De anima*]; F 251,13–14.

5.2.31 Oracula Chaldaica (Chaldean Oracles)

– *Oracula*; frg. ed. and transl. Tardieu, in: Tambrun-Krasker [*39: 157–171].

5.2.32 Plato

See DPhA V s.v. Plato Arabus (Gutas). No dialogue of Plato is known to have been fully translated into Arabic, and none survives. Some portions of the more famous dialogues were literally translated, but for the most part the works of Plato were known in Arabic through (a) the epitomes of Galen (for which see under Galen), (b) citations in the works of other authors who quoted him (notably Galen and Aristotle in *Metaphysics* I and XIII–XIV), and (c) doxographies and gnomologia, the most significant among which is al-ʿĀmirī's (?) *Al-Saʿāda wa-l-isʿād* (for which see Arberry, D 736). Of the dialogues that were known the best, three were known by name, *Laws* (Gutas, D 3808), *Republic* (Reisman, D 7457/4), and *Timaeus* (evidence of an abbreviated translation by Ibn al-Biṭrīq in al-Kindī: Rescher, D 7483), and one anonymously, *Phaedo* (Rowson, D 7660). For the *Symposium*, see Gutas (D 3817); for the *Meno*, see Endress (D 2642). For Plato's sayings see Gutas (D 3809).

5.2.33 Plotinus

- *Enneades* IV–VI; ed. and transl. Dieterici (D 804. 2340); ed. Badawī (D 806); transl. Lewis (D 7155); see Endress 1992 [*50: 30 n. 35] and Adamson (D 218/4S).

5.2.34 Plutarchus

See Gutas [D 3818] 4944n5.

- [*De cohibenda ira*]; F 254,8.
- [*On the Soul* = *De animae procreatione in Timaeo*?]; F 254,8.
- [*De capienda ex inimicis utilitate*]; F 254,7–8.

5.2.35 Pseudo-Plutarchus

- *Placita Philosophorum*; see Aetius.
- [*On training* = Περὶ ἀσκήσεως]; F 254, 8; cf. Gutas (D 3818) 4944n5.

5.2.36 Pseudo-Polemon

- *Physiognomica*; ed. and transl. Hoyland [*47].

5.2.37 Porphyrius

See Walzer (D 9152).

- *Vita Pythagorae*; see Rosenthal (D 7644).
- *Isagoge sive quinque voces*; ed. Badawī (D 7184); ed. Ahwānī (D 7185); GALex I 32*–33*.
- [*In Aristotelis Categorias*]; F 248,20.
- [*Commentary on De Interpretatione*]; F 249,2.
- [*Introduction to Categorical Syllogisms*]; F 253,15–16.
- [*Commentary on Physics*]; F 250,21–22.
- [*On the Elements*]; F 253,17.
- + *On the Soul*; ed. and transl. Kutsch (D 5362).
- [*On the Intellect and the Intelligible* = Ἀφορμαὶ πρὸς τὰ νοητά?]; F 253,16.
- [*Refutation of ? the Intellect and the Intelligible*]; F 253,16–17.
- [*Commentary on the Nicomachean Ethics*]; F 252,2.
- [*Epistula ad Anebonem*]; F 253,16; frg. transl. Gabrieli (D 3261).
- *Fragmenta*; ed. Wasserstein (D 7183).
- [*Historia philosophiae*]; F 253,18; frg. ed. Rosenthal (D 7614).

5.2.38 *Proclus

See Endress 1973 [*36].

- [*In Platonis rem publicam commentaria*]; Endress [*36: 29].
- *Institutio theologica*; ed. Endress [*36]; frg. ed. Badawī (D 7123); Endress 1992 [*50: 30 n. 36]; see also Alexander of Aphrodisias, no. 36. – *De causis*; ed. Badawī

(D 782); ed. and transl. Taylor (D 8565); ed. Badawī (D 7207); Endress 1973 [*36: 18–24].
- [*Institutio physica*]; Endress [*36: 27].
- *In Platonis Timaeum commentaria*; frg. transl. Pfaff (D 7205); Endress [*36: 24].
- [*De decem dubitationibus*]; Endress [*36: 27–28].
- + *De aeternitate mundi*; frg. ed. Badawī (D 7206); transl. Badawī (D 1119); transl. Anawati (D 645); ed. and transl. Maróth (D 5998); Endress [*36: 15–18].
- + *Problemata physica*; ed. Badawī (D 7208); Endress [*36: 26].
- + (Pseudo-Proclus?) *Commentaria in Carmen aureum Pythagorae*; ed. Linley (D 5575); Endress [*36: 26–27]; cf. Westerink 1987 [*53].
- [*In Platonis Gorgiam commentaria*]; Endress [*36: 28].
- [*In Platonis Phaedonem commentaria*]; Endress [*36: 28–29].
- [*In Aristotelis De Interpretatione commentaria*]; Endress [*36: 29–30].
- [*On the Supernal Substances*]; Endress [*36: 30].
- [*On the Atom*]; Endress [*36: 30].

5.2.39 Ptolemy, Claudius
- *Syntaxis mathematica*; GAS VI 88–89; Endress 1992 [*50: 89 n. 23].
- *Tetrabiblos*; GAS VII 43 (#1); Endress 1992 [*50: 105 n. 7].

5.2.40 *Pseudo-Ptolemy
- *Fructus*; GAS VII 44–45 (#2); Endress 1992 [*50: 105 n. 8].

5.2.41 *Ptolemy al-Ġarīb
- + *Vita Aristotelis et pinax*; F 255, 11–12; transl. Plezia (D 7150); cf. Düring (D 2554); Gutas (D 3822).

5.2.42 <Pythagoras>
- *Carmen aureum*; ed. Cheikho (D 7239); ed. Ullmann (D 8820); Endress 1992 [*50: 39 n. 91]; cf. Endress in: D'Ancona 2007 [*104: 331 n. 30].
- > Sayings; ed. and transl. Gutas (D 3809); cf. Gutas (D 3818).

5.2.43 Secundus
See *Vita et Sententiae Secundi*.

5.2.44 <Septem Sapientes>
- >Sayings in Arabic gnomologia; cf. Gutas (D 3818).

5.2.45 Simplicius

See Gätje [D 3399].

– [*In Aristotelis Categorias commentarium*]; F 248,21; cf. Türker (D 87351).
– [*In Aristotelis libros De anima commentaria*]; F 251,15.
– [*Commentary on the Introduction to Euclid's Elements*]; F 268,15.

5.2.46 Socrates

– >Sayings; ed. and transl. Gutas (D 3809); ed. and transl. Alon (D 438. 439).

5.2.47 Stephanus (Alexandrinus, Constantinopolitanus)

– [*Commentary on the Categories*]; F 248,20–21.

5.2.48 *Summaria Alexandrinorum*

– [*On De anima*]; F 251,15–16.

5.2.49 Syrianus

– [*Commentary on Book Beta of the Metaphysics*]; F 251,31.

5.2.50 *Thales

– >Sayings; in Arabic gnomologia, cf. Gutas (D 3818).

5.2.51 *Themistius

– Περὶ φιλίας; Syriac transl. ed. Sachau (D 7759).
– Περὶ ἀρετῆς; Syriac transl. ed. Mach (D 8613).
– [*Commentary on the Categories*]; F 248,21.
– [*In Aristotelis Analyticorum priorum paraphrasis*]; F 249,8.
– *Against Maximus, on the Reduction of the Second and Third Figure to the First*; ed. Badawī (D 8612).
– [*In Aristotelis Analyticorum posteriorum paraphrasis*]; F 249,12–13.
– [*Commentary on Topics*]; F 249,23.
– [*Commentary on Poetics*]; F 250,5.
– [*In Aristotelis physica paraphrasis*]; F 250,22.
– *Commentary on De caelo*; F 250,30; ed. Landauer (D 8604).
– [*Commentary on De generatione et corruptione*]; F 251,6.
– *In Aristotelis libros de anima paraphrasis*; F 251,12–18; ed. Lyons (D 8603); partial transl. Gätje (D 3385).
– + *Epitome of Aristotelian Zoology*; ed. Badawī (D 8608); Ullmann 1972 [*33: 9–10].
– + *Commentary on Book Lambda of the Metaphysics*; F 251, 30; ed. Landauer (D 8606); ed. Badawī (D 8605. 8607).
– [*Commentary on the Nicomachean Ethics*]; F 252,3.
– [*On the Soul = De anima paraphrasis?*]; F 253,27.

- + *Letter to Julian, on Politics*; F 253,26–27 mentions two letters without indication of their identity; ed. Cheikho (D 8609); ed. Sālim (D 8610); ed. Shahid (D 8611).

5.2.52 *Theon Smyrnaeus

- + *Life and Works of Plato*; F 246,4. 255,12–13; ed. in Ibn al-Qifṭī, ed. Lippert (D 7291) 17–25; cf. Lippert (D 5577).

5.2.53 Theon (?)

- [*Commentary on Categories*]; F 248,22.

5.2.54 Theophrastus

- [*De causis plantarum*]; F 252, 9–10; GAS IV 313.
- [*De sensu et sensibilibus*]; F 252,8.
- *De principiis* [*Metaphysica*]; ed. Gutas [*48].
- [*Commentary on Categories*]; F 248,21. 252,10–11.
- [*Commentary on De Interpretatione*]; F 249,3.
- + *Meteorologica*; ed. and transl. Daiber (D 2154); Fragments; ed. and transl. Takahashi (D 8501/6S).
- [*On the Soul*]; F 252,7.
- [*On Education*]; F 252,8.
- + Sayings; ed. Gutas (D 3811).
- + Fragments; ed. and transl. Gutas (D 8617), ed. and transl. Daiber (D 2171).

5.2.55 *Vita et Sententiae Secundi*

- *Vita Secundi*; ed. Perry (D 6991).
- >Sayings; in Arabic gnomologia, cf. Gutas (D 3818).

6 Secondary Literature

6.1 Works of Reference [*1–*10] – 6.2 Studies [*15–*118]

6.1 *Works of Reference*

1 GCAL = Graf, Georg. *Geschichte der christlichen arabischen Literatur*, 5 vols. Vatican City, 1944–1953.

2 EI² = *The Encyclopaedia of Islam: New edition*. Ed. by Clifford Edmund Bosworth et al., 11 vols, 6 suppl. vols. Leiden, 1960–2005.

3 GAS = Sezgin, Fuat. *Geschichte des arabischen Schrifttums*, 17 vols. Leiden, Frankfurt a.M., 1967–2015.

4 WKAS = *Wörterbuch der Klassischen Arabischen Sprache*. Ed. for the Deutsche Morgenländische Gesellschaft by Anton Spitaler and Manfred Ullmann, 2 vols. in 5 parts. Wiesbaden, 1970–2009.

5 EIr = *Encyclopaedia Iranica*. Ed. by Ehsan Yarshater, vols 1 ff. London, 1982 ff.

6 GAP = *Grundriss der arabischen Philologie*, vol. 2: *Literaturwissenschaft*. Ed. by Helmut Gätje. Wiesbaden, 1987; vol. 3: Supplement. Ed. by Wolfdietrich Fischer. Wiesbaden, 1992.

7 DPhA = *Dictionnaire des philosophes antiques*. Ed. by Richard Goulet, vols 1 ff. and Supplément. Paris, 1989 ff.

8 Daiber, Hans. *Bibliography of Islamic Philosophy*, 2 vols. Leiden, Boston, 1999. – Supplement (2007).

9 GALex = *A Greek and Arabic Lexicon: Materials for a Dictionary of the Mediaeval Translations from Greek into Arabic*. Ed. by Gerhard Endress and Dimitri Gutas, vols 1 ff. Leiden, 2002 ff.

10 *Encyclopaedia of Islam*, THREE [EI Three]. Ed. by Marc Gaborieau et al., vols 1 ff. Leiden, 2007 ff.

6.2 *Studies*

15 Steinschneider, Moritz. *Die hebraeischen Übersetzungen des Mittelalters und die Juden als Dolmetscher*. Berlin, 1893. – Repr. Graz, 1956.

16 Bergsträsser, Gotthelf. *Ḥunain ibn Isḥāḳ und seine Schule*. Leiden, 1913.

17 Nallino, Carlo Alfonso. "Tracce di opere greche giunte agli arabi per trafila pehlevica." In *A Volume of Oriental Studies Presented to Edward G. Browne on His 60th Birthday*. Ed. by Thomas Walker Arnold and Reynold Alleyne Nicholson. Cambridge, 1922, 345–363. – Repr. in *Raccolta di scritti editi e inediti*, vol. 6. Ed. by Maria Nallino. Rome, 1948, 285–303.

18 Furlani, Giuseppe. "Di una presunta versione araba di alcuni scritti di Porfirio e di Aristotele." *Rendiconti della Reale Accademia nazionale dei Lincei: Classe di scienze morali, storiche e filologiche*, ser. VI, 2 (1926): 205–213.

19 Gabrieli, Francesco. "L'opera di Ibn al-Muqaffaʿ." *Rivista degli studi orientali* 13 (1931–1932): 197–247.

20 Kraus, Paul. "Zu Ibn al-Muqaffaʿ." *Rivista degli studi orientali* 14 (1934): 1–20. – Repr. in P. Kraus, *Alchemie, Ketzerei, Apokryphen im frühen Islam*. Ed. by Rémi Brague. Hildesheim, 1994, 89–108.

21 Georr, Khalil. *Les Catégories d'Aristote dans leurs versions syro-arabes*. Beirut, 1948.

22 Sourdel, Dominique. *Le vizirat Abbaside*, 2 vols. Damascus, 1959–1960.

23 Walzer, Richard. *Greek into Arabic: Essays on Islamic Philosophy*. Oxford 1962; Cambridge, Mass., 1963 (2nd ed.).

24 Frank, Richard M. "The Neoplatonism of Jahm ibn Ṣafwān," *Le Muséon* 78 (1965): 395–424. – Repr. in Frank, *Philosophy, Theology and Mysticism in Medieval Islam* (Texts and studies on the development and history of *kalām*, I). Ed. by Dimitri Gutas. Aldershot, 2005, no. IX.

25 Rosenthal, Franz. *The Classical Heritage in Islam*. Transl. from the German by Emile and Jenny Marmorstein. London, 1975.

26 Duneau, Jean-François. "Quelques aspects de la pénétration de l'hellénisme dans l'empire perse sassanide (IVe–VIIe siècles)." In *Mélanges offerts à René Crozet*, vol. 1. Ed. by Pierre Gallais and Yves-Jean Riou. Poitiers, 1966, 13–22.

27 Grignaschi, Mario. "Le roman epistolaire classique conservé dans la version arabe de Sālim Abū l-ʿAlāʾ." *Le Muséon* 80 (1967): 211–264.

28 Peters, Francis E. *Aristoteles Arabus*. Leiden, 1968.

29 Pingree, David. *The Thousands of Abu Mashar*. London, 1968.

30 Sournia, Jean Charles and Gérard Troupeau. "Jean Mesue." *Clio Medica* 3 (1968): 109–117.

31 Bosworth, Clifford Edmund. "The Ṭāhirids and Arabic Culture." *Journal of Semitic Studies* 14 (1969): 45–79.

32 Ullmann, Manfred. *Die Medizin im Islam*. Leiden, 1970.

33 Ullmann, Manfred. *Die Natur- und Geheimwissenschaften im Islam*. Leiden, 1972.

34 Strohmaier, Gotthard. "Ḥunayn b. Isḥāk as a Philologist." In *Ephrem-Ḥunayn Festival*. Baghdad, 1974, 529–544.

35 Kunitzsch, Paul. "Über das Frühstadium der arabischen Aneignung antiken Gutes." *Saeculum* 26 (1975): 268–282.

36 Miquel, André. *La géographie humaine du monde musulman jusqu'au milieu du 11e siècle*. Paris, La Haye, 1975.

37 Putman, Hans. *L'église et l'islam sous Timothée I*. Beirut, 1975.

38 Ullmann, Manfred. "Ḫālid ibn Yazīd und die Alchemie: Eine Legende." *Der Islam* 55 (1978): 181–218.

39 Degen, Rainer. "Galen im Syrischen: Eine Übersicht über die syrische Überlieferung der Werke Galens." In *Galen: Problems and Prospects*. Ed. by Vivian Nutton. London, 1981, 131–166.

40 Shaki, Mansour. "The Dēnkard Account of the History of the Zoroastrian Scriptures." *Archív orientální* 49 (1981): 114–125.

41 Troupeau, Gérard. "La logique d'Ibn al-Muqaffaʿ et les origines de la grammaire arabe." *Arabica* 28 (1981): 242–250.

42 Brock, Sebastian. "From Antagonism to Assimilation: Syriac Attitudes to Greek Learning." In *East of Byzantium: Syria and Armenia in the Formative Period, Dumbarton Oaks Symposium 1980*. Ed. by Nina Garsoïan, Thomas Mathews, and Robert Thomson. Washington D.C., 1982, 17–34. – Repr. in Brock, *Syriac Perspectives on Late Antiquity* [*48: no. V].

43 Pingree, David. “Abū Sahl b. Nawbaḵt.” EIr [*5: I 369].
44 Terian, Abraham. “The Hellenizing School: Its Time, Place, and Scope of Activities Reconsidered.” In N. Garsoïan, T. Mathews, R. Thomson 1982 [cf. *42], 175–186.
45 Bosworth, Clifford Edmund. “The Persian Impact on Arabic Literature.” In *Arabic Literature to the End of the Umayyad Period*. Ed. by Alfred Felix Landon Beeston et al. Cambridge, 1983, 483–496.
46 Brock, Sebastian. “Towards a History of Syriac Translation Technique.” In *III Symposium Syriacum 1980: Les contacts du monde syriaque avec les autres cultures*. Ed. by René Lavenant. Rome, 1983, 1–14. – Repr. in Brock, *Studies in Syriac Christianity: History, Literature, Theology*. London, 1992, no. X.
47 Gutas, Dimitri. “Paul the Persian on the Classification of the Parts of Aristotle's Philosophy: A Milestone between Alexandria and Baġdād.” *Der Islam* 60 (1983): 231–267.
48 Brock, Sebastian. *Syriac Perspectives on Late Antiquity*. London, 1984.
49 Pingree, David. “Ḳirān,” EI² [*2: V 130–131].
50 Endress, Gerhard. “Die wissenschaftliche Literatur.” GAP [*6: II 400–506; III 3–152].
51 Frank, Richard M. “The Use of the *Enneads* by John of Scythopolis.” *Le Muséon* 100 (1987): 101–108. – Repr. in R. M. Frank 2005 [cf. *24], no. V.
52 Shaked, Shaul. “Paymān: An Iranian Idea in Contact with Greek Thought and Islam.” In *Transition Periods in Iranian History*. Paris, 1987, 217–240.
53 Westerink, Leendert Gerrit. “Proclus commentateur des Vers d'Or.” In *Proclus et son influence: Actes du colloque de Neuchâtel, 20–23 juin* 1985. Ed. by Gilbert Boss and Gerhard Seel. Zürich, 1987, 62–78.
54 Gutas, Dimitri. “Plato's Symposion in the Arabic Tradition.” *Oriens* 31 (1988): 36–60.
55 Hugonnard-Roche, Henri. “Aux origines de l'exégèse orientale de la logique d'Aristote: Sergius de Rešʿaina (†536), médecin et philosophe.” *Journal asiatique* 277 (1989): 1–17.
56 Haldon, John F. *Byzantium in the Seventh Century: The Transformation of a Culture*. Cambridge, 1990.
57 van Esbroeck, Michael. “La version géorgienne de deux commentaires d'Ammonius fils d'Hermias.” In *Autori classici in lingue del vicino e medio oriente*. Ed. by Gianfranco Fiaccadori. Rome, 1990, 55–64.
58 Brock, Sebastian. “The Syriac Background to Ḥunayn's Translation Techniques.” *Aram* 3 (1991): 139–162.
59 Talmon, Rafael. “Naẓra ǧadīda fī qaḍiyyat aqsām al-kalām: Dirāsa ḥawl kitāb Ibn al-Muqaffaʿ fī l-manṭiq.” *Al-Karmil* 12 (1991): 43–67.
60 van Ess, Josef. *Theologie und Gesellschaft im 2. und 3. Jahrhundert Hidschra: Eine Geschichte des religiösen Denkens im frühen Islam*, 6 vols. Berlin, New York, 1991–1997.

61 Brock, Sebastian. "The Syriac Commentary Tradition." In *Glosses and Commentaries on Aristotelian Logical Texts. The Syriac, Arabic and Medieval Latin Traditions*. Ed. by Charles Burnett. London, 1993, 3–18.
62 Gutas, Dimitri. "Aspects of Literary Form and Genre in Arabic Logical Works." In Ch. Burnett 1993 [cf. *61], 29–76.
63 Hugonnard-Roche, Henri. "Remarques sur la tradition arabe de l'Organon d'après le manuscrit Paris, Bibliothèque nationale, ar. 2346." In Ch. Burnett 1993 [cf. *61], 19–28.
64 Rashed, Roshdi. "Al-Kindī's Commentary on Archimedes' 'The Measurement of the Circle'." *Arabic Sciences and Philosophy* 3 (1993): 7–53.
65 Brentjes, Sonja. "Textzeugen und Hypothesen zum arabischen Euklid." *Archive for History of Exact Sciences* 47 (1994): 53–92.
66 Dhanani, Alnoor. *The Physical Theory of Kalām*. Leiden, 1994.
67 Zakeri, Mohsen. "ʿAlī ibn ʿUbaida ar-Raiḥānī: A Forgotten Belletrist (adīb) and Pahlavi Translator." *Oriens* 34 (1994): 76–102.
68 Endress, Gerhard. "The Circle of al-Kindī: Early Arabic Translations from the Greek and the Rise of Islamic Philosophy." In *The Ancient Tradition in Christian and Islamic Hellenism: Studies on the Transmission of Greek Philosophy and Sciences, Dedicated to H. J. Drossaart Lulofs on His Ninetieth Birthday*. Ed. by Gerhard Endress and Remke Kruk. Leiden, 1997, 43–76.
69 MacMullen, Ramsay. *Christianity and Paganism in the Fourth to Eighth Centuries*. New Haven, London, 1997.
70 Troupeau, Gérard. "ʿAbdīshūʿ ibn Bahrīz et son livre sur les définitions de la logique." In *Les voies de la science grecque*. Ed. by Danielle Jacquart. Genève, 1997, 135–146.
71 Gutas, Dimitri. *Greek Thought, Arabic Culture: The Graeco-Arabic Translation Movement in Baghdad and Early ʿAbbāsid Society (2nd-4th/8th-10th centuries)*. London, 1998.
72 Latham, J. Derek. "Ebn al-Moqaffaʿ." EIr [*5: VIII 39–43].
73 Griffith, Sidney Harrison. "Arab Christian Culture in the Early Abbasid Period." *Bulletin of the Royal Institute for Inter-Faith Studies, Amman, Jordan*, 1 (1999): 25–44.
74 Gutas, Dimitri. "The 'Alexandria to Baghdad' Complex of Narratives: A Contribution to the Study of Philosophical and Medical Historiography Among the Arabs." *Documenti e studi sulla tradizione filosofica medievale* 10 (1999): 155–193.
75 Roueché, Mossman. "Did Medical Students Study Philosophy in Alexandria?" *Bulletin of the Institute of Classical Studies* 43 (1999) 153–169.
76 Daiber, Hans. "Die Aristotelesrezeption in der syrischen Literatur." In *Die Gegenwart des Altertums: Formen und Funktionen des Altertumsbezugs in den*

Hochkulturen der Alten Welt. Ed. by Dieter Kuhn and Helga Stahl. Heidelberg, 2001, 327–345.

77 Luna, Concetta. "Rezension zu Rainer Thiel: Simplikios und das Ende der neuplatonischen Schule in Athen (Stuttgart 1999)." *Mnemosyne* 54 (2001): 482–504.

78 Zuckerman, Constantine. "A Repertory of Published Armenian Translations of Classical Texts." In *Autori classici in lingue del vicino e medio oriente*. Ed. by Gianfranco Fiaccadori. Rome, 2001, 415–448.

79 de Blois, François. "Tardjama 3." EI^2 [*2: X 231–232].

80 Ullmann, Manfred. *Wörterbuch zu den griechisch-arabischen Übersetzungen des 9. Jahrhunderts*. Wiesbaden, 2002. – 2 suppl. vols. Wiesbaden, 2006, 2007.

81 Walker, Joel T. "The Limits of Late Antiquity: Philosophy Between Rome and Iran." *The Ancient World* 33 (2002): 45–69.

82 Endress, Gerhard. "Mathematics and Philosophy in Medieval Islam." In *The Enterprise of Science in Islam: New Perspectives*. Ed. by Jan P. Hogendijk and Abdelhamid I. Sabra. Cambridge, Mass., 2003, 121–176.

83 Teixidor, Javier. *Aristote en syriaque: Paul le Perse, logicien du VIe siècle*. Paris, 2003.

84 Freudenthal, Gad and Tony Levy. "De Gérase à Bagdad: Ibn Bahrīz, al-Kindī, et leur recension arabe de l'Introduction arithmétique de Nicomaque, d'après la version hébraïque de Qalonymos ben Qalonymos d'Arles." In *De Zénon d'élée à Poincaré: Recueil d'études en hommage à Roshdi Rashed*. Ed. by Régis Morelon and Ahmad Hasnawi. Louvain, Paris, 2004, 479–544.

85 Gutas, Dimitri. "Geometry and the Rebirth of Philosophy in Arabic with al-Kindī." In *Words, Texts and Concepts Cruising the Mediterranean Sea: Studies on the Sources, Contents and Influences of Islamic Civilization and Arabic Philosophy and Science: Dedicated to Gerhard Endress on His Sixty-Fifth Birthday*. Ed. by Rüdiger Arnzen and Jörn Thielmann. Leuven, Paris, Dudley, 2004, 195–209.

86 Hugonnard-Roche, Henri. *La logique d'Aristote du grec au syriaque: Études sur la transmission des textes de l'Organon et leur interprétation philosophique*. Paris, 2004.

87 Watt, John W. "Syriac Translators and Greek Philosophy in Early Abbasid Iraq." *Journal of the Canadian Society for Syriac Studies* 4 (2004): 15–26.

88 Watts, Edward J. "Justinian, Malalas, and the end of Athenian Philosophical Teaching in A.D. 529." *The Journal of Roman Studies* 94 (2004): 168–182.

89 Zakeri, Mohsen. "*Ādāb al-falāsifa*: The Persian Content of an Arabic Collection of Aphorisms." *Mélanges de l'Université Saint-Joseph* 57 (2004): 173–190.

90 Bertolacci, Amos. "On the Arabic Translations of Aristotle's *Metaphysics*." *Arabic Sciences and Philosophy* 15 (2005): 241–275.

91 Bettiolo, Paolo. "Scuole e ambienti intellettuali nelle chiese di Siria." In C. D'Ancona 2005 [*92: I 48–100].

92 D'Ancona, Cristina, ed. *Storia della filosofia nell'islam medievale*, 2 vols. Torino, 2005.

93 Schöck, Cornelia. "Aussagenquantifizierung und -modalisierung in der frühen islamischen Theologie." In *Logik und Theologie: Das Organon im arabischen und im lateinischen Mittelalter*. Ed. by Dominik Perler and Ulrich Rudolph. Leiden, 2005, 19–43.

94 Watts, Edward J. "Where to Live the Philosophical Life in the Sixth Century? Damascius, Simplicius, and the Return from Persia." *Greek, Roman, and Byzantine Studies* 45 (2005): 285–315.

95 Becker, Adam H. *Fear of God and the Beginning of Wisdom: The School of Nisibis and Christian Scholastic Culture in Late Antique Mesopotamia*. Philadelphia, 2006.

96 Brentjes, Sonja. "An Exciting New Arabic Version of Euclid's Elements: MS Mumbai, Mullā Fīrūz R.I.6." *Revue d'histoire des mathématiques* 12 (2006): 169–197.

97 Forster, Regula. *Das Geheimnis der Geheimnisse. Die arabischen und deutschen Fassungen des pseudo-aristotelischen Sirr al-asrār/Secretum secretorum*. Wiesbaden, 2006. – PhD Diss., Zurich, 2005.

98 MacMullen, Ramsay. *Voting about God in Early Church Councils*. New Haven, 2006.

99 Maróth, Miklós. *The Correspondence between Aristotle and Alexander the Great: An Anonymous Greek Novel in Letters in Arabic Translation*. Piliscsaba, 2006.

100 Walker, Joel T. *Legend of Mar Qardagh: Narrative and Christian Heroism in Late Antique Iraq*. Berkeley, 2006.

101 Adamson, Peter. *Al-Kindī*. Oxford, 2007.

102 Adamson, Peter. "The Kindian Tradition: The Structure of Philosophy in Arabic Neoplatonism." In C. D'Ancona 2007 [*104: 351–370].

103 Brock, Sebastian. "A Syriac Intermediary for the Arabic Theology of Aristotle? In Search of a Chimera." In C. D'Ancona 2007 [*104: 293–306].

104 D'Ancona, Cristina, ed. *The Libraries of the Neoplatonists: Proceedings of the Meeting of the European Science Foundation Network 'Late Antiquity and Arabic Thought: Patterns in the Constitution of European Culture' held in Strasbourg, March 12–14, 2004*. Leiden, Boston, 2007.

105 Dietrich, Albert. "Ahrun." EI² [*2: XII 52].

106 Endress, Gerhard. "Building the Library of Arabic Philosophy: Platonism and Aristotelianism in the Sources of al-Kindī." In C. D'Ancona 2007 [*104: 319–350].

107 Hadot, Ilsetraut. "Dans quel lieu le néoplatonicien Simplicius a-t-il fondé son école de mathématiques, et où a pu avoir lieu son entretien avec un manichéen?" [and] "Remarque complémentaire." *The International Journal of the Platonic Tradition* 1 (2007): 42–107. 263–269.

108 Hugonnard-Roche, Henri. "Le Corpus philosophique syriaque aux VIe–VIIe siècles." In C. D'Ancona 2007 [*104: 279–291].

109 Kotzia, Paraskevi. *Περὶ τοῦ μήλου ἢ Περὶ τῆς Ἀριστοτέλους τελευτῆς* (*Liber de Pomo*). Thessaloniki, 2007.

110 Vagelpohl, Uwe. *Aristotle's Rhetoric in the East*. Leiden, 2008.

111 van Bladel, Kevin. *The Arabic Hermes: From Pagan Sage to Prophet of Science*. Oxford, 2009.

112 Gutas, Dimitri. "On Graeco-Arabic Epistolary 'Novels'." *Middle Eastern Literatures* 12 (2009): 59–70.

113 Gutas, Dimitri and Kevin van Bladel. "Bayt al-ḥikma." EI Three [*10: 133–137].

114 van Bladel, Kevin. "The Arabic History of Science of Abū Sahl ibn Nawbaḫt (fl. ca. 770–809) and Its Middle Persian Sources." In *Islamic Philosophy, Science, Culture, and Religion: Studies in Honor of Dimitri Gutas*. Ed. by Felicitas Opwis and David Reisman. Leiden 2012, 41–62.

115 Ullman, Manfred. *Die Nikomachische Ethik des Aristoteles in arabischer Übersetzung, part 2: Überlieferung – Textkritik – Grammatik*. Wiesbaden, 2012.

116 King, Daniel. "Why Were the Syrians Interested in Greek Philosophy?" In *History and Identity in the Late Antique Near East*. Ed. by Philip Wood. Oxford, 2013, 61–82.

117 Swain, Simon. *Economy, Family, and Society from Rome to Islam. A Critical Edition, English Translation, and Study of Bryson's 'Management of the Estate'*. Cambridge, 2013.

118 Treiger, Alexander. "Christian Graeco-Arabica." *Intellectual History of the Islamicate World* 3 (2015): 188–227.

CHAPTER 4

Abū Yūsuf al-Kindī

Gerhard Endress and Peter Adamson

1 Primary Sources – 2 Life and Influence – 3 Translations Available in al-Kindī's Time
4 Works – 5 Doctrine – 6 Secondary Literature

1 Primary Sources

1.1 Bio-Bibliographical Testimonies [**1–*19*] – 1.2 Collections of al-Kindī's Works [**25–*35*] – 1.3 Individual Works [**40–*173*]

1.1 *Bio-Bibliographical Testimonies*

1 Ibn ʿAbd-Rabbih, Aḥmad b. Muḥammad (d. 328/940). *Al-ʿIqd al-farīd*. – Ed. by Aḥmad Amīn, Aḥmad al-Zayn, and Ibrāhīm al-Abyārī, vol. 2. Cairo, 1940, 382–383.

2 Ibn al-Dāya, Aḥmad b. Yūsuf (d. between 330/941 and 340/951). *Kitāb Ḥusn al-ʿuqbā*. – Ed. by Maḥmūd Muḥammad Šākir. Cairo, 1940, 130–131. – Repr. Beirut, ca. 1983. – Excerpts in: al-Ṭabarī, *Aḫbār al-rusul wa-l-mulūk*. Ed. by Michael Jan de Goeje et al., vol. 3. Leiden, 1881–1882, 1002.

3 al-Ṣūlī, Abū Bakr Muḥammad b. Yaḥyā (d. 335/947). *Aḫbār Abī Tammām*. Cairo, 1356/1937, 230–232.

4 Ibn Ǧulǧul, Sulaymān b. Ḥassān. *Ṭabaqāt al-aṭibbāʾ wa-l-ḥukamāʾ* [composed 377/987]. – Ed. by Fuʾād Sayyid, *Les générations des médecins et des sages*. Cairo, 1955, 73–74.

5 Ibn al-Nadīm, Abū l-Faraǧ Muḥammad b. Isḥāq (d. 380/990). *Kitāb al-Fihrist*. – Ed. by Gustav Flügel, August Müller and Johannes Roediger, vol. 1. Leipzig, 1871, 255–261. – Repr. Beirut, 1964, Frankfurt a.M., 2005. – Ed. by Ayman Fuʾād Sayyid, vol. 2. London, 2009, 182–195. – Engl. transl. by Bayard Dodge, *The Fihrist of al-Nadīm*, vol. 2. New York, 1970, 615–626.

6 al-Bīrūnī, Abū l-Rayḥān Muḥammad b. Aḥmad (*362/973, d. ca. 442/1050). *Istīʿāb al-wuǧūh al-mumkina fī ṣanʿat al-asṭurlāb* [excerpt], in: Edward Stewart Kennedy, Paul Kunitzsch, and Richard P. Lorch, eds. *The Melon-Shaped Astrolabe in Arabic Astronomy*. Stuttgart, 1999, 184–201.

 DOI 10.1163/9789004323162_006

7 *Ṣiwān al-ḥikma* [attributed to Abū Sulaymān al-Siǧistānī]. – Excerpts ed. by Douglas Morton Dunlop, *The Muntakhab Ṣiwān al-ḥikmah of Abū Sulaimān as-Sijistānī*. The Hague, 1979, 151 §§ 296–302. – Ed. by ʿAbd al-Raḥmān Badawī, *Ṣiwān al-ḥikma wa-ṯalāṯ rasāʾil taʾlīf Abū Sulaymān al-Manṭiqī al-Siǧistānī*. Tehran, 1974, 326–353.

8 Abū Saʿīd ʿUbayd Allāh Ibn Baḫtīšūʿ (d. after 450/1058). *Risāla fī l-Ṭibb wa-l-aḥdāṯ al-nafsāniyya*. – Ed. by Felix Klein-Franke, *Über die Heilung der Krankheiten der Seele und des Körpers*. Beirut, 1977, 52.

9 al-Mubaššir b. Fātik. *Muḫtār al-ḥikam wa-maḥāsin al-kalim* [composed 440/1048–1049]. – Ed. by ʿAbd al-Raḥmān Badawī. Madrid, 1958, 84–85.

10 Ṣāʿid b. Aḥmad al-Andalusī, Abū l-Qāsim (d. 462/1070). *Kitāb (al-Taʿrīf bi-) Ṭabaqāt al-umam*. – Ed. by Luwīs Šayḫū (Louis Cheikho). Beirut, 1912, 51–52. – Ed. by Ḥayāt Bū-ʿAlwān. Beirut, 1985, 134–136. – French. transl. by Régis Blachère, *Kitâb Ṭabaḳât al-umam: Livre des Catégories des nations*, traduction avec notes et indices, précédée d'une introduction. Paris, 1935, 104–106.

11 al-Bayhaqī, Ẓahīr al-Dīn Abū l-Ḥasan ʿAlī b. Zayd Ibn Funduq (d. 565/1169–1170). *Tatimmat Ṣiwān al-ḥikma*. – Ed. by Muḥammad Šafīʿ. Lahore, 1351/1932, 25. – Ed. by Muḥammad Kurd ʿAlī, *Taʾrīḫ ḥukamāʾ al-islām*. Damascus, 1365/1946, 41. – Repr. 1396/1976.

12 Ibn al-Qifṭī, Ǧamāl al-Dīn ʿAlī b. Yūsuf (d. 646/1248). *Taʾrīḫ al-ḥukamāʾ* [*Iḫbār al-ʿulamāʾ bi-aḫbār al-ḥukamāʾ*, epitome by Muḥammad b. ʿAlī al-Zawzanī]. – Ed. by Julius Lippert, *Ibn al-Qifṭī's Taʾrīḫ al-ḥukamāʾ*. Leipzig, 1903, 366.

13 Ibn Abī Uṣaybiʿa, Muwaffaq al-Dīn Aḥmad b. al-Qāsim (d. 668/1270). *ʿUyūn al-anbāʾ fī ṭabaqāt al-aṭibbāʾ*. – Ed. by August Müller, 2 vols. Cairo, 1299/1882, Königsberg, 1884; I 206–214.

14 al-Šahrazūrī, Šams al-Dīn Muḥammad b. Maḥmūd (d. after 687/1288). *Nuzhat al-arwāḥ wa-rawḍat al-afrāḥ fī taʾrīḫ al-ḥukamāʾ wa-l-falāsifa*. – Ed. by Ḫwaršīd Aḥmad, vol. 2. Hyderabad, 1976, 22.

15 al-Ḏahabī, Muḥammad b. Aḥmad (d. 748/1348). *Al-ʿIbar fī ḫabar man ġabar*, vol. 1. Kuwait, 1960, 443.

16 al-Ḏahabī. *Siyar aʿlām al-nubalāʾ*. – Ed. by Šuʿayb al-Arnāʾūṭ et al., vol. 12. Beirut, 1985 (2nd ed.), 337.

17 al-Ṣafadī, Ṣalāḥ al-Dīn Ḫalīl b. Aybak (d. 764/1363). *Al-Wāfī bi-l-wafayāt*. – Ed. by Muḥammad Yūsuf Naǧm, *Das biographische Lexikon des […] aṣ-Ṣafadī*, vol. 8. Wiesbaden, 1971, 415. – Ed. by Ibrāhīm Šabbūḥ, vol. 28. Beirut, Berlin, 2004, 479–488.

18 Ibn Nubāta, Ǧamāl al-Dīn Muḥammad b. Šams al-Dīn al-Miṣrī (d. 768/1366). *Sarḥ al-ʿuyūn fī šarḥ Risālat Ibn Zaydūn*. – Ed. by Muḥammad Abū l-Faḍl Ibrāhīm. Cairo, 1383/1964, 231–234.

19 Ibn Ḥaǧar al-ʿAsqalānī, Abū l-Faḍl Šihāb al-Dīn Aḥmad b. ʿAlī (d. 852/1449). *Lisān al-mīzān*, vol. 6. Hyderabad, 1331/1912, 305.

1.2 *Collections of al-Kindī's Works*

25 *Die philosophischen Abhandlungen des Jaʿqūb ben Isḥāq al-Kindī*, zum ersten Male herausgegeben von Albino Nagy. Münster, 1897.

26 *Rasāʾil al-Kindī al-falsafiyya*. – Ed. by Muḥammad ʿAbd al-Hādī Abū Rīda, vol. 1. Cairo, 1369/1950; vol. 2. Cairo, 1372/1953. – Revised partial ed. of vol. 1. Cairo, 1978.

27 *Rasāʾil al-Kindī al-mūsīqiyya*. – *Al-Kindi's Writings on Music*. Ed. by Zakariyyāʾ Yūsuf. Baghdad, 1962.

28 *Trois épîtres d'al-Kindī*. – Edition and French transl. by Laura Veccia Vaglieri and Giuseppe Celentano, in: *Annali dell'Istituto Orientale di Napoli* 34 = N.S. 24 (1974): 523–562.

29 *Cinq épîtres* / al-Kindî. – Edition and French transl. by Daniel Gimaret et al. Paris, 1976.

30 *Due scritti medici di al-Kindī*. – Edition and Ital. transl. by Giuseppe Celentano. Naples, 1979.

31 *Œuvres philosophiques et scientifiques d'al-Kindī*, vol. 1: *L'Optique et la catoptrique*. – Edition and French transl. by Roshdi Rashed. Leiden, 1997.

32 *Œuvres philosophiques et scientifiques d'al-Kindī*, vol. 2: *Métaphysique et cosmologie*. – Edition and French transl. by Roshdi Rashed and Jean Jolivet. Leiden, 1998.

33 *Obras filosóficas de al-Kindī*. – Span. transl. by Rafael Ramón Guerrero and Emilio Tornero Poveda. Madrid, 1986.

34 *Scientific Weather Forecasting in the Middle Ages: The Writings of al-Kindī: Studies, Editions and Translations of the Arabic, Hebrew and Latin texts*. – Ed. by Gerrit Bos and Charles Burnett. London, 2000.

35 *The Philosophical Works of al-Kindī*. – Engl. transl. by Peter Adamson and Peter E. Pormann. Karachi, 2012.

1.3 *Individual Works*

1.3.1 Introductions to Philosophy

40 *Risāla fī Kammiyyat kutub Arisṭāṭālīs wa-mā yuḥtāǧ ilayhi fī taḥṣīl al-falsafa*. – Edition and Ital. transl. by Michelangelo Guidi and Richard Walzer, *Studi su al-Kindī*, vol. 1: *Uno scritto introduttivo allo studio di Aristotele*. Rome, 1940. – Ed. by Muḥammad ʿAbd al-Hādī Abū Rīda [*26: I 362–384]. – Engl. transl. by Nicholas Rescher, "Al-Kindi's Sketch of Aristotle's *Organon*." *The New Scholasticism* 37 (1963): 44–58.

41 *Risāla fī Ḥudūd al-ašyāʾ wa-rusūmihā.* – Ed. by M. ʿAbd al-Hādī Abū Rīda [**26*: I 165–179; ^{2}113–130]. – Ed. by Yūḥannā Qumayr 1954 [*102: 63–67]. – Ed. by Daniel Gimaret [**29*: 7–69], with French transl. – Ed. by Felix Klein-Franke 1982 [*151: 191–216].

1.3.2 Propaedeutic Ethics

45 *Risāla fī l-Ḥīla li-dafʿ al-aḥzān.* – Ed. and Ital. transl. by Hellmut Ritter and Richard Walzer, *Uno scritto morale inedito di al-Kindī* (*Temistio Περὶ ἀλυπίας?*). Rome, 1938.

1.3.3 Metaphysics

51 *Kitāb al-Kindī ilā l-Muʿtaṣim bi-llāh fī l-Falsafa al-ūlā.* – Ed. by Aḥmad Fuʾād al-Ahwānī. Cairo, 1948. – Ed. by M. ʿAbd al-Hādī Abū Rīda [**26*: I 97–162; ^{2}75–107] (edition quoted below). – Ed. by Muwaffaq Fawzī al-Ǧabr. Damascus, 1997. – Ed. and French transl. by Roshdi Rashed and Jean Jolivet [**32*: 8–111]. – Engl. transl. by Alfred L. Ivry, *Al-Kindi's Metaphysics: A Translation of Yaʿqūb b. Isḥāq al-Kindī's Treatise 'On First Philosophy'* (*fī al-Falsafah al-ūlā*) *with Introduction and Commentary*. Albany, 1974. – Span. transl. by Rafael Ramón Guerrero, Emilio Tornero Poveda [**33*: 46–87]. – Pers. transl. by Aḥmad Ārām, *Nāma-yi Kindī ba-al-Muʿtaṣim bi-llāh dar Falsafa-yi ūlā*. Tehran, 1981.

52 *Risāla fī l-Fāʿil al-ḥaqq al-awwal al-tāmm wa-l-fāʿil al-nāqiṣ allaḏī huwa bi-l-maǧāz.* – Ed. by M. ʿAbd al-Hādī Abū Rīda [**26*: I 182–184; ^{2}134–136]. – Edition and French transl. by Roshdi Rashed and Jean Jolivet [**32*: 167–171].

53 *Risāla fī Iftirāq al-milal fī l-tawḥīd wa-annahum muǧmiʿūn ʿalā l-tawḥīd wa-kull qad ḫālafa ṣāḥibahu* [excerpts], in: Yaḥyā Ibn ʿAdī, *Tabyīn ġalaṭ Abī Yūsuf Yaʿqūb b. Isḥāq al-Kindī fī l-radd ʿalā l-naṣārā*. Edition and French transl. by Augustin Périer [**172*]; French transl. only in: Périer [**171*: 118–128]. – Ed. and French transl. by Roshdi Rashed and Jean Jolivet [**32*: 122–127].

54 *Risāla ilā Aḥmad ibn al-Muʿtaṣim fī l-Ibāna ʿan suǧūd al-ǧirm al-aqṣā.* – Ed. by M. ʿAbd al-Hādī Abū Rīda [**26*: I 244–261]. – Edition and French transl. by Roshdi Rashed and Jean Jolivet [**32*: 176–199]. – Span. transl. by Rafael Ramón Guerrero and Emilio Tornero Poveda [**33*: 117–127].

55 *Liber de quinque essentiis* [Arab., *Kitāb al-Ǧawāhir al-ḫamsa*]. – Ed. by Albino Nagy 1897 [**25*: 28–40]. – Ed. by M. ʿAbd al-Hādī Abū Rīda [**26*: II 8–35], with re-translation into Arabic.

1.3.4 Soul and Intellect

61 *Risāla fī annahu ǧawāhir lā-aǧsām.* – Ed. by M. ʿAbd al-Hādī Abū Rīda [**26*: I 265–269; ^{2}25–107].

62 *al-Qawl fī l-Nafs al-muḫtaṣar min kitāb Arisṭū wa-Falāṭun wa-sā'ir al-falāsifa.* – Ed. by M. ʿAbd al-Hādī Abū Rīda [*26: I 272–280]. – Ital. transl. by Giuseppe Furlani 1922 [*221: 51–58]; excerpts in Ital.: Walzer 1937 [*222: 125–137].

63 *Kalām fī l-Nafs muḫtaṣar waǧīz.* – Ed. by M. ʿAbd al-Hādī Abū Rīda [*26: I 281–282].

64 *Risāla fī Šarḥ mā li-l-nafs ḏikruhu mimmā kāna lahā fī ʿālam al-ʿaql.* – Ed. by Gerhard Endress 1994 [*237]. – Facsimile ed. of MS Tehran, Dāniškada-yi ilāhiyāt 242B, with German transl.

65 *Risāla fī l-ʿAql.* – Ed. by M. ʿAbd al-Hādī Abū Rīda [*26: I 353–362]. – Ed. by al-Ahwānī 1950 [*223: 178–181], Qumayr 1954 [*102: 53–56], McCarthy 1964 [*225], Jolivet 1971 [*227: 158–160]. – Transl. by Albino Nagy [*25: 1–11] (medieval Lat. versions by Gerard of Cremona and Johannes Hispalensis); McCarthy 1964 [*225, Engl.]; Jolivet 1971 [*227, French].

66 *Risāla fī Māhiyyat al-nawm wa-l-ru'yā.* – Ed. by M. ʿAbd al-Hādī Abū Rīda [*26: I 293–311]. – Medieval Lat. version: *De somno et visione.* Ed. by Albino Nagy [*25: 12–27].

67 [*Ǧawāb ʿan su'āl*] *Hal yaǧūzu an yutawahham mā lā yurā.* – Ed. by Giuseppe Celentano [*30: 9]).

1.3.5 Physics and Cosmology

71 *Risāla ilā Muḥammad b. al-Ǧahm fī Waḥdāniyyat Allāh wa-tanāhī ǧirm al-ʿālam.* – Ed. by M. ʿAbd al-Hādī Abū Rīda [*26: I 201–207; ²157–164]. – Edition and French transl. by Roshdi Rashed, Jean Jolivet [*32: 135–147]. – Ed. by Ġulāmriḍā Ǧamšīdnižād, in: *Ganǧīna-yi Bahāristān.* Ed. by ʿAlī Awǧabī [Owjabi]. Tehran, 1379 h.š./2000, 75–96. – Engl. transl. by Fazal Ahmad Shamsi, “Al-Kindi's *Risala Fi Wahdaniyya Allah Wa Tanahi Jirm al-Alam.*” *Islamic Studies* 17 (1978): 185–201; Nicholas Rescher and Haig Khatchadourian, “Al-Kindi's Epistle on the Finitude of the Universe” [*253].

72 *Risāla fī Mā'iyyat mā lā yumkin an yakūna lā-nihāya wa-mā llaḏī yuqālu lā nihāyata lahu.* – Ed. by M. ʿAbd al-Hādī Abū Rīda [*26: I 194–198]. – Edition and French transl. by Roshdi Rashed and Jean Jolivet [*32: 150–155].

73 *Risāla ilā Aḥmad b. Muḥammad al-Ḫurāsānī fī Īḍāḥ tanāhī ǧirm al-ʿālam.* – Ed. by M. ʿAbd al-Hādī Abū Rīda [*26: I 186–192]. – Edition and French transl. by Roshdi Rashed and Jean Jolivet [*32: 157–165].

74 *Risāla fī l-Ibāna ʿan al-ʿilla al-fāʿila al-qarība li-l-kawn wa-l-fasād.* – Ed. by M. ʿAbd al-Hādī Abū Rīda [*26: I 214–237]. – Engl. transl. by Jon McGinnis and David C. Reisman, *Classical Arabic Philosophy: An Anthology of Sources.* Indianapolis, 2007, 1–16.

75 *Risāla fī l-Ibāna ʿan anna ṭabīʿat al-falak muḫālifa li-ṭabāʾiʿ al-ʿanāṣir al-arbaʿa.* – Ed. by M. ʿAbd al-Hādī Abū Rīda [*26: II 40–46].

76 *Risāla ilā Aḥmad b. al-Muʿtaṣim fī anna l-ʿanāṣir wa-l-ǧirm al-aqṣā kuriyyat al-šakl.* – Ed. by M. ʿAbd al-Hādī Abū Rīda [*26: II 48–53]. – Engl. transl. by Nicholas Rescher and Haig Khatchadourian, "Al-Kindī's Epistle on the Concentric Structure of the Universe" [*252].

77 *Risāla fī l-ʿIlla allatī lahā qīla anna l-nār wa-l-hawāʾ wa-l-māʾ wa-l-arḍ ʿanāṣir li-ǧamīʿ al-kāʾina al-fāsida wa-ḫuṣṣat bi-ḏālika dūna ġayrihā min al-kāʾina,* MS Istanbul, Lâleli 2487, no. 4.

78 *Risāla fī l-Sabab allaḏī [lahu] nasabat al-qudamāʾ al-aškāl al-ḫamsa ilā l-usṭuqussāt.* – Ed. by M. ʿAbd al-Hādī Abū Rīda [*26: II 54–63]. – Engl. transl. by Nicholas Rescher, "Al-Kindi's Treatise on the Platonic Solids" [*254].

79 *Risāla fī l-Ǧirm al-ḥāmil bi-ṭibāʿihi [sic leg. pro bi-ṭibāʿat] al-lawn min al-ʿanāṣir al-arbaʿa wa-llaḏī huwa ʿillat al-lawn fī ġayrihi.* – Ed. by M. ʿAbd al-Hādī Abū Rīda [*26: II 64–68].

80 *Risāla fī ʿIllat al-lawn al-lāzuwardī allaḏī yurā fī l-ǧaww fī ǧihat al-samāʾ wa-yuẓann annahu lawn al-samāʾ.* – Ed. by M. ʿAbd al-Hādī Abū Rīda [*26: II 103–108]. – Edition and Engl. transl. by Otto Spies, "Al-Kindī's Treatise on the Cause of the Blue Colour of the Sky." *Journal of the Bombay Branch of the Royal Asiatic Society* N.S. 13 (Bombay 1931): 7–19. – German transl. by Eilhard Wiedemann, in: *Arbeiten aus den Gebieten der Physik, Mathematik, Chemie: Festschrift Julius Elster und Hans Geitel zum 60. Geburtstag gewidmet von Freunden und Schülern.* Braunschweig, 1915, 118.

81 *Kalām fī l-Tarkīb.* – Ed. by Giuseppe Celentano [*30: 8].

1.3.6 Mathematical Sciences

1.3.6.1 *Arithmetic*

85 *Risāla fī Istiḫrāǧ al-aʿdād al-muḍmara,* Istanbul, Süleymaniye, MS Ayasofya 4830, no. 3.

1.3.6.2 *Geometry and Geodesy*

91 *Risāla ilā Yūḥannā b. Māsawayh fī Taqrīb al-dawr min al-watar.* – Ed. by Roshdi Rashed, "Al-Kindī's Commentary on Archimedes' 'The measurement of the circle'." *Arabic Sciences and Philosophy* 3 (1993): 7–54 (text 42–50, Engl. transl. 32–42).

92 *Risāla fī Īḍāḥ wiǧdān abʿād mā bayn al-nāẓir wa-markaz aʿmidat al-ǧibāl wa-ʿuluww aʿmidat al-ǧibāl,* Istanbul, Süleymaniye, MS Ayasofya 4832, fols 66^b–70; cf. Ritter 1932 [*41: 370 no. 31].

1.3.6.3 *Optics*

95 *Kitāb ilā baʿḍ iḫwānihi fī Taqwīm al-ḫaṭaʾ wa-l-muškilāt allatī li-Uqlīdis fī kitābihi al-mawsūm bi-l-Manāẓir.* – Ed. by Roshdi Rashed [*31: 161–358]: "Épître de Abū

Yūsuf Yaʿqūb ibn Isḥāq al-Kindī sur la rectification des erreurs et des difficultés dues à Euclide dans son livre appelé l'Optique." – With French transl. and commentary.

96 *Kitāb fī l-Šuʿāʿāt (al-šamsiyya).* – Ed. by Roshdi Rashed [**31*: 359–422]: Livre de Yaʿqūb ibn Isḥāq al-Kindī sur les rayons solaires. – With French transl. and commentary. – Ed. by Yaḥyā Hāšimī, *al-Kindī, Maṭāriḥ al-šuʿāʿ, aqdam maḫṭūṭa ʿarabiyya fī l-manāẓir (al-marāyā al-muḥriqa).* Aleppo, 1967, 34–55 [Facsimile ed. of a recent copy].

97 *Risāla fī Iḫtilāf al-manāẓir* [Lat.]: *Liber Jacob Alkindi de causis diversitatum aspectus et dandis demonstrationibus geometricis super eas.* – Ed. by Axel Anthon Björnbo, *Alkindi, Tideus und Pseudo-Euklid: Drei optische Werke.* Leipzig, Berlin, 1912, 3–41, [including] explanation by Sebastian Vogl, 42–70. – Ed. by Roshdi Rashed and Henri Hugonnard-Roche [**31*: 437–536]: Livre de Jacob Alkindi sur les causes des diversités de la perspective et sur les démonstrations géométriques qu'il faut en donner, [with] Traduction de Jean Jolivet, Hourya Sinaceur, Henri Hugonnard-Roche, Révision de Roshdi Rashed.

1.3.6.4 *Astronomy*

101 *Kitāb fī l-Ṣināʿa al-ʿuẓmā.* – Ed. by ʿAzmī Ṭāhā al-Sayyid Aḥmad. Cyprus, 1987.

1.3.6.5 *Music*

105 *Kitāb al-Muṣawwitāt al-watariyya min ḏāt al-watar al-wāḥid ilā ḏāt al-ʿašarat al-awtār.* – Ed. by Zakariyyāʾ Yūsuf [*27: 67–92].

106 *Risāla fī Aǧzāʾ ḫabariyya fī l-mūsīqī.* – Ed. by Zakariyyāʾ Yūsuf [*27: 93–110]. – Ed. by Maḥmūd Aḥmad al-Ḥifnī. Cairo, 1963. – Engl. transl. by Henry George Farmer 1956 [*331].

107 *Risāla fī Ḫubr ṣināʿat al-taʾlīf.* – Edition and German transl. by Robert Lachmann and Mahmud el-Hefni, *Risāla fī Ḫubr tāʾlīf* [*sic*] *al-alḥān: Über die Komposition der Melodien,* mit Übersetzung, Einleitung und Kommentar. Leipzig, 1931. – Ed. by Zakariyyāʾ Yūsuf [**27*: 45–66]. – Engl. transl. by Carl Cowl, "The *Risāla fī Ḫubr tāʾlīf* [sic] *al-alḥān* of Jaʿqūb ibn Isḥāq al-Kindī." *The Consort* 23 (1966): 129–166.

108 *Risāla fī l-Luḥūn wa-l-naġam.* – Ed. by Zakariyyāʾ Yūsuf, *Risālat al-Kindī fī l-Luḥūn wa-l-naġam* [*al-Kindi's Treatise on Melodies*]. Baghdad, 1965. – French transl. by Amnon Shiloah 1974 [*336]. – Fragment ed. by Zakariyyāʾ Yūsuf 1962 [*332: 111–120]; under the title: *al-Risāla al-kubrā fī l-Taʾlīf aw al-Kitāb al-aʿẓam fī l-Taʾlīf,* ed. by Zakariyyāʾ Yūsuf 1962 [*332: 121–142], here contaminated with excerpts from Pseudo-Euclid: *Qawl Uqlīdis ʿalā l-luḥūn wa-ṣanʿat al-maʿāzif wa-maḫāriǧ al-ḥurūf;* ibid. [*332: 111–120] further fragments from Pseudo-Euclid under the title *Muḫtaṣar al-mūsīqī fī taʾlīf al-naġam wa-ṣanʿat al-ʿūd* (cf. Shiloah 1979 [*337: 257–260 no. 176–177]).

1.3.7 Astrology, Meteorology, and Magic

1.3.7.1 *Astrology*

111 *Risāla fī Mulk al-ʿArab wa-kammiyyatihi.* – Ed. by Otto Loth, "Al-Kindî als Astrolog." In *Morgenländische Forschungen H. L. Fleischer … gewidmet.* Leipzig, 1875, 261–309 (text 273–279).

112 *Maqāla ʿalā Taḥāwīl al-sinīn*, MS Escurial ²913,2; cf. McCarthy 1962 [*4: 53 no. 326. 72 no. 44]; GAS [*6: VII 132].

113 *Risāla fī Taḥrīr waqt yurǧā fīhi iǧābat al-duʿāʾ wa-l-taḍarruʿ ilā llāh min ǧihat al-tanǧīm.* – Ed. by Muhsin Mahdi: *Nuṣūṣ ġayr manšūra li-l-Kindī wa-l-Fārābī*, in: *Nuṣūṣ falsafiyya muhdāt ilā Ibrāhīm Madkūr.* Ed. by ʿUṯmān Amīn. Cairo, 1976, 53–78 (text 65–68). – Ed. by Mubahat Türker Küyel, in: *Araştırma* 10 (1972): 1–14 (with Turkish transl.).

114 *al-Madḫal ilā ʿilm [aḥkām] al-nuǧūm (al-Arbaʿūn bāban).* – Excerpts ed. by Charles Burnett 1993 [*356].

1.3.7.2 *Astrometeorology*

118 *Risāla fī (ʿIlal) aḥdāṯ al-ǧaww.* – Ed. Yūsuf Yaʿqūb Maskūnī, *Risālat Yaʿqūb b. Isḥāq al-Kindī fī Ḥawādiṯ al-ǧaww.* Baghdad, 1965, 16 (MS Fatih 5411). – Ed. by Franz Rosenthal 1956 [*43: 29–30] (MS Istanbul, Hamidiye 1446; incomplete). – Ed. by Gerrit Bos and Charles Burnett 2000 [*365: 411–419].

119 *al-Risāla al-Kāfiya fī l-āṯār al-ʿulwiyya* [Hebr. and Lat.]. – Ed. by Gerrit Bos and Charles Burnett 2000 [*365: 97–202].

120 *Risāla fī ʿIlal (al-)quwā (al-mansūba ilā) l-ašḫāṣ al-ʿāliya al-dālla ʿalā l-maṭar* [Hebr. and Lat.]. – Ed. by Gerrit Bos and Charles Burnett 2000 [*365: 203–310].

1.3.7.3 *Meteorology*

125 *Risāla fī l-ʿIlla allatī lahā takūn baʿḍ al-mawāḍiʿ lā takād tumṭar.* – Ed. by M. ʿAbd al-Hādī Abū Rīda [*26: II 70–75].

126 *Risāla fī ʿIllat kawn al-ḍabāb.* – Ed. by M. ʿAbd al-Hādī Abū Rīda [*26: II 76–78].

127 *Risāla fī ʿIllat al-ṯalǧ wa-l-barad wa-l-barq wa-l-ṣawāʿiq wa-l-raʿd wa-l-zamharīr.* – Ed. by M. ʿAbd al-Hādī Abū Rīda [*26: II 80–85].

128 *Risāla fī l-ʿIlla allatī lahā yabrud aʿlā l-ǧaww wa-yasḫun mā yaqrub min al-arḍ.* – Ed. by M. ʿAbd al-Hādī Abū Rīda [*26: II 90–100].

129 *Risāla fī ʿIllat al-lawn al-lāzuwardī allaḏī yurā fī l-ǧaww fī ǧihat al-samāʾ.* – Ed. by M. ʿAbd al-Hādī Abū Rīda [*26: II 103–108].

130 *Risāla fī l-ʿIlla al-fāʿila li-l-madd wa-l-ǧazr.* – Ed. by M. ʿAbd al-Hādī Abū Rīda [*26: II 110–133]. – Excerpts in German transl. by Eilhard Wiedemann 1922 [*361].

1.3.7.4 *Magic*

135 *De radiis* [*Maṭraḥ al-šuʿāʿ*, Lat.]. – Ed. by Marie-Thérèse d'Alverny and Françoise Hudry, "Al-Kindi De radiis." *Archives d'histoire doctrinale et littéraire du moyen* âge 41 (1975): 139–260.

136 *Fī l-Mawāḍiʿ allatī yuẓann anna l-dafīn fīhā min kanz aw ġayrihi.* – Ed. by Charles Burnett, Keiji Yamamoto, and Michio Yano 1997 [*375: 57–90].

1.3.8 Medicine and Pharmacology

1.3.8.1 *Physiology*

141 *Risāla fī l-Luṯġa.* – Ed. and Ital. transl. by Giuseppe Celentano [**30*: 47–58].

1.3.8.2 *Pathology*

145 *Risāla fī ʿIllat baḥārīn al-amrāḍ al-ḥādda.* – Ed. by Felix Klein-Franke, "Die Ursachen der Krisen bei akuten Krankheiten, eine wiederentdeckte Schrift al-Kindī's." *Israel Oriental Studies* 5 (1975): 161–188 (Arab. text 171–177, German transl. 180–188).

1.3.8.3 *Pharmacology*

155 *Kitāb fī Maʿrifat quwā l-adwiya al-murakkaba.* – Ed. and French transl. by Léon Gauthier, *Antécédents gréco-arabes de la psychophysique*. Beirut, 1938.

156 *Kitāb fī Kīmiyāʾ al-ʿiṭr wa-l-taṣʿīdāt.* – Ed. by Karl Garbers, *Buch über die Chemie des Parfüms und die Destillationen von Yaʿqūb ibn Isḥāq al-Kindī, ein Beitrag zur Geschichte der arabischen Parfümchemie und Drogenkunde*. Leipzig, 1948 (with German transl.).

157 *al-Iḫtiyārāt li-l-adwiya al-mumtaḥana al-muǧarraba wa-huwa l-Aqrābāḏīn.* – Ed. by Martin Levey, *The Medical Formulary or Aqrābāḏīn of al-Kindī, Translated with a Study of its Materia Medica*. Madison, London, 1966 (with Engl. transl.).

1.3.8.4 *Primary Sources for Greek-Arabic Transmission in the Kindī Circle*

161 *Aristoteles' De Anima, eine verlorene spätantike Paraphrase in arabischer und persischer Überlieferung: Arabischer Text nebst Kommentar, quellengeschichtlichen Studien und Glossaren*. Ed. by Rüdiger Arnzen. Leiden, 1998.

162 *Theologia Aristotelis: Kitāb Arisṭāṭālīs al-musammā bi-Uṯūlūǧiyā wa-huwa l-qawl ʿalā r-rubūbiyya.* – Ed. by Friedrich Dieterici, *Die sogenannte Theologie des Aristoteles*. Leipzig, 1882. – Ed. by ʿAbd al-Raḥmān Badawī, in: *Aflūṭīn ʿind al-ʿArab*. Cairo, 1955, 1–164. – Engl. transl. by Geoffrey Lewis, in: *Plotini Opera*. Ed. by Paul Henry and Hans-Rudolf Schwyzer, vol. 2: *Enneades* IV–V; *Plotiniana Arabica ad codd. fidem anglice vertit G. Lewis*. Paris, Bruxelles, 1959. – Partial edition, Greek-Arabic-Ital., by Cristina D'Ancona 2003 [*81].

163 Pseudo-Aristotle. *Kitāb al-Īḍāḥ fī l-ḫayr al-maḥḍ (maḥḍ al-ḫayr)*. – Ed. by Otto Bardenhewer, *Die pseudo-aristotelische Schrift Über das reine Gute, bekannt unter dem Namen Liber de Causis*. Freiburg im Breisgau, 1882. – Ed. by ʿAbd al-Raḥmān Badawī, *al-Aflāṭūniyya al-muḥdaṯa ʿind al-ʿArab*. Cairo, 1955, 1–33. – Other version of the text, ed. by Pierre Thillet, Saleh Oudaimah 2002 [*80].
See further Pseudo-Ammonius, ed. by Ulrich Rudolph 1989 [*70]; Proclus, ed. by Gerhard Endress 1973 [*61].

1.3.8.5 *Influence of al-Kindī's Works*

171 Périer, Augustin. "Un traité de Yaḥyâ ben ʿAdî: Défense du dogme de la trinité contre les objections d'al-Kindî: Texte arabe publié pour la première fois et traduit." *Revue de l'Orient chrétien* 22 [3. sér., 2] (1920–1921): 3–21. – Contains Edition and French transl. of: Yaḥyā Ibn ʿAdī, *Tabyīn ġalaṭ Abī Yūsuf b. Isḥāq al-Kindī fī l-radd ʿalā l-naṣārā*.

172 Périer, Augustin. *Petits traités apologétiques de Yaḥyâ ben ʿAdî. Texte arabe édité … et traduit en français*. Paris, 1920. – 118–128: Défense du dogme de la Trinité contre les objections d'al-Kindî [transl. only, revised in comparison with *171].

173 Ibn Ḥazm. *Risālat al-Radd ʿalā l-Kindī al-faylasūf*, in: Ibn Ḥazm, *al-Radd ʿalā Ibn al-Naġrīla al-Yahūdī wa-rasāʾil uḫrā*. Ed. by Iḥsān ʿAbbās. Cairo, 1960, 187–216. – Excerpt, edition and French transl. by Roshdi Rashed and Jean Jolivet [*32: 113–117]. – See also Daiber 1986 [*64].

2 Life and Influence

Abū Yūsuf Yaʿqūb b. Isḥāq b. al-Ṣabbāḥ belonged to a family of the ancient Arab tribe of the Kinda. His ancestor al-Ašʿaṯ b. Qays (d. ca. 40/661), a companion of the Prophet Muḥammad, played an important role in early Islamic history. The family line could be traced back to the legendary south-Arabian forefather Qaḥṭān. This gave al-Kindī, the 'Philosopher of the Arabs' (*faylasūf al-ʿArab*), a distinctive nobility amidst the scholars involved in the transmission of the sciences, who were largely of Iranian and Christian-Aramaic descent.

According to our oldest witness (Ibn Ǧulǧul [*4: 73]) he himself hailed from Basra, where his grandfather administered territories of the Banū Hāšim. According to all other biographers, al-Kindī came from Kūfa, where his father served as a high-ranking official in the Abbasid administration; he was among those to hold the governorship of Kūfa under the caliphs al-Mahdī and al-Rašīd, hence, between 158/775 and 193/789 (al-Ṣafadī [*17: VIII 415]; cf. also ʿAbd al-Rāziq 1933 [*13] with further sources on the history of the clan).

At an unknown date al-Kindī came to the court at Baghdad, where he taught the sciences to a son of the caliph al-Muʿtaṣim (regn. 218–227/833–842). This is confirmed by the fact that some of his writings (especially the *rasāʾil*, meaning 'epistles') are dedicated to al-Muʿtaṣim and, above all, his son the prince Aḥmad (cf. Rosenthal 1942 [*14: 265–266]). The author of the *Ṣiwān al-ḥikma* (*The Depository of Wisdom*), possibly Abū Sulaymān al-Siǧistānī himself (even if that work as a whole should not be ascribed to him), gives al-Kindī credit for introducing the epistle (*risāla*) as a literary form to be used in scientific discourse. According to him, al-Kindī wrote most of his works in this form for students at court, and was hence the founder of this style of scientific writing [*7: 113 § 239 Dunlop, 283 Badawī]; on the form and addressees of al-Kindī's *rasāʾil* cf. Endress 2011 [*30].

The most famous dedication is, however, to the caliph himself: al-Kindī's *On First Philosophy for al-Muʿtaṣim* [*51], in which he presents his agenda to legitimize philosophy in the eyes of the Muslim political elite. An optical treatise *On the Sun's Rays* [*96] is also dedicated to a caliph, without however naming him. Another text, on the types (or substances) of swords, was delivered in person to the caliph, who is mentioned as having commissioned the work (ed. Zaki 1952 [*402], ed. Iḥsān-Ilāhī 1962 [*403]).

As a learned member of the court, al-Kindī offered not only philosophical speculation but also practical knowledge. He wrote about the metallurgy of swords for the caliph, and composed an introduction to cryptography for the prince Aḥmad (Marāyātī 1987 [*277: 204–259]). The latter was also the dedicatee of a musical treatise, *On the Composition of Melodies and the Tuning of the Lute* (Ibn Abī Uṣaybiʿa [*13: I 210,23]), and of an introduction to "Indian calculation," meaning decadic arithmetic [*13: I 210,11].

Al-Kindī tutored the caliph's son in philosophy too, demonstrating for him how this discipline could be used to confirm the teachings of Islam, as in a treatise *On the Prostration of the Outermost Sphere* [*54]. The same prince received a mathematical-cosmological demonstration of the spherical form of the elements and the heavenly body [*76]; he was presumably also the recipient of an epistle *Explaining the Proximate Agent Cause of Generation and Corruption* [*74], which has a very similar address though no named recipient.

At court, conflicts inspired by jealousy and ambition led to tensions between al-Kindī and rival scholars. A notorious example is the enmity between him and the two brothers, Muḥammad and Aḥmad b. Mūsā al-Munaǧǧim, significant mathematicians with connections to the Iranian astronomers at the court library. Al-Kindī's horoscope *The Duration of the Rule of the Arabs* [*111] is likely a witness to this conflict. The intrigues of the Banū Mūsā against al-Kindī are reported anecdotally by the Baghdad court historians Ibn al-Dāya [*2: 130–131] and al-Ṣūlī [*3: 230–232]), and later by Ibn Abī Uṣaybiʿa in his medical history [*13: I 207]. After the death of the caliph al-Wāṯiq (232/847) the brothers slandered al-Kindī before the next ruler, al-Mutawakkil, managing to get his private library confiscated and handed over to them (it was later returned to al-Kindī; cf. Hauser 1922 [*12: 185–187]). After the murder of al-Mutawakkil (247/861) the Banū Mūsā supposedly argued against the elevation of Aḥmad b. al-Muʿtaṣim, accusing the latter of seeking to usurp the caliphate under al-Mutawakkil, though in fact they simply hated the prince because he was a student of al-Kindī (Hauser 1922 following al-Ṣūlī [*12: 187–188]; cf. also al-Bīrūnī [*6: 184–185]).

Relations to influential scholars at the court of al-Mutawakkil can also be discerned in a number of dedications. In the preface to a philosophical epistle *On the Oneness of God and the Finiteness of Body of the Universe* [*71], addressed to the poet and scholar Muḥammad b. al-Ǧahm, al-Kindī sought the favour of a successful courtier and powerful official. Muḥammad b. al-Ǧahm, known as a poet but also as an intellectual with connections to the Muʿtazila and to the philosophers, and as an astrologer (GAS [*6: VII 124]; Lecomte 1958 [*16] with references to al-Ǧāḥiẓ and Ibn Qutayba, among others; cf. also Ibn al-Qifṭī [*12: 284]), found success under the caliph al-Maʾmūn, receiving the important governorship of Ǧibāl (ancient Media). (One branch of the text's transmission indicates that al-Kindī addressed the epistle to Muḥammad's brother ʿAlī b. al-Ǧahm, but this seems less likely). Al-Kindī also enjoyed a connection to a circle of Nestorian medical families from Gundishapur, as testified by the dedication in his treatment of a geometrical problem, the relation between circumference and diameter (*On Approximating the Circle* [*91]). This was addressed to Yūḥannā b. Māsawayh (d. 243/857), personal doctor to several caliphs in Baghdad and Samarra (Ullmann 1970 [*5: 112]).

The exact year of al-Kindī's death is unknown. If, as the reports of his conflict with the Banū Mūsā claim, he was still alive at the time of the murder of al-Mutawakkil, then the year 247/861 is a *terminus post quem*. However, consideration of further testimonies shows that he cannot have died much later than 252/866 (ʿAbd al-Rāziq 1933 [*13: 147–148]).

Al-Kindī's influence was varied and far-reaching. According to anecdotes related by his biographers, he "converted" the astrologer Abū Maʿšar of Balkh (d. 272/886; on him see below § 9.3), from a sceptical attitude towards philosophy to an interest in the Greek sciences. Both moved in the same circles, as shown by Balḫī's homage to Muḥammad b. al-Ǧahm (Ibn al-Nadīm [*5: 277,25 Flügel; 336 Taǧaddud]). In his *Great Introduction to Astrology* (*al-Mudḫal* *al-kabīr ilā ʿilm al-nuǧūm*, for which see Lemay 1995 [*26]) Abū Maʿšar shows himself to be an Aristotelian in the tradition of Ptolemy, and hence of a rather different approach than that followed by al-Kindī. This holds especially of his cosmology and his use of the ninth chapter of Aristotle's *On Interpretation* to ground the science of astrology (Baffioni 2002 [*411], but see also Adamson 2002 [*357] for an argument that Abū Maʿšar's views resonate with those of al-Kindī).

The closest student of al-Kindī and a transmitter of his works was Aḥmad b. al-Ṭayyib al-Saraḫsī (d. 286/899). The list of his works includes many titles that match those of treatises by al-Kindī, presumably an indication that he was drawing on the latter's teachings (Rosenthal 1943 [*15]). This is also indicated by a report on the Neoplatonic astrology and philosophy of the Sabians, that is, pagan Greeks, which is presented in the *Fihrist* of Ibn al-Nadīm [*5: 318 Flügel]. Al-Saraḫsī may be identical with the Aḥmad b. Muḥammad al-Ḫurāsānī to whom al-Kindī addressed his *Explanation of the Finiteness of the Universe* [*73].

The philosophy of al-Kindī's school, which we can trace through personal teaching relationships in Baghdad, and later in the Iranian East (cf. Endress 1990 [*112: 24–28], 2003 [*274: 134–135], 2006 [*116: 111–114]), is founded in a commitment to an encyclopedic, mathematical and literary approach to knowledge, which is Hellenizing yet also at home in Arabic and Islamic culture. After al-Saraḫsī and (in North Africa) Isḥāq al-Isrāʾīlī (d. ca. 338/950; on him see Altmann, Stern 1958 [*104]), faithful transmitters of al-Kindī's teachings, it was especially Abū Zayd al-Balḫī (d. 322/934) who furthered this encyclopedic approach, being the first to demonstrate harmony between the Hellenistic and Islamic sciences. Thanks to a philosophical circle at Baghdad in the 4th/10th century, and especially Abū ʿAlī Miskawayh, the Platonist intellectualism of the Kindian tradition was passed on to authors in courtly circles as far as the later Middle Ages. Details on the relevant thinkers and al-Kindī's influence on their doctrines will be presented below in § 5.

3 Translations Available in al-Kindī's Time

Al-Kindī was the first universal thinker to bring the Hellenic legacy into Arabic. He saw himself as a transmitter of the wisdom set forth by the ancients whom he admired as predecessors and role-models (*On First Philosophy* [*51: I 102–104]). Their work had been developed and completed over many generations; now, al-Kindī would present these teachings to 'those who speak our language (*ahl lisāninā*)' (from the commentary on Ptolemy's *Almagest*, cited by

Rosenthal 1956 [*317: 445]; we find the same expression in *On the Prostration of the Outermost Sphere* [*54: I 260]).

Al-Kindī played a certain role in the production of the translations available to him. He was *spiritus rector* of a circle of translators who were responsible for the reception of Aristotle's natural philosophy, Aristotelian and Neoplatonist metaphysics, and Neo-Pythagorean arithmology (Endress 1997 [*76]). On the basis of explicit references in the textual transmission, and of evidence internal to the translations themselves, we know that this circle included Ibn al-Biṭrīq, Ibn Nāʿima and Eustathios (Usṭāṯ). As a natural philosopher and astronomer, al-Kindī had a particular interest in the physical works of Aristotle (*On the Heavens, Meteorologica, Parva Naturalia*) and his *On the Soul*, which al-Kindī placed within a gnostic-Neoplatonic world view. Aristotle's *Metaphysics*, according to Ibn al-Nadīm translated 'for al-Kindī' by Eustathios [*5: 251] offered a conceptual apparatus for his metaphysics, but not its theological content. For this, he turned to the *Theology*, a collection including pseudo-Aristotelian Arabic versions of works by Plotinus and Proclus, along with several treatises by Alexander of Aphrodisias (Endress 2007 [*88]).

Al-Kindī took his views on method and principles from the writings of ancient mathematicians (Endress 2003 [*274: 127–135] Gutas 2004 [*275]). For his Neo-Pythagorean number theory and harmonics, leading to a conception of philosophy as a teaching concerning intelligible reality, al-Kindī could turn to the *Introduction to Arithmetic* of Nicomachus of Gerasa. The early Arabic version of this work, actually more a paraphrase-commentary, was executed in the Kindī circle by the Nestorian metropolitan Ḥabīb (ʿAbdīšūʿ) Ibn Bahrīz, at the behest of the emir Ṭāhir b. al-Ḥusayn (d. 207/822); a further translation was produced by al-Kindī's younger contemporary Qusṭā b. Lūqā (d. ca. 300/912). A redaction of the text by an anonymous student of al-Kindī's, extant only in Hebrew, preserves remarks on the text by al-Kindī himself. These include especially notes on the prologue of the work and its discussion of the propaedeutic status of arithmology (Freudenthal, Lévy 2004 [*281]). The Euclidean geometrical method of proof was more important for al-Kindī than Aristotle's logical hermeneutics and syllogistic theory. Nonetheless Ibn Bahrīz, the translator of Nicomachus' work, did write epitomes of Aristotle's *Categories* and *On Interpretation*, and we are told that al-Kindī also wrote summaries of these two texts (Ibn al-Nadīm [*5: 248,27; 249,4]; cf. also Rashed 1993 [*271: 7–53]).

As concerns the tradition of Platonic works, Harran (ancient Carrhae in upper Mesopotamia) seems to have been especially significant. As late as 336/947, al-Masʿūdī claims to have found quotations of Plato in Aramaic inscriptions there. The exaggerated hypothesis proposed by Tardieu 1986 [*66], 1987 [*67] on the basis of this and other uncertain evidence has, however, been relegated to the realm of legend (on this see above, pp. 53–54).

Through the gnomological tradition, al-Kindī knew Plato's *Symposium*, and the latter's *Timaeus* was first translated in his milieu (Gutas 1988 [*68: 45–46]). Also known were the *Phaedo*, *Sophist* and, from among the political treatises, the *Republic*, insofar as it was an object of Neoplatonic commentary (Ibn al-Nadīm [*5: 246]; Rosenthal 1940 [*51], Walzer 1962 [*53: 236–257]; on the citations in the *Adab al-ṭabīb* of Isḥāq b. ʿAlī al-Ruhāwī cf. Bürgel 1971 [*59]). The contemporary mathematician Ṯābit b. Qurra (d. 288/901) wrote a work displaying knowledge of the *Meno* (Gutas 1988 [*68: 46], cf. below § 9.2; Endress 2003 [*274: 127–128]; on al-Kindī's use of the Platonic idea of recollection cf. Endress 1994 [*237]).

Far more lasting was the influence of the Neoplatonic writings transmitted under the name of Aristotle. The Arabic paraphrase of books IV–VI of Plotinus' *Enneads* [*162], which advertises itself as the true *Theology* of Aristotle, 'explicated by Porphyry,' is connected to the name and authority of al-Kindī (cf. Zimmermann 1986 [*65]; overview of the state of research by Aouad 1989 [*69], D'Ancona 2003 [*81], 2005 [*86]). In addition, there survive shorter parts of the same Plotinus source, called *Sayings of the Greek Sage* (*al-Šayḫ al-Yūnānī*) and the *Epistle on Divine Science* (*Risāla fī l-ʿIlm al-ilāhī*; cf. D'Ancona 2004 [*84] on the various components, D'Ancona 1991 [*72], 2004 [*84] and Adamson 2002 [*90] on the relation to the philosophy of Plotinus); further fragments are extant in the Arabic adaptation of Aristotle's *Parva Naturalia* (ed. and transl. in Hansberger 2011 [*93]).

Also included in the collection called the *Theology* of Aristotle were excerpts from Proclus' *Elements of Theology* (Endress 1973 [*61]). The extant portions derive from a more complete Arabic Proclus source, whose reception may be traced in various texts of the 3rd/9th and 4th/10th centuries (overview in Wakelnig 2006 [*87: 399]; Endress 2011 [*89]). This 'Proclus Arabus' powerfully influenced al-Kindī's metaphysics, and especially his philosophical argument for monotheism (Endress 1973 [*61: 242–245], Jolivet 1979 [*62], Endress 2000 [*79]). However, Proclus' name was not always attached to this tradition. Some of the texts are ascribed to Alexander, presumably because treatises of the two philosophers were transmitted together (Zimmermann 1986 [*65], 1994 [*73]). Furthermore, they share a range of characteristic features of terminology and style with the authentic treatises of Alexander, typical of the translations from the Kindī circle (Endress 1973 [*61], 1997 [*76: 43–76], 2002 [*155], 2007 [*88]).

Another text based on Proclus' *Elements of Theology*, which emerged in the milieu and under the influence of al-Kindī and the Arabic Plotinus, is *On the Pure Good* (*Kitāb Maḥḍ al-ḫayr*), known in Latin as the *Book of Causes* (*Liber de Causis*). The original version is, however, only partly to be found amongst the Arabic Proclus materials (on the transmission history, sources and doctrinal development in relation to the Arabic Proclus and Plotinus see D'Ancona,

Taylor 2003 [*82] and D'Ancona 1995 [*75: 23–52]). D'Ancona has shown that the Arabic Plotinus source, the so-called *Theology of Aristotle*, influenced the prototype of the *Book of Causes*, which was a new redaction of the Arabic Proclus produced in al-Kindī's circle [*82: 624–636]. She has also made a convincing case that certain conceptual and terminological features of the Arabic Proclus itself presuppose influence from the *Theology* (D'Ancona 2000 [*77]). Alongside the version of the *Book of the Pure Good* that found its way into Latin, a second version has been discovered; probably the two versions depend on a common source rather than the second version being an independent development or precursor of the original vulgate of the Arabic Proclus (Thillet, Oudaimah 2001–2002 [*80]). Recently it has been argued that there was a 'proto-*Book of Causes*,' which would have included a larger selection of Proclus texts, which has left traces in other authors, especially Abū l-Ḥasan al-ʿĀmiri (d. 381/992, cf. below § 5.2; cf. Wakelnig 2006 [*87: 395–400] with a conspectus of the Arabic versions of the *Elements of Theology*, and Endress 2011 [*89] for an overview of the whole Arabic Proclus reception).

Another work produced in the same context was the doxography entitled *Opinions of the Philosophers* (*Ārāʾ al-falāsifa*) ascribed to Ammonius. It puts Neoplatonic teachings into the mouths of Presocratics and other Greek authorities. It was put together out of late ancient materials (Rudolph 1989 [*70] establishes as one source among others the *Refutation of all Heresies* of Hippolytus of Rome, d. 235), but received its Arabic form and some original material in the group around al-Kindī.

4 Works

4.1 Introductions to Philosophy – 4.2 Propaedeutic Ethics – 4.3 Metaphysics – 4.4 Soul and Intellect – 4.5 Physics and Cosmology – 4.6 Mathematical Sciences – 4.7 Arithmetic – 4.8 Geometry and Geodesy – 4.9 Optics – 4.10 Astronomy – 4.11 Music – 4.12 Astrology – 4.13 Astrometeorology – 4.14 Meteorology – 4.15 Magic – 4.16 Medicine and Pharmacology – 4.17 Spurious Works

4.1 *Introductions to Philosophy*

Risāla fī Kammiyyat kutub Arisṭūṭālīs wa-mā yuḥtāǧ ilayhi fī taḥṣīl al-falsafa
On the Quantity of Aristotle's Books, and What is Required for the Attainment of Philosophy

Cf. McCarthy 1962 [*4: 8 no. 5. 65 no. 18]; Engl. transl. by Adamson, Pormann [*35: 281–296]. Following the model of the introductions to Aristotle in Alexandrian commentaries (Hein 1985 [*63: 238–387]) the treatise explains the topic of each Aristotelian work, along with introductory remarks on the division of the philosophical sciences as a whole (cf. text and commentary in Guidi, Walzer [*40]): logic (including the *Poetics* and *Rhetoric*), physics (including the *Parva Naturalia*), the *Metaphysics*, and the ethical works along with the *Politics*. The detailed syllabus of Aristotelian works is preceded by an excursus on the relation between human and divine forms of understanding: the former grasps substance and its predicates only through laborious analysis, whereas it is given to the prophets (*rusul*) to grasp the divine knowledge, and to answer all questions concerning hidden truth immediately, with no need of logical or mathematical deduction. Examples are given from the Quran, Sura 36 (cf. also Walzer 1957 [*103], Jolivet 2004 [*156], Janssens 2007 [*158]). The treatment of mathematics (*al-riyāḍiyyāt*) as a propaedeutic of philosophy, and the identification of psychology as the middle-ranked theoretical science, betray the influence of Neoplatonic models. But otherwise al-Kindī follows Peripatetic consensus, as Ibn Sīnā and others will later do: he places the mathematical sciences between physics and metaphysics (or theology) because it studies things abstracted from bodies, and divides mathematics into the quadrivium, following here Nicomachus of Gerasa (cf. Hein 1985 [*63:165–166, 170–181]; she comments on the systematic parallel between mathematics and psychology, following P. Merlan).

Risāla fī Ḥudūd al-ašyā' wa-rusūmihā
On the Definitions and Descriptions of Things

Cf. McCarthy 1962 [*4: 56 no. 344. 67 no. 26]; Engl. transl. by Adamson, Pormann [*35: 300–311]. Al-Kindī's school transmits various versions and additions to this text; cf. Stern 1959 [*142] on the variants in MS British Museum Add. 7473 and the excerpts in Abū Ḥayyān al-Tawḥīdī, *Muqābasāt* [§ 5.3, *184: 325–375]; on a further recension held in Lisbon cf. Klein-Franke 1982 [*151]; also Frank 1975 [*147]. Dependent on al-Kindī's *Definitions* is also the *Book of Definitions* by Isḥāq al-Isrā'īlī (Altmann, Stern 1958 [*104: 3–78]). It is improbable that all the definitions go back to al-Kindī himself, as some are in contradiction to his other works, and the lack of any systematic order suggests a compilation from disparate sources. Yet Kindian authorship of the text need not be entirely rejected (*pace* Gimaret 1976 [*148: 8–13]).

The title differentiates between definitions in the strict sense (*ḥudūd*, which combine a genus with a species, following Aristotle, *Topics* I 8, 103b15) and approximate descriptions (*rusūm*, consisting of a genus with a mere property). Terms from the following areas are considered (numbering and translations taken from Adamson, Pormann 2012 [*35]):

(a) Physics and metaphysics: 1. 'The First Cause (*al-ʿilla al-ūlā*): originator, agent, completer of the universe, unmoved'; 2. 'Intellect (*ʿaql*): a simple substance that perceives things in their true natures'; 3. 'Nature (*ṭabīʿa*): the principle of motion and of rest from motion. It is the first of the faculties of the soul,' cf. 92, 'Discussion of the philosophers on nature,' with alternative definitions; 4. 'Soul (*nafs*): the perfection of the natural, organic body that receives life'; also: 'the first perfection for the natural body having life potentially'; and: 'an intellectual substance, self-moving by means of a harmonious number'; 5. 'Body (*ǧirm*): what has the three dimensions, length, breadth, and depth'; 6. 'Origination (*ibdāʿ*): manifestation of something from non-being'; 7. Matter (*hayūlā*); 8. 'Form (*ṣūrā*): the thing through which something is what it is'; 9. Prime matter or element (*ʿunṣur*), 10. Act (*fiʿl*); 11. 'Action (*ʿamal*): act with deliberation'; 12. Substance (*ǧawhar*), 32. Element (*usṭuquss*); 38. 'Innate [heat] (*ġarīza*): the nature positioned in the heart, set up in it [sc. the heart] in order that through it [sc. the heart] life may be atttained'; 40. Potentiality (*quwwa*); 41. The eternal (*azalī*); 42. The four natural causes (*al-ʿilal al-ṭabīʿiyya*), sc. material cause, formal cause, efficient cause, and final cause.

(b) Logic: 14.–20. Categories: quantity (*kammiyya*), quality (*kayfiyya*), relative (*muḍāf*), time (*zamān*), place (*makān*), and relation (*iḍāfa*); 33. Necessary (*wāǧib*), possible (*mumkin*) and impossible (*mumtaniʿ*); 35. Truth (*ṣidq*); 36. Falsehood (*kaḏib*).

(c) Psychology: 21. Imagination (*tawahhum*) – which is explained with a transliteration of Greek φαντασία; 22. Sense (*ḥāss*); 23. Sensation (*ḥiss*); 24. The sensitive faculty (*al-quwwa al-ḥissiyya*); 25. The sensible object; 26. Reflection (*rawiyya*); 27. Belief (*raʾy*); 34. Knowledge (*ʿilm*); 39. Supposition (*wahm*).

(d) Ethics: 13. Choice (*iḫtiyār*); 29. Will (*irāda*); 30. Love (*maḥabba*); and at 91 a detailed catalogue of the 'human virtues' (*al-faḍāʾil al-insāniyya*).

(e) Mathematics and music: 37. 'Root' (*ǧiḏr*); 31. Rhythm (*īqāʿ*).

(f) At 70 we have traditional definitions of 'philosophy' following the Alexandrian *prolegomena* (cf. Hein 1985 [*63: 105–109]): love of wisdom, becoming similar to God, preparation for death, art of arts, self-knowledge, and knowledge of eternal and universal things.

4.2 *Propaedeutic Ethics*

Risāla fī l-Ḥīla li-dafʿ al-aḥzān
On the Method of How to Dispel Sorrow

Cf. McCarthy 1962 [*4: 31 no. 171. 65 no. 17]; Engl. transl. by Adamson, Pormann [*35: 249–266]. Excerpts (abbreviation of § 6–8 ed. Ritter, Walzer [*45: 37–39] in: Miskawayh, *Tahḏīb al-aḫlāq* [§ 5.4, *273: 219–231], thus in the English transl. of Constantine K. Zurayk, 194–196). The treatise offers a 'consolation of philosophy' on the basis of the Platonism of *Discourse on the Soul* [*62]. The goal of humankind ought not to lie in the world of transitory goods, whose loss leads to sorrow (*ḥuzn*). In order to attain the highest happiness, we must direct our activity to the intelligible world and its eternal good. The one who knows this understands the true causes of suffering and sadness in this world, and can avoid such suffering by grasping the worthlessness of material goods, releasing the rational soul from passions and desire, and aiming attention at the pure Good alone. The philosopher understands that sorrow for lost or unattainable goods is neither necessary nor natural. He consoles himself with the thought that others share the same fate, and that like others before him he will experience joy and happiness again in due course. God has bestowed earthly goods on His creatures and can take them away whenever He likes; to grieve over this would be ingratitude. The best and most precious goods can in any case never be removed: the soul, the understanding, and the virtues (on the late antique sources of these themes and the sources of the anecdotes woven into the text, cf. Ritter, Walzer 1938 [*161: 530]).

Risāla fī Ḫabar iǧtimāʿ al-falāsifa fī l-rumūz al-ʿišqiyya
Report of the Philosophers' Gathering on Allegories of Love

Cf. Ibn al-Nadīm [*5: 259,25 Flügel]; McCarthy 1962 [*4: 31 no. 166]. The treatise is lost apart from excerpts, preserved in (among others) Abū Saʿīd Ibn Baḫtīšūʿ: *Risāla fī l-Ṭibb wa-l-aḥdāṯ al-nafsāniyya* [*8: 52]. On this and one further fragment cf. Gutas 1988 [*68: 37–38. 56–58]. The extant fragments suggest that this was a rather detailed recounting of the core doctrine of the Platonic *Symposium*, on the basis of a translation or paraphrase, which included the names of the Greek interlocutors in the dialogue.

Risāla fī Ḫabar faḍīlat Suqrāṭ
Report on the Virtue of Socrates

Cf. Ibn al-Nadīm [*5: 260,4 Flügel]; McCarthy 1962 [*4: 32 no. 175]. Not extant. Perhaps related to a version of Plato's *Crito*, cf. Gutas 1988 [*68: 46].

Risāla fī Mā ǧarā bayna Suqrāṭ wa-l-Ḥarrāniyyīn
What Passed Between Socrates and the Harranians

Cf. Ibn al-Nadīm [*5: 260,6]; McCarthy 1962 [*4: 32 no. 179]. Not extant. The expression 'Harranians' is probably a synonym for Sabians, i.e. pagan Greeks. The text could thus relate to the *Apology* (Gutas 1988 [*68: 42–46]).

Ḫabar mawt Suqrāṭ
Report of the Death of Socrates

Cf. Ibn al-Nadīm [*5: 260,4]; McCarthy 1962 [*4: 32 no. 178]. A lost adaptation of Plato's *Phaedo*.

Risāla fī Alfāẓ Suqrāṭ
The Sayings of Socrates

Excerpts in MS Istanbul: Köprülü, I, 1608, fols 48ᵇ–51ᵃ, under the title *What al-Kindī Transmitted from the Sayings of Socrates* (*Mā naqalahu l-Kindī min alfāẓ Suqrāṭ*); possibly from the same collection assembled by al-Kindī is the material in the same manuscript, at ibid., fols 21ᵇ11–22ᵃ1: *On Alcibiades* (*Alqibiyādīs*) *and Socrates* (Ibn al-Nadīm [*5: 260,4]; McCarthy 1962 [*4: 32 no. 176]; Engl. transl. by Adamson, Pormann [*35: 268–272]). A gnomology, to judge by the excerpts; see Fakhry 1963 [*54], Alon 1991 [*71: Index s.v. Kindī], Alon 1995 [*74: Index s.v. Kindī]; cf. also Gutas 1975 [*164: 279–281. 284–285. 328–331], Adamson 2007 [*171].

Risāla fī Muḥāwara ǧarat bayna Suqrāṭ wa-Aršīǧānis
A Dialogue Between Archigenes and Socrates

Cf. Ibn al-Nadīm [*5: 260,5]; McCarthy 1962 [*4: 32 no. 177]. Not extant. Consisted of a commentary on gnomological texts, such as found in Mubaššir b. Fātik: *Muḫtār al-ḥikam* (ed. Badawī [Madrid 1958]: 84–85), Ibn Hindū: *al-Kalim al-rūḥāniyya* (ed. Ḫalīfāt [Amman 1995]; 274–277]) and other Socratic collections. The Socratic *Pythagorean Allegories* (*rumūz*) appear in Ibn Hindū as a chapter with the same title (*Muḥāwarāt ǧarat bayna Aršīǧānis* (or *Arsinǧānis*) *wa-Suqrāṭ*); cf. Gutas 1988 [*68: 45–46].

4.3 *Metaphysics*

Kitāb ilā l-Muʿtaṣim bi-llāh fī l-Falsafa al-ūlā (*Kitāb al-Tawḥīd*)
On First Philosophy, for the Caliph al-Muʿtaṣim bi-llāh (*On Oneness*)

Cf. McCarthy 1962 [*4: 56 no. 343. 67 no. 25]; Engl. transl. by Adamson, Pormann [*35: 10–57]. Probably identical with the treatise *Mouth of Gold* (*Fam al-ḏahab*): *On Divine Unity* mentioned by Ṣāʿid al-Andalusī: *Ṭabaqāt* [*10: 52], according to whom al-Kindī follows the teaching of Plato on the atemporal createdness of the world (*ḥudūṯ al-ʿālam fī ġayr zamān*), on the basis of invalid arguments, some sophistical and some rhetorical. Ibn al-Nadīm names a further title on *tawḥīd* (divine oneness), *Epistle on Unity in the Form of Commentaries* (*Risāla fī l-Tawḥīd bi-tafsīrāt*) [*5: 259,19].

The extant text is designated at its conclusion as 'the first part (*al-qism al-awwal*) of the book by Yaʿqūb b. Isḥāq al-Kindī' and ends with a statement by the author that he here concludes this section but will move on to the topic that would naturally follow. Indeed, a series of testimonies allude to other, lost parts of his 'first philosophy':

(a) a reference in al-Kindī's treatment of Ptolemy's *Almagest* to his own *On First, Inner Philosophy* (*Kitāb fī l-Falsafa al-ūlā al-dāḫila*), in which he deals with the nature of the divine, which is separate from all sensible nature (Rosenthal 1956 [*43: 442]); (b) mentions and quotations in Ṣāʿid al-Andalusī: *Ṭabaqāt al-umam* [*10: 52]; Ibn Ḥazm: *Risālat al-Radd ʿalā l-Kindī al-faylasūf* [*173], cf. Daiber 1986 [*64: 285]; Ibn ʿAbd Rabbih: *al-ʿIqd al-farīd* [*1: II 382,11–383,4]. The Andalusian authors know the work under the title *On Oneness* (*Kitāb al-Tawḥīd*). The section pp. 118–122 ed. Abū Rīda is preserved almost verbatim as a separate treatise under the title *On the Oneness of God and the Finiteness of the Body of the Universe* [*71: 199–207].

Despite its only partial survival, *On First Philosophy* is al-Kindī's most important work. The extant first 'part' consists of four 'sections'. The first presents the topic to be considered, namely 'first philosophy' or metaphysics, which is equated with the study of God, the 'first truth who is the cause of all truth'. It is the highest philosophical science, since philosophy is the study of causes, and this science studies the highest cause. The section goes on to a defence of using foreign (i.e. Greek) philosophical materials, on the basis that truth can only be attained over many generations, and by using whatever insights of our predecessors prove to be valid.

The second section begins with a methodological part which apparently sets the stage for what follows, by introducing the idea of purely 'intellectual' investigation that dispenses with the evidence of the senses; this is the type of investigation appropriate to theology (*al-ʿilm al-ilāhī*). Al-Kindī next proceeds to his celebrated proof that the world is not eternal, drawing on arguments from Aristotle and Philoponus (Davidson 1969 [*57]).

The third section begins by arguing that nothing can be its own cause, before proceeding to the topic that will occupy al-Kindī for the rest of the first extant 'part': the problem of (categorial) 'utterances (*maqūlāt*)' and how they apply to God. After setting out the various types of utterance, basing himself in part on Porphyry's *Isagoge*, al-Kindī gives a proof of the existence of a 'true One' who is the cause of unity in all other things.

The fourth section, building on this idea, shows the inapplicability of all types of 'utterance' to this true One, since every type of utterance implies both unity and multiplicity. The true One is also shown to transcend soul and intellect, which presumably reflects the influence of Neoplatonic materials. At the end of the extant text, al-Kindī reveals that the true One he has been describing (or rather, not describing) is God Himself, mentioning several Quranic divine names and arguing that as the bestower of unity, God is also the bestower of being.

The incompletely preserved second part of the work dealt with themes including the transcendence and creative act of the First Cause, and brought forward the views of previous philosophers and schools, just as was done in the first part concerning the subject-matter and basis of first philosophy.

Risāla fī l-Fāʿil al-ḥaqq al-awwal al-tāmm wa-l-fāʿil al-nāqiṣ allaḏī huwa bi-l-maǧāz
On the True, First, Complete Agent and the Deficient Agent Which is Only Metaphorically [an Agent]

Cf. McCarthy 1962 [*4: 29 no. 152. 68 no. 28]; Engl. transl. by Adamson, Pormann [*35: 73–75], under the title 'Against the Trinity.' A brief discussion, which is possibly a fragment from a larger work, contrasting God, the 'True Agent', to created causes which are merely agents in a 'metaphorical' sense. The reasoning for this is that created causes are both agents and acted upon, whereas God is purely an agent. A further distinction is added, between agents whose acts result in a separate effect (e.g. a house) and those whose acts remain dependent upon them (e.g. the walker's walking).

Risāla fī Iftirāq al-milal fī l-tawḥīd wa-annahum muǧmiʿūn ʿalā l-tawḥīd wa-kull qad ḫālafa ṣāḥibahu
On the Disagreement Between Religions Concering [Divine] Oneness: They Agree About Oneness Yet Contradict One Another

Cf. McCarthy 1962 [*4: 52 no. 314. 70 no. 38]; Engl. transl. by Adamson, Pormann [*35: 78–81]. Not extant in its entirety. We do have extensive quotations for the polemic against the Christian doctrine of the Trinity, found in a work of the Christian Aristotelian and Jacobite theologian Yaḥyā Ibn ʿAdī: *Tabyīn ġalaṭ Abī Yūsuf Yaʿqūb b. Isḥāq al-Kindī fī maqālatihi fī l-Radd ʿalā l-naṣārā* [§ 7.2, *132]. According to the title, al-Kindī's work dealt with the views of various religious communities. The quotation in Yaḥyā Ibn ʿAdī begins, 'as for the Christians …,' showing that the treatment of other religions preceded this section (cf. de Boer 1906 [*181], Graf 1910 [*182: 34–36], Périer 1921 [*183], Abel 1961 [*184: 75. 85 n. 2]).

The fragments reported by Yaḥyā Ibn ʿAdī show that al-Kindī explicitly based his argument against the Trinity on Porphyry's *Isagoge*, giving as a rationale for this the fact that his Christian opponents would be familiar with the work. He argues that the supposed Persons can be neither genus, species, common accidents, proper accidents, or individuals. In each case, God would be something composed from a multiplicity, and therefore not eternal (cf. also Schöck 2011 [*206]).

Risāla ilā Aḥmad b. al-Muʿtaṣim fī l-Ibāna ʿan suǧūd al-ǧirm al-aqṣā wa-ṭāʿatihi li-llāh ʿazza wa-ǧalla
To Aḥmad b. al-Muʿtaṣim, Showing that the Outermost [Celestial] Body Prostrates Itself to God, the Exalted, and Obeys Him

Cf. McCarthy 1962 [*4: 22 no. 104. 66 no. 20]; Engl. transl. by Adamson, Pormann [*35: 174–186]. A substantial cosmological work intended as an exegesis of the Quranic verse *wa-l-naǧmu wa-l-šaǧaru yasǧudāni* (Sura 55:5): 'and the stars and the trees prostrate themselves.' As in *On the Proximate Agent Cause of Generation and Corruption* [*74] al-Kindī argues that the heavens bring about the changes and compositions we see here in the sublunary world, and infers that the heavens' motion is out of 'obedience' to the 'command' of God. Preceding this, there is a brief hermeneutic discussion regarding ambiguity: in the present case, 'to prostrate' is argued to have not only the straightforward meaning of laying one's body on the ground, but also the metaphorical one of obeying. Other points of interest in the treatise include a discussion of whether or not the stars possess sensation: al-Kindī concludes that they can hear and see, but lack the other senses. They also have reason. In conclusion al-Kindī describes the entire cosmos as a single animal, echoing such texts as the *Timaeus*.

Fī l-Ǧawāhir al-ḫamsa (*De quinque essentiis*)
On the Five Substances

Extant only in Latin translation; cf. McCarthy 1962 [*4: 51 no. 310. 76 no. 67]; Engl. transl. by Adamson, Pormann [*35: 314–321]. After a propaedeutic introduction concerning the division of philosophy into its theoretical and practical aspects, the treatise deals with five things that 'apply to everything made of the elements,' namely matter, form, place, motion and time. A summary discussion of each is then provided, drawing heavily on Aristotle (for instance the definitions of place and time are closely based on those of the *Physics*).

4.4 *Soul and Intellect*

Risāla fī annahu (tūǧad) ǧawāhir lā-aǧsām
That There Are Incorporeal Substances

Cf. McCarthy 1962 [*4: 56 no. 339. 65 no. 16]; Engl. transl. by Adamson, Pormann [*35: 107–110]. Despite its title, the main goal of the short epistle is to show the immateriality of the human soul, using almost exclusively ideas drawn from Aristotle's *Categories* (cf. Adamson, Pormann 2009 [*243]). Since soul is the source of the living thing's substantiality, it must itself be a substance. Soul is then equated with the 'species' of the living thing, and it is argued that species, including the soul, must be immaterial. Thus, soul is an immaterial substance (cf. also Endress 1994 [*237: 186]).

al-Qawl fī l-Nafs al-muḫtaṣar min kitāb Arisṭū wa-Falāṭun wa-sā'ir al-falāsifa
Discourse on the Soul, Summarized from the Book of Aristotle, of Plato, and of Other Philosophers

Cf. McCarthy 1962 [*4: 51 no. 313. 69 no. 35]; Engl. transl. by Adamson, Pormann [*35: 113–118]. The soul is a simple, noble and perfect substance from the substance of the Creator, as sunlight comes forth from the sun. It is the life-giving form of the bodily substrate, yet separable from it. The perfection of the soul requires the exercise of reason, in order to free it from passions and affections; contemplation of the intelligibles is preparation for the final liberation of the mind from the bodily realm. So long as this is achieved, the soul need not die along with the body, since it is a substantial form that is separable from the body (cf. al-Kindī's treatise on incorporeal substances [*61: I 265–269, esp. 267,10–13]). The same position was held by John Philoponus, and is to be found in the early Arabic paraphrase of Aristotle's *On the Soul*, which was influenced by Philoponus' commentary (Arnzen [*161: esp. 219,17–221,5]; cf. Endress 2000 [*79: 568]). Ultimately, only a few will manage to purify their soul through the perfect refinement of their rational powers, preparing their potential intellects for the reception of pure forms, so as to be able to leave behind the material realm and return to behold the absolute truth in the world of the intellect. Only the true philosopher can share in the understanding of the highest truth and reality (*Discourse on the Soul* [*62: 274,1–6], appealing to the authority of Plato). The true homeland of the soul is the 'world of the mind, the intellect' [275,12] 'beyond the sphere' [277,12], the divine world [278,1]. Only ascetic withdrawal from the satisfaction of desire, and purification of the soul from all impurities of the passions, make this return of the soul possible. Its goal is to return to its origin, and to enjoy blessed contemplation of the intelligible world; this is the highest goal of human existence. The beatific vision is thus the reward of philosophy. Only rational understanding, as the pure activity of the rational soul – which is the substantial form of the human composite – leads to the final end of human activity (cf. Genequand 1987–1988 [*235], Endress 1994 [*237] on the gnostic and Neoplatonic worldview of the text).

Kalām fī l-Nafs muḫtaṣar waǧīz
A Concise and Brief Statement About the Soul

Cf. McCarthy 1962 [*4: 56 no. 341. 66 no. 21]; Engl. transl. by Adamson, Pormann [*35: 120–121]. According to Aristotle, the soul is a simple substance whose actions are shown in bodies. According to Plato, meanwhile, the soul (in the sense of the world soul of *Timaeus* 34c-35a, 37d) unifies (*muttaḥida*) with a body (*ǧism*, which here specifically means 'heavenly body'), and this union (*ittiḥād*) forms a connection (*yattaṣil*) with bodies (*aǧrām*, here meaning specifically 'corruptible bodies'). Both philosophers state that the soul is an unextended substance and, further, that it is connected to the corruptible body, because it shows its actions in and through the body. In this respect, the soul has a place in the world of corruption. See further the commentary of Gimaret et al. 1976 [*148: 71–76].

Risāla fī Šarḥ mā li-l-nafs ḏikruhu mimmā kāna lahā fī ʿālam al-ʿaql
Explanation of What the Soul Remembers of the Things which it Possessed in the World of Intellect

Cf. Endress 1994 [*237]; Engl. transl. by Adamson, Pormann [*35: 101–106]. The soul is the form of a body, but is also a substantial form that needs no body. Before its connection to body, the soul already existed before birth in the world of intellect and beheld the intelligible forms there. From there, it came into the world of the senses, and it will return there once it is liberated from bodily matter. In its bodily existence the soul can be led to the awareness of these principles. 'The soul, inasmuch as it is able to, remembers its state before it used the senses now that it is using the senses; and after it gives up the use of the senses because the common organ of sense perception is destroyed, [the soul remembers] its state while it was using the senses' (Adamson/Pormann transl.). Accordingly, it will retain its recollections after the loss of its sense-organs, recalling 'the intellectual things which [the soul] does not grasp with a corporeal organ but through itself.' By contrast, the objects of sense perception can be grasped only through a bodily organ. These will not be remembered, either from pre-existence or after leaving the bodily world. As soon as the soul gives up use of the body, it will have no more awareness of sensible things, for being reminded of these would require sense perception or imagination.

The Pythagorean model of *anamnesis* is characteristic of the soul's 'middle' position. As the subject of sense perception it belongs to the material world, but as intellect it is the place of eternal forms, and is itself eternal. For al-Kindī, the universal objects of mathematics and metaphysics cannot be learned through sensory experience, because material things provide no basis for grasping them. The soul comes to know them not from external things, but through a sort of self-knowledge. 'We only remember within ourselves those things that are left to us from the beginning of our existence, that is to say, the existence of our souls.' Thus our knowledge of universals is 'intellectual' and 'originary,' and requires no intermediary. It only seems that we need the forms of material things as a means to reach intellective understanding; in reality, this is recollection. – On the sources in Arabic Neoplatonism and especially in the so-called *Theology of Aristotle* and in a work on the soul ascribed to Porphyry (Kutsch 1954 [*52]) see Endress 1994 [*237].

Risāla fī l-ʿAql [also: *fī Māhiyyat al-ʿaql*]
On the Intellect [or *On the Essence of the Intellect*]

Latin *De intellectu*; cf. McCarthy 1962 [*4: 12 no. 22. 33 no. 180. 65 no. 15]; Engl. transl. by Adamson, Pormann [*35: 96–98]. The work takes up the topic of the intellect (*ʿaql*) according to the authorities among the Greeks, especially Aristotle and his teacher Plato. Four 'types' (*anwāʿ*) or levels of the intellect are distinguished. On the one hand there is (1) the universal first intellect, which is always in actuality, on the other hand the intellect in the soul: (2) potential intellect [*65: 353,10. 357,5], the state the soul is in 'as long as it is not actually intellective (*ʿāqila*),' then the (3) acquired intellect as an actual capacity of the soul [353,11. 357,5–358,8] and finally (4) the so-called 'secondary' intellect [354,1. 358,3–9], which is the presence of the intelligible forms in a full-blown act of understanding. Thus al-Kindī distinguishes between (3) intellect as a part of the soul with a disposition for being active and (4) intellect as perfected actuality, in which what it knows is 'displayed,' also called 'secondary' intellect and like (1) the 'first' intellect identical with the objects which it grasps. Hence the thinking part of the soul goes from discursive thought to a preparation of the soul as a capacity, which 'goes from possibility to actuality' [353,11] but is not always in use, and not always actually being displayed. In the (1) first intellect thought is identical to its objects, and it is the 'seat of the species of things' (*nawʿiyyat al-ašyāʾ*) [356,4]. It makes the world of pure forms available to the soul (*ṣāra mufīdan wa-l-nafs mustafīda*) [356,5]. Through this participation of the soul's intellect in the transcendent forms (also called 'contact' or 'conjunction' (*iḏā bāšarathu*), that is, with the first intellect: 356,10, with an analogy drawn to sense perception at 354,7–8. 355,1), the (4) secondary intellect is actualized, which likewise is identical with the intelligible forms within it [356,10–12].

Alexander of Aphrodisias' development of the Peripatetic theory of intellect is an important precursor for al-Kindī, but the latter rejects Alexander's identification of the active intellect with the First Cause. He is more indebted to the commentary of John Philoponus (Jolivet 1971 [*227: 50–73]) and its interpretation of Aristotle, *On the Soul* III 5, according to which active, separate, and unaffected intellect is the highest stage of human thought rather than the divine mind. In Philoponus we also find a distinction between four 'types' of intellect, which could have served as a model for al-Kindī's own classification. Philoponus likewise distinguishes three levels of intellect within the soul – potential, 'habitual' (i.e. second potentiality or first actuality), and in full act – and envisions a fourth 'distinct, speculative intellect' that is always in actuality (Jolivet 1971 [*227: 58–73]). For Philoponus, however, this first, universal intellect is the mind of the divine Creator. Even though al-Kindī too characterizes the first intellect as 'always in act' [353,10. 356,4,13–14], for him the First Cause is the absolute One and not intellect. For the intellect is the form of forms and made plural through the multiplicity of those forms (cf. *On First Philosophy* [*51: 155,9] and Jolivet 1971 [*227: 126–127]).

Risāla fī Māhiyyat al-nawm wa-l-ruʾyā
On the Essence of Sleep and Dream

Latin translation by Gerard of Cremona: *De somno et visione* (McCarthy 1962 [*4: 31 no. 168. 63 no. 6]) = *De Somniorum Visione* (McCarthy 1962 [*4: 79 no. 78])? Engl. transl. by Adamson, Pormann [*35: 124–133]. The chief powers of the soul are sense perception (*al-quwwa al-ḥissiyya*) and intellection (*al-quwwa al-ʿaqliyya*). In sleep, the soul ceases to use the five senses, and in dreams the imagination is able to present the forms of things without their being present to sensation in their material substrates. The more thought concentrates on imagination and separates itself (*taǧarrada*) from sensation, the more clearly the forms appear to it. In sleep the forms of the imagination can appear more clearly, unimpeded by the materiality of sense-objects, so that prophetic dreams are possible. Because thinking in the soul is identical with its object and grasps pure, universal forms without material individuation, the soul – 'knowing, aware, and alive' and purified of accidents – receives symbolic indications of things to come (*turmaz bi-l-ašyāʾ*), or even, when it is prepared for perfect receptivity, beholds the future in prophetic dreams. Only the refined thought of the elite (*ḫāṣṣa*) is capable of contemplating pure forms in the waking state [*66: 296,7–9] (cf. Gätje 1959 [*224: 262–264], Jolivet 1971 [*227: 128–132]).

[Ǧawāb ʿan suʾāl] Hal yaǧūzu an yutawahham mā lā yurā
Whether it is Possible to Imagine What One Does Not See

Cf. McCarthy 1962 [*4: 56 no. 342. 66 no. 23]; Ritter 1932 [*41: 368] on MS Ayasofya 4832, no. 19, fol. 34^{b}-35^{a}; Celentano 1979 [*386: 9]; Engl. transl. by Adamson, Pormann [*35: 324–325] ('Third Fragment'). The word *wahm* has three meanings. (a) The imagination (*al-taṣawwur*), which can present the forms of previously perceived things without their matter; (b) doubtful supposition; (c) an unclear, remembered image. At stake here is the first meaning, *wahm* as *taṣawwur* (corresponding to Greek φαντασία). This goes back to the object of a prior sense perception, but can combine elements of sensation in a way that does not correspond to reality, for instance by imagining a winged man.

4.5 *Physics and Cosmology*

Risāla ilā ʿAlī b. al-Ǧahm fī [l-ibāna ʿan] Waḥdāniyyat Allāh wa-tanāhī ǧirm al-ʿālam
To ʿAlī b. al-Ǧahm, on the Oneness of God and the Finiteness of the Body of the Universe

Cf. McCarthy 1962 [*4: 48 no. 291. 62 no. 2]; Engl. transl. by Adamson, Pormann [*35: 63–68]. Al-Kindī's recension of a section of *On First Philosophy* [*51: 118–122], largely reproduced verbatim. The dedication, presented within an elaborate prologue, to the poet ʿAlī b. al-Ǧahm (d. 249/863) is doubtful, despite the latter's attested interest in philosophy and *kalām*. According to two manuscripts and also Ibn Abī Uṣaybiʿa [*13: I 201] the recipient was rather his brother, the courtier and Muʿtazilite theologian Muḥammad b. al-Ǧahm (see ed. Rashed, Jolivet [*71: 135]; ed. Ǧamšīdnižād [*71: 89]; Lecomte 1991 [*24]; Rosenthal 1942 [*14: 280 n. 5]). Only the concluding sections of the short treatise are significantly different from *On First Philosophy*. These sections draw the inference that, since the world is not eternal, it must be created. Further, the Creator must be purely one, in order to avoid an infinite regress (if the Creator were multiple there would need to be another creator to bring together its multiple parts).

Risāla fī Māhiyyat mā lā yumkin an yakūna lā nihāyata lahu wa-mā llaḏī yuqāl fīhi lā-nihāya
On the Essence of That Which Cannot Be Infinite and of That Which is Called Infinite

Cf. McCarthy 1962 [*4: 11 no. 12. 68 no. 27]; Engl. transl. by Adamson, Pormann [*35: 60–63]. The treatise uses mathematical proofs to show that no body can be infinite in extension. The line of argument follows Aristotle's *On the Heavens* I 5–6: if we suppose an infinite magnitude from which a finite magnitude is removed, then the remainder will be either infinite or finite; but both options lead to absurdity. If there is no infinite body, then there can be nothing actually infinite, neither time that is eternal *a parte ante* nor any infinity in motion, power or other accidents. Infinity exists only potentially, through the incremental increase of numerical series.

Risāla fī Īḍāḥ tanāhī ǧirm al-ʿālam
Explanation of the Finiteness of the Body of the World [to Aḥmad b. Muḥammad al-Ḫurāsānī]

Cf. McCarthy 1962 [*4: 23/49 no. 111/299. 63 no. 8]; Engl. transl. by Adamson, Pormann [*35: 68–72]. The fundamental argument of the treatise is one also found in other treatises by al-Kindī: the idea of an infinite body is absurd, because if something is subtracted from it the result can be neither finite nor infinite. But here simple geometrical diagrams are added, illustrating the definitions which are merely assumed as axioms in *On First Philosophy*.

Kitāb al-Ibāna ʿan al-ʿilla al-fāʿila al-qarība li-l-kawn wa-l-fasād
Explanation of the Proximate Agent Cause of Generation and Corruption

Cf. McCarthy 1962 [*4: 33 no. 181. 66 no. 24]; Engl. transl. by Adamson, Pormann 2012 [*35: 155–172]; Engl. transl. by McGinnis, Reisman [*74]. According to a concluding note, only the first part of a larger work (*al-Fann al-awwal min kitāb al-Kindī fī īḍāḥ al-ʿilla*). Al-Kindī's lengthiest cosmological work, arguing that the reason for the mixture of the four elements, and resulting composition of substances in the sublunary world, is the motion of the heavenly bodies. The spheres are thus the 'proximate' cause of generation and corruption for sublunary substances, whereas God is the 'remote' cause, insofar as it is His providence which directs the motions of the spheres and thus indirectly the changes found in the sublunary world. The mechanism by which the heavenly bodies act is heat: the closer a planet is, the greater its effect (planets also give rise to cold by *not* having an effect, insofar as they are distant). Evidence for the theory is given, emphasizing the particularly powerful effects of the sun: for example, the physical features of people who live closer to the equator show the effects of heat, and the sun's motion gives rise to the seasons. All of this is said to be a sign of divine providence.

Risāla fī l-Ibāna ʿan anna ṭabīʿat al-falak muḫālifa li-ṭabāʾiʿ al-ʿanāṣir al-arbaʿa
Explanation That the Nature of the Celestial Sphere is Different from That of the Four Elements

Cf. McCarthy 1962 [*4: 22 no. 102. 62 no. 3]; Engl. transl. by Adamson, Pormann [*35: 188–193]. Another cosmological treatise influenced by Aristotle's *On the Heavens*. The treatise argues that the heavenly bodies are of a nature different from that of the sublunary elements, as shown by their moving in a circular rather than rectilinear fashion (air, earth, fire and water move either towards or away from the midpoint of the cosmos along straight lines, but the heavens revolve around this midpoint). For this reason, again following Aristotle, the heavenly bodies are ungenerable and incorruptible. Al-Kindī ignores the consequences drawn by Aristotle for the eternity of the world, assuming instead that God can appoint a (limited) time for the persistence of the heavens, despite their incorruptible nature.

Risāla fī anna l-ʿanāṣir wa-l-ǧirm al-aqṣā kuriyyat al-šakl
That the [Four] Elements and the Outermost Body are Spherical in Form [to Aḥmad b. al-Muʿtaṣim]

Cf. McCarthy 1962 [*4: 15/56 no. 44/340. 66 no. 19]; Engl. transl. by Rescher, Khatchadourian [*76]. Like several other treatises, this text uses geometrical arguments in the service of cosmology. It seeks to show that the elements must form concentric spheres, owing to their natural rectilinear motions towards and away from the midpoint of the cosmos. Cf. Aristotle, *On the Heavens* 287b4–20. The outermost heaven must also be spherical, because there is no space outside it through which a protruding portion of it could move.

Risāla fī l-ʿIlla allatī lahā qīla inna l-nār wa-l-hawāʾ wa-l-māʾ wa-l-arḍ ʿanāṣir li-ǧamīʿ al-kāʾina al-fāsida wa-ḫuṣṣat bi-ḏālika dūna ġayrihā min al-kāʾina
On the Reason for the Claim that Fire, Air, Water and Earth are the Elements of All [Substances] Subject to Generation and Corruption, and are Thereby Distinct from All Other Generated Things

Ibn al-Nadīm adds to his version of the title 'and that they and other things mutually transform into one another' (*wa-hiya wa-ġayruhā yastaḥīlu baʿḍuhā ilā baʿḍ*) (McCarthy 1962 [*4: 33 no. 182. 75 no. 58]). Not extant.

Risāla fī l-Sabab allaḏī [*lahu*] *nasabat al-qudamāʾ al-aškāl al-ḫamsa ilā l-usṭuqussāt*
The Reason Why the Ancients Related the Five Geometrical Figures to the Elements

Cf. McCarthy 1962 [*4: 19 no. 80. 64 no. 11]; GAS [*6: V 257 no. 5]; Engl. transl. by Rescher [*78], and by Adamson, Pormann [*35: 196–205]. Another treatise combining geometrical reflection with cosmology. This treatise is based, not on Aristotle's *On the Heavens*, but on Plato's *Timaeus*. Numerological arguments are given for the association of certain figures with certain elements. For example, earth is associated with the cube because the cube has six sides; six is a perfect number; and this reflects the stability of earth. Al-Kindī seems to say that the connection between the polygons and the elements is purely numerological, rather than following the original Platonic view that the smallest parts of the elements are actually shaped like the relevant polygons (e.g. that the smallest part of earth is actually a cube).

Risāla fī l-Ǧirm al-ḥāmil bi-ṭibāʿihi al-lawn min al-ʿanāṣir al-arbaʿa wa-llaḏī huwa ʿillat al-lawn fī ġayrihi
On the Body That, Among the Four Elements, is Because of its Nature [reading *bi-ṭibāʿihi* for *bi-ṭibāʿat*] *Bearer for Colour, and is the Cause of Colour in Other Substances*

Cf. McCarthy 1962 [*4: 24 no. 114. 62 no. 5]; Engl. transl. by Adamson, Pormann [*35: 136–139]. Bodies are coloured only because of the presence of earth in them, because earth alone, among the elements, is 'dense' and thus capable of blocking vision. Here al-Kindī picks up a problem discussed in ancient philosophy, e.g. by Alexander of Aphrodisias, as to which element is responsible for colour. But he gives a new explanation of how earth gives rise to colour, which seems to relate to his geometrical optical works and the theory that vision arises through the contact between visual rays emanating from the eye, and the surface of a suitably dense body (Adamson 2006 [*302]).

Fī ʿIllat al-lawn al-lāzuwardī allaḏī yurā fī l-ǧaww fī ǧihat al-samāʾ wa-yuẓann annahu lawn al-samāʾ
On the Cause of the Blue Colour that is Seen in the Air in the Direction of the Sky, and is Thought to be the Colour of the Sky

Cf. McCarthy 1962 [*4: 23 no. 113. 62 no. 4]; Engl. transl. by Spies [*80]; Engl. transl. by Adamson, Pormann [*35: 139–143]. The treatise presupposes the theory of the one just described, arguing that the sky is only blue because of the earthy exhalations in the atmosphere. Pure air or fire would, by contrast, be perfectly transparent; cf. Spies 1931 [*362].

Kalām fī l-Tarkīb
On Composition

Cf. McCarthy 1962 [*4: 58 no. 357. 66 no. 22]; Engl. transl. by Adamson, Pormann [*35: 323–324] ('Second Fragment'). A short fragment, probably an excerpt of a larger treatise (Celentano 1979 [*386: 8]). There are two kinds of composition: one involving contraries (found in the sublunary elements and substances made up from them), the other not involving contraries (the composition of the heavens). Thus the fragment repeats the view of the treatise *On the Nature of the Celestial Sphere* [*75: II 40–46] and endorses the Aristotelian claim that the heavens are made of a 'fifth element' which has no contraries and is thus incorruptible.

4.6 *Mathematical Sciences*

In addition to the mathematical works listed here and in the following sections, which are those of philosophical relevance, there are further treatises by al-Kindī devoted to the applied mathematical sciences of optics, astronomy, astrology and music; for bibliography see Daiber 1999 [*8], Rashed 1997 [*301: 5–96]. The many lost treatises, whose titles are known only in medieval lists of his works and other testimonies, are itemized in McCarthy 1962 [*4: 9–59].

Risāla fī annahu lā tunāl al-falsafa illā bi-ʿilm al-riyāḍiyyāt
There is No Way to Philosophy Except Through the Knowledge of Mathematics

Title given in Ibn al-Nadīm [*5: 260,27]; not extant. The title of course quotes a famous expression ascribed to Plato, μηδεῖς ἀγεωμέτρητος εἰσίτω.

4.7 *Arithmetic*

Risāla fī l-Ibāna ʿan al-aʿdād allatī ḏakarahā Aflāṭūn fī kitābihi al-Siyāsa
Explanation of the Numbers Mentioned by Plato in His Book on Politics

Title in Ibn al-Nadīm [*5: 34]; cf. McCarthy 1962 [*4: 14 no. 34]. Not extant.

Risāla fī Istiḫrāǧ al-aʿdād al-muḍmara
On the Extraction of Hidden Numbers [i.e. of numbers a partner is thinking of]

Cf. McCarthy 1962 [*4: 54 no. 332. 75 no. 56]. A treatise on a mathematical game.

On the mathematical section of the work *On the Reason Why the Higher Air is Cold*, see below under *Meteorology*; and on the medical-mathematical treatises *On the Causes of Crisis in Acute Illnesses* and *On the Powers of Composite Drugs* see below under *Medicine*.

4.8 *Geometry and Geodesy*

Aġrāḍ kitāb Uqlīdis
The Aims of Euclid's Book [sc. the *Elements*]

Cf. McCarthy 1962 [*4: 19 no. 77]. An introduction to Euclid's foundational treatise of geometry, which probably also dealt with its place within the sciences and propaedeutic value for philosophy. A quote in Ibn al-Nadīm [*5: 266,18–19] transmits the claim that the Euclidean work was written at the behest of the 'King of Phoenicia'. Another possible quote from this treatise is found in the manuscript Istanbul, Ayasofya 2457, no. 3, fol. 41^{b}: 'from al-Kindī, on the translation of the opening of Euclid's book (*li-Yaʿqūb b. Isḥāq* [*al-Kindī*] *fī tarǧamat ṣadr kitāb Uqlīdis*).' Discussed here are key technical terms of Euclid's method of proof, called the seven 'causes of knowledge' (*asbāb al-ʿilm*): *ḫabar* (πρότασις), *miṯāl* (κατασκευή), *ḫalf* (εἰς ἀδύνατον ἀπαγογή), *naẓar* (ἔκθεσις), *faṣl* (διορισμός), *burhān* (ἀπόδειξις), *tamām* (συμπέρασμα) (cf. Luckey 1941 [*286: 108–109. 112]; cf. Endress 2002 [*155: 242–243]).

Risāla ilā Yūḥannā b. Māsawayh fī Taqrīb al-dawr min al-watar
To Yūḥannā b. Māsawayh on Approximating the Circle from the Chord [i.e. approximation of the relation between cirumference and diameter]

A lost commentary on Archimedes' *Measurement of the Circle* (*Dimensio circuli*). Other testimonies call the work *Risāla fī Taqrīb qawl Aršimīdis fī qadr quṭr al-dāʾira min muḥīṭihā* and *Risāla fī Taqrīb watar al-dāʾira*; McCarthy 1962 [*4: 20 no. 81. 83], cf. ed. Rashed [*91: 12–14].

Risāla fī Īḍāḥ wiǧdān abʿād mā bayn al-nāẓir wa-markaz aʿmidat al-ǧibāl wa-ʿuluww aʿmidat al-ǧibāl
Explanation of How to Find the Distance from an Observer to the Base and Peak of a Distant Mountain

Cf. McCarthy 1962 [*4: 54 no. 333. 69 no. 33]; GAS [*6: V 257 no. 2]. Not extant.

For further treatises concerning plane and spherical geometry, the geometrical construction of astronomical instruments, land measurement and surveying, and measurement of time, cf. GAS [*6: V 257–258]; Luckey 1948 [*316: 495–498].

4.9 *Optics*

Kitāb ilā baʿḍ iḫwānihi fī Taqwīm al-ḫaṭaʾ wa-l-muškilāt allatī li-Uqlīdis fī kitābihi al-mawsūm bi-l-Manāẓir [Iṣlāḥ al-Manāẓir]
Treatise for His Brethren on the Correction of Errors and Clarification of Problems Found in the Book of Euclid Called the Optics

Cf. McCarthy 1962 [*4: 53 no. 321]. Following ancient mathematicians from Euclid to Ptolemy, al-Kindī adopts Plato's 'extramission' theory of vision: a 'luminous power' (*quwwa nūriyya* [*95: 163,12]; on which see Rashed 1997 [*301: 337]) in the form of a visual ray extends from the eye to the viewed object. The visual ray forms a cylindrical cone (*maḫrūṭ usṭuwānī*) between eye and field of vision. This model is used to account for the quantitative and qualitative features of eyesight. The author refers to a comprehensive work of his on optics, whose Arabic version does not survive, and restricts himself here to specific problems concerning Euclid's *Optics* (on the Arabic transmission of the *Optics* see the introduction by Rashed [*95: 5–66], Kheirandish 1996 [*91], 1999 [*92]). Where his understanding of the visual cone differs from that of Euclid, al-Kindī refers to Theon of Alexandria, while relating its methodological foundation back to Ptolemy, 'who dealt comprehensively with the science of mathematics, and applied philosophical conditions and proofs (*al-šarāʾiṭ wa-l-barāhīn al-falsafiyya*) to mathematics' [*95: 173,23–25] (cf. also Adamson 2006 [*302]).

Risāla fī ʿIlal iḫtilāf al-manāẓir, also known as *Iṣlāḥ al-manāẓir*
On the Causes of Various [Optical] Perspectives

Extant in Latin as *Liber de causis diversitatum aspectus et dandis demonstrationibus geometricis super eas* (McCarthy 1962 [*4: 19 no. 79. 71 no. 41]). In the introduction to the previous treatise (*Taqwīm al-ḫaṭaʾ wa-l-muškilāt allatī li-Uqlīdis*) al-Kindī mentions a comprehensive presentation of optics (*al-manāẓir*), which may be this treatise that is preserved only in Latin (cf. Rashed 1997 [*301: 67–85]).

The phenomenon of optical parallax is explained using geometrical models of the visual ray and reflected light, both of which are propagated along straight lines. The author situates the topic in the field of the mathematical sciences (*artes doctrinales* = Arab. *ʿulūm al-taʿālīm*), but does begin to develop geometrical optics as a physical science in explaining qualitative features of sensation. Here, as in other works on optics, al-Kindī assumes an extramission model of the visual ray (Rashed 1997 [*301: 84–87]). The treatise touches on the rectilinearity of the visual ray, vision with and without mirrors, and the influence of distance and angle of vision on sight, and on optical illusions (Björnbo, Vogl [*97], Rashed et al. 1997 [*97: 85–96. 437–534.]).

Risāla fī l-Šuʿāʿāt [*al-šamsiyya*]
On the Rays [*of the Sun*]

Cf. McCarthy 1962 [*4: 18 no. 68. 72 no. 47]; Engl. transl. by Adamson, Pormann [*35: 219–234]. A treatise on catoptrics, that is, investigation of the reflection of light rays from mirrored surfaces. In particular, it deals with the construction of burning mirrors on the basis of angles of reflection, again using a geometrical model for the propagation of light, to study conical mirrors and spherical concave mirrors. On al-Kindī's relation to Euclid and the Hellenistic tradition of optics as represented by Anthemius of Tralles cf. Rashed 1997 [*301: 97–152].

4.10 *Astronomy*

Kitāb fī l-Ṣināʿa al-ʿuẓmā
(*On the Great Art* [sc. Ptolemy's Almagest; to his son Aḥmad; also known as *Risāla fī Ṣināʿat Baṭlamyūs al-falakiyya*]

Cf. Ibn al-Nadīm [*5: 258,16]; McCarthy 1962 [*4: 54 no. 328. 73 no. 48]; GAS [*6: VI 153 no. 1]. A commentary on several chapters from the first book of Ptolemy's *Almagest*. Al-Kindī begins by emphasizing the importance of ancient science, which it is his role to pass on, and the significance of the progress of time for the development of scientific knowledge. Drawing on Ptolemy and the commentary of Theon of Smyrna on the place of astronomy within the sciences, he states that a love of knowledge, correct method, and comprehensive knowledge of the philosophical and mathematical sciences are all required for the study of this discipline. Philosophical theology establishes the principles of the cosmos: God is the first, unmoved mover separate from sense perceptible, corporeal substances. Physics meanwhile proves the circular motion of the heavens and the sphericity of the earth (cf. Rosenthal 1956 [*43]).

Risāla fī Taṣḥīḥ qawl Ubisqulāwus fī l-maṭāliʿ
Revision of Hypsicles' Treatise on the Ascensions of the Stars

On the basis of Qusṭā b. Lūqā's Arabic translation; used by Naṣīr al-Dīn al-Ṭūsī in his *Freeing the Book of Hypiscles* (*Taḥrīr kitāb Ubisqulāwus*); cf. de Falco, Krause 1966 [*319: 66]; McCarthy 1962 [*4: 21 no. 92. 75 no. 59].

4.11 *Music*

Kitāb al-Muṣawwitāt al-watariyya min ḏāt al-watar al-wāḥid ilā ḏāt al-ʿašarat al-awtār
On Sounding Instruments with One to Ten Strings

Cf. McCarthy 1962 [*4: 57 no. 351. 74 no. 52]. Five sections are promised in an introduction, but only three are extant (the third only as fragments). Possibly identical with a work *On the Order of Melodies Indicating the Natures of the Exalted Substances, and Analogy in Harmony* (*Risāla fī Tartīb al-naġam al-dālla ʿalā ṭabāʾiʿ al-ašḫāṣ al-ʿāliya wa-tašābuh al-taʾlīf*) which is not extant under this title – cf. Ibn al-Nadīm [*5: 260,4]; McCarthy 1962 [*4: 16 no. 52. 75 no. 55 missing in MS Berlin, 5530 Ahlwardt], Rosenthal 1949 [*42: 150–152], Shiloah 1979 [*337: 254–255]. An introduction to the scientific study of music as one of the mathematical disciplines. Mathematics is an 'intermediate science' between physics and metaphysics and serves as 'training' (*irtiyāḍ*) for both of these branches of theoretical philosophy. It is subdivided into arithmetic, music, i.e. the science of harmony (*ʿilm al-taʾlīf wa-huwa l-mūsīqī*), geometry and astronomy. The position of music as the second discipline, between arithmetic and the further branches of mathematics, corresponds to the 'Pythagorean' system of Nicomachus of Gerasa. After remarking on the priority of knowledge (*ʿilm*) to action (*ʿamal*) al-Kindī passes on to the philosophical study of mathematics as the theoretical basis of rational action.

The extant sections of the work offer an exposition of the Pythagorean-Platonic theory of *ethos*, which makes music a tool for moral education. The idea of the soul as a harmony (put forward by Philolaus and his student Echecrates, according to Plato at *Phaedo* 88d) is accompanied by the notion that musical harmony can influence the soul. There is an analogy and mutual influence between the numerical properties of the tunings in music and the harmonic structure of both the cosmos and the soul. The philosophers explain the tunings of musical instruments as paradigms for cosmic relationships in the physical and intelligible worlds, and further unfold the 'mysteries of natural philosophy' in the alternative form of mathematical relationships, for instance in works on arithmology, on 'congenial' and 'hostile' numbers, on proportional lines and the five polyhedra (*muǧassamāt*, the so-called 'Platonic solids'), which can be fitted within the sphere. After showing that all objects of sense perception are made of the four sublunary elements or the 'fifth nature' (that is, the nature of the heavenly bodies that possess circular motion), the philosophers established the 'sounding instruments' (*ālāt ṣawtiyya watariyya*) as a model of the analogy between the soul and the composition of the elements. They constructed various stringed instruments in correspondence with the composition of living things, and produced from them sounds that correlate with human constitution. To the wise, this is a clear proof of their rank in wisdom (*ḥikma*).

Section (*maqāla*) 1: al-Kindī describes the ethnic and historical forms of string instruments, especially the lute, as models of the universe. He begins with the one-stringed *kinkala* of India, the two-stringed instrument of the Khorasanians and the three-stringed one of the Byzantines. The number of strings is in each case made to correspond to ontological classifications. The four-stringed lute of the Greeks and earlier Arab culture is dealt with in particular detail. Its four strings correspond to a range of four-fold classifications: the elements, the senses, the humours, the cardinal virtues of the four powers of the soul, and in logic, the four primary questions of scientific inquiry following Aristotle's introduction to the *Posterior Analytics*. The classic five-stringed lute is treated similarly. Among the analogies given here are the five 'circles' (*dawāʾir*) of Arabic metrics. The eight-stringed 'instrument of David' is related to the three rhythmic modes (in the terminology of Arab musical practice). Also ascribed to King David is a ten-stringed instrument (this appears at the end of the third chapter in the incomplete manuscript [**105*: 90, with a quotation from the Psalms]). The decadic structures mentioned here include the classes of phonemes in Arabic, the spheres of the heavens, and the Aristotelian categories.

Section 2: what is required for musical mastery, composition (*taʾlīf*), and performance, both vocal and with the lute.

Section 3: (a) the correspondence (*mušākala*) of the four lute strings, namely the *bamm, muṯannā, muṯallaṯ*, and *zīr*, with their analogues in four-fold features of the cosmos; (b) the evocation of psychological character, virtue, vice, temperament and mood through each string (*kayfiyyat iẓhār al-awtār aḫlāq al-nafs*), and (c) how the combination (*tarkīb, mizāǧ*) of two strings, merging their individual properties, evokes a mixture and states of character.

Risāla fī Aǧzāʾ ḫabariyya fī l-mūsīqī
On the Informative Parts of Music

Cf. McCarthy 1962 [*4: 45 no. 264. 73 no. 49]; Farmer 1965 [*333: 9 no. 53bis]; Rosenthal 1966 [*334: 262–265]; Shiloah 1979 [*337: 255–256]. The conclusion of the treatise is missing in the sole surviving manuscript. It deals with the question of rhythm and *ethos* according to the theory of the philosophers, which according to al-Kindī is entirely ignored by contemporary musicians who look only to the tastes of their audience. The treatise displays many similarities to the one just discussed (*On Sounding Instruments*). It is divided into two sections, each of which contains four chapters. Section 1: (a) on the eight rhythmic modes; (b) moving (*intiqāl*) from one type of *īqā*ʿ to another; (c) matching poetic genres to the appropriate rhythm; (d) matching rhythm to the appropriate occasion. As a whole, the doctrines presented agree closely with the previous treatise. Section 2: (a) the doctrine of *ethos*, that is, the correspondence between the musical modes and aspects of the human soul – this is identical with section 3, chapters (a) (b) and (c) of *On Sounding Instruments*; (b) the *ethos* theory as applied to other senses, beginning with the harmony of colours and its effect on the soul; (c) the harmony of scent; (d) precious aphorisms from the philosophers concerning music. The text of the sole surviving manuscript (held in Berlin) breaks off at fol. 35[b], so that this final section includes only seven aphorisms, which agree verbatim with aphorisms found in Paul the Persian, Ḥunayn and the Iḫwān al-Ṣafāʾ (according to Shiloah 1979 [*337: 255–256]).

Risāla fī Ḫubr ṣināʿat al-taʾlīf [= *Risāla fī Ḫubr taʾlīf al-alḥān*]
(*On Experience of the Art of Composition* [*of Melodies*]

Cf. McCarthy 1962 [*4: 16 no. 55; cf. 54 no. 329. 73 no. 50]. The title is absent in the lists of Ibn al-Nadīm and other bibliographical sources, but the work may be mentioned there under a different name. Al-Kindī refers here to a larger work, now lost, entitled *Great Book on Composition* (*al-Kitāb al-aʿẓam fī l-Taʾlīf*), which is summarized in the present treatise (Shiloah 1979 [*337: 256–257 no. 175]).

The text is not divided into chapters or sections, but deals consecutively with (a) fourths, fifths and octaves on the lute; (b) the positions of the notes, the two types of double octaves, the number of notes within the double octave, various expressions for the tetrachord, commonly used notes within the double octave and the octave; (c) the seven modal scales (*ṭanīnāt* = τόνος); (d) 'moving' or transitions (*intiqālāt*), the *ethos* of the modes; (e) composition, definition of melody, and models for imitation; (f) complete mastery in music, the problem of setting poetry to music, the three ethological types of musical composition: *al-basṭī* ('diastalic', exalting), *al-qabḍī* ('systaltic', depressing), *al-muʿtadil* (moderate); types of expression in melody, rhythm and metre (cf. Sawa 2009 [*344: 502–503]).

Risāla fī l-Luḥūn wa-l-naġam
On Melodies and Notes [*of the Scale*]

Written for Aḥmad b. al-Muʿtaṣim; cf. McCarthy 1962 [*4: 44 no. 263; cf. 55 no. 355. 74 no. 51]; Shiloah 1979 [*337: 257–259 no. 176]; complete in MS Manisa 1705: 110[b]–123[a]; for a French transl. cf. Shiloah 1971 [*335: 309–310]. A fragment in MS Berlin, Wetzstein 1240 (5530 Ahlwardt), no. 4, fols 25–31 is contaminated by Pseudo-Euclid's *Discourse on Melodies, the Construction of String Instruments and the Articulation of Letters* (*Qawl Uqlīdis ʿalā l-Luḥūn wa-ṣanʿat al-maʿāzif wa-maḫāriǧ al-ḥurūf*); cf. Rosenthal 1966 [*334: 265–268]. It has also been published under the title *al-Risāla al-kubrā fī l-Taʾlīf aw al-Kitāb al-aʿẓam fī l-Taʾlīf*, ed. Yūsuf 1962 [*332: 121–142]; further fragments of the same Pseudo-Euclidean work are also provided there, on the basis of the same manuscript, fols 22–24. 27–28, under the title *Muḫtaṣar al-mūsīqī fī taʾlīf al-naġam wa-ṣanʿat al-ʿūd* [*332: 111–120]; cf. Shiloah 1979 [*337: 257–260 no. 176–177]. The text of Pseudo-Euclid is completely preserved in MS Manisa 1705, fols 93ᵇ-109ᵇ; cf. GAS [*6: V 120 no. IX]; Shiloah 1979 [*337: 353–355 no. 260]; Neubauer 2004–2005 [*342: 311].

The title *Abbreviated Treatise on Music, on the Composition of Melodies and the Construction of the Lute* (*Muḫtaṣar al-mūsīqī fī taʾlīf al-naġam wa-ṣanʿat al-ʿūd*), written for Aḥmad b. al-Muʿtaṣim (Ibn Abī Uṣaybiʿa [*13: I 210,23]), is perhaps the original one, whereas the bibliographers make no mention of a *Risāla fī l-Luḥūn wa-l-naġam*. In terms of content, the title mentioned in the *Fihrist* (Ibn al-Nadīm [*5: 257 Flügel]), *Epistle on the Arrangement of Notes so as to Indicate Natures* (*Risāla fī Tartīb al-naġam al-dālla ʿalā l-ṭabāʾiʿ*) corresponds to the theme of the second chapter, namely musical *ethos*. Al-Kindī himself refers to another title found in the bibliographers, *Great Book of Harmony* (*kitābunā l-aʿẓam fī l-Taʾlīf*) (McCarthy 1962 [*4: 16 no. 51]) in his *On the Quantity of Aristotle's Books* (*Risāla fī Kammiyyat kutub Arisṭāṭālīs*, ed. Abū Rīda [*26: I 378]) as well as his *On Experience of the Art of Composition* (*Risāla fī Ḫubr ṣināʿat al-taʾlīf*, ed. Yūsuf 1962 [*332: 29]); but it is not possible to know whether this work is identical with any of the extant treatises.

The treatise deals chiefly with the 'instrument of the philosophers', the oud. It is divided into an introduction and three chapters, with the introduction offering a summary of the whole work.

The first chapter deals with the oud and the measurements of its parts, which are given exactly in terms of 'fingers'; the strings and frets; al-Kindī explains that each aspect can be explained with reference to philosophy, geometry, arithmetic or astrology.

The second chapter concerns the four strings, which are made of gut, and their thickness and tuning; the seven notes (*naġam*) of the scale; the two types of third (*wusṭā*): minor (or 'feminine') and major ('masculine'), and on this basis, feminine and masculine melodies and their effect; consonance and dissonance; the second octave, which is identical with the first but at a higher pitch; the first note is also the seventh of the lower octave, so that this note has a double function; the first tuning of the oud and other tunings known to be in use; comparison of notes played on the oud and those that are produced with the voice; aspects of octaves, fifths and fourths; the relation between the parts of the oud and astrological phenomena, and between the four strings and the elements and bodily humours.

The third chapter takes up the variety of musical systems used throughout the world, which reflect differences between human cultures in respect of manners, taste, habits and attitudes; these differences are traced back to atmospheric and astrological causes; in order to illustrate the variety, the Persian modes (*ṭuruq*), the eight Byzantine modes (*ustuḫuṣiyya*), and the eight rhythmic modes of the Arabs are named. The last portion of the treatise contains a practice duet for lute players (for a transcription cf. Shiloah 1974 [*336]), which has been used by Farmer as proof for the existence of notation and polyphony in Arabic music (noted by Shiloah 1979 [*337: 255–256]).

4.12 *Astrology*

Risāla fī Mulk al-ʿArab wa-kammiyyatihi
On the Rule of the Arabs and its Duration

Cf. McCarthy 1962 [*4: 27 no. 142. 48 no. 286. 53 no. 327. 72 no. 45]; GAS [*6: VII 131 no. 2]; Loth 1875 [*351: text 273–379]. Al-Bīrūnī seems to ascribe this treatise to al-Kindī's student al-Saraḫsī (d. 286/899) under the title *Kitāb fī Qirān al-naḥasay fī burǧ intiḥāsihimā*, cf. Fück 1952 [*353: 77,15–16].

Al-Kindī calculates the duration of the Arab caliphate on the basis of an historical horoscope using the Indo-Iranian model of the cosmic year, with a thousand year cycle between great conjunctions of the most distant planets, Saturn and Jupiter. He adopts the Persian theory, but revises previous astrological interpretations of the astronomical data. Whereas Māšāʾ Allāh and others – circles close to the Persian Šuʿūbiyya and, later, to the Ismāʿīliyya – foresee an early end to the Arabic caliphate, he predicts a duration of 693 years. In contrast to the influence of the Iranian faction at the early Abbasid court, al-Kindī's interpretation marks a new alliance between Hellenism and Arabism (Loth 1875 [*351]; for literature on the parameters and models of mundane astrology cf. Endress 1987–1992 [*23: II 414–415; III 106–107]).

Maqāla ʿalā Taḥāwīl al-sinīn
On [Prognostication According to] the Astrological Cylcles of 'Great Years'

Cf. McCarthy 1962 [*4: 53 no. 326. 72 no. 44]; GAS [*6: VII 132]. MS Escurial ²913, 2. A further treatise on mundane astrology.

Risāla fī Taḥrīr waqt yurǧā fīhi iǧābat al-duʿāʾ wa-l-taḍarruʿ ilā llāh min ǧihat al-tanǧīm
On Determining the Moment at Which One May Hope to Have Prayers Answered, and Obeisance to God from the Point of View of Astrology

GAS [*6: VII 132 no. 10]. The heavenly powers, causes of the world of generation and corruption, are beyond time. We may hope to determine the conditions of individual effects and thus to know propitious moments. Philosophers of pre-Islamic monotheistic religions who practiced astrology gave horoscopes for favourable times to have one's prayers answered, choosing certain constellations of the stars, especially involving the planet Jupiter as an intermediary between humankind and God.

al-Madḫal ilā ʿilm [aḥkām] al-nuǧūm [al-Arbaʿūn bāban]
Introduction to Astrology [The Forty Chapters]

Also preserved in medieval Latin, in two versions: *De iudiciis astrorum* and *De astrologia iudiciaria*; McCarthy 1962 [*4: 78 no. 73]; Carmody 1956 [*3: 78]; GAS [*6: VII 133 no. 2]; cf. Burnett 1993 [*356].

A practically oriented handbook of astrological prediction, especially 'elections' (katarchic astrology, *iḫtiyārāt*) and 'questions' (*masāʾil*), with a brief introduction to the astronomical principles of astrology. There are only occasional allusions to the cosmological underpinnings. An appendix to the Latin version of Robert of Ketton reads as follows: 'it is established among wise men that the comings-to-be and the passings-away of things happen by the perpetual movement of the heavenly bodies, whose effect principally proceeds from the nature, condition and order of the luminaries, the other planets and the heavenly sphere when the luminaries are in conjunction and opposition' (transl. in Burnett 1993 [*356: 79]).

4.13 *Astrometeorology*

Risāla fī [ʿilal] Aḥdāṯ al-ǧaww
On the [Causes of] Atmospheric Phenomena

Cf. Ibn al-Nadīm [*5: 260,13 Flügel; 319,18 Taǧaddud], McCarthy 1962 [*4: 19 no. 75. 34 no. 187. 80 no. 83]). An extant Latin treatise called *Prognosticatio aeris* (McCarthy 1962 [*4: 79 no. 79]) deals with the same topic; cf. also *De aeris dispositione* (McCarthy 1962 [*4: 79 no. 80]).

On astrological weather forecasting on the basis of planetary constellations. The positions of Saturn and Jupiter relative to the sun are an indication (*dalīl*) of the weather, concerning the whole year (Jupiter) and the quarter year, in regard to warm vs. cold and dry vs. moist. Prognosis for months and smaller periods of time down to single days are reached on the basis of the 'opening of the greater/smaller door' (*fatḥ al-bāb al-aʿẓam/al-aṣġar*) – a model for the conjunction and aspects of the planets, whose astrological houses lie across from one another (aspect of Saturn relative to the sun in one of the houses of the moon, Jupiter with Mercury, and Venus with Mars). The aspects of the planets in this context are indicators of rain, wind, and changes in the weather (cf. Bos, Burnett 2000 [*365: 409–419; and on *fatḥ al-abwāb* 19]).

al-Risāla al-Kāfiya fī l-āṯār al-ʿulwiyya
On Higher Phenomena [Meteorology]

Extant only in a Hebrew translation, under the title *Epistle on Moisture and Rain, Entitled 'The Sufficient'* (*Iggeret ba-leḥuyyot u-va-maṭar ha-niqre't ha-Iggeret ha-maspeqet*). Written 'for his student Ḥabīb', probably meaning Ḥabīb Ibn Bahrīz, translator of the *Introduction to Arithmetic* of Nicomachus of Gerasa; cf. Freudenthal, Lévy 2004 [*281] as well as Bos, Burnett 2000 [*365: 97. 139. 161]; Ibn Abī Uṣaybiʿa [*13: I 213]. Ed. Bos, Burnett 2000 [*365: 97–135, Letter 1]. A Latin treatise *Liber Alkindii de impressionibus terrae et aeris accidentibus*, also transmitted under the title *Liber Alkindii de mutatione temporum* [*365: 263–323] includes parts of this and the next treatise dealing with the topic of indications of rain [*365: 203–228, Letter 2].

The author seeks to present for his student 'the principles of meteorology, that is, atmospheric phenomena, the winds, and the causes of moisture and dryness' on a scientific basis, following the teachings of the philosophers which are grounded in argument and proof. This will prevent the confusion that has been created by astrologers who were uncritical exegetes of ancient experts like Ptolemy, Dorotheus, etc. Scientific meteorology rests on a sound understanding of the four mathematical disciplines as propaedeutic for philosophy, and also on the philosophers' physical doctrines, especially regarding the elements and their qualities. Chapter 1: On phenomema of the planets, and their causes, mostly following Aristotle's *On the Heavens* and *Meteorology*. The planets cause heat in the sublunar realm, despite themselves lacking any fiery nature; they do so rather through friction exerted by the rotating spheres on the region of air. Chapter 2: On various phenomena caused by the planets in the quadrants of the heavenly sphere. While the sun has a generally warming influence on the sublunar elements, local and seasonal variations arise thanks to the complex relations of the planetary motions, due to both forward and retrograde motion and their varying proximity to the earth as they travel on (cf. Bos, Burnett 2000 [*365: 15]). Chapter 3: On the moist and dry quarters of the year. Prognosis of changes in the weather in the four seasons due to the planets' interrelations in the zodiac. Chapter 4: On moisture and rain, and the conditions for changing weather depending on the seasons and the winds, based on constellations involving the moon, whose effect may be calculated in light of the arithmetic 'proportion' of the sphere of the moon (following the phases of the moon) to the sublunary spheres of earth and water (cf. Bos, Burnett 2000 [*365: 17]). Chapter 5: How to find the times of moisture and rain for each locale; the main topic of practical weather forecasting.

Risāla fī ʿIlal [al-]quwā [al-mansūba ilā] l-ašḫāṣ al-ʿāliya al-dālla ʿalā l-maṭar
On the Causes of the Powers Ascribed to the Higher Bodies, which Indicate Rain

Extant only in Hebrew and Latin translations, but the Arabic title is given by Ibn al-Nadīm [*5: 257,19 Flügel; 317,12 Taǧaddud]; cf. McCarthy 1962 [*4: 19 no. 74]; ed. Bos, Burnett 2000 [*365: 203–228, Letter 2].

The treatise deals with the physical principles of the powers ascribed to the 'higher bodies' of the heavenly spheres, by means of which they affect the 'first qualities' (that is, of the four sublunar elements). In light of these, one can predict weather over the course of the seasons. An explanation of these powers demands expertise in all philosophical sciences: mathematics, physics, and metaphysics (§ 1–18, repeated at § 67–78). The four mathematical disciplines – arithmetic, geometry, astronomy and music – are needed to determine and calculate the aspects, proportions, and harmonic interrelation of the spheres and also for the method of proof used in prediction. Physics supplies an understanding of the proximate efficient causes of sublunary generation and corruption. Metaphysics explains the effect of higher bodies on lower ones.

The nine spheres of the cosmos, in order of distance from the centre, are: 1. the sphere of the heavy elements (earth and water), 2. the sphere of the *meteora* (air and fire), 3. the sphere of the moon, 4. the sphere of Venus and Mercury (at equal distance from the sun), 5. the sphere of the sun, 6.-8. the spheres of Mars, Jupiter, Saturn, 9. the outer sphere of the fixed stars. Their causal roles correspond to their respective natures, and their influence is further determined by aspect and opposition to other heavenly bodies. The moon is watery and earthy, and primarily affects the elements with these characteristics, while Venus has an affinity to moisture and rain, but Mercury to wind and air. The sun, as the largest luminous body, provides motion to the entire world, to which it relates as light does to the soul – the light that actualizes the intelligibles. Mars counteracts coming-to-be, whereas Jupiter promotes generation and life. The complementary and counteracting effects of the planets cause, or prevent, rain in accordance with natural laws, which allows the expert to make accurate forecasts on the basis of their constellations. A special role is given to the relations of the moon and its 'houses' (*anwāʾ*) and 'stations' (*manāzil*), cf. Bos, Burnett 2000 [*365: 18]).

4.14 *Meteorology*

Risāla fī l-ʿIlla allatī lahā takūnu baʿḍ al-mawāḍiʿ lā takād tumṭar
The Reason Why it Hardly Rains in Certain Places

Cf. McCarthy 1962 [*4: 19 no. 76. 63 no. 9]); there is a testimony in al-Kindī's *Risāla fī ʿIllat kawn al-ḍabāb* [*126: II 76,9] giving the more appropriate title *On the Occurrence of Rain in Certain Places, and Its Being Largely Prevented in Other Places* (*Risālatunā fī* *kawn al-maṭar fī baʿḍ al-mawāḍiʿ wa-Imtināʿ kawnihi illā l-aqall fī baʿḍ al-mawāḍiʿ*) – résumé in Sersen 1976 [*363: 146–149. 220–222].

The direction of wind, which is a flow of air as it expands in a warmer region and contracts in a colder region, depends on the position and inclination of the sun, whose warmth causes exhalations (*buḫār*) to rise from the earth. The production and direction of these exhalations is conditioned by waterways and wetlands of low-lying vegetation. The cold in areas further from the sun causes the vapour to condense, resulting in rain. When the vapour flows to a region where it cannot cool and condense, no rain falls but instead the vapour flows on to an area where the ground is moister, and where the conditions are right for the condensation (*inḥiṣār*) and cooling of the vapour and, hence, for rain. This is illustrated with the weather conditions in Egypt, which lies between Ethiopia (the origin of northward-flowing vapours) and the cool regions to the north of the Mediterranean.

On the sources of al-Kindī's meteorological doctrines, cf. Sersen 1976 [*363: 146–149], critiqued by Daiber 1992 [*364: 222 n. 75]: he argues that ideas Sersen traces to Theophrastus can also be found in Aristotle or elsewhere in Greek meteorological literature, as with the definition of wind as a 'flow of air' (*sayalān al-hawāʾ*, 71,8–9).

Risāla fī ʿIllat kawn al-ḍabāb
On the Cause of the Generation of Mist

Cf. McCarthy 1962 [*4: 34 no. 192. 64 no. 10]; résumé in Sersen 1976 [*363: 223–224]. In the previous treatise, it was shown how rising vapour forms clouds under the influence of cold. Mist is produced when wind in the upper air pushes a cloud to the surface of the earth, and this becomes vapour due to the influence of warmer air. Mist can also result when wind is trapped in the lower region of a cloud and sinks towards the earth under the pressure of cold air from above and to the side.

Risāla fī ʿIllat al-ṯalǧ wa-l-barad wa-l-barq wa-l-ṣawāʿiq wa-l-raʿd wa-l-zamharīr [*wa-l-maṭar*]
On the Cause of Snow, Hail, Lightning, Lightning-Bolt, Thunder, and Frost [or: *and Rain*, reading *wa-l-maṭar* in place of *wa-l-zamharīr*, as given by Ibn Abī Uṣaybiʿa and Ibn al-Qifṭī]

Cf. McCarthy 1962 [*4: 41 no. 235. 64 no. 14]); résumé in Sersen 1976 [*363: 225–226]. Rain, snow, and hail are produced from condensing vapours which rise up and cool in the upper atmosphere. Their various forms are due to differences in cooling and proportion of water and air. Lightning is an igniting in a cloud because of violent interior motions; when the spark reaches the earth the result is a lightning bolt (*ṣāʿiqa*). Whereas lightning is perceived immediately as an illumination, thunder lags behind and is perceived afterwards. Again, Sersen 1976 [*363: 188–189] refers to Theophrastus, who explains snow as a frozen mixture of water and air (al-Kindī [*127: II 84–85]); but the ideas have been instead traced to Aristotle (Daiber 1992 [*364: 222 n. 75], cf. Aristotle, *De Generatione animalium* 735 b 21).

Risāla fī l-ʿIlla allatī lahā yabrud aʿlā l-ǧaww wa-yasḫun mā qaruba min al-arḍ
On the Reason Why the Higher Air is Cold, and the Air Closer to the Earth is Warm [and three further questions]

Cf. McCarthy 1962 [*4: 40 no. 233. 63 no. 7]; Engl. transl. by Adamson, Pormann [*35: 208–216]. Three questions whose discussion shows that even fairly trivial problems call for knowledge of natural philosophy and its principles (*al-ʿilm al-ṭabīʿī* [*wa-*] *awāʾiluhu*). Likewise the study of the books of the ancients is useless in the absence of knowledge of their first principles, in their systematic order (*ʿilm al-sawābiq li-tilka l-ʿulūm ʿalā tartībihā*). Philosophy, 'the art of arts and wisdom of wisdoms,' proceeds in stages from the lowest to highest rank, the latter being the 'knowledge of Lordship' (*ʿilm al-rubūbiyya*). No one can attain the next higher stage without mastering the previous one. God alone can select a certain person as a messenger, and illuminate his soul through inspiration (*ilhām*), relieving him of the need to work through basic principles (*yunayyiruhu fī nafsihi bi-lā awāʾil*). This is how He differentiates the prophet from other humans [*128: II 91–93].

Chapter 1: Why does vapour freeze and water cool at higher altitudes, even though air is known to be warm and moist by nature, and to be warmed by the celestial sphere? The qualities of the elements are not absolute, but relative. Air and water, which immediately surround the earth, are warmed by the rotating celestial bodies, but the further away from the earth they are, the more they cool [*128: II 93–98,7].

Chapter 2: When we see clear, cloudless sky above us, can we determine how far the area of clear air reaches? And conversely, can we determine the location and breadth of cloud seen on the horizon? This is impossible, because the observation of weather phenomena is conditioned by the light-rays reflected from moist, warm exhalations. Their behaviour again depends on the distance of warming and cooling factors, which for instance determine the height of the clouds, and on contours of the terrain [*128: II 98,8–99,4].

Chapter 3: Given that numbers are infinite, are counted things also infinite? No, for there is no actual infinity [*128: II 90,5–100,3]. Numbers are composed from unities; every multiplicity made up of finite things is itself finite. Though a multiplicity may be potentially infinite, every addition to it will result in an actually finite magnitude.

Chapter 4 [not mentioned in the introduction]: The ancients' claim that vapour does not rise above an altitude of sixteen stadia was based on observation [*128: II 100,4–14].

Fī ʿIllat al-lawn al-lāzuwardī allaḏī yurā fī l-ǧaww fī ǧihat al-samāʾ
On the Reason for the Blue Colour Seen in the Direction of the Sky

Cf. McCarthy 1962 [*4: 23 no. 113. 62 no. 4]; for a description see above under *Physics*.

Risāla fī l-ʿIlla al-fāʿila li-l-madd wa-l-ǧazr
On the Efficient Cause of Tidal Flow and Ebb

Cf. McCarthy 1962 [*4: 39 no. 225. 62 no. 1]. The swelling of rivers and streams is caused by outflow of water from springs and cavities. By contrast, sea tide is caused by an increase in volume due to warming. This is caused by the rotating celestial body, whose motion warms the surrounding air due to its speed, and thus indirectly heats the surface of the water; cf. Wiedemann 1912 [*251] and 1922 [*361].

4.15 *Magic*

Risāla fī [Maṭraḥ] al-šuʿāʿ
On [the Location Where] Rays [are Cast]

Known by the Latin title *De radiis*; cf. McCarthy 1962 [*4: 17 no. 61. 72 no. 47]; D'Alverny, Hudry 1975 [*354]; Travaglia 1999 [*376]. The cosmos is held together by universal sympathy: a harmony that unifies all existing things and manifests itself in the reciprocal irradiation of the stars and elemental bodies. These regulate natural processes, but also allow for the working of magic.

Fī l-Mawāḍiʿ allatī yuẓann anna l-dafīn fīhā min kanz aw ġayrihi
On Places Suspected to Hold Buried Treasure

A second version of this independently transmitted text is found in chapter 35 of al-Kindī's *Forty Chapters* on astrological 'elections.' On the latter and the medieval Latin reception see Burnett, Yamamoto, Yano 1997 [*375]. The procedure described here calls for the construction of a horoscopic map and identification of a signifying (*dalīl*) ascendant.

Risāla fī ʿIlm al-katif
On the Science of Shoulder-Blade [Prognostication]

Cf. McCarthy 1962 [*4: 55 no. 338. 76 no. 65]. On the science of scapulomancy, that is, prediction based on the shoulder-blade of an animal.

4.16 *Medicine and Pharmacology*

Risāla fī l-Luṯġa
On Luṯġa

Cf. McCarthy 1962 [*4: 47 no. 285. 68 no. 32]. On the speech defects known as *luṯġa*, especially velar pronunciation of the alveolar phoneme *rāʾ*, and other defects (lisp, stammer). The treatise deals with the relation between the physical organs of speech in the mouth and throat on the one hand, and Arabic phonemes on the other. Speech defects are traced to (a) psychological disorders, (b) weakness in the rational soul, which becomes unable to control the organs of speech, (c) physical deficiencies or excess in the use of the organs of speech, hindering correct articulation.

Risāla fī ʿIllat baḥārīn al-amrāḍ al-ḥādda
On the Cause of Crises in Acute Illnesses

Cf. McCarthy 1962 [*4: 25 no. 124]. The author emphasizes the scientific basis of medicine. Only a philosopher who grasps the principles of mathematics and natural philosophy can master this science (ed. Klein-Franke 1975 [*385: 171]). Medical prognosis is based on iatromathematics, in this case Pythagorean arithmology and astrology, following the Hippocratic teaching on hebdomads. Number is the cause of numerable things, while the principle of number is unity. From unity are generated the various types of numbers: even and odd, prime, triangular, square, and the higher orders of polygonal numbers. Numbers may or may not be homogeneous in their relations to each other. Odd numbers imitate 1; for this reason the crises that fall on odd-numbered days help the patient to recover, while those that fall on even days are 'unreliable' and weaken the recuperative powers (on the source material in Hippocrates cf. Klein-Franke 1975 [*385: 164]; on the division of the lunar cycle into eight phases, cf. Weisser 1982 [*387] with corrections of the reconstruction offered by Klein-Franke).

Kitāb fī Maʿrifat quwā l-adwiya al-murakkaba
On Knowledge of the Powers of Compound Drugs

Cf. McCarthy 1962 [*4: 54 no. 330. 74 no. 54]. On the preparation of compound drugs in numerical proportion, on the basis of Neo-Pythagorean arithmology. Al-Kindī reproduces the Galenic teaching on the 'degrees' of simple drugs, and expands on this model by reckoning the effect of compound drugs from their simple ingredients, using geometrical proportion and progression. The numerical speculations may be traced to the *Introduction to Arithmetic* of Nicomachus of Gerasa (see above for al-Kindī's remarks on the text). The influence of this theory, 'based on the arts of number and music,' continued into the 6th/12th century, when it was heavily criticized in Andalusia by Ibn Rušd in his *Kulliyyāt fī l-ṭibb* (known in Latin as *Colliget*). Cf. Gauthier [*155]; on Ibn Rušd's critique, Langermann 2003 [*389].

Kīmiyāʾ al-ʿiṭr wa-l-taṣʿīdāt [or] *Kitāb fī Kīmiyāʾ al-ʿiṭr wa-l-taṣʿīdāt*
[*Book On*] *The Chemistry of Perfume and Distillation*

For the first version of the title cf. McCarthy 1962 [*4: 69 no. 34] (perhaps pseudepigraphical), on the second McCarthy 1962 [*4: 38 no. 219. 69 no. 34]. A collection of recipes, without commentary on their scientific basis. In particular, it offers recipes for substitution of certain drugs by others; instructions for preparing certain types of drugs; recipes for aromatic oils and salves, as well as distillation of scented water; cf. Garbers 1948 [*383], Wiedemann 1916–1917 [*381], Levey 1966 [*384: 6]. For a further text on the making of perfume, under the title *al-Taraffuq fī l-ʿiṭr*, cf. McCarthy 1962 [*4: 55 no. 337. 75 no. 57].

al-Iḫtiyārāt li-l-adwiya al-mumtaḥana al-muǧarraba wa-huwa l-Aqrābāḏīn
Aqrābāḏīn [*Dispensary*], *i.e. Choice of Tested Drugs*

Cf. GAS [*6: III 245]; Levey 1966 [*384]. A practically-oriented, unsystematic collection of recipes. It is doubtful that the extant work is entirely authentic (Ullmann 1970 [*5: 301]).

4.17 *Spurious Works*

Liber introductorius in artem logicae demonstrationis
Introductory Book on the Art of Logical Demonstration

A Latin version is ascribed to al-Kindī; in fact an excerpt from the *Epistles* of the Iḫwān al-Ṣafāʾ; see Nagy [*25]; de Boer 1900 [*140: 177]; Rosenthal 1943 [*15: 57].

5 Doctrine

5.1 Introductions to Philosophy – 5.2 Propaedeutic Ethics – 5.3 Metaphysics – 5.4 Soul and Intellect – 5.5 Physics and Cosmology – 5.6 Mathematical Sciences

5.1 *Introductions to Philosophy*

Al-Kindī's understanding of philosophy and its structure largely follows the precedent of the late ancient commentators on Aristotle (cf. Hein 1985 [*63: 163–87]). Philosophy is divided into practical and theoretical sections, with the theoretical side of philosophy divided into logic and three further parts directed towards different types of objects. The first part studies material things, and consists of physics and the subordinate physical sciences. The second part studies immaterial things that are connected to material things: sometimes this is identified as mathematics, sometimes as psychology. The third part studies wholly immaterial things: this is metaphysics or theology, the two being identical in al-Kindī's view. Al-Kindī is adamant (in section two of *Fī l-Falsafa al-ūlā* [*On First Philosophy*] and elsewhere) that different methods are to be used for different parts of philosophy.

As shown by his *Fī Kammiyyāt kutub Arisṭūṭālīs* (*On the Quantity of Aristotle's Books*), al-Kindī used this system (which is itself derived ultimately from Aristotle, *Metaphysics* VI.1) to organize his understanding of Aristotle's corpus, to the extent that this was known to him. It is also put into practice in his own works, where it becomes clear that the 'purely intellectual' approach commended in *On First Philosophy* is based, above all, on mathematics (for the centrality of mathematics for al-Kindī cf. Endress 2003 [*274], Gutas 2004 [*275], Adamson 2007 [*115: 36–37]). We see this, for instance, in the axiomatic style of argument used to refute the eternity of the world in several parallel works. In these texts ([*71], [*72], [*73], and in *On First Philosophy* itself) al-Kindī sets out premises he considers to be self-evident principles, for instance that 'two bodies, neither of which is larger than the other, are equal' ([*51: 29 Rashed, Jolivet], [*26: 114]). On the basis of these axioms he shows that an actual infinity is impossible. In one case [*73] the argumentative method is explicitly geometrical: simple diagrams are added to the text, to show how the argument applies to linear magnitudes. In these works al-Kindī employs a mathematical approach he would have found in Euclid, to prove a thesis held by Aristotle, namely the impossibility of actually infinite magnitudes (even though al-Kindī will then apply this to temporal magnitude, in order to refute the Aristotelian doctrine of the eternity of the universe).

Alongside this axiomatic style of argument, al-Kindī favours proofs by *reductio* using *modus tollens*: either P or not-P; but if not-P, then either Q or R; not-Q; not-R; therefore P. This does not look much like an Aristotelian syllogism, but it is an argument form found repeatedly in al-Kindī, for instance in a proof that nothing can be the cause of its own existence (in *On First Philosophy* cf. [*32: 41–43; *26: 123]) or that species are incorporeal [*61], cf. Adamson, Pormann 2009 [*243]). In the latter case, his argument is as follows: species is either body or not body. If species were body, then it would be contained as an entirety in its members, or as a part. The species is however in its members neither as a whole nor as a part. Therefore species is not body.

Al-Kindī, as the head of a circle of translators who transmitted numerous works from Greek into Arabic, was unsurprisingly a strong proponent of the use of all the Greek sciences including philosophy. This is clear not only from his explicit defence of using 'foreign' wisdom, in the first part of *On First Philosophy*, and from the extensive use of Greek sources throughout al-Kindī's extant corpus, but also from the attention his circle paid to developing a new Arabic scientific vocabulary to capture Greek technical terms. The most concrete result of this endeavour is *Risāla fī Ḥudūd al-ašyāʾ wa-rusūmihā* (*On the Definitions and Descriptions of Things*), a list of definitions for Arabic technical terms, which is extant in several different versions (cf. Stern 1959 [*142], Allard 1972 [*145], Frank 1975 [*147], Klein-Franke 1982 [*151]).

Only a few intriguing passages shed any light on the question of how al-Kindī thought Greek learning related to the truths of Prophetic revelation. In *On the Quantity of Aristotle's Books* [*26: I 372–373] he praises the completeness and brevity of Prophetic teaching (discussing the famous Quranic verse, 'When He wills something, His command is to say to it: "Be!" and it is' [Sura 36:82]). But he seems to think that the Prophet's teaching simply encapsulates what philosophers too can grasp, albeit over a long period of time and with great effort. The same impression is given by a passage in his *Risāla fī l-ʿIlla allatī lahā yabrud aʿlā l-ǧaww wa-yasḫun mā qaruba min al-arḍ* (*On The Reason Why The Higher Air is Cold*) [*26: II 93]: prophets can grasp immediately that which philosophers need laboriously to establish on the basis of first principles. Similarly, *Risāla fī l-Ibāna ʿan suǧūd al-ǧirm al-aqṣā* (*On the Prostration of the Outermost Sphere*) consists entirely of a philosophical exposition of a Quranic verse (see further Adamson 2003 [*204: 59–66], criticized by Janssens 2007 [*158: 13–14]).

For those who are not blessed with prophetic revelation, a more laborious method is required. In some works, al-Kindī stresses our need to begin from sense-experience in doing philosophy. For instance the beginning of his work on magic and astral causation, *On Rays* (*De radiis*), states that universal concepts derive from sensation, and makes this the starting point for intellection [*135: 215–216]. Similarly in *On the Quantity of Aristotle's Books*, al-Kindī argues that knowledge deals with the primary and the secondary – that is, both particulars and universals, echoing the terminology of *Categories* ch.2. But this knowledge of substance comes only through the understanding of quantity and quality [*40: §VI.1]. This is presumably why Aristotle places his discussion of these two categories early in the *Categories* itself.

In *On First Philosophy*, however, al-Kindī seems more optimistic about the prospects of a 'purely intellectual' approach, at least as regards certain topics. We have already seen that he models this approach on the science of mathematics. And in fact, *On First Philosophy* gives the strong impression that knowledge based on sense-experience is distinctly second-rate. He stresses the fact that bodies are in perpetual flux, and that although our perception (*wuǧūd*) of them is 'prior to us,' it is also 'further from nature' [*51: 19–21]. Intellectual perception grasps universals, that is, species and genera. One might easily enough reconcile this with the more empirical position found in the aforementioned texts, by pointing out that we use sensory perception in order to build up to intellectual perception. But rather than doing this, al-Kindī argues that we can in many cases have a direct intellectual perception 'without an image'. This occurs even in such cases as geometrical figure, which *seems* to be grasped through the senses, but is in fact perceived intellectually *along with* a sensory image [*51: 21]. This methodological issue relates to the aforementioned three-fold distinction between sciences dealing with immaterial things, with immaterial things connected with bodies, and with corporeal things. The example of figure would seem to suggest that, in the case of intermediate sciences like mathematics and psychology, the appropriate method is intellectual rather than empirical (see further Adamson 2007 [*115: 27–35], 2007 [*157: 351–370]).

As we know from the list of his books preserved in the *Fihrist* of Ibn al-Nadīm (cf. McCarthy 1962 [*4]), al-Kindī wrote extensively on the subject of logic. In addition to general introductions to logic, he composed works that, judging by their titles, must have been closely based on the *Isagoge* of Porphyry, the *Categories* and the *Sophistical Refutations*. These works are unfortunately lost, but we can see from the extant corpus how much attention al-Kindī devoted to the *Organon*, especially the first several works (this is unsurprising since we know that in the preceding Syriac tradition, it was standard to study Aristotelian logic only as far as *Prior Analytics* I 7 (Gutas 1999 [*154: 155–193. 181–184]). For instance, al-Kindī discusses the logical works in greater depth than any other part of the Aristotelian corpus in *On the Quantity of Aristotle's Books*. He also, rather more surprisingly, makes use of the *Categories* to prove the immortality of the soul [*61], and uses the *Isagoge* to refute the Christian doctrine of the Trinity [*53].

This latter text is preserved only thanks to a counter-refutation written by the Christian philosopher Yaḥyā Ibn ʿAdī (cf. Adamson 2007 [*115: 41–42], Schöck 2011 [*206: 350]). It provides an interesting insight into the cultural context of al-Kindī's work and his willingness to press logical texts into service in theological contexts. The strategy of this very short work [*53: 123–127] is to consider whether the Persons of the Trinity proposed by the Christians could be understood as any of the Porphyrian predicables, i.e. as genera, species, differentiae, etc. In each case al-Kindī concludes that such an understanding would imply multiplicity in the divine essence and (in an inference which here goes unexplained) compromise God's eternity. There are strong parallels between this reasoning and the arguments in *On First Philosophy* which rule out the application of the Porphyrian predicables to God, the 'true One.' Regarding the cultural context, al-Kindī remarks that he uses the *Isagoge* because it is well-known to his Christian opponents. This is a rare confirmation internal to the Kindian corpus of something we could have inferred from our knowledge of his translation circle: al-Kindī was very familiar with the intellectual world of his Christian contemporaries. Of course, some of his closest collaborators (the translators whose work he oversaw) were Christians. His refutation of the Trinity shows that this did not prevent him from forthrightly attacking their theological doctrines.

As already stated, al-Kindī seems to have followed the Christians in restricting his attention largely to the first four works of the *Organon*. He certainly was aware of the rest of the *Organon* – indeed, as we have seen he wrote works related to the *Sophistical Refutations*, which constitutes an exception to his general focus on the earlier portion of the logical corpus. But al-Kindī makes little use of the *Posterior Analytics*, which will be such a central text in the philosophical formation of al-Fārābī (Adamson 2007 [*157]). Certainly al-Kindī is aware that the sciences should build upon one another in a systematic way. In a meteorological work [*128], he speaks of an ordered progress through the sciences, culminating in theology [*26: II 92]; cf. *On the Quantity of Aristotle's Books* [*26: I 384] and Cortabarría Beitia 1972 [*146: 49–76]. However, we get no detailed account of how, for instance, physics might be a science subordinated to psychology and metaphysics, a preoccupation of later Aristotelian thinkers such as al-Fārābī and Ibn Rušd.

5.2 *Propaedeutic Ethics*

Al-Kindī's output on practical philosophy is largely lost (numerous works are listed in the *Fihrist*, but no longer extant). His most significant work in this area is *Risāla fī l-Ḥīla li-dafʿ al-aḥzān* (*On the Method of How to Dispel Sorrow*) (cf. Ritter, Walzer 1938 [*161], Butterworth 1992 [*165], Druart 1993 [*166]). This treatise consists largely of practical ethical advice, for instance, reminding us to consider the greater misfortunes of others when we undergo misfortune ourselves. A long and striking passage develops a metaphor first found in Epictetus, comparing our earthly life to a temporary disembarkation from a ship [*45: § XI]. Those who are overly concerned with physical possessions and pleasures in this life are like people who stay away from the ship too long, and are punished by getting uncomfortable seats (or no place at all) on the long journey home. The philosophically unchallenging nature of this text suggests that it is 'propaedeutic', that is, a work that can and even should be read prior to any serious philosophical study (esp. Druart 1993 [*166]: 340). On the other hand, the work does begin with some sweeping claims to the effect that the 'world of the intellect' has greater value than this world, which may suggest some appeal to doctrines from al-Kindī's psychological treatises or the Arabic translations of Neoplatonic works (Adamson 2007 [*115: 153–154]).

Indeed, the Neoplatonic works translated in al-Kindī's circle (that is, at least part of the *Enneads* of Plotinus and the *Elements of Theology* of Proclus) seem to have exerted a strong influence on al-Kindī's ethical thought, as well as other areas of his philosophy. As in Plotinus, the 'world of the intellect', i.e. the realm of the intelligibles, constitutes the goal of Kindian ethics. This is shown by al-Kindī's *al-Qawl fī l-Nafs* (*Discourse on the Soul*), which invokes the authority of Plato, Pythagoras and Aristotle to support a psychological doctrine which looks strikingly similar to the one we find in the Neoplatonic translations (this is one of al-Kindī's most thoroughly researched works; cf. Furlani 1922 [*221], Walzer 1937 [*222], Ramón Guerrero 1982 [*232], Genequand 1987–1988 [*235], D'Ancona 1996 [*238], Jolivet 1996 [*239], Adamson 2000 [*241]). The central doctrine of the soul as a 'separate, immaterial substance' which should turn away from the body and towards the world of intellect is straightforwardly Neoplatonic. However, we find traces of a stronger link with Plato himself in a passage dealing with the three parts of the soul (even invoking Plato's proof from *Republic* IV that the soul must have more than one aspect, since it can be in tension with itself). Hermetic and Pythagorean sources have also been detected, e.g. in a passage which states that post-mortem the soul becomes associated with the heavenly bodies (cf. Genequand 1987–1988 [*235]).

Although *Discourse on the Soul* is clearly a work on psychology, it can also be understood as primarily ethical in character. Like *On the Method of How to Dispel Sorrow*, it emphasizes that the soul is an immaterial substance which must direct its focus to the 'world of the intellect,' and measure our ethical development in terms of our engagement with intelligibles rather than objects of sense perception. Likewise, both supplement this doctrine with material apparently drawn from disparate Greek sources. One authority cited in *On the Method of How to Dispel Sorrow* is Socrates, about whom we hear two brief anecdotes that also appear in al-Kindī's gnomological compilation *Risāla fī Alfāẓ Suqrāṭ* (*On the Sayings of Socrates*) (on this see further Adamson 2007 [*115]). Al-Kindī's Socrates is, generally speaking, a supporter of the same ascetic and intellectualist ethics we find in *On the Method of How to Dispel Sorrow* and *Discourse on the Soul*.

5.3 *Metaphysics*

The only partially extant *On First Philosophy* was probably considered by al-Kindī himself to be his most important work: he dedicated it to the caliph al-Muʿtaṣim, and seems to have incorporated smaller epistles into this longer treatise. It is now al-Kindī's best-known work, and is devoted to the subject of metaphysics, hence the title: 'on first philosophy.' But an alternate title is attested: *Fī l-Tawḥīd* (*On Oneness*), and this title captures the goals of the treatise as well. For al-Kindī, philosophy is the study of causes, so that first philosophy is the study of God, the First Cause. But before turning to God, al-Kindī begins by arguing against the eternity of the world. Though this is never explicitly linked to the following, more explicitly theological, discussion, presumably al-Kindī has in mind that the world's non-eternity implies the need for a creating cause. This inference is drawn more explicitly in *Risāla fī* [*l-ibāna ʿan*] *Waḥdāniyyat Allāh wa-tanāhī ǧirm al-ʿālam* (*On the Oneness of God and the Finiteness of Body of the Universe*), one of the short works whose arguments are partially paralleled by the eternity section of *On First Philosophy*.

The arguments against the eternity of the world draw on both Aristotle and Aristotle's fierce critic, John Philoponus. From Aristotle, al-Kindī takes the idea that the body of the cosmos cannot be infinite. Aristotle meant by this only that the cosmos is of finite spatial magnitude. But al-Kindī infers that it is also of finite temporal magnitude: for time is an attribute of body, and if the cosmos' body is finite, so must be each of its attributes. To reinforce this conclusion he appeals to an argument found also in Philoponus, namely that an eternal world *a parte ante* would commit us to an actual (not merely potential) infinity, because an actually infinite number of moments would already have elapsed by now.

This issue of the world's eternity might seem to belong to the realm of physics rather than metaphysics: it is indeed treated by Aristotle in the *Physics* and *On the Heavens*. But al-Kindī's use of the axiomatic, 'purely intellectual' approach announced at the beginning of section two of *On First Philosophy* already suggests that he thinks it can be settled with the more abstract method used by the metaphysician. This is confirmed by the fact that elsewhere, al-Kindī is happy to concede that the heavens are made of a 'fifth element' which is indestructible by nature. Whereas Philoponus went to great lengths to refute this in his *Against Aristotle on the Eternity of the World*, al-Kindī blithely states that this 'indestructible' nature persists only as long as God permits (see *Risāla fī l-Ibāna ʿan anna ṭabīʿat al-falak muḫālifa li-ṭabāʾiʿ al-ʿanāṣir al-arbaʿa* [*On the Nature of the Celestial Sphere*]).

As for God Himself, His existence is proven in *On First Philosophy* not only implicitly by the fact that the world is created, by also explicitly on the basis that created things are always both multiple and unified, and thus stand in need of an external cause of their unity. This cause will be purely one, as the source of the unity, and hence being, of each created thing. In this context al-Kindī gives the impression that God directly creates each thing. But in a very brief work, possibly a fragment, headed *On the True, First, Complete Agent* (*Risāla fī l-Fāʿil al-ḥaqq al-awwal al-tāmm*), we are told that God is the Creator of only one thing 'without an intermediary,' and mediately the Creator of all other things. However, this text and *On First Philosophy* agree in contrasting God to creation in similar terms: God is 'truly' one and an agent, whereas created things are only 'metaphorically' one and agents. The reasoning is also parallel: that which is both one and many is only 'metaphorically' one; that which is both agent and acted upon is only 'metaphorically' an agent.

Apart from the influence of Philoponus in the arguments against the world's eternity, the dominant sources for al-Kindī's metaphysical thought were Neoplatonists and of course Aristotle himself. A good example is the just mentioned *On the True Agent*, which speaks of a single immediate effect of God which gives rise to further effects, and thus seems to endorse the stepwise emanation theory found in the Neoplatonic works produced in his circle (cf. D'Ancona 1992 [*197]). On the other hand one could also understand this in a more Aristotelian way: perhaps the immediate effect of God is the heavens or their motion, which become a cause for the further effects we see below the sphere of the moon (this would bring the little treatise into line with *On the Proximate Agent Cause of Generation and Corruption, Kitāb al-Ibāna ʿan al-ʿilla al-fāʿila al-qarība li-l-kawn wa-l-fasād*). A similar fusion of Aristotelianism and Neoplatonism occurs towards the end of *On First Philosophy*. There, al-Kindī distinguishes the true One from intellect, as Plotinus would. He even remarks, in a very Plotinian passage which however seems rather tentative: 'One may suppose that it [sc. the intellect] is the first multiple, and that it is unified in some way, since it is a whole, as we have said; and that 'one' is said of the whole. But unity in truth is not intellect' [*51: 87]. Yet he also makes sure to show how the same doctrine of God's unity can prove that God is an unmoved mover, that is, He is Himself incorporeal and immune to change, but the source of all change and spatiotemporal motion [*51: 97].

5.4 *Soul and Intellect*

Neoplatonic influence is also apparent in al-Kindī's psychological works. In his view the soul is an immaterial substance; in *That There are Incorporeal*

Substances (*Risāla fī annahu* [*tūǧad*] *ǧawāhir lā-aǧsām*), he argues for this by assimilating soul to the species of Aristotle's *Categories*. While that rather dubious tactic (on which Adamson, Pormann 2009 [*243]) does not appear in other psychological works, he remains consistently committed to the idea that the soul is a substance in its own right, which can survive the death of the body. This is the central theme of the doxographic *Discourse on the Soul*, which describes a broad agreement among ancient philosophers (Pythagoras, Plato, Aristotle) regarding the nature of the soul as a 'divine, immaterial substance'. The same doctrine is presupposed by al-Kindī's discussion of the Platonic theme of recollection (ἀνάμνησις; see Endress 1986 [*234], 1994 [*237]). This work, which takes up a problem found in the Arabic Plotinus, accepts that the soul not only lives on after the death of the body, but also that it already existed before embodiment, in the 'world of the intellect'. This 'world of the intellect' is another prominent theme in al-Kindī's work and as mentioned above, often appears in ethical contexts, where al-Kindī exhorts his reader to turn away from bodily things and towards the intelligible realm.

The same treatise on recollection shows that al-Kindī was, at least sometimes, sceptical about the prospect of achieving intellection on the basis of sense-experience. He argues (as did Plato in the *Phaedo*) that sensation can only prompt us to remember intelligibles, not bring us to grasp them for the first time. We have already seen that al-Kindī gives conflicting signals about the role of sense perception in various works (cf. pp. 191–192 above). He is never more pessimistic about this role than in his discussion of recollection. Obviously he is here influenced by the Platonic tradition. The question of the treatise is what we remember in this life about our pre-existence in the world of intellect, and what we will remember there after death about the life we led here. This can be traced directly to a passage in the Arabic Plotinus (the opening of the second chapter or *mīmar*, in turn based on *Enneads* IV 4,1). Yet al-Kindī builds upon his sources, for instance by giving a clever argument to undermine our conviction that we are learning rather than remembering: usually, when one remembers one can recall the circumstances (e.g. time and place) where the remembered event occurred. But when one remembers intelligible existence, there are no such physical circumstances to call to mind.

When we do achieve intellection, this occurs according to the process laid out in al-Kindī's *On the Intellect* (*Risāla fī l-ʿAql*, cf. Jolivet 1971 [*227], Endress 1980 [*229]). It is the first Arabic work to describe a four-fold scheme of types of intellect, as will later be found in al-Fārābī and Ibn Sīnā. The so-called 'first intellect' is outside the human soul, and is always actual. It has within it all the intelligible forms, and the soul needs to come into contact with this first intellect in order to actualize its own potential for intellection. When this occurs, the human soul passes from the state of 'potential intellect' to that of 'acquired intellect': in al-Kindī, but not in other authors, this phrase means that one has access to the relevant intelligible and can attain it at will. Whenever one actively thinks about an intelligible object, one is in the state of 'active intellect.' Thus the four intellects are: the first intellect which transcends the human soul; and then three states of the human intellect, namely potential, acquired, and actual. These latter three correspond to the Aristotelian levels of first potentiality, second potentiality or first actuality, and second actuality.

Al-Kindī also pays some attention to lower psychological functions, such as would later be grouped by Ibn Sīnā under the rubric of 'internal senses.' We do not find anything quite so systematic in al-Kindī, although in a musical work he associates the four strings of the oud with four psychological capacities which, he says, are situated 'in the head': cognition, imagination, retention and memory, where the last two are not clearly distinguished (cf. Adamson 2007 [*115: 142]).

For more on the imagination, we may turn to al-Kindī's treatise *On Sleep and Dream* (*Risāla fī Māhiyyat al-nawm wa-l-ru'yā*). In this case, it is sensible objects which are to be grasped, rather than intelligible forms – albeit sensible objects which may be in the future. When the soul ceases to use its external senses in sleep, the imagination is able to receive sensible forms of things which are yet to happen. This happens particularly for those whose souls are pure – note that this process of purification is emphasized in both this context of prophetic dreams and in ethical works. If the soul is not completely pure it may see what will occur only in a symbolic way – for instance, a dream about flying may signify a journey – or even by forming an image which is the opposite of what will really happen. This treatise, which draws heavily on an Arabic version of Aristotle's *Parva Naturalia*, also gives a physical account of the mechanism of sleep (cf. Hansberger 2008 [*242: 50–77]).

All the lower psychological functions – sensation, imagination, and related activities such as dreaming – are realized through the soul's connection to body. When unconnected with body, the soul obviously engages solely in intellection. Al-Kindī's eschatological teaching, however, is somewhat murky. Only when he is discussing the theory of recollection does he give the impression of holding that the soul exists *before* its bodily existence, and here one may suspect that he is simply reiterating what he finds in his Plotinian source. On the other hand, unlike Ibn Sīnā al-Kindī gives us no reason why a given soul should have a unique relationship with only one body. In *Discourse on the Soul*, the soul is simply said to come as a 'substance from the substance of the Creator, as light comes from the light of the sun' [*62: 273] – which looks Neoplatonic but does not actually imply that the soul has an existence prior to its embodiment. As for post-mortem existence, this same work invokes Plato for the aforementioned idea that the soul reaches successive spheres of the heavens in a process of purification, before it arrives beyond the spheres in the world of the intellect [*62: 278]. But elsewhere he heaps scorn on the idea that the soul could ever unite with a heavenly body, and explicitly denies that this is Plato's view, since it is unworthy of him [*62: 281–2].

5.5 *Physics and Cosmology*

Al-Kindī's works on natural philosophy emphasize above all the nature and role of the heavenly bodies (cf. Adamson 2007 [*115: 181–206]). Regarding their nature, he argues in *On the Nature of the Celestial Sphere* (cf. p. 171 above) that the heavenly spheres are constituted from a different substance than the four elements. The elements are characterized by rectilinear motion, which has a contrary; thus the elements are corruptible. By contrast, the heavens move in circular fashion, and circular motion has no contrary, so that the heavens are indestructible. All this is faithful to Aristotle and indeed closely based on Aristotle's *On the Heavens*. But whereas John Philoponus had argued forcefully that the heavens are in fact made of the same elements as the sublunary world, in order to avoid Aristotle's conclusion that the heavens (and hence the whole cosmos) are eternal, al-Kindī simply assumes that the 'incorruptible' nature of the heavens merely guarantees their existence for as long as God wills. Thus the original Aristotelian theory is reinterpreted.

Because of the natural motions of the four sublunary elements and the heavens, the cosmos basically consists of five concentric spheres: the heavens surrounding the spheres of fire, air, water and earth. (This is proven geometrically in *That the [Four] Elements and the Outermost Body are Spherical in Form, Risāla fī anna l-ʿanāṣir wa-l-ǧirm al-aqṣā kuriyyat al-šakl.*) The fact that the sublunary elements do not remain as discrete concentric spheres is explained by the influence of the heavens, which impose varying degrees of heat and cold upon the places below them. This results in the transformation and mixture of the sublunary elements, which in turn yields the compound substances of our world. Al-Kindī's fullest treatment of his cosmology, *On the Proximate Agent Cause of Generation and Corruption*, makes clear that the heavens are the cause in question. The 'remote' cause is God, insofar as He directs heavenly motion with His providence. That thesis is further developed and explained in *On the Prostration of the Outermost Sphere* (cf. p. 171 above), which further adds that the heavenly spheres are endowed with rational souls, as well as the capacity for vision and hearing.

Although these Aristotelian cosmological works make no explicit allusion to the science of astrology, they do provide the scientific rationale for that science. Al-Kindī wrote numerous astrological works, describing how the stars indicate specific events like the duration of the political reign of the Arabs, the crisis in a medical illness, or the location of a treasure (cf. Loth 1875 [*351], Bos 1990 [*388], Burnett, Yamamoto, Yano 1997 [*375]). Closely related to these works are his treatises on astrological weather forecasting (Bos, Burnett 2000 [*365]). We can see how these astrological texts connect to the cosmological discussions mentioned above, if we consider the numerous extant works al-Kindī devoted to non-astrological treatments of meteorological phenomena. These explain how the heavenly motions give range to such phenomena as fog, rain and other precipitation. The astrological works on meteorology then show how one can make detailed predictions about the effects of heavenly motions. They are also in harmony with *On the Proximate Agent Cause of Generation and Corruption* in explaining the heavenly influence as the result of friction between the celestial and subcelestial spheres. Thus al-Kindī's corpus as a whole gives us an unusually detailed account of how astrology could be integrated into a fundamentally Aristotelian framework. (In this he is followed by Abū Maʿšar al-Balḫī; cf. Adamson 2002 [*357].)

Another text, which is harder to fit into such an account, is *On Rays* (*Fī* [*Maṭraḥ*] *al-šuʿāʿ*), a magical treatise ascribed to al-Kindī and preserved only in Latin under the title *De radiis*. *On Rays* proposes an ambitious general theory to explain not only how the stars affect the sublunary world, but also how talismans and magical utterances give rise to their supposed effects. More mundane phenomena like colours and sounds are also discussed. In each case, the mechanism invoked is 'rays,' which allow these substances to act at a distance. The divergence between this account and the theory based on friction in the more Aristotelian works may suggest that *On Rays* is not authentic, but it has been pointed out that there are correspondences between the ray theory of *De Radiis* and al-Kindī's works on optics (Travaglia 1999 [*376]).

5.6 *Mathematical Sciences*

Optics were a major interest for al-Kindī, and he wrote a number of treatises on the subject, ranging from a general treatment of the mechanisms of vision, *On Perspectives* (*Risāla fī ʿIlal iḫtilāf al-manāẓir*, Lat. *De Aspectibus*) to more specific works on such topics as mirrors (Rashed 1997 [*301]). In addition there are a pair of Aristotelian works on the subject of colour. One of these presents the claim that of the four sublunary elements, it is only earth that gives rise to colour; different colours result from the admixture of earth into other elemental bodies. The other applies this theory to the case of the sky, which is said to be blue because of earthy and watery exhalations in the atmosphere. There is a connection here to al-Kindī's works on optics, insofar as both postulate the need for a body to be 'dense' in order to intercept vision. But whereas the works on colour are within the Aristotelian tradition, the optical treatises follow such authors as Euclid and Theon of Alexandria (possibly also Ptolemy). His theory supposes that we see when rays emitted from the eye strike illuminated bodies (on the theory and its relation to the works on colour, see Adamson 2006 [*302]).

This is only one area where al-Kindī's mathematical interests were applied to the natural sciences. In addition to several works on pure mathematics (see e.g. Rashed 1993 [*271]) he wrote a treatise on medicines, which tries to establish the arithmetical relationships that underlie the heat, coldness, dryness and moistness of drugs compounded from simple ingredients. This treatise is grounded in medical theories of the Greeks, for example Galen; but al-Kindī emphasizes his own originality in discussing the problem of compound, as well as simple, drugs (cf. Gauthier [*155], Langermann 2003 [*389]). It is striking that al-Kindī thinks that the relationships underlying the intensity of a compound drug can be settled not on empirical grounds, but rather on *a priori* grounds having to do with the primacy of certain ratios.

This betrays Pythagorean commitments that are more evident still in his musical treatises, which for instance establish a correspondence between the four strings of the oud and a range of other four-fold phenomena, like the humours of the body and the seasons of the year (see Adamson 2007 [*115: 174–175] and more generally on music in al-Kindī, Shehadi 1995 [*340: 15–33]). Because it is a mathematical science, al-Kindī considers music to occupy an intermediate position in the hierarchy of sciences (Endress 2003 [*274]: 130, quoting *On Sounding Instruments with One to Ten Strings, Kitāb al-Muṣawwitāt al-watariyya* [*105]). For him, musical theory is thus a study of the proportions which inhere in bodies, for instance the proportions between the lengths of the string on the oud – like psychology or geometry, though, the science of music can abstract these proportions and consider them as such. It is for this reason that, in a work like *On the Informative Parts of Music* (*Risāla fī Aǧzāʾ ḫabariyya fī l-mūsīqī* [*106], transl. in Farmer 1956 [*331]), al-Kindī is able to draw parallels and even a causal connection between, say, the strings of a musical instrument and the humours of the body. In both cases we have a physical object instantiating a four-fold mathematical relationship (four strings on the oud, four humours in the body).

For a treatise applying Pythagorean ideas to cosmology, one can turn to his *The Reason Why the Ancients Related the Five Geometrical Figures to the Elements* (*Risāla fī l-Sabab allaḏī* [*lahu*] *nasabat al-qudamāʾ al-aškāl al-ḫamsa ilā l-usṭuqussāt*, which explains why the 'ancients', in other words Plato, associated the five Platonic solids with the four sublunary elements and the heavens (cf. Baffioni 1984 [*338]). Al-Kindī avoids the sort of geometrical atomism we find in the *Timaeus*; in fact we know from the list of his works in the *Fihrist* that he wrote against atomic theories, presumably those current in *kalām* authors. Instead, al-Kindī explains the relationship between the Platonic solids and the elements by invoking complex geometrical and numerological analysis. For instance, earth is associated by Plato with the cube. The cube has six sides and six is a perfect number (that is, it is equal to the sum of its divisors: 1+2+3). This represents earth's stability and density. It is somewhat startling to note that this sort of symbolic theory accounts for a feature of earth – its 'density' – which in much more naturalistic contexts accounts for earth's role in producing colour, as we have mentioned. Similarly, we find in this treatise an allusion to astrological concepts, which is rare in al-Kindī's non-astrological writings: he says that the dodecahedron is appropriately associated with the heaven, which is divided into the twelve signs of the zodiac.

6 Secondary Literature

6.1 Bibliography and Works of Reference [*1–*8] – 6.2 Biography [*11–*30] – 6.3 Terminology [*36] – 6.4 Textual Transmission of al-Kindī's Works [*41–*44] – 6.5 His Sources, Including Translations from Greek [*51–*93] – 6.6 Introductions and Overviews to al-Kindī in the Context of Arabic Philosophy [*101–*117] – 6.7 Influence [*125–*130] – 6.8 Individual Works. Doctrine: Introductions to Philosophy [*140–*158]; Propaedeutic Ethics [*161–*171]; Metaphysics [*181–*206]; Soul and Intellect [*221–*243]; Physics and Cosmology [*251–*257]; Mathematical Sciences [*271–*277]; Arithmetic [*281]; Geometry [*286]; Optics [*295–*302]; Astronomy [*315–*320]; Music [*331–*343]; Astrology [*351–*357]; Astrometeorology and Meteorology [*361–*365]; Magic [*371–*376]; Medicine and Pharmacology [*381–*389]; Various Works on Natural Philosophy [*402–*403] – 6.9 Influence on Abū Maʿšar [*411–*412]

6.1 *Bibliography and Works of Reference*

1 Rescher, Oskar. "Notizen über einige arabische Handschriften aus Brussaer Bibliotheken." *Zeitschrift der Deutschen Morgenländischen Gesellschaft* 68 (1914): 47–63.

2 GAL = Carl Brockelmann: Geschichte der arabischen Litteratur, 2 vols; 3 suppl. vols. Leiden 1937–1949 (2nd ed.). – Edition adapted to the supplement volumes.

3 Carmody, Francis J. *Arabic Astronomical and Astrological Sciences in Latin Translation*. Berkeley, 1956, 78–85.

4 McCarthy, Richard Joseph. *Al-taṣānīf al-mansūba ilā faylasūf al-ʿArab: Baḥṯ bi-munāsabat iḥtifāl Baġdād wa-l-Kindī*. Baghdad, 1382/1962.

5 Ullmann, Manfred. *Die Medizin im Islam*. Leiden, 1970.

6 GAS = Fuat Sezgin. *Geschichte des arabischen Schrifttums … bis ca. 430 H.*, vol. 3: *Medizin, Pharmazie, Zoologie, Tierheilkunde*. Leiden, 1970; vol. 5: *Mathematik*. Leiden, 1974, 255–259; vol. 6: *Astronomie*. Leiden, 1978; vol. 7: *Astrologie, Meteorologie und Verwandtes*. Leiden, 1979.

7 DPhA = *Dictionnaire des philosophes antiques*. Ed. Richard Goulet, 1 ff. and Supplément. Paris, 1989 ff.

8 Daiber, Hans. *Bibliography of Islamic Philosophy*, vol. 2. Leiden, 1999, 346–354 (Index s.v. Kindī). – Supplement vol. (2007): 380–382.

6.2 *Biography*

11 Flügel, Gustav. *Al-Kindî genannt der Philosoph der Araber, ein Vorbild seiner Zeit und seines Volkes*. Leipzig, 1857.

12 Hauser, Friedrich. *Über das kitâb al ḥijal – das Werk über die sinnreichen Anordnungen – der Benû Mûsâ*. Erlangen, 1922, 185–188.

13 ʿAbd al-Rāziq, Muṣṭafā. "Abū Yūsuf Yaʿqūb b. Isḥāq al-Kindī." *al-Ǧāmiʿa al-Miṣriyya, Maǧallat Kulliyyat al-ādāb* (Cairo 1933): 107–148.

14 Rosenthal, Franz. "Al-Kindî als Literat." *Orientalia* N.S. 11 (1942): 262–288.

15 Rosenthal, Franz. *Aḥmad b. aṭ-Ṭayyib as-Saraḫsî*. New Haven, Conn., 1943.

16 Lecomte, Gérard. "Muḥammad b. al-Ǧahm, gouverneur philosophe." *Arabica* 5 (1958): 263–271.

17 van Riet, Simone. "Le millénaire de Bagdad et d'al-Kindi." *Revue philosophique de Louvain* 61 ([1962] 1963): 111–115.

18 Rescher, Nicholas. *Al-Kindī, an Annotated Bibliography*. Pittsburgh, 1964.

19 Sagadeev, Artur Vladimirovič. "Novye publikatsii traktatov al-Kindi." *Narody Azii i Afriki* (1964): 168–178.

20 Hamarneh, Sami Khalaf. "Al-Kindī, a Ninth-Century Physician, Philosopher, and Scholar." *Medical History* 9 (1965): 328–342.

21 Dagorn, René. "L'histoire d'al-Kindî, extraite du *Kitâb al-buhalâʾ* d'al-Ǧâḥiẓ." *Revue de l'Institut des belles lettres arabes* 38 (1975): 281–298. – Includes the Arabic text.

22 Martin, M. A. "Abu Yusuf Ya`qub al-Kindi (801–873)." In *The Genius of Arab Civilization: Source of Renaissance*. Ed. by John R. Hayes. London, 1983 (2nd ed.), 68–69.

23 Endress, Gerhard. "Die wissenschaftliche Literatur." In *Grundriss der arabischen Philologie,* vol. 2: *Literaturwissenschaft.* Ed. by Wolfdietrich Fischer and Helmut Gätje. Wiesbaden, 1987, 400–506; vol. 3: Supplement. Wiesbaden, 1992, 3–152.

24 Lecomte, Gérard. "Muḥammad ibn al-Djahm." In EI^2 VII (1991) s.v.

25 Butterworth, Charles E. "Al-Kindī." In *Great Thinkers of the Eastern World: The Major Thinkers and the Philosophical and Religious Classics of China, India, Japan.* Ed. by Ian P. McGreal. New York, 1995, 439–442.

26 Lemay, Richard, ed. *Abū Maʿšar al-Balḫī* [Albumasar], *Kitāb al-Mudḫal al-kabīr ilā ʿilm aḥkām al-nuǧūm = Liber introductorii maioris ad scientiam judiciorum astrorum,* 9 vols. Naples, 1995.

27 Klein-Franke, Felix. "Al-Kindī." In *History of Islamic Philosophy,* vol. 1. Ed by Seyyed Hossein Nasr and Oliver Leaman. London, 1996, 165–177.

28 Rudolph, Ulrich. "Abū-Yūsuf Yaʿqūb Ibn-Isḥāq al-Kindī." In *Großes Werklexikon der Philosophie,* vol. 1. Ed by Franco Volpi. Stuttgart, 1999; 2004, 835–837.

29 Travaglia, Pinella. *Magic, Causality and Intentionality: The Doctrine of Rays in al-Kindī.* Florence, 1999, 121–130. – Includes a list of works.

30 Endress, Gerhard. "Höfischer Stil und wissenschaftliche Rhetorik: Al-Kindī als Epistolograph." In *Islamic Philosophy, Science, Culture, and Religion: Studies in Honor of Dimitri Gutas.* Ed by Felicitas Opwis and David Reisman. Leiden, Boston, 2011, 289–306.

6.3 *Terminology*

36 Ǧihāmī, Ǧirār [Gérard Jéhamy]. *Mawsūʿat muṣṭalaḥāt al-Kindī wa-l-Fārābī.* Beirut, 2002.

6.4 *Textual Transmission of al Kindī's Works*

41 Ritter, Hellmut and Martin Plessner. "Schriften Jaʿqūb ibn Isḥāq al-Kindī's in Stambuler Bibliotheken." *Archiv Orientální* 4 (1932): 363–372.

42 Rosenthal, Franz. "From Arabic Books and Manuscripts, II: Kindiana." *Journal of the American Oriental Society* 69 (1949): 149–152.

43 Rosenthal, Franz. "From Arabic Books and Manuscripts, VI: Istanbul Materials for al-Kindî and as-Saraḫsî." *Journal of the American Oriental Society* 76 (1956): 27–31.

44 d'Alverny, Marie-Thérèse. "Kindiana." *Archives d'histoire doctrinale et littéraire du moyen âge* 47 (1980): 277–287.

6.5 His Sources, Including Translations from Greek

51 Rosenthal, Franz. "On the Knowledge of Plato's Philosophy in the Islamic World." *Islamic Culture* 14 (1940): 387–422.

52 Kutsch, Wilhelm. "Ein arabisches Bruchstück aus Porphyrios (?) περὶ ψυχῆς." *Mélanges de l'Université Saint-Joseph* 31 (1954): 265–286.

53 Walzer, Richard. *Greek into Arabic: Essays on Islamic Philosophy*. Oxford, 1962; Cambridge, Mass., 1963 (2nd ed.).

54 Faḫrī, Māǧid [Majid Fakhry]. "Al-Kindī wa-Suqrāṭ." *Al-Abḥāṯ* 16 (1963): 23–24. – Also in: M. Faḫrī, *Dirāsāt fī l-fikr al-ʿarabī*. Beirut, 1977 (2nd ed.), 40–50.

55 Moosa, Matti I. "Al-Kindī's Role in the Transmission of Greek Knowledge to the Arabs." *Journal of the Pakistan Historical Society* 15 (1967): 1–18.

56 Caspar, Robert and Pier Paolo Ruffinengo. "De l'art d'utiliser avec reconnaissance les cultures étrangères, selon al-Kindi, le 'philosophe' (IXe siècle)." *Revue de l'Institut des belles lettres arabes* 31 (Tunis 1968): 295–299.

57 Davidson, Herbert Alan. "John Philoponus as a Source of Medieval Islamic and Jewish Proofs of Creation." *Journal of the American Oriental Society* 89 (1969) 357–391.

58 Allard, Michel. "Comment al-Kindī a-t-il lu les philosophes grecs?" *Mélanges de l'Université Saint-Joseph* 46 (1970–1971): 451–465.

59 Bürgel, Johann Christoph. "A New Arabic Quotation from Plato's *Phaido* and Its Relation to a Persian Version of the *Phaido*." In *IV congresso de estudos árabes e islâmicos, 1968: Actas*. Leiden, 1971, 281–290.

60 Ivry, Alfred L. "Al-Kindi as Philosopher: The Aristotelian and Neoplatonic Dimensions." In *Islamic Philosophy and the Classical Tradition: Essays Presented… to Richard Walzer on His Seventieth Birthday*. Ed by Samuel Miklos Stern, Albert Hourani and Vivian Brown. Oxford, 1972, 117–139.

61 Endress, Gerhard. *Proclus Arabus: Zwanzig Abschnitte aus der Institutio theologica in arabischer Übersetzung*, eingeleitet, herausgegeben und erklärt. Beirut, Wiesbaden, 1973.

62 Jolivet, Jean. "Pour le dossier du Proclus arabe: Al-Kindī et la Théologie platonicienne." *Studia Islamica* 49 (1979): 55–75.

63 Hein, Christel. *Definition und Einteilung der Philosophie: Von der spätantiken Einleitungsliteratur zur arabischen Enzyklopädie*. Frankfurt a.M., Bern, New York, 1985.

64 Daiber, Hans. "Die Kritik des Ibn Ḥazm an Kindīs Metaphysik [nebst] Anhang: Die Auszüge des Ibn Ḥazm aus Kindīs *al-Falsafa l-ūlā* [sic]." *Der Islam* 63 (1986) 284–302.

65 Zimmermann, Friedrich W. "The Origins of the So-Called *Theology of Aristotle*." In *Pseudo-Aristotle in the Middle Ages: The Theology and Other Texts*. Ed. by Jill Kraye, William Francis Ryan and Charles B. Schmitt. London, 1986, 110–240.

66 Tardieu, Michel. "Ṣābiens coraniques et 'Ṣābiens' de Ḥarrān." *Journal asiatique* 274 (1986): 1–44.

67 Tardieu, Michel. "Simplicius et les calendriers de Ḥarrān d'après les sources arabes et le commentaire de Simplicius à la Physique d'Aristote." In *Simplicius, sa vie, son œuvre, sa survie*. Ed. by Ilsetraut Hadot. Berlin, 1987, 40–57.

68 Gutas, Dimitri. "Plato's Symposion in the Arabic Tradition." *Oriens* 31 (1988): 36–60.

69 Aouad, Maroun. "La Théologie d'Aristote et autres textes du Plotinus Arabus." In DPhA [*7: I 541–590].

70 Rudolph, Ulrich. *Die Doxographie des Pseudo-Ammonios: Ein Beitrag zur neuplatonischen Überlieferung im Islam*. Stuttgart, 1989.

71 Alon, Ilai. *Socrates in Medieval Arabic Literature*. Leiden, 1991.

72 D'Ancona, Cristina. "Per un profilo filosofico dell'autore della Teologia di Aristotele." *Medioevo* 17 (1991): 83–134.

73 Zimmermann, Friedrich W. "Proclus Arabus Rides Again." *Arabic Sciences and Philosophy* 4 (1994): 9–51.

74 Alon, Ilai. *Socrates Arabus, Life and Teachings: Sources, Translations, Notes*. Jerusalem, 1995.

75 D'Ancona, Cristina. *Recherches sur le Liber de Causis*. Paris, 1995.

76 Endress, Gerhard. "The Circle of al-Kindī: Early Arabic Translations from the Greek and the Rise of Islamic Philosophy." In *The Ancient Tradition in Christian and Islamic Hellenism: Studies on the Transmission of Greek Philosophy and Sciences, Dedicated to H. J. Drossaart Lulofs on His Ninetieth Birthday*. Ed. by Gerhard Endress and Remke Kruk. Leiden, 1997, 43–76.

77 D'Ancona, Cristina. "L'influence du vocabulaire arabe: 'Causa prima est esse tantum'." In *L'élaboration du vocabulaire philosophique au moyen âge: Actes du colloque international organisé par la SIEPM, Louvain-la-Neuve/Leuven, 12–14 sept. 1998*. Turnhout, 2000, 51–97.

78 Gutas, Dimitri. *Greek Thought, Arabic Culture: The Graeco-Arabic Translation Movement in Baghdad and Early ʿAbbāsid Society (2nd-4th/8th-10th centuries)*. London, 1998.

79 Endress, Gerhard. "The New and Improved Platonic Theology: Proclus Arabus and Arabic Islamic Philosophy." In *Proclus et la théologie platonicienne: Actes du colloque international de Louvain (13–16 mai 1998) en l'honneur de H. D. Saffrey et L. G. Westerink*. Ed. by Alain Philippe Segonds and Carlos G. Steel. Leuven, Paris, 2000, 553–570.

80 Thillet, Pierre and Saleh Oudaimah. "Un nouveau *Liber de Causis*?" *Bulletin d'études orientales* 53–54 (2001–2002): 293–368.
81 D'Ancona, Cristina. *Plotino: La discesa dell'anima nei corpi* (*Enn.* IV 8 [6]): *Plotiniana Arabica* (*pseudo-Teologia di Aristotele, capitoli 1 e 7; 'Detti del Sapiente Greco'*). Padova, 2003.
82 D'Ancona, Cristina and Richard C. Taylor. "Aristote de Stagire, Dubia et spuria: *Liber de Causis*." In DPhA [*7: Supplément (2003): 599–647].
83 Freudenthal, Gad and Tony Lévy. "De Gérase à Bagdad: Ibn Bahrîz, al-Kindî, et leur recension arabe de *l'Introduction arithmétique* de Nicomaque, d'après la version hebraïque de Qalonymos ben Qalonymos d'Arles." In *De Zénon d'Élée à Poincaré: Recueil d'études en hommage à Roshdi Rashed*. Ed. by Régis Morelon and Ahmad Hasnawi. Louvain, Paris, 2004, 479–544.
84 D'Ancona, Cristina. "The Greek Sage, the Pseudo-*Theology of Aristotle* and the Arabic Plotinus." In *Words, Texts and Concepts Cruising the Mediterranean Sea: Studies on the Sources, Contents and Influences of Islamic Civilization and Arabic Philosophy and Science: Dedicated to Gerhard Endress on His Sixty-Fifth Birthday*. Ed. by Rüdiger Arnzen and Jörn Thielmann. Leuven, Paris, Dudley, 2004, 159–176.
85 Adamson, Peter. "Al-Kindī and the Reception of Greek Philosophy." In *The Cambridge Companion to Arabic Philosophy*. Ed. by P. Adamson and Richard Taylor. Cambridge, 2005, 32–51.
86 D'Ancona, Cristina. "Greek into Arabic: Neoplatonism in Translation." In P. Adamson, R. Taylor 2005 [cf. *85] 10–31.
87 Wakelnig, Elvira. *Feder, Tafel, Mensch. Al-ʿĀmirīs Kitāb al-Fuṣūl fī l-Maʿālim al-ilāhīya und die arabische Proklos-Rezeption im 10. Jh*. Leiden, Boston, 2006.
88 Endress, Gerhard. "Building the Library of Arabic Philosophy: Platonism and Aristotelianism in the Sources of al-Kindī." In *The Libraries of the Neoplatonists: Proceedings of the Meeting of the European Science Foundation Network 'Late Antiquity and Arabic Thought: Patterns in the Constitution of European Culture' Held in Strasbourg, March 12–14, 2004*. Ed. by Cristina D'Ancona. Leiden, Boston, 2007, 319–350.
89 Endress, Gerhard. "Proclus, œuvres transmises par la tradition arabe." In DPhA [*7: V s.v. Proclus de Lycie].
90 Adamson, Peter. *The Arabic Plotinus: a Philosophical Study of the "Theology of Aristotle"*. London, 2002.
91 Kheirandish, Elaheh. "The Arabic 'Version' of Euclidean Optics: Transformations as Linguistic Problems in Transmission." In *Tradition, Transmission, Transformation*. Ed. by F. Jamil Ragep and Sally P. Ragep. Leiden, 1996, 227–243.
92 Kheirandish, Elaheh. *The Arabic Version of Euclid's Optics*, 2 vols. New York, 1999.

93 Hansberger, Rotraud. "Plotinus Arabus Rides Again." *Arabic Sciences and Philosophy* 21 (2011): 57–84.

6.6 *Introductions and Overviews to al-Kindī in the Context of Arabic Philosophy*

101 Cabanelas, Dario. "A propósito de un libro sobre la filosofía de al-Kindī." *Verdad y Vida* 10 (Madrid 1952): 257–283. – Review of Abū Rīda, ed., *Rasāʾil al-Kindī al-falsafiyya*, vol. 1. Cairo, 1950.

102 Qumayr, Yūḥannā. *Falāsifat al-ʿArab*, vol. 8: *Al-Kindī*. Beirut, 1954.

103 Walzer, Richard. "New Studies on al-Kindī." *Oriens* 10 (1957): 203–232. – Repr. in: R. Walzer, *Greek into Arabic: Essays on Islamic Philosophy* [*53], 175–205.

104 Altmann, Alexander and Samuel Miklos Stern. *Isaac Israeli: A Neoplatonic Philosopher of the Early Tenth Century*. Oxford, 1958.

105 Atiyeh, George N. *Al-Kindī, the Philosopher of the Arabs*. Rawalpindi, 1966; Delhi, 1994 (2nd ed.).

106 Walzer, Richard. "Early Islamic Philosophy." In *The Cambridge History of Later Greek and Early Medieval Philosophy*. Ed. by Arthur Hilary Armstrong. Cambridge, 1967, 641–669.

107 Cortabarría Beitia, Angel. "A partir de quelles sources étudier al-Kindi?" *Mélanges de l'Institut dominicain d'études orientales du Caire* 10 (1970): 83–108.

108 Walzer, Richard. "L'éveil de la philosophie islamique." *Revue des études islamiques* 38 (1970): 7–42. 207–242, esp. 207–225.

109 Cortabarría Beitia, Angel. "El método de al-Kindī visto a través de sus risālas." *Orientalia Hispanica* (1974): 209–225.

110 Ivry, Alfred L. "Al-Kindī and the Muʿtazila: A Philosophical and Political Reevaluation." *Oriens* 25–26 (1976): 69–85.

111 Pritchett Jackson, David Edward. "Scholarship in Abbasid Baghdad with Special Reference to Greek Mechanics in Arabic." *Quaderni di Studi Arabi* 5–6 (1987–1988) [= *Atti del XIII congresso dell'Union européenne d'arabisants et islamisants, Venezia 29 settembre – 4 ottobre 1986*]: 369–390.

112 Endress, Gerhard. "The Defense of Reason: The Plea for Philosophy in the Religious Community." *Zeitschrift für Geschichte der Arabisch-Islamischen Wissenschaften* 6 (1990): 1–49.

113 Griffith, Sidney Harrison. "The Muslim Philosopher al-Kindi and his Christian Readers: Three Arab Christian Texts on 'The Dissipation of Sorrows'." *Bulletin of the John Rylands University Library of Manchester* 78 (1996): 111–127.

114 Adamson, Peter. "Al-Kindī and the Reception of Greek Philosophy." [*85].

115 Adamson, Peter. *Al-Kindī*. Oxford, 2007.

116 Endress, Gerhard. "The Cycle of Knowledge: Intellectual Traditions and Encyclopaedias of the Rational Sciences in Arabic Islamic Hellenism." In *Organizing Knowledge: Encyclopaedic Activities in the Pre-Eighteenth Century Islamic World*. Ed. by Gerhard Endress. Leiden, Boston, 2006, 103–133.

117 Endress, Gerhard. "Al-Kindī: Arabismus, Hellenismus und die Legitimation der Philosophie im Islam." In *Islamische Grenzen und Grenzübergänge*. Ed. by Benedikt Reinert and Johannes Thomann. Bern, 2007, 35–59.

6.7 *Influence*

125 Cortabarría Beitia, Angel. "Al-Kindi vu par Albert Le Grand." *Mélanges de l'Institut dominicain d'études orientales du Caire* 13 (1977): 117–146.

126 Tornero Poveda, Emilio. "Religión y filosofía en al-Kindī, Averroes y Kant." *Al-Qanṭara* 2 (1981): 89–128.

127 Burnett, Charles. "An Apocryphal Letter from the Arabic Philosopher al-Kindi to Theodore, Frederick II's Astrologer, Concerning Gog and Magog, the Enclosed Nations, and the Scourge of the Mongols." *Viator* 15 (1984): 151–167.

128 Burnett, Charles. "Alkindius Latinus: A Descriptive Catalogue and Study of the Latin Works attributed to al-Kindi in Western Manuscripts." *Islamic Thought and Scientific Creativity* 4 (1993): 73–77.

129 Burnett, Charles. "Al-Kindī in the Renaissance." In *Sapientiam amemus: Humanismus und Aristotelismus in der Renaissance: Festschrift für Eckhard Kessler zum 60. Geburtstag*. Ed. by Paul Richard Blum et al. Munich, 1999, 13–30.

130 González Muñoz, Fernando. "Consideraciones sobre la versión latina de las cartas de al-Hāšimī y al-Kindī." *Collectanea Christiana Orientalia* 2 (2005): 43–70.

6.8 *Individual Works. Doctrine*

6.8.1 Introductions to Philosophy

140 de Boer, Tjitze J. "Zu Kindī und seiner Schule." *Archiv für Geschichte der Philosophie* 13 (1900): 153–178.

141 Guidi, Michelangelo and Richard Walzer. *Uno scritto introduttivo allo studio di Aristotele*. Studi su al-Kindī I. Rome, 1940, 375–419.

142 Stern, Samuel Miklos. "Notes on al-Kindī's Treatise on Definitions." *Journal of the Royal Asiatic Society* (1959): 32–43. – Repr. in: S. M. Stern, *Medieval Arabic and Hebrew Thought*. London, 1983, no. VIII.

143 Ghaussy, Abdul Aziz. *Aufbau und System der Philosophie und der Wissenschaften im Islam nach al-Kindī, al-Fārābī und Ibn Sīnā in ihren systematischen Werken*. PhD Diss., University of Hamburg, 1961.

144 Rescher, Nicholas. "Al-Kindi's Sketch of Aristotle's *Organon*." *New Scholasticism* 37 (1963): 44–58.

145 Allard, Michel. "L'Épître de Kindī sur les définitions." *Bulletin d'études orientales* 25 (1972): 47–83.

146 Cortabarría Beitia, Angel. "La classification des sciences chez al-Kindī." *Mélanges de l'Institut dominicain d'études orientales du Caire* 11 (1972): 49–76.

147 Frank, Tamar Zahara. *Al-Kindī's Book of Definitions: Its Place in Arabic Definition Literature*. PhD Diss., Yale University, New Haven, Conn., 1975.

148 Gimaret, Daniel. "L'Épître des définitions attribuée à al-Kindī." [Arab. and French] In *Al-Kindî: Cinq épîtres*. Ed. by D. Gimaret et al. Paris, 1976, 7–69.

149 Garro, Ibrahim. "Al-Kindī and Mathematical Logic." In *Abḥāṯ al-Nadwa al-ʿĀlamiyya li-Tārīḫ al-ʿUlūm ʿind al-ʿArab = Proceedings of the First International Symposium for the History of Arabic Science, April 5–12*, 1976. Aleppo, 1977–1978, I 379 (Arab. summary); II 36–40 (Engl.).

150 Garro, Ibrahim. "Al-Kindī and Mathematical Logic." *International Logic Review* 9 (1978): 145–149. – Reproduces the English text of [*149].

151 Klein-Franke, Felix. "Al-Kindī's 'On Definitions and Descriptions of Things'." *Le Muséon* 95 (1982): 191–216.

152 al-Aʿsam, ʿAbd al-Amīr. *Al-Muṣṭalaḥ al-falsafī ʿind al-ʿArab*. Baghdad, 1985; Cairo, 1989. – New ed.: *Rasāʾil manṭiqiyya fī l-ḥudūd wa-l-rusūm li-falāsifat al-ʿArab Ibn Ḥayyān, al-Kindī, al-Ḫwārazmī, Ibn Sīnā, al-Ġazālī*. Beirut, 1993. – Contains: al-Kindī, *al-Ḥudūd wa-l-rusūm* (pp. 187–203).

153 Ǧihāmī, Ǧirār [Gérard Jéhamy]. *Al-Iškāliyya al-luġawiyya fī l-falsafa al-ʿarabiyya*. Beirut, 1994. – Contains: al-Kindī, *al-Ḥudūd wa-l-rusūm* (pp. 199–206; reprinted from al-Aʿsam, *Al-Muṣṭalaḥ*).

154 Gutas, Dimitri. "The 'Alexandria to Baghdad' Complex of Narratives: A Contribution to the Study of Philosophical and Medical Historiography Among the Arabs." *Documenti e studi sulla tradizione filosofica medievale* 10 (1999): 155–193.

155 Endress, Gerhard. "The Language of Demonstration: Translating Science and the Formation of Terminology in Arabic Philosophy and Science." *Early Science and Medicine* 7/3 (Leiden 2002): 231–254.

156 Jolivet, Jean. "*L'Épître sur la quantité des livres d'Aristote* par al-Kindi (une lecture)." In *De Zénon d'Élée à Poincaré. Recueil d'études en hommage à Roshdi Rashed*. Ed. by Régis Morelon and Ahmad Hasnawi. Louvain, 2004, 665–683.

157 Adamson, Peter. "The Kindian Tradition: The Structure of Philosophy in Arabic Neoplatonism." In C. D'Ancona 2007 [cf. *88], 351–370.

158 Janssens, Jules. "Al-Kindī: The Founder of Philosophical Exegesis of the Qurʾān." *Journal of Qurʾanic Studies* 9 (2007): 1–21. – On the *Risāla fī Kammiyyat kutub Arisṭūṭālīs*.

6.8.2 Propaedeutic Ethics

161 Ritter, Hellmut and Richard Walzer. "Uno scritto morale inedito di al-Kindī (Temistio Περὶ ἀλυπίας) [Studi su al-Kindī II]." *Reale Accademia nazionale dei lincei: Memorie*, ser. VI, 8 (Rome 1938): 5–63.

162 van Riet, Simone. "Joie et bonheur dans le traité d'al-Kindi sur l'art de combattre la tristesse." *Revue philosophique de Louvain* 61 (1963): 13–23.

163 Riad, Eva. "À propos d'une définition de la colère chez al-Kindī." *Orientalia Suecana* 22 (1973): 62–65.

164 Gutas, Dimitri. *Greek Wisdom Literature in Arabic Translation: A Study of the Graeco-Arabic Gnomologia*. New Haven, 1975.

165 Butterworth, Charles E. "Al-Kindi and the Beginnings of Islamic Political Philosophy," In *The Political Aspects of Islamic Philosophy: Essays in Honor of Muhsin S. Mahdi*. Ed. by Charles E. Butterworth. Cambridge, Mass., 1992, 14–32.

166 Druart, Thérèse-Anne. "Al-Kindi's Ethics." *Review of Metaphysics* 47 (1993): 329–357.

167 Fakhry, Majid. *Ethical Theories in Islam*. Second, expanded edition. Leiden, 1994. – Al-Kindī, *Risāla fī l-Ḥīla li-dafʿ al-aḥzān*, used by Miskawayh, al-Rāġib al-Iṣfahānī and Ibn Sīnā.

168 Druart, Thérèse-Anne. "Philosophical Consolation in Christianity and Islam: Boethius and al-Kindī." In *Medieval Arabic Philosophy and the West*. Ed. by Thérèse Bonin. Dordrecht, 2000, 25–34.

169 Jayyusi-Lehn, Ghada. "The Epistle of Yaʿqūb ibn Isḥāq al-Kindī on the Device for Dispelling Sorrows." *British Journal of Middle Eastern Studies* 29 (2002): 121–135.

170 Mestiri, Soumaya and Guillaume Dye. *Al-Kindi: Le moyen de chasser les tristesses et autres textes éthiques*. Paris, 2004.

171 Adamson, Peter. "The Arabic Socrates: The Place of al-Kindī's Report in the Tradition." In *Socrates from Antiquity to the Enlightenment*. Ed. by Michael Trapp. Aldershot, 2007, 161–178.

6.8.3 Metaphysics

181 de Boer, Tjitze J. "Kindī wider die Trinität." In *Orientalische Studien, Theodor Nöldeke zum siebzigsten Geburtstag gewidmet*, vol. 1. Ed. by Carl Bezold. Gießen, 1906, 279–281.

182 Graf, Georg. *Die Philosophie und Gotteslehre des Jaḥjā ibn ʿAdī: Skizzen nach meist ungedruckten Quellen*. Münster, 1910. – On al-Kindī's refutation of the Christian dogma, preserved in the counter-refutation by Yaḥyā Ibn ʿAdī, ed. by Périer [*171], [*172].

183 Périer, Augustin. "Un traité de Yaḥyâ ben 'Adî: Défense du dogme de la Trinité contre les objections d'al-Kindî." *Revue de l'Orient chrétien* 22 [3. sér., 2] (1920–1921): 3–21.

184 Abel, Armand. "La polémique damascénienne et son influence sur les origines de la théologie musulmane." In *L'élaboration de l'islam*. Paris, 1961, 71–85.

185 Marmura, Michael E. and John M. Rist. "Al-Kindi's Discussion of Divine Existence and Oneness." *Mediaeval Studies* 25 (1963) 338–354.

186 Nucho, Fuad. "The One and the Many in al-Kindī's Metaphysics." *Muslim World* 61 (1971): 161–169.

187 Cortabarría Beitia, Angel. "Un traité philosophique d'al-Kindī." *Mélanges de l'Institut dominicain d'études orientales du Caire* 12 (1974): 5–12. – On al-Kindī, *Risāla fī l-Fāʿil al-ḥaqq al-awwal al-tāmm wa-l-fāʿil al-nāqiṣ allaḏī huwa bi-l-maǧāz.*

188 Ivry, Alfred L. *Al-Kindi's Metaphysics: A Translation of Yaʿqūb b. Isḥāq al-Kindī's Treatise 'On First philosophy' (fī al-Falsafah al-ūlā) with Introduction and Commentary*. Albany, 1974.

189 Ivry, Alfred L. "Al-Kindi's *On First philosophy* and Aristotle's *Metaphysics*." In *Essays on Islamic Philosophy and Science*. Ed. by George F. Hourani. Albany, 1975, 15–24.

190 Jolivet, Jean. "Pour le dossier du Proclus arabe. Al-Kindī et la Théologie platonicienne." [*62].

191 Shamsi, Fazal Ahmad. "Section on World's Finitude and Non-Eternity in al-Kindi's *Kitab al-Falsafah al-Ula*." *Journal of Central Asia* 2, no. 2 (1979): 1–23.

192 Tornero Poveda, Emilio. "Al-Kindī y la *Teología* del Pseudo-Aristóteles." *Miscelánea de estudios árabes y hebraicos* 31 (1982): 111–122.

193 Jolivet, Jean. "L'action divine selon al-Kindī." *Mélanges de l'Université Saint-Joseph* 50 (1984): 311–329.

194 Zimmermann, Friedrich W. "The Origins of the So-Called *Theology of Aristotle*." [*65].

195 Davidson, Herbert Alan. *Proofs for Eternity, Creation and the Existence of God in Medieval Islamic and Jewish Philosophy*. New York, 1987.

196 Staley, Kevin. "Al-Kindi on Creation: Aristotle's Challenge to Islam." *Journal of the History of Ideas* 50 (1989): 355–370.

197 D'Ancona, Cristina. "La doctrine de la création 'mediante intelligentia' dans le Liber de Causis et dans ses sources." *Revue des sciences philosophiques et théologiques* 76 (1992): 209–233.

198 Tornero Poveda, Emilio. *Al-Kindi: La transformación de un pensamiento religioso en un pensamiento racional*. Madrid, 1992.

199 Jolivet, Jean. "Al-Kindī, vues sur le temps." *Arabic Sciences and Philosophy* 3 (1993): 55–75.

200 Janssens, Jules L. "Al-Kindī's Concept of God." *Ultimate Reality and Meaning* 17 (1994): 4–16.

201 D'Ancona, Cristina. "Al-Kindi on the Subject Matter of the First Philosophy: Direct and Indirect Sources of *Falsafa al-ūlā*, Chapter One." In *Was ist Philosophie im Mittelalter?* Ed. by Jan A. Aertsen and Andreas Speer. Berlin, 1998, 841–855.

202 Bertolacci, Amos. "From al-Kindī to al-Fārābī: Avicenna's Progressive Knowledge of Aristotle's *Metaphysics* According to his Autobiography." *Arabic Sciences and Philosophy* 11 (2001): 257–295.

203 Adamson, Peter. "Before Essence and Existence: Al-Kindī's Conception of Being." *The Journal of the History of Philosophy* 40 (2002): 297–312.

204 Adamson, Peter. "Al-Kindī and the Muʿtazila: Divine Attributes, Creation and Freedom." *Arabic Sciences and Philosophy* 13 (2003): 3. 5–6. 45–77.

205 Adamson, Peter. "A Note on Freedom in the Circle of al-Kindī." In *ʿAbbasid Studies: Occasional Papers of the School of ʿAbbasid Studies*. Ed. by James E. Montgomery. Leuven, 2004, 199–207.

206 Schöck, Cornelia. "The Controversy Between al-Kindī and Yaḥyā b. ʿAdī on the Trinity: A Revival of the Controversy Between Eunomius and the Cappadocian Fathers." *Oriens* 40, no. 1 (2012): 1–50.

6.8.4 Soul and Intellect

221 Furlani, Giuseppe. "Una risāla di al-Kindī sull'anima." *Rivista trimestrale di studi filosofici e religiosi* 3 (Perugia 1922): 50–63. – Contains an Ital. transl. of *Risālat al-Kindī fī l-Qawl fī l-Nafs al-muḫtaṣar min Kitāb Arisṭū wa-Falāṭun wa-sā'ir al-falāsifa* [*62].

222 Walzer, Richard. "Un frammento nuovo di Aristotele." *Studi italiani di filologia classica* 14 (1937): 123–137. – Repr. in: R. Walzer, *Greek into Arabic*. [*53], 38–47. – On *Risālat al-Kindī fī l-Qawl fī l-Nafs al-muḫtaṣar min kitāb Arisṭū wa-Falāṭun wa-sā'ir al-falāsifa* [*62].

223 al-Ahwānī, Aḥmad Fu'ād. *Ibn Rušd, Talḫīṣ kitāb al-nafs wa-arbaʿ rasā'il*. Cairo, 1950. – Contains al-Kindī, *Risāla fī l-ʿAql* (178–181).

224 Gätje, Helmut. "Philosophische Traumlehren im Islam." *Zeitschrift der Deutschen Morgenländischen Gesellschaft* 109 (1959): 258–285.

225 McCarthy, Richard Joseph. "Al-Kindī's Treatise on the Intellect." *Islamic Studies* 3 (1964): 119–149.

226 Ṣalībā, Ǧamīl. "Naẓariyyat al-maʿrifa ʿind al-Kindī." In *Al-Dirāsāt al-falsafiyya*, vol. 1. Damascus, 1964, 110–131.

227 Jolivet, Jean. *L'intellect selon Kindi*. Leiden, 1971.

228 Pines, Shlomo. "The Arabic Recension of *Parva Naturalia* and the Philosophical Doctrine Concerning Veridical Dreams According to *al-Risāla al-Manāmiyya* and Other Sources." *Israel Oriental Studies* 4 (1974): 104–153.

229 Endress, Gerhard. Review of J. Jolivet [*227] in: *Zeitschrift der Deutschen Morgenländischen Gesellschaft* 130 (1980): 422–435.

230 Ramón Guerrero, Rafael. "El conocimiento o ciencia profética en al-Kindī y al-Fārābī." In *Actas de las Jornadas de cultura árabe e islámica, 1978*. Madrid, 1981, 353–358.

231 Ramón Guerrero, Rafael. *Contribución a la historia de la filosofía árabe: Alma e intelecto como problemas fundamentales de la misma*. Madrid, 1981. – With an appendix containing the following texts by al-Kindī with Span. transl.: *Risālat al-Kindī fī l-Qawl fī l-Nafs al-muḫtaṣar min Kitāb Arisṭū wa-Falāṭun wa-sā'ir al-falāsifa* (364–381); *Risālat al-Kindī fī l-'Aql* (383–394).

232 Ramón Guerrero, Rafael. "La tradición griega en la filosofía árabe: El tema del alma en al-Kindī." *Al-Qanṭara* 3 (1982): 1–26.

233 Zambelli, Paola. "L'immaginazione e il suo potere: Da al-Kindī, al-Fārābī e Avicenna al Medioevo latino e al Rinascimento." In *Orientalische Kultur und europäisches Mittelalter*. Ed. by Albert Zimmermann. Berlin, 1985, 188–206.

234 Endress, Gerhard. "Al-Kindī's Theory of Anamnesis: A New Text and its Implications." In *Islão e arabismo na Península Ibérica, Actas do* XI *congreso da União europeia de arabistas e islamólogos, 1982*. Ed. by Adel Sidarus. Évora, 1986, 393–402.

235 Genequand, Charles. "Platonism and Hermetism in al-Kindī's *Fī al-Nafs*." *Zeitschrift für Geschichte der Arabisch-Islamischen Wissenschaften* 4 (1987–1988): 1–18.

236 Ramón Guerrero, Rafael. *La recepción árabe del De Anima de Aristóteles: Al-Kindi y al-Farabi*. Madrid, 1992.

237 Endress, Gerhard. "Al-Kindī über die Wiedererinnerung der Seele: Arabischer Platonismus und die Legitimation der Wissenschaften im Islam." *Oriens* 34 (1994): 174–221.

238 D'Ancona, Cristina. "La dottrina neoplatonica dell'anima nella filosofia islamica: Un esempio in al-Kindi." In *Actes del Simposi internacional de filosofia de l'edat mitjana: El pensament antropològic medieval en els àmbits islàmic, hebreu i cristià, Vic-Girona ... 1993*. Ed. by Paloma Llorente et al. Vic, 1996, 91–96.

239 Jolivet, Jean. "La topographie du salut d'après le Discours sur l'âme d'al-Kindī." In *Le voyage initiatique en terre d'islam: Ascensions célestes et itinéraires spirituels*. Ed. by Mohammad Ali Amir-Moezzi. Leuven, 1996, 149–158.

240 Ruffinengo, Pier Paolo. "Al-Kindi, *Trattato sull'intelletto: Trattato sul sogno e la visione." Medioevo* 23 (1997): 337–394.

241 Adamson, Peter. "Two Early Arabic Doxographies on the Soul: Al-Kindī and the 'Theology of Aristotle'." *Modern Schoolman* 77, no. 2 (2000): 105–125.

242 Hansberger, Rotraud. "How Aristotle Came to Believe in God-given Dreams: The Arabic Version of *De divinatione per somnum*." In *Dreaming Across Boundaries:*

The Interpretation of Dreams in Islamic Lands. Ed. by Louise Marlow. Boston, Washington, 2008, 50–77.

243 Adamson, Peter and Peter E. Pormann. "Aristotle's Categories and the Soul: An Annotated Translation of al-Kindī's *That There Are Separate Substances*." In *The Afterlife of the Platonic Soul*. Ed. by John M. Dillon and Maha Elkaisy-Friemuth. Leiden, 2009, 95–106.

6.8.5 Physics and Cosmology

251 Wiedemann, Eilhard. "I. Geographisches von al Bîrûnî. II. Auszüge aus al Schîrâzî's Werk über die Astronomie. III. Über die Größe der Meere nach al Kindî. IV. Geographische Stellen aus den *Mafâtîḥ*." *Sitzungsberichte der Physikalisch-Medizinischen Sozietät in Erlangen* 44 (1912): 1–40.

252 Rescher, Nicholas and Haig Khatchadourian. "Al-Kindī's Epistle on the Concentric Structure of the Universe." *Isis* 56 (1965): 190–195. – Repr. in: N. Rescher, *Studies in Arabic Philosophy*. Pittsburgh, 1967, 1–14.

253 Rescher, Nicholas and Haig Khatchadourian. "Al-Kindī's Epistle on the Finitude of the Universe." *Isis* 56 (1965): 426–433.

254 Nicholas Rescher: Al-Kindi's Treatise on the Platonic Solids, in: N. Rescher: *Studies in Arabic Philosophy* [cf. *252], 15–37.

255 Shamsi, Fazal Ahmad. "Al-Kindī's *Epistle on What Cannot Be Infinite and of What Infinity May Be Attributed*." *Islamic Studies* 14 (1975): 123–144.

256 Shamsi, Fazal Ahmad. "Al-Kindi's *Risala fi wahdaniya Allah wa-tanahi jirm al-ʿalam*." *Islamic Studies* 17 (1978): 185–201.

257 Fazzo, Silvia and Hillary Suzanne Wiesner. "Alexander of Aphrodisias in the Kindī-Circle and in al-Kindī's Cosmology." *Arabic Sciences and Philosophy* 3 (1993): 119–153.

6.8.6 Mathematical Sciences

271 Rashed, Roshdi. "Al-Kindī's Commentary on Archimedes' 'The Measurement of the Circle'." *Arabic Sciences and Philosophy* 3 (1993): 7–53.

272 Garro, Ibrahim. "The Paradox of the Infinite by al-Kindī." *Journal for the History of Arabic Science* 10 (1994): 111–118.

273 Arnzen, Rüdiger. "Wie mißt man den göttlichen Kreis? Phantasievermögen, Raumvorstellung und geometrischer Gegenstand in den mathematischen Theorien Proclus', al-Fārābīs und Ibn al-Haythams." In *Imagination – Fiktion – Kreation: Das kulturschaffende Vermögen der Phantasie*. Ed. by Thomas Dewender and Thomas Welt. Leipzig, 2003, 115–140, esp. 133.

274 Endress, Gerhard. "Mathematics and Philosophy in Medieval Islam." In *The Enterprise of Science in Islam: New Perspectives*. Ed. by Jan P. Hogendijk and Abdelhamid I. Sabra. Cambridge, Mass., 2003, 121–176.

275 Gutas, Dimitri. "Geometry and the Rebirth of Philosophy in Arabic with al-Kindi." In R. Arnzen, J. Thielmann 2004 [cf. *84], 195–209.

276 Mrayati, Mohamad, Yahya Meer Alam and M. Hassan at-Tayyan. *Al-Kindi's Treatise on Cryptanalysis*. Riyadh, 2002. – Contains the Engl. transl. of the treatise ed. in Marāyātī 1987 [*277].

277 Marāyātī, Muḥammad, Muḥammad Ḥassān al-Ṭayyān and Yaḥyā Mīr ʿAlam. *ʿIlm al-taʿmiya wa-stiḫrāǧ al-muʿammā ʿind al-ʿArab*, vol. 1. Damascus, 1987. – 204–259: *Kitāb al-Kindī ilā Abī l-ʿAbbās Aḥmad b. al-Muʿtaṣim fī l-Ḥīla fī Istiḫrāǧ al-muʿammā min al-kutub*, ed. by Mīr ʿAlam (MS Ayasofya 4832).

6.8.7 Arithmetics

281 Freudenthal, Gad and Tony Lévy. "De Gérase à Bagdad: Ibn Bahrîz, al-Kindî, et leur recension arabe de l'*Introduction arithmétique* de Nicomaque, d'après la version hebraïque de Qalonymos ben Qalonymos d'Arles." [*83].

6.8.8 Geometry

286 Luckey, Paul. "Ṯābit b. Qurra über den geometrischen Richtigkeitsnachweis der Auflösung der quadratischen Gleichungen." *Berichte der mathematisch-physikalischen Klasse der Sächsischen Akademie der Wissenschaften zu Leipzig* 93 (1941): 93–114. – Appendix, 108–109, Arab. text, 112: MS Ayasofya 2457, 3, fol. 41b *ʿli-Yaʿqūb b. Isḥāq [al-Kindī] fī tarǧamat ṣadr kitāb Ūqlīdisʾ,* seven *asbāb al-ʿilm* (*ḫabar, miṯāl, ḫalf, naẓar, faṣl, burhān, tamām*).

6.8.9 Optics

295 Lindberg, David Charles. "Alkindi's Critique of Euclid's Theory of Vision." *Isis* 62 (1971): 469–489.

296 Lindberg, David Charles. *Theories of Vision from al-Kindī to Kepler*. Chicago, London, 1976.

297 Aḥmad, Muḫtār al-Dīn. "Al-Kindī and his Treatise on Rays." [Arabic.] In *Abḥāṯ al-Nadwa al-ʿĀlamiyya li-Tārīḫ al-ʿUlūm ʿind al-ʿArab = Proceedings of the First International Symposium for the History of Arabic Sciences, April 5–12, 1976*. Aleppo, 1977–1978, I 83–95 (Arab.); II 3 (summary).

298 Lindberg, David Charles. "The Intromission – Extramission Controversy in Islamic Visual Theory: Alkindi versus Avicenna." In *Studies in Perception: Interrelations in the History of Philosophy and Science*. Ed. by Peter K. Machamer, Robert G. Turnbull. Columbus, 1978, 137–159. – Also in Lindberg 1983 [*299], no. IV.

299 Lindberg, David Charles. *Studies in the History of Medieval Optics*. London, 1983.

300 Rashed, Roshdi. "Le commentaire par al-Kindī de l'Optique d'Euclide: Un traité jusqu'ici inconnu." *Arabic Sciences and Philosophy* 7 (1997): 9–56.

301 Rashed, Roshdi. *Œuvres philosophiques et scientifiques d'al-Kindī*, vol. 1: *L'optique et la catoptrique*. Leiden, 1997.

302 Adamson, Peter. "Vision, Light and Color in al-Kindi, Ptolemy and the Ancient Commentators." *Arabic Sciences and Philosophy* 16 (2006): 207–236.

6.8.10 Astronomy

315 Wiedemann, Eilhard. "Über eine astronomische Schrift von al Kindî (Ergänzung zu Beitrag XVIII)." *Sitzungsberichte der Physikalisch-Medizinischen Sozietät in Erlangen* 42 (1910): 294–302.

316 Luckey, Paul. "Beiträge zur Erforschung der islamischen Mathematik." *Orientalia* 17 (1948): 490–510.

317 Rosenthal, Franz. "Al-Kindī and Ptolemy." In *Studi orientalistici in onore di Giorgio Levi Della Vida*, vol. 2. Rome, 1956, 436–456. – Repr. in: F. Rosenthal, *Science and Medicine in Islam: A Collection of Essays*. Aldershot, 1990, no. IV.

318 Rescher, Nicholas and Haig Khatchadourian. "Al-Kindī's Treatise on the Distinctiveness of the Celestial Sphere." *Islamic Studies* 4 (1965): 45–54.

319 Hypsikles. *Die Aufgangszeiten der Gestirne*. – Ed. and transl. by Vittorio de Falco and Max Krause, with an intro. by Otto Neugebauer. Göttingen, 1966.

320 Celentano, Giuseppe. *L'Epistola di al-Kindī sulla sfera armillare*. Naples, 1982.

6.8.11 Music

331 Farmer, Henry George. "Al-Kindī on the 'Ethos' of Rhythm, Colour and Perfume." *Glasgow University Oriental Society, Transactions* 16 (1956): 29–38.

332 Yūsuf, Zakariyyā'. *Mu'allafāt al-Kindī al-mūsīqiyya*. Baghdad, 1962.

333 Farmer, Henry George. *The Sources of Arabian Music*. Leiden, 1965. – Al-Kindī, 8–10.

334 Rosenthal, Franz. "Two Graeco-Arabic Works on Music." *Proceedings of the American Philosophical Society* 110 (1966): 261–268.

335 Shiloah, Amnon. "Les sept traités de musique dans le ms. 1705 de Manisa." *Israel Oriental Studies* 1 (1971): 303–315.

336 Shiloah, Amnon. "Un ancien traité sur le 'ūd d'Abū Yūsuf al-Kindī: Traduction et commentaire." *Israel Oriental Studies* 4 (1974): 179–205.

337 Shiloah, Amnon. *The Theory of Music in Arabic Writings (c. 900–1900)*. Munich, 1979, 254–260.

338 Baffioni, Carmela. "La scala pitagorica in al-Kindī." In *Studi in onore di Francesco Gabrieli nel suo ottantesimo compleanno*. Ed. by Renato Traini. Rome, 1984, 35–41.

339 Fayzal, Muhammad and Richard Dumbrill. "Arab Musical Theory and Notation During the Abbasid Period, 750–1258 (from al-Kindi to Safi ad-Din)." *Arab Affairs* 1 (1988): 87–99.

340 Shehadi, Fadlou. *Philosophies of Music in Medieval Islam*. Leiden, 1995.

341 Maalouf, Shireen. *History of Arabic Music Theory: Change and Continuity in the Tone Systems, Genres, and Scales*. Jounieh, 2000.

342 Neubauer, Eckhard. "Die Euklid zugeschriebene 'Teilung des Kanon' in arabischer Überlieferung." *Zeitschrift für Geschichte der Arabisch-Islamischen Wissenschaften* 16 (2004–2005): 309–385, esp. 310–311. 314.

343 Wright, Owen. "Al-Kindi's Braid." *Bulletin of the School of Oriental and African Studies* 69 (2006): 1–32.

6.8.12 Astrology

351 Loth, Otto. "Al-Kindî als Astrolog." In *Morgenländische Forschungen H. L. Fleischer… gewidmet*. Leipzig, 1875, 261–309.

352 Wiedemann, Eilhard. "Über einen astrologischen Traktat von al-Kindî." *Archiv für die Geschichte der Mathematik, der Naturwissenschaften und der Technik* 3 (1912): 224–226.

353 Fück, Johann. "Sechs Ergänzungen zu Sachaus Ausgabe von al-Bīrūnīs 'Chronologie orientalischer Völker'." In *Documenta Islamica inedita*. Leipzig, 1952, 69–98.

354 d'Alverny, Marie-Thérèse and Françoise Hudry. "Al-Kindi *De radiis*." *Archives d'histoire doctrinale et littéraire du moyen âge* 41 (1975): 139–260.

355 Muñoz, R. "Una maqāla astrológica de al-Kindī." *Boletín de la Asociación española de orientalistas* 15 (1979): 127–139.

356 Burnett, Charles. "Al-Kindī on Judicial Astrology: The Forty Chapters." *Arabic Sciences and Philosophy* 3 (1993): 77–117.

357 Adamson, Peter. "Abu Maʿshar, al-Kindi and the Philosophical Defense of Astrology." *Recherches de philosophie et théologie médiévales* 69 (2002): 245–270.

6.8.13 Astrometeorology and Meteorology

361 Wiedemann, Eilhard. "Über al-Kindî's Schrift über Ebbe und Flut." *Annalen der Physik* 67 (1922): 374–387. – Repr. in: E. Wiedemann, *Gesammelte Schriften zur arabisch-islamischen Wissenschaftsgeschichte*, vol. 2. Frankfurt a.M., 1984, 1005–1018.

362 Spies, Otto. "Al-Kindī's Treatise on the Cause of the Blue Colour of the Sky." *Journal of the Bombay Branch of the Royal Asiatic Society* N.S. 13 (1931): 7–19. – Contains the Arab. text and Engl. transl. of *Risālat al-Kindī fī ʿIllat al-lawn al-lāzuwardī* [**129*].

363 Sersen, William John. *Arab Meteorology from Pre-Islamic Times to the Thirteenth Century A.D.* PhD Diss., University of London, 1976, 220–226. – Résumé of three meteorological treatises by al-Kindī.

364 Daiber, Hans. "The *Meteorology* in Syriac and Arabic Translation." In *Theophrastus: His Psychological, Doxographical, and Scientific Writings*. Ed. by William W. Fortenbaugh. New Brunswick, London, 1992, 166–293. – 222 n. 75 on al-Kindī.

365 Bos, Gerrit and Charles Burnett. *Scientific Weather Forecasting in the Middle Ages: The Writings of al-Kindī: Studies, Editions, and Translations of the Arabic, Hebrew and Latin Texts*. London, 2000.

6.8.14 Magic

371 d'Alverny, Marie-Thérèse. "Trois opuscules inédits d'al-Kindī." In *Akten des 24. internationalen Orientalisten-Kongresses, München 1957*. Ed. by Herbert Franke. Wiesbaden, 1959, 301–302.

372 Vaglieri, Laura Veccia and Giuseppe Celentano. "Trois épîtres d'al-Kindī (textes et traduction)." *Annali dell'Istituto Orientale di Napoli* 34 = N.S. 24 (1974): 523–562.

373 Autuori, Adele. "Su un trattato di scapulomanzia di al-Kindī." In *Studi arabo-islamici in onore di Roberto Rubinacci nel suo settantesimo compleanno*. Ed. by Clelia Sarnelli Cerqua. Naples, 1985, 15–20.

374 Celentano, Giuseppe. "L'Epistola di al-Kindī sulla smacchiatura." In C. Sarnelli Cerqua 1985 [cf. *373], 141–197.

375 Burnett, Charles, Keiji Yamamoto and Michio Yano. "Al-Kindī on Finding Buried Treasure." *Arabic Sciences and Philosophy* 7 (1997): 57–90. – On al-Kindī's *Fī l-Mawāḍiʿ allatī yuẓann anna l-dafīn fīhā min kanz aw ġayrihi* [*136].

376 Travaglia, Pinella. *Magic, Causality and Intentionality* [*29].

6.8.15 Medicine and Pharmacology

381 Wiedemann, Eilhard. "Parfüms und Drogen bei den Arabern." *Sitzungsberichte der Physikalisch-Medizinischen Sozietät in Erlangen* 48–49 (1916–1917): 329–344. – Repr. in: E. Wiedemann, *Aufsätze zur arabischen Wissenschaftsgeschichte*, vol. 2. Hildesheim, New York, 1970, 415–430.

382 Gauthier, Léon. *Antécédents gréco-arabes de la psycho-physique*. Beirut, 1939.

383 Garbers, Karl. *Buch über die Chemie des Parfüms und die Destillationen von Yaʿqūb ibn Isḥāq al-Kindī, ein Beitrag zur Geschichte der arabischen Parfümchemie und Drogenkunde*. Leipzig, 1948. – German transl.: 31–106.

384 Levey, Martin. *The Medical Formulary or Aqrābāḏīn of al-Kindī, Translated with a Study of its Materia Medica*. Madison, London, 1966.

385 Klein-Franke, Felix. "Die Ursachen der Krisen bei akuten Krankheiten: Eine wiederentdeckte Schrift al-Kindī's." *Israel Oriental Studies* 5 (1975): 161–188.

386 Celentano, Giuseppe. *Due scritti medici di al-Kindī*. Naples, 1979.

387 Weisser, Ursula. "Mondphasen und Krisen nach al-Kindī." *Archiv für Geschichte der Medizin* [Sudhoffs Archiv] 66 (1982): 390–395.

388 Bos, Gerrit. "A Recovered Fragment on the Signs of Death from al-Kindi's 'Medical Summaries'." *Zeitschrift für Geschichte der Arabisch-Islamischen Wissenschaften* 6 (1990): 190–194.

389 Langermann, Y. Tzvi. "Another Andalusian Revolt? Ibn Rushd's Critique of al-Kindī's Pharmacological Computus." In J. P. Hogendijk, A. I. Sabra 2003 [cf. *274], 351–372.

6.8.15 Various Works on Natural Philosophy

402 Zakī, Abd al-Raḥmān. "Risālat al-Kindī fī l-Suyūf wa-aǧnāsihā." *Maǧallat Kulliyyat al-ādāb (Ǧāmiʿat al-Qāhira) = Bulletin of the Faculty of Arts of the University of Egypt* (Fouad I University) 14, no. 2 (1952): 1–36. – Repr. in: Fuat Sezgin, ed. *Technology of Warfare: Texts and Studies*, vol. 8. Frankfurt a.M., 2002, 315–350.

403 Iḥsān-Ilāhī, Rānā M. N. [Ehsan Elahie]. *A Treatise on Swords and their Essential Attributes* [*of al-Kindī*]. Lahore, 1962. – Repr. in: F. Sezgin 2002 [cf. *402], 279–314.

6.9 *Influence on Abū Maʿšar*

411 Baffioni, Carmela. "Una citazione di De Interpretatione, 9 in Abū Maʿšar?" In *Aristotele e Alessandro di Afrodisia nella tradizione araba: Atti del colloquio La ricezione araba ed ebraica della filosofia e della scienza greche, Padova, 14–15 maggio 1999*. Ed. by Cristina D'Ancona and Giuseppe Serra. Padua, 2002, 113–132.

412 Baffioni, Carmela. "Il rapporto astrologia-medicina nelle considerazioni embriologiche del *Kitāb al-Mudḫal al-kabīr* di Abū Maʿšar al-Balḫī." *Oriente Moderno* 24 (2005): 269–285.

CHAPTER 5

The Beginnings of Islamic Philosophy in the Tradition of al-Kindī

1 Al-Kindī's School: From Baghdad to Transoxania – 2 Neoplatonic Developments – 3 The Integration of Philosophical Traditions in Islamic Society in the 4th/10th Century: al-Tawḥīdī and al-Siğistānī – 4 Ancient Ethical Traditions for Islamic Society: Abū ʿAlī Miskawayh – 5 Bridging the Gap between the Kindian Tradition and the Baghdad School: Ibn Hindū – 6 Secondary Literature

1 Al-Kindī's School: From Baghdad to Transoxania

Hans Hinrich Biesterfeldt

1.1 Aḥmad b. al-Ṭayyib al-Saraḫsī – 1.2 Abū Zayd al-Balḫī – 1.3 Ibn Farīġūn

1.1 *Aḥmad b. al-Ṭayyib al-Saraḫsī*

1.1.1 Primary Sources – 1.1.2 Life – 1.1.3 List of Works (LW) – 1.1.4 Doctrine

1.1.1 Primary Sources

1.1.1.1 Bio-bibliographical Testimonies [*1–*5] – 1.1.1.2 Individual Biographical and Doxographical Reports [*8–*17] – 1.1.1.3 Works [*25–*32]

1.1.1.1 *Bio-bibliographical Testimonies*

The two main sources for al-Saraḫsī's life and work are Ibn al-Nadīm's *Fihrist* and Ibn Abī Uṣaybiʿa's biographical collection, which records more titles than the *Fihrist*. Ibn al-Qifṭī's entry in *Kitāb Iḫbār al-ʿulamāʾ bi-aḫbār al-ḥukamāʾ*, as excerpted by al-Zawzanī, and the (derivative) accounts by Barhebraeus and Ibn Faḍl Allāh al-ʿUmarī depend on the *Fihrist*, while Ḥāǧǧī Ḫalīfa's report goes back to Ibn Abī Uṣaybiʿa. The information provided by Yāqūt and, after him, al-Ṣafadī are likely to be based on Ibn ʿAsākir's lost entry in his *Tārīḫ Dimašq*; for details cf. Rosenthal 1943 [*17: 13–15], 1997 [*18]. A number of characteristic *dicta* by al-Saraḫsī are contained in *Kitāb al-Baṣāʾir wa-l-ḏaḫāʾir* by Abū Ḥayyān al-Tawḥīdī.

1 Ibn al-Nadīm, Abū l-Farağ Muḥammad b. Isḥāq (d. 380/990). *Kitāb al-Fihrist* [composed in 377/988]. – Ed. by Gustav Flügel, August Müller and Johannes Roediger, vol. 1. Leipzig, 1871, 261–262. – Repr. Beirut, 1964; Frankfurt a.M., 2005. – Ed. by Riḍā Tağaddud. Tehran, 1350 h.š./1971. – Ed. by Ayman Fu'ād Sayyid, 2 vols. London, 1430/2009. – Engl. transl. by Bayard Dodge, *The Fihrist of al-Nadīm*, 2 vols. New York, 1970.

2 Yāqūt b. ʿAbd Allāh al-Ḥamawī al-Rūmī al-Baġdādī (d. 626/1229). *Iršād al-arīb*. – Ed. by David Samuel Margoliouth, *The Irshād al-arīb ilā maʿrifat al-adīb or Dictionary of Learned Men of Yāqūt*, vol. 1. London, Leiden, 1923 (2nd ed.), 158–160. – Ed. by Iḥsān ʿAbbās, *Muʿğam al-udabā': Iršād al-arīb ilā maʿrifat al-adīb*, vol. 2. Beirut, 1993, 287–292.

3 Ibn al-ʿAdīm, Kamāl al-Dīn ʿUmar b. Aḥmad (d. 660/1262). *Buġyat al-ṭalab fī ta'rīḫ Ḥalab*: *Everything Desirable about the History of Aleppo*, vol. 2. Frankfurt a.M., 1989, 335–349. – Facsimile edition; with an introductory note in English and Arabic by Fuat Sezgin.

4 Ibn Abī Uṣaybiʿa, Muwaffaq al-Dīn Aḥmad b. al-Qāsim (d. 668/1270). *ʿUyūn al-anbā' fī ṭabaqāt al-aṭibbā'*. – Ed. by August Müller, vol. 1. Cairo, 1299/1882; Königsberg, 1884, 214–215.– Repr. Westmead, 1972.

5 al-Ṣafadī, Ṣalāḥ al-Dīn Ḫalīl b. Aybak (d. 764/1363). *Al-Wāfī bi-l-wafayāt*: *Das biographische Lexikon des* [...] *al-Ṣafadī*. – Ed. by Iḥsān ʿAbbās, vol. 7. Wiesbaden, 1969, 5–8. – Cf. also Rosenthal 1943 [*17], 127–131.

1.1.1.2 *Individual Biographical and Doxographical Reports*

8 Moosa, Matti. "A new source on Aḥmad b. al-Ṭayyib al-Sarakhsī: Florentine MS Arabic 299." *Journal of the American Oriental Society* 92 (1972): 19–24. – Introduction to (19–21) and translation of (22–24) a dispute between the bishop of Kashkar and al-Saraḫsī, according to MS Florence, ar. 299, fols 149–156.

9 al-Masʿūdī, Abū l-Ḥasan ʿAlī b. al-Ḥusayn (d. 345/956). *Murūğ al-ḏahab wa-maʿādin al-ğawhar*. – Ed. by Charles B. de Meynard and Abel B. de Courteille, rev. and corr. by Charles Pellat, vol. 5. Beirut, 1974, 161 (§ 3316). – Cf. also *fahāris ʿāmma*, s.v., vol. 6 (1979), 124.

10 Ḥamza al-Iṣfahānī (d. 350 or 360/961 or 971). *Al-Tanbīh ʿalā ḥudūṯ al-taṣḥīf*. – Ed. by Muḥammad Asʿad Ṭalas. Damascus, 1388/1968, 35–36.

11 ʿAlī b. Naṣr al-Kātib (d. probably 377/987). *Ğawāmiʿ al-laḏḏa* (*Compilation on Pleasure*); containing the detailed report of a discussion between al-Saraḫsī and Aḥmad b. Abī Ṭāhir on the topic of a dispute between lovers of boys and lovers of girls, on which group should outrank the other. – Cf. Rosenthal 1956 [*27: 31].

12 Ibn al-Nadīm [*1: 318–320]. – Al-Saraḫsī's description of the religious and philosophical views of the Sabians, based on al-Kindī.

13 al-Tawḥīdī, Abū Ḥayyān ʿAlī b. Muḥammad (d. 414/1023). *Aḫlāq al-wazīrayn*: *Maṯālib al-wazīrayn al-Ṣāḥib Ibn ʿAbbād wa-Ibn al-ʿAmīd*. – Ed. by Muḥammad b.

Tāwīt al-Ṭanǧī. Damascus, 1385/1965, 235–247. – Translation of the text in the version of Yāqūt's *Iršād*, together with the latter's concluding discussion of the authenticity of this report, in: Rosenthal 1943 [*17: 86–94].

14 Abū Ḥayyān al-Tawḥīdī. *Al-Baṣā'ir wa-l-ḏaḫā'ir.* – Ed. by Wadād al-Qāḍī, vol. 6. Beirut, 1408/1988, 7 (*fihris al-a'lām*, s.v.).

15 al-Qāḍī 'Abd al-Ǧabbār, Abū l-Ḥasan (d. 415/1025). *Al-Muġnī fī abwāb al-tawḥīd wa-l-'adl*, vol. 5. – Ed. by Maḥmūd Muḥammad al-Ḫuḍayrī [...]. Cairo, 1962, 152. – A further testimony for the doctrine of the Sabians from al-Saraḫsī.

16 *Ṣiwān al-ḥikma* [ascribed to Abū Sulaymān al-Siǧistānī], excerpts ed. by Douglas Morton Dunlop, *The Muntakhab Ṣiwān al-ḥikmah of Abū Sulaimān as-Sijistānī.* The Hague, 1979, 122. – Cf. Rosenthal 1943 [*17: 134 (edition), 58 (translation)].

17 Ibn Faḍl Allāh al-'Umarī (d. 749/1349). *Masālik al-abṣār fī mamālik al-amṣār: Routes Toward Insight into the Capital Empires*, vol. 9. Ed. by Fuat Sezgin, in collaboration with A. Jokhosha, and Eckhard Neubauer. Frankfurt a.M., 1988, 8–19. – Facsimile edition.

1.1.1.3 *Works: Larger Fragments and a Work of Uncertain Ascription*

None of al-Saraḫsī's works is extant in its entirety, apart from *Kitāb Ādāb al-mulūk*, whose authenticity, however, has not yet been proven (see below, LW °24). The following section records this work as well as seven relatively substantial fragments which are characteristic for the manifold interests and the stylistic approach of this pupil of al-Kindī's. In order to document the scope and proportions of al-Saraḫsī's writing more generally, a list of virtually all titles credited to him – in particular those recorded in the *Fihrist* and in Ibn Abī Uṣaybi'a – is given below. It follows the order given in Rosenthal 1943, while also taking into account the further data collected by Rosenthal from 1951–1995; the items are numbered continuously and furnished with occasional references and additional remarks.

25 *Risāla fī Waṣf maḏāhib al-Ṣābi'īn* (*A Description of the Religious Views of the Sabians*). – Bibliographical notes in Rosenthal 1943 [*17: I A (1), p. 40]; sources, translation and analysis ibid. [*17: 41–51].

26 *Muḫtaṣar* (*Iḫtiṣār*) *Kitāb Qāṭīġūriyās* (*Epitome of the Categories*). – Bibliographical notes in Rosenthal 1943 [*17: III A (7), p. 54]; fragment in MS Ayasofya 4855 (dated on fol. 179ª: 713/1313), heading and incipit: *Min risālat Aḥmad b. al-Ṭayyib al-Saraḫsī: Al-maqūlātu 'ašaratun wa-hiya tanqasimu qismayni* [...]; cf. Daiber 1990 [*35: 96].

27 Report (*Risāla*) on the Expedition of al-Mu'taḍid bi-llāh to al-Ramla against Ḫumārawayh b. Aḥmad b. Ṭūlūn. – Bibliographical notes in Rosenthal 1943 [*17: III A (7), p. 59]; references to the passages in Yāqūt's *Mu'ǧam al-buldān* taken directly from the *Risāla*, with translation and commentary ibid. [*17: 62–80].

28 *Fī anna arkān al-falsafa baʿḍuhā ʿalā baʿḍ wa-huwa Kitāb al-Istīfāʾ* (and variants) (*That the Main Principles of Philosophy are Based One upon the Other, that is, The Book of Completion*). – Bibliographical notes and variants of the title in Rosenthal 1943 [*17: VI A (2), pp. 119–120]; translation and commentary ibid. [*17: 120–121].

29 Works on musical theory. – Titles in Rosenthal 1943 [*17: VIII A (1–4), p. 125]; quotations (without references to the titles) in: al-Ḥasan b. Aḥmad b. ʿAlī al-Kātib, *Kamāl adab al-ġināʾ*. Ed. by Maḥmūd Aḥmad al-Ḥifnī, Ġaṭṭās ʿAbd al-Malik Ḫašaba. Cairo 1395/1975, 19–21 (French transl. in: [...] *La perfection des connaissances musicales* [...], traduction et commentaire d'un traité de musique arabe du XIe siècle par Amnon Shiloah. Paris, 1972, 42–43), 29 (57–58), 64–65 (101–102), 143 (203–204).

30 *On Love*, one passage extant in al-Saraḫsī's *Arkān al-falsafa wa-taṯbīt aḥkām al-nuǧūm*. – Titles in Rosenthal 1943 [*17: VI A (2), pp. 119–120]; identification and translation of the passage (according to MS Topkapı Sarayı, Ahmet III, 3483, fol. 240^{a-b}) in Rosenthal 1961 [*28].

31 *Ādāb al-mulūk* (*The Proper Conduct of Rulers*). – Title in Rosenthal 1943 [*17: II A (20), pp. 56–57]; analysis of the two manuscripts, comparison of the text with *Kitāb Aḫlāq al-mulūk* by Muḥammad b. al-Ḥāriṯ al-Taġlibī / al-Ṯaʿlabī, partial translation of the introduction, notes on the content and discussion of the question of authenticity in Rosenthal 1995 [*37].

32 *Zād al-musāfir wa-ḫidmat al-mulūk* (*Provision of the Traveller and Service to the Rulers*, cf. LW °59). – One passage is extant in Ibn al-ʿAdīm's (d. 660/1262) collection of biographies of people from Aleppo; cf. [*3: 337–339].

1.1.2 Life

The first decades of the life of al-Kindī's most prominent pupil, Abū l-ʿAbbās / Abū l-Faraǧ Aḥmad b. al-Ṭayyib b. Marwān al-Saraḫsī (for the genealogical variants and his *kunya* cf. Rosenthal 1943 [*17: 17–18]), born around 220/835, remain almost entirely in the dark. His *nisba* relates to Saraḫs in Khorasan, about 200 km east of Nishapur; unlike Abū Zayd al-Balḫī he appears to have spent the larger part of his life at the Baghdad court. It was during his early phase at the court in Baghdad, in any case, that he participated, as an envoy of his teacher al-Kindī and accompanied by 'Jews, Muslims and Muʿtazilīs', in a philosophical-theological debate with a Nestorian bishop, which among other things covered the Muslim Arabs' use of the teknonym (*kunya*), as well as the nature of number, and hence the Christian doctrine of the Trinity (Moosa 1972 [*29], Holmberg 1989 [*34], van Ess 1997 [*38: 725]). He began his service at the caliphal court in Baghdad as a tutor to the future caliph al-Muʿtaḍid bi-llāh (regn. 279–289/892–902); this arrangement may have been brokered by al-Kindī. Both the circle around al-Kindī and the milieu at court offered al-Saraḫsī the opportunity to meet a number of illustrious scientists, literary figures, and musicians. We know of connections to al-Ǧāḥiẓ, Ṯābit b. Qurra, and to Ḥammād, son to the famous musician Isḥāq b. Ibrāhīm al-Mawṣilī. In the year 271–272/885 al-Saraḫsī accompanied the prince on his military campaign into southern Palestine, whose itinerary he documented in a journal (fragment 2, LW °32, for a map see Rosenthal 1943 [*17: 64]; on the itinerary and on further geographical works cf. also GAS [*12: XIII 244–245]). Any reports of cultural significance, which we would expect to find in an author like al-Saraḫsī, have in all likelihood been filtered out by the transmitter, Yāqūt, who was not primarily interested in such information. After al-Muʿtaḍid's accession to the throne al-Saraḫsī advanced to the influential office of 'boon-companion' (*nadīm*) to the caliph (cf. LW °37–°40), and, in 282/895, to that of market inspector (*muḥtasib*, cf. LW °34 and °35). However, no more than a year later he fell out of favour with the caliph and was thrown in jail, where he died in 286/899. The reasons for his downfall became the subject of extensive speculation for his contemporaries and later biographers, though no dependable facts could ever be established. His influence on the caliph's religious thinking may have led to courtly intrigues, or may have left the caliph himself in an awkward position once al-Saraḫsī had risen to prominence; and his unorthodox opinions (cf. LW °2, which is reminiscent of a very similar title by Abū Bakr al-Rāzī, who, incidentally, knew al-Saraḫsī's medical works, cf. Rosenthal 1943 [*17: 36 n. 114]; on *maḫārīq* 'fabrications' [of the prophets] cf. also van Ess 1997 [*38: 332–333]) may have placed him under a general suspicion of heresy. In any case the decisive factor will have been a *raison d'état* (for a detailed discussion of the possible causes for al-Saraḫsī's fate see Rosenthal 1943 [*17: 25–38], including references to his relationship to the Muʿtazila [35] and to the Shia [36]; cf. also Glagow 1968 [*13: 152–156]).

1.1.3 List of Works (LW)

1.1.3.1 Religion, History of Religion [°1–°4] – 1.1.3.2 Philosophy, Psychology, Political Theory [°5–°25] – 1.1.3.3 Physics, Geography, Topography [°26–°33] – 1.1.3.4 History, Administration [°34-°36] – 1.1.3.5 Cultural History and *Adab* [°37–°46] – 1.1.3.6 Astronomy, Astrology [°47–°49] – 1.1.3.7 Mathematics [°50] – 1.1.3.8 Music [°51–°54] – 1.1.3.9 Medicine, Cosmetics [°55–°59]

1.1.3.1 *Religion, History of Religion*

°1 *Risāla fī Waṣf maḏāhib al-Ṣābiʾīn* (*Description of the Religious Views of the Sabians*). – Cf. *25.

°2 Books and treatises on the exposure of the secrets of the charlatans, i.e. the prophets.

°3 *Fī Waḥdāniyyat Allāh taʿālā* (*The Unity of God Most High*).
°4 *Risāla fī l-Sālikīn* (*l-Šākkīn*) *wa-ṭarīf* (*wa-ṭarāʾif*) *iʿtiqād al-ʿāmma* (*iʿtiqādihim*) (and variant) (*On the Striding Ones* [*Doubters*] *and the Peculiar Belief of the Populace* [*the Peculiarities of their Belief*]).

1.1.3.2 *Philosophy, Psychology, Political Theory*

°5 *Muḫtaṣar* (*Iḫtiṣār*) *Kitāb Qāṭīġūriyās* (*Epitome of the Categories*).
°6 *Muḫtaṣar* (*Iḫtiṣār*) *Kitāb Bārimīnās* (*Epitome of On Interpretation*).
°7 *Muḫtaṣar* (*Iḫtiṣār*) *Kitāb Anālūṭīqā al-ūlā* (*Epitome of the Prior Analytics*).
°8 *Muḫtaṣar* (*Iḫtiṣār*) *Kitāb Anālūṭīqā al-ṯāniya* (*Epitome of the Posterior Analytics*).
°9 *Kitāb ilā baʿḍ iḫwānihī fī l-Qawānīn al-ʿāmma al-ūlā fī ṣināʿat al-diyālaqṭīqiyya ay al-ǧadaliyya ʿalā maḏhab Arisṭūṭālīs* (*To One of His Friends On the First General Rules of the Art of Dialectics, i.e. of Disputation, According to Aristotle*).
°10 *Iḫtiṣār Kitāb Sūfisṭīqā li-Arisṭūṭālīs* (*Epitome of Aristotle's Sophistical Refutations*).
°11 *al-Nafs* (*The Soul*).
°12 *Fī Māhiyyat al-nawm wa-l-ruʾyā* (*On the Quiddity of Sleep and Dream*).
°13 *Fī l-ʿAql* (*On the Intellect*).
°14 *Fī Waṣāyā Fīṯāġūras* (*On Pythagoras' Legacy*).
°15 *Fī Alfāẓ Suqrāṭ* (*On the Sayings of Socrates*).
°16 *Fī l-ʿIšq* (*On Love*).
°17 *Fī anna l-ǧuzʾ yanqasim ilā mā lā nihāya lahu* (*On the Possibility of Infinite Division*).
°18 *Fī anna l-mubdaʿāt fī ḥāl al-ibdāʿ lā mutaḥarrika wa-lā sākina* (*That at the Moment of their Creation, Created Things are Neither in Motion Nor at Rest*).
°19 *Fī l-Farq bayn naḥw al-ʿArab wa-l-manṭiq* (*On the Difference Between Arabic Grammar and Logic*).
°20 *Fī Adab al-nafs ilā l-Muʿtaḍid* (*On the Education of the Soul, for al-Muʿtaḍid*).
°21 *Sīrat al-insān* (*The Conduct of Human Life*).
°22 *Kitāb al-Siyāsa al-kabīr* (*Great Book on Governance*).
°23 *Kitāb al-Siyāsa al-ṣaġīr* (*Small Book on Governance*).
°24 *Ādāb* (*Adab*) *al-mulūk* (*The Proper Conduct of Rulers*). – Cf. **31*.
°25 *Fī l-Radd ʿalā Ǧālīnūs fī l-maḥall al-awwal* (*On the Refutation of Galen Regarding the Question of the First Station*).

1.1.3.3 *Physics, Geography, Topography*

°26 *Fī Aḥdāṯ al-ǧaww* (*On Atmospheric Phenomena*).
°27 *Fī Kawn al-ḍabāb* (*On the Origin of Fog*).
°28 *Bard ayyām al-ʿaǧūz* (*On Frost during the Days of Late Summer*).
°29 *Manfaʿat al-ǧibāl* (*The Benefit of Mountains*).

°30 *al-Masālik wa-l-mamālik* (*Pathways and Kingdoms*). – Quotations in Ibn al-ʿAdīm's *Buġyat al-ṭalab fī tārīḫ Ḥalab* are referenced in Rosenthal 1951 [*26: 136–138].

°31 Treatises on the Seven Sleepers (*aṣḥāb al-kahf*) and the so-called *aṣḥāb al-raqīm*.

°32 *Risāla* on al-Muʿtaḍid bi-llāh's expedition to al-Ramla against Ḫumārawayh b. Aḥmad b. Ṭūlūn. – Cf. *27. On the transmission of the *Risāla*, in which (Sinān b.) Ṯābit b. Qurra and Ibn al-ʿAdīm had a share, as well as on the question how to differentiate between Yāqūt's quotations from °30 and °32 respectively, cf. Rosenthal 1951 [*26: 138–139].

°33 *Faḍāʾil Baġdād wa-aḫbāruhā* (*The Merits of Baghdad, with Historical Reports*).

1.1.3.4 *History, Administration*

°34 *Kitāb al-Aġšāš wa-ṣināʿat al-ḥisba al-kabīr* (*Great Book on Fraudulence and the Office of Market Inspector*).

°35 *Kitāb Ġišš al-ṣināʿāt wa-l-ḥisba al-ṣaġīr* (*Small Book on Commercial Fraud and the Market Inspectorate*).

°36 A work on history.

1.1.3.5 *Cultural History and Adab*

°37 *al-Lahw wa-l-malāhī* (*wa-nuzhat al-mufakkir al-sāhī*) *fī l-ġināʾ wa-l-muġannīn wa-l-munādama wa-l-muǧālasa wa-anwāʿ al-aḫbār wa-l-mulaḥ* (*Entertainment and Diversions* [*and the Recreation of the Pensive*] *on the Topics of Singing, Singers, Drinking Companionship, Society* [*of High-ranking People*] *and Various Stories and Witty Anecdotes*).

°38 *Risālat Mirāḥ al-rūḥ* (*On the Joyfulness of the Spirit*). – According to Rosenthal 1951 [*26: 141], this epistle is possibly identical with °40 or °37; the title is quoted by al-Tawḥīdī, *Baṣāʾir* IV 206 and VI 106.

°39 *al-Ǧulasāʾ wa-l-muǧālasa* (*On Those Who Keep Company* [*with High-Ranking Persons*], *and On Such Company*).

°40 *Nuzhat al-nufūs* (*Recreation of the Souls*).

°41 *Fī l-Šiṭranǧ al-ʿāliya* (*On the High Game of Chess*).

°42 *al-Ṭabīḫ* (*The Art of Cooking*).

°43 *Risāla ilā Ibn Ṯawāba* (*Letter to Ibn Ṯawāba*).

°44 *al-Rasāʾil* (*The Epistles*).

°45 *Fī l-Faʾl* (*On the Omen*).

°46 *al-Ǧawāriḥ wa-l-ṣayd bihā* (*Birds of Prey and How to Hunt with Them*).

1.1.3.6 *Astronomy, Astrology*

°47 *al-Madḫal ilā ṣināʿat al-nuǧūm* (*Introduction to Astronomy*).

°48   *Fī anna arkān al-falsafa baʿḍuhā ʿalā baʿḍ wa-huwa Kitāb al-Istīfāʾ* (and variants) (*That the Main Principles of Philosophy are Based One upon the Other, that is, The Book of Completion.* – Cf. *28.

°49   *Fī Qirān al-naḥsayn fī burǧ al-saraṭān* (*On the Conjunction of the Two Stars Constituting a Bad Omen within the Sign of Cancer*).

1.1.3.7   Mathematics

°50   *al-Ariṯmāṭīqī fī l-aʿdād wa-l-ǧabr wa-l-muqābala* (*Arithmetic, on Numbers and Algebra*).

1.1.3.8   Music

°51   *Kitāb al-Mūsīqī al-kabīr, maqālatān* (*The Great Book on Music, in Two Parts*).
°52   *Kitāb al-Mūsīqī al-ṣaġīr* (*The Small Book on Music*).
°53   *al-Madḫal ilā ʿilm al-mūsīqī* (*Introduction to the Science of Music*).
°54   *al-Dalāla ʿalā asrār al-ġināʾ* (*Guide to the Secrets of Singing*). For the titles °51–°54 cf. *29.

1.1.3.9   Medicine, Cosmetics

°55   *al-Madḫal ilā ṣināʿat al-ṭibb* (*Introduction to the Art of Medicine*).

°56   *Maqāla fī l-Radd ʿalā Aḥmad b. al-Ṭayyib al-Saraḫsī fīmā radda bihi ʿalā Ǧālīnūs fī amr al-ṭuʿm al-murr* (*Treatise on the Refutation of [the Views of] Aḥmad b. al-Ṭayyib al-Saraḫsī [by Abū Bakr al-Rāzī] in Relation to His Refutation of Galen in Regard of Bitter Food*).

°57   *Maqāla fī l-Namaš wa-l-kalaf* (Treatise on two kinds of rashes [affecting the face in particular]).

°58   *Fī l-Ḥiḍābāt al-musawwida li-l-šaʿr* (*On Tinctures for Dying Hair Black*).

°59   *Zād al-musāfir wa-ḫidmat al-mulūk* (*Provision of the Traveller and Service to the Rulers*). – Cf. *31 (LW °24) and *32. The relation between these two works is yet to be investigated. Besides elements belonging to the 'mirror for princes' genre, the fragment in Ibn al-ʿAdīm also contains medical sections. For the subsumption of the work under al-Saraḫsī's medical writings cf. Rosenthal 1951 [*26: 142]. In al-Tawḥīdī's *Baṣāʾir* [*14: IV 117, no. 381] we find the title mentioned as a source reference for a physiognomical observation, as *Āyīn ḫidmat al-mulūk* (*Rules for the Service to the Rulers*).

1.1.4   Doctrine

The diversity and the general profile of al-Saraḫsī's œuvre can only be gleaned in an indirect fashion from the lists of works in the *Fihrist* and Ibn Abī Uṣaybiʿa's history of physicians (as well as from the fragments and quotations collected above). For the history of Islamic philosophy it obviously is of particular import to note that al-Saraḫsī acted as a transmitter of works by al-Kindī, and occasionally also as his doxographer. How creative he was in this area can perhaps best be seen from those instances where both al-Saraḫsī and al-Kindī are named as authors of philosophical works that go by the same or similar titles. This concerns the epitomes of Aristotle's works (LW °5-°10), astrological speculations about the prospective duration of Islamic rule, in which another pupil of al-Kindī's, Abū Maʿšar, took part as well (LW °49; for al-Bīrūnī's criticism of al-Saraḫsī's ideas cf. Rosenthal 1943 [*17: 122–124]); furthermore testimonies for solutions to geographical and physical problems which mention al-Kindī and al-Saraḫsī in one breath (Rosenthal 1943 [*17: 59–60. 62]); and various themes of material culture (LW °42, °58), for whose Hellenistic context 'Bolus Democritus' (around 200 BC) has been made out to be responsible (cf. Kraus 1942 [*25: 61–62 with n. 3]).

For three of the areas in which al-Saraḫsī's interests coincide with those of his teacher – history of religion, astrology, and music – we are in possession of more substantial extant passages:

(1) The *Fihrist* (for further information see [*25] above) contains a valuable account by al-Saraḫsī, reporting on the authority of (*ʿan*) al-Kindī, concerning the religious views (*maḏāhib*) of the Sabians: they are described as adherents to the principle of an eternal efficient cause (*ʿilla lam yazal*) which is one, not many (*lā yatakaṯṯar*), and which does not admit of any attributes. This cause (God) has sent messengers (*rusul*) to mankind in order to confirm his rule (*al-iqrār bi-rubūbiyyatihi*) and to provide right guidance, promise and admonition, and has selected certain individuals (the text names Arānī, Agathodaemon, Hermes and 'according to some, Plato's maternal grandfather', Solon) who call on people to believe in God and in the *ḥanīfiyya* (true monotheism) and establish an authoritative tradition (*sunna*) as well as religious laws (*šarāʾiʿ*). These include a uniform direction of prayer, three obligatory daily prayers, commandments concerning ritual purity, fasting and animal sacrifice, commandments concerning food, marital laws and laws of inheritance, and others. The philosophical pronouncements of the Sabians (*qawluhum*) are in harmony with Aristotelian doctrine: for natural philosophy the text mentions his *Samʿ al-kiyān* (*Physics*), for the doctrine of the heavens, which constitute an imperishable fifth nature (*ṭabīʿa*) next to the four elements (*ʿanāṣir*), it names his *al-Samāʾ* (*On the Heavens*), for the generation and corruption of the animals and plants that are subjected to the four natures (*ṭabāʾiʿ*), his *al-Kawn wa-l-fasād* (*On Generation and Corruption*), for the influence of heavenly forces on the sublunary phenomena, his book *al-ʿUlwiyya* (*Meteorology*), for his doctrine of the perceptive (*darrāka*), imperishable and incorporeal human soul, his *al-Nafs* (*On the

Soul), for the understanding of veridical dreams (*al-ruʾyā al-ṣādiqa*) and sense perceptions, his *al-Ḥiss wa-l-maḥsūs* (*Parva Naturalia*), for their negative theology his *Maṭāṭāfūsīqā* (*Metaphysics*), and for their demonstrative logic (*barāhīn al-ašyāʾ*) his *Fūdīqṭīqā* (apodictics: *Analytica*). We are thus looking at a construction of a monotheistic community which receives a revelation and quasi-Islamic laws through prophets; a community of people (*ahl*), whose book (*kitāb*) is in fact the canon of Aristotelian philosophy. Together with the philosophical terminology of the report, which is that of the Arabic paraphrases of Plotinus and Proclus, and the at times 'old-style' transliteration of Greek book titles (cf. also LW °5–°10), this construction fits in well with the milieu of the Kindī Circle and its programme of establishing Greek philosophy in Islamic Baghdad, and designing a 'religion for intellectuals' (Endress 1994 [*36: 179]). Al-Saraḫsī's report, which served as a basis for the accounts of al-Muqaddasī, ʿAbd al-Ǧabbār, and perhaps even al-Bīrūnī, in any case does not provide any grounds for speculations about the Sabians as a philosophical school which independently transmitted Greek philosophy to the Muslims. (Nor does the report offer any support for granting the 'Sabian' Ṯābit b. Qurra a role as co-creator or even initiator of this construction of the Kindī Circle, even though he knew al-Saraḫsī personally and may have contributed a few details; cf. also Gutas 1988 [*33: 42 with n. 25].)

(2) The treatise *That the Main Principles of Philosophy are Based One upon the Other, that is, The Book of Completion* [*28 with further information] also contains a passage, transmitted in Ibn Rusta, which is reminiscent of al-Kindī's ideas, in that it proposes a divinely sanctioned contemplation of the heavens and the circular movements of the stars. Besides, the very same treatise includes a theory [*30 with further information] of the lovers' kiss, and of the union of loving souls more generally, which picks up on Hellenistic discussions of *eros*. Al-Saraḫsī's interest in the topic of love (*ʿišq*) furthermore manifests itself in the work *On Love* [LW °16], as well as in the abovementioned discussion between the two Baghdadians al-Saraḫsī and Aḥmad b. Abī Ṭāhir.

(3) We finally need to note al-Saraḫsī's and al-Kindī's shared interest in musical theory. Apart from LW °37 and °40 (?), al-Saraḫsī's expertise in this field is documented mainly by °51-°54; however, the quotations in al-Ḥasan b. Aḥmad b. ʿAlī al-Kātib [*29] cannot be assigned to any specific work. They discuss the inverse relationship of a listener's expertise and his enthusiasm, the necessary preconditions for the practical study of music, the technique of 'ornamentation' (*taḥrīk*) of a melody in 'old' music, the differentiation between linguistic phonemes that must be articulated in a lengthened (*al-ḥurūf al-muṣawwita*) or in a punctual

manner, and the element of unprovability which musical science contains, in contrast to its sister sciences arithmetic and geometry. They also report the legend of the discovery of music by someone who visited the market of the coppersmiths, and who used the categories of proportion, calculation and sense (of hearing) – *nisba, ʿibra, ḥiss* – for his study of the subject matter (cf. Nicomachus of Gerasa, *Harmonicum Enchiridium*, in: *Musici scriptores graeci* [...], rec. [...] Carolus Janus. Leipzig, 1895, 245–246 on Pythagoras).

Apart from the broadly philosophical disciplines mentioned above, al-Saraḫsī contributed to the geographical literature of his time (just as his colleague Abū Zayd al-Balḫī), and left behind numerous testimonies to his knowledge of literature. With respect to the first field we need to mention his traveller's journal [*27, LW °32], his *al-Masālik wa-l-mamālik* (*Pathways and Kingdoms*, LW °30 – a title we also find in the work of his contemporary Ibn Ḫurradāḏbih), as well as further material which he and al-Kindī are said to have collected for the production of a world map (cf. Kropp 1981 [*31; see also the depiction of the world map in GAS [*12: XII 11]; the attribution is discussed in GAS [*12: XIII 243]). The second field is represented by the various titles of section V [°37–°46] of the List of Works, and in a wider sense also by the book *Ādāb al-mulūk* (*The Proper Conduct of Rulers*, LW °24), which is extant in two manuscripts. The Berlin MS names a certain Abū l-Ḥasan ʿAlī b. Razīn as the author, whereas another copy, apparently preserved in Ankara, ascribes the text to al-Saraḫsī. The work presents itself as a critical adaptation and expansion of the so-called *Kitāb al-Tāǧ* (*Book of the Crown*), the mirror for princes formerly ascribed to al-Ǧāḥiẓ. In the absence of any further testimonies for this text, we cannot, of course, put it down as an authentic work by al-Saraḫsī (cf. Rosenthal 1995 [*37]; for authorship and title of *Kitāb al-Tāǧ* cf. Schoeler 1980 [*30]). The relation between works °24 and °59 remains to be examined. The reports collected in Rosenthal 1943 [*17: 94–117], mostly sourced from *Kitāb al-Aġānī*, cast al-Saraḫsī in the role of a connoisseur and transmitter of poems, songs and witty anecdotes and thus reveal him to be well-versed in literature (*adīb*). There is furthermore a report (possibly to be identified with LW °43; for a translation and commentary see Rosenthal 1943 [*17: 86–94]) about al-Saraḫsī playing a trick on an overly pious contemporary who eyed Hellenistic intellectuality with suspicion. In terms of its contents it is a plea for logic and geometry, but in terms of its form it is highly entertaining literature – unless the transmitter of this report, Abū Ḥayyān al-Tawḥīdī, has embellished it, or even invented it himself. The sparse reports concerning al-Saraḫsī show him as a determined representative of Hellenistic scholarship in al-Kindī's footsteps – at a time when this scholarship was not quite established yet – and as a witty participant in the political, intellectual and artistic life of the caliphal court (at least until his fall from grace); as an independent thinker who took part in the discussion about Arabic grammar and universal logic ('grammaire internationale', Kraus 1942 [*25: 251 n. 2, bottom of the page]; cf. also Endress 1986 [*32]; cf. LW °19) and who, according to Ḥamza al-Iṣfahānī's testimony, designed an original 'universal system' for the notation of phonemes of foreign languages (cf. Kraus 1942 [*25: 245 n. 3]).

1.2 *Abū Zayd al-Balḫī*

1.2.1 Primary Sources – 1.2.2 Life – 1.2.3 List of Works (LW) – 1.2.4 Doctrine

1.2.1 Primary Sources

1.2.1.1 Bio-bibliographical Testimonies [*41–*43] – 1.2.1.2 Individual Biographical and Doxographical Reports, Fragments [*48–*70] – 1.2.1.3 Works [*76–*80]

1.2.1.1 *Bio-bibliographical Testimonies*

The *Fihrist* contains a short literary and doxographical characterization of Abū Zayd, as well as a list of his works, comprising 43 titles. Yāqūt's *Iršād* adds 13 further titles; for a number of biographical reports on the author, Yāqūt can refer to a collective biography of three sons of the city of Balkh by Abū Sahl Aḥmad b. ʿUbayd Allāh b. Aḥmad, who in turn made use of Abū Zayd's biography written by the latter's student and companion Abū Muḥammad al-Ḥasan b. Muḥammad al-Wazīrī. Al-Ṣafadī generally follows Yāqūt's account.

41 Ibn al-Nadīm, Abū l-Faraǧ Muḥammad b. Isḥāq (d. 380/990). *Kitāb al-Fihrist* [composed 377/988). – Ed. by Gustav Flügel, August Müller, Johannes Roediger, vol. 1. Leipzig 1871, 138 (ed. quoted below). – Repr. Beirut, 1964; Frankfurt am Main, 2005. – Ed. by Riḍā Taǧaddud. Tehran, 1350 h.š./1971. – Ed. by Ayman Fu'ād Sayyid, 2 vols. London 1430/2009. – Engl. transl. by Bayard Dodge, *The Fihrist of al-Nadīm*, 2 vols. New York, 1970.

42 Yāqūt b. ʿAbd Allāh al-Ḥamawī al-Rūmī al-Baġdādī (d. 626/1229). *Iršād al-arīb*. – Ed. by David Samuel Margoliouth, *The Irshād al-arīb ilā maʿrifat al-adīb or Dictionary of Learned Men of Yāqūt*, vol. 1. London, Leiden, 1923 (2nd ed.), 141–152. – Ed. by Iḥsān ʿAbbās, *Muʿǧam al-udabāʾ: Iršād al-arīb ilā maʿrifat al-adīb*, vol. 2. Beirut, 1993, 274–282.

43 al-Ṣafadī, Ṣalāḥ al-Dīn Ḫalīl b. Aybak (d. 764/1363). *Al-Wāfī bi-l-wafayāt: Das biographische Lexikon des* [...] *aṣ-Ṣafadī*. – Ed. by Sven Dedering, vol. 6. Wiesbaden, 1972, 378; 409–413.

1.2.1.2 *Individual Biographical and Doxographical Reports, Fragments (mostly without source references)*

48 Abū Zayd on the theory of light and colour (MS Oxford, Bodleian Or. Marsh 539, 101[b]). – Text and translation of the passage in Emily Cottrell, "L'Anonyme d'Oxford [...]. Bibliothèque ou commentaire?", in: D'Ancona 2007 [*6: 415–441, ibid.: 438–440]. – Further fragments of Abū Zayd ibid., beginning at 134[a] [lacuna] are not extant, but only announced by the catchwords *qāla Abū Zayd* at the bottom of fol. 133[b]. – Now conveniently accessible in: *A Philosophy Reader from the Circle of Miskawayh*. Ed. and transl. by Elvira Wakelnig. Cambridge, 2014, 282, 10–284, 13 (text); 283, 11–285, 21 (transl.); 452–453 (comm.). For the non-extant passage by Abū Zayd (only hinted at by the catchword on fol. 133[b]), cf. 4 n. 5, and 339 n. 306.

49 al-Rāzī, Abū Bakr Muḥammad b. Zakariyyā' (d. 313/925). *Taqrīr al-Rāzī ḥawl al-zukām al-muzmin 'ind tafattuḥ al-ward.* – Ed. by Friedrun R. Hau, in: *Journal for the History of Arabic Science* 1 (1977): 57–61. – German translation in Hau 1975 [*44].

50 [Pseudo-al-Fārābī]. *Risāla li-Aflāṭūn fī l-Radd 'alā man qāla inna l-insān talāšā wa-fanā ba'd mawtihi,* section 9: Abū Yazīd al-Mu'allim, in: Mubahat Türker, "Un petit traité attribué à al-Fārābī." *Araştırma* 3 (1965): 25–63 (edition of the fragment 63, translation 54–55, discussion 46–47). – *Abū Zayd al-Balḫī (?) on the Senses of Hearing and Sight, with regard to the Celestial Bodies.* For a shorter version of this *risāla,* which does not contain the section by Abū Zayd cf. the edition in Badawī 1974 [*93: 337–339]; cf. furthermore Daiber 1993 [*100: 48–49 with commentary 134–136], *Letter from Abū l-Faḍl Ibn al-'Amīd to 'Aḍud al-Dawla Concerning the Question Whether the Celestial Bodies Possess Souls and Life.*

51 al-Muqaddasī, Šams al-Dīn Abū 'Abd Allāh Muḥammad b. Aḥmad (d. after 380/990). *Aḥsan al-taqāsīm fī ma'rifat al-aqālīm: Descriptio imperii Moslemici* [...]. – Ed. by Michael Jan de Goeje. Leiden, 1906 (2nd ed.), 4. – Description of Abū Zayd's geography as well as an anecdote concerning his refusal to cross the Oxus river. For further quotations from his geography cf. *Bibliotheca Geographorum Arabicorum* IV: Indices, Glossarium et Addenda ad partes I–III. Ed. by Michael Jan de Goeje. Leiden, 1879, s.v. Abū Zayd al-Balḫī, 159.

52 al-'Āmirī, Abū l-Ḥasan Muḥammad b. Yūsuf (d. 381/992). *Kitāb al-Amad 'alā l-abad: A Muslim Philosopher on the Soul and its Fate.* – Ed. by Everett K. Rowson. New Haven, 1988, 76–77. – Abū Zayd as teacher of al-'Āmirī and as pupil of al-Kindī; his relationship to religion (*dīn*) and philosophy/wisdom (*ḥikma*).

53 al-'Āmirī. Paraphrase of a passage from Abū Zayd's *Kitāb al-Siyāsa* (MS Oxford, Bodleian Or. Marsh 539, 127[a]–128[a]). – Text and translation in: Elvira Wakelnig, "Philosophical fragments of al-'Āmirī preserved mainly in al-Tawḥīdī, Miskawayh, and in the texts of the *Ṣiwān al-ḥikma* tradition", in: Peter Adamson, ed., *In the Age of al-Fārābī: Arabic Philosophy in the Fourth/Tenth Century*. London, 2008, 215–238 (234–236 with n. 61). Cf. [*77].

54 Abū l-Ḥasan Ibn Abī Ḏarr. *Al-Saʿāda wa-l-isʿād*. – Facsimile ed. by Mojtaba Minovi (*As-Saʿāda wa-l-isʿād. On Seeking and Causing Happiness*, written by Abū'l-Ḥasan Muḥammad al-ʿĀmirī […]). Wiesbaden, 1957–1958, 407. 419. 224 (?). 413 (?). – Abū Zayd and 'al-šayḫ' on personal opinion (*raʾy*), justice (*ʿadl*), and consensus (*iǧmāʿ*).

55 al-Tawḥīdī, Abū Ḥayyān ʿAlī b. Muḥammad (d. 414/1023). *Al-Baṣāʾir wa-l-ḏaḫāʾir*. – Ed. by Wadād al-Qāḍī, 10 vols. Beirut, 1408/1988, VII 59; VIII 66. – Abū Zayd on intellect as an instrument of worship; Abū Ḥayyān's praise of *Kitāb Naẓm al-Qurʾān* by Abū Zayd (giving a wrong date of death: 'in the years after 330' [940]).

56 Abū Ḥayyān al-Tawḥīdī. *Kitāb al-Imtāʿ wa-l-muʾānasa*. – Ed. by Aḥmad Amīn, Aḥmad al-Zayn, 3 vols. Beirut 1966 (3rd ed.), I 26, 212; II 15, 38. – References to an untitled epistle (*risāla*) (? *Fawāʾid al-ḥadīṯ*) by Abū Zayd and to his *Kitāb Aḫlāq al-umam*; al-Ǧarīrī's polemics against his 'trick' (*kayd*) of declaring philosophy (*falsafa*) compatible with Sharia law; his attitude towards alchemy.

57 Abū Ḥayyān al-Tawḥīdī. *Al-Muqābasāt*. – Ed. by Muḥammad Tawfīq Ḥusayn. Baghdad, 1970, 95.241. – References to Abū Zayd's *Kitāb Aqsām al-ʿulūm, Kitāb Iḫtiyār al-sīra* (= *al-siyar*).

58 al-Ṯaʿālibī, Abū Manṣūr ʿAbd al-Malik b. Muḥammad (d. 961/1038). *Yatīmat al-dahr fī maḥāsin ahl al-ʿaṣr*. – Ed. by Muḥammad Muḥyī l-Dīn ʿAbd al-Ḥamīd, I–IV in 2 vols. Cairo, 1956–1958, IV, 85–86. – Four eminent sons of Balkh, including Abū Zayd.

59 Pseudo(?)-al-Ṯaʿālibī. *Kitāb Tuḥfat al-wuzarāʾ*. – Ed. by Regina Heinecke, *Al-Abḥāṯ* 25 (1972): 3–71, (Arab.) 24, 32. 35. – Abū Zayd on a vizier's qualifications and residence. For further editions of *Tuḥfat al-wuzarāʾ*, and for arguments for its being 'a reworking of al-Thaʿālibī's *Ādāb al-mulūk* and perhaps of another author's work on viziership', cf. Bilal Orfali, "The works of Abū Manṣūr al-Thaʿālibī (350–429/961–1039)." *Journal of Arabic Literature* 40 (2009): 273–318, no. 36, 298–299.

60 al-Šahrastānī, Tāǧ al-Dīn Abū l-Fatḥ Muḥammad b. ʿAbd al-Karīm (d. 548/1153). *Kitāb al-Milal wa-l-niḥal*. – Ed. by Muḥammad Fatḥ Allāh Badrān, vol. 2. Cairo, 1955, 1051. – Abū Zayd appears in a list of 'more recent Muslim philosophers', starting with al-Kindī and ending with al-Fārābī, before a detailed account of Ibn Sīnā's doctrines is given.

61 al-Bayhaqī, Ẓahīr al-Dīn Abū l-Ḥasan ʿAlī b. Zayd Ibn Funduq (d. 565/1169–1170). *Tatimmat Ṣiwān al-ḥikma*. – Ed. by Muḥammad Kurd ʿAlī, *Taʾrīḫ ḥukamāʾ al-islām*. Damascus, 1396/1976 (2nd ed.), 42–43. – Three titles in addition to those in the *Fihrist* and in Yāqūt, as well as ten *dicta* by Abū Zayd.

62 *Ṣiwān al-ḥikma* [ascribed to Abū Sulaymān al-Siǧistānī]. – Excerpts ed. by Douglas Morton Dunlop, *The Muntakhab Ṣiwān al-ḥikmah of Abū Sulaimān as-Sijistānī*. The Hague, 1979, 127. – Abū Zayd as teacher of al-ʿĀmirī.

63 Faḫr al-Dīn al-Rāzī, Muḥammad b. ʿUmar (d. 607/1210). *Lawāmiʿ al-bayyināt, šarḥ asmāʾ Allāh taʿālā wa-l-ṣifāt*. – Ed. by Muḥammad Badr al-Dīn Abū Firās al-Naʿsānī al-Ḥalabī. Cairo, 1323/1905, 56. 79. 145. – Abū Zayd on the non-Arabic origin of Quranic words and names.

64 al-Idrīsī, al-Šarīf Abū Ǧaʿfar Muḥammad b. ʿAbd al-ʿAzīz al-Ḥusaynī (d. 649/1251). *Kitāb Anwār ʿulwī al-aǧrām fī l-kašf ʿan asrār al-ahrām, Das Pyramidenbuch des Abū Ǧaʿfar al-Idrīsī*. – Ed. by Ulrich Haarmann. Beirut, 1991, 60. 88–89. 110–111. 134–135 and *fihrist al-muʾallifīn ilḫ*. s.v. – Quotations from Abū Zayd's geography.

65 al-Šahrazūrī, Šams al-Dīn Muḥammad b. Maḥmūd (d. after 687/1288). *Nuzhat al-arwāḥ wa-rawḍat al-afrāḥ fī taʾrīḫ al-ḥukamāʾ wa-l-falāsifa*. – Ed. by Ḫwaršīd Aḥmad, vol. 2. Hyderabad, 1976, 25.

66 Abū Ḥayyān al-Andalusī, Muḥammad b. Yūsuf b. ʿAlī (d. 745/1344). *Taḏkirat al-nuḥāt*. – Quotes Abū Zayd's *Kitāb al-Muḫtaṣar fī l-luġa* under the title *Kitāb al-Muḫtaṣar fī ʿilm al-ʿarabiyya*; cf. GAS [*42: IX 189].

67 al-Maqrīzī, Taqī l-Dīn Aḥmad b. ʿAlī (d. 845/1441). *Kitāb al-Mawāʿiẓ wa-l-iʿtibār fī ḏikr al-ḫiṭaṭ wa-l-āṯār*, vol. 1. Būlāq, 1270/1854, 115. – Abū Zayd on dating the pyramids on the basis of their building inscription.

68 Ibn Ḥaǧar al-ʿAsqalānī, Abū l-Faḍl Šihāb al-Dīn Aḥmad b. ʿAlī (d. 852/1449). *Lisān al-mīzān*, vol. 1. Beirut, 1390/1971, 183–184.

69 al-Suyūṭī, Ǧalāl al-Dīn ʿAbd al-Raḥmān (d. 911/1505). *Buġyat al-wuʿāt fī ṭabaqāt al-luġawiyyīn wa-l-nuḥāt*. – Ed. by Muḥammad Abū l-Faḍl Ibrāhīm, vol. 1. Cairo, 1384/1964, 311. – Characterization based on Yāqūt, list of works (20 titles).

70 al-Dāwūdī, Šams al-Dīn Muḥammad b. ʿAlī b. Aḥmad (d. 945/1538). *Ṭabaqāt al-mufassirīn*. – Ed. by ʿAlī Muḥammad ʿUmar, vol. 1. Cairo, 1972, 42–44. – Biographical and doxographical details based on Ibn al-Nadīm, al-Tawḥīdī, Yāqūt, Faḫr al-Dīn al-Rāzī; list of works (26 titles).

1.2.1.3 *Works: a Medico-Ethical Work and Four Larger Fragments*

76 *Kitāb Maṣāliḥ al-abdān wa-l-anfus* (*Hygiene of Body and Soul*) (Istanbul, MS Ayasofya 3740, 140 f. [IX/XV]; Ayasofya 3741, 181 f. [884/1479]). – Mūsā b. Yūsuf al-Azharī, *Taḏkira ṭibbiyya muḫtaṣara min Kitāb Maṣāliḥ al-abdān wa-l-anfus li-Abī Zayd al-Balḫī*, (Cairo, MS Dār al-kutub 1832 ṭibb, 20 f. [1315 H.]). – *Sustenance for body and soul: Maṣāliḥ al-abdān wa'l-anfus*, by Abū Zayd al-Balkhī. Frankfurt a.M., 1984. – Facsimile edition. – Edition by Mālik Badrī, Muṣṭafā ʿAšwī. Riyadh, 1424/2003. – Further edition by Maḥmūd Miṣrī. Cairo, 1426/2005. – German transl. of the second part by Zahide Özkan, *Die Psychosomatik bei Abū Zaid al-Balḫī (gest. 934 A.D.)*. Frankfurt a.M., 1990, 89–155.

77 *Kitāb al-Siyāsa al-kabīr* (*Great Book on Governance*), *Kitāb al-Siyāsa al-ṣaġīr* (*Small Book on Governance*), quoted as *Kitāb al-Siyāsa*, in: Abū Ḥayyān al-Tawḥīdī, *al-Baṣāʾir wa-l-ḏaḫāʾir* [*55: IX 146–147]. – Cf. al-ʿĀmirī's paraphrase, cf. fragment no. *53 above. – Translation and discussion of the fragments in Rosenthal 1989 [*99].

78 *Kitāb al-Šiṭranǧ* (on Chess and Backgammon), quoted as *Risālat Ḥikmat waḍʿ al-nard wa-l-šiṭranǧ* (MS Istanbul, Topkapı Sarayı, Ahmet III 1541, fol. 724^{a-b}. Karatay 8683). – Reproduction of the fragment in: Félix M. Pareja Casañas, *Libro del ajedrez, de sus problemas y sutilezas, de autor árabe desconocido* [...], vol. 1. Madrid, 1935, 10–12. – Translation and discussion of the fragment in: Rosenthal 1975 [*94: 165–167].

79 *Kitāb al-Radd ʿalā ʿabadat al-aṣnām* (*Refutation of the Idol Worshippers*), quoted in: Faḫr al-Dīn al-Rāzī, *Kitāb al-Tafsīr al-kabīr*, vol. 30. Cairo, 1352/1933, 143–144. – Translation and discussion of the fragment in: Monnot 1986 [*98: 213–219].

80 [Fragment on a saying ascribed to Plato, concerning the world's having a causal, but not a temporal beginning]: *Kitāb al-Ḥikma* (MS Istanbul, Süleymaniye, Esad Efendi 1933, fols 78^{b}16–79^{b}16 (XI/XVII?; cf. Ritter 1938 [*91: 61–62]). – Edition, translation and notes in: Wakelnig 2009 [*101: 115–119; on the manuscript 86–88, on the identification of the Abū Zayd quoted in the text and on a parallel with al-ʿĀmirī's *Kitāb al-Amad*, 91–92].

1.2.2 Life

Abū Zayd Aḥmad b. Sahl al-Balḫī, born around 235/850 in Šāmistiyān, a village in the vicinity of Balkh in Ḫurāsān, went to Baghdad as a young man, with the purpose of studying Twelver Shiism (the creed he belonged to). During his eight years in Baghdad, he studied theology, philosophy, astrology, astronomy, medicine and natural sciences – not as a direct pupil of al-Kindī (d. between 247/861 and 252/866) (thus *Iršād* [*42: 145 Margoliouth, 277 ʿAbbās]), but nevertheless within his circle. We do not have information about any contacts to the Abbasid court – in contrast to the older pupil of al-Kindī, al-Saraḫsī. He may have undertaken further travels in the West after concluding his studies in Baghdad; in any case, he finally returned to Balkh via Herat, and worked as a schoolteacher. Whether Muḥammad b. Zakariyyāʾ al-Rāzī was amongst the pupils he taught philosophy during that time is a disputed question: the *Fihrist* s.v. al-Rāzī ([*41: 299], followed by Ibn Abī Uṣaybiʿa I 311,4–9) quotes the latter as claiming to have read philosophy with 'al-Balḫī'. The text then goes on to say that this al-Balḫī had travelled widely, was knowledgeable in philosophy and the 'ancient sciences', and that the author, Ibn al-Nadīm, had seen manuscripts in the hand of al-Balḫī, but that none of his works was publicly available in full – unless perhaps in Khorasan. As the *Fihrist*, on the other hand, presents a substantial list of works s.v. Abū Zayd al-Balḫī, which the author is unlikely to have known by hearsay alone, the identification of this particular al-Balḫī with Abū Zayd appears somewhat improbable. In any case al-Rāzī and Abū Zayd were known to each other: thanks to an arrangement by yet another al-Balḫī, the Persian poet and author Šuhayd b. al-Ḥusayn (on him cf. Rowson 1990 [*63: 69], de Blois 1996 [*47: 333–337], Adamson 2008 [*50: 90–92]), al-Rāzī wrote an expertise for Abū Zayd concerning the latter's periodically returning sniffle (*zukām*) at the time of the rose blossom in Balkh – a remarkably early testimony for an allergic disease. At the beginning of this expertise, al-Rāzī refers to Abū Zayd as 'our master' (*šayḫanā*; [*49: 59 Hau]); it remains a question worth pondering whether this is merely a sign of general respect, or may be seen as indicating a teacher-pupil relationship between the two men after all. Beyond this, not much is known about Abū Zayd's activities in Balkh; it is only in 301/914 that we hear, in Abū Zayd's own pointed words (*Fihrist* [*41: 138], *Iršād* [*42: 141–142 Margoliouth, 274 ʿAbbās], translation in Rowson 1990 [*63: 64]), that first the Qarmaṭī general al-Ḥusayn b. ʿAlī al-Marwarrūḏī, and then Abū ʿAlī Muḥammad b. Aḥmad al-Ǧayhānī, minister to the Samanid Naṣr b. Aḥmad, a dualist (*ṯanawī*), had withdrawn their support for dogmatic reasons. The Qarmaṭī was disappointed with Abū Zayd's strictly orthodox Quranic exegesis (LW °64), while the dualist (and perhaps crypto-Manichean, cf. *Fihrist* [*41: 338,12]; on Abū Zayd's *dictum* cf. van Ess 2011 [*67: 380–381], on the problem whether it was al-Ǧayhānī the father or the son, cf. Barthold 1968 [*43: 12. 245–246], Rowson 1990 [*63: 64–65 n. 47], van Ess 2011 [*67: 385–387]) was opposed to Abū Zayd's doctrine about animal sacrifice (LW °74). This testimony certainly ought to be understood as evidence for Abū Zayd's orthodoxy – having left youthful errors behind him –, rather than as evidence for a continued association with heretics; all the more so as all later comments on his life and works – with the exception of al-Ǧarīrī's invectives (cf. pp. 242–243 below) – emphasize his blameless orthodox beliefs. The accusation of heresy (*ilḥād*: *Fihrist* [*41: 138], *Iršād* [*42: 142 Margoliouth, 274 ʿAbbās]) is countered by another 'al-Balḫī' (probably the Muʿtazilite Abū l-Qāsim al-Kaʿbī al-Balḫī, d. 319/931, on him see van Ess 1985 [*45: 359–362], 2011 [*67: 328–375. 376–377]) with the attestation that Abū Zayd professed God's unity – and that the mere fact that both of them, Abū Zayd and Abū l-Qāsim, had studied logic, had not rendered them heretics. The two men seem to have conducted a correspondence of friendly controversy (LW °111), and when Abū l-Qāsim took up the position of a minister at the court of the governor (*amīr*) of Balkh (another Abū Zayd, Abū Zayd Aḥmad b. Sahl b. Hāšim) – an offer which Abū Zayd had rejected, contenting himself, for about a year, with a secretarial position – he offered 100 of his 1000 dirham earnings to Abū Zayd, raising the latter's income from 500 to 600 dirham (*Iršād* [*42: 147 Margoliouth, 278 ʿAbbās]). One of the Samanid rulers in Bukhara invited Abū Zayd to leave Balkh for his court, but

Abū Zayd did not accept; an anecdote (al-Muqaddasī [*51: 4], *Iršād* [*42: 152 Margoliouth, 282 ʿAbbās]) has him shrink back from the torrential waves of the Oxus and return to Balkh, with the ruler's permission. He lived out the last years of his life on an estate in his native Šāmistiyān, which he had been able to buy thanks to the munificence of the emir of Balkh and his minister Abū l-Qāsim al-Kaʿbī. To this late phase we also have to date Abū l-Ḥasan al-ʿĀmirī's (born around 300/912–913, d. 381/992) studies with Abū Zayd (cf. Wakelnig 2006 [*49: 9–11]) – which is how al-Kindī's personal teaching tradition came to span such a remarkably long period, of ca. 200 years: from al-Kindī to al-ʿĀmirī, 'from Baghdad to Bukhara'. Another pupil of Abū Zayd's was Ibn Farīġūn, who, in his sole work, *Ǧawāmiʿ al-ʿulūm*, takes up his teacher's classification of the sciences, *Aqsām al-ʿulūm*. – Abū Zayd al-Balḫī died in Ḏū l-Qaʿda 322/October 934.

1.2.3 List of Works (LW)

1.2.3.1 Quranic Sciences [°60–°65] – 1.2.3.2 Theology [°66–°70] – 1.2.3.3 Religious Studies [°71–°74] – 1.2.3.4 Linguistics [°75–°78] – 1.2.3.5 Classification of the Sciences, Philosophy, Political Science [°79–°88] – 1.2.3.6 Astrology [°89] – 1.2.3.7 Medicine [°90] – 1.2.3.8 (Cultural) Geography [°91–°95] – 1.2.3.9 Cultural History and *Adab* [°96–°104] – 1.2.3.10 Miscellaneous [°105–°110] – 1.2.3.11 Further Correspondence [°111–°119]

In order to demonstrate the areas of Abū Zayd's literary activities as well as their relative proportions, all titles found in the two authoritative catalogues (from the *Fihrist*, composed 377/988, and from Yāqūt's *Iršād*, compiled up to the year of the author's death, 626/1229) are listed. As far as possible, the titles are ordered according to subject areas, with additional comments wherever bibliographical information has been available. Doubtful assignations are flagged by question marks. In case of the *Fihrist* the titles are quoted according to Flügel's edition; occasional variants from Taǧaddud's edition are marked by the siglum T. The titles from the *Iršād* are quoted according to the edition by ʿAbbās; where they constitute variants to Flügel and T they are marked by the siglum Y. The three additional titles found in Ẓahīr al-Dīn al-Bayhaqī have been assigned the siglum Ẓ.

1.2.3.1 *Quranic Sciences*

°60 *Naẓm al-Qurʾān* (*The Order of the Quran*).

°61 *Qawāriʿ al-Qurʾān* (*The Apotropaic Verses of the Quran*).

°62 *Kitāb ǧamaʿa fīhi Mā ġāba ʿanhu min* (*Mā ʿulliqa ʿanhu fī* T, *K. Mā uġliqa min* Y) *ġarīb al-Qurʾān* (*A Collection of the Obscure Passages of the Quran which have Eluded the Author*).

°63 *Fī anna Sūrat al-Ḥamd tanūbu ʿan ǧamīʿ al-Qurʾān* (*That the First Sura is Representative for the Whole Quran*).

°64 *al-Baḥṯ ʿan al-taʾwīlāt* (*Study on [Quranic] Exegesis*).

°65 *Tafsīr al-Fātiḥa wa-l-ḥurūf al-muqaṭṭaʿa fī awāʾil al-suwar* (*Explanation of the First Sura and of the Isolated Letters at the Beginnings of the Suras*).

1.2.3.2 *Theology*

°66 *Kamāl al-dīn* (*The Perfection of Religion*).

°67 *Asmāʾ Allāh ʿazza wa-ǧalla wa-ṣifātuhu* (*The Names and Attributes of God Most High*).

°68 *ʿAṣm* (*ʿIṣmat* TY) *al-anbiyāʾ ʿalayhim al-salām* (*The Sinlessness of the Prophets, Peace be on Them*).

°69 *al-ʿUttāk* (*al-Futtāk* Y) *wa-l-nussāk* (*The Pure and the Ascetics*).

°70 *Bayān wuǧūh al-ḥikma fī l-awāmir wa-l-nawāhī al-šarʿiyya, wa-sammāhu Kitāb al-Ibāna ʿan ʿilal al-diyāna* (*Demonstration of the Aspects of Wisdom Regarding the Commandments and Prohibitions of the Religious Law; Called [by the author] Explication of the Causes of Religion*) Ẓ.

1.2.3.3 *Religious Studies*

°71 *Šarāʾiʿ al-adyān* (*The Laws of the Religions*).

°72 *al-Radd ʿalā ʿabadat al-aṣnām* (*al-awṯān* Y) (*Refutation of the Idol Worshippers*). – Cf. *79.

°73 *al-Šiṭranǧ* (*The Game of Chess*). – Cf. *78.

°74 *al-Qarābīn wa-l-ḏabāʾiḥ* (*Sacrifices and Immolations*).

1.2.3.4 *Linguistics*

°75 *al-Asmāʾ wa-l-kunā wa-l-alqāb* (*Personal Names, Teknonyms and Honorifics*.

°76 *Asāmī* (*Asmāʾ* Y) *al-ašyāʾ* (*The Names of Things*).

°77 *al-Naḥw wa-l-taṣrīf* (*Syntax and Inflection*).

°78 *al-Muḫtaṣar fī l-luġa* (*Outline of Lexicography*). – Quotations are found in Abū Ḥayyān al-Andalusī, *Taḏkirat al-nuḥāt*.

1.2.3.5 *Classification of the Sciences, Philosophy, Political Science*

°79 *Aqsām al-ʿulūm* (*The Parts of the Sciences*). – The title (without naming the author) is also found in al-Tawḥīdī's introduction to his *Risāla fī l-ʿUlūm* 3, line 13 ed. Bergé 1963/64–1968 [*142].

°80 *Risāla fī Ḥudūd al-falsafa* (*On the Definitions of Philosophy*).

°81 *Faḍīlat ʿulūm al-riyāḍiyyāt* (*On the Preeminence of the Mathematical Sciences*).

°82 *Tafsīr ṣuwar* (*ṣadr*) *Kitāb al-Samāʾ wa-l-ʿālam li-* (*ilā*) *Abī Ǧaʿfar al-Ḫāzin* (*Commentary on the Tables [belonging to the first part] of the Book on the Heavens and the Earth [Aristotle's On the Heavens] for [addressed to] Abū Ǧaʿfar al-Ḫāzin*. – Cf. *Fihrist* [*41: 251,1–2 (s.v. Aristotle, *On the Heavens*): *wa-li-Abī Zayd al-Balḫī* *šarḥ ṣadr hāḏā l-kitāb ilā Abī Ǧaʿfar al-Ḫāzin*]; see Rowson 1990 [*63: 70 with n. 68], van Ess 2011 [*67: 378–379 with n. 16 and 17].

°83 *Fī Ifšāʾ* (*Iqtināʿ* T, *Aqsām* Y) *ʿulūm al-falsafa* (*On the Dissemination of the Philosophical Sciences*). Doublet of °79?

°84 *Iḫtiyārāt al-siyar* (*Choosing one's Behaviour*).

°85 *Kitāb al-Siyāsa al-kabīr* (*Great Book of Governance*).

°86 *Kitāb al-Siyāsa al-ṣaġīr* (*Small Book of Governance*). – For °85 and °86, cf. *77.

°87 *al-Amad al-aqṣā* (*The Utmost Limit*) Ẓ.

°88 *Fī l-Aḫlāq* (*On Ethics*) Ẓ. – Perhaps identical with °94?

1.2.3.6 *Astrology*

°89 *Mā yaṣiḥḥu min aḥkām al-nuǧūm* (*Which Parts of Astrology are Valid*). – On this work it is said in *Iršād* [*42: 146 Margoliouth, 277 ʿAbbās] that Abū Zayd does not support the assumption that the celestial bodies – which are subject to God's will alone – exert an effect, even though people who use mathematical calculations (*ḥusbān*) are able to determine a variety of things from their constellations.

1.2.3.7 *Medicine*

°90 *Maṣāliḥ al-abdān wa-l-anfus* (*Hygiene of Body and Soul*). – Cf. *76.

1.2.3.8 *(Cultural) Geography*

°91 *Ṣuwar al-aqālīm* (*The Maps of the Climes*) or *Taqwīm al-buldān* (*The Tablets of the Countries*) or *Ṣifat al-arḍ wa-l-aqālīm* (*Description of the Earth and the Climes*, in al-Idrīsī).

°92 *Faḍāʾil* (*Faḍīlat* T) *Makka ʿalā sāʾir al-biqāʿ* (*The Merits of Mecca over Other Cities*).

°93 *Faḍāʾil Balḫ* (*The Merits of Balkh*).

°94 *Aḫlāq al-umam* (*The Customs of the Nations*).

°95 *Ṣifāt al-umam* (*The Characteristics of the Nations*).

1.2.3.9 *Cultural History and Adab*

°96 *Faḍl ṣināʿat al-kitāba* (*The Merit of the Art of Writing*).

°97 *Ṣināʿat al-šiʿr* (*The Art of Poetry*).

°98 *Faḍīlat ʿilm al-aḫbār* (*The Merit of the Science of [Historical] Reports*).

°99 *al-Nawādir fī funūn šattā* (*Curiosities from Various Disciplines*).

°100 *Munabbih* (*Munyat* TY) *al-kuttāb* (*The Exhortation [The Desire] of the Secretaries*).

°101 *Ṣawlaǧān al-kataba* (*The Scepter of the Secretaries*).

°102 *Adab al-sulṭān wa-l-raʿiyya* (*The Right Conduct of the Ruler and His Subjects*).

°103 *Rusūm al-kutub* (*The Models of the Books*).

°104 *Risāla fī Madḥ al-wirāqa* (*Epistle on the Praise of the Art of Paper*).

1.2.3.10 *Miscellaneous*

°105 *al-Ṣūra wa-l-muṣawwar* (*The Picture and the Depicted*).

°106 *Faḍl al-mulk* (*al-malik?*) (*The Merit of Rulership* [*of the King?*]).

°107 *al-Maṣādir* (*The Origins* [*The Verbal Nouns?*]).

°108 *al-Qurūd* (*The Monkeys*).

°109 *Nuṯārāt min kalāmihi* (*Morsels of His Conversation*).

°110 *Kitāb Waṣiyya* (*Waṣiyyatihi* T) (*Bequest*).

1.2.3.11 *Further Correspondence*

°111 *Aǧwibat Abī l-Qāsim al-Kaʿbī* (*Replies to Abū l-Qāsim al-Kaʿbī*).

°112 *Aǧwibat ahl Fāris* (*Replies to the Iranians*).

°113 *Aǧwibat Abī ʿAlī b. Muḥtāǧ* (*Replies to Abū ʿAlī b. Muḥtāǧ*). – I.e. the ruler of Čaġāniyān, d. 344/955, dedicatee of the *Kitāb Ǧawāmiʿ al-ʿulūm* by Ibn Farīġūn; cf. Bosworth 1981 [*96: 5–10].

°114 *Aǧwibat Abī l-Qāsim* (*Abī Isḥāq* Y) *al-Muʾaddib* (*Replies to Abū l-Qāsim al-Muʾaddib*). – A grammarian who was active around 338/949 in Bukhara (GAS [*42: IX 190]) and the author of *Daqāʾiq al-Taṣrīf*. The terminology of this work shows some conspicuous affinities with the introductory chapter on grammar of Ibn Farīġūn's *Ǧawāmiʿ al-ʿulūm*.

°115 *Aǧwibat masāʾil Abī l-Faḍl al-Sukkarī* (*Replies to Questions from Abū l-Faḍl al-Sukkarī*).

°116 *Ǧawāb risālat Abī ʿAlī Ibn al-Munīr al-Ziyādī* (*Reply to the Epistle of Abū ʿAlī Ibn al-Munīr al-Ziyādī*).

°117 *al-Risāla al-sālifa ilā l-ʿātib* (*ʿalayhi*) (*Previous Epistle to the Censurer*).

°118 *Kitāb katabahu ilā Abī Bakr b. al-Mustanīr ʿātiban wa-muntaṣifan fī ḏammihi al-muʿallimīn wa-l-warrāqīn* (*Letter to Abū Bakr al-Mustanīr, containing a Complaint and an Objection against His Censure of Teachers and Booksellers*).

°119 *Kitāb katabahu ilā Abī Bakr Ibn al-Muẓaffar fī šarḥ mā qīla fī ḥudūd al-falsafa* (*Letter to Abū Bakr Ibn al-Muẓaffar on the Topic of the Definitions of Philosophy*). – Probably the Muḥtāǧid 'Ruler of Khorasan', who is named by al-Ǧarīrī as having charged Abū Zayd with the task of propagating philosophy (*falsafa*) in the guise of the Sharia.

1.2.4 Doctrine

In the eyes of his contemporaries, Abū Zayd achieved prominence first and foremost as a theologian and a stylist; modern scholars regard him as an ancestor of Islamic geography. The only one of his works to have survived in full is a monograph of medico-ethical content; about the philosophical ideas of the author, however, we can only speculate. Ibn al-Nadīm describes the dilemma he was facing due to the diversity of Abū Zayd's literary output with the following words [*41: 138] (paraphrased in *Iršād* [*42: 141 Margoliouth, 274 ʿAbbās]): 'He was excellent in all sciences, old as well as new. In his works (*taṣnīfātihi wa-taʾlīfātihi*) he followed the path of the philosophers, but he was more similar and closer to the men of letters, which is why I have filed him in this section (*al-mawḍiʿ*: reports on rulers, secretaries, orators, writers of epistles, tax and treasury (*dīwān*) magistrates)'. This characterization is apposite in two respects: on the one hand, we can recognize a systematic use of philosophical-theological categories in Abū Zayd's fragments on governance and on chess – topics one may want to assign to *adab*; on the other hand it is a discernible aim of the author of the monograph on the hygiene of body and soul to instruct his educated readership in style – employing syntactic parallelisms, and alternating between his use of technical and non-technical vocabulary etc. The stylistic elegance of this work renders plausible the praise bestowed on it by the great literary figure, al-Tawḥīdī, which Yāqūt (*Iršād* [*42: 124 Margoliouth, 259 ʿAbbās]) quotes from his (lost) *Taqrīẓ al-Ǧāḥiẓ* (*Praise of al-Ǧāḥiẓ*): the three all-time best prose writers were al-Ǧāḥiẓ, Abū Ḥanīfa al-Dīnawarī and Abū Zayd, the 'scholar of scholars' who like none other combined wisdom (or philosophy, *ḥikma*) and religious law. In his *Baṣāʾir* [*55: VIII 66], al-Tawḥīdī praises Abū Zayd's *Naẓm al-Qurʾān* (*The Order of the Quran*), where the latter 'takes on the viewpoint of the philosophers, but discusses the Quran with subtlety and elegance', calling him 'the Ǧāḥiẓ of Khorasan'. The slightly younger al-Ṯaʿālibī (*Yatīma* [*58: IV 85–86]) lists four prominent authors from Balkh: Abū l-Qāsim al-Kaʿbī (distinguished as a theologian), Abū Zayd (on account of his literary and 'compositional skills', *balāġa, taʾlīf*), Šuhayd b. al-Ḥusayn (Sahl b. al-Ḥasan in the text; as Persian poet) and an Arabic poet (cf. Rowson 1990 [*63: 69–70]).

Apart from his ability to integrate *adab* and *falsafa*, it is Abū Zayd's dual competence in the areas of religion (religious law) and philosophy that is mentioned in al-Ǧāḥiẓ' *Taqrīẓ*, and is also pointed out by his readers (cf. Rowson 1990 [*63: 66–67]). It did, however, also attract the criticism of the religious scholar al-Ǧarīrī, whose polemics against the Iḫwān al-Ṣafāʾ as well as against Abū Zayd, Abū Tammām al-Naysābūrī and al-ʿĀmirī have thrown the problem of integrating Sharia and *falsafa* into sharp relief (according to al-Tawḥīdī's report, *Imtāʿ* [*56: II 14–16], reading al-Ḥarīrī; for the context cf. Bergé 1979 [*95: 289–297], for the following translation of the passage concerning Abū Zayd see Rowson 1990 [*63: 68]): 'He [Abū Zayd] claimed that *falsafa* is compatible (*muqāwida*, 15,5; perhaps to be read *muqāwima*? H. H. B.) with the *sharīʿa*, and the *sharīʿa* is similar (*mushākila*) to *falsafa*, and that one of them is a mother and the other a wet nurse. He professed to adhere to the Zaydiyya, and took orders from the amīr of Ḫurāsān, who wrote to him to work at disseminating *falsafa* through the mediation (*šafāʿa*, H. H. B.) of the *sharīʿa*, and to summon people to it with subtlety, solicitude, and enticement'.

Abū Zayd's geographical work is not extant. Even the transmitted versions of its title, *Ṣuwar al-aqālīm* (*The Maps of the Climes*) or *Taqwīm al-buldān* (*The Tablets of the Countries*), are listed neither in the *Fihrist* nor in the *Iršād*. Explicit quotations of the work – and rather brief ones at that – are only found in al-Muqaddasī and in authors of the 7th/13th and the 8th/14th century (cf. GAS [*42: XIV 429. 439; XV 71. 76]), notably the Egyptian geographers al-Idrīsī and al-Maqrīzī. Al-Muqaddasī describes Abū Zayd's work as a series of 20 individual maps (*amṯila*) with attached commentary (*šaraḥa*) and summary (*iḫtaṣara*, *Aḥsan al-taqāsīm* [*51: 4,11]). All in all the work was, as it were, incorporated into the geographical works of al-Iṣṭaḫrī and Ibn Ḥawqal. What was truly epoch-making about Abū Zayd's work, and hence gives rise to the notion of the 'Balḫī School', is the resolute expansion of its interest beyond the narrow boundaries of physical geography, to include climatic data, information on natural products, and their influence on the 'géographie humaine' (cf. Tibbetts 1992 [*75: 110–115], Savage-Smith 2003 [*76: 113–121]).

The only work by Abū Zayd that is extant in its entirety discusses the hygiene of body and soul (*Kitāb Maṣāliḥ al-abdān wa-l-anfus* [*76]). After treating some general themes, like the elements, the physiological and organic structure of man, and climatology, the first part is dedicated to the conventional topics of food, drink, scents, as well as sleep, bathing, gymnastics etc. (including an original chapter on the hygiene and therapeutic value of listening to music); the second part deals mainly with the psychological disorders of wrath (*ġaḍab*), fear (*ḫawf*, *fazaʿ*), sadness (*ḥuzn*, *ǧazaʿ*) and obsessive thoughts (*wasāwis al-ṣadr wa-aḥādīṯ al-nafs*). The basic concept of a correspondence between body and soul, which itself is again embedded in the system of all natural things, is indebted to Galen's physiology, whereas various elements of Abū Zayd's psychology (e.g. the cardinal virtues, the balance of the mean [*iʿtidāl*] between two extremes, or the typology of psychological defects) can be traced back to al-Kindī's reception of Aristotelian and Platonic ideas. Notwithstanding all these elements of the Hellenistic tradition, one should not fail to note Abū Zayd's recurring references to ethos and etiquette of the princely court (following traditional Iranian ideals) and his 'non-technical', pleasing style, geared towards the ideals of Arabic *adab*.

The same triad of (1) indigenous (Arabic-Islamic) components, (2) components that take up Iranian ideas, and (3) categories of primarily Aristotelian provenience can be found in Abū Zayd's fragment on political theory (cf. *Works* [*77]), which may originate in either the *Great* or the *Small Book on Governance*, and is quoted extensively in Abū Ḥayyān al-Tawḥīdī's *Kitāb* *al-Baṣāʾir wa-l-ḏaḫāʾir*. The passage defines governance (*siyāsa*) as an art (*ṣināʿa*) whose aim is the well-being (*ʿimāra*) of a country and the protection of its inhabitants. It names five causes (*ʿilal*) that constitute the creation of the product called 'governance': matter (the subjects' concerns [*umūr*]), form (their well-being [*maṣlaḥa*]), agent (the ruler's solicitude [*ʿināya*] for his subjects' concerns), end (perpetuation of that *maṣlaḥa*), and instrument (use of incentives and deterrents [*tarġīb, tarhīb*]). The combination of the four Aristotelian causes with the Neoplatonic instrumental cause may go back to al-Kindī's or al-Saraḫsī's reception of Proclus' commentaries (cf. *In Tim.*, I 263,19–30 Diehl; further Proclus, *Elem. theol.*, 240–241 Dodds) or the pseudo-Aristotelian *Theology*. Abū Zayd furthermore prepares his analysis of governance with an analogous definition of the causes at work in architecture and in medicine; while these latter two are also regarded as parallel cases in late antiquity (on account of their practical focus, which in fact means that they do not qualify as proper sciences), the (not entirely smooth) parallelization of politics may well be Abū Zayd's own achievement. These late ancient elements dominate his analysis; apart from them one should note, on the one hand, e.g. the use of traditionally Islamic terms of *maṣlaḥa* and *istiṣlāḥ* for the well-being of the community, as well as for measures aimed at its accomplishment; on the other hand, e.g. the emphasis he places on the topic of governance itself, and his exploitation of the two terms *tarġīb* and *tarhīb* (use of incentives and deterrents) for purposes of governance. Both points represent elements of the ancient Iranian tradition, which in any case remained the dominating influence on Islamic political theory up to the 3rd/9th century. How closely al-ʿĀmirī follows his teacher Abū Zayd in this categorization of governance can be gleaned from a passage from MS Oxford Marsh 539 (Wakelnig 2006 [*49: 234–235]; for the differences between both versions cf. ibid., n. 57). A further testimony for al-ʿĀmirī's reception of Abū Zayd's views is provided by a passage in al-ʿĀmirī's *Kitāb al-Amad ʿalā l-abad* [*52: 86,1–3 Rowson] (commentary and investigation of possible sources for the passage, which refers to Plato's *Laws*, ibid., 251–259, in particular 258–259), which assigns a causal beginning (*badʾ ʿillī*), but no temporal beginning (*badʾ zamānī*) to the world; the world has a Creator (*fāʿil*), who has 'produced it not in time', 'for the sake of the self-willed emanation of His generosity'. The distinction between causal and temporal beginning of the world is discussed in more detail in a fragment by Abū Zayd (cf. *Works* [*80]), which likewise relies on Plato's pronouncement that the world is generated (*mukawwan*) or brought about (*mubdaʿ*), without, however, having a temporal beginning (*li-l-ʿālami l-kulliyyi laysa badʾun zamāniyyun* [*80: 116,19 Wakelnig]). For time itself needs the universe as a prerequisite, as it belongs to its concomitants (*lawāḥiq*, line 21). The enumeration and exemplification of the four Aristotelian causes, which are the 'principles of the natural existents' (*mabādiʾ al-akwān al-ṭabīʿiyya*, line 8), are again reminiscent of Abū Zayd's (and al-ʿĀmirī's) definition of politics (see above).

Abū Zayd's fragment on chess and backgammon (cf. *Works* [*78]) first explains the method, employed by 'the sages', of making complicated intellectual facts accessible through the use of instructive examples, and of inventing things which outwardly entertain the common populace, while being inwardly suited to sharpen the minds and the senses of the elite. The invention of the two games, which lend themselves to illustrating the opposition of free will (*qadar*) and determinism (*ǧabr*), falls into this very category. The representatives of determinism localized the determining factor either in God or in the activity of the spheres, whereas the adherents of free will ascribed success and failure of a human being entirely to their good or bad choice – a view, Abū Zayd explains, that was based on dualistic systems like that of the Zoroastrians. The inventor of backgammon had a deterministic model in mind, letting the two dice 'decide'; the inventor of chess, on the other hand, gave both players equal chances to realize their success through prudent choice. It is worth noting that Abū Zayd merely illustrates the two views without judging them explicitly – at least as far as this passage is concerned; nor does he compensate his neutral reference to Zoroastrianism by correlating Islam with determinism (which would, after all, have been a possible option). Granted, within the medieval Islamic discourse chess was usually better tolerated than backgammon; even so the implicit preeminence of chess – which, in passing, is employed as a model for human conduct – could well be interpreted as a Muʿtazilite argument against the deterministic position of a pious Muslim (Rosenthal 1975 [*94: 167]).

Abū Zayd's statements concerning the kinds of idolatry, and the motives for it (cf. *Works* [*79]) are in parts reported in Faḫr al-Dīn al-Rāzī's *Kitāb al-Tafsīr al-kabīr* (*The Large Commentary* [*on the Quran*]). On the one hand, they are a testament to the continuing relevance of the topic in the author's day and age: Abū Zayd does not discuss pre-Islamic antiquities, but testimonies of Indian religions (and especially of Buddhism), which will still have been a visible presence during his life and in his area. On the other hand, the ordered sequence of his all in all seven interpretations (*taʾwīlāt*) of idolatry bear witness to the rational and unprejudiced attitude which is also characteristic of his other writings. In all manifestations of idolatry Abū Zayd diagnoses a common streak, the illicit corporealization (*taǧsīm*) of God, be it as a statue or a talisman, or as a projection onto the stars. Faḫr al-Dīn al-Rāzī summarizes Abū Zayd's report in a twofold verdict: such views were contrary to reason, and banned by revealed law. (We know that Faḫr al-Dīn knew Abū Zayd's other theological writings as well because his *Kitāb al-Lawāmiʿ al-bayyināt* contains quotations from Abū Zayd's *Kitāb Asmāʾ Allāh*).

Due to the small number of extant testimonies from Abū Zayd's voluminous œuvre it is difficult to form a general picture of his thoughts. Like with al-Saraḫsī, Abū Zayd's writing is characterized by its thematic breadth – something that is a feature also of al-Kindī's work, as is their common denominator, *adab*. The biographers seem to hit the nail on the head when they either praise or condemn Abū Zayd's method, with which he managed to cross the boundaries between *adab* and *falsafa* on the one hand, and between *falsafa* and *dīn* or Sharia on the other. Abū Zayd was no pure philosopher, nor was he a freethinker (Kraus 1942 [*25: 251 n. 2]), even if his analysis of Quranic names and concepts, his interest in foreign cultures and religions, and his lack of prejudice within the discussion of free will and determinism was to evoke the censure of later authors. Abū Zayd's writing can be described as eclectic (Rowson 1990 [*63: 74], Adamson 2008 [*50: 364]) and is addressed to a rather diverse audience. Al-Fārābī's works, which come after those of al-Kindī's school and mark off a completely new stage in the history of philosophy, are also addressed to the educated class, but they constitute a system of pure philosophy.

1.3 *Ibn Farīġūn*

1.3.1 Primary Sources – 1.3.2 Biographical Information – 1.3.3 Work and Doctrine

1.3.1 Primary Sources

1.3.1.1 *Manuscripts, Facsimile Edition, Edition*

91 Madrid, Escurial 950, 84 fols. (393/1003).

92 Istanbul, Topkapı Sarayı, Ahmet III 2768, 86 fols. (Ḏū l-Qaʿda 396 / August 1006).

93 Istanbul, Topkapı Sarayı, Ahmet III 2675, 80 fols. (VI / XII).

94 *Compendium of Sciences: Jawāmiʿ al-ʿulūm*, by Ibn Farīʿūn (*sic*). Frankfurt a.M., 1985. – Facsimile edition, with introductory note in English and Arabic, by Fuat Sezgin. – Ed. [based on the aforementioned facsimile edition alone] by Qays Kāẓim al-Ǧanābī, *Kitāb Ǧawāmiʿ al-ʿulūm, taʾlīf Mutaġabbī* (*sic*) *b. Farīʿūn* (*sic*). Cairo, 1428/2007.

1.3.2 Biographical Information

Ibn Farīġūn is known exclusively as the author of a survey of the sciences, entitled *Ǧawāmiʿ al-ʿulūm* (*Summaries of the Sciences*); even his given name (*ism*) cannot be determined with accuracy; in any case neither Šiʿyā (Derenbourg, Renaud 1941 [*121: 82]) nor Mutaġabbī/Mubtaġā (b. Furayʿūn/Farīʿūn) (Ritter 1950 [*122: 83], GAS [*112: I 388]) are likely to be correct readings (of the apparently identical *rasm*). The title pages of all three manuscripts declare Ibn Farīġūn to be the pupil of Abū Zayd al-Balḫī (d. 322/934, himself the author of a – lost – classification of the sciences with the title *Aqsām al-ʿulūm* [*Classification of the Sciences*], cf. § 5.1.2); as addressee of the dedication of the work, the title page of the Escurial MS names a Muḥtāǧid in Čaġāniyān, north of the Oxus river, Abū ʿAlī Aḥmad b. Muḥammad b. al-Muẓaffar (d. 344/955; on the Āl-i Muḥtāǧ cf. Bosworth 1985 [*115]). This places Ibn Farīġūn in the Eastern Iranian milieu of the Kindian tradition, to which his teacher Abū Zayd belonged as well as his co-student Abū l-Ḥasan al-ʿĀmirī and al-Saraḫsī; it furthermore dates his life to the middle of the 4th/10th century. It has been surmised that Ibn Farīġūn was a member of the dynasty of the Āl-i Farīġūn, a family ruling in Gūzgān who paid tribute to the Samanids and, later on, the Ghaznavids (Minorsky 1962 [*127], Bosworth 1985 [*114]). That Ibn Farīġūn is identical with the anonymous author of a Persian geographical work, *Ḥudūd al-ʿālam* (*Boundaries of the World*) (Minorsky 1962 [*127]), is difficult to prove and rather unlikely.

1.3.3 Work and Doctrine

Only a small number of passages of Ibn Farīġūn's *Ǧawāmiʿ* are written in continuous prose. Its bulk is made up from keywords which are arranged in the so-called *tašǧīr* pattern. This is a comparatively rare method of visualizing the progressive diaeresis of superordinate concepts (in this case of various scientific domains with their respective sub-disciplines and professional areas, the respective kinds of expertise required for them, etc.) in the form of 'trees' whose 'branches' are marked by lines in black or red ink. It started to be used in the 3rd/9th century, mainly in teaching materials. This form of presentation is supposed to manifest the unity and interdependency of the various sciences and suggests a more transparent systematization of the subject matter, which is also more easily examined by question and answer – even though it may at times compromise the comprehensibility of the text, as the brief notation of keywords within such tree diagrams (*tašǧīr*) and the placement of lines, which may be difficult to decipher, invite textual corruption.

Two larger blocks mark out the beginning and the end of the *Ǧawāmiʿ*: the first one contains a presentation of Arabic grammar, especially of its morphology, which should probably be understood as an implicit declaration that it is language that makes it possible in the first place to understand all the sciences and professions that will be discussed in the text, and that is the first precondition of the transmission of knowledge. The final block discusses the occult sciences as explicitly inferior disciplines: 'the fields of knowledge on which views may differ as to whether they constitute proper [sciences] or rather deception, fraud, and profiteering', as the headline has it; *Ǧawāmiʿ* [*94: 146]. In between these two blocks, various fields of knowledge are studied in the following sequence: (1) Professional skills of the courtly secretary (*kātib*): Ibn Farīġūn mentions the sub-topics fiscal system, army, messenger service and secret service, law, and a portfolio for representative tasks; he discusses them in terms of calligraphy, official correspondence, and accountancy (cf. Rebstock 1992 [*131: 15–19]), but also in terms of historical knowledge (giving a collection of topics which will be detailed in a different context below); further tasks are added as well as virtues of character when dealing with the ruler and 'people of lower rank'. (2) Ethics and moral instruction (with special consideration to the virtues of the ruler); (3) politics and warfare; (4) theology and religious duties; and as final climax, as it were, (5) sources of knowledge and forms and methods of transmitting knowledge and philosophy. In this context belongs a section on literary genera of communication (*Ǧawāmiʿ* [*94: 134]), where Ibn Farīġūn sketches the respective characteristics and functions of poetry, speech, letter and maxim/saying (*maṯal*) – a quartet which, at its core, goes back to ideas of al-Ǧāḥiẓ and is also found (albeit partially) in authors like Abū Hilāl al-ʿAskarī and Abū l-Ḥusayn Isḥāq b. Ibrāhīm al-Kātib. The same quartet is found in its entirety, in the same order, and with the same emphasis on the specific poignancy and the social function of the *maṯal* in al-ʿĀmirī, in the context of a defence of 'beautiful speech' (*bayān*) against attacks by pious, self-righteous critics who hold it in contempt. It hence constitutes possible evidence for the assumption that both authors studied with Abū Zayd al-Balḫī, and in general for a shared interest in *adab*, in literature as a medium – an aspect which is known to go back to al-Kindī (Rosenthal 1942 [*141]; on this passage see Biesterfeldt 2008 [*132]). This section on forms of communication, which is entitled *lafẓ* (expression), is coupled with a section entitled *maʿnā* (meaning, idea) on the facing page (*Ǧawāmiʿ* [*94: 135]), which, however, discusses in irritatingly asymmetrical fashion the areas of historiography (*ʿilm al-taʾrīḫāt*; see Rosenthal 1968 [*128: 34–36, edition of the passage 539–540]) worth knowing. The division of philosophy into practice (*ʿamal*) and theory (*ʿilm*) and their respective canons of politics, economics and ethics on the one hand and metaphysics (*ilāhī*), mathematics and natural sciences on the other (*Ǧawāmiʿ* [*94: 144]) corresponds to the scheme of the Alexandrian commentaries on Aristotle. The mathematical sciences of arithmetic, geometry, astronomy and music ('composite in a threefold manner, as it utilizes all three aforementioned sciences') are presented as increasingly complex. They correspond to al-Kindī's system (as e.g. found in the latter's *Risāla fī Kammiyyat kutub Arisṭāṭālīs*). Other points that indicate the tradition of al-Kindī, into which his 'grand-pupil' Ibn Farīġūn inscribes himself (Gutas 1988 [*129: 245–248], Adamson 2007 [*152: 351–370]), include the definition of metaphysics as the highest of all sciences which investigates the origin of all things and the rulership (*rubūbiyya*) of the Creator; the definition of logic as a function of intellect and as the instrument of said investigation (*Ǧawāmiʿ* [*94: 145]); as well as the complementarity (if not identification) of metaphysics and Islamic theology (*kalām*) – according to object and method – which Ibn Farīġūn systematizes in another place (facsimile [*94: 136]).

Ibn Farīġūn's survey of the fields of knowledge cultivated in his age is part of a tradition of classifications of the sciences which is rooted in the Alexandrian commentators on Aristotle. Its Arabic transmission begins with al-Kindī (see Cortabarría Beitia 1972 [*144]), continues with his contemporary Qusṭā b. Lūqā (Daiber 1990 [*146]), followed by Abū Zayd al-Balḫī, al-ʿĀmirī, al-Ḫwārazmī, Abū l-Farağ Ibn Hindū (Türker-Küyel 1967 [*143]), Abū Ḥayyān al-Tawḥīdī (Bergé 1963–1964 [*142]), and the Ismaili Abū Yaʿqūb al-Siğistānī (De Smet 2008 [*153]), and finally leads to al-Fārābī's *Enumeration of the Sciences, Iḥṣāʾ al-ʿulūm* (for general information on structure and function of these works see Heinrichs 1995 [*147], Biesterfeldt 2000 [*148], 2002 [*149]). All these classifications share a systematic distinction between Hellenistic sciences (often with the sub-divisions employed by the Greek commentators) and indigenous disciplines (theology, law, and those disciplines that concern the Arabic language), and in several of the authors we also find a systematic correlation of these two areas. In Ibn Farīġūn's *Ǧawāmiʿ*, these two structural principles, differentiation and correlation, are present only implicitly, being scattered loosely across the work. For instance, the physician is, on the one hand, counted among the staff at court (together with the secretary, the gatekeeper, etc.); on the other hand, medicine is listed as part of the curriculum of the natural sciences; also, categories of the Hellenistic doctrine of the virtues are applied to the Muslim ruler, etc. Like the entire œuvres of al-Saraḫsī and Abū Zayd al-Balḫī, Ibn Farīġūn's *Ǧawāmiʿ* displays a pronounced tendency towards integration (under which we may even subsume the mechanically systematic tree-diagram structure [*tašǧīr*]); for they try to combine three traditions: the Hellenistic sciences with their scholarly taxonomy (and with their elements of popular interest in the occult sciences), the religious and linguistic sciences serving the political unity and the continuity of the Muslim community; and, above all, the doctrines of the (originally Sasanian, but then) Abbasid political science concerning the professional skills and ethics of the secretary at court (*kātib*), dressed in the garbs of *adab*. With the end of the 4th/10th century, this tradition of classifying the sciences also finds its end. Ibn Sīnā's momentous outlines of classifications of the sciences are philosophical *summae* which, even though preserving the curricular model of the Aristotelian corpus, settle the relation between metaphysics and Islamic theology in a systematic fashion which prepares the way for a long series of later Arabic and Persian encyclopedias.

2 Neoplatonic Developments

Elvira Wakelnig

2.1 Primary Sources – 2.2 Neoplatonic Philosophy in Textbooks Between al-Balḫī and al-ʿĀmirī – 2.3 Abū l-Ḥasan al-ʿĀmirī

2.1 *Primary Sources*

2.1.1 Neoplatonic Philosophy in Textbooks [*101–*104] – 2.1.2 Abū l-Ḥasan al-ʿĀmirī [*111–*144]

2.1.1 Neoplatonic Philosophy in Textbooks

101 *Kitāb al-Ḥaraka* (MS Ankara, Ankara Üniversitesi dil ve tarih-coğrafya fakültesi kütüphanesi, Ismail Saib I 1696) fols 93^a–108^b (9th/15th cent.). – Cf. Taylor 1982 [*179: 252–258]. – MS Istanbul, Süleymaniye, Hacı Mahmud Efendi 5683, fols 119^a–140^b (13th/19th cent., probably a copy of MS Ankara), cf. Taylor 1982 [*179: 258–259]. – Diplomatic ed. by Elvira Wakelnig at http://www.ancientwisdoms.ac.uk/library/arabicphilos/

102 al-Isfizārī, Abū Ḥāmid. *Kitāb fī Masāʾil al-umūr al-ilāhiyya wa-hiya ṯamāniya wa-ʿišrūn masʾala.* – MS Istanbul, Süleymaniye, Ragıp Paşa 1463, fols 30^a–47^a. – Ed. by D. Gimaret 1984 [*188: 214–52]. – MS Damascus, Ẓāhiriyya 4871, fols 134^b–145^a. – Partial ed. and Engl. transl. by D. C. Reisman 2004 [*189: 279–300], *masʾala* 22; partial Engl. transl. by D. C. Reisman 2008 [*190: 255–264], *masʾala* 8, 9, 11 and 21.

103 Pseudo-Plato. *Ḥuǧaǧ Aflāṭūn ʿalā baqāʾ al-nafs*, in: *Arisṭū ʿind al-ʿArab*. Ed. by ʿAbd al-Raḥmān Badawī. Cairo, 1947, 73–74.

104 Pseudo-Plato. *Ṯamara laṭīfa min maqāyīs Aflāṭūn fī anna l-nafs lā tafsud*, in: *Aflāṭūn fī l-islām*. Ed. by ʿAbd al-Raḥmān Badawī. Beirut, 1980 (2nd ed.), 331–332.

2.1.2 Abū l-Ḥasan al-ʿĀmirī

2.1.2.1 *Bio-bibliographical Testimonies*

111 al-Tawḥīdī, Abū Ḥayyān ʿAlī b. Muḥammad (d. 414/1023). *Aḫlāq al-wazīrayn: Maṯālib al-wazīrayn al-Ṣāḥib Ibn ʿAbbād wa-Ibn al-ʿAmīd.* – Ed. by Muḥammad b. Tāwīt al-Ṭanǧī. Damascus, 1385/1965, 115–116. 344–345. 411–414. 446–447.

112 Abū Ḥayyān al-Tawḥīdī. *Al-Baṣāʾir wa-l-ḏaḫāʾir.* – Ed. by Wadād al-Qāḍī, 10 vols. Beirut, 1408/1988, II 209; III 93–94; IX 148–149.

113 Abū Ḥayyān al-Tawḥīdī. *Kitāb al-Imtāʿ wa-l-muʾānasa.* – Ed. by Aḥmad Amīn, Aḥmad al-Zayn, 3 vols. Beirut, 1953, I 35–36. 222–223; II 15–16. 84–89; III 91–96.

114 Abū Ḥayyān al-Tawḥīdī. *Al-Muqābasāt.* – Ed. by Muḥammad Tawfīq Ḥusayn. Baghdad, 1970, 116–119. 171–172. 177–180. 340–354.

115 Miskawayh, Abū ʿAlī Aḥmad b. Muḥammad (d. 421/1030). *Taǧārib al-umam.* – Ed. by Henry Frederic Amedroz and David Samuel Margoliouth, *The Eclipse of the ʿAbbasid Caliphate*, 4 vols [3–4 = *Continuation of the Experiences of the Nations by Abū Shujāʿ Rūḏrāwarī and Hilāl ibn Muḥassin*]. Oxford, 1920–1921. – Arab. text, ed. H. F. Amedroz. Cairo, 1332–1334/1914–1916, 277.

116 Miskawayh. *Al-Ḥikma al-ḫālida.* – Ed. by ʿAbd al-Raḥmān Badawī. Cairo, 1952, 347–373.

117 *Ṣiwān al-ḥikma* [attributed to Abū Sulaymān al-Siǧistānī]. – Abridgement ed. by Douglas Morton Dunlop, *The Muntakhab Ṣiwān al-ḥikmah of Abū Sulaimān as-Sijistānī.* The Hague, 1979, 5–7. 127–129.

118 al-Sāwī, ʿUmar b. Sahlān (early 6th/12th cent.). *The Mukhtaṣar Ṣiwān al-Ḥikma of ʿUmar b. Sahlān al-Sāwī.* – Ed. by R. Mulyadhi Kartanegara. PhD Diss., University of Chicago, 1996, 264–267.

119 Yāqūt b. ʿAbd Allāh, al-Ḥamawī al-Rūmī al-Baġdādī (d. 626/1229). *Iršād al-arīb.* – Ed. by David Samuel Margoliouth, *The Irshād al-arīb ilā maʿrifat al-adīb or Dictionary of Learned Men of Yāqūt*, vol. 1. London, 1907, 411–412.

120 Ibn Abī Uṣaybiʿa, Muwaffaq al-Dīn Aḥmad b. al-Qāsim (d. 668/1270). *ʿUyūn al-anbāʾ fī ṭabaqāt al-aṭibbāʾ.* – Ed. by August Müller, vol. 2. Cairo, 1299/1882, 20.

2.1.2.2 *Partial Collections*

126 *Rasāʾil Abī l-Ḥasan al-ʿĀmirī wa-šaḏarātuhu al-falsafiyya.* – Ed. by Saḥbān Ḫalīfāt. Amman, 1988.

127 *Abū l-Ḥasan al-ʿĀmirī, Arbaʿ Rasāʾil falsafiyya.* – Ed. by Saʿīd al-Ġānimī. Najaf, 2015.

2.1.2.3 *Individual Works*

131 "El-ʿÂmirî ve Kategoriler'in şerhleriyle ilgili parçalar. Al-ʿĀmirī et les fragments des commentaires des *Catégories* d'Aristote." – Ed. by Mubahat Türker, *Araştırma* 3 (1965): 103–122. – With Turkish transl. 87–102. – Fragments from the commentary on the *Categories* are also ed. by S. Ḫalīfāt [*126: 442–467].

132 *Kitāb al-Iʿlām bi-manāqib al-islām.* – Ed. by Aḥmad ʿAbd al-Ḥamīd Ġurāb. Cairo, 1387/1967. – New, rev. ed., Riyadh, 1408/1988. – Partial German transl. (ch. 1) in: Franz Rosenthal, *Das Fortleben der Antike im Islam.* Stuttgart, 1965, 91–101 (Der Islam und die Wissenschaften). – Engl. in: F. Rosenthal, *The Classical Heritage in Islam*, transl. by Emile and Jenny Marmorstein. London, Berkeley, 1975, 63–70. – Repr. London, New York 1994. – Partial Engl. transl. (ch. 7) in: F. Rosenthal, "State and religion according to Abū l-Ḥasan al-ʿĀmirī." *The Islamic Quarterly* 3/1

(1956): 46–52; also in: F. Rosenthal, *Muslim Intellectual and Social History: A Collection of Essays*. Aldershot 1990, no. VII. – Partial Engl. transl. (chs 1–3) in: Everett K. Rowson, “Knowledge and the Religious Sciences.” In *An Anthology of Philosophy in Persia*, vol 1: *From Zoroaster to ʿUmar Khayyām*. Ed. by Seyyid Hossein Nasr and Mehdi Aminrazavi. Oxford, 1999; London, New York (2nd ed.), 2008, 182–206.

133 *Kitāb al-Amad ʿalā l-abad*. – Ed. by Everett K. Rowson, *A Muslim Philosopher on the Soul and Its Fate: Al-ʿĀmirī's Kitāb al-Amad ʿalā l-abad*, New Haven, Conn. 1988, 52–176. – With Engl. transl. and inventory of al-ʿĀmirī's works, ibid., 52–54. – Ed. by S. al-Ġānimī [**127*].

134 *Inqāḏ al-bašar min al-ǧabr wa-l-qadar*. – Ed. by Kasım Turhan, *Bir ahlak problem olarak kelâm ve felsefe açısından insan fiileri*. Istanbul 1996 [Marmara Üniversitesi İlahiyat Fakültesi vakfı yayınları, 52]. – Arab. text 3–26; with Turkish transl. 139–159. – Ed. by S. Ḫalīfāt [**126*: 249–271]. – Ed. by S. al-Ġānimī [**127*] in two different versions.

135 *Kitāb al-Fuṣūl fī l-maʿālim al-ilāhiyya*. – Ed. by Elvira Wakelnig, *Feder, Tafel, Mensch: Al-ʿĀmirīs Kitāb al-Fuṣūl fī l-maʿālim al-ilāhīya und die arabische Proklos-Rezeption im 10. Jh*. Leiden, Boston, 2006, 82–122; with German transl. – Ed. by S. Ḫalīfāt [**126*: 363–379].

136 *al-Taqrīr li-awǧuh al-taqdīr*. – Ed. by S. Ḫalīfāt [**126*: 303–341]. – Ed. by S. al-Ġānimī [**127*].

2.1.2.4 *Manuscripts*

141 Oxford, Bodleian Library, MS Marsh 539, fols 124ᵃ–133ᵇ (7th/13th cent). – A collection of quotations from Greek and Arabic philosophers, compiled probably in the 5th/11th cent., which contains a long quotation from an unnamed text by al-ʿĀmirī, possibly *al-Itmām li-faḍāʾil al-anām*. – Ed. by Elvira Wakelnig under the title *A Philosophy Reader from the Circle of Miskawayh*. Cambridge, 2014.

142 Istanbul, Süleymaniye, MS Servili 179, fols 110ᵇ–111ᵃ (12th/18th cent). – It contains al-ʿĀmirī's *Kitāb al-Amad*, followed by further, unknown philosophical material which can most probably be ascribed to al-ʿĀmirī.

143 Istanbul, Süleymaniye, MS Ayasofya 4130, p. 26–27. – ʿAlī al-Riyāḍī's *Kitāb Ṣaḥāʾif al-laṭāʾif*, containing Arabic and Persian texts and completed in 882/1477, includes a quotation by al-ʿĀmirī which has a parallel in MS Oxford, Bodleian Library, Marsh 539 [**141*: 324–327 ed. Wakelnig]).

144 Konya, Bölge Yazma Eserle Kütüphanesi, MS 15 Hk 187/2. – According to V. Kaya (2014 [*238: 82 n. 82]), this manuscript contains the text of *al-Taqrīr li-awǧuh al-taqdīr*.

2.2 *Neoplatonic Philosophy in Textbooks Between al-Balḫī and al-ʿĀmirī*

Arabic translations of Greek philosophical texts were not just read, studied and copied; in the course of their reception history they were also adapted, altered, extended, excerpted, and paraphrased. It is this phase of the reception process which generated the texts discussed in this section. The degree to which they have been adapted cannot really be determined in detail, especially since the underlying original translations have not survived. In the final analysis, the bulk of the material goes back to the Neoplatonist Proclus; however, so far it has not been possible fully to establish how exactly Proclus' works were transmitted to the Arabic-Islamic world. All these texts focus mainly on the soul.

Kitāb al-Ḥaraka
Book on Motion

In its extant form, the *Book on Motion* poses a number of riddles. Neither its author nor its compiler are known, and the same goes for its title and date. It makes sense to assume the 6th/12th century as *terminus ad quem* for its date, as both collective manuscripts containing the text must have been compiled by then. At the beginning of the book, its complete title is given as *Book on the Motion by the Heavy, by Aristotle* (*Kitāb al-Ḥaraka min al-ṯaqīl li-Arisṭāṭālīs*), whereas it is referred to as *Book on Motion, with Aristotle's Proof* (*Kitāb al-Ḥaraka bi-l-burhān li-Arisṭāṭālīs*) at the end. The ascription to Aristotle is valid only for those parts of the book (in particular MS Ankara, fols 99[a]–102[b]) which contain quotations from Aristotle's *Physics, On the Heavens, On Generation and Corruption, Meteorology*, and *Metaphysics*, mostly with references to the Aristotelian work in question. Two further important sources are Proclus' *Elements of Theology* (prop. 20, 80, 19, 17, 15 in: MS Ankara, fol. 93[a], and prop. 41, 45, 48, 76, 20, 59, 72, 66 on fols 97[a]–99[a]) and *Elements of Physics* (II 17, 15, 19, 21; I 31; II: 20, 15 ibid., fols 94[b]–97[a]), even though they are used anonymously and occasionally are altered considerably (cf. also Pines 1986 [*180: 288–292]). The exact relation between the material taken over from Proclus' *Elements of Theology* and the other texts of the Arabic Proclus known to date is uncertain (cf. Wakelnig 2006 [*182: 61–66]). The material adopted from the *Elements of Physics* provides unequivocal evidence for the existence of an Arabic version of at least parts of this Proclean work (beside the propositions quoted by Yaḥyā Ibn ʿAdī in his treatise on the *atomon*, cf. Endress 1984 [§ 7.2 *162: 161]). Whether the sections of the *Book on Motion* that are based on these various sources were originally compiled in a single work is questionable (cf. e.g. the fact that *Elem. theol.*, prop. 20 is included twice). In its extant form, the book does not give the impression of having been composed as an integral whole. The title may therefore have been taken from a work from which fragments were integrated into the extant version of the *Book on Motion* – for instance a summary of books v, vi and vii of Aristotle's *Physics*, which were in fact known by the title *On Motion*, or Proclus' *Elements of Physics*, which were seen as a commentary to this same section of Aristotle's *Physics*. Parts of the textual material are very likely to go back to al-Kindī's time, possibly even to his own circle (cf. e.g. the frequent use of the expression *fa-qad istabāna*, which is typical of these translations). – This is further corroborated by the similarity between a particular section from the *Book on Motion* and an excerpt by ʿAbd al-Laṭīf al-Baġdādī which may possibly be based on a *Question* by Alexander of Aphrodisias (Rashed 2004 [*181: 13]).

The *Book on Motion* discusses a number of topics that it loosely strings together, sometimes without any suitable transition. As explained above, they are culled from different sources, and repetitions are frequent. Their underlying common theme is movement, which is discussed from various angles: the soul's self-movement is examined in Proclean fashion; circular movement is juxtaposed to straight movement, and among other things the text demonstrates the continuity of the former and the discontinuity of the latter, using theoretical proofs following Proclus' *Elements of Physics* and various Aristotelian writings. The First Mover is proven to be unmoved, incorporeal, the mover of the spheres, and both final and efficient cause. Sensually perceptible bodies are moreover said not to possess infinity or infinite power. The text furthermore introduces the Neoplatonic ontological scheme One-Intellect-Soul-Body, whereby the First Cause imparts itself to all existing beings, even though its reception remains tied to each recipient's ability to receive it.

Abū Ḥāmid Aḥmad b. Abī Isḥāq al-Isfizārī: *Kitāb fī Masāʾil al-umūr al-ilāhiyya wa-hiya ṯamāniya wa-ʿišrūn masʾala*
28 Questions on Metaphysical Topics

This text is in many ways comparable to the *Book on Motion*. All we know about al-Isfizārī is that he appeared at the Saffarid court in Siǧistān in the 4th/10th cent. (ca. 340–355/950–965), that he was a mathematician and a philosopher of the Neoplatonic tradition (cf. Gimaret 1984 [*188: 209–210], Reisman 2004 [*189: 271–273]), and that Ibn Sīnā mentions him critically several times (Reisman 2004 [*189: 273–275]). The *28 Questions* are the only work by al-Isfizārī known so far, even though the author himself refers, within the text, to three further compositions of his (Reisman 2004 [*189: 275]). Gimaret's edition of the work (1984 [*188: 215–252]) is based on MS Ragıp Paşa 1463, which, according to Reisman (2004 [*189: 263]), however, lacks a lengthy quotation from Plato's *Republic* which is preserved, within the 22nd question, in a second manuscript (Ẓāhiriyya 4871).

The text consists of 28 elaborately phrased questions receiving replies of various lengths. They generally concern the existence of God and His creation, and the possibility of knowing them. Twelve of the questions are concerned explicitly with different aspects of movement, for instance with the movement of the spheres and Aristotle's view on it. Reflections on movement then lead on to the following statements on God, the First Mover: He is incorporeal, eternal, simple, one, the cause of all existing beings. The topics show clear similarities to the *Book on Motion*, even though there are no literal parallels between the two texts. Both works frequently take recourse to Aristotle, explicitly referring to individual works, and furthermore use material from Proclus' *Elements of Theology* (cf. prop. 70 with respect to al-Isfizārī's 21st question). In addition, they both provide good evidence for the use of the concept of movement in the context of metaphysical questions and may provide a possible background for Ibn Sīnā's polemical attack on the attempt to prove God's existence based on the concept of movement.

Pseudo-Plato: *Ḥuǧaǧ Aflāṭūn ʿalā baqāʾ al-nafs*
Plato's Arguments for the Survival of the Soul
Pseudo-Plato: *Ṯamara laṭīfa min maqāyīs Aflāṭūn fī anna l-nafs lā tafsud*
Subtle Fruit from Plato's Logical Proofs That the Soul Does Not Perish

The Arabic Neoplatonic corpus has preserved two short, independent textual units delineating Platonic proofs for the immortality of the soul. One of them, entitled *Plato's Arguments for the Survival of the Soul*, is preserved in the unique Cairo manuscript (Dār al-kutub, MS Ḥikma 6M, 153ᵇ6–18), at the end of Ibn Sīnā's *Commentary on the Theology [of Aristotle]*, *Tafsīr Kitāb Uṯūlūǧiyā* (cf. Hasnawi 1997 [*196: 396 n. 4]). It lists the following five proofs: self-knowledge of the soul (cf. Proclus, *Elements of Theology*, prop. 186–187); the indestructibility of the soul due to its freedom from evil (cf. Plato, *Republic* X, 608c9–611a3); the soul's knowledge of all things that exist through themselves (a variation of the first proof); the life-giving activity of the soul (cf. Plato, *Phaedo*, 105b–107a1); and the essence of the soul (equivalent to the second proof) (cf. Hasnawi 1997 [*196: 396–397]). The other text, bearing the title *Subtle Fruit from Plato's Logical Proofs That the Soul Does Not Perish*, has survived in a marginal gloss of another Neoplatonic treatise, *al-Multaqaṭāt min kalām al-faylasūf al-rabbānī wa-l-ḥakīm al-yūnānī Aflāṭūn al-ilāhī* (cf. Hasnawi 1997 [*196: 399 n. 8]). It presents two proofs only: in its essence, the soul is free from anything bad; the essential activity of the soul is self-knowledge as well as the knowledge of those beings that exist through themselves (αὐθυπόστατα).

Apart from their similarity to each other, these two Neoplatonic texts display a close relationship to Miskawayh's *al-Fawz al-aṣġar*, where three Platonic proofs for the immortality of the soul are given (*al-Fawz* [§5.4 *264: 81–84]), for which the author refers to Proclus' authority. Miskawayh mentions the soul's function as giver of life, its freedom from evil, and its self-movement. The most likely source behind all three versions of the Platonic proofs is, we may assume, Proclus' work *On Plato's Three Proofs for the Immortality of the Soul*, which is lost in Greek, but which we know was translated into Arabic (cf. Hasnawi 1997 [*196: 402] and Westerink 1973 [*195: 296–297]).

2.3 *Abū l-Ḥasan al-ʿĀmirī*

2.3.1 Life – 2.3.2 Works – 2.3.3 Doctrine

2.3.1 Life

Abū l-Ḥasan Muḥammad b. Yūsuf al-ʿĀmirī (about 300–381/912 or 913–992), who was born in Khorasan and studied with Abū Zayd al-Balḫī (d. 322/934, cf. § 5.1.2), saw himself as standing in the Kindian tradition (*Amad* [*133: 76], *Muntaḫab Ṣiwān al-ḥikma* [*117: 127]). Around the year 355/966 he was staying at the court of Abū l-Faḍl Ibn al-ʿAmīd, vizier to the Buyid emir Rukn al-Dawla in Rayy (Abū Ḥayyān al-Tawḥīdī, *Aḫlāq* [*111: 344–345], Miskawayh, *Taǧārib* [*115: II 277]). The vizier was known for his interest in the sciences and for his large library, where Miskawayh worked for seven years as a librarian. There, al-ʿĀmirī may have had access to many Greek philosophical works which he used in his own writings. After Abū l-Faḍl's death in 360/970, al-ʿĀmirī visited Baghdad, probably for the first time (Wakelnig 2006 [*231: 13–25]). Four years later (364/974–975) he returned to Baghdad, this time in the entourage of the vizier's son, Abū l-Fatḥ Ibn al-ʿAmīd Ḏū l-Kifāyatayn (Abū Ḥayyān al-Tawḥīdī, *Baṣāʾir* [*112: III 93]), who organized learned meetings in which al-ʿĀmirī took part. It was on one of these occasions that al-ʿĀmirī asked the famous grammarian Abū Saʿīd al-Sīrāfī a question about the particle *bi-* within the *Basmala* (i.e. the Islamic invocation 'in the name of God'), without, however, receiving an answer (al-Tawḥīdī, *Aḫlāq* [*111: 410–414], Yāqūt, *Iršād* [*119: III 124–125]). Even so this encounter is often referred to as a debate, in parallel to al-Sīrāfī's debate with Abū Bišr Mattā. In any case al-ʿĀmirī does not seem to have been given a friendly reception by the Baghdad scholars, especially not by the philosophers – neither during his first visit in 360/970–971, about which we know no further details, nor during his later visit in 364/974–975 (Abū Ḥayyān al-Tawḥīdī, *Muqābasāt* [*114: 353], *Muntaḫab Ṣiwān al-ḥikma* [*117: 129]). Concerning the period after al-ʿĀmirī's return to Iran we have precious little information. According to the report of a Sufi sheikh (Abū Ḥayyān al-Tawḥīdī, *Imtāʿ* [*113: 91–96]), in 370/980–981 he was travelling as itinerant Sufi in the area of Nīšāpūr (Kraemer 1986 [*214: 238–239]). It is hence plausible to assume that al-ʿĀmirī alternated between a life at court and a life in voluntary retirement, motivated by his Sufi leanings. This may in turn explain why only a few episodes of his life are well documented, whereas larger parts of it remain in the dark, and why we do not find accounts of his life in any of the Arabic standard bio-bibliographies. From al-ʿĀmirī's own pen we learn that he spent some time in Bukhara, first at the court of the Samanid vizier Abū l-Ḥusayn ʿUbayd Allāh b. Aḥmad al-ʿUtbī. In all likelihood he there had access to the very same library Ibn Sīnā praised in his autobiography for being so richly stacked, especially with regard to the ancient sciences. The work *al-Taqrīr li-awǧuh al-taqdīr* (*Establishing the Aspects of Predestination*) is dedicated to this vizier; however, even after the end of the latter's time in office in 375/985–986 we find al-ʿĀmirī still (or again) in Bukhara, putting the finishing touches to his *Kitāb al-Amad ʿalā l-abad* (*On the Afterlife*) (*Taqrīr* [**126*: 303], *Amad* [**133*: 176]; cf. Wakelnig 2006 [*231: 29–30]).

Al-ʿĀmirī died on 27 Šawwāl 381/6 January 992, probably in Nishapur. The only reason why we know about this date is that Abū Bakr Aḥmad b. al-Ḥusayn b. Mihrān al-Muqriʾ died on the same day. He was a scholar who received entries in several biographical dictionaries (e.g. Yāqūt, *Iršād* [**119*: I 411–412], cf. also Wakelnig 2006 [*231: 33–34]), which report that he was saved from hell because al-ʿĀmirī had been his 'ransom from the fire of hell' (*fidāʾuka min al-nār*).

School and impact. – Regarding the impact of our philosopher, one particular remark by Ibn Abī Uṣaybiʿa poses a certain puzzle. Among Ibn Sīnā's works, Ibn Abī Uṣaybiʿa [**120*: II 20] mentions one entitled *Replies to 14 Questions Posed to Him by Abū l-Ḥasan al-ʿĀmirī* (cf. Minovi 1957 [*211: 71–72]). Nothing further is known about this Avicennian work from other sources. However, Kaya (2015 [*239: 2–7]) has recently suggested its identity with (parts of) a text entitled *al-Maǧālis al-sabʿ bayna al-Šayḫ wa-l-ʿĀmirī*. Arguing furthermore that Ibn Sīnā would have been the one posing the questions, while al-ʿĀmirī would have been providing the replies, he suggests that the two may have actually met in Bukhara – assuming Ibn Sīnā to have been born around 363/964 (cf. Gutas 1987/88 [*240: 335]). Yet, Ibn Sīnā did not think much of al-ʿĀmirī's philosophical achievements, as we can infer from his *Kitāb al-Naǧāt* (*Book of Salvation*), where he describes him as stupid (*fadm*) (Rowson 1988 [*227: 28]; cf. Minovi 1957 [*211: 70]). Nevertheless we can find links to al-ʿĀmirī's philosophy in Ibn Sīnā (cf. below, section 3: Doctrine, Metaphysics).

The only personal pupil of al-ʿĀmirī's named by the sources is Abū l-Faraǧ Ibn Hindū (cf. § 5.5), who studied with him in Nishapur in 371–372/981–982.

2.3.2 Works

2.3.2.1 Commentaries on Aristotelian Philosophy – 2.3.2.2 Natural Sciences – 2.3.2.3 Philosophy of Religion – 2.3.2.4 Metaphysics – 2.3.2.5 Documented Works that are Lost or Extant only in Fragments – 2.3.2.6 Further Fragments that Cannot Definitely be Assigned to any of al-ʿĀmirī's Known Works – 2.3.2.7 Works of Uncertain Authorship

2.3.2.1 *Commentaries on Aristotelian Philosophy*

Šarḥ [*Taʿlīq*] *ʿalā Kitāb al-Maqūlāt*
Fragments of a commentary on Aristotle's *Categories*

The epitome of *Tafsīr maʿānī alfāẓ Arisṭūṭālīs fī Kitāb al-Maqūlāt* by Abū Muḥammad ʿAbd Allāh b. Muḥammad al-Wāhibī summarizes the explanations given by Greek and Arabic commentators on select passages of the *Categories* (Rowson 1988 [*227: 13–14]). Among them are 11 passages attributed to al-ʿĀmirī whose main topics are substance, quantity, and relation. Like an interpretation of the Greek term *Qāṭīġūriyās* preserved by al-Tawḥīdī (*al-Baṣāʾir* [*112: II 209]), these comments probably derive from a lost commentary on the *Categories* by al-ʿĀmirī.

2.3.2.2 *Natural Sciences*

al-Ibṣār wa-l-mubṣar
Vision and the Visible

Judging from the preface, al-ʿĀmirī wrote this work during a politically turbulent and difficult time in order to respond to a question posed to him about the sensually perceptible. However, his examination is confined to the sense of sight and the way in which it achieves perception. To this end al-ʿĀmirī discusses select topics like the essence of colour as the essential and original perceptible object of the sense of sight, the anatomical structure of the eye, and the process of seeing as the reception of the coloured rays that traverse the distance from the object to the eye with the help of the transparent air and the rays of light. His explanations are partly based on Aristotle's *On the Soul* as well as on Galenic material transmitted in Ḥunayn b. Isḥāq's *Ten Treatises on the Eye*.

2.3.2.3 *Philosophy of Religion*

Inqāḏ al-bašar min al-ǧabr wa-l-qadar
The Deliverance of Mankind from the Problem of Predestination and Free Will

As announced in the preface (*Inqāḏ* [*126: 249]), al-ʿĀmirī here discusses the various aspects of action, especially the relation between human action and God, since the theologians (*mutakallimūn*) contradict each other on this point. Following Aristotle, al-ʿĀmirī distinguishes four essential causes (matter, agent, form, end) and an indefinite number of accidental causes of an action. With respect to the material, agent, and final cause there is a further distinction to be made between proximate and ultimate cause; thus the Creator can be introduced as ultimate cause of all human actions (*Inqāḏ* [*126: 264]). A one-sided view that focuses on the essential causes without taking into account accidental causes, and on the Creator's munificence without making allowance for the weakness of man, will lead to belief in man's autonomy; a one-sided view focusing on the accidental causes and on human weakness, on the other hand, will lead to the belief in complete predestination. Hence both perspectives must be joined together in order to find a middle way. Having presented this solution to the problem introduced by the title of the book, al-ʿĀmirī adds an appendix on the good and the better (*Inqāḏ* [*126: 270–271]; the relation between the two different, recently edited versions of the text (cf. [*127]) still remains to be established).

al-Taqrīr li-awǧuh al-taqdīr
The Determination of the Various Aspects of Predestination

This rather late work dedicated to the Samanid vizier al-ʿUtbī revisits the subject matter al-ʿĀmirī had discussed years before in *Inqāḏ al-bašar min al-ǧabr wa-l-qadar*. Again al-ʿĀmirī begins by establishing the distinction between the necessary, the possible, and the impossible, not, however, in order to apply it to the problem of action as he did in his earlier work, but in order to utilize it for the classification of all existing things. With respect to its existence, the sublunar realm falls in the category of the possible (*Taqrīr* [*126: 313]), and constitutes al-ʿĀmirī's main focal point (together with the bodies it contains). Following Aristotle's *On the Heavens*, he discusses the four elements as the bodies that move towards or away from the centre, and the ethereal celestial body as moving around the centre. The principles of these bodies are matter, form and receptivity: they are the building blocks out of which all other bodies are formed (as their concomitants, *lawāḥiq*), and the bodies are all subject to predestination (*Taqrīr* [*126: 309]).

As in his earlier work, al-ʿĀmirī does not provide a clear answer to the question of man's autonomy. The one topic on which he expresses himself clearly concerns the celestial influences through which divine predestination is realized in the sublunar world: even though man is subjected to them on account of his corporeal form, he can liberate himself from their influence through the help and guidance of his soul (*Taqrīr* [*126: 321]).

Kitāb al-Iʿlām bi-manāqib al-islām
An Exposition of the Merits of Islam

This work is dedicated to a certain Abū Naṣr who cannot be identified exactly (Wakelnig 2006 [*231: 28–29]). Its purpose is to demonstrate Islam's superiority over the five significant other religions (Judaism, Sabianism, Christianity, Zoroastrianism, and Polytheism). After a detailed description and classification of the philosophical and religious sciences, al-ʿĀmirī turns to those areas for which all religions set up rules and regulations: main tenets of belief, religious practices, life in the social community, and special prohibitions. Since such rules can only partly be grasped by the pure intellect, they need to be revealed by God. Al-ʿĀmirī demonstrates in detail the superiority of the Muslim creed and of the religious practices prescribed by Islam over other religions. Touching only briefly on instructions concerning social interactions within the community (*muʿāmalāt*) and special prohibitions (*al-arkān al-zağriyya*), he explains in sections 7 to 10 that Islam outperforms other religions also when it comes to the relations between political leadership (*al-mulk*) and subjects (*al-raʿāyā*), to relations to other peoples (*ağyāl*), and to learning and the sciences. The epilogue offers an apology of Islam in the face of four frequently raised objections.

2.3.2.4 *Metaphysics*

Kitāb al-Amad ʿalā l-abad
On the Afterlife

This work, which attempts to harmonize the ancient philosophical concept of the soul with the Islamic concept of the hereafter, is addressed to traditional Muslim scholars more than to philosophers (Rowson 1988 [*227: 3]). Al-ʿĀmirī here discusses the immortality of the soul and the question of the hereafter based on an Arabic version of Plato's *Phaedo* whose exact features cannot be established any further (Rowson 1988 [*227: 29–30]; on the Arabic Plato cf. also Arnzen 2009 [*236a]). Having provided an introduction to the different eras and calendars, he proceeds with a chronological account of the development of Greek philosophy from Empedocles to Aristotle, in the course of which he presents doxographical material about Empedocles, Pythagoras, Socrates, Plato and Aristotle. This representation of the history of philosophy, together with the doxography that serves to illustrate it, appears to have secured al-ʿĀmirī's influence more than any other of his works: it was adopted in numerous later works written on the topic in Arabic (Rowson 1988 [*227: 204]). *Kitāb al-Amad ʿalā l-abad* then goes on to investigate in detail the relation between body and soul, that is to say the relation between sensitive and rational soul. Al-ʿĀmirī refutes erroneous views and explains the influence that prayer, magic and celestial bodies may exert on human beings. He also describes the upper, celestial world as well as the resurrection of the dead, the last judgement, paradise and hell; with respect to the latter topics he remains largely in agreement with the standard notions of Islamic religion.

Kitāb al-Fuṣūl fī l-maʿālim al-ilāhiyya
Chapters on Metaphysical Topics

This is a very free paraphrase of about 25 sections of Proclus' *Elements of Theology*. Even though al-ʿĀmirī's paraphrase shows close similarities to the most widely spread Proclean paraphrase, the *Kitāb al-Īḍāḥ fī l-ḫayr al-maḥḍ* (the *Liber de Causis* of the Latin West), it does not seem to go back directly to this work, but to a common ancestor shared by both texts (Rowson 1984 [*226: 193–196], Wakelnig 2006 [*231: 71–73]). Al-ʿĀmirī here describes the structure of the created world based on the Plotinian system of hypostases, God-Intellect-Soul-Nature. He identifies the human intellect as the one substance which may rise from being a substance that exists through matter to being a purely divine substance persisting through its Creator alone (*Fuṣūl* [*126: 112]).

2.3.2.5 *Documented Works that are Lost or Extant only in Fragments*

In one of his later works, *Kitāb al-Amad ʿalā l-abad*, al-ʿĀmirī compiles a catalogue of his own works: on top of seventeen works listed by title he also mentions several brief treatises that are not defined any further, a number of replies to various questions posed to him, explanations of logical principles, commentaries on works on physics, as well as some Persian compositions dedicated to princes and political rulers (*Amad* [*133: 52–55]). Apart from the titles of four extant writings – *Kitāb al-Iʿlām bi-manāqib al-islām, al-Taqrīr li-awǧuh al-taqdīr, Inqāḏ al-bašar min al-ǧabr wa-l-qadar* and *al-Ibṣār wa-l-mubṣar*, the catalogue preserves the titles of thirteen works by al-ʿĀmirī that are either lost or extant in fragments only (Rowson 1988 [*227: 8–13]):

al-Ibāna ʿan ʿilal al-diyāna
Explication of the Causes of Religion

A reference to this work found in *Kitāb al-Iʿlām bi-manāqib al-islām* [*132: 150] suggests that it contained, among other things, comparisons of various religions (Rowson 1988 [*227: 8]; cf. Ḫalīfāt 1988 [*215: 473]).

al-Iršād li-taṣḥīḥ al-iʿtiqād
Guide to the Rectification of Religious Belief

This work likewise seems to have been at least partly dedicated to religious sciences (*Amad* [*133: 162], *Iʿlām* [*132: 145]). Al-ʿĀmirī moreover appears to have used it to discuss the fundamental principles of Quranic exegesis (*Iʿlām* [*132: 199]), the essence (*anniyya*) of God, His unity and attributes (*Taqrīr* [*126: 305]), prophecy (*Ibṣār* [*126: 413]), as well as those things that are linked to divine decrees and spiritual influences, like e.g. magic or talismans (*Taqrīr* [*126: 331]) (Rowson 1988 [*227: 9]; cf. Ḫalīfāt 1988 [*215: 471–472]).

al-Nask al-ʿaqlī wa-l-taṣawwuf al-millī
Intellectual Piety and Institutionalized Ṣūfism

This text is the best documented among all those works by al-ʿĀmirī which are attested but not extant, with Abū Ḥayyān al-Tawḥīdī's *Muqābasāt* being the most important source. The 90th *muqābasa* reports a comment on *al-Nask al-ʿaqlī wa-l-taṣawwuf al-millī*, the major part of which al-Tawḥīdī claims to have heard directly from al-ʿĀmirī [**114*: 340]. In addition, both *Muntaḫab* [**117*: 128–129] and *Muḫtaṣar Ṣiwān al-ḥikma* [**118*: 264–267] adduce, in their respective entries on al-ʿĀmirī, quotations which are explicitly described as culled from the end of *al-Nask al-ʿaqlī wa-l-taṣawwuf al-millī*, and which exhibit some similarities to each other. Thanks to these three sources it is furthermore possible to assign certain sections in Miskawayh's chapter 'From al-ʿĀmirī's Exhortations and [ethical] Aphorisms (*ādāb*)' (in: *al-Ḥikma al-ḫālida* [**116*: 347–373]) to this work by al-ʿĀmirī. We may suppose that Miskawayh records further quotations from *al-Nask al-ʿaqlī wa-l-taṣawwuf al-millī* there, which, however, cannot be identified due to missing references in Miskawayh, and the absence of al-ʿĀmirī's original work. Even in those cases where Miskawayh seems to quote from extant works, i.e. from *Kitāb al-Amad ʿalā l-abad* and *Kitāb al-Iʿlām bi-manāqib al-islām*, his quotations pose some puzzles: both the formulations he uses and, even more so, the contexts in which the quotations appear, deviate so much from their supposed originals that we cannot exclude the possibility that they were in fact taken from other, lost works by al-ʿĀmirī, in which the latter reformulated his thoughts (cf. Wakelnig 2008 [*235]).

Judging from the extant fragments of *al-Nask al-ʿaqlī wa-l-taṣawwuf al-millī*, the work seems to have been a compilation of brief sayings and maxims as well as some lengthier expositions, most of them concerning ethical issues and apparently influenced by Sufism. Al-ʿĀmirī himself refers to this work for an explanation of religious inspiration (*Taqrīr* [**126*: 311]), a discussion on the acquisition of knowledge through the faculty of imagination (*Ibṣār* [**126*: 413]), and a division of mankind into 73 groups, of whom only one will be saved (*Taqrīr* [**126*: 324]; Rowson 1988 [*227: 10]; cf. Ḫalīfāt 1988 [*215: 474]).

Another question attached to *al-Nask al-ʿaqlī wa-l-taṣawwuf al-millī* which cannot be settled definitely is whether it represents the work that made al-ʿĀmirī famous in Sufi circles. The Sufi sheikh who, according to a report by Abū Ḥayyān al-Tawḥīdī (*Imtāʿ* [**113*: 94–96]), met al-ʿĀmirī in 370/980–981 in the area of Nishapur, mentions that al-ʿĀmirī wrote a work on Sufism (*taṣawwuf*), filling it with the knowledge and the intimations of the Sufis (Rowson 1988 [*227: 9]; cf. Ġurāb 1967 [*212: 16 n. 1], who considers the possibility that the work mentioned by the Sufi sheikh was *Minhāǧ al-Dīn*; this, however, would require identifying al-ʿĀmirī with Ibn Abī Ḏarr – for this identification see below).

al-Itmām li-faḍāʾil al-anām
The Perfecting of the Virtues of Man

According to some pronouncements made in *Kitāb al-Iʿlām bi-manāqib al-islām* [**132*: 79], al-ʿĀmirī here investigates the close relationship between knowledge and action (cf. also Rowson 1988 [*227: 10]; cf. Ḫalīfāt 1988 [*215: 474]). This is the very same theme that defines the beginning of a quotation ascribed to al-ʿĀmirī which we find in the philosophical compilation of MS Marsh 539 ([**141*: 322–339 ed. Wakelnig] in the Bodleian Library (Oxford) (see also below, 2.3.2.6). Said quotation is mainly concerned with the virtues, which means it may well stem from *al-Itmām li-faḍāʾil al-anām*.

al-Fuṣūl al-burhāniyya li-l-mabāḥiṯ al-nafsāniyya
Demonstrative Arguments on Psychological Topics

According to information from *al-Taqrīr li-awǧuh al-taqdīr* the questions discussed include the following: (a) How the faculty of thought (*al-quwwa al-fikriyya*) is distracted by its occupation with the (bodily) nature connected with it [**126*: 312]. (b) The relation between the celestial influence of spheres and planets and the emergence of immaterial, psychological powers in man [**126*: 322–323] (Rowson 1988 [*227: 11]; cf. Ḫalīfāt 1988 [*215: 471]). A brief section, preserved in MS Servili 179 (fols. 110^{b}–111^{a}) after *Kitāb al-Amad*, deals with this very topic and hence may well be an excerpt from *al-Fuṣūl al-burhāniyya* (see also below, 2.3.2.6).

Fuṣūl al-taʾaddub wa-uṣūl al-taḥabbub
The Elements of Good Breeding and the Principles of Congeniality

This title is known from al-ʿĀmirī's list only; cf. Rowson 1988 [*227: 11].

al-Ibšār wa-l-išǧār
The Growing of Plants and the Production of Trees

This work is mentioned twice in al-ʿĀmirī's *al-Taqrīr li-awǧuh al-taqdīr*, where he gives many illustrations from the field of biology [**126*: 331. 336] (Rowson 1988 [*227: 11]).

al-Ifṣāḥ wa-l-īḍāḥ
Clarification and Elucidation

In *Kitāb al-Amad ʿalā l-abad* [**133*: 68], al-ʿĀmirī refers to this work for an interpretation of a Quranic verse (Sura 70:4) (Rowson 1988 [*227: 11]).

al-ʿInāya wa-l-dirāya
Care and Study

According to Rowson, this was a larger work on Aristotelian-inspired metaphysics; its title may be derived from a formulation found in the *Nicomachean Ethics* (Rowson 1988 [*227: 11]). Al-ʿĀmirī himself refers to the work for an explanation of why engaging in metaphysics is only possible after having mastered the other scientific disciplines (*Iʿlām* [*132: 93]); for an investigation into the divine forms (*Taqrīr* [*126: 313]); and for a summary of Aristotle's doctrine and his views on God's unity and the hereafter (*Amad* [*133: 88]). With respect to the last reference, Ḫalīfāt (1988 [*215: 471]) considers the alternative possibility that it is supposed to point to al-ʿĀmirī's own work *al-Tawḥīd wa-l-maʿād* (*God's Unity and the Hereafter*) rather than to the report on Aristotle he gives in *al-ʿInāya wa-l-dirāya*.

al-Abḥāṯ ʿan al-aḥdāṯ
Researches into Created Entities

In Rowson's view (1988 [*227: 12]) this work may well have constituted the physical counterpart to the metaphysical treatise *al-ʿInāya wa-l-dirāya*, in which al-ʿĀmirī, among other things, explains that astrological and medical knowledge is based on divine wisdom (*Taqrīr* [*126: 329]) and seeks to explain why the natural and the artificial may deviate from the balance that is accorded to them (*Taqrīr* [*126: 338]).

Istiftāḥ al-naẓar
The Inception of Philosophical Speculation

This title is known from al-ʿĀmirī's list only; cf. Rowson 1988 [*227: 12].

al-Tabṣīr li-awǧuh al-taʿbīr
An Explanation of the Various Aspects of the Interpretation of Dreams

Kaya (2014 [*238: 82 n. 82]) has recently reported a surviving manuscript of this treatise on the interpretation of dreams.

Taking further references in al-ʿĀmirī's *al-Ibṣār wa-l-mubṣar* into consideration, two further titles should be added to this list (Rowson 1988 [*227: 13]; cf. Ḫalīfāt 1988 [*215: 441]):

Šarḥ/Tafsīr Kitāb al-Burhān li-Arisṭūṭālīs
Commentary on Aristotle's Posterior Analytics

Al-ʿĀmirī refers to this commentary twice, once for an account of intellectual insight (*Ibṣār* [*126: 413]); the second time for an explication of the laws of logic (*Ibṣār* [*126: 423]).

Šarḥ Kitāb al-Nafs li-Arisṭāṭālīs
Commentary on Aristotle's On the Soul

It seems that al-ʿĀmirī wanted to dedicate yet another work to the study of the soul and, in particular, the state it finds itself in after death: a commentary on Aristotle's *On the Soul*, which, according to *al-Ibṣār wa-l-mubṣar*, he was hoping to complete with God's help (*Ibṣār* [*126: 414]).

2.3.2.6 *Further Fragments that Cannot Definitely be Assigned to any of al-ʿĀmirī's Known Works*

Apart from the above-mentioned anthology 'From al-ʿĀmirī's Exhortations and (ethical) Aphorisms (*ādāb*)', which is preserved by Miskawayh's testimony (*Ḥikma* [*116: 347–373]), and whose quotations should be assigned to specific treatises by al-ʿĀmirī with caution only, it is first and foremost the writings of his contemporary Abū Ḥayyān al-Tawḥīdī that contain otherwise unknown material of the philosopher. This mainly concerns discussions which al-ʿĀmirī is said to have conducted with several scholars during the periods he spent in Baghdad, and which al-Tawḥīdī is likely to have witnessed in person: the question posed by the Buyid vizier Abū l-Fatḥ Ibn al-ʿAmīd Ḏū l-Kifāyatayn (d. 366/976), concerning the reason why the soul looks for marks of distinction even between similar things, to which al-ʿĀmirī replies (*Aḫlāq* [*111: 446–447]); a discussion with a Manichaean (*al-Maǧūsī*) about the state of the soul after death (*Muqābasāt* [*114: 116–119]); and an explication of the difference between intellect and sense perception laid out by al-ʿĀmirī, together with objections from some unidentified opponents, to whom al-ʿĀmirī replies (*Muqābasāt* [*114: 171–172]). Nevertheless we cannot exclude the possibility that when writing down his reports, al-Tawḥīdī consulted works by al-ʿĀmirī in which the philosopher explored similar topics. Sometimes al-Tawḥīdī abstains from sketching the scene in which a discussion was supposed to have taken place; this seems to suggest that he quotes directly from original works by al-ʿĀmirī. Examples are the account of mostly ethical considerations he gives in *al-Baṣāʾir wa-l-ḏaḫāʾir* [*112: III 93–94; IX 148–149]; the 43rd *muqābasa*, where the relation between physician and astrologer is discussed (*Muqābasāt* [*114: 177–180]); and *Kitāb al-Imtāʿ wa-l-muʾānasa* [*113: 84–89], where al-Tawḥīdī – following a request by the vizier Ibn Saʿdān – offers several tasters of al-ʿĀmirī's doctrine, in particular of his epistemology, and furnishes them with commentaries by the not further identifiable Abū Naḍr Nafīs (cf. Kraemer 1986 [*214: 236 n. 79]). (For a detailed discussion of the individual testimonials for al-ʿĀmirī's works cf. Wakelnig 2008 [*235].)

A further fragment from al-ʿĀmirī's work is found in the philosophical compilation preserved incompletely in MS Marsh 539 ([*141: 322–339. 470–479 ed. Wakelnig]), where it forms the last quotation of the text. This fragment belongs to the field of ethics, its predominant topic being the virtues, which are divided into physical and psychological ones. Further topics that are discussed are knowledge and the art of governance. None of al-ʿĀmirī's works is mentioned by name as a source; however, *al-Itmām li-faḍāʾil al-anām* seems a likely candidate, given its title and the sparse information we have concerning its contents. Apart from that, two sections of the fragment show some similarities to *Kitāb al-Iʿlām bi-manāqib al-islām*. Just as in the earlier case of *al-Nask al-ʿaqlī wa-l-taṣawwuf al-millī*, however, we are not looking here at any verbatim agreement. Thus the similarities may well be explained by the assumption that it was al-ʿĀmirī himself who discussed one and the same topic in several of his works in similar, but not quite identical fashion. In this particular case, this assumption is further supported by the fact that a quotation of al-ʿĀmirī's in ʿAlī al-Riyāḍī's *Kitāb Ṣaḥāʾif al-laṭāʾif* (Süleymaniye, MS Ayasofya 4130, p. 26–27), discovered by Minovi, agrees with the wording of the Oxford MS against that of *Kitāb al-Iʿlām bi-manāqib al-islām* (Minovi (1957 [*211: 74–75]); cf. also Wakelnig 2008 [*235], [*141]). The text moreover contains thematic parallels to *Inqāḏ al-bašar min al-ǧabr wa-l-qadar* [*126: 256] and *al-Taqrīr li-awǧuh al-taqdīr* [*126: 314] concerning the presentation of the four Aristotelian causes on the one hand; and to fragments of al-ʿĀmirī in al-Tawḥīdī (*Baṣāʾir* [*112: III 93–94]) and Miskawayh (*Ḥikma* [*116: 359]) concerning the discussion of the four cardinal virtues on the other. We can furthermore detect a partly literal parallel to al-Balḫī's paragraph on governance, which is preserved in Abū Ḥayyān al-Tawḥīdī's *al-Baṣāʾir wa-l-ḏaḫāʾir* [*112: IX 146–147] (cf. Wakelnig 2008 [*235]).

Following right after the text of *Kitāb al-Amad* in MS Servili 179 (fols 110^b–111^a) we find two short paragraphs and a poem, reported with reference to a certain Sheikh Abū l-Ḥasan ʿAlī b. Muḥammad, which, according to Rowson, are to be ascribed to al-ʿĀmirī (Rowson 1988 [*227: 50]). The first of the two paragraphs (fol. 110^b1–13) again discusses the cardinal virtues, tracing them back to various powers of the soul, just as in the fragment contained in MS Marsh [*141: 324, first paragraph ed. Wakelnig]). However, it does introduce additional powers (growth, sensory, and rational power) from which there will then emerge the desirous, the wrathful, and the critical power as causes of virtues and vices. The second paragraph (fols 110^b13–111^a3, Engl. transl. in Wakelnig 2007 [*233: 49–50]) assigns the various psychological powers of man, which are located in the heart, to the influence of the individual spheres (outermost sphere and zodiacal sphere) and the planets (Sun, Moon, Mercury, Venus, Jupiter, and Saturn). As indicated already, this passage may well stem from the lost work *al-Fuṣūl al-burhāniyya li-l-mabāḥiṯ al-nafsāniyya*. The poem (fol. 111ª3–8) bears the title *On the Property* (*ṣifa*) *of Substance*.

The miscellaneous manuscript Tehran, Kitābḫāna-yi Millī-yi Malik 4694 moreover contains, according to Minovi (1957 [*211: 74]), a chapter entitled *Intellectual Proof which I have Excerpted from the Words of Abū l-Ḥasan al-ʿĀmirī in Some of his Treatises on the Hereafter*.

2.3.2.7 *Works of Uncertain Authorship*

Kitāb al-Saʿāda wa-l-isʿād fī l-sīra al-insāniyya
On Happiness and Its Creation in Human Life

The only extant manuscript of this work, which probably was composed in the first half of the 4th/10th century in an Iranian milieu, names the otherwise unknown Abū l-Ḥasan Ibn Abī Ḏarr as its author. The editor, M. Minovi (1957 [*211: 59]), identified this person with Abū l-Ḥasan Muḥammad b. Yūsuf al-ʿĀmirī, without giving adequate reasons for this, and has been followed in that by several scholars (cf. Wakelnig 2006 [*231: 35–39]). If Ibn Abī Ḏarr were indeed identical with al-ʿĀmirī, this would furthermore make al-ʿĀmirī the author of the (no longer extant) work *Minhāǧ al-Dīn*, which is ascribed to Ibn Abī Ḏarr by al-Kalābāḏī (Minovi 1957 [*211: 68–69], Rowson 1988 [*227: 17]).

There are two further works of undetermined authorship which Minovi (1957 [*211: 56–59.79–81]) counts among al-ʿĀmirī's œuvre: the Persian *Farruḫ-Nāma* and the philosophical treatise which in the Istanbul MS Esad Efendi 1933 (fols 56ª–109ᵇ) is reproduced immediately before al-ʿĀmirī's *Kitāb al-Fuṣūl fī l-maʿālim al-ilāhiyya*, under the title *Kitāb al-Ḥikma* (this title being most certainly a later addition). This latter work, however, is not a self-contained text written by a single anonymous author whom one could perhaps identify as al-ʿĀmirī, but a compilation of passages from mainly four sources, namely Miskawayh's *al-Fawz al-aṣġar*, Aristotle's *Meteorology*, Pseudo-Apollonius, *Kitāb al-ʿIlal*, and ʿAlī b. Rabban al-Ṭabarī's *Firdaws al-ḥikma* (Wakelnig 2009 [*172: 86–88]; see now also the online edition with introduction [*236b]).

2.3.3 Doctrine

Ethics. In the field of ethics, al-ʿĀmirī follows the tradition of al-Kindī's ethics of knowledge: It is up to the human intellect to recognize truth, and to act in accordance with it (*Iʿlām* [*132: 77–78], *Taqrīr* [*126: 306], *Muqābasāt* [*114: 116–117]). Knowledge therefore is the beginning of action, and action is the perfection of knowledge (*Iʿlām* [*132: 78], MS Marsh [*141: 322, passage (213) ed. Wakelnig]). The pursuit of the sciences hence aims at acting correctly. The religious sciences assume a specific role, as they are based on divine revelation and therefore can make pronouncements on issues which cannot be appraised by the intellect alone – for instance the exact form or extent of religious obligations, which moreover may alter in the course of time and under changing conditions (*Iʿlām* [**132*: 102–104]).

Following Platonic tradition, al-ʿĀmirī assigns the four cardinal virtues of temperance, courage, wisdom and justice to the individual parts of the soul and their respective faculties, and understands them as the mean between two vices: Keeping the desire of the faculty of growth in balance, one will achieve temperance; keeping the wrath of the faculty of sense perception in balance, one will become courageous; making use of the critical and discriminating faculty of reason in the proper way, one will reach wisdom. The balance of these three virtues will finally result in justice (MS Servili [**142*: 111b1–12], MS Marsh [**141*: 336 ed. Wakelnig], Abū Ḥayyān al-Tawḥīdī, *Baṣāʾir* [**112*: III 94]). True virtues are justice, wisdom, courage and generosity – the latter replaces temperance in the relevant passage – but only if they are deployed for the sake of others (MS Marsh [**141*: 324 ed. Wakelnig]). Further virtues can be derived from the cardinal virtues; in addition to all these virtues of the soul there are also virtues of the body, which either are useful, for instance by keeping the body in good health, or are of decorative character, so as to bring about a beautiful appearance etc. (MS Marsh [**141*: 336–338 ed. Wakelnig]).

Physics. – For his account of the sublunar realm al-ʿĀmirī takes recourse to Aristotle, and in particular to his *Physics*, *On the Heavens*, and *On Generation and Corruption*. A detailed study of Aristotelian influences in al-ʿĀmirī's work is yet to be conducted.

Everything that happens in the sublunar, i.e. the earthly world is either natural, intellectual, artificial (*al-maʿānī al-mihniyya*), or accidental and occurs through change which may be substantial, quantitative, qualitative, or local (*Taqrīr* [**126*: 310. 316]). The changes which apply to the natural, parts of the artificial, and the accidental, though ultimately being caused by God, the Creator, are imparted to the sublunar world by the influence of the celestial spheres and bodies – that is to say, by nature, which is the divine power operating through the sphere of the sun (*Taqrīr* [**126*: 314. 334]). The intellectual is not subject to such celestial influence, for the power of the thinking soul is higher than the natural power operating through the celestial bodies (*Taqrīr* [**126*: 317], *Amad* [**133*: 102]). To the man who is bent on the higher world, the accidental will only happen according to God's resolution; the man who has fallen for earthly things, on the other hand, will be affected by it according to the workings of natural forces (*Taqrīr* [**126*: 317–318]).

Within this Aristotelian-influenced framework, astrology, similarly to medicine, is understood as a discipline of natural science.

Soul and intellect. – The use of the concept of soul within *Kitāb al-Fuṣūl fī l-maʿālim al-ilāhiyya* [*126: 106] indicates that al-ʿĀmirī first and foremost thinks of the rational part of the soul when speaking of the human soul. Where he does speak of the sensitive soul of man, as he does in *Kitāb al-Amad ʿalā l-abad* [*133: 90–95], he apparently means the vital spirit, i.e. the part of the soul which perishes when the body dies (*Amad* [*133: 133–135]; cf. Rowson 1988 [*227: 266]).

Man consists of two substances, one of earthly origin – the body – and one of celestial origin – the soul (*Amad* [*133: 112], *Taqrīr* [*126: 320–321]). Both substances are separate from each other and independent (*Amad* [*133: 106]). Nevertheless one of them can gain control over the other, as becomes manifest, for instance, in the soul's ability to counter the desires of the body, and to prevent it from giving in to them (*Fuṣūl* [*126: 120], *Amad* [*133: 112]). In another place al-ʿĀmirī introduces a further level, speaking of the dichotomy between intellect and nature: while the former leads the soul to its perfection, i.e. to wisdom and virtue, the latter, in its love for pleasure and comfort, takes the body to *its* perfection, i.e. health and strength. Despite being certainly desirable *per se*, this perfection of the body must under no circumstances be pursued at the expense of the perfection of the soul. In this context al-ʿĀmirī, availing himself of seemingly Sufi terminology, describes the angel as supporting the intellect, and the devil as coming to the aid of nature. Hence a person whose intellect follows his nature is said to be of a devilish disposition, whereas someone whose nature obeys his intellect is of angelic disposition (*Ḥikma* [*116: 352. 354]).

The soul does not suffer any harm in its spirituality by virtue of its association with the body; it is through the body that it is given the possibility to distinguish between good and bad by way of its own experience (*Amad* [*133: 140]), something that is not open to the angels. The essential antagonism between body and soul makes it, however, necessary for God to issue His commands to mankind (*Amad* [*133: 102]). By virtue of religious laws and statutes God compensates this human weakness, which is why man can be defined as religious by nature (*Amad* [*133: 96]).

Thanks to his or her soul, it is possible for a human being to be God's representative in the lower world for a short while, and an adornment in the higher world throughout eternity (*Amad* [*133: 138, cf. also 96]); for through the eternal things it has acquired, and through their intellectual forms the soul is assimilated to the divine and achieves the ability to live for ever (*Amad* [*133: 106]).

Al-ʿĀmirī acknowledges the religious tenet of bodily resurrection on the day of judgement as revealed knowledge, even though the contradiction it poses to his own philosophical belief, according to which the higher world is pure spirituality, causes him obvious discomfort (*Amad* [*133: 166]). Thus he declares in *Kitāb al-Iʿlām bi-manāqib al-islām* [*126: 136–137], that according to Islam, God takes the spirits back to their bodies, together with sense perception and intellect, so that through the intellect they may recognize the right and the wrong they have done during their lives, and may receive reward or punishment by virtue of their sense perception. Nonetheless he immediately adds the qualification that these bodies are different from the earthly ones, and that the sensible pleasures in question are purely spiritual.

Metaphysics. – The most self-contained account of al-ʿĀmirī's metaphysical system can be found in his paraphrase of Proclus' *Elements of Theology*, the *Kitāb al-Fuṣūl fī l-maʿālim al-ilāhiyya*. Based on the Plotinian scheme of hypostases, he distinguishes five different levels of existence: (1) God; (2) the universal forms and the Universal Intellect; (3) the Universal Soul and the sphere of spheres; (4) celestial spheres and celestial bodies; and (5) everything that arises from the four elements (*Fuṣūl* [*126: 84]). All four lower levels of existence receive their existence directly from God, even though each of them does so in a different way, which is expressed by the use of different terms for each act of creation. The Neoplatonic concept of emanation found in the text consulted by al-ʿĀmirī is thus restricted to the constitution of the substance of each existent, or to its essence (cf. *Fuṣūl* [*126: 82–84]). It is yet to be determined to what extent al-ʿĀmirī exerted some influence on Ibn Sīnā in this matter – as well as regarding other philosophical issues, for instance naming God the 'necessary of existence'. It was al-ʿĀmirī who, before Ibn Sīnā, introduced the differentiation between the necessary of existence and the contingent of existence and called God the 'necessary of existence in itself' (*wāǧib al-wuǧūd bi-ḏātihi, Amad* [*133: 78.2]) (cf. Wisnovsky 2003 [*242: 239]).

In contrast to *Kitāb al-Amad ʿalā l-abad*, where the dichotomy of body and soul is the central theme, *Kitāb al-Fuṣūl fī l-maʿālim al-ilāhiyya* focuses on that of body and intellect. It is only the intellect that makes the soul eternal and able to receive the eternal forms (*Fuṣūl* [*126: 114]).

Epistemology. In *Kitāb al-Fuṣūl fī l-maʿālim al-ilāhiyya*, which, as we have just seen, is based on the Neoplatonic system of hypostases, al-ʿĀmirī differentiates between two types of cognition, that of the intellect and that of the soul. Intellectual cognition is always true, as it takes place by virtue of universals and eternal forms (*Fuṣūl* [*126: 88–90]). Cognition of the soul is based on imagination and can be true or false, as the forms of the soul are neither linked to the intellect, nor eternal (*Fuṣūl* [*126: 90]). If the soul is to receive eternal forms, it therefore needs first to be perfected by the intellect (*Fuṣūl* [*126: 114]).

Following Proclus, actual intellect is marked first and foremost by its self-knowledge, through which it becomes subject and object of knowledge at the same time. In addition, al-ʿĀmirī ascribes second-order-knowledge of this very self-knowledge to the actual intellect. (*Fuṣūl* [*126: 104]).

The intellect, which knows itself as well as the things existing above and below it (*Fuṣūl* [*126: 104, 92]), owes its ability to perform its acts of cognition to the divine power alone (*Fuṣūl* [*126: 92], *Amad* [*133: 88]). Al-ʿĀmirī hence seems to assume a certain prefiguration of the intellect by the creator; this can also be gleaned from his statement that God effuses the intellectual forms onto the universal intellect (*Fuṣūl* [*126: 88]).

Problems arise for the interpretation of the expressions 'sublime and lowly intellects' and 'divine and mere [*fa-qaṭ*] intellects', which al-ʿĀmirī takes over from his Proclean source. While al-ʿĀmirī equates the sublime intellects with those of the angels, and the lowly intellects with those of humans, he would like to understand the divine intellects as the prophets, and the mere intellects as the rightly guided leaders. In the context of this second division, people who are neither prophets nor leaders would receive a soul that is merely endowed with intellect (*Fuṣūl* [*126: 94–96]). Thus it is impossible to arrive at an unambiguous interpretation; but in any case we can conclude that al-ʿĀmirī seems to ascribe different intellectual capabilities to individual people.

Both *Kitāb al-Amad ʿalā l-abad* [*133: 168] and *Kitāb al-Iʿlām bi-manāqib al-islām* [*132: 79] focus mainly on the religious insights of man. Here al-ʿĀmirī declares the acceptance of the true belief to be dependent on the intellectual (*ʿāqil*) faculty of the human soul. Imagination, by contrast, can lead to true or false beliefs; unbelief will always be dependent on it.

Philosophy and religion. – In *Kitāb al-Amad ʿalā l-abad*, which discusses the soul and its resurrection, a question really belonging to the domain of religion, al-ʿĀmirī establishes a direct relation between Islam and ancient Greek philosophy. He explains that Empedocles, the first of the Greek sages, received his knowledge from Luqmān, who is credited with wisdom in the Quran.

Even apart from this story, which is meant to underline the justification and necessity of philosophy within Islam, al-ʿĀmirī is convinced of the close relation between religion and philosophy. Thus he explains that the light of the intellect will only be able to help the soul to reach the higher world as long as the light of religion and the light of wisdom (or philosophy) will also lend their support (*Amad* [*133: 140]; cf. also Rowson 1988 [*227: 300]).

In *Kitāb al-Fuṣūl fī l-maʿālim al-ilāhiyya* al-ʿĀmirī strives to produce a correlation between philosophical and religious terminology: the Universal Intellect, the universal forms, the Universal Soul and the sphere of spheres are correlated to the Quranic terms 'pen' (*qalam*), 'command' (*amr*), 'tablet' (*lawḥ*) and ‘throne’ (*ʿarš*) (*Fuṣūl* [*126: 84]; Wakelnig 2006 [*231: 158–162). In *Kitāb al-Amad ʿalā l-abad* he further adds the ‘footstool of the throne’ (*kursī*), corresponding to the sphere of the zodiac (*Amad* [*133: 144]; Wakelnig 2006 [*231: 168–170]).

3 The Integration of Philosophical Traditions in Islamic Society in the 4th/10th Century: al-Tawḥīdī and al-Siǧistānī

Gerhard Endress

3.1 Primary Sources – 3.2 Al-Tawḥīdī’s Life and the Cultural Milieu of 4th/10th Century Baghdad and Western Iran – 3.3 Works: al-Tawḥīdī Reporting on Contemporary Philosophy – 3.4 Al-Siǧistānī’s Life – 3.5 Al-Siǧistānī’s Works – 3.6 Al-Siǧistānī’s Doctrines as Reflected by al-Tawḥīdī’s Reports

3.1 *Primary Sources*

3.1.1 Testimonies for the Historical Context, and for Life and Works of al-Tawḥīdī [*151–*164] – 3.1.2 Works by al-Tawḥīdī [*171–*187] – 3.1.3 Al-Siǧistānī: Bio-bibliographical Testimonies [*201–*209] – 3.1.4 Editions of al-Siǧistānī’s Works [*215–*216]

3.1.1 Testimonies for the Historical Context, and for Life and Works of al-Tawḥīdī

151 Ibn al-Nadīm, Abū l-Faraǧ Muḥammad b. Isḥāq (d. 380/990). *Kitāb al-Fihrist* [composed 377/988]. – Ed. by Gustav Flügel, August Müller and Johannes Roediger, 2 vols. Leipzig, 1871–1872. – Repr. Beirut 1964, Frankfurt a.M., 2005. – Ed. by Riḍā Taǧaddud. Tehran 1350 h.š./1971. – Ed. by Ayman Fuʾād Sayyid, 2 vols. London, 1430/2009. – Engl. transl. by Bayard Dodge, *The Fihrist of al-Nadīm*, 2 vols. New York, 1970.

152 al-Zubaydī, Muḥammad b. al-Ḥasan (d. 379/989). *Ṭabaqāt al-naḥwiyyīn wa-l-luġawiyyīn*. – Ed. by M. Abū l-Faḍl Ibrāhīm. Cairo, 1973.

153 Miskawayh, Abū ʿAlī Aḥmad b. Muḥammad (d. 421/1030). *Taǧārib al-umam = The Eclipse of the ʿAbbasid Caliphate*. – Ed., transl. and elucidated by Henry Frederic Amedroz and David Samuel Margoliouth, 4 vols [vols 3–4 = *Continuation of the Experiences of the Nations by Abū Shujāʿ Rūdhrāwarī and Hilāl ibn Muḥassin*]. Oxford, 1920–1921. – Arab. Text ed. by H. F. Amedroz. Cairo, 1332–1334/1914–1916.

154 Yāqūt b. ʿAbd Allāh, al-Ḥamawī al-Rūmī al-Baġdādī (d. 626/1229). *Iršād al-arīb*. – Ed. by David Samuel Margoliouth, *The Irshād arīb ilā maʿrifat al-adīb or Dictionary of Learned Men of Yāqūt*, 7 vols. London, 1923–1931. – Ed. by Aḥmad Farīd Rifāʿī, *Muʿǧam al-udabāʾ*, 20 vols. Cairo, 1936–1938. – Ed. by Iḥsān ʿAbbās, *Muʿǧam al-udabāʾ. Iršād arīb ilā maʿrifat al-adīb*, 7 vols. Beirut, 1993.

155 Ibn Ḫallikān, Abū l-ʿAbbās Šams al-Dīn Aḥmad b. Muḥammad (d. 681/1282). *Wafayāt al-aʿyān wa-anbāʾ abnāʾ al-zamān*. – Ed. by Iḥsān ʿAbbās, vol. 5. Beirut, 1977, 112–113.

156 al-Ḏahabī, Muḥammad b. Aḥmad (d. 748/1348). *Mīzān al-iʿtidāl fī naqd al-riǧāl*. – Ed. by ʿAlī Muḥammad al-Baǧāwī, vol. 4. Cairo, 1382/1963, 518–519.

157 al-Ṣafadī, Ṣalāḥ al-Dīn Ḫalīl b. Aybak (d. 764/1363). *Al-Wāfī bi-l-Wafayāt, Das biographische Lexikon des* [...] *al-Ṣafadī*, vol. 22. Ed. by Ramzī Baʿalbakkī. Beirut, Wiesbaden, 1983, 39–41.

158 al-Asnawī, Ǧamāl al-Dīn ʿAbd al-Raḥīm (d. 772/1370). *Ṭabaqāt al-Šāfiʿiyya*. – Ed. by ʿAbd Allāh al-Ǧubūrī, vol. 1. Riyadh, 1981, 301–303.

159 al-Subkī, Tāǧ al-Dīn ʿAbd al-Wahhāb b. Taqī al-Dīn (d. 771/1370). *Ṭabaqāt al-Šāfiʿiyya al-kubrā*. – Ed. by Maḥmūd Muḥammad al-Ṭanāḥī and ʿAbd al-Fattāḥ Muḥammad al-Ḥulw, vol. 5. Cairo, 1386/1967, 286–289.

160 Ǧunayd-i Šīrāzī, Muʿīn al-Dīn Abū l-Qāsim b. Naǧm al-Dīn: *Šadd al-izār fī ḥaṭṭ al-awzār ʿan zuwwār al-mazār* [composed 791/1389]. – Ed. by Muḥammad Qazwīnī and ʿAbbās Iqbāl. Tehran, 1328/1949–1950, 53–55.

161 Ibn Ḥaǧar al-ʿAsqalānī. Abū l-Faḍl Šihāb al-Dīn Aḥmad b. ʿAlī (d. 852/1449). *Lisān al-Mīzān*, vol. 7. Hyderabad, 1331/1913, 38–41.

162 al-Suyūṭī, Ǧalāl al-Dīn ʿAbd al-Raḥmān (d. 911/1505). *Buġyat al-wuʿāt fī ṭabaqāt al-luġawiyyīn wa-l-nuḥāt*. – Ed. by Muḥammad Abū l-Faḍl Ibrāhīm, vol. 1. Cairo 1384/1964, 507,14–16.

163 Ṭāšköprüzāde (Aḥmad b. Muṣṭafā Ṭāškobrāzāda (d. 968/1561). *Miftāḥ al-saʿāda wa-miṣbāḥ al-siyāda fī mawḍūʿāt al-ʿulūm*. – Ed. by Kāmil Bakrī and ʿAbd al-Wahhāb Abū-l-Nūr, vol. 1. Cairo, 1968, 234–235.

164 al-Ḫwānsārī, Muḥammad Bāqir b. Zayn al-ʿĀbidīn (d. 1313/1895). *Rawḍāt al-Ǧannāt fī aḥwāl al-ʿulamāʾ wa-l-sādāt*. – Ed. by Asad Allāh Ismāʿīliyān, vol. 8. Tehran, 1972, 92–93.

3.1.2 Works by al-Tawḥīdī

3.1.2.1 *Partial Collections*

171 *Risālatān li-l-ʿallāma al-šahīr Abī Ḥayyān al-Tawḥīdī*. Constantinople, 1883. Contains: *Risāla fī l-Ṣadāqa wa-l-ṣadīq* (2–199); *Risāla fī l-ʿUlūm* (200–208). – Repr. based on this edition under the title: *Kitāb al-Adab wa-l-inšāʾ fī l- ṣadāqa wa-l-Ṣadīq* ([including] *Risāla fī l-ʿUlūm*). Cairo, 1323 H./1905.

172 Abū Ḥayyān al-Tawḥīdī: *Ṯalāṯ rasāʾil.* – Ed. by Ibrāhīm al-Kaylānī. Damascus, 1951. Contains: *Risālat al-Saqīfa* (5–26); *Risāla fī ʿIlm al-Kitāba* (27–48); *Risālat al-Ḥayāt* (48–80).

173 *Rasāʾil Abī Ḥayyān al-Tawḥīdī muṣaddara bi-dirāsa ʿan ḥayātihi wa-āṯārihi wa-adabihi.* – Ed. by Ibrāhīm al-Kaylānī. Damascus, ca. 1970. – Repr. 1980, 1985, 1990.
Contains: *Risālat al-Saqīfa* (207–237); *Risāla fī ʿIlm al-Kitāba* (239–268); *Risālat al-Ḥayāt* (269–318); *Risāla fī l-ʿUlūm* (319–346); *Risāla ilā Abī l-Fatḥ Ibn al-ʿAmīd* (347–358); *Risāla ilā Abī l-Wafāʾ al-muhandis al-Būzaǧānī* (359–367); *Risāla ilā l-wazīr Abī ʿAbd Allāh al-ʿĀriḍ* (369–392); *Risāla ilā l-wazīr Abī ʿAbd Allāh al-ʿĀriḍ wazīr Ṣamṣām al-Dawla al-Buwayhī* (393–399); *Risāla ilā l-Qāḍī Abī Sahl ʿAlī b. Muḥammad* (401–414).

3.1.2.2 *Individual Works*

178 *al-Baṣāʾir wa-l-ḏaḫāʾir.* – Ed. by Wadād al-Qāḍī, 9 vols [including] *Fahāris.* Beirut, 1984–1988. – Older Ed. by Ibrāhīm al-Kaylānī, 4 vols. Damascus 1964–1966. – Ed. by Aḥmad Amīn and al-Sayyid Aḥmad Ṣaqr. Cairo, 1953.

179 Abū Ḥayyān al-Tawḥīdī and Abū ʿAlī Miskawayh. *Al-Hawāmil wa-l-šawāmil.* – Ed. by Aḥmad Amīn and al-Sayyid Aḥmad Ṣaqr. Cairo, 1370/1951.

180 *Risāla fī l-ʿUlūm.* – Ed. by Marc Bergé, “Épître sur les sciences (*Risāla fī l-ʿulūm*) d’Abū Ḥayyān al-Tawḥīdī (310/922[?]-414/1023), introduction, traduction, glossaire technique, manuscrit et edition critique.” In *Bulletin d’études orientales* 18 (1963): 241–300; 21 (1968): 313–346. – Older Ed. in *Risālatān* 1883 [*171: 200–208]. – Ed. by Ibrāhīm al-Kaylānī, *Rasāʾil Abī Ḥayyān al-Tawḥīdī* [*173 (1985): 319–346].

181 *Aḫlāq al-wazīrayn. Maṯālib al-Ṣāḥib Ibn ʿAbbād wa-Ibn al-ʿAmīd.* – Ed. by Muḥammad b. Tāwīt al-Ṭanǧī. Damascus, 1385/1985. – Ed. by Ibrāhīm al-Kaylānī, *Maṯālib al-wazīrayn. Aḫlāq al-Ṣāḥib Ibn ʿAbbād wa-Ibn al-ʿAmīd.* Damascus, 1961.

182 *Risāla fī l-Kitāba.* – Ed. by Franz Rosenthal, *Abū Ḥayyān al-Tauḥīdī on penmanship* (1968 [*315]). – With Engl. transl.

183 *Kitāb al-Imtāʿ wa-l-muʾānasa.* – Ed. by Aḥmad Amīn and Aḥmad al-Zayn, 3 vols. Cairo, 1939–1944; 1953 (2nd ed.).

184 *al-Muqābasāt.* – Ed. by Muḥammad Tawfīq Ḥusayn. Baghdad, 1970. – Repr. Tehran 1987, Beirut 1989. – Further editions: Ed. by al-Mīrzā Ḥusayn al-Šīrāzī. Bombay, 1898. – Ed. by Ḥasan al-Sandūbī. Cairo, 1929. – Repr. Beirut 1978.

185 *Kitāb al-Ṣadāqa wa-l-Ṣadīq.* – Ed. by Ibrāhīm al-Kaylānī. Damascus, 1964. – Ed. by ʿAlī Mutawallī Ṣalāḥ. Cairo, 1972.

186 *Risālat al-Ḥayāt.* – Ed. by Ibrāhīm al-Kaylānī [*172: 48–80]. – French transl. by Claude Audebert, “La Risālat al-Ḥayāt d’Abū Ḥayyān al-Tawḥīdī.” In *Bulletin d’études orientales* 18 (1963/64): 147–195 (with commentary and glossary of terms).

187 *al-Išārāt al-ilāhiyya. Al-ǧuzʾ al-awwal wa-maʿahu mulaḫḫaṣ al-ǧuzʾ al-ṯānī.* – Ed. by Wadād al-Qāḍī. Beirut, 1973.

3.1.3 Al-Siǧistānī: Bio-bibliographical Testimonies

201 Ibn al-Nadīm, Abū l-Faraǧ Muḥammad b. Isḥāq (d. 380/990). *Kitāb al-Fihrist* [composed 377/988]. – Ed. by Gustav Flügel, August Müller and Johannes Roediger, 2 vols. Leipzig, 1871–1872 (ed. quoted below). – Repr. Beirut 1964, Frankfurt am Main, 2005. – Ed. by Riḍā Taǧaddud. Tehran 1350 h.š./1971. – Ed. by Ayman Fuʾād Sayyid, 2 vols. London 1430/2009. – Engl. transl. by Bayard Dodge, *The Fihrist of al-Nadīm*, 2 vols. New York, 1970.

202 Abū Ḥayyān al-Tawḥīdī. *Kitāb al-Imtāʿ wa-l-muʾānasa.* – Ed. by Aḥmad Amīn and Aḥmad al-Zayn, 3 vols. Cairo, 1939–1944, vol. 1, 29–31; vol. 2, 186; *et passim* (Indices, vol. 1, 3b; vol. 2, 3a-b; vol. 3, 3a).

203 Abū Ḥayyān al-Tawḥīdī. *Al-Muqābasāt.* – Ed. by Muḥammad Tawfīq Ḥusayn. Baghdad, 1970. – Passim (cf. Index, 494).

204 Abū Ḥayyān al-Tawḥīdī. *Kitāb al-Ṣadāqa wa-l-Ṣadīq.* – Ed. by Ibrāhīm al-Kaylānī. Damascus, 1964, 55–59 and Index.

205 *Ṣiwān al-ḥikma* [ascribed to Abū Sulaymān al-Siǧistānī], extant in two excerpts: a) *Muntaḫab Ṣiwān al-ḥikma.* – Ed. by ʿAbd al-Raḥmān Badawī, *Ṣiwān al-ḥikma wa-ṯalāṯ rasāʾil.* Tehran, 1974, 227–228. – Ed. by Douglas Morton Dunlop, *The Muntakhab Ṣiwān al-ḥikmah of Abū Sulaimān as-Sijistānī.* Paris, 1979, 140 § 275. – b) ʿUmar b. Sahlān al-Sāwī, *Muḫtaṣar Ṣiwān al-Ḥikma.* – Ed. by R. Mulyadhi Kartanegara. PhD Diss., University of Chicago, 1996 (microfiches, Ann Arbor, Mich: University Microfilms International, 1996).

206 al-Bayhaqī, Ẓahīr al-Dīn Abū l-Ḥasan ʿAlī b. Zayd Ibn Funduq (d. 565/1169–1170): *Tatimmat Ṣiwān al-ḥikma.* – Ed. by Muḥammad Šafīʿ, fasc. 1: Arabic text. Lahore, 1935, 90,6–11. – Ed. by Muḥammad Kurd ʿAlī, *Taʾrīḫ ḥukamāʾ al-islām.* Damascus, 1365/1946. – Repr. 1396/1976. – Excerpts transl. in Max Meyerhof, "ʿAlī al-Bayhaqī's Tatimmat Ṣiwān al-ḥikma, a Biographical Work on Learned Men of the Islam." In *Osiris* 8 (1948): 122–217.

207 Ibn al-Qifṭī, Ǧamāl al-Dīn ʿAlī b. Yūsuf (d. 646/1248). *Taʾrīḫ al-ḥukamāʾ* [*Iḫbār al-ʿulamāʾ bi-aḫbār al-ḥukamāʾ*, epitome by Muḥammad b. ʿAlī al-Zawzanī]. – Ed. by Julius Lippert, *Ibn al-Qifṭī's Taʾrīḫ al-ḥukamāʾ.* Leipzig, 1903, 282–283.

208 Ibn Abī Uṣaybiʿa, Muwaffaq al-Dīn Aḥmad b. al-Qāsim (d. 668/1270). *ʿUyūn al-anbāʾ fī ṭabaqāt al-aṭibbāʾ.* – Ed. by August Müller, 2 vols. Cairo, 1299/1882, Königsberg, 1884, I 321–322. – Cf. I 186,29; II 135,29.

209 Ibn Faḍl Allāh al-ʿUmarī (d. 749/1349). *Masālik al-abṣār fī mamālik al-amṣār. Routes toward Insight into the Capital Empires,* Book 9. – Ed. by Fuat Sezgin, in collaboration with A. Jokhosha and Eckhard Neubauer. Frankfurt a.M., 1988, 28–29. – Facsimile edition.

3.1.4 Editions of al-Siǧistānī's Works

215 Badawī, ʿAbd al-Raḥmān, ed. *Ṣiwān al-ḥikma wa-ṯalāṯ rasāʾil.* Tehran, 1974. – Contains: *Maqāla fī anna l-aǧrām al-ʿulwiyya ḏawāt anfus nāṭiqa* (367–371); *Maqāla fī l-Muḥarrik al-awwal* (372–376); *Maqāla fī l-Kamāl al-ḫāṣṣ bi-nawʿ al-insān* (377–387).

216 Kraemer, Joel L. *Philosophy in the Renaissance of Islam. Abū Sulaymān al-Sijistānī and his Circle* (Leiden 1986). – Part IV: 'Philosophical Treatises' (274–310) contains translations of the following texts: IV § 5 (278–285), *The Supernal Bodies Possess Rational Souls* (*Fī anna l-aǧrām al-ʿulwiyya ḏawāt anfus nāṭiqa*); IV § 6 (285–292), *On the First Mover* (*Fī l-Muḥarrik al-awwal*); IV § 7 (293–304), *On the Specific Perfection of the Human Species* (*Fī l-Kamāl al-ḫāṣṣ bi-nawʿ al-insān*). – Further, in § 8, *Discourse on the Principles of the Existent Beings* (304–310), a resumé of *Kalām fī mabādiʾ al-mawǧūdāt wa-marātib quwāhā* (the attribution to al-Siǧistānī is doubtful).

3.2 *Al-Tawḥīdī's Life and the Cultural Milieu of 4th/10th Century Baghdad and Western Iran*

Al-Tawḥīdī's work reflects a century characterized by various political conflicts, as well as by manifold religious and intellectual movements. It is the century in which the Greek and the Iranian intellectual heritage was first amalgamated with Arabic-Islamic thought. This process, which unfolded through discussion, polemics, and reformation, is portrayed by al-Tawḥīdī in literary stylization; this is why he was called 'philosopher of the littérateurs and littérateur of the philosophers' (*faylasūf al-udabāʾ wa-adīb al-falāsifa*) (Yāqūt [**154*: V 380 Margoliouth]). After a long conflict between Arabic, Kurdish, and Turkish armies and militias, the Arab caliph was reduced to a mere puppet by an Iranian emir of the Buyid dynasty from Northern Iran. The Buyid emirs were followers of the Shia, who regarded ʿAlī and his descendants as the only rightful Imams and leaders of the political community. Nevertheless they needed the Abbasid caliph in order to gain legitimacy; and indeed, the greatest member of the dynasty, ʿAḍud al-Dawla (338–372/949–983), managed to establish the rule of a Persian Great-King, sanctioned by the caliph in a solemn ceremony (367/978). He enlisted the service of the Shiite scholars, who justified their political quietism as well as their legal authority with the occultation of the hidden Imam. For a short period the two worlds, the Sasanian-Iranian on the one hand and the Islamic-Arabic one on the other, were thus united, under Caliph and Great-King ('Kalif und Großkönig', Busse 1969 [*265]).

However, battle lines remained open between Sunna and Shia, between rationalists and traditionalists, philosophers and jurists, grammarians and logicians. Al-Tawḥīdī has given us reports of the debates taking place on the book market of Baghdad, which were joined by Muslims as well as Christians and Jews, by adherents of all confessions and all schools of law, by physicians as well as mathematicians and philosophers. This may well be called the century during which the culture of classical Islam was forged – not because at its end, traditionalism in theology and law would define Islamic orthodoxy by repealing open dispute and freedom of exegesis, but because it produced personalities like the litterateur al-Tawḥīdī, the Transoxanian philosopher al-ʿĀmirī (cf. § 5.2), the Persian historian and moralist Miskawayh (cf. § 5.4), and the scientists, physicians and court secretaries belonging to their circles, who were able to clad the intellectual debate of their day in a language that was listened to and appreciated, offering aesthetic pleasure as well as instruction. Many aspects of the phenomenon, which may be conceived of as an Islamic renaissance (Mez 1922 [*261], Kraemer 1986 [*268]) or as Arabic humanism (Kraemer 1986 [*268], Key 2005 [*355]), are brought to life in al-Tawḥīdī's writings.

We do not know where Abū Ḥayyān ʿAlī b. Muḥammad b. ʿAbbās al-Tawḥīdī came from. He may have been born between 308/920 and 318/930 in Shiraz, the same city to which he withdrew as an old man after saying his final goodbyes to Baghdad (for a survey of all information on al-Tawḥīdī's life available in primary sources see Bergé 1979 [*283]). He himself tells us that he underwent the entire traditional course of education for a Muslim scholar in Baghdad, up to ca. 350/961. This would have comprised Arabic philology – the educated littérateur (*adīb*) is first of all an adept of the Arabic language, and the grammatical and rhetorical hermeneutics of Arabic is needed as an instrument for interpreting the Quran and the traditions which transmit the Sunna, i.e. the instructions and the exemplary acts of the prophet Muḥammad – and furthermore the study and disputation of the orthodox schools of law. Al-Tawḥīdī was taught Šāfiʿī law by Abū Ḥāmid al-Marwarrūḏī (al-Subkī [*159: III 12–13; Ibn Ḫallikān [*155: I 69–70]; mentioned frequently by al-Tawḥīdī, cf. *Baṣāʾir* [*178: I 65 and Index]) and Abū Bakr al-Šāfiʿī. In the field of grammar, his master (*šayḫ*, *Muqābasāt* [*184: 129]) was Abū Saʿīd al-Sīrāfī (368/979), who was the leading authority on systematic grammar in Sībawayh's school, but who had also 'pretended to knowledge in the science of the *Almagest*, of Euclid and of logic' (al-Zubaydī, *Ṭabaqāt* [*152: 119,12]; al-Suyūṭī, *Buġyat al-wuʿāt* [*162: I 507,14–16 [based on al-Tawḥīdī, *Taqrīẓ al-Ǧāḥiẓ*]: 'Abū Saʿīd al-Sīrāfī was the master in the knowledge of grammar … in arithmetic and in geometry'). Al-Sīrāfī defended the traditional Arabic-Islamic sciences against the claims of the 'alien' sciences of the Greeks, in particular against Aristotelian logic and physics. Amongst his colleagues and students were those who made use of definitions and the methods of logic (see pp. 295–296 below: Ibn al-Sarrāǧ [d. 316/928], al-Zaǧǧāǧī [d. 337/949] and al-Rummānī [d. 384/994]). Increasingly, representatives of both schools, the Arabic-Islamic as well as the Greek-philosophical, began to envision a curriculum based on both traditions as their new ideal of learning. Al-Tawḥīdī himself drew up such a syllabus in his *Epistle on the Sciences* (*Risāla fī l-ʿUlūm* [*180]). It was composed during one of his journeys, perhaps in Bukhara, where he spent some time as a young man, around 342–343/952–954 (*al-Baṣāʾir* [*178: VII 52]). A precursor for this endeavour was Abū Zayd from Balkh in Transoxania, a scholar whom he praises warmly, and whose philological and literary knowledge (*adab*) and theological expertise is commended by the chroniclers no less than his scientific knowledge, which he had acquired in the circle of al-Kindī (on Abū Zayd Aḥmad b. Sahl al-Balḫī, d. 322/934, cf. § 5.1.2, and in particular Rowson 1990 [*271]). The central focus of al-Tawḥīdī's catalogue of the sciences, however, is on the Arabic-Islamic disciplines. Of the philosophical disciplines he only lists the instrumental discipline of logic, and rhetoric; as final item of the catalogue he mentions *taṣawwuf*, the internalized piety of Muslim ascetics and mystics (*Risāla fī l-ʿUlūm* [*180: 287–288; Arab. 11–12]).

This last point deserves particular attention. *Taṣawwuf* was no school discipline, even if al-Tawḥīdī mentions his personal master, Abū Muḥammad Ǧaʿfar al-Ḫuldī (d. 348/959, a pupil of Ǧunayd) by name (al-Ḏahabī [*156: IV 518]), and further, less secure reports link him to the adherents of Sufism (cf. Kraemer 1986 [*268: 220–221]). It was the path of the individual's search for God, and of ascetic life, accepted by the official religion of Islam with hesitation only. Al-Tawḥīdī himself describes it in one of his most mature and personal texts, *al-Išārāt al-ilāhiyya* (*Divine Pointers*) [*187], and gives voice to it in numerous stories and *dicta*. It is possible that he was persecuted and even banned from Baghdad by the devout vizier of Muʿizz al-Dawla, al-Muhallabī (d. 352/963), because of his mystical leanings (cf. Massignon 1950 [*262: II 240–241], but doubts are voiced by Stern 1956 [*278: 126] and Kraemer 1986 [*268: 214]). This, at any rate, is claimed by later biographers belonging to the traditionalist schools of law (Ibn Ḥaǧar [*161: VI 369]). Al-Tawḥīdī himself mentions nothing of the kind, but has only praiseworthy things to say about his learned patron (on the latter's circle as reflected by al-Tawḥīdī's reports cf. Bergé 1979 [*283: 60–68], Kraemer 1986 [*268: 54–55]). Thus it seems that al-Tawḥīdī's Sufi tendencies were resented only by later writers, for whom they were reason enough to condemn him as one of the three arch heretics of Islam. It is, however, correct that he advocated the mystical rather than the official version of piety. In one of his works, he thus equated the spiritual pilgrimage of the heart with the pilgrimage to Mecca, one of the canonical duties of each and every Muslim (Yāqūt [*154: V 382,2 Margoliouth]). Al-Tawḥīdī here followed in the steps of the great martyr of early Sufism, al-Ḥallāǧ, who, aware of the mystical union, found the divine 'Thou' in his inner self, and with his ecstatic expression 'I am the Truth', i.e. 'I am God', seemed to challenge the very fundaments of Islam. In consequence he was crucified as a heretic in 309/922. Al-Tawḥīdī, however, did not only undertake the spiritual pilgrimage; in 353–354/964–965, together with a group of Sufis, he also went on the 'proper' pilgrimage to Mecca (*Imtāʿ* [*183: 2,79], about the arduous return journey [*183: 155–156]; cf. also *Aḫlāq al-wazīrayn* [*181: 511–513] on a travel companion, Abū Aḥmad al-ʿAlawī al-ʿAqīqī).

After 354/965 we find al-Tawḥīdī in all circles of intellectual and literary life in Baghdad, as both member and chronicler. In 358/968 he first meets his later patron, the mathematician Abū l-Wafāʾ al-Būzaǧānī (d. 388/998, cf. GAS [*3: V 321–325]), who was active at the Buyid courts of Baghdad and Rayy, and at the court of Qābūs in Ǧurǧān (369/979, cf. *Imtāʿ* [*183: I 51]). He was one of the great mathematicians of the century. As a geometer (*al-muhandis*) he worked on land surveying; as a jurist he concerned himself with practical numeration and algebra for judges and muftis. Later on we encounter al-Tawḥīdī at times in Baghdad, at times in the Buyid residences in Shiraz and in Rayy in northern Iran. Between 358/968 and 362/972 he travelled from Iraq to Fars and al-Ǧibāl (where we find him in 360/970 in the *maǧlis* of the Buyid emir ʿIzz al-Dawla Baḫtiyār, *Aḫlāq* [*181: 202–203], together with al-Rummānī and Abū l-Wafāʾ; cf. Bergé 1979 [*283: 96–97. 101–102]).

Even though al-Tawḥīdī had absolved a thorough course of legal studies and had acquired an encyclopedic body of knowledge, he did not pursue a lucrative career in the offices of the legal scholars, or among the ranks of the official secretaries. Instead he earned his living as a copyist and a bookseller.

The most important of his early works is *The Examples of the Sages and the Treasures of the Ancients* (*Baṣāʾir al-ḥukamāʾ wa-ḏaḫāʾir al-qudamāʾ* [*178]). This four-volume compilation is a classical work of the Arabic literary genre of the so-called *adab*, which denotes good manners and decorum, and the courtly cultivation of intellectual refinement. *Adab* refers to the cultivation of language as well as to a stylistic ideal; it constitutes the purest expression of Arabic-Islamic culture. Al-Tawḥīdī's professed role model is al-Ǧāḥiẓ (d. 255/868–869), the greatest prose author from the heyday of the Abbasid caliphate in the 3rd/9th century. Al-Tawḥīdī's artistic prose is fashioned after the style of *ḫuṭab* and *aḫbār*, the religious-political speeches and the historical narrations that characterized Islamic culture from its early days. He uses it to compose stories and history, as well as the classical repertoire of gnomologia and mirrors for princes. Soon, however, he went further, producing representations of the intellectual discourse of his day, and the topics disputed and fought over by contemporary scholars. With this innovation, al-Tawḥīdī seems to have trespassed into forbidden territory. Jealous contemporaries call him a liar, even an arch liar (*kaḏḏāb*); in the terminology of the traditionalists, this marks him as an unreliable transmitter. Even those authors of later biographical collections who have something commendatory to say about him distance themselves from his *Epistle on the Shelter* (*Risālat al-Saqīfa*) [*172: 5–26]), remarking that what al-Tawḥīdī reports concerning eminent companions of the prophet, like Abū Bakr, Abū ʿUbayda and ʿAlī, was his own free invention, or even plain lies (al-Ḏahabī [*156: IV 518], Ibn Ḥaǧar [*161: VI 369–370]). The events taking place in the 'Saqīfa', the hut of the Banū Sāʿida, concerned the controversial question of the succession of the prophet. Anyone who chose to engage with this topic made himself liable to be judged by the strictest possible standards of transmission.

On closer inspection, however, al-Tawḥīdī's text turns out to be a literary variant on classic historical writing. The high literary style of the artistic prose of the time, the *inšāʾ*, becomes a vehicle for fiction. Even the classic historical tradition can be said to 'lay a claim to truth which is conveyed by the manner of presentation, but does not do justice to the character of the texts' (Leder 1991 [*272: 5]) – even less will it do justice to the *adab* of someone like Abū Ḥayyān. The scholars rejected this fictional game, and demonstrated in grim earnest that the companions of the prophet could never have spoken in this way.

In 362/972, calamity befell Baghdad. In the wake of a Byzantine invasion in Northern Mesopotamia, the capital was forced to cope with a stream of refugees. The situation more and more resembled civil war; in this 'war of all against all' large parts of the city were razed to the ground. Al-Tawḥīdī lost all his possessions and suddenly found himself penniless (for the historical situation cf. Miskawayh, *Taǧārib al-umam* [*153: II 303–307, under 361 AH], Bergé 1979 [*283: 114–119, and cf. the review by Bellamy 769]); Bürgel 1965 [*264: 33–34]). The literary form of *adab* allows him to depict the relationship between scholars and intellectuals on the one hand and those wielding political power on the other, by composing historical anecdotes (*aḫbār*) and literary records of discussions (al-Qāḍī 1981 [*338]). What was there to do, when the caliph had been deprived of power, and the Buyid emir failed to discharge his duties as a ruler? Al-Tawḥīdī reports (*Imtāʿ* [*183: III 150–162]) that a group of judges and scholars approached the emir to impress the plight of the population on him. The emir dismissed the delegation, showering them in abuse and personal insults. From a different source (Miskawayh's *Taǧārib al-ʿumam* [*153: 303–304 Amedroz/Margoliouth]) we know that he demanded funds for the war against Byzantium, and that this request was granted by the caliph; but he squandered the money on other pursuits.

To fend off poverty, al-Tawḥīdī tried to leave behind his constraining profession as a copyist, and sought to obtain a powerful patron. Between 362/972 and 366/976 he moved to Rayy; in 365/975, while the vizier Abū l-Fatḥ Ibn al-ʿAmīd was still in office, he completed the *adab* compilation *al-Baṣāʾir wa-l-ḏaḫāʾir* (*The Examples of* [*the Sages*] *and the Treasures* [*of the Ancients*]) (but cf. al-Qāḍī 1984–1988 [*341: IX 233–234] on the date). In Rayy he met Miskawayh – the author of a philosophical ethics which fuses Plato and Aristotle together with other Hellenistic ethical traditions, and collector of ethical sayings in which ancient Arabic material, Greek gnomologia, and the 'testaments' of the Persian Kings are united as 'eternal wisdom' (*Ǧāwīdān Ḫirad* [§ 5.4 **281*]). The most original testimony to his philosophy emerges from his engagement with al-Tawḥīdī: a philosophical correspondence, in which Miskawayh responds to al-Tawḥīdī's questions – *al-Hawāmil*, 'stray cattle' – with his answers – *al-Šawāmil*, 'secure enclosures' [**179*]. Were one to look for testimonies of an 'Arabic humanism' (which certainly was never conceived of in such terms), one would find them in these questions, and in Miskawayh's replies.

Miskawayh was employed in the service of Abū l-Fatḥ in Rayy, which may well have induced al-Tawḥīdī to try his luck with him, too (around 365–366/975–976, cf. Bergé 1979 [*283: 136–146]). And indeed, Abū l-Fatḥ seems to have regarded him with a benevolent eye; but when the vizier was executed four years later, al-Tawḥīdī returned to Baghdad just as poor as he had left it. One year later (367/977) he travelled again to Rayy, this time to Ibn ʿAbbād who, after the death of his rival Abū l-Fatḥ, had risen to the position of vizier and intimate confidant of Muʾayyid al-Dawla (Bergé 1979 [*283: 146–166]). Al-Tawḥīdī was enticed by the vizier's reputation as a generous man with a taste for scholarship; but he was disappointed. He found employment as a secretary to the vizier, who made him copy his books and epistles; thus he was forced to continue to perform the very kind of activity he loathed so much, lamenting it as the 'craft of doom' (*Aḫlāq* [**181*: 306]). The recognition and lavish remuneration he had hoped for failed to materialize. In 370/980 he broke with al-Ṣāḥib Ibn ʿAbbād and returned to Baghdad. How this came about al-Tawḥīdī describes in his book *On the Character of the Two Viziers* (*Aḫlāq al-wazīrayn* [**181*]), a libel piece he only was able to publish years after his return to Baghdad. He uses the philosophical 'study of character' (*ʿilm al-aḫlāq*), i.e. ethics, as a vehicle for his satire; but it is shaped with the literary tools of *adab*. Collecting comments on the two viziers made by his contemporaries, and tirelessly narrating anecdotes from his own experience, he pulls out all the stops, going to far as to supply astrological and philosophical explanations for Ibn ʿAbbād's having been born a miser, and telling how Ibn al-ʿAmīd became a miser due to his philosophical leanings.

Back in Baghdad, desperate and hopeless, al-Tawḥīdī, against all expectations, finally met an influential patron (Bergé 1979 [*283: 166–204]). In 371/981, the mathematician Abū l-Wafāʾ procured a position for him at the hospital founded by ʿAḍud al-Dawla (*Imtāʿ* [*183: I 19]), and recommended him to the vizier al-ʿĀriḍ Ibn Saʿdān. This proof of friendship prompted al-Tawḥīdī to commence his *Risālat al-Ṣadāqa wa-l-Ṣadīq* (*On Friendship and the Friend*). During the years 373–375/983–985 we find him in the *maǧlis* of the vizier Ibn Saʿdān, who invited al-Tawḥīdī to long evening discussions about various topics. These discussions come to life for us through the reports which al-Tawḥīdī wrote down at Abū l-Wafāʾ's request. This is how the *Kitāb al-Imtāʿ wa-l-muʾānasa* (*Book of Enjoyment and Geniality*) came into being, a most valuable source for the cultural life and the intellectual debates of the 4th/10th century.

In Baghdad, al-Tawḥīdī joined the circles of philosophers linked to the book market (*sūq al-warrāqīn*). His most important partners in conversation he found among the students of the Christian Arabic philosopher Yaḥyā Ibn ʿAdī (cf. § 7.2). At the time, the leading figure within this circle of philosophers was Abū Sulaymān from Sīstān, called al-Manṭiqī, 'the logician'. Al-Tawḥīdī reports at length about his lectures and responses. The school he represents is that of the Baghdad translators and transmitters of Aristotelianism, especially of logic. This is an Aristotelianism which, in the light of Platonic ethics and Neoplatonic cosmology, attempts to reconcile Greek rationalism with Islamic conceptions of God, world, and man. Al-Tawḥīdī praises al-Siǧistānī's erudition, wisdom, and piety, and in his writings largely adopts the latter's attitude towards philosophy.

With al-Siǧistānī (but also with Yaḥyā Ibn ʿAdī and Miskawayh), al-Tawḥīdī saw philosophy as a way to achieve a universal truth and a universal ethics which would leave behind the limitations, the casuistry and the traditionalism of the jurists. This claim, and the intellectual optimism which went with it – the belief that perfect knowledge, and hence the path to immortality, was attainable through the purification of the rational soul, the *tahḏīb al-aḫlāq* ('refinement of character': the title both Ibn ʿAdī and Miskawayh chose for their ethics) – are an expression of the international culture which had emerged from the classical period of Islam, and which was shared by people of all religions and denominations.

However, reality caught up soon with al-Tawḥīdī. After two years in office, the vizier Ibn Saʿdān became involved in a conspiracy against the Buyid emir and was executed. Al-Tawḥīdī lost his income; he sank into poverty and loneliness. Once again he turned to his benefactor Abū l-Wafāʾ (*al-Imtāʿ* [*183: III 226–230]), but his cry for help went unheeded. Al-Tawḥīdī withdrew from public life. In his late works we encounter him as a Sufi: he writes mystical epistles, the *Divine Pointers* (*al-Išārāt al-ilāhiyya* [**187*]), in which he appears as a recluse who looks at fate with a critical eye, but has not given in to cynicism. Dialogue with God remains his last refuge.

After 375/985 we have no precise information about him. He seems to have left Baghdad soon after that time; one of his last works is dedicated to Abū l-Qāsim al-Dalaǧī, who held the office of vizier in Shiraz (Bergé 1979 [*283: 205]). There are further indications that he spent the remainder of his days (from 382/992) in Shiraz, where he took up teaching. During this time he completed the *Kitāb al-Muḥāḍarāt wa-l-munāẓarāt* (*Lectures and Disputations*) – an *adab* compilation of which we only possess excerpts preserved in Yāqūt [**154*: v 382–386 Margoliouth; v 1925–1929 ʿAbbās) – and the philosophical protocols of the *Kitāb al-Muqābasāt* (*Borrowings*).

The last of his extant works is the book about friendship (*Kitāb al-Ṣadāqa wa-l-Ṣadīq* [**185*]), to which he had been inspired by Ibn Saʿdān. It states Ramaḍān 400 (April 1009) as the date of its completion (*al-Ṣadāqa* [**185*: 9]). Al-Tawḥīdī is now an old man: 'My sun has reached the edge of the wall' (*al-Ṣadāqa* [**185*: 69,11–12]; 'in the ninth decade of life', Yāqūt, *Iršād* [**154*: v 388,14 Margoliouth]). His book on friendship, in which he once again unites Arabic, Greek, and Iranian ethics, is the book of a man who has lost all his friends. Soon after its completion al-Tawḥīdī burnt his books, a step he justified in a letter to the Qāḍī Abū Sahl ʿAlī b. Muḥammad (dated Ramaḍān 400 [April 1009], Yāqūt: *Iršād* [**154*: v 386,10–392,1 Margoliouth], cf. Bergé 1979 [*283: 211–215]). A later chronicler (al-Ḫwānsārī [**164*: 93]) discovered his tombstone in Shiraz, dated to the year 414/1023.

3.3 *Works: al-Tawḥīdī Reporting on Contemporary Philosophy*

al-Baṣāʾir wa-l-ḏaḫāʾir or Baṣāʾir al-ḥukamāʾ wa-ḏaḫāʾir al-qudamāʾ
The Examples (of the Sages) and the Treasures (of the Ancients)

Completed in 365/975 (cf. al-Qāḍī, 1984–1988 [**178*: IX 227–317]). A work belonging to the genre of literary culture (*adab*) with numerous texs from Greek, Iranian, and Arabic wisdom literature (gnomologia). The introduction to the work [**178*: I 5–10 al-Qāḍī] al-Tawḥīdī uses to present his programme. As his sources he names the authors of the classic era of literature, the 3rd/9th century; but he also mentions the sources of Islamic culture in a more general sense: Quran and Sunna, 'reason' and 'experience', and finally the princely ethics of the Persians and the philosophy of the Greeks. The Indian-Iranian mirror-for-princes literature and the 'testaments' of the Sasanian kings belong to the earliest non-Arabic sources of *adab*. Later on, not least through al-Tawḥīdī himself, a prominent place was given also to Greek popular philosophy, transmitted through Greek gnomologia which had been translated and compiled to form new Arabic collections.

One of the texts of philosophical import that are mentioned here is Abū Zayd al-Balḫī's *Kitāb al-Siyāsa al-kabīr* (*The Great Book of Governance*) (*al-Baṣā'ir* [**178*: IX 146–148 al-Qāḍī]). The passage defines the art (*ṣināʿa*) of governance, and its five constitutive causes (cf. § 5.1.2). For al-ʿĀmirī's discussion of the Aristotelian causes, for parallels and further testimonies cf. Wakelnig 2009 [*172], for the relation to al-Balḫī cf. Wakelnig 2008 [*171: 215–238, esp. 233–236]. Further philosophical remarks by al-ʿĀmirī can be found in *Baṣā'ir* [**178*: II 209; III 93–94], including a definition of the Greek term *qāṭīġūriyās* (category) (II 209), which perhaps stems from al-ʿĀmirī's commentary, which is extant in fragments. For further *dicta* on virtues and vices in relation to the three faculties of the soul, on name and definition and on the knowledge of God [**178*: III 93–94] cf. Wakelnig 2008 [*171: 216–217].

Taqrīẓ al-Ǧāḥiẓ
Praise of Ǧāḥiẓ

Composed in Rayy after 368/978. The work as a whole is not extant; excerpts are found e.g. in Yāqūt, *Iršād* [**154*: I 124–125 Margoliouth; III 27–29 Rifāʿī (article on Abū Ḥanīfa al-Dīnawarī)]. These and further testimonies from *al-Baṣā'ir wa-l-ḏaḫā'ir*, *Taqrīẓ al-Ǧāḥiẓ*, *Aḫlāq al-wazīrayn* and *al-Imtāʿ wa-l-mu'ānasa* are assembled by Bergé 1965 [*310].

The fragment preserved in Yāqūt is a significant testimony to an ideal of learning which al-Tawḥīdī sees realized in Abū Zayd al-Balḫī – pupil of al-Kindī, secretary, geographer, and philosopher – in al-Ǧāḥiẓ, the master of Arabic language and expert in *kalām*, and in the lexicographer Abū Ḥanīfa al-Dīnawarī.

Risāla fī l-ʿUlūm
On the Sciences

A classificatory exposition of the sciences, motivated perhaps by the lost *Kitāb Aqsām al-ʿulūm* by Abū Zayd al-Balḫī (here [**180*: 296,13] mentioned only by its title, but referred to in *Kitāb al-Muqābasāt* [**184*: 95] in a prominent position under the name of its author).

The text aims at integrating the 'sciences of the ancients'. Apart from the 'Islamic' disciplines (Quran, *ḥadīṯ*, law, theology, Arabic philology, Sufism) it also deals with logic, medicine, astronomy, arithmetic, geometry, and rhetoric.

Risālat al-Ḥayāt
On Life

Composed probably after 400/1010. An ethical treatise explaining the various stages of an ethical life according to the categories of life. The author introduces the topic by defining ten concepts of 'life': 1. the life of the senses and of (physical) movement; 2. the life of knowledge (*ʿilm*) and discernment (*baṣīra*); 3. the life of action and achievement; 4. the life of the natural disposition (*ḫuluq*) of one's character; 5. the life of religious devotion (*dīn, diyāna*) and of rest in God (*sakīna*, illumination through the divine presence, cf. *Imtāʿ* [*183: I 206]); 6. the life of the first perfection (*al-kamāl al-awwal*), i.e. of the perfection of all abovementioned aspects of life to which humans are naturally predisposed; 7. the life of illusion (speculation, *ẓann*, and imagination, *tawahhum*), also: the life of fame which outlasts the human being, as opposed to the truly eternal life; 8. the future life after the separation from the body, in eternal happiness and pure understanding due to the divine light. Above the human sphere are: 9. the life of the angels, the pure spiritual beings, and 10. the life of God.

On the basis of sayings of the sages the various ranks of the ethical life are characterized, in accordance with Platonic ethics, as degrees of purification and of the rational soul's search for truth. Given that man's nature is composed from body and soul, it is the soul's aim to separate itself from the bodily nature and from the world of senses and desires. Here the author presents sayings of the sages belonging to the gnomological tradition: Socrates on the contrast between the natural and the spiritual life; Plato's remark concerning the twofold death, the material death of the body and the 'voluntary death' through which the sage renounces the world of the senses and his bodily desires, thus reaching true life (cf. the topic in Miskawayh, § 5.4 below), and similar sayings according to Homer, Pythagoras, Anaxagoras as well as contemporary philosophers of his circle: Abū Zakariyyā' al-Ṣaymarī, ʿIsā Ibn Zurʿa (cf. § 7.3), Ibn al-Ḫammār (cf. § 7.4), and al-Siǧistānī, providing lengthy explanations [*186: 73–80] about the fear of death and the sage's turn towards the knowledge of unadulterated truth, and on the eternal life in the hereafter.

Aḫlāq al-wazīrayn (also: *Maṯālib al-Ṣāḥib Ibn ʿAbbād wa-Ibn al-ʿAmīd*)
The Character of the Two Viziers (also: *The Ignominy of Ṣāḥib Ibn ʿAbbād and Ibn al-ʿAmīd*)

Composed 370/980. Cf. Bürgel 1965 [*264: 74–84] (on Abū l-Fatḥ Ibn al-ʿAmīd), Bahmanyār 1965 [*263: *qismat* 2, *faṣl* 3, 75–85], Bergé 1979 [*283: 146–166].

[*181: 69–87 Ṭanǧī] Defence of this work of character assassination against Abū l-Fatḥ Ibn al-ʿAmīd and al-Ṣāḥib Ibn ʿAbbād: 'He who attacks puts himself in the wrong; he who retaliates can be excused more easily.' [305–311] Al-Tawḥīdī's first encounter with Ibn ʿAbbād. [366–377] Parsimony and perfidy of the powerful. [492–505] Satire and panegyric: al-Tawḥīdī insults Ibn ʿAbbād; his introductory letter to Ibn al-ʿAmīd.

[234–247] The ignoramus and the rational sciences: Ibn Ṯawāba [Abū l-ʿAbbās Aḥmad b. Yaḥyā, d. 277/890–891 or 273/886–887] and geometry. Quoted by Yāqūt [**154*: II 36–51 Margoliouth; IV 160–174 Rifāʿī], who also discusses the authenticity of the piece (he suspects the *Risāla* to be a fictional work by al-Tawḥīdī, 50–51 Margoliouth; IV 174 Rifāʿī); cf. Rosenthal 1943 [*294: 86–94], Rowson 1988 [*349: 289–293] with Engl. translations.

[115–165] Al-Ṣāḥib Ibn ʿAbbād and the philosopher al-ʿĀmirī (cf. § 5.2.2), whose books he had received from the physician al-Ḥasan al-Ṭabarī. [344–345] The first encounter. [411–414] The debate between Abū Saʿīd al-Sīrāfī and al-ʿĀmirī. [446–447] Philosophical questions posed by Abū l-Fatḥ Ḏū l-Kifāyatayn, on the soul's pursuit of ever more subtle distinctions between similar things (cf. Wakelnig 2008 [*171]).

al-Hawāmil wa-l-šawāmil
Stray Cattle and Secure Enclosures (i.e. random questions [by Abū Ḥayyān al-Tawḥīdī] and exhaustive replies [by his younger friend Abū ʿAlī Miskawayh])

Composed after 370/980. In the introduction, Miskawayh replies to al-Tawḥīdī's complaints 'about the times and the tarrying of the brethren' and exhorts him to be steadfast. The true friend, who according to Aristotle is 'a second self' (*Nicomachean Ethics* IX 4, 1166a31), is rarer than the phoenix or the philosophers' stone [**179*: 2]. While al-Tawḥīdī's reports of contemporary lectures and discussions in *al-Muqābasāt* and *al-Imtāʿ wa-l-muʾānasa* are moulded by his personal style of literary prose, Miskawayh's replies seem to be in his authentic voice, formulated as they are in dry technical language (see § 5.4 below; on the work in general see Arkoun 1973 [§ 5.4 *484: 87–147]).

Besides questions of philology, of *adab* (including music [**179*: 155]), practical [156] and religious [154] political ethics, theology, and the various practices of divination [158], extensive consideration is given to philosophical topics, especially those of anthropology and ethics.

The following section summarizes some philosophically relevant questions which represent al-Tawḥīdī's personal interests. § 47 [**179*: 125]: Questions about the nature of the divinatory dream. § 48 [127–129]: What is a dream, and in particular a divinatory dream? What is its organ and its medium – soul, nature or the human being? (The answer draws on the Aristotelian psychology of the inner senses.) § 49 [129]: Motives for friendship between human beings of different temperaments. § 68 [179–180]: What is the aim of the soul (*multamas al-nafs*) in this world? Does it even have an aim and purpose? If it is characterized by such concepts, it will forgo its high rank and its exalted value, since this would be a mark of deficiency and the beginnings of weakness. What is the soul's relation to man (*mā nisbatuhā ilā l-insān*)? Does the soul's persistence (*qiwām*) rest on the human being, or does it subsist through him? If so, in what way? The human essence is a rather vast subject; 'man is a riddle to man' (*fa-inna l-insān aškala ʿalayhi l-insān*). § 101 [247–248]: Why is laughter contagious? § 116 [268]: Is it possible for man to grasp all sciences, with all their disciplines and methods, and given linguistic diversity and variety of expression? If it is possible, is it also required? If so, does it occur, and has it been known to happen? § 153 [328]: Is there a theological justification for the differences of opinion between legal scholars? § 159 [341]: The four scientific questions (following Aristotle, *Posterior Analytics* II 1), 'whether?', 'what?', 'which?', and 'why?' § 163 [350–352]: When is the soul joined to the body, and after which point (in the embryonic state) will it be in the body? On the human being as hylomorphic compound. § 164 [352]. When the soul leaves the body, will it retain a memory of the knowledge it once had? A philosopher (i.e. Plotinus, cf. the Arabic *Theology of Aristotle*, ed. Badawī, 29.3–30.7, and Plotinus, *Enn.* IV 4: 1.10 ff.; reflected in al-Kindī's treatise on recollection, § 4) has answered that it will remember all intelligible knowledge, but not the knowledge stemming from sense perception. How, then, can one explain that physical illness can lead to a patient forgetting all his knowledge? § 166 [356–357]: Why are the parts of the soul three in number, no more and no less? §§ 165 [354], 167 [357], 168 [359], 171 [361]: Questions on meteorology. § 170 [360]: Every question concerning a certain subject presupposes some knowledge about it; why, then, do we seek knowledge about it (a reflection of Meno's paradox)? § 169 [359]: How come that sleepers can see things (in a dream), without being in command of any instrument of perception? § 172 [363]: The existence of the angels. § 173 [364]: The problem posed by the suffering of children, who lack understanding. § 175 [367]: Error, change of mind, and certainty.

Kitāb al-Muqābasāt
The Borrowings

Completed after 375/985. The 48 *Muqābasāt*, 'adoptions' or 'borrowings' (the name derives from the image of one fire kindled from another) report discussions of the philosophical circles in Baghdad, especially those around Yaḥyā Ibn ʿAdī and al-Siğistānī. For contributions on the text of *Muqābasāt* 4, 5, 8, 11, 13 cf. Muḥyī l-Dīn 1951 [*298].

§ 2 [*184: 57–85]: Discussion of the scholars in the *mağlis* of al-Siğistānī, on the value of astrology (*aḥkām al-nuğūm*). § 9 [95,1–96,5]: Why does every scholar claim his own science to be the most eminent? Reply by ʿĪsā b. ʿAlī b. ʿĪsā (son of the famous vizier and an erudite scribe of the caliph al-Ṭāʾiʿ, d. 391/1001, and well versed in philosophy): since man recognizes the highest idea of knowledge, which is a single one, in each of its manifold forms, he praises the form which he finds in his own soul, and thus praises the First Knowledge. On the hierarchy of higher and lower sciences reference is made to the *Kitāb Aqsām al-ʿulūm* by Abū Zayd al-Balḫī (cf. p. 284 above).

§ 17 [109]: Who can say whether the conduct and the beliefs of the masses are mostly correct, or overall wrong? Reply by Ḥasan b. Suwār (Ibn al-Ḫammār): it is not the majority opinion that is decisive, but one must listen to the consensus of the best, which is well-founded and based on careful judgements. § 20 [116–119]: Al-ʿĀmirī's justification of philosophical speculation about the state of the soul after death; such speculation is not based on mere supposition only (*ẓann wa-tawahhum*). Each object of sense perception carries within it a shadow of the intelligible [118,2]. Intellect is God's representative ('caliph') in this world (*al-ʿaql allaḏī huwa ḫalīfat Allāh fī hāḏā l-ʿālam* 119,3; cf. § 106 [467,5] in Nūšǧānī's lecture: this is an allusion to Quran, Sura 2:30; 38:26 – man is God's *ḫalīfa* in the world). § 22 [121–125]: Given the close relation (*munāsaba*) between logic and grammar, what is the difference between them? Reply by al-Siǧistānī to this question (cf. p. 296 below). § 25 [133–135]: Al-Siǧistānī: human knowledge comprises partly speculation (*ẓann*), partly imagination (*wahm*), perception and reason, knowledge (*ʿilm*) and inspiration (*ḥads*), certainty and doubt, each becoming dominant at different times. Cf. also § 41 [171–173] after al-ʿĀmirī, § 42 [174–176] after Abū l-Ḫayr (Ibn al-Ḫammār): The perceptible world is deceptive and changeable, the light of reason clear and permanent. § 48 [203–206]: Al-Siǧistānī: philosophy is the investigation of everything there is in the world, of external appearances as well as the internal object of intellect. Al-Siǧistānī on the difference between the methods of the theologians (*mutakallimūn*) and the philosophers (*falāsifa*). Yaḥyā Ibn ʿAdī's attack against the arrogance of the theologians. Theology and its ancillary philological sciences are not to be dignified with the name of rational sciences. § 49 [207–208]: Yaḥyā Ibn ʿAdī: the form of movement is one, even though it exists in manifold matters (*mawādd*); their various names. § 50 [209–216]: Al-Siǧistānī on the gift of prophecy (*kahāna*): it is a divine power, and 'the more strongly a soul is shaped by the relevant disposition (*mizāǧ*, 'temperament'), the more luminous and sublime is the light that is received'. Finally, references to al-Siǧistānī's explanations concerning the relation between philosophy and Sharia (cf. below pp. 297–299 and 290 on *Imtāʿ* [**183*: II 2–49]). § 54 [221–230]: ʿIsā b. ʿAlī on the gift of intellect and the value of life. [227, 1]: Al-Siǧistānī against the theologians: the instrument with which they fight so aggressively according to their method is not intellect, but merely resembles it; it may have a shadow of intellect and hence be confused with it, like a phantom. In reality, however, it is ensnared in passion, prejudice, and blind belief in tradition, so that the gate of confusion will open for them, whereas the gate to certainty will close for them. § 61 [241–243]: Al-Siǧistānī studying Aristotle's *On the Soul*, in 370/980: the soul adopts good and bad character traits; the vices of the animal soul are enduring, while the morals of the rational soul lead to the ascent, the purification and the perfection of the character. Reference to Abū Zayd al-Balḫī, *Kitāb Iḫtiyār al-sīra* (*On the Choice of One's Conduct*). § 63 [265–273]: Al-Siǧistānī's reply to the question: why is it not possible to cleanse the religious confession of God's unity from the turbidity of erroneous speculation and linguistic equivocations, so that it would be as purified as it is in philosophy? Speech that is supposed to serve the education of the masses and the unification of the community must employ various means: at times it must be expansive, at other times brief, at times extremely precise and clear, and at times clothed in riddles and allusions; at times it must speak in images, at other times it must be explicit, using arguments and giving reasons. This is the case with everything within the realm of religion (*al-šarʿ*), so that the elite will find satisfactory instruction within it, and the common people a way of expression which is suitable for them. According to the Ancients, not everybody will reach the highest rank; however, as is well-known, the difficulties connected with the translation from the Greek via Hebrew and Syriac are also to blame for a lack of clarity and truth. § 82 [315–319]: Al-Siǧistānī on the meaning of 'being one' (*al-waḥda*), on the basis of a dictation from the year 371/981 (cf. pp. 302–303 below). § 83 [320]: Al-Siǧistānī on the meanings of 'intellect' (*ʿaql*) (cf. p. 304 below). § 95 [355–375]: Definitions of philosophical – logical, scientific, ethical etc. – concepts, partly taken (without reference to the source) from the *Risāla fī Ḥudūd al-ašyāʾ wa-rusūmihā* by al-Kindī and his followers (cf. [§ 4 **41*]), cf. Stern 1959 [§ 4 *142].

Kitāb al-Imtāʿ wa-l-muʾānasa
Book of Enjoyment and Geniality

Composed between 373 and ca. 375/983–985. In 55 nightly conversations (*musāmarāt*, chapters divided by *layālī*, 'nights') al-Tawḥīdī tells the vizier Ibn Saʿdān al-ʿĀriḍ about topics of literature, natural history, philosophy, and other subjects of educated conversation in the circles of Baghdad society.

Night II [**183*: I 29–41]: portraits of contemporary philosophers and their circles of disputation: the philosopher al-Siǧistānī, the Christian Arabic philosophers and translators Yaḥyā Ibn ʿAdī and ʿIsā Ibn Zurʿa, Ibn al-Ḫammār, Ibn al-Samḥ, al-Qūmisī, Miskawayh, the physician and translator Naẓīf, ʿIsā b. ʿAlī b. ʿIsā, the learned son of the vizier ʿAlī b. ʿIsā b. al-Ǧarrāḥ. Night VI [I 206–216, esp. 211–213]: things all peoples have in common, and differences between them; with a reference to Abū Zayd al-Balḫī, *Aḫlāq al-umam* (cf. p. 240 above); on this point cf. also Night XIV [I 211–213], opinions on merit and rank of other peoples compared to the Arabs. Night VII [96–104]: contest between the accountant's numerical art (*Kitābat al-ḥisāb*) and the verbal art of the chancellery clerk (*Kitābat al-balāġa wa-l-inšāʾ wa-l-taḥrīr*); Engl. transl.: van Gelder 1986 [*344]. Night VIII [I 104–143]: Ibn Yaʿīš's critique of scholars who impede access to philosophy, notably the logician Abū Bišr Mattā b. Yūnus. The debate between the grammarian Abū Saʿīd al-Sīrāfī and the logician Mattā (cf. p. 296 below); transl.: Margoliouth 1905 [*291], Taha 1979 [*334], Elamrani-Jamal 1983 [*339], Endress 1986 [*343]). Night IX [I 143–159]: moral character (*aḫlāq*) and states (*aḥwāl*) of human nature (on this, see Bergé 1979 [*283: 305–316]. Nights X–XII [I 159–197]: curious, strange and valuable reports (*nawādir*) on the natural history of animals (annotated Engl. transl.: Kopf

1956 [*301]). Sources include Aristotle's *History of Animals*, a Pseudo-Aristotelian *On the Usefulness of Animals* (*Kitāb Manāfiʿ al-ḥayawān*) and the *Book of Animals* (*Kitāb al-Ḥayawān*) by al-Ǧāḥiẓ. Night XIII [I 198–206]: opinions of the philosophers, esp. of al-Siǧistānī, on the essence of the soul as an incorporeal substance; in parts a literal paraphrase from Miskawayh, *Tahḏīb al-aḫlāq* [§ 5.4: *273: 4,1–5,14], but presented as lecture by al-Siǧistānī. Night XIV [I 206–211]: first part [206–211]: finding rest in God (*sakīna*, Quran, Sura 2:248 et al.) according to pronouncements by al-Siǧistānī and his pupil Abū l-ʿAbbās al-Buḫārī. Second part [I 211–213]: the same circle discussing the various characters and talents of different nations; with a reference to the work *Fī Aḫlāq al-umam* by Abū Zayd al-Balḫī. Night XVI [I 222–226]: free will and determinism, following al-ʿĀmirī, *Inqāḏ al-bašar min al-ǧabr wa-l-qadar* (cf. pp. 258–259 above); comments by al-Siǧistānī. Night XVII [II 2–49]: the relation between philosophy, religion, and politics. First part [II 3–26] (German transl. by Fleischhammer 1988 [*348]): al-Siǧistānī, supported by Abū l-ʿAbbās al-Buḫārī and a certain al-Ǧarīrī (after the legal school of Muḥammad b. Ǧarīr al-Ṭabarī), criticizing the philosophical circle of Basra known as the 'Brethren of Purity' (Iḫwān al-Ṣafāʾ) (cf. § 9.4.2). On the representatives of the Iḫwān whom al-Tawḥīdī mentions by name, including Muḥammad b. Maʿšar al-Bustī, called al-Maqdisī, who features as a disputant, cf. Stern 1964 [*309]. The Iḫwān allege that 'since Greek philosophy and Arabic religion (*šarīʿa*) have been fused [in their doctrine], perfection has come about' [II 5,7]; they are thus able to 'introduce philosophy' – including logic, the doctrine of the categories and all rational sciences – 'into religion, and to include religion within philosophy' [II 6,7–9]. According to al-Siǧistānī, however, the prophet stands above the philosopher; logic and rational sciences have nothing to do with the revealed Sharia. Further contemporaries are included in the criticism: Abū Zayd al-Balḫī, the Shiite Abū Tammām al-Naysābūrī (a member of the entourage of Muṭarrif b. Muḥammad, vizier to the Ziyārid Mardāwīǧ) and Abū l-Ḥasan al-ʿĀmirī, who tried to make their philosophical heresies compatible with the Sharia. Then follow [II 18–22] further lectures by al-Siǧistānī on the relation between philosophy and revealed religion; as well as [II 32–33] a discussion between al-Tawḥīdī and the vizier Ibn Saʿdān about the Greek ideal of the philosopher king. [II 38–40]: opinions of the philosophers – Yaḥyā Ibn ʿAdī, Ibn Zurʿa, Ibn al-Ḫammār, al-Siǧistānī, Abū Zayd al-Balḫī, Miskawayh – on alchemy. Night XXIV [II 104–130]: various topics of natural history. [II 113] The difference between spirit (*rūḥ*) and soul (*nafs*). Night XXV [II 130–147]: comparison and contest between poetry (*naẓm*) and prose (*naṯr*). Opinions of al-Siǧistānī, Abū ʿĀʾiḏ Ṣāliḥ b. ʿAlī al-Karḫī, ʿIsā b. ʿAlī b. ʿIsā, Ibn Hindū and others revolve around the concepts of sensation and reason, spontaneity and reflection, and the priority of these two forms of expression in the language (cf. Hachmeier 2004 [*354]). Night XXXVIII [III 147,11–162,10]: the role of the scholar in society; ruler and subject (ʿIzz al-Dawla Baḫtiyār and the crisis of 362/972, cf. p. 280 above).

3.4 *Al-Siǧistānī's Life*

Not much is known about the life of Abū Sulaymān Muḥammad b. Ṭāhir b. Bahrām al-Siǧistānī al-Manṭiqī. The sources mainly transmit testimonies, and the available biographical data mostly go back to al-Tawḥīdī. Ibn al-Nadīm (d. 380/990), the contemporary bibliographer, offers little information, and in fact had to leave a gap in the text where he hoped to fill in the scholar's date of birth later on – even though al-Siǧistānī was known to him personally (Ibn al-Nadīm [*201: 264 Flügel]).

Al-Siǧistānī was born around the year 300/912 in the South East Iranian province Siǧistān (Sīstān). There he grew up, received his first education, and moved in the court circle of the Saffarid ruler Abū Ǧaʿfar b. Bānūya. As a young man he moved to Baghdad, where he must have arrived in about 327/939. He died probably around the year 374/985; he was still alive when ʿAḍud al-Dawla died in 372/983. Kraemer (1986 [*403: 1–79]) has collected all available data and testimonies about his lifetime and the places where he was active.

At the time when al-Siǧistānī arrived in Baghdad, Mattā b. Yūnus, Yaḥyā Ibn ʿAdī and al-Fārābī were at the height of their activities. There is no indication that al-Siǧistānī ever studied with Mattā b. Yūnus or al-Fārābī; but there is evidence that Yaḥyā Ibn ʿAdī was his teacher (according to al-Tawḥīdī, *Imtāʿ* [*202: II 18,6]); al-Siǧistānī apparently asked him for a translation of Aristotle's *Categories*, with the commentary by Alexander of Aphrodisias (Ibn al-Nadīm, *Fihrist* [*201: 248,24]). His cognomen 'al-Manṭiqī' al-Siǧistānī seems to have picked up in Baghdad, as sign of his ties to the Baghdad Aristotelians (besides his relation to the Kindian tradition). At least once during his time in Baghdad he travelled back to his home province Siǧistān, where he met the mathematician Abū Ǧaʿfar al-Ḫāzin (d. between 350/961 and 360/971) (al-Tawḥīdī, *Muqābasāt* [*203: 332–333]).

It is unknown whether al-Siǧistānī was active in any other profession apart from being a scholar during his time in Baghdad. He enjoyed the patronage of ʿAḍud al-Dawla, whom he venerated, and, in his treatise *On the Specific Perfection of the Human Species* [*215: 377–387] (cf. Kraemer 1986 [*403: 293–304]) glorified as a soteriological figure. After ʿAḍud al-Dawla's death in 372/983 al-Siǧistānī's circumstances took a turn for the worse, since the vizier of the new chief emir, Ṣamṣām al-Dawla, showed no interest in looking after the scholar.

Al-Siǧistānī had al-Tawḥīdī at his side as his confidant and companion, who took his dictations and wrote the protocols of the scholarly assemblies centred around al-Siǧistānī. He did this in such a characteristic and artful style that as a result, most of al-Siǧistānī's philosophical pronouncements (apart from a small number of extant treatises) are known to us only in adapted form, not clearly distinguishable from al-Tawḥīdī's own thoughts. The same applies to other personalities who expressed their opinions on philosophical questions within al-Siǧistānī's circle, like Abū Zakariyyāʾ al-Ṣaymarī (cf. Kraemer 1986 [*403: 45–50]), Abū l-Fatḥ al-Nūšǧānī [50–54]), Abū Muḥammad al-ʿArūḍī [54–56]), and Abū Bakr al-Qūmisī [59–64]). Al-Tawḥīdī's reports are supplemented by the *Ṣiwān al-ḥikma*, which is extant in two large excerpts, the *Muntaḫab* and ʿUmar b. Sahlān al-Sāwī's *Muḫtaṣar* ([*205], cf. al-Qāḍī 1981 [*424], Gutas 1982 [*425], Daiber 1984 [*427] and § 9.1.3). A collection of portraits of scholars, including brief tracts and wise sayings of the featured personalities, it was attributed to al-Siǧistānī (even though it includes a chapter on himself) and is indeed likely to contain a basic stock of materials stemming from his hand; apart from that we find in it, for instance, excerpts from al-Tawḥīdī's *Muqābasāt*. A further source, which in turn makes use of a collection of al-Siǧistānī's gnomologia and aperçus (*Taʿlīqāt*), is the work *Bustān al-aṭibbāʾ wa-rawḍat al-alibbāʾ* (*The Garden of the Physicians and the Meadow of the Intelligent*) by the Christian physician Muwaffaq al-Dīn Ibn al-Muṭrān from Damascus (d. 587/1191, cf. the excerpts in Kraemer 1986 [*403: 91–100]). Despite this collection of scattered texts al-Siǧistānī's personality and work remain somewhat shadowy, a vague reflection in the writings of his epigones.

3.5 *Al-Siǧistānī's Works*

The bulk of doctrines that can be traced back to al-Siǧistānī has to be culled from al-Tawḥīdī's reports and the material gathered in the *Ṣiwān al-ḥikma* [*205]. From his own hand only the following brief treatises are transmitted.

Fī anna l-aǧrām al-ʿulwiyya ḏawāt anfus nāṭiqa
That the Higher Bodies Possess Rational Souls

Engl. transl. in Kraemer 1986 [*216: 278–285]. The work begins with explanations about bodies and their natural motion. Following Aristotle's *On the Heavens*, the heavens are assigned a fifth element and circular motion. In a Neoplatonic interpretation, this leads to the assumption that the heavenly bodies are ensouled and that these souls strive towards the First Cause.

Fī l-Muḥarrik al-awwal
On the First Mover

Text in Kraemer 1986 [*216: 285–292]. The existence of the First Mover follows from the nature of the sphere. The movers of the heavenly spheres, including the first, outermost one (Aristotle, *Physics* VIII), are immanent to their respective spheres, as natural forms which themselves are moved accidentally. The First Mover, by contrast, is a separate substance (sc. the God of Aristotle's *Metaphysics*, book XII) and absolutely motionless. The highest principle *qua* principle of movement is the 'nature of the universe'. The natural forms, or souls, of the heavenly spheres are immanent movers, like the souls of the living beings in their bodies, and as such are moved accidentally. Against the Peripatetics (and their model of the First Mover as final cause) al-Siǧistānī claims that the First Mover of the outermost sphere is immanent to this sphere and is (self-)moved by accident. God, the transcendent, unmoved First Cause, is different from the First Mover (al-Siǧistānī here sides with Themistius and Neoplatonic cosmology, just like al-Fārābī and Ibn Sīnā; cf. Kraemer's comments).

Fī l-Kamāl al-ḫāṣṣ bi-nawʿ al-insān
On the Specific Perfection of the Human Species

Composed for the Buyid ʿAḍud al-Dawla. Text in Kraemer 1986 [*216: 293–304]. Contact with the divine Intellect leads human beings to their highest perfection. The author discusses the opinions of various religions and confessions about the nature of the highest being, and the question whether and how this being can unite with a human individual in order to bring it to the highest perfection. If favoured by divine grace and the stellar constellations, such perfection can indeed be achieved in a human being: so, during his lifetime, in the king of kings, Fanāʾ Ḫusraw ʿAḍud al-Dawla, to whom the author pays homage as the culmination of salvific history. On this topic cf. also the title, documented only by Ibn al-Nadīm (*Fihrist* [*201: 264,17]), *Fī Marātib quwā l-insān wa-kayfiyyat al-inḏārāt allatī tunḏar fīhā l-nafs mimmā yaḥduṯ fī ʿālam al-kawn* (*On the Degrees of the Powers of Man and the Kind of Predictions through Which the Soul is Warned about Events in the World of Generation*).

Kalām fī Mabādiʾ al-mawǧūdāt wa-marātib quwāhā
Treatise on the Principles of the Existing Things and the Ranks of their Powers

Summary and Engl. transl. in Kraemer 1986 [*216: 304–310]. In the Christian Arabic collective manuscript MS Paris, Bibliothèque nationale, ar. 173 the treatise is attributed to 'Abū Sulaymān Ṭāhir'. It also appears in the *Book of Principles* (*Kitāb al-Uṣūl* or *Maǧmūʿ uṣūl al-dīn wa-masmūʿ maḥṣūl al-yaqīn*) by the Coptic scholar al-Muʾtaman Abū Isḥāq Ibrāhīm Ibn al-ʿAssāl (d. around 658/1260; on him cf. Graf, GCAL [*374: II 240–241. 409–410]) alongside his numerous, expansive excerpts from the theological works by Yaḥyā Ibn ʿAdī, followed by the latter's critical comments against the criticism vented by the Muslim Abū Sulaymān. Ibn ʿAssāl remarks, (a) that his brother Hibat Allāh has found the treatise in a book by Abū Sulaymān Ṭāhir b. al-Manṭiqī, and (b) that Faraǧ b. Ǧirǧīs b. Afrām has transmitted it on Yaḥyā Ibn ʿAdī's authority.

Parallels to al-Siǧistānī's definitions of 'nature' and the 'One' in al-Tawḥīdī, *Muqābasāt* [*203: 285. 287] (cf. Troupeau 1969 [*393], Platti 1983 [*381]) confirm his authorship.

In this treatise, al-Siǧistānī deals with the 'existing things, the ranks of their powers and the attributes by which the Christians describe the First Essence, and the question in which way the Christians qualify it as unity and multiplicity, as substantiality (*ǧawhariyya*) and as hypostatization (*uqnūmiyya*)'. He places the views of the Christian theologians in the context of his own Neoplatonic cosmology: the First Cause, at the same time the First Being, is the principle from which all powers emerge, and which bestows being on all existing things by virtue of its emanation. The Intellect is the power which is thought by the First Creator as His first product. It creates and preserves the specific essence of each existing thing. The Soul is the power which gives the highest form, life, to the bodies. Nature is the power which pervades the bodies and thus gives them their specific shape, and leads them to their specific perfection. The Christians characterize the First Cause as life, knowledge and power in analogy to its activity as Intellect, Soul, and Nature. Something al-Siǧistānī regards as inacceptable (afterwards defended by Yaḥyā Ibn ʿAdī) is the justification of the Trinitarian doctrine, which conceives of the single divine substance as three hypostases, corresponding to Intellect, Intellecting and Intellected (each of which, however, is itself substance).

Ṣiwān al-ḥikma
Depository of Wisdom

This work is attributed to al-Siǧistānī. It is a collection of biographical sketches, sayings and excerpts from Greek and Arabic philosophers originating in al-Siǧistānī's school [*205] (cf. also § 9.1.3).

3.6 *Al-Siǧistānī's Doctrines as Reflected by al-Tawḥīdī's Reports*

Other than the few documented treatises, our main sources for al-Siǧistānī's doctrines (and for that of the philosophical circles of his time) are al-Tawḥīdī's reports. However, these reports have been cast into literary form by al-Tawḥīdī and are expressed in his idiosyncratic style, rather than in technical language, and present doctrines and opinions of other authors under al-Siǧistānī's name (for instance, literal quotations from Miskawayh). It is impossible to determine a personal, systematic doctrine proper to al-Tawḥīdī; nor is it possible to fix on a particular philosophical direction to which he would have subscribed. In the following, the views al-Tawḥīdī reports of his teachers and of his partners in conversation will therefore be presented together with other treatises of his time (both authentic and apocryphal). These include Pseudo-Platonic and Pseudo-Aristotelian works as well as a text by the otherwise little known al-Isfizārī (cf. § 5.2), which together with al-Siǧistānī's Neoplatonic metaphysics and psychology are to be classified as belonging to the tradition between al-Kindī and Miskawayh (cf. § 5.4).

Propaedeutics. Following several precursors, including the work *Aqsām al-ʿulūm* (*The Parts of the Sciences*) by Abū Zayd al-Balḫī, al-Tawḥīdī's *Risāla fī l-ʿUlūm* (*Epistle on the Sciences*) describes a predominantly Arabic-Islamic canon of the sciences. Apparently, he was provoked into writing his little encyclopedia by the claim that 'logic had no place in jurisprudence, philosophy had no connection with religion, and wisdom (philosophical ethics) had no influence on the law' [*180: 297,11–13], and that the method of the Ancients (*ṭarīqat al-awāʾil*) was worthless [297,16]. His intention to integrate the 'sciences of the Ancients' is palpable. Having begun with jurisprudence, Quran, prophetic tradition, legal methodology (*qiyās*), theology (*kalām*) and philology (grammar and lexicography), he then proceeds to explain, in detail and with much emphasis, the subject matter and the value of logic. Medicine, astronomy, arithmetic and geometry are dealt with more briefly, whereas he elaborates again on rhetoric. Greek rationalism does not supplant revelation, but serves it through strict rational thinking, both concerning linguistic expression and the subject matter itself. Al-Tawḥīdī closes with *taṣawwuf*, the internalized piety of the Muslim mystics, the Sufis.

Grammar and logic. Competition and antagonism between the propaedeutics of the Arabic-Islamic disciplines, the normative grammar of the Basrian school, and the logical hermeneutics and syllogistics of the philosophical schools are manifest in numerous declarations and discussions of the Baghdad philosophers. The Christian translators and teachers of logic, first and foremost the Nestorian Abū Bišr Mattā, and their students among the contemporaries of al-Tawḥīdī and al-Siǧistānī, i.e. Yaḥyā Ibn ʿAdī and his successors (cf. § 7), impart, teach and propagate logic as the instrument of apodeictic science. With great confidence, Mattā's Christian and Muslim students pit their universal logic against the conventional character of grammar, and their universal metaphysics against the contingency of religious symbols and traditions. The grammarians do not remain unaffected by this. Thus Ibn al-Sarrāǧ (d. 316/928), in his *Uṣūl fī l-naḥw* (*Principles of Grammar*) and above all al-Zaǧǧāǧī (d. 337/949) in his *Īḍāḥ fī ʿilal al-naḥw* (*Explication of Grammatical Causes*) try to show that their sciences sport the same level of scientific conceptualization and logical structure as the logic of the Aristotelians (Versteegh 1995 [*352], Endress 2002 [*353]).

To al-Tawḥīdī we also owe the report – second hand (after the grammarian al-Rummānī, d. 384/994, a student of Ibn al-Sarrāǧ), but in his own ornate style – about a famous debate from the year 326/938, which is representative for the intellectual discussion of the day. It encapsulates the struggle for intellectual supremacy between the hermeneutic sciences of the Islamic scholars (backed by the institutions of the law schools) and the canon of the rational disciplines, of philosophy and the natural sciences. The two disputants are the philologist Abū Saʿīd al-Sīrāfī, al-Tawḥīdī's teacher and the most eminent grammarian of his day, and Abū Bišr Mattā, the leading logician. The logician claims that 'there is no way of distinguishing between right and wrong, truth and lie, good and bad, proof and fallacy, the doubtful and the certain, except by means of our logic' (*Imtāʿ* [*202: I 108]). The grammarian stymies the philosopher by pointing out to him that correct thinking presupposes correct speaking, and that the logic of the Greeks is subject to the conventionalities of their language, and loses cogency when translated into Arabic. Al-Sīrāfī shows that Mattā (a non-Arab) does not understand the Arabic language and its grammar, even though he presumes to be able to judge it. He points out to him that correct thinking is indissolubly linked with correct speech, and that no knowledge can be independent of language. At last he cunningly tricks him into endorsing a contradictory, illogical sentence. Thus exposed, Mattā has to suffer being told that his terminological jargon, the empty phrases of his syllogisms, are no more than hollow words. Targeting his sarcasm with great precision, al-Sīrāfī puts it to the translator of Aristotle's *Poetics* (cf. p. 431 below) that he does not know the first thing about poetry. Not logic, but grammar is the instrument that enables reason to navigate the passage from linguistic signs to intelligible ideas (Elamrani-Jamal 1983 [*400], Endress 1986 [*401]).

Mattā's students defined the relation between grammar and logic carefully, intending also thus to draw the boundaries between the religious and the philosophical disciplines. Yaḥyā Ibn ʿAdī wrote a pedantic tract on the topic (cf. p. 444 below), but al-Siǧistānī, in al-Tawḥīdī's report (*Muqābasāt* § 22 [*203: 121–125]), puts it more concisely: 'grammar is Arabic logic, and logic is intellectual grammar (*al-naḥw manṭiq ʿarabī wa-l-manṭiq naḥw ʿaqlī*). The logician studies meanings first of all, even if he must take care not to make mistakes with respect to words: they are like forms (read *al-ḥulā*?) and ornaments (*maʿāriḍ*, sg. *miʿraḍ*). The grammarian, on the other hand, primarily studies the words, even if he must not make mistakes with respect to their meanings, as they are the essences and substances.' Grammar is confined to the linguistic usage of the Arabs, whereas logic is 'an instrument with he help of which one may establish the difference and decisive distinction between right and wrong with respect to opinion, good and bad with respect to acting, true and false with respect to statements, and beautiful and ugly according to the judgement of reason.' [123,4–7].

Philosophical hermeneutics. Al-Tawḥīdī's discourse is shaped throughout by the linguistic consciousness of the Arabic philologist and littérateur (*adīb*);

this also applies to his reports of the philosophical discussions and lectures of his authorities. Definitions and the philosophical conceptualization of religious, moral and social questions take up ample space in al-Tawḥīdī's *Hawāmil*, *al-Imtāʿ wa-l-muʾānasa*, and *Muqābasāt*, both when it comes to the questions posed by himself and to the lectures he reports as having been given by Ibn ʿAdī and his students, al-Siǧistānī, and others. For instance, *Muqābasāt* § 95 [**203*: 355–375], which is dedicated entirely to the basic concepts of various scientific disciplines, and to establishing their definitions, incorporates an extended excerpt from *Ḥudūd al-ašyāʾ wa-rusūmihā* (*Definitions and Descriptions*), a work of the school of al-Kindī – without citing its source. Topics belonging to natural philosophy are discussed in many variations, adopting the style of philological thesauruses: thus *Muqābasāt* § 49 [**203*: 207–208] on 'motion', § 83 [**203*: 320] on the meanings of 'intellect' (*ʿaql*), § 79 [**203*: 311–312] on 'nature' (*ṭabīʿa*, cf. Kraemer 1986 [*403: 173–177]). In *Muqābasāt* § 60 [**203*: 239–240], but even more so in the 25th Night of *Imtāʿ* [**202*: II 130–147], al-Tawḥīdī, using contributions by al-Siǧistānī and others, develops a theory of discourse relating to the literary forms of poetry and prose, with a number of philosophical contributions to an actual literary debate. Thus he says that poetry is an expression of nature, belonging to the sphere of the composite, whereas prose is an expression of reason, belonging to the sphere of the simple (Kraemer 1986 [*403: 154–158], Hachmeier 2004 [*354]).

Philosophy and religion. The quarrel over methodological supremacy does not go beyond a polite delineation of separate disciplines. (The dispute between al-Sīrāfī and Mattā is an exception: the grammarian was reacting to the 'infection' of his peers by logic, and rising to the defense of his own discipline.) The theologians, by contrast, are seen by the philosophers as incompetent in rational argumentation. Al-Tawḥīdī asks al-Siǧistānī about the difference between the method of the theologians (*al-mutakallimūn*, literally 'the talking ones') and that of the philosophers (*Muqābasāt* § 48 [**203*: 203–206]), exploiting the ambiguity of the word *takallama* (to talk) in order to question the theologians' claim to argumentative proof, given that they did not use philosophical logic.

Al-Tawḥīdī's reports first and foremost focus on the lectures and responses given by al-Siǧistānī, the person who more than anybody else is responsible for his own, al-Tawḥīdī's, attitude towards philosophy. When the emir and king ʿAḍud al-Dawla dies, it is al-Siǧistānī who, together with his companions, recites the same wise sayings which, according to tradition, were intoned by the sages at the funeral of Alexander the Great. This is more than an act of homage to the great Buyid prince: it is also a proclamation of the eternal and universal validity of the doctrine of the Greek sages (al-Rūḏrāwarī, *Ḏayl Taǧārib al-umam* [**153*: *3*: III 75–77]). The apotheosis of the intellect is present everywhere: 'The intellect is the caliph (i.e. representative) of God in this world.' (*Muqābasāt* [*203: 119,3, cf. 467,3]: *al-ʿaql ḫalīfat Allāh fī hāḏā l-ʿālam*). At the same time, al-Siǧistānī insists that rational thought has its limits. He says (in al-Tawḥīdī's phrase) that the mind of man cannot escape the constraints of its natural abode, his material garment, if God does not grant him the garment of grace (*libās al-raḥma*), the coat of purity (*ġišāʾ al-ʿiṣma*) – 'no one has a share in his secret' (*Muqābasāt* [*203: 133,17–134,3]).

More explicit and of greater resonance is al-Siǧistānī's verdict about a group of Shiite intellectuals in Basra, who called themselves the 'Brethren of Purity' (Iḫwān al-Ṣafāʾ), i.e. 'brothers in pure faith' (*Imtāʿ* [*202: II 3–26]; on the Iḫwān cf. § 9.4.2 below). It is, once again, presented to us in the context of a dialogue (with a vizier). Al-Siǧistānī is asked for his opinion on those men who claim that religion is sullied by ignorance and mixed with errors, and that there is no other way to wash and cleanse it than philosophy. Once Greek philosophy and Arabic religious law are in harmony, perfection will be reached (*Imtāʿ* [*202: II 5]). His reply is the most decisive repeal of philosophy's claim to absolute truth ever pronounced by a Muslim philosopher before al-Ġazālī. Reason alone, he says, is not enough; or else revelation would be pointless. Religion has access to the intelligible world just like philosophy, but philosophy has no access to revelation. Philosophy is the work of human beings; the 'light of the intellect' is uncertain, only the light of revelation can offer true guidance (*Imtāʿ* [*202: II 22–23]). With acerbic determination, al-Siǧistānī rejects any attempt to annex the religious law for philospohy. His goal is not intellectual integration, but marking the boundaries between philosophy and religion. Other Muslim thinkers who sought to mediate between religion and philosophy are also criticized explicitly, for instance Abū Zayd al-Balḫī. It is true that al-Tawḥīdī, in his *Baṣāʾir* [*178: VIII 66], praises Abū Zayd's *Naẓm al-Qurʾān* (*The Ordering of the Quran*), where Abū Zayd follows 'the view of the philosophers, but discusses the Quran in a subtle and elegant way'; he even calls Abū Zayd the 'Ǧāḥiẓ of Ḫurāsān'. Nevertheless al-Siǧistānī and his circle reproach him as well as their contemporary Abū l-Ḥasan al-ʿĀmirī for attempting to legitimize philosophical doctrines verging on heresy as concordant with Islam, and thus to vie for the favour of the masses (*Imtāʿ* [*202: II 15]).

This attitude surprised contemporaries and listeners, and it is indeed disconcerting how a philosopher here disavows philosophy. However, for al-Siǧistānī – or for his pupil al-Tawḥīdī – the 'Brethren of Purity' seem to represent all those factions of the Shia who abused philosophy, and the other sciences of the Hellenistic heritage, as an ideological tool in a bid for power. For example, they cited the Neoplatonic concepts of emanation and regression, of cosmic sympathy and of the order of the seven ensouled heavenly spheres as evidence for the renewal of prophetic inspiration through the seven chosen Imams. Thus they devalued God's singular act of grace, the sending of the prophet, and rejected the transmission of His *sunna*. Moreover, to his mind they may well have represented the intellectual background to the virulent sects of the Ismaili Shia who were bent on achieving their goals with the help of the sword, and had become quite dangerous politically, as the Fatimid conquest of Egypt had proved in the recent past. However this may be, al-Siǧistānī's criticism, at least from the vantage point of his spokesman al-Tawḥīdī, has its roots in concrete fears regarding the religious, moral and lastly political implications of a philosophy which was apt to shake state and society to its very core (cf. Endress 1976 [*396]).

Al-Tawḥīdī himself did not see the universal ethics of the philosophers as a negation of Islam's religious duties, but as their confirmation. He was convinced that the philosopher, the 'sage' (we would say: the intellectual), was supposed to advise the politician, and that the politician was indeed in need of such advice. But he also had to experience the futility of such endeavours. The theocratic state of early Islam, whose political leader had also been the Imam, i.e. had led the congregation in worship, had survived as a theoretical postulate only. The spiritual authority of the caliph was a thing of the past, just as the centralized control over the provinces. Here al-Fārābī's philosopher king (cf. p. 635 below) could have served as a model. However, its claim to absolute and universal knowledge placed this kind of philosophy under suspicion, not only with the jurists, but also with political leaders. This becomes clear in the continuation of this very same discussion between the vizier and al-Tawḥīdī: after a long lecture on wise sayings of Cynic-ascetic provenience, al-Tawḥīdī presents the vizier with the Platonic ideal of the philosopher king. (That he puts it into Diogenes' mouth is connected with the fate of Greek gnomologia in late ancient and Arabic transmission). The vizier in turn propagates the well-known Iranian principle, ascribed to the Sasanian Ardašīr, which says that religion and rule are brothers, religion being the foundation, and kingship the guardian. What lacks foundations will cave in, and what has no guardian will perish (*Imtāʿ* [*202: II 33]). In response, al-Tawḥīdī points to the Islamic principle of theocracy: not only the prophet, but also the ruler, i.e. the caliph (representative) of the prophet may enforce God's law in His creation: he has been appointed by God. The answer to the original question on the status of philosophical knowledge within the Islamic state, however, remains open in the end.

Platonic anthropology and ethics. Al-Siǧistānī, 'the logician' (al-Manṭiqī) derives the concepts of Aristotelian logic, ontology, and physics as principles of rational science from the school of the Baghdad Aristotelians. Such principles ensure the intellectual supremacy of the logicians in society. With reference to these principles they challenge the identical claim put forward by the speculative theologians (*mutakallimūn*) – even if (and exactly because) they do not strictly separate the domains of philosophy and religion (including the revealed law of the Sharia) and do not subsume prophecy and revelation under the philosophical doctrine of soul and intellect (in contrast to al-Fārābī). The basic attitude characteristic for the circle of scholars around al-Tawḥīdī and his master al-Siǧistānī resembles that of their older and younger contemporaries al-Balḫī, al-ʿĀmirī and Miskawayh. It is not the scientification of the spiritual life through analysis and demonstration, but Platonic cosmology, anthropology and scientific ethics in the tradition of al-Kindī.

The dominant factor here is Platonic psychology and, following from it, the ethics of purification through reason. The soul is the form of the body, but as such is a self-subsisting, incorporeal, immortal substance. Through purification from all desires and affections attached to the bodily nature it gives the body-soul composite of the human being its specific perfection, and thus its highest happiness (*Imtāʿ* § 13 [**202*: 198–206] according to 'a philosopher' and al-Siǧistānī). Using a Quranic image, this is 'taking rest in God' (*sakīna, Imtāʿ* § 14 [**202*: 206–211] according to al-Siǧistānī). 'According to Socrates' the soul desires the world of the sublime ideas (*al-miṯālāt al-šarīfa*), 'for this is where its true home is; in this world it is a stranger. The human being follows the soul, because through the soul it is a human being' (al-Siǧistānī according to *Imtāʿ* § 14 [**202*: I 215,8–216,2], cf. also Bergé 1979 [*399: 279–280]).

Moral character (*aḫlāq*, ἤθη) and man's ethical perfection are dealt with by the gnomological items in al-Tawḥīdī's *adab* prose and the further sayings found in the *Ṣiwān al-ḥikma*, and in works drawing on the latter. His own philosophical pronouncements touch on the topic too, as do those of his conversational partners and teachers. Al-Tawḥīdī's stance resembles that of his younger contemporary Miskawayh, even if he does not reach the degree of systematization achieved in the latter's ethical treatises (cf. § 5.4 below). As the fifth of several meanings of 'life', al-Tawḥīdī thus records 'the life of the dispositions of character' (*al-aḫlāq*): if a human being purifies them (*haḏḏaba*, as in the title of Miskawayh's *Tahḏīb al-aḫlāq*) and thus purifies himself, rejects ugly habits and adorns himself with beautiful ones, then his life and that of his fellow human beings will be blessed, his inner self will be clean of turbidity, and his endeavours will always be successful, in sweet as well as in bitter circumstances' (*Ḥayāt* [**186*: 57–58]).

Moral and other human states (*aḥwāl*), physical constitution (*ḫalq*) and temperament (*mizāǧ*) make up the moral character (*ḫuluq*) (*Imtāʿ* § 9 [**202*],

cf. Bergé 1979 [*399: 308–311]). In a more systematic fashion, al-Tawḥīdī (in the spirit of al-Siǧistānī) classifies the dispositions of character in accordance with the three psychic faculties of the Platonic tradition, rational, spirited, and appetitive. He draws up a catalogue of virtues and vices, grouped in antithetical pairs. The concepts and diagnoses voiced here are ubiquitous: apart from systematic presentations of philosophical ethics, they are found in the gnomologia of the *Ṣiwān al-ḥikma* [*205], in al-Tawḥīdī's *Al-Baṣāʾir wa-l-ḏaḫāʾir* [*178] and in his questions to Miskawayh (*Hawāmil* [*179]), in the spiteful character sketches of *Kitāb al-Imtāʿ wa-l-muʾānasa* [*202] and in the social satire of *Aḫlāq al-wazīrayn* [*181]. Following Plato, al-Siǧistānī declares 'voluntary death' to be the goal of the sage. Al-Tawḥīdī comments after the fashion of traditional propaedeutics: 'the voluntary death consists in the reigning in of harmful desires. In this state the soul will become free to acquire the degrees of divine perfection' (*Ḥayāt* [*186: 66], French transl. 1963/64 [*306: 162]; cf. Bergé 1979 [*399: 281–282] with further references to the topics of voluntary death and practice for death; on these topics in Miskawayh, cf. p. 314 below). One central topic of Aristotelian ethical discourse is friendship. In al-Tawḥīdī this forms the subject of a monograph belonging to the anecdotal and gnomic genre of *adab*, the *Kitāb al-Ṣadāqa wa-l-Ṣadīq* [*204] mentioned above.

Al-Siǧistānī's systematic positions in physics, metaphysics, and cosmology. In al-Tawḥīdī's reports, we encounter al-Siǧistānī mainly as teaching the philosophical life and creed in the form of ethical wisdom literature. Here as well as in further anthologies of philosophical *adab* we can nevertheless also find expressions of Aristotelian and Neoplatonic physics and metaphysics, in addition to systematic discussions of these topics in the few extant treatises. Their relation to apocryphal texts like the *Kitāb al-Ḥaraka* [*101] (cf. pp. 253–254 above]) is yet to be studied.

However, as far as al-Tawḥīdī's reports allow us to judge, al-Siǧistānī's main interests lay with the semantics of ontological and physical concepts, rather than the science of natural processes (Kraemer 1986 [*403: 165–209]). His discussion of the various kinds of 'cause' is thus composed in the style of works providing lists of definitions. In addition to the four Aristotelian causes from *Physics* 194b16–32 etc. (efficient, material, formal, and final cause) it includes the two 'Platonic' ones, the paradigmatic and the instrumental cause (similarly Yaḥyā Ibn ʿAdī, cf. Kraemer 1986 [*403: 83] according to Ibn al-Muṭrān, *Bustān al-aṭibbāʾ*). Al-Siǧistānī's definitions of 'nature' (*ṭabīʿa*) likewise combines Aristotelian and other concepts (al-Tawḥīdī, *Muqābasāt* § 79 [*203: 311–312], see also Kraemer 1986 [*403: 173–177]): nature as constituent of essence, the composite of form and matter, or (following Aristotle's *Physics* II 1,192b20–23) as 'principle of motion and rest in the things to which they belong properly and essentially, not just accidentally' (cf. Yaḥyā Ibn ʿAdī, *Taʿālīq* [§ 7.2, **121*: 172,11–13] and *Maqāla fī l-Mawǧūdāt* [§7.2, **101*: 269,9–270,14]). In the context of physics furthermore belong explanations of the concepts of 'time' (*Muqābasāt* § 73 [**203*: 301–302, see also Kraemer 1986 [*403: 166–171], featuring the Neoplatonic distinction between time and eternity (*zamān* and *dahr,* χρόνος and αἰών), of the difference between 'unicity' (*waḥda*) and 'point' (*nuqṭa*) (according to *Muqābasāt* § 74 [**203*: 303]; cf. Aristotle, *Posterior Analytics* 87a26, *Topics* 108b24–26, *Metaphysics* 1016b24–26; Kraemer 1986 [*403: 171]), of the meaning of 'substance' (*ǧawhar, Muqābasāt* § 86 [**203*: 324–325]) and of the existence of the vacuum (according to *Muqābasāt* § 84 [**203*: 321–322], cf. Kraemer 1986 [*403: 184–186]).

There are furthermore discussions concerning the various meanings of the homonym 'being'. These closely follow the Aristotelian *Metaphysics*, but also exhibit some Neoplatonic colouring (matter as passive being, form as active, because form-giving, being; and the eternal being that is always being in actuality (*Muqābasāt* § 80 [**203*: 313], Kraemer 1986 [*403: 178–179]). By contrast, the treatise on the manifold meanings of the 'One', which al-Siǧistānī, according to al-Tawḥīdī's *Muqābasāt* § 82 [**203*: 315–317], dictated in his circle in 371/981, is entirely dependent on the Neoplatonic doctrine of emanation. Within the contemporary inter-religious discussion on monotheism, this topic inspired monographs by both al-Fārābī (*al-Wāḥid wa-l-waḥda*; cf. pp. 574–575 below) and Yaḥyā Ibn ʿAdī (*Maqāla fī l-Tawḥīd* [§ 7.2, **104*]). Al-Siǧistānī too touches on the topic's theological implications: among the meanings of 'one', 'absolute unity' (*al-waḥda al-muǧarrada*) which is not in a substrate is the most appropriate one for the First Being. The First, the Creator, cannot be called 'something' (*šayʾ*, ὄν) (thus Abū Zakariyyāʾ in a discussion with al-Siǧistānī, *Muqābasāt* § 30 [**203*: 140–149], cf. Kraemer 1986 [*403: 49–50. 211–212]), nor can it – thus al-Siǧistānī (ibid.) – be termed 'existent' (*mawǧūd*); however, in *Muqābasāt* § 82 He is in fact called the First Being (*awwal mawǧūd*), one of many ambiguities of the text. The First Being is followed by its first product (*mafʿūl*; thus Kraemer instead of *maʿqūl* 318,8), 'the first power, which is the first product of the First's activity'. This is the Intellect, the first created being of Neoplatonic cosmology, and pure unity just like its cause. It is again followed by the second product of that same activity: the Soul. Soul receives existence from the First Being, and form from the second being; by virtue of this form it constitutes the entelechy of every being below it. The human being is the composite which can find a way to reach cognitive union with the First Being, and to profess it (*tawḥīd*). This is possible due to the power that it has received from the monads of the emanation process. (*Muqābasāt* § 82 [**203*: 317–319]; cf. Kraemer 1986 [*403: 219–222]).

Another work strongly influenced by Neoplatonic cosmology is a treatise by al-Siǧistānī in which 'the principles of the existing things' are set in relation to the Christian doctrine of the Trinity (cf. Kraemer 1986 [*403: 304–310]). It is preserved in al-Siǧistānī's own, more clearly phrased words. The First Cause, which is also the First Being, is the principle from which all powers emerge, and which bestows being on all existing things through its emanation. The Intellect is the power which is intellected by the First Creator as His first product; it creates and preserves the specific essence of each and every being. The Soul is the power which confers the highest form onto bodies, life. Nature is the power that pervades bodies and thus gives them their specific shape, and leads them to their specific perfection. The theological relevance of this theory becomes apparent in a discussion with Abū l-Fatḥ al-Nūšǧānī, who denies that the First Cause is directed towards a purpose (*Muqābasāt* § 29 [**203*: 141–145]; in agreement is *Muntaḫab Ṣiwān al-ḥikma* [**205*: 148 Dunlop; 341–342 Badawī], cf. Kraemer 1986 [*403: 50–54]).

Every natural body possesses an essential motion proper to it. Following Aristotle's *On the Heavens*, al-Siǧistānī describes the nature of the heavens as a fifth element whose natural motion is perfect and circular. Its nature, the principle of its motion, therefore must be nobler than that of the four sublunar elements. Consequently the heavenly bodies must be ensouled – according to the Neoplatonic interpretation of the Aristotelian model. For an ensouled body is nobler than one that is not ensouled; and the soul is the principle of its perfect, eternal motion (cf. the treatise: *That the Higher Bodies Possess Rational Souls*; cf. Kraemer 1986 [*403: 278–285]). This soul is the rational soul, which seeks to assimilate itself as far as possible to the unmoved First Cause, the First Mover. (It is the Unmoved Mover of Aristotle's *Metaphysics* XII 12, which acts as final cause; a further Arabic source for this particular elaboration of the topic is also Alexander of Aphrodisias, *On the Principles of the Universe* [*Fī Mabādi' al-kull*]; cf. Endress 2002 [*408]). However, the souls of the stars are (again following the Neoplatonic model) separate forms having their principle of motion within themselves. This means that the movers of the heavenly spheres, including the first, outermost one, are immanent to their spheres, as natural forms which themselves are moved accidentally. By contrast, the First Mover, the mover of the first sphere, is a separate substance and absolutely motionless. The highest principle *qua* principle of motion is the 'nature of the universe'. The natural forms, or souls, of the heavenly spheres are immanent movers, just like the soul of living beings in their bodies; this means they are moved accidentally.

Against the Peripatetics al-Siǧistānī claims that the mover of the outermost sphere is immanent to this sphere and is (self-)moved accidentally. God, the transcendent unmoved First Cause, is different from the First Mover.

In his doctrine of intellect, al-Siǧistānī again follows the synthesis of Aristotelian concepts and Neoplatonic cosmology that was prepared by al-Kindī and his Neoplatonic sources. In a short *Muqābasa* [**203*: § 83,320] al-Tawḥīdī has al-Siǧistānī discuss the meanings of 'intellect' (*ʿaql*), in obvious dependence on al-Kindī's *Risāla fī l-ʿAql* (§ 4 [*65]): the operating principle (*fāʿil*) in everything that possesses reason is the agent intellect (*al-ʿaql al-faʿʿāl*); the receptive substrate (*mafʿūl*) at the other end is constituted by human reason, the material intellect; the acquired intellect (*ʿaql mustafād*) stands between these two, in the process of action (*fiʿl*) that mediates between them, 'in the position of potency that needs to be led to the act' (*tuḫraǧ ilā l-fiʿl*; cf. Endress 1994 [§ 4 *273: 203. 212]).

4 Ancient Ethical Traditions for Islamic Society: Abū ʿAlī Miskawayh

Gerhard Endress

4.1 Primary Sources – 4.2 Life – 4.3 Works – 4.4 Doctrine

4.1 *Primary Sources*

4.1.1 Bio-bibliographical Testimonies [**231*–**242*] – 4.1.2 Greek Source Texts [**245*–**247*] – 4.1.3 Editions [**251*–**254*] – 4.1.4 Individual Works [**259*–**292*]

4.1.1 Bio-bibliographical Testimonies

231 Ibn al-Nadīm, Abū l-Faraǧ Muḥammad b. Isḥāq (d. 380/990). *Kitāb al-Fihrist* [composed 377/988]. – Ed. by Gustav Flügel, August Müller and Johannes Roediger, 2 vols. Leipzig, 1871–1872. – Repr. Beirut 1964, Frankfurt a.M. 2005. – Ed. by Riḍā Taǧaddud. Tehran 1350 h.š./1971. – Ed. by Ayman Fu'ād Sayyid, 2 vols. London 1430/2009. – Engl. transl. by Bayard Dodge, *The Fihrist of al-Nadīm*, 2 vols. New York, 1970.

232 al-Tawḥīdī, Abū Ḥayyān ʿAlī b. Muḥammad (d. 414/1023). *Aḫlāq al-wazīrayn*. – Ed. by Muḥammad b. Tāwīt al-Ṭanǧī. Damascus, 1385/1985, 23, 201, 327, 346, 464.

233 Abū Ḥayyān al-Tawḥīdī. *Kitāb al-Imtāʿ wa-l-muʾānasa*. – Ed. by Aḥmad Amīn and Aḥmad al-Zayn, 3 vols. Beirut, 1953, I 32, 35–36, 48, 136; II 2, 39; III 227.

234 Abū Ḥayyān al-Tawḥīdī. *Al-Muqābasāt*. – Ed. by Muḥammad Tawfīq Ḥusayn. Baghdad, 1970, 103–105, 204–205, 207–208, 334–335.

235 Abū Ḥayyān al-Tawḥīdī. *Kitāb al-Ṣadāqa wa-l-Ṣadīq*. –Ed. by Ibrāhīm al-Kaylānī. Damascus, 1964, 67–68.

236 *Ṣiwān al-ḥikma* [attributed to Abū Sulaymān al-Siǧistānī], excerpts. – Ed. by Douglas Morton Dunlop, *The Muntakhab Ṣiwān al-ḥikmah of Abū Sulaimān as-Sijistānī*. Paris, 1979. 151 §§ 296–302. – Ed. by ʿAbd al-Raḥmān Badawī, *Ṣiwān al-ḥikma wa-ṯalāṯ rasāʾil taʾlīf Abū Sulaymān al-Siǧistānī*. Tehran, 1974, 326–353.

237 al-Sāwī, ʿUmar b. Sahlān (early 6th/12th cent.). *The Mukhtaṣar Ṣiwān al-ḥikma of ʿUmar b. Sahlān al-Sāwī*. – Ed. by R. Mulyadhi Kartanegara. PhD diss., University of Chicago, 1996, 264–267.

238 Yāqūt b. ʿAbd Allāh, al-Ḥamawī al-Rūmī al-Baġdādī (d. 626/1229). *Iršād al-arīb*. – Ed. by David Samuel Margoliouth, *The Irshād al-arīb ilā maʿrifat al-adīb or Dictionary of Learned Men of Yāqūt*, vol. 2. Cairo, 1909, 88–96. – Ed. by A. Farīd Rifāʿī, vol. 5. Cairo, 1936, 5–19.

239 Ibn al-Qifṭī, Ǧamāl al-Dīn ʿAlī b. Yūsuf (d. 646/1248). *Taʾrīḫ al-ḥukamāʾ* [*Iḫbār al-ʿulamāʾ bi-aḫbār al-ḥukamāʾ*, epitome by Muḥammad b. ʿAlī al-Zawzanī]. – Ed. by Julius Lippert, *Ibn al-Qifṭī's Taʾrīḫ al-ḥukamāʾ*. Leipzig, 1903, 331–332.

240 Ibn Abī Uṣaybiʿa, Muwaffaq al-Dīn Aḥmad b. al-Qāsim (d. 668/1270). *ʿUyūn al-anbāʾ fī ṭabaqāt al-aṭibbāʾ*. – Ed. by August Müller, 2 vols. Cairo, 1299/1882, Königsberg, 1884, 235.

241 Ibn al-ʿIbrī, Abū l-Faraǧ Gregorios [Barhebraeus] (d. 685/1286). *Taʾrīḫ muḫtaṣar al-duwal*. – Ed. by Anṭūn Ṣāliḥānī. Beirut, 1890, 1958 (2nd ed.), 176.

242 al-Ṣafadī, Ṣalāḥ al-Dīn Ḫalīl b. Aybak (d. 764/1363). *Al-Wāfī bi-l-wafayāt, Das biographische Lexikon des* [...] *aṣ-Ṣafadī*, vol. 7. – Ed. by Iḥsān ʿAbbās. Wiesbaden, 1969, 298.

4.1.2 Greek Source Texts

245 Porphyry. *Sententiae ad intelligibilia ducentes*. – Ed. by Erich Lamberz. Leipzig, 1975.

246 Proclus. *The Elements of Theology*. A Revised Text with Translation, Introduction, and Commentary. – Ed. by Eric Robertson Dodds. Oxford, 1963 (2nd ed.).

247 *Simplicii in Aristotelis Categorias commentarium*. – Ed. by Carolus Kalbfleisch. Berlin, 1907 [Commentaria in Aristotelem Graeca, VIII].

4.1.3 Editions

251 Miskawayh. *Taǧārib al-umam = The Eclipse of the ʿAbbasid Caliphate*. – Ed., transl., and elucidated by Henry Frederic Amedroz and David Samuel Margoliouth, 4 vols [3–4 = *Continuation of the Experiences of the Nations* by Abū Shujāʿ Rūdhrāwarī and

Hilāl b. Muḥassin]. Oxford, 1920–1921. – Arab. Text, ed. by H. F. Amedroz. Cairo 1332–1334/1914–1916. – Partial facsimile edition, ed. by Leone Caetani, 3 vols (chronicle from the beginnings to 37 AH, and chronicle of the years 284 to 369 AH). Leyden and London, 1909–1917. – Excerpt [preface of the work only], ed. by Mohammed Arkoun, "Textes inédits de Miskawayh." [*253: 203–205 no. XII].

252 Miskawayh and Abū Ḥayyān al-Tawḥīdī. *Al-Hawāmil wa-l-šawāmil*. – Ed. by Aḥmad Amīn and al-Sayyid Aḥmad Ṣaqr. Cairo, 1370/1951.

253 "Textes inédits de Miskawayh" (m. 421). – Ed. by Mohammed Arkoun. In *Annales islamologiques* 5 (1963): 181–205. – Contains: 1. *Waṣiyya* (191–194); 2. [untitled treatise on prayer (*duʿā'*) and grief (*ǧazaʿ*)] (194–195); 3. *Risāla fī l-Ṭabīʿa* (196); 4. *Risāla fī Ǧawhar al-nafs* (197–198); 5. [untitled treatise on the soul: fragment about the Pythagorean number seven, the classification of the stars and the ensouled stars] (198–199); 6. *Kitāb al-ʿAql wa-l-maʿqūl* (199); 7. *al-Maqūlāt al-ṯalāṯ* (200); 8.–10. *Fī Iṯbāt al-ṣuwar al-rūḥāniyya allatī lā hayūlā lahā min kalām Arisṭūṭālīs* [rather: Proclus. *Elementatio theologica*, excerpts] (200); 11. *Mā al-faṣl bayn al-dahr wa-l-zamān* [Proclus. *Elementatio theologica*, excerpts] (202–203); 12. *al-Muqaddima li-Kitāb Taǧārib al-umam* (203–205; French transl. 187–190). – Partial French transl. in G. Cuvelier 1989 [*487] (*al-Maqūlāt al-ṯalāṯ*; *Risāla fī Ǧawhar al-nafs*; *Risāla fī l-Ṭabīʿa*).

254 "Deux épîtres de Miskawayh (mort en 421/1030)." Ed. with intro. and notes by Mohammed Arkoun. In *Bulletin d'études orientales* 17 (1961/62): 7–74. Contains: 1. *Fī l-Laḏḏāt wa-l-ālām* (74–64 = Arab. pages 1–9); 2. *Maqāla fī l-Nafs wa-l-ʿaql* (65–20 = 10–55).

4.1.4 Individual Works

4.1.4.1 *Philosophical Propaedeutics*

259 *Tartīb al-saʿādāt wa-manāzil al-ʿulūm*. – Ed. by ʿAlī al-Ṭūbǧī, *al-Saʿāda li-Ibn Miskawayh fī falsafat al-aḫlāq*. Cairo, 1346/1928 (2nd ed.). – Ed. Abū-l-Qāsim Imāmī, "Tartīb al-saʿādāt wa-manāzil al-ʿulūm." In *Ganǧīna-i Bahāristān*, 1: ḥikmat. Ed. by ʿAlī Awǧabī. Tehran, 1371 h.š. [2000], 97–127.

260 *al-Hawāmil wa-l-šawāmil li-Abī Ḥayyān al-Tawḥīdī wa-Miskawayh*. – Ed. by Aḥmad Amīn and al-Sayyid Aḥmad Ṣaqr. Cairo, 1370/1951.

4.1.4.2 *Metaphysics, Soul, and Intellect*

264 *al-Fawz al-aṣġar* (*al-Masā'il al-ṯalāṯ allatī taštamil ʿalā l-ʿulūm kullihā*). – Ed. by Ṣāliḥ ʿUḍayma, *Le petit livre du salut*, traduction française et notes par Roger Arnaldez. Tunis, 1987. – Older editions: Ṭāhir Efendī al-Ǧazā'irī. Beirut, 1319/1901; Cairo, 1325/1907 (2nd ed.). – Partial edition: ʿAbd al-Raḥmān Badawī, *Aflāṭūn fī l-islām*. Tehran, 1974, 333–336 (mas'ala 2, faṣl 6). – Engl. transl. in: J. Sweetman 1945–1967 [502: I 1, 93–185].

265 *Kitāb [Risālat] al-ʿAql wa-l-maʿqūl.* – Ed. by Mohammed Arkoun, *Miskawayh, De l'intellect et de l'intelligible (Fī l-ʿAql wa-l-maʿqūl).* In *Arabica* 11 (1964): 80–87. – Partial edition in: Arkoun 1963 [*253: 199]. – Engl. transl. in: R. Marcotte 1996 [*521]. – French transl. in: G. Cuvelier 1990 [*518: 115–122].

266 *Maqāla fī l-Nafs wa-l-ʿaql.* – Ed. by Mohammed Arkoun 1961/62 [*480: 20–65]. – Ed. by ʿAbd al-Raḥmān Badawī, *Dirāsāt wa-nuṣūṣ fī l-falsafa wa-l-ʿulūm ʿind al-ʿArab.* Beirut, 1981, 57–97. – Engl. transl. in: Peter Adamson and Peter E. Pormann, "More than Heat and Light: Miskawayh's Epistle on Soul and Intellect." In *Muslim World* 102 (2012): 478–524.

267 *Aḥwāl al-rūḥ.* – Ed. by Hilmi Ziya Ülken, *Ibn Sīnā Risaleleri. Les opuscules d' Ibn Sīnā.* Ankara, Istanbul 1953, 68–70. – Repr. Frankfurt a.M., 1999.

268 *Risāla fī Ǧawhar al-nafs.* – Ed. by M. Arkoun 1963 [*253: 197–198]. – French transl. in: G. Cuvelier 1989 [*487].

269 *Risāla fī l-Ṭabīʿa.* – Ed. by M. Arkoun 1963 [*253: 196].

4.1.4.3 *Ethics*

273 *Tahḏīb al-aḫlāq [wa-taṭhīr al-aʿrāq]. The Refinement of Character.* – Ed. by Qusṭanṭīn Zurayq [Constantine K. Zurayk]. Beirut, 1966. – Older editions: Ed. by Aḥmad Amīn, *al-Fawz al-akbar.* Cairo, 1929. Ed. by ʿAlī Rifāʿa. Cairo [ca. 1950]. Ed. by Ḥasan Tamīm. Beirut, 1978 (2nd ed.); for further editions cf. Daiber 1999 [*5: 650 no. 6351]. – Engl. transl.: *The Refinement of Character.* A Translation from the Arabic of Aḥmad ibn Muḥammad Miskawayh's Tahdhīb al-Akhlāq by Constantine K. Zurayk. Beirut, 1968. – French transl.: *Traité d'éthique,* traduction française avec introduction et notes par Mohammed Arkoun. Damascus, 1969.

274 *Tahḏīb al-aḫlāq* [excerpt]. – Ed. by Louis Cheikho (Šayḫū), "Risāla fī l-ḫawf min al-mawt wa-ḥaqīqatihi wa-ḥāl al-nafs baʿdahu; [with] ʿIlāǧ al-ḥuzn." In *Maqālāt falsafiyya qadīma li-baʿḍ mašāhīr falāsifat al-ʿArab* [Traités inédits d'anciens philosophes arabes]. Beirut, 1911, 103–117. – Corresponds to *Tahḏīb al-aḫlāq,* ed. by Zurayq [*273: 209–221], including al-Kindī's treatise *Fī Dafʿ al-aḥzān,* at 219–221.

275 *Risāla fī l-Laḏḏāt wa-l-ālām.* – Ed. by Mohammed Arkoun 1961/62 [*480: 66–74]. – Ed. ʿAbd al-Raḥmān Badawī, in: *Dirāsāt wa-nuṣūṣ fī l-falsafa wa-l-ʿulūm ʿind al-ʿArab.* Beirut, 1981, 98–104. – Engl. transl. and study in: P. Adamson 2015 [*589].

276 *Risāla fī Māhiyyat al-ʿadl.* – Ed. by M. S. Khan, *An Unpublished Treatise of Miskawayh on Justice, or Risāla fī Māhiyat* [sic] *al-ʿadl li-Miskawaih.* Leiden, 1964 [with Engl. transl.]. – Ed. by Mohammed Arkoun, "Risāla fī Māʾiyyat al-ʿadl wa bayān aqsāmih de Miskawayh." In *Hespéris-Tamuda* 2 (Rabat 1961): 215–230 [edition 223–230].

4.1.4.4 *Gnomologia*

281 *Kitāb Ādāb al-ʿArab wa-l-Furs* (*Ǧāwīḏān ḫirad*). – Ed. by ʿAbd al-Raḥmān Badawī. Cairo, 1952; Beirut 1980 (2nd ed.). – Medieval Persian version by Taqī l-Dīn Muḥammad Šuštarī. – Ed. by Bihrūz Ṯarwatiyān [with French intro. by Mohammed Arkoun]. Tehran, 1976.

282 *Waṣiyya*. – Ed. by Mohammed Arkoun 1963 [*253: 191–194] after *Muntaḫab Ṣiwān al-ḥikma* [*236: 152–155]. – Also in: Miskawayh, *al-Ḥikma al-ḫālida*. Ed. by Badawī 1952 [*281: 285,5–290,7]. – Different text of a *Waṣiyya* in: Yāqūt, *Iršād al-arīb* [*238: II 95–96 Margoliouth]; Engl. version based on this in: Bin Omar 1994 [*576].

4.1.4.5 *Miskawayh's Sources* (*Greek Source Texts in Arabic Translation*)

286 Aristotle. *Nicomachean Ethics* [Arab.]. – Ed. by Anna A. Akasoy and Alexander Fidora, *The Arabic Version of the Nicomachean Ethics*, With an Introduction and Annotated Translation by Douglas M. Dunlop. Leiden, 2005.

287 *Muḫtaṣar Kitāb al-Aḫlāq li-Ǧālīnūs* [*Galenus*: *De moribus*, Arab.]. – Ed. by Paul Kraus, "Dirāsāt fī tārīḫ al-tarǧama fī l-islām I." In *al-Ǧāmiʿa al-miṣriyya, Maǧallat Kulliyyat al-ādāb* (*Bulletin of the Faculty of Arts of the University of Egypt*) 5 (1937): 1–51. – Ed. by ʿAbd al-Raḥmān Badawī, *Dirāsāt wa-nuṣūṣ fī l-falsafa wa-l-ʿulūm ʿind al-ʿArab*. Beirut, 1981, 190–197. – Engl. transl. by John N. Mattock, "A translation of the Arabic Epitome of Galen's Book Περὶ ἠθῶν." In: Samuel Miklos Stern, Albert Hourani and Vivian Brown, eds. *Islamic Philosophy and the Classical Tradition*. Essays Presented … to Richard Walzer on his seventieth Birthday. Oxford, 1972, 235–260. – Excerpts transl. in: Franz Rosenthal, *The Classical Heritage in Islam*. Transl. by Emile and Jenny Marmorstein. London, 1975, 1992, 2004 (2nd ed.), 85–94. – Engl. transl. by Daniel Davies in *Galen. Psychological Writings*. Ed. by P. N. Singer. Cambridge, 2013, 135–172.

4.1.4.6 *Text on the Historical Impact*

291 Abū Naṣr al-Ḥasan Ibn al-Faḍl al-Ṭabarsī. *Makārim al-aḫlāq* [including, incidentally: Miskawayh, *Tahḏīb al-aḫlāq*]. Cairo, 1972.

292 al-Ṭabarsī. *Makārim al-aḫlāq*. – Ed. by Muḥammad Ḥusayn al-Aʿlamī. Beirut, 1972.

4.2 *Life*

The philosopher and historian Abū ʿAlī Aḥmad b. Muḥammad b. Yaʿqūb Miskawayh was born around 320–325/932–936 in Rayy. There he was trained as a secretary, an education which gave him perfect proficiency in Persian and, above all, Arabic. From 340–372/950–983 he served as librarian and secretary at the Buyid courts in Baghdad and Rayy, first under al-Muhallabī (from 340/950 as a secretary, 345–352/956–963 as vizier of the chief emir Muʿizz al-Dawla of Baghdad), later on with the viziers of Rukn al-Dawla and ʿAḍud al-Dawla in Rayy, Abū l-Faḍl Ibn al-ʿAmīd (353–360/951–970) and his son Abū l-Fatḥ (360–366/970–976). His last years were spent in the service of the chief emir and king ʿAḍud al-Dawla (d. 372/983), to whom he dedicated several of his works. For ʿAḍud al-Dawla he wrote his chronicle *Taǧārib al-umam* (*The Experiences of the Nations*), in which he acclaims the years spent in service to the dynasty. In 355/966, under Abū l-Faḍl Ibn al-ʿAmīd in Rayy, Miskawayh commended himself by rescuing the library of his master from the hands of Ḫwārazmī plunderers (*Taǧārib* [*251: II 224–225]). The entry for the year of Ibn al-ʿAmīd's death contains an obituary of the vizier in which Miskawayh describes the realization of perfect intellectual education – in terms of the Arabic-Islamic disciplines as well as the Hellenistic-philosophical ones – in an idealized portrait of a great personality (*Taǧārib* [*251: II 275,1–279,1]).

With the Qāḍī Aḥmad b. Kāmil (260–350/873–961), a student of Muḥammad b. Ǧarīr al-Ṭabarī, Miskawayh studied the former's chronicle *Aḫbār al-rusul wa-l-mulūk* (*History of Prophets and Kings*) (al-Ṣafadī, *al-Wāfī* [*242: VII 298]). This course of study provided the foundations for his own work on early Islamic history, *Taǧārib al-umam* (*Taǧārib* [*251: II 184]). His understanding of philosophical texts was shaped in important ways by Ibn al-Ḫammār (cf. § 7. 4), a pupil of Yaḥyā Ibn ʿAdī, who was highly esteemed by Miskawayh on account of his commentaries on Aristotle (cf. *al-Fawz* [*264: 62.77]). Miskawayh moved within the intellectual circles of Iraq and western Iran. Being a contemporary of al-Siǧistānī, he was, for some time, also a member of the circle of the Baghdad philosophers, as his older friend al-Tawḥīdī reports (cf. *al-Imtāʿ wa-l-muʾānasa* [*233: I 35–36]: he presents a brief portrait of Miskawayh, disparagingly describing him as 'pauper among the rich, and a stammerer among the eloquent' and as incompetent in philosophy; cf. Arkoun 1970 [*452: 39–48] on further pronouncements and quotes in al-Tawḥīdī). With al-Tawḥīdī Miskawayh exchanged ideas about philosophical, in particular ethical questions (*Kitāb al-Hawāmil wa-l-šawāmil* [*252]).

According to an informant of Yāqūt [*238: V 5], Miskawayh died on 9 Ṣafar 421/16 February 1030.

4.3 *Works*

4.3.1 Philosophical Propaedeutics – 4.3.2 Metaphysics and Philosophical Theology. Soul and Intellect – 4.3.3 Ethics – 4.3.4 Gnomologia

4.3.1 Philosophical Propaedeutics

Tartīb al-saʿādāt wa-manāzil al-ʿulūm
The Degrees of Happiness and the Classification of the Sciences

Known also under the title *Kitāb al-Saʿāda fī falsafat al-aḫlāq*. The title *Tartīb al-saʿādāt wa-manāzil al-ʿulūm* is documented by the author's own testimony, *Tahḏīb al-aḫlāq* [*273: 49 Zurayq], and by Ibn Ṭāwūs (d. 664/1266; cf. Kohlberg 1992 [*468: 255]), who under this title preserves an otherwise lost passage from the first part of the work, concerning the measures kings are supposed to take in order to overcome misfortunes (cf. *Farağ al-mahmūm fī tārīḫ ʿulamāʾ al-nuğūm* [Najaf 1949, repr. Tehran, 1985] 208).

Miskawayh composed this treatise by request of the vizier Abū l-Faḍl Ibn al-ʿAmīd, whom he tried to emulate in his striving for knowledge and science, and who had asked him about the 'kinds and degrees of human happiness'.

Everything that exists has its own perfection (*kamāl*, entelechy) that is proper to it. The primary function of the specifically human gift of reason is the initiation of actions based on reflection and rational judgement; but it furthermore serves a highest goal – which is the subject of this treatise – i.e. the specifically human, highest form of happiness, whose attainment puts an end to all quests and pursuits. General happiness (*al-saʿāda al-ʿāmma*) is attainable for all human beings, in accordance with their talents. It consists in the fulfilment of the proximate goals of rational actions, and is classified according to the respective degree of perfection of humanity (*al-insāniyya*), of virtue, or of vice. The specific happiness (*al-saʿāda al-ḫāṣṣa*) of an individual human being is that happiness which he acquires for himself depending on the degree of his knowledge or his skill in a virtuous art. All these degrees of happiness constitute relative happiness, not the highest happiness. For as soon as the lower desires have been satisfied, apathy will follow, and the fulfilment of one goal can be spoilt by the grief caused by the failure to reach another one.

In his discussion of the highest happiness (*al-saʿāda al-quṣwā*) the author presents a division of the three genera of happiness 'according to Aristotle': happiness in the soul, happiness in the body, and a kind of happiness whose cause lies outside the body and the bodily sphere. The happiness of the soul is happiness gained through science and knowledge, with wisdom (*al-ḥikma*) being the final end. This is the highest happiness which is sought after for its own sake (Aristotle, *Nicomachean Ethics* X 7, 1177b). Only the happiness of the soul is perfect; however, it does not occur on its own accord, but only through unceasing endeavour. Not everybody can reach the highest happiness, even if they try. Happiness comes in degrees, and the highest degree opens itself up only gradually and only to few people, thanks to their industrious striving and their emulation of the ancient sages. According to Aristotle, the highest degree of human happiness is attained by virtue of the highest capacity of discernment (*tamyīz*) and the most profound penetration of the noblest subject of reflection (*rawiyya*). Those who reach this degree of happiness will always be serene, hopeful, full of inner peace, and self-contented. They see with the eye of the mind, which will not become weary even with time, but will grow in clarity and certainty of knowledge (cf. Aristotle, *Nicomachean Ethics* III 4, 1112a17).

Directions for achieving this goal are given by the works of Aristotle, which demonstrate theoretical as well as practical knowledge. The classification of sciences here follows an otherwise lost work by Paul the Persian.

al-Hawāmil wa-l-šawāmil
Stray Cattle and Secure Enclosures (i.e. random questions and exhaustive replies)

Questions posed by Abū Ḥayyān al-Tawḥīdī (cf. pp. 286–287 above) are answered in detail by Miskawayh. Since al-Tawḥīdī's questions are stylistically quite elaborate, whereas the replies are phrased in sober scientific language, it stands to reason that the latter were formulated by Miskawayh himself.

Among the philosophical topics under discussion, those belonging to rationalistic ethics, in particular the explication of fundamental features and defects of the human character, are the most prominent. Some of Miskawayh's positions that also surface in other works by him are presented in the context of the following questions:

§ 1 [*252: 5–15]: asked about the meaning of a certain word, Miskawayh explains the relation between name and meaning (synonymy, homonymy, etc.) according to the classification of Aristotle's *Categories* 1. § 5 [*252: 34–36], § 19 [64–66], § 20 [67–68]: on the problem of ascetic renunciation of the world (*zuhd*): Miskawayh replies by pointing out the political nature of human beings, and the necessity of community (*muʿāwana*). Following Aristotle, the philosophers (*falāsifa*) think that the entelechy of the human being, and therefore their happiness, is not to be found outside society. Pious people of all kinds, meanwhile, seek purification of their souls in asceticism (cf. Arkoun 1969 [*556: 46 n. 3]). § 29 [*252: 84–88]: on the essence of tyranny (*ẓulm*): tyranny is the opposite of justice (*ʿadl*). Miskawayh refers to his *Risāla fī l-ʿAdl*, giving a brief synopsis of his explanation of the essence of justice as principle of virtue, which he has presented there as well as in *Tahḏīb al-aḫlāq* ch. IV. § 68 [*252: 179–180]: on the question of the aim of the soul (*multamas al-nafs*) in the world and its attainability, and on the relation between soul and body: according to Aristotle, the soul attains the highest possible perfection in this world, if it receives the forms of the intelligibles and thus turns from an intellect in potentiality into an intellect in actuality. In this way the intellect knows itself and becomes one with itself. § 116 [*252: 268–269]: the question whether man can comprehend all sciences; and if this is possible, whether it is also required. § 159 [*252: 341]: the four scientific questions according to *Posterior Analytics* II 1, 'whether?', 'what?', 'which?' and 'why?' On this topic, see also

§ 170 [360–362]: is it possible to seek knowledge about something one does not know? Yes, depending on the question. § 163 [*252: 350–352]: on the human being as a soul-body composite (cf. Arkoun 1970 [*452: 270–271]). § 164 [*252: 352–353]: on the question about the soul's ability to recollect its existence as a soul-body composite after its separation from the body: 'all powers of the soul which are constituted by the body and the bodily organs are destroyed together with the annihilation of the body; this means that the soul in itself, as simple substance, can do without these organs.' While the body, upon death, disintegrates into its simple elements and loses the abilities that were linked to its organs – like sense perception, imagination and the remembering of perceptible things – the soul, once it is liberated from the body, will be sufficient to itself, thanks to the intelligible forms that it contains, and that are called principles (cf. also Pseudo-Aristotle, *Faḍā'il al-Nafs*, quoted in *Tahḏīb* [*273: 76–90], and Arkoun 1970 [*452: 271–273]). § 166 [*252: 356–357]: why are the parts of the soul three in number, no more and no less? In the evolution of the forms of life the action of the soul is increasingly manifest in the three levels of the vegetative, the animal, and the rational living being; each faculty of the soul occupies the rank that is appropriate to it.

al-Maqūlāt al-ṯalāṯ
The Three Categories

A brief treatise (Arkoun 1963 [*482: 200], Cuvelier 1989 [*487]) discussing the three categories which alone are linked to substance: quantity, quality, and position.

4.3.2 Metaphysics and Philosophical Theology. Soul and Intellect

al-Fawz al-aṣġar
Shorter (*work on*) *Happiness* (or: *The Success*)

This work is also transmitted under the perhaps original title derived from the text's introductory words, *al-Masā'il al-ṯalāṯ allatī taštamilu 'alā l-'ulūm kullihā* (*The Three Questions which Comprehend All Knowledge*); in this form it is also found in the Judaeo-Arabic transmission: anonymous, but with the title *al-Kalām 'alā l-masā'il al-ṯalāṯ*, cf. Langermann 1996 [*469: 159–160], Hasnawi 1997 [*470]).

Besides the manuscripts of the *Fawz* which form the basis of the available editions and which essentially offer the same redaction, there are further textual witnesses which potentially belong to a different, extended version (possibly the work *al-Fawz al-akbar*, which is documented in Miskawayh's work catalogue and announced at the end of *al-Fawz al-aṣġar*? On this point, see Wakelnig 2009 [*529]).

In the introduction, Miskawayh explains the aim he pursues with this work: he wants to discuss the three questions which comprise all knowledge and constitute the centrepiece of wisdom. This was a commissioned task, probably by the chief emir ʿAḍud al-Dawla, who is here praised effusively.

The three topics, divided in three chapters of ten sections each, are: I. God and His essence, II. the human soul and its capacities, III. essence and function of prophecy. In this work, Miskawayh takes recourse to the ancient authors in a particularly pronounced way; but al-Fārābī's influence is also palpable, for instance with respect to the model of nine heavenly spheres (cf. also *al-ʿAql wa-l-maʿqūl* [*265: 85]), to the theory of intellect and the intelligible substances, and to the divine names, even if a number of differences may be noted.

I. God and His essence. 1. Recognizing the true essence of things and the existence and the nature of the Creator requires a gradual formation of one's intellectual capacities through the study of the theoretical sciences according to the Arisotelian syllabus of mathematics, logic, physics, and metaphysics, which constitute the indispensable basis of rational knowledge. 2. The existence of God, Who alone is one, eternal, and incorporeal, according to the consensus of the ancients. 3. Proof of God's existence as that of the First Mover. 4. Everything that moves must be moved by a mover external to it. 5. God, the First Mover, is unique. He only moves through His essence, while the differentiation of secondary causes after Him gives rise to the multiplicity of forms. 6. The First Mover is not a body. 7. He is the necessary of existence (*wāǧib al-wuǧūd*) and unmoved, hence eternal. 8. Knowledge of God allows only for negative, not for positive pronouncements. 9. The being of all things originates in God, beginning with the first existence proceeding from Him, the First Intellect or Agent Intellect, through the hierarchy of the spheres to the existence of the material forms of nature. 10. God has created all things from nothing.

II. The soul and its modes of being. Again Miskawayh refers to the later Greek commentators like Alexander of Aphrodisias and Themistius, following the lead of commentaries by Ibn al-Ḫammār (al-Ḥasan b. Suwār, cf. § 7.4; *al-Fawz* II 1,62, quoted also at section II 4,77), which he commends warmly, even though they were not all directly accessible to him, having been composed in Syriac. 1. The soul exists, even though it is neither body nor accident, nor material form. In contrast to the body, the rational form can receive several forms at once. Whenever it receives an intelligible form, it thereby increases the perfection of its humanity (*akṯar insāniyyatin*). 2. The soul comprehends all existing things, be they accessible to sense perception or comprehensible by reason only, as the genera and species of things. Distinction between abstract concepts which the imagination separates from their material substrate, but which do not subsist without matter; and pure, intelligible substances. 3. The kinds of knowledge of the soul, corresponding to its various objects. 4. On the difference between the soul's rational discernment and its sense perception. 5. The soul is a living substance which survives death and is imperishable. Without being life itself, it bestows life on anything in which it inheres. 6. Doxography of the views of the ancient philosophers (Plato,

Proclus, Galen) on the immortality of the soul, and their proofs for the imperishability of the rational soul. 7.The essence of the soul and the life proper to it. 8. The happiness and unhappiness of the soul: the 'upward' motion leads it towards the Intellect and to the Creator, through Whom unity and perpetuity exist. The 'downward' motion leads to multiplicity, to the alienation from its essence and to unhappiness. Plato defines philosophy as readiness for 'voluntary death', i.e. for the death of natural desires, by contrast to the inevitable natural death. The 'natural life' of the rational soul consists in its movement towards the intellect (cf. Walzer 1985 [*517: 500]). However, man is by nature a political animal; in order to subsist, he needs the cooperation of his fellow human beings, in accordance with the demands of justice. 9. How to achieve happiness, and how to urge others towards it. Instruction through the prophets and the teachings of the sages. The path of finding the truth leads to happiness in three steps: (a) understanding the order of the world, in macro- and microcosmos; (b) understanding another world which is separate, spiritual and simple; (c) vision of a third, higher world of absolute transcendence, which comprises everything below it and rules it as its first mover, the true One and simple. 10. The state of the soul after its separation from the body. The rational soul persists after death. Having reached the level where it recognizes the Highest Being, it will reach the highest happiness, which is ineffable and can only be indicated by allegorical expressions. This section is followed by a sketch of a cosmological tableau of the corporeal and the spiritual world.

III. On the sending of the prophets (*fī l-nubuwwāt*). 1.–2. The order of the hierarchies of being and their interrelation. 3. How the five senses ascend to the common sense and, beyond that, to the spiritual imaginations. 4. The nature of revelation. The path of rational knowledge leads human beings to the highest degree of perfection granted to them. 5. The Intellect has been placed by God on the highest level. In the hierarchy of being it is the king who is obeyed by the orders of nature. 6. Divinatory dreams as elements of prophecy. 7. The difference between prophecy (*nubuwwa*) and divination (*kahāna*). – 8. The difference between a prophet who has been entrusted with a message (*al-nabī al-mursal*), and one who has not. The messenger leads the people to whom he has been sent onto the straight path (*al-ṣirāṭ al-mustaqīm*) of the divine law (*al-šarīʿa*), the 'path to the watering place'. 9. The kinds of revelation correspond to the powers of the soul (sense perception, imagination, reason) on which the emanation descends. 10. The difference between the prophet and the person who pretends to be a prophet (*al-mutanabbī*).

Kitāb [Risāla] fī l-ʿAql wa-l-maʿqūl
On the Intellect and the Intelligible

In the manuscript, the treatise is described as an excerpt from a book of the same title (*min Kitāb al-ʿAql wa-l-maʿqūl*; Arkoun 1964 [*506], Marcotte 1996 [*521]). It discusses the human and the divine intellect.

The treatise begins with a religious doxography concerning the origin and the essence of the human intellect (*ʿaql*), based on passages culled from the Quran and the Islamic tradition, the *ḥadīṯ*. Due to the references to the Quran, Arkoun (1964 [*506: 80–81]) considers this section to be an interpolation, whereas the subsequent parts are most probably authentic; Marcotte (1996 [*521: 1–2]) does not take a clear stance on this point.

The next section differentiates between those human beings who possess intellect, those who endeavour to acquire it (read *ʿaqluhu bi-ʿināya* [*265: 83 Arkoun], *pace* Marcotte 1996 [*521: 4]), and those who lack intellect (*lā ʿaqla lahu*).

The human intellect must remain imperfect if it does not possess ten specific capacities (*ḫiṣāl*). Among other things, it must be firm in its authority, it must not falter in its striving for knowledge, it must be generous towards others, and it must be modest at the same time.

The second part, dedicated to the classification of the intellects, presents the various types of human beings, and the philosophical distinctions made according to the practical and theoretical capacities of a human being. There are four groups, separated according to the strength or weakness of the theoretical faculty (*al-quwwa al-ʿallāma*) and the practical faculty (*al-quwwa al-ʿammāla*) respectively. The group of people in which both types of intellect are equally strong is the one which produces prophets and philosophers.

The third part describes the ten intellects and their spheres. The cosmological model largely corresponds to that of al-Fārābī, in particular regarding the system of the ten spheres and intellects, which corresponds to his *Mabādiʾ ārāʾ ahl al-madīna al-fāḍila*, ch. 7 (ed. Walzer 1985 [*517: 118–134]). Other passages, even though drawing on models described by al-Fārābī, too, differ in terminology and do not offer a systematic explication, as e.g. al-Fārābī's division of the intellect into passive, acquired, and active intellect (*Mabādiʾ*, ch. 15 [*517: 240–244]). In the context of the distinction between theoretical and practical intellect the treatise is conspicuous in its terminology, for instance *al-quwwa al-ʿallāma* as opposed to *al-quwwa al-ʿammāla*. It is true that al-Fārābī also distinguishes between the practical and the theoretical ability of the rational faculty, but his terminology is different (*al-quwwa al-naẓariyya wa-l-ʿamaliyya*).

God has placed the intellects in the centre of microcosm and macrocosm. At the outset He has created the First Intellect as an incorporeal substance. It exists through itself, thinking its own essence and its Creator. The First Intellect gives rise to the highest sphere. The Second Intellect emanates from the First Intellect, and with it the sphere of the fixed stars. The fact that the Second Intellect grasps both its Creator and itself leads to the emanation of the Third Intellect. Thus the process of emanation proceeds until it has reached the Tenth Intellect. The spheres of the fixed stars and planets are concomitants (*lazima ʿanhu*) of the Intellects.

The ten Intellects are always in actuality. The tenth Intellect is the first Intellect with reference to the sublunar world; it mediates between the One Who generates everything (*al-mubdiʿ*), i.e. God, and the nine generated Intellects. They are the angels: they were created as perfect beings, but they differ from each other in the degree of excellence which their respective substances can reach, starting from the First Intellect in descending order.

Thanks to the ten Intellects the human intellect is brought from potentiality to actuality. The actual intellect thus becomes acquired intellect, and the acquired intellect becomes Active Intellect. For only something actual can ever render something potential actual. This means that something emanates from the ten divine Active Intellects to the potential intellects. In comparison with the Active Intellect, the potential intellect is like a fetus in the womb. The emanation of the divine intellect is compared to the light which is present in the air and makes it possible for the eye actually to see visible things. (The author refers [*265: 87] to two of his other, otherwise unknown works: an epistle *On the Mover and the Moved* [*Risāla fī l-Muḥarrik wa-l-mutaḥarrik*] and an epistle *On the Soul* [*Risāla fī l-Nafs*] – not identical with the *Maqāla fī l-Nafs wa-l-ʿaql*, where the relevant remark, that the soul is both essentially knowing and accidentally knowing, is not found.)

The Intellects of the spheres are ten with reference to their genus. In respect to species, however, they are more numerous, since in each sphere there are other spheres which carry out the complex movements assigned to them. Heavenly Intellects are specific individuals (*ašḫāṣ*). The total number of the active Intellects that move the ensouled spheres is fifty-five (cf. Aristotle, *Metaphysics* XII 8, where, however, the calculation has a different foundation). As far as the human intellects are concerned, they are ten in species, whereas their individuals are unlimited in number, since they are actualized one after the other without end.

Maqāla fī l-Nafs wa-l-ʿaql
Treatise on the Soul and the Intellect

On the text cf. Adamson 2007 [*528], Adamson and Pormann 2012 [*530]. Miskawayh replies to ten questions posed by a medically inclined correspondent, who – with reference to the ancient physicians Rufus and Galen – expresses his doubts about the possibilities and limits of an intellectual knowledge that is based on sense perception and is conditioned by the bodily mixtures. Just like the questions, the replies too focus on familiar topics. There are many repetitions, and numerous parallels to other treatises by Miskawayh (especially *al-Fawz*).

1. [*266: 10–22 Arkoun; 57–68 Badawī]: Rational insight into the universal and sensual cognition of the particular require each other; there is no knowledge of universals without sense perception. Is there any valid knowledge which is only based on one of these two sources of knowledge? The physician Rufus says: everybody who strives towards (transcendental) knowledge will be afflicted by melancholy (Rufus of Ephesus,

On Melancholy: cf. Ullmann 1970 [*442: 73], Pormann 2008 [*528a]). The senses are treacherous – how much more so the faculty of imagination (*taḫayyul*, φαντασία)? As this is where reason obtains its information, how are we to acquire certainty about the alleged spiritual substances, with respect to which we cannot perceive particulars and, therefore, cannot discern universals either? Miskawayh replies: according to the opponent's views, reason recognizes only the universals it derives from the particulars obtained through sense perception. In reality, sense perception follows reason, even if to our mind it precedes it in time. However, not all rational knowledge is confined to those things which reason gathers from the particulars of sense perception in order to set them under a unifying concept, i.e. the universals of the particular things. Compared with sense perception, intellect possesses a specific activity, as it has first principles (*awāʾil*) at its disposal, in light of which it assesses sense perception. Intellect has its own kind of cognition: besides the universals obtained by abstraction from particulars of sense perception, there are sublime intelligibles, essential objects of cognition which are not received from the senses, being accessible to purely rational cognition alone. According to Aristotle's *On the Soul* III 4, and Themistius' commentary, the path via sense perception is an indirect one, comparable to seeing something reflected by a mirror (likewise *al-Fawz* II 3). The intellect does not only possess knowledge acquired from particulars, but also self-knowledge, which it draws from itself. In this regard Aristotle (cf. *On the Soul* III 4, 429b5–9, 430a2–5) says that intellect, the intellecting, and the intellected are one. By contrast, the perceiving is different from the perceived. Reason abstracts the material form from the things and prepares it so as to make it intelligible. Once the intelligibles, which are potentially intelligible in the rational soul, become actualized, they will become one with the intellect; this is why one speaks of the potential intellect. Everything that exists in potentiality is led to actuality by something else existing in actuality (cf. *On the Soul* III 5, 430a10–15). This is the the actual intellect; it recognizes the intelligible within itself not through being led into actuality (by another agent), but they belong to it primarily and essentially. These principles are identical with the intellect and the intellected at the same time.

If intellect does not support the senses by confirming the validity or invalidity of sense perception, they will be useless, because sense perception is prone to manifold errors.

Rufus says that anybody who dedicates himself to reflection in a science will end up a melancholic. This amounts to saying that sound views that are the result of prolonged reflection cause severe illness. But it is obvious that many results of reflection in practical sciences, including Rufus' own discipline of medicine, serve the health of the body, which in turn enables sound thinking. The essential difference between humans and animals is, after all, the human capacity to think and to form judgements. Rufus could at best be right with regard to imaginary sorts of knowledge (*al-ʿulūm al-wahmiyya*), to mere phantasms. For such sciences follow sense perception and apply sensual forms to non-sensual imaginations, as if they existed outside of our imagination, as e.g. the existence of a vacuum outside the world, or a sensually perceptible individual imagined to exist beyond the outermost sphere. They indeed spawn invalid ideas and absurd phantasies. However, intellect has nothing to do with such imaginations; on the contrary, it examines sense perceptions and corrects them, even as they rise from the individual senses to the common sense.

With respect to the substances we consider to be spiritual (*rūḥāniyya*), even though we do not know anything about their particular instantiations, Miskawayh says that we can perceive neither particulars nor universals in them without seeing bodies at the same time. They can only be grasped and named with the help of images familiar to us from sense perception, which are able to represent the alien intelligible in an approximate way, even if they can name it only allegorically and by homonymy. He compares this to mirrors which, depending on their form, colour and specific quality, may produce several representations of a single object, without being completely adequate.

2. [*266: 22–25 Arkoun; 68–70 Badawī]: if vital heat is the basis for life in the macrocosm as well as in the microcosm, does not that mean that the soul itself is heat (*ḥarāra*), whose particular we grasp as heat, while comprehending its universal in the upper lights and in the fire (of the heavenly phenomena)? 3. [*266: 25–29 Arkoun; 70–74 Badawī]: if the soul is a spiritual, subtle substance (*ǧawhar rūḥānī laṭīf*), we cannot know it universally or as a particular; is not Rufus right, then, to call it an unreal phantasm? 4. [*266: 29–32 Arkoun; 74–77 Badawī]: if we imagine the intellect in the microcosm as something 'spiritual' (*rūḥānī*), different from the (upper) light, this light and this heat (i.e. the primary forces of the macrocosm) nevertheless remain as the only sources of certainty. However, even if we wanted to go beyond the interaction of sense perception and intellect, we would still only obtain phantasms (*awhām*), which are no reliable representation of intelligible reality.

The questioner quotes a passage from the *Summaria Alexandrinorum* of Galen's works which contains Galen's polemics against the *maššāṭ al-ṣūf* (the 'carder' or 'wool weaver', Greek ἐριουργός; in Miskawayh's reply he is called 'Ṭawusīs'), i.e. Thessalus of Tralles. The son of a wool weaver, who lived in Rome during the reign of Emperor Nero, was the head of the Methodist medical school and as such a frequent subject of Galen's attacks (cf. Diller 1936 [*464: 168–182], on the theoretical foundations of his doctrine 178–179; cf. also Schacht, Meyerhof 1937 [*465: 27; Arab. text 83). The passage is corrupt; apparently Galen polemicized against the misguided Methodist therapies which were derived from mere theoretical models (in Miskawayh's reply: *fasād al-fikr wa-l-taḫayyul* [the corruption of thinking and imagination]).

Miskawayh replies that one cannot say that intellect is imagination (*wahm*); imagination follows sense perception. Intelligibles are not imaginations derived from the senses, which could be adequately represented by the simile of the light. We need not stop at knowledge based on sense perception, because demonstration leads us beyond this point with necessary certainty.

8. [*266: 37–40 Arkoun; 82–84 Badawī]: Hippocrates says that all (physiological) powers arise from the mixture of the bodily humours. Plato says that the mixture is the instrument of an active power external to us – is not this the being in which light and heat originate? – Answer: Hippocrates' doctrine is valid in the context of medical physiology. Being a philosopher, Plato speaks in general terms, about all principles, going beyond the specific principles, up to the principle of principles. The proximate cause of the bodily mixtures cannot be the First Cause.

10. [*266: 42–55 Arkoun; 85–97 Badawī]: if all knowledge is gained through experiences of the soul (that is, through sense perception) and the intellect (through the universals abstracted from sense perception), why does this not apply to the divine powers and to divination (*kahāna*) and other experiences, through which some people at times are able to see what is hidden, and to divine future events? It is impossible to imagine any spiritual things (*rūḥāniyyāt*) that would go beyond the incorporeal accidentals like light and heat; according to Rufus we therefore must content ourselves with (unproven) opinion (*ẓann*). Answer: the topic of 'divine powers' requires a previous clarification of divine activity. God acts outside of time and space. Time is the measure of movement, thus absolute time counts the movement of the highest sphere. The First, however, exists before the body and its movement; as the true One He does not possess plurality or composition. Hence there is no cause that could precede Him. By contrast, He is the Creator of the causes and of all spatio-temporal categories. When we speak of 'divine powers', we therefore refer to an activity that is incorporeal, non-spatial, and outside time. This, however, also applies to the impact of the divine powers on Soul and Intellect. That the phenomena of prophecy are not subject to demonstration does not argue against their validity.

Next follows an account of philosophical psychology in the spirit of the Neoplatonic interpretation of Aristotle which we find in the work *al-Fawz al-aṣġar*. Intellect 'seems to be a genus of soul of its own kind; it alone can separate itself like the eternal from the perishable' (quoting Aristotle, *On the Soul* II 2, 413b25–27; as at *al-Fawz* [*264: II 4,77.II 5,79 ʿUḍayma]). It does not belong to the genus of sense perception; nor is it, like e.g. light or heat, bound to the corporeal substrate whose forms disappear together with its dissolution. According to Aristotle, intellect is eternal and separable from the body, and is the only element/aspect which will outlast human existence, being the substance that subsists through itself (*ǧawhar qāʾim bi-ḏātihi*, αὐθυπόστατος οὐσία). If (and in so far as) there is a balanced mixture (*mizāǧ muʿtadil*, εὐκρασία) of the psycho-somatic nature, intellect can use its body as its instrument and can exert its influence on the body in such a way as to take the mixture to the level of human perfection. Intellect itself persists in its independence of the body and any mixture, for it exists without space and time and other accidents linked to the body [50,8–51,4 Arkoun].

It is only through intellect that intelligibles (*al-maʿānī al-maʿqūla*) can be known. Someone who is weak in this regard compares, with respect to intellectual insight, to the faculty of vision which, after a period of idleness due either to closed eyes or to darkness, will be blinded by sudden brightness. Analogously, someone who has no intellect will not be able to imagine intelligibles merely based on sensory impressions (*awhāmuhu llatī ḥaṣalat fīhā āṯār al-maḥsūsāt*). If a knowledgeable person describes them to him, he will at best be able to gather from this that intellectual imaginations (*mawhūmāt*) are what is at issue [51,6–19]. The path to intellectual knowledge leads via the gradual weaning (*fiṭām*) of the senses, achieved step by step through the study of the four mathematical disciplines (*taʿālīm*), to those things which are increasingly obscure and farther and farther removed from imagination, to the nature of things and then to the things that come after nature (*baʿd al-ṭabīʿa*): to the divine beings, finally to God, the First, the Creator (*mubdiʿ*) of all things, be they intelligible or sensually perceptible [51,21–52,5].

This level can only be reached by (deductive) ascertainment of the causes (*wuǧūd al-sabab*). Only prophets constitute an exception: gifted with a special temperament and favoured by divine providence, this highest power of the intellect is created in them at once (*ibdāʿan*), without gradual practice or effort (*muʿānāt*). They see the divine things in a higher and nobler manner as we do with our clouded spirit; they must, however, fashion similies (*amṯāl*) for those intelligibles which can be grasped by all of us. They also must give pointers (*išārāt*), depending on the circumstances of their people, their rank, and their preparedness for receiving the divine power, in order to guide them on the path to eternal life, to the eternal Spirit (*rūḥ*) and to divine happiness, on God's straight road (quoting Quran, Sura 42:52–53) [52,8–18].

As intellect is incorporeal, it does not have a form that would be proper to it. Instead it is a power that can receive all forms. If it did have a form, this would prevent it from receiving other forms perfectly (like the air that can assume all colours, being colourless itself). Matter, too, can potentially assume all forms; but its essence is altered in the process, and it must give up one form to take on another. The intellect, by contrast, can take on all forms at once, even contrary ones (e.g. the forms of the half and the double, or the status of affirmation and negation; thus according to Alexander's [sc. of Aphrodisias] solution to the question) [52,20–53,16].

The soul is not itself life, but it is a living substance which provides the body with a state similar to itself; or else it would be a corporeal form whose existence is dependent on the body. If the soul were dependent on the body, it would not be repelled by the things that are of use to the body. In reality, however, a soul that seeks perfect virtue disdains and rejects the pleasures of the body. The substance of the soul is different from the substance of the body, just as its specific activity is different from that of the body. This is indicated e.g. by the fact that someone who wants to imagine an intelligible must let go of his senses (*taʿṭīl al-ḥawāss*). It is only when the soul returns to itself, separating itself from the body and its perception, that it can grasp the intelligibles proper to it, and can see with the incorporeal eye of the soul, following the only path to true knowledge open to it.

Socrates says: once the philosopher's soul gains in strength, it will despise the corporeal and its desires, and it will flee the world and seek true being instead. Plato urges us: die by virtue of your will (i.e. voluntary death through extirpating one's desires), and live by virtue of your (psycho-somatic) nature (*mut bi-l-irāda wa-taḥya bi-l-ṭabīʿa*, as it should be read instead of *mut bi-l-ṭabīʿa wa-taḥya bi-l-irāda*; for this topos of philosophical propaedeutics cf. Hein 1985 [*516: 98]). At the end of the *Nicomachean Ethics*, Aristotle says: the specific property of the soul is its self-knowledge. This is the truly human characteristic and the truly virtuous and happy life; herein lies man's peculiar activity. The senses perceive something other than themselves, whereas the intellect thinks itself.

Aḥwāl al-rūḥ
The States of the Spirit

The work is also ascribed to Ibn Sīnā (Mahdawī 1954 [*441: 260]). – Miskawayh's reply to the question: Where did the soul descend from, where was it and where will it get to; what is its form (*qālab*), and how should we imagine it in our minds (*kayfa yutaṣawwar fī l-awhām*)?

As the first of the spiritual beings (*al-arwāḥ*), God created the Intellect (*al-ʿaql*) by virtue of His word (*kalima*). From the Intellect then proceeded the Soul, i.e. the Second Intellect, from which matter was generated, which again gave rise to the generation of the natural form. From natural form, the plurality of being came about through composition: from the spheres to the minerals, plants and other living creatures up to human beings. Hereby, the subtle (*laṭīf*) comprises the crude (*kaṯīf*): Intellect comprises Soul, Soul comprises matter and so on. The soul subsists through itself and is able to perceive future events in its imagination and its dreams, even without separating itself from the body entirely. How much more will it be able to perceive everything that remains hidden to it in this world, once it will return from the corporeal world of darkness to the world of light.

Risāla fī Ǧawhar al-nafs
On the Substance of the Soul (labelled as an 'excerpt from his epistles [*min rasāʾilihi*]' on this topic, followed by another piece '*On the Examination of the Same* [sc. the soul]')

It is not because of their corporeality but because of their possession of a soul that living beings, from plants to animals and human beings, have the capacities of nourishment, growth, and procreation. Due to their animal and spirited soul they share the powers of perception as well as motion, either for pursuit or flight. Within ourselves, we humans recognize the powers of thought, judgement, and of coming to know the hidden from what is manifest, powers that we possess not by virtue of our body, but on account of our rational soul and intellect. Further remarks discuss the insight into hidden things in a dream without taking the usual path via sense perception, as well as psychology ranking higher than the other scientific disciplines: 'whoever knows his soul, knows his Lord'. Self-knowledge is based on the knowledge of the cause of one's essence; and humans are what they are because of their soul.

The soul possesses several parts and powers. According to one doctrine, it is the totality of its powers. The Pythagoreans regard seven as the perfect number, since it is the one number within the first decad which is not generated by another number, and which does not generate another one itself. Therefore this must also be the number of the moved heavenly spheres. According to Plato, the heavenly bodies have a rational soul, and visual and aural perception. According to Aristotle, they only possess intellect as the most perfect form.

Risāla fī l-Ṭabīʿa
On Nature (labelled as an excerpt; MS: *min risālatihi fī l-ṭabīʿa*)

The natural substances are classified into simple and composite ones, with simple ones again subdivided into material ones (constituted from the four elements) and non-material ones (the heavenly bodies). The composite substances are vegetative, animal, or mineral substances, each group being characterized by their various capacities to move. The heavenly bodies only possess locomotion, in fact a particular locomotion that never comes to rest. As a whole, they nevertheless remain stationary around the poles and centres that are always at rest. 'Nature' is more dependent on form than on matter (*ʿunṣur, hayūlā, mādda*), for the natural path of generation leads to perfection by way of impression (*inṭibāʿ, taṭabbuʿ*) through a form (according to Aristotle, against Plato [?]).

4.3.3 Ethics

Tahḏīb al-aḫlāq wa-taṭhīr al-aʿrāq (also: *Kitāb Ṭahārat al-nafs*)
The Refinement of Character and the Purification of Natural Dispositions (also: *The Purity of the Soul*)

Cf. Arkoun 1970 [*452: 115]. The work is divided into six treatises (*maqālāt*) without subheadings. The division given below follows the French translation by Arkoun 1969 [*556].

Introduction: the aim of the work is to produce a moral disposition from which fine actions will arise with ease. The path towards this goal leads via the soul's becoming aware of itself, and the purification of its spiritual nature.

Treatise I [*273: 3–30]: principles of ethics. The soul and its powers. The good and happiness. Virtues and vices. 1 [3–10]: the soul, its powers and its virtues. The soul is not corporeal; it is neither corporeal form nor accident and hence does not stand in need of a corporeal substrate. In fact, it is a simple substance. On one hand, it obtains the principles of knowledge from sense perception; on the other, it also possesses non-sensory principles to which it has its own specific access. The soul's inclination to exercise the actions proper to it, i.e. its inclination towards knowledge and science, and its renunciation of inclinations and actions specific to the body, constitute its virtue. In order to realize the virtues, the soul needs to be cleansed of vices. 2 [10–17]: the virtues. Practical philosophy (*al-falsafa al-ʿamaliyya*) is the study of those voluntary actions which take their direction from a person's thinking and judgement. Good are those modes of behaviour and actions that lead a person towards fulfilling the purpose of his existence, and that he can recognize with the help of the rational faculty that is given to humans alone. The soul has three powers (*quwā*, δυνάμεις) or parts: the rational faculty or soul (*al-quwwa / al-nafs al-nāṭiqa*), the irascible (*al-ġaḍabiyya*, also *al-sabuʿiyya*, 'the lion-like') and the appetitive (*al-šahwiyya*, also *al-bahīmiyya*, 'bestial'). The rational part of the soul is the royal part, for it is up to it to order the other two to be measured and balanced, and hence virtuous. It is localized in the brain. The virtues have value only if they are performed for the sake of another person. 3 [18–24]: each faculty of the soul corresponds to a virtue which arises from the measured use of this faculty, and from an insight into its purpose. The virtue of the rational soul is knowledge (*ʿilm*), followed by wisdom (*ḥikma*); the virtue of the appetitive soul is temperance (*ʿiffa*), followed by generosity (*saḫāʾ*); the virtue of the irascible soul is prudence (*ḥilm*), followed by courage (*šaǧāʿa*). When all three virtues are in perfect balance, the highest cardinal virtue, justice (*ʿadl*), will arise. The four virtues are opposed by four vices: ignorance, greed, cowardice and injustice. The section closes with a catalogue of the specific character traits related to the four cardinal virtues. 4 [24–30]: virtue is the correct mean between two extremes, whereas vice is a deviation from the mean towards one of the extremes. The application of the concept of the correct mean to the catalogue of virtues leads to an analogous compilation of the vices.

Treatise II [*273: 31–74]: the human character and its education. 1 [31–36]: ethical character (*ḫuluq*, ἦθος) is a state (*ḥāl*, διάθεσις) of the soul which conditions its actions without discursive thought. This happens by nature, due to the person's mixture or 'temperament' (*mizāǧ*, κρᾶσις), or through habit (*ʿāda*, ἔθος) and practice (*tadarrub*), which is initiated by thinking and will finally result in the acquisition of a character disposition. Doxography of ancient theories of character: the Stoics and Galen. Character is not an invariable natural disposition; human beings must be directed towards virtue by an education that is oriented at the law (*al-šarīʿa*), at an early age when their character can still be shaped. 2 [36–42]: the art of building character (*ṣināʿat al-aḫlāq*). The perfection that is proper to human beings (*al-kamāl al-ḫāṣṣ bi-l-insān*) is twofold, corresponding to man's twofold potentiality, which is both cognitive and practical. The first potentiality seeks the sciences; the second potentiality seeks to arrange and order things in a rational manner (cf. Aristotle, *Nicomachean Ethics* I 6, 1098a16–17: ψυχῆς ἐνέργειαν καὶ πράξεις μετὰ λόγου; cf. also 1099b26). This has a correlation in the division between theoretical and practical philosophy. When human beings manage to perfect both capacities, they enjoy perfect happiness. 3 [42–46]: the gratification of sensual desires cannot be the highest human good, as some people think. 4 [46–55]: the hierarchy of the faculties of the soul: the highest faculty, the rational soul, is what accounts for the pre-eminence of the human race. The path to the soul's perfection and to perfect happiness is depicted in the authors' work *Tartīb al-saʿādāt wa-manāzil al-ʿulūm* (*The Degrees of Happiness and the Order of the Sciences*). The soul is one in essence, but it has several powers (cf. Aristotle, *On the Soul* II 3, 414a29–415a13), accidents and substrates. Three powers vie for influence; whichever gains the upper hand will determine the degree of happiness. 5 [55–64]: the upbringing of children and adolescents, discussed mainly according to the *Kitāb Burūsun*, i.e. the *Oikonomikos* by a Pythagorean from the 1st (?) century AD, known by the name of Bryson (cf. Swain 2013 [*588]; in its Arabic version, the text is transmitted independently as well; for the text and its reception within the *Tahḏīb al-aḫlāq* cf. Plessner 1928 [*541: 39–52. 139–141 *et passim*]). 6 [64–69]: the various degrees of perfection in the natural and moral realms, according to the respective superiority each higher rank assumes over the next lower one, which is shaped by it and subjected to it: from inanimate (mineral) to animate nature, from the kingdom of plants to that of animals, and finally from the irrational animal to the rational living being, man, who in turn ascends by degrees to the highest perfection of humanity. 7 [69–73]: once man, through studying the sciences, has reached perfection, he will stand on the boundary to the pure intelligences, the angels. Thus he becomes a mediator between the higher and the lower world, either as a perfect philosopher or as a prophet, the recipient of divine revelation. He thus will reach the beatific vision (cf. Quran, Sura 31:17). It is the task of the political rulers of a state to provide all individuals with the guidance appropriate to them, be it to intellectual or to practical perfection, so that everyone is able to reach the specific degree of happiness of which they are capable.

Treatise III [*273: 75–104]: the highest good and happiness. 1 [75–76]: the degrees of happiness. 2 [76–79]: the division of the good: Aristotle's division 'as it is transmitted by Porphyry and others'. It differentiates between the absolute good and the relative good, depending on value and purpose. (The first part of this section corresponds to a Greek synopsis of Aristotelian ethics, which is preserved in Stobaeus as well as in

Arius Didymus, cf. Pines 1956 [*545: 5–6]). 3 [79–86]: happiness: the degrees of happiness follow the grades of the good – health, wealth, honour, success, prudence – and are conditional upon them. Philosophers who preceded Aristotle, 'such as Porphyry, Socrates, Plato and their likes', agreed that all virtues and all instances of happiness belong to the soul alone and can be assigned to its various faculties, and that the following virtues alone are sufficient for happiness: wisdom (*ḥikma, σοφία*), courage (*šaǧāʿa, ἀνδρεία*), temperance (*ʿiffa, σωφροσύνη*) and justice (*ʿadl, δικαιοσύνη*) (for an Arabic source of the passage in Pseudo-Plato, *Iṯbāt faḍāʾil al-nafs*, cf. Daiber 1971 [*558: 37]). The Stoics and some natural philosophers hold a contrary opinion: the body is a constituent part of the human being. Hence the ancients were at variance concerning the question whether the highest happiness can be realized during the psycho-somatic existence in this world. According to Miskawayh only spiritual virtue (*al-faḍīla al-rūḥāniyya*) can yield perfect happiness, which is characterized by perfect wisdom and illumination through the divine light, and which is hence free from the pains and worries which continually endanger corporeal happiness. 4 [86–91]: the degrees of the virtues of the soul and the corresponding degrees of happiness. In this context, the author provides the full text of a treatise ascribed to Aristotle, *The Virtues of the Soul* (*Faḍāʾil al-nafs*, according to the Arabic version by Abū ʿUṯmān al-Dimašqī; cf. Pines 1956 [*545]). The highest happiness, according to the closing words of the treatise, is realized in the highest degree of knowledge. Here the intellect is identical with the first intelligibles, while man's actions, which have reached the highest level of perfection, are divine actions; i.e. his essence is identical with his action and acts for its own sake. 5 [91–103]: the highest degrees of happiness can only be reached by those who have thoroughly studied all parts of philosophy, practical as well as philosophical; for this point the author refers to his work *The Degrees of Happiness and the Order of the Sciences*.

Treatise IV [*273: 105–134]: the practice of true virtue. 1 [105–112]: true virtue and apparent virtue. Aberrations from true virtue: acting according to the external semblance of the ideal, without the internal, moral disposition of the virtue, e.g. the practice of courage, abstinence, generosity and justice merely for the sake of one's reputation among one's fellow human beings. 2 [113–134]: justice is the adherence to equal measure (*musāwāt*), balance, and correct mean; therefore it is the embodiment of all virtue. Division of justice according to Aristotle: observance of duties towards God, towards other human beings, and towards the forebears; duties of worship.

Treatise V [*273: 135–173]: love and friendship. – 1 [135–150]: kinds of love (*maḥabba*). The various forms of love, in respect of depth and constancy, are determined by their purposes: pleasure, benefit, or the good. Pure, unadulterated delight is imparted by divine love alone, which is the desire to become one with God (cf. Aristotle, *Nicomachean Ethics* 1155a32-b8). The inclination to companionship (*uns*), which is innate to human beings, is an important factor that unites society in solidarity; hence law (*al-šarīʿa*) and accepted custom promote regular gatherings for the purpose of worship. Religion thus creates the God-given condition for happiness. 2 [150–155]: the character of the good and the bad person reveals itself in true and false friendship respectively. 3 [155–167]: value and necessity of friendship. How to choose true friends. Duties towards one's friend. 4 [167–172]: the virtues can only be realized in society. The virtues which form the basis for true friendship and pure love (necessary requirements for the happiness of humans, who by nature are political beings) must be fostered by external conditions and social rules.

Treatise VI [**273*: 175–222]: the health of the soul, its preservation, and the therapy of diseases. 1 [175–191]: principles of 'spiritual medicine' and psychic hygiene. Like the body, the soul requires constant training through exposure to role models, self-discipline and introspection. The specific tasks of the ruler. Quotation from a treatise by al-Kindī: we ought to reflect upon our own conduct critically, in order to discipline ourselves, and be an example to others in living virtuously. 2 [191–222]: the therapy of diseases of the soul. The vices, the diseases of the soul: their origin, development and treatment. The fear of death: this is only felt by those who do not know that death is the deliverance from physical defects and sufferings and the path to the highest happiness of the immortal soul. Therefore Plato says: if you die by your will, you will live by your nature'. The death of the will is the relinquishing of desires, whereas natural death is the separation of the soul from the body. The discussion of grief closes [217–221] with a longer excerpt from al-Kindī's *On the Method of How to Dispel Sorrow* (*Risāla fī l-Ḥīla li-dafʿ al-aḥzān*, cf. [§ 4 **45*]); also quoted, after Miskawayh, by al-Rāġib al-Iṣfahānī and Ibn Sīnā, cf. Fakhry 1994 [*577]): he who knows the nature of the true good will stop grieving the loss of material goods and bodily pleasures.

Risāla fī l-Laḏḏāt wa-l-ālām
On Pleasures and Pains

An excerpt (*min risāla* …) according to the dedication, this is nevertheless a self-contained text. Pleasures are moments of fulfilment (*kamālāt*: perfection, entelechy), which are periodically experienced by the living subject; in the essentially perfect being, i.e. in the realm of the divine, they are eternally actual. The perfect is sought either in relation to another or absolutely, for its own sake. Striving is either by nature or voluntary. If its fulfilment grants full perfection, the delight will be true; if the perfection is merely putative, the delight will be merely illusory. If the object sought after is spiritual and intellectual, its fulfilment true and the attraction strong, we speak of passion (*ʿišq*); if the attraction is of medium strength, we speak of love (*maḥabba*), and if it is less strong, of inclination (*nizāʿ*). Absolute and true fulfilment can only be attained through the desire for the absolute good that is loved for its own sake: God the sublime.

Knowledge of God, the highest good, imparts the highest pleasure; in the most perfect act of comprehending the highest object of desire it is permanently actualized. God is the object of desire of the whole universe; to Himself He is the object of the love that is directed to nothing but His essence.

Compared with all other living beings, man is the one who can comprehend his Creator with his reason. In this most noble act of comprehension he fulfils his love for Him and thus obtains the highest pleasure of which any living being is capable. The 'naturalists' (*al-ṭabīʿiyyūn*) say that pleasure is the return to the natural state; but this does not apply to the realm of the divine, since here the natural state is never abandoned. The form of natural things is fair balance (justice, *ʿadl*) in giving and taking; that of divine things is benevolence (*faḍl*) – God gives without taking [101,8–19].

Musical harmonies correspond to the sublime relations of the cosmic order, and the divine foreordinations in spiritual as well as natural things. Their contemplation can convey a vision of the sublime orders to those who truly strive for it. Depending on the degrees of their proximity to the highest end, this will occur in rational perfection or in a mere perceptible analogy of this (on this treatise, see Adamson 2015 [*589]).

Risāla fī Māhiyyat al-ʿadl
On the Essence of Justice

Justice (*ʿadl*) is presented as a principle of cosmology (fair balance), of ontology (symmetry of proportions) and of anthropology (right mixture of the temperaments); as 'voluntative' justice it is the purpose of ethics. Justice is realized in three ways: as natural justice (φύσει), as conventional justice (θέσει, established by statute), and as divine justice. There are two basic premises: (a) the absolute One, the true being without otherness, multiplicity or opposite, is the highest, perfect being, and is the unifying cause within everything that participates in its unity and rank; (b) the pure good (*al-ḫayr al-maḥḍ*) is the perfect existence; it is called the good, because everything that exists strives towards it.

The absolute One cannot exist in a body, because the corporeal is divided in three dimensions and is fragmented into the multiplicity of species and individuals. However, there is a higher order of bodies which are closer to unity: the heavenly bodies which are made up of the eternal, fifth element, whose circular movement is one, and whose nature is one. By contrast, the bodies of the sublunar world are made up of four elements opposed to each other, which are subject to generation and corruption.

The lower bodies, since they lack unity, can only approach the One by virtue of equality (*tasāwin*) in substance, quality, and the other categories. Equality in substance, quantity, and relation (*nisba*, proportion, cf. Aristotle, *Nicomachean Ethics* v 6, 1131a29-b9; 7, 1131b15: τὸ ἀνάλογον, ἀναλογία) is natural justice (*al-ʿadl al-ṭabīʿī*).

Equilibrium in the elemental proportion within a corporeal substance ensures its lasting stability and preserves it from alteration and corruption. Hence the search for the right proportion is what preoccupies the experts in alchemy, the so-called 'science of balances' (*ʿilm al-mawāzīn*).

Even though man is of the highest complexity, he is the noblest being in the world of generation, because he has a unifying element within him: the power of the common sense (*al-ḥāss* [sic] *al-muštarak*). It acts as ruling force (*ḥākim*, regent, ≅ ἡγεμονικόν) over the individual parts, it discards what is false and confirms what is true. Unification (*taʾaḥḥud*), brought about by the gift of this high virtue, enables man to reach the highest happiness in this as well as the coming world.

Conventional justice (*al-ʿadl al-waḍʿī*) is either (a) universal justice of the statutes and agreements concerning commerce and dealings within human society, according to principles that are common to all peoples, or (b) the particular justice of individual countries, nations, cities and groups, which gives them equal rights respectively, through contract and custom.

With reference to the individual human being, we find freely chosen justice (*al-ʿadl al-iḫtiyārī, κατὰ προαίρεσιν*, cf. Aristotle, *Nicomachean Ethics* V 5, 1134a2), i.e. the bringing about of a harmonious cooperation (*musālama*) between the various faculties of the soul, corresponding to the equilibrium of the natural dispositions and the temperament, which is the health of the body.

Divine justice rules the eternal beings, which are beyond the natural things (*mā baʿd al-ṭabīʿiyyāt*). 'Natural' justice is eternal as well, but divine justice exists in the immaterial beings. The Pythagoreans use the pure numbers, which are separable from their material substrate, as well as the geometrical dimensions and their eternal relations as an analogy for this. He who practices mathematics will win insight in the realm of the divine things that are separate from matter.

4.3.4 Gnomologia

Kitāb Ādāb al-ʿArab wa-l-Furs (*Ǧāwīḏān ḫiraḏ*)
Ethical Sayings of Arabs and Persians (*Perennial Wisdom*)

In some testimonials and manuscripts, the work is transmitted under the Persian title *Ǧāwīḏān ḫiraḏ* (*Perennial Wisdom*), after the 'testament' of Hōšang (Ūšhanǧ), which opens the collection, and texts by other Persian sages. Hence it has been printed under the equivalent Arabic title, *al-Ḥikma al-ḫālida* (ed. Badawī 1952 [*281]; on this point see the introduction pp. 54–63, text p. 5]). On the position of the work at the core of wisdom literature cf. also § 9.1.3 'Gnomologia'.

A collection of gnomological wisdom from the literary heritage of the Orient, in five parts. 1: *Ḥikam al-Furs*, i.e. wise sayings of the Persians [1–88], starting with the teaching of Hōšang and other Persian sages, after the *Ǧāwīḏān ḫiraḏ* (cf. Arberry 1963 [*603]). Miskawayh refers to an Arabic translation from the Middle Persian by al-Ḥasan b. Sahl (Ibn Zāḏānfarrūḫ), brother of the vizier al-Faḍl b. Sahl, as Miskawayh reports relying on al-Ǧāḥiẓ [*281: 3] (Arberry 1963 [*603] refers to the astrologer al-Ḥasan b. Sahl b. Nawbaḫt). Al-Ḥasan had made use of a translation that was read and explained to him by al-Ḫiḍr b. ʿAlī [*281: 20–22]. This and other texts of Persian wisdom literature contained in the work are also documented in older strands of transmission, independently of Miskawayh's collection; some of them are transmitted separately, others in different contexts, thus in MS Dublin, Chester Beatty 4819 (ed. Arberry 1963 [*603]), or in Pseudo-Ibn al-Muqaffaʿ, *al-Adab al-ṣaġīr*, perhaps following the Persian-Arabic tradition of ʿAlī b. ʿUbayda al-Rayḥānī (d. 234/819) (cf. Zakeri 1994 [*611: 93–96]). In Miskawayh's collection they were united with other gnomological traditions; but it is not appropriate to describe the whole collection as apocryphal (*pace* Khan 1998 [*614]). 2: *Ḥikam al-Hind* [89–100]. 3: *Ḥikam al-ʿArab* [101–208], including Luqmān, Ḥasan al-Baṣrī and sayings of the Ṣūfiyya. 4: *Ḥikam al-Rūm* [211–282], i.e. wisdom of the Greeks: Socrates, Hermes, Diogenes, Plato and his pupil Aristotle (including the latter's advice to Alexander), Pythagoras' *Golden Verses*, and the *Tablet of Cebes*. 5: *Ḥikam al-islāmiyyīn al-muḥdaṯīn*, i.e. wise sayings by Islamic authors of recent times [285–375], including Ibn al-Muqaffaʿ and al-Fārābī.

Waṣiyya
Testament (*On the Moral Ideal of the Philosopher*)

a) The work is preserved under this title in Miskawayh's *al-Ḥikma al-ḫālida* [*281: 285–290], but it is not described there as his own work. In the *Muntaḫab Ṣiwān al-ḥikma* (ed. Dunlop [*236: 152–155 §§ 297–300]), on the other hand, it is attributed to Miskawayh. It is composed in the language typically associated with gnomologia, characterized by antithesis and grammatical parallelism.

As his testament, the author presents a religiously coloured admonishment to the philosophical life, to the search for wisdom (*ḥikma*), 'God's greatest gift to his servants', and to the pursuit of true virtue through orientating one's mind towards knowledge and true faith.

b) The second 'Waṣiyya', different from the first one in wording and tenor, is the 'testament' ascribed to Miskawayh. It is preserved by Yāqūt (*Iršād* [*238: II 95–96 Margoliouth; II 498–499 ʿAbbās]) and in a longer, albeit anonymous, version in Abū Ḥayyān al-Tawḥīdī's *al-Muqābasāt* [*234: 383–387].

This text bears the hallmarks of al-Tawḥīdī's artistic prose and, like others of his *Muqābasāt*, was perhaps phrased by himself. It contains the 'voluntary commitment' to a programme of education of body and soul; it demands abstinence from base desires and from associating with people of bad character; patient endurance of one's fate, may it bring happiness or sufferings; and confident trust in God; it requires one to offer good advice to everybody, and give honour where it is due; and to praise God when He grants the soul the strength to be virtuous, leads it to its goal and preserves it from the temptations of vice.

Ethical Excerpts

A number of brief remarks, *Faṣl āḫar min kalāmihi* (ed. Arkoun 1963 [*482: 194–195]), about (a) prayers being answered: this does not happen because it moves God to do something he would not otherwise have done, but because it prepares people for the reception of the divine gifts; (b) about the doctrine of personal immortality (*baqāʾ al-nafs bi-l-šaḫṣ*): it is based on a naturalistic-material conception of the soul; (c) the cause of grief (*ǧazaʿ*, λύπη): it is paying excessive attention to particulars and objects of the senses; the philosophers urge us to the 'voluntary death' (*mawt irādī*) of the desires, a well-known topos of ethical propaedeutics (cf. p. 301 above); (d) about the substances (read *al-ǧawāhir* rather than *al-ḫawāṭir*): the soul is imperishable, being an incorporeal substance without intrinsic opposite, life-giving in its essence, self-moved and self-thinking, but nevertheless accidental as it is the perfection of a body.

Taǧārib al-umam wa-ʿawāqib al-himam
The Experiences of the Peoples and the Consequences of Various Ambitions

The programmatic introduction of the chronicle, edited separately in: Arkoun 1963 [*482: 203–205 no. XII]; cf. also *Taǧārib* [*251: II 36–37 Amedroz]: history is presented as moral example according to the 'experiences of the peoples'.

Using the occasion of writing an obituary for his patron, the vizier Abū l-Faḍl Ibn al-ʿAmīd (d. 360/970, *Taǧārib* [*251: II 275,1–279,1]) Miskawayh represents the realization of perfect learning and culture – Islamic-Arabic as well as Hellenistic-philosophical – in the idealised image of a great personality.

4.4 *Doctrine*

Miskawayh was a courtier, a historian of the Iranian dynasty of the Buyids, and a transmitter of gnomological wisdom of the Persians, Greeks and Arabs, all cast into a literary style (*al-Ḥikma al-ḫālida* [*281]). As such he represents the linguistic, literary and philosophical education of the 'classical' Islamic, Arabic-speaking cultural community. As a philosopher, he propagates Greek philosophy, Plato and Aristotle, as a constitutive element of courtly learning, of literary *adab*, which is presented in exemplary Arabic language as universal model of all ethnic and religious communities united under Islam, the same communities whose virtues and vices he illustrated on the basis of the 'experiences of the peoples' (*Taǧārib al-umam* [*251]) in his historical work of the same title.

Philosophy stood in the tradition of those who practised the rational sciences, especially the mathematical sciences and medicine, which had been in the service of the Arabic-Islamic princely courts ever since the Abbasid dynasty first ascended to power in Baghdad. With the advancing Arabization and Islamization of society, these sciences were propagated as serving the Islamic community, and their doctrine – the doctrine of the Greek philosophers – about God, world, and man was justified as a universal rational proof of Islamic belief.

Al-Kindī, the most important precursor and inspirer of Miskawayh's philosophy (as of that of the physician-philosopher Abū Bakr al-Rāzī, even if in a very different way), combined models of Platonic cosmology and theology with Gnostic-Neoplatonic psychology. The latter presents the highest end of man, the genus that is constituted by body and soul, as the ascent to the 'higher', spiritual world. It is this purpose which sanctions ethics, the 'noblest art of all': it indicates the path to the highest happiness as inhering in the purification of the spiritual substance of the soul through the intellect. In Miskawayh, a century after al-Kindī's death, this philosophical theology is based on a systematic basis of Aristotelian epistemology, physics, and positive ethics (supplemented by material from Galen's anthropology). In the Neoplatonic schools of Athens and Alexandria this tradition of ethical propaedeutics indicates the path to the soul's purification through intellect, and hence to the highest happiness. This path leads through the study of the sciences according to the Aristotelian canon and finally to knowledge of the good according to Platonic theology (cf. Simplicius' commentary on Epictetus' *Encheiridion*, ed. and intro. by I. and P. Hadot 2004 [*587], and the commentaries on the Pythagorean *Golden Verses* and on the *Tablet of Cebes*, preserved in Arabic; see Rosenthal 1977 [*607], Linley 1984 [*609], Daiber 1995 [*612]).

The highest happiness is realized in the highest degree of knowledge. Here the intellect is identical with the first intelligibles, and the acts of a human being at the highest level of perfection are divine, i.e. his essence is identical with his actions and it acts for the sake of itself. This highest level can only be reached by those who have thoroughly studied all parts of philosophy, practical as well as theoretical (cf. *Tartīb* [*259], *Tahḏīb* [*273: 91–103]).

Aristotle has pointed out the path to this end in his books: in his works of logic he has indicated the path to correct judgement and to the method of convincing others to turn towards the good, whereas in his ethical books he has shown the happy states of the soul. The advice of the sage leads to happiness through insight into the truth (of the true essence of things, *ḥaqā'iq al-umūr*) and, as a result, to doing what is right. It is therefore two classes of knowledge, practical and theoretical wisdom, which lead to the perfection of humanity (*insāniyya*) and to the realization of the ethos (*ḫuluq*) of the human.

This classification of the rational sciences into the two parts of philosophy, the theoretical and the practical according to Aristotelian doctrine, is represented by Miskawayh (*Tartīb* [*259: 117 Imāmī]) following a work by Būlus (Paulus) for the Sasanian Ḫusraw Anūširwān: an introduction to philosophy in the tradition of the Alexandrian *prolegomena*. In its general structure as well as in details concerning definition and classification it closely follows the schematic tables which, in the Aristotelian commentaries of Olympiodorus' school, were prefixed to Porphyry's *Isagoge* as an introduction, thus for instance in the commentary by Elias. The link between the two was apparently a Middle Persian or Syriac work by Paul the Persian (cf. pp. 59–60 above), which not only had an impact on Miskawayh's *Tartīb* (cf. also Wakelnig 2009 [*529] on a secondary tradition of the *Fawz*) but had already influenced al-Fārābī's catalogue of sciences, *Iḥṣāʾ al-ʿulūm* (§ 8 [*45]) (cf. Pines 1970 [*509], Gutas 1983 [*515]; Hein 1985 [*516: 40]).

Like his predecessors, Miskawayh introduces Aristotle's epistemology as basis for his philosophical system, where it is made to serve spiritual metaphysics of a Neoplatonic bent. However, he also appeals to the harmony of the ancient authorities, with Aristotle in the role of a witness to a universally valid *ḥikma* (wisdom). His ethics in particular is explicitly eclectic, containing numerous references to Plato, Aristotle, and Galen, and even exposing contradictions between the ancient authorities. The method employed by Miskawayh is that of paradigmatic proof, which (like the Platonists of al-Kindī's school) invokes the light of divine intellect for the purification of the spirit. While the Baghdad logicians in the school of Abū Bišr Mattā, Yaḥyā Ibn ʿAdī and, finally, al-Fārābī base their philosophical method on the science of demonstration of the *Analytics*, this does not play a prominent role in Miskawayh's thought, even though he was acquainted with it. In *al-Hawāmil wa-l-šawāmil* [*252: 6–10] we find a small treatise on the relation between word and meaning following *Categories* 1 and an exposé of the four fundamental scientific questions according to *Posterior Analytics* II 1 [341]; the *Tahḏīb al-aḫlāq* [*273: 33–34] contains a single syllogism, supposed to demonstrate that no character is 'natural', because it is subject to alteration.

Metaphysics and noetics. Miskawayh's Platonic theology clearly relies on that of al-Kindī, and in particular on the sources of Arabic Neoplatonism that were translated and adapted in al-Kindī's circle, and reshaped within an Aristotelian framework. Just as in the Kindī-circle texts, Miskawayh's Neoplatonic cosmology appears simplified and brought into harmony with monotheistic theology. The first principle, the pure good, is at the same time the self-thinking First Intellect (νοῦς νοῶν νοητόν, taking up Aristotle's *Metaphysics* XII 7, 1072b21). The cosmological model of nine spheres found in *al-Fawz* I 9 [*264: 54–57] seems to be indebted to al-Fārābī, especially in the elaborated form presented in *Kitāb al-ʿAql wa-l-maʿqūl* [*265: 85] with its emanative triad of Intellect, Soul, and intelligible matter, even though there is no reference to al-Fārābī by name.

For his theology, which professes that God is one only, eternal, and incorporeal (*al-Fawz* I 2 [*264: 40–42]), Miskawayh refers to the consensus of the ancients. He quotes Porphyry (i.e. perhaps his treatise περὶ τοῦ μίαν εἶναι τὴν Πλάτωνος καὶ Ἀριστοτέλους φιλοσφίαν, *That Plato's and Aristotle's Philosophy is One*?) and, above all, Aristotle's *Physics* and *Metaphysics*. Based on the Aristotelian doctrine of motion he establishes a proof for God's existence as the Prime Mover: everything that moves must be moved by a mover external to it (Aristotle, *Physics* VIII 4). God, the Prime Mover, is unique. He moves through His essence alone, whereas the differentiation of secondary causes after Him brings about the multiplicity of forms (according to Porphyry: Aristotle's doctrine *pace* Plato's theory of Forms). He is necessary of existence (*wāǧib al-wuǧūd*) and unmoved, and hence eternal. Knowledge of God allows only negative pronouncements, no positive ones (*bi-ṭarīq al-salb dūna l-īǧāb*). The being of all things comes from God, beginning with the first existence that proceeds from Him, the First Intellect or Agent Intellect, through the ontological hierarchy of the spheres up to the existence of the material forms of nature. God has created everything from nothing; the generation of the created, contingent substance is merely a transformation of forms (*al-Fawz* I 10 [*264: 58], referring to 'Alexander of Aphrodisias'). In the background here, however, is an excerpt from John Philoponus' *Against Proclus On the Eternity of the World*, which in the Arabic tradition was transmitted as a treatise by Alexander, entitled *Refutation of the Doctrine that One Thing can Only be Generated from Another, and Proof that Everything is* [*really*] *Generated from Non-being* (cf. Fazzo 1997 [*582] and in particular Hasnawi 1994 [*519: 107–108]).

Even though the soul appears to us as the 'form of a natural body', in its own, real essence it is pure, substantial form. This is how it can become the formal cause and entelechy of the living body (*al-Fawz* II 7 [*264: 84], following Aristotle, *On the Soul* II 1). It is neither body nor material form, neither part nor accident of a body. It requires no bodily substrate, but subsists in itself (being *ǧawhar qāʾim bi-ḏātihi, al-Nafs wa-l-ʿaql* [*266: 50 Arkoun; 93 Badawī]); for as a pure, spiritual substance its proper activity is its return to itself (cf. *Tahḏīb* [*273: 9]). The movement essential to it is none of the corporeal types of movement, but self-reflection 'outside of space and time, unceasing, akin to the eternity (*dahr*) of the heavenly sphere with its eternal circular motion' (cf. *al-Fawz* [*264: II 7, 84]).

The soul comprehends all existing things, whether or not they are available to sense perception – things that are sensually perceptible as well as those which can only be comprehended by reason, including the genera and species of things. Referring to Aristotle, *On the Soul* III 2, 426b16–23, Miskawayh concludes that the soul does not possess several faculties which perceive sensory particulars on the one hand, and intelligible universals on the other. Instead the rational soul perceives everything with a single faculty, even though it does so in different ways. In order to illustrate this, Miskawayh compares the way we perceive the composite and the simple with a bent and a straight line respectively (reference to Aristotle, *On the Soul* III 4, 429b16; Themistius, *Paraphrase of On the Soul* 96,8–30 Heinze = Arab. 165,16–166,4 Lyons; *Maqāla fī l-Nafs wa-l-ʿaql* [*266: 12 Arkoun; 60 Badawī]).

The soul is neither body nor accident, nor material form. Therefore it does not adopt one particular form to the exclusion of any other; instead it can comprehend all intelligibles, be they strong or weak, at the same time and completely. Being incorporeal, it alone can grasp the first principles and its own essence intellectually (on the identity of intellect and intelligible cf. Aristotle, *On the Soul* III 4, 430a2–5). As it is not bound to the body, the intellect remains untouched by its weakness, aging and corruption. The intellective soul (*al-nafs al-ʿāqila*) is a genus in its own right, eternal and separable from the corporeal (like Abū l-Ḫayr al-Ḥasan b. Suwār, the author refers to Aristotle, *On the Soul* II 2, 413b25–27; cf. *Maqāla fī l-Nafs wa-l-ʿaql* [*266: 50 Arkoun; 93 Badawī]). Miskawayh then backs up his proof for the immortality of the soul with the help of a doxography of ancient philosophers, quoting Plato, Proclus, and Galen, in particular Proclus' treatise *Commentary on Plato's Doctrine of the Immortality of the Soul*, which is lost in the original Greek (cf. Ibn al-Nadīm: *Fihrist* [*231: 252,15–16 Flügel; 313,1 Taǧaddud]; cf. Rosenthal 1940 [*501], Westerink 1973 [*513], Endress 2000 [*526: 553–554]) with the three following arguments: (a) the soul gives life, hence is life in its substance; (b) anything that is perishable only perishes because of an essential defect; and (c) the soul is essentially self-moved. The soul is a living substance which will outlast death and is imperishable. Without being life itself it gives life to everything in which it abides. The soul is an incorporeal substance; according to Plato, its substance is self-movement: 'The substance [*ǧawhar*, in the sense of essential nature] of the self-moved is movement', 'the substance of the soul is movement, and this movement is the life of the soul' (cf. [Pseudo-]Plato, *Kitāb al-Nawāmīs, al-Fawz* [*264: 84]). Its essential movement is none of the corporeal kinds of movement, but it is that of self-reflection, outside of space and time. By virtue of its movement towards the intellect the soul partakes in it; by virtue of its movement towards matter it lets matter partake in life and light. The (First) Intellect, being unmoved, is sufficient to itself. The (universal) Soul is in constant movement in order to seek perfection in its contemplation of the Intellect; its life is called word (*kalima*), idea (*miṯāl*), and seed (*biḏr*). The movement of the soul is imparted to the sphere, from whose movement ours is derived.

The author here relies on the psychology of the Arabic translations of Neoplatonic works and their tradition in the school of al-Kindī. Thus an early paraphrase of Aristotle's *On the Soul* (redacted in the circle of al-Kindī) insists on the definition of the soul as a simple substance (*ǧawhar mabsūṭ*, ἁπλῆ οὐσία), its essential incorporeality, its separability from the body and its imperishability – closely following, and over large stretches of text even adopting the literal wording of John Philoponus' commentary on *On the Soul* (cf. Arnzen 1998 [*471: 212–213. 374]). In the wake of Plotinus' re-definition of substance as that which exists only through itself, and which is determined only through itself, the capacity for self-reversion became the true criterion for substantiality. The eternally existing intelligible is substance (οὐσία) in the full and real sense (Plotinus, *Enn.* V 6 [24]: 6, 18–21; cf. Halfwassen 1998 [*525: 501–502]). This point is taken up in Proclus' theory of the 'subsistent in itself' (αὐθυπόστατον). Miskawayh explicitly quotes Proclus' 'three proofs for the immortality of the soul' (*al-Fawz* [*264: II 6. 82–83]) and will probably have known the Arabic excerpts from the *Elements of Theology* (Endress 2000 [*526]). According to the Proclean text, only something that 'is constituted through itself' (τὰ παρ' ἑαυτῶν ὑφιστάμενα) possesses independent being, i.e. being that 'subsists in itself' (Proclus here turns in particular against the Stoics' material concept of the soul). Only that which has the capability 'to return to itself' (πρὸς ἑαυτὸ ἐπιστρεπτικόν, Arab. *rāǧiʿ ilā ḏātihi*), i.e. the spiritual, is self-subsistent. By virtue of being constitutive of itself it is ungenerated, imperishable, without parts, simple as well as eternal and transcending time (Proclus, *Elements of Theology*, prop. 40–49. 51, cf. prop. 15–17 [*246: 42–50. 16–20]; cf. Halfwassen 1998 [*525: 501–502]; for the Arabic version of prop. 15–17 see Endress 1973 [*511: 202–213]).

In order to reach the highest degree of perfection, the soul must subject the body into which it has been born, which serves it as an instrument, and whose first entelechy it is, to a process of initiation. This process starts from the insights gained through sense perception, and then proceeds, with the help of the Agent Intellect, to the knowledge of universals and, finally, to that of the pure, subsistent forms (Miskawayh uses this topos from *On the Soul* III 5 to argue against the materialism and scepticism of the medical schools, *Maqāla fī l-Nafs wa-l-ʿaql* [*266: 13–14 Arkoun; 60–61 Badawī]).

Besides knowledge based on the senses, reason has a proper activity of its own, because it is in possession of the non-derivative principles (*awāʾil*). Apart from the universals, which are obtained by abstraction from perceptible particulars, but which cannot subsist without matter, there are the simple essential concepts of the pure, intelligible substances, which are not accessible to the senses, but only to purely intellectual knowledge (*Maqāla fī l-Nafs wa-l-ʿaql* 1 [*266: 11–22 Arkoun; 58–68 Badawī]; *al-Fawz* II 2 [*264: 65–66]). The background to this, as to the analogous distinction made by al-Fārābī (*Risāla fī l-ʿAql*, § 25 [§ 8 *105: 20–24 ed. Bouyges], cf. Arnaldez [*264 (1987): 106 n. 9]) is the Neoplatonic redefinition of substance as intellect (νοῦς). Thus Porphyry takes over Alexander's distinction between corporeal and incorporeal substance, but continues to distinguish two kinds of incorporeal substances: ἀσώματα ἀχώριστα are the immanent essential forms of the particulars (εἴδη ἔνυλα), which as in Alexander are supposed to be conceptual abstractions. They are contrasted, as ἀσώματα χωριστά, with the transcendent ideas (εἴδη χωριστά) which, being intelligible substance, constitute the principle of the sensually perceptible substance and are equated with the divine first substance (πρώτη οὐσία) of *Metaphysics* XII (after Halfwassen 1998 [*525: 501–502]); cf. Porphyry, *Sentences* §19. 42 [*245: 10. 53–54]; Simplicius, *In Cat.* [*247: 77–78]).

While his ethics is based on the Platonic conception of the tripartite soul, Miskawayh systematically resorts to Aristotle's *On the Soul* when it comes to the details of the psychic processes and activities, of perception, of the inner senses – imagination, common sense, memory – and their interaction with the intellect. He is furthermore aware of Themistius' commentary and various texts by Alexander of Aphrodisias (*al-Fawz* II 3 [*264: 123–126]); in respect of the localisation of the inner senses in the brain, however, he follows Galen [124–125].

Aristotle is also the authority on whose system the rational sciences rely in paving the way for instruction, practice and purification of the rational soul; it is the classification with which Miskawayh was familiar through the Alexandrian *prolegomena* to Aristotelian philosophy, in particular through the commentaries on Porphyry's *Isagoge* composed in the school of Olympiodorus. These works were available to him in translations and adaptations; he quotes them according to a text by Paul the Persian (*Tartīb*, see above pp. 331–332; cf. Hein 1985 [*516]). As in Paul's text – and as in al-Kindī's Aristotelian syllabus (*Risāla fī Kammiyyat kutub Arisṭāṭālīs* [§ 4 *40]) – the order of the theoretical sciences is justified with reference to the ranking of their objects: those linked to the body (physics), those separable from it (mathematics) and separate substances (metaphysics).

Another topic that belongs in the systematic context of philosophical psychology, and in particular in that of Aristotle's *Parva Naturalia*, is the doctrine of the inner senses, which is drawn on in order to explain veridical dreams, divination, and prophecy. The latter subject provides Miskawayh with the opportunity to include prophetic revelation in his system, and to broach the issue of the message of revelation (in a manner not unrelated to al-Fārābī's model). Whereas the philosopher, through the extertions of his intellect, is himself able to reach a point where 'the divine essences appear in perfect, lucid clarity', so that he no longer requires syllogistic demonstration, these essences will descend to the prophets. In analogy to the process of ascent, the divine ideas, aided by certain temperaments (*amziǧa*, κράσεις) can come down in the descent of emanation (*fayḍ*) and thus operate on the imagination through thinking, and through imagination on the senses, 'so that the human being will see images of the intelligible realities' (*al-Fawz* III 4 [*264: 126–127]): the prophets can now create similes (*amṯāl*) for those intelligibles which any of us are able to grasp, and they need to provide pointers (*išārāt*), according to the circumstances of their people, their rank and their readiness (*Maqāla fī l-Nafs wa-l-ʿaql* [*266: 52 Arkoun; 94 Badawī]).

Ethics. It is Miskawayh who directly affiliates ethics, as a discipline within the Aristotelian system of practical philosophy, with the Platonising metaphysics and theology of the Kindian tradition. As with the ethical propaedeutics of Alexandrian Neoplatonism, there is a twofold function to this: a justification of the prescribed ethical institutions and the individual's attitude which is rooted in them; and 'a mode of life which is not identical with the institutions, but in fact breaks out of them, like that of the philosopher as a cosmopolitan, or that of the person who strives for assimilation with God' (Ritter 1972 [*560: 763] with reference to the Christian philosophy of the early Middle Ages). However, in contrast to al-Kindī's school it draws mainly on the concepts of Aristotelian ethics when it comes to substantiating ethical values and the shaping of lives. Apart from the *Nicomachean Ethics* Miskawayh draws on further texts of the Peripatetic school, which he harmonizes with Platonic premises, as it had already happened in his late ancient sources. Porphyry reports on an Aristotelian classification of the good (*ḫayrāt*, ἀγαθά) (*Tahḏīb* [*273: 76]), while Aristotle himself is quoted extensively as the author of a Pseudo-Platonic-Peripatetic treatise on the 'virtues of the soul' [86–90].

The fundamental ethical concepts were provided by the Platonic model of the psychic faculties and by Miskawayh's Neoplatonic noetics. They serve as the basis for an ethics describing the path to the highest happiness, the perfection of the human being, as purification of the soul from its entanglement with the darkness and the impurities of the corporeal, from bodily desires and passions. In order to serve as adequate instrument of the ruling faculty, reason, a person's character must acquire the required disposition. If it is not an innate disposition, it must achieve this through practice leading to virtue, i.e. the development of a temperate, balanced state (*iʿtidāl al-mizāǧ*, εὐκρασία) of the three 'parts' or (as the Aristotelian would say) 'faculties' of the soul. The doctrine of principles of the *Tahḏīb al-aḫlāq* is based on the Platonic tripartion into the rational, the irascible, and the appetitive soul, and on the Platonic cardinal virtues of wisdom, courage, temperance, and justice. Virtue is embodied by the correct mean; the highest cardinal virtue is justice (*ʿadl*), which has as its model a cosmic principle in the absolute unity of the creator, and which as 'voluntative' justice is the purpose of ethics. Justice is realized in three ways: as natural, as conventional, and as divine justice. The lowly bodies, lacking unity, can approximate themselves to the One only through equality (*tasāwin*) in substance, quality and other categories. Equality with respect to substance, quantity and relation (*nisba*, proportion, cf. Aristoteles *Nicomachean Ethics* V 3, 1131a29-b9; 7, 1131b15: τὸ ἀνάλογον, ἀναλογία) is natural justice (*al-ʿadl al-ṭabīʿī*). Any departure from virtue is a deviation from the balanced mean, while vice is the tendency towards excess (*Tahḏīb* [*273: 15–18], *Risāla fī Māhiyyat al-ʿadl* [*276]).

This conception of the parts of the soul and their virtues is common to Hellenistic and late ancient Greek ethics. As they also appeared under Aristotle's name (thus e.g. in the Pseudo-Aristotelian treatise *On Virtues and Vices*, which was also translated into Arabic), as well as in the Pseudo-Platonic *Iṯbāt faḍāʾil al-nafs* (excerpt preserved in Miskawayh, cf. Daiber 1971 [*558: 35–38]), they were as a matter of course regarded as consensus of ancient wisdom (cf. the references in Walzer 1956 [*546: 221–222]), thus also in al-Kindī's *al-Qawl fī l-Nafs* (*Rasāʾil* [§ 4 *62: 272–275]). Miskawayh's adoption of them is remarkable in its details: to each of the four Platonic virtues he adduces a catalogue of subordinate virtues; next to temperance he puts generosity (*saḫāʾ*) as a special virtue which has further suboardinate virtues assigned to it (for Stoic and other late ancient models cf. Walzer 1956 [*546: 222–223]).

The second chapter of *Tahḏīb al-aḫlāq* begins with the definition of character (*ḫuluq*, ἦθος) from Galen's *De moribus*. The philosophical tradition of ethical propaedeutics is here joined to the medical tradition of ethical anthropology, in particular to its doctrine of the moral disposition shaped by one's character. Hence different ethical models are here juxtaposed; at times their contradictions are discussed by Miskawayh. The philosophers and physicians of antiquity and the Hellenistic era have different principles and pursue different scientific interests. This is why they have different concepts of 'soul' and 'spirit'. Even where both scientific traditions contemplate the physical apparatus of the living being they find different models of explanation for its natural components and functions. The anthropology of the Hellenistic doctors is based on the principle of 'sympathy' (συμπάθεια) between macrocosm (*al-ʿālam al-kabīr*) and microcosm (*al-ʿālam al-ṣaġīr*, cf. *al-ʿAql wa-l-maʿqūl*,

3rd part, see above pp. 314–316), which was developed in detail by Posidonius. At his own specific level, man too represents the structure of the entire universe (cf. *al-Fawz* III 2 [*264: 118–122]). There are four natural substances: homoiomeric ones – the four elements of the sublunar world, and the fifth element of the heavenly bodies with their regular circular movement – and heteromeric ones – plants and animals (*Risāla fī l-Ṭabīʿa* [*269: 196]). To each of the four elements (fire, air, water, earth) there belong two of the four elemental qualities, whose polarity produces affinity and repulsion respectively. Their balanced mixture leads to stability, an imbalanced mixture to disintegration. In the human body, the four elements find their correspondence in the four humours, the four elemental qualities in the temperaments. Throughout the Middle Ages medicine was based on humoural physiology, which was established by the Hippocratics and systematized by Galen.

Galen based his theories on the natural sciences of his time. In numerous questions of embryology, human anatomy, physiology, and the theory of perception he therefore held views different from Aristotle's. New insights into the function of the brain, and above all the discovery of the nerves, had led Galen to localize the ruling organ (the ἡγεμονικόν) together with the higher psychic functions in the brain. Subordinate to it are the affectible soul (located in the heart) and the appetites (here located in the liver); this is how we find it also in Miskawayh's account (*Tahḏīb* [*273: 16]; on the development cf. Harris 1973 [*512]; Manuli, Vegetti 1977 [*514]). Miskawayh incorporates the physiological theory of Galen and his school in order to explain the determining role which the three 'noble organs', i.e. brain, heart, and liver, play in the preservation and perfection of the psycho-somatic being; this is why the brain serves as an interface between soul and body in the human being. By contrast, Aristotle had linked the soul to the vital heat, regarded the heart as the seat of the psychic pneuma, the substrate of the 'innate heat' (σύμφυτον πνεῦμα), and the ruling organ of the nourishing, perceiving and thinking faculties. Thought (νοῦς, intellect), the highest function of the soul, needs no physical organ in order to perform its activity; it has no 'seat' (Müller 1995 [*520: 104–106]). These divergences led to lasting polemics by Peripatetics (as well as Stoics) against Galen's medical physiology. In Arabic Aristotelianism, too, the discussion of body and soul is never free of the discussion with Galen, whose physiology and philosophy dominanted the Hellenistic medical schools. Nevertheless his influence is considerable. In every detail, Miskawayh adheres to the physiology of Galenic writings, especially *De usu partium* and the *Anatomy* (*al-Fawz* [*264: 122], *Tahḏīb* [*273: 121]). Galen's medico-philosophical synthesis integrated the Platonic doctrine of the tripartite soul, Hippocratic physiology, and

Aristotelian physics (Walzer 1949 [*544], and further Arkoun 1970 [*452: 247]). Apart from his work *De moribus*, which was available in an Arabic epitome and exerted great influence on Miskawayh, his treatise on *That the Faculties of the Soul Follow the Mixtures of the Body* (ed. Biesterfeldt 1973 [*510]) left deep traces in Arabic medicine as well as philosophy.

But philosophy, including the philosophy of the physicians, distanced itself from the materialistic and deterministic implications of the Galenic models, be it that the soul was seen as material pneuma or, even though regarded as form, conceived of as a mere function of the physical organism (Moraux 1984 [*486: 773: psychology, Galen's 'naturalism']). In Miskawayh's long discussion with a medically educated adversary about 'soul and intellect' (*Maqāla fī l-Nafs wa-l-ʿaql* [*266]), a duel battled out in ten rounds, this contrahent refers to Rufus of Ephesus, Galen's older contemporary, who in his treatise *On Melancholy* denied the possibility of transcendental knowledge. Even if desires and affections are bound to the body, the rational soul (or so the philosopher says) can still rise above the determination through the body in its act of intellectual perception; it can employ the disposition of the temperaments to further its ends, before finally obtaining the perfect certainty of truth after its separation from the body.

The philosopher agrees with the physician that 'all powers of the soul which are constituted by the body and the bodily organs will expire together with the corruption of the body', but for the philosopher, 'the soul, being a simple substance, in itself can dispense with these organs' (thus Miskawayh in his replies to questions posed by Abū Ḥayyān al-Tawḥīdī, *al-Hawāmil wa-l-šawāmil* [*252: 353]). While the body, upon death, breaks down into its simple elements, and abilities like sense perception, imagination and memory, which are tied to its organs, are lost, 'the soul, liberated from the body, supplies itself sufficiently with the intelligible forms that it contains, and that are called principles' [ibid.]. The survival of the rational soul grants the philosopher the highest activity of the rational power.

Given his strict opposition to the Stoics and 'several natural philosophers' for whom the soul's happiness is not conceivable without the happiness of the body, since the latter is a constituent part of the human being, the philosopher must face up to the question whether the highest happiness is at all realizable during psycho-somatic existence in this world. The philosophers before Aristotle, 'Pythagoras, Socrates, Plato and their likes, agreeing that the virtues generally belong to the soul alone, as does happiness', say that 'the human being will only be able to know the highest happiness when he has been freed from the body and everything natural'; for 'they call this [psychic] substance alone "man", without the body'; furthermore, 'only when it has escaped this impurity [of the body] will the soul become separate, purify itself and liberate itself from ignorance, receiving illumination and divine light, i.e. perfect intellect' (*Tahḏīb* [*273: 80–82, here 80,1–3. 81,4–6. 11–14. 82,2–7]; cf. Walzer 1956 [*546: 224–226]). The other school, that of Aristotle, regards man, in accordance with his essential definition, as a being who is composed of body and soul, rational as well as mortal. They believe that all human beings seek and find their happiness in accordance with their capabilities and needs. The philosopher calls all this happiness, even if he makes distinctions in rank, according to the stipulations of reason. This school (one cannot help thinking of al-Fārābī, even if Miskawayh does not mention him by name) professes the unity of the human being, of the soul and its body. The body contributes constitution, appetite and the ability of self-preservation, as well as procuring contents of knowledge from the substances, for the use of the higher mental faculties, too – imagination, will, and thinking. This is documented by eloquent polemics against a too rigid interpretation of Socrates' example, the Platonic *meditatio mortis* (cf. Dodds 1951 [*504: 207–235, 'Plato and the irrational soul', esp. 212–213], Walzer 1985 [*517: 500]; cf. also Hein 1985 [*516: 98–99] on voluntary death, ϑάνατος προαιρετικός, as a topos of philosophical propaedeutics – in Miskawayh e.g. *al-Fawz* II 8 [*264: 89], *Tahḏīb* VI 2 [*273: 212], *Maqāla fī l-Nafs wa-l-ʿaql* [*266: 55 Arkoun; 96–97 Badawī]). Elements of this criticism can also be found in Miskawayh's ambivalent position, even if for him it is the perfection of the rational soul (the purification of character [*tahḏīb al-aḫlāq*], thus the title of his ethics) which alone can lead to the highest wisdom and to true happiness. By contrast, when speaking of human happiness, Aristotle is thinking of the human being composed of body and soul; hence he reasons 'that human happiness will be obtained by man in this world, if he expends his efforts to strive for it, until he reaches the highest level' (*Tahḏīb* [*273: 82]). With Aristotle, Miskawayh represents an ethics whose ideal of virtue is manifested in people's interactions, and a concept of happiness which man as a political being can seek and experience.

The casuistry of ethical interactions in chapters II to V of *Tahḏīb al-aḫlāq* closely follows Aristotle, whose *Kitāb al-Aḫlāq* (i.e. the *Nicomachean Ethics*, which is the only one of the great ethical works to be translated into Arabic), is more or less excerpted by Miskawayh, considering the numerous quotations. This applies in particular to the detailed description of political ethics – justice in state and society (ch. IV) – and the social ethics of love and friendship (ch. V).

Aristotle's classification of the good is reported 'as transmitted by Porphyry and others'. The classification distinguishes between the absolute good and the relative good according to value and purpose (*Tahḏīb* III 2 [*273:

76–79]). The degrees of happiness follow the grades of the good – health, wealth, honour, success, prudence – and are determined by them. (III 3 [*273: 79–86]).

The path of perfection leads in several steps from the first to the highest perfection, and finally to the utmost happiness, which is beyond the corporeal world. However, even the highest form of happiness needs to be manifested externally in the actions of a virtuous life (Aristotle, *Nicomachean Ethics* 1098a16–17, 1099b26). As long as the happy person lives in the world of generation and corruption he will be subject to the same vicissitudes of fate as everybody else, but he will bear them with equanimity. But can we call a human being in this world truly happy, while his fortune can still turn, or can we do that only after he has died? Happiness presupposes not only ethical perfection, but also the completion of life, so as to bring it to maturity (here the text has a reference to Priam's fate, after *Nicomachean Ethics* I 10, 1100a4–14). Aristotle seems to presuppose the immortality of the soul and the completion of its happiness after death, when he asserts that true happiness is by definition permanent and unchangeable, yet during their lifetime, humans inevitably experience changes and misfortunes – so that no one ought to be called happy as long as he lives. On the other hand, it would be absurd to say that a human being will only be absolutely happy once he dies. No, the truly happy person, who always puts virtue into practice, preserves the foundations of happiness even when misfortunes arise (*Nicomachean Ethics* I 12, 1100b18–1101a14; *Tahḏīb* III 4 [*273: 86–91]).

The cardinal virtue of justice is nothing but the adherence to equal measure (*musāwāt*), which is a reproduction of unity, and ultimately of divine unity. Absolute justice is seldom put into practice; oftentimes we can only observe a fixed, even proportion, for instance in the execution of external justice in the apportionment of reward, in the recompense of deserts, in trade, and as reparation for injustice (*Nicomachean Ethics* V 4–5, 1130a30–1131a9). According to Aristotle, the law (*nāmūs*, νόμος) is threefold: first there is the light coming from God; then the law of the ruler; and thirdly, the νόμος of money as quantitative measurement of commensurable mutual service (νόμισμα, *Nicomachean Ethics* V 8, 1133a30–31). With respect to the observance of one's duties towards God, as well as towards one's fellow human beings, justice is fair balance and correct mean, and hence the epitome of all virtue. It is a disposition of the soul, not an action or a capability, but a habit which enables one to act justly (*Tahḏīb* IV 1 [*273: 105–119]).

The manifestations of love (*maḥabba*; *Tahḏīb* V 1 [*273: 135–137]), its depth and its constancy are determined by its purpose: pleasure, benefit, or the good. Friendship (*ṣadāqa*) is a special kind of love [137], it is the affection (*mawadda*) between individuals; by contrast, amorous passion (*ʿišq*) is excessive love, bent on pleasure and hence reprehensible. In addition to their psycho-somatic nature, human beings also have a simple, divine substance in them which alone bestows pure, unadulterated pleasure: this is divine love [138–139], the desire to become one with God (referring to Aristotle, *Nicomachean Ethics* VIII 2, 1155a32-b8). Once a man liberates himself from the turbidities of his corporeal nature, he will see the First and Pure Good with the eye of reason, and the light of the First Good will stream upon him and will give him unequalled pleasure (cf. al-Kindī, *al-Qawl fī l-Nafs*; on this point see p. 166 above).

Humans' innate inclination to society (*uns*) is an important factor of social cohesion. Here, within the context of friendship rather than that of ethical principles or religious instruction of any kind, we find passages referring to Islamic religion as means of strengthening the community: law (*al-šarīʿa*) and custom promote regular gatherings, like the daily five prayers in the mosque and the obligatory convention of all people of a city or a quarter for Friday prayers, in order to unite in the praise of God and the surrender to His law. Thus religion creates the God-given conditions for happiness. The leader of the religious community (*imām*) hence corresponds in his significance to that of the king as the guardian of this community (here Miskawayh quotes the famous saying of the Sasanian Ardašīr: 'Religion and kingship are twin brothers. Religion is the fundament, kingship the guardian'). An analysis of the various forms of love – between members of a family, of social and political groups – closes with the first love of God, followed by the love of one's parents and the philosopher's love to his teacher (*Tahḏīb* V 1 [*273: 135–150]).

The virtues, which are necessary foundations for pure friendship and unadulterated love – preconditions for the happiness of man as a by nature political animal – must be fostered by external circumstances and social rules. They can only be realized within a community. Above the human virtues, which man forms and exercises within society, there stands divine virtue, which originates from the love of the highest good and the emulation of its activity. Only instruction and the constant aspiration to come closer to God and to become worthy of His love prepare the way to the highest happiness (*Tahḏīb* V 4 [*273:167–172]).

As Miskawayh adds, however, there are two degrees of virtue, and hence also two degrees of happiness: corporeal and spiritual (*rūḥānī*) happiness, of which only the latter is perfect [82–86]. Aristotle's scale of values, which lists the virtues and vices of the various parts of the soul, those looking towards the body, and the spiritual-rational ones, thus becomes part of the Platonic view of man. The chief witness of Miskawayh's synthesis is once again none other than Aristotle, or rather a treatise ascribed to him, *On the Virtues of the Soul* (*Faḍāʾil al-nafs*), which the author quotes extensively according to the Arabic version by Abū ʿUṯmān al-Dimašqī [86–90], for instance as follows: 'Once the actions of man have all become divine, they will arise from his innermost core and his real essence (*ʿan lubābihi wa-ḏātihi l-ḥaqīqiyya*). This is his divine intellect, his true essence. Therefore all calls of his bodily nature will ebb away' [88,9–12]; for the text cf. Pines 1956 [*545: here 12 / 164; cf. 32–33 / 184–185]). This is the Aristotle of the spirit of the age, as he can be heard in numerous texts by Miskawayh and other thinkers of his milieu. His spokesman, significantly, is Porphyry, who reports on Aristotle's classification of the good (*Tahḏīb* [*273: 76–77]) and in a contemporary book on *On Happiness and Its Creation in Human Life* (al-ʿĀmirī [?], *Kitāb al-Saʿāda wa-l-isʿād*) is quoted with definitions of 'human' and 'divine' happiness: 'Happiness is the entelechy of the human being with reference to its form; the perfection of a human being as human being is constituted by his voluntary acts, while his perfection as angel (*malak*) and intellect will be achieved by speculative thought' (*al-Saʿāda wa-l-isʿād* [§ 5.2.3 *211: 5–6]; cf. Porphyry, *Sentences* § 32. 35 [*245: 22–35. 39–41]; Walzer 1965 [*553: 293]).

5 Bridging the Gap between the Kindian Tradition and the Baghdad School: Ibn Hindū

Cleophea Ferrari

5.1 Primary Sources – 5.2 Life – 5.3 Works – 5.4 Doctrine

5.1 *Primary Sources*

5.1.1 Bio-bibliographical Testimonies [*301–*311] – 5.1.2 Collection of Works [*315] – 5.1.3 Individual Works [*321–*324]

5.1.1 Bio-bibliographical Testimonies

301 Miskawayh, Abū ʿAlī Aḥmad b. Muḥammad (d. 421/1030). *Taǧārib al-umam*. – Ed. by Henry Frederic Amedroz and David Samuel Margoliouth, *The Eclipse of the ʿAbbasid Caliphate*, 4 vols [3–4 = *Continuation of the Experiences of the nations by Abū Shujāʿ Rūḏrāwarī and Hilāl ibn Muḥassin*], Oxford 1920–1921. – Arab. text, ed. by H. F. Amedroz, Cairo 1332–1334/1914–1916.

302 al-Ṯaʿālibī, Abū Manṣūr ʿAbd al-Malik b. Muḥammad (d. 429/1038). *Yatīmat al-dahr fī maḥāsin ahl al-ʿaṣr*. – Ed. by Muḥammad Muḥyī l-Dīn ʿAbd al-Ḥamīd, vol. 3. Cairo 1956 (2nd ed.), 397.

303 al-Ṯaʿālibī. *Tatimmat al-Yatīma*. – Ed. by ʿAbbās Iqbāl, vol. 1. Tehran 1953, 134.

304 al-Bāḫarzī, ʿAlī b. al-Ḥasan (d. 467/1075). *Dumyat al-qaṣr wa-ʿuṣrat ahl al-ʿaṣr*. – Ed. by Sāmī Makkī al-ʿĀnī, vol. 2. Baghdad, Najaf 1971, 62–71.
305 Yāqūt b. ʿAbd Allāh, al-Ḥamawī al-Rūmī al-Baġdādī (d. 626/1229). *Iršād al-arīb*. – Ed. by David Samuel Margoliouth, The *Irshād al-arīb ilā maʿrifat al-adīb or Dictionary of Learned Men of Yāqūt*, vol. 5. London 1911, 168–173.
306 Ibn al-Naǧǧār, Muḥibb Allāh b. Maḥāsin al-Baġdādī (d. 643/1245). *Ḏayl Taʾrīḫ Baġdād*. – Ed. by Caesar E. Farah, vol. 18. Hyderabad 1402/1982, 354.
307 Ibn al-Qifṭī, Ǧamāl al-Dīn ʿAlī b. Yūsuf (d. 646/1248). *Taʾrīḫ al-ḥukamāʾ* [*Iḫbār al-ʿulamāʾ bi-aḫbār al-ḥukamāʾ*, epitome by Muḥammad b. ʿAlī al-Zawzanī]. – Ed. by Julius Lippert, *Ibn al-Qifṭī's Taʾrīḫ al-ḥukamāʾ*. Leipzig 1903, 233.
308 Ibn Abī Uṣaybiʿa, Muwaffaq al-Dīn Aḥmad b. al-Qāsim (d. 668/1270). *ʿUyūn al-anbāʾ fī ṭabaqāt al-aṭibbāʾ*. – Ed. by August Müller, vol. 1. Cairo 1299/1882, Königsberg 1884, 323–327.
309 al-Šahrazūrī, Šams al-Dīn Muḥammad b. Maḥmūd (d. after 687/1288). *Rawḍat al-afrāḥ wa-nuzhat al-arwāḥ* (MS Berlin, Staatsbibliothek, arab. 6215 Ahlwardt) fols 57^a30–57^b22. – French summary in: Emily Cottrell, *Le Kitâb Nuzhat al-arwâḥ wa-rawḍat al-afrâḥ de Shams al-Dîn al-Shahrazûrî al-Ishrâqî, composition et sources*. PhD Diss., École des hautes études pratiques, Paris 2004, section IV, no. 24.
310 Ibn Faḍl Allāh al-ʿUmarī (d. 749/1349). *Masālik al-abṣār fī mamālik al-amṣār*. – Ed. by Fuat Sezgin, in collaboration with A. Jokhosha and Eckhard Neubauer, *Routes Toward Insight into the Capital Empires*, book 9. Frankfurt a.M. 1988, 30–33.
311 al-Kutubī, Abū ʿAbd Allāh Muḥammad b. Šākir (d. 764/1363). *Fawāt al-wafayāt*. – Ed. by Iḥsān ʿAbbās, vol. 3. Beirut 1974, 9–14.

5.1.2 Collection of Works

315 Saḥbān Ḫalīfāt (Khalifat). *Ibn Hindū: Sīratuhu, ārāʾuhu al-falsafiyya, muʾallafātuhu, dirāsa wa-nuṣūṣ*, 2 vols [Ibn Hindu. Biography, philosophy, and his works, a critical edition with study]. Amman 1995.

5.1.3 Individual Works

321 *Muqtaṭafāt min al-Risāla al-mušawwiqa fī l-falsafa*. – Ed. by S. Ḫalīfāt [**315*: I 195–201].
322 *Maqāla fī Waṣf al-maʿād al-falsafī*. – Ed. by S. Ḫalīfāt [**315*: I 227–251].
323 *Al-Kalim al-rūḥāniyya min al-ḥikam al-yūnāniyya*. – Ed. by S. Ḫalīfāt [**315*: I 307–480]. – Ed. Muṣṭafā al-Qabbānī al-Dimašqī. Cairo 1318/1900.
324 *Miftāḥ al-Ṭibb wa-minhāǧ al-ṭullāb*. – Ed. by Muḥammad Muḥaqqiq, Muḥammad Taqī Dānišpažūh. Tehran 1368/1989. – Ed. by S. Ḫalīfāt [**315*: II 571–785]. – Partial Engl. transl. by A. Shiloah 1972 [*682].

5.2 *Life*

Abū l-Farağ ʿAlī b. al-Ḥusayn Ibn Hindū was born into a a Shiite family tracing their origins back to ʿAlī's younger son al-Ḥusayn in Qum in the year 335/946. In 342/953 the family moved to Rayy, where Ibn Hindū spent many years, and where he returned time and again during the course of his life. Frequent changes of place in any case were a determining factor in his biography: always in search for a prestigious position to earn his living, he sold his services at the courts of various rulers (cf. the references in Ḫalīfāt 1995 [*672: I 11–95]).

Initially he worked in Arrağān, as a secretary (*kātib al-inšāʾ*) in the administration of the Buyid ʿAḍud al-Dawla (from 338/944 sovereign ruler of Fārs) – to be exact, in the services of his vizier Abū l-Faḍl Ibn al-ʿAmīd (Miskawayh, *Tağārib al-umam* [*301: II 279,7]). In 369/979 Ibn Hindū returned to Rayy and took a position with the vizier of Muʾayyid al-Dawla, al-Ṣāḥib Ibn ʿAbbād (al-Ṯaʿālibī, *Yatīma* [*302: I 142]). There he began to be educated in literary *adab*, poetry and the art of writing (*Yatīma* [*302: III 397]). In 372–373/982–983 he left this position with the Ṣāḥib, which had become endangered by intrigues, and moved to Nishapur, where he devoted himself, among other things, to studying philosophy with Abū l-Ḥasan al-ʿĀmirī (§ 5.2.3). Between 375/985 and 380/990 he went on to Baghdad; here, Abū l-Ḫayr al-Ḥasan b. Suwār Ibn al-Ḫammār (cf. § 7.4) became his teacher in medicine and philosophy (Ibn Abī Uṣaybiʿa, *ʿUyūn* [*308: I 323,26]).

In 380/990 Ibn Hindū moved again to Nishapur in order to take up an official position with the Ziyārid Šams al-Maʿālī Qābūs b. Wušmgīr. He also followed Šams al-Maʿālī to Ğurğān in 388/998, but any expectations he may have had of being given a higher position were disappointed. When Bahāʾ al-Dawla, the son of ʿAḍud al-Dawla, had become emir of Fārs and overlord of the entire East (388/991), Ibn Hindū, in 391/994, went to Shiraz; but the Buyid ruler did not fulfil his hopes either. It took Ibn Hindū until 403/1012 to seek out yet another opportunity: Faḫr al-Mulk, whom he had met in Fārs, was installed as the vizier of the chief emir, Sulṭān al-Dawla. Ibn Hindū followed him to Baghdad, but once again the panegyric odes he dedicated to the vizier fell on deaf ears (Yāqūt, *Iršād* [*305: V 169] after Abū Ğaʿfar Aḥmad b. Muḥammad b. Sahl al-Harawī; al-Kutubī, *Fawāt* [*311: III 309]).

Further stages took him to Ğurğān, Nishapur, Qazwīn, Rayy, again Ğurğān and, finally, Daylam. In Daylam he dedicated a panegyric poem to Nāṭiq bi-l-Ḥaqq Sayyid Abū Ṭālib Yaḥyā, Shiite imam of the province from 421/1030, on the occasion of his taking office. According to his son, Abū l-Šaraf ʿImād, Ibn Hindū died in 423/1032 in Astarābāḏ (Ibn al-Nağğār, *Ḏayl* [*306: XVIII 354]; according to al-Kutubī, *Fawāt* [*311: III 13] he died already in 420/1029).

Even though a well-known scholar in philosophy, logic, and medicine, Ibn Hindū was very much at home in the administrative milieu and 'dressed in the fashion of the secretaries' (*yalbas al-durrāʿa ʿalā rasm al-kuttāb*, Yāqūt, *Iršād* [**305*: v 169]; al-Kutubī, *Fawāt* [**311*: III 9–14]). While being a court official, he gained fame also as a man of letters (*adīb*), in poetry, philology and literary prose. His poetical work ensured him a place in the anthologies compiled by al-Ṯaʿālibī and his successor al-Bāḫarzī.

Ibn Hindū encountered many famous scholars of the Islamic East, for instance the *Qāḍī l-quḍāt* ʿAbd al-Ǧabbār, who lived in Rayy from 360/970–971 up to his death in 415/1025. The historian Abū Naṣr al-ʿUtbī (author of the Ghaznavid chronicle *al-Taʾrīḫ al-Yamīnī*) worked together with Ibn Hindū in the service of the Ziyārid Qābūs in Ǧurǧān. There he also met the astronomer Abū l-Rayḥān al-Bīrūnī, who during the years 389–400/998–1010 was working in Ǧurǧān, and who cites Ibn Hindū in several of his medico-scientific writings.

5.3 *Works*

5.3.1 Philosophical Propaedeutics – 5.3.2 Philosophical Theology – 5.3.3 Medical Theory

5.3.1 Philosophical Propaedeutics

al-Risāla al-mušawwiqa fī [*al-madḫal ilā ʿilm*] *al-falsafa*
Epistle Promoting Philosophy [or: *Promoting the Introduction to the Science of Philosophy*]

The longer form of the title follows Ibn Hindū's own reference to the work in *Miftāḥ al-ṭibb* [**324*: 572]). The text is only preserved in excerpts (*multaqaṭāt*) in manuscript form.

The epistle serves as an introduction to Aristotelian philosophy. It is divided in seven chapters (largely following the 'headings' of the introductory literature of the Alexandrians), dealing with the fundament of and the reason for philosophical thought, definition and division of philosophy, and, above all, logic.

Philosophy is possible for human beings because they alone among the living beings possess the ability for rational thought. Philosophy is defined as the furthest assimilation to the divine ability of discerning good and bad, as well as the corresponding actions, that is possible in accordance with human capabilities. It is divided into practical philosophy (ethics, economics, politics) and theoretical philosophy (physics, metaphysics, mathematics). Logic is the instrument of philosophy, which helps to distinguish the false from the true in the sciences, and the good and the bad in the realm of action. It is called *manṭiq* because it trains the ability to articulate oneself (*al-quwwa al-nuṭqiyya*) and in this way develops reason as the true property of a human being. The rank of man is defined by the art of logic, which itself takes up the highest rank among the arts. The last two chapters are concerned with the enumeration and classification of the Aristotelian writings; here Ibn Hindū counts all eight books of the *Organon* among the logical works.

5.3.2 Philosophical Theology

Maqāla fī Waṣf al-maʿād al-falsafī
Philosophical Description of the Hereafter

The text consists of twelve chapters on the soul and its fate in the hereafter. The particular topics Ibn Hindū discusses are the nature of the soul (its existence is presupposed), its influence, the differences between the human soul and other souls, and the question which souls will be able to live on after death, and under which conditions.

5.3.3 Medical Theory

Kitāb Miftāḥ al-ṭibb
The Key to Medicine

Introductory work for students (GAS [*663: III 334–335. 414]; Ullmann 1970 [*664: 152]) in ten chapters, whose design closely follows the so-called *prolegomena* of late ancient commentaries on Aristotle's works, in particular the *Categories*.

The text discusses the definition of medicine as well as its rank, its parts, its various schools and the requirements a capable physician will have to fulfil. Chapter 9 explains the medical curriculum and presents an account of the *Summaria Alexandrinorum* of the Galenic canon, i.e. of Galen's *Sixteen Books*, which goes back to Ibn Hindū's teacher Ibn al-Ḫammār (cf. § 7.4) (*mā tarǧama lī ustāḏī Abū l-Ḫayr Ibn al-Ḫammār min maḏhabihim fī ḏālika*; Dietrich 1966 [*662: 198–202]; ed. Ḫalīfāt [*324: 632–640]).

Both the theory of science presented in the introductory chapter and the pharmacological doctrine in chapter 8 contain intriguing remarks about the therapeutic use of music (ed. Ḫalīfāt [*324: 630. 742–743]; cf. Shiloah 1972 [*682]). Also important is the long final chapter (ch. 10: *fī l-ʿibārāt wa-l-ḥudūd*, ed. Ḫalīfāt [*324: 641–785]) on the basic concepts and technical terms of logic and medicine.

5.4 *Doctrine*

Ibn Hindū studied with the Baghdad Aristotelians; his introductory writings are part of their – i.e. the Alexandrian – tradition. With his Platonic intellectualist ethics and his Neoplatonic psychology he is at the same time indebted to the Kindian tradition as it was carried on by the Eastern philosophers: by his teacher al-ʿĀmirī (§ 5.2.2) and his contemporary Miskawayh (§ 5.4, like he himself working within the circle of the Buyid administration).

Propaedeutics. – As Ibn Hindū points out in his introductory work *al-Risāla al-mušawwiqa fī l-falsafa* (*Epistle Promoting Philosophy*), humans are the only living beings capable of thought. Hence the exercise of philosophical thinking is the noblest activity they can pursue, as in doing so they will draw closer to the divine sphere. In making the assimilation to God the decisive criterion, Ibn Hindū's definition of philosophy here deviates from the Aristotelian approach transmitted in the Arabic tradition. Gifted with logic, man possesses the instrument for distinguishing truth from falsehood; therefore he will also need logic to do the good, since it is only with its help that he can recognize the good in the first place.

Ibn Hindū had a profound knowledge of logic, especially of Aristotle's *Categories*; this may well be linked to the fact that his teachers were active as commentators in this field. His teacher Ibn al-Ḫammār, for instance, composed commentaries on Porphyry's *Isagoge* and the *Categories* (Georr 1948 [*681: 361–386], cf. also § 7.4); from al-ʿĀmirī's pen we also have some annotations to the *Categories*, which his pupil would have been able to consult (Türker 1965 [§ 5.2 **131*], Wakelnig 2006 [§ 5.2 *231: 42]).

Philosophical theology. – In his *Maqāla fī Waṣf al-maʿād al-falsafī* (*Philosophical Description of the Hereafter*) Ibn Hindū studies the properties of the soul, in particular the rational soul. In contrast to the embodied organisms, which consist of mixtures, the soul is unmixed, of one substance. Its existence is not disputed, as it is obvious; what is discussed is merely its form and its mortality. Ibn Hindū emphasizes that the soul is not constituted from the four elements and their mixtures. He shares the Aristotelian view that the soul can be neither body nor accident, but in contrast to Aristotle he holds the view that it is an incorporeal substance.

As souls need to produce some effect in order to exist, it stands to reason that they cannot subsist without a body. While this applies to all those souls that are not rational, it does not apply to the rational soul. Its specific activity allows it to grasp the reality of existent things, be they limited (if material) or unlimited (if immaterial). This means that in occupying itself with the rational sciences (*al-ʿulūm al-ʿaqliyya*) it will reach its perfection, as it will receive things that will remain with it and will not perish. In contrast, its occupation with knowledge based on sense perception (*al-ʿulūm al-ḥissiyya*) only ever elicits sensual impressions in the soul, like images in a mirror which will naturally disappear again. This is what characterizes the human soul. The animal soul does not possess equal possibilities, which is why a donkey cannot learn philosophy, or rule over cities (*Maqāla* [**315*: I 236]).

A return, i.e. a continued existence, of the rational soul is possible, but not in the sense that it will wander from one place to another. For once the body has dissolved, the soul will be free from all corporeal accidents. It does, however, retain a disposition for the good or the bad, and accordingly will feel joy or pain, receiving reward or punishment.

Medical theory. – Given that man is the noblest of the living beings due to his rationality, while at the same time being the subject of the physician's art, this art must be the noblest of them all, because the rank of an art depends on its foundations as well as its end. Ibn Hindū here puts the art of medicine on the same level as logic, which he also claims to be an art of the highest rank. In his *Kitāb Miftāḥ al-ṭibb* (*The Key to Medicine*) we can see him follow the late ancient Greek school tradition: the foundations of medical science are the Greek authors, of which he names Hippocrates and Galen, as well as Soranus. Medicine is furthermore embedded in the late ancient curriculum as a whole, whose most important instrument is Aristotelian logic.

Ibn Hindū thus continues the school tradition of his teachers. His teacher in Baghdad, Ibn al-Ḫammār (cf. § 7.4) composed *prolegomena* on Aristotle's *Categories* (Georr 1948 [*681: 361–386]), while at the same time engaging with medical topics and discussing Galen's famous dictum that a physician ought to be a philosopher. He turned this postulation on its head, however, arguing that a philosopher ought to be a physician, since medicine was a part of philosophy (ed. Ḫalīfāt [*324: 627]). His pupil Ibn Hindū reports this discussion in *Miftāḥ al-ṭibb*, and takes the side of his teacher.

6 Secondary Literature

6.1 Works of Reference [*1–*7] – 6.2 Al-Kindī's School [*11–*153] – 6.3 Neoplatonic Developments [*171–*242] – 6.4 The Integration of Philosophical Traditions in Muslim Society in the 4th/10th Century [*260–*429] – 6.5 Abū ʿAlī Miskawayh [*441–*644] – 6.6 Ibn Hindū [*661–*684]

6.1 *Works of Reference*

1 GAL = Brockelmann, Carl. *Geschichte der arabischen Litteratur*, 2 vols, 3 suppl. vols. Leiden, 1937–1949 (2nd ed.). – Edition adapted to the supplementary volumes.

2 EI² = *The Encyclopaedia of Islam: New edition*. Ed. by Clifford Edmund Bosworth et al., 11 vols, 6 suppl. vols. Leiden, 1960–2005.

3 GAS = Sezgin, Fuat. *Geschichte des arabischen Schrifttums*, 17 vols. Leiden, Frankfurt a.M., 1967–2015.

4 EIr = *Encyclopaedia Iranica*. Ed. by Ehsan Yarshater, vols 1 ff. London, 1982 ff.

5 Daiber, Hans. *Bibliography of Islamic Philosophy*, 2 vols. Leiden, Boston, 1999. – Supplement (2007).

6 D'Ancona, Cristina, ed. *The Libraries of the Neoplatonists: Proceedings of the Meeting of the European Science Foundation Network 'Late Antiquity and Arabic Thought: Patterns in the Constitution of European Culture' held in Strasbourg, March 12–14, 2004*. Leiden, Boston, 2007.

7 *Encyclopaedia of Islam*, THREE [EI Three]. Ed. by Marc Gaborieau et al., vol. 1 ff. Leiden, 2007 ff.

6.2 *Al-Kindī's School*

6.2.1 Aḥmad b. al-Ṭayyib al-Sarahsī [*11–*38] – 6.2.2 Abū Zayd al-Balhī [*41–*101] – 6.2.3 Ibn Farīġūn [*111–*153]

6.2.1 Aḥmad b. al-Ṭayyib al-Sarahsī

6.2.1.1 *Bibliography and Biography*

11 GAL [*1: I 231–232; S I 375].

12 GAS [*3: III 259; V 263; VI 162–163; VII 137. 269; IX 233; X 136. 316. 323. 560. 563; XII 11 (map 2); XIII 242–245. 414. 415; XIV 180. 220. 439. 440].

13 Glagow, Rainer. *Das Kalifat des al-Muʿtaḍid billāh (892–902)*. PhD Diss., University of Bonn, 1968) 152–159. – On al-Sarahsī's downfall under al-Muʿtaḍid bi-llāh.

6.2.1.2 *General Surveys*

17 Rosenthal, Franz. *Aḥmad b. aṭ-Ṭayyib as-Sarahsī*. New Haven, Conn., 1943.

18 Rosenthal, Franz. "al-Sarakhsī." In EI^2 [*2: IX 35].

6.2.1.3 *Individual Works and Topics*

25 Kraus, Paul. *Jābir ibn Ḥayyān: Contribution à l'histoire des idées scientifiques dans l'Islam*, vol 2: *Jābir et la science grecque*. Cairo, 1942, repr. Paris, 1986, 61–62 n. 2. 171–172 n. 2. 245 n. 2. 251–252 n. 2. – Al-Sarahsī's remarks (after Ḥamza al-Iṣfahānī's *Kitāb al-Tanbīh fī ḥudūṯ at-taṣḥīf*) on the geographical distribution of the philosophical schools; on his 'universal alphabet' for recording the sounds of foreign languages; on the difference between Arabic grammar and logic (LW °19).

26 Rosenthal, Franz. "From Arabic Books and Manuscripts, IV: New Fragments of as-Sarahsī." *Journal of the American Oriental Society* 71 (1951): 135–142. – On two geographical works by al-Sarahsī (LW °30, 32) as well as his *Ris. Mirāḥ al-rūḥ* (LW °38).

27 Rosenthal, Franz. "From Arabic Books and Manuscripts, VI: Istanbul Materials for al-Kindī and as-Sarahsī." *Journal of the American Oriental Society* 76 (1956):

27–31, here 29 and 31. – Four *dicta* by al-Saraḫsī from ʿUmar b. Sahlān al-Sāwī's (ca. 1145) *Muḫtaṣar Ṣiwān al-ḥikma*; reference to *Kitāb Ǧawāmiʿ al-laḏḏa* by ʿAlī b. Naṣr al-Kātib [**11*].

28 Rosenthal, Franz. "From Arabic Books and Manuscripts, VIII: As-Saraḫsī on Love." *Journal of the American Oriental Society* 81 (1961): 222–224. – Cf. LW °16.

29 Moosa, Matti. "A New Source on Aḥmad ibn al-Ṭayyib al-Sarakhsī: Florentine Ms Arabic 299." *Journal of the American Oriental Society* 92 (1972): 19–24. – On al-Saraḫsī's debate with the bishop of Kashkar.

30 Schoeler, Gregor. "Verfasser und Titel des dem Ǧāḥiẓ zugeschriebenen sog. Kitāb at-Tāǧ." *Zeitschrift der Deutschen Morgenländischen Gesellschaft* 130 (1980): 217–225. – On the model for *Kitāb Ādāb al-mulūk* (LW °24).

31 Kropp, Manfred. "Kitāb al-Badʾ wa-t-taʾrīḫ von Abū l-Ḥasan ʿAlī ibn Aḥmad ibn ʿAlī ibn Aḥmad aš-Šāwī al-Fāsī und sein Verhältnis zu dem Kitāb al-Ǧaʿrafiyya von az-Zuhrī." In *Proceedings of the Ninth Congress of the Union européenne des arabisants et islamisants, Amsterdam* […] *1978*. Ed. by Rudolph Peters. Leiden, 1981, 153–168. – On al-Kindī's and al-Saraḫsī's world map for the caliph al-Maʾmūn; reproduction of a late copy of the map facing p. 160, its description p. 166–167.

32 Endress, Gerhard. "Grammatik und Logik: Arabische Philologie und griechische Philosophie im Widerstreit." In *Sprachphilosophie in Antike und Mittelalter*. Ed. by Burkhard Mojsisch. Amsterdam, 1986, 163–299 (esp. 189 with n. 51 and 52). – On al-Saraḫsī's treatise on the difference between Arabic grammar and logic (LW °19) and his 'universal alphabet'.

33 Gutas, Dimitri. "Plato's Symposion in the Arabic Tradition." *Oriens* 31 (1988): 36–60 (esp. 42 with n. 25). – Repr. in: D. Gutas, *Greek Philosophers in the Arabic Tradition*. Aldershot, 2000, no. IV. – On al-Saraḫsī's description of the religious view of the Sabians (LW °1).

34 Holmberg, Bo. *A Treatise on the Unity and Trinity of God by Israel of Kashkar (d. 872): Introduction, edition and word index*. Lund, 1989, 50–56. – On al-Saraḫsī's debate with the bishop of Kashkar.

35 Daiber, Hans. "Qosṭā Ibn Lūqā (9. Jh.) über die Einteilung der Wissenschaften." *Zeitschrift für Geschichte der Arabisch-Islamischen Wissenschaften* 6 (1990): 93–129.

36 Endress, Gerhard. "Al-Kindī über die Wiedererinnerung der Seele: Arabischer Platonismus und die Legitimation der Wissenschaften im Islam." *Oriens* 34 (1994): 174–221.

37 Rosenthal, Franz. "From Arabic Books and Manuscripts, XVI: As-Saraḫsī (?) on the Appropriate Behavior of Kings." *Journal of the American Oriental Society* 115 (1995): 105–109. – Cf. LW °24.

38 van Ess, Josef. *Theologie und Gesellschaft im 2. und 3. Jahrhundert Hidschra: Eine Geschichte des religiösen Denkens im frühen Islam*, vol. 4. Berlin, New York, 1997,

332–333. 725. – Cf. LW °2, on the term *maḫāriq*, 'fabrications'; on al-Saraḫsī's debate with the bishop of Kashkar.

6.2.2 Abū Zayd al-Balḫī

6.2.2.1 *Bibliography and Biography*

41 GAL [*1: S I 408].

42 GAS [*3: III 274–275. 287–288; IV 291; VI 190–191; VII 24; IX 97. 189; X 346; XIV 15–19. 189–191. 192–196. 429. 439; XV 55. 68. 71. 76].

43 Barthold, Wilhelm. *Turkestan Down to the Mongol Invasion*. London, 1968 (3rd ed.), 12. 245–246. – On Abū Zayd's patron, the Samanid vizier Muḥammad b. Aḥmad al-Ǧayhānī.

44 Hau, Friedrun R. "Razis Gutachten über Rosenschnupfen." *Medizinhistorisches Journal* 10 (1975): 94–102.

45 van Ess, Josef. "Abu'l-Qāsem al-Balḵī al-Kaʿbī." In EIr [*4: I 359–362]. – On the prominent Muʿtazilite, correspondent and friend of Abū Zayd.

46 Ḫalīfāt, Saḥbān. *Rasāʾil Abī l-Ḥasan al-ʿĀmirī wa-šaḏarātuhū l-falsafiyya*. Amman, 1988, 163–172. – Cf. also ed. Ḫalīfāt, *Fihris al-aʿlām* s.v. al-Balḫī, p. 531. – Abū Zayd's influence on his pupil al-ʿĀmirī; Abū Zayd's remarks on the office and the virtues of the vizier and on politics (*siyāsa*).

47 de Blois, François. "Shuhayd al-Balkhī, a Poet and Philosopher of the Time of Rāzī." *Bulletin of the School of Oriental and African Studies* 59 (1996): 333–337. – On a companion of Abū Zayd.

48 Bungy, Gholam Ali et al. "Razi's Report about Seasonal Allergic Rhinitis (Hay Fever) from the 10th Century A.D." *International Archives of Allergy and Immunology* 110 (1996): 219–224.

49 Wakelnig, Elvira. *Feder, Tafel, Mensch: Al-ʿĀmirīs Kitāb al-Fuṣūl fī l-Maʿālim al-ilāhīya und die arabische Proklos-Rezeption im 10. Jh.* Leiden, Boston, 2006, 9–11. – Abū Zayd as teacher of al-ʿĀmirī.

50 Adamson, Peter. "Platonic Pleasures in Epicurus and al-Rāzī." In *In the Age of al-Fārābī. Arabic Philosophy in the Fourth/Tenth Century*. Ed. by Peter Adamson. London, 2008, 71–94. – For Šuhayd b. al-Ḥusayn al-Balḫī, a companion of Abū Zayd, cf. 90–92.

51 Marlow, Louise. "Abū Zayd al-Balkhī and the *Naṣīḥat al-mulūk* of Pseudo-Mawārdī." *Der Islam* 93 (2016): 35–64. Abū Zayd's and Abū l-Qāsim al-Balkhī's 'close associations' with a 10th-century mirror for princes usually ascribed to al-Māwardī.

6.2.2.2 *General Surveys*

61 Dunlop, Douglas Morton. "al-Balkhī, Abū Zayd Aḥmad b. Sahl." In EI^2 [*2: I 1002–1003].

62 Watt, William Montgomery. "Abū Zayd Aḥmad b. Sahl Balḵī." In EIr [*4: I 399–400].

63 Rowson, Everett K. "The Philosopher as Littérateur: Al-Tawḥīdī and his Predecessors." *Zeitschrift für Geschichte der Arabisch-Islamischen Wissenschaften* 6 (1990): 50–92. – On Abū Zayd: 61–70.

64 Kutluer, İlhan. "Belhî, Ebû Zeyd." In *Türkiye Diyanet Vakfı İslam Ansiklopedisi*, vol. 5. Istanbul, 1992, 412–414.

65 Muwaḥḥid, Ṣamad. "Abū Zaid-i Balḫī." In *Dā'irat al-ma'ārif-i buzurg-i islāmī*, vol. 5. Tehran, 1372 h.š./1993, 502–505 [Pers.].

66 Biesterfeldt, Hans Hinrich. "al-Balkhī, Abū Zayd." In EI Three [*7: I/4 32–33].

67 van Ess, Josef. *Der Eine und das Andere: Beobachtungen an islamischen häresiographischen Texten*, vol. 1. Berlin, New York, 2011, 328–385.

6.2.2.3 *Geography*

71 de Goeje, Michael Jan. "Die Iṣṭaḫrī-Balḫī-Frage." *Zeitschrift der Deutschen Morgenländischen Gesellschaft* 25 (1871): 42–58.

72 Kramers, Johannes Hendrik. "La question Balḫī – Iṣṭaḫrī – Ibn Ḥawqal et l'Atlas de l'Islam." *Acta Orientalia* 10 (1932): 9–30.

73 Bartol'd [Barthold], Vasilij Vladimirovič. Preface to: *Ḥudūd al-'ālam: 'The Regions of the World': A Persian Geography 372 A.H. – 982 A.D.: Translated and explained by V. Minorsky*. London, 1937, 15–23.

74 Miquel, André. *La géographie humaine du monde musulman jusqu'au milieu du 11e siècle*, vol. 1. Paris, La Haye, 1973, 80–85.

75 Tibbetts, Gerald R. "The Balkhī School of Geographers." In *The History of Cartography*, vol. 2.1. Ed. by John Brian Harley and David Woodward. Chicago, 1992, 108–136.

76 Savage-Smith, Emilie. "Memory and Maps." In *Culture and Memory in Medieval Islam: Essays in Honour of Wilferd Madelung*. Ed. by Farhad Daftary and Josef W. Meri. London, New York, 2003, 109–127.

6.2.2.4 *Maṣāliḥ al-abdān wa-l-anfus*

81 Biesterfeldt, Hans Hinrich. "Notes on Abû Zayd al-Balḫî's Medico-ethical Treatise Maṣâliḥ al-abdân wa-l-anfus." In *La signification du bas moyen âge dans l'histoire et la culture du monde musulman: Actes du 8me congrès de l'Union européenne des arabisants et islamisants, Aix-en-Provence 1976*. Aix-en-Provence, 1978, 29–34.

82 Waines, David. "Abū Zayd al-Balkhī on the Nature of Forbidden Drink: A Medieval Islamic Controversy." In *La alimentación en las culturas islámicas*. Ed. by Manuela Marín and David Waines. Madrid, 1994, 111–127. – Repr. in D. Waines, ed. *Patterns of Everyday Life*. Aldershot, 2002, 329–344.

83 Biesterfeldt, Hans Hinrich. "Ein Philosoph trinkt Wein." In *Alltagsleben und materielle Kultur in der arabischen Sprache und Literatur. Festschrift für Heinz Grotzfeld zum 70. Geburtstag*. Ed. by Thomas Bauer and Ulrike Stehli-Werbeck. Wiesbaden, 2005, 89–103.

6.2.2.5 *Miscellaneous*

91 Ritter, Hellmut. "Philologika, IX. Die vier Suhrawardī." *Der Islam* 24 (1937): 270–286; 25 (1938) 35–86. – Repr. in *Beiträge zur Erschließung der arabischen Handschriften in Istanbul und Anatolien*, vol. 2. Ed. by Fuat Sezgin et al. Frankfurt a.M., 1986, 94–162. – For *75 cf. p. 61–62 (repr. 137–138).

92 Wieber, Reinhard. *Das Schachspiel in der arabischen Literatur von den Anfängen bis zur zweiten Hälfte des 16. Jahrhunderts*. Walldorf, 1972, 27. 38. 151. 491. – On LW °73.

93 Badawī, ʿAbd al-Raḥmān, ed. *Aflāṭūn fī l-islām: Nuṣūṣ*. Tehran 1353 h.š./1974, 337–339. – Cf. [*50].

94 Rosenthal, Franz. *Gambling in Islam*. Leiden, 1975, 165–167. – On LW °73.

95 Bergé, Marc. *Pour un humanisme vécu: Abū Ḥayyān al-Tawḥīdī*. Damascus, 1979, 289–297. – Cf. also 433: Index général s.v. Balḫī. – On Abū Zayd's position within the polemics concerning philosophy and religion.

96 Bosworth, Clifford Edmund. "The Rulers of Chaghāniyān in Early Islamic Times." *Iran (Journal of the British Institute of Persian Studies)* 19 (1981): 1–20 (esp. 5–10). – On the Muḥtāǧid Abū ʿAlī, addressee of a letter from Abū Zayd (LW °113).

97 Kraemer, Joel L. *Humanism in the Renaissance of Islam: The Cultural Revival during the Buyid Age*. Leiden, 1986, 1992 (2nd ed.). – Cf. 306: Index s.v. al-Balkhī, a. Zayd.

98 Monnot, Guy. *Islam et religions*. Paris, 1986, 213–219. – On LW °71.

99 Rosenthal, Franz. "Abū Zayd al-Balkhī on Politics." In *The Islamic World, from Classical to Modern Times: Essays in Honor of Bernard Lewis*. Ed. by Clifford Edmund Bosworth et al. Princeton, 1989, 287–301. – On LW °85 and 86.

100 Daiber, Hans. *Naturwissenschaft bei den Arabern im 10. Jahrhundert n. Chr.: Briefe des Abū l-Faḍl Ibn al-ʿAmīd (gest. 360/970) an ʿAḍudaddaula*. Leiden, New York, Cologne, 1993, 48–49. 134–136. – Cf. *50.

101 Wakelnig, Elvira. "A New Version of Miskawayh's *Book of Triumph*: An Alternative Recension of *al-Fawz al-aṣghar* or the Lost *Fawz al-akbar*?" *Arabic Sciences and Philosophy* 19 (2009): 83–119.

6.2.3 Ibn Farīġūn

6.2.3.1 *Bibliography and Biography*

111 GAL [*1: S I 435].

112 GAS [*3: I 384. 388].

113 Bosworth, Clifford Edmund. “Ibn Farīghūn.” In EI² [*2: Supplement 386–387].
114 Bosworth, Clifford Edmund. “Āl-e Farīġūn.” In EIr [*4: I 756–758].
115 Bosworth, Clifford Edmund. “Āl-e Moḥtāj.” In EIr [*4: I 764–766].

6.2.3.2 *Textual Transmission and Textual History*

121 Derenbourg, Hartwig and Henri Paul Joseph Renaud. *Les manuscrits arabes de l'Escurial: Tome II, fascicule 3: Sciences exactes et sciences occultes*. Paris, 1941, 82–83.
122 Ritter, Hellmut. “Philologika, XIII: Arabische Handschriften in Anatolien und İstanbul (Fortsetzung).” *Oriens* 3 (1950): 83–85.

6.2.3.3 *On Ibn Farīġūn's Ǧawāmiʿ al-ʿulūm*

126 Dunlop, Douglas Morton. “The *Ǧawāmiʿ al-ʿulūm* of Ibn Farīġūn.” In *Zeki Velidi Togan'a armağan*. Istanbul, 1955, 348–353.
127 Minorsky, Vladimir. “Ibn Farīghūn and the *Ḥudūd al-ʿālam*.” In *A Locust's Leg: Studies in Honour of S. H. Taqizadeh*. Ed. by Walter Bruno Henning and Ehsan Yarshater. London, 1962, 189–196. – Repr. in: V. Minorsky, *Iranica: Twenty Articles*. Tehran, 1964, 327–332.
128 Rosenthal, Franz. *A History of Muslim Historiography*. Leiden, 1968 (2nd ed.), 34–36. 539–540.
129 Gutas, Dimitri. *Avicenna and the Aristotelian Tradition: Introduction to Reading Avicenna's Philosophical Works*. Leiden, 1988, 245–249. – Revised ed. Leiden, 2014, 278–282.
130 Biesterfeldt, Hans Hinrich. “Ibn Farīġūn's Chapter on Arabic Grammar in his Compendium of the Sciences.” In *Studies in the History of Arabic Grammar*, vol. 2. Ed. by Kees Versteegh and Michael G. Carter. Amsterdam, Philadelphia, 1990, 49–56.
131 Rebstock, Ulrich. *Rechnen im islamischen Orient: Die literarischen Spuren der praktischen Rechenkunst*. Darmstadt, 1992, 15–19.
132 Biesterfeldt, Hans Hinrich. “Ibn Farīghūn on Communication.” In P. Adamson 2008 [cf. *50], 265–276.
133 Biesterfeldt, Hans Hinrich. “Ibn Farīghūn's *Jawāmiʿ al-ʿulūm*: Between Classification of Sciences and Mirror for Princes.” In *Global Medieval Mirrors for Princes Reconsidered*. Ed. by Regula Forster and Neguin Yavari. Boston, Washington, 2015, 11–25.

6.2.3.4 *On the Classification of the Sciences in the Tradition of al-Kindī*

141 Rosenthal, Franz. “Al-Kindî als Literat.” *Orientalia*, N.S. 11 (1942): 262–288. – Repr. in: F. Rosenthal, *Muslim Intellectual and Social History: A Collection of Essays*. Aldershot, 1990, no. VI.

142 Bergé, Marc. "Épître sur les sciences (*Risāla fī l-ʿulūm*) d'Abū Ḥayyān at-Tawḥīdī (310/922(?)-414/1023): Introduction, traduction, glossaire technique, manuscrit et édition critique." *Bulletin d'études orientales de l'Institut français de Damas* 18 (1963/64): 241–300; 21 (1968) 313–346.

143 Türker-Küyel, Mübahat. "La classification des sciences selon Cumal al-Falsafa d' İbn Hindī." *Araştırma* 5 (1967): 47–53.

144 Cortabarría Beitia, Angel. "La classification des sciences chez al-Kindī." *Mélanges de l'Institut dominicain d'études orientales du Caire* 11 (1972): 49–76.

145 Hein, Christel. *Definition und Einteilung der Philosophie: Von der spätantiken Einleitungsliteratur zur arabischen Enzyklopädie*. Frankfurt a.M., Bern, New York, 1985.

146 Daiber, Hans. "Qosṭā Ibn Lūqā (9. Jh.) über die Einteilung der Wissenschaften." *Zeitschrift für Geschichte der Arabisch-Islamischen Wissenschaften* 6 (1990): 93–129.

147 Heinrichs, Wolfhart. "The Classification of the Sciences and the Consolidation of Philology in Classical Islam." In *Centres of Learning: Learning and Location in Pre-Modern Europe and the Near East*. Ed. by Jan Willem Drijvers and Alasdair A. Macdonald. Leiden, New York, Cologne, 1995, 119–139. – 129–130: On Ibn Farīġūn's *Ǧawāmiʿ*.

148 Biesterfeldt, Hans Hinrich. "Medieval Arabic Encyclopedias of Science and Philosophy." In *The Medieval Hebrew Encyclopedias of Science and Philosophy: Proceedings of the Bar-Ilan University Conference*. Ed. by Steven Harvey. Dordrecht, Boston, London, 2000, 77–98. – 83–86: On Ibn Farīġūn's *Ǧawāmiʿ*.

149 Biesterfeldt, Hans Hinrich. "Arabisch-islamische Enzyklopädien: Formen und Funktionen." In *Die Enzyklopädie im Mittelalter vom Hochmittelalter bis zur frühen Neuzeit: Akten des Kolloquiums des Projekts D im Sonderforschungsbereich 231 (29.11.–1.12.1996)*. Ed. by Christel Meier. Munich, 2002, 43–83.

150 Heck, Paul L. "The Hierarchy of Knowledge in Islamic Civilization." *Arabica* 49 (2002): 27–54.

151 Endress, Gerhard. "The Cycle of Knowledge: Intellectual Traditions and Encyclopaedias of the Rational Sciences in Arabic Islamic Hellenism." In *Organizing Knowledge: Encyclopaedic Activities in the Pre-Eighteenth Century Islamic World*. Ed. by G. Endress. Leiden, Boston, 2006, 103–133.

152 Adamson, Peter. "The Kindian Tradition: The Structure of Philosophy in Arabic Neoplatonism." In: C. D'Ancona 2007 [*6: 351–370].

153 De Smet, Daniel. "Une classification ismaélienne des sciences: L'apport d'Abū Yaʿqūb al-Siǧistānī à la 'tradition d'al-Kindī' et ses liens avec Abū 'l-Ḥasan al-ʿĀmirī." In *Islamic Thought in the Middle Ages. Studies in Text, Transmission*

and Translation, in Honour of Hans Daiber. Ed. by Anna Akasoy and Wim Raven. Leiden, Boston, 2008, 77–90.

6.3 *Neoplatonic Developments*

6.3.1 Neoplatonic Philosophy in Textbooks between al-Balḫī and al-ʿĀmirī [*171–*196] – 6.3.2 Abū l-Ḥasan al-ʿĀmirī [*205–*242]

6.3.1 Neoplatonic Philosophy in Textbooks between al-Balḫī and al-ʿĀmirī

6.3.1.1 *General*

171 Wakelnig, Elvira. "Philosophical Fragments of al-ʿĀmirī Preserved Mainly in al-Tawḥīdī, Miskawayh, and in the Texts of the *Ṣiwān al-ḥikma* Tradition." In P. Adamson 2008 [cf. *50], 215–238.

172 Wakelnig, Elvira. "A new version of Miskawayh's *Book of Triumph*: An Alternative Recension of *al-Fawz al-aṣghar* or the Lost *Fawz al-akbar*?" [*101].

6.3.1.2 *Book on Motion*

179 Taylor, Richard. "Neoplatonic Texts in Turkey: Two Manuscripts Containing Ibn Ṭufayl's *Ḥayy Ibn Yaqẓān*, Ibn al-Sīd's *Kitāb al-Ḥadāʾiq*, Ibn Bājja's *Ittiṣāl al-ʿAql bi-l-Insān*, the *Liber de Causis* and an Anonymous Neoplatonic Treatise on Motion." *Mélanges de l'Institut dominicain d'études orientales du Caire* 15 (1982): 251–264.

180 Pines, Shlomo. "Hitherto Unknown Arabic Extracts from Proclus' *Stoicheōsis Theologikē* and *Stoicheiōsis Physikē*." In: S. Pines, *Studies in Arabic Versions of Greek Texts and in Mediaeval Science*. Jerusalem, Leiden, 1986, 287–293.

181 Rashed, Marwan. "Priorité de l'εἶδος ou du γένος entre Andronicos et Alexandre: Vestiges arabes et grecs inédits." *Arabic Sciences and Philosophy* 14 (2004): 9–63.

182 Wakelnig, Elvira. *Feder, Tafel, Mensch: Al-ʿĀmirīs Kitāb al-Fuṣūl fī l-Maʿālim al-ilāhīya und die arabische Proklos-Rezeption im 10. Jh.* [*49].

183 Wakelnig, Elvira. "Proclus in Aristotelian Disguise. Notes on the Arabic Transmission of Proclus' *Elements of Theology*." In *Universalità della Ragione. Pluralità delle Filosofie nel Medioevo.* XII *Congresso Internazionale di Filosofia Medievale. Palermo, 17–22 settembre 2007*. Vol. 3: *Comunicazioni Orientalia*. Ed. by Alessandro Musco. Palermo, 2012, 165–176.

6.3.1.3 *Abū Ḥāmid al-Isfizārī*

188 Gimaret, Daniel. "Un traité théologique du philosophe musulman Abū Ḥāmid al-Isfizārī (IVe/Xe s.)." In *Mélanges in memoriam Michel Allard, S.J. (1924–1976), Paul Nwyia, S.J. (1925–1980)*. Ed. by Louis Pouzet. Beirut, 1984, 207–252.

189 Reisman, David C. “Plato’s Republic in Arabic: A Newly Discovered Passage.” *Arabic Sciences and Philosophy* 14 (2004): 263–300.
190 Reisman, David C. “An Obscure Neoplatonist of the Fourth/Tenth Century and the Putative Philoponus Source.” In P. Adamson 2008 [cf. *50], 239–264.
191 Wakelnig, Elvira. “Die Philosophen in der Tradition al-Kindīs. Al-ʿĀmirī, al-Isfizārī, Miskawayh, as-Siǧistānī und at-Tawḥīdi.” In *Islamische Philosophie im Mittelalter. Ein Handbuch*. Ed. by Heidrun Eichner, Matthias Perkams, and Christian Schäfer. Darmstadt, 2013, 233–252.
192 Wakelnig, Elvira. “Al-Anṭākī’s Use of the Lost Arabic Version of Philoponus’ *Contra Proclum*.” *Arabic Sciences and Philosophy* 23 (2013): 291–317.

6.3.1.4 *Pseudo-Plato on the Immortality of the Soul*

195 Westerink, Leendert Gerrit. “Proclus on Plato’s Three Proofs of Immortality.” In *Zetesis, aangeboden aan Prof. Dr. Emile de Strijcker*. Antwerpen, Utrecht, 1973, 296–306. – Repr. in: L. G. Westerink, *Texts and Studies in Neoplatonism and Byzantine Literature*. Amsterdam, 1980, 345–355.
196 Hasnawi, Ahmad. “Deux textes en arabe sur les preuves platoniciennes de l’immortalité de l’âme.” *Medioevo* 23 (1997): 395–408.

6.3.2 Abū l-Ḥasan al-ʿĀmirī

6.3.2.1 *Bibliography*

205 Daiber, Hans. *Bibliography of Islamic Philosophy* [*5: II 25–26].

6.3.2.2 *Biography*

211 Minovi, Mojtaba. “Az ḫazā’in-i Turkiyya 2.” *Maǧalla-yi Dāniškada-yi adabiyyāt*, Dānišgāh-i Ṭihrān [*Revue de la Faculté des lettres*, Université de Téhéran] 4/3 (1957): 53–89. – For references to al-ʿĀmirī in later authors cf. 68–76.
212 Ġurāb, Aḥmad ʿAbd al-Ḥamīd. *Kitāb al-Iʿlām bi-manāqib al-islām*. Cairo 1387/1967, 5–19.
213 Rowson, Everett K. “al-ʿĀmirī.” In EI² [*2: XII 72–73].
214 Kraemer, Joel L. *Humanism in the Renaissance of Islam: The Cultural Revival during the Buyid Age*. Leiden, 1986, 1992 (2nd ed.), 233–241.
215 Ḫalīfāt, Saḥbān. *Rasā’il Abī l-Ḥasan al-ʿĀmirī wa-šaḏarātuhū l-falsafiyya*. Amman, 1988, 5–215.
216 Rowson, Everett K. “The Philosopher as Littérateur: Al-Tawḥīdī and his Predecessors.” *Zeitschrift für Geschichte der Arabisch-Islamischen Wissenschaften* 6 (1990): 50–92.
217 Rowson, Everett K. “Al-ʿĀmirī.” In *History of Islamic Philosophy*, vol. 1. Ed. by Seyyed Hossein Nasr and Oliver Leaman. London, 1996, 216–221.
218 Turhan, Kasim. *Âmirî ve felsefesi*. Istanbul, 1992.

6.3.2.3 *Individual Works and Topics*

221 Vadet, Jean-Claude. "Le souvenir de l'ancienne Perse chez le philosophe Abū l-Ḥasan al-ʿĀmirī (m. 381 H.)." *Arabica* 11 (1964): 257–271.

222 Arkoun, Mohammad. "Logocentrisme et vérité religieuse dans la pensée islamique d'après *al-Iʿlām bi-manāqib al-islām* d'al-ʿĀmirī." *Studia Islamica* 35 (1972): 5–51. – Repr. in: M. Arkoun, *Essais sur la pensée islamique*. Paris 1973, 1984 (2nd ed.), 185–231.

223 Vadet, Jean-Claude. "Une défense philosophique de la Sunna: Les *Manāqib al-islām* d'al-ʿĀmirī." *Revue des études islamiques* 42 (1974): 245–276; 43 (1975): 77–96.

224 Allard, Michel. "Un philosophe théologien: Muḥammad b. Yūsuf al-ʿĀmirī." *Revue de l'histoire des religions* 187 (1975): 57–69.

225 Biesterfeldt, Hans Hinrich. "Abū l-Ḥasan al-ʿĀmirī und die Wissenschaften." *Zeitschrift der Deutschen Morgenländischen Gesellschaft*, Supplement III/1 (1977): 335–341.

226 Rowson, Everett K. "An Unpublished Work by al-ʿĀmirī and the Date of the Arabic *De Causis*." *Journal of the American Oriental Society* 104 (1984): 193–199.

227 Rowson, Everett K. *A Muslim Philosopher on the Soul and its Fate: Al-ʿĀmirī's Kitāb al-Amad ʿalā l-abad*. New Haven, Conn., 1988.

228 Abū Zayd, Munā Aḥmad. *Al-Insān fī falsafat al-ʿĀmirī*. Beirut, 1993.

229 D'Ancona, Cristina. "The Topic of the 'Harmony between Plato and Aristotle': Some Examples in Early Arabic Philosophy." In *Wissen über Grenzen. Arabisches Wissen und lateinisches Mittelalter*. Ed. by Andreas Speer, Lydia Wegener. Berlin, New York, 2006, 379–405. – Cf. 382–399.

230 Heck, Paul L. "The Crisis of Knowledge in Islam (I): The Case of al-ʿĀmirī." *Philosophy East & West* 56/1 (2006): 106–135.

231 Wakelnig, Elvira. *Feder, Tafel, Mensch: Al-ʿĀmirīs Kitāb al-Fuṣūl fī l-Maʿālim al-ilāhīya und die arabische Proklos-Rezeption im 10. Jh.* [*49].

232 Wakelnig, Elvira. "Al-ʿĀmirī's Paraphrase of the Proclean *Elements of Theology*: A Search for Possible Sources and Parallel Texts." In C. D'Ancona 2007 [*6: 457–569].

233 Wakelnig, Elvira. "Metaphysics in al-ʿĀmirī: The Hierarchy of Being and the Concept of Creation." In *Nature and Object of the Metaphysics in Medieval Arabic Authors and Texts*. Ed. by Cecilia Martini Bonadeo. Padova, 2007 [*Medioevo: Rivista di storia della filosofia medievale* 32], 39–59.

234 Wakelnig, Elvira. "Al-ʿĀmirī on Vision and the Visible: Variations on Traditional Visual Theories." In *Islamic Thought in the Middle Ages: Studies in Text, Transmission and Translation, in Honour of Hans Daiber*. Ed. by Anna Akasoy and Wim Raven. Leiden, Boston, 2008, 413–430.

235 Wakelnig, Elvira. "Philosophical Fragments of al-ʿĀmirī Preserved Mainly in al-Tawḥīdī, Miskawayh, and in the Texts of the *Ṣiwān al-ḥikma* Tradition." In P. Adamson 2008 [cf. *50], 215–238.

236 De Smet, Daniel. "Une classification ismaélienne des sciences. L'apport d'Abū Yaʿqūb al-Sijistānī à la 'tradition d'al-Kindī' et ses liens avec Abū 'l-Ḥasan al-ʿĀmirī." In *Islamic Thought in the Middle Ages: Studies in Text, Transmission and Translation, in Honour of Hans Daiber*. Ed. by Anna Akasoy and Wim Raven. Leiden, Boston, 2008, 77–90.

236a Arnzen, Rüdiger. "Arabisches Mittelalter." In *Platon-Handbuch: Leben – Werk – Wirkung*. Ed. by Christoph Horn, Jörn Müller and Joachim Söder. Stuttgart, Weimar, 2009, 439–45.

236b Anonymous. *Kitāb al-Ḥikma*. – Online ed. by Elvira Wakelnig (Sharing Ancient Wisdoms / SAWS, 2013), www.ancientwisdoms.ac.uk .

237 Heck, Paul L. *Skepticism in Classical Islam. Moments of Confusion*. London, New York, 2014.

238 Kaya, Veysel. "Kalām and Falsafa Integrated for Divine Unity. Saʿīd b. Dādhurmuz's (5th/11th century) *Risāla fī l-Tawḥīd*." *Studia Graeco-Arabica* 4 (2014): 65–123.

239 Kaya, M. Cüneyt. "A New Source for Al-ʿĀmirī Studies: *al-Majālis al-sabʿ bayna al-Shaykh wa al-ʿĀmirī*." *Nazariyat. Journal for the History of Islamic Philosophy and Sciences* 1/2 (2015): 1–34.

6.3.2.4 *Influence*

240 Gutas, Dimitri. "Avicenna's *maḏhab* with an Appendix on the Question of his Date of Birth." *Quaderni di Studi Arabi* 5/6 (1987/88): 323–336.

241 Ḫalīfāt, Saḥbān (Sahban Khalifat). *Ibn Hindū: Sīratuhu, ārāʾuhu al-falsafiyya, muʾallafātuhu*. Amman, 1995.

242 Wisnovsky, Robert. *Avicenna's Metaphysics in Context*. Ithaca, N.Y., 2003, 239–243. 251–252. 262.

6.4 *The Integration of Philosophical Traditions in Muslim Society in the 4th/10th Century*

6.4.1 Historical Context. Philosophical and Literary Traditions [*260–*273] – 6.4.2 Abū Ḥayyān al-Tawḥīdī [*278–*354] – 6.4.3 Abū Sulaymān al-Siǧistānī [*371–*429]

6.4.1 Historical Context. Philosophical and Literary Traditions

260 Mez, Adam. *Abulḳāsim, ein bagdâder Sittenbild von Muḥammad ibn aḥmad abulmuṭahhar alazdî*. Heidelberg, 1902.

261 Mez, Adam. *Die Renaissance des Islâms*. Heidelberg, 1922.

262 Massignon, Louis. "Interférences philosophiques et percées métaphysiques dans la mystique hallagienne: Notion de l'essentiel désir." *Mélanges J. Maréchal* 2 (Bruxelles 1950): 263–296. – Repr. in: L. Massignon, *Opera Minora*, vol. 2. Beirut, 1963, 226–253, esp. 240–241.

263 Bahmanyār, Aḥmad. *Ṣāḥib-i Ibn-i ʿAbbād: Šarḥ-i aḥwāl wa āṯār: Ba-kūšiš-i Muḥammad Ibrāhīm Bāstānī Pārīzī*. Tehran, 1344 h.š./1965.

264 Bürgel, Johann Christoph. *Die Hofkorrespondenz ʿAḍud ad-Daulas und ihr Verhältnis zu anderen historischen Quellen der frühen Būyiden*. Wiesbaden, 1965.

265 Busse, Heribert. *Chalif und Großkönig: Die Būyiden im Iraq (945–1055)*. Beirut, Wiesbaden, 1969.

266 Glassen, Erika. *Der mittlere Weg: Studien zur Religionspolitik und Religiosität der späten Abbasiden-Zeit*. Wiesbaden, 1981. – Cf. esp. ch. II (9–62): Die traditionalistische Religionspolitik unter den Abbasidenchalifen al-Qādir und al-Qāʾim in der ersten Hälfte des 5./11. Jahrhunderts: Programm und Wirklichkeit.

267 Mottahedeh, Roy P. *Loyalty and Leadership in an Early Islamic Society*. Princeton, 1982. – West Iran and Iraq in the 10th and 11th centuries.

268 Kraemer, Joel L. *Humanism in the Renaissance of Islam: The Cultural Revival during the Buyid Age*. Leiden, 1986, 1992 (2nd ed.).

269 Kraemer, Joel L. *Philosophy in the Renaissance of Islam: Abū Sulaymān al-Sijistānī and his Circle*. Leiden, 1986.

270 Rowson, Everett K. "Religion and Politics in the Career of Badîʿ al-Zamân al-Hamadhânî." *Journal of the American Oriental Society* 107 (1987): 653–673.

271 Rowson, Everett K. "The Philosopher as Littérateur: Al-Tawḥīdī and his Predecessors." *Zeitschrift für Geschichte der Arabisch-Islamischen Wissenschaften* 6 (1990): 50–92.

272 Leder, Stefan. *Das Korpus al-Haiṯam ibn ʿAdī (st. 207/822): Herkunft, Überlieferung, Gestalt früher Texte der Aḫbār-Literatur*. Frankfurt a.M., 1991.

273 Daiber, Hans. *Naturwissenschaft bei den Arabern im 10. Jahrhundert n. Chr.: Briefe des Abū l-Faḍl Ibn al-ʿAmīd (gest. 360/970) an ʿAḍudaddaula*. Leiden, New York, Cologne, 1993.

6.4.2 Abū Ḥayyān al-Tawḥīdī

6.4.2.1 *Bibliography, Biography, General Surveys*

278 Stern, Samuel Miklos. "Abū Ḥayyān al-Tawḥīdī." In EI[2] [*2: I 126–127].

279 Murādyān, Ḫudāmurād. *Bar-rasī dar aḥwāl wa āṯār-i Abū Ḥayyān ʿAlī b. Muḥammad b. ʿAbbās Tawḥīdī Šīrāzī, 312–414 hiǧrī*. Tehran, 1352 h.š./1974.

280 Bergé, Marc. "Continuité et progression des études tawḥīdiennes modernes de 1883 à 1965." *Arabica* 22 (1975): 267–279.

281 Bergé, Marc. "Le Corpus Tawḥīdien: Essai d'inventaire et de classement." *Annales islamologiques* 13 (1977): 43–72.

282 Bergé, Marc. "Les écrits d'Abū Ḥayyān al-Tawḥīdī: Problèmes de chronologie." *Bulletin d'études orientales* 29 (1977): 53–63.

283 Bergé, Marc. *Pour un humanisme vécu: Abū Ḥayyān al-Tawḥīdī*. Damascus, 1979. – Cf. the review by James A. Bellamy, *Journal of the American Oriental Society* 103 (1983): 768–770.

6.4.2.2 *Individual Works and Exemplary Texts*

291 Margoliouth, David Samuel. "The discussion between Abū Bishr Mattā and Abū Saʿīd al-Sīrāfī on the merits of logic and grammar." *Journal of the Royal Asiatic Society* (1905): 79–129. – After Abū Ḥayyān al-Tawḥīdī, *al-Imtāʿ wa-l-muʾānasa*.

292 Wiedemann, Eilhard. "Definitionen verschiedener Wissenschaften und über diese verfaßte Werke." *Sitzungsberichte der Physikalisch-Medizinischen Sozietät zu Erlangen* 50/51 (1918/19): 1–32. – Repr. in: E. Wiedemann, *Aufsätze zur arabischen Wissenschaftsgeschichte*, vol. 2. Hildesheim, 1970, 431–462. – Cf. 30–32: v. From al-Tawḥīdī's work *On the Sciences*.

293 Margoliouth, David Samuel. "Some extracts from the Kitāb al-Imtāʿ wal-Muʾānasah of Abū Ḥayyān Tauḥīdī." *Islamica* 2 (1926): 380–390.

294 Rosenthal, Franz. *Aḥmad b. aṭ-Ṭayyib as-Saraḫsî*. New Haven, Conn., 1943. – 86–94 on *Aḫlāq al-wazīrayn* [*181: 235–247].

295 Stern, Samuel Miklos. "The authorship of the Epistles of the Ikhwān al-Ṣafāʾ." *Islamic Culture* 20 (1946): 367–372; 21 (1947): 403–404 (Additional notes).

296 Muḥyī l-Dīn, ʿAbd al-Razzāq. *Abū Ḥayyān al-Tawḥīdī: Sīratuhu, āṯāruhu*. Cairo, 1949, Beirut, 1979 (2nd ed).

297 Kaylānī, Ibrāhīm. Abū Ḥayyān at-Tauḥīdī: *Essayiste arabe du IV*e *s. de l'hégire (X*e *s.): Introduction à son œuvre*. Beirut, 1950.

298 Muḥyī l-Dīn, ʿAbd al-Razzāq. "Taḥqīq naṣṣ kitāb al-Muqābasāt." *Maǧallat al-Maǧmaʿ al-ʿilmī al-ʿirāqī* 2 (1951): 329–337. – Contribution on the text of *Muqābasāt* 4, 5, 8, 11 and 13.

299 Fariq, K. A. "Abu-Hayyan at-Tauhidi and his Kitabul-Muqabasat." *The Islamic Quarterly* 28 (1954): 372–388.

300 ʿAbbās, Iḥsān. *Abū Ḥayyān al-Tawḥīdī*. Beirut, 1956.

301 Kopf, Lothar. "The Zoological Chapter of the *Kitāb al-Imtāʿ wal-Muʾānasa* of Abū Ḥayyān al-Tauḥīdī (10th century), translated from the Arabic and annotated." *Osiris* 12 (1956): 390–466. – Repr. in: L. Kopf, *Studies in Arabic and Hebrew Lexicography*. Jerusalem, 1976, 47–123.

302 Stern, Samuel Miklos. "Notes on al-Kindī's Treatise on Definitions." *Journal of the Royal Asiatic Society* (1959): 32–43. – Repr. in: S. M. Stern, *Medieval Arabic and Hebrew Thought*. London, 1983, no. VIII. – On al-Kindī's *Fī Ḥudūd al-ašyāʾ wa-rusūmihā*, quoted in Abū Ḥayyān al-Tawḥīdī, *Muqābasāt*; influence on later Arabic authors.

303 Bergé, Marc. "Une anthologie sur l'amitié d'Abū Ḥayyān at-Tawḥīdī." *Bulletin d'études orientales* 16 (1960): 15–60. – On *Kitāb al-Ṣadāqa wa-l-ṣadīq*.

304 Mushtak, Hazim T. *Al-Fārābī's Risāla on the One and the Many: First Edition, English Translation and Notes*. B.L. Thesis, University of Oxford, 1960. – Including Appendix I: The eighty-second *Muqābasa* from the *Kitāb al-Muqābasāt* of Abū Ḥayyān al-Tauḥīdī (text and translation, 133–141).

305 Arkoun, Mohammed. "L'humanisme arabe au IVe/Xe siècle, d'après le Kitâb al-Hawâmil wal-Šawâmil." *Studia Islamica* 14 (1961): 73–108. – Repr. in: M. Arkoun, *Essais sur la pensée islamique*. Paris, 1973, 1984 (2nd ed.), 87–147.

306 Audebert, Claude. "La Risālat al-Ḥayāt d'Abū Ḥayyān al-Tawḥīdī." *Bulletin d'études orientales* 18 (1963/64): 147–195.

307 Bergé, Marc. "Épître sur les sciences (Risāla fī l-ʿulūm) d'Abū Ḥayyān at-Tawḥīdī (310/922(?)-414/1023): Introduction, traduction, glossaire technique, manuscrit et édition critique." *Bulletin d'études orientales de l'Institut français de Damas* 18 (1963/64): 241–300.

308 Mahjoub, Zadi. "Abū Ḥayyān at-Tawḥīdī, un rationaliste original." *Revue de l'Institut des belles-lettres arabes* 27 (1964): 317–344. – Contains at 341–344 a translation of the sections on Abū Sulaymān al-Siǧistānī, Ibn Zurʿa, Ibn al-Ḫammār, Ibn al-Samḥ, al-Qūmisī, ʿĪsā b. ʿAlī and Yaḥyā Ibn ʿAdī from *al-Imtāʿ wa-l-muʾānasa*.

309 Stern, Samuel Miklos. "New Information about the Authors of the 'Epistles of the Sincere Brethren'." *Islamic Studies* 3 (1964): 405–428.

310 Bergé, Marc. "Al-Tawḥīdī et al-Ǧāḥiẓ: Recensement des textes tawḥīdiens sur la filiation ǧāḥiẓienne d'Abū Ḥayyān al-Tauḥīdī, homme de lettres musulman du IVe /Xe siècle." *Arabica* 12 (1965): 188–195.

311 Vajda, Georges. "Brèves notes sur la Risāla fī l-ʿulūm d'Abū Ḥayyān al-Tauḥīdī." *Arabica* 12 (1965): 196–199. – Review of Marc Bergé: Épître sur les sciences (1963–1964).

312 Bergé, Marc. "Tawḥīdī, un humaniste arabe du IVe/Xe siècle." *Travaux et jours, Université Saint Joseph, Beyrouth* 23 (1967): 43–61.

313 Pomezny, Waltraud. *Zu Abū Ḥayyān at-Tauḥīdī und seinem Kitāb al-baṣāʾir wa ḏ-daḫāʾir*. PhD Diss., University of Vienna, 1967. – On *al-Baṣāʾir wa-l-ḏaḫāʾir*; *Taqrīẓ al-Ǧāḥiẓ*.

314 Bergé, Marc. "Épître sur les sciences (Risāla fī l-ʿulūm) d'Abū Ḥayyān al-Tawḥīdī (310/922 (?) 414/1023): Glossaire et index analytique." *Bulletin d'études orientales* 21 (1968): 313–346.

315 Rosenthal, Franz. "Abū Ḥayyān al-Tawḥīdī on Penmanship." *Ars Islamica* 13/14 (1968): 1–30. – Includes a translation of Abū Ḥayyān al-Tawḥīdī's *Risāla fī l-Kitāba*.

316 Bergé, Marc. "Conseils politiques à un ministre: Épître d'Abū Ḥayyān al-Tawḥīdī au vizir Ibn Saʿdān al-ʿÀrid: Introduction, traduction partielle et analyse." *Arabica* 16 (1969): 269–278. – On *al-Imtāʿ wa-l-muʾānasa* [**183*: III 210–225].

317 Bergé, Marc. "Espoirs et rancœurs d'un homme de lettres: Deux épîtres d'Abū Ḥayyān al-Tawḥīdī, l'une adressée au ministre Ibn Saʿdān al-ʿārid et l'autre au

mathématicien Abū l-Wafāʾ: Introduction, traduction partielle et analyse." *Bulletin d'études orientales* 22 (1969): 127–132.

318 al-Qāḍī, Wadād. *Muǧtamaʿ al-qarn al-rābiʿ fī muʾallafāt Abī Ḥayyān al-Tawḥīdī.* Beirut, 1969.

319 Bergé, Marc. "Justification d'un autodafé de livres: Introduction et traduction de la Risāla ilā l-Qāḍī Abī Sahl." *Annales islamologiques* 9 (1970): 65–85.

320 Bergé, Marc. "Une profession de foi politico-religieuse sous les apparences d'une pièce d'archive: La Riwāyat al-Saqīfa d'Abū Ḥayyān al-Tawḥīdī (m. 414/1023)." *Annales islamologiques* 9 (1970): 87–95.

321 Mahdi, Muhsin. "Language and Logic in Classical Islam." In *Logic in Classical Islamic Culture.* Ed. by Gustave Edmund von Grunebaum. Wiesbaden, 1970, 51–83.

322 al-Qāḍī, Wadād. "Al-Rakāʾiz al-fikriyya fī naẓrat Abī Ḥayyān al-Tawḥīdī ilā l-muǧtamaʿ." *Al-Abḥāṯ* 23 (1970): 15–32.

323 Giffen, Lois Anita. *Theory of Profane Love among the Arabs: The Development of the Genre.* New York, London, 1971. – On *Risālat al-Ṣadāqa wa-l-ṣadīq.*

324 Bahnasī, ʿAfīf. *ʿIlm al-ǧamāl ʿinda Abī Ḥayyān al-Tawḥīdī wa-masāʾil fī l-fann.* Baghdad [ca. 1972].

325 Bergé, Marc. "Genèse et fortune du Kitāb al-Imtāʿ wa l-muʾānasa d'Abū Ḥayyān al-Tawḥīdī (m. en 414/1023)." *Bulletin d'études orientales* 25 (1972): 97–104.

326 Bergé, Marc. "Mérites respectifs des nations selon le Kitāb al-Imtāʿ wa-l-muʾānasa d'Abū Ḥayyān al-Tawḥīdī (m. en 414/1023)." *Arabica* 19 (1972): 165–176. – On *al-Imtāʿ wa-l-muʾānasa* [**183*: I 70,11–96,12. 211,9–213,9].

327 Bergé, Marc. "Structure et signification du Kitāb al-Baṣāʾir wa l-ḏaḫāʾir d'Abū Ḥayyān al-Tawḥīdī (m. 414/1023)." *Annales islamologiques* 10 (1972): 53–62.

328 Endress, Gerhard. "The Limits To Reason: Some Aspects of Islamic Philosophy in the Būyid Period." In *Akten des VII. Kongresses für Arabistik und Islamwissenschaft, Göttingen 1974.* Ed. by Albert Dietrich. Göttingen, 1976, 120–125.

329 Bergé, Marc. "Abu Hayyan al-Tawhidi." *Études philosophiques et littéraires* [= Dirāsāt falsafiyya wa-adabiyya, 2] (Rabat 1977): 130–146. – With an outline of the contents of *Kitāb al-Imtāʿ wa-l-muʾānasa* and a few sample texts from the work.

330 Bergé, Marc. "Les écrits d'Abū Ḥayyān al-Tawḥīdī: Problèmes de chronologie." *Bulletin d'études orientales* 29 (1977): 53–63.

331 al-Aʿsam, ʿAbd al-Amīr. *Abū Ḥayyān al-Tawḥīdī fī kitāb al-Muqābasāt.* Beirut, 1978, 1983 (2nd ed.). – French title: *Essais sur les Muqābasāt d'Abū Ḥayyān al-Tawḥīdī: Conférences sur l'histoire de la philosophie arabe au IVe siècle de l'Hégire: cours professé en 1978 à l'université de Paris IV-La Sorbonne.*

332 Hamdani, Abbas. "Abū Ḥayyān al-Tawḥīdī and the Brethren of Purity." *International Journal of Middle East Studies* 9 (1978): 345–353. – Against

al-Tawḥīdī's report about the authors of the *Rasāʾil Iḫwān al-Ṣafāʾ* the author suggests an earlier date of composition.

333 Bergé, Marc. *Pour un humanisme vécu: Abū Ḥayyān al-Tawḥīdī*. Damascus, 1979.

334 Taha, Abderrahmane. *Langage et philosophie: Essai sur les structures linguistiques de l'ontologie, avec la traduction de la discussion rapporté par Abū Ḥayyān at-Tawḥīdī entre le logicien Mattā Ibn Yūnus et le grammairien Abū Saʿīd as-Sīrāfī et de deux autres textes*. Rabat, 1979.

335 al-Takrītī, Nāǧī. *Al-falsafa al-aḫlāqiyya al-Aflāṭūniyya ʿind mufakkirī al-islām*. Beirut, 1979. – Engl. title: *The Platonic Moral Philosophy*.

336 al-Takrītī, Nāǧī. "Al-maʿnā al-aḫlāqī li-l-ṣadāqa." *Maǧallat al-Maǧmaʿ al-ʿilmī al-ʿirāqī* 31.4 (1980): 325–361.

337 al-Qāḍī, Wadād. "ʿAlāqat al-mufakkir bi-l-sulṭān al-siyāsī fī fikr Abī Ḥayyān al-Tawḥīdī." In *Studia Arabica et Islamica: Festschrift for Iḥsān ʿAbbās on his Sixtieth Birthday*. Beirut, 1981, [Arab. part] 221–238.

338 al-Qāḍī, Wadād. "*Kitāb Ṣiwān al-ḥikma*: Structure, Composition, Authorship and Sources." *Der Islam* 58 (1981): 87–124. – On Miskawayh, *al-Ḥikma al-ḫālida*; here also on the gnomological tradition in al-Tawḥīdī's *al-Baṣāʾir wa-l-ḏaḫāʾir*; *al-Imtāʿ wa-l-muʾānasa*; *al-Muqābasāt*; *al-Ṣadāqa wa-l-ṣadīq*.

339 Elamrani-Jamal, Abdelali. *Logique aristotélicienne et grammaire arabe, étude et documents*. Paris, 1983.

340 Frolov, Dmitrij Vladimirovič. "Abu Chajjan at-Tauchidi, Kniga Uslady i Razvlečeniya, čestaja glava." *Narody Azii i Afriki* 5 (1984): 100–110 (Summary, 213). – Al-Imtāʿ wa-l-muʾānasa, laila 6 (rank of the ʿArab in relation to the ʿAǧam).

341 al-Qāḍī, Wadād. "Dirāsa fī Kitāb al-baṣāʾir wa-l-ḏaḫāʾir." In *Abū Ḥayyān al-Tawḥīdī, al-Baṣāʾir wa-l-ḏaḫāʾir*. Ed. by Wadād al-Qāḍī, 1984–1988 [= *178: IX 252–256].

342 Kaylānī, Ibrāhīm. *Rasāʾil Abī Ḥayyān al-Tawḥīdī muṣaddaratan bi-dirāsa ʿan ḥayātihi wa-āṯārihi wa-adabihi*. Damascus, 1985.

343 Endress, Gerhard. "Grammatik und Logik: Arabische Philologie und griechische Philosophie im Widerstreit." [*32].

344 van Gelder, Geert Jan. "Man of letters v. man of figures: The seventh night from al-Tawḥīdī's al-Imtāʿ wa-l-muʾānasa." In *Scripta Signa Vocis: Studies about scripts, scriptures, scribes and languages in the Near East, presented to J. H. Hospers by his pupils, colleagues and friends*. Ed. by Herman L. J. Vanstiphout et al. Groningen, 1986, 53–63.

345 Kraemer, Joel L. *Humanism in the Renaissance of Islam: The Cultural Revival during the Buyid Age*. Leiden, 1986, 1992 (2nd ed.).

346 Kraemer, Joel L. *Philosophy in the Renaissance of Islam: Abū Sulaymān al-Sijistānī and his Circle*. Leiden, 1986.

347 Kühn, Wilfried. "Die Rehabilitierung der Sprache durch den arabischen Philologen as-Sirafi." In B. Mojsisch 1986 [cf. *32], 301–402.

348 Fleischhammer, Manfred. *Altarabische Prosa*. Leipzig, 1988. – Contains 288–307: "Abū Ḥaijān at-Tauḥīdī. Ein Streitgespräch über die "Lauteren Brüder" von Basra und über das Verhältnis von Philosophie und Religion."

349 Rowson, Everett K. *A Muslim Philosopher on the Soul and its Fate: Al-ʿĀmirī's Kitāb al-Amad ʿalā l-abad*. New Haven, Conn. 1988. – Cf. 289–293 on *Aḫlāq al-wazīrayn* [*181: 235–247].

350 Rowson, Everett K. "The Philosopher as Littérateur: Al-Tawḥīdī and his Predecessors." *Zeitschrift für Geschichte der Arabisch-Islamischen Wissenschaften* 6 (1990): 50–92.

351 Niewöhner, Friedrich. "Zum Ursprung der Lehre von der doppelten Wahrheit: Eine Koran-Interpretation des Averroes." In *Averroismus im Mittelalter und in der Renaissance*. Ed. by F. Niewöhner, Loris Sturlese. Zürich, 1994, 23–41. – On the dispute between Abū Sulaymān al-Siǧistānī and the Iḫwān al-Ṣafāʾ according to Abū Ḥayyān al-Tawḥīdī, *al-Imtāʿ wa-l-muʾānasa*.

352 Versteegh, Kees. *The Explanation of Linguistic Causes: Az-Zaǧǧāǧī's Theory of Grammar. Introduction, translation, commentary*. Amsterdam, Philadelphia, 1995.

353 Endress, Gerhard. "The Language of Demonstration: Translating Science and the Formation of Terminology in Arabic Philosophy and Science." *Early Science and Medicine* 7.3 (Leiden 2002): 231–254.

354 Hachmeier, Klaus. "Rating *adab* – al-Tawḥīdī on the Merits of Poetry and Prose: The 25th Night of the *Kitāb al-Imtāʿ wa-l-muʾānasa*, translation and commentary." *Al-Qanṭara* 25 (2004): 357–385.

355 Key, Alexander. "The applicability of the term 'humanism' to Abū Ḥayyān al-Tawḥīdī." *Studia Islamica* 100–101 (2005 [(2007]): 71–112.

6.4.3 Abū Sulaymān al-Siǧistānī

6.4.3.1 *Bibliography and Biography*

371 Meyerhof, Max. "Von Alexandrien nach Bagdad: Ein Beitrag zur Geschichte des philosophischen und medizinischen Unterrichts bei den Arabern." In *Sitzungsberichte der Preussischen Akademie der Wissenschaften: Philologisch-historische Klasse*. Berlin, 1930, 389–429 (esp. 420–421).

372 Ibn ʿAbd al-Wahhāb Qazwīnī, Muḥammad-Ḫān. *Šarḥ-i ḥāl-i Abū Sulaymān-i Manṭiqī-i Siǧistānī* [Abū Sulaïman Manṭiqi Sidjistani, savant du IVe siècle de l'Hégire]. Chalon-sur-Saône, 1933. – Repr. in: M. Qazwīnī, *Bīst maqāla*, vol. 2. Tehran 1332/1954, 128–133.

373 GAL [*1: I 236; S I 377].

374 Graf, Georg. *Geschichte der christlichen arabischen Literatur* [GCAL], vol. 2. Vatican City, 1947, 160–176.

375 Dunlop, Douglas Morton. "Biographical Material from the *Ṣiwān al-ḥikmah.*" *Journal of the Royal Asiatic Society* 89.1–2 (1957): 82–89.

376 Kaḥḥāla, ʿUmar Riḍā. *Muʿǧam al-muʾallifīn: Tarāǧim muṣannifī l-kutub al-ʿarabiyya*, vol. 10. Damascus, 1960, 96.

377 Stern, Samuel Miklos. "Abū Sulaymān Muḥammad b. Ṭāhir b. Bahrām al-Sidjistānī al-Manṭiḳī." In EI[2] [*2: I 151–152].

378 al-Ziriklī, Ḫayr al-Dīn. *Al-Aʿlām: Qāmūs tarāǧim li-ašhar al-riǧāl wa-l-nisāʾ min al-ʿArab wa-l-mustaʿribīn wa-l-mustašriqīn*, vol. 7. Beirut, 1969 (3rd ed.), 41.

379 Badawī, ʿAbd al-Raḥmān, ed. *Muntaḫab Ṣiwān al-ḥikma wa-ṯalāṯ rasāʾil taʾlīf Abū Sulaimān al-Manṭiqī al-Siǧistānī.* Tehran, 1974; taṣdīr, 5–74.

380 Endress, Gerhard. *The Works of Yaḥyā Ibn ʿAdī: An Analytical Inventory.* Wiesbaden, 1977, §§ 1.21; 8.11; 8.74.

381 Platti, Emilio. *Yaḥyā ibn ʿAdī, théologien chrétien et philosophe arabe: Sa théologie de l'incarnation.* Leuven, 1983.

6.4.3.2 *Studies*

391 Amīn, Aḥmad. "Abū Sulaymān al-Manṭiqī kamā yuṣawwiruhu Abū Ḥayyān al-Tawḥīdī." In A. Amīn, *Fayḍ al-ḫāṭir*, vol . 7. Cairo, 1953, 329–341.

392 Arkoun, Mohammed. "L'humanisme arabe au IVe/Xe siècle, d'après le *Kitâb al-Hawâmil wal-Šawâmil.*" *Studia Islamica* 14 (1961): 73–108. – Repr. in: M. Arkoun, *Essais sur la pensée islamique.* Paris, 1973, 1984 (2nd ed.), 87–147. – On Abū Sulaymān al-Siǧistānī: 102–105.

393 Troupeau, Gérard. "Un traité sur les principes des étres attribué à Abū Sulaymān al-Siǧistānī." *Pensamiento* 25 (1969): 259–270. – On Abū Sulaymān al-Siǧistānī [?], *Kalām fī Mabādiʾ al-mawǧūdāt wa-marātib quwāhā.*

394 Türker Küyel, Mübahat. "Le traité inédit de Siǧistānī sur la perfection humaine." *Pensamiento* 25 (1969): 207–224. – Also in: *Araştırma* 7: 1969 (Ankara 1971): 72–117; *Iran Şehinşahlığının 2500: Kuruluş Yıldönümü Armağan* (Istanbul 1971): 329–337. – On the treatise *Fī l-Kamāl al-ḫāṣṣ bi-nawʿ al-insān.*

395 Jadaane, Fehmi. "La philosophie de Sijistānī." *Studia Islamica* 33 (1971): 67–95.

396 Endress, Gerhard. "The Limits To Reason: Some Aspects of Islamic Philosophy in the Būyid Period." In *Akten des VII. Kongresses für Arabistik und Islamwissenschaft, Göttingen 1974.* Ed. by Albert Dietrich. Göttingen, 1976, 120–125.

397 Arnaldez, Roger. "Histoire de la pensée grecque vue par les Arabes." *Bulletin de la société française de philosophie* 72 (1978): 117–168. – Esp. on the *Muntaḫab Ṣiwān al-ḥikma.*

398 Badawī, ʿAbd al-Raḥmān. "Abū Sulaymān al-Sidjistānī al-Manṭiqī, grand humaniste du 4e siècle de l'Hégire." In ʿA. Badawi, *Quelques figures et thèmes de la philosophie islamique.* Paris, 1979, 95–136.

399 Bergé, Marc. *Pour un humanisme vécu: Abū Ḥayyān al-Tawḥīdī*. Damascus, 1979.

400 Elamrani-Jamal, Abdelali. *Logique aristotélicienne et grammaire arabe, étude et documents*. Paris, 1983.

401 Endress, Gerhard. “Grammatik und Logik: Arabische Philologie und Griechische Philosophie im Widerstreit.” [*32].

402 Kraemer, Joel L. *Humanism in the Renaissance of Islam: The Cultural Revival during the Buyid Age*. Leiden, 1986, 1992 (2nd ed.).

403 Kraemer, Joel L. *Philosophy in the Renaissance of Islam: Abū Sulaymān al-Sijistānī and his Circle*. Leiden, 1986.

404 Jolivet, Jean. “L’idée de la sagesse et sa fonction dans la philosophie des 4e et 5e siècles.” *Arabic Sciences and Philosophy* 1 (1991): 31–65.

405 De Smet, Daniel. “Sijistānī.” In *Encyclopédie philosophique universelle*, vol. 3: *Les œuvres philosophiques*, t. 1. Ed. by Jean-François Mattéi. Paris, 1992, 837–838.

406 Niewöhner, Friedrich. “Averroismus vor Averroes? Zu einer Theorie der doppelten Wahrheit im 10. Jahrhundert.” *Mediaevalia Philosophica Polonorum* 32: 1994 (1995): 33–39.

407 Endress, Gerhard. “Abū Sulaymān al-Sijistānī.” In *Encyclopedia of Arabic Literature*, vol. 1. Ed. by Julie Scott Meisami and Paul Starkey. London, New York, 1998, 47.

408 Endress, Gerhard. “Alexander of Aphrodisias on the First Cause: Aristotle’s First Mover in an Arabic Treatise Attributed to Alexander of Aphrodisias.” In *Aristotele e Alessandro di Afrodisia nella tradizione araba: Atti del colloquio ‘La Ricezione araba ed ebraica della filosofia e della scienza greche’, Padova, 14–15 maggio 1999*. Ed. by Cristina D’Ancona and Giuseppe Serra. Padova, 2002, 19–74.

6.4.3.3 *On the Ṣiwān al-Ḥikma (Ascribed to Abū Sulaymān al-Siǧistānī, cf. § 9.1.3)*

421 Dunlop, Douglas Morton. “Biographical Material from the *Ṣiwān al-ḥikmah*.” *Journal of the Royal Asiatic Society* (1957): 82–89.

422 Dunlop, Douglas Morton. “Philosophical Discussions in Sijistan in the 10th Century A.D.” In A. Dietrich 1976 [cf. *396], 108–114.

423 Dunlop, Douglas Morton. *The Muntakhab Ṣiwān al-ḥikmah of Abū Sulaimān as-Sijistānī: Arabic Text, Introduction and Indices*. The Hague, 1979.

424 al-Qāḍī, Wadād. “*Kitāb Ṣiwān al-ḥikma*: Structure, Composition, Authorship and Sources.” *Der Islam* 58 (1981): 87–124.

425 Gutas, Dimitri. “The *Ṣiwān al-Ḥikma* Cycle of Texts.” *Journal of the American Oriental Society* 102 (1982): 645–650.

426 Dunlop, Douglas Morton. "The Arabic Tradition of the *Summa Alexandrinorum*." *Archives d'histoire doctrinale et littéraire du moyen âge* 49 (ann. 57: 1982) (1983): 253–263.

427 Daiber, Hans. "Der *Ṣiwān al-ḥikma* und Abū Sulaimān al-Manṭiqī as-Siǧistānī in der Forschung." *Arabica* 31 (1984): 36–68. – Doubles as review of D. M. Dunlop, ed., *The Muntakhab Ṣiwān al-ḥikmah* [*205].

428 Tornero Poveda, Emilio. "La 'Vida de Platón' del Muntajab Ṣiwān al-ḥikma." *Ciudade de Dios* 199 (1986): 105–117.

429 García-Junceda, José and Rafael Ramón Guerrero. "La Vida de Aristoteles de Abū Sulaymān al-Siŷistānī." *Anales del Seminario de historia de la filosofía* 7 (1989): 25–36.

6.5 *Abū ʿAlī Miskawayh*

6.5.1 Bibliography [*441–*443] – 6.5.2 General Surveys and Biography [*451–*457] – 6.5.3 Textual Tradition and Sources [*464–*471] – 6.5.4 Individual Works and Topics [*480–*489] – 6.5.5 Epistemology. Metaphysics. Soul and Intellect. [*501–*530] – 6.5.6 Ethics [*541–*589] – 6.5.7 Gnomological Writings. *Ādāb al-ʿArab wa-l-Furs* (*Ǧāwīḏān Ḫiraḏ*) [*601–*614] – 6.5.8 Reception and Influence [*631–*644]

6.5.1 Bibliography

441 Mahdawī, Yaḥyā. *Fihrist-i nusḫahā-yi muṣannafāt-i Ibn-i Sīnā*. Tehran, 1333 h.š./1954, 260.

442 Ullmann, Manfred. *Die Medizin im Islam*. Leiden, 1970.

443 Daiber, Hans. *Bibliography of Islamic Philosophy* [*5: II 25–26].

6.5.2 General Surveys and Biography

451 Badawī, ʿAbd al-Raḥmān. "Miskawayh." In *A History of Muslim Philosophy*, vol. 1. Ed. by M. M. Sharif. Wiesbaden, 1963, 469–479. – Repr. in: ʿA. Badawi, *Quelques figures et thèmes de la philosophie islamique*. Paris, 1979, 137–147. – Discusses, among other things, Miskawayh, *al-Fawz al-aṣġar*; *al-Masāʾil al-ṯalāṯ allatī taštamil ʿalā l-ʿulūm kullihā*; *Tahḏīb al-aḫlāq*.

452 Arkoun, Mohammed. *Contribution à l'étude de l'humanisme arabe au IVe/Xe siècle: Miskawayh (320/325–421=932/936–1030), philosophe et historien*. Paris 1970, 1982 (2nd ed.).

453 Kraemer, Joel L. *Humanism in the Renaissance of Islam: The Cultural Revival during the Buyid Age*. Leiden, 1986, 1992 (2nd ed.).

454 Rowson, Everett K. "The Philosopher as Littérateur: Al-Tawḥīdī and his Predecessors." *Zeitschrift für Geschichte der Arabisch-Islamischen Wissenschaften* 6 (1990): 50–92.

455 Leaman, Oliver. “Ibn Miskawayh.” In S. H. Nasr, O. Leaman 1996 [*217], 252–257.
456 Endress, Gerhard. “Miskawayh.” In J. Scott Meisami, P. Starkey 1998 [cf. *407], 529–530.
457 Hoffmann, Gerhard. “Miskawaih – ein Kronzeuge bujidischer Fremdherrschaft? Annäherung an das Fremde.” In *36. Deutscher Orientalistentag 1995 in Leipzig. Vorträge*. Stuttgart, 1998. [*Zeitschrift der Deutschen Morgenländischen Gesellschaft*, Supplement XI], 291–298.

6.5.3 Textual Tradition and Sources

464 Diller, Hans. “Thessalos von Tralleis.” In *Paulys Realencyclopädie der Classischen Altertumswissenschaft*, VI, A, 1 [= A 11]. Stuttgart, 1936, 168–182.
465 Schacht, Joseph and Max Meyerhof. *The Medico-Philosophical Controversy between Ibn Butlan of Baghdad and Ibn Ridwan of Cairo: A Contribution to the History of Greek Learning among the Arabs*. Cairo, 1937.
466 Rundgren, Frithiof. “Das Muxtaṣar min Kitāb al'Axlāq des Galenos, einige Bemerkungen.” *Orientalia Suecana* 23–24 (1974–1975): 84–105.
467 Cranz, F. Edward et al., eds. *Catalogus translationum et commentariorum: Mediaeval and Renaissance Latin Translations and Commentaries: Annotated Lists and Guides*, VI 3. Washington, 1986. – Cora E. Lutz: bibliography on the *Tabula Cebetis*, Arab. version in Miskawayh, *al-Ḥikma al-ḫālida* [**281*: 229–262].
468 Kohlberg, Etan. *A Medieval Muslim Scholar at Work: Ibn Ṭāwūs and his Library*. Leiden, New York, 1992.
469 Langermann, Y. Tzvi. “Arabic Writings in Hebrew Manuscripts: A Preliminary Relisting.” *Arabic Sciences and Philosophy* 6 (1996): 137–160. – Discusses, among other things, an anonymous Judeo-Arabic manuscript of *Kalām ʿalā l-masāʾil al-ṯalāṯ* [= *al-Fawz al-aṣġar*].
470 Hasnawi, Aḥmad. “Une transcription en caractères hébraïques non identifiée d'al-Fawz al-aṣghar de Miskawayh (Oxford, Bodl., Pococke 181).” *Mélanges de l'Institut dominicain d'études orientales du Caire* 23 (1997): 447–453. – A Judeo-Arabic manuscript of Miskawayh, *al-Fawz al-aṣġar*, anonymous, under the title: *al-Kalām ʿalā l-masāʾil al-ṯalāṯ*.
471 Arnzen, Rüdiger. *Aristoteles' De Anima: Eine verlorene spätantike Paraphrase in arabischer und persischer Überlieferung: Arabischer Text nebst Kommentar, quellengeschichtlichen Studien und Glossaren*. Leiden, 1998.

6.5.4 Individual Works and Topics

480 Arkoun, Mohammed. “Deux épîtres de Miskawayh (mort en 421/1030), édition avec introduction et notes.” *Bulletin d'études orientales* 17 (1961/62): 7–74. – Miskawayh, *Risāla fī l-Laḏḏāt wa-l-ālām*; *Maqāla fī l-Nafs wa-l-ʿaql*.

481 Arkoun, Mohammed. "L'humanisme arabe au IVe/Xe siècle d'après le Kitâb al-Hawâmil wal-Šawāmil." *Studia Islamica* 14–15 (1961–1962): 73–108. – Repr. in: M. Arkoun 1973 [*484: 87–148].

482 Arkoun, Mohammed. "Textes inédits de Miskawayh (m. 421)." *Annales islamologiques* 5 (1963): 181–205.

483 Siddiqi, Bakhtyar Husain. "Miskawayh on the purposes of historiography." *Muslim World* 61 (1971): 21–27.

484 Arkoun, Mohammed. *Essais sur la pensée islamique*. Paris, 1973, 1984 (2nd ed.).

485 Preissler, Holger. "Ibn Sīnā und Miskawaih: Bemerkungen zu ihren gegenseitigen Beziehungen." In *Avicenna/Ibn Sīnā, 980–1036*, vol. 2. Ed. by Burchard Brentjes. Halle an der Saale, 1980, 35–42.

486 Moraux, Paul. *Der Aristotelismus bei den Griechen*, vol. 2. Berlin, 1984.

487 Cuvelier, Grégoire. "Les 'Textes inédits' attribués à Miskawayh: Présentation et traduction." *Revue philosophique de Louvain* 87 (1989): 215–234. – *Al-Maqūlāt al-ṯalāṯ; Risāla fī Ǧawhar al-nafs; Risāla fī l-Ṭabīʿa.*

488 Black, Deborah L. *Logic and Aristotle's Rhetoric and Poetics in Medieval Arabic Philosophy*. Leiden, 1990. – Includes discussion of Miskawayh, *Tartīb al-saʿādāt wa-manāzil al-ʿulūm.*

489 Endress, Gerhard. "L'Aristote arabe: Réception, autorité et transformation du Premier Maître." *Medioevo* 23 (1997): 1–42.

6.5.5 Epistemology. Metaphysics. Soul and Intellect.

501 Rosenthal, Franz. "On the Knowledge of Plato's Philosophy in the Islamic World." *Islamic Culture* 14 (1940): 387–422.

502 Sweetman, James. *Islam and Christian Theology*, I/1. Birmingham, 1945, 93–185. – Contains the Engl. transl. of Miskawayh's *al-Fawz al-aṣġar.*

503 Abdul Hamid, Khwaja. *Ibn Maskawaih* [sic], *a study of his al-Fauz al-asghar*. Lahore, 1946.

504 Robertson Dodds, Eric. *The Greeks and the Irrational*. Cambridge, 1951.

505 Abdul Haq, Muḥammad. "Miskawaih's Conception of God, the Universe and Man." *Islamic Culture* 37 (1963): 131–144. – On *al-Fawz al-aṣġar.*

506 Arkoun, Mohammed. "Miskawayh, *De l'intellect et de l'intelli*gible (*Fī l-ʿaql wa-l-maʿqūl*)." *Arabica* 11 (1964): 80–87.

507 Siddiqi, Bakhtyar Husain. "Al-Fārābī and Miskawayh on the Classification of Sciences." *Iqbal* 12.3 (Lahore 1964): 55–63. – Discusses *Tartīb al-saʿādāt wa-manāzil al-ʿulūm.*

508 Rist, John Michael. *Stoic Philosophy*. Cambridge, 1969.

509 Pines, Shlomo. "Aḥmad Miskawayh and Paul the Persian." *Īrān-šināsī* 2 (Tehran 1970): 121–129. – Repr. in: S. Pines, *Studies in the History of Arabic Philosophy*. Ed.

by Sarah Stroumsa. Jerusalem, 1996, 208–216. – On the source of *Tartīb al-saʿādāt wa-manāzil al-ʿulūm.*

510 Biesterfeldt, Hans Hinrich. *Galens Traktat "dass die Kräfte der Seele den Mischungen des Körpers folgen" in arabischer Übersetzung.* Wiesbaden, 1973.

511 Endress, Gerhard. *Proclus Arabus: Zwanzig Abschnitte aus der Institutio theologica in arabischer Übersetzung, eingeleitet, herausgegeben und erklärt.* Beirut, Wiesbaden, 1973.

512 Harris, Charles Reginald Schiller. *The Heart and the Vascular System in Ancient Greek Medicine from Alcmaeon to Galen.* Oxford, 1973.

513 Westerink, Leendert Gerrit. "Proclus on Plato's Three Proofs of Immortality." In *Zetesis, aangeboden aan Prof. Dr. Emile de Strijcker.* Antwerpen, Utrecht, 1973, 296–306. – Repr. in: L. G. Westerink, *Texts and Studies in Neoplatonism and Byzantine Literature.* Amsterdam, 1980, 345–355. – Proclus as source of Miskawayh, *al-Fawz al-aṣġar.*

514 Manuli, Paola and Mario Vegetti. *Cuore, sangue e cervello: Biologia e antropologia nel pensiero antico.* Milan, 1977.

515 Gutas, Dimitri. "Paul the Persian on the Classification of the Parts of Aristotle's Philosophy: A Milestone between Alexandria and Baġdād." *Der Islam* 60 (1983): 231–267. – On the source of *Tartīb al-saʿādāt wa-manāzil al-ʿulūm.*

516 Hein, Christel. *Definition und Einteilung der Philosophie: Von der spätantiken Einleitungsliteratur zur arabischen Enzyklopädie.* Frankfurt a.M., Bern, New York, 1985.

517 Walzer, Richard. *Al-Farabi on the Perfect State: Abū Naṣr al-Fārābī's Mabādiʾ ārāʾ ahl al-madīna al-fāḍila: A revised text with introduction, translation, and commentary.* Oxford, 1985.

518 Cuvelier, Grégoire. "Le 'Livre de l'intellect et de l'intelligible' de Miskawaih: Présentation et essai de traduction." *Arabica* 37 (1990): 115–122.

519 Hasnawi, Ahmad. "Alexandre d'Aphrodise vs Jean Philopon: Notes sur quelques traités d'Alexandre 'perdus' en grec, conservés en arabe." *Arabic Sciences and Philosophy* 4 (1994): 53–109. – Passages from John Philoponus' *De aeternitate mundi,* transmitted in Arabic under the name of Alexander of Aphrodisias, *Maqāla fī Ibṭāl qawl man qāla innahu lā yakūn šayʾ illā min šayʾ,* source of Miskawayh, *al-Fawz al-aṣġar, masʾala* 1, *faṣl* 10.

520 Müller, Irmgard. "Seelensitz." *Historisches Wörterbuch der Philosophie,* vol. 11. Ed. by Joachim Ritter and Karlfried Gründer. Basel, 1995, 105–110.

521 Marcotte, Roxanne. "The *Risālah fī al-ʿaql wa al-maʿqūl* of Ibn Miskawayh: An Epistle on the Intellect and the Intelligible." *Islamic Culture* 70 (1996): 1–17. – Also under the title: "The *Book of the Intellect and the Intelligible*: An Abstract from *Kitāb al-ʿaql wa al-maʿqūl.*" *Al-Tawḥīd* 13 (1996): 137–148.

522 Marcotte, Roxanne. “Imagination et révélation chez Miskawayh.” *Luqmān* 13 (1996/97): 45–55.

523 Hasnawi, Ahmad. “Deux textes en arabe sur les preuves platoniciennes de l’immortalité de l’âme.” *Medioevo* 23 (1997): 395–408.

524 Marcotte, Roxanne. “Ibn Miskawayh, Imagination and Prophecy (*nubuwwah*).” *Islamic Culture* 71 (1997): 1–13.

525 Halfwassen, Jens. “Substanz,” “Substanz/Akzidens.” In *Historisches Wörterbuch der Philosophie*, vol. 10. Ed. by Joachim Ritter and Karlfried Gründer. Basel, 1998, 501–502.

526 Endress, Gerhard. “The New and Improved Platonic Theology: Proclus Arabus and Arabic Islamic Philosophy.” *In Proclus et la théologie platonicienne: Actes du colloque international de Louvain (13–16 mai 1998) en l’honneur de H. D. Saffrey et L. G. Westerink*. Ed. by Alain Philippe Segonds and Carlos G. Steel. Leuven, Paris, 2000, 553–570.

527 Mohamed, Yasien. “The Cosmology of Ikhwān al-Ṣafāʾ, Miskawayh and al-Iṣfahānī.” *Islamic Studies* 39 (2000): 657–679.

528 Adamson, Peter. “Miskawayh’s Psychology.” In *Classical Arabic Philosophy: Sources and Reception*. Ed. by P. Adamson. London, 2007, 39–54.

528a Pormann, Peter E., ed. *Rufus of Ephesus: On Melancholy.* Tübingen, 2008.

529 Wakelnig, Elvira. “A New Version of Miskawayh’s *Book of Triumph*: An Alternative Recension of *al-Fawz al-aṣghar* or the lost *Fawz al-akbar*?” [*101].

530 Adamson, Peter and Peter E. Pormann. “More than Heat and Light: Miskawayh’s *Epistle on Soul and Intellect*.” *Muslim World* 102 (2012): 478–524.

6.5.6 Ethics

541 Plessner, Martin. *Der Οἰκονομικός des Neupythagoreers ‘Bryson’ und sein Einfluss auf die islamische Wissenschaft: Edition und Übersetzung der erhaltenen Versionen, nebst einer Geschichte der Ökonomik im Islam mit Quellenproben in Text und Übersetzung*. Heidelberg, 1928. – Exemplary study of the sources and the history of transmission of economics (Arab. *tadbīr al-manzil*, doctrine of the management of the household) within ethical literature, esp. Miskawayh’s *Tahḏīb al-aḫlāq*.

542 ʿIzzat, ʿAbd al-ʿAzīz. *Ibn Miskawayh, falsafatuhu l-aḫlāqiyya wa-maṣādiruhā*, 2 vols. Cairo, 1946.

543 Mulder, Dirk Cornelis. *Openbaring en rede in de islamietische filosofie van al-Fārābī tot Ibn Rušd*. Amsterdam, 1949.

544 Walzer, Richard. “New Light on Galen’s Moral Philosophy (from a Recently Discovered Arabic Source).” *The Classical Quarterly* 43 (1949): 82–96. – Repr. in: R. Walzer, *Greek into Arabic: Essays on Islamic Philosophy*. Oxford, Cambridge, Mass., 1962, 1963 (2nd ed.), 142–163.

545 Pines, Shlomo. "Un texte inconnu d'Aristote en version arabe." *Archives d'histoire doctrinale et littéraire du moyen âge* 23 (1956): 5–43. – Addenda, ibid., 26 (1959) 295–299. – Repr. in: S. Pines 1986 [cf. *180], 196–200. – Aristotle, *Faḍāʾil al-nafs*, quoted in Miskawayh, *Tahḏīb al-aḫlāq* [*273: 86–91].

546 Walzer, Richard. "Some Aspects of Miskawaih's *Tahdhīb al-akhlāq*." In *Studi orientalistici in onore di Giorgio Levi Della Vida*, vol 2. Rome, 1956, 603–621. – Repr. in: R. Walzer 1962 [cf. *544], 220–235.

547 Rosenthal, Franz. *The Muslim Concept of Freedom Prior to the Nineteenth Century*. Leiden, 1960, 81–119. – Philosophical positions on free will, e.g. in Miskawayh, *Tahḏīb al-aḫlāq*.

548 Walzer, Richard and Hamilton A. R. Gibb. "Akhlāḳ: i. Survey of Ethics in Islam. ii. Philosophical Ethics." In EI² [*2: I 325–329].

549 Arkoun, Mohammed. "*Risāla fī māʾiyyat al-ʿadl wa-bayān aqsāmih* de Miskawayh." *Hespéris-Tamuda* 2 (Rabat 1961): 215–230. – Edition (223–230), introduction and commentary.

550 Arkoun, Mohammed. "À propos d'une édition récente du *Kitāb Tahḏīb al-ʾaḫlāq*." *Arabica* 9 (1962): 61–73. – Review of Miskawayh, *Tahḏīb al-aḫlāq*, ed. Cairo 1959.

551 Abdul Haq, Muḥammad. *The Ethical Philosophy of Miskawayh*. Aligarh, 1964.

552 Khan, M. S. *An Unpublished Treatise of Miskawayh on Justice, or Risāla fī māhiyyat al-ʿadl li Miskawaih*. Leiden, 1964. – Ed. with notes, annotations, English translation and an introduction.

553 Walzer, Richard. "Porphyry in the Arabic Tradition." In *Porphyre*. Vandœuvres-Genève, 1965, [Entretiens sur l'Antiquité classique 12], 273–299.

554 Arkoun, Mohammed. "Éthique et histoire d'après les Tajarib al-Umam." In *Atti del III congresso di studi arabi e islamici, Ravello 1966*. Naples, 1967, 83–112. – Repr. in: M. Arkoun 1973 [*484: 51–86].

555 Jadaane, Fehmi. *L'influence du stoïcisme sur la pensée musulmane*. Beirut, 1968.

556 Arkoun, Mohammed. "Contribution à l'étude du lexique de l'éthique musulmane." *Bulletin d'études orientales de l'Institut français de Damas* 22 (1969): 205–237. – Repr. in: M. Arkoun 1973 [*484: 319–351]. – *Tahḏīb al-aḫlāq*, terminology.

557 Pines, Shlomo. "Aḥmad Miskawayh and Paul the Persian." *Īrān-šināsī* 2 (Tehran 1970): 121–129. – Repr. in: S. Pines, *Studies in the History of Arabic Philosophy*. Ed. by Sarah Stroumsa. Jerusalem, 1996, 208–216.

558 Daiber, Hans. "Ein bisher unbekannter pseudoplatonischer Text über die Tugenden der Seele in arabischer Überlieferung." *Der Islam* 47 (1971): 25–42; Addendum in: *Der Islam* 49 (1972): 122–123. – On Miskawayh, *Tahḏīb al-aḫlāq*; echo of Pseudo-Plato: *Maqāla fī Iṯbāt faḍāʾil al-nafs = ʿādāt al-nafs*.

559 Riad, Eva. "Miskawayh sur la colère, quelques remarques." *Orientalia Suecana* 21 (1972): 34–52.

560 Ritter, Joachim. "Ethik." In *Historisches Wörterbuch der Philosophie*. Ed. by J. Ritter, vol. 2. Basel, 1972, 759–795.

561 Fakhry, Majid. "Justice in Islamic Philosophical Ethics: Miskawayh's Mediating Contribution." *Journal of Religious Ethics* 3 (1975): 243–254. – Repr. in: M. Fakhry, *Philosophy, Dogma and the Impact of Greek Thought in Islam*. Aldershot, 1994, no. XX.

562 Fakhry, Majid. "The Platonism of Miskawayh and its Implications for his Ethics." *Studia Islamica* 42 (1975): 39–57. – Repr. in: M. Fakhry 1994 [cf. *561], no. VIII. – Discusses Miskawayh, *Tahḏīb al-aḫlāq*; *al-Fawz al-aṣġar*; *Tartīb al-saʿādāt wa-manāzil al-ʿulūm*.

563 al-Takrītī, Nāǧī. *Al-falsafa al-aḫlāqiyya al-Aflāṭūniyya ʿind mufakkirī al-islām*. Beirut, 1979. – Engl. title: *The Platonic Moral Philosophy*.

564 al-Takrītī, Nāǧī. "Al-Maʿnā al-aḫlāqī li-l-ṣadāqa." *Maǧallat al-Maǧmaʿ al-ʿilmī al-ʿirāqī* 31/4 (1980): 325–361.

565 Muḥammad, M. A. M. *An Inquiry into the Utilitarian Tendencies in the Ethics of Miskawayh*. Edinburgh, 1982.

566 Hourani, George F. *Reason and Tradition in Islamic Ethics*. Cambridge, 1985.

567 Hovannisian, Richard G., ed. *Ethics in Islam*. Malibu, 1985.

568 Kraemer, Joel L. *Humanism in the Renaissance of Islam: The Cultural Revival during the Buyid Age*. Leiden, 1986, 1992 (2nd ed.).

569 Arkoun, Mohammed. "L'unité de l'homme dans la pensée islamique." *Diogène* 140 (1987): 46–65.

570 Borrmans, Maurice. "Un principe d'éthique aristotélicien: In medio stat virtus, à travers les traditions musulmane et chrétienne." In *Individu et societé: L'influence d'Aristote dans le monde méditerranéen, Actes du colloque d'Istanbul 1986*. Ed. by Thierry Zarcone. Istanbul, 1988, 83–97.

571 Makdisi, George. *The Rise of Humanism in Classical Islam and the Christian West, with Special Reference to Scholasticism*. Edinburgh, 1990. – Influence of philosophy on literature and religious tradition.

572 Muḥaqqiq, Mahdī (Mehdi Mohaghegh). "Mabānī-yi aḫlāq-i falsafī dar islām." In *Duwwumīn bīst guftār dar mabāḥiṯ-i adabī wa-tārīḫī wa-falsafī wa-kalāmī wa-tārīḫ-i ʿulūm dar islām*. Ed. by M. Muḥaqqiq. Tehran, 1990, 71–89.

573 Jolivet, Jean. "L'idée de la sagesse et sa fonction dans la philosophie des 4e et 5e siècles." *Arabic Sciences and Philosophy* 1 (1991): 31–65.

574 Bin Omar, Mohammed Nasir. *A Study of How to Attain Happiness as Reflected in the Works on* Tahdhīb al-akhlāq *by Yaḥyā Ibn ʿAdī (d. 974) and Miskawayh (d. 1030)*. PhD Diss., University of Nottingham, 1992.

575 ʿUwayḍa, Kāmil. *Ibn Miskawayh, maḏāhib aḫlāqiyya*. Beirut, 1993.

576 Bin Omar, Mohammed Nasir. "Miskawayh's Theory of Self-Purification and the Relationship between Philosophy and Sufism." *Journal of Islamic Studies* 5 (1994): 35–51. – Includes discussion of Miskawayh's *Waṣiyya*.

577 Fakhry, Majid. *Ethical Theories in Islam.* 2nd, expanded ed. Leiden, 1994.
578 Vadet, Jean-Claude. *Les idées morales dans l'islam*. Paris, 1995.
579 Bin Omar, Mohammed Nasir. "Sources of Muslim Ethics: Miskawayh's Experience." *Studia Islamica* 70 (1996): 83–90.
580 Al-Azmeh, Aziz. *Muslim Kingship: Power and the Sacred in Muslim, Christian, and Pagan Polities*. London, 1997.
581 Bin Omar, Mohammed Nasir. "Preliminary Remarks on Greek Sources of Muslim Ethics: Miskawayh's Experience." *Islamic Quarterly* 41 (1997): 270–283.
582 Fazzo, Silvia. "L'Alexandre arabe et la génération à partir du néant." In *Perspectives arabes et médiévales sur la tradition scientifique et philosophique grecque: Actes du colloque de la SIHSPAI (Société internationale d'histoire des sciences et de la philosophie arabes et islamiques), Paris, 31 mars–3 avril 1993*. Ed. by Ahmad Hasnawi, Abdelali Elamrani-Jamal and Maroun Aouad. Leuven, Paris, 1997, 277–287. – On *al-Fawz al-aṣġar*; *creatio ex nihilo*.
583 Akalay, Omar. *Histoire de la pensée économique en islam du 8e au 12e siècle*. Paris, Montréal, 1998.
584 ʿIrāqī, Muḥammad ʿĀṭif. *Al-Falsafa al-ʿarabiyya wa-l-ṭarīq ilā l-mustaqbal: Ruʾya ʿaqliyya naqdiyya*. Cairo, 1998. – On the concept of man in the Iḫwān al-Ṣafāʾ, al-Fārābī, Abū Ḥayyān al-Tawḥīdī, Miskawayh, al-Ġazālī, Ibn Bāǧǧa, Ibn Ṭufayl; on Ibn Sīnā's and Ibn Rušd's physics; on al-Fārābī's *Kitāb al-Ḥurūf* and al-Ġazālī's *Tahāfut al-falāsifa*.
585 Bin Omar, Mohammed Nasir. "Preliminary Remarks on Christian Sources of Muslim Ethics: Miskawayh's Experience." *Hamdard Islamicus* 23 (2000): 53–56.
586 Arkoun, Mohammed and M. S. Khan. "Ethics and History According to the *Tajârib al-Umam* of Miskawaih." *Islamic Culture* 75 (2001): 1–40.
587 Hadot, Ilsetraut and Pierre Hadot. *Apprendre à philosopher dans l'antiquité: L'enseignement du «Manuel d'Épictète» et son commentaire néoplatonicien*. Paris, 2004.
588 Swain, Simon. *Economy, Family and Society from Rome to Islam: a Critical Edition, English Translation, and Study of Bryson's "Management of the Estate"*. Cambridge, 2013.
589 Adamson, Peter. "Miskawayh on Pleasure." *Arabic Sciences and Philosophy* 25 (2015): 199–223.

6.5.7 Gnomological Writings. *Ādāb al-ʿArab wa-l-Furs* (*Ǧāwīḏān Ḫiraḏ*)

601 Anawati, Georges C. "'La sagesse éternelle' de Miskawayh." *Revue du Caire* 30 (1952/53): 59–81. – *Ādāb al-ʿArab wa-l-Furs* (*Ǧāwīḏān ḫiraḏ*).
602 Henning, Walter Bruno. "Eine arabische Version mittelpersischer Weisheitsschriften." *Zeitschrift der Deutschen Morgenländischen Gesellschaft* 106 (1956) 73–77. – Engl.

transl. by M. S. Khan, "The Jawidan Khirad of Miskawaih." *Islamic Culture* 35 (1961): 238–243. – On a passage from *Ādāb al-ʿArab wa-l-Furs* (*Ǧāwīḏān ḫiraḏ*).

603 Arberry, Arthur John. "Javidhan Khiradh." *Journal of Semitic Studies* 8 (1963): 145–158.

604 Arberry, Arthur John. "Plato's 'Testament to Aristotle'." *Bulletin of the School of Oriental and African Studies* 34 (1971): 475–490. – From Miskawayh, *Ādāb al-ʿArab wa-l-Furs* (*Ǧāwīḏān ḫiraḏ*). Ed. by ʿA. Badawī, 217–219, on its adaptation in Naṣīr al-Dīn al-Ṭūsī, *Aḫlāq-i Nāṣirī*, and on the reception in Mubaššir Ibn Fātik, *Muḫtār al-ḥikam*.

605 Arkoun, Mohammed. "Comment lire le Javidan Khirad." In *Miskawayh, Javidan Khirad. Traduction persane de T. M. Shushtari*. Tehran, 1976, 1–24. – Repr. in: M. Arkoun, *Pour une critique de la raison islamique*. Paris, 1984, 273–296. – *Al-Ḥikma al-ḫālida*.

606 ʿAbbās, Iḥsān. "Naẓra ǧadīda fī baʿḍ al-kutub al-mansūba li-Ibn al-Muqaffaʿ." *Maǧallat Maǧmaʿ al-luġa al-ʿarabiyya = Maǧallat al-Maǧmaʿ al-ʿilmī* 52 (1977): 538–580. – Texts from Miskawayh, *Ǧāwīḏān ḫiraḏ* compared with the transmission in Pseudo-Ibn al-Muqaffaʿ, *al-Adab al-ṣaġīr*.

607 Rosenthal, Franz. "The Symbolism of the *Tabula Cebetis* according to Abū l-Faraǧ ibn aṭ-Ṭayyib." In *Recherches d'islamologie: Recueil d'articles offert à Georges C. Anawati et Louis Gardet*. Louvain, 1977, 273–283.

608 al-Qāḍī, Wadād. "*Kitāb Ṣiwān al-ḥikma*: Structure, Composition, Authorship and Sources." *Der Islam* 58 (1981): 87–124.

609 Linley, Neil. *Ibn aṭ-Ṭayyib: Proclus' Commentary on the Pythagorean Golden Verses: Arabic Text and Translation*. Buffalo, 1984.

610 de Fouchécour, Charles-Henri. *Moralia: Les notions morales dans la littérature persane du 3e/9e au 7e/13e siĝcle*. Paris, 1986. – Contains a study of *Kitāb al-Ḥikma al-ḫālida*.

611 Zakeri, Mohsen. "ʿAlī ibn ʿUbaida ar-Raiḥānī: A Forgotten Belletrist (*adīb*) and Pahlavi Translator." *Oriens* 34 (1994): 76–102. – Parallel transmissions of Persian wisdom literature in Pseudo-Ibn al-Muqaffaʿ's *al-Adab al-ṣaġīr*, Miskawayh's *Ǧāwīḏān ḫiraḏ* and other gnomologies go back to the Persian-Arabic tradition of ʿAlī b. ʿUbayda al-Rayḥānī (d. 234/819).

612 Daiber, Hans. *Neuplatonische Pythagorica in arabischem Gewande: Der Kommentar des Iamblichus zu den Carmina Aurea*. Amsterdam, 1995.

613 Marcotte, Roxanne. "An Early Anonymous Persian Moral Text: The *Jāvidan Khirad*." *Islamic Studies* 36 (1997): 77–87. – Comparison with the anonymous *Nuktahā-yi kitāb-i Ǧāwīḏān ḫiraḏ*.

614 Khan, M. S. "An Apocryphal Work – the *Jāvidān Khirad* of Miskawayh." *Islamic Studies* 37 (1998): 371–380.

6.5.8 Reception and Influence

631 Plessner, Martin. *Der Οἰκονομικός des Neupythagoreers 'Bryson' und sein Einfluss auf die islamische Wissenschaft*. [*541].

632 Abul Quasem, Muhammad. "Al-Ghazali's Rejection of Philosophical Ethics." *Islamic Studies* 13 (1974): 111–127.

633 Madelung, Wilferd. "Ar-Rāġib al-Iṣfahānī und die Ethik al-Ġazālīs." In *Islamwissenschaftliche Abhandlungen Fritz Meier zum sechzigsten Geburtstag*. Ed. by Richard Gramlich. Wiesbaden, 1974, 152–163.

634 Cole, Juan Ricardo. "Rifāʿa al-Ṭahṭāwī and the Revival of Practical Philosophy." *Muslim World* 70 (1980): 29–46. – On *Tahḏīb al-aḫlāq*.

635 al-Takrītī, Nāǧī. *Al-falsafa al-siyāsiyya ʿinda Ibn Abī l-Rabīʿ maʿa taḥqīq kitābihī Sulūk al-malik fī tadbīr al-mamālik*. Beirut, 1980 (2nd ed.).

636 Madelung, Wilferd. "Naṣīr al-Dīn al-Ṭūsī's Ethics Between Philosophy, Shiʿism, and Sufism." In R. G. Hovannisian 1985 [*567], 85–101.

637 Bhat, Badruddin. "Miskawayh on Social Justice, Education and Friendship." *Islamic Studies* 25 (1986): 197–210. – Influence of Miskawayh's ethics on al-Ġazālī, Naṣīr al-Dīn al-Ṭūsī, Rifāʿa al-Ṭahṭāwī and Muḥammad ʿAbduh.

638 Cole, Juan Ricardo. "Ideology, Ethics and Philosophical Discourse in Eighteenth Century Iran." *Iranian Studies* 22.1 (1989): 7–34. –Miskawayh's influence on Narāqī.

639 Sourdel, Janine. "Reflexions sur les 'facultés' de l'âme chez al-Ghazali." In *Mélanges en hommage au professeur et au penseur libanais Farid Jabre*. Beirut, 1989, 237–240.

640 Daiber, Hans. "Griechische Ethik in islamischem Gewande: Das Beispiel von Rāġib al-Iṣfahānī (11. Jh.)." In *Historia Philosophiae Medii Aevi: Studien zur Geschichte der Philosophie des Mittelalters: Festschrift für Kurt Flasch*. Ed. by Burkhard Mojsisch and Olaf Pluta. Amsterdam, 1991, 181–192. – The relation of Rāġib al-Iṣfahānī's *al-Ḏarīʿa ilā makārim al-šarīʿa* to Miskawayh's *Tahḏīb al-aḫlāq*.

641 Harvey, Steven. "A new Islamic Source of the *Guide of the Perplexed*." *Maimonidean Studies* 2 (1991): 31–59. – Miskawayh's *Tahḏīb al-aḫlāq* as source of Ibn Falaquera's *Šelemūt ha-maʿaṣīm* and Maimonides' *Guide for the Perplexed* (*Dalālat al-ḥāʾirīn*).

642 Mohamed, Yasien. "The Ethical Philosophy of al-Rāghib al-Iṣfahānī." *Journal of Islamic Studies* 6.1 (1995): 51–75.

643 Mohamed, Yasien. "The Concept of Justice in Miskawayh and Iṣfahānī." *Journal for Islamic Studies* 18–19 (1998): 51–111.

644 Mohamed, Yasien. "Knowledge and Purification of the Soul: An Annotated Translation of Iṣfahānī's *Kitāb al-Dharīʿa ilā Makārim al-sharīʿa* (58–76; 89–92)." *Journal of Islamic Studies* 9 (1998): 1–34. – In comparison with Miskawayh's *Tahḏīb al-aḫlāq*.

6.6 *Ibn Hindū*

6.6.1 Bibliography and Biography [*661–*665] – 6.6.2 Life, Work, and Historical Context [*671–*672] – 6.6.3 Individual Works and Topics [*681–*684]

6.6.1 Bibliography and Biography

661 GAL [*1: I 240, S I 425].

662 Dietrich, Albert. *Medicinalia Arabica: Studien über arabische medizinische Handschriften in türkischen und syrischen Bibliotheken*. Göttingen, 1966, 198–202 (no. 92).

663 GAS [*3: III 334–335. 414].

664 Ullmann, Manfred. *Die Medizin im Islam*. Leiden, 1970, 152.

665 Rowson, Everett K. *A Muslim Philosopher on the Soul and its Fate: Al-ʿĀmirī's Kitāb al-Amad ʿalā l-abad*. New Haven, Conn., 1988, 27.

6.6.2 Life, Work, and Historical Context

671 Kraemer, Joel L. *Philosophy in the Renaissance of Islam: Abū Sulaymān al-Sijistānī and his Circle*. Leiden, 1986.

672 Ḫalīfāt, Saḥbān (Sahban Khalifat). *Ibn Hindū: Sīratuhu, ārāʾuhu al-falsafiyya, muʾallafātuhu*. Amman, 1995.

6.6.3 Individual Works and Topics

681 Georr, Khalil. *Les Catégories d'Aristote dans leurs versions syro-arabes*. Beirut, 1948.

682 Shiloah, Amnon. "Ibn Hindū, le médecin et la musique." *Israel Oriental Studies* 2 (1972): 447–462.

683 Dānišpažūh, Muḥammad Taqī. "Sar-guḏašt-i Ibn-i Hindū Ṭabaristānī wa Risāla-yi Mušawwiqa-yi ū." *Ǧāwīdān Ḫirad = Sophia Perennis* 3.2 (1977): 26–33.

684 Rowson, Everett K. "The Philosopher as Littérateur: Al-Tawḥīdī and his Predecessors." *Zeitschrift für Geschichte der Arabisch-Islamischen Wissenschaften* 6 (1990): 50–92.

CHAPTER 6

Abū Bakr al-Rāzī

Hans Daiber

1 Primary Sources – 2 Translations Available in al-Rāzī's Time – 3 Life – 4 Works – 5 Doctrine – 6 Secondary Literature

1 Primary Sources

1.1 Sources for al-Rāzī's Life, Work, and Influence [*1–*22] – 1.2 Sources Used by al-Rāzī [*31–*35] – 1.3 Works [*41–*51]

1.1 *Sources for al-Rāzī's Life, Work, and Influence*

1 al-Ṭabarī, Abū Ǧaʿfar Muḥammad b. Ǧarīr (d. 310/923). *Aḫbār al-rusul wa-l-mulūk*. – Ed. by Michael Jan de Goeje, *Annales quos scripsit Abu Djafar Mohammed Ibn Djarir at-Tabari*, 15 vols. Leiden, 1879–1901.

2 Abū Ḥātim al-Rāzī, Aḥmad b. Ḥamdān (d. 322/933–934). *Aʿlām al-nubuwwa*. – Ed. by Ṣalāḥ al-Ṣāwī and Ġulāmriḍā Aʿwānī, with Engl. intro. by Seyyed Hossein Nasr. Tehran, 1397/1977. – Partial French transl. by Fabienne Brion, "Philosophie et révélation: Traduction annotée de six extraits du *Kitāb Aʿlām al-nubuwwa* d'Abū Ḥātim al-Rāzī." *Bulletin de philosophie médiévale* 28 (1986): 134–162. – Partial French transl. by Fabienne Brion, "Le temps, l'espace et la genèse du monde selon Abū Bakr al-Rāzī: Présentation et traduction des chapitres I, 3–4 du *Kitāb aʿlām al-nubuwwa* d'Abū Ḥātim al-Rāzī." *Revue philosophique de Louvain* 87 (1989): 139–164. – Complete English transl. with parallel Arabic text by Tarif Khalidi, *The Proofs of Prophecy*. Provo, 2012.

3 al-Balḫī, Abū Zayd Aḥmad b. Sahl (d. 322/934). *Maṣāliḥ al-abdān wa-l-anfus*. – Facsimile ed. Frankfurt a.M., 1984. – German transl. by Zahide Özkan, *Die Psychosomatik bei Abū Zaid al-Balḫī (gest. 934 A.D.)*. Frankfurt a.M., 1990.

4 al-Masʿūdī, Abū l-Ḥasan ʿAlī b. al-Ḥusayn. *Kitāb al-Tanbīh wa-l-išrāf* [composed 345/956] – Ed. by Michael Jan de Goeje, *Kitâb at-tanbîh wa'l-ischrâf auctore al-Masûdî*. Leiden, 1894. – Ed. by ʿAbd Allāh Ismāʿīl al-Ṣāwī. Cairo, 1357/1938.

5 Ibn al-Nadīm, Abū l-Faraǧ Muḥammad b. Isḥāq (d. 380/990). *Kitāb al-Fihrist* [composed 377/988]. – Ed. by Gustav Flügel, August Müller and Johannes Roediger, 2 vols. Leipzig, 1871–1872. – Repr. Beirut, 1964; Frankfurt a.M., 2005. – Ed. by Riḍā Taǧaddud. Tehran, 1350/1971. – Ed. by Ayman Fuʾād Sayyid, 2 vols.

 | DOI 10.1163/9789004323162_008

London, 1430/2009. – Engl. transl. by Bayard Dodge, *The Fihrist of al-Nadīm*, 2 vols. New York, 1970.

6 Ibn Ǧulǧul, Sulaymān b. Ḥassān (d. around 384/994). *Ṭabaqāt al-aṭibbāʾ wa-l-ḥukamāʾ*. – Ed. by Fuʾād Sayyid, *Les générations des médecins et des sages*. Cairo, 1955.

7 Ibn al-Ǧazzār, Abū Ǧaʿfar Aḥmad b. Ibrāhīm (d. 395/1004–1005). *Ṭibb al-fuqarāʾ wa-l-masākīn*. – Ed. by Waǧīha Kāẓim Āl Ṭūʿma, with Pers. and Engl. intro. by Mehdi Mohaghegh. Tehran, 1996.

8 al-Kirmānī, Ḥamīd al-Dīn (d. after 411/1020–1021). *Al-Aqwāl al-ḏahabiyya*. – Ed. by Ṣalāḥ al-Ṣāwī, with Pers. intro. by Ġulāmriḍā Aʿwānī, Engl. intro. by Seyyed Hossein Nasr. Tehran, 1977.

9 Miskawayh, Abū ʿAlī Aḥmad b. Muḥammad (d. 421/1030). *Tahḏīb al-aḫlāq*. – Ed. by Constantine Zurayk. Beirut, 1967. – Engl. transl. by Constantine Zurayk, *The Refinement of Character*. Beirut, 1968.

10 al-Bīrūnī, Abū l-Rayḥān Muḥammad b. Aḥmad (d. after 442/1050). *Risāla fī Fihrist kutub Muḥammad b. Zakariyyāʾ al-Rāzī*. – Ed. by Mehdi Mohaghegh, *Fihrist-i kitāb-hā-yi Rāzī wa nām-hā-yi kitāb-hā-yi Bīrūnī*. Tehran, 1366/1987. – Older ed. by Paul Kraus, *Risāla li-l-Bīrūnī fī fihrist kutub Muḥammad b. Zakariyyāʾ al-Rāzī*, Paris, 1936. – German transl. by Julius Ruska, "Al-Bīrūni als Quelle für das Leben und die Schriften al-Rāzi's." *Isis* 5 (1923): 26–50. – Engl. transl. by Nurdeng Deuraseh, "*Risālah al-Bīrūnī fī Fihrist kutub al-Rāzī*: A comprehensive bibliography of the works of Abū Bakr al-Rāzī (d. 313/925) and al-Bīrūnī (d. 443/1051)." *Afkār: Journal of ʿAqīdah & Islamic Thought* 9 (2008): 51–99.

11 Ṣāʿid b. Aḥmad Abū l-Qāsim al-Andalusī (d. 462/1070). *Ṭabaqāt al-umam*. – Ed. by Louis Cheikho. Beirut, 1912. – Ed. by Ġulāmriḍā Ǧamšīdnižād-i Awwal, *al-Taʿrīf bi-ṭabaqāt al-umam*. Tehran, 1997.

12 Ibn ʿEzra (d. 532/1138). *Kitāb al-Muḥāḍara wa-l-muḏākara*. – Ed. by Montserrat Abumalham Mas, with Span. transl., 2 vols. Madrid, 1985.

13 al-Bayhaqī, Ẓahīr al-Dīn Abū l-Ḥasan ʿAlī b. Zayd Ibn Funduq (d. 565/1169–1170). *Tatimmat Ṣiwān al-ḥikma*. – Ed. by Rafīq al-ʿAǧam. Beirut, 1994.

14 Faḫr al-Dīn al-Rāzī, Abū ʿAbd Allāh Muḥammad b. ʿUmar (d. 607/1210). *Al-Maṭālib al-ʿāliya min al-ʿilm al-ilāhī*. – Ed. by Aḥmad Ḥiǧāzī al-Saqqā, 9 vols. Beirut, 1407/1987.

15 Yāqūt b. ʿAbd Allāh al-Rūmī al-Baġdādī al-Ḥamawī (d. 626/1229). *Iršād al-arīb*. – Ed. by David Samuel Margoliouth, *The Irshād al-arīb ilā maʿrifat al-adīb or Dictionary of Learned Men of Yāqūt*, 7 vols. London, 1923–1926.

16 Yāqūt. *Muʿǧam al-buldān*. – Ed. by Ferdinand Wüstenfeld, *Jacut's Geographisches Wörterbuch aus den Handschriften zu Berlin, St. Petersburg und Paris*, 6 vols. Leipzig, 1867. – Repr. Tehran, 1965.

17 Ibn al-Qifṭī, Ǧamāl al-Dīn ʿAlī b. Yūsuf (d. 646/1248). *Taʾrīḫ al-ḥukamāʾ* [*Iḫbār al-ʿulamāʾ bi-aḫbār al-ḥukamāʾ*, epitome by Muḥammad b. ʿAlī al-Zawzanī]. – Ed.

by Julius Lippert, *Ibn al-Qifṭī's Taʾrīḫ al-ḥukamāʾ, auf Grund der Vorarbeiten August Müllers*. Leipzig, 1903.

18 Ibn Abī Uṣaybiʿa, Muwaffaq al-Dīn Aḥmad b. al-Qāsim (d. 668/1270). *ʿUyūn al-anbāʾ fī ṭabaqāt al-aṭibbāʾ*. – Ed. by August Müller, 2 vols. Cairo, 1299/1882; Königsberg, 1884. – Repr. Westmead, 1972.

19 Ibn Ḫallikān, Aḥmad b. Muḥammad (d. 681/1282). *Wafayāt al-aʿyān*. – Ed. by Iḥsān ʿAbbās, 8 vols. Beirut, 1968.

20 Ibn al-ʿIbrī, Abū l-Farağ Gregorios [Barhebraeus] (d. 685/1286). *Taʾrīḫ muḫtaṣar al-duwal*. – Ed. by Anṭūn Ṣāliḥānī. S.l., 1890; Beirut, 1958 (2nd ed.).

21 al-Šahrazūrī, Šams al-Dīn Muḥammad b. Maḥmūd (d. after 687/1288). *Nuzhat al-arwāḥ wa-rawḍat al-arwāḥ fī taʾrīḫ al-ḥukamāʾ wa-l-falāsifa*. – Ed. by Ḫwaršīd Aḥmad, 2 vols. Hyderabad, 1976.

22 Ibn Faḍl Allāh al-ʿUmarī (d. 749/1349). *Masālik al-abṣār fī mamālik al-amṣār*. – Ed. by Fuat Sezgin, in collaboration with A. Jokhosha and Eckhard Neubauer, *Routes Toward Insight into the Capital Empires Book 9*. Frankfurt a.M., 1988. – Facsimile.

1.2 *Sources Used by al-Rāzī*

31 Galen. *Compendium Timaei Platonis aliorumque dialogorum synopsis quae exstant fragmenta* [*Plato Arabus* 1]. – Ed. by Paul Kraus and Richard Walzer. London, 1951.

32 Galen. *De moribus* [Arabic Epitome: *Fī l-Aḫlāq*]. – Ed. by Paul Kraus, "Dirāsāt fī Taʾrīḫ al-tarğama fī l-islām, I." *Bulletin of the Faculty of Arts* 5 (1937 [1939]): 1–51. – Also in *Dirāsāt wa-nuṣūṣ* [*35], 190–211. – Engl. transl. by Daniel Davies, "Character Traits." In: *Galen. Psychological Writings*. Ed. by Peter N. Singer. Cambridge, 2013, 135–150.

33 Galen. *Galens Abhandlung darüber, dass der vorzügliche Arzt Philosoph sein muss* [*Kitāb fī anna al-ṭabīb al-fāḍil faylasūf*]. – Ed. by Peter Bachmann, with German transl. Göttingen, 1965.

34 al-Ğāḥiẓ. *Fī Ṣināʿat al-kalām*. – Ed. by ʿAbd al-Salām Hārūn, *Rasāʾil al-Ğāḥiẓ*, vol. 4. Cairo, 1979, 241–250.

35 *Dirāsāt wa-nuṣūṣ fī l-falsafa wa-l-ʿulūm ʿind al-ʿArab*. – Ed. by ʿAbd al-Raḥmān Badawī. Beirut, 1981.

1.3 *Works*

For further editions cf. Daiber, *Bibliography of Islamic Philosophy*, vol. 2 [*3], 4–6.

1.3.1 Collections

41 *Rasāʾil falsafiyya li-Abī Bakr Muḥammad b. Zakariyyāʾ al-Rāzī*. Ed. by Paul Kraus. Cairo, 1939. – Contents summarized in Bausani [*31].

1.3.2 Individual Editions

45 *Kitāb al-Muršid aw al-fuṣūl*. – Ed. by Albert Zakī Iskandar. Cairo, 1995.

46 *Kitāb al-Sīra al-falsafiyya*. – Ed. by Paul Kraus in *Rasā'il falsafiyya* [*41] 97–111. – Engl. transl. by Arthur John Arberry, "Rhazes on the philosophic life." *Asiatic Review* 45 (1949): 703–713; also in Arberry, *Aspects of Islamic Civilization*. London, 1964, 120–130. – Engl. transl. by Charles E. Butterworth, "The Book of the Philosophic Life." *Interpretation* 20, no. 3 (1993): 227–236 (cf. ibid., p. 237–257 the comments by Butterworth: The origins of al-Rāzī's political philosophy). – French transl. by Paul Kraus, "Raziana I. La conduite du philosophe: Traité d'éthique d'Abū Muḥammad b. Zakariyya al-Rāzī." *Orientalia* N.S. 4 (1935): 300–334; repr. in Kraus, *Alchemie, Ketzerei, Apokryphen im frühen Islam: Gesammelte Aufsätze*. Ed. by Rémi Brague. Hildesheim, Zurich, New York, 1994, 221–255. – Span. transl. by Emilio Tornero, *La conducta virtuosa del filósofo al-Rāzī: Traducción, introducción y notas*. Madrid, 2004, 95–104.

47 *Kitāb al-Šukūk ʿalā Ǧālīnūs*. – Ed. by Mehdi Mohaghegh. Tehran, 1993.

48 *Kitāb al-Ṭibb al-rūḥānī*. – Ed. by Paul Kraus in *Rasā'il falsafiyya* [*41], 1–96. – Repr. in Mehdi Mohaghegh, *al-Dirāsāt al-taḥlīliyya: Analytical Studies on the Spiritual Physic of Rāzī*. Tehran, 1999, 67–164. – Engl. transl. by Arthur John Arberry, *The Spiritual Physick of Rhazes*. London, 1950. – French transl. by Rémi Brague, *Muhammad Ibn Zakariyyā Al-Razi (Rhazès): La médecine spirituelle*. Paris, 2003. – Span. transl. by Emilio Tornero, *La conducta virtuosa del filósofo al-Rāzī: Traducción, introducción y notas*. Madrid, 2004, 27–91.

49 *Maqāla fī Amārāt al-iqbāl wa-l-dawla*. – Ed. by Paul Kraus in *Rasā'il falsafiyya* [*41], 135–138.

50 *Maqāla fī Mā baʿd al-ṭabīʿa*. – Ed. by Paul Kraus in *Rasā'il falsafiyya* [*41], 113–134. – Ital. transl. by Giulio A. Lucchetta [*87], 359–378.

51 *al-Mudḫal al-ṣaġīr ilā ʿilm al-ṭibb*. – Ed. by ʿAbd al-Laṭīf al-ʿAbd. Cairo, 1397/1977.

2 Translations Available in al-Rāzī's Time

Abū Bakr al-Rāzī's comprehensive collection of medical excerpts, *Kitāb al-Ḥāwī* (translated into Latin under the title *Continens*), provides us with an idea of the vast number of medical texts which were available in Arabic translation in the 3rd/9th century. The decisive texts from the Greek medical corpus (Sezgin 1970 [*1: 20–171], Ullmann 1970 [*2: 25–100]) were the translations of Hippocrates, available already in the early 3rd/9th century, and, later on, those of Galen in particular. The Arabic and Syriac versions of Galen's texts, which in part were based on compendia, i.e. the so-called *Summaria Alexandrinorum* (Endress 1992 [*32: 118–119]), were produced or commissioned by arguably the most eminent translator, Ḥunayn b. Isḥāq (d. 260/873, cf. § 9.2.1

below); sometimes earlier translations were utilized or consulted in the process (cf. Endress 1987 [*32: 424–426]). Al-Rāzī's medical works are fundamentally based on the Arabic Galenic corpus, even though he also draws on other Greek authors (Ullmann 1970 [*2: 128–135]). Thus he was the first to compose systematic textbooks to replace the Galenic corpus (Endress 1992 [*32:121–122]).

Among the rare philosophical works translated by Ḥunayn (or his school) that are relevant in the present context is Galen's *Compendium of Plato's Timaeus* (lost in the original Greek), which may well have been known to al-Rāzī (see below p. 405). Ḥunayn's son Isḥāq b. Ḥunayn (830–910) continued his father's translation activities, though focusing more on Aristotle's physical and scientific works. He translated Aristotle's *Physics* into Arabic, thus creating the basis for the study of the *Physics* in the Baghdad school under Yaḥyā b. ʿAdī (d. 363/974) (Lettinck 1994 [*108: 3–33]; on Yaḥyā cf. § 7.2 below). A roughly contemporary version by Qusṭā b. Lūqā (ca. 204–300/820–912), which apparently incorporated parts of the commentaries by John Philoponus and Alexander of Aphrodisias, is not extant; nor is the translation produced by Abū ʿUṯmān al-Dimašqī (d. after 302/914). In his treatise on metaphysics, al-Rāzī appears to have drawn upon Qusṭā's version: in his definition of nature he refers to Aristotle's *Physics* book II, shortly before (*Maqāla* [*50: 117,11. 118,1. 121,4. 123,9; Ital. transl. 360–361. 364. 367]) mentioning John Philoponus and his commentary on the *Physics* several times (cf. Lettinck, Urmson 1994 [*109: 210: 684,34]). That al-Rāzī was furthermore familiar with Qusṭā's translation of the *Placita philosophorum*, a Greek doxography ascribed to Plutarch, is confirmed by a reference to Metrodorus and Seleucus in his treatise on metaphysics (*Maqāla* [*50: 132,13–15. 133,13–18; Ital. transl. 376–377]; Daiber 1980 [*78: 81, on I 5,4; 377–378, on II 1,5]). Al-Rāzī will also have benefitted from Ibn al-Biṭrīq's translation activity: the fact that he mentions Aristotle's *On the Heavens* (*Maqāla* [*50: 133,1–12; Ital. transl. 376–377]) as well as Proclus (*Maqāla* [*50: 128,16; Ital. transl. 372]) indicates that he knew the translations of the Aristotelian corpus and of some Neoplatonic works by Proclus which were produced in the early 3rd/9th century by Yaḥyā b. al-Biṭrīq (or his school) under the auspices of the philosopher al-Kindī (d. between 247/861 and 252/866). This applies in particular to the translation of Proclus' *Elements of Theology* (Endress 1973 [*68: 185–193]), which, together with further works of a Neoplatonic bent, e.g. the so-called *Theology of Aristotle* and the *Liber de Causis*, had a lasting influence on the way in which Aristotle was perceived during the Islamic era. This is in fact exemplified by al-Rāzī, who took a critical stance towards Aristotle and sympathized with John Philoponus, whose works *Against Proclus On the Eternity of the World, Against Aristotle On the Eternity of the World* and *On the Contingency of the World* may well have been known to him. He professes himself explicitly to be a follower of Plato's, whose *Timaeus* was supposedly translated by Yaḥyā b. al-Biṭrīq (Dunlop 1959 [*54: 144]). By contrast, Aristotle's *Organon* does not play any significant role in al-Rāzī's philosophy, even though it was available to him in translations produced by Ḥunayn and his school (Peters 1968 [*59: 7–30]) and he himself composed summaries of its individual books, including Porphyry's *Isagoge* (see LW °24–°28 below). It seems that he regarded logic as indispensable for theologians (cf. LW °30).

3 Life

Abū Bakr al-Rāzī earned his fame first and foremost as a physician; from the 6th/12th century onwards, some of his medical works were translated into Latin (Sezgin 1970 [*1: 274–294], Ullmann 1970 [*2: 128–135], Richter-Bernburg 1994 [*8: 377–392]). The few extant remains of his philosophical and scientific writings were collectively edited by Kraus in 1939. Any further material from al-Rāzī's pen that has since been discovered belongs to the field of medicine. The most noteworthy case is al-Rāzī's book on his *Doubts on Galen* (*al-Šukūk ʿalā Ǧālīnūs*), which was edited by Mohaghegh in 1993 [*47] and is still awaiting proper study (Pines 1953 [*52: 256–263], Bürgel 1968 [*57: 284–286], Strohmaier 1998 [*114: 263–287]).

Our knowledge of al-Rāzī's life is just as fragmentary as that of his work. The scholar al-Bīrūnī (d. ca. 442/1050) reports, in his *Risāla fī Fihrist kutub Muḥammad b. Zakariyyāʾ al-Rāzī* ([*10: 4,8–5,10] Mohaghegh), that he was born on 1 Šaʿbān 251/28 August 865 in Rayy, a suburb of today's Tehran, where he died on 5 Šaʿbān 313/26 October 925 (cf. Ṣāʿid [*11: 53,3–4 Cheikho; 222,2 Ǧamšīdnižād-i Awwal]; Barhebraeus [*20: 158,4]). Apart from that, al-Bīrūnī is merely able to report that al-Rāzī had first been interested in chemistry, and switched to medicine because his occupation with chemistry had harmed his eyes. When exactly this happened, however, he does not tell us.

According to Ibn Abī Uṣaybiʿa, though [*18: I 309,16–18], al-Rāzī came to Baghdad aged about 30, i.e. in 282/895, after first (*min ṣiġarihi*) having studied philosophy (*al-ʿulūm al-ʿaqliyya*), literature (*ʿilm al-adab*), and poetry, and it was only after his arrival there that he turned to medicine. This is already reported by Ibn Ǧulǧul (*Ṭabaqāt* [*6: 77–78]), and later by Ibn Ḫallikān [*19: V 158,1–3] and Ibn Faḍl Allāh [*22: 27,3–4], albeit coupled with the somewhat different and not entirely consistent remark that al-Rāzī first concerned himself with music, before later turning to medicine and philosophy (thus also Barhebraeus [*20: 158,4–5]). Ṣāʿid al-Andalusī (5th/11th century), on the other hand, tells us that al-Rāzī turned to philosophy after first having pursued music (Ṣāʿid [*11: 52,22–23 Cheikho; 221,10–11 Ǧamšīdnižād-i Awwal]).

Deviating from these reports, Ẓahīr al-Dīn al-Bayhaqī (d. 565/1169–1170) relates in an anecdotal account (*Tatimma* [*13: 34,10–35,5]; cf. Meyerhof 1948

[*13: 136]) that al-Rāzī used to be a goldsmith who practiced alchemy (*ʿilm al-iksīr*) and contracted an inflammation of the eyes, on account of which he turned to medicine. The same story appears again in the 7th/13th century in al-Šahrazūrī (*Nuzha* [*21: II 7,2–10]).

After studying medicine in Baghdad he seems to have returned to Rayy, since he first became head of the hospital in Rayy, before being appointed to the same position in Baghdad'. Without giving a specific date, Ibn Ǧulǧul reports: 'He was head of the hospital in Rayy, and after that, for some time (*zamānan*), of the hospital in Baghdad (*Ṭabaqāt* [*6: 77,3–4]; likewise Barhebraeus [*20: 158,6]). Some excerpts from Ibn Ǧulǧul, however, deviate from this text: Ibn al-Qifṭī writes *ṭawīlan* 'for a long time' instead of 'for some time' (*Taʾrīḫ* [*17: 272,6; cf. 271,21]). Ibn Abī Uṣaybiʿa (*ʿUyūn* [*18: I 310,22–23]) modifies the statement so as to report that Abū Bakr al-Rāzī 'was head of the hospital in Rayy for some time' before taking up his post at the hospital in Baghdad. In the same excerpt from Ibn Ǧulǧul, Ibn Ḫallikān (*Wafayāt* [*19: V 157, ult.]) replaces *zamānan* by *fī ayyām al-Muktafī*, 'in the days of al-Muktafī'.

Al-Muktafī bi-llāh was the governor of Rayy and other cities between 281/894 and 286/899, and after that of Mesopotamia, before becoming caliph for the six years leading up to his death in 295/908. If Ibn Ḫallikān's information is correct, we can interpret it to mean that Abū Bakr al-Rāzī probably was head of the hospital in Baghdad during al-Muktafī's caliphate, i.e. between 289/902 and 295/908. Al-Rāzī dedicated his two books *al-Ṭibb al-Manṣūrī* and *al-Ṭibb al-rūḥānī* to the Samanid prince al-Manṣūr b. Ismāʿīl, who apparently was a friend of his (Ibn al-Nadīm [*5: 299,3–4 Flügel; 356,25 Taǧaddud; Engl. transl. II 704; cf. there n. 169 on variants of al-Manṣūr's name]); if we can trust Yāqūt's report (*Muʿǧam* [*16: II 901,15–16]), this prince had arrived in Rayy in 290/902–903 and was governor there for six years, i.e. up to 296–297/908–909. Perhaps al-Rāzī wanted to secure his return to Rayy with the help of these dedications, or generally by means of his friendship to al-Manṣūr (for a different view, see Sezgin 1970 [*1: III 274–275]). In any case, *al-Manṣūrī* and *al-Ṭibb al-rūḥānī* must have been composed before 296–297/908–909.

Al-Rāzī may well have alternated several times between positions in Baghdad and Rayy, before he finally settled in Rayy. Perhaps this is what the Baghdad bookseller Ibn al-Nadīm alludes to in his *Fihrist* (completed in 377/988) when he notes that al-Rāzī 'travelled around in the countries' (*intaqala fī l-buldān*) (*Fihrist* [*5: 299,3 Flügel; 356,25 Taǧaddud]; following him al-Šahrazūrī [*21: II 8,1]). We do not know when exactly al-Rāzī ultimately settled in Rayy, i.e. whether it was during the reign of the governor (before 296–297/908–909), or afterwards. The biographies transmit various anecdotes (Ullmann 1970 [*2: 128]), in particular about his eye disease and the resulting blindness at the end of his life. According to Ibn al-Nadīm, Abū Bakr al-Rāzī had wet eyes because he always ate beans, and he became blind at the end of his life. Ibn al-Nadīm furthermore reports that he treated people in a polite, friendly, and respectful manner (*karīm mutafaḍḍil bārr*), that he was particularly kind to the poor (cf. Ibn al-Ǧazzār [*7: 38,6–39,8]) and the sick, generously sending them food every day or nursing them. One would always find him busy writing (thus also Barhebraeus [*20: 158,11–12], Šahrazūrī [*21: II 8,3–4]).

At the end of his entry on al-Rāzī, Ibn al-Nadīm adds that he had studied philosophy with a man named al-Balḫī (*Fihrist* [*5: 299,10–11 Flügel; 357,4–5 Taǧaddud; Engl. transl. II 701–702]; following him, Šahrazūrī [*21: II 8,5–6]). He follows up this remark with a brief entry on this scholar, who was proficient in philosophy and the ancient sciences. At this point Ibn al-Nadīm adds the intriguing note which prompted Kraus and Pines (1936 [*22: III 1225a]) to suggest an identification of this person with al-Rāzī's role model Īrānšahrī: *wa-qad yuqālu inna l-Rāziya ddaʿā kutubahu fī ḏālika* 'people allege sometimes that al-Rāzī claimed his (al-Balḫī's) books on this (sc. on philosophy and ancient sciences) as his own'. He, Ibn al-Nadīm, had seen many works of his, notably drafts and sketches that were not meant for publication.

Ibn al-Nadīm follows this up with a chapter on a man called Šahīd b. al-Ḥusayn, known by the *kunya* Abū l-Ḥasan, whom he reports to have published books, and to have engaged in disputes with al-Rāzī (*Fihrist* [*5: 299,17–19 Flügel; 357,10–12 Taǧaddud; Engl. transl. II 701–702]). He is probably identical with a person named Šuhayd (or Šahīd) al-Balḫī (de Blois 1996 [*15: 333–337]), who is mentioned shortly afterwards (*Fihrist* [*5: 301,5 Flügel; 358,22 Taǧaddud, who, incorrectly, has 'Suhayl']), and whose critique of the treatise on pleasure (*al-laḏḏa*) – the title probably refers to al-Rāzī's work of the same name (*Fihrist* [*5: 299,25 Flügel; 357,18 Taǧaddud]) – al-Rāzī is said to have refuted [*5: 301,5–6 Flügel; 358,22 Taǧaddud], along with two further works by Šuhayd/Šahīd al-Balḫī, namely a critique of al-Rāzī's theology (*al-ʿilm al-ilāhī*) and a work on eschatology (*Taṯbīt al-maʿād*) [*5: 301,10–11. 14 Flügel; 358,26. 29 Taǧaddud]. Ibn al-Nadīm rightly assumes that this Šuhayd/Šahīd al-Balḫī is not identical with the subsequently mentioned Abū Zayd al-Balḫī, another contemporary of al-Rāzī's [*5: 301,10–11. 14 Flügel; 358,26. 29 Taǧaddud] (on Abū Zayd al-Balḫī cf. § 5.1.2 above).

Apart from the two refutations of al-Rāzī and the eschatological work, no further writings by Šuhayd/Šahīd al-Balḫī are known to us. This is different in the case of Abū Zayd: his long list of works is presented by Ibn al-Nadīm elsewhere (*Fihrist* [*5: 138,14-ult. Flügel; 153,12-ult. Taǧaddud; Engl. transl. I 303–304]; based on that, Yāqūt [*15: I 142,4–143,6]; Rowson 1990 [*14: 61–70]).

However, Ibn al-Nadīm does not discuss whether this Abū Zayd al-Balḫī might be identical with the al-Balḫī whom he mentions as al-Rāzī's teacher. If we compare the list of works of Abū Zayd al-Balḫī with that of al-Rāzī himself, we will notice that both write on psychology, on prophets, and on theology.

Only one of Abū Zayd al-Balḫī's works is extant today: the psychosomatic treatise *Maṣāliḥ al-abdān wa-l-anfus* (*Hygiene of Body and Soul*, [*3]). In an appendix to this work (*Maṣāliḥ* [*3: 360,11–14]), al-Balḫī's now lost writings *Kitāb al-Amad al-aqṣā fī l-ḥikma*, *Kitāb Bayān wuǧūh al-ḥikma fī l-awāmir wa-l-nawāhī al-šarʿiyya*, also known as *Kitāb al-Ibāna ʿan ʿilal al-diyāna*, *Kitāb fī l-Ḫilāf*, and *Kitāb al-Siyāsa* are mentioned. A few reverberations of the latter, *Kitāb al-Siyāsa* (*Book on Politics*) (see also *Fihrist* [*5: 138,15 Flügel; 153,13–14 Taǧaddud]; based on that, Yāqūt [*15: I 142,5]) have been preserved in later literature; they have been investigated by Rosenthal (1989 [*91]). Al-Balḫī's poltitical thought is informed not so much by al-Kindī's Platonic-Aristotelian notion of politics as religious ethics as by the Persian literary tradition of 'mirrors for princes', where religion takes second place and the common good of society assumes priority over the interest of the individual (Daiber 1996 [*111: 844–845]).

Abū Zayd al-Balḫī's view of religion as of secondary importance provides us with a point of comparison with al-Rāzī and his rationalistic attitude towards religion. On the whole, it therefore does not seem too fanciful to contemplate the possibility that Abū Zayd al-Balḫī's critical stance on religion may have stimulated al-Rāzī's thought (for a different view, see Kraus, Pines 1936 [*22: III 1225a]). In this context it is intriguing to note that al-Rāzī's medical corpus includes a treatise addressed to Abū Zayd al-Balḫī, advising him on the topic of hay fever (al-Bīrūnī [*10: 8,1 (no. 38)], Ibn Abī Uṣaybiʿa [*18: I 319,19]).

4 Works

4.1 List of Works (LW) – 4.2 Description of Works

4.1 *List of Works (LW)*

The following list of al-Rāzī's philosophical writings, including those lost to us, comprises works on ethics, political philosophy, Aristotelian logic, metaphysics, theology, cosmology, physics, psychology, as well as commentaries on Greek works, in which al-Rāzī took a critical stance towards Aristotle and Proclus. The few surviving works provide us with a relatively clear idea about his sources. They are, in the main, Platonic and can often be traced back to Plato's *Timaeus* (Fakhry 1994 [*107: 70–77]), but they also comprise Aristotelian-Alexandrian traditions – including Aristotle's *Physics* and its commentary by John Philoponus (Lucchetta 1987 [*87: 35–38]) –, as well as Galenic (Bar-Asher 1989 [*89: 130–142], Zonta 1995 [*110: 84–85; cf. 116. 119–120]) and Presocratic traditions (Aetius: see LW °21 below). Gnostic-Manichean and Iranian material recedes into the background (Pines 1937 [*49: 54–60], Corbin 1951/1982 [*50: 185–188/41–43], Pines 1955 [*53: 58–60], Peters 1990 [*93: 207–209]).

The list below mainly follows Pines (1997 [*39: 99–107]), whose annotated compilation of al-Rāzī's works is based on the catalogues assembled by al-Bīrūnī (*Risāla* [**10*: 9–18]), Ibn al-Nadīm (*Fihrist* [**5*: 299–302 Flügel; 357–359 Tağaddud; Engl. transl. II 703–709), Ibn Abī Uṣaybiʿa (*ʿUyūn* [**18*: I 315,14–321,20]) and Ibn al-Qifṭī (*Ṭabaqāt* [**17*: 273,9–277,7]), as well as on some data retrieved from al-Rāzī's autobiography (*al-Sīra* [**46*: 108–109]). Ibn Ǧulǧul's catalogue (*Ṭabaqāt* [**6*: 77,4–78,1]), which since has come to light, does not add anything of significance.

The list begins with the extant works and fragments, edited by Kraus, and enumerates them according to their sequence in Kraus' edition.

°1 *Kitāb al-Ṭibb al-rūḥānī* (*The Spiritual Medicine*). – On ethics. Ed. by Kraus [**41*: 1–96]. This edition is reprinted in Mohaghegh 1999 [**48*: 67–164], followed by a facsimile edition of the oldest manuscript, which was not used by Kraus for his edition. It dates from 636/1238–1239, and is in possession of Yaḥyā Mahdawī, Tehran [165–228]. Further editions (Daiber 1999 [*3: II 6]) are based on Kraus' edition. On a manuscript (fragment) that has not been considered in any of the editions, cf. Gutas 1977 [*7]. – For translations cf. [**48*]. Al-Rāzī's *Kitāb al-Ṭibb al-rūḥānī* was criticized by the Ismāʿīlī Ḥamīd al-Dīn al-Kirmānī, *al-Aqwāl al-ḏahabiyya* [**8*]; al-Kirmānī here often continues discussions developed by Abū Ḥātim al-Rāzī in *Aʿlām al-nubuwwa* (see p. 407 below; on al-Kirmānī and Abū Ḥātim al-Rāzī cf. § 9.4.1 below). Similarities between *al-Ṭibb al-rūḥānī* and the ethical treatise *Tahḏīb al-aḫlāq* by the later Christian philosopher Yaḥyā b. ʿAdī (d. 363/974 aged 84 years; on him cf. § 7.2 below) are listed by al-Takrītī 1978 [*74: 207–208]. According to al-Masʿūdī, *al-Tanbīh* [**4*: 106,3–4] Yaḥyā b. ʿAdī was an adherent of al-Rāzī's doctrine.

°2 *Kitāb al-Sīra al-falsafiyya* (*The Philosophical Life*). – An apologetical autobiography, which al-Rāzī composed at the end of his life; due to the advancing weakness of his eyesight and muscles he had to dictate it rather than writing it down himself. – Ed. Kraus [**41*: 97–111]; for Engl. and French transl. cf. [**46*].

°3 *Maqāla fī Mā baʿd al-ṭabīʿa* (*Metaphysics*). – Ed. by Kraus 1939 [**41*: 113–134]. – Ital. transl. Lucchetta 1987 [*87: 359–378].

°4 *Maqāla fī Amārāt al-iqbāl wa-l-dawla* (*Treatise on the Signs of Well-Being and of Political Success*). – On political philosophy. – Ed. Kraus [**41*: 135–138]. – Ital. summary in Bausani 1981 [*31: 21–22]; cf. Daiber 1996 [*111: 846].

°5 *Kitāb al-Laḏḏa* (*On Pleasure*). – This also formed the topic of a dispute with Šuhayd/Šahīd al-Balḫī (Bīrūnī [*10: 10 no. 65]). The Persian fragments in Nāṣir-i Ḫusraw, *Zād al-musāfirīn*, have been edited by Kraus 1939 [*41: 148–164] together with an Arabic transl. Cf. Bausani 1981 [*31: 23–26].

°6 *Kitāb al-ʿIlm al-ilāhī* (*On Theology*). – The Arabic and Persian (Nāṣir-i Ḫusraw, *Zād al-musāfirīn*) fragments have been edited by Kraus 1939 [*41: 165–190] (partial Engl. transl. in Pines 1997 [*39: 100–101]). Cf. Bausani 1981 [*31: 27–32]. It is possible that the next item (LW °7) also belongs to this work (Kraus [*41: 166]). The titles given in the work catalogues alternate, but it is not possible to establish whether they refer to different works of different scope (Pines 1997 [*39: 101]). It remains uncertain whether the title *Kitāb al-ʿIlm al-ilāhī ʿalā raʾy Aflāṭūn* (*On Theology According to Plato*), which is only mentioned by Ibn Abī Uṣaybiʿa (*ʿUyūn* [*18: I 317,1–2]) and was included by Pines on that basis (1997 [*39: 103 no. 6]), represents an independent work by al-Rāzī. – Ibn Abī Uṣaybiʿa (*ʿUyūn* [*18: I 317,1–2]) further refers to a poem (*qaṣīda*) on theology. Moreover, the biographies mention, by various titles, refutations composed by the Muʿtazilī Abū l-Qāsim al-Balḫī, to which al-Rāzī is said to have responded in writing (Kraus [*41: 166–168], Pines 1997 [*39: 104 nos 13, 14, 15]): *Kitāb al-Radd ʿalā Abī l-Qāsim al-Balḫī fī naqḍihi al-maqāla al-ṯāniya min al-ʿilm al-ilāhī* (*On the Objection against Abū l-Qāsim al-Balḫī on account of his Refutation of the Second Treatise of the Theology* [*by al-Rāzī*]) (Pines 1997 [*39: 104 no. 13) seems to be identical with the title *Kitāb Naqḍ al-naqḍ ʿalā l-Balḫī fī l-ʿilm al-ilāhī* (Pines 1997 [*39: 104 no. 14]), recorded by Ibn al-Qifṭī and Ibn al-Nadīm. Also, both works are probably identical with the titles *Kitāb ilā Abī l-Qāsim al-Balḫī fī l-Ziyāda ʿalā ǧawābihi wa-ʿalā ǧawāb hāḏā l-ǧawāb* (*Against Abū l-Qāsim al-Balḫī concerning the Addition to his Response, and to the Response to that Response*) (Pines 1997 [*39: 104 no. 15]) and *Mā ǧarā baynahu wa-bayna Abī l-Qāsim fī l-zamān* (*On* [*the Disputes*] *between him and Abū l-Qāsim al-Balḫī concerning Time*) (Pines 1997 [*39: 104 no. 16], based on al-Bīrūnī). Fragments are extant in Faḫr al-Dīn al-Rāzī, *al-Maṭālib al-ʿāliya* [*14: IV 413–419] (Rashed 2000 [*117: 39–54]; see now also Vallat 2015 [*128: 183–200], who adds Abū l-Qāsim al-Balkhī al-Kaʿbī's reports on al-Rāzī in Muṭahhar Ibn Ṭāhir al-Maqdisī [4th/10th cent.], *Kitāb al-Badʾ wa-l-taʾrīkh*).

The work *Kitāb Munāqaḍat al-Ǧāḥiẓ fī kitābihi fī faḍīlat al-kalām*, mentioned by Ibn al-Nadīm (*Fihrist* [*5: 300,24–25 Flügel; 328,14 Tağaddud; Engl. transl. II 705]) and, based on him, by Ibn Abī Uṣaybiʿa (*ʿUyūn* [*18: I 316,22], slightly extended), by Ibn al-Qifṭī (*Taʾrīḫ* [*17: 274,19]) and Pines (1997 [*39: 104 no. 17]) does not belong to this group of titles. Al-Bīrūnī (*Fihrist* [*10: 11 no. 89]) has *Fīmā waqaʿa li-l-Ǧāḥiẓ min al-tanāquḍ fī faḍīlat ṣināʿat al-kalām* instead. From this it clearly emerges that the work in question is a treatise on the inconsistencies which al-Ǧāḥiẓ falls into in *Fī Ṣināʿat al-kalām*, a work that is available in print [*34*] and is concerned with rhetoric. Al-Bīrūnī classifies it as belonging to the category of *ṭabīʿiyyāt* (works on physics), while Ibn Abī Uṣaybiʿa appears to have regarded it as a work 'against the philosophers', just as did his Latin translator Salomon Negri (d. 1728 or 1729) (Graf 1951 [*51: 279]). The Latin translation of the entry on al-Rāzī was published by Ranking (1914 [*11]); there the relevant passage runs as follows: '*Liber contradictionibus Giahezi in libro suo de metaphysica et de iis quae Philosophis perperam attribuit*'.

°7 *Kitāb fī Naqḍ kitāb Anābū ilā Furfūriyūs fī šarḥ maḏāhib Arisṭūṭālīs fī l-ʿilm al-ilāhī* (*On the Refutation of Anebo's Letter to Porphyry, Commenting on Aristotle's Doctrines on Metaphysics*). – Cf. Ibn Abī Uṣaybiʿa [**18*: I 317,9–10], Ranking 1914 [*11: 254 no. 85], al-Bīrūnī [**10*: 14 no. 128], Peters 1973 [*69: 291–292]).

°8 *al-Qawl fī l-Qudamāʾ al-ḫamsa* (*On the Five Eternals*), i.e. Creator, Soul, Matter, Space, and Time. – This may have been a part of al-Rāzī's *Kitāb al-ʿIlm al-ilāhī* (cf. LW °6). The Arabic fragments of the work have been edited by Kraus 1939 [**41*: 191–216]. Al-Rāzī seems to have discussed his five principles individually as well; they form the topic of a dispute between Abū Bakr al-Rāzī and the Ismaili Abū Ḥātim al-Rāzī, which the latter recorded in his *Aʿlām al-nubuwwa* (ed. Kraus [**41*: 300,21–313]; this corresponds to Abū Ḥātim [*2: 10–27,15] al-Ṣāwī). Cf. Bausani 1981 [*31: 33–36].

°9 *al-Qawl fī l-Hayūlā* (*On Matter*). – Quotations and testimonies are assembled in Kraus [**41*: 217–240], where the various titles of the work are listed as well. Cf. Bausani 1981 [*31: 37–39]. The *Kitāb al-Hayūlā al-kabīr*, mentioned by Pines 1997 [*39: 103 no. 5], is classified by Kraus – and probably rightly so – as a variant of *Kitāb al-Hayūlā al-muṭlaqa wa-l-ǧuzʾiyya*. – Al-Bīrūnī is the only bibliographer to mention (after the *Kitāb al-Hayūlā al-kabīr*) a further work by the title of *al-Hay(y)ūlā al-ṣaġīr* (no. 59) (= Pines 1997 [*39: 104 no. 18]). We may assume that al-Rāzī will furthermore have discussed the topic in his *Theology* (*Kitāb al-ʿIlm al-ilāhī*) (Kraus [**41*: 173]), as well as in his *Reply to the Theologian al-Mismaʿī concerning his Refutation of the Materialists* (Pines 1997 [*39: 105 no. 19]) and his *Reply to Ibn al-Yammān* (or: *Tammār*) *concerning his Refutation of al-Mismaʿī on Matter* (Pines 1997 [*39: 105 no. 20]). The latter may possibly have formed a part of al-Rāzī's *Reply* to the theologian al-Mismaʿī.

°10 *Kitāb fī l-Mudda wa-hiya l-zamān wa-fī l-ḫalāʾ wa-l-malāʾ wa-humā l-makān* (*On Duration, i.e. on Time; on Filled and Vacant Space, i.e. on Space*). – Quotations and references are compiled in Kraus [**41*: 241–279] (Meier 1992 [*101: 15–16]). Cf. Bausani 1981 [*31: 40–44]. The topic was also discussed in al-Rāzī's *Theology*. Perhaps the text entitled *Fī l-Farq bayna ibtidāʾ al-mudda wa-btidāʾ al-ḥarakāt* (*On the Difference Between the Beginning of Time and the Beginning of Movement*), only mentioned in al-Bīrūnī (*Fihrist* [*10: 9 no. 63]; cf. Pines 1997 [*39: 103 no. 4]), was part of this work.

°11 *Kitāb fī anna l-Nafs laysat bi-ǧism* (*On the Fact that the Soul is Not a Body*); *Kitāb al-Nafs al-kabīr* (*Long Book on the Soul*); *Kitāb fī l-Nafs al-ṣaġīr* (*Short Book on the Soul*). – Cf. *Fihrist* [*5: 301,15–16 Flügel; 358, ult. Tağaddud], Ibn Abī Uṣaybiʿa [*18: I 320,12–13], Ranking 1914 [*11: 263 no. 164–165].

°12 *Kitāb ʿIllat ǧaḏb ḥaǧar al-maġnāṭīs li-l-ḥadīd* (*On Why a Magnetic Stone Attracts Iron*). – Pines 1997 [*39: 104 no. 10; cf. 162–164]. According to Ibn Abī Uṣaybiʿa [*18: I 320,11], the treatise contained an extensive discussion of the vacuum.

°13 *Kitāb fī anna li-l-insān ḫāliqan mutqinan ḥakīman* (*On the Fact that Man has a Perfect, Wise Creator*). – Pines 1997 [*39: 105 no. 23]. The work seems to have an alternative title, *Kitāb fī anna li-l-ʿālam ḫāliqan ḥakīman* (Pines 1997 [*39: 105 no. 24]). A fragment of the latter is preserved by Nāṣir-i Ḫusraw, in *Zād al-musāfir*: cf. Kraus [*41: 282–286]. It shows that the discussion included the issue of soul and matter (cf. also the fragments edited in Kraus [*41: 286–290]).

°14 *Maqāla fīmā istadrakahu min al-faṣl fī l-kalām fī l-qāʾilīn bi-ḥudūṯ al-aǧsām wa-ʿalā l-qāʾilīn bi-qidamihā* (*On the Section He has Added to the Treatise on Those Who Teach the Temporal Generation of Bodies, and Against Those Who Claim their Eternity*). – Pines 1997 [*39: 106 no. 26]; *Fihrist* [*5: 302,8–9 Flügel; 359,18 Tağaddud; Engl. transl. II 708]. This might be part of al-Rāzī's *Kalām ǧarā baynahu wa-bayna l-Masʿūdī fī ḥudūṯ al-ʿālam* (*Dispute between him and al-Masʿūdī on the Temporal Generation of the World*) (only in Ibn Abī Uṣaybiʿa [*18: I 321,6]; cf. Pines 1997 [*39: 107 no. 29]). Another work that possibly belongs in this context is mentioned by Ibn Abī Uṣaybiʿa [*18: I 319,26–28] (cf. Ranking 1914 [*11: 262 no. 140]) and, in shorter form, by al-Bīrūnī (*Fihrist* [*10: 15 no. 143]): *Kitāb fī anna l-munāqaḍa llatī bayna ahl al-dahr wa-ahl al-tawḥīd fī sabab iḥdāṯ al-ʿālam innamā ǧāza min nuqṣān al-sima* [al-Bīrūnī: *al-qisma*] *fī asbāb al-fiʿl – baʿḍuhu ʿalā l-Tamādiyya* (= *Māddiyya*?) *wa-baʿḍuhu ʿalā l-qāʾilīn bi-qidam al-ʿālam* (*That the Contradiction between Materialists and Monotheists concerning the Cause of the Origin of the World is only Possible because the Efficient Causes have not been sufficiently Specified; against the Tamādiyya* [= *Māddiyya*: *'materialists'*?], *and all those who profess the eternity of the world*).

°15 *Kitāb fī an lā yumkin al-ʿālam an yakūna lam yazal ʿalā miṯāl mā nušāhiduhu* (*That it is not Possible for the World Continuously to Be as we Perceive it*). – Pines 1997 [*39: 104 no. 9].

°16 *Kitāb al-Intiqād wa-l-taḥrīr ʿalā l-Muʿtazila* (*Critique and Clarification directed against the Muʿtazila*). – Pines 1997 [*39: 104 no. 11]. This is probably identical with a further title listed by Ibn Abī Uṣaybiʿa [*18: I 319,32], *Kitāb al-Intiqād ʿalā ahl al-Muʿtazila* (*Critique of the Muʿtazila*). Part of this critique may well have been constituted by the treatise *On the Proof of Transformation* (*istiḥāla*), *and of* *this being inconsistent with the claim that transformation equals latency and manifestation* (*kumūn wa-ẓuhūr*), mentioned by al-Bīrūnī [*10: 10 no. 66], which evidently is directed against the Muʿtazilite al-Naẓẓām (cf. van Ess 1986 [*84]).

°17 *Kitāb mā ǧarā baynahu wa-bayna Sīsin al-Manānī* (*or: al-Ṯanawī*) *yurīhi ḫaṭaʾ mawḍūʿātihi wa-fasād nāmūsihi fī sabʿ mabāḥiṯ* (*On* [*the Dispute*] *between him and the Manichaean* [*or: dualist*] *Sīsin, for the sake of demonstrating to him the defectiveness of his hypotheses and the inadequacy of his law; in seven studies*). – Cf. Ibn Abī Uṣaybiʿa [*18: I 315,29–30], Ranking 1914 [*11: 248 no. 10], Pines 1997 [*39: 105 no. 21].

°18 *Kitāb Samʿ al-kiyān* (*On Physics*). – Pines 1997 [*39: 105 no. 22]. The book is mentioned by al-Rāzī in his *Šukūk ʿalā Ǧalīnūs* (*Doubts about Galen*) [*47: 30,14–15]. In his *Sīra al-falsafiyya* he also calls it *Introduction to the Natural Sciences* (*al-Mudḫal ilā l-ʿilm al-ṭabīʿī*) (*al-Sīra* [*46: 109,1]). Apparently, his *Risāla yabḥaṯu fīhā ʿan al-arḍ al-ṭabīʿiyya: ṭīn hiya am ḥaǧar? Dāḫil Samʿ al-kiyān* (*Treatise in which he investigates whether the natural earth is clay or stone; a component of* [*his work on*] *Physics*) (Ibn Abī Uṣaybiʿa [*18: I 319,2–3], Ranking 1914 [*11: 259 no. 111]) also forms a part of this work. Three further titles al-Rāzī mentions in *al-Sīra al-falsafiyya* [*46: 109,2–4] may conceivably belong to the work, although this cannot be proved: *Fī Šakl al-ʿālam* (*On the Shape of the World*), *Sabab qiyām al-arḍ fī wasaṭ al-falak* (*The Cause of the Earth's Position in the Middle of the Heavenly Sphere*); *Sabab taḥarruk al-falak ʿalā istidāra* (*The Cause of the Circular Motion of the Heavenly Sphere*).

°19 *Kitāb fī anna l-ǧism yataḥarraku min ḏātihi wa-anna l-ḥaraka mabdaʾ ṭabīʿatihi* (*That a Body moves on its own accord, and that motion is a principle of its nature*). – *Fihrist* [*5: 301,3 Flügel; 358,20 Taǧaddud]; cf. Ibn al-Qifṭī [*17: 275,2]; Ibn Abī Uṣaybiʿa [*18: I 316,32–33]; al-Bīrūnī [*10: 10 no. 9]; al-Sīra [*46: 109,4–5]. As we can see from al-Rāzī's *Maqāla fī Mā baʿd al-ṭabīʿa* [*50: 116–134], he polemicizes against the Peripatetic notion (cf. Aristotle, *Physics* III.1) of nature as a source of motion (Pines 1997 [*39: 105 n. 172]; cf. Lucchetta 1987 [*87: 49–55]). Motion appears as something temporary and transient in a treatise mentioned by al-Bīrūnī [*10: 10 no. 72], *On the Fact that Rest* (*sukūn*) *and* [*the state of*] *Separation* (*iftirāq*) *may be Everlasting, but not so Motion* (*ḥaraka*) *and Conjunction* (*iǧtimāʿ*).

°20 *Kitāb al-Šukūk ʿalā Buruqlus* (*Doubts about Proclus*). – Pines 1997 [*39: 106 no. 27]. This work is obviously directed against Proclus' doctrine of the eternity of the world; al-Rāzī seems to refer to it in his *Maqāla fī Mā baʿd al-ṭabīʿa* [*50: 128,6–17. 129,11–12].

°21 *Kitāb al-Ārāʾ al-ṭabīʿiyya* (*Opinions on Natural Science*). – Pines 1997 [*39: 106 no. 28]. The title is formulated in an identical manner to the beginning of the title of the Arabic translation of Pseudo-Plutarch (i.e. Aetius), *Placita philosophorum*, which was produced by the Syriac Christian Qusṭā b. Lūqā (d. ca. 299/912) and was used by al-Rāzī several times (Daiber 1980 [*78: Index s.v. Rāzī, Abū Bekr]; Lucchetta 1987 [*87: Index s.v. Aezio; Ps.-Plutarco]). Perhaps we are looking at an excerpt from al-Rāzī's hand.

°22 *Mā qālat al-qudamāʾ fī l-mabādiʾ wa-l-kayfiyyāt* (*What the Ancients taught on Principles and Qualities*). – Al-Bīrūnī [**10*: 11 no. 87].

°23 *Kitāb fī Tafsīr Kitāb Aflūṭarḫūs fī tafsīr Kitāb Tīmāwūs* (*Commentary on Plutarch's Commentary on the Timaeus*). – According to Pines (1997 [*39: 103 n. 169]), this must be either a commentary on Plutarch's *On the Generation of Soul in the Timaeus* (Περὶ τῆς ἐν Τιμαίῳ ψυχογονίας), or on his *On the World's Having Come into Being According to Plato* (Περὶ τοῦ γεγονέναι κατὰ Πλάτονα τὸν κόσμον). It may be the work al-Rāzī sought to complement in writing his *Supplement to Plutarch's Book* (*Kitāb fī Itmām Kitāb Aflūṭarḫūs*) (Pines 1997 [*39: 103 no. 8]).

°24 *Kitāb Īsāġūǧī wa-huwa l-Mudḫal ilā l-manṭiq* (*Isagoge, i.e. Introduction to Logic*). – Ibn Abī Uṣaybiʿa [**18*: I 315,20]; cf. Ranking 1914 [*11: 247 no. 6]; al-Bīrūnī [**10*: 11 no. 90]. Probably a summary of Porphyry's *Isagoge* to Aristotle's *Organon*. This is indicated by the works listed in the following.

°25 *Ǧumal maʿānī Qāṭīġūriyās* (*Compendium of the contents of* [*Aristotle's*] *Categories*). – Ibn Abī Uṣaybiʿa [**18*: I 315,23]; cf. Ranking 1914 [*11: 247 no. 6]. The treatise *Kitāb fī Ǧawāhir al-aǧsām* (*On the Substances of Bodies*), mentioned by Ibn Abī Uṣaybiʿa [**18*: I 321,13]; cf. Ranking 1914 [*11: 267 no. 221], may possibly be part of this work.

°26 *Ǧumal maʿānī Bārīmīniyās* (*Compendium of the Contents of* [*Aristotle's*] *On Interpretation*). – Ibn Abī Uṣaybiʿa [**18*: I 315,23–24]; cf. Ranking 1914 [*11: 247 no. 6].

°27 *Ǧumal maʿānī Anālūṭīqā l-ūlā ilā tamām al-qiyāsāt al-ḥamliyya* (*Compendium of the Contents of* [*Aristotle's*] *Prior Analytics up to the end of* [*the Chapter on*] *Categorical Syllogisms* [Aristotle, *An. pr.* I 7]). – Ibn Abī Uṣaybiʿa [**18*: I 315,23–24]; cf. Ranking 1914 [*11: 247 no. 6]. On this restriction, which is already found in Syriac Aristotelianism and seems to be based on the fact that the section on the three figures of the syllogism accepted by Aristotle forms a self-contained part of the text, cf. Daiber 2001 [*118: 330–335].

°28 *Kitāb al-Mudḫal al-burhānī* (*Introduction to Demonstration* [*i.e. in Aristotle's Posterior Analytics*]). – Ibn Abī Uṣaybiʿa [**18*: I 316,6]; cf. Ranking 1914 [*11: 248 no. 21]; cf. al-Bīrūnī [**10*: 11 no. 93] and al-Rāzī, *al-Sīra* [**46*: 108,20].

°29 *Qaṣīda fī l-Manṭiqiyyāt* (*Poem on Logical Topics*). – Ibn Abī Uṣaybiʿa [**18*: I 317,1]; cf. Ranking 1914 [*11: 254 no. 73].

°30 *Kitāb fī l-Manṭiq yaḏkuru fīhi ǧamīʿ mā yuḥtāǧu ilayhi minhu bi-alfāẓ mutakallimī l-islām* (*On Anything that is Required in the Field of Logic, in the Terminology of Muslim Theologians*). – Ibn Abī Uṣaybiʿa [**18*: I 318,31–32]; cf. Ranking 1914 [*11: 259 no. 108]; more briefly al-Bīrūnī [**10*: 11 no. 92]

°31 *Kitāb al-Maḥabba* (*On Love*). – Ibn Abī Uṣaybiʿa [**18*: I 316,9]; cf. Ranking 1914 [*11: 249 no. 30].

°32 *Kitāb fī l-Ṯubūt fī l-ḥikma* (*On Certainty in Philosophy*). – Ibn Abī Uṣaybiʿa [*18: I 317,14–15]; cf. Ranking 1914 [*11: 254 no. 92].

°33 *Kitāb Mīzān al-ʿaql* (*On the Criterion of the Intellect*). – Ibn Abī Uṣaybiʿa [*18: I 320,13]; cf. Ranking 1914 [*11: 264 no. 266]; al-Bīrūnī [*10: 14 no. 121] has the variant *Maydān al-ʿaql* (*The Domain of the Intellect*).

°34 *Kitāb Naqḍ kitāb al-wuǧūd li-Manṣūr b. Ṭalḥa* (*Refutation of Manṣūr b. Ṭalḥa, On Existence*). – Ibn al-Nadīm [*5: 301,18–19 Flügel; 359,2 Taǧaddud]; Ibn Abī Uṣaybiʿa [*18: I 320,16]; cf. Ranking 1914 [*11: 264 no. 172]. Manṣūr b. Ṭalḥa was the son of Ṭalḥa b. Ṭāhir (d. 213/828–829), who, like his father Ṭāhir b. al-Ḥusayn, was governor of Khorasan (Ṭabarī [*1: III 1064–1065. 1099]).

°35 *Kitāb Maḫārīq al-anbiyāʾ* (*The Fabrications of the Prophets*), also called *Ḥiyal al-mutanabbiyīn* (*The Tricks of Those Who Claim to be Prophets*), probably identical to the treatise *Fī l-nubuwwāt* (*On the Prophetic Religions*), which is supposedly identical with al-Rāzī's *Naqḍ al-adyān* (*Refutation of the Religions*) and extant in quotations within Abū Ḥātim al-Rāzī's refutation, *Aʿlām al-nubuwwa*. – Ibn al-Nadīm [*5: 301,19 Flügel; 359,2–3 Taǧaddud; Engl. transl. II 707]; al-Bīrūnī [*10: 17 no. 173–174]; cf. Meier 1992 [*101: 14], Stroumsa 1999 [*116: 93–107], Dodikhudoev 2013 [*125]. Ibn Abī Uṣaybiʿa doubts al-Rāzī's authorship of the book and attributes the information to the polemical stance of the Egyptian ʿAlī b. Riḍwān [*18: I 320,16–20]; cf. Ranking 1914 [*11: 264 no. 173].

4.2 *Description of Works*

The following description is limited to the three philosophical works by al-Rāzī that alone are extant in their entirety; the first two of them are briefly sketched in *Großes Werklexikon der Philosophie* [*34: 1260–1261]. Their main concern is ethics. – Medical works are excluded here, including those which occasionally contain philosophical remarks and criticism of Galen's logical argumentation, as e.g. al-Rāzī's *Kitāb al-Šukūk ʿalā Ǧālīnūs* (cf. Mohaghegh's English introduction to [*47]; Strohmaier 1998 [*114: 263–287]), or are of a primarily doxographical nature, as e.g. *Maqāla fī Mā baʿd al-ṭabīʿa* [*50]. Treatises extant in fragments (cf. § 6.4, °5, °8, °9, °10 and °13 above) are briefly summarized by Bausani [*31: 23–45].

Kitāb al-Sīra al-falsafiyya
The Philosophical Life

In the opening paragraphs of this small and rather late work, al-Rāzī justifies its composition by referring to the criticism he was subjected to by the intellectual circles of his day on account of his claim to be leading a philosophical life: due to his preoccupation with his fellow human beings and the care for his livelihood (so they said) he departed from the Socratic ideal of a philosopher, who was supposed to lead an ascetic, and solitary life and to adhere to a vegetarian diet. Moreover, the Socratic ideal of an ascetic and abstemious life was unnatural in the first place, since it would lead to the extinction of mankind.

Al-Rāzī concedes this last point to his critics, and then goes on to criticize his opponents' image of Socrates. He points out that later in life, Socrates had left the ascetic way of life behind, leading a moderate life like other people; he had eaten good food – with the exception of meat – and had fathered daughters. Al-Rāzī thus sets out the principle of the mean, to which Socrates himself – after initial exaggeration – finally came to aspire. Socrates nevertheless remained the good example with whom he, al-Rāzī, shared his quest for a just life, knowledge, and the suppression of desire; even though he could never reach Socrates' level of achievement in these respects. Referring to several of his earlier works, in particular to his *Spiritual Medicine* (*al-Ṭibb al-rūḥānī*), al-Rāzī establishes six hypotheses concerning the 'philosophical life':

(1) Praise and blame in the afterlife are determined by our conduct in this world.
(2) The supreme goal does not consist in bodily pleasures, but in the attainment of knowledge and in acting justly. This is how we are freed from this world for the sake of another, where there is neither death nor pain.
(3) Our reason urges us to give up the delights of this world, but not so 'nature' and 'desire'.
(4) God, to whom we look for our reward and whose punishment we fear, objects to causing pain and detests injustice and ignorance in us.
(5) One ought not to tolerate pain for the sake of a greater pleasure.
(6) God has charged us with the particulars of daily life that are inevitable for our continuing existence.

The permanent delights of the hereafter are to be preferred to the ephemeral and transient delights of this world, because the latter cannot liberate us to the world of the soul. Pain in this world derives from nature, not from God. This is how al-Rāzī justifies his maxim that human beings may only ever cause pain to other living beings if it means that greater pain is avoided. Maximising pleasures, for instance through hunting animals or through utilizing domesticated animals, is only permissible in moderation and when serving reasonable and just intentions. Here al-Rāzī gives the example of a man who spurs on a horse, thereby hurting it, for the sake of a higher goal, namely the rescue of the man from the hands of his enemy – in particular if the man is good, intelligent and beneficial to his fellow human beings. Animals may only be hunted and killed if they destroy other animals and eat the flesh of other animals, if they cause harm and do not offer any benefit, or if their numbers are getting out of control. Socrates himself already had banned hunting animals for the sake of eating their meat.

Reason and justice demand that no pain may be inflicted on anyone, including oneself. In this context, al-Rāzī explicitly criticizes Hindus who burn their bodies or throw them onto shards of iron, Manichaens who castrate themselves and chasten themselves through hunger and thirst, as well as Christians who live a monastic life and Muslims who do nothing but pray in the mosque and content themselves with the bare necessities. Such behaviour, al-Rāzī says, constitutes an injustice against one's own self, as it causes pain without extinguishing other pain. It is the way of life which Socrates abandoned in his later years.

Al-Rāzī then goes on to discuss the various degrees of sensitivity towards pain that are found in different people, depending on how much they are accustomed to it. This is why not everybody and everything can be judged according to the same standard. Nevertheless there is unanimous agreement that pleasures must not be sought through injustice and murder, or through contravening God's will. Likewise it is not permitted to overstep a certain limit within asceticism and abstinence, for instance if someone leads a life that is harmful to him and makes him ill. What is permitted is the mean between extreme pleasure and extreme pain: it represents the temperate life of the philosopher, who is just, does not cause unnecessary pain to anyone, and does not act against the will of God. God is the source of reason, dispels sorrow and fear, and guides and supports human beings in everything that brings them closer to Him.

Since God is omniscient and just, his servants, who are closest to him, will possess the highest possible degree of knowledge, justice, and compassion. Hence 'philosophy makes people God-like, as far as this is possible for human beings'. Al-Rāzī here once again refers to his earlier work *The Spiritual Medicine*, which (he points out) explains in detail to what extent the soul ought to liberate itself from bad habits, and to what extent a person striving towards philosophy ought to devote himself to the demands of daily life, and of governing others. Producing a list of some of his works, al-Rāzī then demonstrates that more than anybody among his contemporaries he possesses knowledge that deserves the name of 'philosophy'. The same goes for his actions: he only ever mixed with rulers in order to heal them, or to advise them on what was beneficial for them and their followers. He has not accumulated wealth, he has been just to his fellow human beings, and more than once has relinquished claims and entitlements. He has occupied himself incessantly with writing, so much so that he now is no longer able to read or write, due to fading eyesight and failing strength.

Al-Rāzī concludes his apology by calling on his opponents to conduct an open dispute with him. He concedes that in his actions, he may not have fulfilled every possible expectation; but his knowledge is a different matter. His opponents could not but profit from it, so as to implement it later on in their actions.

Kitāb al-Ṭibb al-rūḥānī
The Spiritual Medicine

This is the only one of al-Rāzī's more extensive works that is extant in its complete form, comprising 20 chapters. Containing frequent repetitions and occasionally drifting off tangentially into digressions which do not reach the level of maturity found in *Kitāb al-Sīra al-falsafiyya*, it presents us with an ethics that does not lay any claim to being heavy philosophical fare, and frequently includes examples taken from Greek anecdotal literature, or from the author's own experience. Addressing the healing of the soul, the book appears to be a companion volume to al-Rāzī's medical work on the healing of the body, *al-Kitāb al-Manṣūrī*, and is likely to have been dedicated to the same person, i.e. the governor of Kirmān and Khorasan, Abū Ṣāliḥ al-Manṣūr b. Isma'īl b. Aḥmad b. Nūḥ.

Al-Rāzī begins with a praise of reason, God's gift to mankind. Reason is what distinguishes man, in his thinking and desiring, from the animals: it is by reason that man is able to reign in his natural instincts and his passions and develop discipline. It is the philosopher who attains this to the greatest extent. Reflection enables a human being to weigh up pleasure and pain against each other. Someone who only follows his pleasures will, in the hereafter, suffer extremely harsh and long-lasting pain once his soul will have left his body, and hence will come to regret his actions. For al-Rāzī, pleasure and desire are expressive of the inability of man to attain everything. However, philosophers are able to rise above this. They are described as people who do not seek wealth and affluence, in some cases even retiring to locations that have been deserted by others. Their arguments refer to the state of the soul, which is striving to liberate itself from the body. Hence any discussion of the soul must deal with the 'improvement of character'. Here al-Rāzī mentions Plato's doctrine (*Rep.* IV) of the tripartite soul, where the rational part of the soul directs the two others, i.e. the appetitive and the spirited parts; a theory which he claims was held by Socrates, too. Controlling one's desires always involves pain, which, however, will be followed by even greater delights. Besides, the suppression of desire becomes easier once one grows accustomed to discipline, and when the resulting delights increase. This, however, presupposes that a human being recognizes his own vices, be it through his own efforts or with the help of others. Here al-Rāzī refers to an unknown work by Galen on the question of 'how one can recognize one's own mistakes' (but compare the material in *On the Affections and Errors of the Soul*, V.8–14 Kühn, 244–250 transl. Singer [cf. **32*]). Chapters 5 to 16 follow this up with a detailed description of the vices: passionate love (*hawā*), whose excesses reveal lack of self-control and intelligence (ch. 5); arrogance is denounced as a consequence of the inability to assess one's own capabilities (ch. 6); envy (which usurps the place of modest competitiveness) is presented as a combination of meanness and avarice, and as a sign of spitefulness. In truth it will never bring any joy; on the contrary, it is detrimental for body and soul: it robs the soul of rational thought, deprives the body of sleep and induces it to take in insufficient amounts of food (ch. 7); anger is explained as the feeling of revenge against somebody who has inflicted harm on the one who takes revenge; it points to a lack of reason when this passion escalates and ends up causing the angry person even more grief than before (ch. 8); mendacity is interpreted as a consequence of the lust for power; reason demands that we be wary of liars (ch. 9); avarice that results from passion alone and does not have any rational justification is frowned upon (ch. 10); solicitousness and anxiousness lead to success, as long as they are kept to the rational mean rather than becoming too much or too little. Al-Rāzī cites philosophy as an example, whose illustrious representatives Socrates, Plato, Aristotle, Theophrastus, Eudemus, Chrysippus, Themistius and Alexander remain for ever beyond reach, irrespective of one's greatest efforts, of one's having relinquished food and sleep, or of unrivalled study (ch. 11); grief, caused for instance by the loss of a loved one, should be reigned in by previous training and strengthening of the rational soul and its awareness of the changeability and transitoriness of all things (ch. 12); greed and gluttony do nothing but cause pain and harm; they are a product of the appetitive soul which lacks the corrective of the rational soul and hence procures more pain for itself than pleasure (ch. 13); drunkenness harms the body, especially by virtue of its excessiveness, and leads to the loss of reason (ch. 14); excessive sexual intercourse for the sake of pleasure weakens the body and causes premature ageing, which is why reason demands moderation through the control of one's passions (ch. 15); obsessiveness and hypersensitivity, by affecting a person's behaviour or, for instance, giving rise to a fixation upon cleanliness, render life unbearable in an irrational way (ch. 16). The following two chapters first demonstrate how reason demands us to exercise moderation in acquiring good and necessary things, as well as in spending our money. In this pursuit, human beings are dependent on each other and support each other through the exchange of goods. After that, al-Rāzī discusses people's striving to attain ever higher positions, which on the one hand affords them pleasure, but on the other hand saddles them with new burdens. Thus they do not gain anything in terms of their passions, but nevertheless they will have done what according to reason is preferable, more excellent, and more salutary. Ch. 19 summarizes the virtuous life (led by all great philosophers in the past) as consisting in acting justly towards people. To be just and moderate, and to treat other people with peacefulness and benevolence, is a precondition for being accepted in society. The last chapter establishes why one should not fear death: after death, the human souls reach a better state in which they feel no pain. Such freedom of pain cannot be compared to the pleasure that follows pain in this world. Hence no rational person needs to be grieved by death, or to give much thought to it. Anybody who is just and virtuous, and adheres to the rules of the true religious law, will attain tranquillity (*rāḥa*) and eternal happiness (*naʿīm*).

Maqāla fī Amārāt al-iqbāl wa-l-dawla
Treatise on the Signs of Well-Being and Political Success

This brief treatise, which may have been composed for a ruler of his time, transfers some basic ideas of al-Rāzī's ethics onto politics: it sketches the qualities a political leader ought to have. First of all, he needs to have knowledge that will come to him in a sudden inspiration due to 'a divine or a natural cause'. This will afford him an eminent position, because his attention will be focused on happiness. Further signs of well-being and political success, which al-Rāzī lists in prosaic manner, are: (1) harmony and continuity of things; (2) harmony between the soul's character and leadership, which is hereby strengthened; (3) an exclusive love of leadership, which cannot be impaired by anything; (4) insight (*ḥilm*) and thoughtfulness (*tu'ada*) in respect of problematic matters, which will result in the avoidance of mistakes and the detection of truth; (5) truthfulness and sensitivity of the soul, as well as the ability to remember things and to judge them correctly; this presupposes right guidance by a 'divine force' and hence makes it possible to lead those who are in need of an excellent, knowledgeable leader who is in harmony with them; (6) harmony among companions and followers, and a predilection for their well-being; (7) the well-being of the servants and their deferential conduct; (8) the banishment, from the heart of the leader, of hate and malice against his peers and noblemen; (9) the heart's predilection for justice and its abhorrence of violence (*ǧawr*), even in trying times. All these signs point to the presence of a supporting divine power.

5 Doctrine

5.1 Al-Rāzī's Basic Philosophical Principles and Ethics – 5.2 Epistemology: Philosophy versus Revelation – 5.3 The Doctrine of the Creation of the World

5.1 *Al-Rāzī's Basic Philosophical Principles and Ethics*

It was primarily as a physician that al-Rāzī won his fame; the tradition hails him as the 'unsurpassed physician of the Muslims' (Ṣāʿid [**11*: 52,21 Cheikho; 221,9 Ǧamšīdnižād-i Awwal]). Knowing his Galen, he will most certainly have followed a maxim Galen discussed in a monograph that was also translated into Arabic: that 'the best physician must be a philosopher' (*De moribus* [*32]). In his *Book on the Philosophical Life* (*Kitāb al-Sīra al-falsafiyya*), which has autobiographical traits and should be read together with his earlier work *al-Ṭibb al-rūḥānī* (Druart 1997 [*113]), al-Rāzī defends himself against the allegation of having strayed from the path of the philosophical life as it was led by Socrates, due to his constant dealings with people (apparently in his role as a physician) and his engagement in activities designed to earn a living (*al-Sīra* [**46*: 99,3–10; transl. Butterworth 227]). Here al-Rāzī is taking up the traditional image of Socrates as a pious ascetic, as we find it sporadically in a handful of Platonic dialogues (e.g. *Apology* 23b7–c1), but more particularly in Stoic and Cynic literature, as well as in works of the Islamic era, where it was very widely spread (Alon 1991 [*94: 47–52], Döring 1979 [*76: 17. 25. 33. 59. 96. 98. 117.

121–122. 132]). What is new in al-Rāzī, however, is his claim that Socrates later on gave up his initially ascetic lifestyle, because he realized that in its excessive form, the ascetic life – that is to say, people who do not procreate – will lead to the demise of the world and of mankind (*al-Sīra* [*46: 100,19–101,4; transl. Butterworth 228–229]). Therefore he, al-Rāzī, differs from Socrates only with regard to the extent of his pursuit of a just life, knowledge, and suppression of the passions [*46: 100,11–14; 228 § 6].

The principles of a philosophical life [*46: 101,5–102,4; 229 § 9] that connects knowledge (*ʿilm*) with practice (*ʿamal*) [*46: 108,16; 234 § 30] (cf. Daiber 1980 [*78: 330]), do not consist in the pursuit of bodily pleasure, but in the acquisition of knowledge and the exercise of justice on one's way to the hereafter, to a world which knows neither pain nor death. 'Our Lord, by Whom we hope to be rewarded and fear to be punished, watches over us and is merciful to us. He does not want us to cause pain, and He hates injustice and ignorance on our part, loving our knowledge and justice' [*46: 101,19–20; 229]. However, nature (*al-ṭabīʿa*) and passion (*al-hawā*) induce people to prefer 'immediate pleasure' (*al-ladda al-ḥāḍira*), whereas reason (*al-ʿaql*) urges them towards the opposite [*46: 101,17–18; 229].

Any pain that is not caused voluntarily by human beings originates in the necessity of nature; thus al-Rāzī uses examples from the human and the animal kingdom to argue that one ought not cause pain to any being equipped with sensory faculties (*muḥiss*) – unless this is done to prevent even greater pain. In this respect one ought to act according to 'intention, custom, approach and policy that conform to reason and justice'. The considerations which al-Rāzī here follows are quite utilitarian, as it were: should there be only enough water left for one person on a trip through the desert, one must save the person who is of the most benefit for society [*46: 103,14–104,14; 231 § 15. 16]. Carnivorous animals and those that create more harm than benefit, cause pain and cannot be put to use by humankind (e.g. snakes, scorpions, wasps) may be killed – this in the additional hope that their souls may attain 'more suitable' bodies [*46: 105,6; 232] (cf. Adamson 2012 [*123]). Shortly before this reference to metempsychosis (only) in animals (Walker 1991 [*98: 224–225], Sorabji 1993 [*106: 188–189. 197], Alexandrin 2002 [*134]) al-Rāzī has said explicitly that only human souls could be liberated from their bodies (*taḫlīṣ*), which was 'like paving and smoothing the way to deliverance (*ḫalāṣ*) (from the body)' [*46: 105,4; 231].

Al-Rāzī does not explain this liberation of the soul from the body – to which he already alludes in the earlier *al-Ṭibb al-rūḥānī* [*48: 27,9–11; transl. 29], – any further, but later on, in his concluding discussion of the true philosophical life, he emphasizes the necessity for 'virtuous souls' to adhere to a mean between extreme asceticism and extreme dissipation (in keeping with the example of Socrates). Furthermore, 'it is better to tend (*mayl*) towards the lower, rather than the upper, limit' (*al-Sīra* [*46: 107,13; cf. Butterworth 233 § 27]). In this, people must let themselves be guided by the judgement and principles of reason (*al-ʿaql*) and justice (*al-ʿadl*) [*46: 107,1; 233 § 25].

Al-Rāzī creatively fashions a parallel [*46: 108,4–13; 234 § 29] between said principles of reason and justice and the divine attributes of knowledge (*ʿilm*) and justice, to which he adds the attribute of mercy (*raḥma*). He compares the relation between God and man to that between a master and his servants: 'because the servants who are most beloved of their lords are those who adopt their way of life and conduct themselves according to their customs, thus the servant who is closest to God, the exalted and mighty, is the one among them who is most knowing, most just, most merciful, and most compassionate.' According to al-Rāzī, this leads us straight to the philosophers' affirmation that 'philosophy is the assimilation to God in accordance with human capacity'; this is exactly what is meant by the 'philosophical life' as described in his *The Spiritual Medicine* (*al-Ṭibb al-rūḥānī*), a book that al-Rāzī had written as a 'companion volume' to his well-known work *al-Kitāb al-Manṣūrī* (translated into Latin under the title *Liber Almansoris*). This latter book al-Rāzī had composed for the sake of the 'improvement of character' (*iṣlāḥ al-aḫlāq*) (*al-Ṭibb* [*48: 44,3; transl. 18]); he called it *The Spiritual Medicine* because it intends to show how the soul, by increasing its knowledge and acting justly, can liberate itself from the rule of the passions. The person who improves his character in this way is the philosopher, the 'sage' (*ḥakīm*), who is familiar with the 'conditions and fundamental rules of logical demonstration, and is able to comprehend and attain mathematics, physics, and theology (*al-ʿilm al-ilāhī*) in accordance with human capacity' [*48: 43,7–8; 45] (Druart 1997 [*113: 49]).

This late work of al-Rāzī's is significant in several respects.

(1) God holds a firm position in his philosophy; his attributes of knowledge and justice are reminiscent of the very same attributes featuring within the Quranic theology of the Muʿtazilites (Sura 21:47; 35:38) (van Ess 1991–1997 [*99: IV 442. 507–512]; cf. Rashed 2000 [*117: 49]). They place a high value on reason and rationality, even if the definition of *ʿaql* occurs rather late (van Ess 1991–1997 [*99: III 251; IV 205]). Again, the attribute of 'mercy' should not be traced back to the Quranic attribute alone, but also to the ideas of the Muʿtazilite Bišr b. al-Muʿtamir (beginning of the 3rd/9th century), who held that God is free to afford human beings demonstrations of His grace (*lutf*), or to grant them 'benefits' (*ṣalāḥ*) (van Ess 1991–1997 [*99: III 123–124; IV 509–510]).

(2) The thought that God's attributes of omniscience, justice and mercy are parallel to the attributes of knowledge, justice and sympathy or gentleness as ways in which man can assimilate himself to God within a 'philosophical life' is original with al-Rāzī. In order to support his idea, he refers to the Platonic doctrine of the assimilation to God 'as far as it is possible for man' (cf. *Theaetetus* 176b), which was later picked up by Galen (*De moribus* [*32: 40,6–41,4], *Dirāsāt* [*35: 201,12–202,4]; cf. Mattock 1972 [*65: 248–249]); just as in Neoplatonism and in Islamic thought since al-Kindī in the early 3rd/9th century (Druart 1993 [*104: esp. 336–357]) it here appears recast as a doctrine of the soul's liberation from the body, through increasing intellectual insight acquired in the course of the ascension to the divine, as well as through good actions (cf. Daiber 1980 [*78: 327–328]).

(3) The interpretation of 'nature' (Genequand 1984 [*82: 123–125]) as the necessity to prefer present pleasure – a necessity which obtains in this world and is dictated by passion, and which man ought to counter with his reason – evokes the Platonic thought of a conflict between reason and desire (cf. Plato, *Phaedrus* 246a-257a; al-Rāzī, *al-Ṭibb* [*48: 20–32, esp. 27,14–31,3; transl. 22–34, esp. 30–33]; Druart 1997 [*113: 49–50]). Like the Platonic notion of the assimilation to God outlined above, it went on, in the 5th/11th century, to serve as a basis for the philosophical ethics of Miskawayh and, after him, of Rāġib al-Iṣfahānī (Daiber 1991 [*96: 182–187]). Miskawayh dedicates a separate chapter to the virtue of justice (*Tahḏīb* [*9: 105–134; transl. 95–119]); following the Platonic tradition, Aristotle's doctrine of the mean, as well as Plotinus (cf. *Enn.* III 6,2 and II 3,8) he describes it as the mean between two extremes and as harmony of the parts of the soul, united in their obedience to reason (Daiber 1971 [*61: 39]); cf. p. 337 above.

(4) This principle of the mean is also brought to mind when al-Rāzī emphasizes the virtue of justice and condemns the philosophical life of pure asceticism, because excessive asceticism will lead to the demise of the world and of mankind. One text that Miskawayh used – a work ascribed to Plato which only survives in Arabic and as Syriac fragments (cf p. 84 above) – therefore ends with the conclusion that the perfection of happiness requires not only the goods of the soul but also those of the body and 'of what surrounds the body'. Someone who has them all is more excellent than 'all those who possess virtue (only) on account of asceticism, poverty, separation and exile. (For) giving up the body and relinquishing one's possessions may well be a magnificent thing, but at the same time it is something entirely imperfect' (Daiber 1971 [*61: 34 = Arab. text 31,58–60; comm. 39–40]). This text, which follows the Platonic-Aristotelian tradition, has evoked criticism (Fakhry 1994 [*107: 71–77]; Adamson 2008 [*121]) of Goodman's (1971 [*63: 5–26], 1972 [*64: 26–48], 1996 [*38: 207], 2015 [*126]) classification of al-Rāzī as an 'Epicurean'. For despite structural parallels it is

more plausible to assume that al-Rāzī's pronouncements on pleasure and pain were first and foremost inspired by Plato's *Timaeus* – possibly the only work by Plato which he actually knew (Pines 1955 [*53: 60–61]). According to our bio-bibliographical sources, al-Rāzī apparently wrote an interpretation of this text, together with Plutarch's commentary (see above, LW °23). We do not, as a matter of fact, know any Arabic version of such a commentary by Plutarch. However, in his medical writings al-Rāzī quotes Galen's commentary on the *Timaeus* (Pines 1997 [*39: 86 n. 116]); hence it is quite conceivable that he may have encountered the views Plato expresses in the *Timaeus* on these matters in a compendium by Galen which is only extant in Arabic.

Just as Plato's *Timaeus*, the compendium emphasizes the balance between body and soul (Plato, *Tim.* 88b5-c6; Galen [**31*: 32,5–33,6]), while a lack of reason (ἄνοια), divided into two types, 'insanity' (μανία) and 'ignorance' (ἀμαθία), is explained as one of the diseases of the soul, among which excessive pleasure (ἡδοναί) and excessive pain (λύπαι) rank supreme (Plato, *Tim.* 86b2–7; Galen [**31*: 31,15–32,4]). A sudden impression that is contrary to nature is painful, whereas a sudden return to the natural state is pleasant (Plato, *Tim.* 64c7-d2; Galen [**31*: 19,10–14]).

Al-Rāzī would have encountered the same Platonic thought in Galen's treatise *De moribus*, a work lost in the original Greek, which would have been accessible to him in Ḥunayn b. Isḥāq's Arabic translation. Here again the topic of pain and pleasure is discussed in a Platonic vein: the Arabic epitome which is extant to us – perhaps from the pen of Abū ʿUṯmān al-Dimašqī (first half of the 4th/10th century) – takes up Plato's tripartition of the soul into a rational or thinking, an irascible or animalistic, and an appetitive or vegetative soul (Rundgren 1974–1975 [*71: 88–98]), and describes pleasure as part of the appetitive soul, which God has given to mankind since it is necessary for life and procreation (*De moribus* [*32: 26,6–27,5], *Dirāsāt* [**35*: 190,22–191,20]; cf. Rosenthal 1965 [*55: 121–122], Mattock 1972 [*65: 237]). If it becomes excessive, it will cause harm, and hence it must be kept under regulation of the rational soul which 'must love the beautiful [and] hunger for truth' (*De moribus* [*32: 28,7, Engl. transl. 141,7–8], *Dirāsāt* [**35*: 192,11–12]; cf. Rosenthal 1965 [*55: 124], Mattock 1972 [*65: 238]). Galen mentions Socrates and Plato as examples of people who 'have dedicated their lives entirely to the rational soul' rather than to pleasure (*De moribus* [*32: 35,18–19], *Dirāsāt* [**35*: 192,19–20]; cf. Mattock 1972 [*65: 245]). – There is no doubt that al-Rāzī knew Galen's *De moribus* (probably in the unabridged translation by Ḥunayn), since in his *Kitāb al-Šukūk ʿalā Ǧālīnūs* he mentions the work and, taking up the discussion in his *al-Ṭibb al-rūḥānī*, [**48*: 36,12–39,1; transl. 39–40] emphasizes in a critical tone that pleasure is not 'the intended good' (*al-Šukūk* [**47*: 17,18–19]).

5.2 *Epistemology: Philosophy versus Revelation*

A good philosopher is someone whose soul strives for knowledge, and who, in his conduct, increasingly assimilates himself to God in justice and mercy, thus liberating his soul from the shackles of the body and letting it return to its divine origins. This is, first of all, reminiscent of Aristotle's distinction between theory and practice (Aristotle, *Metaphysics* 1026a19; *Topics* 145a14–18; *Nicomachean Ethics* 1178b20–21). In accordance with Aristotle's view, 'practice' is here identified with acting ethically (*Nicomachean Ethics* X 8). In a Neoplatonic vein, the aim of such ethical actions is said to be the liberation of the soul from the body – Plotinus (*Enn.* I 6) spoke of the 'purification' of the soul. It is also termed the 'assimilation to God, as far as this is possible for a human being'. This combination of Aristotle, Plato and Plotinus follows in the footsteps of the Alexandrian philosophers of the 5th and 6th centuries, who, in this respect, also inspired a short treatise on the classification of the sciences by Qusṭā b. Lūqā (Daiber 1990 [*92: 114. 116–117. 118–119]).

It is remarkable that al-Rāzī only mentions logic ('logical demonstration'), mathematics, physics and theology in his definition of philosophy (see above), without providing an analysis of the practical part of philosophy; in urging the reader to act justly he only addresses ethics, while leaving out economics and politics. Here al-Rāzī deviates from the Alexandrians, who, following Aristotle (*Metaphysics* 1064b1–3; cf. Daiber 1990 [*92: 120]), divided philosophy into a theoretical part on the one hand, whose subdivisions, progressing from the visible to the invisible, comprised physics, mathematics and theology, and into a practical part on the other, which was sub-divided into ethics, economics, and politics (Gutas 1983 [*81: 261]).

Apart from the marginally different order given to the subdivisions of the theoretical part there is yet another aspect in which al-Rāzī notably deviates from the Alexandrian classification of philosophy: in *al-Ṭibb al-rūḥānī* [*48: 43,5–6; transl. 45] he explicitly rejects 'grammar, poetry, correctness of speech (*faṣāḥa*) and eloquence' as proper parts of philosophy. This is a consequence arising from the Alexandrian division of the syllogism into five kinds, i.e. the demonstrative, the dialectical, the rhetorical, the sophistical, and the poetical, of whom only the first one is said to be true in every respect (Gutas 1983 [*81: 264], Daiber 1990 [*92: 115–116]).

Al-Rāzī therefore modifies the Alexandrian concept of a 'philosopher': he possesses theoretical knowledge, since he 'knows the conditions and fundamental rules of logical demonstration and is able to grasp and attain knowledge of mathematics, physics, and theology (*al-ʿilm al-ilāhī*) in accordance with human capacity'; in addition, he is guided in his actions by 'the judgement and principle of reason (*al-ʿaql*) and justice (*al-ʿadl*)' (see p. 404 above).

The 'excellent philosopher' (*al-rağul al-faylasūf al-fāḍil*), who is superior to the majority of people, will, according to al-Rāzī, achieve the control of reason over passion to the greatest extent (*al-Ṭibb* [*48: 21,3–5; transl. 23]; cf. also Vallat 2015 [*128: 208–211]). 'He who reflects (*naẓara*) and exerts oneself (*iğtahada*) is walking on the path of truth (*muḥiqq*), even if he will not reach its furthest limit', as al-Rāzī declares according to the report of his Ismaili opponent, Abū Ḥātim al-Rāzī (*Aʿlām* [*41: 303,2–3; *2: 12,18–19]); even a small amount of reflection is capable of liberating the soul from its unhappy state (*kudūra*) (*Aʿlām* [*41: 302,13–14; *2: 12,7–8]; cf. Gutas 1988 [*88: 207–209]). In his dispute with Abū Bakr al-Rāzī, Abū Ḥātim had reached a different conclusion: from the dissimilarity of people who can be separated in leaders and followers, teachers and learners, he had deduced the necessity for a prophet sent by God, to lead and instruct the people (*Aʿlām* [*41: 299,17–300,4; *2: 8,7–16]; cf. Daiber 1989 [*90: 91–92], 1996 [*111: 846–847]). Abū Bakr al-Rāzī, on the other hand, had replaced people's need for guidance and their submissiveness to authority by active initiative, reflection, and the striving endeavour of the individual – the emulation of God, the assimilation to God in accordance with the capacity of a human being.

As can be seen from this, al-Rāzī's denial of prophecy within this argument does not involve any 'atheism'. What he says here does not sound so much like a 'rebellion against Islam' (Stroumsa 1999 [*116: 93]), as like the criticism of a 'free thinker' who does not deny the existence of a God. Al-Rāzī arrived at a different, negative assessment of prophecy, which provoked the criticism of his opponent Abū Ḥātim al-Rāzī. Following Ibn al-Rāwandī, who lived in the 3rd/9th century (van Ess 1991–1997 [*99: IV 322–326]), Abū Ḥātim had defended Muḥammad's prophethood and prophecy as a source of knowledge in his book on *Signs of Prophecy* (*Aʿlām al-nubuwwa*), within which he quotes from Abū Bakr al-Rāzī's *Maḫārīq al-anbiyāʾ* (*On the Fabrications of the Prophets*) (see above LW °35). He explained that people need prophetic guidance because of their dissimilarity in their natural ability and behaviour. An evaluation of prophecy as source of knowledge backed by this type of justification prefigures al-Fārābī's (d. 339/950–951) formulation that religion, based on the divine revelation of the prophet, is a symbolic image and metaphorical 'imitation' of philosophical truth; the ruler and philosopher is also a prophet (Daiber 1989 [*90: 90–92], 1991 [*96: 144–145], 1999 [*115: 35]).

Al-Rāzī dismissed the idea that any such prophetic quality should constitute a precondition for leading people, on the grounds that this would mean that God had favoured those with a prophetic gift over the others; they would take over the leadership of the people, which would involve conflict and enmity between different groups who were only prepared to accept their own leader (*imām*). 'What is most fitting for the wisdom of the Wise and the mercy of the Merciful is to give all His servants (without discrimination) His knowledge (*maʿrifa*) about those things which will be beneficial or harmful to them on this earth as well as in the hereafter' (Abū Ḥātim [*2: 3,11–12]). In al-Rāzī's view, differences between people only exist because they focus their zeal (*himma*), their sagacity (*fiṭna*) and their intellect (*ʿaql*) on different things (Abū Ḥātim [*2: 4,19–6,12]). However, when people blindly follow tradition (*taqlīd*) and avoid or even ban the reflection (*naẓar*) about, and the investigation (*baḥṯ*) of the principles of religion, as is the case with the adherents of revealed religions (*ahl al-šarāʾiʿ*) – here al-Rāzī will have been thinking of certain people among the followers of Islam, as well as of intolerant and tyrannical religious authorities (Stroumsa 1999 [*116: 97–98. 105]) – truth will be oppressed (Abū Ḥātim [*2: 31,12–32,3]; cf. Stroumsa 1999 [*116: 97–98]).

Al-Rāzī's criticism extends to other revealed religions; one issue he criticizes extensively is the prophets' claim to be performing miracles (Abū Ḥātim [*2: 191,3–4]; cf. Stroumsa 1999 [*116: 102–103]). In this context he opposes the doctrine of the inimitability of the Quran and its status as a miracle. There are, al-Rāzī says, better compositions, in terms of literary form as well as content (Abū Ḥātim [*2: 228,4–7]; cf. Stroumsa 1999 [*116: 103–104]); al-Rāzī designates the Quran by an expression which, in the Quran itself (Sura 6:25), is used by the unbelievers to challenge the revelation received by the prophet: *asāṭīr al-awwalīn* 'the fairy tales of the ancient ones' (transl. Arberry); it is 'full of contradictions, without any information (*fāʾida*) or clear (*bayyina*) directions' (Abū Ḥātim [*2: 228,5–6]).

5.3 *The Doctrine of the Creation of the World*

Three important elements of al-Rāzī's thought appear as the foundation for his doctrine of the creation of the world: (1) the soul, which returns to its divine origin through increasing knowledge (following Neoplatonic tradition) and through acting justly (following the tradition of Aristotelian ethics); (2) the characterization of this increasing knowledge as 'reflection' and as 'endeavour', as 'imitation' of God, i.e. as 'the assimilation to God in accordance with human capacity'; (3) the denial of prophecy as a source of knowledge and the dismissal of the Quran as divine miracle and as source of divine revelation.

These three elements are components of an essentially Neoplatonic view of the world, even though the attempt to bridge the gap between the transcendent God and creation through a mediating process of emanation has been abandoned. The only connecting link is the soul of the reflecting human being, which endeavours to assimilate itself to God through knowledge and just action. In al-Rāzī's account, the soul's divinity is tarnished by the body, i.e. by matter, which is why it strives to return to its divine origin.

Here we can begin to discern a certain contradiction that al-Rāzī had to deal with. How can the divine soul be something divine, uncreated and primordial, as well as something that has been created by God and presupposes the categories of space, time, and matter? Can anything ever emerge from God that is not equal to him? Let us first quote a report by Nāṣir-i Ḫusraw from the 5th/11th century (*Zād al-musāfirīn*, in: *Rasāʾil* [*41: 282,3–284,3]; German transl. Meier 1992 [*101: 8–9]):

'He taught: The existence of the world can relate to the wise Creator in two ways only: either the world has been generated from [His] nature (*ṭabʿ*), and thus is a thing of nature (*maṭbūʿ*) and created (*muḥdaṯ*). In that case, however, the creator must be created too, because this [creative] nature will never cease to act [or to make something]. But when a being that arises from the giver of being is of the nature of the giver of being, then there must be a finite period of time between the giver of being and the being that was generated from [his] nature, in which it is possible (*mumkin*) that the thing exists which has been generated from the other thing, from which it comes into being... From this follows that the world must have come into being later than its Creator, by one finite period of time. However, if He is older than a created thing by a finite period of time, He must be created too. Therefore the Creator of the world, from whom, and through whose nature the world came into being, would have to be created.

[Or else], if the world has come into being from the Creator through His will (*ḫwāst*) [rather than automatically through His nature] and there was nothing in being beside Him throughout sempiternity which could have moved Him from that will which He had had throughout sempiternity, i.e. not to create the world, to this will, i.e. to create the world – [if it was like that], why then did He create the world after all?' Al-Rāzī concludes: 'Since we see that God has made a transition from the will not to create the world, to the will to create it, something else that is uncreated must have been with God which induced him to this action.'

This text is revealing in several respects. First of all, it indicates the equality that obtains between the divine cause and its effect: if the created being has come to be a certain period of time after the Creator, the Creator of the world must be created too, especially as the world has been generated from God, through God's nature. Furthermore, al-Rāzī points out that God's sempiternal will was not originally bent on creating the world (cf. Plotinus, *Enn.* VI 8,13,37–38 and VI 8,18,49). Since this will has changed, another uncreated being must have existed before God's act of creation, in order to provoke him to this act.

This further uncreated thing al-Rāzī identifies as 'the soul, which was alive and ignorant' (Nāṣir-i Ḫusraw [*41: 284,6–7]). He explains this with a creation myth which is available to us in two similar versions, in Nāṣir-i Ḫusraw, *Zād al-musāfirīn* (*Rasāʾil* [*41: 284,7–286,6]), and in Abū Ḥātim al-Rāzī, *Aʿlām al-nubuwwa* [*2: 20,3–24,16] (cf. Meier 1992 [*101: 10–11. 16–17]; Goodman 1975 [*72: 25–40], Daiber 1999 [*3: 36–37]): the ignorant, primordial soul falls in love with matter, which is equally uncreated and, before its formation into bodies and elements, consists in atoms and empty space (Pines 1997 [*39: 49]; cf. Pines 1970 [*25: 802]; Baffioni 1982 [*80: 115–141]). Following Aristotle's example (Aristotle, *On Generation and Corruption* II 1,329a26), it is called *al-ha(y)yūlā al-muṭlaqa*, 'absolute matter'. Driven by lust, the soul wants to shape forms out of matter. As it fails to do so, since the primordial matter is resisting this treatment and the soul only manages to move it about in 'irregular and confused movements without any order', God takes pity on it (cf. Abū Ḥātim [*2: 24,17–27,1]; Meier 1992 [*101: 18–20]) and helps the soul to create the world. Thus the soul becomes a cause for the creation of the world. Nāṣir-i Ḫusraw's report [*41: 285,2–12] (Meier 1992 [*101: 10]) adds a note about the human soul, which says that when man was created, God sent him reason (*ʿaql*) in order to 'awake his soul from sleep', so that the soul might liberate itself from matter through knowledge of the superlunary world, and return to its original world, to the seat of joy and happiness. The instrument for this, however, was philosophy. In the style of al-Rāzī's *al-Sīra al-falsafiyya*, the report adds: 'Whoever studies philosophy, recognizes his world, does not harm anybody as far as possible, and acquires knowledge, will liberate himself from the present adversity'; thus the souls are able to return to their original worlds, the lower world can dissolve itself and 'matter is released from being bound up [in forms], just as it was from eternity' [*41: 285,12–286,6] (Meier 1992 [*101: 10–11]).

Al-Rāzī's creation myth stands opposed to *creatio ex nihilo* (Davidson 1987 [*86: 9–16]) as well as the Aristotelian doctrine of the eternity of the world (Lucchetta 1987 [*87: 231–241]; Koetschet 2015 [*127]). It assumes the uncreatedness of God, soul and matter, to which al-Rāzī adds space and time; on this point Abū Ḥātim al-Rāzī's *Aʿlām al-nubuwwa* transmits a dispute between himself and Abū Bakr al-Rāzī (Abū Ḥātim [*2: 14,3–24,16]; cf. Meier 1992 [*101: 14–16]). According to this report, absolute time (*al-zamān al-muṭlaq*), which is duration (*al-mudda*) and eternity (*al-dahr*) (Meier 1992 [*101: 15]), as opposed to limited time (*maḥṣūr*), which is measured by the heavenly motions, is uncreated (*qadīm*) (Walker 1978 [*75: 360–361], Goldman 1981 [*79: 61. 66. 68], Goodman 1992/1993 [*100: 11–13/151–154], Pines 1997 [*39: 57–64]). The same goes for space (*al-makān*), where al-Rāzī distinguishes between absolute and relative (*muḍāf*) space. Absolute space 'does not have a body which could be pointed to, but can only be conceived of in the imagination' (Abū Ḥātim [*2: 19,6–7]). Al-Rāzī here refers to Plato, distancing himself from the Aristotelian concept of time and space (*Phys.* VIII 8, 256a11–12; IV 14, 223b21–23; cf. Daiber

1980 [*78: 365–366]; *Phys.* IV 4, 212a20–21) of his opponent Abū Ḥātim al-Rāzī. What he says about time partly follows a Neoplatonic pattern (Pines 1986 [*85: 368–369], 1997 [*39: 57–60]; on a comparison with Galen see Adamson 2012 [*124]; on a comparison with Ibn Ḥazm cf. Escobar Gómez 2010 [*122]).

In Nāṣir-i Ḫusraw's report, al-Rāzī justifies his introduction of absolute space and absolute time pointing out that matter, which is as such uncreated, needs space; hence space must be uncreated as well [**41*: 259,7] (cf. Meier 1992 [*101: 13]). The uncreatedness of God, soul, matter and space presupposes a concept of time which is not related to motion or, more specifically, to generation and corruption, but is something eternal and unmeasurable.

With his doctrine of five uncreated, primordial beings, i.e. God, soul, matter, space, and time, al-Rāzī modifies the teachings of his predecessor Īrānšahrī (2nd half of the 3rd/9th century). As far as we can glean his doctrine from later reports, Īrānšahrī took four uncreated and eternal things as basic principles: time, space, motion, and body, which signified God's knowledge (*ʿilm*), power (*qudra*), act (*fiʿl*), and strength (*quwwa*) respectively, and were subordinated to God (Nāṣir-i Ḫusraw [**41*: 266,7–267,5]; cf. Meier 1992 [*101: 11]). In al-Rāzī's account, this subordination is not expressed in an equally pronounced fashion, which is why he was criticized in Nāṣir-i Ḫusraw's report, if not with perfect justification (Nāṣir-i Ḫusraw [**41*: 255,10–257,3]; cf. Meier 1992 [*101: 12]).

Nor did al-Rāzī adopt Īrānšahrī's idea of God's unceasing creative activity; instead, he held the view that God's will only creates when prompted to it by something else equally uncreated. On account of this, al-Rāzī incurred censure from Nāṣir-i Ḫusraw, who remarks that Īrānšahrī deduced from God's unceasing creative activity that 'that in which [God's] work manifests itself must be uncreated, and that His work manifests itself in matter' (Nāṣir-i Ḫusraw [**41*: 258,11–12]; cf. Meier 1992 [*101: 12]). On al-Rāzī's view a direct creative act by God (*ibdāʿ*) was impossible, since something cannot be created from nothing. This criticism is aimed at al-Rāzī's model of the soul which, through its conjunction with matter, prompts God to help it create the world.

With this move, al-Rāzī, in contrast to Īrānšahrī, had tried consciously to create some distance between God and His creation, in order to avoid the accusation, resting on the alleged equality of the divine cause and its effect, that the Creator must be created, if the world had been generated from him and through his nature, and if God's creative nature then did not cease to create. Here al-Rāzī shows himself to be a Neoplatonist much more than Īrānšahrī. He introduces soul, matter, and space as intermediate entities, as it were. Comparable to the Neoplatonic emanations, they stand between God and His creation, and ensure that the world has not been generated from God or through His nature, thus implying God's createdness. Contrary to Nāṣir-i Ḫusraw's criticism that al-Rāzī had 'joined the Creator and His creatures together in a single genus' [*41: 257,2–3] (cf. Meier 1992 [*101: 12]), his account in fact takes a new approach, whereby the Aristotelian model of equality between cause and effect (ἄνθρωπος ἄνθρωπον γεννᾷ, 'man begets man' *Met.* 1032a25) is replaced by the notion of the ancillary causes soul, matter, space, and time, which mediate between God and the world He creates. This account, which differs essentially from John Philoponus' proof for the creation of the world in time (Troupeau 1984 [*83: 79–88], Pines 1986 [*85: 294–320]), modifies the Neoplatonic (and later, Avicennian) model of a differentiation between the divine One, the intellect, and the soul which led to a hierarchy of causes and effects, and prompted Ibn Sīnā to introduce his distinction between essence and existence (Daiber 2004 [*120: 32–33]). Here again al-Rāzī presents himself as an independent and critical spirit, who felt free to draw on his Platonic, Neoplatonic, Aristotelian, and Gnostic-Manichaen heritage, and combine it with his own insights as a physician and an expert on Galen. His criticism of some of the fundamentals of Islamic religion is part of his generally critical attitude towards all religions – an attitude which led him to a concept of God which essentially has Neoplatonic features, without departing from the Quranic-Islamic belief in God when he characterizes human knowledge and ethical conduct as an increasing 'assimilation to God'. Nevertheless it does not come as a surprise that, a few exceptions notwithstanding, al-Rāzī's thoughts did not receive much appreciation from his contemporaries, especially among the Ismailis, nor from later thinkers up to and including Mošeh ben Maimon (Maimonides) (Peters 1968 [*60: 172], Meier 1992 [*101], Bar-Asher 1995 [*36: 110–111]). Writing in the 6th/12th century, Maimonides, in his *Guide for the Perplexed* (book III, ch. 12), calls al-Rāzī's pronouncements in his theological work *Kitāb al-ʿIlm al-ilāhī* (see LW °6 above) 'senseless jabber' (*hadayān*) (Stroumsa 2001 [*119: 146–152]). However, in another work he used al-Rāzī's *Šukūk ʿalā Ǧālīnūs* (*Doubts about Galen*) [*47: 87,3–12] as a source for Galen, in particular for his statements about the most perfect language (Schreiner 1983 [*131: 224–225]), as did Mošeh Ibn ʿEzra before him in his *Kitāb al-Muḥāḍara wa-l-muḏākara* [*12: I 44,14–45,6; Span. transl. II 44–45]. – In the Latin Middle Ages, again only a fraction of al-Rāzī's philosophy was known, in stark contrast to his medical work. We find evidence of it in Petrus Alfonsi (ca. 1060–1140) and Ramón Martí (ca. 1230–1285). Both had mastered Arabic and knew al-Rāzī's *Doubts about Galen* (*al-Šukūk ʿalā Ǧālīnūs*) or quoted from it (Burnett 1998 [*132: 979–981]). In the 20th century, it seems that al-Rāzī's psychology held some fascination for Thomas Mann, who came across it in a 1925 article by Schaeder on 'Die islamische Lehre vom vollkommenen Menschen' ('The Islamic Doctrine of the Perfect Man') [*21: 232–235]; it found an echo in Mann's tetralogy *Joseph und seine Brüder* (*Joseph and his Brothers*) (Tornero 2001 [*133: 746–750]).

6 Secondary Literature

6.1 Bibliographies [*1–*3] – 6.2 Textual Transmission and Textual History [*7–*8] – 6.3 Biography [*11–*15] – 6.4 Introductions, General Accounts [*21–*41] – 6.5 Individual Groups of Works, Writings, Problems, and Concepts [*48–*128] – 6.6 Reception [*131–*134]

6.1 *Bibliographies*

1 Sezgin, Fuat. *Geschichte des arabischen Schrifttums*, vol. 3: *Medizin, Pharmazie, Zoologie, Tierheilkunde*. Leiden, 1970.

2 Ullmann, Manfred. *Die Medizin im Islam*. Leiden, 1970.

3 Daiber, Hans. *Bibliography of Islamic Philosophy*, 2 vols. Leiden, Boston, 1999. – Supplement vol., 2007.

6.2 *Textual Transmission and Textual History*

7 Gutas, Dimitri. "Notes and Texts from Cairo Mss. I." *Arabica* 24 (1977): 91–93.

8 Richter-Bernburg, Lutz. "Abū Bakr Muḥammad al-Rāzī's (Rhazes) Medical Works." *Medicina nei secoli: Arte e scienza* 6 (1994): 377–392.

6.3 *Biography*

11 Ranking, George S. A. "The Life and Works of Rhazes (Abū Bakr Muḥammad Bin Zakariyā Ar-Rāzī)." In *17th International Congress of Medicine, London 1913, Section XXIII*. London, 1914, 237–268.

12 Ruska, Julius. "Al-Bīrūnī als Quelle für das Leben und die Schriften al-Rāzī's." *Isis* 5 (1923): 26–50.

13 Meyerhof, Max. "ʿAlī al-Bayhaqī's *Tatimmat Ṣiwān al-ḥikma*." *Osiris* 8 (1948): 122–217.

14 Rowson, Everett K. "The Philosopher as Litterateur: Al-Tawḥīdī and His Predecessors." *Zeitschrift für Geschichte der Arabisch-Islamischen Wissenschaften* 6 (1990): 50–92.

15 de Blois, François. "Shuhayd al-Balkhī, a Poet and Philosopher of the Time of Rāzī." *Bulletin of the School of Oriental and African Studies* 59 (1996): 333–337.

6.4 *Introductions, General Accounts*

21 Schaeder, Hans Heinrich. "Die islamische Lehre vom vollkommenen Menschen." *Zeitschrift der Deutschen Morgenländischen Gesellschaft* 79 (1925): 192–268.

22 Kraus, Paul and Shlomo Pines. “al-Rāzī, Abū Bakr Muḥammed b. Zakarīyā’.” In *Enzyklopaedie des Islām*, vol. 3. Leiden, 1936, 1225–1227.

23 Gaudefroy-Demombynes, Maurice. “Er Razi philosophe d’après des ouvrages récents.” *Revue de l’histoire des religions* 124 (1941): 142–190.

24 Meyerhof, Max. “The Philosophy of the Physician ar-Râzî.” *Islamic Culture* 15 (1941): 45–58. – Summaries of the contents of al-Rāzī’s writings ed. by Kraus, *Rasā’il falsafiyya*, Cairo, 1939. – Repr. Frankfurt a.M., 1999.

25 Pines, Shlomo. “Philosophy.” In *The Cambridge History of Islam*, vol. 2. Ed. by Peter Malcolm Holt, Ann K. S. Lambton, and Bernard Lewis. Cambridge, 1970, 780–823.

26 Muḥaqqiq, Mahdī (Mehdi Mohaghegh). *Failasūf-i Raiy Muḥammad ibn-i Zakariyyā-yi Rāzī*. Tehran, 1974 (2nd ed.).

27 Bazmee Ansari, A. S. “Abū Bakr Muḥammad b. Yaḥyā al-Rāzī, Universal Scholar and Scientist.” *Islamic Studies* 15/3 (1976): 155–166.

28 al-ʿAbd, ʿAbd al-Laṭīf Muḥammad. *Uṣūl al-fikr al-falsafī ʿind Abī Bakr al-Rāzī*. Cairo, 1977.

29 Bazmee Ansari, A. S. “Philosophical and Religious Views of Muḥammad ibn Zakariyyā al-Rāzī.” *Islamic Studies* 16, no. 3 (1977): 157–177.

30 Badawī, ʿAbd al-Raḥmān. *Quelques figures et thèmes de la philosophie islamique*. Paris, 1979. – Contains 79–94: repr. of “Muḥammad b. Zakariyyā’ al-Rāzī,” from *A History of Muslim Philosophy*, vol. 1. Ed. by M. M. Sharif. Wiesbaden, 1963, 434–449.

31 Bausani, Alessandro. *Un filosofo ‘laico’ del medioevo musulmano: Abū Bakr Muḥammad ben Zakariyyā’ Rāzī*. Rome, 1981.

32 Endress, Gerhard. “Die wissenschaftliche Literatur.” In *Grundriss der arabischen Philologie*, vol. 2: *Literaturwissenschaft*. Ed. by Wolfdietrich Fischer and Helmut Gätje. Wiesbaden, 1987, 400–506. – Vol. 3: *Supplement*, 1992, 3–152.

33 Iskandar, Albert Z. “Al-Rāzī.” In *Religion, Learning and Science in the ʿAbbasid Period*. Ed. by M. J. L. Young, John D. Latham and Robert B. Serjeant. Cambridge, New York, 1990, 370–377.

34 Brague, Rémi. “Abu Bakr Muḥammad Ibn-Zakarīyā ar-Rāzī.” In *Grosses Werklexikon der Philosophie*, vol. 2. Ed. by Franco Volpi. Stuttgart, 1991, 1260–1261.

35 Escobar Gómez, Santiago. “Abū Bakr Zakariyyā Al-Rāzī, un filósofo de una antigüedad tardía.” *Revista española de filosofía medieval* 0 [sic] (1993): 57–60.

36 Bar-Asher, Meir M. “Abū Bakr al-Rāzī (865–925).” In *Klassiker der Religionsphilosophie*. Ed. by Friedrich Niewöhner. Munich, 1995, 99–111; 356–358.

37 Escobar Gómez, Santiago. “Orígenes y evolución de la filosofía ética de Abū Bakr al-Rāzī.” In *Actas del II congreso nacional de filosofía medieval*. Ed. by J. M. Ayala Martinez. Zaragoza, 1996, 265–270.

38 Goodman, Lenn E. "Muḥammad ibn Zakariyyā' al-Rāzī." In *History of Islamic Philosophy*, vol. 1. Ed. by Seyyed Hossein Nasr and Oliver Leaman. London, 1996, 198–215.

39 Pines, Shlomo. *Studies in Islamic Atomism* [= *Beiträge zur islamischen Atomenlehre*, Berlin 1936]. Transl. from Germ. by Michael Schwarz. Ed. by Tzvi Langermann. Jerusalem, 1997.

40 Ḥamd, Muḥammad ʿAbd al-Ḥamīd. *Muḥammad b. Zakariyyā' al-Rāzī al-ṭabīb wa-l-faylasūf: Dirāsa*. Damascus, 1999.

41 Adamson, Peter. "Abū Bakr ar-Rāzī." In *Islamische Philosophie im Mittelalter. Ein Handbuch*. Ed. by Heidrun Eichner, Matthias Perkams and Christian Schäfer. Darmstadt, 2013, 199–217.

6.5 *Individual Groups of Works, Writings, Problems, and Concepts*

48 de Boer, Tjitze J. *De 'Medicina mentis' van den arts Razi*. Amsterdam, 1920. – Repr. in *Muḥammad ibn Zakariyā' al-Rāzī (d. 313/925): Texts and Studies*, vol. 2. Ed. by Fuat Sezgin. Frankfurt, 1996, 137–153.

49 Pines, Shlomo. "Some Problems of Islamic Philosophy." *Islamic Culture* 11 (1937): 66–80. – Repr. in Pines, *Studies in the History of Arabic Philosophy*. Ed. by Sarah Stroumsa. Jerusalem, 1996, 47–61.

50 Corbin, Henry. "Le temps cyclique dans le mazdéisme et dans l'ismaélisme." *Eranos-Jahrbuch* 20 (1951 [1952]): 149–217. – Repr. in Corbin, *Temps cyclique et gnose ismaélienne*. Paris, 1982.

51 Graf, Georg. *Geschichte der christlichen arabischen Literatur*, vol. 4. Vatican City, 1951.

52 Pines, Shlomo. "Rāzī critique de Galien." In *Actes du VIIe congrès international d'histoire des sciences*. Paris, 1953, 480–487. – Repr. in Pines, *Studies in Arabic Versions of Greek Texts and in Mediaeval Science* [see *85], 256–263.

53 Pines, Shlomo. *Nouvelles études sur Awḥad al-Zamān Abu'l-Barakāt al-Baghdādī*. Paris, 1955. – Repr. in Pines, *Studies in Abu'l-Barakāt al-Baghdādī. Physics and Metaphysics*. Jerusalem, 1979, 96–173.

54 Dunlop, Douglas Morton. "The Translations of al-Biṭrīq and Yaḥyā (Yuḥannā) Ibn al-Biṭrīq." *Journal of the Royal Asiatic Society* (1959): 140–150.

55 Rosenthal, Franz. *Das Fortleben der Antike im Islam*. Zurich, 1965.

56 Mohaghegh, Mehdi. "Notes on the 'Spiritual Physic' of al-Razi." *Studia Islamica* 26 (1967): 5–22. – Also in Mohaghegh [*26; Engl. part], 5–27.

57 Bürgel, Johann Christoph. *Averroes "contra Galenum": das Kapitel von der Atmung im Colliget des Averroes als Zeugnis mittelalterlich-islamischer Kritik an Galen*. Göttingen, 1968, 284–286.

58 Fakhry, Majid. "A Tenth-Century Arabic Interpretation of Plato's Cosmology." *Journal of the History of Philosophy* 6 (1968): 15–22. – Repr. in Fakhry, *Philosophy, Dogma and the Impact of Greek Thought in Islam*. Aldershot, 1994, no. IV.

59 Peters, Francis E. *Aristoteles Arabus: The Oriental Translations and Commentaries on the Aristotelian Corpus*. Leiden, 1968.

60 Peters, Francis E. *Aristotle and the Arabs: The Aristotelian Tradition in Islam*. New York, 1968.

61 Daiber, Hans. "Ein bisher unbekannter pseudoplatonischer Text über die Tugenden der Seele in arabischer Überlieferung." *Der Islam* 47 (1971): 25–42. – Addendum in *Der Islam* 49 (1972): 122–123.

62 Giffen, Lois Anita. *Theory of Profane Love Among the Arabs: The Development of the Genre*. New York, 1971. – 141–142: analysis of al-Rāzī's *al-Ṭibb al-rūḥānī*, ch. 5.

63 Goodman, Lenn E. "The Epicurean Ethic of Muḥammad ibn Zakariyāʾ ar-Rāzī." *Studia Islamica* 34 (1971): 5–26.

64 Goodman, Lenn E. "Rāzī's Psychology." *The Philosophical Forum* 4, no. 1 (N.S.) (1972): 26–48.

65 Mattock, John N. "A Translation of the Arabic Epitome of Galen's Book Περὶ ἠθῶν." In *Islamic Philosophy and the Classical Tradition: Essays Presented by his Friends and Pupils to Richard Walzer on His Seventieth Birthday*. Ed. by Samuel Miklos Stern, Albert Hourani, and Vivian Brown. Oxford, 1972, 235–260.

66 Pines, Shlomo. "An Arabic Summary of a Lost Work of John Philoponus." *Israel Oriental Studies* 2 (1972): 320–359. – Repr. in Pines, *Studies in Arabic Versions of Greek Texts and in Mediaeval Science* [*85], 294–326.

67 Mohaghegh, Mehdi. "Rāzī's *Kitāb al-ʿilm al-ilāhī* and the Five Eternals." *Abr-Nahrain* 13 (1972/73): 16–23. – Also in Mohaghegh, *Failasūf-i Raiy Muḥammad ibn-i Zakariyyā-yi Rāzī* [*26; Engl. part], 28–35.

68 Endress, Gerhard. *Proclus Arabus: Zwanzig Abschnitte aus der Institutio theologica in arabischer Übersetzung*, eingeleitet, herausgegeben und erklärt. Beirut, 1973.

69 Peters, Francis E. *Allah's Commonwealth: A History of Islam in the Near East, 600–1100 A.D.* New York, 1973.

70 Pines, Shlomo. "Philosophy, Mathematics and the Concepts of Space in the Middle Ages." In *The Interaction Between Science and Philosophy*. Ed. by Yehuda Elkana. Atlantic Highlands: Humanities Press, 1974, 165–174. – Repr. in Pines, *Studies in Arabic Versions of Greek Texts and in Mediaeval Science* [*85], 359–374.

71 Rundgren, Frithiof. "Das Muxtaṣar min Kitāb al'Axlāq des Galenos, einige Bemerkungen." *Orientalia Suecana* 23–24 (1974–1975): 84–105.

72 Goodman, Lenn E. "Rāzī's Myth of the Fall of Soul: Its Function in His Philosophy." In *Essays on Islamic Philosophy and Science*. Ed. by George F. Hourani. Albany, 1975, 25–40.

73 Mohaghegh, Mehdi. "Maqām-i falsafī-yi Muḥammad Ibn Zakariyā'-i Rāzī." In Mohaghegh, *Bīst Guftār dar mabāḥiṯ wa falsāfī wa kalāmī wa firāqi islāmī*, with an Engl. intro. by Josef van Ess. Tehran, 1976, 301–318.

74 al-Takrītī, Nāǧī. *Yahya Ibn 'Adi: A Critical Edition and Study of his Tahdhib al-akhlaq*. Beirut, 1978.

75 Walker, Paul E. "Eternal Cosmos and the Womb of History: Time in Early Ismaili Thought." *International Journal of Middle East Studies* 9 (1978): 355–366.

76 Döring, Klaus. *Exemplum Socratis: Studien zur Sokratesnachwirkung in der kynisch-stoischen Popularphilosophie der frühen Kaiserzeit und im frühen Christentum*. Wiesbaden, 1979.

77 al-Takrītī, Nāǧī. *Al-Falsafa al-aḫlāqiyya al-Aflāṭūniyya 'ind mufakkirī l-islām*. Beirut, 1979. – 152–164: on al-Rāzī's ethics.

78 Daiber, Hans. *Aetius Arabus: Die Vorsokratiker in arabischer Überlieferung*. Wiesbaden, 1980.

79 Goldman, Steven Louis. "On the Beginnings and Endings of Time in Medieval Judaism and Islam." In *The Study of Time*, vol. 4. Ed. by Julius Thomas Fraser, Nathaniel Lawrence, David Park. New York, 1981, 59–72.

80 Baffioni, Carmela. *Atomismo e antiatomismo nel pensiero islamico*. Naples, 1982.

81 Gutas, Dimitri. "Paul the Persian on the Classification of the Parts of Aristotle's Philosophy: A Milestone between Alexandria and Baġdād." *Der Islam* 60 (1983): 231–267.

82 Genequand, Charles. "Quelques aspects de l'idée de nature, d'Aristote à al-Ghazālī." *Revue de théologie et de philosophie* 116 (1984): 105–129.

83 Troupeau, Gérard. "Un épitomé arabe du 'de contingentia mundi' de Jean Philopon." In *Mémorial André-Jean Festugière: antiquité païenne et chrétienne: vingt-cinq études*. Ed. by Enzo Lucchesi and Henri Dominique Saffrey. Geneva, 1984, 77–88. – Ed. of the Arabic text transl. by Pines [see *66].

84 van Ess, Josef. "Kumūn." In *The Encyclopaedia of Islam: New Edition*. Ed. by Clifford Edmund Bosworth, vol. 5. Leiden, 1986, 384–385.

85 Pines, Shlomo. *Studies in Arabic Versions of Greek Texts and in Mediaeval Science*. Jerusalem, 1986.

86 Davidson, Herbert Alan. *Proofs for Eternity, Creation and the Existence of God in Medieval Islamic and Jewish Philosophy*. New York, 1987.

87 Lucchetta, Giulio A. *La natura e la sfera: La scienza antica e le sue metafore nella critica di Rāzī*. Lecce, 1987.

88 Gutas, Dimitri. *Avicenna and the Aristotelian Tradition: Introduction to Reading Avicenna's Philosophical Works*. Leiden, 1988.

89 Bar-Asher, Meir M. "Quelques aspects de l'éthique d'Abū-Bakr al-Rāzī et ses origines dans l'œuvre de Galien." *Studia Islamica* 69 (1989): 5–38; 70 (1989): 119–147.

90 Daiber, Hans. "Abū Ḥātim ar-Rāzī (10th century A.D.) on the unity and diversity of religions." In *Dialogue and Syncretism: an Interdisciplinary Approach*. Ed. by Jerald Gort et al. Grand Rapids, Mich., Amsterdam, 1989, 87–104.

91 Rosenthal, Franz. "Abū Zayd al-Balkhī on Politics." In *The Islamic World, From Classical to Modern Times: Essays in Honor of Bernard Lewis*. Ed. by Clifford Edmund Bosworth et al. Princeton, 1989, 287–301.

92 Daiber, Hans. "Qosṭā Ibn Lūqā (9. Jh.) über die Einteilung der Wissenschaften." *Zeitschrift für Geschichte der Arabisch-Islamischen Wissenschaften* 6 (1990): 93–129.

93 Peters, Francis E. "Hermes and Harran: The Roots of Arabic-Islamic Occultism." In *Intellectual Studies on Islam: Essays Written in Honor of Martin B. Dickson*. Ed. by Michel M. Mazzaoui and Vera B. Moreen. Salt Lake City, 1990, 185–215.

94 Alon, Ilai. *Socrates in Medieval Arabic Literature*. Jerusalem, 1991.

95 Daiber, Hans. "Griechische Ethik in islamischem Gewande: Das Beispiel von Rāġib al-Iṣfahānī (11. Jh.)." In *Historia philosophiae medii aevi: Studien zur Geschichte der Philosophie des Mittelalters: Festschrift für Kurt Flasch*. Ed. by Burkhard Mojsisch and Olaf Pluta. Amsterdam, 1991, 181–192.

96 Daiber, Hans. "The Ismaili Background of Fārābī's Political Philosophy." In *Gottes ist der Orient, Gottes ist der Okzident: Festschrift für Abdoljavad Falaturi zum 65. Geburtstag*. Ed. by Udo Tworuschka. Cologne, 1991, 143–150.

97 Mohaghegh, Mehdi. "The *Kitāb al-Shukūk ʿalā Jālīnūs* of Muḥammad Ibn Zakariyya al-Rāzī." In *Islamic Studies Presented to Charles J. Adams*. Ed. by Wael B. Hallaq and Donald P. Little. Leiden, 1991, 107–116. – Also in *Études orientales: Dirāsāt šarqiyya* 9–10 (Paris 1991): 18–26 as well as in the intro. to Mohaghegh's ed. of al-Rāzī's *Kitāb al-Šukūk ʿalā Ǧālīnūs*.

98 Walker, Paul E. "The Doctrine of Metempsychosis in Islam." In *Islamic Studies Presented to Charles J. Adams* [cf. *97], 219–238.

99 van Ess, Josef. *Theologie und Gesellschaft im 2. und 3. Jahrhundert Hidschra: Eine Geschichte des religiösen Denkens im frühen Islam*, 6 vols. Berlin, 1991–1997.

100 Goodman, Lenn E. "Time in Islam." *Asian Philosophy* 2 (1992): 3–19. – Also in *Religion and Time*. Ed. by Anindita Niyogi Balslev and Jitendra Nath Mohanty. Leiden, 1993, 138–162.

101 Meier, Fritz. "Der 'Urknall': Eine Idee des Abū Bakr ar-Rāzī." *Oriens* 33 (1992): 1–21.

102 Walker, Paul E. "The Political Implications of al-Rāzī's Philosophy." In *The Political Aspects of Islamic Philosophy: Essays in Honor of Muhsin Mahdi*. Ed. by Charles E. Butterworth. Cambridge, Mass., 1992, 61–94.

103 Butterworth, Charles E. "The Book of the Philosophic Life." *Interpretation* 20, no. 3 (1993): 227–236.

104 Druart, Thérèse-Anne. "Al-Kindī's Ethics." *Review of Metaphysics* 47 (1993): 329–357.

105 Druart, Thérèse-Anne. "Al-Rāzī (Rhazes) and Normative Ethics." In *Tradition and Renewal: Philosophical Essays Commemorating the Centennial of Louvain's Institute of Philosophy*, vol. 2. Ed. by David A. Boileau and John A. Dick. Leuven, 1993, 167–181.

106 Sorabji, Richard. *Animal Minds and Human Morals: The Origins of the Western Debate*. Ithaca, 1993.

107 Fahkhry, Majid. *Ethical Theories in Islam*, second expanded edition. Leiden, 1994.

108 Lettinck, Paul. *Aristotle's Physics and Its Reception in the Arabic World*. Leiden, 1994.

109 Lettinck, Paul and James Opie Urmson, transl. *Philoponus on Aristotle's Physics 5–8 with Simplicius: On Aristotle on the Void*. London, 1994.

110 Zonta, Mauro. *Un interprete ebreo della filosofia di Galeno: gli scritti filosofici di Galeno nell'opera di Shem Tob ibn Falaquera*. Turin, 1995.

111 Daiber, Hans. "Political Philosophy." In *History of Islamic Philosophy*, vol. 2. Ed. by Seyyed Hossein Nasr and Oliver Leaman. London, 1996, 841–885.

112 Druart, Thérèse-Anne. "Al-Rāzī's Conception of the Soul: Psychological Background to His Ethics." *Medieval Philosophy and Theology* 5 (1996): 245–263.

113 Druart, Thérèse-Anne. "The Ethics of al-Razi (865–925?)." *Medieval Philosophy and Theology* 6 (1997): 47–71.

114 Strohmaier, Gotthard. "Bekannte und unbekannte Zitate in den *Zweifeln an Galen* des Rhazes." In *Text and Tradition: Studies in Ancient Medicine and its Transmission, Presented to Jutta Kollesch*. Ed. by Klaus-Dietrich Fischer, Diethard Nickel and Paul Potter. Leiden, 1998, 263–287.

115 Daiber, Hans. "Rebellion gegen Gott: Formen atheistischen Denkens im frühen Islam." In *Atheismus im Mittelalter und in der Renaissance*. Ed. by Friedrich Niewöhner, Olaf Pluta. Wiesbaden, 1999, 23–44.

116 Stroumsa, Sarah. *Freethinkers of Medieval Islam: Ibn al-Rāwandī, Abū Bakr al-Rāzī, and Their Impact on Islamic Thought*. Leiden, 1999. – Repr. (paperback) 2016.

117 Rashed, Marwan. "Abû Bakr al-Râzî et le kalâm." *Mélanges de l'Institut dominicain d'études orientales du Caire* 24 (2000): 39–54.

118 Daiber, Hans. "Die Aristotelesrezeption in der syrischen Literatur." In *Die Gegenwart des Altertums: Formen und Funktionen des Altertumsbezugs in den Hochkulturen der Alten Welt*. Ed. by Dieter Kuhn and Helga Stahl. Heidelberg, 2001, 327–345.

119 Stroumsa, Sarah. "'Ravings': Maimonides' Concept of Pseudo-Science." *Aleph: Historical Studies in Science and Judaism* 1 (2001): 141–163.

120 Daiber, Hans. "The Limitations of Knowledge According to Ibn Sīnā: Epistemological and Theological Aspects and the Consequences." In *Erkenntnis und Wissenschaft: Probleme der Epistemologie in der Philosophie des Mittelalters*.

Ed. by Matthias Lutz-Bachmann, Alexander Fidora and Pia Antolic. Berlin, 2004, 25–34.

121 Adamson, Peter. "Platonic Pleasures in Epicurus and al-Rāzī." In *In the Age of al-Fārābī: Arabic Philosophy in the Fourth/Tenth Century*. Ed. by Peter Adamson. London, 2008, 71–94. – Repr. in: P. Adamson, *Studies on Early Arabic Philosophy*. Farnham, Surrey, 2015, no. VI.

122 Escobar Gómez, Santiago. "Los conceptos de tiempo y espacio en Ibn Hazm de Córdoba en su relación con Abū Bakr Al-Rāzī y Newton." In *El pensamiento politico en la Edad Media*. Ed. by Pedro Roche Arnas. Madrid, 2010, 419–422.

123 Adamson, Peter. "Abū Bakr al-Rāzī on Animals." *Archiv für Geschichte der Philosophie* 94 (2012): 249–273. – Repr. in P. Adamson 2015 [cf. *121], no. VII.

124 Adamson, Peter. "Galen and al-Rāzī on Time." In *Medieval Arabic Thought: Essays in Honour of Fritz Zimmermann*. Ed. by Rotraud Hansberger, M. Afifi al-Akiti, and Charles Burnett. London, 2012, 1–14. – Repr. in: P. Adamson 2015 [cf. *121], no. IV.

125 Dodikhudoev, Khayolbek. "The Polemic between the Two Razis." *Ishraq* 4 (2013): 140–161 (in Russian; Engl. summary p. 624).

126 Goodman, Lenn E. "How Epicurean was al-Rāzī?" *Studia graeco-arabica* 5 (2015): 247–280.

127 Koetschet, Pauline. "Galien, al-Rāzī, et l'éternité du monde. Les fragments du traité sur la démonstration, IV, dans les *Doutes sur Galien*." *Arabic Sciences and Philosophy* 25 (2015): 167–198.

128 Vallat, Philippe. "Between Hellenism, Islam, and Christianity: Abū Bakr al-Rāzī and His Controversies with Contemporary Muʿtazilite Theologians as Reported by the Ashʿarite Theologian and Philosopher Fakhr al-Dīn al-Rāzī." In *Ideas in Motion in Baghdad and Beyond*. Ed. by Damian Janos. Leiden, Boston, 2016, 178–220.

6.6 *Reception*

131 Schreiner, Martin. *Gesammelte Schriften*. Ed. by Moshe Perlmann. Hildesheim, 1983.

132 Burnett, Charles. "Encounters with Rāzī the Philosopher: Constantine the African, Petrus Alfonsi and Ramón Martí." In *Pensamiento medieval hispano. Homenaje a Horacio Santiago-Otero*. Ed. by M. Soto Rábanos. Madrid, 1998, 973–992.

133 Tornero, Emilio. "Filosofía árabe y literatura del siglo XX." *Anaquel de estudios árabes* 12 (2001) 743–750.

134 Alexandrin, Elizabeth R. "Rāzī and His Mediaeval Opponents: Discussions Concerning *tanāsukh* and the Afterlife." In *Iran, questions et connaissances: Actes du IVe congrès européen des études iraniennes*, vol. 2. Ed. by Philip Huyse and Maria Szuppe. Paris, 2002, 397–409.

CHAPTER 7

The Baghdad Aristotelians

1 The Arabic Aristotle and the Transmission of Aristotelian Philosophy in Baghdad: Abū Bišr Mattā b. Yūnus – 2 Yaḥyā Ibn ʿAdī – 3 ʿĪsā Ibn Zurʿa – 4 Ibn al-Ḫammār – 5 Ibn al-Samḥ – 6 Abū l-Faraǧ Ibn al-Ṭayyib – 7 Secondary Literature

1 The Arabic Aristotle and the Transmission of Aristotelian Philosophy in Baghdad: Abū Bišr Mattā b. Yūnus

Gerhard Endress

1.1 Primary Sources – 1.2 Arabic Aristotelianism and the Transmission of the *Organon* in the 3rd/9th and the 4th/10th Centuries – 1.3 Abū Bišr Mattā and the Reception of the *Organon* in the 4th/10th Century – 1.4 Translations from Mattā's School – 1.5 Doctrine and Influence

1.1 *Primary Sources*

1.1.1 Bio-bibliographical Testimonies [*1–*7] – 1.1.2 Works [*11–*19] – 1.1.3 Additional Source Texts [*23–*24] – 1.1.4 Textual Evidence for the Reception History [*27–*28]

1.1.1 Bio-bibliographical Testimonies

1 Ibn al-Nadīm, Abū l-Faraǧ Muḥammad b. Isḥāq (d. 380/990). *Kitāb al-Fihrist* [composed in 377/988]. – Ed. by Gustav Flügel, August Müller and Johannes Roediger, 2 vols. Leipzig, 1871–1872, vol. 1, 248–251. 263–264 (ed. quoted below). – Repr. Beirut 1964, Frankfurt a.M. 2005. – Ed. by Riḍā Taǧaddud. Tehran, 1350 h.š./1971. – Ed. by Ayman Fu'ād Sayyid, 2 vols (I\1–2 - II\1–2). London, 1430/2009, vol. 2, 160–167. 197–202. – Engl. transl. by Bayard Dodge, *The Fihrist of al-Nadīm*, 2 vols. New York, 1970.

2 al-Masʿūdī, Abū l-Ḥasan ʿAlī b. al-Ḥusayn. *Kitāb al-Tanbīh wa-l-išrāf* [composed in 345/956]. – Ed. by Michael Jan de Goeje, *Kitâb al-tanbîh wa'l-ischrâf auctore al-Masûdî*. Leiden, 1894, 122.

3 al-Tawḥīdī, Abū Ḥayyān ʿAlī b. Muḥammad (d. 414/1023). *Kitāb al-Imtāʿ wa-l-muʾānasa*. – Ed. by Aḥmad Amīn and Aḥmad al-Zayn, 3 vols. Cairo, 1939–1944, vol. 1, 107–129 and Indices.

 | DOI 10.1163/9789004323162_009

4 al-Bayhaqī, Ẓahīr al-Dīn Abū l-Ḥasan ʿAlī b. Zayd b. Funduq (d. 565/1169). *Tatimmat Ṣiwān al-ḥikma*. – Ed. by Muḥammad Šafīʿ, fasc. 1: Arabic text. Lahore, 1935, no. 14. – Ed. by Muḥammad Kurd ʿAlī, *Taʾrīḫ ḥukamāʾ al-islām*. Damascus, 1365/1946, 28–29. – Repr. 1396/1976. – Engl. transl. by Max Meyerhof, "ʿAlī al-Bayhaqī's *Tatimmat Ṣiwān al-Ḥikma*: A Biographical Work on Learned Men of the [sic] Islam." *Osiris* 8 (1948): 139–140, no. 14.

5 Ibn al-Qifṭī, Ǧamāl al-Dīn ʿAlī b. Yūsuf (d. 646/1248). *Taʾrīḫ al-ḥukamāʾ* [*Iḫbār al-ʿulamāʾ bi-aḫbār al-ḥukamāʾ*, epitome by Muḥammad b. ʿAlī al-Zawzanī]. – Ed. by Julius Lippert, *Ibn al-Qifṭī's Taʾrīh al-ḥukamāʾ*. Leipzig, 1903, 323.

6 Ibn Abī Uṣaybiʿa, Muwaffaq al-Dīn Aḥmad b. al-Qāsim (d. 668/1270). *ʿUyūn al-anbāʾ fī ṭabaqāt al-aṭibbāʾ*. – Ed. by August Müller, 2 vols. Cairo, 1299/1882, Königsberg, 1884, vol. 1, 235.

7 Ibn Ḫallikān, Abū l-ʿAbbās Šams al-Dīn Aḥmad b. Muḥammad (d. 681/1282). *Wafayāt al-aʿyān wa-anbāʾ abnāʾ al-zamān*. – Ed. by Iḥsān ʿAbbās, 8 vols. Beirut, 1968–1972, vol. 5, 153–154.

1.1.2 Works (Translations of Works by Aristotle with Commentaries and Glosses)

1.1.2.1 *Partial Collection*

11 Aristotle. *Organon* [Arab.]. – Ed. by ʿAbd al-Raḥmān Badawī, *Manṭiq Arisṭū*. Cairo, 1948–1952. – Repr. [partly with different pagination]: Kuwait, Beirut 1980. – Ed. by Farīd Ǧabr, Ǧirār Ǧihāmī and Rafīq al-ʿAǧam, *al-Naṣṣ al-kāmil li-Manṭiq Arisṭū*. Beirut, 1999. – Contains the Arab. transl. of Aristotle's *Categories, On Interpretation, Prior Analytics, Posterior Analytics, Topics, Sophistical Refutations*, and (only in Badawī's ed.) Porphyry's *Isagoge* ('Introduction'), as well as scholia from the hands of Arabic transmitters and translators of the 3rd/9th and 4th/10th centuries, based on MS Paris, BnF, ar. 2356.

1.1.2.2 *Individual Editions*

15 Aristotle. *Poetics* [Arab.] = *Kitāb al-Šiʿr*. – Ed. by David Samuel Margoliouth, *Analecta Orientalia ad poeticam Aristoteleam*. London, 1887. – Repr. Hildesheim, 2000. – Lat. transl. of this edition: D. S. Margoliouth, *The Poetics of Aristotle, Translated from Greek into English and from Arabic into Latin, with a Revised Text, Introduction, Commentary, Glossary and Onomasticon*. London, 1911. – Ed. by Jaroslaus Tkatsch: *Die arabische Übersetzung der Poetik des Aristoteles und die Grundlage der Kritik des griechischen Textes*, 2 vols. Vienna, 1928–1932. – Ed. by ʿAbd al-Raḥmān Badawī, *Arisṭūṭālīs: Fī l-Šiʿr*. Cairo, 1953. – Ed. by Šukrī Muḥammad ʿAyyād, *Kitāb Arisṭūṭālīs fī l-Šiʿr: naql Abī Bišr Mattā b. Yūnus al-Qunnāʾī*. Cairo, 1967.

16 Aristotle. *Physics* [Arab.]. – Ed. by ʿAbd al-Raḥmān Badawī, *Arisṭūṭālīs: al-Ṭabīʿa: tarǧamat Isḥāq b. Ḥunayn, maʿa šurūḥ Ibn al-Samḥ wa-Ibn ʿAdī wa-Mattā b. Yūnus wa-Abī l-Faraǧ Ibn al-Ṭayyib*, 2 vols. Cairo, 1384–1385/1964–1965.

17 Aristotle. *Metaphysics*, Book XII [Arab.]. – Ed. by M. Bouyges [*28: III 1406–1736].

18 Alexander of Aphrodisias. *Maqāla fī l-Fuṣūl* [*On Specific Differences*]. – Ed. by ʿAbd al-Raḥmān Badawī, *Arisṭū ʿind al-ʿArab*. Cairo, 1947, 295–308. – With interspersed commentary (*šarḥ*) by Abū Bišr Mattā.

19 Abū Muḥammad ʿAbd Allāh b. Muḥammad al-Wāhibī. *Iḫtiṣār Tafsīr maʿānī alfāẓ Arisṭūṭālīs fī Kitāb al-Maqūlāt*. Istanbul, Süleymaniye, MS. Ayasofya 2483. – Ed. [excerpts] in Türker 1965 [*67: 103–122].

1.1.3 Additional Source Texts

23 Elias. *Eliae in Porphyrii Isagogen et Aristotelis Categorias commentaria*. – Ed. by Adolfus Busse. Berlin, 1900 [Commentaria in Aristotelem Graeca XVIII,1].

24 Simplicius. *Simplicii in Aristotelis Categorias commentarium*. – Ed. by Carolus Kalbfleisch. Berlin, 1907 [Commentaria in Aristotelem Graeca VIII].

1.1.4 Textual Evidence for the Reception History

27 Pseudo-Maǧrīṭī. *Picatrix: Das Ziel des Weisen*. – Ed. by Hellmut Ritter. Leipzig, Berlin, 1933. – German transl. by Hellmut Ritter and Martin Plessner. London, 1962.

28 Ibn Rušd, Abū l-Walīd Muḥammad b. Aḥmad (d. 595/1198). *Tafsīr Mā baʿd al-ṭabīʿa*. – Ed. by Maurice Bouyges, 3 vols. Beirut, 1938–1967.

1.2 *Arabic Aristotelianism and the Transmission of the Organon in the 3rd/9th and the 4th/10th Centuries*

The final phase of the Arabic reception of Aristotle lasted from the end of the 3rd/9th to the beginning of the 5th/11th century, and was sustained mainly by the labours of Christian-Arabic translators working from Syriac versions of Aristotle's texts. This phase establishes the Arabic Aristotle as the basis of Arabic-Islamic philosophy. It is the Aristotle of the first principles of the *Metaphysics*, of the hermeneutics and the syllogistics found in the *Organon*, and in particular of the epistemology of the *Posterior Analytics* (*Kitāb al-Burhān* in Arabic, meaning 'Book of Demonstration'). This is the basis on which Aristotle becomes the 'first teacher' of Arabic-Islamic philosophy, the master of demonstrative science – later superseded, with the advent of al-Fārābī and Ibn Sīnā, by a new philosophical theology which integrates prophecy and the language of revelation into a universal cosmology and epistemology. In Aristotle's name,

Graeco-Arabic transmission and translation activities had been paving the way for this development for two centuries, appealing to an Aristotelianism which based the authority of the Stagirite on his agreement with Platonic theology, in accord with the commentators of the late antique schools and in particular of the school of Alexandria and its Christian heirs. However, Aristotle's towering authority was not, at first, grounded in the *Organon* so much as in his cosmic and sublunar physics. Above all, there was the pseudepigraphical *Theology*, based on Neoplatonic sources but transmitted under Aristotle's name.

The readers of ancient philosophy, the initiators and sponsors of its Arabic translations and adaptations, belonged to various circles of scientific activity devoted to mathematics, astronomy, medicine, and theological-juridical hermeneutics – the latter occurring at first merely in Christian, but later on also in Muslim milieus. For the mathematicians and 'physicists' around al-Kindī (cf. § 5) Aristotle was the embodiment of true philosophy; but his name was attached to authentic as well as apocryphal writings, to Platonic, Peripatetic, and Neoplatonic doctrines. It was in this guise that, following the demise of the old schools within the Christian milieu, Aristotle entered into the service of the Islamic administration. Only later did a readership emerge whose interest in the hermeneutical disciplines in Islam led them to demand that rational deduction be put on a secure footing, using the complete *Organon* of logic.

1. The Arabic reception of Aristotle in the early Abbasid era. However, the authorities on logic, on whom the authority of this tradition ultimately rested in the 4th/10th century (*ilayhi ntahat riʾāsat al-manṭiqiyyīn fī ʿaṣrihi*, Ibn al-Nadīm says of Abū Bišr Mattā [**1*: 363,25], and *fī ʿaṣrinā hāḏā* of his pupil Yaḥyā Ibn ʿAdī [**1*: 264,6]; similarly al-Masʿūdī [*2: 122]) were preceded by a tradition of similar orientation. Already in the first half of the 2nd/8th century, the Iranian ʿAbd Allāh (Rōzbih) b. al-Muqaffaʿ (d. 137/755 or 139/756), or perhaps his son Muḥammad b. ʿAbd Allāh, composed a compendium of the *Organon*, picking up where the Iranian adherents of the Alexandrian school tradition had left off. However, his analysis of types of propositions according to *On Interpretation* left no traces in the further history of philosophical logic; at best we may find some parallels in the hermeneutics of early grammarians and exegetes of the Quran (cf. Schöck 2006 [*50: 119–151]).

The early reception of Aristotelian logic, by Christian theologians on the payroll of courtly patrons and of dignitaries of the Abbasid administration, was of much wider scope than we may be led to believe by al-Fārābī. He dismissively remarked, '[In the Christian schools] they used to call everything that comes after the figures of the categorical syllogism [sc. after *An. pr.* I 7] the part of logic which one does not read' (*Fī Ẓuhūr al-falsafa*, Ibn Abī Uṣaybiʿa [**6*: II 135,21]). At best, this may be true of the reading habits of Christian theologians who confined themselves to studying the Syriac compendia of the *Organon*, and from whom the Muslim Aristotelians sought to distance themselves as adepts in the Greek-Syriac tradition as a whole. Syriac translations of the entire *Analytics*, the *Topics*, and the *Sophistical Refutations* – by Athanasius of Balad (d. 686), Theophilus of Edessa (d. 785), and others – are well attested (cf. Watt 2009 [*52]). The caliph al-Mahdī (regn. 158–169/775–785) and his son and successor Hārūn al-Rašīd (regn. 170–193/786–809) held the Nestorian Catholicos, Timothy I (728–823, Rescher 1964 [*16: 93]), in high esteem. One of the two caliphs, al-Rašīd, commissioned him to procure a translation of the *Topics* from the Syriac. The Patriarch had the translation carried out by Abū Nūḥ al-Anbārī, a *kātib* of the governor of Mosul who seems to have translated yet further parts of the *Organon* (cf. Hugonnard-Roche 1990 [*40], 1993 [*47]). We get a vivid impression of the enthusiasm which animated the protagonists of this activity from two letters written by Patriarch Timothy. They furthermore reveal that in order to support his activity, he strove to obtain evidence for commentaries on Aristotle's *Topics*, *Sophistical Refutations*, *Rhetorics*, and *Poetics*, as well as copies of further philosophical texts (Brock 1999 [*45: 233–246], Berti 2007 [*51: 56]).

Some of the translations from the *Organon* which had been produced by Christian scholars in the environment of the Baghdad court during the early Abbasid period were still circulating in the 4th/10th century, as we are informed by glosses in a Paris manuscript of the *Organon* (1950–1952 Badawī; 1999 Ǧabr et al. [*11]). This concerns the Syriac versions of the *Prior Analytics* and the *Sophistical Refutations*, translated by Theophilus of Edessa (d. 785) during the caliphate of al-Mahdī (cf. also Ibn al-Nadīm, *Fihrist* [*1: I 249,22], Baumstark 1922 [*11: 341–342], Georr 1948 [*33: 30–31], Walzer 1962 [*34: 69. 81–94]), as well as the even older renderings of the *Prior Analytics* and the *Topics* from the pen of the Jacobite Athanasius of Balad (Patriarch of Antioch, d. 686, cf. Baumstark 1922 [*11: 256–257], Georr 1948 [*33: 26], Walzer 1962 [*34: 68. 82–83. 85–86. 88. 113]). They continued to be quoted in order to provide further aspects of textual criticism and interpretation, even once they were surpassed by more recent translations. For instance, the oldest Arabic version of the *Prior Analytics*, by Yaḥyā Ibn al-Biṭrīq (known as Yūḥannā before his conversion; a client (*mawlā*) of the caliph al-Ma'mūn who was active in the circle of al-Kindī), is used in a marginal gloss of the standard translation by Theodore (Taḏārā) Abū Qurra [*11: 112 n. 5 Badawī, 141 no. 2 and 3]: Abū Bišr Mattā dismisses Ibn al-Biṭrīq's translation in favour of Theodore's, etc. (cf. Walzer 1962 [*34: 78. 85]).

2. *Mathematicians and Astronomers. The circle of al-Kindī.* Al-Kindī's worldview was defined by Aristotle's physics and metaphysics – albeit in the service of a Platonic theology adapted to monotheism. His all-embracing curiosity led

him to engage with the entire scientific heritage of the Alexandrian canon, including topics of Aristotelian logic according to the books of the *Organon* (or rather: according to their paltry school compendia). Yet his logical works are known only by their titles, evidently having found no readership. Rather than the syllogism of Aristotle's propositional logic, he adopted as his models Euclidian analysis and Pythagorean arithmology (cf. § 4).

3. Abū Maʿšar al-Balḫī (171–272/787–886, cf. also § 9.3), was an orthodox Aristotelian after the fashion of Ptolemy, even though, in his role as astrologer, he transmitted Iranian models and parameters from the Iranian tradition. It is not only al-Balḫī's cosmology, in his *Great Introduction to Astrology* (*al-Mudḫal al-kabīr ilā ʿilm aḥkām al-nuǧūm*), that follows Aristotle (esp. *On the Heavens*), but he himself too is firmly rooted in the Alexandrian school tradition. His introduction to astrology, as one of the ancient encyclopedic sciences, follows the Alexandrian commentators in its traditional pattern of introductory headings (*kephalaia*) – purpose, benefit, and division of the work, name of author (or authority), title, position within the order of the sciences – and the four types of question from the beginning of the *Posterior Analytics*, which enquire into existence, essence, quality and cause. A subtle philosophical investigation is applied to the subject matter and to the justification of astrology, drawing on the discussion of future contingents in Aristotle's *On Interpretation* (ch. 9) – it is unclear which translation or paraphrase he used (*al-Mudḫal al-kabīr, qawl* 1, *ṣinf* 3; see Baffioni 2002 [*49] with references to the testimonies of Aristotelian compendia in the Ǧābir corpus).

4. Ḥunayn b. Isḥāq and his circle. Another figure firmly rooted in the scientific tradition is the physician Ḥunayn b. Isḥāq (d. 260/873 or 264/877, cf. § 9.2.1), whose extensive translation activity, sponsored by Syriac and Arab physicians as well as prominent courtiers and their learned entourage (such as the mathematician brothers Banū Mūsā), focused primarily on ancient medicine. Philosophy he only cultivated to the extent of the Hippocratic exhortation that 'the best doctor must also be a philosopher', confining himself to Galen's compendia of Plato's works. In the field of logic, he followed not Aristotle, but Galen's *On Demonstration* (cf. Zimmermann 1981 [*78: lxxvi. ciii–cviii]).

Within Ḥunayn's school, it was first and foremost his son Isḥāq b. Ḥunayn (d. 289/910–911) who, apart from a few translations of medical works, commenced the translations of Aristotelian logic, physics and ethics from Greek originals. The resulting corpus was to become authoritative for a whole era. After his conversion to Islam, he served as a court physician to several Baghdad caliphs, and in particular as the advisor of al-Muktafī (289–295/902–908); he was closely associated with the latter's vizier al-Qāsim b. ʿUbayd Allāh. His translations of Aristotle's *Categories* and *On Interpretation* are transmitted in the edition of the *Organon* that was compiled and annotated by al-Ḥasan b. Suwār (Ibn al-Ḫammār, cf. § 7.4) on the basis of Yaḥyā Ibn ʿAdī's copy of Isḥāq's authograph. Like those two translations, his versions of the *Physics* and of book II (α) of the *Metaphysics* supplanted other versions. His translation of *On the Soul* is now lost, but was still used by Ibn Sīnā. In the case of other fundamental writings, such as the *Nicomachean Ethics*, and of Aristotelian commentaries, such as Themistius' commentary on *On the Soul*, he was the first to produce a translation. In the course of his translation activity he created a unified and coherent terminology of logic and ontology. In his work on mathematical sources he was supported by Ṯābit b. Qurra (cf. § 9.2.2), himself known as an adept in Aristotelian philosophy.

Another translator with close ties to this circle was Abū ʿUṯmān Saʿīd b. Yaʿqūb al-Dimašqī. A leading physician of his time, he enjoyed the favour of the powerful vizier ʿAlī b. ʿĪsā b. al-Ǧarrāḥ (d. 334/946). He became chief physician in the hospital which the vizier founded in the al-Ḥarbiyya district in Baghdad (302/914–915), and was made superintendent of further hospitals in Baghdad, Mecca, and Medina (see Ibn Abī Uṣaybiʿa [*6: I 234]; cf. Meyerhof 1930 [*13: 424], Walzer 1962 [34: 67 and index] and Endress 1995 [*43] with further references to his translations). Leaving aside his work on important medical and mathematical sources, his lasting significance as a translator rests on his philosophical œuvre, which – as with Isḥāq – comprises the logical, physical, and ethical works of Aristotle as well as his commentators. His translation of Aristotle's *Topics*, book I–VII, was to become the authoritative Arabic version of this fundamental textbook of logical argumentation (*Manṭiq Arisṭū* [*11: 467–689, ²487–725 Badawī; 635–891 Ǧabr et al.]). According to the date of a manuscript that was produced from Abū ʿUṯmān's own copy, it was completed before 298/910–911 [*11: 532]. His version of Porphyry's introduction to Aristotle's *Categories*, the *Isagoge*, circulated even more widely (*Manṭiq Arisṭū* [*11: 1019–1068, ²1055–1104]). Of particular interest are his renderings of numerous treatises by the leading Peripatetic commentator of Aristotle, Alexander of Aphrodisias, on questions arising from the *Categories*, and on ontology and physics.

With Isḥāq b. Ḥunayn and Abū ʿUṯmān al-Dimašqī the translation activity of Ḥunayn's circle left behind the narrow constraints of medicine and the philosophical horizon of Galenism. They addressed themselves to a new and larger audience who had an increasing interest in Aristotle's doctrine of demonstration. By now, the hermeneutical disciplines of Islam were being presented as 'scientific', something we first see with the grammarians of the Basran school, and soon thereafter with the 'principles of jurisprudence' (*uṣūl al-fiqh*). The Arabic-Islamic scientific tradition and its Greek counterpart were now locked in a contest for intellectual supremacy within Islamic society. The battle was all the more fierce in the wake of the *miḥna*, an 'inquisition' geared towards the interests of rational theology, which was put to an end by al-Mutawakkil (234/848): for the time being, the attempt to integrate both sides had failed.

1.3 *Abū Bišr Mattā and the Reception of the Organon in the 4th/10th Century*

As a translator and commentator of Aristotle, especially of his logical works, Abū Bišr Mattā (Matthew) b. Yūnus (Yūnān) al-Qunnāʾī was among the most important initiators of the reception of Peripatetic philosophy via translations from the Syriac in its final period. A Nestorian Christian, he initially studied and taught in Dair Qunnā in Mesopotamia (Fiey 1968 [*17: III 187–193]), in the school (*uskūl*) of the monastery Mār Mattā. He came to Baghdad during the caliphate of al-Rāḍī (i.e. after 322/934). His translation and teaching activities were so successful with Christians as well as Muslims that he was able to live off the fees he charged for his instruction in logic (as we may glean from the polemically tainted report of a contemporary, he used to dicate for one *Muqtadirī* dirham per leaf; see Abū Ḥayyān al-Tawḥīdī, *al-Imtāʿ wa-l-muʾānasa* [*3: I 14]). He died on 11 Ramaḍān 328/20 June 940 (Ibn Abī Uṣaybiʿa [*6: 317]).

The Christian transmitters and translators who provided the source texts of the Arabic Aristotle and his commentators in the last period of the translation movement – now working primarily from Syro-Aramaic versions – are mentioned by name in a report ascribed to al-Fārābī and entitled *On the Emergence of Philosophy* (in Ibn Abī Uṣaybiʿa [*6: 134,30–135,29]). The same report is also incorporated by the historian al-Masʿūdī (*al-Tanbīh wa-l-išrāf* [*2: 122]), though without referring to any source and with several variants. The history of the philosophical tradition, in particular of Aristotelian logic, is here construed as a continuous school tradition from Alexandria via Antioch to Baghdad. Like similar texts from the medical tradition, this presentation is meant on the one hand to establish the coherence and authenticity of the doctrine, and on the other hand to emphasize the importance of Arabic-Islamic scholarship. As the history of a continuous scholarly tradition 'from Alexandria to Baghdad' the report cannot lay claim to historical truth. But as far as the names of Mattā's and al-Fārābī's immediate teachers and their textual transmission are concerned, it is likely to be more reliable (cf. Meyerhof 1930 [*13: 405–407. 413–414], Zimmermann 1981 [*78: cv–cviii], Gutas 1999 [*46]; cf. also § 8 below).

Among Mattā's (and hence, al-Fārābī's) teachers, the report names the following, some of whom are also mentioned in Ibn al-Nadīm's *Fihrist*, followed by later bibliographers:

Abū Yaḥyā Ibrāhīm al-Marwazī was a physician and a teacher of logic in Syriac language. With him, Mattā and al-Fārābī read Aristotle's *Posterior Analytics*, which means that he can be regarded as having initiated the renewal of logical studies in Baghdad, a process completed by Mattā (Ibn Abī Uṣaybiʿa [*6: II 135], Ibn al-Nadīm [*1: 249,4. 263,15]; Meyerhof 1930 [*13: 405–407], Walzer 1962 [*34: 100–101], Rescher 1964 [*16: 110 no. 17]). A gloss (from the Syriac?) on *Posterior Analytics* I 23, 84b26 can be found in the margins of the Paris *Organon* manuscript [*11: 517 n. 17 Ǧabr].

Abū Isḥāq Ibrāhīm Quwayrā (Cyrus) was one of Mattā's personal teachers and is quoted as the author of commentaries on Aristotle's logic: on the *Organon* (*Fihrist* [*1: I 262]); in particular on *Prior Analytics* I 1–7 and on *Sophistical Refutations* I 1–11 (cf. the Arabic scholia on the *Organon*, *Manṭiq Arisṭū* [*11: 951]); we furthermore find mention of commentaries on the *Categories*, on *On Interpretation*, and on the *Prior Analytics* that were 'structured like a tree' (*mušaǧǧar*), i.e. composed in the form of schematic graphic patterns (according to Ibn al-Qifṭī [*5: 88]).

Yūḥannā b. Ḥaylān (who, according to al-Masʿūdī, died in Baghdad during the reign of al-Muqtadir, 295–320/908–932) is mentioned in al-Fārābī's report as the teacher with whom he read the *Organon* up to the end of the *Book of Demonstration* (i.e., of the *Posterior Analytics*; see Ibn Abī Uṣaybiʿa [*6: II 135,20]).

Abū ʿAmr al-Ṭabarī is mentioned only as Mattā's pupil and, though documented as a transmitter, he is is not known to us from his own works (Hasnawi 1966 [*69]). According to Abū Bišr he was the author of the scholia on Alexander of Aphrodisias' *Maqāla fī l-Fuṣūl* (see p. 432 below).

1.4 *Translations from Mattā's School*

The translations produced by Abū Bišr Mattā and his school were based on Syriac versions mainly from the 2nd/8th and the 3rd/9th centuries, most of which are now lost. They went far beyond the repertoire of Aristotelian studies that had been at the disposal of the Arabic scholars belonging to the earlier reception period. In fact, they constituted a veritable renaissance of Aristotelian studies, assembling, on the basis of all available texts of the Aristotelian corpus as well as the associated commentaries by Alexander of Aphrodisias and Themistius, the most complete and most authentic Aristotle available at any time in the Arabic Middle Ages. Of Mattā's own translations, the following were known to the bookseller and bibliographer Ibn al-Nadīm (*Fihrist* [*1: I 249–251. 263–264]): the *Posterior Analytics*, including Alexander's lemmatized commentary, as well as Themistius' paraphrase of 'the three last books'; the *Sophistical Refutations* (the revision of an older version, cf. *Manṭiq*

Arisṭū [**11*: 785 n. 2; 1018]); the *Poetics*; *On the Heavens* ('a part of book I', later revised by Yaḥyā Ibn ʿAdī) and its paraphrase by Themistius (revised by Yaḥyā Ibn ʿAdī); *On Generation and Corruption*, together with the commentaries by Alexander and Olympiodorus; the *Meteorology*, together with Olympiodorus' commentary; and book XII of the *Metaphysics*, together with Alexander's commentary as well as Themistius' paraphrase.

Scholia and philological marginal notes on Aristotelian philosophy. As far as they are extant, the commentaries of Mattā and his school took the form of more or less extensive annotations, either written in the margins or appended to the lemmata of the text (*taʿālīq*). Other commentaries of the Peripatetic school and of Alexandrian Neoplatonism appear next to his in glosses and in compilations of commentaries of the school – without it being possible to ascertain who was responsible for the individual translations. For instance, Iamblichus' *On the Categories* shows up in the scholia of al-Ḥasan b. Suwār (Georr 1948 [*33: 371,6]), and in al-Wāhibī's hypomnemata (see below under Arist., *Cat.*).

The only textual witnesses of those translation and transmission activities extant today are the following:

1.4.1 Aristotle: *Organon*

A significant number of philological and commentatorial scholia from Mattā's school can be found in the Paris manuscript of the Arabic *Organon*. Some are ascribed to Yaḥyā Ibn ʿAdī (see § 7.2 below) and the 'editor' of the manuscript, Ibn ʿAdī's pupil al-Ḥasan b. Suwār (Ibn al-Ḫammār, cf. § 7.4). They relate to the *Prior Analytics* (cf. Walzer 1962 [*34: 66. 77–78. 99–100. 102), the *Posterior Analytics* (cf. ibid., 102), and Porphyry's *Isagoge* (ibid., 1046 n. 1. 1048 n. 1 and 3. 1053 n. 2. 1054 n. 1).

A catena commentary on the *Categories* from the 4th/10th century, Istanbul, Süleymaniye, MS Ayasofya 2483 (partially edited in Türker 1965 [*67: 103–122]), entitled *Tafsīr maʿānī alfāẓ Arisṭūṭālīs fī Kitāb al-Maqūlāt* and surviving as an excerpt by one al-Wāhibī, contains, in addition to excerpts from Greek commentators, glosses by Mattā, al-Fārābī (Ibn al-Ḏahabī?), al-ʿĀmirī, and Abū Sulaymān al-Siǧistānī. As Rowson suspects, it might go back to a pupil of Abū l-Ḥasan al-ʿĀmirī's (cf. § 5.2) named Abū l-Qāsim al-Kātib (Rowson 1988 [*36: 14], cf. Reisman 2002 [*423: 169–170], citing Abū Ḥayyān al-Tawḥīdī, *al-Imtāʿ* [**3*: I 35]: al-Tawḥīdī presents Miskawayh with a copy of Abū l-Qāsim's *Ṣafw al-šarḥ li-Īsāġūǧī wa-Qāṭīġūriyās*); cf. ibid., pp. 109, 110, 111, Abū Bišr Mattā on *Cat.* 5, 3b10–23. 34–38 (primary and secondary substances, substance and property), p. 119, and MS fol. 130ª (not in Türker) on *Cat.* 7. 8a27–35 and 8a35–8b15 (substance and relation).

Further glosses by Mattā are quoted by his pupil Yaḥyā Ibn ʿAdī (Endress 1977 [*18: 52. 93]); others were known to Ibn al-Nadīm (*Fihrist* [**1*: I 264], and, even later, to the physician Ibn al-Muṭrān (d. 587/1191; cf. al-Šabībī 1923 [*12: 7 no. 9. 19, 20]: glosses on *Isag.*, *Cat.*, *De int.*) and to the physician and philosopher ʿAbd al-Laṭīf al-Baġdādī (d. 629/1231, *Risāla fī Muǧādalat al-ḥakīmayn al-kīmiyāʾī wa-l-naẓarī*, MS Bursa, Hüseyin Çelebi 823, fol. 113ᵇ, lines 5–7, cf. Stern 1962 [*65: 55. 66]).

1.4.2 Aristotle: *Posterior Analytics* (*Kitāb al-Burhān*)

The Paris manuscript of the Arabic *Organon* (Bibl. nat., ar. 2346) contains the *Posterior Analytics* in Mattā's translation, copied from a holograph of his pupil Yaḥyā Ibn ʿAdī (ed. Badawī [*11: 309–465]). For the revision of book I on which Ibn Rušd based his *Long Commentary*, and which consequently was translated into Latin by Gerard of Cremona, cf. Gätje, Schoeler (1980 [*35: 564–583]). Ibn al-Nadīm mentions two introductory treatises to the *Analytics* (*Fihrist* [*1: I 264]).

1.4.3 Aristotle: *Poetics* (*Kitāb al-Šiʿr*)

Mattā and his teachers continued the late Alexandrian tradition of Aristotelian studies. It was only within such a context that the difficult (and ultimately unsuccessful) project of an Arabic translation of the *Poetics* could be undertaken in the first place: that is to say, within the framework of a complete transmission of the Aristotelian corpus, and in particular of the *Organon*, to which the *Poetics* was thought to belong (Walzer 1962 [*34: 129–136]). Like the *Rhetoric*, the *Poetics* offered, to the logician, an analysis of certain forms of discourse that were non-syllogistic and particular. It thus complemented the forms of demonstration treated in the other books of the *Organon*.

Hampered by a lack of direct knowledge of the Greek literary heritage, and working from a Syriac translation from the early Abbasid period (cf. Schrier 1997 [*87], Berti 2007 [*51: 312–315]), the translator was confronted by unsurmountable problems in attempting this task. Some of his more serious mistakes in rendering the literary terminology, whose cultural background – Greek theatre – was unknown to him, have become notorious: 'tragedy' is translated by *madīḥ* (panegyrical poem), comedy by *hiǧāʾ* (satirical poem), and ὄψις (scenery, stage setting) by *naẓar*, which, to philosophers, meant 'speculative thinking' (Heinrichs 1978 [*75: 109]; cf. also Gabrieli 1929 [*64]; Tarán and Gutas 2012 [*91a]).

Far-reaching consequences for the understanding of the text were furthermore incurred by Abū Bišr's terminological choice for the foundational concept of Aristotelian poetics, μίμησις, which he rendered by the hendiadys *tašbīh wa-muḥākāt* (simile and imitation). Taken out of its context within the analysis of 'logical' discourse, the concept provided al-Fārābī with the notions of representation, imitation and persuasion which he used within his theory of religious language (Heinrichs 1978 [*75]; for al-Fārābī cf. also § 8 below).

1.4.4 Aristotle: *Physics* (*Kitāb al-Samāʿ al-Ṭabīʿī*)

Several quite substantial remarks penned by Mattā on *Physics* II,3-III,4 have survived in the commentary compilation of MS. Leiden, Or. 1433 (together with Isḥāq b.

Ḥunayn's Arabic translation and comments by Greek and Arabic authors, redacted in 395/1004 by Abū l-Ḥusayn al-Baṣrī on the basis of lectures by Yaḥyā Ibn ʿAdī's pupil Abū ʿAlī Ibn al-Samḥ (ed. Badawī [*16]) (cf. § 7.5) see Janos 2016 [*95]).

1.4.5 Aristotle: *Metaphysics* (*Kitāb Mā baʿd al-ṭabīʿa*)

Abū Bišr's Arabic version of Alexander of Aphrodisias' commentary on *Metaphysics* XII, ch. 1–7 (1069a18–1072b16), which contains the lemmata of Aristotle's text, served as basis for Ibn Rušd's *Long Commentary* (*Tafsīr Mā baʿd al-ṭabīʿa* [*28: III, cf. 'Notice' cxxx–cxxxi]). The Arabic text, which is extant nowhere else, goes back to Alexander's authentic commentary, whereas the Greek tradition preserves a Pseudo-Alexandrian text for books VI–XIV, probably by Michael of Ephesus (Freudenthal 1885 [*61]; cf. also Luna 2001 [*48]).

Pseudo-Mağrīṭī, *Picatrix* (ed. Ritter 1933, transl. Ritter, Plessner [*27]) quotes from a commentary by Abū Bišr Mattā – or, more likely, from his translation of Alexander's commentary – on *Metaphysics* II, III and XII; to be specific: a) on *Metaphysics* III 1, 995a27–30, concerning the dissolution of doubts through knowledge, illustrated by an anecdote about Mazdak and Anūširwān (*Picatrix* [*27: 282–283; transl. 290–291]); b) on a 3, 995a3, concerning the treatment of myths, and their importance for law and order (*Picatrix* [*27: 283–284; transl. 292–293]); c) on *Metaphysics* I within a passage on the scope of metaphysics (*Picatrix* [*27: 355; trans. 351]), containing a dictum by Ṯābit b. Qurra about the relationship between theology and mathematics (from a gloss by Mattā?).

1.4.6 Alexander of Aphrodisias: *Maqāla fī l-Fuṣūl*

Alexander's treatise on specific differences is only extant in Arabic. Its translation by Abū ʿUṯmān al-Dimašqī is explicated by inserted scholia (*taʿālīq*, introduced at their specific locations by the word *šarḥ*) by Abū ʿAmr al-Ṭabarī, according to the teaching (*ʿan*) of Abū Bišr Mattā, cf. *Maqāla fī l-Fuṣūl*, ed. by ʿA. Badawī [*18: 295–308]; cf. van Ess 1966 [*68: 154–158]; see here also for information on another translation of the treatise, ed. Dietrich 1964 [*66]; for Abū ʿAmr al-Ṭabarī cf. Hasnawi 1966 [*69].

1.5 *Doctrine and Influence*

Abū Bišr Mattā was unanimously held to be the leading expert of logic during his time (Ibn al-Nadīm, *Fihrist* [*1: I 263,25]; al-Masʿūdī, *al-Tanbīh* [*2: 122]). Al-Fārābi studied the *Organon* with Mattā (or alongside him with Mattā's teachers; cf. § 8, p. 539); and through his closest pupil, the Jacobite Christian Yaḥyā Ibn ʿAdī (§ 7.2), his doctrine was passed on to subsequent generations of Christian and Muslim philosophers in Baghdad, and further on to the Islamic East.

Mattā was a transmitter and interpreter of logic, but did not write any treatises on specific topics in which he would offer his own presentations or doctrines of logical method. In Abū Ḥayyān al-Tawḥīdī's brilliant, albeit biased, report [*3: I 107–128] (cf. also § 5.3) of a disputation with the grammarian Abū Saʿīd al-Sīrāfī (d. 368/979), to which he was challenged by the vizier Ibn al-Furāt in 326/937–938, he appears as the defender of logic. He extols it as 'a tool of speech by which correct ('sound') speech can be distinguished from incorrect ('unsound') speech, invalid from valid meaning, just as I distinguish, with the help of scales, the excessive from the deficient, the superior from the inferior'. Mattā is following here the *prolegomena* of the Alexandrian commentary tradition (cf. Elias, *In Cat.* ed. Busse [*23: 117,9–14. 119,16–14], similarly Simplicius, *In Cat.* ed. Kalbfleisch [*24: 20,10–12]).

However, Mattā cannot ward off the grammarian's attack in the Arabic language. The grammarian confronts the non-Arab logician with the claim that correct thinking is preceded by correct speaking, and that Greek logic is thus inevitably subject to the conventions of the Greek language. When cast into the linguistic form of an Arabic translation, logic no longer has its force: 'logical discourse' (*nuṭq*, cf. the term used by philosophers: *manṭiq*, λογική) always needs to be based on the grammar of a particular, conventional language. The backdrop to this controversy is a growing polemic against the logical paradigms that were infiltrating the hermeneutics (*uṣūl al-naḥw*) of the Basrian grammarians, like Ibn al-Sarrāǧ (d. 316/928) and his pupil ʿAlī b. ʿĪsā al-Rummānī (d. 384/994, cf. *Fihrist* [*1: I 62]), who was al-Tawḥīdī's source for the disputation (for further information cf. Elamrani-Jamal 1983 [*79], Endress 1986 [*81], 2002 [*89]). It was left to Mattā's pupils to determine the position of logic – and hence of the rational sciences altogether – more adequately and more effectively in its relation to grammar and to the hermeneutics of the religious law that characterized the Islamic disciplines, and thus to defend logic as a universal grammar of logical thinking (on al-Fārābī, cf. Zimmermann 1981 [*78: cxxvi–cxxxix], Endress 2015 [*93]; on Yaḥyā Ibn ʿAdī, Endress 1977 [*18: 45–46], see § 7.2 below).

Even in Mattā's commentaries belonging to the fields of categorical doctrine and physics, independent philosopical opinions can only be identified in rare individual cases. His view of nature as an immanent, creative force (*al-ṭabīʿa al-faʿʿāla*, *Physics* [Arab.] ed. Badawī [*16: 151], cf. John Philoponus, *In Phys.*, 317,18 Vitelli) is explicitly attacked by Ibn Sīnā (cf. Brown 1972 [*72: 43–45], Genequand 1984 [*80], Janos 2016 [*94]).

In his roles as a translator of Aristotelian works and as a teacher of Aristotelian philosophy, and of logic in particular, Mattā laid the foundations for the leading philosophical school of 4th/10th century Baghdad. The most important of his pupils and successors will be introduced below in their own specific sections: Christian Arabic translators and teachers of Aristotelian philosophy, starting with Yaḥyā Ibn ʿAdī (§ 7.2) and his circle of Christian translators and teachers of Aristotelian logic (§ 7.3 ʿĪsā Ibn Zurʿa, § 7.4 Ibn al-Ḫammār, § 5.5 Ibn Hindū, § 7.5 Ibn al-Samḥ), as well as the Muslim Abū Sulaymān al-Siǧistānī (§ 5.3).

Indebted to him too are those who were to become the creators of an Islamic philosophy in its own right, among them the most eminent Muslim pupil of the circle of the Baghdad transmitters of philosophy: al-Fārābī, who used the *Posterior Analytics* in Mattā's translation as a foundation on which to build the highest kind of philosophy, originally established by Aristotle, as a science based on demonstration. He reports with great satisfaction that the book on demonstration, *Kitāb al-Burhān*, which had always been considered the centrepiece and crown of logic, yet was no longer studied in the Christian schools, had for the first time become available to him again (Ibn Abī Uṣaybiʿa [*6: II 135,20]). His full commentary on this work appears to be lost, but his hermeneutical and systematical works impart a new concept of philosophy as an apodeictic science, which takes its direction from the Aristotelian *Analytics*.

2 Yaḥyā Ibn ʿAdī

Gerhard Endress

2.1 Primary Sources – 2.2 Life and Influence – 2.3 Works – 2.4 Doctrine

2.1 *Primary Sources*

2.1.1 Bio-bibliographical Testimonies [*31–*41] – 2.1.2 Works [*46–*132] – 2.1.3 Additional Source Texts [*141–*142]

2.1.1 Bio-bibliographical Testimonies

31 al-Masʿūdī, Abū l-Ḥasan ʿAlī b. al-Ḥusayn. *Kitāb al-Tanbīh wa-l-išrāf* [composed 345/956]. – Ed. by Michael Jan de Goeje, *Kitâb at-tanbîh wa'l-ischrâf auctore al-Masûdî.* Leiden, 1894, 122,10–14.

32 Ibn al-Nadīm, Abū l-Farağ Muḥammad b. Isḥāq (d. 380/990). *Kitāb al-Fihrist* [composed 377/988]. – Ed. by Gustav Flügel, August Müller and Johannes Roediger, 2 vols. Leipzig, 1871–1872, 264.5–14. – Repr. Beirut 1964, Frankfurt a.M. 2005. – Ed. by Riḍā Tağaddud, Tehran 1350 h.š./1971, 322,18–25. – Ed. by Ayman

Fuʾād Sayyid, 2 vols (I\1–2- II\1–2). London, 1430/2009, vol. 2, 202,3–203,4. – Engl. transl. by Bayard Dodge, *The Fihrist of al-Nadīm*, 2 vols. New York, 1970.

33 al-Tawḥīdī, Abū Ḥayyān ʿAlī b. Muḥammad (d. 414/1023). *Al-Baṣāʾir wa-l-ḏaḫāʾir*. – Ed. by Wadād al-Qāḍī, vol. 1. Beirut, 1988, 145.

34 Abū Ḥayyān al-Tawḥīdī. *Al-Muqābasāt*. – Ed. by Muḥammad Tawfīq Ḥusayn. Baghdad, 1970, 103–105. 204–205. 207–208. 334–335.

35 Abū Ḥayyān al-Tawḥīdī. *Kitāb al-Imtāʿ wa-l-muʾānasa*. – Ed. by Aḥmad Amīn and Aḥmad al-Zayn, 3 vols. Cairo, 1939–1944, vol. 1, 37. 376–379. 381; vol. 2, 18. 38.

36 *Ṣiwān al-ḥikma* [ascribed to Abū Sulaymān al-Siǧistānī]. – Ed. by ʿAbd al-Raḥmān Badawī, *Ṣiwān al-ḥikma wa-ṯalāṯ rasāʾil*. Tehran, 1974, 227–228. – Excerpts ed. by Douglas Morton Dunlop, *The Muntakhab Ṣiwān al-ḥikmah of Abū Sulaimān as-Sijistānī*. The Hague, 1979, 140 § 275.

37 al-Bayhaqī, Ẓahīr al-Dīn Abū l-Ḥasan ʿAlī b. Zayd Ibn Funduq (d. 565/1169–1170). *Tatimmat Ṣiwān al-ḥikma*. – Ed. by Muḥammad Šafīʿ, fasc. 1: Arabic text. Lahore, 1935, 90,6–11. – Ed. by Muḥammad ʿAlī, *Taʾrīḫ ḥukamāʾ al-islām*. Damascus, 1365/1946. – Repr. 1396/1976. – Engl. transl. by Max Meyerhof, "ʿAlī al-Bayhaqī's *Tatimmat Ṣiwān al-ḥikma*: A Biographical Work on Learned Men of the Islam." *Osiris* 8 (1948): 122–217, here 97,4–11.

38 Ibn al-Qifṭī, Ǧamāl al-Dīn ʿAlī b. Yūsuf (d. 646/1248). *Taʾrīḫ al-ḥukamāʾ* [*Iḫbār al-ʿulamāʾ bi-aḫbār al-ḥukamāʾ*, epitome by Muḥammad b. ʿAlī al-Zawzanī]. – Ed. by Julius Lippert, *Ibn al-Qifṭī's Taʾrīh al-ḥukamāʾ*. Leipzig, 1903, 361–364.

39 Ibn Abī Uṣaybiʿa, Muwaffaq al-Dīn Aḥmad b. al-Qāsim (d. 668/1270). *ʿUyūn al-anbāʾ fī ṭabaqāt al-aṭibbāʾ*. – Ed. by August Müller, 2 vols. Cairo, 1299/1882, Königsberg, 1884, vol. 1, 241.

40 Ibn al-ʿIbrī, Abū l-Faraǧ Gregorios [Barhebraeus] (d. 685/1286). *Taʾrīḫ muḫtaṣar al-duwal*. – Ed. by Anṭūn Ṣāliḥānī. Beirut, 1890, 1958 (2nd ed.), 55. 170.

41 Ibn Faḍl Allāh al-ʿUmarī (d. 749/1349). *Masālik al-abṣār fī mamālik al-amṣār: Routes Toward Insight into the Capital Empires*, book 9. – Ed. by Fuat Sezgin, in collaboration with A. Jokhosha and Eckhard Neubauer. Frankfurt a.M., 1988, 25–26. – Facsimile edition.

2.1.2 Works

2.1.2.1 *Bibliographical Inventories*

46 Endress, Gerhard. *The Works of Yaḥyā Ibn ʿAdī: An Analytical Inventory*. Wiesbaden, 1977.

47 Wisnovsky, Robert. "New Philosophical Texts of Yaḥyā ibn ʿAdī: A Supplement to Endress' Analytical Inventory." In *Islamic Philosophy, Science, Culture, and Religion: Studies in Honor of Dimitri Gutas*. Ed. by Felicitas Opwis and David Reisman. Leiden, 2012, 307–326. – Treatises in MS Tehran, Madrasa-yi Marwī 19 [*56].

2.1.2.2 *Partial Collections*

51 Périer, Augustin, ed. and transl. *Petits traités apologétiques de Yaḥyâ ben ʿAdî. Texte arabe, éd. pour la première fois d'après les manuscrits de Paris, de Rome et de Munich et traduit en français*. – PhD Diss., University of Paris, 1920.

52 Sbath, Paul, ed. *Vingt traités philosophiques et apologétiques d'auteurs arabes chrétiens du IXe au XIVe siècle, publiés pour la première fois, avec corrections et annotations*. Cairo, 1929.

53 Ḫalīfāt, Saḥbān, ed. *Maqālāt Yaḥyā Ibn ʿAdī al-falsafiyya*. Amman, 1988.

54 Platti, Emilio, ed. and transl. *La grande polémique antinestorienne de Yaḥyā ibn ʿAdī*, 2 vols. Leuven, 1981–1982 [Corpus Scriptorum Christianorum Orientalium 427–428. 437–438 = Scriptores Arabici 36–39].

55 Endress, Gerhard. "Yaḥyā Ibn ʿAdī's Critique of Atomism: Three Treatises on the Indivisible Part, Edited with an Introduction and Notes." *Zeitschrift für Geschichte der Arabisch-Islamischen Wissenschaften* 1 (1984), 155–179.

56 [Collection of treatises in:] *An Anthology of Classical Arabic Philosophy: A Facsimile Edition of Manuscript Tehran, Madrasa-yi Marwī 19*. – Ed. by Ahmedreza Rahimirise and Robert Wisnovsky. Tehran, forthcoming. – On the treatises contained in the manuscript cf. Wisnovsky [*47].

2.1.2.3 *Translations of and Commentaries on Greek Works*

61 Aristotle. *Kitāb Sūfisṭīqā = Kitāb Tabkīt al-sūfisṭāʾiyyīn li-Arisṭūṭālīs* [*Sophistical Refutations*, Arab.]. – Ed. by ʿAbd al-Raḥmān Badawī, *Manṭiq Arisṭū*, vol. 3. Cairo, 1952, 737–1014; Kuwait, Beirut, 1980 (2nd ed.), 773–1050. – Ed. by Cyrille Haddad, *Trois versions inédites des Réfutations sophistiques d'Aristote, études et vocabulaire*. – PhD Diss., University of Paris, 1952. – Ed. by Farīd Ǧabr [Ferid Jabre], Ǧirār Ǧihāmī and Rafīq al-ʿAǧam, *al-Naṣṣ al-kāmil li-manṭiq Arisṭū*, vol. 2. Beirut, 1999, 905–1195.

62 *Tafsīr* [*li-l-maqāla al-ūlā min Kitāb Arisṭūṭālīs fī Mā baʿd al-ṭabīʿa wa-hiya al-mawsūma bi-*] *al-Alif al-ṣuġrā*. – Ed. by Muḥammad Miškāt, *Arisṭāṭālīs-i ḥakīm: Naḫustīn maqāla-i Mā baʿd al-ṭabīʿa mawsūm ba-Maqālat al-Alif al-ṣuġrā, tarǧama-i Isḥāq b. Ḥunayn bā Tafsīr-i Yaḥyā Ibn ʿAdī wa tafsīr-i Ibn-i Rušd*. Tehran, 1346 h.š./1967; with Pers. transl. – Ed. by ʿAbd al-Raḥmān Badawī, *Rasāʾil falsafiyya li-l-Kindī wa-l-Fārābi wa-Ibn Bāǧǧa wa-Ibn ʿAdī*. Beirut, 1981 (2nd ed.) [Benghazi 1393/1973], 168–203. – *Tafsīr al-Alif al-ṣuġrā* (ed. S. Ḫalīfāt [*53: 220–262]). – Literal commentary on Arist. *Met.* II.

63 Aristotle. *Physics* [Arab.]. – Ed. by ʿAbd al-Raḥmān Badawī, *Arisṭūṭālīs: al-Ṭabīʿa: tarǧamat Isḥāq b. Ḥunayn, maʿa šurūḥ Ibn al-Samḥ wa-Ibn ʿAdī wa-Mattā b. Yūnus wa-Abī l-Faraǧ Ibn al-Ṭayyib*, 2 vols. Cairo, 1384–1385/1964–1965. – Ed. by Wilhelm Kutsch and Khalil Georr, "Texte arabe du grand commentaire de la Physique d'Aristote, par Abū ʿAlī b. as-Samḥ: 1er livre." [The only one to appear.] *Mélanges de l'Université Saint Joseph* 39 (Beirut 1963): 266–310.

64 *Šarḥ maʿānī maqālat al-Iskandar al-Afrūdīsī fī l-farq bayn al-ǧins wa-l-mādda.* – Ed. by S. Ḫalīfāt [*53: 280–298].

2.1.2.4 *Isagoge and Logic*

71 *Maqāla fī l-Mabāḥiṯ al-ḫamsa ʿan al-ruʾūs al-ṯamāniya.* – Ed. by R. Wisnovsky 2012 [*153], with Engl. transl.

72 *Maqāla fī l-Buḥūṯ al-arbaʿa al-ʿilmiyya ʿan ṣināʿat al-manṭiq wa-hiya Hal hiya wa-Mā hiya wa-Ayy šayʾ hiya wa-Limā hiya = al-Hidāya li-man tāha ilā sabīl al-naǧāt.* – Ed. by Nicholas Rescher and Fadlou Shehadi, "Yaḥyā ibn ʿAdī's Treatise 'On the Four Scientific Questions Regarding the Art of Logic'." *Journal of the History of Ideas* 25 (1964): 572–578. – Repr. in: N. Rescher, *Studies in Arabic Philosophy*. Pittsburgh, 1967, 38–47. – Ed. by Mubahat Türker, "Yaḥyā ibn ʿAdī ve neşredilmemiş bir risalesi." *Ankara Üniversitesi dil ve tarih-coğrafya fakültesi dergisi* 14 (1956): 87–102, suppl. ibid., 16 (1958) 163.

73 *Qawl fīhi Tafsīr ašyāʾ ḏakarahā ʿinda ḏikrihi faḍl ṣināʿat al-manṭiq.* – Ed. by S. Ḫalīfāt [*53: 201–205].

74 *Maqāla fī Tabyīn al-faṣl bayna ṣināʿatay al-manṭiq al-falsafī wa-l-naḥw al-ʿarabī.* – Ed. by Gerhard Endress, in: *Maǧallat tārīḫ al-ʿulūm al-ʿarabiyya (Journal for the History of Arab Science)* 2 (Aleppo 1978): 38–50. – Ed. by S. Ḫalīfāt [*53: 414–424]. – German transl. in Endress 1986 [*81: 272–296].

75 *Mā kataba bihi ilā Abī Ḥātim Aḥmad b. Ǧaʿfar al-Siǧistānī fī l-ḥāǧa ilā maʿrifat māhiyyat al-ǧins wa-l-faṣl wa-l-nawʿ wa-l-ḫāṣṣa wa-l-ʿaraḍ fī maʿrifat al-burhān.* – Ed. by S. Ḫalīfāt [*53: 263–265].

76 *Maqāla fī Tabyīn anna al-šaḫṣ ism muštarak.* – Ed. by S. Ḫalīfāt [*53: 208–211].

77 *Munāqaḍa fī anna l-ǧism ǧawhar wa-ʿaraḍ.* – Ed. by S. Ḫalīfāt [*53: 165–166].

78 *Maqāla fī anna l-ʿAraḍ laysa huwa ǧinsan li-l-tisʿ al-maqūlāt al-ʿaraḍiyya.* – Ed. by S. Ḫalīfāt [*53: 144–147].

79 *Maqāla fī l-ʿAdad wa-l-iḍāfa (Kitāb fī Tabyīn anna li-l-ʿadad wa-l-iḍāfa ḏātayn mawǧūdatayn fī l-aʿdād)*, MS Tehran, Kitābḫāna-i Millī 1382, 382–389.

2.1.2.5 *Physics and Mathematics*

85 *Maqāla fī l-Kull wa-l-aǧzāʾ.* – Ed. by S. Ḫalīfāt [*53: 212–219].

86 *Maqāla fī Tabyīn anna kull muttaṣil innamā yanqasim ilā munqasim wa-ġayr mumkin an yanqasim ilā mā lā yanqasim.* – Ed. by G. Endress 1984 [*162: 164–167]. – Ed. by S. Ḫalīfāt [*53: 141–143].

87 *al-Qawl fī anna kull muttaṣil fa-innahu munqasim ilā ašyāʾ tanqasim dāʾiman bi-ġayr nihāya.* – Ed. by G. Endress 1984 [*162: 167–175]. – Ed. by S. Ḫalīfāt [*53: 275–279].

88 *Qawl fī l-Ǧuzʾ allaḏī lā yataǧazzaʾ.* – Ed. by G. Endress 1984 [*162: 175–179]. – Ed. by S. Ḫalīfāt [*53: 160–164] (under the title *Fī Tazyīf al-qāʾilīna bi-tarkīb al-aǧsām min aǧzāʾ lā tataǧazzaʾ*, see [*89]).

89 *Maqāla fī Tazyīf qawl al-qā'ilīn bi-tarkīb al-aǧsām min aǧzā' lā tataǧazza'*. – Ed. by D. Bennett, R. Wisnovsky 2015 [*170].

90 *Maqāla fī Ṯalāṯat buḥūṯ 'an ġayr al-mutanāhī.* – Ed. by S. Ḫalīfāt [*53: 425–432].

91 *Maqāla fī Ġayr al-mutanāhī.* – Ed. by S. Ḫalīfāt [*53: 135–140].

92 *Ǧawāb 'an faṣl min kitāb Abī l-Ǧayš al-naḥwī fī mā ẓannahu min anna l-'adad ġayr mutanāhin.* – Ed. by S. Ḫalīfāt [*53: 299–302].

93 *Maqāla fī Istiḫrāǧ al-'adad al-muḍmar min ġayr an yus'al al-muḍmir 'an šay'.* – Ed. by S. Ḫalīfāt [*53: 407–413].

94 *Maqāla fī Tafsīr faṣl min al-maqāla al-ṯāmina min al-Samā' al-ṭabī'ī.* – Ed. by Peter Adamson and Robert Wisnovsky, "Yaḥyā Ibn 'Adī on the Location of God." *Oxford Studies in Medieval Philosophy* 1 (2013): 205–28, with Engl. transl. and study.

2.1.2.6 *Metaphysics*

101 *Maqāla fī l-Mawǧūdāt* (= *Maqāla fīmā intaza'ahu min kitāb al-Samā' al-ṭabī'ī wa-ġayrihi li-Arisṭū*). – Ed. by Mubahat Türker, "Yahyâ ibn-i 'Adî'nin varlıklar hakkındaki makalesi." *Ankara Üniversitesi dil ve tarih-coğrafya fakültesi dergisi* 17 (1959): 145–157 (with Turkish transl. 147–151). – Ed. by S. Ḫalīfāt [*53: 266–274].

101a *Maqāla fī l-Buḥūṯ al-'ilmiyya al-arba'a 'an aṣnāf al-wuǧūd al-ṯalāṯa al-ilāhī wa-ṭabī'ī wal-manṭiqī.* – Ed. by R. Wisnovsky, S. Menn 2012 [*196].

102 *Maqāla fī Tabyīn wuǧūd al-umūr al-'āmmiyya wa-l-naḥw allaḏī 'alayhi takūn maḥmūla wa-l-naḥw allaḏī taḫruǧ bihi min an takūna maḥmūla.* – Ed. by S. Ḫalīfāt [*53: 148–159]

103 *Ru'yā [fī ta'rīf al-nafs]*. – Ed. by S. Ḫalīfāt [*53: 206–207].

104 *Maqāla fī l-Tawḥīd.* – Ed. by Samīr Ḫalīl, *Maqāla fī l-Tawḥīd li-l-šayḫ Yaḥyā Ibn 'Adī.* Ǧūniya, Rome, 1980 [al-Turāṯ al-'arabī al-masīḥī, 2]. – Ed. by S. Ḫalīfāt [*53: 375–406].

105 *Maqāla fī Iṯbāt ṭabī'at al-mumkin wa-naqḍ ḥuǧaǧ al-muḫālifīn li-ḏālika wa-l-tanbīh 'alā fasādihā.* – Ed. by Carl Ehrig-Eggert, "Über den Nachweis der Natur des Möglichen, Edition und Einleitung." *Zeitschrift für Geschichte der Arabisch-Islamischen Wissenschaften* 5 (1989): 283–297 (= Arab. text 63–97). – German transl. of this edition by Carl Ehrig-Eggert, *Die Abhandlung über den Nachweis der Natur des Möglichen von Yaḥyā ibn 'Adī (gest. 974 A.D.)*. Frankfurt a.M., 1990. – Ed. by S. Ḫalīfāt [*53: 337–374].

106 *Kitāb Naqd al-ḥuǧaǧ fī nuṣrat qawl al-qā'ilīn bi-anna l-af'āl ḫalq li-llāh wa-ktisāb li-l-'ibād.* – Ed. by S. Ḫalīfāt [*53: 303–313].

2.1.2.7 *Ethics*

111 *Tahḏīb al-aḫlāq.* – Ed. by Samīr Ḫalīl [Qusaym] (Cairo, Beirut 1994). – Ed. by Marie-Thérèse Urvoy, *Traité d'éthique d'Abū Zakariyyā' Yaḥyā ibn 'Adī, introduction,*

texte et traduction. Paris, 1991; with French transl. – Ed. by Sidney H. Griffith, *Yaḥyā ibn ʿAdī, The Reformation of Morals: A Parallel English-Arabic Text, Translated and Introduced*. Provo, 2002; Arab. text following the ed. by Samīr Ḫalīl 1994. – Ed. by Nāǧī al-Takrītī, *Yahyā Ibn ʿAdi: A Critical Edition and Study of His Tahdhib al-Akhlaq*. Beirut, Paris, 1978. – Ed. by ʿAbd al-Raḥmān Badawī, "Maqāla fī l-Aḫlāq li-l-Ḥasan b. al-Hayṯam (?) aw li-Yaḥyā Ibn ʿAdī." In *Dirāsāt wa-nuṣūṣ fī l-falsafa wa-l-ʿulūm ʿind al-ʿArab*. Beirut, 1981, 104–145, Benghazi, 1973 (1st ed.). – Ed. by Ǧād Ḥātim, *Yaḥyā Ibn ʿAdī, Tahḏīb al-aḫlāq, dirāsa wa-naṣṣ*. Beirut, 1985. – For further editions cf. Endress 1977 [*126: 82–84, § 6.1].

112 Traité sur la continence de Yahya ibn ʿAdi. – Ed. by Vincent Mistrih, in: *Studia Orientalia Christiana, Collectanea* 16 (1981): 3–137 (with French transl.).

2.1.2.8 *Philosophical Questions*

121 *Taʿālīq ʿidda fī maʿānin kaṯīra*. – Ed. by S. Ḫalīfāt [*53: 167–200].

122 *al-Aǧwiba ʿan masāʾil Bišr al-Yahūdī*. – Ed. by S. Ḫalīfāt [*53: 314–363].

2.1.2.9 *Christian Theology and Apologetics*

This list only contains the apologetic works against Abū ʿĪsā al-Warrāq and al-Kindī. For further titles see Endress 1977 [*126: 99–123, § 8], Platti 1983 [*128: 54–75].

131 *Tabyīn ġalaṭ Muḥammad b. Hārūn al-maʿrūf bi-Abī ʿĪsā al-Warrāq ʿammā ḏakarahu fī kitābihi fī l-Radd ʿalā l-ṯalāṯ firaq min al-naṣārā*. – Ed. by Emilio Platti, *Abū ʿĪsā al-Warrāq, Yaḥyā ibn ʿAdī, De l'incarnation*. Leuven, 1987 [Corpus Scriptorum Christianorum Orientalium 490 = Scriptores Arabici 46]. – With French transl. by Emilio Platti. Leuven, 1987 [Corpus Scriptorum Christianorum Orientalium 491 = Scriptores Arabici 47].

132 *Tabyīn ġalaṭ Abī Yūsuf Yaʿqūb b. Isḥāq al-Kindī fī maqālatihi fī l-Radd ʿalā l-naṣārā = Un traité de Yaḥyâ ben ʿAdî: Défense du dogme de la Trinité contre les objections d'al-Kindî*. – Ed. by Augustin Périer 1920/21 [*234] (with French transl.). – Revised transl. in Périer 1920 [*232: 118–128]. – Excerpt (restricted to the arguments from al-Kindī, *Risāla fī Iftirāq al-milal fī l-tawḥīd*), ed. by Roshdi Rashed and Jean Jolivet, *Yaʿqūb b. Isḥāq al-Kindī, Œuvres philosophiques et scientifiques*, vol. 2: *Métaphysique et cosmologie*. Leiden, 1998, 122–127 (with French transl.).

2.1.3 Additional Source Texts

141 Proclus. *The Elements of Theology: A Revised Text with Translation and Commentary*. – Ed. by Eric Robertson Dodds. Oxford, 1963 (2nd ed.).

142 Elias. *Eliae in Porphyrii Isagogen et Aristotelis Categorias commentaria*. – Ed. by Adolfus Busse. Berlin, 1900 [Commentaria in Aristotelem Graeca XVIII,1].

2.2 *Life and Influence*

Yaḥyā Ibn ʿAdī, a Jacobite Christian whose full *nasab* was Abū Zakariyyāʾ Yaḥyā b. ʿAdī b. Ḥamīd b. Zakariyyāʾ, was born in 279/893 or 280/894. In a number of manuscripts of his works (e.g. the *Maqāla fī l-Mawǧūdāt* [*101]), all copied in Iran, his descent is traced back to an Iranian ancestor named Buzurǧmihr; the same manuscripts claim that he belonged 'to the sons of Iran, being called Buzurǧmihr b. Abī Manṣūr b. Farrukhānshāh al-Munaǧǧim'. The *nisba* al-Takrītī points to Takrīt in Mesopotamia as his birthplace (Ibn al-ʿIbrī, *Tārīḫ mukhtaṣar al-duwal* [*40: 170,18]); other *nisab* are documented but uncertain (Troupeau 1994 [*105]). He spent most of his life in Baghdad, earning his living as a book dealer and copyist (*warrāq*). He died on 21 Ḏū l-Qaʿda 363/ 13 August 974 (cf. Ibn al-Qifṭī [*38: 363,18–364,2]).

The majority of testimonials name Abū Bishr Mattā b. Yūnus (d. 328/940, cf. § 7.1), the head of the Baghdad logicians, as Yaḥyā's teacher in Aristotelian philosophy. Study with al-Fārābī is not equally well documented; there is no testimony from Ibn ʿAdī himself that would vouch for it. Ẓahīr al-Dīn al-Bayhaqī [*37: 17 Šafīʿ; 31 Kurd ʿAlī] calls Ibn ʿAdī al-Fārābī's 'most outstanding pupil' and ascribes to him otherwise unknown compendia of his works. He writes that he had seen 'some of the rarest books by Abū Naṣr al-Fārābī' in the library of Rayy, 'most of which were copied in his own hand, or in that of his pupil, Yaḥyā Ibn ʿAdī'. Yaḥyā's brother Ibrāhīm Ibn ʿAdī – who is also known as the dedicatee of two of his treatises (Endress 1977 [*126: § 3.33. 7.4]) – is described by al-Bayhaqī as a close intimate of al-Fārābī's who undertook a redaction of the latter's works (*mudawwin taṣānīf Abī Naṣr* [*37: 102 Šafīʿ; 109 Kurd ʿAlī]). According to Ibn Abī Uṣaybiʿa [*39: II 139,19] Ibrāhīm studied with al-Fārābī in Aleppo, and al-Fārābī dictated his full commentary on the *Posterior Analytics* to him.

In keeping with the tradition established by Mattā and his predecessors, Ibn ʿAdī became a prolific writer in the field of the reception and translation (from Syriac) of Aristotelian philosophy and its commentary tradition (mainly Alexander of Aphrodisias, Themistius, and the Alexandrians Olympiodorus and John Philoponus); in particular, he played a leading role in the transmission and dissemination of logical methodology in philosophy and theology.

His contemporaries unanimously regarded Ibn ʿAdī as the head of the Baghdad *falāsifa* (Ibn al-Nadīm [*32: 264,4]; Abū Ḥayyān al-Tawḥīdī [*33: I.37,7]). Al-Masʿūdī claimed he did not know any living authority in philosophy and logic except the Baghdad Christian Abū Zakariyyāʾ Ibn ʿAdī, adding: 'His work, his theory and his system was based on the study of the system (*ṭarīqa*) of Muḥammad b. Zakariyyāʾ al-Rāzī, i.e. the Pythagoreans' theory of First Philosophy' (*Kitāb al-Tanbīh wa-l-išrāf* [*31: 122,10–14]) – an unusual and otherwise unknown appraisal of Ibn ʿAdī's philosophical position (see Urvoy 2008 [*136]). However, Ibn ʿAdī is linked to Abū Bakr al-Rāzī not only by his contempt for *kalām*, the speculative theology of the contemporary Islamic schools, which he shared with the religious critic, but also by the promotion of the philosophical way of life prominent within his ethics.

Ibn ʿAdī's school. Ibn ʿAdī was held in high esteem by his contemporaries as a teacher of logic and Aristotelian philosophy, and as the centre of a circle of Muslim as well as Christian adepts of philosophy, who joined him in defending Aristotle's demonstrative doctrine against the dialectics of the theologians. In smooth prose style Abū Ḥayyān al-Tawḥīdī recorded the discussions of the circle around Ibn ʿAdī and, after him, around Abū Sulaymān al-Siǧistānī (cf. § 5.3). He criticizes Ibn ʿAdī's language and style as a translator and as an author, and claims that he did not have an adequate understanding of metaphysics (*al-ilāhiyyāt*). Nevertheless he praises the spirit and the high standard of his circle (*al-Imtāʿ* [*35: I 37,6–9]).

Among Ibn ʿAdī's personal pupils who continued his teaching tradition the following should be named along with al-Tawḥīdī:

(1) Abū Sulaymān Muḥammad b. Ṭāhir b. Bahrām al-Siǧistānī al-Manṭiqī (d. around 374/985), the Muslim philosopher who succeded Ibn ʿAdī as the leading figure of the Baghdad *falāsifa* (cf. § 5.3.4–6).

(2) Abū ʿAlī ʿĪsā b. Isḥāq Ibn Zurʿa (331–398/942–1008), like Ibn ʿAdī a Jacobite Christian and the pupil closest to him, continued his work both in the field of philosophy and in that of Christian theology (cf. § 7.3).

(3) Abū l-Ḫayr al-Ḥasan b. Suwār b. Bābā b. Bihnām, called Ibn al-Ḫammār (born 331/942, d. after 407/1017), was also a Christian, but in old age converted to Islam; he transmitted the school tradition in logic and philosophical propaedeutics (cf. § 7.4).

(4) Abū ʿAlī Ibn al-Samḥ (d. 418/1027), another Christian philosopher, commented on Aristotelian logic and physics; his bookshop at the Bāb al-Ṭāq served as a meeting point for the circle of Ibn ʿAdī's students (cf. § 7.5).

(5) Abū Isḥāq Ibrāhīm Ibn Bakkūs (Bakkūš?) was a physician at the Baghdad hospital which had been founded by ʿAḍud al-Dawla in 372/982 (al-Bīmāristān al-ʿAḍudī; cf. Ibn Abī Uṣaybiʿa [*39: I 205. 236 and esp. 244]); after Ibn ʿAdī's death he belonged to the circle of his pupil ʿĪsā Ibn Zurʿa (*al-Imtāʿ* [*35: I 38,4]) He translated medical texts as well as works on logic and natural philosophy, for instance Aristotle's *Sophistical Refutations* (a revision of Ibn Nāʿima's version), Aristotle's *On Generation and Corruption*, and Theophrastus' *On Sense Perception* (according to Ibn al-Nadīm [*32: 249. 251. 252. 316 Flügel; 601. 604. 607. 742 Taǧaddud]).

(6) ʿĪsā b. ʿAlī b. ʿĪsā (302/914–915 - 391/1001) was one of the most prominent personalities among Ibn ʿAdī's students. Son to the famous vizier ʿAlī b. ʿĪsā b. al-Ǧarrāḥ (d. 334/946), who was respected for his scholarly interests, he was educated in the conventional subjects of the Arabic-Islamic tradition, to which he seems to have turned his full attention in his later years. In addition, he studied philosophy with Ibn ʿAdī and participated in the discussions of his circle. ʿĪsā b. ʿAlī b. ʿĪsā's refutation of astrology, *Risāla fī Ibṭāl aḥkām al-nuǧūm*, is preserved within *Miftāḥ dār al-saʿāda* by the Ḥanbalite Ibn Qayyim al-Ǧawziyya (Ḫalīfāt 1987 [*255], 1988 [*256]).

(7) Abū Bakr b. al-Ḥasan al-Qūmisī is mentioned several times as one of Yaḥyā Ibn ʿAdī's students (Kraemer 1986 [*130: 59–64]). None of his works are extant, but a short astronomical tract, translated by Ibn ʿAdī from the Syriac, has been transmitted from his autograph; it contains a comparison of cosmic and terrestial dimensions (cf. Endress 1977 [*126: § 1.72]).

(8) The poet Abū l-Ḥasan ʿAlī b. Muḥammad al-Badīhī was one of the participants in Ibn ʿAdī's circle. We know this through Abū Ḥayyān al-Tawḥīdī's *Muqābasāt* (Kraemer 1992 [*129: 136–139), which preserves Ibn ʿAdī's answer to al-Badīhī's question about the meaning of priority (*qabla*) within temporal, causal, and other relations (Abū Ḥayyān al-Tawḥīdī, *Muqābasāt* [*34: § 13, 103–104]), as well as al-Badīhī's rendition of a lecture which he had heard Ibn ʿAdī give in 361/972, and which discussed the conceptual principles of substance and the categories (*Muqābasāt* [*34: § 14, 104–105]).

(9) Abū Bakr al-Ādamī al-ʿAṭṭār is the addressee of several works by Ibn ʿAdī (cf. Endress 1977 [*126: 98]); he seems to be the same Abū Bakr who copied Ibn ʿAdī's autograph of the *Prior Analytics* (*Manṭiq Arisṭū* [*11: 127 n. 3. 129 n. 4. 133 n. 3]).

2.3 *Works*

2.3.1 Translations of and Commentaries on Greek Texts – 2.3.2 Propaedeutics and Logic – 2.3.3 Physics and Mathematics – 2.3.4 Metaphysics – 2.3.5 Ethics – 2.3.6 Collections of Philosophical Questions – 2.3.7 Christian Theology and Apologetics

2.3.1 Translations of and Commentaries on Greek Texts

On Ibn ʿAdī's translations of works by Greek authors, as well as his commentaries and glosses on their texts cf. Endress 1977 [*126: § 1.11–2.41]; on the transmission of

Aristotle's *Organon* in Ibn ʿAdī's textual and doctrinal tradition cf. § 7.3 on his student ʿĪsā Ibn Zurʿa. Preserved are his translation of the *Sophistical Refutations*, his commentary on *Metaphysics* II, and his commentary on *Question* II 28 (*fī l-Farq bayn al-ǧins wa-l-mādda*) by Alexander of Aphrodisias.

Tafsīr al-Alif al-ṣuġrā min kutub Arisṭūṭālīs fī Mā baʿd al-ṭabīʿa
(Commentary on Book II (α) of the Metaphysics by Aristotle)

This is a literal commentary on book II (α), which in the Arabic tradition is the first book of the *Metaphysics*. The lemmata of the text, which are presented in Ḥunayn b. Isḥāq's Arabic translation, are collated by Ibn ʿAdī with a Syriac and another Arabic version (Martini 2003 [*187], Martini 2007 [*192]).

2.3.2 Propaedeutics and Logic

2.3.2.1 *Extant Works*

Maqāla fī l-Mabāḥiṯ [*v.l. al-Buḥūṯ, al-Maṭālib*] *al-ḫamsa ʿan al-ruʾūs al-ṯamāniya*
On the Eight Headings [*of the prolegomena on Aristotle's books*]

Endress [*46: § 3.11]; Wisnovsky [*47: § 3.11]; ed. Wisnovsky 2012 [*153], with transl. and commentary. Five investigations on the eight headings, i.e. the eight headings (κεφάλαια) of the traditional introductions (προλεγόμενα or προτεχνολογούμενα) found in the Alexandrian commentaries on Aristotle's works, explicated in the introductions to Porphyry's *Isagoge*: subject matter (ὁ σκοπός), benefit (ἡ χρῆσις), title of the work (ἡ ἐπιγραφή), authenticity (τὸ γνήσιον), arrangement (ἡ τάξις), division into chapters (ἡ εἰς κεφάλαια διαίρεσις), didactic method (ὁ διδασκαλικὸς τρόπος), and 'the branch of philosophy to which the work belongs' (ἡ ὑπὸ τί μέρος τῆς φιλοσοφίας ἀναφορά). The five investigations discuss the term 'headings' (*ruʾūs*), the eight specific topics, the aim of inquiry, and the reasons for the arrangement and a justification of the number of those headings.

Maqāla fī l-Buḥūṯ al-arbaʿa al-ʿilmiyya ʿan ṣināʿat al-manṭiq wa-hiya Hal hiya wa-Mā hiya wa-Ayy šayʾ hiya wa-Limā hiya = al-Hidāya li-man tāha (v.l. taʾattā) ilā sabīl al-naǧāt
On the Four Scientific Questions of the Art of Logic: 'whether', 'what', 'which', and 'why' = The Right Guidance for Those Who are Going Astray on the Path to Salvation

Endress [*46: § 3.12]. Aristotle's four questions (cf. *An. Post.* II 1, 89b24–25) according to the arrangement of the Alexandrian prolegomena to philosophy.

Maqāla fī Tabyīn faḍl ṣināʿat al-manṭiq bi-waṣf mā yufīduhu ahlahā min al-quwā l-muʿǧiza li-sāʾir al-ṣināʿāt al-kalāmiyya siwāhā [along with appendix:] *Qawl fīhi Tafsīr ašyāʾ ḏakarahā ʿinda ḏikrihi faḍl ṣināʿat al-manṭiq*
Explanation of the Excellence of the Art of Logic, Demonstrating How it Awards its Adepts with Abilities Dumbfounding all other Arts of Disputation; [along with an appendix:] *Commentary on several points which he has dealt with in his discussion of the excellence of the art of logic*

Endress [*46: § 3.14, 3.14.1]. Logic is an instrument serving to defend the truth against equivocation, deception and fallacies. As a highlight of what the art of logic can achieve, the author shows that the statement *al-qāʿid ġayr al-qāʾim*, 'the standing is other than / different from the sitting' admits of 16380 different significations, in view of the equivocal meanings of the sentence and its components. In the concluding section, he exposes four sophismata, further explained in the Appendix, viz. the 'liar paradox' of the Megarian sophists (cf. Arist. *Soph. El.* ch. 25; Prantl 1855 [141: 50 n. 83], and three examples of fallacy of accident.

Maqāla fī Tabyīn al-faṣl bayna ṣināʿatay al-manṭiq al-falsafī wa-l-naḥw al-ʿarabī
Explanation of the Difference between the Art of Philosophical Logic and the Art of Arabic Grammar

Endress [*46: § 3.15]; on the content cf. Endress 1986 [*150]. Both disciplines, grammar as well as logic, are arts (*ṣināʿa* = τέχνη). The specific difference between them consists in their subject matters (*al-mawḍūʿ* – τὸ ὑποκείμενον) and their aims (*al-ġaraḍ* – τὸ τέλος). Subject matter of grammar are the utterances or sounds (*al-alfāẓ* – αἱ φωναί) of the language, while its end is their inflexion 'as the Arabs inflect them' (i.e., in accordance with the conventions of the linguistic community concerned). However, grammar does not have anything to do with meaning (*al-maʿnā* – τὸ [σημαινόμενον] πρᾶγμα) and with symbolic utterances (*al-alfāẓ al-dālla ʿalā l-maʿānī* = φωναὶ σημαντικαί) in so far as they carry meaning.

Symbolic utterances are the subject matter of logic – though only those that denote universals, as they are the only ones that form a constitutive part of logical demonstration (cf. Arist. *An. Post.* I 25, 86a4–8). A valid demonstration requires a combination of utterances (*taʾlīf* [συμπλοκή, cf. Arist. *De int.* 16a12–13]) within one proposition, in agreement with the actual reality that they denote. Hence we differentiate between correct and incorrect propositions: this is the aim of logic. The higher rank of logic is left implicit: subjecting meaningful and meaningless words alike to the formalism of inflection (*iʿrāb*), grammar has at best a merely subordinate share in the attainment of truth.

ʿIddat masāʾil fī maʿānī kitāb Īsāġūǧī
Questions on the Subject Matter of [Porphyry's] Isagoge

Endress [*46: § 3.21]; Wisnovsky [*47: § 3.21]. On the definition of the concepts of genus, species, difference, property and accident, and their logical correlations.

Taʿālīq ʿidda ʿanhu ʿan Abī Bišr Mattā fī umūr ǧarat baynahumā fī l-manṭiq (Aǧwibat šayḫinā Abī Bišr Mattā b. Yūnus al-Qunnāʾī ʿan masāʾil saʾalahu Yaḥyā Ibn ʿAdī b. Ḥumayd b. Zakariyyāʾ ʿanhā fī maʿānī Īsāġūǧī li-Furfūriyūs)
Abū Bišr Mattā's Answers to Yaḥyā Ibn ʿAdī's Questions on Topics of the 'Isagoge'

Endress [*46: § 3.52]; Wisnovsky [*47: § 3.52]. Various notes on problems of logic, partly arising from discussions with Abū Bišr Mattā. Questions on the ontological relationship between the Porphyrian universals, in particular concerning the relation between genus and accident; futhermore, among those addressed to Mattā, questions regarding the syllogism (reduction of various arguments to basic syllogistic figures).

Mā kataba bihi ilā Abī Ḥātim Aḥmad b. Ǧaʿfar al-Siǧistānī fī l-Ḥāǧa ilā maʿrifat māhiyyāt al-ǧins wa-l-faṣl wa-l-nawʿ wa-l-ḫāṣṣa wa-l-ʿaraḍ fī maʿrifat al-burhān
Why Knowledge of Genus, Difference, Species, Property and Accident is Necessary for the Knowledge of Demonstration, written at the request of Abū Ḥātim Aḥmad b. Ǧaʿfar al-Siǧistānī

Endress [*46: § 3.22]). On the *quinque voces*, the subject matter of Porphyry's *Isagoge*, which form the basis of apodeictic knowledge.

Maqāla fī Tabyīn anna l-šaḫṣ ism muštarak
Explanation that 'Indiviual' is a Homonym

Endress [*46: § 3.23]. According to Porphyry's definition, individuals must differ from each other in substance, given that their constitutive properties are different. The individuals do not correspond to the definition of synonyms (as laid down in *Cat.* 1, 1a6); therefore *šaḫṣ* (individual, ἄτομον) must be a homonym (*ism muštarak*).

Maqāla fī anna l-Maqūlāt ʿašr lā aqall wa-lā akṯar
That There are 10 Categories, No More and No Less

Endress [*46: § 3.31]; Wisnovsky [*47 : § 3.31]. A justification of the doctrine that the categories are 10 in number. The same topic is discussed in *Taʿālīq*, no. 25 (ed. Ḫalīfāt [*121: 180–181]): *al-Sabab fī wuǧūd al-maqūlāt ʿašr.*

Maqāla fī Ibānat anna ḥarārat al-nār laysat ǧawharan li-l-nār
Explanation that the Heat of Fire does Not Belong to its Substance

Endress [*46: § 3.32]; Wisnovsky [*47: § 3.32]. This problem was discussed by the Aristotelian commentators in the context of the definition of 'in a substrate' (ἐν ὑποκειμένῳ), *Cat.* 2, 1a24–25: are the essential attributes of a substance (συμπληρωτικὰ τῆς οὐσίας), like the heat of fire, in a substance 'like in a substrate' (ὡς ἐν ὑποκειμένῳ), as inseperable accidents, or rather as part of the substance (ὡς μέρος τῆς οὐσίας)? Ibn ʿAdī held the first view (perhaps connected to his Monophysite interpretation of the Trinity?), whereas his student al-Ḥasan b. Suwār Ibn al-Ḫammār – together with the majority of the Greek commentators – supported the latter (see § 7.4 below on Ibn al-Ḫammār, pp. 488–489, with further references).

Nusḫat mā atā bihi li-Abī Bakr al-Ādamī al-ʿAṭṭār
Notes Addressed to Abū Bakr al-Ādamī al-ʿAṭṭār

Perhaps identical with the work *Risāla katabahā li-Abī Bakr al-Ādamī al-ʿAṭṭār fīmā taḥaqqaqa min iʿtiqād al-ḥukamāʾ baʿd al-naẓar wa-l-taḥqīq*, attested in Ibn al-Qifṭī [*38: 363.16] (Endress [*46: § 7.3]; Wisnovsky [*47: § 7.3 and n. on § 3.32]). Arguments relating to the problem of inherent essential attributes discussed in the previous treatise, brought forward during a disputation with Abū l-Qāsim ʿĪsā b. ʿAlī b. ʿĪsā.

Maqāla fī l-Ḥukūma bayna Ibrāhīm Ibn ʿAdī al-Kātib wa-munāqaḍihi fīmā ḫtalafā fīhi min anna l-ǧism ǧawhar wa-ʿaraḍ
Verdict in the Controversy between [his brother] Ibrāhīm Ibn ʿAdī al-Kātib and his Opponent, on whether the genus is substance or accident

Endress [*46: § 3.33]; Wisnovsky [*47: § 3.33]. The body as such is substance, but *qua* quantity (spacial extension) it is an accident. The question was originally posed by the Ḥamdānid emir Sayf al-Dawla, to whom the answer was presented by Ibn ʿAdī.

Maqāla fī anna l-ʿaraḍ laysa huwa ǧinsan li-l-tisʿ al-maqūlāt al-ʿaraḍiyya
Treatise on That Accident is Not a Genus of the Nine Accidental Categories

Endress [*46: § 3.34]. Even though the nine accidental categories all denominate accidents, the concept 'accident' is not their genus in the sense of a definition ('a genus is what is predicated, in answer to "What is it?", of several items which differ in species': Porphyry, *Isag.* 2, 15–16 Busse: τὸ κατὰ πλειόνων καὶ διαφερόντων τῷ εἴδει ἐν τῷ τί ἐστι κατηγορούμενον, transl. Barnes). Every substance to which one of the nine categories applies will receive the attribute of an accident (in the linguistic form of a derivation from the concept of the accident concerned: spatial, temporal, etc.). This attribute is in the substance in so far as the substance is its substrate, but without constituting a part of it (*Cat.* 2, 1a24–25). Thus, even though the substance participates in all categorical genera of accidents that apply to it, it does not participate in the (concept of) accident as such (it is not possible to say: 'the substance is accident'). Hence none of the genera of accidents that apply to a substance are 'accident'. And *vice versa*, the accident is none of the genera of accidents applying to a substance.

Maqāla fī Qismat al-sitt al-maqūlāt (v.l.: al-aǧnās al-sitta) allatī lam yaqsimhā Arisṭūṭālīs ilā l-aǧnās wa-l-anwāʿ allatī taḥtahā (v.l.: ilā aǧnāsihā al-mutawassiṭa wa-anwāʿihā wa-ašḫāṣihā)
Division of the Six Categories which Aristotle did not Divide into Intermediary Genera, Species, and Individuals

Endress [*46: § 3.35]; Wisnovsky [*47: § 3.35]. At issue are the categories acting, being acted upon, being in a position, sometime, somewhere, and having (*Cat.* 9, 11b1–16) as opposed to substance, quantity, relation, and quality (cf. Simpl. *In Cat.* 298,27).

Maqāla fī anna l-kam laysa fīhi taḍādd
That There is No Contrary in Quantity

Endress [*46: § 3.36]; Wisnovsky [*47: § 3.36]. On Arist. *Cat.* 6, 5b11: 'quantity does not have a contrary'.

Kitāb fī Tabyīn anna li-l-ʿadad wa-l-iḍāfa ḏātayn mawǧūdatayn fī l-aʿdād
Explication that Both Number and Relation are Essentially Present in the Numbers

Endress [*46: § 3.37]. Number falls under the category of quantity, here: number (discrete quantity, *Cat.* 6), as well as under that of relation (*Cat.* 7).

Maqāla fī Nahǧ al-sabīl ilā taḥlīl al-qiyāsāt
The Open Path to the Solution of Syllogisms

Endress [*46: § 3.41]; Wisnovsky [*47: § 3.41]. The topic of the text is the reduction of second- and third-figure syllogisms to first-figure syllogisms.

2.3.2.2 *Lost but Attested Writings*

Maqāla fī l-Muḥrisāt al-mubṭila li-Kitāb al-Qiyās
On the Stunning Arguments Refuting the Prior Analytics

This lost work is attested in Ibn ʿAdī's school, for instance in Ibn Buṭlān (d. 458/1066) and his opponent Ibn Riḍwān (d. 460/1068); Endress [*46: § 3.42].

2.3.3 Physics and Mathematics

2.3.3.1 *Extant Works*

Maqāla fī Tafsīr faṣl min al-maqāla al-ṯāmina min al-Samāʿ al-ṭabīʿī
Interpretation of a Section of Aristotle's Physics VIII

Endress [*46: § 2.21]; Wisnovsky [*47: § 2.21]. – Ed. by Adamson and Wisnovsky [*94: 225–226]. *On Phys.* VIII 10, 267b6–9, about the question whether the First Mover is active in the centre or at the periphery of the universe; according to Ibn ʿAdī, the Mover is active at the periphery. See also Endress 2015 [*137: 236–7].

Maqāla fī l-Kull wa-l-ağzāʾ
On the Whole and the Parts

Endress [*46: § 4.1.1]. Definition of the various classes of whole and part, like substance (consisting of matter and form), essential definition or defined essence (consisting of genus and specific difference), quantity (consisting of its discrete or continuous parts). This is followed by a diaeresis of essential and accidential qualities (*lawāḥiq*, concomitants) of the respective 'wholes made up of parts'. The author regards wholeness as form, characterized by the divisibility of the continuous whole.

Maqāla fī Tabyīn anna kull muttaṣil innamā yanqasim ilā munqasim wa-ġayr mumkin an yanqasim ilā mā lā yanqasim
Explication that Every Continuum can be Divided into Divisible Parts, whereas it is Impossible to Divide it into Indivisible Parts

Endress [*46: § 4.2.1]. A rejection of atomism following Aristotle, e.g. *Phys.* VI 1, 231b16.

al-Qawl fī anna kull muttaṣil fa-innahu munqasim ilā ašyāʾ tanqasim dāʾiman bi-ġayr nihāya
Every Continuum can be Divided into Divisible Things ad infinitum

Endress [*46: § 4.22]. A supplement to the previous treatise.

Qawl fī l-Ğuzʾ allaḏī lā yatağazzaʾ
On the Indivisible Part

Endress [*46: § 4.23]. The adherents of atomism argued in the following way: if it were possible to divide continuous bodies infinitely, then even the smallest particle, like the proverbial mustard seed (*ḫardala*), could be divided into so many parts they would cover the entire celestial sphere; which is absurd.

Ibn ʿAdī counters that division can be understood in more than one way. Infinite division exists potentially in the imagination, inasmuch as a spatial magnitude may be infinitely divided according to a constant ratio (cf. Arist. *Phys.* III 6, 206a17); but there is no infinite division in actuality. On the contrary, for every species there is a smallest part demarcating the limit below which no part of the species may ever fall (cf. *Phys.* I 4, 187b22–188a2); therefore the mustard seed cannot actually be divided into infinitely many parts 'which would cover the entire celestial sphere'.

Maqāla fī Tazyīf qawl al-qāʾilīn bi-tarkīb al-aǧsām min aǧzāʾ lā tataǧazzaʾ
Proof that Those Who Claim that Bodies are Constituted from Indivisible Parts (atoms) *Fall into Absurdity*

Among other things, the text discusses the argument that refers to the fact that a sphere touches an even surface in a single point in each instance, even while it moves across it (*bi-ḥtiǧāǧihim bi-mulāqāt al-kura al-basīṭa al-musaṭṭaḥa ʿalā nuqṭatihi wa-ḥarakatihā ʿalayhi*) (Endress [*46: § 4.24]; Wisnovsky [*47: § 4.24]; Endress 2015 [*137: 245]). The movement of the sphere's periphery across an even surface in discrete, atomic points implies the 'leap' (*ṭafra*) from point to point; a continuous movement would therefore be impossible. This argument for a refutation of atomism stems from the theologian al-Naẓẓām.

Maqāla fī Ṯalāṯat buḥūṯ ʿan ġayr al-mutanāhī
Three Studies on the Infinite

Endress [*46: § 4.31]. In the introduction, the infinite is defined as a quantity 'which is such that after each part which has been taken away from it, there is another part that can be taken away' (cf. Arist. *Phys.* III 6, 207a7).

1) The existence of a subsequent infinity is concomitant and coexclusive with the existence of a preceding infinity: if there is an infinite essence, both a preceding and a subsequent infinity can exist. If there is no such essence, neither of the two is possible.
2) Everything that is infinite *a parte ante* must be infinite *a parte post*, and *vice versa*.
3) For any given species of individuals that fall under generation and corruption, each individual of the species can be preceded and succeeded by another one.

Maqāla fī anna l-ʿadad laysa huwa ḏā nihāya min tilqāʾ awwalihi wa-ġayr mutanāhī min tilqāʾ āḫirihi
Refutation of the View that Number is Infinite a parte post, but Finite a parte ante

Endress [*46: § 4.32]. Ibn ʿAdī refers to his *Ṯalāṯat buḥūṯ ʿan ġayr al-mutanāhī* (cf. the previous entry), where he has demonstrated that every infinity must be infinite in both directions. Since there is no actually infinite number, infinity does not exist within the universal species of number (cf. Arist. *Cat.* 2a35–2b6).

Ǧawāb ʿan faṣl min kitāb Abī l-Ǧayš [?] al-Naḥwī fī-mā ẓannahu [fī] anna l-ʿadad ġayr mutanāhī
Reply to a Letter from Abū l-Ǧayš [?] al-Naḥwī, Regarding his View that Number is Infinite

Endress [*46: § 4.33]. The claim that 'absolute' number is infinite is refuted, among other points, with the argument that there is no actually infinite number.

Maqāla fī annahu laysa šayʾ mawǧūd ġayr mutanāhī lā ʿadadan wa-lā ʿiẓaman
That there is Nothing Infinite, neither in Number nor in Magnitude

Endress [*46: § 4.34]; Wisnovsky [*47: § 4.34]. There is no actually infinite magnitude, cf. Arist. *Phys.* III 5, 204b5–8; cf. further Ibn ʿAdī's *Maqāla fī anna l-ʿadad laysa huwa ḏā nihāya* (Endress [*46: § 4.32]).

Maqāla fī l-Radd ʿalā man qāla bi-anna l-aǧsām muḥdaṯa ʿalā ṭarīq al-ǧadal
Refutation of Those that Claim that Bodies Came into Being [in Time], Dialectically Argued

Endress [*46: § 4.41]; Wisnovsky [*47: § 4.41]. Ed. and transl. in P. Adamson and R. Wisnovsky, "Yaḥyā Ibn ʿAdī on a *Kalām* Argument for Creation," forthcoming in Oxford Studies in Medieval Philosophy. A refutation of the classic *kalām* argument, apparently first put forward by Abū l-Huḏayl (see J. van Ess, *Theologie und Gesellschaft im 2. und 3. Jahrhundert Hidschra: eine Geschichte des religiösen Denkens im frühen Islam.* Berlin, 1991–5, vol. 5, § XXI.42): since bodies cannot exist without accidents, and accidents are created, bodies too must be created rather than eternal. Applying this to the case of the body of the universe, the *kalām* argument infers that the universe has a Creator. Ibn ʿAdī finds the argument unconvincing, in part because body is indeed "prior" to its accidents in the sense that their existence requires the existence of the bodies to which they belong. The polemic against the *kalām* argument was continued by Ibn ʿAdī's student Ibn al-Ḫammār: see pp. 485–486 below on his treatise comparing Philoponus' proof against the eternity of the world to that of the *mutakallimūn*.

Maqāla fī anna l-Quṭr ġayr mušārik li-l-ḍilaʿ
That the Diagonal [of a square or a cube] is Incommensurable with its Sides

Endress [*46: § 4.51]); Wisnovsky [*47: § 4.51]. A geometrical theorem which is used by Aristotle as well, cf. *An. Pr.* I 23, 41a26; *De caelo* I 12, 281a7, etc., see Th. L. Heath:

Mathematics in Aristotle (Oxford 1949) 169. Ibn ʿAdī's interest in the matter has to be seen in context with his refutation of atomism, cf. Endress [*46: § 4.22].

2.3.3.2 *Lost but Attested Work*

Ǧawāb ʿan masāʾil li-Abī ʿAlī ʿĪsā Ibn Zurʿa
Reply to Questions from Abū ʿAlī ʿĪsā Ibn Zurʿa

An excerpt from the lost treatise on a question concerning Arist. *De cael.* III 8, 306b3–8 (which regular polyhedra can fill space with no gaps?) is quoted by the mathematician Ibn al-Ṣalāḥ (d. 548/1153); Endress [*46: § 4.52].

2.3.4 Metaphysics

2.3.4.1 *Extant Works*

Maqāla fī l-Mawǧūdāt (= *Maqāla fīmā intazaʿahu min kitāb al-Samāʿ al-ṭabīʿī wa-ġayrihi li-Arisṭū*)
Treatise on the [classes of] Beings

The alternative title is only preserved in MS Damascus, Ẓāhiriyya 4871 ʿāmm (Türker 1959 [*176]; cf. Endress [*46: § 5.11]). Compendium on a number of basic concepts of metaphysics and physics: 1. the Creator (*al-bāriʾ*), 2. intellect (*al-ʿaql*), 3. soul (*al-nafs*), 4. nature (*al-ṭabīʿa*), 5. matter (*al-hayūlā*), 6. form (*al-ṣūra*), 7. eternity (*al-dahr*), 8. motion (*al-ḥaraka*), 9. time (*al-zamān*), 10. space (*al-makān*), 11. void (*al-ḫalāʾ*).

Maqāla fī l-Buḥūṯ al-ʿilmiyya al-arbaʿa ʿan aṣnāf al-mawǧūd al-ṯalāṯa al-ilāhī wa-l-ṭabīʿī wa-l-manṭiqī
The Four Scientific Investigations Concerning the Three Classes of Beings: Divine, Natural, and Logical Being

Endress [*46: 5.12]; Wisnovsky [*47: § 5.12]; Wisnovsky and Menn 2012 [*196]. The four scientific investigations are 'whether', 'what', 'how', and 'why' (εἰ ἔστι, τί ἐστιν, ὁποῖον τί ἐστι, διὰ τί ἐστι, cf. *An.Post.* II.1). The three classes of being are also discussed in the treatise *Fī Tabyīn wuǧūd al-umūr al-ʿāmmiyya* (cf. the next entry): the natural existence of material substances; the logical existence of the universals as conceptions in the mind; and the essential (*al-wuǧūd al-ḏātī*) or divine existence, i.e. the existence of the absolute essence according to its definition (that is, God's existence is necessary on account of His own essence). A large section of the treatise is reproduced in Ibn ʿAdī's christological treatise *On the Necessity of the Incarnation* (*Maqāla fī Wuǧūb* [*v.l. wuǧūd* 'existence'] *al-taʾannus*, Endress [*46: 8.21]), explaining that the union in Christ between the human knower and the form of God is complete (Wisnovsky and Menn 2012 [*197: 75–76]).

Maqāla fī Tabyīn wuǧūd al-umūr al-ʿāmmiyya wa-l-naḥw allaḏī ʿalayhi takūn maḥmūla wa-l-naḥw allaḏī taḫruǧ bihi min an takūn maḥmūla
Explication of the Existence of the Common Things, in Which Way they Can be Used as Predicates, and in Which Way they Cannot be Predicates

Endress [*46: § 5.13]. Ibn ʿAdī refutes the opinion of those Peripatetics who claim that universals (*al-kulliyyāt*) or common things (*al-ašyāʾ al-ʿāmmiyya*), when separated from matter and accidents, only exist as forms imagined in the soul (*ṣūra mutaṣawwara fī l-nafs*).

There are three kinds of existence which apply to universals: natural (*ṭabīʿī*) existence in material substances; logical (*manṭiqī*) existence, as conceived in the mind; and essential (*ḏātī*) or divine (*ilāhī*) existence, i.e. the existence of the species in its mere essence as denoted by its definition. The absolute essences exist without inhering in an individual substrate (referring to Arist. *Phys.* I 2, 185b32; I 8, 191b19–23); on Ibn ʿAdī's position with regard to Aristotle and Alexander of Aphrodisias' commentary cf. Rashed 2004 [*190], Adamson 2007 [*191].

Ǧawāb masʾala waradat min al-Rayy fī Ḏī l-Qaʿda min sanat iḥdā wa-ṯalāṯimiʾa
Reply to a Question from Rayy in Ḏū l-Qaʿda, 301 H. [= *May-June 914 AD*]

Endress [*46: § 5.21]. The text discusses the question whether an individual, Zayd, who is made up of a sum of properties and accidents which are not found in any other individual, could ever have a second existence, or whether he only exists at the present point in time. Ibn ʿAdī refers to the idea of resurrection as it is taught by the religions, and cites Aristotle's assertion that unrealized potentialities do not exist (*De cael.* I 12, 283a24–9). Despite being perishable, the individual remains possible and will be realized again; next time, however, in perpetuity.

Ruʾyā
Dream [*on the Nature of the Soul*]

Endress [*46: § 5.22]. Ibn ʿAdī heard the following words in a dream, spoken in Syriac: 'The soul is a dispersion of the rational soul'. He names ten reasons why it is a 'dispersion' (*niṯāra*) rather than an 'impression' (*ḫitāma*) of the rational soul.

Maqāla fī l-Tawḥīd
On God's Unity, dictated in the month of Rağab, 328 H. [= *April-May 940 AD*]

Endress [*46: § 5.31]. After a detailed set of distinctions concerning the concept 'One' (following Arist. *Met.* I 6) Ibn ʿAdī explains that the One, the First Cause, is one neither as a genus, nor as a species, nor with reference to a relation, nor as a continuous (*muttaṣil* – συνεχές) or indivisible (*ġayr munqasim* – ἀδιαίρετον) being, but by being one by definition (*wāḥid al-ḥadd*): He is one as the word (λόγος, *qawl*) which defines its own existence.

Subsequently, Ibn ʿAdī shows that the First Cause possesses plurality only by virtue of the constitutive parts of His definition, namely by virtue of the attributes that can be predicated of the divine essence. These three attributes may be deduced from His creation; even though His substance is hidden, His essence is evident from His activity: goodness (*ǧūd* – ἀγαθότης), power (*qudra* – δύναμις), and wisdom (*ḥikma* – γνῶσις). Everything that is created, individuals as well as universals, are brought into being from non-being; this happens through the power of the Creator. Since He existed before they were transformed into being, this spontaneous and voluntary act of creation reveals His goodness. Lastly, His wisdom manifests itself in the order and perfection of His creation. See Lizzini 2009 [*195], Lizzini 2016 [*198].

Mā kataba bihi ilā Abī Bakr Aḥmad b. Muḥammad b. ʿAbd al-Raḥmān b. al-Ḥasan b. Qurayš fī Iṯbāt ṭabīʿat al-mumkin wa-naqḍ ḥuǧaǧ al-muḫālifīn li-ḏālika wa-l-tanbīh ʿalā fasādihā
What He Wrote to Abū Bakr Aḥmad b. Muḥammad b. ʿAbd al-Raḥmān b. al-Ḥasan b. Qurayš, Endorsing the Existence of what is Potential in the Nature of Things, and Refuting the Arguments of Those Who Deny this, and Exposing their Untenability

Endress [*46: § 5.32]. While there is unanimous agreement concerning the necessity of past and present existents, there is controversy about future contingents. The two main arguments of those who deny future contingents rely on God's foreknowledge on the one hand, and on the universal validity of the law of non-contradiction on the other. Ibn ʿAdī rebuts the assumption that the existence (or non-existence) of things follows necessarily from divine foreknowledge; for the refutation of the second argument he invokes Aristotle's discussion of future contingents in *De int.* 9, 18a28–19b4. This is followed by a detailed commentary on that chapter (cf. edition, translation and commentary by C. Ehrig-Eggert [**105*]).

Ǧawāb Abī ʿAbd Allāh al-Dārimī wa-Abī l-Ḥasan ʿAlī b. ʿĪsā al-Mutakallim ʿan al-masʾala fī Ibṭāl al-mumkin
Reply to Abū ʿAbd Allāh al-Dārimī and Abū l-Ḥasan ʿAlī b. ʿĪsā Concerning the Question of Denying the Possible

Endress [*46: § 5.33]; Wisnovsky [*47: 5.33]. *Question* concerning Ibn ʿAdī's criticism of the position of Muslim theologians (*mutakallimūn*) who deny potentiality as being incompatible with God's omnipotence and omniscience. The eponymous ʿAlī b. ʿĪsā is better known as a grammarian, under the name of ʿAlī b. ʿĪsā al-Rummānī (d. 384/994). On this topic, see the treatise *Fī Iṯbāt ṭabīʿat al-mumkin* above.

al-Šubha fī ibṭāl al-mumkin [*along with*] *Ǧawāb Abī Bakr al-Daqqāq ʿan al-šubha fī ibṭāl al-mumkin*
On a Sophism [*šubha, 'specious argument', ἀπάτη, sc. of the theologians*] *concerning the Possible, along with a Reply to Abū Bakr al-Daqqāq* (= Abū Bakr al-Ādamī, see p. 442 above)

Endress [*46: § 5.34], Wisnovsky 2012 [*47: § 5.34]. On this topic, cf. the two treatises listed previously.

Maqāla fī Tabyīn ḍalālat man yaʿtaqid anna ʿilm al-Bārīʾ bi-l-umūr al-mumkina qabla wuǧūdihā mumtaniʿ
Explication of the Error of Those Who Believe that it is Impossible for the Creator to have Foreknowledge of Possible Events Before they Come into Existence

Endress [*46: § 5.35], Wisnovsky [*47: § 5.35]. On this topic, cf. the previously listed treatises; cf. also Endress [*46: 77–78]).

Maqāla fī Tabyīn ḍalālat man yaẓunnu anna l-ašḫāṣ al-kāʾina al-fāsida laysa min šaʾnihā an yuʿlama l-battata
Explication of the Error of Those Who Believe that the Particulars Falling under Generation and Corruption cannot at all be Known [*in advance*] by *their Creator*

According to Ibn al-Qifṭī's testimony [*38: 362]: *Taʿlīq āḫar fī hāḏā l-maʿnā*, 'further remarks on this issue', sc. on the previous treatise (Endress [*46: § 5.35]; Wisnovsky [*47: supplement to § 5.35]). Another refutation of those who deny God's foreknowledge, especially concerning particulars.

Mā kataba ilā Abī ʿAmr Saʿd b. al-Zaynabī [?] b. Saʿīd fī Naqḍ al-ḥuǧaǧ allatī anfaḏahā ilayhi fī nuṣrat qawl al-qāʾilīn anna l-afʿāl ḫalq Allāh wa-ktisāb li-l-ʿibād
What He Wrote to Abū ʿAmr Saʿd b. al-Zaynabī [?] b. Saʿīd: a Critique of the Arguments the Latter put before him in Support of Those Who Claim that Actions are Created by God and Acquired by Man

Endress [*46: § 5.36]. At the outset, the otherwise unknown addressee of the letter presents to Ibn ʿAdī the arguments of an unnamed supporter of the doctrine of Islamic *kalām* which claims that man acquires his deeds (*iktisāb*) but is not able to create them, given that he cannot 'recreate' them. God alone is able to effect initial creation (*ibtidāʾ*) as well as recreation (*iʿāda*); in respect of creation there furthermore is no difference to be made between substance (*ǧawhar*) and act (*fiʿl*). The possible objection that God cannot create evil is rebutted by referring to the existence of Iblīs, the hellfire, and harmful creatures like snakes and predatory animals.

Ibn ʿAdī criticizes the lack of any differentiation between substance and act within the doctrine of *iktisāb*; the term 'act' can really only be applied to accidents which are brought into being in an already existing substance. Thus, while God may have created Iblīs and the harmful creatures in their essence, he did not create their evil acts; while he may have created hellfire, he did not create the sinful acts of those who will be punished in it. Even though man cannot 'recreate' his acts, he does create them; and again, although God is able to recreate, He will not reproduce every single substance He has ever brought into being. For the position of this treatise within the discussion between *falsafa* and *kalām* cf. Pines 1973 [*178: 119–122]; Pines, Schwarz 1979 [*179], Platti 2004 [*189].

2.3.4.2 *Lost but Attested Work*

Maqāla fī Māhiyyat al-ʿilm
On the Quiddity of Knowledge

Endress [*46: § 5.23].

2.3.5 Ethics

Tahḏīb al-aḫlāq
The Refinement of Character

This compendium of philosophical ethics is attributed to Ibn ʿAdī by most manuscripts, but is not mentioned by the bibliographers under this title; it is, however, possible that the title *Maqāla fī Siyāsat al-nafs*, which Ibn Abī Uṣaybiʿa [*39: I 235,25] lists among Ibn ʿAdī's works, in fact refers to this treatise. Other manuscripts name various Arabic-Islamic writers as its author: al-Ǧāḥiẓ (d. 255/868–869), Muḥyī l-Dīn Ibn al-ʿArabī (d. 638/1240), Abū ʿAlī al-Ḥasan Ibn al-Hayṯam (d. 430/1039) (Endress [*46: § 6.1]; on the transmission see Samir 1974 [*207]). There are notably close parallels in the ethical chapter of the scientific encyclopedia *Ǧawāmiʿ al-ʿulūm* by Abū Zayd al-Balḫī's pupil Ibn Farīġūn (written before 344/955, cf. § 5.1.3), which deserve a detailed investigation.

(1) Definition of ἦθος (*ḫuluq*). Deficiencies of man's inborn character and the necessity of moral education aiming at the perfection of the soul.

(2) Tripartition of the soul (*al-nafs al-šahwāniyya, al-ġaḍabiyya, al-nāṭiqa*) [the Platonic partition into appetitive (ἐπιθυμητικόν), spirited (θυμοειδές), rational (λογιστικόν)] as the basis of ethics; virtues and deficiencies of each part.

(3) Catalogue of virtues and vices (and some ambivalent characteristics).

(4) The path to perfection of character: how the appetitive and spirited parts of the soul can be subjected to the rule of reason.

(5) The character of the perfect human being, who is an example for those who strive towards cleansing their souls.

Cf. bibliographical references in Endress [*46: 85], Takrītī 1978 [*208], Griffith 2002 [*218: xxviii–xlvi].

Iǧābat ṣadīqinā ʿammā staftaynāhu fīhi min al-masāʾil al-ṯalāṯ al-wārida fī Muḥarram sanat 353.
Three questions on abstinence, procreation, and the upbringing of children

Dated 10 Muḥarram 353 [= 28 January 964]; cf. Endress [*46: § 6.3, 8.65.1]; Mistrih [*112].

2.3.6 Collections of Philosophical Questions

Taʿālīq [*Taʿālīq ʿidda fī maʿānī kaṯīra*]
Comments [*on various questions*]

Endress [*46: § 7.1]. Most of the 60 *Questions* refer to Arist. *Cat.* and *De int.*

[*Aǧwiba ʿan masāʾil Ibn Abī Saʿīd b. ʿUṯmān b. Saʿīd al-Yahūdī*]
[*Replies to Questions Posed by Ibn Abī Saʿīd*]

Endress [*46: § 7.2]. Fourteen questions on Aristotelian physics, on the doctrine of the categories, and on metaphysics (no. 12 on providence).

2.3.7 Christian Theology and Apologetics

Only the two apologetical treatises addressed against Abū ʿĪsā al-Warrāq and al-Kindī are listed here; for further works on Christian theology by Ibn ʿAdī cf. GCAL [*102: 239–249], Endress [*46: § 8, 99–120], Platti 1983 [*240: 54–75].

Tabyīn ġalaṭ Muḥammad b. Hārūn al-maʿrūf bi-Abī ʿĪsā al-Warrāq ʿammā ḏakarahu fī kitābihi fī l-Radd ʿalā l-ṯalāṯ firaq min al-naṣārā
Explication of the Error of Muḥammad b. Hārūn, also known as Abū ʿĪsā al-Warrāq, based on what he said in his book on the refutation of the three sects of Christianity

The work is in two parts: 1. on Trinity (*al-taṯlīṯ*); 2. on union and incarnation (*al-ittiḥād wa-l-wilād*); Endress [*46: § 8.11]; on Abū ʿĪsā al-Warrāq cf. GAL [*1: S I 341–342], Stern 1955 [*123]. Cf. further Abel 1961 [*236: 75–80]; ed. Platti [*131], Introduction.

The first part of Ibn ʿAdī's reply defends the Christian doctrine of God's unicity and trinity: God is a single substance, but with regard to His essence as a substantial intellect that knows itself He is manifest in three aspects or hypostases (*aqānīm*): *ʿaql* (intellect) 'Father', *ʿāqil* (intellecting) 'Son' and *maʿqūl* (intelligible) 'Spirit', to which we refer with the three attributes goodness, wisdom, and power. In the second part Ibn ʿAdī discusses the dogma of incarnation with reference to the specific doctrines of the three confessions (Jacobites, Nestorians, and Melkites); he explains the incarnation in terms of the Monophysite doctrine as substantial union of the eternal, divine nature with the temporal, human nature.

Tabyīn ġalaṭ Abī Yūsuf Yaʿqūb b. Isḥāq al-Kindī fī maqālatihi fī l-Radd ʿalā l-naṣārā
Explication of the Error of Abū Yūsuf Yaʿqūb b. Isḥāq al-Kindī in his Refutation of the Christians

Written in Ramaḍān 350/October-November 961; GCAL [*102: II 243 no. 13], Endress [*46: § 8.12].

Against the Christian doctrine that God consists in three 'persons' (hypostases, *aqānīm*), i.e. individuals (*ašḫāṣ*), and in a single substance, al-Kindī had objected that each of these 'persons' must necessarily be composed of the common substance and the respective hypostasis as its determination. But every composite requires a cause for its composition; hence the 'persons' of the Trinity cannot be eternal.

Against this, Ibn ʿAdī argues as follows: the divine substance is a single substance, whereas the hypostases are properties (*ḫawāṣṣ*). The hypostases are not individuals of congeneric substance, which result from the composition of this substance with three specific differences. Instead, the names of the hypostases describe the divine being by virtue of being its essential attributes (*ṣifāt*) (*Tabyīn ġalaṭ al-Kindī* [*132: 4–5]; see Escobar, González 2006 [*243], Schöck 2012 [*244]).

2.4 *Doctrine*

2.4.1 Logic and Theory of Science – 2.4.2 Ontology – 2.4.3 Metaphysics and Theology – 2.4.4 Creation, Causality, and Determination – 2.4.5 Ethics

Ibn ʿAdī was a teacher of Aristotelian logic, but also of the philosophical way of life, and of the philosophical cognition of the truth and of God. This knowledge should guide man, by virtue of his reason, along the universally valid path to perfection, no matter which religious or linguistic community he belongs to. For his methodology and his doctrine of first principles he drew on the Greek philosophers, whose works he translated and commented on. Thus he continued the tradition of the – mostly Nestorian and Jacobite – Christians of the 3rd/9th and the 4th/10th centuries, and in particular followed in the steps of his teacher Abū Bišr Mattā. Neither 'pagan', nor Christian, nor Islamic, this tradition took the Aristotelian doctrine of demonstration of the *Posterior Analytics*, and the Aristotelian critique of rhetorical, dialectical, and eristic methods (*Rhetoric*, *Topics*, *Sophistical Refutations*) as the standard for rational discourse. His logical analysis of ontological, theological, and ethical doctrines claims universal validity, and is addressed to the Christian factions to which he is justifying his Monophysite creed, as well as to the Muslim polemics against which he is defending the Trinitarian doctrine of Christian theology. Many of his writings are dedicated to the interpretation of Aristotelian philosophy in the tradition of the Peripatetic, and especially the Alexandrian, commentaries, without touching on any polemical or apologetical topics; but even there Ibn ʿAdī cannot hide the fact that he is preparing weapons for the defense of his convictions. The system of apodeictic science had been absorbed and developed by mathematicians and scientists along with Aristotelian philosophy. In discussions conducted by Ibn ʿAdī and his peers, and also by those among his predecessors, contemporaries, and students who were of Islamic persuasion, it was now taken up as a tool and an emblem of universal authority, and was developed into a universalistic interpretation of the religious view of the world and its divine First Cause.

2.4.1 Logic and Theory of Science

Logical analysis, the reduction of traditional and contemporary topics to syllogistical figures, and the adroit use of the *reductio ad absurdum* as a tool in discussion are characteristic features of Ibn ʿAdī's entire work. Just like his teacher Abū Bišr Mattā, Ibn ʿAdī confronts the argumentative forms of Islamic law and hermeneutics and clothes his criticism of *kalām*, the conceptualization and disputation technique of Islamic dogmatics, with the sober (if at times insipid) technique of syllogistic. Fierce attacks against the theologians' (*aṣḥāb al-kalām*) attempt to claim for themselves the proper use of 'rational discourse (*kalām*)', are not expressed in his works, although they are manifest in the reports about his disputation circle by Abū Ḥayyān al-Tawḥīdī (*al-Muqābasāt* [**34*: 204,9–205,4]).

In his treatise *On the Difference between Philosophical Logic and Arabic Grammar* [**74*] Ibn ʿAdī deals with the grammatical sciences as they were systematized and taught by Arabic philologists, who modelled their hermeneutical method on jurisprudence. He identifies the subject matter of grammar as the phonemes of the Arabic language (and no other language). The subject matter of logic, according to his definition, is by contrast the meanings and their universal categories and relations, as they can be expressed in any language. In its basic features, this definition was to be found already in the Alexandrian *prolegomena* to logic, but in the context of the contemporary discussion it acquired further significance. Ibn ʿAdī contrasts *ʿilm*, science as defined by Islamic theology, with his own *ʿilm*, which is defined as Aristotelian demonstrative science. It is the method found in Aristotle's *Analytics*, the method of determining an essence by definition, by a deduction from major premise, minor premise, and middle term – a method which confers the absolute and universal authority of rational science on the theology of both Christians and Muslims. On the one hand Ibn ʿAdī is warding off Islamic attacks against Christian theology, against Jesus' divinity, and against the Trinitarian doctrine of the – not exactly unanimous – Christian denominations. On the other hand he is devising a universal theology which, by using the tools of apodeictic demonstration, presents itself as a rational science and defeats the claims of its critics – the *kalām* theologians – with the weapons of logic.

2.4.2 Ontology

A hierarchy of being follows from his theistic, creationistic world-view. There are three classes of being: (a) the natural (*ṭabīʿī*) existence of the material substances with their accidents; (b) the logical (*manṭiqī*) existence of universals as representations in the mind (*ṣuwaran fī l-nafs*); and (c) the essential (*al-wuǧūd al-ḏātī*) or 'divine' (*ilāhī*) existence, i.e. the existence of the absolute essence in accordance with its definition, i.e. the existence of the species in the quality of its pure essence, as determined by its definition: God's existence is necessary by virtue of His own essence (*Maqāla fī Tabyīn wuǧūd al-umūr al-ʿāmmiyya* [*53: 154,17–20]; see also Wisnovsky and Menn 2012 [*196] on Ibn ʿAdi's treatise *On the Four Scientific Questions Regarding the Three Categories of Existence: Divine, Natural and Logical*).

This Middle Platonic and Neoplatonic doctrine, as it is known to us from the Alexandrian commentaries on Aristotle, is a tripartition of universals (e.g.

Elias, *In Isag.* 48,16 et al.); here it instead appears as a division of being. Ibn ʿAdī refutes the view of those Peripatetics who claim that universals (*al-kulliyyāt*) or common things (*al-ašyāʾ al-ʿāmmiyya*), when separated from matter and accidents, only exist as a form that is imagined in the soul (*ṣūra mutaṣawwara fī l-nafs*). The absolute essences (*maʿānī*, sc. things *qua* objects of thought or speech) exist without inhering in any individual substrate (with reference to Arist. *Phys.* I 2, 185b32; I 8, 191b19–23; on the difference between this interpretation and that of Alexander of Aphrodisias, cf. Rashed 2004 [*190: 135–142]). Ibn ʿAdī emphasizes the ontological priority of the universal, and can appeal to Aristotle himself as a witness: there is no absolute proof of the particular and transient; such a proof only exists for the necessary and eternal [*53: 156,3–9]. This is a 'Platonism' that remains firmly grounded in Aristotelian metaphysics. In Aristotle, form plays the same metaphysical role as it had in Plato: it determines quiddity in respect of both logic and ontology – it is true being. Eternal like the Platonic idea, it governs all unfolding events – which for the Christian Aristotelian means the events of creation – and therefore it is the cause of all phenomena, even though it is manifest in a body. Form is present in the perceptible world, and through its being determines the being and the events of the perceptible world, so that this perceptible world is what it is through the form alone. Thus even 'natural' being becomes a universal concept of the being of everything that participates in the same essence (οὐσία); as such it can be an object of the divine knowledge of universals as well as an object of human knowledge of particulars (Adamson 2007 [*191], cf. also Ehrig-Eggert 2008 [*193]). The hierarchy of knowledge is analogous to the hierarchy of being: empirical knowledge of particulars constitutes the lowest level; above it we find absolute knowledge of logical being, gained from the knowledge of universals; and finally, in the highest position, the divine representation (*taṣawwur*) in the intellection (νόησις) of the First Cause, which creates by thinking (*ʿālim bi-ḫalāʾiqihi fa-huwa iḏan mutaṣawwir bi-ṣuwarihā* [*51: 83], cf. Ehrig-Eggert 2008 [*193: 57–61], Endress 2015 [*137]).

2.4.3 Metaphysics and Theology

Christians and Muslims shared a fundamental philosophical question, whether they approached it in the context of the controversy surrounding the nature of the Trinity or in the dispute as to whether God's attributes introduced multiplicity into His oneness: 'What is the One?'

In his treatises on rival conceptions of the Trinity, Ibn ʿAdī names his interlocutors and opponents, in particular Nestorian Christians, who had always constituted the strongest faction in Mesopotamia, built upon institutions established since Sasanian times. In his apologetical works he gives explicit answers to Islamic criticisms. The critique voiced in the Quran (Sura 5:73, 75:

'They are unbelievers who say, "God is the Third of Three." No god is there but One God. [...] The Messiah, son of Mary, was only a Messenger' [transl. Arberry]) had been already systematically elaborated by Muslim theologians in the 3rd/9th century. Ibn ʿAdī himself refuted the attacks launched by the philosopher al-Kindī and the theologian Abū ʿĪsā al-Warrāq. By contrast, in those of his treatises in which he discusses general questions of philosophical theology by means of the Aristotelian doctrine of demonstration, he does not mention any addressee by name. All the same, the most important of his treatises are no less 'political', for the universals they discuss happen to be concepts of Islamic theology, and the questions they are meant to solve are the problems of *kalām* (Endress 2015 [*137]).

The treatise *Maqāla fī l-Tawḥīd* (*On Unity* [*104]) is marked by its title as a diatribe against the Islamic profession of God's unity, *al-tawḥīd*. At the same time it constitutes an apology of the Christian doctrine of the triune God: Christian monotheism needed to be defended against the criticism of Islamic religion. Nevertheless, in both its approach and its aims the treatise does not belong to Ibn ʿAdī's Christian apologetical writings. Just as his works on the principles of the categorical doctrine and on logic, it was included, together with further treatises on various theological tenets of *kalām*, in codices of the Islamic tradition.

Ibn ʿAdī opens with an exposition of various views on God's unicity. (1) The predicate 'one' is merely a negation of plurality, rather than an affirmation of God's unity. Ibn ʿAdī does not say who he is thinking of, but it is clear that he is describing the Islamic creed: 'There is no god but God'. (2) The expression 'The One' means that He has no equal. This also corresponds to the Islamic formula: 'He has no partner'. (3) Oneness, as applied to God, is the principle of number. This is Aristotelian doctrine (*Met.* v 6, 1016b18: τὸ δὲ ἑνὶ εἶναι ἀρχῇ τινί ἐστιν ἀριθμοῦ εἶναι), but Ibn ʿAdī ascribes the phrase to one of the contemporary Islamic theologians (*mutakallimūn*), claiming that he does not know anybody else who shared this opinion, nor any precursor to it. (4) In the profession of God's unity, we use the expression 'one' in the same, general sense used in other contexts. People furthermore differ with respect to the question whether and to what extent plurality, i.e. a multiplicity of attributes, can be predicated of the Creator. This question of the divine attributes (*ṣifāt*) is a topic in Islamic theology as well. The exegesis of the Quranic statements about God and the question whether to interpret them rationally, as metaphors, was indeed a pivotal point of contention. All this belonged to debate over *al-tawḥīd*, the profession of unity.

Ibn ʿAdī dismisses these concepts of unity as being applicable to the one and first divine cause, and rejects the predication of other concepts that would imply an unacceptable plurality in the essentially One. After a detailed division of the concept of 'one' (following Arist. *Met.* v 6), he introduces his own doctrine: The Creator, the one and first cause, is one – neither as a genus, nor as a species, nor because of a relation, nor as a continuous or indivisible quantity. The One is one, insofar as there is only one defining determination of His essence: the λόγος (*qawl*) that determines His essence is one. The formulation appears to hark back to Aristotle (*Met.* V 6, 1016a33: ὅσων ὁ λόγος ὁ τὸ τί ἦν εἶναι ὁ λέγων ἀδιαίρετος πρὸς ἄλλον δηλοῦντα τὸ πρᾶγμα, one in the fullest sense is that 'of which the *logos* which states the essence of one is indivisible from another *logos* which shows the essence of the other' [transl. after Ross], and further: 'does not admit separation in time or in space, or in *logos* [1016b2–3; transl. after Ross]). The One is one *qua* substance.

Among the philosophers writing in Arabic, Ibn ʿAdī had two Muslim predecessors in this matter, or rather one predecessor and one contemporary. The older one was al-Kindī, who, in the fourth decade of the 3rd/9th century, strove to legitimize the tradition of Greek rationalism as a service to the Islamic profession of God's unicity – the very same man whose criticism of the Christian Trinitarian doctrine Ibn ʿAdī refuted in a small polemical treatise. Al-Kindī's *On First Philosophy* demonstrates the absolute unity of the First Cause, using an elaborate deduction which is indebted to Proclus' Platonic theology, perhaps indirectly. The many is not without the One; everything that is one participates in the absolute One; every plurality, and hence everything there is, depends logically and ontologically on the One. Al-Kindī's discourse is therefore different from Ibn ʿAdī's: rather than an analysis of the meanings of the concept 'one', it is a Neoplatonic metaphysics of the One. In contrast, al-Fārābī's treatise *al-Wāḥid wa-l-waḥda* (*The One and Unity*) [§ 8 *111] shares the same Aristotelian fundament as Ibn ʿAdī's treatise, and offers a similar analysis: al-Fārābī assigns to each concept of unity a concept of plurality, without, however, attempting an ontological or even cosmological deduction of the many from the one as al-Kindī had done before him, and as, indeed, he himself did in his philosophical summa *The Principles of the Opinions of the Inhabitants of the Virtuous City*.

In respect of the question whether, and to what extent a plurality can be predicated of the One, Ibn ʿAdī follows a different approach. On the one hand, he is taking aim at the Islamic doctrine of attributes, on the other, at Islamic polemics against the Christian doctrine of the Trinity. His approach is the same as that on which he bases his Monophysite persuasion as against other Christological positions (GCAL [*102: II 235–236]). God's essence has its cause in itself. God's self-causation implies that He is one only, and that He is absolute, substantial intellect. Of all possible definitions of the concept 'one', it is only unity of substance that can be applied to God. The First Cause possesses plurality only in the constitutive parts of the definition of its essence, i.e. in the attributes (*ṣifāt*) which can be predicated of the divine essence.

These attributes are three in number: goodness (*ǧūd*, ἀγαθότης), power (*qudra*, δύναμις) and wisdom (*ḥikma*, σοφία). These essential attributes can be deduced from God's creation. Even though His substance is hidden, in His actions His essence manifests itself to the eye of reason (*ḫafiyy al-ǧawhar ẓāhir al-aṯar*): all created beings – individuals as well as universals (which subsist in the particulars) – are brought from non-existence to existence, by the *power* of the Creator alone. Since the Creator existed before they came into being, His free and spontaneous act of creation shows His *goodness*. Finally, His *wisdom* is revealed in the order and perfection of His work (*Maqāla fī l-Tawḥīd* [**104*: 242–247 Samir], cf. Lizzini 2009 [*195]; Lizzini 2016 [*197]).

Even though we cannot find any of the elements of the Neoplatonic doctrine of emanation in Ibn ʿAdī's text, and he argues for *creatio ex nihilo*, whereas Peripatetics as well as Neoplatonists support the idea of a *creatio ex aeterno*, the crucial attributes benevolence, omnipotence, and wisdom (ἀγαθότης, δύναμις, σοφία) can be traced back to Proclus and his Christian adept Pseudo-Dionysius Areopagita. In Proclus' philosophy, goodness, power, and knowledge (γνῶσις) constitute the first divine triad (*Theologia Platonica*, I.xvi.44 [**141*: 264, on Procl. *Elem. theol.*, prop. 121]), which contains the germ of the second hypostasis, i.e. being, life, and intellect. This goes back to the interpretation of the Platonic demiurge and of providence as conceived by the Middle and Late Platonists. The triad is used by Pseudo-Dionysius as well in this context, but he replaces knowledge (γνῶσις) with wisdom (σοφία), following, in this instance, not Proclus but the Patristic tradition: the Christian application of the triad benevolence, omnipotence, and wisdom had first been formulated explicitly by the Church Father Irenaeus (Whittaker 1987 [*183: 277–291, esp. 285–286]).

The polemical and apologetical concepts go back to the Church Fathers. Within the old Church, Trinitarian theology was the chief topic over which the various denominations parted ways, in particular the Monophysites of the West Syrian Church, and the Nestorian Christians of Iran and Mesopotamia. However, the old arguments were also launched against Islamic monotheism. The doctrine of Christ's nature being ὁμοούσιος, i.e. of the same essence as, and consubstantial with the Father, won the day at the Council of Nicaea in 325. In opposition to it, the Eastern Fathers in particular argued for the doctrine that regarded God Father, Son and Holy Spirit as the three 'hypostases' of the one God. After a long period of ecclesiastical conflict, the formula 'one essence, three hypostases' (μία οὐσία, τρεῖς ὑποστάσεις) was finally adopted by the adherents of the Nicene creed. This development was led by Basil of Caesarea, who is largely responsible for integrating the distinction between substance (οὐσία) and hypostasis (ὑπόστασις), which had not been customary before. It was provided with theological foundations by the three Cappadocian Fathers

Basil, Gregory of Nazianzus, and Gregory of Nyssa. Thanks to their authority and wide influence, this gradually became the accepted dogma everywhere (cf. Pannenberg 1957 [*235: 1767], Kettler 1962 [*237: 1029]). As it had happened at first in the West, the three hypostases soon were equated with Tertullian's 'three persons' (Greek πρόσωπον, Arab. *uqnūm*, pl. *aqānīm*) in the East as well. Naturally, this was grist to the mill of Ibn ʿAdī's Monophysite doctrine. However, in the face of the mono-*physite* theology of Severus of Antioch Ibn ʿAdī does not speak of the one nature (φύσις, *ṭabīʿa*) of the *logos* incarnate in Christ's person, but of the one substance or the one essence (*maʿnā* in the sense of τὸ τί ἦν εἶναι) constituted of both divine and human essence (*Maqāla fī l-Tawḥīd* [*104: 230–232]; cf. Platti 1983 [*240: 87–90], Ehrig-Eggert 1994 [*241: 315]).

The main objection of the Muslim opponents had first been articulated by al-Kindī: while one in substance, the 'persons' each have a property (*ḫāṣṣa*) that constitutes them. Hence each person possesses its own individual substantiality, composed from the shared substance and its own property. Composition, however, presupposes a cause; thus the Trinitarian God could not be eternal. Ibn ʿAdī counters as follows: the hypostases are not individuals of a uniform substance which are constituted by combining that substance with their respective specific differences; rather, the names of the hypostases describe the divine being as its essential attributes (*ṣifāt*). The divine substance is a single one, whereas the hypostases are properties (*ḫawāṣṣ*), through which the one substance in its eternal essence can be described as good (Father), wise (Son) and powerful (Holy Spirit) (*Tabyīn ġalaṭ al-Kindī* [*132: 4–5]; Schöck 2012–2014 [*244]).

In several of his apologetic works directed against Islamic criticism, albeit not in his treatise on God's unity, Ibn ʿAdī interprets the God of Trinitarian theology as a self-thinking, self-identical intellect. The hypostases or 'persons' (*aqānīm*, sing. *uqnūm*) of the Trinity are aspects of this act of thinking: the Father is intellect (νοῦς, *ʿaql*), the incarnation in the Son is that which is engaging in intellection (νοῶν, *ʿāqil*), and the Holy Spirit is the intelligible (νοούμενον, *maʿqūl*). The substance of the intellect is the essence of the cognizant subject as well as that of the intelligible object – the three aspects are inseparable within the One, since the intellect is inseparable from its knowledge and from the object of its knowledge, even though the three can be distinguished conceptually. Ibn ʿAdī here makes use of the Aristotelian concept of the First Mover, which, in its eternal contemplation, is nothing but the thinking of thinking (νόησις νοήσεως; Arist. *Met.* XII 9, 1074b34; cf. GCAL [*102: II 236], Platti 1983 [*240: 107–114]).

Being a Christian theologian, Ibn ʿAdī cannot allow the idea that God is detached from any knowledge of the spatio-temporal universe, any more than the Neoplatonists before him could have admitted this (cf. Dodds 1963 [*177: 289, on Procl. *Elem. theol.*, prop. 173]). We find a theological use of Platonist reflection on the providential workings of the divine demiurge with his three attributes, as for example in Proclus: an intelligence's 'existence' or 'substance' is identical with its intelligible content (νοητόν); its 'power' is the intellectual faculty (νοῦς); its 'activity' is the act of thinking (νόησις); all these aspects are co-eternal [*177: 288, on Procl. *Elem. theol.*, prop. 169].

However, according to Christian as well as Islamic belief the creation is the product of a divine act of will, which originates movement and also time, which is the measure of motion. In contrast to the entire *falsafa* tradition after al-Fārābī, Ibn ʿAdī (like al-Kindī before him) follows the Christian Aristotelianism of the Alexandrian John Philoponus, whose commentary on Aristotle's *Physics* was transmitted in his school (cf. § 7.5 on Ibn al-Samḥ), and whose works *Against Proclus* and *Against Aristotle* were well-known. The act of creation correlates with the divine attributes of benevolence and power: being benevolent (*ǧawād*) and powerful (*qādir*), God has brought His creatures into being (*īǧād*) after they did not exist (*baʿd al-ʿadam*); not by a necessary process emerging from the nature of His essence, but as 'an act of a Creator who has the power to act or not' (*fiʿla qādirin ʿalā fiʿlihi aw tark fiʿlihi*) (*Maqāla fī l-Mawǧūdāt* [*101: 266–267 Ḫalīfāt]; *Maqāla fī l-Tawḥīd* [*104: 330–331, 334 Samīr]; cf. Lizzini 2009 [*195]).

2.4.4 Creation, Causality, and Determination

Ibn ʿAdī employs logical analysis in order to solve the aporias of *kalām* theology, or rather, in order to show the futility of its claims, in particular with respect to certain topics that were at the centre of discussions among Ašʿarite theologians: creation, causality, and contingency in the spatio-temporal world, especially as it impacts on the freedom of human agency in the face of God's omnipotence.

Thus Ibn ʿAdī turned against those who denied future contingents by invoking God's omniscience and the universal validity of the law of non-contradiction. The existence (or non-existence) of things does not follow necessarily from the fact that God knows about them even before they exist. If God's previous knowledge rendered them necessary, it would have to be one of the six kinds of cause. But it is neither material cause (*sabab ʿunṣurī* – αἴτιον ὑλικόν), nor formal cause (*ṣūrī* – εἰδικόν), nor efficient cause (*fāʿil* – ποιητικόν), nor final cause (*kamālī* – τελικόν), nor instrumental cause (*ʿadawī* – ὀργανικόν), nor paradigmatic cause (*miṯālī* – παραδειγματικόν) of a thing's being necessary or not necessary. The denial of future contingents is furthermore based on the universal validity of the law of non-contradiction. Since each element of a pair of contradictory statements is either true or false, it must be the case that either the affirmation or the negation of a future event is true. What is predicted veridically cannot but come to pass – therefore everything that happens does so by necessity. In his refutation of this argument, Ibn ʿAdī refers to Aristotle's remarks on future contingents in *De int.* 9, 18a 28–19b4, which he quotes extensively and comments on in detail. In his view, those who deny future contingents commit a twofold error: they do not differentiate between the existence of things that have being, and the existence of things *tout court* (*ʿalā l-iṭlāq* – ἁπλῶς, *De int.* 9, 19a26); and they conclude that the truth of a proposition will necessarily cause the affirmed matter to occur, and the negated matter not to occur (*Maqāla fī Iṯbāt ṭabīʿat al-mumkin* [*105]; cf Ehrig-Eggert 1990 [*165]). The problem of future contingents is also treated by al-Fārābī, *Šarḥ fī l-ʿIbāra* [§ 8 *65: 83–100 (esp. 97–100)] (cf. Rescher 1963 [*145: 43–54]; on the problem more generally, see Bruns 1889 [*142: 613–30] and Frede 1970 [*147]).

Ibn ʿAdī furthermore rejects another doctrine developed by Ašʿarite *kalām*: that man is not able to create his own deeds, but acquires them (*iktisāb*) – since God is the only Creator there is. According to Ibn ʿAdī, actions are brought about by those who perform them (*mūǧidūhā fāʿilūhā*). True, it is God alone who is able to restore (*iʿāda*), but any re-creation of individual actions that occurred at a particular time can only ever take place at a second time: the 'first time' cannot be restored. Again, the Creator will not restore every single substance that He has brought into being; but even if the 're-creation' of a particular thing is not possible, it is impossible to deny its original creation, and God's power to bring it about. If this applies to the Creator, then other agents must also be able to create their actions, even if they cannot reproduce them. Finally, the concept of *iktisāb* leads to internal contradictions. The 'acquisition' of an action through a human being is yet another action, which mediates between God's creation of the action and its possible execution through the person acquiring it. If the advocate of *iktisāb* remains true to the maxim that there is no creator of actions except God, he will be forced to admit that this very act of acquisition must again be created by God, and acquired by man – which will lead to an infinite regress [*53: 303–313] (cf. Pines 1973 [*178], Pines, Schwarz 1979 [*179]).

2.4.5 Ethics

The final goal of acting ethically is the attainment of happiness through perfecting one's moral qualities (*ḫuluq*, pl. *aḫlāq*, Greek ἦθος; cf. Galen, *De moribus*, Arab. *Kitāb al-Aḫlāq* [*206: 236]). The moral qualities are constituted by the behaviour (*aḥwāl*) of the three faculties of the soul according to Plato's division: the appetitive, the spirited, and the rational parts of the soul (ἐπιθυμητικόν, θυμοειδές, λογιστικόν μέρος, Arab. *al-quwwa al-šahwāniyya*, *al-ġaḍabiyya, al-nāṭiqa*). The dispositions or habits (*ʿādāt*) of those parts of the soul are either good or bad, either virtues (*faḍāʾil*) or vices (*raḏāʾil*). The rational soul is able to differentiate between those qualities and to rein in and refine the appetites and passions according to its judgement. By this process of 'refinement' or 'education of character' (*tahḏīb* or *taʾdīb al-aḫlāq*) man is able to reach the highest degree of humanity (*insāniyya*), i.e. become a perfect human being (*insān kāmil, insān tāmm*). The virtues and vices, each of them twenty in number, are presented systematically in their allocation to the respective parts of the soul (*Tahḏīb*, ed. Samīr [*111: 49–84]). Amongst the 'good character traits' (*aḫlāq ḥasana*), i.e. virtues, he counts chastity (*ʿiffa*), moderation (*qanāʿa*), forbearance (*ḥilm*), friendship (*wudd* in the sense of *maḥabba muʿtadila*, well-balanced love), mercy (*raḥma*), faithfulness (*wafāʾ*), humility (*tawāḍuʿ*), generosity (*saḫāʾ*), high-mindedness (*ʿiẓam al-himma*) and justice (*ʿadl*); they are contrasted by the corresponding vices, including profligacy (*fuǧūr*), greed (*šarah*), irascibility (*safah*), passionate love (*ʿišq*, i.e. exessive love, *ifrāṭ al-ḥubb*), mercilessness (*qasāwa*), perfidy (*ġadr*), arrogance (*kibr*), avarice (*buḫl*), faint-heartedness (*ṣiġar al-himma*) and injustice (*ǧawr*). Apart from giving definitions of the moral qualities, the author weighs them with respect to the social position of the agent. Some of them are ambivalent in that they need to be judged positively or negatively depending on the higher or lower station of the person concerned: love of honour (*ḥubb al-karāma*), love of pomp (*ḥubb al-zīna*), paying for praise (*al-muǧāzāt ʿalā l-madḥ*), and asceticism (*zuhd*); the latter becomes scholars and teachers of the religious community, but not kings and other members of the political elite (Griffith 2002 [*218: xxxvi]).

Ibn ʿAdī's programme of character refinement (*al-irtiyāḍ bi-makārim al-aḫlāq*) is meant to cultivate the habit (*ʿāda*) of virtue in the soul; to this end the rational soul has to bring the appetitive and spirited parts of the soul under its control. Personal role models and didactic tracts will provide guidance. First and foremost, however, it is the rational sciences (*al-ʿulūm al-ʿaqliyya*) that point the rational soul in the right direction (*taqwīm*); for this purpose, Ibn ʿAdī recommends the 'books of ethics and of [moral] guidance' (*kutub al-aḫlāq wa-l-siyāsa*) (*Tahḏīb al-aḫlāq* ed. Samīr [*111: § 12.2, 118]). Following the example of the propaedeutics of the Greek philosophical schools, ethics means practicing the ideal of the 'perfect human being', guided by the models of science and wisdom: 'The path that leads man to perfection and keeps him in this state consists in directing his attention to the true sciences (*al-ʿulūm al-ḥaqīqiyya*) and in seeking his goal in the comprehension of the essences of all things, in the discovery of their origins and causes, and in the search for their purposes and ends' [*111: 131]. The philosopher's form of life (βίος) thus leads to true happiness. Ibn ʿAdī here stands in the tradition of ancient ethics (Griffith 2002 [*218: xxxix]) and its adherents in the school of al-Kindī and al-Rāzī (cf. the latter's *al-Sīra al-falsafiyya* [§ 6 *46: 99–111]; *al-Ṭibb al-rūḥānī* [§ 6 *48: 43–44]).

The theoretical life, however, can fully be achieved only by those who renounce the active life: scholars (*ahl al-ʿilm*), monks (*ruhbān*), and ascetics (*zuhhād*) – addressees of the treatise on abstinence (Mistrih 1981 [*212]). While the king is more than anybody called upon to act as an exemplary, public representative of a virtuous life, and to consult the best possible advisors to this purpose, he is not free to turn his back on the political life, on its material foundations, and on the exercise of power. Therefore it is difficult if not impossible for him to reach the level of a perfect philosopher (*Tahḏīb* [*111: 132. 153–163 Samīr]; cf. Hatem 1985 [*213]). However, Ibn ʿAdī's image of the perfect king also seems to integrate traditions from the *adab al-mulūk* (i.e. the literature on the proper behaviour of kings), which had established a canon of princely virtues, drawing on Hellenistic as well as Iranian mirrors for princes. The success of Ibn ʿAdī's account is indicated by the fact that the list of virtues of his *Tahḏīb al-aḫlāq* was incorporated into the *Survey of the Sciences* (*Ǧawāmiʿ al-ʿulūm*) of al-Balḫī's student Ibn Farīġūn (cf. § 5.1.3).

3 ʿĪsā Ibn Zurʿa

Gerhard Endress

3.1 Primary Sources – 3.2 Life – 3.3 Works – 3.4 Doctrine

3.1 *Primary Sources*

3.1.1 Bio-bibliographical Testimonies [*151–*161] – 3.1.2 Works [*171–*186]

3.1.1 Bio-bibliographical Testimonies

151 Ibn al-Nadīm, Abū l-Farağ Muḥammad b. Isḥāq (d. 380/990). *Kitāb al-Fihrist* [composed 377/988]. – Ed. by Gustav Flügel, August Müller and Johannes Roediger, 2 vols. Leipzig, 1871–1872, 264 (ed. quoted below). – Repr. Beirut, 1964, Frankfurt a.M., 2005. – Ed. by Riḍā Tağaddud. Tehran, 1350 h.š./1971, 323. – Ed. by Ayman Fu'ād Sayyid, 2 vols (I\1–2 - II\1–2). London, 1430/2009. – Engl. transl. by Bayard Dodge, *The Fihrist of al-Nadīm*, 2 vols. New York, 1970.

152 al-Tawḥīdī, Abū Ḥayyān ʿAlī b. Muḥammad (d. 414/1023). *Risālat al-Ḥayāt*. – Ed. by Ibrāhīm Kaylānī, in: *Ṯalāṯ rasā'il li-Abī Ḥayyān al-Tawḥīdī: Trois épîtres d'Abū Ḥaiyān at-Tauḥīdī*. Damascus, 1951, 51–80, at 70. – French transl. by Claude

Audebert, “La Risālat al-Ḥayāt d’Abū Ḥayyān al-Tawḥīdī.” *Bulletin d’études orientales* 8 (1963/64): 147–195, at 165.

153 Abū Ḥayyān al-Tawḥīdī. *Kitāb al-Imtāʿ wa-l-muʾānasa*. – Ed. by Aḥmad Amīn, Aḥmad al-Zayn, 3 vols. Cairo, 1939–1944, vol. 1, 33.

154 Abū Ḥayyān al-Tawḥīdī. *Al-Muqābasāt*. – Ed. by Muḥammad Tawfīq Ḥusayn. Baghdad, 1970, 164. 165. 274. 436.

155 al-Tawḥīdī, Abū Ḥayyān. *Kitāb al-Ṣadāqa wa-l-ṣadīq*. – Ed. by Ibrāhīm al-Kaylānī. Damascus, 1964, 64–65.

156 *Ṣiwān al-ḥikma* [ascribed to Abū Sulaymān al-Siǧistānī]. – Excerpts ed. by Douglas Morton Dunlop, *The Muntakhab Ṣiwān al-ḥikmah of Abū Sulaimān as-Sijistānī*. The Hague, 1979, § 283,144–145; § 303,156–158. – Ed. by ʿAbd al-Raḥmān Badawī, *Ṣiwān al-ḥikma wa-ṯalāṯ rasāʾil taʾlīf Abū Sulaymān al-Siǧistānī*. Tehran, 1974, 333–335.

157 al-Bayhaqī, Ẓahīr al-Dīn Abū l-Ḥasan ʿAlī b. Zayd Ibn Funduq (d. 565/1169–1170). *Tatimmat Ṣiwān al-ḥikma*. – Ed. by Muḥammad Šafīʿ. Lahore, 1935, 66–69. – Ed. by Muḥammad Kurd ʿAlī. *Taʾrīḫ ḥukamāʾ al-islām*. Damascus, 1976, 75–78.

158 Ibn Abī Uṣaybiʿa, Muwaffaq al-Dīn Aḥmad b. al-Qāsim (d. 668/1270). *ʿUyūn al-anbāʾ fī ṭabaqāt al-aṭibbāʾ*. – Ed. by August Müller, 2 vols. Cairo, 1299/1882, Königsberg 1884, vol. 1, 235.

159 Ibn al-Qifṭī, Ǧamāl al-Dīn ʿAlī b. Yūsuf (d. 646/1248). *Taʾrīḫ al-ḥukamāʾ* [*Iḫbār al-ʿulamāʾ bi-aḫbār al-ḥukamāʾ*, epitome by Muḥammad b. ʿAlī al-Zawzanī]. – Ed. by Julius Lippert, *Ibn al-Qifṭī’s Taʾrīh al-ḥukamāʾ*. Leipzig, 1903, 245.

160 Ibn al-ʿIbrī, Abū l-Faraǧ Gregorios [Barhebraeus] (d. 685/1286). *Taʾrīḫ muḫtaṣar al-duwal*. – Ed. by Anṭūn Ṣāliḥānī. Beirut, 1890, 1958 (2nd ed.), 277.

161 Ibn Faḍl Allāh al-ʿUmarī (d. 749/1349). *Masālik al-abṣār fī mamālik al-amṣār: Routes Toward Insight into the Capital Empires*, book 9. – Ed. by Fuat Sezgin, in collaboration with A. Jokhosha and Eckhard Neubauer. Frankfurt a.M., 1988, 25–26. – Facsimile edition.

3.1.2 Works

An inventary of works is available in Haddad 1971 [*272].

3.1.2.1 *Collection*

171 Sbath, Paul, ed. *Vingt traités philosophiques et apologétiques d’auteurs arabes chrétiens du IXe au XIVe siècle, publiés pour la première fois, avec corrections et annotations*. Cairo, 1929. – Contains: *Risāla ṣannafahā fī maʿānī saʾalahu ʿanhā baʿḍ iḫwānihi* (6–19); *Maqāla ʿamilahā ilā baʿḍ al-Yahūd wa-huwa Bišr b. Pinḥās b. Šuʿaib al-Ḥāsib* (19–52); [*al-Iǧāba*] *ʿan radd Abī l-Qāsim ʿAbd Allāh b. Aḥmad al-Balḫī ʿalā l-naṣārā fī kitābihi al-musammā Awāʾil al-adilla* (52–58); *Maqālat*

Yaḥyā Ibn ʿAdī b. Ḥamīd b. Zakariyyā allatī awʿazahā bi-l-ruʾyā ilā tilmīḏihi wa-šayḫinā Abī ʿAlī ʿĪsā Ibn Zurʿa (68–75).

3.1.2.2 *Translations from the Syriac (after the Greek)*

176 Aristotle. *Kitāb Sūfisṭīqā* [*Sophistical Refutations*, Arabic] *naql Abī ʿAlī ʿĪsā b. Isḥāq Ibn Zurʿa min al-suryānī bi-naql Aṯānis min al-yūnānī*. – Ed. by ʿAbd al-Raḥmān Badawī, *Manṭiq Arisṭū*. Cairo, 1948–1952, 739–1015; Kuwait, 1980 (2nd ed.), 775–1051. – Ed. by Farīd Ǧabr, Ǧirār Ǧihāmī and Rafīq al-ʿAǧam, *Al-Naṣṣ al-kāmil li-manṭiq Arisṭū*, vol. 2. Beirut, 1999, 908–1195.

177 Themistius. *Risālat Ṯāmisṭiyūs ilā Yūliyān al-Malik fī l-siyāsa wa-tadbīr al-mamlaka*. – Ed. by Muḥammad Salīm Sālim. Cairo, 1970, 51. – Ed. by Louis Cheikho, *Risālat Dāmisṭiyūs fī l-siyāsa*, in: Cheikho, *Maǧmūʿat arbaʿ rasāʾil li-qudamāʾ falāsifat al-Yūnān wa-li-Ibn al-ʿIbrī*. Beirut, 1920–1923, 3–11. – Ed. [with Lat. transl.] by Irfan Shahid, *Epistula de re publica gerenda*, in: *Themistii orationes quae supersunt*. Ed. by H. Schenkl et al., vol. 3. Leipzig, 1974, 73–119.

3.1.2.3 *Authored Works*

181 *Aġrāḍ Arisṭūṭālīs al-manṭiqiyya*. –Ed. by Ǧirār Ǧīhāmī (Gérard Jéhamy) and Rafīq al-ʿAǧam, *Manṭiq ʿĪsā Ibn Zurʿa*. Beirut, 1994. – Contains: *Kitāb Bārmīnās wa-huwa l-kalām fī l-ʿibāra* (Arist. *De int.*) (23–79); *Kitāb al-Qiyās* (Arist. *An. Pr.*) (93–200); *Kitāb al-Burhān* (Arist. *An. Post.*) (215–284).

182 *Maqāla yubayyin fīhā barāʾat al-nāẓirīn fī l-manṭiq wa-l-falsafa mimmā yaʿrifūna min fasād al-dīn*. – Ed. by N. Rescher 1963 [*293] (with Engl. transl.).

183 *Risāla ṣannafahā fī maʿānī saʾalahu ʿanhā baʿḍ iḫwānihi*. – Ed. by P. Sbath [**171*: 6–19].

184 *Maqāla ʿamilahā ilā baʿḍ al-Yahūd wa-huwa Bišr b. Pinḥās al-Ḥāsib*. – Ed. by P. Sbath [**171*: 19–52]. – Ed. by P. Starr 2000 [*295].

185 [*Al-Iǧāba*] *ʿan radd Abī l-Qāsim ʿAbd Allāh b. Aḥmad al-Balḫī ʿalā l-naṣārā fī kitābihi al-musammā Awāʾil al-adilla*. –Ed. by P. Sbath [**171*: 52–58].

186 *Maqālat Yaḥyā Ibn ʿAdī b. Ḥamīd b. Zakariyyā allatī awʿazahā bi-l-ruʾyā ilā tilmīḏihi wa-šayḫinā Abī ʿAlī ʿĪsā b. Zurʿa*. –Ed. by P. Sbath [**171*: 68–75].

3.2 *Life*

ʿĪsā b. Isḥāq Ibn Zurʿa, a Jacobite Christian, was born in Ḏū l-Ḥiǧǧa 331/August-September 943 in Baghdad, where he died on 6 Šaʿbān 398/16 April 1008. (Ibn Abī Uṣaybiʿa mentions 371 and 448 as further possible years of his death, but in the light of contemporary testimonies given by Ibn al-Nadīm and Abū Ḥayyān al-Tawḥīdī neither of them appears credible.) In his working life he was a merchant – Abū Ḥayyān al-Tawḥīdī criticizes him for his mercantile pettiness – a profession that also took him to the Byzantine West. Due to a lack of experience, and to envious competitors who denounced him for allegedly having plotted intrigues with the Byzantines, his business failed eventually. His wealth was confiscated, and he suffered bad health as a consequence of his misfortune. Even though he was no physician himself, he was closely acquainted with the doctors at the Bīmāristān al-ʿAḍudī in Baghdad (the hospital founded in 372/982 by the Buyid prince ʿAḍud al-Dawla), who duly strove to establish a diagnose for his ailment – those mentioned (Ibn Abī Uṣaybiʿa [*158: I 236]) are Ibn Bakkūs (also Bakkūš, Bak[ku]s, a translator of medical works, cf. *158: I 244); Abū l-Ḥusayn Ibn Kaškarāyā (a student of Sinān b. Ṯābit, *158: I 238) and Abū Manṣūr Ṣāʿid b. Bišr Ibn ʿAbdūs [*158: I 232].

Ibn Zurʿa was the most prominent among Yaḥyā Ibn ʿAdī's (d. 363/974, cf. § 7.2) students. Like his teacher, he was a Christian theologian and apologist who translated Aristotelian works into Arabic, occupied himself with the composition of introductions to philosophy and logic, and discussed individual problems of epistemology, physics, and theology.

3.3 *Works*

3.3.1 Translations and Summaries of Greek Philosophical Works (from the Syriac) – 3.3.2 Philosophical Introductions and Logic – 3.3.3 Physics – 3.3.4 Christian Dogmatics and Apologetics

3.3.1 Translations and Summaries of Greek Philosophical Works (from the Syriac)

Ibn Zurʿa was the last notable translator to emerge from Abū Bišr Mattā's and Yaḥyā Ibn ʿAdī's school; this seems to have been apparent already to his contemporaries (cf. Abū Ḥayyān al-Tawḥīdī [*153: I 33]; *Muntaḫab Ṣiwān al-ḥikma* [*156: 143 Dunlop]). In the main, he translated philosophical works by Aristotle and his commentators, from existing Syriac versions.

3.3.1.1 *Aristotle: Sophistical Refutations*

Arabic translation based on the Syriac version by Athanasius of Balad and improving on an earlier translation made by Yaḥyā Ibn ʿAdī, adducing additional Syriac material, transl. by Theophilus of Edessa (cf. Hugonnard-Roche 1991 [*281: 193–210]): *Kitāb Sūfisṭīqā naql Abī ʿAlī ʿĪsā b. Isḥāq Ibn Zurʿa min al-suryānī bi-naql Aṯānis min al-yūnānī.* The manuscript Paris ar. 2346 was copied from Ḥasan b. Suwār's copy, which in turn was copied from the translator's autograph (*dustūr*).

3.3.1.2 *Aristotle: Nicomachean Ethics* (*Summa Alexandrinorum?*)

Ibn al-Nadīm (*Fihrist* [*151: I 264]) documents a translation of an anonymous treatise on ethics (*Maqāla fī l-Aḫlāq*); it may possibly refer to the Arabic original of the *Summa Alexandrinorum*, which only survives in Latin. An Aristotelian *dictum* about humanity as an ethical ideal (*al-insāniyya ufuq*) which can be reached only through education that improves on human nature, is quoted by Abū Ḥayyān al-Tawḥīdī (*al-Muqābasāt* [*154: § 37, 164]) and in the *Muntaḫab Ṣiwān al-ḥikma* [*156: 143 Dunlop], while also being found in the Latin *Summa* (cf. Dunlop 1982 [*279: 261–263]; Akasoy, Fidora 2005 [*282: 68–72]).

[Pseudo-]Aristotle: Iḫtiṣār kitāb al-Maʿmūr min al-arḍ
Epitome of Aristotle's Book on the Oikumene

Attested only by Ibn Abī Uṣaybiʿa [*158: 236].

3.3.1.3 *Nicolaus of Damascus: Compendium of Aristotle's Philosophy*

According to Ibn al-Nadīm (*Fihrist* [*151: I 251,23]), Yaḥyā Ibn ʿAdī had produced an epitome of Nicolaus' *Kitāb al-Ḥayawān*, which Ibn Zurʿa had begun to translate. However, among Ibn Zurʿa' s works listed in the *Fihrist* [*151: I 264,26] are 'Five treatises from Nicolaus' book *On Aristotle's Philosophy*, as well as a translation of Aristotle's *Book of Animals* (*Kitāb al-Ḥayawān*)' (cf. Drossaart Lulofs 1965 [*330: 9–10. 12–13. 39]).

In addition, Ibn al-Nadīm (*Fihrist* [*151: I 264]) attests further Arabic versions of Aristotle's [or Nicolaus'? see above] *History of Animals*, and of Proclus' *Commentary on Plato's Phaedo*, 'on the soul', as well as two anonymous texts of ethical content. For translations of commentaries by John the Grammarian (or rather: John of Alexandria?), of the *Summa Alexandrinorum*, of Galen's *To Glaucon, The Elements according to Hippocrates, Anatomical Procedures*, and *The Function of the Parts of the Body* cf. GAS [*4: III 147–148], Ullmann 1970 [*265: 90].

Themistius: Risālat Dāmisṭiyūs (v.l. Ṯāmisṭiyūs) ilā Yūliyān(ūs) al-Malik fī l-siyāsa
Themistius: Letter to Julian on Governance

In MS Cairo, Dār al-kutub, Taymūr aḫlāq 290, the text, entitled *Risālat Dāmisṭiyūs wazīr ʾlyān wa-huwa Yūliyānūs al-Malik fī l-siyāsa*, is identified as a translation by Ibn Zurʿa. By contrast, the text transmitted in MS Istanbul, Köprülü under the title *Risālat Ṯāmisṭiyūs al-ḥakīm ilā ʾllyān* [*Yūliyān*] *al-Malik fī l-siyāsa wa-tadbīr al-mamlaka* names Abū ʿUṯmān al-Dimašqī as translator of the same version (cf. ed. Sālim [*177: 14–18]).

3.3.2 Philosophical Introductions and Logic

Maqāla yubayyin fīhā barāʾat al-nāẓirīn fī l-manṭiq wa-l-falsafa mimmā yuʿrafūna min fasād al-dīn
A Demonstration Exonerating Those Who Cultivate the Sciences of Logic and Philosophy from being Considered Irreligious

Excerpts in al-Bayhaqī [*157: 66–69 Šafīʿ; 75–78 Kurd ʿAlī] under the title *Risāla fī anna ʿilm al-ḥikma aqwā l-dawāʿī ilā mutābaʿat al-šarāʾiʿ* (*Epistle Demonstrating that Philosophical Science Constitutes the Strongest Incitement to Abiding by the Religious Law*) (GCAL [*2: II 256 no. 10], Rescher 1963 [*293], Haddad 1971 [*272: 50–52 no. 10]).

Religious law and rational sciences are not in conflict with each other. It would be unwarranted to claim that religion cannot withstand rational scrutiny: religion itself prohibits fallacies and prejudices. In the second part the author argues that in order to demonstrate the truth of religion, reason is necessary: the cornerstone of true religion is the miracle, but we need reason in order to distinguish, with the help of philosophical logic, between what is possible and what is impossible according to the laws of nature – and hence to recognize the divine miracle and the gift of prophecy.

Aġrāḍ Arisṭūṭālīs al-manṭiqiyya
The Aims [i.e. essential tenets] of Aristotelian Logic

An epitome of the *Organon* (*On Interpretation* and *Analytics* only). Contains: 1. *Maʿānī Īsāġūǧī* (Porphyr. *Isag.*; not contained in the edition by al-ʿAǧam et al. [*181]). 2. *Kitāb Bārmīnās wa-huwa l-kalām fī l-ʿibāra* (Arist. *De int.*). 3. *Kitāb al-Qiyās* (variant title: *Ǧawāmiʿ Anūlūṭīqā al-ūlā wa-l-ṯāniya wa-humā l-qiyās wa-l-burhān*) (Arist. *An. Pr.*). 4. *Kitāb al-Burhān* (Arist. *An. Post.*). The author discusses each of the texts in an introductory fashion, using the eight headings (*kephalaia*) familiar from the Alexandrian commentators (subject matter, usefulness, title, authorship, place in the curriculum, division, didactical method, and place within the classification of philosophy).

The only commentator quoted by name is John Philoponus, on *An. Post.* I 9, 75b37, concerning the inappropriate use of principles in certain demonstrations. Ibn Zurʿa adopts Philoponus' explanation of Aristotle's criticism of a geometrical construction undertaken by the Megarian thinker Bryson [*181: 238]. There follows a presentation of *An. Post.* I 9, 76a16–25 – on the indemonstrability of the specific principles of a science – where Ibn Zurʿa professes the traditional view that 'the science which explains the remaining principles that are accepted as given in the individual disciplines, is the renowned science of metaphysics' [*181: 239].

3.3.3 Physics

Maʿnā qiṭʿa min al-maqāla al-ṯāliṯa min kitāb al-Samāʾ
On the Meaning of a Certain Section from the Third Book of On the Heavens

Ibn Zurʿa had asked his teacher Yaḥyā Ibn ʿAdī about Arist. *De cael.* III 5, 306b3–8 concerning regular polyhedra: why there is no regular solid corresponding to the hexagon. Ibn ʿAdī's answer is reported by the mathematician Abū l-Futūḥ Aḥmad b. al-Sārī (Ibn al-Ṣalāḥ, d. 548/1153) (cf. Endress 1977 [*126: § 2.2.2; § 4.52; § 8.63.1]).

Kitāb fī ʿIllat istinārat al-kawākib maʿa annahā wa-l-kurāt al-ḥāmila lahā min ǧawhar wāḥid basīṭ
On the Reason why the Stars [as opposed to the spheres] are Luminous, even though both they and the spheres that carry them consist of the same simple substance

According to Ibn Abī Uṣaybiʿa [**158*: I 235]; not extant.

3.3.4 Christian Dogmatics and Apologetics

In addition to the philosophically relevant texts listed below, cf. further theological writings recorded in GCAL [*2: II 252–256], Haddad 1971 [*272: 43–53], Starr 2000 [*295: 330–370].

Maqāla fī Maʿnā l-ab wa-annahu murakkab [Ruʾyā fī amr al-ʿaql]
On the Concept 'Father', and on Its Being Composite [Dream Concerning the Intellect]

This is the title given in MS Vatic. ar. 127: *Maqālat Yaḥyā Ibn ʿAdī* [...] *allatī awʿaza bi-l-ruʾyā ilā tilmīḏihi wa-šayḫinā Abī ʿAlī ʿĪsā b. Isḥāq Ibn Zurʿa bi-taṣnīfihā ʿanhu, Treatise which Yaḥyā Ibn ʿAdī advised his pupil, our master Ibn Zurʿa, to write down in a dream* (title of ed. Sbath [**171*]). Ibn Zurʿa attributes the origin of the treatise to having seen his teacher Yaḥyā Ibn ʿAdī, who had died in 363/974, in a dream; it was composed in the night of 8 Ramaḍān 368 (8 Nīsān 1290 post Alex. = 8 April 979). GCAL [*2: II 252 no. 1], Haddad 1971 [*272: 42 no. 1], Starr 2000 [*295: 336–341].

Following Yaḥyā Ibn ʿAdī, Ibn Zurʿa interprets the Trinity of Father, Son, and Holy Spirit as intellect, intellecting, and intelligible (*ʿaql, ʿāqil, maʿqūl*). The Creator's essence is intellect and hence simple; however, the hypostasis of the Father (*qunūm al-ab*) is composed (*murakkab*) of the eternal substance (*al-ǧawhar al-azalī*) and paternity (*maʿnā l-ubuwwa*), like intellect and its subject. The first object of intellect is its own essence. The Creator is truly simple and ineffable, whereas the Intellect is the first matter, which can be described as 'simple'; then follows the soul, whose description requires more than one attribute.

Risāla ṣannafahā fī maʿānī saʾalahu ʿanhā baʿḍ iḫwānihi
On Topics about Which He had been Asked by a Friend

Letter to a Muslim friend, concerning the unicity of the Creator and the Trinity of the divine attributes, composed in Ḏū l-Ḥiǧǧa 378/March-April 989 (GCAL [*2: II 253 no. 2], Haddad 1971 [*272: 43 no. 2], Starr 2000 [*295: 338–340]).

Not only God's unity, but also the Trinity of His essential attributes can be established by logical necessity. Even the divine attributes acknowledged by Muslims converge on three – benevolent (*ǧawād*), wise (*ḥakīm*), and powerful (*qādir*). They are in fact different states (*aḥwāl*) of the one essence. Following a cosmological argument for God's existence, the author talks about essential attributes (*ṣifāt al-ḏāt*) which are predicated of the Creator, to wit: benevolence, wisdom, and power; from them the functional attributes (*ṣifāt al-fiʿl*) derive. Employing the intellect analogy for the Trinity (intellect, intellecting, intelligible), he justifies the symbolic expression used by Christian doctrine when naming the divine persons, referring to the use of language adopted in Scripture (Mt 7,6; 13,34–35) and by the Church Fathers (Gregory of Nazianzus, Pseudo-Dionysius the Areopagite). With even more determination than Yaḥyā Ibn ʿAdī, Ibn Zurʿa emphasizes that any attribute predicated of the divine being that is chosen by human reason and language must ultimately be inadequate; for this point he again refers to Gregory of Nazianzus.

3.3.4.1 *Answer to 12 Questions from Abū Ḥakīm Yūsuf Ibn al-Buḥayrī*

Composed in 387/997. The addressee, Ibn al-Buḥayrī of Mayyāfāriqīn, is mentioned in *Muntaḫab Ṣiwān al-ḥikma* [*156: 144 Dunlop; 335 Badawī]: 'al-Buḫārī'; there he asks Ibn Zurʿa how it is possible to know 'the point, the now, and unity' even though they do not fall under any of the ten categories (GCAL [*2: II 254 no. 4], Haddad 1971 [*272: 44 no. 4], Starr 2000 [*295: 344–349]).

1. Christ's historical existence. 2. Why did the Eternal create the world? (Answer: because of his perfect benevolence [*ǧūd*]). 7. The existence of the angels. (Answer: in addition to the beings of the noblest form, i.e. reason, but of mortal matter, God needed to create beings that combine the form of reason with the noblest, imperishable substrate). 8. The reason for the incarnation (*taʾannus*) of God's word. 9. God's Trinity (an outline of Ibn Zurʿa's doctrine of God's essence as thought thinking itself). 10. The immortality of the rational soul after its separation from the body (the rational soul has a separate existence, with reference to Plato and Aristotle; according to St. Paul, 1 Cor 15,12–19, Christ gives Himself up to death in the rationally justified knowledge that He has an everlasting home).

[al-Iǧāba] ʿan radd Abī l-Qāsim ʿAbd Allāh b. Aḥmad al-Balḫī ʿalā l-naṣārā fī kitābihi al-musammā Awāʾil al-adilla
Reply to the Refutation of the Christian Doctrine in the Book Awāʾil [also: ʿUyūn] al-adilla [fī uṣūl al-dīn] (Principles [or core issues] of the Proofs [concerning the foundations of religion]) by Abū l-Qāsim ʿAbd Allāh b. Aḥmad al-Balḫī

Composed in Ḏū l-Qaʿda 387/November–December 997) (GCAL [*2: II 254 no. 5], Starr 2000 [*295: 350–354]).

The treatise is addressed to Abū l-Qāsim al-Balḫī (d. 319/931), a leading Muʿtazilī theologian of the time (cf. van Ess 1985 [*294]). At the beginning of the text, three contentious points are marked out as the main differences between Christianity and Islam: 1. the Trinity – Ibn Zurʿa gives reasons for his distinction between God's one essence and the plurality of the essential states (*aḥwāl*) or attributes; 2. the alleged anthropomorphism (*tašbīh*) of the Christian concept of God – God does not share the corporeal nature of his creatures, but His creatures may participate in some of His attributes, e.g. in existence; 3. the prophethood of Muḥammad – this is rejected by the Christians on the grounds that with Christianity, God has already revealed the most perfect religion and the perfect moral law; hence he has also laid out the most excellent course of action for each of the three parts of the soul, as well as the disposition (*taqwīm*) of the lower faculties towards reason.

Maqāla ʿamilahā ilā Bišr b. Pinḥās
Epistle to Bišr b. Pinḥās

Composed 387/997. It is addressed to the Jew Bišr b. Pinḥās b. Šuʿayb al-Ḥāsib ('the calculator', i.e. a mathematician who conducts astronomical calculations).

According to Ibn Abī Uṣaybiʿa this is an 'epistle he dictated for one of his friends in 387; it concerns a few points in which he refutes the Jews. I found an epistle by Bišr b. Bīšī, also known as Ibn ʿAnāyā [or ʿUnāba? ʿAtābā?] al-Isrāʾīlī, in which he refutes ʿĪsā b. Isḥāq Ibn Zurʿa; to which the latter replies in this present epistle' (Ibn Abī Uṣaybiʿa [*158: I 236]; GCAL [*2: II 255 no. 6], Pines 1961 [*292]). The Jacobite author al-Muʾtaman Ibn al-ʿAssāl (d. ca. 658/1260), who inserts an excerpt into his theological *Maǧmūʿ*, calls him 'Bišr b. Bīsā, also known as Ibn ʿAtābā' (Starr 2000 [*295: 21]).

The inquirer and addressee, Bišr b. Pinḥās b. Šuʿayb, reports questions posed by other Jewish scholars as well, including Abū l-Ḫayr Dāwūd b. Mūsaǧ, who is also known from Abū Ḥayyān al-Tawḥīdī's *al-Muqābasāt* § 106, 466,4 (whereas the Abū l-Ḫayr mentioned there at § 42, 174,2 appears to be Ibn ʿAdī's pupil al-Ḥasan b. Suwār, also called Ibn al-Ḫammār; cf. § 7.4). The epistle has the purpose to convince the Jew of the truth of the Christian message, and possibly to convert him. (Text, translation and analysis in Starr 2000 [*295]).

The treatise is divided in four 'points of difference between us and the Jews' (*al-mawāḍiʿ allatī baynanā wa-bayna l-Yahūd*), and deals with the following questions:

1. On the abolition of the Mosaic law through Christian law. The law of nature (*sunna ṭabīʿiyya*) and the law of reason (*sunna ʿaqliyya*) are accompanied by the positive law (*sunna waḍʿiyya*) that has been instituted (*tawqīf*) by the Creator. The Jewish (and implicitly, the Islamic) law of justice (*sunnat al-ʿadl*) is presented as surpassed and abolished by the Christian law, which is the law of eminence (*sunnat al-tafaḍḍul*).

2. On the arrival of Christ the Messiah, as it was predicted by the prophets and announced by signs.

3. On God's unity and the Trinity. The author argues that it is valid to say: 'The Creator's essence (*ḏāt*) is one, but it is characterized by three different attributes (*ṣifāt*), which require a predication of plurality'. Notwithstanding the one single essence, several individually different predications are required, since attribution is different from essence. A second argument refers to the concept of God as thought thinking itself, being at the same time intellect, intellecting, and intelligible, which, in religious language, translates as 'benevolent', 'wise', and 'powerful'.

4. On the hypostatic union of divine and human nature in Christ. In Christ, two essences become one: a human, natural, temporal and created one (*ḏāt insāniyya*), and a divine, eternal, uncreated, atemporal and imperishable one (*ḏāt ilāhiyya*); He is constituted from the Eternal Son and the son born to Mary. The union (*ittiḥād, ittiṣāl*) of God and man is possible only in the Son, not in the Father, who is separate intellect, nor in the Holy Spirit, who is the absolute object of intellection (on the interpretation of the union in this text cf. Haddad 1971 [*272: 270–278]).

A further, appended question deals with the resurrection of the dead, in particular the general resurrection of all mankind; the author reports on a disputation with the Jew Abū l-Ḫayr Dāwūd b. Mūsaǧ (Pines 1961 [*292: 156 n. 10]).

The methods of proof employed in the text are called 'rational demonstration' (*qiyāsiyya ʿaqliyya*) and 'scriptural proof' (*kitābiyya ṣaḥafiyya*). Among the ancient personages called upon as witnesses, Galen appears several times (Pines 1961 [*292: 163–172]).

Maqāla fī l-Mabāḥiṯ al-arbaʿa ʿan al-ittiḥād allaḏī yaqūlu bihi l-naṣārā
On the Four Scientific Questions applied to the Union [of the three hypostases] in which the Christians Believe

Starr 2000 [*295: 360–364]. In the Alexandrian commentary tradition, the four questions (1) whether something is the case, (2) why it is the case, (3) whether a thing exists, and (4) what kind of thing it is (after Arist. *An. Post.* II 1, 89b24–5: Ζητοῦμεν δὲ τέτταρα, τὸ ὅτι, τὸ διότι, εἰ ἔστι, τί ἐστιν) are prefixed to the philosophical *prolegomena*. Here they are applied to the union of the two essences in Christ, following the conventional sequence of (1) existence, (2) essence, (3) cause, and (4) quality, and taking into account the various doctrines of the Nestorians, Melkites, and Jacobites. The author uses scriptural proofs (*adilla kitābiyya*) and syllogistic demonstrations (*adilla burhāniyya*), especially for the purpose of justifying the Monophysite doctrine.

3.4 *Doctrine*

In his role as translator of Aristotelian writings, as transmitter and teacher of logic, and as defender of Christian doctrine by means of philosophical concepts and logical analysis, Ibn Zurʿa follows in the footsteps of his teacher Yaḥyā Ibn ʿAdī. However, he directs his services more exclusively to the Christian faith in its dispute with the Islamic and Jewish communities, and takes up scriptural proofs and the (Neo-)Platonic conceptualization of theological topics found in the Church Fathers in a more consistent manner than Ibn ʿAdī.

As a teacher of Aristotelian logic and author of an elementary book on logic according to the *Organon*, Ibn Zurʿa remains within the framework, and on the grounds of the Alexandrian tradition. His choice to translate the *Sophistical Refutations* anew indicates how much importance he assigned to this work within the debate between philosophy and theology. Few works on natural philosophy are attested; a number of remarks reported by Abū Ḥayyān al-Tawḥīdī (e.g. *al-Muqābasāt* [*154: § 37] on the six types of movement after Arist. *Cat.* 14; *al-Imtāʿ* [*153: § 37, 132–136] with a few definitions of moral qualities) show him to be profoundly knowledgeable about Aristotle, but lacking Ibn ʿAdī's polemical bite.

In contrast to the propaedeutical handbooks written by Yaḥyā Ibn ʿAdī, Ibn al-Ḫammār, and Ibn al-Samḥ, Ibn Zurʿa's defence of apodeictic philosophy is decidedly meant to serve the application of logical methodology to theological questions. It shows 'that those who cultivate the sciences of logic and philosophy do not deserve to be accused of irreligiosity', and that reason is necessary to demonstrate the truth of religion.

Christian theology as a rational science. Like Ibn ʿAdī, Ibn Zurʿa defines the hypostases of the Christian Trinity, God Father, Son, and Holy Spirit (in the language of the Church Fathers: πρόσωπα, *personae*, Arabic *aqānīm*) as aspects of the one divine Spirit who thinks itself and is identical with itself (*ʿaql, ʿāqil, maʿqūl*; cf. also Haddad 1971 [*272: 180–197] based on Ibn Zurʿa, *Maqāla ilā Bišr b. Pinḥās*).

In terms of his philosophical conceptualization of the Trinitarian dogma in the tradition of the Nicene Council and the Cappadocian Fathers – where the Trinity is 'one substance, three hypostases', μία οὐσία, τρεῖς ὑποστάσεις – Ibn Zurʿa refines Ibn ʿAdī's account in some respects. The hypostases (persons) of the Trinity are defined as attributes (*ṣifāt*) of the divine essence (*ḏāt*). The attributes of the three hypostases are understood as states (*aḥwāl*) of the divine substance (*ǧawhar*) *qua* subject (*mawḍūʿ*) of thought; a hypostasis (*uqnūm*) is one, eternal substance, each having one attribute and each identical to the Godhead. It is pure intellect (according to Ibn ʿAdī, 'our teacher' [*171: 69]), and therefore – according to the ancient philosophers – simple. However, while the simple substance remains identical, each hypostasis is composed of the substance and of one of the three attributes: that of the Father (*qunūm al-ab*) is composed from the eternal substance (*al-ǧawhar al-azalī*) and the element of fatherhood (*maʿnā l-ubuwwa*). The substrate of the intellect corresponds to the substance in the Father, his 'fatherhood' to the power of intellectual representation (*al-quwwa ʿalā taṣawwur sāʾir al-maʿqūlāt* [*171: 70–71]). The aspect of the person-hypostasis thus relates to the divine substance as an essentially concomitant accident (*lazimahu*) (*al-Iǧāba ʿan radd al-Balḫī* [*171: 53–54]).

In his discussion of the 'attributes' of the persons of the Trinity, Ibn Zurʿa – like Ibn ʿAdī before him – takes up the debate about attributes familiar from *kalām* (where we also find the difference between *ṣifāt al-ḏāt* and *ṣifāt al-fiʿl*, just as in the *Risāla ṣannafahā fī maʿānī saʾalahu ʿanhā baʿḍ iḫwānihi* [*171: 13–14]), and connects it with the Aristotelian doctrine of substance (Starr 2000 [*295: 40]). However, we are not dealing with inherent accidents of the 'eternal substance', but with inseparable states (*aḥwāl*, also aspects, *ǧihāt*). The names of the three hypostases God Father, Son, and Holy Spirit are, like the traditional epithets 'benevolent, 'wise', and 'powerful' (*ǧawād, ḥakīm, qādir*), nothing but metaphors of religious language, which can never be entirely appropriate. This in contrast to the concepts of philosophical language: the close relationship between intellect and intellecting justifies their designation as 'Father' and 'Son', while the 'Spirit' denotes the intelligible as 'something that goes forth' (*al-šayʾ al-mufāriq*) and 'is, as it were, outside of the one that possesses spirit' (*kaʾannahu ḫāriǧ ʿan ḏī l-rūḥ wa-huwa abʿad minhu*), even though the intelligible is not really separated from the intellect. Ultimately, no linguistic expression can convey the perfect simplicity of the divine being [*171: 9–10. 17–18].

Ethics. Ibn Zurʿa's ethical propaedeutics are based on Plato's soul-body dualism as also found in al-Kindī and al-Rāzī. He, however, presents it as the doctrine of Christian thinkers (according to Abū Ḥayyān al-Tawḥīdī [*152: 70]). In order to return (*maʿād*, to eternal spiritual life), the rational soul needs to liberate itself from its imprisonment by the body's desires and affections. For Ibn Zurʿa, ethics as defined by Plato and Aristotle is yet another subject that has found its highest perfection in Christianity. Religion places the positive law (*sunna waḍʿiyya*) that has been granted by God (*tawqīf*) above the natural law (*sunna ṭabīʿiyya*) and the law of reason (*sunna ʿaqliyya*). The natural ethics of self-preservation and desire-satisfaction does not allow people to reach moral perfection and true happiness (this topic is also discussed in an excerpt from the so-called *Summa Alexandrinorum* which was translated by Ibn Zurʿa [see pp. 471–472 above]). The law established by revelation acts as an instruction in the right way to live for those who are unable to recognize the good by deducing it from the law of reason. The Mosaic law is but a first step to moral perfection, replacing nature's rule that the strongest prevail with a law of equality (*musāwāt*). Ultimately, the Jewish (and implicitly, the Islamic) 'law of justice' (*sunnat al-ʿadl*) is surpassed and abolished by the Christan 'law of eminence (*sunnat al-tafaḍḍul*; a different interpretation is found in Pines 1961 [*292: 175 with n. 1]: overflowing 'grace'). This is borne out not only by scriptural proof but also by rational demonstration (Starr 2000 [*295: 26–33]; cf. also Pines 1961 [*292]). Given His benevolence, God is bound to grant mankind the highest possible good. Nothing but the teaching of the Messiah can convey the highest virtues of each of the three parts of the soul (i.e. the appetitive, the spirited, and the rational faculty of the soul), and in particular of the rational soul, as well as the subordination of the non-rational parts of the soul to reason.

4 Ibn al-Ḫammār

Gerhard Endress

4.1 Primary Sources – 4.2 Life – 4.3 Works – 4.4 Doctrine

4.1 *Primary Sources*

4.1.1 Bio-bibliographical Testimonies [*201–*209] – 4.1.2 Redaction and Annotation of Greek Works in Arabic Translation [*215] – 4.1.3 Edited Works [*221–*223] – 4.1.4 Other Greek and Arabic Sources [*228–*234]

4.1.1 Bio-bibliographical Testimonies

201 Ibn al-Nadīm, Abū l-Farağ Muḥammad b. Isḥāq (d. 380/990). *Kitāb al-Fihrist* [composed 377/988]. – Ed. by Gustav Flügel, August Müller and Johannes Roediger, 2 vols. Leipzig, 1871–1872, 265. – Repr. Beirut, 1964, Frankfurt a.M., 2005. – Ed. by Riḍā Tağaddud. Tehran, 1350 h.š./1971, 323. – Ed. by Ayman Fu'ād Sayyid, 2 vols (I\1–2 - II\1–2). London, 1430/2009. – Engl. transl. by Bayard Dodge, *The Fihrist of al-Nadīm*, 2 vols. New York, 1970.

202 al-Tawḥīdī, Abū Ḥayyān ʿAlī b. Muḥammad (d. 414/1023). *Risālat al-Ḥayāt*. – Ed. by Ibrāhīm Kaylānī, in: *Ṯalāṯ rasāʾil li-Abī Ḥayyān al-Tawḥīdī: Trois épîtres d'Abū Ḥaiyān at-Tauḥīdī*. Damascus, 1951, 51–80, esp. 70–71. – French transl. by Claude Audebert, "La Risālat al-Ḥayāt d'Abū Ḥayyān al-Tawḥīdī." *Bulletin d'études orientales* 8 (1963/64): 147–195, esp. 165–166.

203 Abū Ḥayyān al-Tawḥīdī. *Al-Muqābasāt*. – Ed. by Muḥammad Tawfīq Ḥusayn. Baghdad, 1970, § 42,174.

204 Abū Ḥayyān al-Tawḥīdī. *Kitāb al-Imtāʿ wa-l-muʾānasa*. – Ed. by Aḥmad Amīn and Aḥmad al-Zayn. Cairo, 1939–1944, vol. 1, 33.

205 al-Bīrūnī, Abū l-Rayḥān Muḥammad b Aḥmad (*362/973, d. ca. 442/1050). *Kitāb al-Ṣaydana fī l-ṭibb*. – Ed. by ʿAbbās Zaryāb. Tehran, 1370 h.š./1991, 29, 31.

206 *Ṣiwān al-ḥikma* [ascribed to Abū Sulaymān al-Siǧistānī]. – Excerpts ed. by Douglas Morton Dunlop, *The Muntakhab Ṣiwān al-ḥikmah of Abū Sulaimān as-Sijistānī*. The Hague, 1979, § 283,144–145; § 303,156–158. – Ed. by ʿAbd al-Raḥmān Badawī, *Ṣiwān al-ḥikma wa-ṯalāṯ rasāʾil taʾlīf Abū Sulaymān al-Siǧistānī*. Tehran, 1974, 335–336. 353–355.

207 al-Bayhaqī, Ẓahīr al-Dīn Abū l-Ḥasan ʿAlī b. Zayd Ibn Funduq (d. 565/1169–1170). *Tatimmat Ṣiwān al-ḥikma*. – Ed. by Muḥammad Šafīʿ, fasc. 1: Arabic text. Lahore, 1935, 13. – Ed. by Muḥammad Kurd ʿAlī, *Taʾrīḫ ḥukamāʾ al-islām*. Damascus, 1365/1946, 26–28. – Repr. 1396/1976. – Engl. transl by Max Meyerhof, "ʿAlī al-Bayhaqī's *Tatimmat Ṣiwān al-ḥikma*: A Biographical Work on Learned Men of the Islam." *Osiris* 8 (1948): 122–217, at 138–139.

208 Ibn al-Qifṭī, Ǧamāl al-Dīn ʿAlī b. Yūsuf (d. 646/1248). *Taʾrīḫ al-ḥukamāʾ* [*Iḫbār al-ʿulamāʾ bi-aḫbār al-ḥukamāʾ*, epitome by Muḥammad b. ʿAlī al-Zawzanī]. – Ed. by Julius Lippert, *Ibn al-Qifṭī's Taʾrīh al-ḥukamāʾ*. Leipzig, 1903, 164.

209 Ibn Abī Uṣaybiʿa, Muwaffaq al-Dīn Aḥmad b. al-Qāsim (d. 668/1270). *ʿUyūn al-anbāʾ fī ṭabaqāt al-aṭibbāʾ*. – Ed. by August Müller, 2 vols. Cairo, 1299/1882, Königsberg, 1884, vol. 1, 322–323.

4.1.2 Redaction and Annotation of Greek Works in Arabic Translation

215 [Glosses on Arist. *Cat.*:] *Les Catégories d'Aristote dans leurs versions syro-arabes*. – Ed. by Khalil Georr. Beirut, 1948, 149–182 [French transl.], 361–386 [Arabic text]. – Ed. by Farīd Ǧabr, Ǧirār Ǧihāmī and Rafīq al-ʿAǧam, *al-Naṣṣ al-kāmil li-Manṭiq Arisṭū*. Beirut, 1999, 15–96.

4.1.3 Edited Works

221 *Maqāla fī anna dalīl Yaḥyā al-Naḥwī ʿalā ḥadaṯ al-ʿālam awlā bi-l-qabūl min dalīl al-mutakallimīn aṣlan*. – Ed. by ʿAbd al-Raḥmān Badawī, in: *Al-Aflāṭūniyya al-muḥdaṯa ʿind al-ʿArab*. Cairo, 1955, 243–247.

222 *Maqāla fī Ṣifat al-raǧul al-faylasūf*, MS Istanbul, Ragıp Paşa, 1463, fols 63^b-65^a. – French transl. by Bernhard Lewin, "L'idéal antique du philosophe dans la tradition arabe: Un traité d'éthique du philosophe bagdadien Ibn Suwār." *Lychnos* 1954/55 (Uppsala 1955): 267–284.

223 *Maqāla fī l-Āṯār al-mutaḫayyila fī l-ǧaww*. – Ed. by Paul Lettinck, *Aristotle's Meteorology and its Reception in the Arab World, with an edition and translation of Ibn Suwār's Treatise on Meteorological Phenomena and Ibn Bājja's Commentary on the Meteorology*. Leiden, 1999.

4.1.4 Other Greek and Arabic Sources

228 *Theologia Aristotelis: Kitāb Arisṭāṭālīs al-musammā bi-Uṯūlūǧiyā wa-huwa l-qawl ʿalā l-rubūbiyya.* – Ed. by Friedrich Dieterici, *Die sogenannte Theologie des Aristoteles.* Leipzig, 1882. – Ed. by ʿAbd al-Raḥmān Badawī, *Aflūṭīn ʿind al-ʿArab.* Cairo, 1955, 1–164. – Engl. transl. by Geoffrey Lewis, in: *Plotini Opera.* Ed. by Paul Henry and Hans-Rudolf Schwyzer, II: Enneades IV–V; Plotiniana Arabica ad codd. fidem Anglice vertit G. Lewis. Paris, Brussels, 1959.

229 *Themistii Orationes.* – Ed. by Wilhelm Dindorf. Leipzig, 1832. – Repr. Hildesheim, 1961.

230 Proclus. *The Elements of Theology: A Revised Text with Translation and Commentary.* – Ed. by Eric Robertson Dodds. Oxford, 1963 (2nd ed.). – Arab.: *Proclus Arabus: Zwanzig Abschnitte aus der Institutio theologica in arabischer Übersetzung, eingeleitet, herausgegeben und erklärt von Gerhard Endress.* Beirut, Wiesbaden, 1973.

231 *The Greek Commentaries on Plato's Phaedo*, vol. 1: *Olympiodorus.* – Ed. by Leendert Gerrit Westerink. Amsterdam, Oxford, New York, 1976.

232 *Simplicii in Aristotelis Categorias commentarium.* – Ed. by Carolus Kalbfleisch. Berlin, 1907 [Commentaria in Aristotelem Graeca VIII].

233 *Simplicii in Aristotelis Physicorum libros quattuor priores commentaria.* – Ed. by Hermannus Diels. Berlin, 1882 [Commentaria in Aristotelem Graeca IX].

234 *Averroes' De substantia orbis: Critical Edition of the Hebrew text, with English Translation and Commentary by Arthur Hyman.* Cambridge, Mass., 1986.

4.2 *Life*

Abū l-Ḫayr al-Ḥasan b. Suwār b. Bābā b. Bihnām Ibn al-Ḫammār (born 331/942, died after 407/1017) grew up in Baghdad. He studied Aristotelian logic and Christian theology with Yaḥyā Ibn ʿAdī (§ 7.2), the head of the school of the Baghdad Aristotelians. Like Ibn ʿAdī, he was a Monophysite (*pace* GCAL [*313: II 156], of Nestorian denomination; cf. Platti 1983 [*333: 137 n. 1]).

His medical studies resulted in a considerable number of (nowadays lost) writings, and he seems to have earned his living as a physician. When he was already advanced in years he joined the service of the Ḫwārazm-Šāh Abū l-ʿAbbās Maʾmūn II of Gurgānǧ (regn. 399–407/1009–1017), to whom he dedicated his physiological work *On Man's Physique and the Composition of the Parts of His Body* (*Fī Ḫalq al-insān wa-tarkīb aʿḍāʾihi*). When Maḥmūd of Ġazna conquered Ḫwārazm in 407/1017, he shared the same fate as the astronomer al-Bīrūnī and other scholars: he was deported to Ġazna (al-Bayhaqī [*207*: 26–27 Kurd ʿAlī]), where he spent his last years at the court of the conqueror and is said to have converted to Islam (al-Bayhaqī [**207*: 26 Kurd ʿAlī]). Amongst his pupils in medicine as well as in philosophy was the Iranian Abū l-Faraǧ Ibn Hindū (§ 5.5; cf. Ḫalīfāt 1995 [*318: 81–87]).

4.3 *Works*

4.3.1 Transmission and Annotation of Greek Philosophy – 4.3.2 Ethical Propaedeutics – 4.3.3 Physics – 4.3.4 Christian Apologetics – 4.3.5 Medicine

4.3.1 Transmission and Annotation of Greek Philosophy

Aristotle: Organon

MS Paris, Bibliothèque nationale, ar. 2346 provides a record of the Arabic version of Aristotle's *Organon* reflecting the tradition of Yaḥyā Ibn ʿAdī's school. The direct source of the manuscript containing Aristotle's *Categories, On Interpretation, Prior Analytics, Posterior Analytics, Topics,* and *Sophistical Refutations,* was a copy produced by Ibn al-Ḫammār from the personal copies of Yaḥyā Ibn ʿAdī and his pupil ʿĪsā Ibn Zurʿa. It is, effectively, a 'critical edition' of the *Organon* according to the state of knowledge of Ibn ʿAdī's school, and is accompanied by numerous annotations that critically discuss both text and translation (at times on the basis of the Syriac versions), and explanatory glosses based on Ibn al-Ḫammār's lectures. (Walzer 1953/²1962 [*326: 70–84], Hugonnard-Roche 1992 [*338]).

Porphyry: Isagoge (Introduction). Aristotle: Categories

Ibn Abī Uṣaybiʿa [*209: 323] mentions among Ibn al-Ḫammār's introductory and logical works:

a) a literal commentary on Porphyry's *Isagoge* (*Tafsīr Īsāġūǧī mašrūḥ*), and a shorter commentary (*Tafsīr Īsāġūǧī muḫtaṣar*);
b) *Taqāsīm Īsāġūǧī wa-Qāṭāġūriyās li-Al[l]īnūs al-Iskandarānī, mimmā naqalahu min al-suryānī, wa-šaraḥahu ʿalā ṭarīq al-ḥawāšī*, i.e. a structured epitome of Porphyry's *Isagoge* and Aristotle's *Categories*, translated from a Syriac version of the Greek commentator Allīnūs' (Hellenos?) text (only known from the Arabic tradition), together with commenting glosses by Ibn al-Ḫammār. Ibn Abī Uṣaybiʿa adds that he has copied the work himself from Ibn al-Ḫammār's autograph (on Allīnūs and the testimony concerning him cf. Rosenthal 1972 [*331: 339]).

Ibn al-Ḫammār's glosses on the *Categories* (ed. Georr [*215]), contained in MS Paris, Bibliothèque nationale, ar. 2346 provide the following:

(a) an introduction into the *Categories* modelled on the *Kephalaia* of the Alexandrian *Prolegomena*; e.g. subject, benefit, disposition and structure, method (cf. Hein 1985 [*334: 385–386]);
(b) definitions and explications of basic terms: *maqūla* = κατηγορία; *al-muttafiqa asmāʾuhā* = ὁμώνυμα and their subdivisions; *tuqāl* = λέγεται *Cat.* 1a6, *qawl* = λόγος *Cat.* 1a7; *al-mutawāṭiʾa asmāʾuhā* = συνώνυμα, *al-muštaqqa asmāʾuhā* = παρώνυμα;
(c) on *Cat.* 2, 1a20–1b9 τὰ ὄντα, οὐσία, συμβεβηκός: explanations concerning the position of the essential attributes in relation to substance, based on the author's

treatise *Fī Ṣūrat al-nār* (see below); furthermore numerous critical annotations on text and translation.

4.3.2 Ethical Propaedeutics

Maqāla fī Ṣifat al-rağul al-faylasūf
Description of the [true] Philospher

An introduction to the philosophical way of life in the spirit of Plato's intellectualistic ethics, with close references to Plato, *Rep.* 485–486 and the Platonic motifs from ethical propaedeutics and wisdom literature, here from the tradition of the Neoplatonic authors of Late Antiquity and their Arabic recipients (Lewin 1954/55 [*327]).

Philosophy is love of wisdom; wisdom (*ḥikma*) is knowledge of the things as they really are. The true philosopher is characterized by his rational soul's unconditional quest for truth (cf. Plato, *Rep.* 485a–c). To him, satisfaction of bodily desires merely serves self-preservation (*Rep.* 485d). In respect of all other objects of bodily and material appetites, he shows temperance (cf. Plato, *Rep.* 485e). Animated by his desire to know 'divine and human matters' (one of the traditional definitions of philosophy, cf. Plato, *Rep.* 486a), he uses both his intellectual and his moral excellence towards that end, in small just as in large matters. The philosopher's wisdom is perfect virtue, towards which he may advance either by living as a recluse, away from society, or by associating only with people of the highest spiritual qualities. In his seclusion he will remain unaffected by the struggle of passions and material desires; in his state of abstemiousness, his soul will be able to see the forms in their true reality (*ṣuwar al-ašyā' 'alā ḥaqā'iqihā*) as if in a polished mirror in bright daylight (cf. Plato, *Phaedr.* 255d). Examples of this way of life have been provided by Socrates, Diogenes, and other ascetics among the philosophers. However, the virtues of the soul may also be strengthened by associating with great minds, just as bright sunlight enhances the reflection in a mirror. This is confirmed by the authority of such philosophers as Plato and Aristotle. If a philosopher is unable to earn the favour of a ruler and an appropriate position in his service, he should nevertheless earn his keep in a dignified manner and in the service of the public good; in this way he can control and govern the sphere of his influence himself. An example of such an occupation is that of the farmer (recommended also by Socrates), for it creates the preconditions for a noble, frugal and selfless life. (Lewin 1954/55 [*327: 278–279] here refers to sayings ascribed to Socrates in Xenophon's *Oeconomica* and in other Hellenistic authors; also in particular to Themistius' speech in the praise of agriculture, *Orationes*, ed. Dindorf [*229]).

4.3.3 Physics

Maqāla fī anna dalīl Yaḥyā al-Naḥwī ʿalā ḥadaṯ al-ʿālam awlā bi-l-qabūl min dalīl al-mutakallimīn aṣlan
That John Philoponus' Proof for the Createdness of the World is Rather to be Accepted than that of the [*Islamic*] *Theologians*

That the world has a beginning in time is argued for by the Islamic theologians (*mutakallimūn*) as follows: the body, – in the sense of a three-dimensional substance – is inseparable from contingently arising affections (*ḥawādiṯ*) or accidents (*aʿrāḍ*), and does not precede them; anything that is inseparable from contingent phenomena is itself contingent; hence every body is contingent. In order to refute this, Ibn al-Ḫammār asserts (a) that it is not necessary to assume a continuous succession of accidents – in the case of the body, instances of movement and rest – that are created in each instance (as in the case of the celestial body with its eternal circular movement, and the body of the earth, which is eternally at rest); (b) that the substance of the body can exist without accidents, even if accidents cannot exist without a bodily substrate; (c) that it is still possible for the succession of accidents to proceed eternally, without a beginning in time, even if one were to assume inseparable, inherent accidents. The fact that the argument is incorrect, in Ibn al-Ḫammār's view, does not suggest that the hypothesis itself is wrong; just that John Philoponus' (Arab. Yaḥyā al-Naḥwī) argument is to be preferred, since it is not based on accidents, but on essential features: every body is limited; the world is a body; hence the world is limited. Every limited body possesses limited power, whereas the power of unlimited essences is unlimited; hence the world is not eternal (cf. Joh. Philop. *Against Aristotle*, in Simplicius, *Comm. in Arist. Phys.*, 1327 Diels [*233]). 'Contingent' (*muḥdaṯ*) can be understood either in the sense of a temporal, or in the sense of an atemporal relation of states; here it is to be understood in the sense that there is a cause that brings about the existence of the substance in question as opposed to its non-existence. In this sense Aristotle, too, is said by Ibn al-Ḫammār to describe the world as contingent, insofar as the Creator has brought it into existence – 'He spoke, and it came into being' (thus alluding to the Quranic statement as being in harmony with Aristotle) – not in temporal succession as in a natural process of generation (*takwīn ṭabīʿī*) which is preceded temporally by something else, but 'in one stroke' (*dufʿatan wāḥidatan*; Lewin 1964 [*329: 87] finds this expression in Pseudo-Aristotle, *Uṯūlūǧiyā* X 2 [*228*: 142 Dieterici; 139 Badawī], cf. Plot. *Enn.* VI 7, 2, 53 ὁμοῦ, for the creation of the First Intellect together with the forms that subsist in it). Together with the movement of the sphere, the very act of creation also creates time as the measure of movement. The Creator is prior not in time, but in rank: thus Proclus says that in relation to the Creator, 'eternal' means an eternity beyond time (*dahr*, αἰών);

whereas in relation to the world, 'eternal' is to be understood as referring to the temporality of becoming (Procl. *Elem. theol*. [*230: prop. 5 Dodds; Arab. Endress: 271]). On the treatise, cf. Lewin 1964 [*329], Wolfson 1976 [*332: 374–382]; on the problem as it is discussed in Yaḥyā Ibn ʿAdī, see Pines 1955 [*328: 110–118].

Maqāla fī l-Āṯār al-mutaḫayyila fī l-ǧaww [al-ḥādiṯa ʿan al-buḫār al-māʾī, wa-hiya l-hāla wa-l-qaws wa-l-šumūs wa-l-quḍbān]
Treatise on the Phenomena that are Imagined in the Atmosphere [due to watery vapour, i.e. halo, (rain-)bow, (par-)helia, and (light) shafts]

In order to explain physical, and in particular meteorological phenomena, first their causes and principles (*ʿilal wa-mabādiʾ*) ought to be presented, starting with the most remote cause and finishing with the proximate one (*causa proxima*). Following Aristotle's *On Generation and Corruption*, the author explains that the four elements of the sublunar world, during the process of changing into each other, pass through an intermediate state which invariably is a form of vapour, either a smoky vapour (as when earth is turned into fire), or a watery vapour (as when water changes into air). The phenomena discussed in the work are all based on watery vapour. Referring to Aristotle, Nicolaus of Damascus (*De Aristotelis philosophia*, book VI?; cf. Drossaart Lulofs 1965 [*330: 11. 12–13]), and to Olympiodorus' *In Aristotelis meteorologica*, the author explains the phenomena in question as imaginary perceptions (*ḫayāl*) which result when the visual power (*al-quwwa al-bāṣira*) is reflected (*inʿikās*) back from a cloud onto a luminous object. They are realized in various forms depending on differences in the refraction (*inkisār*) of the visual ray according to the positions of the cloud, the luminous object, and the observer in relation to each other (Lettinck 1999 [*341: 10. 312–379]).

Taṣaffuḥ mā ǧarā bayna Abī Zakariyyāʾ Yaḥyā Ibn ʿAdī wa-bayna Abī Isḥāq Ibrāhīm Ibn Bakkūs fī ṣūrat al-nār wa-tabyīn fasād mā ḏahaba ilayhi Abū Sulaymān Muḥammad b. Ṭāhir fī ṣuwar al-usṭuqussāt
Examination of the Discussion between Abū Zakariyyāʾ Yaḥyā Ibn ʿAdī and Abū Isḥāq Ibrāhīm Ibn Bakkūs about the Form of Fire, along with an Explanation of the Invalidity of the Views of Abū Sulaymān Muḥammad b. Ṭāhir (al-Siǧistānī) on the Forms of the Elements

This work, which is mentioned by Ibn Abī Uṣaybiʿa [*209: 323,17], is lost, as is Ibn ʿAdī's treatise on the topic (cf. § 7.2); the author's glosses on the *Categories*, however, preserve a summary of his argument [*215: 373–377 Georr] 373,20.

Concerning the essential qualities of the elements, al-Ḥasan b. Suwār holds the view that is prevalent in the Greek commentaries on the *Categories*, i.e. that they are not inseparable accidents – the position taken by Yaḥyā Ibn ʿAdī – but part of the substance. In his glosses on Aristotle's *Categories* [*215: 376,9–377,15 Georr], he includes a long quotation from Simpl. *In Cat.* [*232: 48,11–49,8] relating to this point. It is based on Porphyry's interpretation, which supports Ibn Suwār's view (cf. also Porphyry, *In Cat.* 95,2–8. 99,8; Ammon. *In Cat.* 461,4). The same problem is discussed in a treatise entitled *Aǧwibat al-masāʾil al-wārida min balad al-šayḫ al-fāḍil al-ḥakīm Abī l-Ḫayr al-Ḥasan b. Suwār*, MS Damascus, Ẓāhiriyya 4871 ʿāmm, fol. 123ᵇ. 39ᵇ, lines 1–15.

4.3.4 Christian Apologetics

Kitāb al-Wifāq bayna raʾy al-falāsifa wa-l-naṣārā
On the Agreement between the View of the Philosophers and that of the Christians

This treatise is the only one among Ibn al-Ḫammār's writings in which Yaḥyā Ibn ʿAdī's apologetic tradition manifests itself (Ibn Abī Uṣaybiʿa [*209: 323,7]; GCAL [*313: II 156]; according to Paul Sbath: *Al-Fihris. Catalogue de manuscrits arabes* [Cairo 1938–1940] no. 297, 2258, preserved together with a further treatise on the Trinity in a manuscript whose current whereabouts are unknown).

4.3.5 Medicine

Ibn al-Ḫammār's medical writings are lost to us. Among the works mentioned in bibliographical sources is a treatise on the examination of the physician (*Maqāla fī Imtiḥān al-aṭibbāʾ*), composed for the Ḫwarazm-Šāh Abū l-ʿAbbās Maʾmūn II b. Maʾmūn (Ibn Abī Uṣaybiʿa [*209: 323]), and a *Kitāb fī Ḫalq al-insān wa-tarkīb aʿḍāʾihi* (*On Man's Physique and the Composition of the Parts of His Body*, Ibn Abī Uṣaybiʿa, ibid.). In addition, Ibn al-Ḫammār is to be credited with the explications on the *Summaria Alexandrinorum* of the Galenic works which his pupil Ibn Hindū integrated into his work *Miftāḥ al-ṭibb*, making use of his teacher's translation (cf. § 5.5).

In his *Kitāb al-Ṣaydana*, al-Bīrūnī quotes from Ibn al-Ḫammār's glosses on the *Hypomnema* (*Kunnāš*) by Paul of Aegina (al-Bīrūnī [*205: 29,14. 31,13]), and also evaluates his *Kitāb al-Aġḏiya* [*205: Index s.v.]. In *Kitāb al-Ṣaydana* [*205: 536] as well as in *Kitāb al-Ǧamāhir fī maʿrifat al-ǧawāhir* (cf. Ullmann 1970 [*316: 85]) al-Bīrūnī mentions a translation or annotation by Abū l-Ḫayr of the medical handbook composed by Aetius of Amida.

4.4 *Doctrine*

Ibn al-Ḫammār was an Aristotelian, following in the footsteps of his teacher Yaḥyā Ibn ʿAdī (§ 7.2). For him, the concepts of Aristotle's doctrine of the categories and of his hermeneutics, together with the methodology of syllogistical demonstration, make it possible to understand and solve philosophical problems. Philosophy's claim to authority is based on their universal validity, especially with regard to those questions that are contested between Aristotelians and theologians, and between Christians and Muslims. In respect of the question whether the knowledge of God was necessary or acquired by deduction (a question that was controversial among Islamic theologians), Abū Ḥayyān al-Tawḥīdī quotes Ibn al-Ḫammār as saying: 'It is necessary from the perspective of reason, but a deduction from the perspective of sense perception; each object of knowledge is determined either by reason on the basis of intelligibles, or by sense perception on the basis of the perceptible, and thus leads us from the apparent to the hidden' [according to the formula for inductive proofs familiar from Islamic law and *kalām*: *qiyās al-šāhid ʿalā l-ġāʾib*] (*al-Muqābasāt* [*203: § 42, 174], based on this *Ṣiwān al-ḥikma* [*206: 156 Dunlop; 353 Badawī]).

Ethical propaedeutics. With his treatise on the philosophical life Ibn al-Ḫammār follows the Platonic ideal of the rational soul that is guided towards the contemplation of truth by temperance (σωφροσύνη). In this, he relies more closely on Plato's *Republic* and *Phaedrus* than did his predecessors (al-Kindī, Abū Bakr al-Rāzī) and contemporaries (cf. § 7.2 on Yaḥyā Ibn ʿAdī, § 7.5 on Ibn al-Samḥ, § 5.4 on Miskawayh). Man's composite nature places him in the world of the senses, but he may gain perfection through wisdom: the realization that he owes his being to the intelligible One will free him from the fear of death; and it is death which deprives him of the ability to perceive himself as a composite being (according to Abū Ḥayyān al-Tawḥīdī, *Risālat al-Ḥayāt* [*202: 70; transl. Audebert 165–166]. The philosophical life does not preclude an active life, as long as it preserves its self-sufficiency, as it would be the case with the self-reliant life of the farmer; however, it is not as a philospher-king that the philosopher can be of service to society, but at best through gaining favour with the noble elite.

Logic and epistemology. Of this part of Ibn al-Ḫammār's work we only possess glosses on the *Organon* and treatises on individual questions. The introduction to Aristotle's *Categories* is closely connected to the *Prolegomena* of the Alexandrian commentaries from the school of Ammonius and Olympiodorus. One topic is of more consequence than the others: the question of the ontological status that ought to be assigned to essential accidents, which was discussed between Yaḥyā Ibn ʿAdī, Ibrāhīm Ibn Bakkūs and Abū Sulaymān al-Siǧistānī in the context of the definition of 'in the substrate' (ἐν ὑποκειμένῳ) (Arist. *Cat.* 2, 1a24–25). Ibn al-Ḫammār restates it, together with his own evaluation of the problem, in a work entitled *On the Form of Fire* [*215: 373–377 Georr, esp. 373,20]. Siding with Porphyry and most of the older commentators, and against Ibn ʿAdī, Ibn al-Ḫammār regards the essential properties of a substance (συμπληρωτικὰ τῆς οὐσίας), like the heat of fire, as a part of the substance (ὡς μέρος τῆς οὐσίας). It seems Yaḥyā Ibn ʿAdī held that they inhered in the substance as in a substrate (ὡς ἐν ὑποκειμένῳ, i.e. as an inseparable accident, perhaps in order to support his Monophysite view of the Trinity as three hypostases of one substance, which in turn would have served to defend Christian monotheism. The question reappears in a different context within the dispute about the temporal creation of the world (see below).

Natural philosophy and cosmology. Within natural philosophy, Ibn al-Ḫammār again remains firmly on Aristotelian ground, basing himself on Aristotelian doctrines regarding principles, elements, and movement. His small treatise on optical phenomena in the sublunar atmosphere is remarkable mainly because of his choice to deal with a topic that was barely ever dealt with between al-Kindī and Ibn al-Hayṯam.

The problem of the temporal creation of the world is connected to a dispute which first emerged between the various schools of Alexandrian Aristotelianism, and later was carried on between philosophers on the one hand and adherents of the Christian or Islamic doctrine of creation on the other. The question of creation is the point concerning which the Neoplatonist commentators on Aristotle especially insist on the unity of philosophical truth, on the harmony between Plato and Aristotle. This is the expression of an attitude of compromise, which may not exactly propagate philosophy as a scientific interpretation of monotheistic religion, but nevertheless makes this role available to it as an option. This tendency had been prepared by Aristotelian commentators such as Themistius, but most notably by Porphyry, and in particular by his work Περὶ τοῦ μίαν εἶναι τὴν Πλάτωνος καὶ Ἀριστοτέλους αἵρεσιν (*On the School of Plato and Aristotle Being One*). The topos of this Alexandrian 'philosophy of compromise' (cf. Westerink 1976 [**231*: 24–25]) then shows up in the *prolegomena* of the commentaries on the *Categories*, within the framework of an introduction to Aristotle: Aristotle's First Intellect is at the same time final cause and efficient cause, and is identified with the demiurge of Plato's *Timaeus*. The Arabs knew that Ammonius made God, i.e. Aristotle's unmoved mover, the efficient cause of the universe. While Arabic Aristotelians since al-Fārābī argued for the unity of the Aristotelian world view and hence for eternal creation, the early Islamic authors (al-Kindī) and the Christians of the Baghdad school in the 4th/10th century sided with John Philoponus' refutation of the eternity of the world. Both his *Against Proclus* and his *Against Aristotle* were known in Arabic translations; Ibn ʿAdī's school furthermore transmitted large parts of Philoponus' commentary on Aristotle's *Physics* (cf. § 7.5 on Ibn al-Samḥ). Two of his arguments for the contingency of creation remain part of the discussion: the first argues that the present cannot possibly be preceded by an infinite series of events; the second argues that a finite body cannot have infinite power, and hence has the possibility of non-existence (passing away), which is why it could not have possibly existed eternally *ex parte ante* (cf. Davidson 1987 [*336: 86–116] on the reception of Philoponus, in particular by al-Kindī and the Jewish theologian Saʿadya).

The same argument is discussed in Yaḥyā Ibn ʿAdī's replies to questions posed by the Jewish scholar Ibn Abī Saʿīd al-Mawṣilī. Ibn ʿAdī dismisses Philoponus' position, pointing out that even though Aristotle (*Phys.* VIII 10) speaks about the limited power of a finite body, he does not rule out that this body could be of infinite duration, as long as it remains under the influence of an infinite efficient cause (see Pines 1955 [*328: 114–115]; on sources and context cf. Davidson 1987 [*336: 36] (Philoponus), on the further discussion in Ibn Rušd, *De substantia orbis* et al., cf. Hyman [*234], Davidson 1987 [*336: 321–331], Endress 1995 [*340]).

Ibn al-Ḫammār agrees with Philoponus' argument and declares it as preferable to the line of argument taken by the theologians: a flawed argument must not be allowed to stand in the way of truth. The argument he refers to (without associating it with a specific theologian) is based on *kalām* physics as it was represented (perhaps under the influence of Philoponus?) by the Muʿtazilī Abū l-Huḏayl (d. 235/849), later by ʿAbd al-Ǧabbār (d. 415/1025) and the Ašʿarite al-Bāqillānī (d. 403/1013) and others. It deduces the temporal creation of the corporeal world from the contingency of the accidents (*aʿrāḍ*) that constitute every body (van Ess 1992 [*337: III 229–232]; cf. also Davidson 1987 [*336: 134–143]). In his argument against the Muslim theologian, Ibn al-Ḫammār denies that the argument has any force against the possibility of an infinite sequence of contingencies *a parte ante*, and objects in particular to the assumption that accidents are inseparable (*lā yanfakk*) from the substance. As he has shown elsewhere in a comment on Arist. *Cat.* 2, essential attributes are not really accidents, but are part of the substance. In an original contribution to the topic, Ibn al-Ḫammār shows familiarity with the Pseudo-Aristotelian Neoplatonic writings: creation takes place 'in one stroke'; along with the origination of the corporeal world and its physical processes of motion it simultaneously creates time, the measure of motion.

5 Ibn al-Samḥ

Gerhard Endress

5.1 Primary Sources – 5.2 Life – 5.3 Works – 5.4 Doctrine

5.1 *Primary Sources*

5.1.1 Bio-bibliographical Testimonies [*241–*244] – 5.1.2 Works [*251–*262]

5.1.1 Bio-bibliographical Testimonies

241 al-Tawḥīdī, Abū Ḥayyān ʿAlī b. Muḥammad (d. 414/1023). *Kitāb al-Imtāʿ wa-l-muʾānasa.* – Ed. by Aḥmad Amīn and Aḥmad al-Zayn, 3 vols. Cairo, 1939–1944, vol. 1, 34.

242 Abū Ḥayyān al-Tawḥīdī. *Al-Muqābasāt.* – Ed. by Muḥammad Tawfīq Ḥusayn. Baghdad, 1970, 85,8. 109,2.

243 Ibn al-Qifṭī, Ǧamāl al-Dīn ʿAlī b. Yūsuf (d. 646/1248). *Taʾrīḫ al-ḥukamāʾ* [*Iḫbār al-ʿulamāʾ bi-aḫbār al-ḥukamāʾ*, epitome by Muḥammad b. ʿAlī al-Zawzanī]. – Ed. by Julius Lippert, *Ibn al-Qifṭī's Taʾrīh al-ḥukamāʾ*. Leipzig, 1903, 411–412.

244 Ibn Abī Uṣaybiʿa, Muwaffaq al-Dīn Aḥmad b. al-Qāsim (d. 668/1270). *ʿUyūn al-anbāʾ fī ṭabaqāt al-aṭibbāʾ*. – Ed. by August Müller, 2 vols. Cairo, 1299/1882, Königsberg, 1884, vol. 1, 240. 242.

5.1.2 Works

5.1.2.1 *Translations and Commentaries*

251 Aristotle. *Rhetorica: Aristotle's Ars Rhetorica, the Arabic Version, a New Ed., with Commentary and Glossary by Malcolm C. Lyons*. Cambridge, 1982. – Ed. by ʿAbd al-Raḥmān Badawī, *Arisṭūṭālīs, al-Ḫiṭāba*. Cairo, 1959. – Redaction of the Arabic translation; Ibn al-Samḥ's authorship is doubtful.

252 Aristotle. *Physica* [commentary]. – Ed. by ʿAbd al-Raḥmān Badawī, in: *Arisṭūṭālīs, al-Ṭabīʿa, tarǧamat Isḥāq b. Ḥunayn, maʿa šurūḥ Ibn al-Samḥ wa-Ibn ʿAdī wa-Mattā b. Yūnus wa-Abī l-Farağ Ibn al-Ṭayyib*, 2 vols. Cairo, 1384–1385/1964–1965.

5.1.2.2 *Independent Writings*

261 *Ǧawāb* [*ʿan masʾalat sāʾil*]: *Mā l-ġāya allatī yanḥū l-insān naḥwahā bi-l-tafalsuf?* Ed. Mahdī Muḥaqqiq: *Risāla-yi Ibn al-Samḥ dar ġāyat-i falsafa*, in Muḥaqqiq 1976 [*373: 319–332, text 327–332].

262 *Qawl fī l-Aḫbār allatī yuḫbir bihā kaṯīrūn.* – Ed. Marie Bernand-Baladi 1969 [*371a]. – Ed. Muḥammad Taqī Dānišpažūh 1970–1971 [*372]. – Based on MS London, British Library, Add. Or. 7473, fols 33^{b}-40^{a}.

5.2 *Life*

Abū ʿAlī Ḥasan b. Sahl b. Ġālib Ibn al-Samḥ was a Christian (he is mentioned as being Christian, together with ʿĪsā Ibn Zurʿa, by Abū l-ʿAlāʾ al-Maʿarrī; cf. Stern 1956 [*361: 32]). He owned a bookstore (*dukkān*) at Bāb al-Ṭāq in Baghdad (cf. Abū Ḥayyān al-Tawḥīdī, *al-Muqābasāt* [*242: § 3, 85,8. § 17, 109,2]), and died in 418/1027.

As a philosopher, he was a student of the Baghdad logicians around the Jacobite Yaḥyā Ibn ʿAdī (§ 7.2), and, later on, of the Nestorian Abū l-Farağ Ibn al-Ṭayyib (§ 7.6). In his portrayals of contemporary literary and scholarly circles [*241: I 34; *242: 85. 109], Abū Ḥayyān al-Tawḥīdī mentions Ibn al-Samḥ's contributions to the debates of this philosophical circle (*mutaḥazzimūn bi-l-falsafa*, 'those who gird themselves with the study of philosophy'; *al-Muqābasāt* [*242: 85,9]) centered around Yaḥyā Ibn ʿAdī and around Abū Sulaymān al-Siğistānī, together with Ibn al-Ḫammār (§ 7.4), ʿĪsā Ibn Zurʿa, al-Qūmisī, the physician Naẓīf b. Ayman al-Rūmī and the vizier's son, ʿĪsā b. ʿAlī b. ʿĪsā. On one occasion, when Ibn al-Ḫammār was presented with an ethical problem, Abū Ḥayyān al-Tawḥīdī [*242: 109,2] reports that the group met 'in his [book?]store'.

5.3 *Works*

5.3.1 Translations of and Commentaries on Aristotle – 5.3.2 Philosophical Propaedeutics and Logic

5.3.1 Translations of and Commentaries on Aristotle

Kitāb Arisṭūṭālīs al-musammā Rīṭūrīqā ay al-Ḫiṭāba
Aristotle: Rhetoric

Redaction of the Arabic translation after a Syriac translation from the Greek. The only extant manuscript of the Arabic *Rhetoric* (Paris, Bibliothèque nationale, ar. 2346) is in all likelihood based on Ibn al-Samḥ's copy, even though the exact wording and the dating of the transmission statement cannot be determined with certainty. According to the holographic colophon he collated two defective copies, and additionally consulted the Syriac translation (Stern 1956 [*361: 42], ed. Lyons [*251: iv–vi]; ed. Vagelpohl 2008 [*366: 39–58]).

Šarḥ al-Samāʿ al-ṭabīʿī
Commentary on the Physics

Cf. Ibn al-Qifṭī [*243: 39,19–20]. A complete literary commentary on the *Physics*. The Leiden manuscript of the *Physics* (ed. Badawī [*252]) preserves the lemmata of Aristotle's text in Isḥāq b. Ḥunayn's Arabic translation (transcribed after Yaḥyā Ibn ʿAdī's copy), as well as Ibn al-Samḥ's comments on books I–VI,5. In addition to Ibn al-Samḥ's comments, the manuscript also contains notes by other authors, in particular by John Philoponus ('Yaḥyā', sc. al-Naḥwī), as well as by Alexander of Aphrodisias, Abū Bišr Mattā, and Yaḥyā Ibn ʿAdī. (The second half of book VI [i.e. ch. 5–10] and books VII and VIII are accompanied solely by the commentary by Abū l-Farağ b.

al-Ṭayyib [d. 435/1043], in addition to a number of excerpts from John Philoponus; cf. § 7.6 on Ibn al-Ṭayyib). An analytical overview of the comments relating to Ibn al-Samḥ is provided in Lettinck 1994 [*377: 38. 41–42. 49–52. 57–58. 61. 121–122. 125. 128–129. 131. 136–137. 141. 151. 155. 195–196. 201. 238. 286. 330–332. 415. 446. 456. Index locorum 775].

The entire corpus of text and commentary is transmitted according to an autograph of the Muʿtazilī theologian Abū l-Ḥusayn Muḥammad b. ʿAlī b. al-Ṭayyib al-Baṣrī (d. 436/1044), who was also responsible for its redaction. Al-Baṣrī, a pupil of Ibn al-Samḥ's, arranges his teacher's comments, which he extracted from his lectures, together with those of other authorities (*qaraʾahu Muḥammad b. ʿAlī al-Baṣrī ʿalā Abī ʿAlī al-Ḥasan Ibn al-Samḥ, wa-ʿallaqahu ʿanhu Muḥammad b. ʿAlī al-Baṣrī* [*252: 77 Badawī]; in certain places he reproduces his own questions together with his master's replies. Abū l-Farağ b. al-Ṭayyib also was a teacher of his; to him, he poses questions concerning various passages in books I–V, before making him take Ibn al-Samḥ's place within the commentaries on books VI 5–10, VII and VIII (Stern 1956 [*361: 33–41], Brown 1972 [*362], Giannakis 1993 [*363: 256–257], Lettinck 1994 [*377: 775. Index s.v.]).

Ibn al-Samḥ further composed a *Commentary Akin to the Compendia* (Ibn al-Qifṭī [*243: 39,19]: *šarḥ ka-l-ğawāmiʿ*) on the *Physics*.

5.3.2 Philosophical Propaedeutics and Logic

Ğawāb [*ʿan masʾalat sāʾil*]*: Mā l-ġāya allatī yanḥū l-insān naḥwahā bi-l-tafalsuf*
Answer [*to the question*]*: To Which End do Human Beings Devote Themselves to the Study of Philosophy?*

An introduction to philosophy: true rational insight will guide any willing human being towards his perfection and hence towards the reward of true virtue, i.e. the highest form of happiness.

Qawl fī l-Aḫbār allatī yuḫbir bihā kaṯīrūn
On Statements Which Many People Pronounce [*in agreement with each other*]

The treatise is concerned with the conditions of truth for statements that are pronounced by many people on the same topic, i.e. with the correctness (or otherwise) of the claim: 'If many people say something, its truth counts as confirmed' (*inna kull ḫabar yuḫbir bihi kaṯīrūn yağib al-taṣdīq bihi lā maḥālata*; cf. the accepted opinions [ἔνδοξα] as defined by Arist. *Top.* 100b20).

The author examines the validity of statements with regard to opinions which are pronounced by 'many', but where these 'many' are constituted by adherents of various groups, so that the statements in fact contradict each other. As examples he quotes statements made by various religious communities or peoples about prophets and religio-historical traditions. Such statements need to be subjected to logical analysis in order to find out whether their respective general principles and particular premises and deductions have a claim to validity, or can be verified by rational (logical) demonstration (*dalīl ʿaqlī*). 'Statements that rest on such premises [i.e. belonging to the type discussed] refer either to something universal or to something particular. If they refer to something universal, such premises must be based on statements which are common (*mustafīḍa*) amongst many peoples [as has been illustrated by examples], or else they must be based on statements which can be reduced to such statements by way of analysis; in this category there are again statements that in principle are strong and will withstand scrutiny [or can be reduced to such statements, or will turn out to be weak].' Particular statements, i.e. statements that claim validity in one of the sciences (*ʿilm*), arts (*ṣināʿa*) or religious communities (*šarīʿa*), must be judged according to the criteria that are prevalent and generally accepted in each instance [*262: 254].

The number of witnesses (*al-kaṯra al-muḫbira bihā*) is without consequence for a statement whose validity can be deduced according to the criteria of rational deduction. This primacy of logical demonstration is emphasized, in the last paragraph of the work, with respect to those people who refer to a tradition (*naql*) passed on by their closest predecessors (*salafuhum al-qarīb*), the more remote predecessors of the latter, and so on, who eventually combine to make up an overall majority of witnesses. Here the author is clearly targeting the truth criteria of religious tradition, in particular that of Islamic *ḥadīṯ*.

5.4 *Doctrine*

Philosophical propaedeutics. In keeping with the tradition of his teacher Yaḥyā Ibn ʿAdī, Ibn al-Samḥ conceives of philosophy as the rational cognition of the First Principle, the pure good, and the highest good. Both the theoretical and the practical parts of philosophy are based on rational cognition through demonstrative proofs (*burhān*), and through a process of purifying the philosopher's soul, will lead him to true happiness. Ibn al-Samḥ's treatise on the purpose of studying philosophy [*261] is perfectly in tune with the ethical propaedeutics pursued in al-Kindī's school by contemporaries like Abū Sulaymān al-Siǧistānī and Miskawayh.

The study of philosophy helps a human being towards perfection. The best feature of the human being, the feature that actually makes one a human being, and for the sake of which God has created humans, is reason. On the one hand, reason is theoretical and geared towards knowledge; on the other hand, it is practical and geared towards doing good. Perfection of theoretical reason occurs through the certain knowledge (*al-ʿilm al-yaqīn*) of the best of beings, i.e. God, the pure good (*al-ḫayr al-maḥḍ*, the name for God used in the Arabic translations of Neoplatonism). The life of a human being whose rational faculty is filled with certain knowledge about God's essence is the best and most beautiful life.

Certain knowledge of God is attainable to us in the science of divinity, which examines things that are neither bodies nor subsist in bodies, according to their order of perfection. At the top of that order there is a being which has no equal and which is not preceded by anything else; it does not derive its being from any other, and therefore is unique and absolutely eternal. This One and First bestows being on everything apart from itself; within it, there can be no plurality, relation, or attribute. Through philosophy we come to understand how other beings emerge from the First, and how they derive their being from it (*istafādat*, i.e. through participation [μέθεξις]); and further, how all beings, arranged in their respective orders, proceed under the influence of God, in whom there is no deficiency or evil.

Once a human being's reason reaches the level where it attains these insights with certainty, he will achieve the most perfect and happy life. The perfection of practical reason is the subject matter of the practical part of philosophy. It analyses the difference between good and bad and establishes that the good is to be preferred, since it keeps the substance of the soul in its best possible condition. Practical philosophy explains the essence of virtue by reference to the relation between reason, passion (*ġaḍab*) and desire (*šahwa*), and clarifies the path to acquiring virtue through the refinement of character. A sensible human being realizes through self-examination where they have strayed from virtue, and thus need to train their character to be virtuous, just as one straightens a crooked piece of wood. Conditions that are required for the acquisition of a virtuous character include one's upbringing by family and society; willingness to acquire the virtues; diligence in practising virtue, and finally the intellectual insight, 'through demonstrations', that the good is appropriate for the substance of the soul, and for its improvement and ascent. Whether someone has been gifted with true virtue, they can tell from the fact that virtue causes them true joy, whereas vice causes them pain. True knowledge of values is guided by reason, which leads the right way in the face of the aberrations of desire and passion. The aim of philosophy hence consists in aiding human beings in bringing themselves to perfection, and making their lives better, more beautiful, and happier.

Natural philosophy. Ibn al-Samḥ's commentary on Aristotle's *Physics* is heavily influenced by John Philoponus, in particular by his interpretation of books III to VI. Together with other comments – by Alexander of Aphrodisias, and, on the Arabic front, by Abū Bišr Mattā – this interpretation was introduced into a literal commentary (i.e. consisting of lemmata and comments) of the *Physics* as derived from Ibn al-Samḥ's lecture, and in this form was transmitted by Ibn al-Samḥ's pupil, the Muʿtazilī theologian Abū l-Ḥusayn al-Baṣrī.

However, the Arabic comments by Yaḥyā (sc. al-Naḥwī, John Philoponus), are transmitted here in a rather free paraphrase that at times deviates from the Greek text in content as well (Lettinck 1994 [*377: 192–195, cf. Index locorum s.v. Yaḥyā]). Ibn al-Samḥ follows him, for instance, with regard to the scope of physics in relation to mathematics (Lettinck 1994 [*377: 125]), the doctrine of causation [ibid., 128], and other points; but Ibn al-Samḥ's explications, like those by Abū Bišr Mattā which he reports, tend to be much briefer than Philoponus' analyses (cf. Lettinck 1994 [*377: 155]; both authors' comments on the doctrine of causation are somewhat more elaborate, cf. id. [*377: 128–129]).

In the face of Philoponus' criticism of Aristotle's theory of propulsion, Ibn al-Samḥ defends the Aristotelian model (Lettinck 1994 [*377: 20–21. 331]). A propelled body requires a mover not just at the origin of its movement, but throughout its entire course; this mover is the surrounding air (hence a propelling motion is not possible in a vacuum, Arist. *Phys.* IV 8). Philoponus, on the other hand, claimed that the propelled body was moved by an internal motive power, an 'impetus' (ῥοπή, Arab. *mayl*), which it received from the original cause of the propelling motion, without a material medium like air being necessary. This concept was also to influence Ibn Sīnā's theory of inanimate motion (cf. Pines 1953 [*371], Zimmermann 1987 [*376]).

6 Abū l-Farağ Ibn al-Ṭayyib

Cleophea Ferrari

6.1 Primary Sources – 6.2 Life – 6.3 Works – 6.4 Doctrine and Influence

6.1 *Primary Sources*

6.1.1 Bio-bibliographical Sources [*271–*274] – 6.1.2 Edited Works [*281–*303] – 6.1.3 Testimonies [*311]

6.1.1 Bio-bibliographical Sources

271 Ibn Sīnā, Abū ʿAlī al-Ḥusayn b. ʿAbd Allāh (d. 428/1037). *Al-Mubāḥaṯāt.* – Ed. by Muḥsin Bīdārfār (Qum, 1992).

272 al-Bayhaqī, Ẓahīr al-Dīn Abū l-Ḥasan ʿAlī b. Zayd Ibn Funduq (d. 565/1169–1170). *Tatimmat Ṣiwān al-ḥikma.* – Ed. by Muḥammad Šafīʿ. Lahore, 1935, 66–69. – Ed. by Muḥammad Kurd ʿAlī: *Taʾrīḫ ḥukamāʾ al-islām,* Damascus, 1976, 43–45.

273 Ibn al-Qifṭī, Ǧamāl al-Dīn ʿAlī b. Yūsuf (d. 646/1248). *Taʾrīḫ al-ḥukamāʾ* [*Iḫbār al-ʿulamāʾ bi-aḫbār al-ḥukamāʾ*, epitome des Muḥammad b. ʿAlī al-Zawzanī]. – Ed. by Julius Lippert, *Ibn al-Qifṭī's Taʾrīh al-ḥukamāʾ*. Leipzig, 1903, 223.

274 Ibn Abī Uṣaybiʿa, Muwaffaq al-Dīn Aḥmad b. al-Qāsim (d. 668/1270). *ʿUyūn al-anbāʾ fī ṭabaqāt al-aṭibbāʾ*. – Ed. by August Müller, 2 vols. Cairo, 1299/1882, Königsberg 1884, vol. 1, 239–241.

6.1.2 Edited Works

Compared with the number of attested works, only a small proportion of Ibn al-Ṭayyib's philosophical commentaries are extant. Much more has been transmitted in the fields of medicine and exegesis, but in any case the author has generally received little attention from editors.

6.1.2.1 *Partial Collections*

281 *Kitāb al-Nukat wa-l-aṯmār al-ṭibbiyya wa-l-falsafiyya*, MS Istanbul, Nuru Osmaniye, 3610 [new shelfmark: 3095], 149 fols (1076/1665–1666), cf. Daiber 1996 [*407: 630–631 n. 8]. It contains: 1. *Masāʾil al-Iskandar* (fols 1^{b}–21^{b}); 2. *Ṯimār al-masāʾil al-ṭibbiyya ʿalā waǧh āḫar* (fols 22^{a}–33^{b}); 3. *Ṯimār masāʾil Arisṭūṭālīs al-maʿrūfa bi-Mā bāl* (fols 34^{a}–86^{b}); 4. *Ṯimār min kalām Ǧālīnūs fī l-tiryāq* (fols 86^{b}–92^{a}); 5. *Ṯamarat kalām li-ʿĪsā Ibn Māsawayh fī l-ǧimāʿ wa-mā yataʿallaqu bihi* (fols 92^{b}–94^{a}); 6. *Ṯimār al-masāʾil al-ṭibbiyya ʿalā waǧh āḫar* (fols 94^{b}–99^{b}); 7. *Šurūṭ ilqāʾ al-adwiya* (fols 99^{b}–121^{a}); 8. *Ṯimār masāʾil ṭibbiyya* (fols 121^{a}–125^{a}); 9. *Fī l-rūḥ wa-l-nafs* (fol. 125^{a-b}); 10. *al-ʿAṭaš* (fols 125^{b}–126^{b}); 11. Galen: *Fī l-ḥuqan* [*De clisteribus*] (fols 126^{b}–127^{a}); 12. *Fī l-rawāʾiḥ* (fols 127^{a}–128^{b}); 13. *Qawānīn ḥasana fī l-adwiya wa-l-aġḏiya* (fols 128^{b}–134^{b}); 14. *Fī l-šarāb* (fols 134^{b}–137^{b}); 15. *Ṯimār maqālat Arisṭūṭālīs fī tadbīr al-manzil* (fols 138^{a}–140^{b}); 16. *Masāʾil fī l-ḥayawān* (fols 141^{a}–148^{b}).

282 *Kitāb al-Nukat wa-l-aṯmār al-ṭibbiyya wa-l-falsafiyya*, MS Escurial 2888, cf. Henri Paul Joseph Renaud: *Les manuscrits arabes de l'Escurial*, vol. II, fasc. 3 (Paris 1941) 100–104 no. 888. It contains: 1. *Ṯamarat kalām Ibuqrāṭ fī l-mawlūd li-ṯamāniyat ašhur* (fols 2^{b}–14^{a}); 2. *Kitāb al-Nabāt* (fols 14^{a}–76^{b}); 3. *Ṯamarat maqālat fī l-rawāʾiḥ* (fols 76^{b}–82^{b}); 4. *Kalām fī l-šaʿr* (fols 82^{b}–85^{a}); 5. *al-Farq bayn al-rūḥ wa-l-nafs* (fols 85^{b}–86^{b}) (= MS Istanbul, Nuru Osmaniye, 3610 [3095], fol. 125^{a-b}); 6. *Kalām fī l-ʿaṭaš* (fols 86^{b}–88^{b}) (= MS Istanbul, Nuru Osmaniye, 3610 [3095], fols 125^{b}–126^{b}); 7. *Kalām Ǧālīnūs fī l-ḥuqan* (fols 88^{b}–91^{a}) (= MS Istanbul, Nuru Osmaniye, 3610 [3095], fols 126^{b}–127^{a}); 8. *Istiṯmār li-maqālat Fīṯāġūrus al-maʿrūfa bi-l-ḏahabiyya tafsīr Buruqlus* (fols 91^{a}–114^{a}) [edition: *285]; 9. *Ṯimār kalām fī l-bawl wa-l-nabḍ* (fols 114^{b}–130^{a}); 10. *Min kalām Aflāṭūn fī l-nawāmīs* (fols 130^{a}–145^{a}); 11. *Ṯimār maqālat Arisṭūṭālīs fī tadbīr al-manzil* (fols 145^{b}–149^{b}) (= MS Istanbul, Nuru Osmaniye, 3610 [3095], fols 138^{a}–140^{b}) [edition: *293]; 12. *Kalām li-ʿĪsā b. Māsawayh fī l-ǧimāʿ wa-mā yataʿallaqu bihi* (fols 149^{a}–157^{a})

(= MS Istanbul, Nuru Osmaniye, 3610 [3095], fols 92[b]–94[a]); 13. *Maqāla fī l-Ḥurūf wa-mā yatarakkabu minhā* (fols 157[a]–167[a]); 14. *Tafsīr luġz Qābus ʿalā ṭarīq al-istiṯmār* (fols 167[b]–170[a]).

6.1.2.2 *Individual Works*

Greek Philosophy: Translations and Commentaries

285 *Istiṯmār maqālat Fīṯāġūras al-maʿrūfa bi-l-ḏahabiyya.* – Ed. by Neil Linley, *Ibn al-Ṭayyib: Proclus' Commentary on the Pythagorean Golden Verses: Arabic Text and Translation*. Buffalo, 1984.

286 *Tafsīr luġz Qābūs ʿalā ṭarīq al-istiṯmār.* – Ed. by F. Rosenthal 1977 [*413]. – With Engl. transl.

287 *Ibn al-Tayyib's commentary on Porphyry's* Eisagoge. – Arabic text edited with introduction and a glossary of Greek-Arabic logical terms by Kwame Gyekye. Beirut, 1975. – Engl. transl. by K. Gyekye, *Arabic Logic: Ibn al-Ṭayyib's Commentary on Porphyry's Eisagoge*. Albany, 1979.

288 *Tafsīr kitāb al-Qāṭīġūriyās li-Arisṭūṭālīs fī l-manṭiq.* – Ed. by Cleophea Ferrari, *Der Kategorienkommentar von Abū l-Faraǧ ʿAbd Allāh ibn aṭ-Ṭaiyib: Text und Untersuchungen*. Leiden, 2006. – Ed. ʿAlī Ḥusayn al-Ǧābirī, *al-Šarḥ al-kabīr li-Maqūlāt Arisṭū*. Baghdad, 2002 (inadequate).

289 *Epitome of the Commentary on the Categories*, MS London, British Library, India Office or. 3832, fols 252[a]–286[a].

290 *Epitome of the Commentary on the Posterior Analytics*, MS London, British Library, India Office or. 3832, fols 286[a]–309[a].

291 Aristotle. *Physics* [commentary]. – Ed. by ʿAbd al-Raḥmān Badawī, in: *Arisṭūṭālīs, al-Ṭabīʿa, tarǧamat Isḥāq b Ḥunayn, maʿa šurūḥ Ibn al-Samḥ wa-Ibn ʿAdī wa-Mattā b. Yūnus wa-Abī l-Faraǧ Ibn al-Ṭayyib*, 2 vols. Cairo, 1384–1385/1964–1965.

292 *Maqāla ṣannafahā Aristūṭāṭālīs fī l-faḍīla* [*De virtutibus et vitiis* and further texts on ethics]. – Ed. by Mechthild Kellermann: *Ein pseudo-aristotelischer Traktat über die Tugend: Edition und Übersetzung der arabischen Fassungen des Abū Qurra und des Ibn aṭ-Ṭaiyib*. PhD Diss., University of Erlangen-Nürnberg, 1965, 46–96.

293 *Ṯimār maqālat Arisṭūṭālīs fī tadbīr al-manzil* [Pseudo-Aristotle, *Oeconomica*, excerpts]. – Ed. by ʿĪsā Iskandar al-Maʿlūf, in: *Maǧallat al-Maǧmaʿ al-ʿilmī al-ʿarabī* 1 (1921): 377–385. – German transl. in: Ulrich Victor, *Aristoteles, Oikonomikos: Das erste Buch der Ökonomik: Handschriften, Text, Übersetzung und Kommentar, und seine Beziehungen zur Ökonomikliteratur*. Königstein im Taunus, 1983, 66–73.

294 Aristotle. *De Caelo* [commentary]. – Fragment ed. by Gerhard Endress, "Abū l-Faraǧ Ibn al-Ṭayyib's Commentary (*Tafsīr*) and Short Annotation (*Taʿlīqāt*) on Aristotle's *De caelo*." *Studia Graeco-Arabica* 7 (2017). – Containing further information on Ibn al-Ṭayyib's Arabic translation of *De caelo*, witnesses and testimonies of his work.

Independent Monographs

297 *Risālat al-Quwā al-ṭabīʿiyya*. – Ed. by Hilmi Ziya Ülken, in: *Ibn Sînâ risâleleri = Les opuscules d'Ibn Sina, éd. et annoté*, vol. 1: *Les opuscules d'Ibn Sina. Uyun al-hikma et l'opuscule d'Abu'l Faraj et la réfutation d'Ibn Sina*. Ankara, 1953. – Repr. Frankfurt a.M., 1999 [Islamic Philosophy, 43], 57–65.

6.1.2.3 *Works on Christian Theology and Canon Law*

301 Ibn al-Ṭayyib. *Commentaire sur la Genèse*. – Ed. and French transl. by Joannes Cornelis Josephus Sanders, 2 vols. Louvain, 1967 [Corpus Scriptorum Christianorum Orientalium 274–275 = Scriptores Arabici 24. 25].

302 Ibn al-Ṭaiyib. *Fiqh al-naṣrāniyya: Das Recht der Christenheit*. – Ed. and German transl. by Wilhelm Hoenerbach, Otto Spies, 2 vols. Louvain, 1956–1957 [Corpus Scriptorum Christianorum Orientalium 161. 162. 167. 168 = Scriptores Arabici 16–19].

303 *Traité sur la science et le miracle et fragments du Traité sur les fondements de la religion de ʿAbd Allāh ibn al-Tayyib*. – Ed. by Gérard Troupeau, in: *Études de civilisation médiévale (IXe–XIIe siècles): Mélanges offerts à Edmond-René Labande*. Poitiers, 1974, 675–679.

6.1.3 Testimonies

311 Ibn Rušd, Abū l-Walīd Muḥammad b. Aḥmad (d. 595/1198). *Averrois Cordubensis Commentum magnum super libro De celo et mundo Aristotelis, ex recognitione Francis James Carmody in lucem edidit Rüdiger Arnzen, editioni praefatus est Gerhard Endress*, 2 vols. Leuven, 2003.

6.2 *Life*

The Nestorian Abū l-Farağ ʿAbd Allāh Ibn al-Ṭayyib al-ʿIrāqī worked as a physician at the hospital founded by the Buyid ʿAḍud al-Dawla (al-Bīmāristān al-ʿAḍudī) in Baghdad. He also held high ecclesiastical offices within the Nestorian Church in Mesopotamia, for instance that of Patriarchal Secretary (*kātib al-ğāṯalīq*) under the Nestorian catholicus Yūḥannā b. Nāzūk (1012–1022). He died in 435/1043 and was laid to rest in the chapel of the ancient monastery Dair Durtā on the Tigris (GCAL [*391: II 160], Allard 1962 [*392: 378], Kellermann [*292: 15]).

Ibn al-Ṭayyib's literary activity was manifold and extensive; he composed theological, philosophical and medical commentaries. However, only a small part of his œuvre has been edited and studied (Ferrari 2006 [*426: 17–22]).

6.3 *Works*

6.3.1 Philosophical Propaedeutics – 6.3.2 Commentaries and Compendia on Aristotelian Philosophy – 6.3.3 Commentary on Platonic Philosophy – 6.3.4 Theoretical Medicine

6.3.1 Philosophical Propaedeutics

Istiṯmār li-maqālat Fīṯāġūras al-maʿrūfa bi-l-ḏahabiyya
Epitome of Pythagoras' Carmen aureum

This ethico-propaedeutical treatise describes the fundamental principles of a successful life, based on strict discipline and order of body and soul. This means that the soul will renounce greed, wrath and related affections, but also that the body is cared for by eating moderately, and by providing sufficient amounts of sleep and of physical exercise. These conditions are what renders the spirit prepared for the performance of its proper activity. Misfortunes should not be lamented, but ought to be borne with composure, given that they are sent by God.

Even though the tenor of the brief work is Neoplatonic, it is unlikely that Ibn al-Ṭayyib had access to a commentary by Proclus; nor is it likely that he had a commentary by Hierocles at his disposal (Linley 1984 [*414: 6–11]).

Tafsīr luġz Qābūs ʿalā ṭarīq al-istiṯmār
Epitome of an Explication of the Tablet of Cebes

The allegorical *Tablet of Cebes* (*Tabula Cebetis*), ascribed to a pupil of Socrates, was also meant to provide ethical instruction. It points out the path to happiness, which can be reached by means of a virtuous life and the pursuit of true knowledge. Within the Arabic tradition, Ibn al-Ṭayyib's abbreviated explication of the image is also known through Miskawayh's *al-Ḥikma al-ḫālida* (ed. Badawī, § 5.4 [*281: 229–262]; cf. Rosenthal 1977 [*413]).

6.3.2 Commentaries and Compendia on Aristotelian Philosophy

Not all of Ibn al-Ṭayyib's commentaries on Aristotelian philosophy that are mentioned in the sources survive to this day. Of his commentaries on the *Organon*, for instance, we only possess the commentary on the *Categories* and a paraphrase of the *Posterior Analytics*. Several important commentaries, among them the long commentary on the *Metaphysics* – whose existence is attested by Ibn Buṭlān, one of Ibn al-Ṭayyib's pupils (Ibn Abī Uṣaybiʿa [*274: 240–243]), and by further sources (Ibn Sīnā [*271: 82]; cf. Mahdawī 1333/1954 [*401: 206–210]) – are not extant (Ferrari 2006 [*426: 20–27]).

Taʿlīq Īsāġūǧī ʿalā Furfūriyūs
Commentary on Porphyry's Isagoge

A literal commentary following the model familiar from extant Greek commentaries like those of Ammonius, Elias, Pseudo-Elias and David (Gyekye 1975 [*287]). The commentary on the *Isagoge* is structured in the same way as that devoted to the *Categories*. After an introduction, the text is divided into 18 chapters (πράξεις, Arab. *taʿālīm*). Each of these chapters comprises a general introduction (θεωρία) and a commentary section based on the lemmatized text of the *Isagoge* (λέξις). Aporias are discussed within the body of the text.

Tafsīr Qāṭīġūriyās
Commentary on the Categories

A literal commentary on Aristotle's *Categories*, following the methodological model of the Alexandrian tradition as it was common in the school of Ammonius (Ferrari 2006 [*426: 43–92]). Corresponding to the structure of its Greek models from late antiquity (of which no Arabic translations are extant), it begins with a discussion of the *prolegomena*, i.e. of the ten introductory questions (Ferrari 2006 [*426: 45–49]). Then follows the commentary, which is divided into 25 chapters (πράξεις, Arab. *taʿālīm*).

Introductory passages (θεωρία) are followed by the commentary section (λέξις), which consists of the lemmatized text of the *Categories* and the commentator's explications. In its division of the text into didactic units the structure of the commentary resembles the model employed by Olympiodorus. A characteristic typical of the Arabic commentary is its heavy systematization of the subject matter, not just in respect of its division of the text into chapters and subchapters, but also in terms of the content, which is arranged by means of systematically ordered questions. More often than not, the explanations refer back to the Aristotelian text, so that Aristotle is in fact being explained through Aristotle (cf. Ferrari 2006 [*426: 92–94]).

Kitāb Qāṭīġūriyās
Epitome of the *Commentary on the Categories*

Except for its beginning, this epitome [*289] is composed without any lemmata of the text commented upon. Both form and content leave no doubt that this work is an abridged version of the long commentary by Ibn al-Ṭayyib (Ferrari 2006 [*426: 31]).

Kitāb al-Burhān Arisṭāṭālīs (*sic*)
Epitome of the *Commentary on the Posterior Analytics*

The existence of this epitome [*290] is documented by Ibn Abī Uṣaybiʿa [*274: 240]. The corresponding long commentary, however, is not extant. Structure and presentation of the text correspond to the epitome of the commentary on the *Categories*.

[*Tafsīr*] *al-Samāʿ al-ṭabīʿī*
Literal Commentary on the Physics

This commentary on Aristotle's *Physics*, which is preserved in MS Leiden, Bibliotheek der Rijksuniversiteit or. 583, is based on lecture notes taken by Abū l-Ḥusayn al-Baṣrī (d. 436/1044). Al-Baṣrī compiled notes by various authors (in particular by John Philoponus), using a collection of commentaries assembled by Ibn al-Samḥ (cf. § 7.5); starting from book VI 6, he resorted to Ibn al-Ṭayyib's explications (cf. Lettinck 1994 [*416: 459–472. 514. 527. 564–593]).

The text consists in part of summaries of Aristotle's arguments, but in a number of places Ibn al-Ṭayyib actually disagrees with Aristotle – very prominently so in respect of the question of the First Mover. In contrast to Aristotle, who claims that motion has always existed, Ibn al-Ṭayyib asserts that the things which are in motion come into being outside of time, through an act of the Creator. They are not associated with motion by nature. (*Physics* [*291: 809]; cf. Lettinck 1994 [*416: 564]). Obviously, the Aristotelian model could not be brought into harmnoy with the Christian beliefs held by its commentator. Here and in other places Ibn al-Ṭayyib mentions arguments which we also find in Philoponus (cf. e.g. Lettinck 1994 [*416: 577]), whose commentaries were probably known to him.

Tafsīr Kitāb al-Samāʾ wa-l-ʿālam
Commentary on On the Heavens

The commentary is not extant, nor is it mentioned in the bibliographical sources. Its existence is documented on the one hand by a letter from one of Ibn Sīnā's pupils (Mahdawī 1333/1954 [*401: 201–210], Ibn Sīnā [*271: 82], Reisman 2002 [*423: 124]), on the other hand by a testimony contained in Ibn Rušd's commentary on *On the Heavens*, which is preserved in a Latin version. In his commentary, Ibn Rušd appeals to Ibn al-Ṭayyib's authority as the translator of the Aristotelian text (Averroes, *Commentum magnum* [*311: III c. 52, p. 599; III c. 56, p. 612: 74; III c. 58, p. 616: 49]). Extant pieces are the following: (a) explanatory annotations (*taʿlīqāt*) in the margins of Ibn al-Ṭayyib's Arabic translation of the work, a long fragment of which (book I, ch. 9–book II, ch. 6) is preserved in MS Paris, Bibliothèque nationale, ar. 2281, fols 63–124. His authorship is suggested by the composition and structure of the extant text (a division in *taʿālīm*, πράξεις), which correspond to those of Ibn al-Ṭayyib's surviving commentaries (Ferrari 2006 [*426: 25–27]). (b) A fragment of the author's *Large Commentary* (*al-Tafsīr al-kabīr*), referred to in the Paris excerpts of his shorter exposition, is contained in three folios from the Jewish Geniza in Cairo, Cambridge University Library, Taylor-Schechter Ar. 40.18 (cf. Langermann 1996 [*403: 252–253]); it is explicitly identified as the end of the last *taʿlīm* on book II of *Tafsīr al-šayḫ al-faylasūf al-fāḍil Abī l-Farağ ʿAbd Allāh Ibn al-Ṭayyib ʿalā ṭarīq al-ṯamar wa-l-iḫtiṣār* (see Endress 2017 [*292] for further information on Ibn al-Ṭayyib's translation and comments).

Kitāb al-Nabāt
On Plants

Several different topics from the field of botany are treated in an unsystematic fashion in this book, by way of collecting various philosophical and scientific texts. An analysis of the text reveals that Ibn al-Ṭayyib intended to gather together the available knowledge on plants, in order to make up for the loss of the book on plants by Aristotle (Daiber 1996 [*402: 631–642]). To this purpose he combined at least three texts: (1) a compilation of topics from *On Generation and Corruption* and *Meteorology*; (2) arguments from Ibn Sīnā's book on plants (even though there does not seem to be any dependency); (3) a late ancient compilation which was available to Ibn al-Ṭayyib, and to which he added, in chapters 25–30, a paraphrase from book I of Nicolaus' paraphrase of Aristotle's treatise on plants.

These compilations and paraphrases are complemented by explanations from Ibn al-Ṭayyib's own hand, in which he refers back to Aristotelian topics, as e.g. the theory of growth, or the assertion that living beings retain their substance (cf. *Generation of Animals* I 2, 715a19-b17; II 8, 747b30–748a7, cf. Daiber 1996 [*402: 640 n. 74]). Ibn al-Ṭayyib's book on plants exerted no influence on later texts on the topic.

Masāʾil fī l-ḥayawān
On Animals (*De animalibus*)

In both the Latin and the Arabic tradition, the title *On Animals* comprises all three Aristotelian books on animals (*History of Animals*, *Parts of Animals*, and *Generation of Animals*). A 'long commentary' on *On Animals* from Ibn al-Ṭayyib's pen is mentioned by Ibn Abī Uṣaybiʿa, but is not extant in Arabic (Ullmann 1972 [*394: 27]); however, it is preserved in a Hebrew version (Zonta 1991 [*415: 235–247]). Apparently, when writing his *Long Commentary*, Ibn al-Ṭayyib made use of a version of *History of Animals* that had been revised by Ḥunayn b. Isḥāq (Zonta 1991 [*415: 243]). The *Long Commentary* was widely used particularly in medieval Spain, within Hebrew literature, possibly also within Arabic literature (Ibn Rušd), and finally within Latin literature (Petrus Gallegus).

The *Masāʾil fī l-ḥayawān* [*281: no. 16] are a collection of individual questions concerning the *History of Animals*. It is an eclectic compilation whose main focus is the human being. Examples from the animal kingdom are mainly cited for the sake of a comparison with human beings. The order of the chosen passages follows the Aristotelian text, even though the individual questions are discussed without any reference to their thematic context.

Ṯimār masāʾil Arisṭūṭālīs al-maʿrūfa bi-Mā bāl
Epitome of the [Pseudo-]Aristotelian Problemata physica

For his adaptation, Ibn al-Ṭayyib used the Arabic translation of the *Problemata physica* attributed to Ḥunayn b. Isḥāq (Filius 1999 [*422: xlv]; but see Ullmann's review, which calls the attribution into question).

Maqāla ṣannafahā Aristūṭālīs fī l-faḍīla
A version of [Pseudo-]Aristotle, *On Virtues and Vices* [and further texts on ethics]

This three-part compilation, which is also preserved in a translation by Theodore Abū Qurra, contains (Kellermann [*292: 4–7]): (a) a version of the Pseudo-Aristotelian *On Virtues and Vices*, (b) a section on virtue as a mean, following Aristotle's *Magna moralia*, followed by a diaeretic analysis of the good featuring elements from the *Magna moralia* and parallels to Stobaeus' *Anthology* (see Pines 1956 [*411] regarding the quotations in Miskawayh, *Tahḏīb al-aḫlāq*; cf. Cacouros 1997 [*418: 292–296]); (c) the division of the virtues called *divisiones Aristoteleae*, transmitted in Greek in Diogenes Laertius' biography of Plato (III 80–81).

Ṯimār maqālat Arisṭūṭālīs fī tadbīr al-manzil
Epitome of Aristotle's Economics

The beginning of this short Arabic epitome ascribed to Ibn al-Ṭayyib [*281: no. 15] is a fairly exact paraphrase of the Greek original; further on, however, the text turns out to be a rather free summary. Given the brevity of the text it is difficult to verify Ibn al-Ṭayyib's authorship. A phrase stating that the part has to be considered before the whole may well point to Ibn al-Ṭayyib (fol. 138^a, line 13), whereas misconstructions of Greek sentences speak against the attribution.

6.3.3 Commentary on Platonic Philosophy

Min kalām Aflāṭūn fī l-Nawāmīs
Epitome of Plato's Laws

This epitome is preserved in MS Escurial[2] 888, fols 130ª-145ª. It is ascribed to Ibn al-Ṭayyib, but this attribution is uncertain. It is probably safe to assume that the epitome is not based on that by al-Fārābī ([*Talḫīṣ*] *Ǧawāmiʿ kitāb al-Nawāmīs li-Aflāṭūn*) but instead goes back to an older, common source, possibly the Galenic *Synopsis of Plato's Dialogues* (Ullmann 1970 [*393: 63–64], Gutas 1997 [*419: 117–118], Druart 1998 [*420: 112. 117], Gutas 1998 [*421]; for a different view see Harvey 2003 [*424], who assumes the text to be a version revised by al-Fārābī himself).

6.3.4 Theoretical Medicine

Risāla fī l-Quwā al-ṭabīʿiyya
On the Natural Faculties

This text is also known under the title *Risāla fī anna l-quwā al-arbaʿ* [...] *quwwa wāḥida bi-l-ḏāt* (*On the Four Faculties* [...] *being one faculty in essence*). It contains an account of the Galenic doctrine of the natural faculties (δυνάμεις) of nutrition and growth (following Galen, *De temperamentis* III 1; Ullmann 1978 [*395: 60–61]): the attractive faculty (*al-quwwa al-ǧāḏiba*), the retaining or digesting faculty (*al-māsika, al-hāḍima*), the transforming faculty (*al-muġayyira al-ṯāniya*, the 'second' one after the first one, which assembles the fetus out of its components), and the expelling faculty (*al-dāfiʿa*). In terms of substrate, Ibn al-Ṭayyib claims, it is one and the same faculty which works in four different ways.

Ibn Sīnā composed a refutation (*radd*) of this treatise; both texts are frequently transmitted together (cf. Mahdawī 1333/1954 [*401: 116 no. 76]). Ibn Sīnā, who, as he writes at the outset, appreciates Ibn al-Ṭayyib's medical works – in contrast to his works on logic and natural philosophy – criticizes, in the case of this particular text, that Ibn al-Ṭayyib treats the faculties as a function of mixture (*mizāǧ*) and the spirits (*arwāḥ*).

6.4 *Doctrine and Influence*

Doctrine. As the author of commentaries on works by Aristotle, Hippocrates and Galen, as well as on Porphyry's *Isagoge*, Ibn al-Ṭayyib belongs to the school tradition that goes back to Mattā b. Yūnus and Yaḥyā Ibn ʿAdī. He is one of the last proponents of a scholarly tradition that cultivated and continued the Greek intellectual heritage. His writings represent an encyclopaedic attempt to collect the entire body of knowledge on certain topics that was available at the time. In doing so, he first and foremost remains a faithful commentator, aiming at a systematization rather than a critical reception of Aristotelian philosophy. His understanding of Aristotle is shaped by the Neoplatonic school tradition of the late ancient commentators.

Influence. Evidently, Ibn al-Ṭayyib's efforts in the field of medicine had a much bigger influence than his philosophical works. As one of the earliest commentators on Hippocratic and Galenic works, he holds an important position within medieval Christian as well as medieval Islamic medicine (Ullmann 1970 [*393: 157]). Among his contemporaries he was highly regarded as a learned commentator, a reputation he is also credited with in the bibliographical literature by Ibn Abī Uṣaybiʿa (*ʿUyūn* [*274: 239]) and Ibn al-Qifṭī (*Taʾrīḫ* [*273: 223]); on the other hand, he also attracted scathing criticism by Ibn Sīnā (Ferrari 2006 [*426: 23–25]).

It is mainly thanks to Ibn al-Ṭayyib's most prominent pupil, al-Muḫtār b. al-Ḥasan b. ʿAbdūn Ibn Buṭlān, that his teacher's fame was preserved for posterity. A Christian like his teacher, he left Baghdad in 440/1049 in order to travel – to Aleppo, Antioch, Laodicea, Jaffa, Cairo, and Constantinople (Conrad 2001 [*438: 131–158]). The last years of his life he spent in a monastery in Antioch, where he died some time after 455/1063 (Ullmann 1970 [*393: 157–158]; cf. also GCAL [*391: II 191–194]). Ibn Buṭlān was primarily interested in hygiene, dietetics, and medical ethics. His *Kitāb Taqwīm al-ṣiḥḥa* (*Almanac of Health*) was translated into German already in the 16th century (Ullmann 1970 [*393: 158]). In Cairo he met ʿAlī Ibn Riḍwān (d. 453/1061 or 460/1068). The two doctors got locked into a controversy about which one of them was to be regarded as the true representative of their science (Schacht, Meyerhof 1937 [*436]). The major point of contention was related to medico-philosophical education and concerned the question whether a course of study based purely on reading books could possibly lead to success, or whether it was indispensable to have a teacher. The two opponents follow very different methods of argument. Ibn Riḍwān usually argues polemically, while Ibn Buṭlān bases his defense of the institution of the teacher on the rich funds of the knowledge he acquired through his training with Ibn al-Ṭayyib, and responds with informed substantial arguments (see Conrad 1995 [*437: 84–100]).

7 Secondary Literature

7.1 Works of Reference [*1–*7] – 7.2 The Arabic Aristotle and the Transmission of Aristotelian Philosophy in Baghdad [*11–*23] – 7.3 Textual Transmission and Textual History. The Translations from Greek and from Syriac (especially of the 'Organon') [*32–*52] – 7.4 Abū Bišr Mattā: Translation Activity, Doctrine and Influence [*61–*94]

– 7.5 Yaḥyā Ibn ʿAdī [*101–*256] 7.6 ʿĪsā Ibn Zurʿa [*261–*295] – 7.7 Ibn al-Ḫammār [*311–*341] – 7.8 Ibn al-Samḥ [*355–*377] – 7.8 Abū l-Faraǧ Ibn al-Ṭayyib [*391–*438]

7.1 *Works of Reference*

1 GAL = Brockelmann, Carl. *Geschichte der arabischen Litteratur*, 2 vols; 3 suppl. vols. Leiden, 1937–1949 (2nd ed.). – Edition adapted to the supplement volumes.

2 GCAL = Graf, Georg. *Geschichte der christlichen arabischen Literatur*, 5 vols. Vatican City, 1944–1953.

3 EI² = *The Encyclopaedia of Islam: New edition*. Ed. by Clifford Edmund Bosworth et al., 11 vols, 6 suppl. vols. Leiden, 1960–2005.

4 GAS = Sezgin, Fuat. *Geschichte des arabischen Schrifttums*, 17 vols. Leiden, Frankfurt a.M., 1967–2015.

5 EIr = *Encyclopaedia Iranica*. Ed. by Ehsan Yarshater, vols 1 ff. London, 1982 ff.

6 DPhA = *Dictionnaire des philosophes antiques*. Ed. by Richard Goulet, vols 1 ff. and Supplément. Paris, 1989 ff.

7 Daiber, Hans. *Bibliography of Islamic Philosophy*, 2 vols. Leiden, Boston, 1999. – Supplement vol., 2007.

7.2 *The Arabic Aristotle and the Transmission of Aristotelian Philosophy in Baghdad*

7.2.1 Bibliography and Prosopography

11 Baumstark, Anton. *Geschichte der syrischen Literatur: Mit Ausschluss der christlich-palästinensischen Texte*. Bonn, 1922. – Repr. Berlin, 1968.

12 al-Šabībī, Muḥammad Riḍā. "*Bustān al-aṭibbāʾ wa-rawḍat al-alibbāʾ*, aw Dimašq fī ʿaṣrihā l-ḏahabī." *Maǧallat al-Maǧmaʿ al-ʿilmī al-ʿarabī* 3 (1923): 2–8. – On Ibn al-Muṭrān, *Bustān al-aṭibbāʾ*.

13 Meyerhof, Max. "Von Alexandrien nach Bagdad: Ein Beitrag zur Geschichte des philosophischen und medizinischen Unterrichts bei den Arabern." In *Sitzungsberichte der Preussischen Akademie der Wissenschaften: Philologisch-historische Klasse*. Berlin, 1930, 389–429.

14 GAL [*1: I 328; S I 370].

15 GCAL [*2: II 153–154. 160–176]. – On Abū Bišr Mattā.

16 Rescher, Nicholas. *The Development of Arabic Logic*. Pittsburgh, 1964, 119–122.

17 Fiey, Jean-Maurice. *Assyrie chrétienne*, vol. 3. Beirut, 1968, 187–193. – On the monastery Dair Qunnā.

18 Endress, Gerhard. *The Works of Yaḥyā Ibn ʿAdī: An Analytical Inventory*. Wiesbaden, 1977. – Cf. 5–6. 52, Index s.v. Abū Bišr Mattā.

19 Ullmann, Manfred. *Islamic Medicine*. Edinburgh, 1978.

20 Endress, Gerhard. "Mattā ibn Yūnus." In EI² [*3: VI 844–846].

21 Endress, Gerhard. "Abū Bišr Mattā ibn Yūnus." In *Religion in Geschichte und Gegenwart*, vol. 1. Tübingen, 1998 (4th ed.), 91.

22 Endress, Gerhard. "Mattā b. Yūnus." In *Encyclopedia of Arabic Literature*, vol. 2. Ed. by Julie Scott Meisami and Paul Starkey. London, New York, 1998, 517.

23 Daiber, Hans. *Bibliography of Islamic Philosophy* [*7], Index II s.v. Abū Bishr.

7.3 *Textual Transmission and Textual History The Translations from Greek and from Syriac (especially of the 'Organon')*

32 Walzer, Richard. "Zur Traditionsgeschichte der aristotelischen Poetik." *Studi italiani di filologia classica*, n.s. 11 (1934): 5–14. – Repr. in: R. Walzer 1962 [*113], 129–136.

33 Georr, Khalil. *Les Catégories d'Aristote dans leurs versions syro-arabes*. Beirut, 1948.

34 Walzer, Richard. "New Light on the Arabic Translations of Aristotle." *Oriens* 6 (1953): 91–142. – Rev. repr. in R. Walzer 1962 [*113], 60–113.

35 Gätje, Helmut and Gregor Schoeler. "Averroes' Schriften zur Logik: Der arabische Text der zweiten Analytiken im Großen Kommentar des Averroes." *Zeitschrift der Deutschen Morgenländischen Gesellschaft* 130 (1980): 556–585.

36 Rowson, Everett K. *A Muslim Philosopher on the Soul and Its Fate: Al-ʿĀmirī's Kitāb al-Amad ʿalā l-abad*. New Haven, 1988.

37 Aouad, Maroun. "La Rhétorique, tradition syriaque et arabe." In DPhA [*6: I 455–472].

38 Hugonnard-Roche, Henri. "Aristote de Stagire, l'Organon, tradition syriaque et arabe;" "Le De interpretatione, tradition syriaque et arabe;" "Les Premiers analytiques, tradition syriaque et arabe;" "Les Réfutations sophistiques, tradition syriaque et arabe." In DPhA [*6: I 502–507. 513–516. 516–520. 526–528].

39 Hugonnard-Roche, Henri and Abdelali Elamrani-Jamal. "Aristote de Stagire, les Catégories, tradition syriaque et arabe;" "Les Seconds analytiques, tradition syriaque et arabe;" "Les Topiques, tradition syriaque et arabe." In DPhA [*6: I 507–513. 520–524. 524–526].

40 Hugonnard-Roche, Henri. "Les traductions du grec au syriaque et du syriaque à l'arabe (à propos de l'Organon d'Aristote)." In *Rencontres de cultures dans la philosophie médiévale: Traductions et traducteurs de l'antiquité tardive au XIVᵉ siècle*. Ed. by Jacqueline Hamesse, Marta Fattori. Louvain-la-Neuve, Cassino, 1990, 133–147.

41 Hugonnard-Roche, Henri. "Une ancienne 'édition' arabe de l'Organon d'Aristote: Problèmes de traduction et de transmission." In *Les problèmes posés par l'édition*

critique des textes anciens et médiévaux. Ed. by Jacqueline Hamesse. Louvain-la-Neuve, 1992, 139–157.

42 Hugonnard-Roche, Henri. "Remarques sur la tradition arabe de l'Organon d'après le manuscrit Paris, Bibliothèque nationale, ar. 2346." In *Glosses and Commentaries on Aristotelian Logical Texts: The Syriac, Arabic and Medieval Latin Traditions*. Ed. by Charles Burnett. London, 1993, 19–28.

43 Endress, Gerhard. "Saʿīd b. Yaʿḳūb al-Dimashḳī." In EI² [*3: VIII 858–859].

44 Hugonnard-Roche, Henri. "La traduction arabe des Premiers analytiques d'Aristote." In *Perspectives arabes et médiévales sur la tradition scientifique et philosophique grecque: Actes du colloque de la SIHSPAI (Société internationale d'histoire des sciences et de la philosophie arabes et islamiques), Paris, 31 mars – 3 avril 1993*. Ed. by Ahmad Hasnawi, Abdelali Elamrani-Jamal, and Maroun Aouad. Leuven, Paris, 1997, 395–407.

45 Brock, Sebastian. "Two Letters of the Patriarch Timothy from the Late Eighth Century on Translations from Greek." *Arabic Sciences and Philosophy* 9 (1999): 233–246.

46 Gutas, Dimitri. "The 'Alexandria to Baghdad' Complex of Narratives: A Contribution to the Study of Philosophical and Medical Historiography Among the Arabs." *Documenti e studi sulla tradizione filosofica medievale* 10 (1999): 155–193.

47 Hugonnard-Roche, Henri. "Les traductions du syriaque." In *Les traducteurs au travail: Leurs manuscrits et leurs méthodes: Actes du Colloque international organisé par le Ettore Majorana Centre for Scientific Culture (Erice, 30 septembre-6 octobre 1999)*. Ed. by Jacqueline Hamesse. Turnhout, 2001, 19–49.

48 Luna, Concetta. *Trois études sur la tradition des commentaires anciens à la Métaphysique d'Aristote*. Leiden, Boston, Cologne, 2001.

49 Baffioni, Carmela. "Una citazione di De Interpretatione, 9 in Abū Maʿšar?" In *Aristotele e Alessandro di Afrodisia nella tradizione araba: Atti del colloquio La ricezione araba ed ebraica della filosofia e della scienza greche, Padova, 14–15 maggio 1999*. Ed. by Cristina D'Ancona and Giuseppe Serra. Padova, 2002, 113–132.

50 Schöck, Cornelia. *Koranexegese, Grammatik und Logik: Zum Verhältnis von arabischer und aristotelischer Urteils-, Konsequenz- und Schlusslehre*. Leiden, 2006. – 119–158 (Ibn al-Muqaffaʿ's doctrine of judgement).

51 Berti, Vittorio. "Libri e biblioteche cristiane nell'Iraq dell'VIII secolo: Una testimonianza dell'epistolario del patriarca siro-orientale Timoteo I (727–823)." In *The Libraries of the Neoplatonists: Proceedings of the Meeting of the European Science Foundation Network 'Late Antiquity and Arabic Thought: Patterns in the Constitution of European Culture' Held in Strasbourg, March 12–14, 2004*. Ed. by Cristina D'Ancona. Leiden, Boston, 2007, 307–317.

52 Watt, John W. *Al-Farabi and the History of the Syriac Organon*. Piscataway, 2009.

7.4 *Abū Bišr Mattā: Translation Activity, Doctrine, and Influence*

61 Freudenthal, Jakob. *Die durch Averroes erhaltenen Fragmente Alexanders zur Metaphysik des Aristoteles, unters. und übers. mit Beiträgen zur Erläuterung des arabischen Textes von S. Fränkel.* Berlin, 1885, 134.

62 Margoliouth, David Samuel. "The Discussion Between Abū Bishr Mattā and Abū Saʿīd al-Sīrāfī on the Merits of Logic and Grammar." *Journal of the Royal Asiatic Society* (1905): 79–129. – After Abū Ḥayyān al-Tawḥīdī, *al-Imtāʿ wa-l-muʾānasa*.

63 Tkatsch, Jaroslaus. *Die arabische Übersetzung der Poetik des Aristoteles und die Grundlage der Kritik des griechischen Textes*, vol. 1. Vienna, 1928, 126–128.

64 Gabrieli, Francesco. "Intorno alla versione araba della Poetica di Aristotele." *Rendiconti della Reale Accademia nazionale di Lincei: Classe di scienze morali, storiche e filologiche*, ser. VI, 5 (1929): 224–235.

65 Stern, Samuel Miklos. "A Collection of Treatises by ʿAbd al-Laṭīf al-Baghdādi." *Islamic Studies* 1 (1962): 53–70.

66 Dietrich, Albert. *Die arabische Übersetzung einer unbekannten Schrift des Alexander von Aphrodisias über die Differentia specifica.* Göttingen, 1964 [Nachrichten der Akademie der Wissenschaften zu Göttingen, 1964, no. 2], 85–148.

67 Türker, Mübahat. "El-ʿÂmirî ve Kategoriler'in şerhleriyle ilgili parçalar = Al-ʿÂmiri et les fragments des commentaires des Catégories d'Aristote." *Araştırma* 3 (1965): 65–122. – Includes Mattā's glosses on Aristotle's *Categories*.

68 van Ess, Josef. "Über einige neue Fragmente des Alexander von Aphrodisias und des Proklos in arabischer Übersetzung." *Der Islam* 42 (1966): 148–168.

69 Hasnawi, Ahmad. "Un élève d'Abū Bišr Mattā b.Yūnus: Abū ʿAmr al-Ṭabarī." *Bulletin d'études orientales* 48 (1966): 35–55.

70 Heinrichs, Wolfhart. *Arabische Dichtung und griechische Poetik: Ḥāzim al-Qarṭāǧannīs Grundlegung der Poetik mit Hilfe aristotelischer Begriffe*. Beirut, Wiesbaden, 1969. – 105–123 on the Arabic tradition of Aristotle's *Poetics* and Mattā's translation.

71 Mahdi, Muhsin. "Language and Logic in Classical Islam." In *Logic in Classical Islamic Culture*. Ed. by Gustave Edmund von Grunebaum. Wiesbaden, 1970, 51–83.

72 Brown, H. Vivian B. "Avicenna and the Christian Philosophers in Baghdad." In *Islamic Philosophy and the Classical Tradition: Essays Presented… to Richard Walzer*. Ed. by Samuel Miklos Stern, Albert Hourani and Vivian Brown. Oxford, 1972, 35–48.

73 Lindberg, David Charles. *Theories of Vision from al-Kindī to Kepler*. Chicago, London, 1976. – German transl. by Matthias Althoff, *Auge und Licht im Mittelalter: Die Entwicklung der Optik von Alkindi bis Kepler*. Frankfurt a.M., 1987.

74 Mattock, John N. "The Supposed Epitome by Themistius of Aristotle's Zoological Works." In *Akten des VII. Kongresses für Arabistik und Islamwissenschaft, Göttingen* 1974. Ed. by Albert Dietrich. Göttingen, 1976, 260–267.

75 Heinrichs, Wolfhart. "Die antike Verknüpfung von phantasia und Dichtung bei den Arabern." *Zeitschrift der Deutschen Morgenländischen Gesellschaft* 128 (1978): 252–298.

76 Taha, Abderrahmane. "Discussion entre Abū Saʿīd al-Sīrāfī, le grammairien et Mattā b. Yūnus, le philosophe." *Arabica* 25 (1978): 310–323.

77 Taha, Abderrahmane. *Langage et philosophie: Essai sur les structures linguistiques de l'ontologie, avec la traduction de la discussion rapporté par Abū Ḥayyān at-Tawḥīdī entre le logicien Mattā Ibn Yūnus et le grammairien Abū Saʿīd as-Sīrāfī et de deux autres textes.* Rabat, 1979.

78 Zimmermann, Friedrich W. *Al-Farabi's Commentary and Short Treatise on Aristotle's De interpretatione, Translated with an Introduction and Notes.* Oxford, 1981. – Repr. 1987. – On Abū Bišr Mattā esp. ciii–cviii. cxxii–cxxxix.

79 Elamrani-Jamal, Abdelali. *Logique aristotélicienne et grammaire arabe, étude et documents.* Paris, 1983.

80 Genequand, Charles. "Quelques aspects de l'idée de nature, d'Aristote à al-Ghazālī." *Revue de théologie et de philosophie* 116 (1984): 105–129. – Among other things, on a comment by Abū Bišr Mattā on Aristotle's *Physics*.

81 Endress, Gerhard. "Grammatik und Logik: Arabische Philologie und griechische Philosophie im Widerstreit." In *Sprachphilosophie in Antike und Mittelalter*. Ed. by Burkhard Mojsisch. Amsterdam, 1986, 163–299.

82 Kühn, Wilfried. "Die Rehabilitierung der Sprache durch den arabischen Philologen as-Sirafi." In *Sprachphilosophie in Antike und Mittelalter*. Ed. by Burkhard Mojsisch. Amsterdam, 1986, 301–402.

83 Hugonnard-Roche, Henri and Abdelali Elamrani-Jamal. "Aristote de Stagire, les Seconds analytiques, tradition syriaque et arabe." In DPhA [*6: I 520–524].

84 Kemal, Salim. *The Poetics of Alfarabi and Avicenna.* Leiden, New York, København, 1991.

85 Kemal, Salim. "Debate between Mattā and Sīrāfī." In *Democracy in the Middle East: Proceedings of the Annual Conference of the British Society for Middle Eastern Studies 1992*. St. Andrews, 1992, 189–198.

86 Lettinck, Paul. *Aristotle's Physics and Its Reception in the Arabic World: With an Edition of the Unpublished Parts of Ibn Bājja's Commentary on the Physics.* Leiden, New York, Cologne, 1994.

87 Schrier, Omert J. "The Syriac and Arabic Versions of Aristotle's Poetics." In *The Ancient Tradition in Christian and Islamic Hellenism: Studies on the Transmission of Greek Philosophy and Sciences, Dedicated to H. J. Drossaart Lulofs on His Ninetieth Birthday.* Ed. by Gerhard Endress and Remke Kruk. Leiden, 1997, 259–278.

88 Versteegh, Kees. "The Arabic tradition." In *The Emergence of Semantics in Four Linguistic Traditions: Hebrew, Sanskrit, Greek, Arabic*. Ed. by Wout van Bekkum et al. Amsterdam, 1997, 225–284.

89 Endress, Gerhard. "The Language of Demonstration: Translating Science and the Formation of Terminology in Arabic Philosophy and Science." *Early Science and Medicine* 7.3 (Leiden 2002): 231–254.

90 Hugonnard-Roche, Henri. "Aristote de Stagire, la Poétique, tradition syriaque et arabe." In DPhA [*6: Suppl. 208–218].

91 Perkams, Matthias. "Das Prinzip der Harmonisierung verschiedener Traditionen in den neuplatonischen Kommentaren zu Platon und Aristoteles." In *Antike Philosophie verstehen: Understanding Ancient Philosophy.* Ed. by Marcel van Ackeren and Jörn Müller. Darmstadt, 2006, 332–347.

91a Tarán, Leonardo and Dimitri Gutas. *Aristotle Poetics: Editio Maior of the Greek Text with Historical Introductions and Philological Commentaries*, Mnemosyne: Supplements, 338. Leiden, 2012.

92 Adamson, Peter and Alexander Key. "Philosophy of Language in the Medieval Arabic Tradition." In *Linguistic Content: New Essays in the History of the Philosophy of Language*. Ed. by Margaret Cameron and Robert J. Stainton. Oxford, 2015, 74–99.

93 Endress, Gerhard. "'This Is Clear Arabic Speech': God's Speech and Prophetic Language in Early Islamic Hermeneutics, Theology and Philosophy." In *Transcending Words: The Language of Religious Contact Between Buddhists, Christians, Jews, and Muslims in Premodern Times*. Ed. by Görge K. Hasselhoff, Knut Martin Stünkel. Bochum, 2015, 27–42.

94 Janos, Damien. "'Active Nature' and Other Striking Features of Abū Bišr Mattā Ibn Yūnus's Cosmology as Reconstructed from His Commentary on Aristotle's Physics." In *Ideas in Motion in Baghdad and Beyond: Philosophical and Theological Exchanges Between Christians and Muslims in the Third/Ninth and Fourth/Tenth Centuries*. Ed. by D. Janos. Leiden, Boston, 2016, 135–77.

7.5 *Yaḥyā Ibn ʿAdī*

7.5.1 Bibliography and Biography

101 GAL [*1: I 228; S I 370].

102 GCAL [*2: II 233–249].

103 GAS [*4: III 303–304; V 309].

104 Endress, Gerhard. *The Works of Yaḥyā Ibn ʿAdī* [*18].

105 Troupeau, Gérard. "Quelle était la *nisba* de Yaḥyā ibn ʿAdī?" *Arabica* 41 (1994): 416–418.

106 Daiber [*7] II 543–545; Supplement 422.

7.5.2 Textual Transmission and Textual History

111 Périer, Augustin. *Petits traités apologétiques de Yaḥyâ ben ʿAdî: Texte arabe édité pour la première fois d'après les manuscrits de Paris, de Rome et de Munich et traduit en français*. PhD Diss., University of Paris, 1920.

112 Meyerhof, Max. "Von Alexandrien nach Bagdad" [*13].

113 Walzer, Richard. *Greek into Arabic: Essays on Islamic philosophy*. Oxford, 1962 Cambridge, Mass., 1963 (2nd ed.), 7. 21. 33. 66–102. 165 n. 1. 194 n. 2. 222.

114 Platti, Emilio. "Deux manuscrits théologiques de Yaḥyā b. ʿAdī." *Mélanges de l'Institut dominicain d'études orientales du Caire* 12 (1974): 215–229.

115 Hugonnard-Roche, Henri. "Une ancienne 'édition' arabe de l'Organon d'Aristote" [*41].

116 Hugonnard-Roche, Henri. "Remarques sur la tradition arabe de l'Organon" [*42].

7.5.3 General Studies. Yaḥyā Ibn ʿAdī in the Context of Arabic Philosophy

121 Graf, Georg. *Die Philosophie und Gotteslehre des Jaḥjâ ibn ʿAdî und späterer Autoren: Skizzen nach meist ungedruckten Quellen*. Münster, 1910.

122 Périer, Augustin. *Yaḥyâ ben ʿAdî, un philosophe arabe chrétien du Xe siècle*. PhD Diss., University of Paris, 1920. – Review by Richard Hartmann, in: *Der Islam* 12 (1922): 307–313.

123 Stern, Samuel Miklos. "Abū ʿĪsā al-Warrāḳ." In EI² [*3: I 130].

124 Mahjoub, Zadi. "Abū Ḥayyān at-Tawḥīdī, un rationaliste original." *Revue de l'Institut des belles-lettres arabes* 27 (1964): 317–344.

125 Fakhry, Majid. *A History of Islamic Philosophy*. New York, London, 1970, 216–227.

126 Endress, Gerhard. *The Works of Yaḥyā Ibn ʿAdī* [*18].

127 Bergé, Marc. *Pour un humanisme vécu: Abū Ḥayyān al-Tawḥīdī*. Damascus, 1979.

128 Platti, Emilio. *Yaḥyā ibn ʿAdī, théologien chrétien et philosophe arabe: sa théologie de l'incarnation*. Leuven, 1983.

129 Kraemer, Joel L. *Humanism in the Renaissance of Islam: The Cultural Revival During the Buyid Age*. Leiden, 1986, 1992 (2nd ed.).

130 Kraemer, Joel L. *Philosophy in the Renaissance of Islam: Abū Sulaymān al-Sijistānī and His Circle*. Leiden, 1986.

131 Ḫalīfāt, Saḥbān. *Maqālāt Yaḥyā Ibn ʿAdī al-falsafiyya: dirāsa wa-taḥqīq*. Amman, 1988.

132 Netton, Ian Richard. *Al-Fārābī and His School*. London, New York, 1992.

133 Maróth, Miklós. *Die Araber und die antike Wissenschaftstheorie*. Leiden, New York, Cologne, 1994.

134 Bin Omar, Mohammed Nasir. "Christian Translators in Medieval Islamic Baghdad: The Life and Works of Yaḥyā Ibn ʿAdī (d. 974)." *Islamic Quarterly* 39 (1995): 167–181.

135 Endress, Gerhard. "Yaḥyā ibn ʿAdī." In EI² [*3: XI 245–246].
136 Urvoy, Dominique. "Abū Bakr al-Rāzī and Yaḥyā ibn ʿAdī." In *In the Age of al-Fārābī: Arabic Philosophy in the Fourth/Tenth Century*. Ed. by Peter Adamson. London, 2008, 51–61.
137 Endress, Gerhard. "Theology as a Rational Science: Aristotelian Philosophy, the Christian Trinity and Islamic Monotheism in the Thought of Yaḥyā Ibn ʿAdī." In *Ideas in Motion in Baghdad and Beyond. Philosophical and Theological Exchanges between Christians and Muslims in the Third / Ninth and Fourth / Tenth Centuries*. Ed. by Damien Janos. Leiden, Boston, 2016, 221–52.

7.5.4 Propaedeutics and Logic

141 Prantl, Carl. *Geschichte der Logik im Abendlande*, vol. 1. Leipzig, 1855.
142 Bruns, Ivo. "Studien zu Alexander von Aphrodisias, I: Der Begriff des Möglichen und die Stoa." *Rheinisches Museum für Philologie* N.F. 44 (1889): 613–630.
143 Georr, Khalil. *Les Catégories d'Aristote dans leurs versions syro-arabes*. Beirut, 1948.
144 Türker, Mubahat. "Yaḥyā ibn ʿAdī ve neşredilmemiş bir risalesi." *Ankara Üniversitesi dil ve tarih-coğrafya fakültesi dergisi* 14 (1956): 87–102, [with] corrigenda, ibid., 16 (1958) 163. – On *Maqāla fī l-Buḥūṯ al-arbaʿa*.
145 Rescher, Nicholas. "An Interpretation of Aristotle's Doctrine of Future Contingency and Excluded Middle." In Rescher, *Studies in the History of Arabic Logic*. Pittsburgh, 1963, 43–54.
146 Rescher, Nicholas and Fadlou Shehadi. "Yaḥyā ibn ʿAdī's treatise 'On the Four Scientific Questions Regarding the Art of Logic'." *Journal of the History of Ideas* 25 (1964): 572–578. – Repr. in: N. Rescher, *Studies in Arabic Philosophy*. Pittsburgh, 1967, 38–47.
147 Frede, Dorothea. *Aristoteles und die 'Seeschlacht': Das Problem der contingentia futura in De interpretatione IX*. Göttingen, 1970. – With bibliography, 126–181.
148 Zimmermann, Friedrich W. *Al-Farabi's Commentary and Short Treatise on Aristotle's De interpretatione* [*78].
149 Elamrani-Jamal, Abdelali. *Logique aristotélicienne et grammaire arabe, étude et documents*. Paris, 1983.
150 Endress, Gerhard. "Grammatik und Logik" [*81].
151 Black, Deborah L. "Aristotle's 'Peri Hermeneias' in Medieval Latin and Arabic Philosophy: Logic and the Linguistic Arts." In *Aristotle and His Medieval Interpreters*. Ed. by Richard Bosley and Martin Tweedale. Calgary, 1992, 25–83.
152 Ǧihāmī, Ǧirār (Gérard Jéhamy). *Al-Iškāliyya al-luġawiyya fī l-falsafa al-ʿarabiyya*. Beirut, 1994.
153 Wisnovsky, Robert. "Yaḥyā ibn ʿAdī's Discussion of the Prolegomena to the Study of a Philosophical Text." In *Law and Tradition in Classical Islamic Thought*. Ed. by Michael Cook et al. Basingstoke, Hampshire, 2012, 161–171.

7.5.5 Physics and Mathematics

161 Türker, Mubahat. "İbnü 'ṣ-Ṣalaḥ'ın De Coelo ve onun şerhleri hakkındaki tenkitleri." *Araştırma* 2 (1964): 1–79.

162 Endress, Gerhard. "Yaḥyā Ibn ʿAdī's Critique of Atomism: Three Treatises on the Indivisible Part, Edited with an Introduction and Notes." *Zeitschrift für Geschichte der Arabisch-Islamischen Wissenschaften* 1 (1984): 155–179.

163 Genequand, Charles. "Quelques aspects de l'idée de nature, d'Aristote à al-Ghazālī." *Revue de théologie et de philosophie* 116 (1984): 105–129.

164 Ehrig-Eggert, Carl. "Über den Nachweis der Natur des Möglichen: Edition und Einleitung." *Zeitschrift für Geschichte der Arabisch-Islamischen Wissenschaften* 5 (1989): 283–297 (= Arab. 63–97).

165 Ehrig-Eggert, Carl. *Die Abhandlung über den Nachweis der Natur des Möglichen von Yaḥyā ibn ʿAdī (gest. 974 A.D.): Übersetzung und Kommentar*. Frankfurt a.M., 1990.

166 Lettinck, Paul. *Aristotle's Physics and Its Reception in the Arabic World* [*86].

167 Giannakis, Elias. "Yaḥyā ibn ʿAdī Against John Philoponus on Place and Void." *Zeitschrift für Geschichte der Arabisch-Islamischen Wissenschaften* 12 (1998): 245–302.

168 Baffioni, Carmela. "Archimedean Influences on Yaḥyā ibn ʿAdī." *Parole de l'Orient* 24 (1999): 367–376.

169 Baffioni, Carmela. "The Concept of 'Nature' in Yaḥyā ibn ʿAdī (a Comparison with the Ikhwān al-Ṣafāʾ)." In *Studies on the Christian Arabic Heritage in Honour of Father Prof. Dr. Samir Khalil Samir S. I. at the Occasion of His Sixty-fifth Birthday*. Ed. by Rifaat Ebied and Herman Teule. Leuven, 2004, 199–204.

170 Bennett, David, and Robert Wisnovsky. "A Newly Discovered Yaḥyā Ibn ʿAdī Treatise Against Atomism." In D. Janos 2016 [cf. *137], 298–311.

7.5.6 Ontology, Metaphysics, Doctrine of the Intellect

175 Pines, Shlomo. "La doctrine de l'intellect selon Bakr al-Mawṣilī." In *Studi orientalistici in onore di Giorgio Levi Della Vida*, vol. 2. Rome, 1956, 350–364.

176 Türker, Mubahat. "Yahyâ ibn-i ʿAdî'nin varlıklar hakkındaki makalesi." *Ankara Üniversitesi dil ve tarih-coğrafya fakültesi dergisi* 17 (1959): 145–157. – On *Maqāla fī l-Mawǧūdāt*.

177 Dodds, Eric Robertson, ed. *Proclus: The Elements of Theology: A Revised Text with Translation, Introduction and Commentary*. Oxford, 1963 (2nd ed.).

178 Pines, Shlomo. "Some Traits of Christian Theological Writing in Relation to Moslem Kalām and to Jewish Thought." *Proceedings of the Israel Academy of Sciences and Humanities* 5, no. 4 (1973): 105–125.

179 Pines, Shlomo and Michael Schwarz. "Yaḥyā Ibn ʿAdī's Refutation of the Doctrine of Acquisition (*iktisāb*): Edition, Translation and Notes on Some of His Other

Treatises." In *Studia Orientalia memoriae D. H. Baneth dedicata*. Jerusalem, 1979, 49–94.

180 Samir, Khalil (Ḫalīl Samīr). *Le Traité de l'unité de Yaḥyā ibn ʿAdī (893–974) (Maqāla fī l-Tawḥīd li-Yaḥyā Ibn ʿAdī* [Arab. text.]). Ǧūniya, Rome, 1980.

181 Platti, Emilio. "Intellect et révélation chez Ibn ʿAdī: Lecture d'une page d'un petit traité." *Orientalia Christiana Analecta* 226 [Actes du deuxième congrès international d'études arabes chrétiennes. Ed. by Khalil Samir] (Rome 1986): 229–234.

182 Samir, Khalil. "Science divine et théorie de la connaissance chez Yaḥyā ibn ʿAdi. Textes édités et traduits." *Annales de philosophie* 7 (1986): 75–115.

183 Whittaker, John. "Proclus and the Middle Platonists." In *Proclus, lecteur et interprète des anciens*. Ed. by Jean Pépin and Henri Dominique Saffrey. Paris, 1987, 277–291.

184 Holmberg, Bo. *A Treatise on the Unity and Trinity of God by Israel of Kashkar (d. 872): Introduction, Edition and Word Index*. Lund, 1989, 50–56. – Argues against the ascription to Yaḥyā Ibn ʿAdī.

185 Boualwan, Kamal. "Yaḥyā ibn ʿAdī's Conception of 'the One'." *Parole de l'Orient* 28 (2003): 485–495. – In the context of Trinitarian theology (comparison with Thomas Aquinas).

186 Lizzini, Olga. "Le traité sur l'unité (Maqâlah fî l-Tawḥîd) de Yaḥyā ibn ʿAdī et la troisième maqâlah de la Métaphysique du Kitâb al-Shifâʾ d'Avicenne: Deux finalités différentes dans l'analyse de l'Un." *Parole de l'Orient* 28: *Actes du IIème Symposium Syro-Arabicum, études arabes chrétiennes*, vol. 2 (2003): 497–529.

187 Martini Bonadeo, Cecilia. "Un commento ad Alpha Elatton 'sicut litterae sonant' nella Baġdād del x secolo." *Medioevo* 28 (2003): 69–96.

188 Platti, Emilio. "Yaḥyā ibn ʿAdī and the Theory of *iktisāb*." In *Christians at the Heart of Islamic Rule: Church Life and Scholarship in Abbasid Iraq*. Ed. by David Thomas. Leiden, Boston, 2003, 131–157.

189 Platti, Emilio. "Yaḥyā ibn ʿAdī, réflexions à propos de questions du *kalām* musulman." In R. Ebied, H. Teule 2004, [cf. *169], 177–197.

190 Rashed, Marwan. "Ibn ʿAdī et Avicenne, sur les types d'existants." In *Aristotele e i suoi esegeti neoplatonici: Logica e ontologia nelle interpretazioni greche e arabe: Atti del convegno internazionale Roma, 19–20 ottobre 2001*. Ed. by Vincenza Celluprica and Cristina D'Ancona. Naples, 2004, 107–171.

191 Adamson, Peter. "Knowledge of Universals and Particulars in the Baghdad School." *Documenti e studi* 18 (2007): 141–164.

192 Martini Bonadeo, Cecilia. "The Arabic Aristotle in the 10th Century Baġdād: The Case of Yaḥyā ibn ʿAdī's Commentary on Metaph. Alpha Elatton." *Veritas* 52, no. 3 (Porto Alegre 2007): 7–20.

193 Ehrig-Eggert, Carl. "Yaḥyā ibn ʿAdī on Universals and the Intellect." In P. Adamson 2008 [cf. *136], 51–61.

194 Baffioni, Carmela. "Le cosidette 'mawǧūdāt' in Yaḥyā Ibn ʿAdī." In *La letteratura arabo-cristiana e le scienze nel periodo abbaside (750–1250 d.C.): Atti del 2° convegno di studi arabo-cristiani, Roma 9–10 marzo 2007*. Ed. by Davide Righi. Turin, 2008, 245–271.

195 Lizzini, Olga. "Critica dell'emanatismo e creazione dal nulla in Yaḥyā ibn ʿAdī." In D. Righi 2008 [cf. *194], 23–42.

196 Wisnovsky, Robert, and Stephen Menn. "Yaḥyā ibn ʿAdī's *Essay on the Four Scientific Questions Regarding the Three Categories of Existence: Divine, Natural and Logical*. Editio princeps and translation." *MIDEO* 29 (2012): 73–96.

197 Lizzini, Olga. "What does *Tawḥīd* mean? Yaḥyā ibn ʿAdī's Treatise on the Affirmation of the Unity of God between Philosophy and Theology." In D. Janos 2016 [cf. *137], 253–80.

7.5.7 Ethics

205 Donaldson, Dwight M. *Studies in Muslim Ethics*. London, 1953.

206 Mattock, John N. "A Translation of the Arabic Epitome of Galen's Book Περὶ ἠθῶν." In *Islamic Philosophy and the Classical Tradition*. Ed. by Samuel Miklos Stern, Albert Hourani and Vivian Brown [cf. *72], 235–260.

207 Samir, Khalil. "Le Tahḏīb al-aḫlāq de Yaḥyā b. ʿAdī (m. 974) attribué à Ǧāḥiẓ et à Ibn al-ʿArabī." *Arabica* 21 (1974): 111–138.

208 al-Takrītī, Nāǧī. *Yahya Ibn ʿAdi: A Critical Edition and Study of His Tahdhib al-akhlaq*. Beirut, Paris, 1978.

209 Samir, Khalil. "Nouveaux renseignements sur le Tahḏīb al-aḫlāq de Yaḥyā Ibn ʿAdī et sur le 'Taymūr aḫlāq 290'." *Arabica* 26 (1979): 158–178.

210 al-Takrītī, Nāǧī. *Al-falsafa al-aḫlāqiyya al-Aflāṭūniyya ʿind mufakkirī l-islām*. Beirut, 1979.

211 al-Takrītī, Nāǧī. "Al-maʿnā al-aḫlāqī li-l-ṣadāqa." *Maǧallat al-Maǧmaʿ al-ʿilmī al-ʿirāqī* 31, no. 4 (1980): 325–361.

212 Mistrih, Vincent. "Traité sur la continence de Yaḥyā ibn ʿAdī: Introduction, texte et traduction." *Studia Orientalia Christiana, Collectanea* 16 (1981): 3–137.

213 Hatem, Jad. "Que le roi ne peut être parfait selon Yaḥyā ibn ʿAdī." *Annales de philosophie de l'Université Saint-Joseph* 6 (1985): 89–104. – Arabic version: Ǧād Ḥātim, "Fī anna l-malik lā yastaṭīʿ an yakūn insānan tāmman: Qirāʾa fī kitāb *Tahḏīb al-aḫlāq* li-Yaḥyā ibn ʿAdī." *Al-Mašriq* 66 (1992): 161–177.

214 Hatem, Jad. "La dialectique des mœurs dans l'éthique de Yaḥyā ibn ʿAdī." *Orientalia Christiana Analecta* 226 [Actes du deuxième congrès international d'études arabes chrétiennes. Ed. by Khalil Samir] (Rome 1986): 215–228.

215 Bin Omar, Mohammed Nasir. *A Study of How to Attain Happiness as Reflected in the Works on Tahdhīb al-akhlāq by Yaḥyā ibn ʿAdī (d. 974) and Miskawayh (d. 1030)*. Nottingham, 1992.

216 Fakhry, Majid. *Ethical Theories in Islam*. Leiden, 1994 (2nd ed.).
217 Vadet, Jean-Claude. *Les idées morales dans l'islam*. Paris, 1995.
218 Griffith, Sidney Harrison. *Yaḥyā ibn ʿAdī: The Reformation of Morals: A Parallel English-Arabic Text, Translated and Introduced*. Provo, 2002.
219 Griffith, Sidney Harrison. "The 'Philosophical Life' in Tenth-Century Baghdad: The Contribution of Yaḥyā ibn ʿAdī's *Kitāb Tahdhīb al-Akhlāq*." In *Christians at the Heart of Islamic Rule: Church Life and Scholarship in Abbasid Iraq*. Ed. by David Thomas. Leiden, Boston, 2003, 129–151.
220 Raad, Samih. "L'homme parfait dans le 'Traité d'éthique' de Yaḥyā ibn ʿAdī." *Parole de l'Orient* 28 (2003): 531–536.
221 Zilio-Grandi, Ida. "Il 'kitāb tahḏīb al-aḫlāq' di Yaḥyā Ibn ʿAdī († 974/363): Riflessioni sul tema dell'etica nel periodo abbaside." In D. Righi 2008 [cf. *194], 273–283.

7.5.8 Various Philosophical Questions

225 Furlani, Giuseppe. "Le 'Questioni filosofiche' di Abū Zakarīyā Yaḥyā b. ʿAdī." *Rivista degli studi orientali* 8 (1919/20): 157–162.
226 Pines, Shlomo. "A Tenth Century Philosophical Correspondence." *Proceedings of the American Academy for Jewish Research* 24 (1955): 103–136.

7.5.9 Christian Theology and Apologetics

231 de Boer, Tjitze J. "Kindī wider die Trinität." In *Orientalische Studien, Theodor Nöldeke zum siebzigsten Geburtstag gewidmet*, vol. 1. Ed. by Carl Bezold. Gießen, 1906, 279–281.
232 Périer, Augustin. *Petits traités apologétiques de Yaḥyâ ben ʿAdî* [*111].
233 Périer, Augustin. *Yaḥyâ ben ʿAdî* [*122].
234 Périer, Augustin. "Un traité de Yaḥyâ ben ʿAdî: Défense du dogme de la trinité contre les objections d'al-Kindî: Texte arabe publié pour la première fois et traduit." *Revue de l'Orient chrétien* 22 [3. sér., 2] (1920/21): 3–21. – Includes ed. and transl. of Yaḥyā Ibn ʿAdī, *Tabyīn ġalaṭ Abī Yūsuf b. Isḥāq al-Kindī fī l-radd ʿalā l-naṣārā*.
235 Pannenberg, Wolfhart. "Christologie, II: Dogmengeschichtlich." In *Die Religion in Geschichte und Gegenwart*, vol. 1. Tübingen, 1957 (3rd ed.), 1762–1777.
236 Abel, Armand. "La polémique damascénienne et son influence sur les origines de la théologie musulmane." In *L'élaboration de l'islam*. Paris, 1961, 71–85.
237 Kettler, Franz-Heinrich. "Trinität, III: Dogmengeschichtlich." In *Die Religion in Geschichte und Gegenwart*, vol. 6. Tübingen, 1962 (3rd ed.), 1025–1032.
238 Devalve, Robert Henry. *The Apologetic Writings of Yaḥyā b. ʿAdī (Tenth century), Their Significance in the History of the Muslim-Christian Encounter and Their Impact on the Historical Development of Muslim and Christian Theology*. PhD Diss., University of Hartford, Conn., 1973.

239 Wolfson, Harry Austryn. *The Philosophy of the Kalam*. Cambridge, Mass.; London, 1976.

240 Platti, Emilio. *Yaḥyā ibn ʿAdī* [*128].

241 Ehrig-Eggert, Carl. "John Philoponus, Yaḥyā ibn ʿAdī and Tritheism." *Parole de l'Orient* 19 [Actes du 4e congrès international d'études arabes chrétiennes (Cambridge, sept. 1992), vol. 2. Ed. by Samir Khalil Samir] (1994): 313–318.

242 Turcescu, Lucian. *Gregory of Nyssa and the Concept of Divine Persons*. Oxford, New York, 2005.

243 Escobar Gómez, Santiago and Juan Carlos González López. "La polémica trinitaria entre Yaḥyā ibn ʿAdī y al-Kindī." *Anales del Seminario de historia de la filosofía* 23 (2006): 75–97.

244 Schöck, Cornelia. "The Controversy Between al-Kindī and Yaḥyā b. ʿAdī on the Trinity, Part One: A Revival of the Controversy Between Eunomius and the Cappadocian Fathers." *Oriens* 40, no. 1 (2012): 1–50. – "Part Two: Gregory of Nyssa's and Ibn ʿAdī's Refutations of Eunomius' and al-Kindī's Error." *Oriens* 42 (2014): 220–253.

7.5.10 School and Influence

251 Riedel, Wilhelm. "Der Katalog der christlichen Schriften in arabischer Sprache [*Miṣbāḥ al-ẓulma wa-īḍāḥ al-ḫidma*] von Abū 'l-Barakāt, hg. und übersetzt." In *Nachrichten von der Kgl. Gesellschaft der Wissenschaften zu Göttingen. Phil.-hist. Kl.* Göttingen, 1902, 635–706.

252 Graf, Georg. "Die koptische Gelehrtenfamilie der Aulād-al-ʿAssāl und ihr Schrifttum." *Orientalia* 1 (1932): 34–56. 129–148. 193–204.

253 Hasnawi, Ahmad. "Abū ʿAmr al-Ṭabarī." *Bulletin d'études orientales* 48 (1966): 35–55.

254 al-Takrītī, Nāǧī. *Al-falsafa al-siyāsiyya ʿind Ibn Abī l-Rabīʿ maʿa taḥqīq kitābihi Sulūk al-malik fī tadbīr al-mamālik*. Beirut, 1980 (2nd ed.).

255 Ḫalīfāt, Saḥbān. "*Risāla fī Ibṭāl aḥkām al-nuǧūm* li-l-faylasūf al-baġdādī Abī l-Qāsim ʿĪsā b. ʿAlī." *Maǧallat Maǧmaʿ al-luġa al-ʿarabiyya al-urdunnī* 11/32 (1987): 121–146.

256 Ḫalīfāt, Saḥbān. "ʿĪsā b. ʿAlī b. ʿĪsā: Sīratuhu wa-ārāʾuhu l-falsafiyya." *al-Maǧalla al-ʿarabiyya li-l-ʿulūm al-insāniyya* 8 (1988): 166–197.

7.6 *ʿĪsā Ibn Zurʿa*

7.6.1 Bibliography and Biography

261 GAL [*1: I 208; S I 371].

262 GCAL [*2: II 252–256].

263 Meyerhof, Max. *Von Alexandrien nach Bagdad* [*13], 422 (36).

264 GAS [*4: III 137. 148. 351. 352].

265 Ullmann, Manfred. *Die Medizin im Islam*. Leiden, 1970, 90.

266 Endress, Gerhard. *The Works of Yaḥyā Ibn ʿAdī* [*18], §§ 1.23. 2.11. 2.12. 2.13. 10.

267 Kraemer, Joel L. *Humanism in the Renaissance of Islam: The Cultural Revival During the Buyid Age*. Leiden, 1986, 1992 (2nd ed.).

268 Daiber [*7], II 306. 329. Index s.v. Ibn Zurʿa, ʿĪsā Ibn Zurʿa. Supplement, 376.

7.6.2 General Studies

271 EI² 1971 [*3: III 979–980].

272 Haddad, Cyrille. *ʿĪsā ibn Zurʿa, philosophe arabe et apologiste chrétien*. Beirut, 1971.

7.6.3 Textual Transmission and Textual History

276 Walzer, Richard. *New Light on the Arabic Translations of Aristotle* [*34].

277 Drossaart Lulofs, Hendrik Joan. *Nicolaus Damascenus on the Philosophy of Aristotle: Fragments of the First Five Books Translated from the Syriac with an Introduction and Commentary*. Leiden, 1965.

278 Dānišpažūh, Muḥammad Taqī. *Al-Manṭiq li-Ibn al-Muqaffaʿ*. Tehran, 1357 h.š./1978. – Includes an introduction to the texts of Arabic logic and their manuscript tradition.

279 Dunlop, Douglas Morton. "The Arabic Tradition of the *Summa Alexandrinorum*." *Archives d'histoire doctrinale et littéraire du moyen âge* 49 (ann. 57: 1982) (1983): 253–263.

280 Dunlop, Douglas Morton. "Divine Ascriptions in the *Summa Alexandrinorum*." *Hamdard Islamicus* 6, no. 3 (1983): 43–45.

281 Hugonnard-Roche, Henri. "Contributions syriaques aux études arabes de logique à l'époque abbaside." *Aram* 3 (1991): 193–210.

282 Akasoy, Anna A. and Alexander Fidora, eds. *The Arabic Version of the Nicomachean Ethics*, with an introd. and annot. transl. by Douglas M. Dunlop. Leiden, 2005.

7.6.4 Individual Works and Topics

291 Thomson, Herbert Fergus. *Four Treatises by ʿĪsā b. Zurʿa, Tenth Century Jacobite Christian*. PhD Diss., New York, 1952.

292 Pines, Shlomo. "La loi naturelle et la société. La doctrine politico-théologique d'Ibn Zurʿa, philosophe chrétien de Bagdad." In *Studies in Islamic History and Civilization*. Ed. by Uriel Heyd. Jerusalem, 1961, 154–190.

293 Rescher, Nicholas. "A Tenth-Century Arab-Christian Apologia for Logic." *Islamic Studies* 2 (1963): 1–16. – Ed. of the Arab. text. – Repr. in N. Rescher 1963 [cf. *145], 55–63. – Ed. of the Arabic text with Engl. transl.

294 van Ess, Josef. "Abu 'l-Qāsem." In *EIr* [*5: I 359–363].

295 Starr, Peter. *The 'Epistle to Bišr b. Finḥās (Maqālah ʿamilahā ilā Bišr b. Finḥās)' of Ibn Zurʿah (m. A. H. 398/A.D. 1008): Edition, Translation and Commentary*. PhD Diss., University of Cambridge, 2000.

7.7 *Ibn al-Ḫammār*

7.7.1 Bibliography and Biography

311 GAL [*1: I 236; S I 378].

312 Meyerhof, Max. *Von Alexandrien nach Bagdad* [*13], 421 (35).

313 GCAL [*2: II 156–157].

314 GAS [*4: III 322–323].

315 Daiber [*7], II Index s.v. Ibn al-Khammār.

316 Ullmann, Manfred. *Die Medizin im Islam*. Leiden, 1970, 85. 95. 227.

317 Endress, Gerhard. *The Works of Yaḥyā Ibn ʿAdī* [*18], §§ 1.23. 2.10. 2.11–13. 2.15. 3.32. 8.33.

318 Ḫalīfāt, Saḥbān (Sahban Khalifat). *Ibn Hindū: Sīratuhu, ārāʾuhu al-falsafiyya, muʾallafātuhu*. Amman, 1995, 81–87.

7.7.2 Studies

325 Georr, Khalil. *Les Catégories d'Aristote dans leurs versions syro-arabes*. Beirut, 1948.

326 Walzer, Richard. "New light on the Arabic Translations of Aristotle" [*34].

327 Lewin, Bernhard. "L'idéal antique du philosophe dans la tradition arabe: Un traité d'éthique du philosophe bagdadien Ibn Suwār." *Lychnos* 1954/55 (Uppsala 1955): 267–284.

328 Pines, Shlomo. *A Tenth Century Philosophical Correspondence* [*226].

329 Lewin, Bernhard. "La notion de muḥdaṯ dans le kalām et dans la philosophie." In *Donum natalicium H. S. Nyberg oblatum*. Ed. by Erik Gren et al. Uppsala, 1964, 84–93.

330 Drossaart Lulofs, Hendrik Joan. *Nicolaus Damascenus on the Philosophy of Aristotle* [*277].

331 Rosenthal, Franz. "A Commentator of Aristotle" In S. M. Stern, A. Hourani, V. Brown 1972 [cf. *72], 337–353.

332 Wolfson, Harry Austryn. *The Philosophy of the Kalam* [*239], 374–382. – Cf. esp.: Arguments for creation, 1. Argument from finitudes and the reconstruction of its original form in John Philoponus.

333 Platti, Emilio. *Yaḥyā ibn ʿAdī* [*128].

334 Hein, Christel. *Definition und Einteilung der Philosophie: Von der spätantiken Einleitungsliteratur zur arabischen Enzyklopädie*. Frankfurt a.M., Bern, New York, 1985.

335 Kraemer, Joel L. *Philosophy in the Renaissance of Islam: Abū Sulaymān al-Sijistānī and His Circle*. Leiden, 1986.

336 Davidson, Herbert A. *Proofs for Eternity, Creation and the Existence of God in Medieval Islamic Philosophy*. New York, Oxford, 1987.

337 van Ess, Josef. *Theologie und Gesellschaft im 2. und 3. Jahrhundert Hidschra. Eine Geschichte des religiösen Denkens im frühen Islam*, 6 vols. Berlin, New York, 1991–1997.
338 Hugonnard-Roche, Henri. "Une ancienne 'édition' arabe de l'Organon d'Aristote" [*41].
339 Hugonnard-Roche, Henri. "Remarques sur la tradition arabe de l'Organon" [*42].
340 Endress, Gerhard. "Averroes' *De caelo*: Ibn Rushd's Cosmology in His Commentaries on Aristotle's *On the Heavens*." *Arabic Sciences and Philosophy* 5 (1995): 9–49.
341 Lettinck, Paul. *Aristotle's Meteorology and Its Reception in the Arab World* [*86].

7.8 *Ibn al-Samḥ*

7.8.1 Bibliography and Biography

355 GCAL [*2: II 160–176].

7.8.2 Textual Transmission and Textual History

361 Stern, Samuel Miklos. "Ibn al-Samḥ." *Journal of the Royal Asiatic Society* (1956): 31–44. – Repr. in: S. M. Stern, *Medieval Arabic and Hebrew Thought*. London, 1983, no. XVI.
362 Brown, H. Vivian B. "Avicenna and the Christian Philosophers in Baghdad" [*72].
363 Giannakis, Elias. "The Structure of Abū l-Ḥusayn al-Baṣrī's Copy of Aristotle's *Physics*." *Zeitschrift für Geschichte der Arabisch-Islamischen Wissenschaften* 8 (1993): 251–258.
364 Giannakis, Elias. "Fragments from Alexander's Lost Commentary on Aristotle's *Physics*." *Zeitschrift für Geschichte der Arabisch-Islamischen Wissenschaften* 10 (1996): 157–187.
365 Giannakis, Elias. "Yaḥyā ibn ʿAdī Against John Philoponus on Place and Void." *Zeitschrift für Geschichte der Arabisch-Islamischen Wissenschaften* 12 (1998): 245–302.
366 Vagelpohl, Uwe. *Aristotle's Rhetoric in the East:The Syriac and Arabic Translation and Commentary Tradition*. Leiden, 2008.

7.8.3 Individual Works and Topics

371 Pines, Shlomo. "Un précurseur bagdadien de la théorie de l'impetus." *Isis* 44 (1953): 247–251. – Repr. in S. Pines, *Studies in Arabic Versions of Greek Texts and in Mediaeval Science*. Jerusalem, Leiden, 1986, 418–422.
371a Bernand-Baladi, Marie. "Des critères de la certitude: un opuscule de Ḥasan Ibn Sahl sur la crédibilité du dire transmis par un grand nombre." *Journal Asiatique* 257 (1969): 95–124.

372 Dānišpažūh, Muḥammad Taqī. "*Qawl al-Ḥasan b. Sahl Ibn al-Samḥ b. Ġālib fī l-aḫbār allatī yuḫbir bihā kaṯīrūn.*" *Maqālāt wa bar-rasīhā, Našriyya-yi Dāniškada-yi ilāhiyyāt wa maʿārif-i islāmī*, 3, no. 4 (Tehran, 1349 h.š./1970–1971): 239–257.

373 Muḥaqqiq, Mahdī. "*Risāla-yi Ibn al-Samḥ dar ġāyat-i falsafa.*" In Mahdī Muḥaqqiq, *Bīst guftār dar mabāḥiṯ-i ʿilmī wa-falsafī wa-kalāmī wa firaq-i islāmī*. Tehran, 1976, 319–332.

374 Kraemer, Joel L. *Humanism in the Renaissance of Islam: The Cultural Revival During the Buyid Age*. Leiden, 1986, 1992 (2nd ed.).

375 Kraemer, Joel L. *Philosophy in the Renaissance of Islam: Abū Sulaymān al-Sijistānī and His Circle*. Leiden, 1986.

376 Zimmermann, Fritz. "Philoponus' Impetus Theory in the Arabic Tradition." In *Philoponus and the Rejection of Aristotelian Science*. Ed. by Richard Sorabji. London, 1987, 121–129.

377 Lettinck, Paul. *Aristotle's Physics and Its Reception in the Arabic World* [*86].

7.9 *Abū l-Farağ Ibn al-Ṭayyib*

7.9.1 Biography and Bibliography

391 GCAL [*2: II 160–176].

392 Allard, Maurice. "Les chrétiens à Baġdād." *Arabica* 9 (1962): 375–388.

393 Ullmann, Manfred. *Die Medizin im Islam*. Leiden, 1970.

394 Ullmann, Manfred. *Die Natur- und Geheimwissenschaften im Islam*. Leiden, 1972.

395 Ullmann, Manfred. *Islamic Medicine*. Edinburgh, 1978.

396 Daiber, Hans. *Bibliography of Islamic Philosophy* [*7].

7.9.2 Textual Transmission and Textual History

401 Mahdawī, Yaḥyā. *Fihrist-i nusḫahā-yi muṣannafāt-i Ibn-i Sīnā*. Tehran, 1333 h.š./1954, 206.

402 Daiber, Hans. "Abū l-Farağ Ibn aṭ-Ṭayyib 'On plants': An Inquiry into His Sources." *Erdem* 9 (1996): 629–642. – According to MS Esc. 2 888, fols 14^{a}–75^{b}. Includes (630 n. 8) a survey of contents of MS Istanbul, Nuruosmaniye, 3610 (new: 3095) with works by Ibn al-Ṭayyib.

403 Langermann, Y. Tzvi. "Transcriptions of Arabic Treatises into the Hebrew Alphabet: An Underappreciated Mode of Transmission." In *Tradition, Transmission, Transformation: Proceedings of Two Conferences on Pre-Modern Science Held at the University of Oklahoma*. Ed. by F. Jamil Ragep and Sally P. Ragep. Leiden, 1996, 247–260.

404 Zonta, Mauro. "Fonti antiche e medievali della logica ebraica nella provenza del trecento." *Medioevo* 23 (1997): 515–594.

7.9.3 Individual Works and Topics

411 Pines, Shlomo. "Un texte inconnu d'Aristote en version arabe." *Archives d'histoire doctrinale et littéraire du moyen âge* 23 (1956): 5–43. – Addenda, ibid., 26 (1959) 295–299. – Repr. in S. Pines 1986 [cf. *371], 157–195. 196–200.

412 Stern, Samuel Miklos. "Ibn al-Ṭayyib's Commentary on the *Isagoge*." *Bulletin of the School of Oriental and African Studies* 19 (1957): 419–425.

413 Rosenthal, Franz. "The Symbolism of the *Tabula Cebetis* According to Abû l-Farağ ibn aṭ-Ṭayyib." In *Recherches d'islamologie: Recueil d'articles offert à Georges C. Anawati et Louis Gardet*. Louvain, 1977, 273–283. – Repr. in: F. Rosenthal, *Greek Philosophy in the Arab World*. London, 1990, no. VI.

414 Linley, Neil. *Ibn aṭ-Ṭayyib. Proclus' Commentary on the Pythagorean Golden Verses: Arabic Text and Translation*. Buffalo, 1984.

415 Zonta, Mauro. "Ibn al-Ṭayyib Zoologist and Ḥunayn Ibn Isḥāq's Revision of Aristotle's *De animalibus*: New Evidence from the Hebrew Tradition." *Aram* 3 (1991): 235–247.

416 Lettinck, Paul. *Aristotle's Physics and Its reception in the Arabic World* [*86].

417 Daiber, Hans. "Abū l-Farağ Ibn aṭ-Ṭayyib 'On plants'" [*402].

418 Cacouros, Michel. "La division des biens dans le Compendium d'éthique par Abū Qurra et Ibn al-Ṭayyib et ses rapports avec la Grande Morale et le Florilège de Stobée." In A. Hasnawi, A. Elamrani-Jamal, M. Aouad 1997 [cf. *44], 289–318.

419 Gutas, Dimitri. "Galen's Synopsis of Plato's *Laws* and Fārābī's *Talḫīṣ*." In G. Endress, R. Kruk 1997 [cf. *87], 101–119. – On the epitome of the *Laws* in MS Esc.2.

420 Druart, Thérèse-Anne. "Le sommaire du livre des Lois de Platon (*Ǧawāmiʿ Kitāb al-nawāmīs li-Aflāṭūn*) par Abū Naṣr al-Fārābī: Édition critique et introduction." *Bulletin d'études orientales* 50 (1998): 109–155.

421 Gutas, Dimitri. "Fārābī's knowledge of Plato's *Laws*". – Review of Joshua Parens, *Metaphysics as Rhetoric: Alfarabi's Summary of Plato's Laws*. Albany, 1995, in: *International Journal of the Classical Tradition* 4, no. 3 (1998): 405–411.

422 Filius, Lou S. *The Problemata Physica Attributed to Aristotle: The Arabic Version of Ḥunain ibn Isḥāq and the Hebrew version of Moses ibn Tibbon*. Leiden, 1999. – Review by Manfred Ullmann, in *Zeitschrift der Deutschen Morgenländischen Gesellschaft* 153 (2003): 470–473.

423 Reisman, David C. *The Making of the Avicennan Tradition: The Transmission, Contents, and Structure of Ibn Sīnā's al-Mubāḥaṯāt (The Discussions)*. Leiden, 2002.

424 Harvey, Steven. "Did Alfarabi Read Plato's *Laws*?" *Medioevo* 28 (2003): 51–68.
425 Ferrari, Cleophea. "Der Duft des Apfels: Abū l-Farağ Ibn aṭ-Ṭayyib und sein Kommentar zu den Kategorien des Aristoteles." In *Aristotele e i suoi esegeti neoplatonici: Logica e ontologia nelle interpretazioni greche e arabe: Atti del convegno internazionale Roma, 19–20 ottobre* 2001. Ed. by Vincenza Celluprica and Cristina D'Ancona. Naples, 2004, 85–106.
426 Ferrari, Cleophea. *Der Kategorienkommentar von Abū l-Farağ ʿAbdallāh ibn aṭ-Ṭayyib: Text und Untersuchungen*. Leiden, 2006.
427 Ferrari, Cleophea. "Die Kategorie der Relation in der griechischen und arabischen Aristoteles-Kommentierung." In C. D'Ancona, 2007 [cf. *51], 471–479.
428 Reisman, David C. "Two Medieval Arabic Treatises on the Nutritive Faculties." *Zeitschrift für Geschichte der Arabisch-Islamischen Wissenschaften* 18 (2008/09): 288–342.

7.9.4 School and Influence

436 Schacht, Joseph and Max Meyerhof. *The Medico-Philosophical Controversy Between Ibn Butlan of Baghdad and Ibn Ridwan of Cairo: A Contribution to the History of Greek Learning Among the Arabs*. Cairo, 1937.
437 Conrad, Lawrence. "Scholarship and Social Context: A Medical Case from the Eleventh-Century Near East." In *Knowledge and the Scholarly Medical Traditions*. Ed. by Donald George Bates. Cambridge, 1995, 84–100.
438 Conrad, Lawrence. "Ibn Buṭlān in Bilād al-Shām: The Career of a Travelling Christian Physician." In *Syrian Christians Under Islam: The First Thousand Years*. Ed. by David Thomas. Leiden, Boston, Cologne, 2001, 131–158.

CHAPTER 8

Abū Naṣr al-Fārābī

Ulrich Rudolph

1 Primary Sources – 2 Life and Influence – 3 Works – 4 Doctrine – 5 Secondary Literature

1 Primary Sources

1.1 Bio-bibliographical Testimonies [**1–*11*] – 1.2 Partial Collections [**20–*34*] – 1.3 Editions of Individual Works [**45–*130*] – 1.4 Doubtful and Spurious Writings [**140–*156*]

1.1 *Bio-bibliographical Testimonies*

1 al-Masʿūdī, Abū l-Ḥasan ʿAlī b. al-Ḥusayn. *Kitāb al-Tanbīh wa-l-išrāf* [composed 345/956]. – Ed. by Michael Jan de Goeje: *Kitâb at-tanbîh wa'l-ischrâf auctore al-Masûdî.* Leiden, 1894. – Ed. by ʿAbd Allāh Ismāʿīl al-Ṣāwī. Cairo, 1357/1938.

2 Ibn al-Nadīm, Abū l-Farağ Muḥammad b. Isḥāq (d. 380/990). *Kitāb al-Fihrist.* – Ed. by Gustav Flügel, August Müller, and Johannes Roediger, 2 vols. Leipzig, 1871–1872. – Repr. Beirut, 1964, Frankfurt a.M., 2005. – Ed. by Riḍā Tağaddud. Tehran, 1350 h.š./1971. – Ed. by Ayman Fu'ād Sayyid, 2 vols (I\1–2 – II\1–2). London, 1430/2009. – Engl. transl. by Bayard Dodge, *The Fihrist of al-Nadīm*, 2 vols. New York, 1970.

3 Ibn Ḥawqal, Abū l-Qāsim b. ʿAlī (d. 2nd half of the 4th/10th cent.). *Kitāb Ṣūrat al-arḍ.* – Ed. by Johannes Hendrik Kramers. Leiden, 1938. – French transl. by J. H. Kramers and Gaston Wiet, *Configuration de la terre*, 2 vols. Beirut, 1964.

3a al-Ṭabarī, Abū l'Ḥasan (d. 2nd half of the 4th/10th cent.). *Al-Muʿālağāt al-buqraṭiyya.* – Ed. and Engl. transl. of the relevant passages by P. E. Pormann 2015 [*60: 216. 222–223].

4 al-Andalusī, Abū l-Qāsim Ṣāʿid b. Aḥmad (d. 462/1070). *Kitāb* (*al-Taʿrīf bi-*) *Ṭabaqāt al-umam.* – Ed. by Louis Šayḫū (Cheikho). Beirut, 1912. – Ed. by Ḥayāt Bū-ʿAlwān. Beirut, 1985. – French transl. by Régis Blachère, *Kitâb Ṭabaḳât al-Umam. Livre des Catégories des nations*. Traduction avec notes et indices, précédée d'une introduction. Paris, 1935.

 | DOI 10.1163/9789004323162_010

5 al-Bayhaqī, Ẓahīr al-Dīn Abū l-Ḥasan ʿAlī b. Zayd Ibn Funduq (d. 565/1169–1170). *Tatimmat Ṣiwān al-ḥikma*. – Ed. by Rafīq al-ʿAǧam. Beirut, 1994. – Ed. by Muḥammad Šafīʿ under the title: *Taʾrīḫ ḥukamāʾ al-islām*. Lahore, 1935. – Ed. by Muḥammad Kurd ʿAlī. Damascus, 1946, 1976 (2nd ed.). – Ed. by Mamdūḥ Ḥasan Muḥammad. Cairo, 1996. – Abbreviated Engl. transl. by Max Meyerhof, "ʿAlī al-Bayhaqī's *Tatimmat Ṣiwān al-ḥikma*. A Biographical Work on Learned Men of the Islam." *Osiris* 8 (1948): 122–217.

6 Ibn Ṭufayl, Abū Bakr b. ʿAbd al-Malik b. Muḥammad (d. 581/1185). *Ḥayy Ibn Yaqẓān*. – Ed. by Léon Gauthier. Beirut, 1936. – Engl. transl. by Lenn E. Goodman, *Ibn Tufayl's Hayy Ibn Yaqzān*. New York, 1972. – German transl. by P. Schaerer 2004 [*99: 1–115].

7 Ibn al-Qifṭī, Ǧamāl al-Dīn ʿAlī b. Yūsuf (d. 646/1248). *Taʾrīḫ al-ḥukamāʾ* [*Iḫbār al-ʿulamāʾ bi-aḫbār al-ḥukamāʾ*, epitome by Muḥammad b. ʿAlī al-Zawzanī]. – Ed. by Julius Lippert, *Ibn al-Qifṭī's Taʾrīḫ al-ḥukamāʾ*. Leipzig, 1903.

8 Ibn Abī Uṣaybiʿa, Muwaffaq al-Dīn Aḥmad b. al-Qāsim (d. 668/1270). *ʿUyūn al-anbāʾ fī Ṭabaqāt al-aṭibbāʾ*. – Ed. by August Müller, 2 vols. Cairo, 1299/1882, Königsberg, 1884.

9 Ibn Ḫallikān, Abū l-ʿAbbās Šams al-Dīn Aḥmad b. Muḥammad (d. 681/1282). *Wafayāt al-aʿyān wa-anbāʾ abnāʾ al-zamān*. – Ed. by Iḥsān ʿAbbās, 8 vols. Beirut, 1968–1972. – Engl. transl. by William MacGuckin de Slane, *Ibn Khallikan's Biographical Dictionary*, 4 vols. Paris, 1842–1871.

10 al-Qazwīnī, Zakariyyāʾ b. Muḥammad (d. 682/1283). *Āṯār al-bilād wa-aḫbār al-ʿibād*. Beirut, 1380/1960.

11 al-Ṣafadī, Ṣalāḥ al-Dīn Ḫalīl b. Aybak (d. 764/1363). *Al-Wāfī bi-l-wafayāt. Das biographische Lexikon des* [...] *aṣ-Ṣafadī*, vol. 1. – Ed. by Hellmut Ritter. Istanbul, Leipzig 1931; Wiesbaden, 1949 (2nd ed.).

1.2 *Partial Collections*

20 *Alfārābī's Philosophische Abhandlungen*, aus Londoner, Leidener und Berliner Handschriften hg. von Friedrich Dieterici. Leiden, 1890. – Contains: *al-Ǧamʿ bayna raʾyay al-ḥakīmayn Aflāṭūn al-ilāhī wa-Arisṭūṭālīs; Fī Aġrāḍ al-ḥakīm fī kulli maqāla min al-Kitāb al-mawsūm bi-l-Ḥurūf; Maqāla fī Maʿānī al-ʿaql; Risāla fīmā yanbaġī an yuqaddama qabla taʿallum al-falsafa; ʿUyūn al-masāʾil; Risālat Fuṣūṣ al-ḥikam; Risāla fī Ǧawāb masāʾil suʾila ʿanhā; Fīmā yaṣiḥḥu wa-lā yaṣiḥḥu min aḥkām al-nuǧūm; Qiṭʿa min tarǧamat al-Fārābī wa-hiya maʾḫūḏa min Taʾrīḫ al-ḥukamāʾ*. – Repr. Frankfurt a.M., 1999 [Islamic Philosophy, 12].

21 *Alfārābī's Philosophische Abhandlungen*, aus dem Arab. übers. von Friedrich Dieterici. Leiden, 1892. – Contains: Harmonie zwischen Plato und Aristoteles;

Tendenz der aristotelischen Metaphysik; Der Intellect; Die Vorstudien zur Philosophie; Die Hauptfragen; Die Petschafte der Weisheitslehre; Die Antworten auf vorgelegte Fragen; Wert der Astrologie; Alfārābī's Schriften von Al-Ḳifti. – Repr. Frankfurt a.M., 1999 [Islamic Philosophy, 13].

22 *Rasāʾil al-Fārābī*. Hyderabad, 1340–1349 H. [1921–1930]. – Repr. Frankfurt a.M., 1999 [Islamic Philosophy, 16].

23 *Alfarabi*: *Philosophy of Plato and Aristotle*, translated with an introduction by Muhsin Mahdi. Glencoe, 1962. – Revised ed. Ithaca, 1969. – Revised ed. with a foreword by Charles E. Butterworth and Thomas L. Pangle. Ithaca, 2001.

24 *Kitāb al-Milla wa-nuṣūṣ uḫrā*. – Ed. by Muhsin Mahdi. Beirut, 1968. – Repr. Beirut, 1991.

25 *Al-Fārābī*: *Deux ouvrages inédits sur la rhétorique*, vol. 1: *Kitāb al-Ḫaṭāba*; vol. 2: *Didascalia in Rhetoricam Aristotelis ex glosa Alpharabii*. – Ed. by J. Langhade, M. Grignaschi. Beirut, 1971.

26 *Traités philosophiques par al-Kindī, al-Fārābī, Ibn Bājjah, Ibn ʿAdyy*. – Ed. by ʿAbd al-Raḥman Badawī. Benghazi, 1973.

27 *al-Manṭiq ʿinda al-Fārābī*. – Ed. by Rafīq al-ʿAǧam, 3 vols. Beirut, 1985–1986.

28 *al-Manṭiq ʿinda l-Fārābī*: *Kitāb al-Burhān wa-Kitāb Šarāʾiṭ al-yaqīn maʿa Taʿālīq Ibn Bāǧǧa ʿalā l-Burhān*. – Ed. by Majid Fakhry. Beirut, 1987.

29 *al-Manṭiqiyyāt li-l-Fārābī*. – Ed. by Muḥammad Taqī Dānišpažūh, vol. 1: *al-Nuṣūṣ al-Manṭiqiyya*; vol. 2: *al-Šurūḥ al-Manṭiqiyya*; vol. 3: *al-Šurūḥ ʿalā l-nuṣūṣ al-Manṭiqiyya*. Qom, 1408–1410 h.š. [1987–1989].

30 *Farabi*: *Deux traités philosophiques. L'Harmonie entre les opinions des deux sages, le divin Platon et Aristote et De la religion*. Introduction, traduction et notes par Dominique Mallet. Damascus, 1989.

31 *al-Aʿmāl al-falsafiyya*. – Ed. by Ǧaʿfar Āl Yāsīn, vol. 1. Beirut, 1992.

32 *Alfarabi*: *The Political Writings*, vol. 1: *Selected Aphorisms and Other Texts*, translated and annotated by Charles E. Butterworth. Ithaca, 2001.

33 *al-Fārābī*: *Philosopher à Bagdad au Xe siècle*. Présentation et dossier par Ali Benmakhlouf. Traduit de l'arabe par Stéphane Diebler. Glossaire par Pauline Koetschet. Paris, 2007. – Contains: Le livre de la religion [Arab. and French.] as well as [French] Les préliminaires indispensables à l'étude de la philosophie; Discours d'al-Fārābī sur la proportion et l'agencement; Le livre de la poésie; Traité sur les règles de l'art des poètes par le Second Maître; Le Compendium des Lois de Platon.

34 *Alfarabi: The Political Writings*, vol. 2: *Political Regime* and *Summary of Plato's Laws*, translated, annotated and with introductions by Charles E. Butterworth. Ithaca, 2015.

1.3 *Editions of Individual Works*

1.3.1 General Theory of Science

45 *Iḥṣāʾ al-ʿulūm*. – Ed. by ʿUṯmān Amīn. Cairo, 1931. – 2nd, revised ed.: Cairo, 1949; repr. Frankfurt a.M., 1999 [Islamic Philosophy, 10], 1–148. – 3rd ed.: Cairo, 1968. – Ed. with Latin and Spanish transl. by Angel González Palencia, *Catálogo de las ciencias*. Madrid, 1932, 1953 (2nd ed.). – Engl. excerpt in: Fauzi M. Najjar, "On Political Science: Canonical Jurisprudence and Dialectical Theology." *Islamic Culture* 34 (1960): 233–241; repr. Frankfurt a.M., 1999 [Islamic Philosophy, 11], 373–381; also printed in F. M. Najjar: "The Enumeration of the Sciences." In *Medieval Political Philosophy: A Sourcebook*. Ed. by Ralph Lerner and Muhsin Mahdi. New York, 1972, 1991 (7th ed.): 22–30. – German transl. of the Latin version by Gerard of Cremona: F. Schupp 2005 [*102]. – German transl. of the Latin version by Dominicus Gundissalinus: J. H. J. Schneider 2006 [*103].

46 *Kitāb al-Ḥurūf*. – Ed. by Muhsin Mahdi under the title: *Alfarabi's Book of Letters (Kitāb al-Ḥurūf). Commentary on Aristotle's Metaphysics*. Arabic text, edited with introduction and notes. Beirut, 1970. – Repr. Beirut, 1990, 2004. – French transl. by A. Hilal 1997 [*41: II]. – Span. excerpt in: J. A. Paredes Gandía 2004 [*45]. – Engl. excerpt in: M. A. Khalidi 2005 [*48: 1–26].

1.3.2 Propaedeutics

51 *al-Tanbīh ʿalā sabīl al-saʿāda*. – Ed. by Āl Yāsīn [*31: 227–265] [ed. quoted below]. – Ed.: Hyderabad, 1346 [1927]. In *Rasāʾil* [*22]; repr. Frankfurt a.M., 1999 [Islamic Philosophy, 16], 75–100. – French transl. by D. Mallet 1987–1988 [*34: 120–140]. – Span. transl. by Rafael Ramón Guerrero, *El camino de la felicidad*, Madrid, 2002. – Engl. transl. by J. McGinnis and D. Reisman, 2007 [*52: 104–122].

52 *Fīmā yanbaġī an yuqaddama qabla taʿallum al-falsafa*. – Ed. by F. Dieterici [*20: 49–55]. – Ed. by M. T. Dānišpažūh 1987 [*29: I 1–10]. – German transl. by F. Dieterici [*21: 82–91] – French transl. by S. Diebler [*33: 97–106].

53 [*Fī Ẓuhūr al-falsafa*] fragment, preserved in: Ibn Abī Uṣaybiʿa, *ʿUyūn al-anbāʾ* [*8: II 134,30–135,24].

1.3.3 Logic

58 *al-Tawṭiʾa fī l-Manṭiq*. – Ed. by R. al-ʿAǧam 1985 [*27: I 55–62]. – Ed. by M. T. Dānišpažūh [*29: I 11–17]. – Ed. with Engl. transl. by Douglas Morton Dunlop, "Al-Fārābī's Introductory Risālah on logic." *The Islamic Quarterly* 3 (1956): 224–235; repr. Frankfurt a.M., 1999 [Islamic Philosophy, 11], 246–257.

59 *Fuṣūl taštamil ʿalā ǧamīʿ mā yuḍtarr ilā maʿrifatihi man arāda al-šurūʿ fī ṣināʿat al-Manṭiq (al-Fuṣūl al-ḫamsa)*. – Ed. by R. al-ʿAǧam [*27: I 63–72]. – Ed. by

M. T. Dānišpažūh [*29: I 18–27]. – Ed. with Engl. transl. by Douglas Morton Dunlop, "Al-Fārābī's Introductory Sections on Logic." *The Islamic Quarterly* 2 (1955): 264–282; repr. Frankfurt a.M., 1999 [Islamic Philosophy, 11], 204–222.

60 *Al-Alfāẓ al-mustaʿmala fī l-Manṭiq*. – Ed. by Muhsin Mahdi. Beirut, 1968. – Repr. Beirut, 1982. – Partial French transl. by A. Elamrani-Jamal 1983 [*164: 198–220].

61 *Īsāġūǧī ay al-Madḫal*. – Ed. by R. al-ʿAǧam [*27: I 75–87]. – Ed. by M. T. Dānišpažūh [*29: I 28–40]. – Ed. with Engl. transl. by Douglas Morton Dunlop, "Al-Fārābī's Eisagoge." *The Islamic Quarterly* 3 (1956): 117–138; repr. Frankfurt a.M., 1999 [Islamic Philosophy, 11], 223–244. – Engl. transl. by J. McGinnis and D. C. Reisman 2007 [*52: 55–63].

62 *Qāṭāġūriyās ay al-Maqūlāt*. – Ed. by R. al-ʿAǧam [*27: I 89–131]. – Ed. by M. T. Dānišpažūh [*29: I 41–82]. – Ed. with Engl. transl. by Douglas Morton Dunlop, "Al-Fārābī's Paraphrase of the Categories of Aristotle." *The Islamic Quarterly* 4 (1958): 168–197; 5 (1959): 21–54. – Repr. Frankfurt a.M., 1999 [Islamic Philosophy, 11], 258–322.

63 [*Šarḥ al-Maqūlāt*]. Ed. of the Hebrew fragments; new edition of the Arabic fragments already published by M. Türker 1965 [*156: 103–122], with Engl. transl. by M. Zonta 2006 [*187: 195–254].

64 *Bārī Armīniyās ay al-ʿIbāra*. – Ed. by R. al-ʿAǧam [*27: I 133–163]. – Ed. by M. T. Dānišpažūh [*29: I 83–114]. – Engl. transl. by F. W. Zimmermann 1981 [*163: 220–247].

65 *Šarḥ al-Fārābī li-Kitāb Arisṭūṭālīs fī l-ʿIbāra*. – Ed. by Wilhelm Kutsch and Stanley Marrow. Beirut, 1960, 1971 (2nd ed.). – Ed. by M. T. Dānišpažūh [*29: II 1–259]. – Engl. transl. by F. W. Zimmermann 1981 [*163: 1–219].

66 *al-Qiyās* (*al-Madḫal ilā l-qiyās*). – Ed. by R. al-ʿAǧam [*27: II 11–64]. – Ed. by M. T. Dānišpažūh [*29: I 115–151].

67 *Kitāb al-Qiyās al-ṣaġīr ʿalā ṭarīqat al-mutakallimīn*. – Ed. by R. al-ʿAǧam [*27: II 65–93 without the last two ch.]. – Ed. by M. T. Dānišpažūh [*29: I 152–194]. – Engl. transl. (with intro. and notes) by Nicholas Rescher, *Al-Fārābī's Short Commentary on Aristotle's Prior Analytics*. Pittsburgh, 1963.

68 [*Šarḥ al-Qiyās*] (fragment). – Ed. by M. T. Dānišpažūh [*29: II 261–553].

69 *al-Burhān*. – Ed. by M. Fakhry [*28: 17–96]. – Ed. by M. T. Dānišpažūh [*29: I 265–349]. – Partial Engl. transl. by J. McGinnis and D. Reisman 2007 [*52: 63–68].

70 *Šarāʾiṭ al-yaqīn*. – Ed. by M. Fakhry [*28: 97–104]). – Ed. by M. T. Dānišpažūh [*29: I 350–357].

71 *al-Ǧadal*. – Ed. by R. al-ʿAǧam [*27: III 13–107]. – Ed. by M. T. Dānišpažūh [*29: I 358–455].

72 *al-Taḥlīl*. – Ed. by R. al-ʿAǧam [*27: II 95–129]. – Ed. by M. T. Dānišpažūh [*29: I 229–264].

73 *al-Amkina al-muġliṭa.* – Ed. by R. al-ʿAǧam [*27: II 131–164]. – Ed. by M. T. Dānišpažūh [*29: I 195–228].

74 *al-Ḫiṭāba.* – Ed. with French transl. by J. Langhade [*25: 30–121]. – Ed. by M. T. Dānišpažūh [*29: I 456–492].

75 *Didascalia in Rethoricam [sic] Aristotelis ex glosa Alpharabii.* – Ed. by M. Grignaschi [*25: 149–252].

76 *al-Šiʿr.* – Ed. by Muhsin Mahdi. In *Shiʿr* 3/12 (1959): 91–95. – Ed. by M. T. Dānišpažūh [*29: I 500–503]. – French transl. by S. Diebler [*33: 112–118]. – Engl. transl. by G. van Gelder and M. Hammond 2008 [*190: 15–18].

77 *Risāla* (or *Maqāla*) *fī Qawānīn ṣināʿat al-šuʿarāʾ.* – Ed. by M. T. Dānišpažūh [*29: I 493–499]. – Ed. with Engl. transl. by Arthur J. Arberry, "Fārābī's Canons of Poetry." *Rivista degli studi orientali* 17 (1938): 266–278; repr. Frankfurt a.M., 1999 [Islamic Philosophy, 9], 296–308. – French transl. by S. Diebler [*33: 119–129].

78 *Qawl al-Fārābī fī l-tanāsub wa-l-taʾlīf.* – Ed. by M. T. Dānišpažūh [*29: I 504–506]. – French transl. by S. Diebler [*33: 107–111].

1.3.4 Mathematics

85 *Šarḥ al-mustaġlaq min muṣādarāt al-maqāla al-ūlā wa-l-ḫāmisa min Uqlīdis.* – Ed. by G. Freudenthal 1988 [*209: 184–192. 204–207] with French transl. [*209: 174–183. 209–211]. – Ed. by M. T. Dānišpažūh under the title: *Šarḥ ṣadr al-maqāla al-ūlā min Kitāb Uqlīdis* (and *al-ḫāmisa minhu*) [*29: III 414–424]. – Engl. transl. by F. A. Shamsi 1984 [*208: 35–45].

86 *Šarḥ al-Maǧisṭī.* – Partial Russian transl. (books I–V) by Audanbek Kubesov and Jamal al-Dabbagh. Alma-Ata, 1975; cf. Rosenfeld, İhsanoğlu 2003 [*213: 570 no. 36].

87 *al-Lawāḥiq.* – Russian transl. by Audanbek Kubesov. In *Matematičeskie traktaty.* – Ed. by A. Kubesov and B. Rosenfeld. Alma-Ata, 1971, 52–89.

88 *Maqāla fīmā yaṣiḥḥu wa-mā lā yaṣiḥḥu min aḥkām al-nuǧūm.* – Ed. by F. Dieterici [*20: 104–114]. – Ed. (without the preface by Abū Isḥāq Ibrāhīm b. ʿAbd Allāh al-Baġdādī) under the title: *Risāla fī Faḍīlat al-ʿulūm wa-l-ṣināʿāt.* Hyderabad, 1340 H. [1921]. In *Rasāʾil* [*22: no. 10]; repr. Frankfurt a.M., 1999 [Islamic Philosophy, 16], 1–14. – Ed. by Ǧ. Āl Yāsīn [*31: 281–301]. – German transl. by F. Dieterici [*21: 170–186].

89 *Risāla fī Faḍīlat al-ʿulūm wa-l-ṣināʿāt*: cf. *88.

90 *Maqāla fī al-Ǧiha allatī yaṣiḥḥu ʿalayhā al-qawl fī aḥkām al-nuǧūm.* – Ed. by Muhsin Mahdi. In *Nuṣūṣ falsafiyya muhdāt ilā l-duktūr Ibrāhīm Madkūr.* Ed. by ʿUṯmān Amīn. Cairo, 1976, 69–74.

91 *Kitāb al-Mūsīqā* [sic] *al-kabīr.* – Ed. by Ġaṭṭās ʿAbd al-Malik Ḫašaba and Maḥmūd Aḥmad al-Ḥifnī. Cairo, s.a. [1967]. – French transl. by Rodolphe d'Erlanger, ʿAbd al-ʿAzīz Bakkūš and al-Manūbī al-Sanūsī. In *La musique arabe*, 6 vols. Ed. by

Rodolphe d'Erlanger. Paris, 1930–1959, I. II 1–104. – Engl. excerpt in: G. van Gelder and M. Hammond 2008 [*190: 19–28].

92 *al-Īqāʿāt*. Facsimile ed. of the Arabic MS Ahmet III, 1878, fols 160b-167a, and German transl. by E. Neubauer 1998 [*211: 132–183].

93 *Iḥsāʾ al-īqāʿāt*. Facsimile ed. of the Arabic MS Manisa, Il Halk Kütüphanesi 1705, fols 59a–81b, 88a–89b, and German transl. by E. Neubauer 1998 [*212: 213–308].

1.3.5 Physics

99 [*Distinctio super librum Aristotelis de naturali auditu*]. – Ed. by A. Birkenmajer 1935 [*236: 475–481].

100 *al-Radd ʿalā Yaḥyā al-Naḥwī*. – Ed. by M. Mahdi 1972 [*244: 271–284]. – Ed. by A. Badawī [*26: 108–115]. – Engl. transl. by M. Mahdi 1967 [*243: 253–260].

101 *Maqāla fī Al-Ḫalāʾ*. – Ed. by N. Lugal and A. Sayılı 1951 [*237: 2–16 Arab. text] [= 49–64 acc. to the pagination of the reprint 1999].

102 *Risāla fī Wuǧūb ṣināʿat al-kīmiyāʾ*. – Ed. by A. Sayılı 1951 [*240: 74–79]. – German transl. by E. Wiedemann 1907 [*235: 117–122].

103 *Risāla fī l-Radd ʿalā Ǧālīnūs fīmā nāqaḍa fīhi Arisṭūṭālīs li-aʿḍāʾ al-insān*. – Ed. by ʿA. Badawī [*26: 38–107].

104 *Risāla fī l-Ṭibb*. – Ed. by M. Plessner 1972 [*245: 312–314] = excerpt from [*103].

105 *Risāla fī l-ʿAql*. – Ed. by Maurice Bouyges. Beirut, 1948, 1983 (2nd ed. [ed. quoted below]). – Ed. by F. Dieterici [*20: 39–48]. – German transl. by F. Dieterici 1892 [*21: 61–81]. – Partial Engl. transl. by Arthur Hyman, "The Letter Concerning the Intellect." In *Philosophy in the Middle Ages. The Christian, Islamic, and Jewish Traditions*. Ed. by A. Hyman and James J. Walsh. Indianapolis, 1973, 215–221. – Ital. transl. by Francesca Lucchetta, *Epistola sull'intelletto*. Padova, 1974. – French transl. by Dyala Hamza, *L'Epître sur l'intellect*. Paris, 2001. – Engl. transl. by J. McGinnis and D. Reisman 2007 [*52: 68–78]. – French transl. by Philippe Vallat 2012 [*256: 1–63]. – Ed. of the medieval Latin transl. with French transl. of the Latin by E. Gilson 1929 [*71].

1.3.6 Metaphysics

110 *Fī Aġrāḍ al-Ḥakīm fī kull maqāla min al-Kitāb al-mawsūm bi-l-Ḥurūf*. – Ed. by F. Dieterici [*20: 34–38] [ed. quoted below]. – Ed. Hyderabad, 1349 H. [1926]. In *Rasāʾil* [*22: no. 2]. – German transl. by F. Dieterici [*21: 54–60]. – French transl. by Th.-A. Druart 1982 [*274 : 38–43]. – Engl. transl. by J. McGinnis and D. Reisman 2007 [*52: 78–81].

111 *Kitāb al-Wāḥid wa-l-waḥda*. – Ed. by Muhsin Mahdi. Al-Dār al-bayḍāʾ, 1989. – Unpublished ed. and Engl. transl. by Mushtak 1960 [*270].

1.3.7 Ethics and Politics

116 *Fuṣūl muntazaʿa.* – Ed. by Fawzī M. Naǧǧār. Beirut, 1971. – Repr. Tehran, 1985; Beirut, 1993 (2nd ed. [ed. quoted below]). – Ed. and Engl. transl. by Douglas Morton Dunlop, *Al-Fārābī. Fuṣūl al-madanī. Aphorisms of the Statesman.* Cambridge, 1961. – Engl. transl. by Ch. Butterworth 2001 [*32: 11–67]. – French transl. by Soumaya Mestiri and Guillaume Dye, *Abū Naṣr al-Fārābī. Aphorismes choisis.* Paris, 2003.

117 *al-Milla.* – Ed. by M. Mahdi 1968 [*24: 41–66]. – French transl. by D. Mallet [*30: 117–145]. – Engl. transl. by Ch. Butterworth [*32: 93–113]. – French transl. by S. Diebler [*33: 42–93] [with reproduction of the Arabic text according to Mahdi's edition].

118 (*Talḫīṣ*) *Ǧawāmiʿ Kitāb al-Nawāmīs li-Aflāṭūn.* – Ed. by Th.-A. Druart 1998 [*324: 124–153]. – Ed. and Latin transl. by Franciscus Gabrieli. London, 1952 [*Corpus Platonicum Medii Aevi. Plato Arabus* III: *Alfarabius, Compendium Legum Platonis*]. – French transl. by S. Diebler [*33: 138–187]. – Engl. transl. by Ch. Butterworth [*34].

1.3.8 Philosophical Summae

125 *Mabādiʾ ārāʾ ahl al-madīna al-fāḍila*: *Al-Farabi on the Perfect State.* A Revised text with Introduction, Translation, and Commentary by Richard Walzer. Oxford, 1985. – Repr. 1998 [ed. quoted below]. – Ed. by Friedrich Dieterici. Leiden, 1895. – German transl. by F. Dieterici, *Der Musterstaat von Alfārābī.* Leiden, 1900. – Repr. of edition and transl. by F. Dieterici, Hildesheim, 1985. – French transl. by R. P. Jaussen, Youssef Karam and J. Chlala, *Al-Fārābī: Idées des habitants de la cité vertueuse.* Cairo, 1949. – French transl. by Tahani Sabri, *Traité des opinions des habitants de la cité idéale.* Paris, 1990. – Ital. transl. by Massimo Campanini, *La città virtuosa.* Milano, 1996. – German transl. by Cleophea Ferrari, *Die Prinzipien der Ansichten der Bewohner der vortrefflichen Stadt.* Stuttgart, 2009. – Ed. and French transl. by Amor Cherni, *Opinions des habitants de la cité vertueuse.* Beirut, 2011.

126 (*Kitāb*) *al-Siyāsa al-madaniyya* (*al-mulaqqab bi-*) *Mabādiʾ al-mawǧūdāt.* – Ed. by Fawzi M. Naǧǧār. Beirut, 1964. – Repr. Beirut, 1993 [ed. quoted below]. – Ed. Hyderabad, 1346 [1927]. In *Rasāʾil* [*22]; repr. Frankfurt a.M., 1999 [Islamic Philosophy, 16], 149–224. – German transl. by Friedrich Dieterici, *Die Staatsleitung von Alfārābī.* Dt. Bearbeitung mit einer Einl. 'Ueber das Wesen der arabischen Philosophie', aus dem Nachlasse des Geh. Regierungsrats Dr. F. Dieterici herausgegeben mit einem Gedenkblatt von Paul Brönnle. Leiden, 1904; repr. Frankfurt a.M., 1999 [Islamic Philosophy, 7], 131–275. – Partial Engl. transl. by F. M. Najjar [Naǧǧār], "The political Regime." In R. Lerner and M. Mahdi 1972 [cf. *45], 31–57.

– Partial Engl. transl. by J. McGinnis and D. Reisman 2007 [*52: 81–104]. – Engl. transl. by Ch. Butterworth [*34]. – French transl. by Phillipe Vallat 2012 [*346].

127 *Taḥṣīl al-saʿāda*. – Ed. by Ǧ. Āl Yāsīn [*31: 119–197] [ed. quoted below]. – Ed. Hyderabad, 1345 [1926]. In *Rasāʾil* [*22]; repr. Frankfurt a.M., 1999 [Islamic Philosophy, 16], 101–147. – Engl. transl. by M. Mahdi [*23: 13–50]. – French transl. by Olivier Seydeyn and Nassim Lévy, *Al-Fārābī: De l'obtention du bonheur*. Paris, 2005.

128 *Falsafat Aflāṭūn wa-aǧzāʾuhā wa-marātib aǧzāʾihā min awwalihā ilā āḫirihā*. – Ed. with Latin transl. by Franz Rosenthal and Richard Walzer. London, 1943 [*Corpus Platonicum Medii Aevi. Plato Arabus*, vol. 2: *Alfarabius, De Platonis Philosophia*]; repr. Nendeln/Liechtenstein, 1973. – Ed. by ʿAbd al-Raḥmān Badawī: *Aflāṭūn fī l-islām*. Tehran, 1974, 3–33. – Engl. transl. by M. Mahdi [*23: 51–67]. – French transl. by Olivier Seydeyn and Nassim Lévy, *Al-Fārābī: La philosophie de Platon*. Paris, 2002.

129 *Falsafat Arisṭūṭālīs wa-aǧzāʾ falsafatihi wa-marātib aǧzāʾihā wa-l-mawḍiʿ allaḏī minhu ibtadaʾa wa-ilayhi intahā*. – Ed. by Muhsin Mahdi. Beirut, 1961. – Engl. transl. by M. Mahdi [*23: 69–130].

130 *Al-Ǧamʿ bayna raʾyay al-Ḥakīmayn Aflāṭūn al-ilāhī wa-Arisṭūṭālīs*. – Ed. with Ital. transl. by Cecilia Martini Bonadeo, in *Al-Fārābī: L'armonia delle opinioni di due sapienti il divino Platone e Aristotele*, introduzione, testo arabo, traduzione e comment. Pisa, 2008. – Ed. by F. Dieterici [*20: 1–33]. – Ed. by Fawzi Mitri Najjar, in *L'Harmonie entre les opinions de Platon et d'Aristote*, texte arabe et traduction, Fawzi Mitri Najjar and Dominique Mallet. Damascus, 1999; the French transl. by D. Mallet had already been published separately in 1989 [*30: 55–115]. – German transl. by F. Dieterici [*21: 1–53]. – Engl. transl. by Ch. Butterworth [*32: 125–167].

1.4 *Doubtful and Spurious Writings*

140 *Duʿāʾ ʿaẓīm*. – Ed. by M. Mahdi [*24: 87–92].

141 *Fuṣūl Mabādiʾ ārāʾ ahl al-madīna al-fāḍila*. – Ed. by M. Mahdi [*24: 77–86].

142 *Ǧawābāt li-masāʾil (mutafarriqa) suʾila ʿanhā al-Fārābī*. – Ed. by F. Dieterici 1890, under the title: *Risāla fī Ǧawāb masāʾil suʾila ʿanhā* [*20: 84–103]. – Ed. under the title: *Risāla fī Masāʾil mutafarriqa*. Hyderabad, 1344 H. [1925]. In: *Rasāʾil* [*22: no. 17]; repr. Frankfurt a.M., 1999 [Islamic Philosophy, 16], 15–40. – Ed. Ǧ. Āl Yāsīn 1992, under the title: *Ǧawābāt suʾila ʿanhā* [*31: 313–350]. – German transl. by F. Dieterici [*21: 139–169].

143 *Ǧawāmiʿ al-siyar al-marḍiyya fī iqtināʾ al-faḍāʾil al-insiyya*. – Ed. by H. Daiber 1986 [*310: 745–746; with German transl.: 747–748].

144 *al-Ḥiyal al-rūḥāniyya wa-l-asrār al-ṭabīʿiyya fī daqāʾiq al-aškāl al-handasiyya*. – Russ. transl. by Svetlana Krasnova and Audanbek Kubesov. In *Matematičeskie*

traktaty. Ed. by A. Kubesov and B. Rosenfeld. Alma-Ata, 1971, 91–231. – Turkish transl. by Mehmet Bayrakdar, *Fârâbî teknik geometri*. Ankara, 1989.

145 *Maqālāt al-rafīʿa fī uṣūl ʿilm al-ṭabīʿa*. – Ed. by N. Lugal and A. Sayılı 1951 [*238: 103–122].

146 *Min al-Asʾila al-lāmiʿa wa-l-aǧwiba al-ǧāmiʿa*. – Ed. by M. Mahdi [*24: 93–115].

147 *Risāla fī l-ʿIlm al-ilāhī*. – Ed. by ʿAbd al-Raḥmān Badawī, in *Aflūṭīn ʿind al-ʿArab*. Cairo, 1955, 167–183.

148 *Risāla fī Iṯbāt al-mufāraqāt*. – Ed. Hyderabad, 1345 H. [1926]. In *Rasāʾil* [*22: no. 1]; repr. Frankfurt a.M., 1999 [Islamic Philosophy, 16], 41–48. – The same text was published also as ascribed to Bahmanyār b. Marzubān, under the title: *Risāla fī Marātib al-mawǧūdāt*.

149 *Risāla fī Māhiyyat al-nafs*. – Reproduction of the Hebrew transl. from the 13th century (after the first print by Zvi Hirsch Edelmann [Königsberg 1856]) and French transl. by G. Freudenthal 2003 [*44: 227–237. 185–206].

150 *Risāla fī l-Milla al-fāḍila*. – Ed. by ʿA. Badawī [*26: 33–36].

151 *Risāla fī l-Siyāsa*. – Ed. by Louis Cheikho, "Risālat Abī Naṣr al-Fārābī fī l-siyāsa." *Al-Mašriq* 4 (1901): 648–653. 689–700. – Repr. in: *Maqālāt falsafiyya qadīma li-baʿḍ mašāhīr falāsifat al-ʿArab*. Ed. by Louis Malouf, Ḫalīl Eddé, and Louis Cheikho. Beirut, 1911, 18–34. – German transl. by Georg Graf, "Farabis Traktat 'Über die Leitung'." *Jahrbuch für Philosophie und spekulative Theologie* 16 (1902): 385–406. – Repr. of the edition and transl. Frankfurt a.M., 1999 [Islamic Philosophy, 7], 276–293. 295–316.

152 *Risālat Fuṣūṣ al-ḥikam*. – Ed. by F. Dieterici [*20: 66–83]. – Ed. by M. Horten 1904–1905 [*70: 272–294]. – Ed. ʿAlī Awǧabī, Tehran, 1381 h.š./2003. [together with the commentary by Ismāʿīl al-Ḥusaynī al-Šanbġāzānī and glosses by Mīr Dāmād]. – German transl. by F. Dieterici [*21: 108–138].

153 *Šarḥ Risālat Zīnūn al-kabīr*. – Ed. Hyderabad, 1349 H. [1930]. In *Rasāʾil* [*22: no. 7]. – Repr. Frankfurt a.M., 1999 [Islamic Philosophy, 16], 225–234. – Span. transl. and analysis by Josep Puig Montada: "Un tratado de Zenon el Mayor. Un comentario atribuido a al-Fārābī." *La Ciudad de Dios* 201 (1988): 287–321.

154 *Taǧrīd Risālat al-daʿāwā al-qalbiyya*. – Ed. Hyderabad, 1349 [1930]. In *Rasāʾil* [*22: no. 6].

155 *al-Taʿlīqāt*. – Ed. by Ǧaʿfar Āl Yāsīn. Beirut, 1988. – Repr. with different pagination in Ǧ. Āl Yāsīn [*31: 371–406]. – Ed. Hyderabad, 1346 [1927]. In *Rasāʾil* [*22: no. 4]; repr. Frankfurt a.M., 1999 [Islamic Philosophy, 16], 49–74.

156 *ʿUyūn al-masāʾil*. – Ed. by F. Dieterici [*20: 56–65]. – German transl. by F. Dieterici [*21: 92–107].

2 Life and Influence

2.1 Biographical Sources – 2.2 Life – 2.3 Influence

2.1 *Biographical Sources*

Our medieval sources contain precious few reports on al-Fārābī's life, which moreover tend to be rather scant, and at times even contradict each other. Nevertheless these testimonials have acquired a certain significance in the history of the field, since they have been used time and again as a basis for hypotheses about al-Fārābī's person, his convictions, and his philosophical outlook.

The material was collected some time ago by Maḥfūẓ (1975 [*27]) but still awaits critical historical analysis. The beginnings of such an analysis can be found in Mahdi (1990 [*314: 693–694. 705–707. 712–713]) and above all in Gutas (1999 [*42: 208–209]), who was the first to try to identify and assess the various strands of transmission. On the basis of his deliberations we can distinguish between the following types of testimonies:

(1) Occasional remarks contained in the manuscripts that transmit al-Fārābī's works. Such testimonies are rare, but all the more valuable because of their documentary character. This was pointed out already by Walzer (1985 [*276: 20]), who was able to extract evidence from them regarding the genesis and date of the *Mabādiʾ* [*125].

(2) Biographical statements by al-Fārābī himself which are scattered across his report on the transmission of Aristotelian philosophy and its route 'from Alexandria to Baghdad' (*Ẓuhūr* [*53]). Even though their primary purpose is to legitimate al-Fārābī's position as heir and reformer of this tradition, they can tell us a number of interesting details about al-Fārābī's studies and the environment in which he worked.

(3) Reports provided by authors of the 4th/10th and the 5th/11th centuries. They are likewise rather prosaic and brief, but for precisely this reason they may lay claim to a certain amount of plausibility. More specifically, we have remarks by Masʿūdī (*Tanbīh* [*1: 122]; Engl. transl. in Stern 1960 [*21: 39–41]), Ibn al-Nadīm (*Fihrist* [*2: I 263, 8–14 Flügel; II\1 199,1–9 Sayyid; Engl. transl. 629]), Ibn Ḥawqal (*Ṣūra* [*3: 510–511]), and Abū l-Ḥasan al-Ṭabarī (*al-Muʿālaǧāt al-buqraṭiyya*; Arabic text and Engl. transl. in Pormann 2015 [*60: 216. 222–223]), who were younger contemporaries of al-Fārābī. In addition, there is a bio-bibliographical entry in the scientific history of Ṣāʿid al-Andalusī (*Ṭabaqāt* [*4: 53–54; French transl. 107–109]), who, writing in the 5th/11th century, was able to witness the beginnings of the reception of al-Fārābī's works in Spain.

(4) Later accounts, either in works on the history of science, or in biographical collections. They differ markedly from the older testimonies in that they not only embellish the pronouncements of earlier authors with respect to their literary style, but also supplement them with numerous details that have never been mentioned before. This material, which exhibits increasingly tendentious and legendary traits, can, according to Gutas (1999 [*42: 208–209]), be separated into three different strands of transmission: (a) the 'Eastern', i.e. Iranian tradition, which apparently can be discounted as it does not contribute any factual additions to the data found in earlier authors; it manifests itself for the first time in the 6th/12th century in a work by Bayhaqī (*Tatimma* [*5: 41–44]); (b) the 'Syrian' tradition, whose main representative is Ibn Abī Uṣaybiʿa (*ʿUyūn* [*8: II 134–140]); he is said to have collected all testimonies on al-Fārābī that were circulating in the 7th/13th century in Syria; (c) the 'pro-Turkish' tradition, which likewise becomes discernible in the 7th/13th century, this time in Ibn Ḫallikān (*Wafayāt* [*9: V 153–157; Engl. transl. III 307–311]); his extensive account of al-Fārābī's life and merits was apparently aimed at presenting the philosopher as a prominent representative of the Turkish ethnic community. It is, however, difficult to reach an exact classification of the source material since the different lines of transmission cannot always be neatly separated from each other. Thus Ibn al-Qifṭī (*Taʾrīḫ* [*7: 277–280]), for instance, combines statements he finds in Ṣāʿid al-Andalusī with certain traditions of 'Syrian' provenience. Again, Ibn Ḫallikān (who lived in Syria) did not restrict himself to propagating the 'pro-Turkish' hypothesis, but also integrated quotations from Ṣāʿid al-Andalusī in his account, as well as further traditions which were circulating in his home country at the time.

2.2 *Life*

These findings suggest that in describing al-Fārābī's life, it is advisable to base oneself on information stemming from the first three types of sources (Gutas 1999 [*42: 209–210], Reisman 2005 [*50: 52–53]). They only mark a few distinctive points in his biography, and hence can be considered beyond any suspicion of spreading a tendentious image of his person and work. These testimonies indicate that Abū Naṣr Muḥammad b. Muḥammad al-Fārābī's family probably came from Fārāb, a district on the mid Syr Darya (Jaxartes); however, Ibn al-Nadīm holds a contrary view, claiming his native city to be Fāryāb in North Eastern Iran (*Fihrist* [*2: I 263,9 Flügel; II\1 199,2 Sayyid; Engl. transl. 629]). Al-Fārābī's date of birth is unknown. The early sources divulge no information on this point, until we reach Ibn Ḫallikān, who claims that al-Fārābī died at the age of 80 (*Wafayāt* [*9: v 157,10; Engl. transl. iii 310]), which would mean that he was born around 256/870.

We possess no information on al-Fārābī's youth and early education. The reports only pick up again at a point when he had already left his home country and settled in Iraq. Here he visited Abū Yaḥyā Ibrāhīm al-Marwazī (cf. p. 429 above) and, most importantly, Yūḥannā b. Ḥaylān, with whom he wanted to study Aristotelian logic. As al-Fārābī tells us himself (*Ẓuhūr* [*53: 135,20–25]), they read the *Organon* together, up to and including the *Posterior Analytics*, ignored in Christian circles for centuries. In all likelihood this took place in Baghdad, as this is where Yūḥannā b. Ḥaylān was active (according to information from Masʿūdī, he died there during the reign of Caliph al-Muqtadir [regn. 295–320/908–932]), while al-Fārābī himself demonstrably spent many years in the city. This is attested by the fact that he dedicated two of his works to important Baghdad personalities: his *Maqāla fīmā yaṣiḥḥu wa-mā lā yaṣiḥḥu min aḥkām al-nuǧūm* (*Treatise on Admissible and Inadmissible Judgements* [*Based on the Observation*] *of the Stars*) was composed in reply to the entreaty of the Christian scholar Abū Isḥāq Ibrāhīm b. ʿAbd Allāh al-Baġdādī (*Maqāla* [*88: 104–105; German transl. 170–171]); whereas his *Great Book on Music* bears a dedication to the vizier Abū Ǧaʿfar Muḥammad b. al-Qāsim al-Karḫī (*Mūsīqī* [*91: 30,15–16. 35 n. 1]. Besides, we know that in later years, al-Fārābī had his own students in Baghdad, the most famous one being the Jacobite scholar Yaḥyā Ibn ʿAdī.

In 331/942–943, however, al-Fārābī left the Abbasid capital and turned towards Damascus. This can be gleaned from certain notes in the manuscripts of the *Mabādiʾ* (Walzer 1985 [*276: 20]), which are quoted or otherwise confirmed by Ibn Abī ʿUṣaybiʿa (*ʿUyūn* [*8: ii 138,30–139,3]). According to these, the book was begun at the end of the year 330/in September 942 in Baghdad, and completed during the year 331/by September 943 in Damascus.

Al-Fārābī spent the following years in Syria. Details of his time there remain obscure, but we know for sure that he did not live in Damascus only, but also at the court of the Ḥamdānid prince Sayf al-Dawla in Aleppo. Ibrāhīm Ibn ʿAdī (a brother of Yaḥyā Ibn ʿAdī) studied with him there. As we learn from a further manuscript note recorded by Ibn Abī Uṣaybiʿa (*ʿUyūn* [*8: ii 139,19–20]), al-Fārābī apparently dictated a commentary on the *Posterior Analytics* to him.

Later on al-Fārābī also travelled to Egypt, where, it seems, the final editing of the *Mabādiʾ* was accomplished. At least the aforementioned manuscript notes claim that the division of the work into six large sections (*fuṣūl*) was undertaken in the year 337/July 948–June 949 in Egypt (Walzer 1985 [*276: 20]). Nevertheless he cannot have been there for long, as he was back in Damascus soon after. There he died in the month of Raǧab 339/14 December

950–12 January 951, possibly 'under the protection' (*fī kanaf*) of Sayf al-Dawla, as reported for the first time in the biographical note by Ṣāʿid al-Andalusī (*Ṭabaqāt* [*4: 54,10]).

Al-Fārābī's life, then, seems to have been rather uneventful. The authors closest to him in time, i.e. writing in the 4th/10th and the 5th/11th centuries, have nothing much to say about it (cf., however, the remarks on his alleged melancholy highlighted by Pormann 2015 [*60]). This alone makes the elaborate descriptions we encounter in later sources look suspicious. In addition, many of the themes that writers enlarge on from the 6th/12th and especially the 7th/13th century onwards (for instance, al-Fārābī's purported modesty and reclusiveness, his close relation to Sayf al-Dawla, the cause of his death etc.), are quite irrelevant from a philosophical point of view. This also applies to the much-discussed question of al-Fārābī's origins. Scholars have tended to answer this question by assuming a Turkish genealogy (still to be found in Black 1996 [*40: 178] and Fakhry 2002 [*43: 6]), invoking the statements of Ibn Ḫallikān (*Wafayāt* [*9: V 153,5–11; Engl. transl. III 307]). However, his account seems to be programmatic in character, and could well be understood as a conscious response to Ibn Abī Uṣaybiʿa's claim that al-Fārābī's father was Persian by origin (*ʿUyūn* [*8: II 134,3]). This is why Gutas (1999 [*42: 211]) comes to the conclusion that the question cannot be decided on the basis of the available sources, though Vallat (2004 [*47: 11]) argues decidedly for a Persian ancestry.

Some of the reports that emerge in the later sources nevertheless do touch on questions that belong to the sphere of philosophy. It is therefore not surprising that they have been taken up and discussed repeatedly by modern scholars. In particular:

(1) The claim that al-Fārābī studied not only with Yūḥannā b. Ḥaylān, but also with other famous teachers, goes back to two authors of the 7th/13th century: according to Ibn Ḫallikān, al-Fārābī read Aristotelian logic with Abū Bišr Mattā (*Wafayāt* [*9: V 153,13–154,5; Engl. transl. III 307]); according to Ibn Abī Uṣaybiʿa he acquired the intricacies of Arabic grammar from Ibn al-Sarrāǧ, to whom he in turn gave lessons in logic (*ʿUyūn* [*8: II 136,23–24]). Both suggestions are possible, since Abū Bišr Mattā (d. 328/940) and Ibn al-Sarrāǧ (d. 316/928) lived in Baghdad and were acclaimed experts in said disciplines. Therefore al-Fārābī may well have sought their acquaintance, especially given that his deep interest in grammar and logic is well-attested (thus Vallat 2004 [*47: 11. 16–17]). However, one may equally look at the connection the other way round and regard the statements made by Ibn Ḫallikān and Ibn Abī Uṣaybiʿa as having been construed in retrospect. This is Gutas' argument (1999 [*42: 211]): he assumes that the two authors were simply led to these conclusions by al-Fārābī's

stupendous knowledge of both disciplines, inferring that he must have studied with the greatest masters of his time.

(2) The claim that al-Fārābī spoke several languages has, again, been passed on with regularity since the 7th/13th century. Thus we can read in Ibn Ḫallikān that al-Fārābī only learnt Arabic after his arrival in Baghdad (his mother tongue having been Turkish), but in total spoke more than 70 languages (*Wafayāt* [*9: V 153,10–12. 155,15–16; Engl. transl. III 307. 309]). Al-Qazwīnī (d. 682/1283) reports that al-Fārābī translated Aristotle from Greek into Arabic (*Āṯār* [*10: 548,9]). Al-Ṣafadī (d. 764/1363) goes as far as to claim that he studied philosophy in Greek, being as fluent in Greek as in other languages (*Wāfī* [*11: I 106,11–12]). Modern scholarship has rejected these claims, and with good reason. There are no serious indications that al-Fārābī knew any languages besides his mother tongue (be it Persian or Turkish) and Arabic. The most we can say with confidence is that he was alert to the differences between languages with regard to lexis, syntax, etc. Notes and glosses to this effect can be found in several works from his pen, concerning the Sogdian, Syriac (*Ḥurūf* [*46: 111]), Persian and Greek languages (*Ḥurūf* [*46: 111–112]; *Šarḥ fī l-ʿIbāra* [*65: 46; Engl. transl. 37–38]). Some of his comments on Greek, incidentally, clearly prove that al-Fārābī was not familiar with this language (e.g. the wrong etymologies of *philosophia* and *sophistikē*).

(3) The claim, probably linked to (2), that al-Fārābī travelled 'to the Greeks' goes back to a text preserved in a Kabul manuscript, which, however, has not been edited or made accessible in any way to date (notes concerning the MS can be found in De Laugier de Beaurecueil 1964 [*24: 293 no. 40]). This text allegedly contains a variant version of al-Fārābī's well-known report on the transmission of philosophy 'from Alexandria to Bagdhad' (*Ẓuhūr* [*53]). According to Mahdi (1971 [*26: 523–524]), and to Langhade, Grignaschi (1971 [*25: 136–137 n. 2]) it says: 'After that [i.e. after studying with Yūḥannā b. Ḥaylān] he [i.e. al-Fārābī] travelled to the Greeks and remained in their lands for eight years, until he had finished [studying] the science and had acquired the entire philosophical curriculum.' This remark, which stands alone within our corpus of sources (unless one wanted to associate it with the demonstrably false claims, made by al-Qazwīnī and al-Ṣafadī, that al-Fārābī studied Aristotle in Greek), has been interpreted in various ways by modern scholars. At first it spawned the thesis that al-Fārābī spent some time in Constantinople (Mahdi 1971 [*26: 524], Butterworth [*32: IX–X], 2006 [*51: 247], Parens 2006 [*339: 3]); however, this never was widely accepted due to its lack of support in other source texts (Gutas 1999 [*42: 212]). More recently, Vallat (2004 [*47: 17–19]) suggested interpreting the journey 'to the Greeks' as a stay in

Harran (which is furthermore mentioned by Ibn Ḫallikān, *Wafayāt* [*9: v 153,6–7; Engl. transl. iii 307]). He links this claim to a string of further hypotheses: on the one hand he assumes (partly in line with Tardieu 1986 [*32]), that at the time in question, there was still a continuous Platonic tradition reaching back to late antiquity in Harran. On the other hand he considers al-Fārābī's philosophy itself to be essentially Platonic; which Vallat (2004 [*47: 19–26]) wants to explain in historical terms by pointing out that during his sojourn in Harran, al-Fārābī got to know, and to appreciate, a living tradition of Platonism. However, this interpretation does not seem very plausible, given that we must regard its foundation – Tardieu's assumption of a Platonist academy in Harran – as entirely speculative and improbable (cf. pp. 53–54 above).

(4) Finally there is the claim that al-Fārābī was a follower of the Twelver Shia, and aligned his political philosophy in accordance with their doctrine of the Imamate. This assumption is nowhere to be found in our medieval sources, but could be linked to certain remarks we find there. For there are authors (in particular among the later ones) who report that al-Fārābī was a close associate of the Ḥamdānid ruler Sayf al-Dawla (hinted at in Ṣāʿid al-Andalusī, *Ṭabaqāt* [*4: 54,10–11; French transl. 109]; more detailed in Ibn al-Qifṭī, *Taʾrīḫ* [*7: 279,2–5], Ibn Abī Uṣaybiʿa, *ʿUyūn* [*8: ii 134,12–18], and Ibn Ḫallikān, *Wafayāt* [*9: v 155–156; Engl. transl. iii 308–310]); and we know that Sayf al-Dawla openly professed adherence to the Twelver Shia. Some scholars, as e.g. Corbin (1964 [*23: 223. 228–231]) and Walzer (1985 [*276: 15. 441–449]) therefore believed that al-Fārābī sought out the Ḥamdānid ruler because he shared his religious convictions. They proposed that al-Fārābī's concept of an ideal ruler (especially *Mabādiʾ* [*125: ch. 15 §§ 11–14]) did not only reflect the Platonic notion of the philosopher-king, but was also inspired by the doctrine of the Imamate held by the Twelver Shia. The arguments which were put forward to this effect, however, remained rather speculative, which is why this thesis has not prevailed in more recent scholarship. Moreover, it has since been established that al-Fārābī's move from Baghdad to Syria could never have been instigated by an invitation from Sayf al-Dawla, since al-Fārābī had already left Baghdad by the year 331/942–943, whereas Sayf al-Dawla only entered Aleppo two years later (Vallat 2004 [*47: 16]).

2.3 *Influence*

Al-Fārābī belongs to the thinkers known as the 'Baghdad Aristotelians', who are presented in § 7 above. It was in this circle that he received his instruction (cf. p. 429 above), and that his own doctrines and writings were first received. Amongst his direct pupils were, for instance, Yaḥyā Ibn ʿAdī (§ 7.2; cf.

also Netton 1992 [*86: 8–11]) and his brother (?) Ibrāhīm Ibn ʿAdī, who edited al-Fārābī's writings and apparently served as his secretary (Walzer 1985 [*276: 20 n. 8], Rashed 2009 [*57: 71–72]). However, al-Fārābī's influence went beyond this circle early on, as is evidenced by a large number of quotations and testimonies which we find in other authors. They suggest that in the second half of the 4th/10th century, his writings were read by virtually all philosophically inclined people in the central areas of the Islamic world.

Examples include Abū Sulaymān al-Siǧistānī (d. around 374/985; cf. § 5.3 above), Abū l-Ḥasan al-ʿĀmirī (d. 381/992; cf. § 5.2.3), Abū Ḥayyān al-Tawḥīdī (d. 414/1023; cf. § 5.3), and Abū ʿAlī Miskawayh (d. 421/1030; cf. § 5.4) (Netton 1992 [*86: 11–18]). They all built on al-Fārābī as well as on al-Kindī, which seems to have been a characteristic feature of the philosophical debates of the time. Apart from that, al-Fārābī also had readers amongst the Ismailis (i.e. readers who belonged to the 'Sevener Shia'). This may already apply to the authors of the *Rasāʾil Iḫwān al-Ṣafāʾ* (*The Epistles of the Brethren of Purity*) – assuming that they were active between 359/970 and 369/980 and came from an Ismaili milieu (on the problem concerning their historical placement cf. § 9 below; on quotations of and testimonies to al-Fārābī found in the *Rasāʾil*, cf. Walzer 1985 [*276: 246–248. 446], Abouzeid 1987 [*83], Baffioni 2002 [*94]). Most certainly, though, it applies to Ḥamīd al-Dīn al-Kirmānī (d. after 411/1020–1021), who integrated essential elements of al-Fārābī's cosmology and noetics into his Ismaili conceptual system (De Smet 2008 [*104]). In light of this, some scholars have assumed a deeper, personal connection between al-Fārābī and the Ismāʿīliyya. Thus Daiber (1991 [*316]) thinks that al-Fārābī's political theory was already influenced by Ismaili models, whereas Steigerwald even deems it probable that al-Fārābī was himself 'secrètement Ismaélien' (1999 [*92: 476]). However, the arguments they present are not cogent. In the final analysis they only prove that al-Fārābī explored Ismaili ideas – which is not surprising, given his interest in the various intellectual currents of his day (cf. pp. 607–609 and 621–622 below) as well as the Ismailis' political import. Therefore it remains advisable not to assume a particular affinity between al-Fārābī and contemporary Shiite ideas and groups. This applies to the Twelver Shia, which had already been suggested as his potential ideological background by Corbin and Walzer (cf. p. 541 above), as well as for their Ismaili competitors.

It is undeniable that Ibn Sīnā (d. 428/1037; cf. vol. II, § 1) was to play a crucial role in the further proliferation of al-Fārābī's ideas. He was indebted to the latter's philosophy in many aspects and even expressed this connection in a now famous passage of his autobiography (Gutas 1988 [*84: 28. 238–254]). This ensured that al-Fārābī would enjoy lasting influence. Anybody who studied Ibn Sīnā in later centuries was likely to be led back to al-Fārābī in one way or the other. At the same time this meant that al-Fārābī was not always read as a thinker significant in his own right, but as a mere precursor to Ibn Sīnā, providing complementary reading material to the latter's works.

This does not equally apply to the reception al-Fārābī enjoyed in the Western regions of the Islamic world, especially in Spain. Here many of al-Fārābī's works earned recognition in the 5th/11th century at the latest (Ṣāʿid, *Ṭabaqāt* [*4: 53,5–54,12; French transl. 107–109]). From then onwards, all prominent Andalusian authors would quote and discuss his writings: Ibn Bāǧǧa (d. 533/1139), for whom he represented the most authoritative predecessor (Fakhry 2002 [*43: 136–139]; cf. Puig Montada 2005 [*101: 157–165]), Ibn Ṭufayl (d. 581/1185), who judges him much more critically in his philosophical novel, *Ḥayy b. Yaqẓān* (*The Living, Son of the Waking*) (Schaerer 2004 [*99: XXI–XXIX. 8. 10–11]) and, last but not least, Ibn Rušd (d. 595/1198). The latter reacted extensively and with great subtlety to al-Fārābī's writings. In his works we find critical statements which usually are employed in the context of his criticism of Ibn Sīnā (Fakhry 2002 [*43: 140–146]; but cf. now Menn 2012 [*106]), along with passages in which he explicitly takes up al-Fārābī's interpretation of Aristotle, and his deliberations concerning political communities (on this last point, see Mahdi 1978 [*79] and in particular Endress 1986 [*82], 1992 [*38: 45–47], who follows the development of political philosophy through Ibn Bāǧǧa and Ibn Ṭufayl up to Ibn Rušd).

The Andalusian philosophers' interest in al-Fārābī ran so deep that an author as late as Ibn Ḫaldūn (d. 808/1406) repeatedly mentions his name in the same breath as theirs (Rosenthal 1958 [*76: II 371. III 272]; cf. Larcher 2006 [*185: 121 n. 20]). It moreover meant that al-Fārābī's writings were transmitted, through the mediation of the Spanish Muslims, to two further circles of readers: firstly to Jewish thinkers (first in Spain, later on also in other parts of Europe), whose intense engagement with al-Fārābī began in the 6th/12th century. One famous example is Moses Maimonides (Mošeh ben Maimon, d. 601/1204) (Berman 1974 [*78], Brague 1996 [*89: 19–22], Daiber 2005 [*100]), another is Šem Ṭov Ibn Falaquera (d. 694/1295) (Zonta 1995 [*88: 362–363. 368–371], Harvey 2002 [*97]). Furthermore, many works of al-Fārābī were translated into Hebrew (cf. the overview provided by Robinson 2012 [*107: 61–66] and Zonta 2016 [*108: ch. 4]), some of them even several times, such as the *Risāla fī l-ʿAql* (*Epistle on the Intellect*), which enjoyed particular attention in these circles (Freudenthal 2002 [*96]).

In a parallel development, several of al-Fārābī's works were translated into Latin. This process seems to have started in the early 6th/12th century with the translation of *Iḥṣāʾ al-ʿulūm* (*The Enumeration of the Sciences*) (for the various Latin versions cf. Schupp 2005 [*102], Schneider 2006 [*103]), which was to have a lasting impact. The *Risāla fī l-ʿAql*, which also had many readers in the Latin world (Gilson 1929 [*71], Schneider 1995 [*87]) followed suit soon after that. Apart from that, the number of translations remained rather limited. Nevertheless the corpus of 'Farabi Latinus' (for overviews of the translated works see Salman 1939 [*73], Schneider 1994 [*177: 697–703], 2006 [*103: 37–46]; cf. also Bédoret 1938 [*72], Salman 1940 [*74], 1948 [*75]) does preserve some textual material which appears to be lost in Arabic, as e.g. certain quotations from al-Fārābī's commentary on the *Nicomachean Ethics* (Fakhry 2002 [*43: 149]) or the brief work on Aristotle's *Physics* which was edited by Birkenmajer (1935 [*236]) under the title *Distinctio super librum Aristotelis de naturali auditu*.

In the central regions and in the East of the Islamic world, al-Fārābī's impact remained, however, more closely tied to the reception of Ibn Sīnā's philosophy. This applies to authors who engaged critically with Ibn Sīnā (or with both of them), as e.g. Abū Ḥāmid al-Ġazālī (d. 505/1111) (Marmura 1997 [*90: XIX–XX. 4. 83]), as well as for those who followed him in essential points. Beginning with the 7th/13th century, the latter group became rather numerous, which may well suggest that the increased interest that al-Fārābī receives in the biographical literature of the 7th/13th century (cf. p. 539 above), could be explained by a more general upsurge in philosophical studies. This does not mean to say, however that he was henceforth read merely as a supplementary voice to Ibn Sīnā.

Instead, the manner of his reception will have differed according to topic and subject area. It needs to be added that assessments of this kind must remain provisional, since reading habits and the formation of traditions during this time have not been extensively studied so far. Nevertheless it is beyond dispute that al-Fārābī's remarks on political communities (from the *Mabādiʾ* and from *al-Siyāsa al-madanīya*) form a separate field of reception; they were picked up and expanded within the so-called '*aḫlāq*' (ethics) tradition, whose most important representatives are Naṣīr al-Dīn al-Ṭūsī (d. 672/1274) and Ǧalāl al-Dīn al-Dawānī (d. 908/1502) (Rosenthal 1958 [*303: 210–223], Lambton 1965 [*77], Madelung 1985 [*81], Gutas 1999 [*42: 222]; cf. also Crone 2004 [*334: 222–224]) and, later on, eagerly studied (along with other works by al-Fārābī) by the Iranian thinkers of the 10th/16th and 11th/17th centuries (Endress 1992 [*38: 45 n. 132], 2001 [*93: 22–23]). Further clearly distinct areas are constituted by logic, where al-Fārābī's ideas were taken up by several later thinkers despite Ibn Sīnā's general predominance (examples can be found in El-Rouayheb 2010 [*105: 74. 146–148]), and, of course, by music (Sawa 1999 [*42: 225]). Apart from that, the doctrine that religion or theology is but a symbolic representation of philosophy remained tied to al-Fārābī's name for a long time, as we can see e.g. from a testimony from Saʿd al-Dīn al-Taftāzānī (d. 793/1390) (*Šarḥ al-Maqāṣid* [*91: 93]).

Within the central field of metaphysics, however, al-Fārābī's influence was shaped and superceded by the reception of Ibn Sīnā's philosophy, which may also explain the origin of several inauthentic works, including the *Risāla Fuṣūṣ al-ḥikam* (*Epistle on the Bezels of Wisdom*), the *Risāla fī Iṯbāt al-mufāraqāt* (*Epistle on the Proof of the Existence of the Separate Entities*) and the *ʿUyūn al-masāʾil* (*The Principal Questions*), which foist some of Ibn Sīnā's metaphysical core theses onto al-Fārābī (cf. pp. 591–594 below). This became an influential aspect of al-Fārābī's legacy, since such texts were studied and interpreted over centuries, under the assumption they were genuine (Endress 2001 [*93: 22]). Some of the later commentaries on the *Fuṣūṣ al-ḥikam* have now been made accessible, either in excerpts or in their entirety (Horten 1904–1914 [*70], Dānišpažūh 1979 [*80], Awǧabī 2003 [*98]). But it is to be assumed that this material is much more extensive, and that its full assessment remains a task for future scholarship.

3 Works

3.1 Lists of Works – 3.2 General Theory of Science – 3.3 Propaedeutics – 3.4 Logic – 3.5 Mathematics – 3.6 Physics – 3.7 Metaphysics – 3.8 Ethics and Politics – 3.9 Philosophical *Summae* – 3.10 Lost Works – 3.11 Disputed and Spurious Works

3.1 *Lists of Works*

Even though several medieval sources contain inventories of al-Fārābī's works, it is not possible to reconstruct his œuvre exactly: the data proffered by the various authors differ considerably. As a rule – which also applies to the biographical reports – the older sources (4th/10th and 5th/11th cent.) provide rather brief but reliable information, whereas later accounts unfurl extensive material which often does not withstand closer scrutiny.

The first list of works we owe to Ibn al-Nadīm. In the course of his explanatory remarks on the Arabic translations of, and commentaries on the *Organon* (*Fihrist* [*2: I 248–250 Flügel; II\1 161–164 Sayyid; Engl. transl. 598–602]) as well as on al-Fārābī himself (I 263 Flügel; II\1 199 Sayyid; Engl. transl. 629) he mentions twelve titles in total: epitomes of the *Categories, Posterior Analytics, Topics, Sophistical Refutations* and *Rhetoric*, commentaries on the *Categories, On Interpretation, Posterior Analytics, Topics, Rhetoric*, and (*Nicomachean*) *Ethics*, as well as *Marātib al-ʿulūm* (*The Steps of the Sciences*). Without exception, they denote works that can be assumed to be genuine, even if they are partly lost. This applies in a similar manner to the remarks by Ṣāʿid al-Andalusī (*Ṭabaqāt* [*4: 53–54; French transl. 107–109]). Beyond making the general remark that al-Fārābī explained the five domains of logic, he names only four individual titles: *Iḥṣāʾ al-ʿulūm*, *Kitāb fī Aġrāḍ falsafat Aflāṭūn wa-Arisṭāṭālīs*, *al-Siyāsa al-madaniyya* and *al-Sīra al-fāḍila*, which is probably meant to refer to the work *Mabādiʾ ārāʾ ahl al-madīna al-fāḍila* (see Daiber 1986 [*310: 742]).

With al-Bayhaqī (*Tatimma* [*5: 41,12–42,2]) we arrive at a group of inventories which are more extensive but must be approached with caution. Al-Bayhaqī, it is true, does not record more than 32 titles; but beside genuine works by al-Fārābī, his list also contains texts whose authenticity is disputed (e.g. the *Risāla fī l-Siyāsa*), as well as a third category of works which are, in fact, only mentioned by him (e.g. an alleged *Risāla fī l-Adwiya*). Such imponderabilities are the hallmarks of all bibliographical lists produced after the 6th/12th century. Some of them are very extensive, which may well be explained by the fact that al-Fārābī had, by that time, gained an indisputable reputation, with the result that his works were recorded more extensively than before. The increased interest in his person also led people to ascribe numerous new texts to him which followed the 'mainstream' philosophy of the time, i.e. Avicennian ideas. This observation applies in the first instance to those three authors who have received the greatest amount of scholarly attention so far: Ibn al-Qifṭī, who, in his account, first repeats the information recorded by Ṣāʿid (*Taʾrīḫ* [*7: 277–278]) before adding his own work list, containing 73 titles [*7: 279,7–280,11]; Ibn Abī Uṣaybiʿa, who compiles various sources before listing more than 100 titles at the end of his chapter on al-Fārābī (*ʿUyūn* [*8: II 138,14–140,6]; for a comparison of both lists see Steinschneider 1869 [*15: 214–220]); and al-Ṣafadī, who merely assembles older material, including the long inventory taken over from Ibn Abī Uṣaybiʿa (*Wāfī* [*11: I 108,15–111,2]).

3.2 *General Theory of Science*

Iḥṣāʾ al-ʿulūm
The Enumeration of the Sciences

This text, which is probably identical with the work which Ibn al-Nadīm (*Fihrist* [*2: I 263,10 Flügel; II\1 199,4 Sayyid; Engl. transl. 629]) and others call *Marātib al-ʿulūm* (*The Steps of the Sciences*), describes the subject matter of the individual sciences, thereby marking off their domains. This gives rise to a dichotomy between the universally valid discipline of philosophy (with the sub-disciplines of logic, mathematics, physics, metaphysics and politics/ethics) and those disciplines with a more limited scope of application (grammar, law, and theology). The enumeration of the chapters follows Amīn's edition.

Introduction: purpose, division, and benefit of the work. I: Linguistics (*ʿilm al-lisān*). Semantics (applied to individual words as well as to compound expressions); morphology; syntax; orthography; recitation; prosody/metrics. II: Logic (*ʿilm al-manṭiq*). Subject matter: the rules of thinking; benefit: the evaluation of statements; field of application: all intelligibles, or rather the terms that denote them; universal validity (in contrast to grammar, which always refers to a specific language); division according to the eight parts of the *Organon*; primacy of the *Posterior Analytics*. III: Mathematics (*ʿilm al-taʿālīm*). Arithmetics; geometry; optics; astrology (which is a skill, not a science) and astronomy; music; statics; engineering. IV: Physics (*al-ʿilm al-ṭabīʿī*) and metaphysics (*al-ʿilm al-ilāhī*). Subject matter of physics: bodies and their properties; method: asking about material, formal, efficient, and final cause; division in eight parts in accordance with Aristotle's *Physics*, *On the Heavens*, *On Generation and Corruption*, *Meteorology* I–III, *Meteorology* IV, *On Stones* (Ps.), *On Plants* (Ps.), *History of Animals*. Subject matter of metaphysics: (1) being *qua* being, (2) the principles of proof in the individual theoretical sciences and (3) incorporeal being, which exists, and is manifold but not infinite in number, ordered hierarchically, and originating from God, who is the First, One, and Perfect Being. V: Science of the community (*al-ʿilm al-madanī*), law (*ʿilm al-fiqh*) and theology (*ʿilm al-kalām*). Subject matter of the science of the community (on this phrase, see below pp. 633–635): actions and character traits which will lead to true happiness (in the hereafter) and are to be met with in polities that enjoy excellent leadership (*siyāsa* or *riʾāsa*). Excellent leadership is based on (1) knowledge of the general rules (*al-qawānīn al-kulliyya*) and (2) experience (comparison with medicine). Philosophy (*al-falsafa al-madaniyya*) imparts (1), by virtue of identifying happiness and the actions belonging to it, and by defining how a given community and its leaders are supposed to be constituted in order for the citizens to reach this goal. This polity is demarcated from ignorant communities who pursue erroneous ideas of happiness and do not use knowledge but merely experience to orient themselves. The role of jurisprudence: deriving judgements from statements contained within the religious law (*šarīʿa*); field of application: a religion (*milla*) or a community (*umma*); division into one part that is concerned with opinions (*ārāʾ*), and one that is concerned with actions (*afʿāl*). Subject matter of theology: the same opinions and actions, which go back to a founder of religion (*wāḍiʿ al-milla*); the theologian, however, does not derive conclusions from them as the legal scholar does; his task is instead to ensure or enforce (*nuṣra*) these opinions and to refute opposed opinions; examples for the arguments which are employed by the various theological schools in furtherance of this task.

Kitāb al-Ḥurūf
The Particles

Another text on the sciences, albeit one in which al-Fārābī goes beyond a mere description and classification of the various disciplines, and engages with the more fundamental question of the basis of scientific thinking, both from a systematic and from a historical perspective. The systematic perspective comes to the fore in sections I and III, where al-Fārābī investigates the connection between language use, in particular the posing of questions (with special regard to the interrogative particles), and the various forms of thinking (especially conceptual thinking). The historical perspective dominates section II, where al-Fārābī explains how different forms of thinking and scientific disciplines emerge as stages of progress in people's (or humankind's) linguistic and reflective capacity.

Al-Fārābī's argument is complex, and apart from aspects of logic, philosophy of language, and theory of science also touches on central ontological questions. Moreover, since the Arabic term *ḥurūf* does not only denote 'particles', but also 'letters', and since in Arabic, Aristotle's *Metaphysics* bore (among others) the title *Book of* (i.e. *known by*) *Letters* (due to the fact that its individual books are named after the letters of the alphabet), Mahdi edited the work under the title *The Book of Letters*, arguing that the text was a (free) commentary on the *Metaphysics* (Mahdi [*46: 30–34 of the Arabic introduction]). However, this view has not prevailed. Instead, there is now a long-standing consensus that al-Fārābī's deliberations take their cue from the meanings and functions of the particles, which is why the title of the book correctly translates as *The Particles* (cf. e.g. Diebler 2005 [*181: 276]). A short while ago, however, Menn (2008 [*284: 62–71]) pointed out that this diagnosis need not preclude a proximity to important concerns of the *Metaphysics* (and in particular to *Metaphysics* V), and hence suggested that the title is at the same time an allusion to the Aristotelian work [*284: 59. 63. 71].

The enumeration of chapters follows Mahdi's edition. One needs to remember, however, that the available text, which is based on a single Arabic manuscript, contains occasional breaks (especially in the transition from section I to II) and is not likely to represent the original version of the text. An improved edition (based on three manuscripts) was being prepared by Mahdi, but never reached completion. For thoughts on the original order of the text cf. Menn (2008 [*284: 66]), on a testimonial preserved in Ǧalāl al-Dīn al-Suyūṭī (d. 911/1505), cf. Larcher (2006 [*185]). A complete French translation is provided by Hilal (1997 [*41: II]), a detailed analytical overview of the contents by Diebler (2005 [*181: 295–305]).

I: Language and conceptual thinking (particles and categories). 1: That (*anna*). 2: When (*matā*). 3: Questions lead to categorical propositions. 4–6: The categories as first intelligibles; their division; their being called *maqūlāt* ([types of] predication). 7–10: First and second intelligibles; the impossibility of third intelligibles. 11–18: The conceptualized object as subject matter of the sciences. 19–26: Relations between name and object (homonymy, synonymy, paronymy etc.); the ten categories and their linguistic representations. 27–36: Linguistic terms (*alfāẓ*): basic forms, derivations, abstractions etc.; their use within the sciences and within various languages. 37–55: *Nisba* (relationship, ratio, proportion etc.) and *iḍāfa* (relation) and their different meanings within the sciences and within ordinary language. 56–61: Accident (*ʿaraḍ*). 62–73: Substance (*ǧawhar*). 74–79: Essence (*ḏāt*). 80–103: Being (*mawǧūd*).

104–105: Thing (*šay'*). 106: For-the-sake-of-which (*allaḏī min aǧlihi*). 107: From/out of (*'an*).

II: The development of the sciences (vernacular and philosophical language). 108–113: Provisional résumé: dialectics, sophistics, philosophy, religion, theology and law originated one after another and constitute a hierarchy of knowledge. The elite and the masses. 114–119: Man as rational being; the necessity of communication; the formation of phonemes and words. 120–122: The generation of vocabulary through convention (*iṣṭilāḥ*) and a 'giver of language' (*wāḍiʿ lisān*). 123–128: The differentiation and standardization of vocabulary. 129–139: Generation of the 'general', i.e. generally comprehensible, disciplines (rhetoric, poetics, the art of narration and mnemonics, linguistics [i.e. lexicography and grammar], and the art of writing). 140: The search for causes leads to the development of mathematics and physics. 141: Formation of dialectics (and sophistics). 142: Perfection of dialectics; development of politics (= state of philosophy during Plato's time). 143: Perfection of philosophy through Aristotle's theory of demonstration. 144: Instruction of the masses through religion (*milla*). 145: Theology and jurisprudence serve religion. 146: The described order of process will unfold within each culture, as long as it enjoys an autonomous development. 147–153: Possible interferences and conflicts, if the development is influenced by external factors (e.g. exposure to other cultures). 154–158: Possibilities for the development of a religious and philosophical terminology (including 156: examples from the Greek-Arabic reception).

III: Questions and conceptual thinking (particles and forms of speech or discourse). 159–161: Definitions and forms of speech or discourse. 162: Scientific language is composed of questions and categorical propositions. 163: Interrogative pronouns. 164–165: Literal and metaphorical usage in poetics, rhetoric, sophistics, dialectics, and philosophy. 166–182: What (*mā*). 183–199: Which (*ayyun*). 200–209: How (*kayfa*). 210–214: The yes-no question (*hal*). 215–225: Philosophical questions (whether, what, why) and the quest for the four Aristotelian causes; differences between apodeictics, dialectics, rhetoric, and sophistics. 226–244: The use of interrogative pronouns in philosophy (apodeictics). 245–247: Their use in dialectics. 248: Their use in sophistics. 249–251: Their use in rhetoric and poetry.

3.3 *Propaedeutics*

al-Tanbīh 'alā sabīl al-sa'āda
Exhortation to the Path to Happiness

Popular introduction to ethics, which al-Fārābī, following the late antique tradition, construes in the manner of a propaedeutics for philosophical instruction. Sections I and II treat of the basic concepts and the ethical virtues, referring extensively to the *Nicomachean Ethics* (cf. especially its books I–III). Section III has a transitional function. It starts with the dianoetic virtues (again following the *Nicomachean Ethics*) and goes on to classify the objects of cognition (i.e. the sciences), before finally referring to the proper beginning of the curriculum, i.e. the study of logic. The following enumeration of the chapters does not follow any of the available Arabic editions, but Mallet's French translation (1987–1988 [*34: 120–140]), which is structured more adequately.

I: Happiness and virtue. 1: Happiness as ultimate human perfection (*nihāyat al-kamāl al-insānī*). 2–3: The path to happiness leads through actions, affections of the soul, and rational discernment (*al-tamyīz bi-l-ḏihn*), all of which must be praiseworthy and the result of our free decision (*ṭawʿ wa-ḫtiyār*). 4: All this is based on our innate capacity (*quwwa*), which we can develop into an ethical disposition (*ḫulq*) and into the capability to think. 5: This is how, finally, good character and intellectual habit (*malaka*) will come about; together they constitute human virtue (*al-faḍīla al-insāniyya*). II: Ethical virtues. 6: Through repetition of praiseworthy actions, a good character will transform into a good habit (comparison with the art of writing). 7: Praiseworthy actions must always aim for the mean (*tawassuṭ*) and avoid extremes (comparison with medicine). 8: Criteria for determining the mean. 9: Catalogue of ethical virtues, together with the corresponding extremes. 10: The necessity to analyse and improve one's own character (comparison with medical diagnosis and therapy). 11: In order to find the mean we need to counterbalance our tendencies towards certain extremes with their opposites. 12: Criteria for knowing that we lie in the mean. 13: The role played by pleasure (*laḏḏa*) and pain (*aḏan*) in the formation of one's character. 14: Implementation of these insights in one's interactions with various types of people, and in the upbringing of children. III: Dianoetic virtues. 15: Discernment (*tamyīz*) enables us to grasp things and to separate good actions from bad ones. In both cases the aim of the learning process is a good (*ǧamīl*). There are further disciplines (e.g. medicine) that aim at the useful (*nāfiʿ*). 16: Together, the mental activities aiming at a good constitute philosophy; division into theoretical and practical philosophy with further subdivisions. 17: Since each mental activity must heed the rules of logic, the study of logic ought to form the beginning of the curriculum. 18: Explanations of certain concepts (*ʿaql, nuṭq, manṭiq*); differences between, and common characteristics of logic and grammar. 19: The first intelligibles as starting point of logic. 20: In order to become aware of our knowledge of the first intelligibles we need linguistic expressions which indicate them (*alfāẓ dālla*). Hence grammar, as science of language, can be useful to logic.

Fīmā yanbaġī an yuqaddama qabla taʿallum al-falsafa
On What Must Proceed the Study of [*Aristotelian*] *Philosophy*

The work is entirely inscribed in the tradition of the late ancient 'Introductions to Aristotle's Philosophy' (Προλεγόμενα πρὸς τὴν Ἀριστοτελικὴν φιλοσοφίαν). Al-Fārābī's account is peculiar only in that he reduces the classical scheme of subjects in need of explanation from ten to nine. He discusses (1) the origins of the names of the philosophical schools; (2) the division of Aristotle's works; (3–5) the beginning, the final aim and the path of philosophical studies; (6) the various methods used by Aristotle in explicating his subjects; (7) why Aristotle at times used a method of explication that is difficult to understand; (8) what are the prerequisites expected from students of philosophy; and (9) what one needs to know about the individual works by Aristotle (aim, benefit, partition etc.). Brief information on these points with regard to the first four books of the *Organon* is supplied at the end of the work.

Despite certain doubts that have been expressed occasionally (Zimmermann 1981 [*163: 258–259]), the small treatise can be regarded as an authentic work by al-Fārābī. A short analysis and contextualisation of the text is provided by Gutas (1985 [*30]; cf. also Reisman 2005 [*50: 54]).

Fī Ẓuhūr al-falsafa
On the Emergence of Philosophy

This is a treatise on intellectual history, in which al-Fārābī describes the history of philosophy as a continuous tradition of teaching from Aristotle up to his own time. The work became known through an extensive testimonial in Ibn Abī Uṣaybiʿa (*ʿUyūn* [*8: II 134,30–135,24]), but a primary witness is still lacking, even though the text is said to be transmitted in a Kabul manuscript (for information on this see Gutas 1999 [*137: 158] and p. 540 above). For this reason the fragment transmitted by Ibn Abī Uṣaybiʿa has commanded even more attention. Among other things, it depicts philosophy's journey 'from Alexandria to Baghdad'; on which account it has been discussed in numerous scholarly contributions (cf. pp. 51–53 above) and has been translated into several languages (into English most recently by Gutas 1999 [*137: 158–167]; into German most recently by Strohmaier 1987 [*136: 381–382]). It has been noted that al-Fārābī's account is not isolated but belongs to a narrative complex which is manifest in several Arabic authors, and which broaches the transmission of ancient philosophy or medicine to the Arabs in different variants (Gutas 1999 [*137]).

Al-Fārābī's account, however, is limited to the tradition of philosophical teaching, which he divides into the following stages: the continuation of philosophical teaching after Aristotle's death in Alexandria up to the reign of Cleopatra (at which point Andronicus is said to have been in charge of the school). The take-over of the tradition by the Romans: Augustus has Aristotle's books copied, as well as those of his students, and orders them to be used for teaching in Alexandria and in Rome. With the advent of Christianity (i.e. with Constantine), philosophical instruction comes to an end in Rome, continuing in Alexandria only. Restriction of philosophical teaching also in Alexandria: in accordance with a resolution of the Christian bishops, the *Organon* may only be read 'up to and including the figures of the categorical syllogisms' (i.e. up to and including *Prior Analytics* I 7). Transfer of teaching activities (with said restriction) from Alexandria to Antioch during the early Islamic era. Activities of scholars from Harran and Marw. The arrival of philosophy in Baghdad, where logic can once again be studied without any restriction.

3.4 *Logic*

al-Tawṭiʾa fī l-manṭiq
Introduction to Logic

This text is also known by the title *al-Risāla allatī suddira bihā l-manṭiq* (*The Treatise with which Logic Opens*). It begins with some explanations which, with respect to their structure, are dependent on the late ancient *Introductions to the Whole of Philosophy* (Προλεγόμενα πρὸς τὴν πᾶσαν φιλοσοφίαν) (ch. 1–4). They are followed by a set of remarks designed to lead on to the first part of the curriculum, i.e. Porphyry's *Isagoge* (ch. 5). The following enumeration of chapters follows the edition and translation by Dunlop.

1: Logic is the touchstone of thinking (*ʿiyār al-ʿaql*), in contrast to grammar, which is concerned with a single language only. 2: Differentiation between syllogistic and non-syllogistic disciplines (e.g. medicine, agriculture) and, within the syllogistic disciplines, between those that are demonstrative (philosophy) and those that are dialectical, sophistical, rhetorical, or poetical. 3: Division of the *Organon* in three general books (*Categories*, *On Interpretation*, *Prior Analytics*) and five books that each deal with a specific syllogism; division of philosophy as a whole. 4: (Demonstrative) logic provides the philosopher with a guarantee of certain knowledge (*al-ʿilm al-yaqīn*); its subject matter is the universally valid 'inner language' (*al-nuṭq al-dāḫil*). 5: Simple (universal and individual) predicates; the five simple universal predicables: genus, species, difference, proprium, accident. 6: Composite predicates; definitions (*ḥadd*), descriptions (*rasm*) and characterizations by means of the indication of accidents.

Fuṣūl taštamil ʿalā ǧamīʿ mā yuḍtarr ilā maʿrifatihi man arāda l-šurūʿ fī ṣināʿat al-manṭiq [*al-Fuṣūl al-ḫamsa*]
Chapters Containing Everything a Beginner in the Art of Logic Needs to Know [*The Five Chapters*]

This treatise does not follow the established patterns of late ancient 'prolegomena' but explains a number of basic requirements and concepts of logic in a rather unconventional manner. Its fourth section is modelled on the twelth chapter of the *Categories*, the fifth section on certain parts of *On Interpretation*. The enumeration of chapters follows Dunlop's system.

1: Each discipline has its own technical terms. 2: Propositions or mental content not based on syllogistic reasoning: those that are adopted (from trustworthy people) (*maqbūlāt*); those that are universally recognized (*mašhūrāt*), e.g. ethical principles; sense perceptions (*maḥsūsāt*); primary intelligibles (*maʿqūlāt uwal*). 3: Differentiation between essential and accidental connections. 4: The five kinds of priority: time; nature; sequence; rank; causality. 5: Simple expressions with simple meanings: noun (*ism*), word (*kalima*) or verb (*fiʿl*) and instrument (*adāt*) or particle (*ḥarf*). Composite expressions (a) with simple meanings: composites; (b) with composite meanings: phrases and sentences; their use within definitions and descriptions.

al-Alfāẓ al-mustaʿmala fī l-manṭiq
Linguistic Expressions Used in Logic

This is a third introductory text to logic, surpassing the two previous ones in size as well as in significance. Its starting point is the insight (hinted at several times already) that logic deals not only with (universal) intelligibles but also with those (Greek, Arabic, etc.) words which denote those intelligibles. Therefore al-Fārābī strives to present the basic concepts and assumptions of the *Organon* in clear and comprehensible form, and thus makes a major contribution to the conceptualization and development of Arabic terminology, so as to render it fit for the representation of philosophical ideas. The enumeration of sections and chapters follows Mahdi's edition.

I: Simple linguistic expressions which indicate something (*alfāẓ dālla*), comprise (1) noun (*ism*), verb (*kalima*) and (2) particle (*ḥarf*). (3) It is the aim of this investigation to determine the signifying function which each of them possesses within logic. II: Five kinds of particles: (4) representatives (*ḫawālif*), i.e. pronouns; (5) connectives (*wāṣilāt*), i.e. articles and other determinants; (6) intermediaries (*wāsiṭāt*), i.e. prepositions; (7) fillers (*ḥawāšin*) as e.g. confirmations, negations, restrictions and interrogative pronouns; (8) connections (*rawābiṭ*), i.e. conjunctions. III: (9) The sentence (*qawl*) as combination of simple expressions; the simple nominal clause, i.e. the categorical statement, as proper subject matter of logical investigation. (10) The combination of expressions within language corresponds to the combination of meanings within the soul. (11) Universals and individual concepts. IV: (12) Universals can be predicated on their own or together. (13–14) In the latter case they possess a general, a specific, or an equal extension; (15) in the former case they are exclusive. (16) Absolute and non-absolute predication. (17) Degrees of universality. V: Simple universals: (18) the question about quiddity as starting point. (19–25) Genus and species. (16–29) Difference. (30) Proprium. (31) Accident. VI: Composite universals: (32) Definitions. (33) Descriptions. (34) Congruity between definition and species. (35) Relation between definition and name. VII: Definitions can also be reached through (36–37) diaeresis (*qisma*) and (38) composition (*tarkīb*). (39) Diaeresis by accidents and propria.

VIII: Instruction ought to rely on teaching and imitation. The student needs to form concepts (*taṣawwur*) and make judgements concerning existence and the truth of predications (*taṣdīq*). (41) Means of instruction: (a) characterizations, definitions, particular and universal concepts, descriptions, propria, accidents, similarity, (b) opposition, diaeresis, example, induction, syllogism, concrete illustration. (42–44) Various applications of (a). (45) Aristotle's method. (46) Critique of the Pythagoreans, Empedocles and in particular Plato (with reference to Aristotle); allegories (*rumūz*) and riddles (*alġāz*) ought to be confined to rhetoric and political speech. (47) The application of opposites, (48) of diaeresis, (49) of induction, of the example and (50) of illustration. IX: (51) The student needs to know the aim, benefit, division, relation, rank, title, author and method of a book. (52–55) What he will gain through logic; five forms of logical instruction (poetical, rhetorical, sophistical, dialectical, certain [demonstrative]); what they have in common (syllogism) and what differentiates them from each other (five kinds of syllogism). (56) Syllogisms do not connect words but intelligible concepts. (57) Structure of the syllogism. X: Introduction to logic: (58) aim, (59) benefit, (60) division (i.e. a description of the *Organon*), (61) relation (to philosophy and grammar), (62) rank (within the curriculum), (63) author (i.e. Aristotle, as is shown in a brief summary of the history of logic), (64) types of instruction. (65) Transition to reading the texts proper, which must begin with the *Categories*.

Īsāġūğī ay al-Madḫal
Isagoge, i.e. Introduction

Epitome of Porphyry's *Isagoge* (= part II of the text), supplemented by a short introduction (= I) and a section on composite universals, corresponding, in terms of contents, to ch. 6 of the *Tawṭi'a* (= III). The enumeration of chapters follows Dunlop.

I: Introduction. 1: The subject matter of the book is formed by the expressions which are used in judgements (*qaḍāyā*) as subjects or predicates. 2: Differentiation between individual concepts (used, among other things, in rhetoric and poetics) and universals (used especially within the sciences). 3: Simple and composite universals. II: Simple universals. 4–5: Genus and species. 6–13: Difference; its relation to genus; the application of both within definitions. 14: Proprium. 15: Accident. 16: Different options for subdividing genera. III: Composite universals. 17: Definitions. 18: Descriptions; Characterizations based on indicating species and/or accidents.

Qāṭāġūriyās ay al-Maqūlāt
Categories, i.e. the [Types of] Predication[s]

Epitome of the *Categories*. Al-Fārābī covers the central themes of the treatise at length, in parts even more extensively than Aristotle. On the other hand, he leaves out of his account the questions Aristotle addresses at the beginning (homonyms, synonyms, paronyms) and towards the end of the text (the types of movement). The enumeration of chapters follows Dunlop.

1–2: Universal (*kullī*) and individual (*šaḫṣ*) substances and accidents; the ten categories/highest genera (*aǧnās ʿāliya*) as (types of) predication(s) about things. 3–5: Substance (*ǧawhar*). 6–15: Quantity (*kam*). 16–20: Quality (*kayfiyya*). 21–28: Relation and the relative (*al-iḍāfa wa-l-muḍāf*). 29–31: When (*matā*). 32–33: Where (*ayna*). 34–35: Position (*waḍʿ*). 36: Possession (*lahu*). 37–38: Affection (*yanfaʿil*). 39–40: Action (*yafʿal*). 41: The categories may be understood logically or ontologically. 42: Transition to the post-predicaments. 43: Distinction between 'essential' and 'accidental'. 44–55: The four kinds of opposites. 56–58: Essential and accidental concomitants (*al-mutalāzimāt*). 59: 'Earlier' and 'later'. 60: 'At the same time'.

[*Šarḥ al-Maqūlāt*]
[*Commentary on the Categories*]

For a long time, a few brief Arabic quotations surviving in a commentary on the *Categories* by a certain ʿAbd Allāh al-Ḏahabī (4th/10th or 5th/11th cent.?) were all that was known of al-Fārābī's commentary on the *Categories* (Türker 1965 [*156: 103–122]). Meanwhile, however, more extensive fragments have been discovered in Hebrew. They can be found in a supercommentary on Ibn Rušd's *Middle Commentary* on the *Categories* penned by the 9th/15th century author Yehuda ben Yiṣḥaq ben Mošeh Kohen (Zonta 2006 [*187: 188–192]). In detail, Yehuda quotes al-Fārābī's explanations on the following topics: aim, title, benefit, division, position within the curriculum, and method of the work; *Cat.* 1a1–15 (homonyms, synonyms, paronyms); 1a16 and 1a20–1b9 (words within and outside a sentence; individual and general substances); 1b16–24 (scope of a predication in the case of higher- and lower-order terms); 1b25–2a10 (table of categories); 2a11–31 (explanations concerning substance).

Bārī Armīniyās ay al-ʿIbāra
Peri hermeneias, i.e. On Interpretation

Epitome of *On Interpretation*. Even more than in his epitome of the *Categories* al-Fārābī breaks away from his model, altering the focus through transpositions, additions and a systematic structuring of the problems under discussion. None of the available Arabic editions, nor the English translation, contains a systematic division of the text (the sub-headings in al-ʿAǧam are misleading).

1: Forms of linguistic expression: simple expressions with simple meanings (noun, verb, particle). Composite expressions with simple meanings (composites). Composite expressions with composite meanings (phrases, sentences); five types of sentences:

(true and false) statement, order, request, wish, interjection. Different types of meaning: metaphorical (*mustaʿār*), transposed (*manqūl*), equivocal (*muštarak*), univocal (*mutawāṭiʾ*), common (*ʿāmm*), specific (*ḫāṣṣ*), distinct (*mutabāyin*), synonymous (*mutarādif*), derivative (*muštaqq*). Their application to the ten categories.

II: The declarative sentence: categorical and conditional judgements. Affirmations and negations containing definite and indefinite nouns: simple (*basīṭ*), privative (*ʿadamī*), metathetical (*maʿdūl*). Their application in contrary and contradictory sentences. Affirmation and negation in modal statements. Three primary modes (*ǧihāt*): necessary (*ḍarūrī*), possible (*mumkin*), absolute, i.e. not specified (*muṭlaq*). Contradictory sentences about necessary, absolute, and possible (also: future) things. Possible *per se* and possible for us (i.e. depending on our knowledge).

Šarḥ al-Fārābī li-Kitāb Arisṭūṭālīs fī l-ʿIbāra
Al-Fārābī's Commentary on Aristotle's On Interpretation

This is the only lemmatized commentary ('great commentary') written by al-Fārābī on a work by Aristotle to be extant in its entirety. It consists of the lemmata of the base text together with detailed comments. Following the Alexandrian tradition, al-Fārābī divides his discussion of the fourteen chapters of *On Interpretation* in five larger sections (*fuṣūl*).

Introduction: purpose, division, title, classification, and benefit of the text; its position within the curriculum. I: The relation between language and thought; noun and verb; sentence; simple categorical judgements (commenting on ch. 1–6 of the base text). II: Contrarily and contradictorily juxtaposed statements; opposites in statements comprising two components; their truth value (ch. 7–10 [to 19b19]). III: opposites in statements containing a third component (copula); their truth value (ch. 10 [from 19b19]-11). IV: Modal statements (ch. 12–13). V: Opposition of subject and predicate (ch. 14).

al-Qiyās [al-Madḫal ilā l-Qiyās]
The Syllogism [Introduction to the Syllogism]

Epitome of the *Prior Analytics*. Its account focuses on assertoric syllogistics. The enumeration of chapters follows al-Fārābī's own specifications in the introduction to the work.

Introduction: purpose and division of the book. 1: Assertoric sentences; the distinction between categorical and conditional judgements. 2: Modes of propositions. 3: Criteria for the investigation of opposed and non-opposed sentences. 4: Forms of opposed sentences. 5: The truth value of opposed sentences. 6. The inversion of sentences. 7: Statements/epistemic contents that are not based on syllogisms: adopted (from trustworthy people); commonly accepted; sense perceptions; primary intelligibles. 8: Definition and purpose of the syllogism; categorical and conditional syllogisms. 9: Structure of the categorical syllogism: premises, terms, three figures. 10: Conjunctions of the premises in each of the three figures. 11: The modes of the first figure. 12: The modes of the second figure. 13: The modes of the third figure. 14: Conditional syllogisms (conjunctive and disjunctive). 15: *Reductio* arguments (*ḫalf*). 16: Induction (*istiqrāʾ*) and its transformation into a categorical syllogism. 17: The paradigm (literally: the analogy, *tamṯīl*) and its transformation into a categorical syllogism. 18: Examples for the application of syllogisms within an argument.

The two chapters on inferences in theology and jurisprudence, which al-ʿAǧam adds after ch. 18 of his edition (based on isolated findings relating to some late manuscripts) do not belong to this work but to *Kitāb al-Qiyās al-ṣaġīr*, described immediately below (where they are missing in al-ʿAǧam's edition).

Kitāb al-Qiyās al-ṣaġīr [*or*] *al-Muḫtaṣar al-ṣaġīr fī Kayfiyyat al-qiyās* [*or*] *al- Muḫtaṣar al-ṣaġīr fī l-manṭiq ʿalā ṭarīqat al-mutakallimīn*
Short Book on the Syllogism [or] *Short Summary on the Form of the Syllogism* [or] *Short Summary of Logic as Practiced by the Theologians*

A further account of syllogistics, with numerous parallels to the epitome of the *Prior Analytics* (*al-Qiyās*) described in the previous section. However, this text serves a different purpose: al-Fārābī attempts to present the Aristotelian doctrine of logical deduction as a reference point for all forms of argument that were cultivated in the various scholarly disciplines (and especially the religious ones). To this end he illustrates every syllogism explained in the text with an example from Islamic theology or jurisprudence. The concluding chapters (9 and 10) are furthermore designed to explain whether and in what respect the inferential deductions of the theologians and jurists might themselves be subsumed under Aristotelian syllogistics. The enumeration of chapters follows the editions by al-ʿAǧam and Dānišpažūh (whose divisions do not, however, agree entirely).

Preface: division and purpose of the book. Introduction: it is the author's aim to explain the rules of Aristotelian syllogistics to an Arabic readership, or rather 'to our contemporaries', with the help of examples. 1: Assertoric statements; the distinction between categorical and conditional propositions/premises; the quantification of categorical propositions. 2: Opposed sentences, their characteristics and truth value; propositions that are opposed to each other individually and generally; the latter's subdivision into contrary, subcontrary, and contradictory statements. 3: Propositions/epistemic contents that are not based on syllogisms: adopted; commonly accepted; sense perceptions; primary intelligibles. 4: Definition of the syllogism; categorical syllogisms; description of the fourteen valid modes. 5: Conditional syllogisms (conjunctive and disjunctive). 6: *Reductio*. 7: Composite syllogisms. 8: Induction and its transformation into a categorical syllogism. 9: The inference (commonly used in theology) from the visible/observable to the invisible/hidden (*al-istidlāl bi-l-šāhid ʿalā l-ġāʾib*): form and application; relation to the categorical syllogism; methods for verifying the utilized premises. 10: Legal inferences (*maqāyīs fiqhiyya*), understood as figures of rhetorical syllogism; their relation to the categorical syllogism.

[*Šarḥ al-Qiyās*]
[*Commentary on the* (*Book on the*) *Syllogism*]

A lemmatized commentary on the *Prior Analytics*, preserved incompletely and without its title. Formally, the work resembles the *Great Commentary* on *On Interpretation*. However, the presentation is limited to a continuous explication of the lemmata and does not contain any additional structuring of the text.

The extant fragment begins in the chapter on the *reductio ad impossibile* (II 11, 61b7) and breaks off shortly before the end of the entire text (II 27, 70a22). For further quotations that have been identified to date cf. Lameer 1994 [*175: 8–9].

al-Burhān
Demonstration

Epitome of the *Posterior Analytics*, complemented (in ch. 5) by a topic which al-Fārābī borrows from the *Sophistical Refutations* (cf. there sections 2 and 11). The chapter enumeration follows Fakhry's and Dānišpažūh's editions.

1: Demonstrations are based on concept (*taṣawwur*) and judgement (*taṣdīq*); the grasping of the definition (*ḥadd*) as perfect concept; certainty (*yaqīn*) as perfect truth judgement; distinction between necessary certainty (i.e. secure knowledge about immutable things) and non-necessary certainty (i.e. secure knowledge about changeable things); necessary universal judgements as premises of the apodeictic syllogism. 2: Demonstrations aim to show that something is, why something is, or that and why something is; scope of application of premises and demonstrations; forms of demonstration. 3: Definitions: composition, types, application, verification of their elements; discussion of the doctrines of definition of Xenocrates (via demonstration) and Plato (via diaeresis). 4: Forms of application of demonstrations and definitions within the theoretical sciences; subject matter, questions and principles of these sciences. 5: Four types of demonstrations (really: arguments) used in disputation (*muḫāṭaba burhāniyya*): (apodeictic) instruction (*taʿlīm*); (sophistical) contradiction (*ʿinād*); (dialectical) inference, combining instruction and contradiction (*al-ištirāk fī l-istinbāṭ*); examination (*imtiḥān*).

Šarāʾiṭ al-yaqīn
Conditions for Certainty

This text is intended as supplement to *al-Burhān*: it expands on statements presented in the latter, furnishing them with more detailed arguments. Thus it can claim a key position within al-Fārābī's epistemology. The enumeration of chapters follows Dānišpažūh's edition.

I: Preconditions for certain knowledge. 1: Absolute certainty (*al-yaqīn ʿalā l-iṭlāq*) comes about when six conditions are fulfilled: (1) A person has a conviction (*iʿtiqād*) concerning a certain subject matter. (2) Conviction and facts are in agreement. (3) The person is aware of this agreement. (4) It is impossible for conviction and facts not to agree, or to contradict each other. (5) Not even a temporary contradiction obtains between them. (6) All this is based on essence, not on accidents. 2: Explanation of (1). 3: Explanation of (2). 4–9: Explanation of (3). 10–11: Explanation of (4). 12: Explanation of (5). 13–15: Explanation of (6).

II: Content and irrefutability of certain knowledge. 16–17: It is based on the primary intelligibles and can be expanded through (demonstrative) syllogisms. 18–22: It consists of necessary universal judgements, against which no true objection is possible, only sophistical fallacies referring to specific disciplines or general ideas. 23–28: Certain knowledge within a given scientific discipline is constituted by (a) the primary intelligibles, the principles of this discipline, and (b) proven conclusions derived from them. Neither of these admits of contradiction. Only propositions that are based on commonly accepted (*mašhūr*), but unverified premises, can be denied. However, they do not express certainty, but merely opinion (*ẓann*). 29–31: Apart from absolute certainty, there is (a) certainty that is limited in time; it relates to changeable things and has its application in rhetoric and many practical disciplines; (b) opinions that are taken for certainties, but have arisen by accident; they are the result of errors, inattentiveness, and deception and are used for various purposes in rhetoric, poetry, and sophistics.

al-Ǧadal
Dialectical Disputation

Epitome of the *Topics*. The presentation highlights in particular the general characteristics and rules of dialectics (often in contrast to apodeictics, rhetoric, and sophistics). The individual topoi (from the accidents etc.), whose discussion constituted the focus of Aristotle's text, take second stage by comparison. The enumeration of paragraphs follows al-ʿAǧam's edition (deviating only where his division does not suit the content of the sections).

I: Characterization of dialectics. 1: Dialectics as argumentative technique of disputation. 2: Forms of question. 3: Starting point: commonly accepted (*mašhūr*) premises. 4: Selection and formation of sentences. 5: The form of dialectical disputation. 6–7: Distinction between dialectics, apodeictics, and sophistics. 8: Benefit of dialectics. II: The application of dialectics. 1: Practice and perfection. 2: The principles of questions. 3: The roles of questioner and respondent. 4: The types of question. 5: Dialectics as general method of discourse, as opposed to instruction (*taʿlīm*) and examination (*imtiḥān*) in a specific discipline. 6: Shortcomings in establishing proof. 7: Links between dialectics, apodeictics, rhetoric and sophistics. III: Elements of dialectics. 1: The positing (*waḍʿ*) of premises. 2: The positing of opposed views. 3: Various meanings of *waḍʿ* (position, convention, positing of a hypothesis); commonly accepted premises are found in the domains of ethics and sense perception. 4: Possible doubts about premises. 5: General (*ʿāmm*) and specific (*ḫāṣṣ*) aims of argumentation (*maṭlūbāt*) as predicates of a dialectical premise. 6: Definitions/descriptions and the five universal predicables as specific aims of argumentation. IV: The use of terms within dialectics. 1: Determination through definition, description, proprium, genus, difference, species and accident. 2: Topoi arising from definition and description. 3: Topoi arising from genus, species, difference, proprium and accident. 4: The subject of a premise falls under one of the ten categories. V: The use of judgements within dialectics. 1: Their application within syllogism, induction, and *reductio ad impossibile*. 2: Objection (*tabkīt*) of the questioner and contradiction (*ʿinād*) of the respondent within dialectial argumentation.

al-Taḥlīl
Analysis

A further work on the wider theme of dialectics, which can likewise be understood as an epitome of (parts of) the *Topics* (in particular *Top.* II–VII). It mainly focuses on the discussion of the individual topoi, which is only hinted at in the treatise on disputation (*al-Ǧadal*). The enumeration of paragraphs follows Dānišpažūh's edition, where the text is more appropriately subdivided than in al-ʿAǧam's edition.

Introduction: It is the aim of the treatise to show how, through knowing the topoi, one can find the premises and syllogisms that are appropriate for a certain argumentative purpose. 1: Topoi arising from subdivision (diaeresis). 2: Topoi arising from composition (*tarkīb*). 3: Topoi arising from definition. 4: Topoi arising from consequences/implications (*lawāzim*). 5: Topoi arising from opposites (*mutaqābilāt*). 6: Topoi arising from contraries (*aḍdād*). 7: Topoi arising from consequences and opposites, which are known to us as opinions or as modes of behaviour. 8: Topoi arising from morphological changes (conjugations and declinations). 9: Topoi arising from similarity. 10: Topoi arising from inequality and equality. 11: Topoi arising from increase and decrease.

Al-Amkina al-muġliṭa
Deceptive Topoi

Epitome of the *Sophistical Refutations*. Al-Fārābī focuses on the main topic of the work: fallacies, both linguistic and non-linguistic. The latter group are presented with a number of additions in comparison with Aristotle's account, the former with numerous new distinctions accommodating the specific features of the Arabic language.

1: Introduction: Having examined the doctrine of demonstration as well as dialectics, it is now necessary to investigate fallacies. 2: Fallacies based on linguistic expression (*min al-alfāẓ*): differentiation between a) *muštarak* (here: ambiguous), which is again subdivided into homonymous, equivocal, metaphorical, figurative, and resulting from identical formation (of individual words as well as composite speech), and b) *muġayyar* (altered), comprising alterations in the expression itself (e.g. replacement of words, change of inflection), in its position or construction within the sentence, in its presentation in speaking (e.g. facial expressions) or writing (e.g. punctuation, vocalization), as well as in the addressee. 3: Fallacies based on meaning (*min al-maʿānī*): differentiation between errors due to accident, consequence (*lāḥiq*), wrong application of absolute (*muṭlaq*) and qualified (*muqayyad*) propositions, subsumption of several questions under one question (including a dispute with the Eleatics), the wrong understanding of oppositions, begging the question (*petitio principii*), conceiving of something that is not a cause as a cause, and transposition (*naqla*) to an incongruent concept or conceptual domain.

al-Ḫiṭāba
Rhetoric

Epitome of Aristotle's *Rhetoric*. It is characteristic for al-Fārābī's approach to the text that he thinks of rhetoric primarily as a syllogistic discipline, and only secondarily as a theory of public speaking. This leads to considerable alterations in the presentation of the material. The general characterization of rhetoric (as opposed to apodeictics, dialectics, and sophistics) and the explication of its argumentative evidence (enthymeme and example) constitute the focal point of the entire work. By contrast, the psychological means of persuasion (*Rhet.* II) are discussed only briefly, whereas the various forms of speech (*Rhet.* I 4–15) are barely touched upon at all, and stylistics (*Rhet.* III) is not even mentioned. The enumeration of paragraphs is based on the outline of the text which Langhade has prefixed to his edition [*25: 11–21], even though his thesis that the text is incompletely transmitted [*25: 9–10] is not adopted here.

I: Characterization of rhetoric. 1: It is a syllogistic discipline aimed at the persuasion of others (*iqnāʿ*); persuasion as change in opinion (*ẓann*), knowledge as certainty (*yaqīn*); both belong to the genus of belief (*raʾy*). 2: (Problematic) pronouncements by earlier authors concerning belief. 3: Five types of opinion; their respective degrees of certainty. 4: Rhetoric, dialectics (including sophistics) and apodeictics as stages in the development of thinking, in respect of individual people as well as of mankind as a whole; it was Plato who introduced apodeictics, whereas Aristotle systematized it. 5: Rhetoric as general discipline (not tied to a specific subject matter), which takes already existing common opinions as its starting points; its premises in comparison to the premises of dialectics and sophistics; its evidence and addressees.

II: Means of persuasion and proof. 1: List of twelve means of persuasion (with repeated references to their misuse by Galen): enthymeme and example, moral authority, psychological influence, arousing of enthusiasm or perplexity, dramatization or marginalization of a topic, reference to written records, reference to oral testimonies, desires and fears of the orator, wagers and agreements with the audience, oaths, facial expression and gesture, mode of speaking and intonation. 2: Enthymeme and example stick out in this list as they are means of persuasion as well as means of proof; though the enthymeme is more closely related to the syllogism. 3. The enthymeme (*ḍamīr*): types; similarity to the syllogism; persuasive force based on form (categorical, hypothetical, conjunctive and disjunctive; the role of opposites); persuasive force based on the subject matter (commonly adopted premises; proof and sign). 4: The paradigm (literally: the analogy, *tamṯīl*): characterization; differentiation between similarity in expression, and similarity in meaning; structure and premises of a paradigm.

Didascalia in Rethoricam [*sic*] *Aristotelis ex glosa Alpharabii*
[i.e. a fragment of *Šarḥ Kitāb al-Ḫiṭāba*, the commentary on the *Rhetoric*]

Al-Fārābī's *Great Commentary* on Aristotle's *Rhetoric* is documented more than once in Arabic as well as Latin sources. According to information from Herman the German it covered the text up to *Rhet.* III 9. The only section that is extant, however, is a fragment in Latin translation which was revised by Herman the German between 1243 and 1253, and published under the title cited above. It comprises the extensive introduction to the work (which may well have circulated as an independent treatise in its Arabic version already, under the title *Ṣadr li-Kitāb al-Ḫiṭāba*), as well as the first lemma of the text, together with al-Fārābī's commentary. The enumeration of paragraphs follows Grignaschi.

Prooemium by Herman the German. Introduction: (1) Exposition of al-Fārābī's intention. (2–12) The various meanings of *credulitas* (*taṣdīq*), i.e. of making something believable or plausible. (13–33) Characterization and division of rhetoric; title, purpose, and benefit of the work. (34–38) The position of rhetoric within the *Organon*; the means of proof used. (39–56) Synopsis of the contents of the *Rhetoric*. (57) Résumé.

Main part: (58) a lemma (*Rhet.* I 1, 1354a 1–4) with commentary.

al-Šiʿr
Poetics

Epitome of the *Poetics*. The number of topics which al-Fārābī picks up from the Aristotelian treatise (imitation, rhythm, music; taken from *Poet.* 1–5) is strikingly small. This shows that he had considerable difficulties in understanding this work, or in applying it to the field of Arabic literature and poetry. Again, the conceptual integration in the *Organon* is the most relevant point for al-Fārābī. This integration is accomplished by assuming a poetic syllogism, an assumption which is neither justified nor explicated, but simply presupposed in this text. It can be found in other works by al-Fārābī as well; for instance it is already present in his introductory work to logic (*al-Tawṭiʾa fī l-manṭiq*, ch. 2 and 3). In the final analysis, however, it goes back to late ancient authors, as Walzer (1934 [*155]) and Heinrichs (1969 [*159: 130–131. 138–140; cf. there 141–145 for an analysis of the text]) have shown.

1: Criteria for the quality of poems: selection of words; consistency of order, rhythm, and metre (in Arabic also: matching verse-endings); imitation of things through language; setting to music. Excursus on the role of music in the poetry of the Arabs and of other nations. 2: (Contemporary) audiences and poets claim that a text is a poem if it possesses a metre and the ends of verses rhyme (which was not the case in Homer!). The element of imitation (*muḥākāt*), on the other hand, would not give rise to poetry, but only to a poetic statement (*qawl šiʿrī*). 3. The ancients (*al-qudamāʾ*), however, teach us the opposite: for them, imitation was the primary constitutive element of poetry. Division and metre were indispensable, too; everything else was regarded as merely complementary. 4: In practice rhetoric and poetry often touch upon each other, because both arts use persuasion (which really belongs to rhetoric) and imitation (which properly belongs to poetry). 5: Imitation is achieved by action (fine art) and by speech (poetry). 6: Imitation within poetry aims at evoking the imagination (*taḫyīl*). It is related to poetics as knowledge is related to apodeictic demonstration, opinion to dialectics, and persuasion to rhetoric. 7: The aim of evoking the imagination is to influence people in their attitudes and actions. Many people let themselves be guided by their imagination, even ignoring their own opinions and insights. 8: It is possible to combine several imitations (comparison taken from fine art: human being – picture of a human being – mirror image of the picture) and imaginative evocations with each other. People favour the imitation of the most remote thing the most (in poetry).

Risāla [or Maqāla] fī Qawānīn ṣināʿat al-šuʿarāʾ
Epistle on the Laws of the Art of the Poets

Another compendium on the art of poetry, which according to al-Fārābī is based on his reading of several ancient authors (Aristotle, Themistius, ‘and other ancients and commentators') and on oral information from connoisseurs of Greek poetry. Heinrichs (1969 [*159: 129. 145–146. 149]) gives good reasons for dating the work before *Kitāb al-Šiʿr*, describing it as an 'unsystematic compilation of ideas which al-Fārābī found in the writings of the ancients, first and foremost the Alexandrian commentators, and regarded as important' [*159: 137]. The following outline is based on his analysis of the text [132–137], although it occasionally combines several points which are listed separately by Heinrichs.

I. Definitions. 1: Purpose of the treatise is to provide pointers for a better understanding of the *Poetics*. These pointers must, however, remain incomplete since not even Aristotle was able to present either the *Sophistical Refutations* or the *Poetics* in a comprehensive manner, due to the lack of previous preparatory work (cf. *Soph. El.* 24, 183b?). 2: Definition of poetry as signifying (*dāll*), composite, assertoric, untrue (*kāḏib*) speech (by means of diaeresis); poetic statements are untrue, because they only imitate what is meant; the varying perfection of the imitation is examined by poets and scholars of poetics of the various languages. 3: Distinction between the aim of the sophist and the aim of the imitator (poet). 4: Definition of poetry as analogy (*tamṯīl*), i.e. as a potential assertoric syllogism (by means of a second diaeresis). 5. Definition of poetry as untrue speech as opposed to sophistics (mostly untrue), rhetoric (as untrue as it is true), dialectics (mostly true) and apodeictics (true). All five are syllogistic disciplines. II. Classifications. 1: The classification of poetic statements rests upon metre and content; in contrast to Arabs, Persians, and other peoples, the Greeks assigned specific metres to certain contents. 2: Description of twelve poetic forms (each with its own content and metre), which were cultivated in Greece (with reference to the sources named above): tragedy, dithyramb, comedy, etc. 3: Three types of poets: natural talents, trained poets (i.e. experts in poetics and hence in the syllogism), and epigones. 4: Poems originate spontaneously (in the area the poet has mastered most fully) or by compulsion (in any other area). 5: The quality of poems (by the same author) varies depending on his inner disposition and the chosen subject matter; sometimes even amateurs manage to produce something great. 6. The quality of poetic comparisons varies depending on the subject matter and on the poet's compository skill. 7: Comparison between poetry and the art of painting. Final remarks.

Qawl al-Fārābī fī l-tanāsub wa-l-taʾlīf
Al-Fārābī's Doctrine of Harmony and Composition

A third, very brief treatise on the art of poetry. The text repeats various motifs which are discussed more extensively in the two other works. In one important point, however, it goes beyond them: it does not just postulate the existence of poetical syllogisms, but gives two examples (Aouad, Schoeler 2002 [*179: 189–193]). It therefore becomes the earliest piece of evidence for the practical application of this form of syllogism, which otherwise appears for the first time in Ibn Sīnā.

1: Our soul is well-proportioned and has a propensity towards harmonic proportions, in all sense-perceptible things including linguistic expressions (*qawl*); hence the latter should possess metre (*wazn*), musical composition (*ta'līf al-alḥān*) and rhythm (*īqā'*), if they are supposed to influence people (which is important for political leaders!). 2: Taking that into consideration, the ancients (*al-qudamā'*) devised twelve types of metre and poetry for their various communities, which in each case match the meaning of what is said. 3: Those who want to understand this in detail must study mathematics and physics. However, it is also possible to apply the adequate forms in a practical manner by means of taste (*ḏawq*) and experience (*taǧriba*) during performances of music and dancing. 4: Metre, rhythm and composition constitute a common natural language (*nuṭq ṭabīʿī ʿāmm*) for all people, even for many animals. 5: The sophistic syllogism turns a matter of fact into its opposite. The poetic syllogism, through referring, by means of images, to similarities, evokes a mental image; two examples for poetic syllogisms; the soul is influenced by the agreement between metre (linguistic rhythm) and content. 6: Therefore, poetry cannot only be grasped with the help of the categories of truth and untruth. It can be defined as 'composite speech which evokes mental images and is determined ... by a harmonious rhythm'.

3.5 *Mathematics*

Šarḥ al-mustaġlaq min muṣādarāt al-maqāla al-ūlā wa-l-ḫāmisa min Uqlīdis
Explanation of the Difficulties Connected with the Postulates of the First and Fifth Books by Euclid

This two-part text, which Ibn Abī Uṣaybiʿa (*ʿUyūn* [*8: II 139,10–11]) records under this title, is designed as a commentary on the opening parts of books I and V of the *Elements*. In the first section al-Fārābī investigates the ontological status of basic geometrical concepts (point, line, etc.); in the second section he focuses on the interpretation of the concept of relation. The enumeration of chapters follows the division devised by Freudenthal (1988 [*209: 111–113.212–213]). The extant textual witnesses (1 Arab. MS, 4 MSS of the Hebrew translation by Mošeh Ibn Tibbon) contain no division.

Commentary on book I. 1: Body, plane and point as subjects of physics and geometry. 2: In geometry, these subjects (e.g. a line) are grasped in isolation, even if in reality they are connected with others (e.g. as the limit of a plane). 3: Geometry can be grasped through the analysis of sensible objects (Aristotle's method) or through the synthesis of intelligible concepts (Euclid's method). 4: Analysis and various definitions of bodies; their definitive characteristic is their being extended (*imtidād*) in all directions.

5: Exension as 'length' (*ṭūl*) (taken generally); 'length' as generic term; line, plane and body as species; length (in its specific sense), breadth and depth as specific differences. 6: The point as end/extreme limit of a line (as understood within physics). 7: The point as indivisible entity (as understood within geometry); the relation between these two definitions. 8: Further definitions from the first book of Euclid.

Commentary on book V. 1: Equal (*ǧuzʾ*) and unequal (*baʿḍ*) parts of the whole. 2: The specific relation (*nisba*) obtaining between magnitudes within the same dimension. 3: General relation between magnitudes of different dimensions. 4: Justification of Euclid's distinction between these two types of relation.

Šarḥ al-Maǧisṭī
Commentary on the Almagest

That al-Fārābī commented on the *Almagest*, is documented by Ibn al-Qifṭī [*7: 279,17–18], Ibn Abī Uṣaybiʿa [*8: 138,14] and al-Ṣafadī [*11: 108,15–16]. In Ibn Abī Uṣaybiʿa's list of al-Fārābī's works the commentary is even given as the very first entry (cf. also Steinschneider 1869 [*15: 78. 214]). However, for a long time there was no certain evidence for the work, and the known manuscript tradition is problematic in several respects.

According to Sezgin we are in possession of two manuscripts: a longer one in Tehran (Maǧlis 10945), and a shorter one in London (British Library, MS Or. 7368), which he describes as an 'abbreviated recension by Ibn Sīnā' (GAS 1978 [*2: VI 195]; cf. also Dhanani (2007 [*214: 357]). Neither of the texts is edited, though the London text has served as basis for the partial Russian translation produced by Kubesov and al-Dabbagh ([*86]; the reference, in GAS (1978 [*2: VI 195]), to a 1959 Russian translation by B. Rosenfeld is erroneous and ought to be deleted).

Soon after Sezgin's publication, however, doubts were raised concerning the attribution of the London manuscript. As B. Goldstein writes in his review of the sixth volume of GAS (in: *Isis* 71 [1980] 341–342), the British Library text shows such extensive correspondences with the commentary on the *Almagest* contained in *Kitāb al-Šifāʾ* that it should be credited to Ibn Sīnā (even if al-Fārābī's name is mentioned twice on the first pages of the text). In the meantime, this assessment has been emphatically confirmed by Janos (2010 [*216: 238–239]), so that the London manuscript can no longer be regarded as a witness to al-Fārābī's commentary on the *Almagest*.

The Tehran manuscript, on the other hand, was long believed to be lost, because none of the texts in the Maǧlis library could be identified with the call number indicated by Sezgin (Janos 2010 [*216: 239]). Meanwhile, however, Thomann (2010–2011 [*218]) has been able to show that the manuscript does in fact exist, albeit under a different number (Maǧlis 6531). His preliminary investigations have shown that the text is indeed the last part of a commentary on the *Almagest* (book X–XIII), credited to al-Fārābī on the flyleaf, which was added later. In addition there are two further testimonies, which Thomann (2015 [*221]) has only recently brought to attention: (a) another Tehran manuscript (Maǧlis 6430), which transmits the same commentary mentioned above, albeit more extensively (book X–XIII); (b) a text transmitted in another manuscript (MS Mašhad Riḍā 5593), in which Aḥmad Ibn al-Ṣalāḥ (d. 548/1154) subjects al-Fārābī's *Commentary on the Almagest* to detailed criticism. The latter text contains lengthy quotations from the commentary (here on book V of the *Almagest*), mentions al-Fārābī explicitly as its author, and shares terminological parallels with both Tehran manuscripts. All in all, this suggests the conclusion that al-Fārābī certainly did compose a *Commentary on the Almagest*, and that the two Tehran manuscripts most likely represent parts of it.

al-Lawāḥiq
The Supplements

Supplement to the commentary on the *Almagest*, which mainly discusses trigonometry and its application in astronomy (cf. Rosenfeld, İhsanoğlu 2003 [*213: 76]). However, the text seems to be transmitted only in the problematic London manuscript mentioned in the previous entry (British Library, MS Or. 7368, as part II), which renders its attribution to al-Fārābī unlikely. It has not been edited to date, though it has been translated into Russian [*87].

Maqāla fīmā yaṣiḥḥu wa-mā lā yaṣiḥḥu min aḥkām al-nuǧūm
Treatise on Admissible and Inadmissible Judgements [Based on the Observation] of the Stars

A brief treatise which draws a clear distinction between astronomical calculations and astrological predictions. It is extant in two versions: (a) an extensive one (bearing the abovementioned title), which was transmitted by the Christian scholar Abū Isḥāq Ibrāhīm b. ʿAbd Allāh al-Baġdādī, who, in his preface, states that he had been looking for information on the possibility of astrological predictions, discussed the issue with al-Fārābī, and was presented by him with this treatise; (b) an abbreviated one, which was transmitted and published under the (misleading) title *Risāla fī Faḍīlat al-ʿulūm wa-l-ṣināʿāt*, and has no preface. The enumeration of chapters follows Āl Yāsīn's edition.

1: Preface by Abū Isḥāq. 2–3: Al-Fārābī says: the science of the stars (*ʿilm al-nuǧūm*) is valued because of its subject matter (not because of its demonstrative power or its benefit); but many people tend to overestimate it. 4: Two things may be similar due to essential or accidental causes. 5: Two events may be simultaneous due to a cause, or by mere accident. Accidental coincidences cannot be scientifically investigated. 6: If there were no accidents, we would not be worried about, nor take care of our life.

7: Predictions are only possible in the fields of exact knowledge (*ʿulūm muḥaṣṣala*). 8–10: Forms of the indefinite: the possible and the probable (= object of experience). Even natural effects are merely probable (rather than necessary), because their occurrence depends on whether the objects they encounter are susceptible to being influenced by them. 11–12: Distinction between 'possible' and 'unknown' (in the sense of 'not yet known', 'knowable'). 13: The equivocal use of 'judgement' in the context of astronomy/astrology: judgements about the dimensions and distances of stars are necessary; judgements about the natural effect of stars (e.g. the effect the sun has on the earth due to its heat) are probable; judgements about the effects of the stars on our life are pure speculation. 14–16: Stars only exert an influence through their rays; different views on this point. 17–18: Proximate and remote causes. 19–20: Only immature people or those who are in the grip of their passions seek for signs relating to their life in natural events or in the movements of the heavens. 21–29: Examples for such speculations (each with its own critique). 30: Sometimes, speculations hit the mark (by accident). 31: Astrologers do not themselves believe in their predictions, but act from selfish motives.

Maqāla fī l-Ǧiha allatī yaṣiḥḥu ʿalayhā al-qawl fī aḥkām al-nuǧūm
Treatise on the Sense in which it is Admissible to Speak of Judgements [Based on the Observation] of the Stars

A second text on astronomy and astrology, which, though independent of the previous text in its wording, nevertheless does not really go beyond it in terms of content. The work is basically confined to explaining in greater detail a topic that had already been mentioned in the other work, i.e. the effect the celestial bodies have on the earth due to their heat. The enumeration of chapters follows Mahdi's edition.

1–2: Depending on their position, celestial bodies exert various influences on earthly bodies. 3: The observation and assessment of such effects is the task of the astronomer. 4: The astronomers' claims, however, come with a qualification: the effects of the celestial bodies may be impeded by other natural influences and by actions or effects generated by human beings, animals, or plants. 5: Since time immemorial humans have believed to be recognizing mysterious signs in the stars that would be relevant for their lives. This has led to many mistakes. If anything, the warmth of the celestial bodies may affect our bodily mixtures and thus some of our behaviour. Acts that result from our deliberations and our will cannot be influenced by the stars.

Kitāb al-Mūsīqī al-kabīr
The Great Book on Music

A significant work of musical theory, based on the Greek tradition. Originally, the treatise consisted of two books. According to al-Fārābī's own information, book II, which is considered lost, contained a doxography of ancient and Arabic authors. Book I, which has been edited and translated, comprises the following main parts:

I: Introduction (*madḫal*) to musical theory: definition and classification; theoretical principles, fundamental concepts. II: Musical theory (*ṣināʿat al-mūsīqī*). 1: Elements (*usṭuqussāt*): note; interval; modes (*aǧnās*) of tetrachords and of scales (*ǧamāʿāt*) exceeding them; rhythmics. 2: Instruments: lute (*ʿūd*); further string instruments and wind instruments. 3: Composition: melody; metres and rhythms; singing. Epilogue on the effect music has on human beings.

al-Īqāʿāt
The Musical Metres

Having discussed musical metre and rhythm already within the framework of *Kitāb al-Mūsīqī al-kabīr*, al-Fārābī dedicated three further independent treatises to the topic, two of which are extant. The apparently earlier one of the two is the work that has been published under the title *al-Īqāʿāt* (on the title of the treatise and on the chronology of the works see Neubauer 1998 [*211: 130]). It begins with an explanation of the terms used in the treatise and continues with a description of the different genera (*aǧnās*) and classes (*aṣnāf*) of musical metre.

Iḥṣāʾ al-īqāʿāt
Enumeration of Musical Metres

The last (extant) and at the same time most detailed discussion of rhythmics penned by al-Fārābī (introduced and transl. into German by Neubauer 1998 [*212]). After a brief terminological introduction the different metres are described in greater detail and with more references to musical practice than in the previous works. Al-Fārābī furthermore adds a final section, in which he critically discusses the theories of his predecessors Isḥāq al-Mawṣilī, Manṣūr al-Ṭāhirī, and in particular al-Kindī.

3.6 *Physics*

[Distinctio super librum Aristotelis de naturali auditu]
[Exposition of (or: Chapter on) Aristotle's Book on Physics]

A brief text, extant only in Latin, which has been edited by Birkenmajer (1935 [*236: 475–481]). It was translated from the Arabic by Gerard of Cremona and is unanimously ascribed to al-Fārābī by all manuscripts. Title and form of the Arabic original can no longer be reconstructed with certainty. Steinschneider (1869 [*15: 135]) assumed that Lat. *distinctio* might render Arab. *tabyīn* (exposition, explanation). Birkenmajer (1935 [*236: 474 n. 8]) instead suggested translating *distinctio* as 'chapter'; this he linked to the hypothesis that the work may originally have been part of al-Fārābī's lemmatized commentary on the *Physics*.

In its extant Latin version, the text at any event gives the impression of being incomplete. It begins with a brief reference to the topics Aristotle has discussed in the first four books of the *Physics* ('Postquam narrauit Aristotiles in tractatibus quatuor libri De auditu naturali ...'), before embarking on a more detailed description of the contents of books V–VIII. Its style is clear and the presentation well-informed. Therefore the text can be regarded as a companion piece to al-Fārābī's synopsis of Aristotle's *Metaphysics* (*Fī Aġrāḍ al-ḥakīm fī kull maqāla min al-Kitāb al-mawsūm bi-l-Ḥurūf*; cf. pp. 573–574 below), as Birkenmajer [*236: 474] has rightly pointed out.

al-Radd ʿalā Yaḥyā al-Naḥwī
Refutation of John the Grammarian [*Philoponus*]

This brief text targets John Philoponus' (lost) treatise *Against Aristotle on the Eternity of the World*. However, al-Fārābī does not address the entire work (Mahdi 1967 [*243: 236]), but limits himself to commenting on, and rejecting, Philoponus' claims about the doctrine of the elements (which refer to *On the Heavens* I. 2–4). He is particularly concerned with showing that Philoponus (a) does not succeed in refuting Aristotle's claim that certain movements are associated with certain elements; and (b) wrongly imputes to Aristotle that he wanted to prove the eternity of the world by means of his elemental doctrine (inferring from the eternal circular movement to the eternity of the corresponding element). For a further dispute with John Philoponus in the lost work *Fī l-Mawǧūdāt al-mutaġayyira* cf. p. 586 below. The enumeration of chapters follows Mahdi's edition.

I: Introduction. 1: None of Aristotle's claims attacked by Philoponus was ever meant to prove the eternity of the world. Aristotle merely intended them to explain the existence and nature of the simple bodies. 2: Bodies consist of matter and form (as demonstrated in physics). 3: The celestial body is different from all other simple bodies. 4: Aristotle speaks about simple bodies in a different sense from his predecessors. 5: Philoponus' criticism addresses *On the Heavens* and *On Generation and Corruption*. 6: He thereby overlooks the fact that Aristotle has established the theoretical principles in the *Physics*. 7: He accuses Aristotle of transferring claims about the heavens to the entire world. 8: His own pronouncements can be understood in light of religious concerns. II: Philoponus' argument. 9: Aristotle's allocation of certain movements to certain elements is not consistent. 10–12: Since earth and water on the one hand, and fire and air on the other, perform the same kind of movement, according to Aristotle they would have to be the same kind of element. 13: But they are of different kinds. 14: Hence, if elements of different kinds can perform the same kind of movement, one and the same element must also be able to perform different kinds of movement. 15: This is substantiated by earth and water, which perform the same kind of movement.

III: Al-Fārābī's reply. 16: Earth and water do not perform the same movement, since their (natural) places are different. 17: Sometimes different elements travel a certain overlapping distance; however, each of them will be moving towards its (natural) place, which is why it has its own kind of movement. 18: Neither does water sink as far down as the middle of the cosmos, as Philoponus claims, but only up to its own place. 19: Therefore different kinds of elements do not perform the same kind of movement.

Maqāla fī l-Ḫalāʾ
Treatise on the Void

This work, which takes up late ancient discussions, has the basic purpose of defending Aristotle's rejection of the void using arguments of the Alexandrian Pneumatists. Nevertheless al-Fārābī reveals that he was also familiar with the contemporary debate on the topic, which was conducted between the various representatives of the Muʿtazila (al-Kaʿbī *versus* al-Ǧubbāʾī), as well as Abū Bakr al-Rāzī (Daiber 1983 [*248]). The argument unfolds in four steps:

1: Description of two experiments, which formed the basis for claiming the existence of the void. 2: (Dialectical) refutation of this claim. 3: Discussion of the properties of the material and instruments used in the experiments. 4: Proof that the correct interpretation of the experiments confirms the rejection of the void.

Risāla fī Wuǧūb ṣināʿat al-kimiyāʾ
Epistle on the Necessity of the Science of Alchemy

The purpose of the text is to prove that alchemy, being the science of the transformation of material ingredients, falls under physics. In his argument, al-Fārābī refers extensively to the Pseudo-Aristotelian treatise *On Stones* (*De lapidibus*).

1: One ought neither to reject alchemy altogether, nor to overestimate its significance. 2: Alchemical texts are written in code, in order to keep knowledge away from unauthorized people, who might harm the community. 3: Alchemy is a science (with concepts and judgements) and belongs to physics; those who study it must know logic, mathematics and other sub-disciplines within physics. 4: Why substances can be transformed is explained by Aristotle in his book on minerals.

Risāla fī l-Radd ʿalā Ǧālīnūs fīmā nāqaḍa fīhi Arisṭūṭālīs li-aʿḍāʾ al-insān
Epistle on the Refutation of Galen Concerning That in Which He Contradicts Aristotle Regarding the Parts of the Human Body

This text, which has been edited by Badawī, consists of three parts. They build on each other, despite a number of repetitions and redundancies. Part I offers a general characterization of medicine, focusing especially on its relation to physics. In this context al-Fārābī brings up his famous division of medicine into seven sub-domains; it was later also transmitted independently of the text as a whole (cf. the following entry on the so-called *Risāla fī l-Ṭibb*) and aroused the interest of Ibn Rušd and Maimonides. Part II, which has its own title, *Risāla fī Aʿḍāʾ al-insān* (*Epistle on the Parts of the Human Body*), names the conditions under which Aristotle's and Galen's views on human anatomy may be compared with each other. In part III, which apparently was revised by one of al-Fārābī's students (Richter-Bernburg 2008 [*255: 120 n. 6]), this comparison is carried out under the sub-heading *Risāla fī Aʿḍāʾ al-ḥayawān wa-afʿālihā wa-quwāhā* (*Epistle on the Parts of the Bodies of Living Beings, their Effects and their Powers*), coming to the conclusion that Aristotle had advanced the superior doctrine.

I: The subject matter of the text is those parts of the human body which were examined both by Aristotle and by Galen. Galen's examination was carried out within the framework of medicine, Aristotle's within that of physics. Physics is a theoretical science which imparts certain knowledge about the existence, the composition and the causes of natural bodies, by rendering its subject matter intelligible to our souls. Medicine is a practical art (*ṣināʿa fāʿila*), whose purpose it is to bring about certain effects on objects, for the sake of certain ends (comparison with the art of the smith). Since a physician needs criteria in order to proceed, medicine must gain knowledge in seven areas: (1) the parts of the human body; (2) the types of health; (3) the types of disease; (4) diagnosis from accidents; (5) nutriments and drugs; (6) measures for the preservation of health; (7) measures for the restoration of health. Areas (1) to (3) are subject matter of physics, too (as they are cases of universal knowledge).

II: The objective is to compare Galen's and Aristotle's statements about the parts of the body. Aristotle examines the body from the perspective of physics: definition and classification of living beings; insights about living beings by means of observation or analogical reasoning; the inquiry into the causes (in particular: the final cause) of the structure of the body and its organs; knowledge as the goal of physics. Galen examines the body and its organs from the perspective of medicine; health as the goal of medicine; the seven fields of medical knowledge (as in part I). Shared characteristics and differences within their pronouncements on the parts of the body. Galen exhibits a tendency towards unduly criticizing Aristotle, and unduly defending Hippocrates. Criteria for correctly deciding between Aristotle and Galen, where they differ from each other.

III: The objective is to prove the superiority of Aristotle's view. Aristotle on vital heat and its relation to heart, liver, reproductive organs and faculties of the soul; the heart as highest, ruling organ. Timaeus and Plato (and Galen) on the distribution of the ruling functions between brain, heart, and liver. For Aristotle, brain and liver are subordinate to the heart with regard to their functions (comparison with the ruling hierarchies within a community). Examinations of the statements which Aristotle presents as arguments; their demonstrative character. Examination of the statements which Galen produces as arguments against Aristotle; their faultiness. Galen misunderstands Aristotle and is unduly lenient towards Hippocrates.

[*Risāla fī l-Ṭibb*]
[*Epistle on Medicine*]

Under this title, Plessner published a short text found in an Istanbul manuscript, which he – following the information given in the MS – identified as the preface to a *Risāla fī l-Ṭibb* (Plessner 1972 [*245: 308–309]). In fact, however, it is no independent work, but represents an excerpt from Part I of the *Epistle on the Refutation of Galen Concerning That in Which He Contradicts Aristotle Regarding the Parts of the Human Body*. It comprises the general characterization of medicine and its division into seven fields (cf. p. 312–313 in Plessner with p. 40,8–42 ult. in Badawī's edition).

Risāla fī l-ʿAql
Epistle on the Intellect

This treatise is part of the intense debate about Aristotle's doctrine of the intellect (*On the Soul* III 4–8), which had already developed in late antiquity, and had found its way into Arabic philosophy through al-Kindī's work bearing the same title. Al-Fārābī, however, places the discussion within a larger context, as he combines the specific problem of interpreting the passage from *On the Soul* with a more general semantic investigation. This investigation concerns the word *ʿaql*, which in Arabic can denote the various forms or powers of thinking, and in Greek-Arabic translations usually renders the word νοῦς.

The text begins with the declaration that the noun *ʿaql* is 'said in many ways'. Then al-Fārābī lists six different meanings (assigning them to certain speakers or texts), which are going to form the subject matter of the then following investigation. These are the linguistic usage of (1) the masses, (2) the theologians, (3) in the *Posterior Analytics*, (4) in the sixth book of the (*Nicomachean*) *Ethics*, (5) in *On the Soul*, and (6) in the *Metaphysics*.

3.7 *Metaphysics*

Fī Aġrāḍ al-ḥakīm fī kull maqāla min al-Kitāb al-mawsūm bi-l-Ḥurūf
On the Aims of the 'Philosopher' in Each Treatise of the Book Marked by Letters [i.e. the *Metaphysics*]

A brief but influential work on the subject matter of metaphysics. The text was highly esteemed by Ibn Sīnā, and has left its marks on the latter's own conception of metaphysics (Gutas 1988 [*84: 238–254]).

Problem: Many people believe that Aristotle's *Metaphysics* (only) discusses theological questions (Creator, intellect, soul). This misunderstanding is supported by the fact that only commentaries on *Met.* XII are available in Arabic: that by Alexander of Aphrodisias (incomplete) and that by Themistius (complete). Clarification: one ought to distinguish between the various particular sciences and the one universal science. The former concern themselves with delimited areas of being (examples: physics, geometry, arithmetic, medicine), while the latter investigates (1) what pertains to all beings (i.e. being itself and the general concepts of thinking/principles of thinking), and (2) the common origin of all being (i.e. God). Thus philosophical theology (*al-ʿilm al-ilāhī*) is part (but not the whole) of universal science. Ranking of the theoretical sciences: physics, mathematics, universal science (i.e. metaphysics); the subject matter of metaphysics, e.g. One, Many, the ten categories, potentiality and actuality. Survey of the topics which are dealt with in the individual books of the *Metaphysics* (omitting *Met.* I and *Met.* XIV).

Al-Wāḥid wa-l-waḥda
The One and Oneness

This text stands in the tradition of Aristotle's *Metaphysics*: al-Fārābī explains the 'one' and the 'many' with reference to *Met.* V 6 and *Met.* I 1; though he expands the thematic scope by introducing further distinctions (in particular in respect of the 'many'), and emphasizes the logical and semantical perspective in addition to the ontological one. The enumeration of chapters and the sub-headings follow Mahdi's edition.

I: What is described as 'one'. 1–5: Multiplicities which are in agreement with respect to genus, species, definition, accident, or matter; or which may be linked by a shared predicate or subject. 6–8: One according to number. 9–16: Divisible 'ones': continuum; composite. 17–26: 'One' due to its separate essence. II: What is described as 'many'. 27–29: Unities that have no multiplicity opposed to them. 30–36: Unities that have a multiplicity opposed to them. 37–49: Multiplicities that originate in a unity. 50–54: What must be multiple, if unity is predicated of it (e.g. a preface). 55–60: What must not be many/multiple, if unity is predicated of it (e.g. a point). 61: What can be many/multiple, if unity is predicated of it (separate essences). III: Multiplicity and unity. 62–65: Multiplicities which have a unity opposed to them. 66–71: Multiplicities that have originated in a unity. IV: Unity and multiplicity. 72–76: Unities which are part of a multiplicity. 77–82: Unities which are not part of a multiplicity. 83–90: Forms of unity. V: Summary. 91: One with respect to genus, species, matter, definition, accident, or purpose. 92: One according to number. 93: Continuum and composite. 94: The absolutely indivisible (point) and the essentially one. 95: Indivisibility as characteristic of unity.

3.8 *Ethics and Politics*

Fuṣūl [*muntazaʿa*]
[*Selected*] *Aphorisms*

A compilation of 96 (or 100) remarks on questions of ethics and politics, some aphoristic and some more extended. The textual tradition is uncertain in two places: (a) Dunlop (1961 [*116: 103]) gives the title as *Fuṣūl al-madanī*, whereas Naǧǧār (1971 [*116: 23]), following earlier authors, records it as *Fuṣūl muntazaʿa*. Both variants are problematic, as the former is only documented in a single late manuscript, whereas the second one (which is now commonly used) is derived from the incipit of a number of older manuscripts. (b) Sections 97 to 100 are only mentioned in a single manuscript, and exhibit certain peculiarities in form. Hence there are good reasons not to regard them as part of the original text (Naǧǧār 1971 [*116: 100]). The enumeration of chapters follows Naǧǧār's edition, which also forms the basis for the textual division in Butterworth's English translation.

1–2: Analogy between body and soul. 3–5: Analogy between physician and statesman. 6: Each body possesses matter and form. 7: The five faculties of the soul. 8: Distinction between ethical and dianoetical virtues. 9–13: Ethical virtues; disposition and habit as their preconditions. 14–15: Distinction between virtue and self-discipline. 16: Combating evil. 17: The possibility to conquer one's habits. 18–21: Ethical virtues as 'mean' between extremes. 22–27: State and household; their comparability with bodies. 28: Excellent communities aim at happiness. 29: Keeping the 'mean' contributes to happiness. 30–32: Kingship. 33: Distinction between theoretical and practical intellect. 34–37: Theoretical intellect; knowledge, certainty, wisdom. 38–46: Practical intellect; prudence (*taʿaqqul*) *versus* cleverness; forms of prudence. 47–49: Forms of deficiency in prudence. 50: Acumen (*ḏakāʾ*). 51: Prudence as realization of a disposition. 52–53: Distinction between prudence and wisdom. 54–56: The meaning of rhetoric and poetics. 57–61: The excellent community: structure and cohesion. 62–64: Justice. 65: Division of labour. 66: Care for the poor. 67: Just and unjust wars. 68–71: Modes of being; genera of beings. 72–73: Perfect (= self-sufficient) and imperfect being. 74: Good and evil. 75: The affections of the soul. 76: True happiness. 77–80: The virtuous person's attitude towards death. 81: Separation of body and soul (or intellect). 82: Composition as imperfect form of being. 83–84: Forms of causation. 85: Human thinking. 86: God's thinking. 87: God's providential care. 88–89: Excellent guidance of the community. 90–92: Ignorant communities. 93: The influence of the community on the soul of the individual. 94: The uses of theoretical philosophy in practical philosophy. 95: The benefit of reflective virtue. 96: Limited possibilities of educating the soul.

(97: The improbability of perfect dispositions in an individual human being. 98: Theoretical knowledge is not yet philosophy. 99: Only communities which exist for the sake of virtue are free of disagreements. 100: Negligence leads to ruin.)

al-Milla
Religion

This text first sketches the properties of (an excellent) religion, before discussing the connection between religious and social/political community that is so characteristic of al-Fārābī. Many questions raised here are discussed in a very similar manner in the *Mabādiʾ* (especially in section V). The enumeration of chapters follows Mahdi's edition, which also forms the basis for the textual divisions in Mallet's and Butterworth's translations.

1: Religion as system of opinions (*ārāʾ*) and actions (*afʿāl*), which a community has received from its first leader; the religion of an excellent leader or community is based on revelation. 2: Opinions of an excellent religion. 3: Actions of an excellent religion. 4: Terms for 'religion', 'law', etc.; excellent *versus* erroneous religion. 5: Religion as particular representation of philosophy. 6: Usefulness of dialectics and rhetoric. 7: The first leader does not always leave complete instructions. 8: Successors who are equal to him will supplement his instructions or will adapt them to the requirements of the times. 9: Other successors will preserve the tradition by means of jurisprudence. 10: Division of jurisprudence; its subordination to theoretical and practical philosophy (= the science of the community). 11–12: The science of the community aims at human happiness and therefore analyses people's actions and the properties of their characters. 13: In a community, division of labour is necessary (because of the different distribution of abilities). 14: True and alleged virtue. 14a: Excellent and bad communities, rulers, and citizens. 14b: Independent rulers, and rulers that follow custom (*sunna*). 14c: The true physician knows the universals of medicine and is experienced in the particulars of treatment. 14d: The true ruler knows the universals of philosophy and, thanks to his prudence (*taʿaqqul*), is able to grasp the particulars of a given community. 15: The science of the community therefore consists of two parts. 16: Wrong forms of government. 17: Reasons for the decline and paths towards the preservation of an excellent community. 18: Relation of the various forms of government to philosophy. 19–20: The hierarchy of being (up to the First One). 21–22: The hierarchy of the faculties of the soul and the organs of the body. 23–25: The hierarchy of the members of an excellent community. 26–27: Analogy between cosmos/God and excellent community/ruler (= recipient of divine revelation).

[Talḫīṣ] Ǧawāmiʿ Kitāb al-Nawāmīs li-Aflāṭūn
[Detailed Explication] of the Epitome of Plato's Book of Laws

The treatise consists of (1) a preface which explains that Plato presented his views partly encoded or allegorically, and partly overtly; (2) a main part, which summarizes chapters 1–6 and 8–9 of the *Laws*, and (3) a brief epilogue, which offers certain information about purpose and genesis of the text. In the main part, al-Fārābī does not simply sum up Plato's views, but, by means of certain omissions and additions, sets his own agenda. In secondary literature, this has often lead to the accusation that he was ignorant of the ancient tradition, whereas it in fact corresponds to the literary form of the text, which we also encounter in his epitomes on Aristotle's *Organon*.

By contrast to the logical works, however, it does remain unclear in the case of the *Laws* paraphrase whether or not al-Fārābī was directly familiar with the Platonic dialogue. Several authors believe that he was (decidedly so Mahdi 1961 [*304: 4–6]; following him Parens 1995 [*319: XXVIII–XXXI]; cautiously agreeing Druart 1998 [*324: 112]). Gutas, however, holds that al-Fārābī only knew Galen's epitome of the *Laws* (1997 [*321: 103. 117], 1998 [*325]; similarly Harvey 2003 [*332]). With reference to the manuscript tradition (MS Kabul) he therefore argues that al-Fārābī's text did not bear the title *Ǧawāmiʿ Kitāb al-Nawāmīs li-Aflāṭūn* (as used by Druart in her edition), but was called *Talḫīṣ Ǧawāmiʿ Nawāmīs Aflāṭūn* (*Detailed Explication of* [*Galen's*] *Epitome of Plato's Book of Laws*).

3.9 *Philosophical Summae*

Mabādiʾ ārāʾ ahl al-madīna al-fāḍila
The Principles of the Opinions of the Inhabitants of the Excellent City

This treatise is the only one among al-Fārābī's works for which we have detailed medieval reports concerning its composition. According to this information, al-Fārābī started to work on the text in 330/942 in Baghdad, and completed it in 331/943 in Damascus. Its definitive structure, however, it was to receive only later, in the course of two revisions: first, al-Fārābī is said to have inserted the division in nineteen chapters (*abwāb*); finally he also added the arrangement in six large sections (*fuṣūl*) (Walzer 1985 [*276: 20]). This unusual editorial effort was not expended without reason: the *Mabādiʾ* takes up a key position within al-Fārābī's œuvre, given that it brings together his positions on various central topics of metaphysics, physics (including psychology and prophetology), ethics, and politics (omitting logic and mathematics). Thus it may well be called the first 'summa' in the history of philosophy. Interestingly, though, the structure of the work and the selection of topics seems to be determined not so much by the philosophical tradition as by contemporary Islamic theology and its systematic presentation of the principles of religion (*uṣūl al-dīn*) (Rudolph 2008 [*285]).

In most manuscripts, the text is preceded by a brief summary, which is based on the division of the text into 19 chapters. Two manuscripts furthermore contain a number of addenda (Walzer 1985 [*276: 38–55]). These passages are likely to have been produced quite early on; Walzer dates them with good reason to the second half of the 4th/10th century. Nevertheless he leaves no doubt that they were not penned by al-Fārābī himself, which is why they will not be taken into consideration in the now following survey. On the Hebrew strand of transmission, which preserves a few variants of text-critical interest, cf. Chiesa (1986 [*31], 1989 [*85]).

Section I: The First Cause. Ch. 1: It is (1) perfect, eternal, and unchangeable, (2) without likeness, (3) without opposite, (4) indivisible, (5) one, (6) actual intellect, (7) knowing, (8) wise and (9) true. (10–13) It possesses life, greatness, majesty, beauty and other attribute in a perfect manner which transcends our human attributes. (14) It thinks itself in perfect bliss. (15) It is the First Loved (*al-maʿšūq al-awwal*), subject and object of perfect love. Ch. 2: (1) It is the origin of all things (excepting those that go back to decisions of the human will). It causes all being through emanation (*fayḍ*), without itself being affected by it. (2) Its justice is manifest in the meaningful order of things, (3) which are interconnected in manifold ways. (4) It is indivisibly one, even if its different aspects are designated by different names (*asmāʾ*). (5) If such a name (e.g. 'just') implies a relation to other beings, this relation will not be constitutive for the essence of the First Cause.

Section II: Cosmology. Ch. 3: (1–10) The thinking of the First Cause has generated an intellect from all eternity; the thinking of this intellect (by virtue of knowing its origin) has yielded a further intellect and (by virtue of knowing itself) a sphere. By repetition of this process, the eternal and perfect cosmic hierarchy has come into being; it consists of ten intellects and nine spheres (diurnal sphere, sphere of the fixed stars, Saturn, Jupiter, Mars, Sun, Venus, Mercury, Moon).

Section III: The sublunar world. Ch. 4: (1–3) The sublunar things are perishable; since they are generated in a defective state, they always need the their potentialities to be actualized. Ch. 5: (1–6) The reason for this lies in their being composed from matter and form. Ch. 6: (1) The order of the beings in the sublunar world. (2) The hierarchy of the ten separate intellects and the nine spheres in the supralunar world. Each separate intellect (3) is unique and (4) without opposite; (5) it thinks itself and the First Cause and (6) thereby experiences bliss (in proportion to the excellence of the object of its thought). Ch. 7: (1) The celestial bodies are arranged in nine spheres, (2) each of which constitutes a separate species, (3) though they all together belong to the genus of bodies. (4) All of them have actualized forms (intellects of the spheres, which al-Fārābī assumes alongside with the separate intellects), (5) experience bliss and (6) possess an excellent form. (7–9) Due to their motions they change place and find themselves in various relations. (10) Therefore they have opposites. (11) However, they also share a common nature, which manifests itself in that they complete one circular movement in the course of one day. Ch. 8: (1) These different aspects are mirrored in the influence the celestial bodies exert on the sublunar world. They result in the generation of commonalities (e.g. a common 'prime matter'; regular recurrence of processes) and differences (the plurality of substances, forms, alterations, etc.) in the sublunar world, too. (2) First the elements and kindred bodies are generated. (3) Then the more complex mixtures arise: (4) minerals, plants, animals, human beings. (5) Each of these species is provided with its own characteristic activities, so that in the end, supralunar and sublunar forces are mixed in this world. Ch. 9: (1–7) The sublunar things are subject to alteration, because both the simple and the more complex bodies keep adopting different forms time and again. Due to this change, all possibilities of combination are brought about in an equitable manner. Generation and corruption only concern the individuals, while species and genera are being preserved.

Section IV: Humankind. Ch. 10: (1) The faculties of the soul: (2) the nutritive faculty (*al-quwwa al-ġāḏiya*); (3) the perceptive faculty (*al-quwwa al-ḥāssa*); (4) the imaginative faculty (*al-quwwa al-mutaḫayyila*); (5) the rational faculty (*al-quwwa al-nāṭiqa*); (6) the appetitive faculty (*al-quwwa al-nuzūʿiyya*). (7) The distribution of faculties of the soul within the body. (8) Their co-operation in/with respect to cognition, perceptions, and imaginations. (9) The nutritive, perceptive, imaginative and rational faculties constitute a hierarchy and stand in the same relation to each other as matter and form; the appetitive faculty accompanies them as heat accompanies fire. Ch. 11: The organs of the body: (1–5) the heart as the first, and the brain as the second ruling organ; their functions and operation by means of vital heat (heart), or coldness and moisture (brain); the nerves and the spinal marrow; (6) liver, spleen and reproductive organs; (7) the lung. (8) The organs are generated in order of their significance. Ch. 12: Reproduction: (1–2) it is controlled by the heart and carried out by the specific organs. The female makes the material contribution (i.e. the blood in the womb), whereas the male makes the formative contribution (i.e. the added semen). (3) Generation and route of the semen. (4) The semen as 'instrument' of the man. (5) After fertilization the first organ to develop is the heart, then follow the others; the sex of the foetus is determined by the predominance of blood (= female) or semen (= male). (6) In plants and in some animals, the material and the formative principles of reproduction are united. (7) In human beings, they are distributed between woman and man. There are further differences between women and men (vital heat, certain properties of character). (8) With respect to their perceptive, imaginative, and rational faculties, however, they are equal. Ch. 13: Thinking: (1) division of intelligibles into pure forms (e.g. intellects) and forms in matter; the exceptional position of the human potential intellect: being at first a mere disposition in a body (*hayʾa fī mādda*), it becomes itself intellect through the process of thinking. (2) The Active Intellect guides the thinking process;

comparison of its activity to that of the sun, which, by virtue of its light, enables us to see. (3) Starting point of our thinking: the primary intelligibles (i.e. the principles of all sciences). (4) What instigates our thinking is our will (*irāda*) or choice (*iḫtiyār*). (5–7) The goal of our thinking is happiness (*saʿāda*). It is identified by our theoretical faculty (*al-quwwa al-naẓariyya*), pursued by our will, and attained by good actions, which are determined by our deliberation (*rawiyya*), supported by good dispositions and habits. Ch. 14: Imagination and prophecy: (1–6) imagination is responsible for three things: (a) mediating between the other faculties of the soul (during waking); (b) dreams (during sleep); (c) imitating (*muḥākāt*) insights, sense perceptions, psychological and physical states. (7–11) Due to these abilities it is able to receive intelligibles and sensibles (which it will imitate) from the Active Intellect. This leads to (a) true dreams, (b) divinations, (c) the gift of prophecy in the sense of predicting events, and in the sense of insight into the divine (in people of extraordinarily powerful imagination) and (d) false imaginings (in people with psychological or physiological defects).

Section v: Human society. Ch. 15: The significance of excellent communities: (1) the necessity of communities. (2) Three kinds of perfect (*kāmil*) communities: global community, nation, city; all smaller associations (village etc.) must be part of a larger unity. (3) Excellent communities promote the happiness of their members. (4–6) They are hierarchically structured and are similar to the functioning body on the one hand, and the cosmos on the other (ruling entities: heart-ruler-First Cause). The founder and ruler of such a community (7) must be made suitable for this task by his nature and his habits; (8–9) needs to have an extraordinary faculty of imagination and a perfectly actualized (i.e. acquired) theoretical and practical intellect; (10) receives divine revelation from the Active Intellect, through which he becomes a philosopher (theoretical intellect), wise (practical intellect), and a prophet (faculty of imagination); and (11) will then know how happiness can be achieved; (12) by birth he possesses twelve preeminent qualities. (13) His successors will need only part of these qualities (in order to continue his principles and apply them by analogy), (14) and if necessary can share the rule (though such rulers always must include a philosopher). (15) The excellent community is contrasted to (16–18) the ignorant communities (having ignorant rulers), (19) the corrupted communities (with corrupted rulers) and the erring communities, which have been led astray by knowledgeable but deceitful rulers. Ch. 16: Reward and punishment in the hereafter: (1) The souls of the rulers of an excellent communities are as one soul; the same applies to each class (*martaba*) of their citizens. (2) They all approach happiness through their insights and their good actions, which are partly common to all, partly specific to a certain class. (3–5) After death they achieve the state of happiness (which is experienced in varying intensity). (6) In other communities, the souls of the citizens suffer deformations, with disastrous consequences: (7) perishability in the ignorant communities; (8) eternal punishment in corrupted communities; and (9–10) perishability (for the citizens) and punishment (for the ruler) in erring communities. (11) If a citizen of an excellent community is forced to live in a bad community, he can preserve his soul from harm. Ch. 17: Philosophy and religion: (1) The citizens of an excellent community ought to know everything that has been delineated so far. (2) The philosophers know it as it is (i.e. by means of their intellect) and possess universally valid proofs for it. Other human beings can only grasp it through symbols and analogies (i.e. by means of their imaginative faculty); this leads to different representations (among various peoples). (3) Proofs are unassailable, whereas symbols can be rejected. (4) Some do this for a good purpose, i.e. in order to find more appropriate symbols. (5–6) Others do it because they are following selfish goals (honour, wealth, pleasure) or because they lack understanding.

Section VI: The views of the citizens of deficient communities. Ch. 18: Ignorant communities: (1) Just as in the erring communites, here religion is based on wrong assumptions transmitted by the ancestors. (2–3) Examples for such assumptions: (a) being is constantly in flux and does not have a substantial structure; (b) it consists of opposed powers locked in constant battle; (4–14) in ignorant communities this model of conflict is often transferred to the sphere of human society. (15–18) Some also assume that human beings love peace, without having real insight into our nature. Ch. 19: Erring communities: (1–4) Even though they seek happiness (in the hereafter), they fail to achieve it in various ways. Some reject the life of this world (i.e. the soul's connection to a body) on principle. (5–7) Others reject the affections of the soul. (8–9) Yet another group claim that there is no certain knowledge about the world surrounding us (i.e. about substances, their natures and their effects).

(Kitāb) al-Siyāsa al-madaniyya (al-mulaqqab bi-) Mabādiʾ al-mawǧūdāt
[Book on] Ruling the Community [also called:] The Principles of the Existing Things

This text treats of the same topics as the *Mabādiʾ*, exhibiting numerous parallels in its wording. Nevertheless it seems to have played a minor role within the œuvre, given that al-Fārābī did not revise it with the same degree of care. One consequence of his negligence is the rather confusing presentation of the work in the editions, including the one prepared by Naǧǧār. Therefore the now following survey introduces a division which does not refer to any enumeration present in the printed editions.

1: Six grades of being: First Cause, secondary causes, Active Intellect (all belonging to the spiritual sphere); soul, form, matter (to be found in bodies). Six kinds of bodies: celestial bodies, human beings, animals, plants, minerals, elements. 2: Characterization of the grades of being: the First Cause as God; the secondary causes as celestial intellects; the Active Intellect; the different souls and the grades of thinking; forms; matter. With the exception of the First Cause, no grade of being is perfect. 3: The First Cause and its properties. 4: The secondary causes and their properties; celestial intellects and spheres. 5: The Active Intellect; how the supralunar world affects the sublunar world;

generation and structure of the sublunar world. 6: Human society; various nations or communities; the specific abilities of human beings; natural dispositions and their actualization; in order to achieve happiness, people must depend on cooperation and good guidance. 7: The excellent community: its ruler; its orientation towards happiness; knowledge of the truth (in the few) and representation of the truth (in the many). 8: Deficient communities: their types; rulers; values; defective people within excellent communities.

Taḥṣīl al-saʿāda
The Attainment of Happiness

According to Mahdi [*23: 4], who has studied and translated the text, it is divided in three parts: part A, which bears the title *Taḥṣīl al-saʿāda*, determines the problems, methods and goals of philosophy from al-Fārābī's own perspective; part B explains Plato's view, and part C that of Aristotle (in each case with reference to several works), though the views put forward by all three are claimed to be in agreement. The Arabic bibliographers, however, are ignorant of any such work. Beginning with Ṣāʿid al-Andalusī (*Ṭabaqāt* [*4: 53,14; French transl. 108]) they only mention a *Kitāb fī Aġrāḍ falsafat Aflāṭūn wa-Arisṭūṭālīs* (or similar titles), without connecting it to the title *Taḥṣīl al-saʿāda*. The enumeration of chapters follows Mahdi's translation.

A: *Taḥṣīl al-saʿāda*
The Attainment of Happiness

I: Philosophy as theoretical (conceptual) knowledge. 1: Four things lead to happiness in this world and in the hereafter: theoretical knowledge (*naẓar*), discursive thinking (*fikr*), ethical virtues and practical skills. 2–4: Theoretical knowledge as goal of science, which is not always attained due to uncertainties of method. 5: Certain knowledge demonstrates the existence of something, and its cause. 6–9: The four causes. 10–12: Structure of the philosophical curriculum: Mathematics. 13–15: Physics. 16: Cosmology leads to the question about metaphysical causes. 17: Psychology. 18: Politics. 19: Metaphysics as science of the highest causes (First Cause). 20: Ethics. 21: Reaching theoretical perfection. II: Further points concerning theoretical knowledge. 22–25: What knowledge grasps in (unchanging) concepts appears in reality with (changing) accidents. 26–28: These alterations are grasped by discursive thought, which has several functions (political, economical, military, advisory). 29–31: The hierarchy of the virtues which correspond to these faculties. 32: Hierarchy of practical skills. 33: Criteria for the hierarchization. 34: The highest form of the thinking faculty, virtue and skill, ought to unite with theoretical knowledge. 35–37: Different predispositions in individual people. III: The communication of knowledge.

38–39: A human being who possesses all these abilities ought to pass them on through instruction (*taʿlīm*) and education (*taʾdīb*). 40: Forms of instruction (for both the educated and the non-elite). 41–44: Forms of education. 45–49: Knowledge should be passed on in different ways to the different groups within a community (demonstration, persuasion, analogy, or mixtures of the three). IV: The hierarchy of knowledge serving the happiness of all people. 50: The hierarchy of the forms of knowledge corresponds to the hierarchy of the citizens/groups within a community. 51–52: The philosopher king as ideal ruler. 53: Transmission of the sciences from the Chaldeans via the Egyptians, Greeks, and Syrians to the Arabs. 54–55: The philosopher king passes on his knowledge by means of concepts and demonstrations (= philosophy) and by means of imagination and persuasion (= religion); religion as image of philosophy. 56–58: He issues practical instructions and therefore is a legislator, too. 59–61: True and false philosophers. 62: Even the true philosopher can be prevented from fulfilling his task. 63–64: True philosophy has its origins in Plato and Aristotle.

B: *Falsafat Aflāṭun wa-aǧzāʾuhā wa-Marātib aǧzāʾihā min awwalihā ilā āḫirihā*
Plato's Philosophy, its Parts and their Ranks, from the Beginning to the End

1–2: Human perfection and happiness are not based on external goods, but on knowledge and a certain way of life (*Alcibiades I*). 3–4: This means substantial knowledge (*Theaetetus*) and the virtuous way of life (*Philebus*). 5: Defence of the possibility of true knowledge (*Protagoras*). 6: The knowability and teachability of knowledge (*Meno*). 7–11: Incomplete approximation to knowledge: religion (*Euthyphro*), grammar (*Cratylus*), poetics (*Ion*), rhetoric (*Gorgias*), and sophistics (*The Sophist* and *Euthydemus*). 12: Dialectics makes essential contributions to knowledge, without being able to guarantee it (*Parmenides*). 13: Practical skills and proficiencies do not aim at knowledge but at the useful. 14: The good and the useful according to the many (*Alcibiades II*). 15–16: The truly good and useful (*Hipparchus*). 17: The apparent good of the sophists (*Hippias I* and *II*). 18: True and false pleasure (*Symposium*). 19: Philosophy leads to correct knowledge and the correct way of life (*Theages*). 20: It is useful and necessary (*Amatores*). 21: Politics as the knowledge of how to live. 22: The philosopher king. 23: Prudence (*Charmides*) and courage (*Laches*). 24: Love. 25: Eros and madness; soul. 26: Methods of investigation. 27: Instruction through rhetoric and dialectics. 28: Priority of the oral over the written word (*Phaedrus*). 29: Even if the philosopher is isolated, he should not content himself with commonly held opinions (*Crito* and *Apology*). 30: Death ought to be preferred to an immoral life (*Apology* and *Phaedo*); if a community prevents a moral way of life, a better community is necessary. 31–32: Excellent and bad communities (*Republic*). 33: Natural philosophy within the excellent community (*Timaeus*). 34: The way of life that is correct for its members (*Laws*). 35: The ruler of the community unites theoretical and practical knowledge

(*Critias*) and issues laws (*Epinomis*). 36: Theoretical instruction (according to Socrates) for selected persons; character formation (according to Thrasymachus) for the many. 37: Rank and appreciation of the select (*Menexenus*). 38: The alarming state of contemporary communities (letters).

C: *Falsafat Arisṭūṭālīs wa-aǧzāʾ falsafatihi wa-Marātib aǧzāʾihā wa-l-mawḍiʿ allaḏī minhu ibtadaʾa wa-ilayhi intahā*
The Philosophy of Aristotle, the Parts of his Philosophy, their Ranks, and the Position from which he Started and at which he Ended

1–2: Since human perfection (which Aristotle describes just like Plato) is not directly comprehensible and provable, Aristotle begins his investigation with that which is immediately available to us: each human being strives for the integrity of his body and his senses; possibilities and limits of perception. 3: Further sources of knowledge: primary intelligibles and syllogisms; the search for knowledge as specific human property; the conditions of human life are determined partly by human nature, partly by human will; hence the necessity for several sciences. 4: Distinction between logic (= forms of instruction and argumentation), physics, and the science of the will or of human beings; determination of the highest genera (categories). 5: Judgement (*On Interpretation*). 6: Syllogism (*Prior Analytics*). 7–12: Demonstrations and certainty as fundament of the sciences (*Posterior Analytics*). 13–14: Dialectical discovery of syllogisms (*Topics*) and fallacies (*Sophistical Refutations*). 15–16: Communication of knowledge through persuasion (*Rhetoric*) and the evocation of images (*Poetics*). 17–18: What is grasped conceptually manifests itself in perceptible things in manifold shape; substances and properties. 19: Critique of the Eleatic doctrine of being. 20–36: Matter and form; potency and act; four causes; nature; bodies and their properties; movement, space and time (*Physics*). 37–38: The elements (*On the Heavens*). 39–53: Generation and corruption (*On Generation and Corruption*). 54–63: Effects on the elements in the sublunar realm (*Meteorology* I–III). 64–66: Composite bodies and their transformation (*Meteorology* IV). 67–68: Minerals (*On Stones*). 69–71: Plants. 72–73: Animals. 74: Inanimate and ensouled beings. 75–77: General investigation of the soul; the nutritive faculty. 78–89: Further faculties of the soul and characteristics of living beings: health and disease (*On Health and Disease*); old age (*On Length and Shortness of Life*); life and death; sense perception (*On Sense Perception and the Perceived*); movement of animals (*Progression of Animals*); breath; sleep and waking; dreams; memory. 90–97: The intellect as specific property of the human soul; practical and theoretical intellect; potential and actualized intellect. 98: The Active Intellect. 99: The influence of the Active Intellect and the celestial bodies on the sublunar world; further questions cannot be clarified by physics; the necessity for another type of investigation (*Metaphysics*). Thus it has become clear that knowledge of the intelligibles will lead a human being to perfection.

al-Ǧamʿ bayna raʾyay al-ḥakīmayn Aflāṭūn al-ilāhī wa-Arisṭūṭālīs
The Harmony Between the Two Sages, Divine Plato and Aristotle

Another text on Plato's and Aristotle's philosophy, which at first sight connects to the one described above. In contrast to *Taḥṣīl al-saʿāda*, however, *al-Ǧamʿ* claims that Plato and Aristotle were in agreement not only with respect to their intentions, but also in their opinions (*raʾy*, δόξα). In order to prove this thesis, the text posits the assumption (portrayed as widely accepted) that there were manifold differences between the two thinkers, and then tries dialectically to resolve these (in its view) merely apparent divergences, first in a more general manner (= part I), later by discussing individual theses (= part II).

Al-Fārābī was long assumed to be the author of the text as a matter of course; now, however, his authorship is disputed. Lameer was the first to present numerous objections against it (1994 [*175: 30–39]); they were rejected by Mallet in the preface to his French translation of the text ([*130: 37–40]). Further doubts were raised by Rashed (2004 [*46: 133 n. 56], 2008 [*254: 55–58]), whereas Martini Bonadeo, in her new edition and Italian translation of the work, maintained its authenticity (2008 [*55: 28–30]). In this context Endress, in the preface to Martini Bonadeo's edition, expressed the assumption that *al-Ǧamʿ* could be an early work by al-Fārābī, which might explain certain discrepancies with his later works (2008 [*55: X–XI]). This gave rise to another round of discussion, articulated in two simultaneously published contributions by Rashed and Janos. Rashed (2009 [*57: 44–66]) points out that *al-Ǧamʿ* contradicts al-Fārābī's convictions on four important topics (divine providence, Platonic ideas, temporality of the world, God's will), and suggests ascribing the text to a post-Farabian, Christian author interested in al-Kindī's doctrine – possibly to a specific person, Ibrāhīm Ibn ʿAdī [*57: 66–75]. Janos (2009 [*56: 2–13]) argues that the cosmological claims of *al-Ǧamʿ* do not correspond to al-Fārābī's usual doctrine, but takes the view that it is not possible to deduce a definite answer to the authorship question from this. In his opinion, *al-Ǧamʿ* could be by Yaḥyā Ibn ʿAdī (a brother of Ibrāhīm Ibn ʿAdī; both were students of al-Fārābī), or an early work by al-Fārābī himself [*56: 13–17]. The latter is argued for decidedly by Genequand (2012 [*58: 195–211]), who criticizes Rashed's arguments in detail, concluding that *al-Ǧamʿ* was composed 'au début de la carrière d'al-Fārābī'. The enumeration of chapters follows the edition of Najjar and Mallet, which, unlike that by Martini Bonadeo, numbers the sections of the text.

I: Principles of the argumentation. 1: It is the purpose of the text to prove the harmony between Plato's and Aristotle's opinions, contrary to allegations claiming the opposite. 2: Possible reasons for such allegations: (a) philosophy does not lead to knowledge of things; (b) the high appreciation of Plato and Aristotle as the masters of philosophy is unfounded; (c) the general knowledge of their philosophy is inadequate. 3: Elimination of (a). 4: Elimination of (b). 5: Proof of (c). 6–7: Possible reasons for (c). 11: Discussion and dissolution of the alleged differences. 8–11: Plato's disregard of this world *versus* Aristotle's disregard for the hereafter. 12–16: Allegorical *versus* systematical presentation. 17–20: Priority of the universals *versus* priority of the first substances. 21–23: Diaeresis *versus* synthesis. 24–30: Different views on opposed propositions. 35–41: Emission of a visual ray *versus* affection of the eye as explanation of vision. 42–46: Nature *versus* habit as origin of the virtues of the soul. 47–52: Recollection *versus* sense perception as basis for learning. 53–62: Createdness *versus* eternity of the world. 63–76: Assertion *versus* rejection of the existence of separate spiritual forms. 77–79: Both thinkers are unjustly presumed to reject the recompense in the hereafter. 80–81: Conclusion: he who studies Plato and Aristotle diligently will raise no false accusations against them.

3.10 *Lost Works*

Given that most extant lists of works (cf. p. 545–546 above) are unreliable, it is not possible to ascertain the exact number and titles of al-Fārābī's lost works. Nevertheless we can reconstruct the approximate extent of those losses, by (a) using the information supplied by the oldest bio-bibliographers as a basis, (b) taking quotations of al-Fārābī in works by other philosophers into consideration, and (c) only including those statements of later bio-bibliographers which are confirmed by several testimonies. Observing these criteria, we arrive at the following picture:

(1) In the field of logic it appears that several 'Great Commentaries' have been lost. Al-Fārābī presumably composed lemmatized commentaries like the extant commentary on *On Interpretation* on all texts of the *Organon* (including the *Isagoge*, but perhaps excepting the *Poetics*) (for an overview of the quotations and fragments identified so far see Zonta 1998 [*178: 231–232]).

(2) This is similar for the discipline of physics. There probably existed commentaries on the *Physics*, *On the Heavens*, *On Generation and Corruption*, and the *Meteorology* (Steinschneider 1869 [*15: 135–138]). In addition, al-Fārābī composed an independent treatise *Fī l-Mawǧūdāt al-mutaġayyira* (*On Changeable Things*) (Steinschneider 1869 [*15: 119–123], Mahdi 1967 [*243: 236]), of which we have testimonies transmitted by Ibn Bāǧǧa, Ibn Rušd and Maimonides. It used to be said that this text was possibly identical with the commentary on the *Physics* (Lettinck 1994 [*251: 2]). However, it has now been shown by Rashed (2008 [*254]) that it was in all likelihood an independent treatise on the question of the eternity of the world, which took its starting point from Aristotle's *Physics* VIII 1, and critically discussed the opposing arguments in John Philoponus' *Against Aristotle On the Eternity of the World* VI, as well as in al-Kindī. In this respect the text seems to connect to the extant work *al-Radd ʿalā Yaḥyā al-Naḥwī* (cf. pp. 570–571 above).

(3) In the field of ethics we are missing the commentary on the *Nicomachean Ethics* which is quoted by many later Arabic as well as Latin authors (cf. Fakhry 2002 [*43: 149]; on newly discovered fragments see now Neria 2013 [*347]). According to Ibn al-Nadīm (*Fihrist* [*2: I 263,11 Flügel; II\1 199,4–5 Sayyid; Engl. transl. 629]) it only covered a part (*qiṭʿa*) of the Aristotelian work.

(4) Apart from that al-Fārābī is likely to have composed further propaedeutical works. This includes his well-known report *Fī Ẓuhūr al-falsafa* (*On the Emergence of Philosophy*), of which we have at least an extant fragment. Lesser known, by contrast, is another work which, entitled *Fī Ism al-falsafa* (or something similar), discusses the name of philosophy. Ibn Abī Uṣaybiʿa unfortunately only quotes a brief passage from it (*ʿUyūn* [*8: II 134,25–30]). However, a longer quotation, in Hebrew translation, has been identified in Šem Ṭov Ibn Falaquera (Chiesa, Rigo 1993 [*39: 8–9]). Among other things, this implies that the two texts should probably be regarded as independent works rather than as two parts of the same treatise, as had long been assumed.

(5) There is finally the possibility that al-Fārābī composed two further refutations (in addition to his tracts against Galen and John Philoponus). These would have been critiques of Ibn al-Rāwandī (concerning the art of disputation) and Abū Bakr al-Rāzī (concerning metaphysics) (Steinschneider 1869 [*15: 116–117. 119]). It would be highly interesting to know these works, since it would enable us to place al-Fārābī more exactly within the intellectual debates of his day. However, so far the reports about these two texts must be considered as uncertain since they are only found in Ibn al-Qifṭī and Ibn Abī Uṣaybiʿa, who moreover provide divergent information (on the reports about Ibn al-Rāwandī see van Ess 1980 [*28: 3–6]).

3.11 *Disputed and Spurious Works*

Buġyat al-āmāl fī ṣināʿat al-raml wa-taqwīm al-aškāl
The Aim of the Hopes in the Art of [Divination through] Sand and of the Erection of Figures

A so far unedited work on geomancy (Kubesov, Rosenfeld 1969 [*205]). The text is transmitted in an Oxford manuscript which (apparently wrongly) names al-Fārābī as its author (GAS 1974 [*2: V 296]).

Duʿāʾ ʿaẓīm
Great Prayer

This brief text, edited by Mahdi, is preserved in three places: in MS Şehit Ali Paşa 537, in Ibn Abī Uṣaybiʿa (*ʿUyūn* [*8: II 136,27–138,1]) and in al-Ṣafadī (*Wāfī* [*11: I 111,3–113,2]).

These textual witnesses are not, however, independent from each other, because al-Ṣafadī explicitly refers to Ibn Abī Uṣaybiʿa, and the manuscript mentioned above is so young that Mahdi ([*24: 33]) conceded that this version might well go back to Ibn Abī Uṣaybiʿa, too. In terms of content, the text presents an invocation of God, in which many of the terms used by al-Fārābī ('Cause of causes', 'Active Intellect') are employed. This is why some scholars have postulated al-Fārābī's authorship (Mahdi 1968 [*24: 32]), or have declared it possible (Vallat 2004 [*47: 386]). There are, however, weighty reasons against such an attribution: (a) The context of transmission: Ibn Abī Uṣaybiʿa quotes the text among other dubious traditions (an anecdote, several alleged poems by al-Fārābī), but does not mention it in his list of al-Fārābī's works. (b) Terminology: in one place [*24: 89,4], the text refers to God as *wāǧib al-wuǧūd* (the Necessary of existence), which would presuppose knowledge of Ibn Sīnā's philosophy; in another place [89,13] it contains the wish that the praying person may belong to the *iḫwān al-ṣafāʾ* (the Brethren of Purity), which would imply that the text was composed after the *Rasāʾil Iḫwān al-Ṣafāʾ*. (c) The intention of the text: it combines poetical language with philosophical terminology. While this might, at first sight, echo al-Fārābī's stance on religion, it in fact contradicts it. For al-Fārābī always draws a clear distinction between the level of apodeictics and that of religious poetics and rhetoric.

Fuṣūl Mabādiʾ ārāʾ ahl al-madīna al-fāḍila
Sections of the Principles of the Opinions of the Inhabitants of the Excellent City

A short text which has been edited by Mahdi [*24: 77–86], who attributed it to al-Fārābī; since then it has occasionally been listed among his works. In fact it is probably a later composition, which should be seen in the context of the manuscript tradition of the *Mabādiʾ*. The *Mabādiʾ* were composed in a drawn-out process (cf. p. 577 above), within which two sub-divisions of the text, put in place retrospectively by al-Fārābī, play a certain role (first a division into nineteen chapters [*abwāb*], secondly a division in six larger sections [*fuṣūl*]). Both divisions are documented in the manuscripts and apparently motivated several transmitters to produce summaries of the extensive text structured in an analogous way. A nineteen-part summary is found already in the oldest manuscripts; Walzer, who prepended it to his edition of the *Mabādiʾ*, dates it to the 4th/10th century. The six-part summary published here by Mahdi was probably written later. In its published form it goes back to an Istanbul manuscript (Kılıç Ali Paşa 674; see Mahdi [*24: 29]), which apparently stems from the 11th/17th or the 12th/18th century (Walzer 1985 [*276: 28–29. 36]).

Ǧawābāt li-masāʾil [mutafarriqa] suʾila ʿanhā al-Fārābī
Replies to [several] Questions Posed to al-Fārābī

A sequence of brief sections of text, within each of which one question (about a topic of physics or logic) is recorded together with al-Fārābī's reply. The number of sections is not certain. Ibn Abī ʿUṣaybiʿa (*ʿUyūn* [*8: II 140,2–3]) mentions the title of the work, claiming that it comprises 32 questions; this may well be the reason why a corresponding arrangement can be encountered in the manuscript tradition as well as in the Hyderabad edition. It does not really fit the transmitted text, however, which discusses a larger number of topics. Therefore Dieterici and Āl Yāsīn had good reason to divide the text up differently in their editions (42 and 43 sections respectively). Such disparities, in conjunction with several internal characteristics of the text, have prompted Lameer (1994 [*175: 25–30]) and (less emphatically) Janos (2009 [*56: 13. 16]) to argue for the inauthenticity of the text. This is a likely assumption, not least because in the Arabic tradition the text is not even ascribed to al-Fārābī himself, but seems to go back to an author (a student?) who, based on oral traditions or written records, noted down various pronouncements by al-Fārābī (among others?) in the form of questions and answers. The following survey is limited to listing the topics treated. The enumeration of chapters follows Dieterici's edition.

1–2: Origin and definition of colour. 3: Mixture. 4: The Ǧinn (in contrast to human beings and angels). 5: Loose and dense. 6: Rough and smooth. 7: Hard and soft. 8: Reason and memory. 9: Generation/perishability of the world. 10: The existence of universals. 11: The category 'affection'. 12: The ambiguity of nouns. 13: Predication of accidents. 14: Predication of substances. 15: Finding premises. 16: Existential propositions. 17: Contradictory propositions. 18–20: 'Action', 'affection', and 'relation'. 21: Movement. 22: Subjects and predicates in syllogisms. 23: Specific difference. 24: 'Quantity' and 'quality'. 25: 'Possession'; the ten categories. 26: Demonstrations are based on necessary propositions. 27: Formation of concepts. 28: Forms (in matter, and as objects of sense perception and thinking). 29: Determination of the undetermined. 30: Potentiality, habit, and actions. 31: Will and free choice. 32: The soul according to Aristotle. 33: Substance and body. 34: The elements. 35: Matter. 36: The celestial spheres. 37: Knowing about opposites. 38: Forms of opposites. 39: Universals. 40: Individual concepts; opposed propositions. 41: Indefinite nouns. 42: The 'paradigm' in rhetoric.

Ǧawāmiʿ al-siyar al-marḍiyya fī iqtināʾ al-faḍāʾil al-insiyya
Survey of the Ways of Life which are Praiseworthy with regard to the Acquisition of Human Virtue

Brief, anonymously transmitted treatise on several main questions of ethics (faculties of the soul; major and minor virtues; the means of acquiring the virtues; effects of the virtues). The text has occasional parallels with al-Fārābī's doctrine, which is why it has repeatedly been ascribed to him in the secondary literature. Several considerations, however, speak against such an attribution: (a) the work also contains claims that deviate from al-Fārābī's known positions; (b) several passages exhibit parallels with other famous authors (in particular Miskawayh); and (c) the text closes with a *ḥadīṯ* (tradition of the Prophet Muḥammad), which is presented as the quintessence of the doctrine of the virtues. A further problem is that the text, which is extant in a single manuscript, might be incompletely transmitted; at least the inner logic of the argument suggests a possibly extensive lacuna (fol. 61b, line 9 = 745,10–11 in Daiber's edition [**143*]).

al-Ḥiyal al-rūḥāniyya wa-l-asrār al-ṭabīʿiyya fī daqāʾiq al-aškāl al-handasiyya
The Spiritual Devices and the Natural Secrets Concerning the Subtleties of the Geometrical Figures

A ten-part treatise on geometrical constructions (for a survey of contents and literature cf. Rosenfeld, İhsanoğlu 2003 [*213: 76]). The text has been translated into Russian and Turkish and has been subject of several studies. To date it nevertheless has not been possible to show whether it can indeed be attributed to al-Fārābī or not (Endress 1992 [*38: 76 n. 88]).

Maqālāt al-rafīʿa fī uṣūl ʿilm al-ṭabīʿa
Select Remarks on the Principles of the Science of Physics

A brief treatise on the properties of intellect (*ʿaql*), spirit/pneuma (*rūḥ*), and soul (*nafs*). The work combines popular ideas with numerous scriptural quotations (Quran, *ḥadīṯ*) and shows no relation to al-Fārābī's doctrine. Nor can we find, contrary to Vallat's assumption (2004 [*47: 384]), any textual overlaps between this text and the likewise apocryphal *Risāla fī Māhiyyat al-nafs*.

Min al-Asʾila al-lāmiʿa wa-l-aǧwiba al-ǧāmiʿa
From the Brilliant Questions and Comprehensive Replies

A collection of traditions and stories about prophets (from Adam to Muḥammad), transmitted in an Istanbul manuscript, where it is ascribed to al-Fārābī. However, the text shows no points of contact with the philosopher's doctrine. Therefore the editor has suggested attributing it to a certain Abū Naṣr al-Fārābī al-Ǧawharī, who is also said to have lived in the 4th/10th century (Mahdi [**24*: 37–38]).

Risāla fī l-ʿIlm al-ilāhī
Epistle on Divine Science

This text is part of the Arabic Plotinus corpus, which also includes the better-known *Theology of Aristotle* as well as the *Sayings of the Greek Sage* (*al-Šayḫ al-yūnānī*). Hence its attribution to al-Fārābī, as found in the manuscript evidence, is misleading, as was already observed by Kraus (1940–1941 [*18]).

Risāla fī Iṯbāt al-mufāraqāt
Epistle on the Proof of the Existence of the Separate Entities

Concise explanation of the spiritual entities, which in the manuscript tradition is not attributed to al-Fārābī alone, but also to two students of Ibn Sīnā (al-Maʿṣūmī and Bahmanyār b. Marzubān). In addition, several claims found in the text make it more likely to have originated in Ibn Sīnā's environment, or among his successors: (a) the proof of God's existence, which is designed as a proof of the existence of the Necessary of existence [*28: no.1: 3,13–4,5]; (b) the statement that in God, essence and existence are one [4,8–11]; (c) the strict separation of celestial intellects and celestial souls [4,13–6,11 *vs.* 6,12–7,3]; (d) the demonstration of the extistence of individual human souls by means of self-perception [7,13–16]. The available textual edition is not divided into chapters.

1: Four classes of separate entities: the First Cause, the agent intellects, the celestial powers (= souls), the human souls. 2: All four are incorporeal and imperishable, they grasp themselves and participate in spiritual happiness. 3: Proofs for the existence and separateness of the First Cause. 4: Proofs for the existence and separateness of the agent intellects. 5: Proofs for the existence and separateness of the celestial souls. 6: Proofs for the existence and separateness of the human soul. 7: Once our soul has actualized its intellect, it will gain a permanent share in spiritual happiness.

Risāla fī Māhiyyat al-nafs
Epistle on the Essence of the Soul

A brief treatise on the existence, the essence and the properties of the soul, which is extant in a Hebrew translation only, entitled *Maʾamar be-mahut ha-nefeš*. Even though Ibn Abī Uṣaybiʿa (*ʿUyūn* [*8: II 140,6]) mentions a text of this title among al-Fārābī's works, this treatise is not likely to be by him, as Freudenthal (2003 [*44: 182–84]) has convincingly argued.

Risāla fī l-Milla al-fāḍila
Epistle on the Excellent Religion

This text, published in 1973 by Badawī, is another piece of evidence showing that in parts of the manuscript tradition of the *Mabādiʾ*, a six-part summary was transmitted together with the work itself. It comes from a Tashkent manuscript of the *Mabādiʾ* (dated to 1075/1664), which Walzer, though mentioning it, did not use in his edition [**125*: 29]. The text combines, without transition, two originally separate elements: the beginning of the six-part summary, which was edited by Mahdi ([**24*: 77–86]) under the title *Fuṣūl Mabādiʾ ārāʾ ahl al-madīna al-fāḍila* (cf. p. 588 above), and the beginning of the *Mabādiʾ* proper, with Badawī [**150*: 33,3–35,11] corresponding to Mahdi [**24*: 79,9–81,18], and Badawī [**150*: 35,11–36 ult.] corresponding to Walzer/*Mabādiʾ* [**125*: 56,2–60,7].

Risāla fī l-Siyāsa
Epistle on Governance

In older scholarship, this text was considered to be by al-Fārābī, because it was with this attribution (and under the abovementioned title) that it was edited by Louis Cheikho in 1901, and translated into German by Georg Graf in 1902 [**151*]. As emerged later on, however, the attribution is untenable, since the text (1) does not manifest any proximity to al-Fārābī's doctrine, and (2) is transmitted in numerous manuscripts under various titles (e.g. *Risāla fī l-Aḫlāq* or *Kalām fī Waṣāyā*), and under the names of different authorities (Daiber 1986 [*310: 742–743]).

This diffuse manuscript evidence is matched by the rather blurry contents of the text. It contains observations of popular philosophy, which are divided in three parts: part I deals with questions of anthropology and theology (placement/classification and faculties of the human being; proof of God's existence; necessity of revelation and prophecy); part II, which is reminiscent of a mirror for princes, provides rules for proper ethical conduct (towards one's superiors, peers, subordinates, and oneself); part III consists of a collection of aphorisms concerning the right way of life, which, in the version edited by Cheikho, are put into Plato's mouth.

Risālat Fuṣūṣ al-ḥikam [*or al-ḥikma*]
Epistle on the Bezels of Wisdom

A speculative, partly even meditative text, which has long since been considered spurious by scholars. The text begins with ontological observations (ch. 1–7 in Dieterici), which are probably stimulated by Ibn Sīnā's philosophy. After that, the discussion focuses entirely on God, and on man's relation to Him. Passages of religious or devotional character (e.g. ch. 11–16) alternate with sections presenting well-known theoretical elements of the philosophical tradition (e.g. ch. 56, on definition).

Šarḥ Risāla Zīnūn al-kabīr
Commentary on the Epistle by Zeno the Older

A brief treatise on the following topics: existence of the First Principle; its attributes; its origination of all things; prophecy; religious law; our destiny in the hereafter.

Individual passages represent al-Fārābī's doctrine quite accurately, in particular the description of how the cosmic intellects emerge from the First Principle. Nevertheless it is likely to be an apocryphal work, rather than having flowed from his pen. This is indicated (a) by the fact, that several passages presuppose knowledge of Ibn Sīnā's philosophy (ontology, proof of God's existence); (b) by the religious language of the text (God as *al-bāriʾ* etc.); (c) by the repeated reference to an authoritative transmission of knowledge (from Socrates via Plato and Aristotle, to the latter's alleged pupil Zeno the Older), which appears to belong in the genre of popular wisdom literature.

Taǧrīd Risālat al-Daʿāwā al-qalbiyya
Excerpt from the Epistle on the Demands of the Heart

According to the introduction of the text, it is a work by Aristotle (*Epistle on the Demands of the Heart*) in an adaptation by al-Fārābī. In reality it is another version of the text known by the title *ʿUyūn al-masāʾil* (*The Principal Questions*) (see below). Ch. 1–2 of the *ʿUyūn* are omitted, ch. 3–22 are represented completely, if often in divergent wording.

al-Taʿlīqāt
Notes

A collection of explanatory remarks on various areas of philosophy, which originated in the context of instruction. The *Taʿlīqāt* which have come down to us under the name of al-Fārābī do not appear to go back to him, since they exhibit numerous references to Ibn Sīnā's philosophy, and are all contained in the latter's own collections of *Taʿlīqāt* (Michot 1982 [*29: 234–244]).

ʿUyūn al-masāʾil
The Principal Questions

A compilation of fundamental theses concerning the origin and the structure of being. Its attribution to al-Fārābī is highly problematic. Several factors speak against it: (a) the manuscript tradition, which names not just al-Fārābī, but also Ibn Sīnā and one further person (Abū l-Barakāt al-Baġdādī?) as its author; (b) several positions taken in the text, like its assumption of primary concepts (ch. 1), the development of its ontology out of the distinction between possible and necessary (ch. 3. 7 etc.) and its assumption of an intellect '*in habitu*' (ch. 21), which all presuppose familiarity with Ibn Sīnā's philosophy; and (c) the fact that large parts of the text were also transmitted under a different title (cf. the information on *Taǧrīd risālat al-daʿāwā al-qalbiyya* above). For a long time now scholars have worked on the assumption that the text is not by al-Fārābī. A contrary opinion was last advanced by Lameer (1994 [*175: 24–25]), whose arguments, however, are not convincing.

1–2: Knowledge consists of concepts and judgements, which can all be traced back to primary concepts (existence, necessity, possibility) and first judgements. 3: Possible and necessary existence; existence of the Necessary Existent. 4–5: Description of the Necessary Existent. 6: Its thinking brings about all things. 7: The Coming-to-be of the First Intellect. 8: Second intellect; celestial sphere, soul. 9: Further intellects, down to the Active Intellect, which affects the material world. 11: Generation of the material world under the influence of the stars. 12–13: Motion; time. 14: Space; impossibility of vacuum. 15: No atoms; no actual infinity. 16: Natural place. 17: The celestial bodies (fifth element; motion; soul; intellect). 18: Primary qualities. 19: Forms of mixture. 20: Intellect as specific property of human beings; further faculties of the soul. 21: Practical and theoretical intellect (with its different stages). 22: The human body as such, and as substrate for the soul; destiny of the soul in the hereafter; God's providence.

4 Doctrine

4.1 General Theory of Science. Definition and Classification of Philosophy – 4.2 Logic – 4.3 Mathematics and Physics – 4.4 Metaphysics – 4.5 Ethics and Politics

4.1 *General Theory of Science. Definition and Classification of Philosophy*

What al-Fārābī considered philosophy to be, and how he classified his own contribution to it, is indicated in various contexts. His most explicit comments on this question can be found in *Fī Ẓuhūr al-falsafa* (*On the Emergence of Philosophy* [*53]), a work that is extant in fragments only, and has become known under the title *From Alexandria to Baghdad*. As we know now, it belongs to a larger narrative complex which can be traced also in al-Masʿūdī (345/956), Ibn Riḍwān (460/1068) and Ibn Ǧumayʿ (594/1198) (cf. pp. 51–53 above). The version we find in al-Fārābī can nevertheless be considered as a testimony to his own personal views, and to his own self-image. Describing how Aristotle's doctrine was transmitted over generations of students, until it would finally reach him, he emphasizes various stages in the process: the continual and comprehensive instruction in ancient Alexandria (first under Ptolemaic, later under Roman rule); the resolution of the Christian bishops (in late antiquity) to read the books of the *Organon* up to and including the figures of the categorical syllogisms (*Prior Analytics* I 7) only; the relocation of philosophical instruction (with this limitation in place) from Alexandria to Antioch in the early Islamic era; the activities of scholars from Harran and Marw and, finally, the arrival of philosophy in Baghdad, where logic once again could be studied without restriction (cf. most recently Rudolph 2015 [*142]).

Al-Fārābī's description is not a reliable historiographical report, but it does shed light on how he positioned his own philosophical activity. Placing himself in the tradition of the Alexandrian school, he simultaneously declares that this implies taking up the Aristotelian philosophical project.

Both claims have now been confirmed by research. It has been possible to demonstrate, with various examples, how closely al-Fārābī connects to the late ancient tradition of commenting on Aristotle (e.g. Zimmermann 1981 [*163], Streetman 2014 [*257]). Scholars have moreover been able to determine a specific route of transmission (besides many other lines of transmission, cf. pp. 59–61 above), which seems to have led from Alexandria to Baghdad via the Sasanian and Syriac milieus (Gutas 1983 [*134]).

Nevertheless it is plain to see that al-Fārābī knew other philosophical currents apart from Aristotelianism; this applies in particular to (Neo-)Platonism, which influenced parts of his philosophy to such an extent that some scholars have called him a downright (Neo-)Platonist. This view was prevalent especially in older secondary literature (for an overview see Galston 1977 [*133]), but was revived by Fakhry (2002 [*43]) and Vallat (2004 [*47]); the latter added the supposition that al-Fārābī harked back to a so far unknown Platonic tradition which had existed in Harran since the 6th century (Vallat 2004 [*47: 17–23]). The Harran hypothesis, which ultimately goes back to Tardieu (1986 [*32]), is, however, highly speculative and controversial (on this debate, including the many critical voices, cf. pp. 53–54 above). Moreover, it appears superfluous. Platonic doctrine was in any case transmitted by the known late ancient schools. This also applied to Alexandria, where the study of Aristotle was accompanied by the reading of Platonic texts. Hence there is no reason to doubt al-Fārābī's claim that he orientated himself first and foremost towards the Alexandrian tradition. This meant that he was able to get to know the views of both schools, even if, judging from his own account, Aristotelianism was the defining element of the tradition.

Apart from that it is not enough to mention Aristotle and Plato as al-Fārābī's philosophical paragons: the intellectual background to the development of his philosophy was much broader. It included Galen, whom he criticized several times by name (Zimmermann 1981 [*163: lxxxi–lxxxiv]), as well as some Stoic provocations, which, however, are rather diffuse and not easy to locate historically (Gätje 1971 [*160: 12–13], Lameer 1994 [*175: 44–46. 76–77]). Moreover, one must not forget that al-Fārābī did not live in late antiquity, but in 4th/10th century Baghdad. Thus he was also familiar with those sciences that had originated in the Arabic-Islamic context, and had long since given rise to new debates. Being part of his intellectual horizon, they influenced the way in which he took up and interpreted the late ancient heritage (for examples from logic cf. Schöck 2006 [*186: 285–372]). In this respect the path 'from Alexandria to Baghdad' marks not only an historical process of transmission taken up by al-Fārābī, but also an intellectual process which was his very own achievement.

How this unfolded in practice can be gleaned from his attempts to define and classify philosophy. We encounter them in several of his works, each of which marks a certain stage in his engagement with the Alexandrian *Prolegomena* literature. Starting point of this process is the small treatise *Fīmā yanbaġī an yuqaddama qabla taʿallum al-falsafa* (*On What Must Proceed the Study of [Aristotelian] Philosophy* [*52]). It discusses the ten questions (here only nine are mentioned) whose explication is traditionally used as an introduction to Aristotelian philosophy; given that the text follows the Alexandrian formula very closely, it really is less an original work than an adaptation of an ancient prototype. *Al-Tanbīh ʿalā sabīl al-saʿāda* (*Exhortation to the Path to Happiness* [*51]) leads one step further. Here al-Fārābī combines two elements of the tradition: an introduction to ethics, which in late antiquity also belonged to philosophical propaedeutics, and a brief classification of philosophy [*51: 256,7–257,10], which already bears the features of his own thoughts on the theory of science. In order fully to perceive his own conception, however, we must consult a third text: the famous work *Iḥṣāʾ al-ʿulūm* (*The Enumeration of the Sciences* [*45]). With this text, al-Fārābī at last rewrites the late ancient *Prolegomena* for his own purposes, taking into account not only philosophy itself, but also other disciplines original to Arabic-Islamic culture, and integrating them in a complete system of sciences.

This system is divided in five areas: (1) grammar (*ʿilm al-lisān*), (2) logic (*ʿilm al-manṭiq*), (3) mathematics (*ʿilm al-taʿālīm*), (4) physics (*al-ʿilm al-ṭabīʿī*) and metaphysics (*al-ʿilm al-ilāhī*), and (5) the 'science of the community' (*al-ʿilm al-madanī*: literally 'civic science' or 'political science' in the original sense of the science of the city-state, Greek *polis*). The latter in fact comprises ethics and politics, supplemented by jurisprudence (*ʿilm al-fiqh*) and theology (*ʿilm al-kalām*). All these disciplines are given a brief description by al-Fārābī: he names their tasks, their sub-disciplines, sometimes even their fundamental texts (Mahdi 1975 [*132]). In this respect, the *Iḥṣāʾ* is first and foremost a propaedeutical work introducing beginners to the study of philosophy (for the curricular background to the text cf. Günther 2009 [*138: 16–17]). However, its descriptive method is linked to a normative purpose. The description of the disciplines implicitly reveals their separation in two groups. The first group comprises logic, mathematics, physics and the science of the community, whereas grammar, jurisprudence, and theology are counted as parts of the second group.

The difference is one of scope. Only the sciences of the first group can claim universality. Striving for universally true, conceptual knowledge, they together constitute philosophy, which in another work (*Tanbīh* [*51: 256,3]) is also called 'absolute wisdom' (*al-ḥikma ʿalā l-iṭlāq*). It needs to be pointed out, however, that it is only in the *Iḥṣāʾ* that al-Fārābī counts logic as part of philosophy proper. In other texts, for instance in *al-Alfāẓ al-mustaʿmala fī l-manṭiq* (*Linguistic Expressions Used in Logic*) [*60: 107,12–108,3], he separates it from philosophy, explaining that it is a mere instrument of thought, and that the study of logic is a precondition for the study of philosophy (Diebler 2005 [*181: 289], Druart 2007 [*282: 19–23]).

The disciplines of the second group are particular; their areas of competence are tied to specific, culturally determined conditions. This goes for grammar, which deals with a specific language, just as for jurisprudence and theology, whose interest is directed towards a specific religious tradition. Nevertheless the two types of inquiry are linked. For every object that is treated by a particular discipline can be examined with respect to its universal properties – albeit in a different way. This leads to the assumption that each particular discipline (grammar, theology, jurisprudence) corresponds to a universal science (logic, metaphysics, ethics) (Endress 1992 [*38: 50]); but it also raises the question why knowledge is structured in these two parallel tiers, and how the entire system of sciences has come about.

This question al-Fārābī does not address within the *Iḥṣāʾ* but in another work, entitled *al-Ḥurūf* (*The Particles* [*46]). Here he describes an historical process which, in his view, has led to the emergence of the various disciplines. According to al-Fārābī it can be divided in the following main stages (*Ḥurūf* [*46: § 114–146]): human beings gathered together and thus wanted to communicate with each other. They formed sounds and words and, finally, a set of vocabulary which was defined by convention, and by the activity of a 'giver of language'. The further differentiation of their means of expression, which occurred mainly through various forms of expansion and transposition (*naqla*) of meaning (de Vaulx d'Arcy 2010 [*139: 130–146. 173–176]), resulted in the successive generation of the 'generally comprehensible' arts of rhetoric, poetics, the art of narration and mnemonics, linguistics (i.e. lexicography and grammar), and the art of writing. The search for causal explanations subsequently led to the development of mathematics and physics; after that, the wish to refine the technique of argumentation resulted in the formation of dialectics (including sophistics). Plato completed dialectics and drew up the science of the community; Aristotle completed the entire development of scientific (i.e. philosophical) thought by devising the rules of demonstration. However, since only few people are able to grasp the truth in its demonstrative form, two further steps were required. Thus religion came into being in order to proclaim (the same) truth with the means of poetry and rhetoric. Finally, jurisprudence and theology were developed in order to defend and to interpret the claims of religion with dialectical arguments (for details see Vajda 1970 [*130: 250–256], Mahdi 1972 [*131: 5–12]; Druart 2010 [*140]; French transl. by Hilal 1997 [*41: II 123–147], Span. transl. by Paredes Gandía 2004 [*45], Engl. transl. by Khalidi 2005 [*48: 4–20]).

This 'idealist systematization of cultural history' (Gutas 1983 [*134: 259 n. 70]) becomes the basis for all further developments. Al-Fārābī is aware that the actual historical processes often deviate from his presentation, as emerges from his subsequent remarks in which he enumerates several disruptions and modifications which may occur during the process (*Ḥurūf* [*46: § 147–153]; cf. Mahdi 1972 [*131: 12–23]). Nevertheless he regards the process, as described by him, as the normative standard that indicates how the human spirit will ideally unfold. This applies to the community (which forms the focus of attention here) as well as the individual, which is equally supposed to learn first the rhetorical, then the dialectical, and finally the demonstrative methods of argument (*Ḫiṭāba* [*74: 55,6–57,9 Langhade; 456,13–466,11 Dānišpažūh]).

Therefore the passage summed up above can be regarded as a key text within al-Fārābī's work. It contains numerous hints and germs of explanation which are illuminating not only in respect of his conception of science, but also of other areas of his thought. Three of them carry particular weight: (1) the linguistic aspect: as al-Fārābī emphasizes, language plays a decisive role in the development of the mind. Its differentiation is a motor of development, in consequence of which the temporally prior, particular methods of expression and communication (i.e. the subject of grammar) gradually turn into consideration of universals (i.e. the subject of logic) (Diebler 2005 [*181: 291–292]). Remarkably, al-Fārābī describes the cultural development specifically as following the path from 'poetry' to 'philosophy'. In doing so, he probably takes up ideas which in similar form can be found in early Arabic historiographers like al-Yaʿqūbī or Abū ʿĪsā Ibn al-Munaǧǧim (both late 3rd/9th cent.). They repeatedly refer to parallels between Greek and Arabic cultural history, inasmuch as the development in both cases had led from an early blossoming of poetry (on the side of the Greeks: Homer; on that of the Arabs: Imruʾ al-Qays) to a later formation of philosophical thinking (Rudolph 2011 [*141: 309–311]).

(2) The pragmatic aspect: despite the teleological character of this process it is not exclusively directed towards the highest form of thinking, i.e. philosophical demonstration. Al-Fārābī in fact takes it for granted that most people will never be able to reach this level, and therefore have to be addressed with the help of less advanced forms of argument (poetry, rhetoric, at best dialectics). Here religion holds a decisive function, as it is able to transform the demonstrative, universally valid results of philosophy into particular modes of expression (symbols, allegories). (3) The epistemological aspect: it is furthermore characteristic of the process that people put each new grade of knowledge into practice first, before mastering it intellectually (arithmetic, for example, comes about by first counting real objects, before one learns to calculate with absolute numbers). They therefore perform a process of abstraction which leads from practice to theory. This prompts al-Fārābī to initiate a new understanding of 'practical' and 'theoretical', which deviates from the traditional Aristotelian view and anticipates our usage of these two terms today (Schramm 1986 [*135]).

It is furthermore remarkable that al-Fārābī identifies the authorities he intends to follow by name. For he describes cultural history as an intellectual process which lasted over many generations, until it was finally advanced properly by Plato, and completed by Aristotle. Similar characterizations (with Plato as pioneer and Aristotle as the one responsible for mature science) are to be found in several other works. This also applies to *al-Ǧamʿ bayna raʾyay al-ḥakīmayn Aflāṭūn al-ilāhī wa-Arisṭūṭālīs* (*The Harmony Between the Two Sages, the Divine Plato and Aristotle*) – whether or not the work was composed by al-Fārābī himself or by one of his students (for the state of discussion cf. p. 585 above). Even in this text, which is supposed to emphasize the agreement between both philosophers, Plato takes on the role of the precursor, while Aristotle is characterized as the one who completes the development (Endress 1991 [*37: 249–251]). This again confirms the prominent position which al-Fārābī assigned to the Stagirite, and helps us understand why his own philosophical programme, with few exceptions, is structured along the lines of the Aristotelian curriculum.

4.2 *Logic*

Propaedeutics having been dealt with, the programme begins with an explication of logic, which al-Fārābī undertakes within three different genres: (1) A series of epitomes which sum up the entire material of the *Organon*, including the *Isagoge*, the *Rhetoric*, and the *Poetics*. They seem to have been studied and passed on as a unit from early on, with the result that the sources and manuscripts occasionally present them as a single work (Gutas 1993 [*174: 49–50]). (2) A number of lemmatized commentaries; extant are the commentary on *On Interpretation* [*65] and parts of al-Fārābī's notes on the *Categories*

[*63], the *Prior Analytics* [*68] and the *Rhetoric* [*75]. However, according to the bio-bibliographical sources, al-Fārābī composed a 'great commentary' on each of the parts of the *Organon*, with the exception of the *Poetics* (Gutas 1993 [*174: 48], Zonta 1998 [*178]). (3) A few smaller treatises which supplement the logical curriculum. These either serve the purpose of a general introduction, like *al-Tawṭiʾa fī l-manṭiq* (*Introduction to Logic* [*58]), *Fuṣūl taštamil ʿalā ǧamīʿ mā yuḍtarr ilā maʿrifatihi man arāda l-šurūʿ fī ṣināʿat al-manṭiq* (*Chapters Containing Everything a Beginner in the Art of Logic Needs to Know* [*59]) and *al-Alfāẓ al-mustaʿmala fī l-manṭiq* (*Linguistic Expressions Used in Logic* [*60]), or are meant to round off a specific topic (like the two additional treatises on the art of poetry [*77], [*78]). Individual problems which al-Fārābī apparently considers to be of particular importance are occasionally discussed in dedicated works, as e.g. in *Šarāʾiṭ al-yaqīn* (*Conditions for Certainty* [*70]) and in *Kitāb al-Qiyās al-ṣaġīr* (*Short Book on the Syllogism*), also known as *al-Muḫtaṣar al-ṣaġīr fī kayfiyyat al-qiyās* (*Short Summary on the Form of the Syllogism*) or *al-Muḫtaṣar al-ṣaġīr fī l-manṭiq ʿalā ṭarīqat al-mutakallimīn* (*Short Summary of Logic as Practiced by the Theologians* [*67]).

The size of this corpus of texts shows how highly al-Fārābī rated the significance of logic. For him, logic is the indispensable 'touchstone of intellect' (*ʿiyār al-ʿaql*) (*Tawṭiʾa* [*58: 56,1–2 al-ʿAǧam; 11,13 Dānišpažūh]), as it mediates the rules that will help us find our path to what is 'correct' (*ṣawāb*) and to 'truth' (*ḥaqq*), and avoid all errors (*Iḥṣāʾ* [*45: 67,5–9], *Tawṭiʾa* [*58: 55,7–9 al-ʿAǧam; 11,5–7 Dānišpažūh]). Thus it becomes the central instrument of philosophy and in some sense takes the place of mathematics, which al-Kindī had regarded as the definitive philosophical method (cf. pp. 118–119 and 190 above). Nevertheless al-Fārābī's works do not present a coherent logical system, but instead document his continuous engagement with the fundamental Aristotelian texts, which perhaps never reached a final conclusion. This is evident, on the one hand, from striking vacillations in terminology (Lameer 1994 [*175: 202. 265–266. 274–280]), and on the other, from al-Fārābī's attitude towards individual Aristotelian tenets, which seems to have changed over time. Both factors make it difficult to arrive at an overall assessment, which has led some to conclude that we will probably never be in a position to describe al-Fārābī's logic with certitude (Street 2004 [*180: 537]).

Notwithstanding such limitations, his achievements in this area remain enormous. They consist not so much in the elaboration of a logical system as in the systematic discussion of individual elements and topics of logical theory. Thereby al-Fārābī was able to interrelate the Aristotelian tradition with problems that were discussed in his day. This contributed decisively to the widespread adoption of the *Organon* as a study text, and to its gaining a permanent place in the philosophy and, moreover, the general scientific tradition of the Islamic world.

(1) One such topic was the question of the relation between grammar and logic or, differently put, between language and thinking. In the early 4th/10th century it was subject of a lively debate, as we can infer from the reports about the discussion between Abū Bišr Mattā (d. 328/940) and Abū Saʿīd al-Sīrāfī (d. 368/979). In this discussion, Abū Bišr championed the pre-eminence of logic, claiming that logic alone was able to distinguish right from wrong and truth from falsehood, since it dealt with the concepts and laws of thought, which were independent of their particular linguistic manifestations. Al-Sīrāfī was of the opposite opinion. According to him, thinking is always bound to the linguistic signs through which it is expressed. In order to distinguish between right and wrong propositions, one therefore would have to determine whether the rules of the language used were followed correctly. Hence a logical examination could never amount to anything but an inspection of grammar (Elamrani-Jamal 1983 [*164: 61–71], Endress 1986 [*166: 194–200. 235–270], Hasnaoui 1988 [*169: 221–223]).

In principle, al-Fārābī shares Abū Bišr Mattā's position: he likewise maintains a clear separation between the conceptual level (i.e. the subject matter of logic) and the level of linguistic signs (i.e. the subject matter of grammar). This is appositely expressed in his often-quoted claim that logic is related to the intellect and the intelligibles as grammar is related to language and linguistic expressions (*alfāẓ*). For every rule concerning linguistic expressions there exists a corresponding law concerning the intelligibles, taught to us by logic (*Iḥṣāʾ* [*45: 68,4–7]; cf. *Tawṭiʾa* [*58: 55,11–56,2 al-ʿAǧam; 11,11–13 Dānišpažūh], *Tanbīh* [*51: 260,12–20]; on this point see Zimmermann 1981 [* 163: xliii], Hasnaoui 1988 [*169: 220]). All the same al-Fārābī recognizes a connection between the two levels. Anyone who wants to mention concepts or describe thought processes will need to use linguistic signs for this purpose. Therefore the logician must be clear on the expressions he uses; and thus al-Fārābī explains that the subject matter of logic, i.e. the things about which it legislates, consists in 'intelligibles, inasmuch as they are signified by linguistic expressions; and linguistic expressions, inasmuch as they signify intelligibles' (*Iḥṣāʾ* [*45: 74,10–12]).

Accordingly, language is not just an auxillary device of logic; it also forms one of its subject matters. For the logician cannot confine himself to establishing a relation between concepts and real objects. He rather 'considers thought as relating to both sides, namely, to the entities (*mawǧūdāt*) outside the soul and to speech' (*Šarḥ fī l-ʿIbāra* [*65: 24,4–6 Kutsch, Marrow; 9,5–6 Dānišpažūh; Engl. transl. 10]). This insight inspires al-Fārābī to extensive deliberations about the relationship between language and thinking, sounding the various relations that obtain between the particular objects of sense perception (*mušār ilayhi*), our statements about them (*maqūl*), and the contents of our thoughts (*maʿqūl*) (Arnaldez 1977 [*161], Schneider 1994 [*177: 711–720], Diebler 2005 [*181: 280–281]). These reflections are of intrinsic philosophical interest, but also serve a particular purpose arising from the specific historical context within which al-Fārābī was writing: with their help he intends to prove that the contents of the *Organon* (which he studied with Abū Bišr Mattā in Baghdad) possess universal validity and are adequately expressed not only in the Greek original, but also in its Arabic translation.

The proof itself unfolds in several steps. First al-Fārābī undertakes to produce his own classification of all linguistic signs that are employed in the Arabic language. It is not oriented at the grammatical, but at the logical function of the words; thus, for instance, *kull* (each, every) is not listed under the nouns, but under the particles (*Alfāẓ* [*60: 41–56]; cf. Gätje 1971 [*160], Eskenasy 1988 [*168], Langhade 1994 [*176: 327–341], Schöck 2006 [*186: 327–329]). Then al-Fārābī discusses those linguistic signs in detail which are used as terms in logical contexts. Here it is important for him to show that the Arabic words are used adequately in each case. Logic, or philosophy, does not develop its own language that would be based on transferred meanings or metaphors; rather, it is characterized by the very fact 'that within it, each expression is used in the same meaning for which it was originally laid down' (*Ḥurūf* [*46: 165,3–5]; on the issue in general cf. Abed 1991 [*171: 1–34. 171]). Finally, al-Fārābī turns to a discussion of syntax. Here he needs to explain several peculiarities of the Arabic language, for example the lack of a copula (*Ḥurūf* [*46: 112,1–3]; on this point see Zimmermann 1981 [*163: xlxv–xlv. lx–lxiii], Schneider 1994 [*177: 720–734]). But even this does not impede the ability of Arabic to render all the points of logic set down by Aristotle unequivocally, so that nothing will stand in the way of accepting and applying the *Organon* in Arabic (Abed 1991 [*171: 119–141]).

Behind these reflections lies al-Fārābī's conviction that the various forms of expression are connected in terms of content as well as historically, a conviction that is already manifest in his ideas concerning 'cultural history' (cf. pp. 597–598 above), which show that he assumes a continuous process during which language and thinking are progressively differentiated. This process is not just formulated as a general postulate, but is illustrated with specific examples. In *al-Ḥurūf*, al-Fārābī produces meticulous observations which belong to the most original passages in his entire œuvre, and which in recent times have increasingly moved into the focus of research. There have been various individual studies, which step by step have contributed to unlocking the complex work, and to establishing an overall interpretation. For instance, scholars have examined how al-Fārābī connects the meanings of *ǧawhar* in colloquial language (jewel, ore) and in philosophical terminology (substance) (Druart 1987 [*167], Langhade 1994 [*176: 358–363]; cf. Druart 2007 [*282: 35–36]); or how he creates a link between commonly used questions (whether?, how?, which?, what?) and the project of finding definitions (Abed 1991 [*171: 59–67]), or in general between the different sorts of question (in everyday life as well as in the various forms of pre-scientific and scientific thinking) and the Aristotelian formation of categories (Diebler 2005 [*181: 279. 281–291]). It has furthermore been established that his analysis of the categories serves the additional purpose of setting metaphysics apart from all other parts of philosophy; for in contrast to them, it investigates matters that lie 'beyond' the categories (like the Divine Cause), or concern all categories at once (like being) and hence are transcategorial (Druart 2007 [*282: 16. 32–37]). Finally, a recent study has shown that al-Fārābī's analysis of the meanings of 'being(s)' goes noticeably beyond Aristotle (Menn 2008 [*284]). Among other things, this is demonstrated by the discovery that al-Fārābī apparently was the first thinker to understand 'being', in one of its meanings, as a second intelligible (*maʿqūl ṯānī*), i.e. as second intention or as second-order concept (Menn 2008 [*284: 81–82]).

(2) A further topic that receives particular attention from al-Fārābī is syllogistics. It is of eminent importance for him insofar as it determines his approach to the *Organon*, indeed his understanding of the tasks and applications of logic in general. According to al-Fārābī, the *Organon* is divided in two large parts. The first one consists of the *Categories, On Interpretation*, and the *Prior Analytics*, treatises that examine concept, proposition, and the general rules of the syllogism, thus producing the fundament on which every logical investigation must be built. The other five books, i.e. the *Posterior Analytics, Topics, Sophistical Refutations, Rhetoric*, and *Poetics*, have more specific tasks: they each discuss a certain type of logical discourse, and each require their own investigation, because they are based on premises with different epistemic content. Their formal structure, however, is comparable, for they all use syllogisms. Hence the subject matter of these five books can be defined respectively as the demonstrative, dialectical, sophistical, rhetorical, and poetical syllogism (*Tawṭiʾa* [*58: 56,8–58,16 al-ʿAǧam; 12,2–13,22 Dānišpažūh; Engl. transl. 230–232], *Alfāẓ* [*60: 104,18–106,7]).

The opinion advanced here by al-Fārābī is called 'context theory' in modern scholarship (Black 1990 [*170: 1–16. 247–258], Street 2004 [*180: 538]). He did not develop it himself; it was among the doctrines that he adopted from the Alexandrian commentators on Aristotle (Gutas 1983 [*134: 256–257. 264–267]).

However, al-Fārābī did not just take over this theory as it was, but modified and developed it, led by two major concerns.

(a) First, he tries to supplement the theory whenever necessary. There are several examples for this, e.g. his theory of conditional propositions and conditional syllogisms (Karimullah 2014 [*197]), but none perhaps as instructive as those found in the 'last' two books of the *Organon*, which deal especially with phenomena that are defined by language and culture. This applies to the area of rhetoric on the one hand, to which al-Fārābī made several original contributions (Black 1990 [*170: 106–108. 171–178], Würsch 1991 [*172: 76–78. 87–93], Aouad 1992 [*173], 2008 [*188], 2009 [*194], Woerther 2008 [*193], 2009 [*195], 2015 [*198]). On the other hand, this point also relates to poetics, a field within which very different presuppositions had to be considered in an Arabic, as opposed to a Greek, cultural environment. It is therefore unsurprising that al-Fārābī dedicated several independent compendia to it. In these texts he combined different theoretical segments known from late antiquity (Heinrichs 1969 [*159: 127–155]), but also added new elements, as can be seen from the example of the poetical syllogism (Aouad, Schoeler 2002 [*179], Schoeler 2013 [*196]); more generally Black 1990 [*170: 209–246], Schoeler 2005 [*182]). By contrast, in the case of the Aristotelian *Poetics*, al-Fārābī seems to have abstained from writing a lemmatized commentary of the sort he had composed for all other parts of the *Organon*. This could be linked to the fact that the text contained too many topics and examples that would have been unfamiliar to an Arabic readership.

(b) The second, ultimately more important decision concerned the transfer of syllogistics to the realm of noetics and ontology (Gutas 1999 [*42: 221]). This was possible for al-Fārābī because he was convinced that the aforementioned types of syllogisms (from the demonstrative to the poetical one) did not just form the subject matter of the last five books of the *Organon*, but presented an adequate and complete description of all human intellectual capacities (*Alfāẓ* [*60: 96,1–97,3]). Working with this assumption, he was able to establish a relation between the various forms of human knowledge and the Aristotelian texts, which is hierarchically structured and confirms the classificatory system we have already encountered in his theory of science. According to this classification, only philosophers are able to understand and apply the demonstrative syllogism (to which the *Posterior Analytics* are assigned). The theologians confine themselves to dialectical syllogisms (i.e. the subject matter of the *Topics*), while religious revelation deploys the methods of persuasion (*Rhetoric*), and of imitation and the evocation of images (*Poetics*) (Heinrichs 1978 [*162], Schoeler 2005 [*182: 52–56]; cf. p. 598 above). This thesis has numerous implications that reach beyond logic (in particular to metaphysics and politics). However, its consequences for logic itself are already considerable, with the

Organon acquiring an entirely new function and meaning. Having shed its role as a mere 'instrument' with whose help the philosophers may determine their own method, it is now the central epistemological work, which takes account of every form of rationality possible for human beings, and analyses it in a valid manner.

(3) Despite this broadened perspective, al-Fārābī insists that the different texts of the *Organon* are arranged around a common centre: for him the doctrine of demonstration remains 'the highest aim' (*al-maqṣūd al-aʿẓam*) of logic (*Alfāẓ* [*60: 99,13–14]). It forms the methodological foundation of philosophy, and against every doubt – even against the apparent *aporia* known as 'Meno's paradox' (Black 2008 [*189: 23–34]) – ensures philosophy's exclusive claim to forming apodeictic and universally true propositions. This is why it is treated so elaborately by al-Fārābī, in his epitome of the *Posterior Analytics* as well as in the work *Šarāʾiṭ al-yaqīn* (*Conditions for Certainty*), in which he analyses one particular feature of apodeictics in depth.

The starting point for his observations is a dichotomy which would later become part of the standard repertoire of epistemological discussions in the Arabic world. It marks the two aspects that are at the basis of each act of cognition: *taṣawwur*, i.e. the 'concept', or rather the act with which we form the concept of each individual thing; and *taṣdīq*, literally 'assent': a judgement about the existence of something, or about states of affairs (*Burhān* [*69: 19,7 Fakhry; 266,5 Dānišpažūh]; cf. *Didascalia* [*75: 154,11–14], where *taṣawwur* is rendered as *formatio* and *taṣdīq* as *assertio seu creditio*). Both elements are central to the doctrine of demonstration, and hence are examined by al-Fārābī from various points of view. Thus he describes *taṣawwur* as (among other things) an act (a) through which we understand the meaning (*maʿnā*) of what we have heard from a teacher (*Alfāẓ* [*60: 87,1–3]); (b) through which we understand (*fahima*) what a name/noun (*ism*) means (*Burhān* [*69: 80,1–3 Fakhry; 329,22–330,1 Dānišpažūh]; cf. *Fuṣūl taštamil* [*59: 68,2–6 al-ʿAǧam; 22,16–19 Dānišpažūh]); (c) which can also be called knowing (*ʿarafa*) or grasping (*ʿaqala*) (*Ḥurūf* [*46: 173,2–3]); and (d) which occurs in perfect form when we have grasped a thing in accordance with its definition (*Burhān* [*69: 20,2–3. 45,5 Fakhry; 266,12–13. 293,3 Dānišpažūh]). *Taṣdīq*, on the other hand, happens when we assent to the existence of that which we have grasped conceptually (*taṣawwara*) and understood (*fahima*) due to what we have heard from a teacher (*Alfāẓ* [*60: 87,3]). It means 'generally that a human being believes about a certain thing on which he has formed a judgement, that it is, in its existence outside of the mind, as he believes it to be in his mind' (*Burhān* [*69: 20,4–5 Fakhry; 266,14–16 Dānišpažūh]). If this is the case, it is an instance of truth; but it is also possible that we assent to something false. Therefore one must distinguish different grades of *taṣdīq*. They go from 'false assent' (*taṣdīq kāḏib*) through the vague sensation of 'rest of the soul' (*sukūn al-nafs*; cf. pp. 608–609 below) up to the state which can be identified as 'certainty' (*yaqīn*) [*69: 20,6–10 Fakhry; 266,16–21 Dānišpažūh]. The latter is modelled on the certainty which 'is prior according to time and nature', namely our knowledge about the 'first intelligibles, which are the principles of the theoretical sciences' (*Šarāʾiṭ* [*70: 101,13–17 Fakhry; 354,1–5 Dānišpažūh]).

It is likely that al-Fārābī was the first to use the terms *taṣawwur* and *taṣdīq* in this sense and, moreover, as a contrasted pair. No similar use can be found either in earlier authors or in the Arabic translation of the *Posterior Analytics*, which was produced by his teacher Abū Bišr Mattā. In essence, however, his deliberations are not new, but take up some ideas which are already found in Aristotle. As the latter explains at the very beginning of the *Posterior Analytics*, the antecedent knowledge necessary for a demonstration needs to be gained in two ways: of some things one must already believe 'that' they are (ὅτι ἔστι); of others one must grasp 'what' the thing said is (τί. . .ἐστι); in yet other cases, both things apply (*Anal. Post.* I 1, 71a11–13). Later Aristotle specifies that by this kind of antecedent knowledge, we are supposed to understand axioms and hypotheses ('that') as well as definitions ('what') (*Anal. Post.* I 1, 72a14–24; on all this see van Ess 1966 [*157: 103–113], Lameer 1994 [*175: 266–268. 275]).

For a demonstration to be valid, both basic elements must be present in perfect form. This prompts al-Fārābī to look more closely into definition (as perfect *taṣawwur*) and certainty (as perfect *taṣdīq*). The first topic is discussed within the framework of his epitome of the *Posterior Analytics*; here he analyses the various possibilities of obtaining and verifying definitions (*Burhān* [*69: 45–57 Fakhry; 292–306 Dānišpažūh]), also mentioning Platonic diaeresis (*qisma*) and classification (*tarkīb*) in the process [*69: 53,13–57,13 Fakhry; 302,11–306,21 Dānišpažūh]. They play an important role in al-Fārābī's methodical deliberations (Gutas 1999 [*42: 220]), even if he does not recognize them as fully valid methods for obtaining a definition (Abed 1991 [*171: 95–100]).

The question of certainty forms the central topic of the second study mentioned above (*Šarāʾiṭ al-yaqīn*). Here al-Fārābī first explains that in order to obtain absolute certainty (*al-yaqīn ʿalā l-iṭlāq*), six conditions need to be fulfilled: (a) the presence of a conviction (*iʿtiqād*) concerning a particular thing; (b) the agreement between conviction and fact; (c) knowledge about this agreement; (e) the perpetual duration of this agreement; (f) all this must follow from the essence and not from the accidents of the thing concerned (*Šarāʾiṭ* [*70: 98,1–4 Fakhry; 350,3–7 Dānišpažūh]). In explaining these conditions, al-Fārābī develops further differentiations. They include the distinction between absolute certainties which can only occur with respect to inalterable, necessary facts (and consequently can only be obtained in science); temporarily limited certainties which apply to contingent things (these are important in rhetoric as well as in practical disciplines); and mere opinions, which are wrongly assumed to be certainties (*Šarāʾiṭ* [*70: 102,2–103,10. 104,6–20 Fakhry; 354,13–355,20. 356,15–357,7 Dānišpažūh]). The most interesting point here is perhaps his explanation concerning the third (c) of the abovementioned conditions (knowledge about the agreement). Al-Fārābī brings a new aspect to bear on the matter, which is not found in the traditional Aristotelian deliberations on this topic. According to him, our certainty does not only depend on our complete knowledge of the facts of the matter, but also on our being aware of having this knowledge (*Šarāʾiṭ* [*70: 98,20–99,23 Fakhry; 351,3–352,8 Dānišpažūh]; cf. *Burhān* [*69: 20,11–14 Fakhry; 267,1–4 Dānišpažūh). Therefore a perfectly certain judgement can only be accomplished if the cognitive act is supplemented by a moment of self-reflection (for all this, see Black 2006 [*184]).

(4) As should by now be clear, al-Fārābī used the *Organon* for various concerns and purposes. On the one hand it enabled him methodically to safeguard philosophy's claim to being an apodeictic science. On the other hand he used it as foundation for his observations about non-philosophical disciplines. They promote the idea that there are several forms of rationality, which are hierarchically ordered and can be captured completely using the description of the different types of syllogisms. This latter claim, however, was a precarious one, for there clearly were disciplines which used different forms of argumentation. This applies to theology, which traditionally employed the 'inference from the visible/observable to the invisible/hidden' (*al-istidlāl bi-l-šāhid ʿalā l-ġāʾib*), as well as to jurisprudence, where the 'inference from analogy' (*qiyās fiqhī*) had become common practice. Both forms of argumentation presented a challenge for the all-embracing claim of syllogistics, and in response al-Fārābī had to demonstrate that both forms of inference could be traced back to a syllogistic structure, and that they nevertheless could not lay claim to demonstrative power, since theologians and legal scholars often applied them under the wrong conditions (e.g. using misconstrued premises).

This question is discussed in the brief text mentioned above, entitled *Kitāb al-Qiyās al-ṣaġīr* (*Short Book on the Syllogism*) or *al-Muḫtaṣar al-ṣaġīr fī kayfiyyat al-qiyās* (*Short Summary on the Form of the Syllogism*) or *al-Muḫtaṣar al-ṣaġīr fī l-manṭiq ʿalā ṭarīqat al-mutakallimīn* (*Short Summary of Logic as Practiced by the Theologians* [*67]). For the most part it seems to be a general introduction to syllogistics, but it ends with an appendix which is explicitly dedicated to the two abovementioned forms of argument. In this appendix al-Fārābī first turns to the *istidlāl bi-l-šāhid ʿalā l-ġāʾib* used by the theologians, which he examines as to its form, and compares with other types of inferences. Al-Fārābī concludes that it has no independent structure of its own, but in essence corresponds to the argument which Aristotle has called 'paradigm' (*Kitāb al-Qiyās al-ṣaġīr* [*67: 175–183 Dānišpažūh; missing in al-ʿAǧam]; see also Lameer 1994 [*175: 204–232; cf. 185–193]). Then follows the analysis of the legal *qiyās*. It needs to be carried out in several steps, because the jurists use 'inference by analogy' in various ways. Nevertheless al-Fārābī finally arrives at a comparable result: *qiyās*, as used in the Islamic context, again shares structural similarities with the 'Aristotelian' syllogisms, in this case as they are applied in rhetoric [*67: 184–194 Dānišpažūh; missing in al-ʿAǧam] (see also Lameer 1994 [*175: 233–258]).

These brief remarks had major consequences, as they initiated a lively discussion about the relation between the methods of theology (or jurisprudence) and those of Aristotelian logic. It later led to most Muslim scholars adopting the *Organon* in their disciplines, because the two methods of argumentation appeared compatible to them. Al-Fārābī did not go this far. He merely pointed to a certain similarity between the two methods. According to his view, the arguments of the theologians and jurists might well be convertible into syllogistic structures; but this happened at a level which did not reach the status of demonstration, and would always remain bound to the techniques of rhetoric.

One reason for this is the fact that the theologians often lack adequate understanding of the premises on which an inference is built. This becomes apparent in the context of a problem which al-Fārābī mentions in *Kitāb al-Qiyās al-ṣaġīr* as well as in further writings on the *Prior Analytics* and *On Interpretation*: the question how propositions should be understood which are not unequivocally (or only apparently unequivocally) quantified and modalized. This question arises, for instance, when reading the Quran, e.g. where it says, in Sura 82/14, that 'the libertines shall be in a fiery furnace' (transl. Arberry), where neither 'the' is quantified specifically, nor 'shall be' is further modalized. Al-Fārābī discusses this problem in a general way (i.e. without directly referring to the Quran) and confines himself to analysing the logical meaning of the linguistic expressions used in such propositions (articles, indefinite pronouns, general concepts, oppositions, etc.). However, there are good reasons to assume that he is here taking a stand in a current theological debate. For what he writes can be interpreted not just as a logical study, but also as an enumeration of objections against central positions of the Muʿtazila – which at the same time would mean that he was implicitly taking the side of the (Murǧiʾite-Ḥanafite) opposition (Schöck 2006 [*186: 285–372]; on al-Fārābī's analysis of indefinite nouns in general cf. Thom 2008 [*191]).

A further problem facing the theologians is their lack of a reliable criterion of truth. They are in this position because they fail to adopt the Aristotelian doctrine of demonstration, including the 'conditions of certainty' connected to it, which were of such importance for al-Fārābī (cf. pp. 606–607 above). Lacking an infallible standard, al-Fārābī says, they try to apply doubtful criteria in their quest for truth. One of those is, for instance, the so-called 'rest of the soul' (*sukūn al-nafs*), which indeed played a major role in the epistemology of several prominent Muʿtazilites, from al-Naẓẓām (d. before 232/847) to Abū Hāšim al-Ǧubbāʾī (d. 321/933). Al-Fārābī criticizes it severely in various places, which also indicates that he regarded the Muʿtazila with a particularly sceptical eye (*Ǧadal* [*71: 71,11–72,7 al-ʿAǧam; 417,13–418,10 Dānišpažūh], *Burhān* [*69: 20,7–21,12 Fakhry; 266,18–268,7 Dānišpažūh]; see also Vajda 1967 [*158: 388–389. 391–393], Rudolph 2007 [*283: 72–75]).

This criticism, on the other hand, also points to a certain interest. Al-Fārābī did not ignore the teachings of the theologians of his day, but responded to their ideas – as soon as they touched upon his own theories. Nor was he always dismissive in doing so. At times one gets the impression that he was stimulated by their ideas, and that he picked up on certain points raised in *kalām*, and incorporated them into his own account. A case in point is his original explications on the topic of future contingents (*Šarḥ fī l-ʿIbāra* [*65: 97,27–100,25 Kutsch, Marrow; 103,9–107,2 Dānišpažūh]; cf. Hasnawi 1985 [*165: 28–29]; on the topic in general see Adamson 2006 [*183]).

4.3 *Mathematics and Physics*

Unlike al-Fārābī's logical texts, his works on mathematics have not received much attention in the secondary literature on his philosophy. This has to do with the fact that they constitute a discrete body of work which was transmitted separately and in terms of content does not easily join up with the other areas of his work. Nevertheless this neglect of mathematics in studies on al-Fārābī is problematic: it means that we tend to look at al-Fārābī's œuvre and his conception of philosophy from a one-sided perspective, rather than perceiving it in a balanced manner. As significant contributions to theoretical philosophy are suppressed, other areas, like logic or politics, automatically move into the foreground, so that his interest in them is often given disproportionate weight.

In fact, al-Fārābī was intensely engaged with theoretical philosophy, including mathematics, as is already indicated by the elaborate introduction to this field which he provides in his catalogue of the sciences (*Iḥṣāʾ* [*45: 93–110]; cf. Schramm 1986 [*135: 22–40]). Details, however, only come to light once one considers the relevant works. Here, three topics constitute the focus of interest: (1) geometry, represented by a commentary on parts of Euclid's *Elements* [*85], possibly also by *al-Ḥiyal al-rūḥaniyya wa-l-asrār al-ṭabīʿiyya fī daqāʾiq al-aškāl al-handasiyya* (*The Spiritual Devices and the Natural Secrets Concerning the*

Subtleties of the Geometrical Figures), whose attribution to al-Fārābī is, however, uncertain; (2) astronomy, represented by a commentary on Ptolemy's *Almagest* [*86] and two critical reports on astrology ([*88], [*90]); (3) last but not least, music, a topic on which we have the *Great Book on Music* [*91] and two specialized studies on rhythm [*92, *93].

In geometry, al-Fārābī is mainly concerned with reconciling Euclid's approach with Aristotle's epistemology. He deems this necessary because the two thinkers had chosen quite different paths in order to obtain the basic geometrical concepts. Aristotle had opted for the analytical method, which meant that he took the perceptible, three-dimensional body as his starting point and established its constitutive elements (plane, line, point) by means of several processes of abstraction. Euclid did the reverse. He first defined the point, it being what was most congenial to the intellect, in order then to obtain the other concepts by way of synthesis. The two approaches seem to exclude each other, but one can also see them as complementary, as al-Fārābī explains. For in his view they signify two phases of geometrical thinking: the grasping of concepts, which are obtained by means of analysing perceptible bodies; and their application within geometrical science, which is based on distinctive objects that are completely abstracted from matter, and on their synthesis (*Šarḥ al-mustaġlaq* [*85: no. 32–41]). Beyond that al-Fārābī studies the definitions that are used within Euclidean geometry. Formally, they do not correspond to the rules which Aristotle has established for defining things. Nevertheless Euclid's definitions are admissible, as they can be interpreted in an Aristotelian way. Thus, 'extension' or 'length', which is supposed to be a property of all geometrical objects (with the exception of the point), can be understood as a generic concept, with line, plane and body being assigned to it as species (*Šarḥ al-mustaġlaq* [*85: no. 63–78]; on all this see Freudenthal 1988 [*209: 124–132. 137–143], 1990 [*210]).

In the field of astronomy, al-Fārābī's ideas are only partly accessible to us. This is due to the fact that his extensive commentary on the *Almagest* has neither been edited nor studied so far – although the extant text seems to be by him (for question of authenticity cf. pp. 566–567 above). What al-Fārābī understood astronomy to be must therefore, according to the present state of research, be deduced from other writings. Here, *Kitāb al-Musīqī al-kabīr* (*The Great Book on Music*) and *Kitāb al-Burhān* (i.e. the epitome of the *Posterior Analytics*) are particularly significant. As Janos (2010 [*216: 243–265]) has shown, these texts contain illuminating passages on the subject matter, method and theory of astronomy, which indicate that al-Fārābī's approach is much more indebted to the Aristotelian tradition and certain authors like Geminus and Ptolemy than to the Neoplatonic concept of astronomy. Of importance are furthermore two small treatises on the question which conclusions or judgements (*aḥkām*) one may infer from the observation of the stars. They make clear that in contrast to many other thinkers of his day, al-Fārābī was a decided opponent of astrology, or at least of astrological prognosis. His line of argument is also interesting: he does not confine himself to voicing his criticism, but takes the opportunity to explore more fundamental questions, concluding that our ability to pass judgements on a certain situation, be it concerning the stars or any other area, always depends on the causal context, i.e. on our ability to give a causal explanation. Some things are necessary and unchangeable; therefore they are the subject of necessary judgements and definite knowledge (e.g. the size of stars, which can be determined astronomically). Others, in al-Fārābī's words, are 'possible for the most part' (*mumkin ʿalā l-akṯar*); they belong to the realm of the probable, which is the domain of empirical knowledge (e.g. the earth being warmed by sunrays, which occurs as a rule, but may be suspended due to an obstacle; on this topic see Druart 1981 [*272: 39]). Yet others are also possible, but in a different sense. These are processes which occur simultaneously with others, without there being a discernible causal nexus between them. They include the accidental coincidences between occurrences in the heavens and events in our lives, which are used by the astrologers as pretext for their prognoses (*Maqāla fīmā yaṣiḥḥu wa-mā lā yaṣiḥḥu min aḥkām al-nuǧūm* [*88: no. 5. 7–10. 13 Āl Yāsīn]; cf. Druart 1978 [*206], 1979 [*207]; for the context see also Janos 2010 [*216: 240–243]).

In the area of music, al-Fārābī made several seminal contributions, the most important one being the already mentioned *Kitāb al-Musīqī al-kabīr* (*The Great Book on Music*), where he links the fundamental principles of Greek musical theory to the musical practice of Arabic-Islamic society (instruments, keys, rhythmics). Many topics that are discussed there are relevant within the immediate subject area only; but as we have just seen, some explanations are of interest also for other areas, and for philosophy in general. This in particular applies to the prologue, in which al-Fārābī establishes substantive relations to geometry, astronomy, physics, poetics, and rhetoric, but also to the epilogue, where he explains the significance of music for the ethical disposition of human beings (Endress 1992 [*38: 111. 113–114]).

In the second area of theoretical philosophy, i.e. physics, the situation is less auspicious, as we are missing several important sources: the lemmatized commentaries al-Fārābī composed on Aristotle's most important works of natural philosophy (cf. p. 586 above). Though they are mentioned by several later authors (for details see Lettinck 1994 [*251: 782]), the information concerning them is brief and of little value. This is all the more regrettable as the works themselves are apparently lost. In order to reconstruct al-Fārābī's physics, we must therefore rely on a number of shorter and substantively incomplete accounts. They are found in two textual genres in particular: in various extant treatises on individual topics (the void [*101]; chemistry [*102]) and on polemical issues (against John Philoponus [*100]; against Galen [*103]); and in al-Fārābī's main work, *Mabādiʾ ārāʾ ahl al-madīna al-fāḍila* (*The Principles of the Opinions of the Inhabitants of the Excellent City* [*125]), which provides a brief survey of natural philosophy. In addition we possess some testimonies concerning the lost work *Fī l-Mawǧūdāt al-mutaġayyira* (*On Changeable Things*) (cf. p. 586 above). It was apparently meant to defend the thesis of the eternity of the world against the objections of John Philoponus and al-Kindī (Rashed 2008 [*254]).

These testimonies show that al-Fārābī in principle followed Aristotelian doctrine. This diagnosis extends to all areas for which his views are documented. In detail, the following topics are concerned: the idea of the existence of 'prime matter' (*Mabādiʾ* [*125: III.8.1]); the doctrine of the elements, which is briefly alluded to in one place [*125: III.8.2], and is discussed more elaborately in another (*al-Radd ʿalā Yaḥyā al-Naḥwī* [*100: no. 4. 16–18]; cf. Mahdi 1967 [*243]), though in the second case, al-Fārābī again utilizes it as an argument to defend the thesis of the eternity of the world against the attacks by John Philoponus; the doctrine that all bodies consist of matter and form (*Mabādiʾ* [*125: III.5], *al-Radd ʿalā Yaḥyā* [*100: no. 2]) and possess potentiality as well as actuality (*Mabādiʾ* [*125: III.4.2]); the characterization of the sublunar realm as a world of generation and corruption [*125: III.9]; the claim that there are 'chemical' processes of transformation taking place in this world, which we can describe scientifically (*Risāla fī Wuǧūb ṣināʿat al-kīmiyāʾ* [*102]); and finally, the rejection of the existence of void (*Maqāla fī l-Ḫalāʾ* [*101]). The latter is not just a continuation of the Aristotelian thesis, but is to be located within the context of a contemporary debate on physical models (like atomism or the doctrine of the existence of primordial 'natures' [*ṭabāʾiʿ*]), in which both philosophers and Islamic theologians took part (Daiber 1983 [*248]).

If we add al-Fārābī's pronouncements on biology, a similar picture emerges. Here, too, he in principle follows Aristotle's ideas; examples include his doctrine of reproduction (*Mabādiʾ* [*125: IV.12]), and his claim that the heart, rather than the brain is the leading organ of our body [*125: IV.11.1–5]. In order to add authority to this view, he explicitly defends it against the objections raised by Galen (*Risāla fī l-Radd ʿalā Ǧālīnūs* [*103]; cf. Bürgel 1967 [*242: 286–289], Zimmermann 1976 [*246]). In the course of this, al-Fārābī also discusses the more fundamental question whether medicine is a science at all (see generally Richter-Bernburg 2008 [*255: 120–124]). He shows some reticence here, since in his opinion, there are only three parts of medicine which can lay claim to striving for universal knowledge (to wit, the study of the parts of the human body, the study of the types of health, and the study of the types of diseases); four other parts, by contrast, seek knowledge which merely concerns particulars (diagnosis, nutrition and drugs, measures for preserving health, and measures for restoring health) (*Risāla fī l-Radd ʿalā Ǧalīnūs* [**103*: 41,9–42,11. 53,21–54,9]). Therefore it is wrong to apply the term 'science' to medicine as a whole. It is rather a 'practical art' (*ṣināʿa fāʿila*), whose task it is to exert influence on its objects for certain purposes [**103*: 40,16–41,9].

The ideas which al-Fārābī developed on the soul, finally, are likewise indebted to the Aristotelian heritage. This already emerges from the way in which he opens the topic, introducing the various psychological faculties (nutritive faculty [*al-quwwa al-ġāḏiya*], sensitive faculty [*al-quwwa al-ḥāssa*], imaginative faculty [*al-quwwa al-mutaḫayyila*], rational faculty [*al-quwwa al-nāṭiqa*], appetitive faculty [*al-quwwa al-nuzūʿiyya*]; on all this, see *Mabādiʾ* [**125*: IV.10.1–6]; cf. *Siyāsa* [**126*: 32,14–15], *Fuṣūl muntazaʿa* [**116*: no. 7]). In comparison with Aristotle, the imaginative faculty clearly increases in significance; it is given not only mimetic, but also creative capabilities. This will later help al-Fārābī to develop his theory of prophecy (Walzer 1957 [*241]). The most important point, however, is that we are able to think, the rational faculty being the one that characterizes human beings as such. It therefore occupies a central role within al-Fārābī's philosophy, being not only addressed in several texts with broad thematic content (*Mabādiʾ* [**125*: IV.13], *Fuṣūl muntazaʿa* [**116*: no. 33–46]), but also discussed in a treatise dedicated to it specifically.

This is the brief, but famous work *Risāla fī l-ʿAql* (*Epistle on the Intellect*) [**105*]; cf. now the detailed discussion in Vallat 2012 [*256]). Here al-Fārābī combines the task of interpreting Aristotle (cf. Streetman 2014 [*257]) with his own semantic interests. The text is designed as a reply to a question concerning the different ways the Arabic word *ʿaql* is used. One after the other, six different possibilities are introduced:

(1) The meaning which the masses (*al-ǧumhūr*) assign to the word *ʿaql* when they call somebody 'intelligent' (*ʿāqil*). They primarily mean that this person possesses the 'intelligence' (*taʿaqqul*) to decide correctly when it comes to choosing an action. This, however, implies a moral judgement. For ultimately the masses are only prepared to call those people 'intelligent' whose actions are not directed towards their own advantage (this would rather be 'cunning'), but towards virtue (*Fī l-ʿAql* [**105*: no. 2–6]; cf. *Fuṣūl muntazaʿa* [**116*: no. 85]).

(2) The meaning assigned to the word by the theologians when they claim that *ʿaql* (here: 'reason') prescribes the good and forbids the bad. This claim is explicitly criticized by al-Fārābī. For according to his view, the

theologians base their (allegedly rational) value judgements not on established premises, but merely on opinions which at first sight are accepted by the general public (*Fī l-ʿAql* [*105: no. 7]; cf. *Fuṣūl muntazaʿa* [*116: no. 85, end]; cf. Rudolph 2007 [*283: 69–72]).

(3) The meaning which the word *ʿaql* (here: 'intellect') is given in the *Posterior Analytics*. According to al-Fārābī, Aristotle understands by this a certain faculty innate to each of us, through which we know the 'universal, true and necessary premises' (*Fī l-ʿAql* [*105: no. 8]; cf. *Fuṣūl muntazaʿa* [*116: no. 34]).

(4) The meaning which *ʿaql* has in the sixth book of the [*Nicomachean*] *Ethics*. What is meant is 'prudence' (*taʿaqqul*), by means of which we gain insight into the principles of the practical sciences. It is not an inborn ability, but will increase during our entire life through our actions and the experiences we gain by acting (*Fī l-ʿAql* [*105: no. 9–12], *Fuṣūl muntazaʿa* [*116: no. 38]).

(5) The meaning of *ʿaql* (here again: 'intellect') in Aristotle's *On the Soul*. This point al-Fārābī discusses more elaborately than all other questions, again claiming to do nothing but repeat the genuine view of Aristotle. In fact, however, he presents a doctrine that goes far beyond Aristotle's statements in *On the Soul* and draws on Alexander of Aphrodisias' *On Intellect* (Geoffroy 2002 [*253]), as well as al-Kindī's ideas (cf. pp. 197–198 above). For al-Fārābī wants to distinguish the following stages: (a) Potential intellect (*al-ʿaql bi-l-quwwa*), i.e. the human capacity to think. It is described as that part (or capacity) of the soul whose essence (*ḏāt*) is disposed to abstract the forms of material things. (b) Actual intellect (*al-ʿaql bi-l-fiʿl*). It is characterized by the fact that it has been able to abstract the forms that beforehand were potential objects of thought only, and has turned them into actual objects of its thought (*maʿqūlāt bi-l-fiʿl*). (c) Acquired intellect (*al-ʿaql al-mustafād*), the highest stage of knowledge for human beings. It surpasses the actual intellect insofar as it knows the forms not only as they are joined to matter, but also as those pure, already abstracted objects of thought as which they are present in the actual intellect. This knowledge enables the acquired intellect to recognize even those separate, spiritual entities which are always pure forms and have no connection to matter at all (e.g. the celestial intellects). (d) The Active Intellect (*al-ʿaql al-faʿʿāl*), which al-Fārābī interprets as one of those separate spiritual entities. It is assigned a series of key functions: it knows all forms, together and, unlike us, beginning with the most perfect one; it gives us these forms – and in contrast to what he says in other texts (*Mabādiʾ*, *Siyāsa*), al-Fārābī here seems to claim that the Active Intellect does not only give them to the human intellects, but also to matter (on this

problem, see Druart 1981 [*272: 35], 1987 [*277: 32]); it guides human beings towards recognizing the forms by the method just described, and thus enables us to realize our real, spiritual self (*taǧawhara*). Nevertheless the Active Intellect cannot be the highest spiritual being, because it is dependent on the activity of other beings. In addition, it is in immediate contact with the world of generation and corruption, that is, with an imperfect area of being, which forces it to assume changing relations with the changeable things (*Fī l-ʿAql* [*105: no. 13–49]; cf. *Mabādiʾ* [*125: IV.13], deviating in a few details; see Jolivet 1977 [*247], 1997 [*252: 579–581]; cf. Davidson 1992 [*250: 48–53. 66–68]).

(6) The meaning of *ʿaql* ('intellect') in Aristotle's *Metaphysics*. Here, finally, the celestial intellects are at issue. They constitute a hierarchy, with the First Intellect at the top. Its effect, the cosmic system, however, is merely hinted at by al-Fārābī in this context, rather than being described in detail (*Fī l-ʿAql* [*105: no. 50–55]; cf. Druart 1987 [*277: 32–33]; Davidson 1992 [*250: 65]).

4.4 *Metaphysics*

It is probably for a good reason that the celestial intellects are mentioned only briefly in *Fī l-ʿAql*: with the Active Intellect, a boundary is reached which marks the end of physical investigation. For physics is concerned exclusively with nature, that is, with things that can be subsumed under the categories (*Falsafat Arisṭūṭālīs* [*129: 77,22–73,1. 130,11–12]). The Active Intellect and all entities above it, however, transcend the Aristotelian categories [*129: 130,12–14]. They are more perfect than the natural things, which is why they are the subject of metaphysics (*Ḥurūf* [*46: 69,17–18]), which precedes physics in rank – despite coming after it in the curriculum (*Taḥṣīl* [*127: 136,10–137,3]) – and cultivates an approach which is more general (*aʿamm*) than physical theory (*Falsafat Arisṭūṭālīs* [*129: 130,15–16]).

However, al-Fārābī nowhere describes systematically how metaphysical investigations ought to be conducted. In order to trace his views in this area one needs to take a number of works into consideration which approach the topic in different ways. Apart from several smaller treatises dedicated to specific topics, they also include two comprehensive texts, in which al-Fārābī outlines his view in general. These are *Mabādiʾ ārāʾ ahl al-madīna al-fāḍila* (*The Principles of the Opinions of the Inhabitants of the Excellent City*) and *al-Siyāsa al-madaniyya* (*Ruling the Community*), which are counted among his most famous works.

In both texts the 'principles of the existing things' (thus the subtitle of *al-Siyāsa al-madaniyya*) are delineated in detail. Both presentations begin with the highest principle, which al-Fārābī calls the 'First Cause' (*al-sabab* *al-awwal*). It has several attributes: it is perfect, eternal and unchangeable, without equal and without opposite, indivisible, actual intellect, omniscient and wise (*Mabādiʾ* [**125*: I.1.1–9]; cf. *Siyāsa* [**126*: 42,14–46,3]). It is most deserving of being called 'one', 'being' and 'true', and is also named 'God' by us (*Iḥṣāʾ* [**45*: 122,6–9], *Fī l-ʿAql* [**105*: 36,2–3], *Siyāsa* [**126*: 31,12]). We know moreover that it is the origin of a harmonious order of being; this is why we may describe it as 'just' and 'benevolent'. In doing so, however, we must be aware that in the case of the Highest Principle, such names do not signify multiplicity or various forms of perfection, but are already implied in its absolute perfection (*Mabādiʾ* [**125*: I.2.1–5]; on all this see Walzer 1985 [*276: 333–362]).

The activity of the First Cause consists in thinking itself from eternity (*Siyāsa* [**126*: 34,13]). In this, al-Fārābī follows a famous thesis which was already put forward by Aristotle. He, however, interprets it differently; in contrast to the Stagirite he thinks that the divine reflection has creative power, even though it consists of self-thinking. For from it there emerges, by way of emanation (*ʿalā ǧihati fayḍin*; *Mabādiʾ* [**125*: I.2.1]), a second being, which, due to its origin, is again a pure intellect. This intellect also thinks, but its activity is directed towards two objects. It intelligizes not only itself (leading to its substantialization [*taǧawhur*]), but also the cause from which it has sprung. The latter results in the emanation of a further intellect, while the former entails the generation of something corporeal, a heaven, which al-Fārābī identifies with the diurnal sphere. This process repeats itself, until a series of ten intellects and nine spheres has been brought about. They are ordered so as to form a cosmic system which comprises all the celestial bodies that were presupposed in al-Fārābī's time (the diurnal sphere, and the spheres of the fixed stars, Saturn, Jupiter, Mars, the Sun, Venus, Mercury, and the Moon), assigning each of them to an intellect (*Mabādiʾ* [**125*: II.3]). All celestial spheres move, partly along shared, partly in divergent courses. This leads to the birth of our sublunar world, as the common movements generate matter ('prime matter'), while the divergent ones result in various forms arising in that matter (*Siyāsa* [**126*: 55,13–56,12]). Even after its generation the sublunar world remains under the influence of the celestial spheres. This is due to the heat exuded by the spheres, which has a complex variety of effects on our world (Druart 1981 [*272]). These effects, however, only affect it at the level of bodies. For our intellects are connected with a higher entity: the Active Intellect, which guides our thinking, and which itself takes the place of the tenth and last celestial intellect within the cosmic system (Davidson 1992 [* 250: 46–47]).

Many aspects of al-Fārābī's account are reminiscent of older metaphysical (or cosmological) systems. The most important parallels have been mentioned repeatedly in modern scholarship: they include Aristotle's metaphysics, Ptolemy's astronomical model, and the Neoplatonic doctrine of emanation (thus most recently Reisman 2005 [*50: 56]). The latter was known to al-Fārābī not only through the Arabic Plotinus, but also through the Arabic Proclus, as has now been shown (Janos 2010 [*217]). Apart from that there are good reasons to believe that some of his ideas go back to Alexander of Aphrodisias, or rather to the treatise *Fī Mabādiʾ al-kull* (*On the Principles of the Universe*) which is attributed to Alexander and extant in Arabic (Maróth 1995 [*278: 105–108], Genequand 1997 [*279: 275–276], 2001 [*280: 21–22]). Nevertheless the outlined scheme seems to be an original achievement of al-Fārābī: as far as we know, the heterogeneous elements of this theory were never combined by an earlier author in similar form and with a similar degree of systematization. In addition, al-Fārābī does not describe the cosmological model with complete consistency across the two texts in which it is presented. It seems, therefore, that he was still struggling with his ideas, for instance concerning the question how the process of emanation is structured in detail. The *Mabādiʾ* tell us that each intellect gives rise to (1) a further intellect and (2) a heaven(ly body) (*Mabādiʾ* [*125: II.3]). This suggests that al-Fārābī – unlike Ibn Sīnā and other later authors – presupposed a dyadic model (thus Black 1996 [*40: 189. 194]). In *Siyāsa*, however, we find not only (1) cosmic intellects and (2) celestial bodies, but also (3) celestial souls, which are described as rational, always in actuality, and the cause of the motions of the spheres (*Siyāsa* [*126: 33,18–34,10; cf. 53,7–10]). From this we can infer that al-Fārābī already had a triadic model (thus Druart 1999 [*42: 218], Reisman 2005 [*50: 57. 60]).

More serious than such differences, however, is the question how the cosmological scheme as a whole should be integrated within al-Fārābī's philosophy (on the entire topic see Janos 2012 [*219]). For even if the model was quite popular, or was to become so later on, its relation to the other parts of al-Fārābī's philosophy is not really clear. On the one hand it is remarkable that the doctrine of the emanation of the ten celestial intellects is only described in the *Mabādiʾ* and in the *Siyāsa*, and hence is only found in two works which present their subject matter in form of a survey, without arguing for it in detail. On the other hand al-Fārābī composed further texts on metaphysics, in which he chooses a different approach to the questions that are dealt with in this area, so that the sum-total of his various works do not provide a systematic account of his metaphysics.

(1) The most famous amongst these treatises is entitled *Fī Aġrāḍ al-Ḥakīm fī kull maqāla min al-Kitāb al-mawsūm bi-l-Ḥurūf* (*On the Aims of the 'Philosopher' in Each Treatise of the Book Marked by Letters* [i.e. the *Metaphysics*]). It has been the subject of scholarly attention for some time now, which is reflected in the publication of several (partial) translations and analytical studies (Druart 1982 [*274], Ramón Guerrero 1982 [*275], Gutas 1988 [*84: 238–242]), and in an attempt to trace the work back to a late antique source (Bertolacci 2005

[*281: 293–300]). The purpose of the treatise is to reveal the aim or aims which Aristotle pursued in composing the *Metaphysics*. Such a clarification appears necessary to al-Fārābī: as he states at the beginning, the *Metaphysics* are particularly often misunderstood. Many readers expect it to contain theological discussions of the Creator, the intellect, the soul and other related topics, and hence are confused when they find, upon reading the text, that it does not address anything like that, with the exception of book XII (*Aġrāḍ* [*110: 34,6–13]; on the identification of those readers with the school of al-Kindī cf. Gutas 1988 [*84: 243–249]). In order to confront this misunderstanding, al-Fārābī refers to a fundamental distinction which sets the various individual sciences, which each are concerned with a partial area of being (e.g. physics, geometry, arithmetic, medicine), apart from the one universally valid science (i.e. metaphysics). The latter investigates (1) what applies to all beings, and (2) the common origin of all things (*Aġrāḍ* [*110: 34,21–35,12]). From this point of view it is correct to class philosophical theology (*al-ʿilm al-ilāhī*), which asks about the origin of all things, with metaphysics [*110: 35,16–19]. It does not, however, constitute its totality, and, most notably, it is not the starting point of metaphysical investigation. For metaphysics is primarily ontology. Its primary subject matter (*al-mawḍūʿ al-awwal*) is absolute being (*al-wuǧūd al-muṭlaq*) and the One (*al-wāḥid*), which equals being in terms of universality [*110: 36,9–10].

(2) This provides a link to the second work of interest in this context. It carries the title *al-Wāḥid wa-l-waḥda* (*The One and Oneness*) and examines in detail in which different ways 'One' and 'Many' can be said, closely following *Met.* V. 6 and *Met.* X 1. Therefore we can say that al-Fārābī takes up an important concern of Aristotle's *Metaphysics* (Mushtak 1960 [*270], Druart 1999 [*42: 217]). However, in doing so he confines himself exactly to the specific problem at issue. The text contains no indication of how the ontological (and logical) investigations undertaken here are supposed to relate to the above-mentioned theological problems. This is rather surprising insofar as a treatise on the 'One' and the 'Many' would indeed have allowed for a closer look at the origin of being, and in particular at the doctrine of emanation.

(3) The situation is similar in the case of the third work, the book *al-Ḥurūf*, which we have encountered already in various contexts. Despite not being a metaphysical treatise as such, it nevertheless examines questions relevant to metaphysics. This applies first and foremost to the (Aristotelian) categories, which are addressed here in their logical as well as in their ontological dimension (Druart 1999 [*42: 217–218]). This leads to many illuminating reflections which, however, are again restricted to the general doctrine of being and to concepts used within ontology, meaning that they provide no specific indications concerning the principles of being.

It is therefore not possible to locate the idea that ten cosmic intellects and nine celestial spheres have emanated from the First Cause within al-Fārābī's philosophy with the degree of clarity one would wish for. This has led several scholars to reject this doctrine, or the texts in which it is described (i.e. the *Mabādiʾ* and the *Siyāsa*), as expressions of his personal views, even though they hold such a prominent place within al-Fārābī's œuvre. Various reasons have been advanced in support for this sceptical attitude.

(a) The most famous one, which has commanded the greatest influence in the scholarly literature, is based on the assumption that the two works react to a certain political situation, as al-Fārābī (like other thinkers, too) was supposedly subjected to political constraints. At the same time he wanted to influence his own community with texts like the *Mabādiʾ* and the *Siyāsa*; this is why he consciously composed them in a language that was easy to understand, and made far-reaching concessions to the religious sensibilities of the general public (as e.g. the doctrine of emanation), something that was not necessary in other texts addressed to philosophical experts. This hypothesis goes back to Leo Strauss, who phrased it as a distinction between an 'exoteric' and an 'esoteric' presentation of philosophy (e.g. Strauss 1952 [*300: 9. 14–18]; on the Straussian theory and al-Fārābī's role within his thinking cf. Tamer 2001 [*329: 100–123. 207–262. 270–287], Kraemer 2009 [*345: 142. 156. 158–164]). Since then this approach has been repeated many times, for instance by Mahdi ([*23: 3–4. 5–6. 9 of the intro. to the transl.], 2001 [*328: 3–4. 8–11]), who drew a distinction between 'popular' and 'scientific-philosophical' writings. There were also attempts at formulating the thesis in an even more pointed manner; this was aimed at by Parens (1995 [*319: XIII–XIV. 18–21], 2006 [*339: 5–7]), who described al-Fārābī's metaphysics simply as 'rhetoric' and attested him to have been a 'masterly manipulator of Neoplatonism' [*319: 24].

(b) A completely different argument is given by Pines. He was of the opinion that al-Fārābī's epistemology implied that he could not have put forward the emanation of the cosmic intellects as a scientific theory, since it claimed that our cognitive faculty was limited to sensually perceptible things. To grasp purely spiritual entities or even their emergence from God, by contrast, al-Fārābī would have regarded as impossible. The corresponding statements in *Mabādiʾ* or *Siyāsa*, which presuppose a different epistemological stance, could therefore not be part of a philosophically-grounded doctrine (Pines 1981 [*273: 217–219]). This argument did not meet with similar success, but it did have a certain resonance in the scholarly community. One example is Colmo, who bases a whole theory on the epistemological caveat articulated by Pines. Colmo (2005 [*338: 1–3. 120–130. 167]) not only presupposes that al-Fārābī regarded the metaphysical principles as beyond cognition, but also claims to find a generally anti-metaphysical understanding of philosophy in his texts which prefigures modern attitudes. It is supposedly characterized by al-Fārābī having performed the change 'from metaphysics to method' [*338: 1] long before Descartes and Hobbes, thanks to his insight in the epistemic limitations of human beings.

The suspicion that al-Fārābī's statements about God and the cosmic intellects were merely functional in character has found several supporters since the 1950s. Nevertheless it has not remain unchallenged. The majority of scholars still assume that both the doctrine of emanation and the cosmological model do represent al-Fārābī's philosophical convictions, being integral parts of his metaphysics. In order to be able to hold this view, however, one needs to link the two concepts to other statements within his work. In more specific terms: one has to explain how these ideas that are articulated in the *Mabādiʾ* and the *Siyāsa* relate to the metaphysical thoughts developed in other works. In recent years, this question has been the focus of a number of studies. The most elaborate discussion was published by Druart, who suggested explaining the discrepancies between the various texts on the grounds of 'the amount of Aristotelian loyalty al-Fārābī wants to show in different contexts' (1987 [*277: 24]). Al-Fārābī had indeed advanced the doctrine of emanation in his own philosophy, but had been aware of the fact that he was deviating from Aristotle in this point. Therefore it was possible to distinguish three types of work in his metaphysical œuvre: the 'Aristotelian' texts, in which he limited himself to an exegesis of the Stagirite's works (e.g. *Aġrāḍ*); the 'programmatic' texts, in which he developed his own views within the conceptual framework of Aristotelianism (e.g. *Taḥṣīl al-saʿāda*); and, finally, the 'emanationist' texts (e.g. *Mabādiʾ*), which discussed all those theological questions which were only briefly mentioned in Aristotle, or had been suppressed entirely in the first place (Druart 1987 [*277: 24–43]; and following her Black 1996 [*40: 187–189]). This thesis has since been developed further, in this case by Druart herself, who took the topic up again, this time emphasizing much more strongly that certain texts (like *Aġrāḍ* and *Taḥṣīl al-saʿāda*) mainly focus on general metaphysics, while others (as the *Mabādiʾ*) were dedicated to special metaphysics (Druart 1999 [*42: 216–218]). Apart from this there were other suggestions for modifying the thesis, among them a proposal by Reisman. He thought that one may need to differentiate between al-Fārābī's 'curricular' texts, in which he summarized and commented on the philosophical heritage, and those in which he expressed his own synthesis (Reisman 2005 [*50: 69 n. 9]).

Even these explanations which, in principle, assume al-Fārābī's œuvre to be coherent, cannot provide answers to all the questions that arise in the context of his metaphysics. They may claim in their support, however, that their attempt to bridge the gap between 'ontological' and 'theological' deliberations can already be found in the texts themselves. This is already indicated in the passages from *Aġrāḍ* which were briefly touched upon above: they are not confined to highlighting ontology as the true subject matter of Aristotelian metaphysics. In fact, al-Fārābī explains even there that theology also belongs to metaphysics, and that its subject matter comprises God, the intellect, and the soul (*Aġrāḍ* [**110*: 34,8–10. 35,16–19]). This passage can be supplemented by several others. Thus it is said in *Falsafat Arisṭūṭālīs* [**129*: 130,9–10] that one ought to investigate whether the celestial bodies are nature, soul, intellect, or something more perfect. In *al-Ḥurūf* [**46*: 69,18–19; cf. 119,1–7] al-Fārābī states that metaphysics (*ʿilm mā baʿd al-ṭabīʿiyyāt*) analyses the natural things, insofar as they are caused by higher things. In *Taḥṣīl al-saʿāda* [**127*: 140,4–141,8] the metaphysical discussion is interpreted as search for principles and as ascent to the First Principle (*al-mabdaʾ al-awwal*). In *Iḥṣāʾ*, finally, al-Fārābī explains that metaphysics deals with three topics: (1) being in general, (2) the principles of the theoretical sciences, and (3) the incorporeal beings. The latter is subsequently discussed in a particularly elaborate manner. We learn of several details which may be understood as hints at the doctrine of emanation: the incorporeal beings are limited in number and ordered hierarchically (*Iḥṣāʾ* [**45*: 121,5–8]); the pinnacle of the hierarchy is God [**45*: 122,9]; therefore one ought to examine how being (or rather: beings) emanate from him (*istafāḍat* [122,11–12]).

Such expressions suggest that al-Fārābī was striving to establish a systematic connection between his deliberations about ontology and his doctrine of emanation. That he did not accomplish this entirely is indisputable. But this is not an isolated case, given that al-Fārābī endeavoured to connect several approaches systematically in various areas (apart from metaphysics for instance in logic; cf. pp. 599–600 above), without being able to avoid certain inconsistencies completely (for further divergences between al-Fārābī's works cf. Janos 2009 [*56: 15–16]). And there is a further point that also speaks for taking his espousal of the emanationist doctrine seriously: it is expounded in his most prominent works, i.e. in the *Siyāsa* and especially in the *Mabādiʾ*. The latter is not just any part of his œuvre, but the work that al-Fārābī composed more carefully than any other. According to our sources, he revised and redacted the text several times. This may have contributed to the enthusiastic response that the *Mabādiʾ* received, and to its considerable influence on many later philosophers (cf. p. 544 above). First and foremost, this applies to Ibn Sīnā, who accepted fundamental positions advanced in the text as integral parts of al-Fārābī's thought, among them the doctrine of emanation and the cosmological model, and even adopted them in his own philosophy.

Nevertheless it is fair to ask why al-Fārābī would have composed the *Mabādiʾ* in its current form, given that the work displays a highly peculiar and unusual structure, compared with the rest of his œuvre. It begins with explications concerning the First Cause, before successively discussing the generation and the structure of the world (supralunar and sublunar); humankind; the human faculties of cognition and imagination; prophethood; the community; and the fate of human beings in the hereafter. This sequence of topics cannot be explained with reference to the philosophical tradition (Walzer 1985 [*276: 5]). Instead there is good reason to believe that al-Fārābī took up an agenda which originally had been developed in Islamic theology, and which in particular served as a method to present the principles of religion (*uṣūl al-dīn*). This does not turn the *Mabādiʾ* into a theological text (for the relationship between al-Fārābī's ideas and the theology of his time cf. Frank 1977 [*271: 132–135], for his criticism of the theologians cf. Rudolph 2007 [*283], Brague 2009 [*286: 65. 67–71]). On the contrary: it rather appears to be a philosophical reply to certain 4th/10th century works belonging to the genre of *uṣūl al-dīn*. Its purpose probably was to pick up all the topics which were discussed in the systematic accounts of the theologians – but not just on the level of mere opinions (*ārāʾ*), as (in al-Fārābī's view) was the usual practice in theology, but with reference to the principles which can only be known through philosophy (Rudolph 2008 [*285], Wain 2012 [*288]; on parallels and differences between religion and philosophy more generally cf. also Mahdi 1997 [*323: 590–600]). This is exactly what makes the *Mabādiʾ* such a central work. It apparently summarizes what al-Fārābī thought about the major questions discussed in his day. Consequently it seems that one ought not to regard the individual theses which are put forward in this text (including the emanationist doctrine) as marginal, but should rather consider them as authoritative expressions of his thought.

4.5 *Ethics and Politics*

Al-Fārābī's remarks on practical philosophy have received much attention in scholarship, ever since the work of Leo Strauss (cf. p. 619 above). This applies in particular to al-Fārābī's ideas concerning political communities, which many authors consider to be the second major focal point of his philosophy, alongside logic (Rosenthal 1974 [*307: 65], Black 1996 [*40: 190], Mahdi 2001 [*328: 56]). This assessment, however, is not borne out by a correspondingly large number of political works. Apart from some rather brief passages in *Iḥṣāʾ al-ʿulūm* and *al-Ḥurūf*, the corpus of al-Fārābī's texts on this topic is limited to five works, which moreover only partly deal with the topic. The most famous among them are, without doubt, the *Mabādiʾ* and *al-Siyāsa*, which both contain extensive discussions of the community. In addition there are three smaller texts, *Fuṣūl muntazaʿa* ([*Selected*] *Aphorisms*), a collection of separate, partly aphoristic remarks on ethics and politics; *al-Milla* (*Religion*), an account of the nature of religion and the significance it has within a community; and finally, the epitome *Ǧawāmiʿ Kitāb al-Nawāmīs li-Aflāṭūn* ([*Detailed Explication*] *of the Epitome of Plato's Book of Laws*), which sums up (parts of) Plato's *Laws*.

The positions which al-Fārābī puts forward in these texts do not agree with each other in every detail (Rosenthal 1974 [*307: 66. 69–70], Galston 1990 [*313: 3]), leaving us with problems similar to those we have encountered already in logic, cosmology, and metaphysics. This again has left scholars pondering whether al-Fārābī may consciously have used various argumentative strategies, leading to a discussion of whether it was possible to differentiate between 'exoteric' and 'esoteric' writings (cf. p. 619 above), but also to the development of the hypothesis that he tried alternative, contrasting types of argument in different texts. More specifically, there was the assumption that he had cultivated a form of 'dialectical multilevel writing' (Galston 1990 [*313: 10–11. 35–54. 200–221]). However, this interpretative model has not met with general approval, either – probably due to the fact that it is possible to read al-Fārābī's explications without prejudging the issue with such assumptions. What will be decisive when reading al-Fārābī is to weigh the different texts according to their ambitions and their significance. This is something the scholarly community seems always to have done, by focusing especially on the *Mabādiʾ* and on *al-Siyāsa*, thus assigning philosophical priority to them. Both texts have long been considered as authoritative, or at least as the most significant testimonies for al-Fārābī's political ideas. Not only do they very likely belong to his latest works, they also sum up the entire topic in a manner that is both systematically structured, and coherent in content (thus most recently Crone 2004 [*334: 217. 225–228]).

An account of these ideas (on the briefer presentation of the same topic which al-Fārābī offers within his *Kitāb al-Milla*, cf. Mahdi 1997 [*323: 584–590]) needs to be based on the fundamental question how al-Fārābī explained the existence of political communities, or their necessity. It finds its most precise answer in the *Mabādiʾ*, where he states that in order to survive and to reach the most excellent of their perfections (*afḍal kamālātihi*), all human beings by nature (*mafṭūr ʿalā*) need many things which they cannot provide for themselves on their own (*Mabādiʾ* [*125: 228,2–4]). This is why we depend on communities. Only within them we can reach the perfection which is the aim of our natural disposition (*fiṭra ṭabīʿiyya*). However, a distinction has to be made between perfect (or complete, Arab. *kāmil*) and imperfect (or incomplete) forms of communities. Amongst the former, al-Fārābī counts the global community (*maʿmūra*), the nation (*umma*) and, most importantly, the city (*madīna*), which is accorded the largest space in his account. The incomplete forms include the village, the urban district, the street and the house. They are not autonomous, but serve the communities mentioned before [*125: 228,5–230,2].

The (complete) community is of immense importance for the people who belong to it. Not only does it guarantee their physical survival; it also enables them to find the perfection (*kamāl*) and happiness (*saʿāda*) towards which they are directed by nature. This, however, can only happen under particular circumstances. It presupposes communities which, beyond their functional completeness, are furthermore 'excellent' (*fāḍil*), that is, directed towards virtue (*faḍīla*) [230,7–11]. The task of practical philosophy therefore consists in establishing the principles that will serve such communities as points of orientation, and, through this investigation, in defining the institutional framework within which human beings can reach their perfection.

To this effect al-Fārābī compares the excellent city (*al-madīna al-fāḍila*) first with an intact and healthy body (*al-badan al-tāmm al-ṣaḥīḥ*) [230,12–13]. This analogy already allows him to determine a number of characteristics which he considers constitutive of an ideal community. They include: a structure comprising different organs, ordered hierarchically according to their aptitudes and abilities; cooperation between these organs; the existence of a ruling organ (*al-ʿuḍw al-raʾīs*; in the body, this is the heart), which exceeds all others in perfection; and finally the stipulation that this ruling organ permanently rules all other parts of the body, by giving them the aim (*ġaraḍ*) for the sake of which they perform their activities [230,12–232,4. 234,6–14. 236,1–4].

In contrast to the body, however, we cannot speak of natural processes with regard to the community. For people do not act by being forced, but due to disposition (*hayʾa*) and habit (*malaka*), which are determined by their intention and will (*irādiyya*) [232,13–234,5. 234,14–16]. Therefore it makes sense for al-Fārābī to supplement the deliberations about the state with a second comparison, between the city and the cosmos, which can also serve as a model for political structures (*Mabādiʾ* [*125: 236,13–238,10]; cf. *Taḥṣīl al-saʿāda* [*127: 142,7–143,7]). Here, too, we encounter a hierarchical order with several levels. However, the preeminent position held by the ruling entity (within the cosmos, this is the First Cause) in erecting and ruling the entire order becomes even clearer. This is where al-Fārābī sees a decisive analogy with the community; therefore he declares that the relation of the First Cause to the other beings corresponds to that of the ruler of an excellent city to its other parts. Later on he makes this even more explicit: 'The excellent city ought to be arranged in the same way [i.e., as the cosmos, U.R.]): all its parts ought to imitate in their actions the aim of their first ruler according to their rank' (*Mabādiʾ* [*125: 236,13–14. 238,9–10. 239 (transl.); on the possibility of creating further analogies, e.g. to music, see now al-ʿAyyādī 2016 [*349]).

The ruler, or more precisely, the founder and first ruler of a community thus becomes the central figure in al-Fārābī's conception; therefore the qualities and abilities this ruler ought to possess are discussed in particular detail. They include (1) aptitude to rule, both natural (*bi-l-fiṭra wa-l-ṭabʿ*) and based on a voluntarily developed disposition (*bi-l-hayʾa wa-l-malaka al-irādiyya*) [238,11–14]; (2) a perfect intellect which has become actual thought and actual object of thought (*ʿaqlan bi-l-fiʿl wa-maʿqūlan bi-l-fiʿl*) and thus has reached the stage of the acquired intellect (*al-ʿaql al-mustafād*) [240,11. 240,15–242,5]; as well as (3) a perfect faculty of imagination which is also able to connect with the Active Intellect in order to receive particulars and intelligibles from it, albeit in the form of imitations [240,12–15]. The first ruler moreover ought (4) to be a good orator, and to possess a range of other attributes – like health and physical strength, strong powers of comprehension, love of truth, justice, and resolution [246,2–5. 246,8–248,14] – which traditionally were ascribed to good rulers in mirrors for princes and political literature.

The central items on this list are, doubtless, the stipulations concerning intellect and imaginative faculty. They make clear that a political community can only ever be excellent if its founder is in possession of comprehensive knowledge. In order to attain this, his rational faculties must be perfectly actualized, and the Active Intellect must inhere in him (*ḥalla fīhi al-ʿaql al-faʿʿāl* [244,6]). For if this is the case with respect to both parts of his rational faculty, the theoretical as well as the practical, and with respect to his imaginative faculty, then revelation will be bestowed on him (*yūḥā ilayhi*). God will grant him a revelation, using the Active Intellect as a mediator. Through it the divine emanation (*mā yufīḍu*), mediated through the acquired intellect, is passed on to the passive intellect and the imaginative faculty, thus producing a twofold effect. By virtue of the emanation of the Active Intellect onto the passive intellect, the human being concerned becomes a 'a wise man and a philosopher (*ḥakīman faylasūfan* [in theoretical matters]) and an accomplished thinker (*mutaʿaqqilan ʿalā l-tamām* [in practical matters])'; by virtue of the emanation of the Active Intellect onto his imaginative faculty he becomes 'a prophet (*nabiyyan*): who warns of things to come and tells of particular things which exist at present' (*Mabādiʾ* [*125: 244,11–14. 245 (transl.); cf. 224,2–8]; on this issue cf. Gutas 2004 [*336: 271–272]; on the question whether ideas like this can be found already in the (Arabic) Aristotelian corpus, cf. Hansberger 2008 [*341a] and Streetman 2008 [*343]).

The ideal founder of a community must therefore be a philosopher and a prophet. Only this double qualification will enable him not merely to grasp the truth conceptually, but also to express it in images and symbols which are intelligible to all, and accessible for people lacking philosophical education and knowledge. This twofold approach mirrors the general division of labour al-Fārābī envisages to obtain between philosophy and religion. It has been mentioned before in the context of his cultural theory (cf. pp. 597–598 above); but it is here, in the context of his deliberations about the excellent community, that it is explained in detail. The most striking elaboration is once again found in the *Mabādiʾ*. In its often-quoted 17th chapter it is claimed that truths may be known in two ways: either they are impressed on people's souls as they really are, or by analogy (*munāsaba*) and representation (*tamṯīl*), i.e. such that certain similes (*miṯālāt*) will arise in their souls which imitate (*tuḥākī*) those things [*125: 278,8–10]. It remains the privilege of the philosophers to gain knowledge of these things through proofs (*barāhīn*) and their own insights (*baṣāʾir*) (and to pass this knowledge on to their immediate students). All others, however, are dependent on similes, 'because neither nature nor habit has provided their minds with the gift to understand them as they are' [278,13–14. 279 (transl)]. In addition, those similes differ from each other in respect of their form and the extent to which they represent things as they really are. For of those people who have this type of knowledge, '[s]ome [...] know them through symbols which are near to [the things, U.R.], and some through symbols slightly more remote, and some through symbols which are even more remote than these, and some through symbols which are very remote indeed' [278,10–280,1. 279–281 (transl.)]. In practice this means that every nation (*umma*) uses different similes, because their members or founders resort to symbols which are best known (*aʿraf*) within their respective traditions and surroundings. This is how the divergences between the individual religions can be explained: they are due to the fact that each community expresses its convictions through different similes: 'Therefore it is possible that excellent nations and excellent cities exist whose religions (*milal*) differ, although they all have as their goal one and the same felicity (*saʿāda*) and the same aims (*maqāṣid*)' (*Mabādiʾ* [*125: 280,4–6. 281 (transl.)]; on this point cf. Endress 1990 [*35: 20]).

This passage throws the relation between philosophy and religion into sharp relief. Both may lay claim to communicating knowledge to people. But only philosophy recognizes the things 'as they really are'. Religion, by contrast, makes this knowledge accessible to people by virtue of clothing it in symbols, imitations, and similes. In doing so, it always uses those similes which are 'best known' to its respective addressees; this leads to different religious symbolic systems being generated in various cultural contexts, which moreover may be internally inconsistent and provoke dissent (Heck 2008 [*342]). Nevertheless al-Fārābī regards the correspondence between conceptual knowledge and symbolic representation as guaranteed, as they both go back to a common author, the first ruler. Guided by the Active Intellect, he gains philosophical insight. Thanks to his exceptional faculty of imagination he is, however, also able to receive from the Active Intellect the images and similes with which to represent his knowledge, passing it on to all those which depend on such forms of representation (cf. also *Taḥṣīl* [*127: 184,6–186,8]; Engl. transl. in Mahdi 1969 [*23: 44–45]; on this point cf. Griffel 2000 [*326: 245–246]; for references to Plato and Aristotle see Lameer 1997 [*322]; on the late ancient background cf. O'Meara 2002 [*331]).

Once philosophy and religion are established, the preconditions for an excellent community will be fulfilled on a permanent basis. The rulers who succeed the founder therefore need no longer possess the same all-encompassing qualities. It suffices if they are philosophers and, with respect to religion, ensure compliance with and expedient supplementation of the revealed law (on the role of laws and legislation cf. Butterworth 2008 [*340], Genequand 2008 [*341]). If circumstances dictate, the governance of the state may even be distributed amongst several persons, even though al-Fārābī emphasizes that there always has to be at least one philosopher among them (*Mabādi'* [*125: 248,15–252,149]). For it is the philosopher who will guarantee the preservation of the principles according to which the excellent community was established in the first place. He will take care that the state keep the hierarchical order which it was first given, and thus grant each of its members their participation in knowledge. In this way the excellent community fulfils its noblest task: it enables its citizens – even if there may be dissenters who keep themselves apart from the community (cf. Alon 1990 [*312]) – to lead a virtuous life and to perfect their souls, and thus to show them the path to joy (*iltiḏāḏ*) and happiness (*sa'āda*) (*Mabādi'* [*125: 260,7–262,6]).

Things look very different if the principles of governance are not determined by philosophy. This leads to the generation of communities that suffer from deficiencies, as al-Fārābī also elaborates in detail. He distinguishes three basic types: (1) the ignorant community (*madīna ǧāhiliyya*), where neither the ruler nor the citizens have ever gained knowledge; (2) the community that has gone astray (*madīna ḍālla*), whose rulers do possess knowledge, but are not prepared to share it with their subjects; and (3) the wicked or immoral community (*madīna fāsiqa*); characteristic here is that its members – rulers and citizens – would have access to knowledge, but out of base motives neglect doing what is good, striving for the bad instead (*Mabādi'* [*125: 270,6–276,1]; cf. Mahdi 1999 [*42: 226]). However, this distinction, which is highly reminiscent of categories used in Islamic theology (Arfa 2015 [*348]), only marks the three basic forms of deformation. In reality al-Fārābī's classification is much more detailed. This becomes evident as soon as one compares his explications in *Fuṣūl muntaza'a*, *Iḥṣā' al-'ulūm*, *al-Milla*, *al-Ḥurūf*, *Mabādi'*, and *al-Siyāsa*, placing all types of imperfect states which are mentioned and discussed in these texts next to each other (Crone 2004 [*334: 192–208]). Such a comparison shows that al-Fārābī's thoughts are not limited to the general classification of communities along the lines of ethical criteria. Sometimes he mentions quite real forms of governance, with which he was obviously familiar through the political philosophy of antiquity, like tyranny (*madīnat al-taġallub*), oligarchy (*madīnat al-naḏala*), timocracy (*madīnat al-karāma*) and democracy (*madīnat al-ǧamāʿiyya*; cf. the table in Crone 2004 [*334: 228]). Such references, however, do not ultimately alter the fundamental direction of his argument. Even where historically documented forms of governance are mentioned, he does not show any interest in their constitution or political institutions. The only thing he takes to be relevant is whether and in what way a community promotes knowledge and upright conduct in its members. In this respect all those states that deviate from the ideal described above are equal, in that they do not direct their citizens to the attainment of perfection and to happiness.

The passages summarized above certainly belong to the most accessible in al-Fārābī's œuvre. Therefore it is not surprising that they were taken up time and again by later authors like Ibn Rušd, Naṣīr al-Dīn al-Ṭūsī and Ǧalāl al-Dīn al-Dawānī, and are still counted among the best-known parts of his work today. Nevertheless it is not always clear how they should be understood. What al-Fārābī so vividly describes sometimes turns out to be problematic upon closer inspection. This is also confirmed by the various debates about his practical philosophy that have arisen in recent scholarship.

(1) One of them centres on the question whether al-Fārābī's thoughts concerning political communities include the idea of the immortality of human beings, and of an afterlife. The question arises because his pronouncements on this topic are contradictory to some extent. On the one hand there is a series of remarks which irrefutably seem to imply the idea of a hereafter: (a) The best-known among them is a chapter of the *Mabādiʾ* to which Walzer (1985 [*276: 259]) gave the heading 'After-life'. It explains the fate that will be awaiting the citizens of the various communities. As the reader is told, the citizens of the excellent community will receive everlasting reward (*Mabādiʾ* [*125: 266,2–4]), and the citizens of immoral communities everlasting punishment [274,7–8], while people who have remained ignorant and have never actualized their intellect will simply perish [270,6–272,3. 274,11–13]. (b) In *Iḥṣāʾ al-ʿulūm*, al-Fārābī distinguishes between real happiness (*mā hiya fī l-ḥaqīqa saʿāda*) and that which is only taken to be happiness. He emphasizes that real happiness cannot be reached in this life, but only in another life in the hereafter (*Iḥṣāʾ* [*45: 124,9–13]). (c) Even more specific indications are found in the *Fuṣūl muntazaʿa*. They not only point to the afterlife (*al-ḥayāt al-aḫīra*) in general, but also link it to the decidedly religious idea that after their death, human beings will be awaited by the 'beatific vision' (*ruʾya*) (*Fuṣūl muntazaʿa* [*116: 87,6–7. 92,7–12]). (d) In the work on the harmony between Plato and Aristotle, finally, a fourth aspect is brought into play. Here al-Fārābī (if indeed he is the author;

cf. p. 585 above), argues that Plato and Aristotle also had maintained the notion of recompense in the hereafter, even if they were often said to hold the opposite view (*al-Ǧamʿ* [*130: 75,7–76,6 Martini Bonadeo; 157,1–159,3 Najjar, Mallet]).

On the other hand, there is also evidence for the opposite tendency, beginning with a passage in the *Mabādiʾ* which lends itself to a rather different interpretation. Here al-Fārābī explains that a community will stray from its path if it focuses on the happiness after this life (*baʿda ḥayātihā hāḏihi*), i.e. in the hereafter (*Mabādiʾ* [*125: 258,4–8]). Even more important in this case are, however, the external voices. They belong to three well-known Andalusian authors (Ibn Bāǧǧa, Ibn Ṭufayl, and Ibn Rušd), who in their works declare more or less explicitly that al-Fārābī had rejected the idea of human immortality. These claims are made with reference to his lost commentary on the *Nicomachean Ethics*, though it is not possible to reconstruct the original stance from the way in which the three authors quote this commentary. Ibn Bāǧǧa rather gives the impression that he does not regard the quoted passage as al-Fārābī's real or definite view. Ibn Ṭufayl, on the other hand, seems to be convinced of exactly that. Ibn Rušd, finally, shares this conviction and even goes beyond Ibn Ṭufayl by supplementing the latter's thesis with further claims (for details see Davidson 1992 [*250: 70–73]; cf. Vallat 2004 [*47: 102–123] and Neria 2013 [*347]). Despite these uncertainties the testimony of the three authors carries some weight, in particular as two of them express it in a very incisive way. For Ibn Ṭufayl and, following him, Ibn Rušd condensed their view in the pithy and, since then, often repeated formula that al-Fārābī regarded the belief in the hereafter as 'old wives' tale' (*ḫurāfāt ʿaǧāʾiz*) (*Ḥayy Ibn Yaqẓān* [*6: 14,4]; see Davidson 1992 [*250: 71]; cf. Vallat 2004 [*47: 122]).

In view of this ambivalent evidence, scholars have been forced to weigh the different statements up against each other. In doing so, they have developed various strategies of interpretation: it is possible that al-Fārābī revised his views on immortality and the hereafter in the course of his life (this hypothesis is hinted at in Crone 2004 [*334: 213]); it is also possible that he phrased his true beliefs on this topic – and on metaphysics in general – in an indirect way only (e.g. Colmo 2005 [*338: 110. 119]); but it is also conceivable that he held a more complex position, rejecting the immortality of the individual while ascribing everlasting life to the common intellect of humankind (Endress 1992 [*38: 41], Black 1996 [*40: 191]).

This last assumption holds a certain appeal in that it would enable us to establish a continuous line of development within the history of philosophy. It assigns al-Fārābī a view which would directly lead to the position later championed by Ibn Rušd. Nonetheless some degree of caution is in order: what al-Fārābī says is not unambiguous – not even concerning the question of individual immortality. At some point he declares that upon their separation from the body, the souls of the deceased will join themselves (*ittaṣala*) to other souls resembling them (*Mabādiʾ* [*125: 264,4–266,4]), which would support the idea of a 'collective' immortality. However, immediately afterwards he adds that even after their separation from matter, the souls will experience no uniform perfection but a diversity of states of happiness (*saʿādāt*) [266,5–268,3]. The question about the hereafter is thus beset with multiple difficulties. This in fact already applies to the attempt to determine al-Fārābī's concept of happiness or felicity (Galston 1990 [*313: 55–94], 1992 [*318: 95–99. 148–151]). The only clear point in this context is that he tied both human immortality and human happiness to the act of cognition. Only in the act of cognition are human beings able to actualize their own self, which is at the same time a precondition for perfection, and the path leading up to it. Though addressed in several texts, this is perhaps nowhere as clearly expressed as in *Fī l-ʿAql* (*On Intellect*). In a rather short passage, which may well be regarded as a key text for the entire topic, al-Fārābī tells us that upon reaching the highest level of cognition, the substance of the human being, or rather the human being insofar as he or she becomes substance (*bimā yataǧawharu bihi*), will become the being that is closest in rank to the Active Intellect. This is supreme happiness (*al-saʿāda al-quṣwā*) and the afterlife, meaning 'that the ultimate thing by which man becomes a substance comes about for him, and he attains his final perfection, which is that the final thing through which he becomes a substance performs the final action by virtue of which he becomes a substance. This is what is meant by the afterlife' (*wa-hāḏā maʿnā al-ḥayāt al-āḫira*; *Fī l-ʿAql* [*105: 31,4–9; Engl. transl. 76]; on the connection between cognition and eternity cf. Vallat 2008 [*192: *passim*, esp. 120–121]).

(2) The second scholarly debate focuses on the question how to contextualize al-Fārābī's discussions of political communities. This can mean their reference to a specific historical context on the one hand, and the place of his views within the history of philosophy on the other.

With respect to the first aspect of the question, only one major hypothesis has been advanced within the scholarly community. Originally, it stems from Najjar, and found two prominent adherents in Corbin and Walzer. In their opinion, al-Fārābī's political ideas were closely connected to the notion of governance developed by the Imāmī Shiites. One argument cited in support of this view refers to al-Fārābī having spent the last years of his life at the court of the Ḥamdānids in Aleppo, known for their Imāmī leanings (Najjar 1961 [*305], Corbin 1964 [*23: 223. 228–231], Walzer 1970 [*25: 240–241], 1985 [*276: 15. 441–442. 456]). This hypothesis, however, was widely rejected (already by Rosenthal 1974 [*307: 71]). This applies not only to its specific reference to the Imāmīs, but more generally to any attempt at interpreting al-Fārābī's views as directly partisan to the religio-political conflicts of his time. This type of interpretation is obviously inadequate. Al-Fārābī was not interested in day-to-day politics nor in the religious legitimation of a specific dynasty; he was concerned with philosophical reflection about the community based on fundamental principles. He thus followed a tradition which had already been avidly cultivated in antiquity; which is also why it seems more apposite to focus on the second question, how his ideas can be located within the history of philosophy.

On this point another scholarly debate arose, which for a long time was dominated by the thesis that al-Fārābī's views on the community were, unlike all other parts of his philosophy, indebted to Platonism (e.g. Walzer 1970 [*25: 233], Black 1996 [*40: 190], Fakhry 2002 [*43: 104–105]). There are indeed good arguments for this, as many statements about the ideal ruler and the various forms of communities we encounter in the *Mabādiʾ* or in the *Siyāsa* are reminiscent of thoughts Plato puts forward in the *Republic* and in the *Laws*. The only question left to answer seemed to be how al-Fārābī was supposed to have learnt of these views, given that the transmission situation of Plato's 'political' writings is rather obscure: the *Republic* seems to have been transmitted in a disparate manner (Reisman 2004 [*337]), whereas the *Laws* apparently were known to al-Fārābī through a later paraphrase only (cf. p. 577 above). Apart from that it is questionable whether there was a continuous school tradition for him to carry on: many modern interpreters assume that the political aspects of Plato's thought were consciously suppressed or at least neglected by the late ancient commentators.

Scholars therefore tried to close this apparent gap in the Platonic tradition. To this end, three hypotheses were developed. Walzer argued for assuming a further philosophical strand in late antiquity, over and above the known Neoplatonic schools; it supposedly aligned itself more with Middle Platonism and hence had kept a genuine interest in politics alive (Walzer 1970 [*25: 234–239], 1985 [*276: 9. 424–429]). According to O'Meara, Neoplatonism was itself much more 'political' than modern scholarship usually assumes, so that al-Fārābī might well have received inspiration from that quarter (2003 [*333: 185–197]). Vallat, finally, developed the hypothesis mentioned already, that al-Fārābī possessed comprehensive knowledge of Platonism (in all its aspects) because he had been to Harran, where an uninterrupted Platonic tradition had been preserved far into the Islamic era (2004 [*47: 17–23. 46–83]; rooting al-Fārābī in the ancient pagan tradition even leads Vallat 2008 [*344: 118–129, esp. 122] to conclude that al-Fārābī did not recognize Islam as realization of the Platonically conceived 'religion' described by him, but saw it critically, as Proclus used to see Christianity.

Independently of the specific problem of transmission it became clear, however, that it was not enough to point to Platonism in order to determine the philosophical horizon of al-Fārābī's ideas; for his deliberations concerning the community contain several theoretical elements which cannot be deduced from, nor meaningfully located in, this context. Hence more recent scholarship has increasingly taken Aristotelianism into account, even in questions of politics. This first brought to light that some statements found in the *Mabādiʾ* and in the *Siyāsa* presuppose a certain familiarity with Aristotle's *Politics* – in whatever form of transmission (Pines 1975 [*308: 156–160], Maróth 1978 [*309: 465–467]). Subsequently, further links to the Aristotelian corpus were discovered. Thus it was explained by Daiber that certain elements in the description of the excellent community go back to *On the Soul* (theory of mimesis) and to the *Nicomachean Ethics* (doctrine of the virtues) (1986 [*310: 729–741]). Galston confirmed the significance of the *Nicomachean Ethics* (1990 [*313: 13–14]), while also pointing to other relevant texts [*313: 235 s.v. Aristotle]. Gutas finally made the case for broadening the question even further, since al-Fārābī had been inspired by Aristotle not just at the level of individual motifs and theoretical elements, but more generally in his fundamental understanding of the doctrine of the community (2004 [*336: 262–269]).

These different pieces of evidence do not deny the relevance of the Platonic tradition, but do reveal the complexity of transmission and reception in this case. Evidently, al-Fārābī knew texts from both schools where practical philosophy was concerned (as argued already by Pines 1975 [*308: 160]). Moreover, he may well have encountered further ideas that had originated in late ancient Christianity (Crone 2004 [*334: 220–222]). Nevertheless it makes particular sense at this point to juxtapose Platonism and Aristotelianism. For what is of interest with respect of al-Fārābī's ideas is not first and foremost the source of individual theoretical elements. More fundamental is his general aim in formulating his practical philosophy. This recently has become the subject of a third scholarly debate, which can be boiled down to a dispute between two alternatives: whether his thoughts on this topic really ought to be understood as political philosophy at all, or rather as a contribution to ethics.

(3) For a long time, the answer to this question appeared to be a foregone conclusion. After all, the texts concerned were not about individuals, but about political communities. For decades it was therefore assumed as a matter of course that they ought to be designated as political writings (e.g. Butterworth 2001 [*32] in the title of his Engl. transl.); which in consequence led to the claim that al-Fārābī was the founder of political philosophy within the culture of Islam (in particular Mahdi 1963 [*306: 160], 1991 [*317: 9–10], 1997 [*323: 583–584. 607–608], 2001 [*328]; cf. Fakhry 2002 [*43: 101]; more finely nuanced Rosenthal 1955 [*301], 1974 [*307: 65]). This assessment, however, has since been called into question. More recent scholarship increasingly

emphasizes the fact that within his discussion of the community, al-Fārābī also addresses topics which belong to other philosophical disciplines. Thus Galston has highlighted close connections to metaphysics and psychology (1990 [*313: 183–188. 192–199]). Crone noted that the texts deal neither with constitutions, nor with political leadership, but with ethical norms and the guidance of the soul (2004 [*334: 191. 217]). Gutas argued for a fundamentally new interpretation of al-Fārābī's ideas on the community, by subjecting the term *madanī*, which plays a central role in this context, to a detailed investigation (2004 [*336] following preliminary work in 1999 [*42: 221–222] and 2002 [*330: 23–24]).

In order to support this new interpretation, he appealed to three main bodies of evidence: (a) The testimony of Ibn Ḫaldūn (d. 808/1406), who denies that al-Fārābī was interested in questions of public welfare and politics in the proper sense of the word; instead, his *siyāsa madaniyya* (and the eponymous work, *Ruling the Community*) had only one goal: to determine the dispositions of the souls and characters of human beings that live in a community (Gutas 2004 [*336: 260]). (b) The philological evidence which can be deduced from the Greek-Arabic translations from the 3rd/9th and the 4th/10th centuries; here *politikos* is usually translated as *madanī* (meaning 'belonging to the city' or 'belonging to the community'), whereas in several key passages of the *Nicomachean Ethics*, *politeia* is rendered by *sīra* (i.e. not by 'politics' but by 'way of life') [*336: 261–267]. (c) The philosophical evidence; according to Gutas, this confirms that al-Fārābī was not interested in political structures. His concern was rather to assign the community a place within the metaphysically based overall structure of being, the citizens' proper conduct of life, and the governance of the state by philosophers (under the guidance of the Active Intellect). Therefore it is not appropriate to speak of 'political philosophy' where al-Fārābī is concerned, but rather of a doctrine which was developed together with his metaphysics and ethics, and was directly linked to his noetics [*336: 270–279].

Gutas' thoughts are yet awaiting a wider reception and discussion within the scholarly community (so far cf. Reisman 2005 [*50: 68]). However, it is already clear that they open up a new perspective, and reveal important correlations between several parts of al-Fārābī's œuvre. This is not to deny that al-Fārābī occasionally touches on specific problems that unequivocally belong to the political sphere, for example the question when and under what conditions a state would be justified in waging war (*ǧihād*) (Kraemer 1987 [*311: 297–318], Brague 2001 [*327: 80–83]). But even comments of this kind gain their full meaning only within a larger context; this in particular applies to discussions concerning the community in general. Rather than constituting an autonomous segment within al-Fārābī's thought which could be defined as politics in the narrow sense, they are part of an all-embracing philosophical conception which as a whole is directed towards human happiness.

As it happens, al-Fārābī has pointed this out himself in several places. First indications can already be found in writings he designed as *Prolegomena* to the study of philosophy. Thus we read in *al-Tawṭiʾa fī l-manṭiq* (*Introduction to Logic*), in the context of a brief description of philosophy, that *ʿilm madanī* (the science of the community) studies true happiness (*al-saʿāda allatī hiya bi-l-ḥaqīqa saʿāda*), those things that are merely taken to be happiness, and the things by which people are prevented from reaching happiness. As all these things are connected to our will, the science investigating these matters is also called 'the philosophy of humankind' (*al-falsafa al-insāniyya*) or 'practical philosophy' (*al-ʿamaliyya*) (*Tawṭiʾa* [*58: I 59,5–8 al-ʿAǧam; 14,5–9 Dānišpažūh]). In *al-Tanbīh ʿalā sabīl al-saʿāda* (*Exhortation to the Path to Happiness*) al-Fārābī explains once more how philosophy is to be subdivided, and how its various disciplines are characterized. *Falsafa madaniyya* (philosophy of the community), he tells us, is not one science, but is divided in two parts: one of them confers knowledge about good actions (*al-afʿāl al-ǧamīla*), about traits of character (*al-aḫlāq*) which result in good actions, and about the ability (*al-qudra*) to produce good actions and to acquire the good (*qunya*); this part is called the discipline of ethics (*al-ṣināʿa al-ḫuluqiyya*). The second part, on the other hand, investigates in which way members of a community partake in the good, and teaches us how to effectuate and preserve the good for them; this part is called the philosophy of (political) governance (*al-falsafa al-siyāsiyya*) (*Tanbīh* [*51: 257,4–10]). A similar division is met with, finally, in the philosophical summa *Taḥṣīl al-saʿāda* (*The Attainment of Happiness*). Here again al-Fārābī distinguishes two areas within *ʿilm madanī* (science of the community) or *ʿilm insānī* (science of humankind): while one determines the perfection (*kamāl*) of the human being and the actions and virtues (*faḍāʾil*) through which an individual may reach this goal (*ġaraḍ*), the other specifies how a community must be governed so that even those human beings which do not possess such knowledge may partake in happiness 'according to the measure in which they are naturally disposed to it' (*bi-miqdāri mā lahu uʿidda bi-l-fiṭra*) (*Taḥṣīl al-saʿāda* [*127: 141,9–142,7]).

In the face of such statements it is idle to define *falsafa madaniyya* (philosophy of the community) exclusively as either politics or ethics. Rather it seems that characteristically, it comprises both areas and investigates all things that belong to the sphere of humankind. In this al-Fārābī pursues an idea that evidently goes back to Aristotle, who already had defined ethics and politics as complementary parts of one comprehensive science of all things human. His view can be summed up as follows: 'Ethics and politics represent themselves as two branches of one and the same science, called πολιτική, which Aristotle also identifies as 'the philosophy that is concerned with all things human', with politics being understood as the natural supplement of ethics, 'in order to bring the philosophy of all things human to its completion' (Flashar 2004 [*335: 293] with reference to *Eth. Nic.* I 1, 1094b11 and X 9, 1181b15).

The similarities to al-Fārābī's account are striking, not only concerning the basic understanding of practical philosophy, but also the individual terms that are used: al-Fārābī's *madanī* obviously renders Aristotle's πολιτική, while the compound *falsafa insāniyya* will reflect 'the philosophy that is concerned with all things human'. It is therefore possible to locate *falsafa madaniyya* – even while giving full recognition to all its Platonic elements – in the Aristotelian tradition. Even this, though, does not fully clarify its position within the context of al-Fārābī's thought, for in one important point al-Fārābī goes beyond Aristotle. This concerns the epistemic status that should be awarded to practical philosophy, linked to the problem how its relation to theoretical philosophy and its general position within the framework of philosophical knowledge ought to be determined.

As is well known, Aristotle was of the opinion that the science which he called πολιτική did not aim at theoretical knowledge, but at action. Hence he did not assign the cognitive part of the soul (ἐπιστημονικόν) to it, but the deliberative part (βουλευτικόν), and in particular 'practical wisdom' or 'prudence' (φρόνησις) (*Eth. Nic.* VI 2–3). Al-Fārābī was well familiar with this classification (cf. *Fī l-ʿAql* [*105: 9,4–11,9; Engl. transl. 70–71; French transl. 67–70], with explicit reference to *Eth. Nic.* VI) but he did not consider it adequate for establishing practical philosophy. According to his view, *ʿilm madanī* (the science of the community) also holds the rank of a demonstrative science. Like theoretical philosophy, it is based on first intelligibles. Anybody who has mastered it should therefore be able to recognize universals and to form judgements which can be regarded as proven according to the rules of the *Posterior Analytics* (Druart 1997 [*320: 406–409. 415–423]).

On the face of it, it may well be surprising that al-Fārābī should have taken this view. However, it essentially arose from the metaphysical context in which he placed his practical philosophy. He did, after all, claim that knowledge of the good and its communication to the community was not dependent on a process of practical calculation and collecting experience. Both can be achieved immediately, once the state is ruled by a philosopher king who has placed himself under to the guidance of the Active Intellect. Connection to the Active Intellect or, more generally, integration into the emanative scheme makes it possible to recognize the good and to found an excellent community. Practical and theoretical philosophy have the same source of knowledge and hold the same epistemic rank. This also means that both are indispensable if all human beings want to reach the goal assigned to them. This goal is nothing but the 'attainment of happiness': *Taḥṣīl al-saʿāda*, as al-Fārābī calls the philosophical *summa* within which he has summarized his path to knowledge, documenting both his self-confidence and his programmatic ambitions.

5 Secondary Literature

5.1 Works of Reference [*1–*6] – 5.2 General Accounts. Life and Works [*15–*60] – 5.3 Influence [*70–*108] – 5.4 Terminology [*120–*121] – 5.5 General Theory of Science. Definition and Classification of Philosophy [*130–*142] – 5.6 Logic [*155–*198] – 5.7 Mathematics [*205–*221] – 5.8 Physics [*235–*257] – 5.9 Metaphysics [*270–*288] – 5.10 Ethics and Politics [*300–*349]

5.1 *Works of Reference*

1 EI² = *The Encyclopaedia of Islam: New edition*. Ed. by Clifford Edmund Bosworth et al., 11 vols, 6 suppl. vols. Leiden, 1960–2005.

2 GAS = Sezgin, Fuat. *Geschichte des arabischen Schrifttums*, 17 vols. Leiden, Frankfurt a.M., 1967–2015.

3 EIr = *Encyclopaedia Iranica*. Ed. by Ehsan Yarshater, vols 1 ff. London, 1982 ff.

4 GAP = *Grundriss der arabischen Philologie*, vol. 2: *Literaturwissenschaft*. Ed. by Helmut Gätje. Wiesbaden, 1987; vol. 3: *Supplement*. Ed. by Wolfdietrich Fischer. Wiesbaden, 1992.

5 Daiber, Hans. *Bibliography of Islamic Philosophy*, 2 vols. Leiden, Boston, 1999. – Supplement (2007).

6 *Encyclopaedia of Islam*, THREE [EI Three]. Ed. by Marc Gaborieau et al., 1 ff. Leiden, 2007 ff.

5.2 *General Accounts. Life and Works*

15 Steinschneider, Moritz. *Al-Farabi (Alpharabius): Des arabischen Philosophen Leben und Schriften mit besonderer Rücksicht auf die Geschichte der griechischen Wissenschaft unter den Arabern*. St. Petersburg, 1869. – Repr. Amsterdam, 1966.

16 ʿAbd al-Rāziq, Muṣṭafā. "Al-ḥakīm Abū Naṣr al-Fārābī." [Arab.] *Maǧallat al-Maǧmaʿ al-ʿilmī al-ʿarabī* 12 (1932): 385–397. – Repr. Frankfurt a.M., 1999 [Islamic Philosophy, 8], 364–376.

17 Madkūr, Ibrāhīm. *La place d'al-Fārābī dans l'école philosophique musulmane*. Paris, 1934.

18 Kraus, Paul. "Plotin chez les Arabes: Remarques sur un nouveau fragment de la paraphrase arabe des Ennéades." *Bulletin de l'Institut d'Égypte* 23 (1940–1941):

263–295. – Repr. in: P. Kraus, *Alchemie, Ketzerei, Apokryphen im frühen Islam*. Hildesheim, 1994, 313–345.

19 Fackenheim, Emil L. "Al-Farabi: His Life, Times, and Thought: On the Occasion of the Millenary Anniversary of his Death." *Middle Eastern Affairs* 2 (1951): 54–59. – Repr. Frankfurt a.M., 1999 [Islamic Philosophy, 9], 408–413.

20 Madkūr, Ibrāhīm. "Abū Naṣr al-Fārābī (259–339 h) = (870–950 m)." [Arab.] *Maǧallat Kulliyyat al-ādāb* 19 (1957 [1961]): 69–92. – Repr. Frankfurt a.M., 1999 [Islamic Philosophy, 11], 338–361.

21 Stern, Samuel Miklos. "Al-Masʿūdī and the Philosopher al-Fārābī." In *Al-Masʿūdī Millenary Commemoration Volume*. Ed by S. Maqbul Ahmad and A. Rahman. Aligarh, 1960, 28–41. – Repr. Frankfurt a.M., 1999 [Islamic Philosophy, 11], 382–395.

22 Walzer, Richard. *Greek into Arabic: Essays on Islamic Philosophy*. Oxford 1962; Cambridge, Mass., 1963 (2nd ed.).

23 Corbin, Henri. *Histoire de la philosophie islamique*, vol. 1: *Des origines jusqu'à la mort d'Averroës (1198)*. Avec la collaboration de Seyyed Hossein Nasr et Osman Yahya. Paris, 1964. – Engl. transl. in: H. Corbin, *History of Islamic Philosophy*, translated by Liadain Sherrard with the assistance of Philip Sherrard. London, New York, 1993, 1–252.

24 de Laugier de Beaurecueil, Serge. *Manuscrits d'Afghanistan*. Cairo, 1964.

25 Walzer, Richard. "L'éveil de la philosophie islamique." *Revue des études islamiques* 38 (1970): 7–42. 207–242. – Repr. as *Hors série* 1. Paris, 1971.

26 Mahdi, Muhsin. "Al-Farabi." In *Dictionary of Scientific Biography*, vol. 4. Ed. by Charles Coulston Gillispie. New York, 1971, 523–526.

27 Maḥfūẓ, Ḥusayn ʿAlī. *Al-Fārābī fī l-marāǧiʿ al-ʿarabiyya*. Baghdad, 1975.

28 van Ess, Josef. "Al-Fārābī and Ibn al-Rēwandī." *Hamdard Islamicus* 3 (1980): 3–15.

29 Michot, Jean. "Tables de correspondance des 'Taʿlīqāt' d'al-Fārābī, des 'Taʿlīqāt' d'Avicenne et du 'Liber aphorismorum' d'Andrea Alpago." *Mélanges de l'Institut dominicain d'études orientales du Caire* 15 (1982): 231–250.

30 Gutas, Dimitri. "The Starting Point of Philosophical Studies in Alexandrian and Arabic Aristotelianism." In *Theophrastus of Eresus: On His Life and Work*. Ed. by William W. Fortenbaugh. New Brunswick, London, 1985, 115–123. – Repr. in: D. Gutas, *Greek Philosophers in the Arabic Tradition*. Aldershot, 2000, no. X.

31 Chiesa, Bruno. "Note su al-Fārābī, Averroè e Ibn Bāǧǧa (Avempace) in traduzione ebraica." *Henoch* 8 (1986): 79–86.

32 Tardieu, Michel. "Ṣābiens coraniques et 'Ṣābiens' de Ḥarrān." *Journal asiatique* 274 (1986): 1–44.

33 Endress, Gerhard. "Die wissenschaftliche Literatur." In GAP 1987 [*4: I 400–506].

34 Mallet, Dominique. "Le rappel de la voie à suivre pour parvenir au bonheur de Abū Naṣr al-Fārābī: Intr., trad. et notes." *Bulletin d'études orientales* 39–40 (1987–1988): 113–140.

35 Endress, Gerhard. "Der arabische Aristoteles und die Einheit der Wissenschaften im Islam." In *Die Blütezeit der arabischen Wissenschaft*. Ed. by Heinz Balmer and Beat Glaus. Zurich, 1990, 3–39.

36 Endress, Gerhard. "'Der erste Lehrer': Der arabische Aristoteles und das Konzept der Philosophie im Islam." In *Gottes ist der Orient, Gottes ist der Okzident: Festschrift für Abdoljavad Falaturi zum 65. Geburtstag*. Ed. by Udo Tworuschka. Cologne, Vienna, 1991, 151–181.

37 Endress, Gerhard. "'La Concordance entre Platon et Aristote', l'Aristote arabe et l'émancipation de la philosophie en islam médiéval." In *Historia philosophiae medii aevi: Studien zur Geschichte der Philosophie des Mittelalters: Festschrift für Kurt Flasch*. Ed. by Burkhard Mojsisch and Olaf Pluta. Amsterdam, 1991, 237–257.

38 Endress, Gerhard. "Die wissenschaftliche Literatur." In GAP [*4: III 3–152].

39 Chiesa, Bruno and Caterina Rigo: "La tradizione manoscritta del ספר המעלות di Shem Tob Ibn Falaquera e una citazione ignorata della *Risāla fī ism al-falsafa* di al-Fārābī." *Sefarad* 53 (1993): 3–15.

40 Black, Deborah L. "Al-Fārābī." In *History of Islamic Philosophy*, vol. 1. Ed. by Seyyed Hossein Nasr and Oliver Leaman. London, 1996, 178–197.

41 Hilal, Aziz. *Le livre des Lettres de Farabi* (*Kitāb al-Ḥurūf*). Intr., trad. et commentaires, 3 vols. PhD Diss., University of Bordeaux, 1997.

42 "Fārābī, Abū Naṣr." In EIr [*3: IX 208–229] (Dimitri Gutas [Biography], Deborah L. Black [Logic], Thérèse-Anne Druart [Metaphysics], Dimitri Gutas [Fārābī and Greek philosophy], George Sawa [Music], Muhsin Mahdi [Political philosophy]).

43 Fakhry, Majid. *Al-Fārābi: Founder of Neoplatonism: His Life, Works and Influence*. Oxford, 2002.

44 Freudenthal, Gad. "La quiddité de l'âme, traité populaire néoplatonisant faussement attribué à al-Fárābī: Traduction annotée et commentée." *Arabic Sciences and Philosophy* 13 (2003): 173–237.

45 Paredes Gandía, José Antonio. *Abū Naṣr al-Fārābī: El libro de las letras: El origen de las palabras, la filosofía y la religión*. Madrid, 2004.

46 Rashed, Marwan. "Ibn ʿAdī et Avicenne sur les types d'existants." In *Aristotele e i suoi esegeti neoplatonici: Logica e ontologia nelle interpretazioni greche e arabe: Atti del convegno internazionale, Roma, 19–20 ottobre 2001*. Ed. by Vincenza Celluprica and Cristina D'Ancona. Naples, 2004, 107–171.

47 Vallat, Philippe. *Farabi et l'école d'Alexandrie: Des prémisses de la connaissance à la philosophie politique*. Paris, 2004.

48 Khalidi, Muhammad Ali, ed. *Medieval Islamic Philosophical Writings*. Cambridge, 2005.

49 Martini Bonadeo, Cecilia and Cleophea Ferrari. "Al-Fārābī." In *Storia della filosofia nell'islam medievale*, vol. 1. Ed. by Cristina D'Ancona. Turin, 2005, 380–448.

50 Reisman, David C. "Al-Fārābī and the Philosophical Curriculum." In *The Cambridge Companion to Arabic Philosophy*. Ed. by Peter Adamson and Richard Taylor. Cambridge, 2005, 52–71.

51 Butterworth, Charles E. "Al-Farabi (Alfarabius or Avennasar)." In *Medieval Islamic Civilization: An Encyclopaedia*, vol. 1. Ed. by Josef W. Meri. New York, Abingdon, 2006, 247–248.

52 McGinnis, Jon and David C. Reisman. *Classical Arabic Philosophy: An Anthology of Sources:* Translated with Introduction, Notes, and Glossary. Indianapolis, Cambridge, 2007.

53 Adamson, Peter, ed. *In the Age of al-Fārābī: Arabic Philosophy in the Fourth/Tenth century*. London, 2008.

54 Aydınlı, Yaşar. *Fârâbî*. Istanbul, 2008. – With a synopsis of al-Fārābī's works and information on Turkish translations.

55 Martini Bonadeo, Cecilia, ed. *Al-Fārābī: L'armonia delle opinione di due sapienti il divino Platone e Aristotele:* Introduzione, testo arabo, traduzione e commento: Prefazione di Gerhard Endress. Pisa, 2008.

56 Janos, Damien. "Al-Fārābī, Creation Ex Nihilo, and the Cosmological Doctrine of *K. al-Jamʿ* and *Jawābāt*." *Journal of the American Oriental Society* 129 (2009): 1–17.

57 Rashed, Marwan. "On the Authorship of the Treatise *On the Harmonization of the Opinions of the Two Sages* attributed to al-Fārābī." *Arabic Sciences and Philosophy* 19 (2009): 43–82.

58 Genequand, Charles. "Théologie et philosophie: La providence chez al-Fārābī et l'authenticité de l'Harmonie des opinions des deux sages." *Mélanges de l'Université Saint-Joseph* 64 (2012): 195–211.

59 Gleede, Benjamin. "*Creatio ex nihilo* – a Genuinely Philosophical Insight Derived from Plato and Aristotle? Some Notes on the *Treatise of the Harmony between the Two Sages*." *Arabic Sciences and Philosophy* 22 (2012): 91–117.

60 Pormann, Peter E. "Al-Fārābī, the Melancholic Thinker and Philosopher Poet." *Journal of the American Oriental Society* 135 (2015): 209–224.

5.3 *Influence*

70 Horten, Max. "Das Buch der Ringsteine [*Risālat al-Fuṣūṣ*] Fârâbî's: Mit Auszügen aus dem Kommentar des Emîr Ismâʿîl el-Ḥoseinî el-Fârânî." *Zeitschrift für Assyriologie und verwandte Gebiete* 18 (1904–1905): 257–300; 20 (1907): 16–48. 303–354; 28 (1914): 113–146. – Repr. Frankfurt a.M., 1999 [Islamic Philosophy, 8], 1–164.

71 Gilson, Etienne. "Les sources gréco-arabes de l'augustinisme avicennisant." *Archives d'histoire doctrinale et littéraire du moyen âge* 2 (1929): 5–149. – Repr. Paris, 1981; Frankfurt a.M., 1999 [Islamic Philosophy, 8], 209–353.

72 Bédoret, H. “Les premières traductions tolédanes de philosophie: Œuvres d’Alfarabi.” *Revue néoscolastique de philosophie* 41 (1938): 80–97. – Repr. Frankfurt a.M., 1999 [Islamic Philosophy, 9], 278–295.
73 Salmon [= Salman], Dominique H. “The Mediaeval Latin Translations of Alfarabi’s Works.” *The New Scholasticism* 13 (1939): 245–261. – Repr. Frankfurt a.M., 1999 [Islamic Philosophy, 9], 321–337.
74 Salman, Dominique H. “Le ‘Liber exercitationis ad viam felicitatis’ d’Alfarabi.” *Recherches de théologie ancienne et médiévale* 12 (1940): 33–48. – Repr. Frankfurt a.M., 1999 [Islamic Philosophy, 9], 339–354.
75 Salman, Dominique H. “Fragments inédits de la logique d’Alfarabi.” *Revue des sciences philosophiques et théologiques* 32 (1948): 222–225. – Repr. Frankfurt a.M., 1999 [Islamic Philosophy, 9], 356–359.
76 Rosenthal, Franz, ed. *Ibn Khaldûn: The Muqaddimah: An Introduction to History, Translated from the Arabic*, 3 vols. New York, 1958. – Second, revised ed. London, 1967. – Repr. Princeton, 1980.
77 Lambton, Ann K. S. “al-Dawānī.” In EI² [*1: II 174].
78 Berman, Lawrence V. “Maimonides, the Disciple of Alfārābī.” *Israel Oriental Studies* 4 (1974): 154–178.
79 Mahdi, Muhsin. “Alfarabi et Averroès: Remarques sur le commentaire d’Averroès sur la République de Platon.” In *Multiple Averroès. Actes du colloque international organisé à l’occasion du 850ᵉ anniversaire de la naissance d’Averroès: Paris 20–23 septembre 1976*. Paris, 1978, 91–103.
80 Dānišpažūh, Muḥammad Taqī, ed. *Šarḥ Fuṣūṣ al-ḥikma, mansūb ba-Abū Naṣr al-Fārābī, az Muḥammad Taqī Astarābādī*. Tehran [McGill], 1358 h.š./1979.
81 Madelung, Wilferd. “Naṣīr al-Dīn al-Ṭūsī’s Ethics between Philosophy, Shiʿism, and Sufism.” In *Ethics in Islam*. Ed by Richard G. Hovannisian. Malibu, 1985, 85–101.
82 Endress, Gerhard. “Wissen und Gesellschaft in der islamischen Philosophie des Mittelalters.” In *Pragmatik: Handbuch pragmatischen Denkens*, vol. 1: *Pragmatisches Denken von den Ursprüngen bis zum 18. Jahrhundert*. Ed. by Herbert Stachowiak. Hamburg, 1986, 219–245.
83 Abouzeid, Ola Abdelaziz. *A Comparative Study between the Political Theories of al-Farabi and the Brethren of Purity*. PhD Diss., University of Toronto, 1987.
84 Gutas, Dimitri. *Avicenna and the Aristotelian Tradition: Introduction to Reading Avicenna’s Philosophical works*. Leiden, 1988, 2014 (2nd, revised and enlarged edition).
85 Chiesa, Bruno. “Shem Tob ibn Falaquera traduttore di al-Fārābī e di Averroè.” *Sefarad* 49 (1989): 21–35.
86 Netton, Ian Richard. *Al-Fārābī and His School*. London, New York, 1992.
87 Schneider, Jakob Hans Josef. “Le parallélisme de la raison pratique et théorique: S. Thomas d’Aquin et al-Farabi.” In *Les philosophies morales et politiques au moyen âge: Actes du IXᵉ congrès international de philosophie médiévale: Ottawa, du 17 au*

22 août 1992. Ed. by B. Carlos Bazán, Eduardo Andújar, and Léonard G. Sbrocchi. Ottawa, 1995, 567–580.

88 Zonta, Mauro. "The Reception of al-Fārābī's and Ibn Sīnā's Classifications of the Mathematical and Natural Sciences in the Hebrew Medieval Philosophical Literature." *Medieval Encounters* 1 (1995): 358–382.

89 Brague, Rémi, ed. *Maïmonide: Traité de logique*. Traduction, présentation et notes. Paris, 1996.

90 Marmura, Michael E., ed. *Al-Ghazālī: The Incoherence of the Philosophers*: A parallel English-Arabic text translated, introduced, and annotated. Provo, 1997, 2000 (2nd ed.).

91 al-Taftāzānī, Saʿd al-Dīn. *Šarḥ al-Maqāṣid*, vol. 5. Beirut, 1998.

92 Steigerwald, Diane. "La pensée d'al-Fārābī (259/872–339/950): Son rapport avec la philosophie ismaélienne." *Laval théologique et philosophique* 55 (1999): 455–476.

93 Endress, Gerhard. "Philosophische Ein-Band-Bibliotheken aus Isfahan." *Oriens* 36 (2001): 10–58.

94 Baffioni, Carmela. "*Al-madīnah al-fāḍilah* in al-Fārābī and in the Ikhwān al-Ṣafāʾ: A Comparison." In *Studies in Arabic and Islam: Proceedings of the 19th Congress of the Union européenne des arabisants et islamisants, Halle 1998*. Ed. by Stefan Leder et al. Leuven, 2002, 3–12.

95 Fakhry, Majid. *Al-Fārābi* 2002 [*43: 128–150].

96 Freudenthal, Gad. "*Ketav ha-daʿat* or *Sefer ha-sekhel we-ha-muskalot*: The Medieval Hebrew Translations of al-Fārābī's *Risāla fī l-ʿAql*: A Study in Text History and in the Evolution of Medieval Hebrew Philosophical Terminology." *The Jewish Quarterly Review* 93 (2002): 29–115.

97 Harvey, Steven. "Falaquera's Alfarabi: An Example of the Judaization of the Islamic *falâsifa*." *Trumah: Studien zum jüdischen Mittelalter* 12 (2002): 97–112.

98 Awǧabī, ʿAlī, ed. *Al-Fārābī: Fuṣūṣ al-ḥikma*. Tehran, 1381 h.š./2003. – Contains the commentary by Ismāʿīl al-Ḥusaynī al-Šanbġāzānī and glosses by Mīr Dāmād.

99 Schaerer, Patric O., ed. *Abū Bakr Ibn Ṭufail: Der Philosoph als Autodidakt: Ḥayy ibn Yaqẓān: Ein philosophischer Inselroman*: Übersetzung, mit einer Einleitung und Anmerkungen herausgegeben. Hamburg, 2004.

100 Daiber, Hans. "Das Fārābī-Bild des Maimonides: Ideentransfer als hermeneutischer Weg zu Maimonides' Philosophie." In *The Trias of Maimonides: Jewish, Arabic, and Ancient Culture of Knowledge*. Ed by Georges Tamer. Berlin, New York, 2005, 199–209.

101 Montada, Josef Puig. "Philosophy in Andalusia: Ibn Bājja and Ibn Ṭufayl." In P. Adamson, R. Taylor 2005 [cf. *50], 155–179.

102 Schupp, Franz, ed. *Al-Fārābī: Über die Wissenschaften: De scientiis*: Nach der lat. Übers. Gerhards von Cremona, mit einer Einleitung und kommentierenden Anmerkungen. Hamburg, 2005. – Latin text with German transl.

103 Schneider, Jakob Hans Josef, ed. *Al-Fārābī: De scientiis: Über die Wissenschaften*: Die Version des Dominicus Gundissalinus, übersetzt und eingeleitet. Freiburg, 2006. – Latin text with German transl.

104 De Smet, Daniel. "Al-Fārābī's Influence on Ḥamīd al-Dīn al-Kirmānī's Theory of Intellect and Soul." In P. Adamson 2008 [*53: 131–150].

105 El-Rouayheb, Khaled. *Relational Syllogisms and the History of Arabic Logic 900–1900*. Leiden, Boston, 2010.

106 Menn, Stephen. "Fārābī in the Reception of Avicenna's Metaphysics: Averroes against Avicenna on Being and Unity." In *Arabic, Hebrew and Latin Reception of Avicenna's Metaphysics*. Ed. by Dag Nikolaus Hasse and Amos Bertolacci. Berlin, 2012, 51–96.

107 Robinson, James T. "Al-Farabi, Avicenna, and Averroes in Hebrew: Remarks on the Indirect Transmission of Arabic-Islamic Philosophy in Medieval Judaism." In *The Judeo-Christian-Islamic Heritage: Philosophical and Theological Perspectives*. Ed. by Richard C. Taylor and Irfan A. Omar. Milwaukee, 2012, 59–87.

108 Zonta, Mauro. "Influence of Arabic and Islamic Philosophy on Judaic Thought." In *Stanford Encyclopedia of Philosophy*. Ed. by Edward N. Zalta. Revised Version, May 2016. URL = <http://plato.stanford.edu/archives/spr2011/entries/arabic-islamic-judaic/>.

5.4 *Terminology*

120 Ǧihāmī, Ǧirār (Gérard Jéhamy). *Mawsūʿat muṣṭalaḥāt al-Kindī wa-l-Fārābī*. Beirut, 2002.

121 Alon, Ilai and Shukri B. Abed. *Al-Fārābī's Philosophical Lexicon*, vol. 1: *Arabic Text*; vol. 2: *English Translation*. Cambridge, 2007.

5.5 *General Theory of Science. Definition and Classification of Philosophy*

130 Vajda, Georges. "Langage, philosophie, politique et religion d'après un traité récemment publié d'Abū Naṣr al-Fārābī." In *Journal asiatique* 258 (1970): 247–260.

131 Mahdi, Muhsin. "Alfarabi on Philosophy and Religion." *The Philosophical Forum* 4 (1972): 5–25. – Revised version in M. Mahdi 2001 [*328: 208–228].

132 Mahdi, Muhsin. "Science, Philosophy, and Religion in Alfarabi's Enumeration of the Sciences." In *The Cultural Context of Medieval Learning*. Ed by John Emery Murdoch and Edith Dudley Sylla. Dordrecht, 1975, 113–147. – Revised version in M. Mahdi 2001 [*328: 65–96].

133 Galston, Miriam. "A Re-examination of al-Fārābī's Neoplatonism." *Journal of the History of Philosophy* 15 (1977): 13–32.

134 Gutas, Dimitri. "Paul the Persian on the Classification of the Parts of Aristotle's Philosophy: A Milestone between Alexandria and Baġdād." *Der Islam* 60 (1983): 231–267. – Repr. in D. Gutas 2000 [cf. *30] no. IX.

135 Schramm, Matthias. "Theoretische und praktische Disziplin bei al-Fārābī." *Zeitschrift für Geschichte der Arabisch-Islamischen Wissenschaften* 3 (1986): 1–55. – Repr. Frankfurt a.M., 1999 [Islamic Philosophy, 11], 403–457.

136 Strohmaier, Gotthard. "'Von Alexandrien nach Bagdad' – eine fiktive Schultradition." In *Aristoteles: Werk und Wirkung*, vol. 2: *Kommentierung, Überlieferung, Nachleben*. Ed. by Jürgen Wiesner. Berlin, New York, 1987, 380–389. – Repr. in: G. Strohmaier, *Von Demokrit bis Dante: Die Bewahrung antiken Erbes in der arabischen Kultur*. Hildesheim, Zürich, New York, 1996, 313–322.

137 Gutas, Dimitri. "The 'Alexandria to Baghdad' Complex of Narratives: A Contribution to the Study of Philosophical and Medical Historiography Among the Arabs." *Documenti e studi sulla tradizione filosofica medievale* 10 (1999): 155–193.

138 Günther, Sebastian. "The Principles of Instruction are the Grounds of our Knowledge: Al-Fārābī's Philosophical and al-Ghazālī's Spiritual Approaches to Learning." In *Trajectories of Education in the Arab World: Legacies and Challenges*. Ed. by Osama Abi-Mershed. London, New York, 2009, 15–35.

139 de Vaulx d'Arcy, Guillaume. "La naqla: Étude du concept de transfert dans l'œuvre d'al-Fārābī." *Arabic Sciences and Philosophy* 20 (2010): 125–176.

140 Druart, Thérèse-Anne. "Al-Fârâbî: An Arabic Account of the Origin of Language and of Philosophical Vocabulary." *Proceedings of the American Catholic Philosophical Association* 84 (2010): 1–17.

141 Rudolph, Ulrich. "Die Deutung des Erbes: Die Geschichte der antiken Philosophie und Wissenschaft aus der Sicht arabischer Autoren." In *Entre Orient et Occident: La philosophie et la science gréco-romaines dans le monde arabe*. Ed. by Richard Goulet and Ulrich Rudolph. Vandœuvres-Genève, 2011, 279–320.

142 Rudolph, Ulrich. "Al-Farabi und die Neubegründung der Philosophie in der islamischen Welt." In *Bedeutende Lehrerfiguren: Von Platon bis Hasan al-Banna*. Ed. by Tobias Georges, Jens Scheiner, and Ilinca Tanaseanu-Döbler. Tübingen, 2015, 269–293.

5.6 *Logic*

155 Walzer, Richard. "Zur Traditionsgeschichte der aristotelischen Poetik." *Studi italiani di filologia classica*, N.S. 11 (1934): 5–14. – Repr. in: R. Walzer 1962 [*22: 129–136].

156 Türker, Mübahat. "El-ʿÂmirî ve Kategoriler'in Şerhleriyle ilgili parçalar = Al-ʿÂmiri et les fragments des commentaires des Catégories d'Aristote." *Araştırma* 3 (Ankara 1965): 65–122.

157 van Ess, Josef. *Die Erkenntnislehre des ʿAḍudaddīn al-Īcī: Übersetzung und Kommentar des ersten Buches seiner Mawāqif.* Wiesbaden, 1966.

158 Vajda, Georges. "Autour de la théorie de la connaissance chez Saadia." *Revue des études juives* 126 (1967): 135–189. 375–397.

159 Heinrichs, Wolfhart. *Arabische Dichtung und griechische Poetik: Ḥāzim al-Qarṭāǧannīs Grundlegung der Poetik mit Hilfe aristotelischer Begriffe.* Beirut, Wiesbaden, 1969.

160 Gätje, Helmut. "Die Gliederung der sprachlichen Zeichen nach al-Fārābī." *Der Islam* 47 (1971): 1–24.

161 Arnaldez, Roger. "Pensée et langage dans la philosophie de Fārābī (à propos du *Kitāb al-Ḥurūf*)." *Studia Islamica* 45 (1977): 57–65.

162 Heinrichs, Wolfhart. "Die antike Verknüpfung von phantasia und Dichtung bei den Arabern." *Zeitschrift der Deutschen Morgenländischen Gesellschaft* 128 (1978): 252–298.

163 Zimmermann, Friedrich W. *Al-Farabi's Commentary and Short Treatise on Aristotle's De Interpretatione.* Oxford, 1981. – Repr. 1982; paperback edition 1987.

164 Elamrani-Jamal, Abdelali. *Logique aristotélicienne et grammaire arabe, étude et documents.* Paris, 1983.

165 Hasnawi, Ahmad. "Fārābī et la pratique de l'exégèse philosophique: Remarques sur son commentaire au De interpretatione d'Aristote." *Revue de synthèse* 106 (1985): 27–59.

166 Endress, Gerhard. "Grammatik und Logik: Arabische Philologie und griechische Philosophie im Widerstreit." In *Sprachphilosophie in Antike und Mittelalter.* Ed. by Burkhard Mojsisch. Amsterdam, 1986, 163–299.

167 Druart, Thérèse-Anne. "Substance in Arabic Philosophy: Al-Farabi's Discussion." In *The Metaphysics of Substance.* Ed. by Daniel O. Dahlstrom. Washington, 1987, 88–97.

168 Eskenasy, Pauline E. "Al-Fārābī's Classification of the Parts of Speech." *Jerusalem Studies in Arabic and Islam* 11 (1988): 55–82.

169 Hasnaoui, Ahmad. "Les théories du langage dans la pensée arabo-musulmane." In *Aristote aujourd'hui: Études réunies sous la direction de M. A. Sinaceur à l'occasion du 2300e anniversaire de la mort du philosophe.* Paris, 1988, 218–240.

170 Black, Deborah L. *Logic and Aristotle's Rhetoric and Poetics in Medieval Arabic Philosophy.* Leiden, 1990.

171 Abed, Shukri B. *Aristotelian Logic and the Arabic Language in Alfārābī.* New York, 1991.

172 Würsch, Renate. *Avicennas Bearbeitungen der aristotelischen Rhetorik: Ein Beitrag zum Fortleben antiken Bildungsgutes in der islamischen Welt.* Berlin, 1991.

173 Aouad, Maroun. "Les fondements de la rhétorique d'Aristote reconsidérés par Fārābī, ou le concept de point de vue immédiat et commun." *Arabic Sciences and Philosophy* 2 (1992): 133–180.

174 Gutas, Dimitri. "Aspects of Literary Form and Genre in Arabic Logical Works." In *Glosses and Commentaries on Aristotelian Logical Texts. The Syriac, Arabic and Medieval Latin Traditions*. Ed. by Charles Burnett. London, 1993, 29–76.

175 Lameer, Joep. *Al-Fārābī and Aristotelian Syllogistics: Greek Theory and Islamic Practice*. Leiden, 1994.

176 Langhade, Jacques. *Du Coran à la philosophie: La langue arabe et la formation du vocabulaire philosophique de Farabi*. Damascus, 1994.

177 Schneider, Jakob Hans Josef. "Al-Farabis Kommentar zu 'De interpretatione' des Aristoteles: Ein Beitrag zur Entwicklung der Sprachphilosophie im Mittelalter." In *Scientia und ars im Hoch- und Spätmittelalter*. Ed. by Ingrid Craemer-Ruegenberg and Andreas Speer. Berlin, New York, 1994, 687–738.

178 Zonta, Mauro. "Al-Fārābī's Commentaries on Artistotelian Logic: New Discoveries." In *Philosophy and Arts in the Islamic World: Proceedings of the Eighteenth Congress of the Union européenne des arabisants et islamisants held at the Katholieke Universiteit Leuven, September 3 – September 9, 1996*. Ed. by Urbain Vermeulen and Daniel De Smet. Leuven, 1998, 219–232.

179 Aouad, Maroun and Gregor Schoeler. "Le syllogisme poétique selon al-Fārābī: Un syllogisme incorrect de la deuxième figure." *Arabic Sciences and Philosophy* 12 (2002): 185–196.

180 Street, Tony. "Arabic Logic." In *Handbook of the History of Logic*, vol. 1. Ed. by Dov M. Gabbay and John Woods. Elsevier, 2004, 523–596.

181 Diebler, Stéphane. "Catégories, conversation et philosophie chez al-Fārābī." In *Les Catégories et leur histoire*. Ed. by Otto Bruun and Lorenzo Corti. Paris, 2005, 275–305.

182 Schoeler, Gregor. "Poetischer Syllogismus – Bildliche Redeweise – Religion: Vom aristotelischen Organon zu al-Fārābīs Religionstheorie." In *Logik und Theologie: Das Organon im arabischen und im lateinischen Mittelalter*. Ed. by Dominik Perler and Ulrich Rudolph. Leiden, Boston, 2005, 45–58.

183 Adamson, Peter. "The Arabic Sea Battle: Al-Fārābī on the Problem of Future Contingents." *Archiv für Geschichte der Philosophie* 88 (2006): 163–188.

184 Black, Deborah L. "Knowledge (*ʿilm*) and Certitude (*yaqīn*) in al-Fārābī's Epistemology." *Arabic Sciences and Philosophy* 16 (2006): 11–45.

185 Larcher, Pierre. "Un texte d'al-Fārābī sur la 'langue arabe' réécrit?" In *Grammar as a Window onto Arabic Humanism: A Collection of Articles in Honour of Michael G. Carter*. Ed. by Lutz Edzard and Janet Watson. Wiesbaden, 2006, 108–129.

186 Schöck, Cornelia. *Koranexegese, Grammatik und Logik: Zum Verhältnis von arabischer und aristotelischer Urteils-, Konsequenz- und Schlusslehre*. Leiden, 2006.

187 Zonta, Mauro. "Al-Fārābī's Long Commentary on Aristotle's *Categoriae* in Hebrew and Arabic: A Critical Edition and English Translation of the Newly-found Extant Fragments." In *Studies in Arabic and Islamic Culture*, vol. 2. Ed. by Binyamin Abrahamov. Ramat-Gan, 2006, 185–254.

188 Aouad, Maroun. "Les lois selon les *Didascalia in Rethoricam* (*sic*) *Aristotelis* ex glosa Alpharabii." *Mélanges de l'Université de Saint-Joseph* 61 (2008): 453–470.

189 Black, Deborah L. "Al-Fārābī on Meno's Paradox." In P. Adamson 2008 [*53: 15–34].

190 van Gelder, Geert Jan and Marlé Hammond, eds. *Takhyīl: The Imaginary in Classical Arabic Poetics,* vol. 1: *Texts:* Selected, translated and annotated by G. J. van Gelder, M. Hammond, intr. Wolfhart Heinrichs, pref. Anne Sheppard; vol. 2: *Studies*. Cambridge, 2008.

191 Thom, Paul. "Al-Fārābī on Indefinite and Private Names." *Arabic Sciences and Philosophy* 18 (2008): 193–209.

192 Vallat, Philippe. "Du possible au nécessaire: La connaissance de l'universel selon Farabi." *Documenti e studi sulla tradizione filosofica medievale* 19 (2008): 89–121.

193 Woerther, Frédérique. "L'interprétation de l'ēthos aristotélicien par al-Fārābī." *Rhetorica* 26 (2008): 392–416.

194 Aouad, Maroun. "Al-Fārābī critique des traditions non aristotéliciennes de la rhétorique." In *Literary and Philosophical Rhetoric in the Greek, Roman, Syriac, and Arabic Worlds*. Ed. by Frédérique Woerther. Hildesheim, 2009, 155–183.

195 Woerther, Frédérique. "The philosophical rhetoric, between dialectics and politics: Aristotle, Hermagoras, and al-Fārābī." In F. Woerther 2009 [cf. *194], 55–72.

196 Schoeler, Gregor. "The 'Poetic Syllogism' Revisited." *Oriens* 41 (2013): 1–26.

197 Karimullah, Kamran. "Alfarabi on Conditionals." *Arabic Sciences and Philosophy* 24 (2014): 211–267.

198 Woerther, Frédérique. "Al-Fārābī and the *Didascalia*." In *Aristotle and the Arabic Tradition*. Ed. by Ahmed Alwishah and Josh Hayes. Cambridge, 2015, 92–104.

5.7 *Mathematics*

205 Kubesov, Audanbek and Boris Rosenfeld. "On the Geometrical Treatise of al-Farabi." *Archives internationales d'histoire des sciences* 22 (1969): 50.

206 Druart, Thérèse-Anne. "Astronomie et astrologie selon Fārābī." *Bulletin de philosophie médiévale* 20 (1978): 43–47.

207 Druart, Thérèse-Anne. "Le second traité de Fārābī sur la validité des affirmations basées sur la position des étoiles." *Bulletin de philosophie médiévale* 21 (1979): 47–51.

208 Shamsi, Fazal Ahmad. "Al-Fārābī's Treatise on Certain Obscurities in Books I and V of Euclid's Elements." *Journal for the History of Arabic Science* 8 (1984): 31–58.

209 Freudenthal, Gad. "La philosophie de la géométrie d'al-Fārābī: Son commentaire sur le début du Ier et le début du Ve livre des Eléments d'Euclide." *Jerusalem Studies in Arabic and Islam* 11 (1988): 104–219.

210 Freudenthal, Gad. "Al-Fārābī on the Foundations of Geometry." In *Knowledge and the Sciences in Medieval Philosophy: Proceedings of the Eight International Congress of Medieval Philosophy (S.I.E.P.M), Helsinki 24–29 August 1987*, vol. 3. Ed. by Monika Asztalos, John E. Murdoch and Ilkka Niiniluoto. Helsinki, 1990, 52–61. – Repr. in: G. Freudenthal, *Science in the Medieval Hebrew and Arabic Traditions*. Aldershot, 2005, no. X.

211 Neubauer, Eckhard. "Die Theorie vom *īqāʿ*, I: Übersetzung des *Kitāb al-Īqāʿāt* von Abū Naṣr al-Fārābī; Anhang: Faksimile der Handschrift des *Kitāb al-īqāʿāt*." In E. Neubauer, *Arabische Musiktheorie von den Anfängen bis zum 6./12. Jahrhundert:* Studien, Übersetzungen und Texte in Faksimile. Frankfurt a.M., 1998, 128–184. – First published, without appendix, in: *Oriens* 21–22 (1968–1969): 196–232.

212 Neubauer, Eckhard. "Die Theorie vom *īqāʿ*, II: Übersetzung des *Kitāb Iḥsāʾ al-īqāʿāt* von Abū Naṣr al-Fārābī; Anhang: Faksimile der Handschrift des *Kitāb Iḥsāʾ al-īqāʿāt*." In E. Neubauer, *Arabische Musiktheorie von den Anfängen bis zum 6./12. Jahrhundert*: Studien, Übersetzungen und Texte in Faksimile. Frankfurt a.M., 1998, 185–310. – First published, without appendix, in: *Oriens* 34 (1994): 103–173.

213 Abramovič Rozenfel'd [Rosenfeld], Boris and Ekmeleddin İhsanoğlu. *Mathematicians, Astronomers, and Other Scholars of Islamic Civilization and Their Works (7th–19th c.)*. MAO. Istanbul, 2003.

214 Dhanani, Alnoor. "Fārābī: Abū Nasr Muhammad ibn Muhammd ibn Tarkhān al-Fārābī." In *The Biographical Encyclopedia of Astronomers: Springer Reference*. Ed. by Thomas Hockey et al. New York, 2007, 356–357.

215 Klein, Yaron. "Imagination and Music: *Takhyīl* and the Production of Music in al-Fārābī's *Kitāb al-musīqī al-kabīr*." In G.J. van Gelder, M. Hammond 2008 [*190: 179–195].

216 Janos, Damien. "Al-Fārābī on the Method of Astronomy." *Early Science and Medicine* 15 (2010): 237–265.

217 Janos, Damien. "The Greek and the Arabic Proclus and al-Fārābī's Theory of Celestial Intellection and Its Relation to Creation." *Documenti e studi sulla tradizione filosofica medievale* 21 (2010): 19–44.

218 Thomann, Johannes. "Ein al-Fārābī zugeschriebener Kommentar zum Almagest (Hs. Tehran Mağlis 6531)." *Zeitschrift für Geschichte der Arabisch-Islamischen Wissenschaften* 19 (2010–2011): 35–76.

219 Janos, Damien. *Method, Structure, and Development in al-Fārābī's Cosmology*. Leiden, 2012.

220 Thomann, Johannes. "From Lyrics by al-Fazārī to Lectures by al-Fārābī: Teaching Astronomy in Baghdād (750–1000 C.E.)." In *The Place to Go: Contexts of Learning in Baghdād, 750–1000 C.E.* Ed. by Jens Scheiner and Damien Janos. Princeton, 2014, 503–525.

221 Thomann, Johannes. "Al-Fārābīs Kommentar zum Almagest in sekundärer Überlieferung bei Ibn al-Ṣalāḥ: Ein vorläufiger Bericht." *Asiatische Studien* 69 (2015): 99–113.

5.8 *Physics*

235 Wiedemann, Eilhard. "Zur Alchemie bei den Arabern." *Journal für praktische Chemie*, Neue Folge 76 (1907): 65–87. 105–123.

236 Birkenmajer, Alexander. "Eine wiedergefundene Übersetzung Gerhards von Cremona." In *Aus der Geisteswelt des Mittelalters: Studien und Texte Martin Grabmann zur Vollendung des 60. Lebensjahres von Freunden und Schülern gewidmet*, 1. Halbband. Münster, 1935, 472–481. – Repr. Frankfurt a.M., 1999 [Islamic Philosophy, 8], 384–393.

237 Lugal, Necati and Aydın Sayılı. *Ebû Nasr il-Fârâbî'nin halâ üzerine makalesi* [Engl. title: *Fârâbî's Article on Vacuum*]. Ankara, 1951. – Contains 36 p. [Turk. and Engl.], 8 p. [facsimile], 16 p. [Arab.]. – Repr. Frankfurt a.M., 1999 [Islamic Philosophy, 11], 1–64.

238 Lugal, Necati and Aydın Sayılı. "Fârâbî'nin tabiat ilminin kökleri hakkında yüksek makaleler kitabı." *Belleten* 15 (1951): 83–122. – Repr. Frankfurt a.M., 1999 [Islamic Philosophy, 11], 117–156.

239 Sayılı, Aydın. "Fârâbî'nin halâ hakkında risâlesi." *Belleten* 15 (1951): 123–174. – Turk. and Engl. – Repr. Frankfurt a.M., 1999 [Islamic Philosophy, 11], 65–116.

240 Sayılı, Aydın. "Fârâbî'nin simyanın lüzûmu hakkında risâlesi." *Belleten* 15 (1951): 65–79.

241 Walzer, Richard. "Al-Fārābī's Theory of Prophecy and Divination." *Journal of Hellenic Studies* 77 (1957): 142–148. – Repr. in R. Walzer 1962 [*22: 206–219]; Frankfurt a.M., 1999 [Islamic Philosophy, 11], 330–336.

242 Bürgel, Johann Christoph. "Averroes 'contra Galenum': Das Kapitel von der Atmung im Colliget des Averroes als ein Zeugnis mittelalterlich-islamischer Kritik an Galen, eingeleitet, arabisch herausgegeben und übersetzt." *Nachrichten der Akademie der Wissenschaften in Göttingen: Philologisch-historische Klasse* (Göttingen 1968): 263–340.

243 Mahdi, Muhsin. "Alfarabi Against Philoponus." *Journal of Near Eastern Studies* 26 (1967): 233–260.

244 Mahdi, Muhsin. "The Arabic Text of Alfarabi's *Against John the Grammarian*." In *Medieval and Middle Eastern Studies in Honor of Aziz Suryal Atiya*. Ed. by Sami A. Hanna. Leiden, 1972, 268–284.

245 Plessner, Martin. "Al-Fārābī's Introduction to the Study of Medicine." In *Islamic Philosophy and the Classical Tradition: Essays presented … to Richard Walzer on his seventieth birthday*. Ed. by Samuel Miklos Stern, Albert Hourani and Vivian Brown. Oxford, 1972, 307–314.

246 Zimmermann, Friedrich W. "Al-Farabi und die philosophische Kritik an Galen von Alexander zu Averroes." In *Akten des VII. Kongresses für Arabistik und Islamwissenschaft, Göttingen 1974*. Ed. by Albert Dietrich. Göttingen, 1976, 401–414.

247 Jolivet, Jean. "L'intellect selon al-Fārābī: Quelques remarques." *Bulletin d'études orientales* 29 (1977): 252–259. – Repr. in: J. Jolivet, *Philosophie médiévale arabe et latine*. Paris, 1995, 211–220.

248 Daiber, Hans. "Fārābīs Abhandlung über das Vakuum: Quellen und Stellung in der islamischen Wissenschaftsgeschichte." *Der Islam* 60 (1983): 37–47.

249 Strohmaier, Gotthard. "Al-Fārābī über die verschollene Schrift 'Über Gesundheit und Krankheit' und über die Stellung der Medizin im System der Wissenschaften." In *Aristoteles als Wissenschaftstheoretiker*. Ed. by Johannes Irmscher and Reimar Müller. Berlin, 1983, 202–205. – Repr. in G. Strohmaier 1996 [cf. *136], 34–37.

250 Davidson, Herbert Alan. *Alfarabi, Avicenna, and Averroes, on Intellect: Their Cosmologies, Theories of the Active Intellect, and Theories of Human Intellect*. New York, Oxford, 1992.

251 Lettinck, Paul. *Aristotle's Physics and Its Reception in the Arabic World: With an Edition of the Unpublished Parts of Ibn Bājja's Commentary on the Physics*. Leiden, New York, Cologne, 1994.

252 Jolivet, Jean. "Étapes dans l'histoire de l'intellect agent." In *Perspectives arabes et médiévales sur la tradition scientifique et philosophique grecque: Actes du colloque de la SIHSPAI (Société internationale d'histoire des sciences et de la philosophie arabes et islamiques), Paris, 31 mars – 3 avril 1993*. Ed. by Ahmad Hasnawi, Abdelali Elamrani-Jamal, and Maroun Aouad. Leuven, Paris, 1997, 569–582.

253 Geoffroy, Marc. "La tradition arabe du Περὶ νοῦ d'Alexandre d'Aphrodise et les origines de la théorie farabienne des quatre degrés de l'intellect." In *Aristotele e Alessandro di Afrodisia nella tradizione araba: Atti del colloquio La ricezione araba ed ebraica della filosofia e della scienza greche, Padova 14–15 maggio 1999*. Ed. by Cristina D'Ancona and Giuseppe Serra. Padova, 2002, 191–231.

254 Rashed, Marwan. "Al-Fārābī's lost treatise *On Changing Beings* and the Possibility of a Demonstration of the Eternity of the World." *Arabic Sciences and Philosophy* 18 (2008): 19–58.

255 Richter-Bernburg, Lutz. "Abū Bakr al-Rāzī and al-Fārābī on Medicine and Authority." In P. Adamson 2008 [*53: 119–130].

256 Vallat, Philippe. *Al-Fārābī, Épître sur l'intellect : Introduction, traduction et commentaires, suivis de Onto-noétique : L'intellect et les intellects chez Fārābī*. Paris, 2012.

257 Streetman, W. Craig. "Al-Fārābī: Legitimate 'Second Teacher' after Aristotle on Matters Relating to the Intellect." *Documenti e studi sulla tradizione filosofica medievale* 25 (2014): 85–129.

5.9 *Metaphysics*

270 Mushtak, Hazim T. *Al-Fārābī's Risāla on the One and the Many:* First edition, English translation and notes. B. L. Thesis, University of Oxford, 1960.

271 Frank, Richard M. "Reason and Revealed Law: A Sample of Parallels and Divergences in Kalâm and Falsafa." In *Recherches d'islamologie: Recueil d'articles offert à Georges C. Anawati et Louis Gardet*. Louvain, 1977, 123–138.

272 Druart, Thérèse-Anne. "Al-Fārābī's Causation of the Heavenly Bodies." In *Islamic Philosophy and Mysticism*. Ed. by Parviz Morewedge. Delmar, New York, 1981, 35–45.

273 Pines, Shlomo. "Les limites de la métaphysique selon al-Fārābī, Ibn Bājja et Maïmonide: Sources et antithèses de ces doctrines chez Alexandre d'Aphrodise et chez Thémistius." In *Sprache und Erkenntnis im Mittelalter: Akten des VI. internationalen Kongresses für mittelalterliche Philosophie der Société internationale pour l'étude de la philosophie médiévale, 29. August – 3. September 1977 in Bonn,* 1. Halbband. Ed. by Jan P. Beckmann et al. Berlin, 1981, 211–225. – Engl.: "The Limitations of Human Knowledge According to al-Farabi, Ibn Bajja, and Maimonides." In *Studies in Medieval Jewish History and Literature*. Ed. by Isadore Twersky. Cambridge, Mass.; London, 1979, 82–109.

274 Druart, Thérèse-Anne. "Le traité d'al-Fārābī sur les buts de la Métaphysique d'Aristote." *Bulletin de philosophie médiévale* 24 (1982): 38–43.

275 Ramón Guerrero, Rafael. "Al-Fārābi y la 'Metafisica' di Aristoteles." *La Ciudad de Dios* 196 (1982): 211–240.

276 Walzer, Richard. *Al-Farabi on the Perfect State: Abū Naṣr al-Fārābī's Mabādi' ārā' ahl al-madīna al-fāḍila*. A Revised Text with Introduction, Translation, and Commentary. Oxford, 1985. – Repr. 1998.

277 Druart, Thérèse-Anne. "Al-Farabi and Emanationism." In *Studies in Medieval Philosophy*. Ed. by John F. Wippel. Washington, 1987, 23–43.

278 Maróth, Miklós. "The Ten Intellects Cosmology and Its Origin." In *Proceedings of the 14th Congress of the Union européenne des arabisants et islamisants, Budapest, 29th August – 3rd September 1988,* vol. 1. Ed. by Alexander Fodor. Budapest, 1995, 103–111.

279 Genequand, Charles. "Vers une nouvelle édition de la *Maqāla fī mabādi' al-kull* d'Alexandre d'Aphrodise." In A. Hasnawi, A. Elamrani-Jamal, M. Aouad 1997 [cf. *252], 271–276.

280 Genequand, Charles. *Alexander of Aphrodisias on the Cosmos*. Leiden, Boston, Cologne, 2001.

281 Bertolacci, Amos. "Ammonius and al-Fārābī: The Sources of Avicenna's Concept of Metaphysics." *Quaestio* 5 (2005): 287–305.

282 Druart, Thérèse-Anne. "Al-Fārābī, the Categories, Metaphysics, and the Book of Letters." *Medioevo* 32 (2007): 15–37.

283 Rudolph, Ulrich. "Al-Fārābī und die Muʿtazila." In *A Common Rationality: Muʿtazilism in Islam and Judaism*. Ed. by Camilla Adang, Sabine Schmidtke, and David Sklare. Würzburg, 2007, 59–80.

284 Menn, Stephen. "Al-Fārābī's *Kitāb al-Ḥurūf* and his Analysis of the Senses of Being." *Arabic Sciences and Philosophy* 18 (2008): 59–97.

285 Rudolph, Ulrich. "Reflections on al-Fārābī's *Mabādiʾ ārāʾ ahl al-madīna al-fāḍila*." In P. Adamson 2008 [*53: 1–14].

286 Brague, Rémi. "La philosophie contre le 'kalâm'." In *Philosophie et théologie au moyen âge: Anthologie*, vol. 2. Ed. by Olivier Boulnois. Paris, 2009, 63–74.

287 Vallat, Philippe. "Al-Fārābī's Arguments for the Eternity of the World and the Contingency of Natural Phenomena." In *Interpreting the Bible and Aristotle in Late Antiquity: The Alexandrian Commentary Tradition between Rome and Baghdad*. Ed. by Josef Lössl and John W. Watt. Farnham, Surrey, 2011, 259–323.

288 Wain, Alexander. "A Critical Study of the *Mabādiʾ ārāʾ ahl al-madīna al-fāḍila:* The Role of Islam in the Philosophy of Abū Naṣr al-Fārābī." *Journal of Islamic Philosophy* 8 (2012): 45–78.

5.10 *Ethics and Politics*

300 Strauss, Leo. *Persecution and the Art of Writing*. Glencoe, 1952. – Repr. Westport, 1973; Chicago, 1980.

301 Rosenthal, Erwin I. J. "The Place of Politics in the Philosophy of al-Farabi." *Islamic Culture* 29 (1955): 157–178. – Repr. Frankfurt a.M., 1999 [Islamic Philosophy, 10], 399–420.

302 Najjar, Fauzi M. "Al-Fārābī on Political Science." *The Muslim World* 48 (1958): 94–103. – Repr. Frankfurt a.M., 1999 [Islamic Philosophy, 11], 362–371.

303 Rosenthal, Erwin I. J. *Political Thought in Medieval Islam: An Introductory Outline*. Westport, 1958, 1968 (2nd ed.), 1985 (3rd ed.).

304 Mahdi, Muhsin. "The Editio Princeps of Fārābī's *Compendium legum Platonis*." *Journal of Near Eastern Studies* 20 (1961): 1–24.

305 Najjar, Fauzi M. "Farabi's Political Philosophy and Shi'ism." *Studia Islamica* 14 (1961): 57–72.

306 Mahdi, Muhsin. "Alfarabi." In *History of Political Philosophy*. Ed. by Leo Strauss and Joseph Cropsey. Chicago, 1963, 160–180. – Revised version in M. Mahdi 2001 [*328: 125–146].

307 Rosenthal, Erwin I. J. "Some Observations on al-Fārābī's 'Kitāb al-Milla'." In *Études philosophiques offertes au Dr. Ibrahim Madkour*. Ed. by Osman Amine. Cairo, 1974, 65–74.

308 Pines, Shlomo. "Aristotle's *Politics* in Arabic Philosophy." *Israel Oriental Studies* 5 (1975): 150–160. – Repr. in: S. Pines, *The Collected Works of Shlomo Pines*, vol. 2: *Studies in Arabic Versions of Greek Texts and in Mediaeval Science*. Leiden, 1986, 146–156; also in: S. Pines, *The Collected Works of Shlomo Pines*, vol. 3: *Studies in the History of Arabic Philosophy*. Jerusalem, 1996, 251–261.

309 Maróth, Miklós. "Griechische Theorie und orientalische Praxis in der Staatskunst von al-Fārābī." *Acta antiqua Academiae Scientiarum Hungaricae* 26 (1978): 465–469.

310 Daiber, Hans. "Prophetie und Ethik bei Fārābī (gest. 339/950)." In *L'homme et son univers au moyen âge*, vol. 2. Ed. by Ch. Wenin. Louvain-la-Neuve, 1986, 729–753.

311 Kraemer, Joel L. "The Jihād of the Falāsifa." *Jerusalem Studies in Arabic and Islam* 10 (1987): 288–324.

312 Alon, Ilai. "Fārābī's Funny Flora: al-Nawābit as 'Opposition'." *Arabica* 37 (1990): 56–90.

313 Galston, Miriam. *Politics and Excellence: The Political Philosophy of Alfarabi*. Princeton, 1990.

314 Mahdi, Muhsin. "Al-Fārābī's Imperfect State." *Journal of the American Oriental Society* 110 (1990): 691–726.

315 Butterworth, Charles E. "Al-Fārābī's Statecraft: War and the Well-Ordered Regime." In *Cross, Crescent and Sword: The Justification and Limitation of War in Western and Islamic Tradition*. Ed. by James T. Johnson and John Kelsay. New York, 1991, 79–100.

316 Daiber, Hans. "The Ismaili Background of Fārābī's Political Philosophy: Abū Ḥātim ar-Rāzī as a Forerunner of Fārābī." In U. Tworuschka 1991 [cf. *36], 143–150.

317 Mahdi, Muhsin. "Philosophy and Political Thought: Reflections and Comparisons." *Arabic Sciences and Philosophy* 1 (1991): 9–29. – Revised version in M. Mahdi 2001 [*328: 29–46].

318 Galston, Miriam. "The Theoretical and Practical Dimensions of Happiness as Portrayed in the Political Treatises of al-Fārābī." In *The Political Aspects of Islamic Philosophy: Essays in Honor of Muhsin S. Mahdi*. Ed. by Charles E. Butterworth. Cambridge, Mass., 1992, 95–151.

319 Parens, Joshua. *Metaphysics as Rhetoric: Alfarabi's Summary of Plato's 'Laws'*. Albany, 1995.

320 Druart, Thérèse-Anne. "Al-Fārābī, Ethics, and First Intelligibles." *Documenti e studi sulla tradizione filosofica medievale* 8 (1997): 403–423.

321 Gutas, Dimitri. "Galen's Synopsis of Plato's *Laws* and Fārābī's *Talḫīṣ*." In *The Ancient Tradition in Christian and Islamic Hellenism: Studies on the Transmission of Greek Philosophy and Sciences, Dedicated to H. J. Drossaart Lulofs on His*

Ninetieth Birthday. Ed. by Remke Kruk and Gerhard Endress. Leiden, 1997, 101–119. – Repr. in D. Gutas 2000 [cf. *30], no. v.

322 Lameer, Joep. "The Philosopher and the Prophet: Greek Parallels to al-Fārābī's Theory of Religion and Philosophy in the State." In A. Hasnawi, A. Elamrani-Jamal, M. Aouad 1997 [cf. *252], 609–622.

323 Mahdi, Muhsin. "Remarks on Alfarabi's Book of Religion." In A. Hasnawi, A. Elamrani-Jamal, M. Aouad 1997 [cf. *252], 583–608.

324 Druart, Thérèse-Anne. "Le sommaire du livre des Lois de Platon (*Ǧawāmiʿ Kitāb al-Nawāmīs li-Aflāṭūn*) par Abū Naṣr al-Fārābī: Édition critique et introduction." *Bulletin d'études orientales* 50 (1998): 109–155.

325 Gutas, Dimitri. "Fārābī's Knowledge of Plato's *Laws*." *International Journal of the Classical Tradition* 4, no. 3 (1998): 405–411.

326 Griffel, Frank. *Apostasie und Toleranz im Islam: Die Entwicklung zu al-Ġazālīs Urteil gegen die Philosophie und die Reaktionen der Philosophen*. Leiden, Boston, Cologne, 2000.

327 Brague, Rémi. "Der Dschihad der Philosophen." In *Krieg im Mittelalter*. Ed. by Hans-Henning Kortüm. Berlin, 2001, 77–91.

328 Mahdi, Muhsin. *Alfarabi and the Foundation of Islamic Political Philosophy*. Chicago, London, 2001. – French transl.: *La cité vertueuse d'Alfarabi: La fondation de la philosophie politique en islam*. Paris, 2000.

329 Tamer, Georges. *Islamische Philosophie und die Krise der Moderne: Das Verhältnis von Leo Strauss zu Alfarabi, Avicenna und Averroes*. Leiden, 2001.

330 Gutas, Dimitri. "The Study of Arabic Philosophy in the Twentieth Century: An Essay on the Historiography of Arabic Philosophy." *British Journal of Middle Eastern Studies* 29 (2002): 5–25.

331 O'Meara, Dominic J. "Religion als Abbild der Philosophie: Zum neuplatonischen Hintergrund der Lehre al-Farabis." In *Metaphysik und Religion: Zur Signatur des spätantiken Denkens: Akten des Internationalen Kongresses vom 13.-17. März 2001 in Würzburg*. Ed. by Theo Kobusch and Michael Erler. Munich, Leipzig, 2002, 343–353.

332 Harvey, Steven. "Did Alfarabi read Plato's *Laws*?" *Medioevo* 28 (2003): 51–68.

333 O'Meara, Dominic J. *Platonopolis: Platonic Political Philosophy in Late Antiquity*. Oxford, 2003.

334 Crone, Patricia. "Al-Fārābī's Imperfect Constitutions." *Mélanges de l'Université Saint-Joseph* 57 (2004): 191–228.

335 Flashar, Hellmut. "Aristoteles." In *Grundriss der Geschichte der Philosophie: Die Philosophie der Antike*, vol. 3: *Ältere Akademie – Aristoteles – Peripatos*. Ed. by H. Flashar. Basel, 2004 (2nd ed.), 167–492.

336 Gutas, Dimitri. "The Meaning of *madanī* in al-Fārābī's 'Political' Philosophy." *Mélanges de l'Université Saint-Joseph* 57 (2004): 259–282.

337 Reisman, David C. "Plato's Republic in Arabic: A Newly Discovered Passage." *Arabic Sciences and Philosophy* 14 (2004): 263–300.

338 Colmo, Christopher A. *Breaking with Athens: Alfarabi as Founder*. Lanham, 2005.

339 Parens, Joshua. *An Islamic Philosophy of Virtuous Religions: Introducing Alfarabi*. New York, 2006.

340 Butterworth, Charles E. "What Might We Learn from al-Fārābī about Plato and Aristotle with Respect to Lawgiving?" *Mélanges de l'Université Saint-Joseph* 61 (2008): 471–489.

341 Genequand, Charles. "Loi morale, loi politique: Al-Fārābī et Ibn Bāǧǧa." *Mélanges de l'Université Saint-Joseph* 61 (2008): 491–514.

341a Hansberger, Rotraud. "How Aristotle Came to Believe in God-given Dreams: The Arabic Version of *De divination per somnum*." In *Dreaming Across Boundaries: The Interpretation of Dreams in Islamic Lands*. Ed. by Louise Marlow. Cambridge, Mass., 2008, 50–77.

342 Heck, Paul L. "Doubts about the Religious Community (*milla*) in al-Fārābī and the Brethren of Purity." In P. Adamson 2008 [*53: 195–213].

343 Streetman, W. Craig. "'If it Were God Who Sent them ...': Aristotle and al-Fārābī on Prophetic Vision." *Arabic Sciences and Philosophy* 18 (2008): 211–246.

344 Vallat, Philippe. "Vrai philosophe et faux prophète selon Fārābī: Aspects historiques et théoriques de l'art du symbole." In *Miroir et savoir: La transmission d'un thème platonicien, des Alexandrins à la philosophie arabo-musulmane: Actes du colloque international tenu à Leuven et Louvain-la-Neuve, les 17 et 18 novembre 2005*. Ed by Daniel De Smet, Meryem Sebti, and Godefroid de Callataÿ. Leuven, 2008, 117–143.

345 Kraemer, Joel L. "The Medieval Arabic Enlightenment." In *The Cambridge Companion to Leo Strauss*. Ed by Steven B. Smith. Cambridge, 2009, 137–170.

346 Vallat, Philippe. *Al-Fārābī, Le livre du régime politique*. Introduction, traduction et commentaires. Paris, 2012.

347 Neria, Chaim Meir. "Al-Fārābī's Lost Commentary on the Ethics: New Textual Evidence." *Arabic Sciences and Philosophy* 23 (2013): 69–99.

348 Arfa, Mokdad. "La connaissance vraie comme cause possible de souffrance perpétuelle chez al-Fārābī." In *The Pleasure of Knowledge = Quaestio* 15 (2015). Ed. by Pasquale Porro and Loris Sturlese. Turnhout, Bari, 2015, 223–234.

349 Al-ʿAyyādī, D. Sālim (Ayadi, Salem). *Siyāsat al-ḥaqīqa fī falsafat al-Fārābī: Al-Mītāfīzīqā wa-l-mūsīqā*. Sfax, 2016.

CHAPTER 9

The Dissemination of Philosophical Thought

1 Popular Ethics, Practical Politics – 2 Scholars as Transmitters of Philosophical Thought – 3 Philosophy and Natural Science – 4 The Religious Application of Philosophical Ideas – 5 Secondary Literature

1 Popular Ethics, Practical Politics

Dimitri Gutas

1.1 Primary Sources – 1.2 Introduction – 1.3 Gnomologia – 1.4 Doxographies – 1.5 Mirrors for Princes – 1.6 *Liber de Pomo*

1.1 *Primary Sources*

1.1.1 Sources on History and Transmission [*1–*2] – 1.1.2 Gnomologia, Doxographies, Mirrors for Princes [*6–*32] – 1.1.3 Pseudepigraphic Collections [*35–*36] – 1.1.4 *Liber de Pomo* [*51–*71]

1.1.1 Sources on History and Transmission

1 Ibn al-Nadīm, Abū l-Farağ Muḥammad b. Isḥāq (d. 380/990). *Kitāb al-Fihrist* [composed 377/988]. – Ed. by Gustav Flügel, August Müller and Johannes Roediger, 2 vols. Leipzig, 1871–1872 (ed. quoted below). – Repr. Beirut, 1964, Frankfurt a.M. 2005. – Ed. by Riḍā Tağaddud. Tehran, 1350 h.š./1971. – Ed. by Ayman Fu'ād Sayyid, 2 vols. London, 1430/2009. – Engl. transl. by Bayard Dodge, *The Fihrist of al-Nadīm*, 2 vols. New York, 1970.

2 Ibn Abī Uṣaybiʿa, Muwaffaq al-Dīn Aḥmad b. al-Qāsim (d. 668/1270). *ʿUyūn al-anbāʾ fī ṭabaqāt al-aṭibbāʾ*. – Ed. by August Müller, 2 vols. Cairo, 1299/1882. Königsberg, 1884. – Repr. Westmead, 1972.

1.1.2 Gnomologia, Doxographies, Mirrors for Princes

6 Menander. *Monostichoi*. – Ed. by Manfred Ullmann, *Die arabische Überlieferung der sogenannten Menandersentenzen*. Wiesbaden, 1961.

7 Pseudo-Plutarch. *Placita philosophorum*. – Ed. by Hans Daiber, *Aetius Arabus: Die Vorsokratiker in arabischer Überlieferung*. Wiesbaden, 1980.

 | DOI 10.1163/9789004323162_011

8 Cebes. *Tabula*. – Ed. by ʿAbd al-Raḥmān Badawī, *Miskawaih: al-Ḥikma al-ḫālida*. Cairo, 1952, 229–262. – Cf. the commentary by Abū l-Farağ [*28].

9 Porphyry. "Philosophos historia: Fragments." In *Porphyrii philosophi fragmenta*. Ed. by Andrew Smith and David Wasserstein. Stuttgart, Leipzig, 1993.

10 *ʿAhd Ardašīr*. – Ed. by Iḥsān ʿAbbās. Beirut, 1967.

11 Boyce, Mary. *The Letter of Tansar*. Rome, 1968.

12 Pseudo-Ǧāḥiz. *Kitāb al-Tāğ fī aḫlāq al-mulūk*. – Ed. by Aḥmad Zakī Bāšā. Cairo, 1914. – French transl. by Charles Pellat, *Le livre de la couronne*. Paris, 1954.

13 Grignaschi, Mario. "Quelques spécimens de la littérature sassanide conservés dans les bibliothèques d'Istanbul." *Journal asiatique* 254 (1966): 1–142.

14 Pseudo-Maximus Confessor. *Loci communes: Erste kritische Edition einer Redaktion des sacro-profanen Florilegiums Loci communes*. Ed. by Sibylle Ihm. Stuttgart, 2001.

15 al-Rayḥānī, ʿAlī b. ʿUbayda. *Ǧawāhir al-kilam wa-farāʾid al-ḥikam*. – Ed. and transl. by Mohsen Zakeri, *Persian Wisdom in Arabic Garb: ʿAlī b. ʿUbayda al-Rayḥānī (d. 219/834) and His Jawāhir al-kilam wa-farāʾid al-ḥikam*, 2 vols. Leiden, 2007.

16 Ḥunayn b. Isḥāq. *Ādāb al-falāsifa: iḫtaṣarahu Muḥammad b. ʿAlī b. Ibrāhīm b. Aḥmad b. Muḥammad al-Anṣārī*. – Ed. by ʿAbd al-Raḥmān Badawī. Kuwait, 1406/1985. – Medieval Hebrew transl. by al-Ḫarīzī (Ḫarizi). *Sefer musre ha-filosofim*. – Ed. by Albert Loewenthal. Frankfurt a.M., 1896. – German transl. by Albert Loewenthal, *Honein Ibn Ishāk, Sinnsprüche der Philosophen*. Berlin, 1896. – Medieval Span. transl.: ed. by Hermann Knust, "Libro de los buenos proverbio." *Mittheilungen aus dem Eskurial, Bibliothek des Litterarischen Vereins in Stuttgart* 141 (1879): 1–65. 519–536. – Ed. by Harlan Sturm, *The libro de los buenos proverbios*. Lexington, Kentucky, 1970.

17 al-Kindī. *Alfāẓ Suqrāṭ*. – Ed. by Māğid Faḫrī, "Al-Kindī wa-Suqrāṭ." *Al-Abḥāṯ* 16 (1963): 23–34. – Engl. transl. by Peter Adamson, "The Arabic Socrates: The Place of al-Kindī's Report in the Tradition." In *Images and Uses of Socrates from Antiquity to the Present*. Ed. by Michael Trapp. Aldershot, 2007, 161–178. – Engl. transl. by Peter Adamson and Peter E. Pormann, "The Sayings of Socrates." In *The Philosophical Works of Al-Kindī*. Karachi, 2012, 267–275.

18 Isḥāq b. Ḥunayn. "*Nawādir falsafiyya*: Nawādir falsafiyya tarğamahā Isḥāq b. Ḥunayn." Ed. by Ṣalāḥ al-Dīn ʿAbd Allāh, in: *Mağallat Maʿhad al-maḫṭūṭāt al-ʿarabiyya* 42, no. 2 (1998): 65–108.

19 Ibn Durayd. "*Bāb min nawādir kalām al-falāsifa*: Sayings of the Ancients from Ibn Durayd's *Kitāb al-Mujtanā*." – Ed. by Franz Rosenthal, in: *Orientalia* 27 (1958): 150–183. – Engl. transl. by F. Rosenthal, "Sayings of the Ancients: From Ibn Durayd's *Kitāb al-Mujtanā*." *Orientalia* 27 (1958) 29–54. – Repr. in: F. Rosenthal 1990 [*52: no. VII and 'Additional Notes' p. 3].

20 Ibn Abī ʿAwn. "Ǧuzʾ min ǧawābāt al-falāsifa wa-l-Ḥukamāʾ." In *al-Aǧwiba al-muskita: Das Buch der schlagfertigen Antworten von Ibn Abī ʿAwn: Ein Werk der klassisch-arabischen Adab-Literatur*. Einleitung, Edition und Quellenanalyse. Ed. by May A. Yousef. Berlin, 1988, no. 664–770. – Engl. transl. by Franz Rosenthal, "Witty Retorts of Philosophers and Sages from the *Kitāb al-Ajwibah al-muskitah* of Ibn Abī ʿAwn." *Graeco-Arabica* 4 (1991): 179–221.

21 Abū l-Ḥasan b. Abī Ḏarr [= al-ʿĀmirī?]. *Al-Saʿāda wa-l-isʿād*. – Ed. by Mojtaba Minovi. Wiesbaden, 1957–1958. – Ed. by Aḥmad ʿAbd al-Raḥīm ʿAṭiyya, *al-Fikr al-siyāsī wa-l-aḫlāqī ʿinda l-ʿĀmirī*. Cairo, 1991.

22 Pseudo-Apollonius of Tyana. *Sirr al-ḫalīqa: Buch über das Geheimnis der Schöpfung und die Darstellung der Natur (Buch der Ursachen) von Ps.-Apollonios von Tyana*. – Ed. by Ursula Weisser. Aleppo, 1979. – Partial German transl. by Ursula Weisser, *Das 'Buch über das Geheimnis der Schöpfung' von Ps.-Apollonios von Tyana*. Berlin, 1989.

23 al-Ḥātimī, Muḥammad b. al-Ḥasan. *Al-Risāla al-Ḥātimiyya*. – For manuscripts and editions cf. GAS [*3: II 488]. – German transl. by Oskar Rescher, "Die Risālet el-Ḥātimijje." *Islamica* 2 (1926): 439–473. – Study by B. Gruendler 2012 [*74].

24 *Ṣiwān al-ḥikma*: (a) *Muḫtaṣar Ṣiwān al-ḥikma*, MS Istanbul, Fatih 3222. – Text in R. Mulyadhi Kartanegara, *The Mukhtaṣar Ṣiwān al-Ḥikma of ʿUmar b. Sahlān al-Sāwī: Arabic Text and Introduction*. PhD diss., University of Chicago, 1996. – (b) *Muntaḫab Ṣiwān al-ḥikma*. Ed. ʿAbd al-Raḥmān Badawī, *Ṣiwān al-ḥikma wa-ṯalāṯ rasāʾil*. Tehran, 1974. 75–364. – Ed. by Douglas Morton Dunlop, *The Muntakhab Ṣiwān al-ḥikmah of Abū Sulaimān as-Sijistānī*. The Hague, 1979. – Review D. Gutas 1982 [*37], H. Daiber 1984 [*39]. – Study on the identity of the compiler: F. Griffel 2013 [*75]. – (c) *Muḫtār min kalām al-ḥukamāʾ al-arbaʿ al-akābir*. – Ed. by Dimitri Gutas 1975 [*28].

25 al-Tawḥīdī. *Al-Baṣāʾir wa-l-ḏaḫāʾir*. – Ed. by Wadād al-Qāḍī, 10 vols. Beirut, 1408/1988.

26 Miskawayh. *Al-Ḥikma al-ḫālida*. – Ed. by ʿAbd al-Raḥmān Badawī. Cairo, 1952.

27 Ibn Hindū. *Al-Kalim al-rūḥāniyya fī l-ḥikam al-yūnāniyya li-Abī l-Faraǧ Ibn Hindū*. – Ed. by Muṣṭafā al-Qabbānī. Cairo, 1318/1900. – Ed. by Muḥammad Ǧallūb al-Farḥān. Beirut, 2001. – Ed. by Saḥbān Ḫalīfāt, *Ibn Hindū: Sīratuhu, ārāʾuhu al-falsafiyya, muʾallafātuhu*, vol 1. ʿAmmān, 1995, 252–480, the only reliable edition.

28 Abū l-Faraǧ Ibn al-Ṭayyib. "*Tafsīr luġz Qābūs ʿalā ṭarīq al-istiṯmār*: The Symbolism of the *Tabula Cebetis* according to Abû l-Faraǧ ibn aṭ-Ṭayyib." – Ed. by Franz Rosenthal, in: *Recherches d'islamologie: Recueil d'articles offert à Georges C. Anawati et Louis Gardet*. Louvain, 1977, 273–283. – Repr. in: F. Rosenthal 1990 [*52: no. VI].

29 al-Mubaššir b. Fātik. *Muḫtār al-ḥikam wa-maḥāsin al-kalim*. – Ed. by ʿAbd al-Raḥmān Badawī. Madrid, 1958. – Medieval Span. transl. "Bocados de oro." Ed.

by Hermann Knust, in: *Mittheilungen aus dem Eskurial*. Bibliothek des Litterarischen Vereins in Stuttgart, vol. 141. Tübingen, 1879, 66–395, 537–612. – Ed. by Mechthild Crombach. *Bocados de oro: Kritische Ausgabe des altspanischen Textes*. Bonn, 1971. – Medieval Lat. transl. "Liber philosophorum moralium antiquorum." Ed. by Ezio Franceschini, in: *Atti del Reale Istituto Veneto di scienze, lettere ed arti* 91, no. 2 (1932): 393–597. – Medieval French transl. "Dits moraulx: Tignonvillana inedita." Ed. by Robert Eder, in: *Romanische Forschungen* 33 (1915): 851–1022. – Medieval Engl. transl. *The Dicts and Sayings of the Philosophers*. Ed. by Curt F. Bühler. Oxford, 1941. – Partial Engl. transl. by F. Rosenthal 1975 [*19: 124–144].

30 al-Šahrastānī. *Kitāb al-Milal wa-l-niḥal: Book of Religious and Philosophical Sects*. – Ed. by William Cureton, 2 vols. London, 1846. – Repr. Leipzig, 1923. – German transl. by Theodor Haarbrücker, *Abu-'l-Fath' Muh'ammad asch-Schahrastâni's Religionspartheien und Philosophenschulen*. Halle, 1850–1851. – French transl. of the second part by Jean-Claude Vadet, *Les dissidences de l'islam*. Paris, 1984. – Engl. transl. of the second part by A. K. Kazi, J. G. Flynn, *Muslim Sects and Divisions*. London, Boston, 1984. – Ital. transl. of the Presocratics, as well as Socrates, Plato, and Aristotle in: C. Baffioni 1990 [*49] and there p. 15–16. – French transl. by Daniel Gimaret, Jean Jolivet and Guy Monnot, *Shahrastani: Livre des religions et des sectes*, 2 vols. Leuven, 1986–1996.

31 Ibn Abī Uṣaybiʿa [*2]. – French transl. of the Greek gnomologia by Beniamino Raffaello Sanguinetti: "Cinquième extrait de l'ouvrage arabe d'Ibn Aby Ossaibi'ah." *Journal asiatique* 8 (1856): 175–196.

32 al-Šahrazūrī. *Nuzhat al-arwāḥ wa-rawḍat al-afrāḥ fī tāʾrīḫ al-ḥukamāʾ wa-l-falāsifa*. – Ed. by Ḫwaršīd Aḥmad, 2 vols. Hyderabad, 1976. – Ed. by ʿAbd al-Karīm Abū Šuwayrib. Tripoli, 1398/1978. – Ed. by Muḥammad ʿAlī Abū Rayyān. Alexandria, 1414/1993.

1.1.3 Pseudepigraphic Collections

35 *Turba philosophorum: Ein Beitrag zur Geschichte der Alchemie*. Ed. by Julius Ruska. Berlin, 1931. – Repr. Berlin, Heidelberg, 1970.

36 *Die Doxographie des Pseudo-Ammonios: Ein Beitrag zur neuplatonischen Überlieferung im Islam*. Ed. and transl. by Ulrich Rudolph. Stuttgart, 1989.

1.1.4 Liber de Pomo

1.1.4.1 *Manuscripts, Editions, Translations*

Arabic Version

51 MS Istanbul, Nuruosmaniye 4931, dated 1275, fols 76^{b}–85^{a} (Aristotle) (Bielawski 1974 [*95: 129], Aouad 1989 [*103: 540], GAS [*104]).

52 MS Istanbul, Köprülü 1608, not dated: 16th cent. (?), fols 170b–181b (Aristotle) (Kraemer 1956 [*89: 489–492], Gutas 1975 [*97: 42–50. 425–426], Aouad 1989 [*103: 539], GAS [*104]).

53 MS Cairo, Taymūriyya, Aḫlāq 290, not dated: 14th/15th cent. (?) (short version / Socrates) (Kraemer 1956 [*89: 488]). – Ed. by ʿAlī Sāmī al-Naššār and ʿAbbās al-Širbīnī. *Fīdūn wa-Kitāb al-Tuffāḥa al-mansūb li-Suqrāṭ*. Cairo, 1965, 6 and 218–231 (Aouad 1989 [*103: 539], GAS [*104]).

54 MS Damascus, Library of the Greek Orthodox Patriarchate of Antioch (Socrates). – Ed. by Amīn Ẓahīr Ḫayr Allāh, in: *al-Muqtaṭaf* 55 (1919): 475–484 and 56 (1920): 18–22. 105–110. 217–221. 295 (Kraemer 1956 [*89: 488–489], Bielawski 1974 [*95: 128], Aouad 1989 [*103: 539], GAS [*104]).

55 MS Tashkent 2213, dated 1344, fols 82b-88b (Aristotle) (GAS [*104]).

56 MS Kabul, Royal Library, dated 1600, fols 12–16 (Aristotle) (Aouad 1989 [*103: 540], GAS [*104]).

Persian Version

61 MS Oxford, Bodleian Library, 1422/Ouseley 95, VIII. – Ed. with Engl. transl. by D. S. Margoliouth, "The Book of the Apple, Ascribed to Aristotle." *Journal of the Royal Asiatic Society* (1892): 187–252 (=187–192 and 230–252).

62 MS Istanbul, Nuruosmaniye 4931, dated 1275, fols 126b-136a, transl. by Afḍal al-Dīn-i Kāšānī (12th/13th cent.). – Ed. by M. Minowi and Y. Mahdawi, *Muṣannafāt-i Afḍal al-Dīn-i Muḥammad-i Maraqī-i Kāšānī*, vol 1. Tehran, 1952, 113–144 (Bielawski 1974 [*95: 129], Aouad 1989 [*103: 540]).

Hebrew Version

66 Information on manuscripts and prints of the Hebrew version in Steinschneider 1893 [*82: 268 and xxvii]; cf. also Margoliouth 1892 [*81: 187], Hertz 1905 [*83: 372 n. 4]. – Lat. transl. by Johann Justus Losius, *Biga dissertationum*. Gießen, 1706. – German transl. by Joachim Musen, *Hatapuach*. Lemberg, 1873. – Engl. transl. by Isidor Kalisch, *Ha-Tapuach: The Apple: A Treatise on the Immortality of the Soul by Aristotle, the Stagyrite*. New York, 1885. – Engl. transl. by Hermann Gollancz, *The Targum to the 'Song of Songs': The Book of the Apple: The Ten Jewish Martyrs: A Dialogue on Games of Chance*. Translated from the Hebrew and Aramaic. London, 1908, 91–117.

Latin Version

71 For the manuscripts, cf. Schmitt, Knox 1985 [*99: 52], Plezia 1960 [*91: 24–32, 72–78], Mazzantini 1964 [*92: 33–36]. – Critical editions: Marian Plezia, "Aristotelis qui ferebatur Liber de Pomo: Versio Latina vetusta interprete Manfredo duce." *Eos* 47 (1954): 191–217. – M. Plezia, *Aristotelis qui ferebatur 'Liber*

de Pomo': Versio Latina Manfredi, Varsoviae, 1960. – Paolo Mazzantini, in *Il canto di Manfredi e il liber de pomo sive de morte Aristotilis*. Ed. by Bruno Nardi and P. Mazzantini. Turin, 1964, 40–51. – Swedish transl. by Ingemar Düring, "Boken om äpplet." In *Florilegium amicitiae till Emil Zilliacus*. Helsingfors, 1953, 65–76. – Engl. transl. with detailed introduction and notes by Mary F. Rousseau, *The Apple or Aristotle's Death* (*De pomo sive De morte Aristotilis*). Milwaukee, Wisconsin, 1968. – German transl. with introduction and commentary by Elsbeth Acampora-Michel, *Liber de pomo/Buch vom Apfel*. Frankfurt a.M., 2001. – Greek transl. by Paraskevi Kotzia, Περὶ τοῦ μήλου ἢ Περὶ τῆς Αριστοτέλους τελευτῆς (*Liber de Pomo*). Thessaloniki, 2007. – With introduction, commentary and detailed discussion of the question of the work's provenance.

1.2 *Introduction*

The social and intellectual factors at the beginning of the 3rd/9th century in Baghdad which produced the rebirth of philosophy in Arabic (cf. above, § 3.3) were not only confined to those intellectuals who were actually engaged in sponsoring and doing philosophy but were operative also for all literate classes. Given the social and theological (i.e., in the context of 3rd/9th century Baghdad, political) motivation behind much of the demand for these intellectual developments, there was broad interest in wisdom that would address itself to the practical aspects of the sciences in general and to ethical and political concerns in particular. Philosophical thinking and philosophical argumentation accordingly spread throughout most of the learned disciplines, and educated laymen kept commissioning treatises from scholars, requesting discussions of all sorts of subjects. The scholars who responded were not all philosophers, but they had a good philosophical education and were thus able to contribute to the widening spread of philosophical literature. It is not possible, for the purposes of this volume, to discuss all these scholars who in one way or another contributed to this development, so I will concentrate on two of them, arguably the most famous and significant among them, Ḥunayn b. Isḥāq and Ṯābit b. Qurra. Though not philosophers by profession or by main preoccupation, they helped spread philosophical learning both by their numerous translations into Syriac and Arabic, and by the philosophical discussions of a number of subjects in medicine, mathematics, and theology. As such, they serve as perfect examples of the philosophically minded intellectual of early Abbasid society.

The broad interest in ethical and social concerns and in questions of proper governance – which interest, as a matter of fact, predated the beginnings of the translation movement and the formal origins of philosophy in the emergent Muslim societies in the Near East – was naturally re-oriented in the

3rd/9th century toward the new discipline of philosophy and its new figures of authority. This gave rise to the translation of material whose nature is best characterized as popular ethical and practical political, i.e., as distinct from the formal disciplines of ethics and politics which were part of practical philosophy (namely, in essence, whatever was known of Aristotle's *Politics* and Plato's *Republic* and *Laws*, and the well-studied *Nicomachean Ethics* by Aristotle). The literary genres to which this material belongs, both with regard to the translated sources and the compilations in Arabic, can be usefully discussed under the categories of gnomologia, doxographies, and mirrors for princes, though in the case of the productions in Arabic, it is difficult to maintain strict boundaries among these categories which, in any case, were not those used by the Arabic writing authors themselves. However, they are convenient for the purposes of analysis and will be so used here.

Similar to these works with regard to the hortatory character of its contents, but quite different in its formal aspects, is a dialogue between the dying Aristotle and his disciples. It became known under the title *Liber de Pomo* ('Book of the Apple'), named after the fruit whose scent kept the philosopher alive until he had spoken his last words of wisdom. This book was widely known, in Arabic, Persian, Hebrew, and Latin versions. Even though *prima facie* it appears to be a work originally written in Arabic, it contains elements that point to a Greek original of some kind (cf. § 9.1.6 below).

In Arabic, most of these writings would fall under the general category of *adab*, that indigenous genre of literature that combined instruction and entertainment in aesthetically pleasing forms (cf. Fähndrich 1990 [*50]). Because of the popularity of *adab* literature in Muslim societies, the gnomologia, the doxographies, and mirrors for princes were read to the full extent of literacy and were responsible for the widest possible dissemination of philosophical ideas – albeit in a popularized form – in Islamic societies. Their popularity can be gauged from the mere fact that they continued to be produced throughout the ages in numerous adaptations in Arabic, and in translations into the other main languages of the Islamic world, Persian and Turkish (Gutas 1990 [*51]). In this way they both expressed and were fed by some fundamental attitudes that were characteristic of these societies regarding ethical and social or political behaviour. The main sources of this popular ethical and practical political wisdom were in essence two, pre-Islamic Greek and Persian. However, late antique Greek compilations had absorbed some of the world-view of the peoples belonging to the Eastern churches, and the Persian Sasanian material was broadly representative also of the wisdom of the Semitic-speaking indigenous population of the Near East as well as of certain aspects of Indian wisdom acquired through translations from Sanskrit into Middle Persian. To this extent, then, the gnomic material that eventually appeared in Arabic was a distillation of the experiences of the people of the Near East from the earliest stages of their long-lasting civilization.

1.3 *Gnomologia*

The practice of compiling anthologies of sayings by Greek philosophers, or gnomologia as they are properly called, began already in classical antiquity and continued throughout the centuries with increasing regularity into medieval times and beyond (for the terminology and literary types of sayings see Overwien 2005 [*72: 27–35], but cf. also the remarks by Searby 1998 [*60: 28 n. 2]). Linguistically, the practice was not confined only to Greek, but it also flourished in other languages in which Greek letters made a significant impact, particularly in Latin, Syriac, and Arabic. Always a popular genre, it was adapted to meet various needs by the societies, or classes within societies, that used it to express themselves. Perhaps originally intended for school-room instruction (Barns 1950–51 [*14]), the compilation of gnomologia gained a new and significant function during Hellenistic and early Imperial times as the main medium for the propagation of the tenets of philosophical schools that owed their popularity and wider appeal to their ethical content. The Epicureans to a certain extent (the preservation of Epicurus' own *Kyriai Doxai* in the form of a gnomologium comes immediately to mind), the Stoics certainly (Chrysippus is one of the founders of the genre), and particularly the Cynics (whose characteristic "unrestrained speech" or *parrhesia* could be well captured with the quick repartee of an apophthegm) made sustained use of gnomologia in their teaching.

In late antiquity, during the confrontation of Hellenic with Christian ideologies, proponents of the old *paideia* used the gnomologia both to preserve it in a most convenient fashion and promote it in a least provocative way. As a reaction to this trend, Christians themselves began to compile anthologies of the sayings of the Greek Church Fathers. Christians of the Eastern churches followed suit by translating into Syriac both Christian and pagan collections, although in the latter case they were selective; they tended to prefer those sayings and philosophers who could be either Christianized or presented as models of ascetic and pious conduct (cf. Brock 1982 [*36: 28 and 34 n. 132]). For the Arabs, gnomologia were a priori adoptable. In pre-Islamic times, pithy sayings, tersely expressed, by tribal wise men or leaders constituted one of the staples of a national literature that was almost exclusively oral. With the advent of Islam, greater literacy, and the contact with Hellenism, Greek gnomologia offered themselves to Arabic authors as the natural candidates for translation and wide-spread use (Gutas 1981 [*33]).

A natural characteristic of the genre, in all languages, is its fluidity. It is fluid with regard to three basic things: the extent of each individual collection, the text of the sayings contained in each collection, and the attribution of the sayings to individual authorities. In the first case, a particular gnomologium may have a greater or smaller number of sayings in each of the various manuscripts in which it is preserved, and it may vary substantially in extent if it happens to have survived in more than one recension, as happens relatively frequently. Second, the very wording of a discrete saying may vary from one manuscript of a particular collection to the next, let alone from one collection to another. The reasons are self-evident. Since the very point of a maxim or witticism depends heavily on its form, on the precise wording, attempts to improve upon a perceived imperfection by a transmitter or even scribe must be responsible for many of the textual variants. Furthermore, given the longevity of the collections and the sayings they contain, the development of a language and the aesthetic rules that govern its expression are also factors in considering textual variations. To take Greek as an example, the particular wording of a saying that made the point perfectly in the fourth century BC in Athens no longer fulfilled the same function twelve centuries later in Constantinople due to the changes in the language, and it was accordingly recast in a more immediately intelligible linguistic form. Third, and in some ways most important, is the matter of pseudepigraphy. Sayings can be attributed just as easily to one author as to the next, given the difficulty of identifying any specific teaching or sentiment expressed in the sayings with a particular author. The reason is that gnomologies are not doxographies: gnomic sayings express general and worldly wisdom in memorable form, and any philosopher could have uttered any one of them. It is true that certain attitudes or subjects may have been identified in the mind of the audiences with a particular philosopher – like political wisdom with Plato or misogyny with Diogenes – but the vast majority of subjects touched upon in the gnomologies are common to all. Now pseudepigraphy can be accidental, due to the hazards of manuscript copying and transmission, or deliberate. Deliberate pseudepigraphy is difficult to study because its causes are specific to the time, place, and cultural orientation of the society in which it occurs, and most gnomologia, anonymous as they are – at most we may know the names of derivative compilers, not original authors – do not easily lend themselves to such analysis. There has been considerable discussion of pseudepigraphy and its many forms in various literatures (for Greek see von Fritz 1972 [*25]), including some in the case of Arabic philosophy (Reisman 2004 [*70], with many references), but very little specifically addressed to the gnomologia. All these characteristics just discussed, as well as the problems affiliated with them, also apply to the Arabic collections, with an added complication introduced by the fact of translation. The translators as a rule gave literal renditions of the sayings. To the Arab men of letters who collected these sayings in new compilations or cited them incidentally in related works, the style of the translations frequently seemed awkward and verbose and they recast the maxims in a form better suited to their aesthetic sensibilities; at times they even recast them in verse (cf. Rescher [*23]; Rosenthal 1975 [*19: 261–263]).

The Greek collections are available in a bewildering variety of recensions and traditions extant in a seemingly unmanageable plethora of manuscripts. (For lists of Greek gnomologia and secondary literature cf. Gutas 1975 [*28: 4–5. 9–33], Kindstrand 1981 [*34: 99–105], Searby 1998 [*60: 43–70], Ihm [*14: III–LXXIV on Pseudo-Maximus Confessor]). Classical scholarship in the nineteenth century concentrated on delineating the main lines of transmission from the Hellenistic to Byzantine times and on the anthologies of Stobaeus. In the last quarter of the 20th century the emphasis was primarily on editions of the sayings of individual philosophers as well as on manuscript research. The beginnings of the 21st saw a return to publications of the major gnomologia and a renewed interest in the history of transmission, Greek and Arabic (Funghi 2003–2004 [*68], Overwien 2005 [*72]). These various aspects of the study of Greek gnomologia, however, are interdependent, and a comprehensive work on the Greek gnomologia, their transmission, and internal relationships remains to be written (cf. Gutas 1975 [*28: 34–35], Strohmaier 1998 [*61], and especially Searby 1998 [*60: 28–42], to be complemented by Overwien 2005 [*72: 39–93]). The more recent research points forward to more sophisticated and detailed analyses. The collections of sayings in Syriac, though what is extant of them is more limited in extent, also need to be related to their Greek archetypes and subsequent Arabic collections, as well as to be studied on their own (cf. Zeegers-Vander Vorst 1978 [*32], Brock 2003 [*65], Bettiolo 2004 [*67]).

The Arabic gnomologia came into being through a complicated series of stages whose exact nature is not yet fully understood. The difficulty arises from the complex nature of the earliest stages of the translation movement itself (cf. § 3), but also from the fluid nature of the gnomologia and their textual unit, the single saying, which cannot be easily confined in strict categories of authorship, as just mentioned. In broad outline it may be possible to posit two major stages in the generation of the Arabic gnomologia, the first represented by translations into Arabic of gnomic material from the original sources, and the second by original compilations, in Arabic this time, from the material translated during the first stage. On occasion it is observed that the translator belonging to the first stage is the same person as the compiler belonging to the second, like Ḥunayn b. Isḥāq (see § 9.2.1 below) and Miskawayh (see § 5.4 above).

The original sources from which gnomic material was translated into Arabic during the first stage are primarily Greek and Persian, and possibly also Syriac, though this has yet to be documented in connection with gnomologia; in addition, some Indian material may have passed into Arabic by way of Middle Persian rather than by direct translation. The Greek sources are similar to those briefly enumerated above, though it must be emphasized that none of the extant Greek collections has been identified as having been translated into Arabic, even if numerous individual sayings from these collections have. The translated Greek collections belonging to the first stage are for the most part not extant independently, but only to the extent that they have been incorporated in the compilations of the second stage. A significant exception is constituted by the small gnomologium translated by Isḥāq b. Ḥunayn. It consists of two parts; the first, and by far the longest, contains sayings by Hesiod, Basil, Solon, Socrates, Plato, Melissus, Democritus, Zeno, Thales, Aristotle, Anacharsis, Homer, Timaeus, Zeno and Pythagoras, and the second has the maxims inscribed on the signet rings of the philosophers (cf. Gutas 1975 [*28: 43. 48–49]; published from this manuscript by ʿAbd Allāh 1998 [*18 = Isḥāq]). A similar collection under the title *Nawādir al-Yūnāniyyīn* (*Anecdotes of the Greeks*) is recorded by the bibliographers (*Fihrist* [*1: 295,18]) as having been translated by Qusṭā b. Lūqā, but it has not survived.

The Middle Persian sources consist of the vast range of Sasanian wisdom literature, collections of Sasanian emperors' edicts (including the *tawqīʿāt*: Zakeri 2002 [*64]), sayings, and political practice, and general books of social and political etiquette which were translated into Arabic in the course of the parallel Perso-Arabic translation movement during the early Abbasid era. Ibn al-Muqaffaʿ may be assumed to have translated from this material for his gnomic collection entitled *al-Adab al-Kabīr* (cf. § 9.1.5 below on mirrors for princes), as is ʿAlī b. ʿUbayda al-Rayḥānī for his numerous compilations, some of which actually survive (cf. Zakeri 1994 [*57], 2004 [*71]). Most of this material is not extant in the original Middle Persian, and much of it in Arabic translation has been lost, but enough survives to give us an excellent idea of the range of this literature, its various genres, and basic contents (cf. the detailed exposition in the article on *adab* [*40] and *andarz* [*45] in EIr [*5], and the extensive extant compilation by al-Rayḥānī, ed. Zakeri 2007 [*15]). It becomes clear that with regard to general ideas about popular ethics and practical politics, the Persian material was more widespread and influential in Arabic than the Greek.

In the second stage we see original compilations in Arabic made on the basis of the already translated collections of the first stage; this constitutes the indirectly transmitted material (for discussion of the details of the textual transmission, both direct and indirect, of Greek material into Arabic cf. Gutas 1985 [*41: 64–67]). However, in a few cases, we may have the two stages represented by the same person, when the translator may be also the compiler. This would appear to be the case with the work entitled *Anecdotes of the Philosophers* (*Nawādir al-falāsifa*) attributed to the famous translator and physician Ḥunayn b. Isḥāq (cf. § 9.2.1 below). The work is divided into two major parts. The first contains introductory material to the history of philosophy: its Greek origin and the description of the various philosophical schools, the transmission of philosophy and its significance, and the story of Ibycus' death and the cranes which helped identify his murderers. The second part contains three sections, one on the sayings on the signet rings of the philosophers, a second on the gatherings of philosophers in the courts of various kings discussing sundry subjects, and a third containing the sayings of the philosophers proper, with the chapter on Alexander containing significant excerpts from the pseudepigraphous correspondence between Alexander and Aristotle and Alexander and his mother Olympias.

The work as we have it is not from Ḥunayn himself but exists in three later recensions, the debt of each of which to the pen of Ḥunayn has yet to be determined. The first of these, representing the only recension extant in Arabic, is due to an otherwise unknown compiler named Muḥammad al-Anṣārī (Ḥunayn, ed. Badawī [*16]), who in all likelihood put together his collection some time in the 6th/12th century; the second is the Hebrew translation made in Andalus around 1200 by Yehuda ben Šelomo al-Ḥarīzī (Ḥarizi) (ed. Loewenthal [*16]); and the third is an old Spanish translation, itself also made in the 6th/12th or 7th/13th century (ed. Knust, Sturm [*16]). The contents of these three recensions partially overlap but also show some significant variations (Merkle 1921 [*12: 3–15. 59–61]). To these there is to be added a gnomological Arabic manuscript preserved in Istanbul (Köprülü 1608) which contains numerous sections attributed to Ḥunayn but also additional material especially of Persian provenance (Gutas 1975 [*28: 42–50], Zakeri 2004 [*71: 187–190]). The manuscript itself dates from the 10th/16th or 11th/17th century, but its archetype, with this particular set of contents, clearly goes back to the 4th/10th century (Zakeri 2004 [*71: 190]). The contents of all three recensions, as we have them, are both of Greek and Persian origin (Overwien 2003 [*66], Zakeri 2004 [*71]), a mixture of gnomic material precisely like the one we see in the Köprülü manuscript. Ḥunayn could not have deliberately included Persian material in a compilation which he said in his introduction was to contain the sayings of Greek and Byzantine sages (Badawī [*16: 43], Overwien 2003 [*66: 96]). It thus appears most likely that the unknown al-Anṣārī put together the collection which has come down to us from such a gnomological manuscript which included, in addition to large parts of Ḥunayn's original work on *The Anecdotes of the Philosophers*, also Persian material. For the Greek material in his original collection Ḥunayn did not apparently translate all the texts himself but freely used pre-existing translations, as in the case of Alexander's correspondence and the Pythagorean *Golden Verses* (Gutas 1975 [*28: 447]).

A similar situation, this time with regard to Persian material, obtains with the collection entitled *al-Ḥikma al-ḫālida* ('Eternal Wisdom') by the courtier and historian Miskawayh (ed. Badawī [*26]). It contains some texts that are translations, apparently his, from Middle Persian, but it also includes material derived from Indian, Arab, and Greek sources translated during the first stage. The section on Greek philosophers is characterized by an emphasis on ethical and political subjects and by its inclusion of longer texts in addition to sayings and anecdotes, most notably the *Tablet of Cebes*, on which his younger contemporary, the Baghdadi philosopher Abū l-Farağ Ibn al-Ṭayyib, was to write a commentary (Rosenthal 1977[*28]).

The earliest extant Arabic compilation belonging to the second stage is the very short collection by al-Kindī of the sayings of Socrates (ed. Faḫrī, transl. Adamson [*17]). Al-Kindī was Ḥunayn's contemporary, but it does not seem that he drew his material from the Socrates section in Ḥunayn's gnomologium discussed above. But if al-Kindī drew his Socratic material primarily from Sabian sources (Gutas 1988 [*48: 42–47]), it is likely that this collection also derives from there. It consists of 39 sayings alternating between anecdotes of a Cynic and Stoic colouring and moralizing maxims with a Neoplatonic flavour.

In contrast with al-Kindī's collection, which is brief and concerned with just one philosopher, two other early compilations belonging to the second stage give ample indication of the variety and quality of material that was available in the first stage. The first is the section on Greek philosophers in the anthology of *al-Ağwiba al-muskita* ('Dumbfounding Repartees') by the littérateur Ibn Abī ʿAwn (d. 321/933) (ed. Yousef, transl. Rosenthal [*20]), while the second is a similar section in the gnomologium of the philologist and lexicographer Ibn-Durayd (d. 321/933), entitled *al-Muğtanā* (*Harvest*) (Rosenthal [*19]). They both draw upon translations of Greek gnomologia that survive neither in Greek nor in Arabic as they were first translated, although the same sources were used by subsequent compilers. Rosenthal [*19: 158] is of the opinion that Ibn-Durayd's source was a single Greek collection translated into Arabic; Yousef [*20: 57] points to Ibn Abī ʿAwn's use of Ḥunayn's *Nawādir* and suggests that he may have drawn, in addition to other sources, upon the earlier compilation of his grandfather, Aḥmad b. Abī l-Naǧm, entitled *Aqāwīl* [or *Aqwāl*] *al-falāsifa* ('The Sayings of the Philosophers'). This work is not extant and hence its sources and their translator(s) remain unknown.

Later than these early compilations but fully within the second stage are three Arabic gnomologia which collectively contain most of the Greek gnomic material extant in Arabic. They were all compiled within fifty years of each other, but in different parts of the Muslim world, from sources that had been translated in the first stage and only partially overlap.

The *Ṣiwān al-ḥikma* ('Depository of Wisdom Literature') was compiled around 390/1000 in the Eastern provinces of the Islamic world, most likely by a minor philosopher who appears to have belonged to the circle of Abū Sulaymān al-Siǧistānī (al-Qāḍī 1981 [*35]). The original *Ṣiwān al-ḥikma* itself is not extant, and it has therefore to be pieced together on the basis of its later recensions and secondary transmission. The major recensions are two significant abridgments (the first edited by Dunlop and Badawī, the second transcribed only in a doctoral dissertation) and a shorter selection from the sayings of Pythagoras, Socrates, Plato, and Aristotle (Gutas 1975 [*28]). In the secondary tradition it was drawn heavily upon by both al-Šahrastānī and al-Šahrazūrī. For each philosopher treated, these sources for the most part provide only partially overlapping material so that a future edition has the possibility to recreate it almost in its entirety. The significance of the *Ṣiwān al-ḥikma* has been remarked upon a number of times; it lies in the fact that it contains not only sayings and maxims of a great number of philosophers, but also important biographical data (Dunlop 1957 [*15], Gutas 1986 [*43: 15–22]). The philosophers anthologized are representatives of all philosophical schools, and this makes the Arabic gnomologia, and this one in particular, the most important source of information available in Arabic for the views of pre-Plotinian philosophers and the various schools other than the Aristotelian (cf. Gutas 1994 [*56]). The *Ṣiwān al-ḥikma* contains specifically 137 names of pre-Islamic philosophers and sages, with a significant proportion of them still unidentified. A list of these names is provided by Rosenthal (1975 [*19: 36–38]), and again by Dunlop in his edition of the *Muntaḫab Ṣiwān al-ḥikma* (Dunlop 1979 [*24: xxxiii–xxxvi]). A comparison of the discrepancies between the two lists well illustrates the difficulties of identification facing the editor. As Rosenthal suggests (ad loc.), however, the Greek collections should prove helpful in identifying most, if not all of them, especially after a comprehensive edition of the Arabic gnomologia has been prepared.

The gnomologium of Ibn Hindū, a scholar and physician who died in 423/1032 (cf. above § 5.5 [*323]), bears the title *Al-Kalim al-rūḥāniyya min al-ḥikam al-yūnāniyya* ('The Spiritual Sayings among Greek Maxims') and is extant in two recensions, a longer and a shorter one (cf. Rosenthal 1963 [*18], review of Ullmann [*6] = Menander 365), both of which are now available in print (Qabbānī, Ḫalīfāt [*27]). It contains sayings by numerous Greek philosophers, a number of whom cannot be easily identified. This gnomologium, together with the *Ṣiwān al-ḥikma*, has been successfully used in the edition of the Arabic translation of Menander's *Monostichoi* which they include (Ullmann 1959 [*16: 57–59], 1961 [*6: 7–12]), and it appears, on the basis of this and other evidence, that they have both used some of the same sources translated during the first stage of the transmission of the gnomologia.

The third major gnomologium is *Muḫtār al-ḥikam wa-maḥāsin al-kalim* ('Choice Maxims and Best Sayings') by the scholar and bibliophile al-Mubaššir b. Fātik, compiled in 440/1048–49 (cf. Rosenthal 1960–1961 [*17], Gutas 1975 [*28: 50–51]). This work, like the *Ṣiwān al-ḥikma* which it uses as a source, contains both biographies and sayings, and is characterized by al-Mubaššir's desire to be comprehensive. Although it includes few philosophers in comparison with the preceding two, the sections devoted to each philosopher contain apparently all the information that al-Mubaššir could find in his sources, which also include Christian gnomologia. This makes for entries of dubious ascription in some cases, as well as for a source of confusion to the scholar who would disentangle the sources (cf. Gutas 1986 [*43: 25–28]). The work contains the following entries: Seth, Hermes, Sab, Asclepius, Homer (= Menander), Solon, Zeno, Hippocrates, Pythagoras, Diogenes, Socrates, Plato, Aristotle, Alexander the Great, Ptolemy, Luqmān, Mahadarǧis (= Mihr Āḏarǧušnašp, according to Zakeri 1994 [*57: 96–101]), [St.] Basil, Gregory the Theologian, Galen, a chapter on 'Sayings by a number of philosophers known by name for none of whom enough sayings are recorded to make a special chapter possible' (translated by Rosenthal 1965 [*19: 124–144]), and a final chapter on anonymous sayings.

Two later gnomologia that contain sizeable material on Greek authors are *al-Milal wa-l-niḥal* (*Religions and Sects*) by al-Šahrastānī, written in 521/1127, and *Rawḍat al-afrāḥ* (*Garden of Delights*) by al-Šahrazūrī, dating from the second half of the 7th/13th century. They drew upon the immediately preceding gnomologia – and in particular on the *Ṣiwān al-ḥikma* and on al-Mubaššir's *Muḫtār* – as well as on other doxographies such as that of Pseudo-Ammonius (see § 9.1.4 below). Because they had at their disposal the original *Ṣiwān al-ḥikma* and not the subsequent recensions that have survived, they are valuable witnesses for its reconstruction (see above). Al-Šahrastānī's work, which is more of a doxography than a gnomologium, is primarily haeresiographic in nature and is divided in two parts, the first of which deals with Muslim sects and the second with Greek and Muslim philosophers (French transl. by

Gimaret, as well as by Jolivet and Monnot [*30]). It is a markedly tendentious compilation and has to be used with caution; the value to be attached to those parts of it which preserve material not extant elsewhere is to be assessed only after al-Šahrastānī's editorial intrusions and alterations have been thoroughly studied on the basis of a comparison of other passages with his sources that have survived (cf. Gutas 1985 [*41: 86–87 no. 5]; but see also, for a different perspective that lends greater credibility to his works, Baffioni 1990 [*49], and her articles listed there on pp. 15–16).

Al-Šahrazūrī's work appears not to have these shortcomings (from the point of view of the historian of ancient philosophy), but it has not been studied as extensively. His main sources are the *Ṣiwān al-ḥikma* and al-Mubaššir's *Muḫtār*, which he follows closely. In the printed edition, the personages treated are the following: Adam, Seth, Empedocles, Hermes, Thoth, Asclepius, Pythagoras, Socrates, Plato, Aristotle, Diogenes, Hippocrates, Homer, Solon, Zeno, Alexander the Great, Anaxagoras, Theophrastus, Eudemus, ʾsḫwlws [an unidentified student of Aristotle along with Eudemus], Democritus, Cebes, ʾrsṭys, Plutarch, Sfyd's, Themistius, Alexander of Aphrodisias, The Greek Sage [Plotinus], Zoroaster, Ptolemy, Mahadarǧis (= Mihr Āḏarǧušnašp, according to Zakeri 1994 [*57: 96–101]), Gregory the Theologian, Basil, Luqmān, and Galen.

1.4 *Doxographies*

The lively interest in Greek philosophy exhibited by the educated classes in general and by scholars and philosophers in particular during the translation movement also led to the translation into Arabic of Greek works with a doxographic character. Those that are known to have been translated are the following, in chronological order of their authors:

- Pseudo-Plutarch, *Placita Philosophorum* (ed. Daiber [*7]), a major source of information about Greek philosophers; it was used repeatedly in Arabic literature.
- Hippolytus, *Refutatio omnium haeresium* (φιλοσοφούμενα; written after 222 AD), was used extensively in the doxography of Pseudo-Ammonius (ed. Rudolph [*36]) and in the alchemical *Turba Philosophorum.*
- Diodorus of Tarsus, *The Book of Reflection,* is not extant either in the original Greek or in its Arabic translation, though extracts are quoted in the Pseudo-Ǧāḥiẓian *Kitāb al-ʿIbar* (Gibb 1948 [*13: 153–154]).
- Porphyry, *History of Philosophy,* of which there was a Syriac translation, of unknown extent, and an Arabic translation, possibly by Ibn al-Ḫammār, of

two sections of the first book. The extant Arabic fragments are translated in Smith, Wasserstein [*9: 220–248].
- Nemesius of Emesa, *De natura hominis*, was a very popular work, of which there apparently exist four different Arabic translations (Samir 1986 [*44]). The one attributed to Isḥāq b. Ḥunayn has been edited (Weisser [*22: 537–632]).
- Theodoretus of Cyrus, *De providentia*, the Arabic translation of which has not yet been located. Extracts therefrom are also quoted in the work by Pseudo-Ǧāḥiẓ (Gibb 1948 [*13: 154–156]).

Christian authors who included philosophical information of a doxographic nature in their works – information based on some of the sources just mentioned – were read and excerpted by Syriac theologians who may thus have acted as intermediaries for the transmission of some of this material into Arabic. Eusebius' *Praeparatio evangelica* and Epiphanius' *Panarion* may have been two such works which possibly appear in the work of Theodore bar Konai, a Nestorian theologian, who wrote around 791 a Bible commentary that included a brief account of Greek philosophy (Daiber 1994 [*55: 4978], following Baumstark 1905 [*11]).

In Arabic, the doxographies drawing on these and other sources contained both longer and shorter pieces attributed to the philosophers, following the style of the indigenous literary genre of *adab*, as discussed above. Thus some of the works discussed in the previous section (§ 9.1.3), such as al-Šahrastānī's *al-Milal wa-l-niḥal*, could easily have been listed under this rubric as well.

Several collections that were compiled in the 3rd/9th and 4th/10th centuries contain significant philosophical material. Gabriel b. Nūḥ, a Christian who lived during the time of the caliph al-Mutawakkil (regn. 232–247/847–861), put together a doxography of cosmological passages, entitled *Fikar fī l-dalāʾil ʿalā l-ḫāliq* ('Thoughts on the Evidence for the Creator'). It drew from the Pre-Socratics and Aristotle, but apparently through the mediation of Pseudo-Plutarch (Aetius) and others, with the purpose of demonstrating that the philosophers did not arrive at the truth (Daiber 1994 [*55: 4976]). An equally early and very influential doxography that has survived only in fragmentary form in later authors is *Opinions and Religions* (*Kitāb al-Ārāʾ wa-l-diyānāt*) by the Shiite author al-Nawbaḫtī (d. between 299/912 and 309/922). The work apparently contained a comprehensive section on Greek philosophy; the fragments that survive indicate that it included discussion of the scepticism of the sophists, Socrates, the Stoics, and logic (see van Ess 1987 [*47]). From the 4th/10th century dates the most important sourcebook we have on practical philosophy, compiled by a certain Abū l-Ḥasan b. Abī Ḏarr and entitled *al-Saʿāda wa-l-isʿād* ('On Being and Making Happy'). Abū l-Ḥasan, who, if his identification with al-ʿĀmirī is correct, was not an insignificant thinker, included in this book voluminous extracts from Greek political, economical, and ethical works. Plato and Aristotle are naturally the most frequently quoted authorities, but the book, still insufficiently studied, contains substantial passages from other authors as well (cf. Pohl 1997 [*58]).

The popularity of philosophical ideas and their wide dissemination among intellectuals of various stripes in the 3rd/9th and 4th/10th centuries gave rise also to pseudepigraphic compilations in Arabic. These compilations are characterized by the fact that, although ultimately dependent on some sort of Greek doxography, they rework the material in ways which makes it in the end unrecognizable. Three such compilations, which arose around 900, are the *Turba Philosophorum* (ed. Ruska [*35], cf. Rudolph 1990 [*53], with further bibliography), the doxography by Pseudo-Ammonius (ed. and comm. Rudolph [*36]), as well as an anonymous doxography on the natural philosophy of the ancients (*Kitāb fīhi ārāʾ al-ḥukamāʾ fī l-Ṭabīʿiyyāt wa-fīhi l-ārāʾ wa-l-kalimāt al-rūḥāniyya li-l-mutaqaddimīn, Book of the Opinions of the Philosophers on Natural Things and of the Spiritual Opinions and Sayings of the Ancients*), extant in the Istanbul MS Ayasofya 2450, fols 72–106, which contains mostly passages attributed to Aristotle and Ptolemy on questions of meteorology, astronomy, and the soul (Daiber 1994 [*55: 4980–4981]).

1.5 *Mirrors for Princes*

The origins of the Arabic mirror-for-princes literature lie in pre- and early Islamic wisdom literature together with the speeches, reports, and correspondence of the early Arab rulers and their functionaries. This genre of literature experienced a vast expansion in its scope among the hands of the administrative elite of both the Umayyad and Abbasid courts. The initiative for compositions of counsel more comprehensive in their coverage and more sustained in their extent than the occasional pieces of political wisdom among the early Muslim Arabs came from the Umayyad chancellery secretaries, who were themselves the immediate successors of their Byzantine colleagues in Damascus.

The person credited with initiating the genre as well as the Arabic prose style appropriate to it is ʿAbd al-Ḥamīd b. Yaḥyā (d. 132/750), secretary to the last Umayyad caliphs, among whose extant correspondence there exist a famous letter, giving counsel to his fellow secretaries, and other incidental pieces addressed to the last Umayyad caliph Marwān b. Muḥammad (al-Qāḍī 1992 [*54]). More important for the ultimate influence they were to exert, however, seem to be the activities of ʿAbd al-Ḥamīd's brother- (or father-) in-law and senior colleague, Sālim Abū l-ʿAlāʾ, secretary to the caliph Hišām b. ʿAbd al-Malik (regn. 105–125/724–743). It appears that Sālim was responsible for instigating the translation, apparently from Greek, of a series of Pseudo-Aristotelian letters to Alexander on the general subjects of politics and the craft of government (according to the thesis of Grignaschi 1965–1966 [*20]). These letters, one of which has been claimed by Stern (1970 [*23]) as authentic, derive primarily from Byzantine manuals on administration and warfare (the *Tactica*), with accretions from Greek material from the classical and Hellenistic periods, and from so-called Hermetic material deriving from sundry sources (Manzalaoui 1974 [*26: 194–219]). Significant portions of the contents of these letters were re-worked and augmented in Arabic with the addition of further material from Persian sources until, by the end of the 4th/10th century, they appeared under the title *Sirr al-asrār* ('Secret of Secrets'), an encyclopedic mirror for princes of immense influence both in Islam and, in its European translations (the famous *Secretum Secretorum*), in the medieval and early modern West (cf. the collection of articles in Ryan and Schmitt 1982 [*38], and Forster 2006 [*73]; for the Persian background see Grignaschi 1975 [*27: 224–233]). In its fullest recension, the Arabic *Sirr al-asrār* contains in ten chapters a veritable political encyclopedia of information on all subjects that a ruler would conceivably need to know, as follows: (1) kinds of kings; (2) conduct of kings and proper behaviour; defense of astrology; physical and spiritual health and its preservation; physiognomy and its uses; (3) justice; (4) ministers; (5) secretaries; (6) ambassadors; (7) governors; (8) generals; (9) wars; (10) occult sciences.

If the Umayyad bureaucracy to which ʿAbd al-Ḥamīd b. Yaḥyā and Sālim Abū l-ʿAlāʾ belonged, because of its immediate links with Byzantine administration, was responsible for the transmission of many Greek ideas on politics into the Arabic mirrors for princes, Persian functionaries in similar positions under both the late Umayyads and especially the early Abbasids formed their counterpart with regard to Sasanian material translated from Middle Persian. Ibn al-Muqaffaʿ stands unrivalled as the translator of Sasanian wisdom and related texts into Arabic, and as the author, based on these, of a collection of (anonymous) maxims under the title *al-Adab al-kabīr* (*The Great Adab Book*), and of an advisory epistle to the Abbasid caliph al-Manṣūr, *Fī l-Ṣaḥāba* (*On the [Caliph's] Entourage*), in which he advocated the centralized authority of the caliph over all governmental institutions and the enforcement of an 'orthodox' religious code (cf. Latham 1998 [*59]). But his most famous work is doubtless his translation of *Kalīla wa-Dimna*, a mirror for princes in the form of a fable book, translated from a Middle Persian version of an originally Sanskrit work, the *Pañcatantra* (Brockelmann 1978 [*31]).

The translation of Middle Persian texts on these subjects into Arabic in the 2nd/8th and 3rd/9th centuries was extensive and included such classics as *ʿAhd Ardašīr* (*The Testament of Ardašīr*, ed. ʿAbbās [*10], Grignaschi [*13]), the *Letter of Tansar* (ed. Boyce [*11]), and the *Kitāb al-Tāǧ* (*Book of the Crown*, ed. Zakī [*12]), which became available in Arabic between 232/847 and 247/861; as a result, Sasanian material in the mirrors-for-princes literature tended to predominate in Arabic letters. This situation eventually led, after the re-emergence of Persian as a literary language in the 5th/11th century, to the composition of mirrors for princes in Persian. Within a period of less than thirty years during the rise of the Seljuks in Iraq and Iran, there were written in Persian at least *three* such works: the *Qābūsnāma* (*The Book* [*in honour*] *of Qābūs*), composed in 1082 by Kay Kāʾus, the Ziyārid prince of Ṭabaristān, for his son and heir, Gīlānšāh; the *Siyāsatnāma* ('The Book of Government'), written for the Seljuk sultan Malikšāh by his famous vizier Niẓām al-Mulk shortly before his assassination in 485/1092; and *Naṣīḥat al-mulūk* ('Counsel for Kings') by none other than al-Ġazālī himself, addressed to the Seljuk ruler Muḥammad b. Malikšāh, though it appears that only the first part of the work, consisting of a treatise on faith, is by al-Ġazālī, and not the second part, which is the mirror for princes proper (according to Crone 1987 [*46]). Be that as it may, al-Ġazālī incorporated a chapter on this subject, but on a smaller scale and with Sufi coloring, in his Persian work *Kīmiyā-yi saʿādat, Elixir of Happiness* (Hillenbrand 2004 [*69]). These works eventually occupied a central position among Islamic mirrors for princes and determined to a large extent the later development of the genre. The first was translated into Ottoman Turkish, while the third was translated both into Arabic and Turkish. Al-Ġazālī's work also prompted a similar effort on the part of the Andalusian al-Ṭurṭūšī (d. 520/1126 or 525/1131), whose *Sirāǧ al-mulūk* ('Lamp for Kings') was studied by Ibn Ḫaldūn. Al-Ṭurṭūšī's intention was to surpass al-Ġazālī; as it turned out, he fell quite short of the mark, but it was precisely his failures that gave Ibn Ḫaldūn much food for thought. The ideas implicit in the long series of encyclopedic mirrors for princes and *adab* works about the nature of government, the qualities, duties, and conduct of the ruler, and the causes of the rise and fall of dynasties found their theoretical formulation, like so many other concepts constitutive of the fabric of Islamic civilization, in Ibn Ḫaldūn's masterpiece, the *Muqaddima* ('Introduction') to his historical work, *Kitāb al-ʿIbar* (*The Book of Examples*). Ibn Ḫaldūn himself tells us in his preliminary remarks that it was works such as these that he considered to have been the predecessors of his own researches: he mentions among them the statements of the Sasanian rulers and dignitaries, the *Sirr al-asrār* (*The Secret of Secrets*) which is 'ascribed to Aristotle and has wide circulation', the *adab* books of Ibn al-Muqaffaʿ, and *Sirāǧ al-mulūk* (*The Lamp for Kings*) of al-Ṭurṭūšī. In this way the practical political ideas that were based on Greek and Persian sources, as they developed in medieval Islamic civilization, became one of the sources that inspired Ibn Ḫaldūn (cf. Gutas 1990 [*51: 355–358]).

1.6 *Liber de Pomo*

Paraskevi Kotzia †

The *Book of the Apple, or The Death of Aristotle*, known as *Liber de Pomo* due to a Latin translation that was widely circulated in the Middle Ages, is a Pseudo-Aristotelian work allegedly recording the last discussion between the dying Aristotle and a group of his disciples. Like Socrates in Plato's *Phaedo*, Aristotle, lying on his death-bed, pronounces his final 'exhortation to philosophy', delineating his views on the attitude of the true philosopher towards death, but also towards life as preparation for the eventual liberation of the immortal soul from the body. Aristotle acquires the strength to extend his life long enough to deliver these teachings in full by breathing in the scent of an apple he is holding in his hand, hence the title of the pseudepigraphic text.

According to the prologue attached to the Latin translation by King Manfred of Sicily (1232–1266, a son of Frederick II of Hohenstaufen), who names himself as the translator, this text is but the final link in a long chain of translations: a Greek work was first translated into Arabic, then from Arabic into Hebrew, and finally from Hebrew into Latin (for the text of the prologue see Plezia 1960 [*91: 37–42] and Mazzantini 1964 [*92: 37–39]). While there is no other testimony to the Greek original, all the translations mentioned in the text are extant.

A comparison with the Hebrew translation (*Sefer ha-Tappuaḥ*), composed by Abraham Ibn Ḥasday around 1235 in Barcelona, confirms this information. The existence of an Arabic version of the *Book of the Apple* came to light only in 1892, through an anonymous Persian text which Margoliouth 1892 [*81] found in a manuscript of the Bodleian Library, and identified as a translation of the Arabic *Book of the Apple*. About 60 years later Kraemer (1956 [*89]) discovered and published the Arabic basis (*Kitāb al-Tuffāḥa*) of the Persian translation.

A comparison of the four 'translations' of the *Book of the Apple* reveals that we are in fact dealing with two different traditions, an Arabic-Persian and a Hebrew-Latin one. The text of the Hebrew-Latin version comprises only about a third of the Arabic-Persian version. Differences in content rule out that it is a translation made from the extant Arabic-Persian version.

According to the current state of research, all extant versions go back to an Arabic work composed in the 3rd/9th century. The existence of a now lost

Greek original cannot, however, be ruled out (Schmitt, Knox 1985 [*99: 51], Schmitt 1986 [*101: 5]; cf. Bielawski 1974 [*95: 128], Kraemer in Bielawski 1974 [*95: 132–133], Gutas 1986 [*100: 31. 36 n. 63], Aouad 1989 [*103: 537]; cf. also Flashar 2004 [*106: 276]). The Hebrew-Latin version is furthermore likely to be a free adaptation of the extant Arabic-Persian version; ideas and doctrines that are missing in the Arabic-Persian version can be regarded as insertions by the 13th century Hebrew 'translator' (Margoliouth 1892 [*81: 191], Kraemer 1956 [*89: 495], Plezia 1959 [*90: 193], 1960 [*91: 67], Rousseau 1968 [*94: 23–25 and 55 n. 7], Bielawski 1974 [*95: 127], Acampora-Michel 2001 [*105: 34. 36. 109–111. 117–118. 124]).

All extant versions of the *Book of the Apple* contain a common core which links them to Greek literature in two ways: first, the setting of the scene refers to Plato's *Phaedo*, as do the topic of the last discussion and the names of two of 'Aristotle's' interlocutors, which, despite some distortions, are reminiscent of two of Socrates' interlocutors (Simmias, Crito); second, in two (albeit younger) manuscripts of the Arabic text the dying philosopher is called Socrates rather than Aristotle. A further Greek source is alluded to by the brief extension of Aristotle's life by means of breathing in the scent of an apple: the death of Democritus as attested in multiple sources since Hellenistic times (Hermippus frg. 31 Wehrli = 60 Bollansée).

The obvious similarities to Plato's *Phaedo*, together with the fact that the strict dualism of body and soul and the belief in the immortality of the soul sound entirely un-Aristotelian, have led to the now commonly accepted conclusion that the *Book of the Apple* is really an imitation of the *Phaedo*. Consequently, the study of its transmission would belong to the field of *Plato Arabus* rather than that of Aristotle (Gutas 1986 [*100: 31]). The presence of the apple in the text can be explained as the transfer of a motif from the anecdote about Democritus' death (Hertz 1905 [*83: 387], Wehrli 1974 [*96: 65]); in addition, scholars have drawn on various ethnological and literary material related to the symbolism of the apple (Hertz 1905 [*83: 387–395], Kraemer 1956 [*89: 498], Plezia 1960 [*91: 66], Rousseau 1968 [*94: 12 n. 5], Acampora-Michel 2001 [*105: 107–109]).

However, Aristotle is cast in the role of the dying philosopher by the best and oldest Arabic manuscripts, as well as by the Arabic authors who mention the *Book of the Apple* (Iḫwān al-Ṣafāʾ, Ibn Ǧulǧul, Ibn Sabʿīn); and as already noted, a Greek origin of the work cannot be excluded. Therefore it seems necessary to examine the possibility of a distant Greek predecessor of the common core shared by all extant versions of this Pseudo-Aristotelian text, referring to Aristotle. As is well known, in Hellenistic times Aristotle's name was already attached to an alarming number of pseudepigrapha, obliging the ancient commentators to verify the authenticity of Aristotle's writings. This practice is attested even for the first editor of the Aristotelian corpus, Andronicus of Rhodes (Ammonius, *In De interpr.* 5,28–6,4); with the Alexandrian commentators belonging to the school of Ammonius it assumed the form of a standardized question (κεφάλαιον), which had to be clarified in each case before any of the Aristotelian works could be commented on (τὸ γνήσιον; cf. e.g. Ammonius, *In Cat.* 8,2–6; Philoponus, *In Cat.* 7,16–18; Simplicus, *In Cat.* 8,10–12; Olympiodorus, *Proleg.* 13,4–14,4).

The question whether it is possible to assume a Greek original of the *Book of the Apple* should not aim at identifying specific Greek sources, but first and foremost should take into account the traditions referring to Aristotle and his reception in antiquity. There are several commonly accepted assumptions that may serve as points of departure:

(1) The defining influence of Plato's *Phaedo* on Greek literature (an instructive example being the now lost Aristotelian dialogue *Eudemus or On the Soul*), which on the one hand spawned a string of imitations (e.g. the pseudo-Platonic *Axiochus*, which is transmitted in the Platonic corpus and shares certain similarities with all extant versions of the *Book of the Apple*), and on the other hand served as model for the 'death of the philosopher', which became a topos of Greek biographical literature (Stauffer 1941 [*87: 29], Ronconi 1966 [*93: 1258–1259], Döring 1979 [*98: 37–38]).

(2) The ancient evidence for Aristotle in the role as interlocutor, both in his own dialogues (Cicero, *Letters to Quintus* frg. 3.5.1 [= frg. 34 Gigon], *Letters to Atticus* 13.19.4 [= frg. 1000 Gigon]) and in those written by others. Of decisive significance for evaluating Aristotle as *dramatis persona* in a Greek dialogue is a fragment from the dialogue *On Sleep* by the Peripatetic Clearchus (frg. 6 Wehrli).

(3) The 'Socratification' of Aristotle in the Greek biographical tradition, by transferring Socrates' manner of death (poison cup) and his continuing to live on for a while (Eumelus in Diogenes Laertius V 6) after an accusation of impiety (Favorinus in Diogenes Laertius V 5; cf. Hermippus frg. 48 Wehrli = 30 Bollansée), as well as by the comparison of his own fate to that of Socrates, which Aristotle is alleged to have drawn himself (Origen, *Against Celsus* I 380, *Vita Marciana* 41, Aelian, *Various Histories* 3.36).

(4) The existence of texts whose topic was the death of Aristotle is confirmed, for instance, by a deathbed anecdote in Gellius (*Attic Nights* 13.5,1–2) which has an uncanny resemblance to the introductory scene of the *Book of the Apple*; or by the information, provided by Plutarch, that

> Antipater emphasized Aristotle's powers of persuasion in a letter *On the Death of Aristotle* (*Comparison of Alcibiades and Coriolanus* 3,3; cf. *Comparison of Aristides and Cato the Elder* 2,5).

Much more important than these rather general points, however, is the fact that the Platonic portrait of Aristotle drawn in the *Book of the Apple* (in particular the endorsement of the immortality of the soul) does not necessarily indicate an imitation of the *Phaedo*. A Platonic Aristotle appears in fragments of his lost exoteric works (cf. e.g. *Eudemus* frg. 37a Rose = 56 Gigon, frg. 44 Rose = 65 Gigon, frg. 45 Rose = 59–62 Gigon, *Protrepticus* frg. 60 Rose = 106–107 Düring) as well as in the Greek exegesis of Aristotle's extant writings; to be exact, in those commentators who apply the so-called συμφωνία τῶν φιλοσόφων, the harmonization of Plato's and Aristotle's philosophy, as an interpretative principle. This is a tendency whose beginnings can be observed soon after Aristotle's death (cf. Gerson 2005 [*108], Karamanolis 2006 [*109]), and which was consolidated as a principle in Ammonius' school. It usually means that Aristotle is interpreted in a way that will make him agree with Plato. An example is the harmonization of Aristotelian psychology with that of Plato's *Phaedo* (cf. Kotzia 2007 [*110: 203–222 and 174–187. 257–264]).

The most direct link between the *Book of the Apple* and the Greek Aristotelian tradition, however, seems to be the very presence of the apple itself: it refers to the main topic of the Pseudo-Aristotelian work, the nature of the soul. For the apple and its scent constitute a frequent motif of philosophical texts, since at least the 2nd century AD, e.g. in the Sceptic τρόποι τῆς ἐποχῆς (tropes of the suspension of judgement, cf. Sextus Empiricus, *Outlines of Pyrrhonism* I 94–99, Diogenes Laertius IX 80) or in the debate between Stoics and Peripatetics about the corporeality or incorporeality of qualities (Alexander of Aphrodisias, *Mantissa* 123,23–35, [Galen], *On Incorporeal Qualities* 6,17–8,5). The most important point is, though, that for the Greek commentators of Aristotle, the scent of the apple serves as a typical example (1) within the discussion of a philosophical *aporia* specifying problems of the important ontological differentiations, established in the *Categories* (2, 1a20-b9), between substances and accidents, i.e. between the independent being of a thing and the 'being-in-a-subject' (for the same issue in Ibn al-Ṭayyib cf. Ferrari 2004 [*106a]); and (2) in reference to the various faculties (δυνάμεις) of the soul, which, in *On the Soul*, Aristotle assumes instead of the traditional 'parts of the soul'. A detailed analysis of the function of the scent of the apple within the Aristotelian exegetical tradition (cf. Kotzia 2007 [*110: 129–159]) shows that this example (which may have originated in the post-Aristotelian Peripatetic school [cf. Lykon frg. 18 Wehrli]) was used by the Neoplatonists in their interpretation of Aristotelian psychology, in order to defend Aristotle against 'false' interpretations. According to these interpretations the soul, being the perfection (ἐντελέχεια) of the body (Aristotle, *On the Soul* II 1), belongs to the category of quality and consequently is an accident existing 'in a subject' (the body) (cf. e.g. Nemesius, *On the Nature of Man* 2. 26,10–11 Morani). This would mean, however, that it does not have an independent existence, cannot detach itself from the body, and therefore must be mortal.

All this means that it is very likely, or in any case not to be ruled out, that all extant versions of the *Book of the Apple* share a common Greek core referring to Aristotle. It remains to be determined, however, which of the two traditions, the Arabic-Persian or the Hebrew-Latin one, is closer to this hypothetical Greek archetype, and how exactly these two traditions relate to each other. The commonly accepted verdict which regards the Hebrew-Latin tradition as a free adaptation of the Arabic-Persian one may be plausible, but only on the assumption that it goes back to the Arabic-Persian tradition known to us. However, several indications suggest that a further comparative study ought to be undertaken, which will perhaps lead to a revision of the scholarly consensus.

In the Hebrew-Latin version, and only there, we encounter exegetical topoi current in the Greek Neoplatonic commentaries, as well as characteristic features of the image of the Arabic Aristotle (cf. Kotzia 2007 [*110: 281–296]); the Arabic-Persian tradition does not refer to any Greek ideas apart from the core common to all four versions (cf. Plezia 1959 [*90: 192]). Even those passages of the Hebrew-Latin version which are to be regarded as insertions fit into this Greek-Arabic image of Aristotle, being topoi associated with the topic of the *Book of the Apple* (e.g. the passage on the nature of the soul). Particularly illuminating is the refutation of the specifically Aristotelian doctrine of the eternity of the world in favour of a 'creation from nothing' (*creatio ex nihilo*), conducted by 'Aristotle' himself. For several scholars, this statement by 'Aristotle', which is missing in the Arabic-Persian version, constituted the decisive reason for attributing the (extant) Arabic 'original' to al-Kindī (Massignon 1929 [*85: 178. 186], GAL 1937 [*86: S I 373], Abel 1944 [*88: 71]; cf. Kraemer 1956 [*89: 505–506], Plezia 1959 [*90: 194], Rousseau 1968 [*94: 34], Bielawski 1974 [*95: 134], Gutas 1988 [*102: 45–46 n. 39]). That there once was an Arabic version of the *Book of the Apple* in which 'Aristotle' argues against the eternity of the world, however, can be seen from information given by Ibn Sabʿīn, who invokes this Pseudo-Aristotelian work in order to prove that Aristotle had given up this doctrine towards the end of his life (Ibn Sabʿīn, *The Sicilian Questions*; cf. Akasoy 2005 [*107: 95. 139]).

The points made above lead to the assumption that the Hebrew-Latin tradition represents a different Arabic version which is closer to the hypothetical Greek original, and which is lost or has not yet been identified; to this it may be added that the Hebrew version probably is a summary, as was customary with the Jewish translators from Arabic into Hebrew (cf. Niese 1912 [*84: 507–508]). If this assumption were found to be correct, the extant Arabic-Persian version would then represent a free adaptation of the Arabic archetype. This, however, is yet to be investigated.

2 Scholars as Transmitters of Philosophical Thought

Dimitri Gutas

2.1 Ḥunayn b. Isḥāq – 2.2 Ṯābit b. Qurra

2.1 *Ḥunayn b. Isḥāq*

2.1.1 Primary sources – 2.1.2 Life – 2.1.3 Works (W) – 2.1.4 Doctrine.

2.1.1 Primary Sources

2.1.1.1 Bio-bibliographical Testimonies [*81–*88] – 2.1.1.2 Works [*101–*137]

2.1.1.1 *Bio-bibliographical Testimonies*

81 al-Masʿūdī, Abū l-Ḥasan ʿAlī b. al-Ḥusayn. *Kitāb al-tanbīh wa-l-išrāf* [composed 345/956]. –Ed. by Michael Jan de Goeje, *Kitâb at-tanbîh wa'l-ischrâf auctore al-Masûdî.* Leiden, 1894. – Ed. by ʿAbd Allāh Ismāʿīl al-Ṣāwī. Cairo, 1357/1938.

82 al-Masʿūdī. *Murūǧ al-ḏahab wa-maʿādin al-ǧawhar*. –Ed. by Charles Pellat, 7 vols. Beirut, 1966–1979.

83 Ibn al-Nadīm, Abū l-Faraǧ Muḥammad b. Isḥāq (d. 380/990). *Kitāb al-Fihrist* [composed 377/988]. – Ed. by Gustav Flügel, August Müller and Johannes Roediger, 2 vols. Leipzig, 1871–1872 (ed. quoted below). – Repr. Beirut, 1964, Frankfurt a.M., 2005. – Ed. by Riḍā Taǧaddud. Tehran, 1350 h.š./1971. – Ed. by Ayman Fu'ād Sayyid, 2 vols. London, 1430/2009. – Engl. transl. by Bayard Dodge, *The Fihrist of al-Nadīm*, 2 vols. New York, 1970.

84 Ibn Ǧulǧul, Sulaymān b. Ḥassān (d. around 384/994). *Ṭabaqāt al-aṭibbā' wa-l-ḥukamā'*. – Ed. by Fu'ād Sayyid: *Les générations des médecins et des sages.* Cairo, 1955.

85 al-Andalusī, Abū l-Qāsim Ṣāʿid b. Aḥmad (d. 462/1070). *Ṭabaqāt al-umam*. – Ed. by Louis Šayḫū (Cheikho). Beirut, 1912.

86 Ibn al-Qifṭī, Ǧamāl al-Dīn ʿAlī b. Yūsuf (d. 646/1248). *Taʾrīḫ al-Ḥukamāʾ* [*Iḫbār al-ʿulamāʾ bi-aḫbār al-Ḥukamāʾ*: epitome by Muḥammad b. ʿAlī al-Zawzanī]. – Ed. by Julius Lippert, *Ibn al-Qifṭī's Taʾrīḫ al-Ḥukamāʾ*. Leipzig, 1903.

87 Ibn Abī Uṣaybiʿa, Muwaffaq al-Dīn Aḥmad b. al-Qāsim (d. 668/1270). *ʿUyūn al-anbāʾ fī ṭabaqāt al-aṭibbāʾ*. – Ed. by August Müller, 2 vols. Cairo, 1299/1882; Königsberg, 1884. – Repr. Westmead, 1972.

88 Ibn al-ʿIbrī, Abū l-Faraǧ Gregorios [Barhebraeus] (d. 685/1286). *Taʾrīḫ muḫtaṣar al-duwal*. – Ed. by Anṭūn Ṣāliḥānī. Beirut, 1890, 1958 (2nd ed.).

2.1.1.2 *Works*

Collections of Reprints

101 Sezgin, Fuat et al., eds. *Ḥunayn ibn Isḥāq (d. 260/873): Texts and Studies*. Islamic Medicine, 23. Frankfurt a.M., 1996.

102 Sezgin, Fuat et al., eds. *Ḥunayn ibn Isḥāq (d. 260/873): Texts and Studies*. Islamic Philosophy, 17. Frankfurt a.M., 1999.

Autobiography, Correspondence, Bibliography

105 *Ḥunain ibn Isḥāq über die syrischen und arabischen Galen-Übersetzungen, zum ersten Mal herausgegeben und übersetzt von Gotthelf Bergsträsser*. Leipzig, 1925. – Repr. Nendeln, Liechtenstein, 1966.

106 *Neue Materialien zu Ḥunain ibn Isḥāq's Galen-Bibliographie von Gotthelf Bergsträsser*. Leipzig, 1932. – Repr. Nendeln, Liechtenstein, 1966.

107 "*Maqāla fī Ṯabat al-kutub allatī lam yaḏkurhā Ǧālīnūs fī Fihrist kutubihi, waṣafa fīhā ǧamīʿ mā wuǧida li-Ǧālīnūs min al-kutub allatī lā yušakku annahā lahu*." In G. Bergsträsser [*106: 84–91]. – German transl. ibid., 91–98.

108 *Mā aṣābahu min al-miḥan wa-l-šadāʾid*. – Arab. Text in Ibn Abī Uṣaybiʿa [*87: I 191,1–197,23]. – Engl. transl. by Michael Cooperson, in D. Reynolds 2001 [*149: 109–118].

109 *Une correspondance islamo-chrétienne entre Ibn al-Munaǧǧim, Ḥunayn ibn Isḥāq et Qusṭā ibn Lūqā*. Introduction, édition, divisions, notes et index par Khalil Samir; introduction, traduction et notes par Paul Nwyia. Turnhout, 1981.

Physics

116 [Ḥunayn] Pseudo-Avicenna. *Liber celi et mundi*. Ed. by Oliver Gutman. Leiden, 2003.

117 *Fī anna l-ḍawʾ laysa bi-ǧism*. (a) Ed. by Louis Cheikho: "Notice sur un ancien manuscrit arabe." In *Actes du onzième congrès international des orientalists*. Paris, 1897. Troisième section, 125–142, text and French transl. – (b) Ed. by Louis Cheikho: "Fī l-ḍawʾ wa-ḥaqīqatihi." *Al-Mašriq* 24 (1899): 1105–1113, text only. – Repr. of both in F. Sezgin 1996 [*101: 1–18. 20–28]. – German transl. by Curt Prüfer

and Max Meyerhof, "Die aristotelische Lehre vom Licht bei Ḥunain b. Isḥāq." *Der Islam* 2 (1911): 117–128. – Repr. in F. Sezgin 1996 [**101*: 75–86].

118 Daiber, Hans. *Ein Kompendium der aristotelischen Meteorologie in der Fassung des Ḥunain ibn Isḥāq*. Amsterdam, Oxford, 1975.

Medicine

121 *The Book of the Ten Treatises on the Eye, Ascribed to Hunain ibn Ishaq (809–877 A.D.): The Earliest Existing Systematic Text-Book of Ophthalmology*. The Arabic Text Edited from the only two Known Manuscripts, with an English Translation and Glossary by Max Meyerhof. Cairo, 1928. – Repr. in F. Sezgin 1996 [**101*]). – Partial German transl. by Max Meyerhof and Curt Prüfer, "Die Lehre vom Sehen bei Ḥunain b. Isḥāq." *Archiv für Geschichte der Medizin* 6 (1913): 21–33. – Repr. in F. Sezgin 1996 [**101*: 87–99].

122 *Le Livre des questions sur l'œil de Honain ibn Isḥāq, par Paul Sbath et Max Meyerhof*. Cairo, 1938. – Arab. text and French transl. – Repr. in F. Sezgin 1996 [**101*: 113–263].

123 *Masāʾil fī l-Ṭibb li-l-mutaʿallimīn li-Ḥunayn b. Isḥāq*. – Ed. and study by Muḥammad ʿAlī Abū Rayyān, Mursī Muḥammad ʿArab, Ǧalāl Muḥammad Mūsā. Cairo, 1978. – Engl. transl. by Paul Ghalioungui, *Questions on Medicine for Scholars by Ḥunayn ibn Isḥāq*. Translated into English, with a Preface and Historical Note. Cairo, 1980.

Theology and Religion

131 *Maqāla fī Kayfiyyat idrāk ḥaqīqat al-diyāna*. – (a) Ed. by Louis Cheikho: "Un traité inédit de Ḥonein." In *Orientalische Studien, Theodor Nöldeke zum siebzigsten Geburtstag gewidmet*, vol. 1. Ed. by Carl Bezold. Gießen, 1906, 283–291. – Repr. in F. Sezgin 1999 [**102*: 235–243]. – (b) Ed. by Paul Sbath, *Mabāḥiṯ falsafiyya dīniyya li-baʿḍ al-qudamāʾ min ʿulamāʾ al-naṣrāniyya*. Cairo, 1929, 171–175. – (c) Ḫalīl Samīr, "Maqālat Ḥunayn b. Isḥāq fī kayfiyyat idrāk ḥaqīqat al-diyāna." *Al-Mašriq* 71 (1997): 345–363.

132 *Maqāla fī l-Āǧāl*. Ed. by Ḫalīl Samīr, "Maqāla fī l-Āǧāl li-Ḥunayn b. Isḥāq." *Al-Mašriq* 65 (1991): 403–425.

Popular Ethics

136 *Ādāb al-falāsifa* – see above [**16*] under gnomologia.

137 *Qiṣṣat Salāmān wa-Absāl*. In *Tisʿ rasāʾil fī l-ḥikma wa-l-ṭabīʿiyyāt, taʾlīf Abī ʿAlī al-Ḥusayn b. ʿAbd Allāh Ibn Sīnā, wa-fī āḫirihā Qiṣṣat Salāmān wa-Absāl tarǧamahā min al-yūnānī Ḥunayn b. Isḥāq*. Constantinople, 1298/1880–1881. – Repr. in *Rasaʾil fī l-falsafa, Abū ʿAlī al-Ḥusayn b. ʿAbd allāh Ibn Sīnā*. Frankfurt a.M., 1999.

2.1.2 Life

Ḥunayn b. Isḥāq, Abū Zayd al-ʿIbādī, was born in 192/808: in his *Risāla*, an autobibliographical essay which he addressed to his colleague and patron ʿAlī b. Yaḥyā (Bergsträsser [*105: 52/43]), he says that he was 48 years old in the year 1167 of the Seleucid era; he was accordingly born in year 1119 of the same era, corresponding to 1 October 807–30 September 808 AD, which covers most of the Hijra year 192. He came from a Nestorian Arab family in al-Ḥīra, a city in the south of Iraq close to the Euphrates (just south of Islamic Kufa), where his father was an apothecary. Though al-Ḥīra, which had been the capital of the pre-Islamic Arab dynasty of the Lakhmids (a tribe in federation with the Sasanian Persians against the Byzantines), had lost much of its former splendor at the time Ḥunayn was born, the schools of the Nestorian community there must have been good enough to have provided the basic education and attitude to learning that we can witness in Ḥunayn. We have no details about his early education, though it is clear that he must have been trilingual, speaking Arabic at home and studying Syriac and Greek at school, the latter two being the languages of Nestorian and Orthodox Christianity.

Ḥunayn moved to Baghdad by the time he was sixteen and apparently benefited, in earning his living, from contacts with his Nestorian co-religionists in the Abbasid capital. By the time he was seventeen years old, he says in the *Risāla* (Bergsträsser [*105: 11,3. 15,16–17]) – that is, by 209/825 – he had already translated two books by Galen into Syriac for Ǧibrīl b. Baḫtīšūʿ (d. 211/827), the senior member of the most powerful medical family in Baghdad and the personal physician of the caliph al-Maʾmūn. This indicates that so great was the need in Baghdad for skilled translators from Greek into Syriac and Arabic that even a provincial youth of seventeen could find commissions from the highest echelons of the society. He then went to study medicine with Yūḥannā b. Māsawayh, a renowned physician active at the court of the caliph, but apparently he had to interrupt his studies when Yūḥannā rebuffed him for his insufficient knowledge of Greek. Ḥunayn left Baghdad and re-appeared some two years later, commanding Greek to such an extent as to be able to recite Homer by heart. One report mentions that he learned his Greek in Alexandria (Ibn Ǧulǧul [*84: 69,7]), whereas another has him visit and study in the lands of the Byzantines (Ibn al-Qifṭī [*86: 173,7]); but these reports cannot be verified. He returned to Baghdad in 211/827 – just before the death of Ǧibrīl b. Baḫtīšūʿ (cf. Ibn Abī Uṣaybiʿa [*87: 186,1] for the temporal reference) – was reconciled with Yūḥannā b. Māsawayh, and resumed his studies.

Ḥunayn soon made a name for himself as a translator of Greek works into both Syriac and Arabic, and found powerful sponsors and patrons in Baghdad.

Apparently the first sponsors after his studies were the Banū Mūsā (Ibn al-Qifṭī [*86:173,8]), the three sons of a wealthy adventurer who befriended al-Ma'mūn, for whom he worked on a regular basis, receiving a princely 'monthly salary of 500 dinars for translation and living expenses' (*Fihrist* [*83: 243,18–20]; see also below in the life of Ṯābit). He is reported to have been sent by his employers to Byzantium on expeditions in search of Greek manuscripts for translation and to have returned with rare and precious texts (*Fihrist* [*83: 243,15–17]). This report is difficult to verify; in his *Risāla* Ḥunayn himself does not say anything about visiting Byzantium when he was looking for specific manuscripts but the only names he mentions are ancient Greek cities within the Islamic world (Antioch, Alexandria, etc.). Among his other sponsors were family members of the Abbasid elite, various high standing government officials, and numerous scholars and professionals, including his teacher, Yūḥannā, Ṭayfurī the physician (*Fihrist* [*83: 298,2]), and, as already mentioned, the influential Baḫtīšūʿ family of Nestorian physicians.

Ḥunayn worked with a group of associates and students with whom he shared the various translation tasks. Among his students there are counted, first and foremost, his son, Isḥāq b. Ḥunayn, his nephew Ḥubayš al-Aʿṣam, ʿĪsā b. ʿAlī, and ʿĪsā b. Yaḥyā b. Ibrāhīm (*Fihrist* [*83: 297,19–27. 298,16–22]). Ḥunayn's success aroused the envy of his Christian colleagues, who calumniated against him to the caliph. Ḥunayn was imprisoned and his library confiscated, as he himself reports in an autobiographical account, but was eventually released with many compensations, including an appointment as chief physician to the court, a post he held until his death (Ibn Abī Uṣaybiʿa [*87: 191,1–197,23]). The accuracy of this text has been doubted (Strohmaier 1965 [*127: 528–530]) just as more recent research points to its literary and stylized character (Reynolds 2001 [*149: 108]), as well as to its dependence on Galen. On the whole, though, it is certain that some such event did take place: in the *Risāla*, Ḥunayn makes reference to the loss of his books (Bergsträsser [*105: 2,5 Arabic text]. The precise details and circumstances of the incident may not be clear. Ḥunayn died in Baghdad on Tuesday, 6 Ṣafar 260/ 1 December 873, corresponding to 1 December (Kānūn I) 1185 of the Seleucid Era. This date is given in the *Fihrist* and repeated by others. Ibn Abī Uṣaybiʿa's deviating information, on the other hand, is incorrect (Graf 1947 [*125: 123 n. 2]).

Ḥunayn's own scientific activities were mostly in the area of medicine and especially ophthalmology. In general medicine he composed an introductory handbook in the form of questions and answers, named *Questions on Medicine* (*Masāʾil fī l-Ṭibb*), which met with great popularity both in Arabic (though it was criticized by al-Kindī's student, al-Saraḫsī [*Fihrist* [*83: 262, 16]) and, in its

Latin version (*Isagoge Johannitii*), in the medieval West. In ophthalmology his major work is *The Book of the Ten Treatises on the Eye*, also translated into medieval Latin, and an introductory work, *Questions on the Eye*. Ḥunayn's scholarly interests were broad, and he wrote treatises on sundry subjects, including philosophy, meteorology, Christian theology, and the maxims of Greek philosophers, some of which are extant. But his greatest contribution was doubtless his skilful translation of classical Greek works into Syriac and Arabic.

2.1.3 Works (W)

2.1.3.1 Own Works: Autobiography – Bibliography [°1–°5]; Introduction to Philosophy and the Sciences [°6–°8]; Logic [°9–°13]; Physics [°14–°15]; Astronomy/Astrology [°16]; Meteorology [°17–°21]; Mineralogy [°22–°23]; Optics [°24–°25]; History [°26]; Theology and Religion [°27–°30]; Popular Ethics [°31]; Grammar [°32–°33]. – 2.1.3.2 Translations: Aristotle [°34–°43]; Plato [°44–°46]; Galen [°47–°59]; Others [°60–°62].

In the following survey, individual works are referred to by W °1, W °2, W °3 etc.

The works of Ḥunayn have not yet received a detailed and critical inventory. Information about his works is found in four main sources: (a) manuscripts which ascribe the works they contain to Ḥunayn, (b) medieval bibliographers who list his works, and who compiled these lists both from previous lists, which may go back to students and relatives of the author, and from the manuscripts mentioned in (a); (c) incidental references to or quotations from Ḥunayn's works in subsequent literature; and (d) the critical work of modern scholars trying to evaluate the information from all these sources and assess its reliability. An inventory of Ḥunayn's works that would coordinate and rationalize all this information remains to be done. The works that are available do little more than present the lists of the medieval bibliographers (cf. al-Sāmarrāʾī, al-ʿAlūǧī 1974 [*135], Ḥabbī 1974 [*133], Samīr [*132: 405–414]).

The analytical discussion of Ḥunayn's works is further complicated by the fact that he was both a translator and an author in his own right. In the case of medieval Arabic authors, however, the distinction between author, compiler, abridger, and 'original' composer is sometimes difficult to draw. Many of the works ascribed to Ḥunayn are described as *ǧawāmiʿ*, epitomes, or *ṯamara*, anthology, of works by Galen and others. Even if the Arabic translations of the epitomized Greek works in question are assumed to have been made by Ḥunayn himself – something which is not a given – the work of abridging or epitomizing involved in the production of these titles may be considered as original, though even in this case it is not clear whether these works should be considered as Ḥunayn's own or as part of his translations.

This is not the place to attempt such an inventory. For the purposes of the present volume, it is important to have an idea of the extent to which philosophical literature in general had penetrated into scholarly writing, using the term 'philosophical literature' in the broadest sense to encompass all the sciences that were included in the late Alexandrian curriculum of higher studies. Accordingly, in the list below I will present all the works by Ḥunayn, whether translations or his own, on all subjects except medicine, pharmacology, and veterinary medicine (for which see GAS [*3: III 247–256], and Ullmann 1970 [*128: 115–119]), and biology and agriculture (for which cf. GAS [*3: IV 337–338]).

In the case of his translations, for which we have the same sources as those I mentioned above, I have been conservative. It should be noted that manuscripts containing Arabic translations of Greek works frequently name Ḥunayn as the translator. These ascriptions are rarely reliable, being for the most part due to the wish of scribes or scholars to increase the authority (and possibly price?) of the work they are copying by ascribing the translation to the most famous translator. I have not taken them into consideration; the interested reader can find them, e.g., in the volumes of GAS dealing with the translated sciences by looking at the references to Ḥunayn in the indices. The list below includes only those translations which can be ascribed to Ḥunayn with relative certainty, either because Ḥunayn himself claims to have translated them or because serious philological evidence has been presented for their authenticity on linguistic and stylistic grounds.

2.1.3.1 *Own Works*

Autobiography – Bibliography

°1 *Risālat Ḥunayn b. Isḥāq ilā ʿAlī b. Yaḥyā fī ḏikr mā turǧima min kutub Ǧālīnūs bi-ʿilmihi wa-baʿḍ mā lam yutarǧam*

Ḥunayn b. Isḥāq's Epistle to ʿAlī b. Yaḥyā, on the Books by Galen that he knows to have been translated, and on some of those that have not been translated

Ibn Abī Uṣaybiʿa [*87: 198,26] = *Fihrist* [*83: 294,30–295,1 = *Fihrist* 295,3–4]. This autobibliography – a unique extant document about the Graeco-Arabic translations by one of the principal participants – was written for the gentleman courtier and patron of the arts and sciences, ʿAlī b. Yaḥyā b. al-Munaǧǧim (d. 275/888–889), who asked Ḥunayn to compile a bibliography of the Galenic translations (Bergsträsser [*105] and [*106]). ʿAlī came from a prominent Zoroastrian family which had converted in the meantime to Islam; it was his father, as a matter of fact, Yaḥyā b. Abī Manṣūr al-Munaǧǧim, who had professed Islam when invited to do so by the caliph al-Maʾmūn (cf. Fleischhammer 1993 [*139]).

°2 *Maqāla li-Ḥunayn b. Isḥāq fī ḏikr al-kutub allatī lam yaḏkurhā Ǧālīnūs fī Fihrist kutubihi*
A Treatise by Ḥunayn b. Isḥāq on the Books that Galen did not mention in the Index of his own Works

Ibn Abī Uṣaybiʿa [*87: 198,27–29]; GAS [*3: III 77]; Ullmann 1970 [*128: 36]. This brief essay is a continuation of the preceding, 'and in it Ḥunayn described all the extant undisputed books written by Galen after Galen had compiled the Index of his own works', according to Ibn Abī Uṣaybiʿa. Ed. and transl. by Bergsträsser [**106*: 84–98].

°3 *Ǧawāmiʿ Kitāb Ǧālīnūs fī kutub Buqrāṭ al-ṣaḥīḥa wa-ġayr al-ṣaḥīḥa*
Epitome of Galen's Book on the Authentic and Inauthentic Books by Hippocrates

Ibn Abī Uṣaybiʿa [*87: 199,2]; GAS [*3: III 26. 256]; Ullmann 1970 [*128: 26–27.53]. In the *Risāla* Ḥunayn mentions (no. 104) that he translated this piece into Syriac and then prepared an epitome of it. It was later that Isḥāq translated it into Arabic. Not extant.

°4 *Risāla ilā Salmawayh b. Bunān ʿammā saʾalahu min tarǧamat Maqālat Ǧālīnūs fī l-ʿĀdāt*
Epistle to Salmawayh b. Bunān, Replying to his Question about the Translation of Galen's treatise On Character Traits

Ibn Abī Uṣaybiʿa [*87: 200,7]. The letter survives in the same manuscript (Süleymaniye, MS Ayasofya 3725, fols 193b-194b) which also has the translation of the Galenic text itself (Ritter, Walzer 1934 [*123: 816 no. 25; 829 no. 7]). In his *Risāla* (no. 45) Ḥunayn mentions that he had translated the Galenic work for Salmawayh into Syriac, and that Ḥubayš had translated that version into Arabic. The letter accordingly should be discussing the Syriac translation in relation to the Greek original. The text remains unpublished and unstudied (cf. Klein-Franke 1979 [*137: 125–150]).

°5 *Mā aṣābahu min al-miḥan wa-l-šadāʾid*
On his Trials and Tribulations

Ibn Abī Uṣaybiʿa [*87: 200,20]. Autobiographic account of his trials at the hands of his calumniators, all Christian doctors in Baghdad, who falsely charged him with impiety to the caliph. Ḥunayn was imprisoned for some time, but in the end he was freed and his good name restored. Text in Ibn Abī Uṣaybiʿa [*87: I 191,1–197,23]. Engl. transl. by Cooperson in Reynolds 2001 [*149: 109–118].

Introduction to Philosophy and the Sciences

°6 *Ǧawāmiʿ Kitāb Ǧālīnūs fī anna l-ṭabīb al-fāḍil yaǧibu an yakūna faylasūfan ʿalā ṭarīq al-masʾala wa-l-ǧawāb*
Epitome in the Form of Questions and Answers regarding Galen's Book That the Best Physician is also a Philosopher

Ibn Abī Uṣaybiʿa [*87: 198,31–199,1]. Not extant.

°7 *Ǧawāmiʿ Kitāb Ǧālīnūs fī l-ḥaṯṯ ʿalā taʿallum al-ṭibb ʿalā ṭarīq al-masʾala wa-l-ǧawāb*
Epitome in the Form of Questions and Answers regarding Galen's Book On the Exhortation to Study Medicine

Ibn Abī Uṣaybiʿa [*87: 199,2]. Not extant.

°8 *Kitāb fīmā yuqraʾu qabla kutub Falāṭun*
On What is read before [the study of] Plato's books

Ibn Abī Uṣaybiʿa [*87: 200,2]. Not extant.

Logic

°9 *Masāʾil istaḫraǧahā min kutub al-manṭiq al-arbaʿa*
Questions Derived from the Four Books on Logic

Ibn Abī Uṣaybiʿa [*87: 199,22]. These books are apparently the *Categories*, *On Interpretation*, *Prior* and *Posterior Analytics*, though it is possible that the set may have included Porphyry's *Isagoge* and excluded the *Posterior Analytics*. It is not extant. The word 'Questions' in the title indicates not that the book treated difficult problems in these Aristotelian treatises but that it was cast in the form of questions and answers, an instructional format for beginners much beloved and used by Ḥunayn; cf. his *Masāʾil fī l-ṭibb li-l-mutaʿallimīn* (*Questions on Medicine for Beginners*) [*123].

°10 *Kitāb fī l-Manṭiq*
Book on Logic

Ibn al-Qifṭī [*86: 171,17] = Ibn Abī Uṣaybiʿa [*87: 200,1] = Ibn Ǧulǧul [*84: 69,12] = Ṣāʿid [*85: 37,6]. Ibn Ǧulǧul calls it *Kitāb fī Ṣināʿat al-manṭiq* (*Book on the Craft* [τέχνη] *of Logic*), and adds that it was unparalleled among similar books by his predecessors for its orderly and skilful arrangement (*lam yasbiqhu ilā miṯlihi ġayruhu li-ḥusni taqsīmihi wa-barāʿati niẓāmihi*), which Ibn al-Qifṭī copies but abbreviates to *aḥsana fīhi al-taqsīm* ('he arranged it very well'). This work, not extant, would also appear to have been an introductory account of logic, in all likelihood treating only the first three or four treatises of the *Organon*, together with Porphyry's *Isagoge* (*Introduction*).

°11 *Masāʾil muqaddama li-kitāb Furfuriyūs al-maʿrūf bi-l-Madḫal*
Preliminary Questions to Porphyry's Isagoge

Ibn Abī Uṣaybiʿa [*87: 200,24]. These questions, which, Ibn Abī Uṣaybiʿa adds, are to be read before Porphyry's book (manifestly the *Isagoge*), are not extant. Apparently a primer for students, in the form of preliminary questions and answers (see above), on the subject of Porphyry's work. Ṣāʿid al-Andalusī mentions an *Introduction to Logic* by Ḥunayn, which must be referring to this book (*kitābuhu fī Madḫal al-manṭiq* [*85: 37,7]).

°12 *Kitāb Qaṭīġūriyās ʿalā raʾy Ṭāmisṭiyūs, maqāla*
The Categories, according to Themistius; one book

Fihrist [*83: 295,1] = Ibn al-Qifṭī [*86: 174,1–2] = Ibn Abī Uṣaybiʿa [*87: 200,10]. Not extant. This would appear to be an epitome of Themistius' paraphrase of the *Categories*, apparently known in Arabic according to the *Fihrist* [*83: 248,21]. Ḥunayn relied considerably on Themistius for his Aristotelian works, as is apparent also from his epitome of *On the Heavens*, based on Themistius (see below under Physics, W °14).

°13 *Muḫtaṣar* [*Kitāb fī l-ʿIbāra*]
Abridgment of *On Interpretation*

Fihrist [*83: 249,4]. Not extant.

Physics

°14 *Ǧawāmiʿ Tafsīr al-qudamāʾ al-yūnāniyyīn li-kitāb Arisṭūṭālīs fī l-Samāʾ wa-l-ʿālam*
Epitome of Ancient Greek Commentaries on Aristotle's On the Heavens and the Earth

Ibn Abī Uṣaybiʿa [*87: 200,23–24 = 200,1] = *Fihrist* [*83: 251,1] = Ibn al-Qifṭī [*86: 40,4]. This particular title is found in Ibn Abī Uṣaybiʿa only. Ibn Abī Uṣaybiʿa cites the work a second time under a slightly different title, *Ǧawāmiʿ Kitāb al- Samāʾ wa-l-ʿālam* (*Epitome of On the Heavens and the Earth*). The *Fihrist* has a different description of the book. In its entry on Aristotle's *On the Heavens*, and after mentioning Ḥunayn's correction of Ibn al-Biṭrīq's translation and Themistius' commentary, he adds that Ḥunayn has 'something' on the Aristotelian work which consists of sixteen questions (*Fihrist* [*83: 250,28–29. 250,30–251,1] = Ibn al-Qifṭī [*86: 40,4]). The work is lost in Arabic but it has been apparently preserved in a Latin translation and a heavily edited Hebrew translation of the Latin (Glasner 1996 [*140]). In a remarkable piece of scholarly detective work, Alonso Alonso 1951 [*126] was able to identify the Latin translation, circulating in the extant manuscripts either anonymously or under the name of Ibn Sīnā, as the work of Ḥunayn. The text is in fact in sixteen chapters and it does rely on the Greek commentators of the Aristotelian treatise, including the paraphrase by Themistius (which is extant only in a Latin and a Hebrew translation of the Arabic, ed. in CAG V, iv, by Landauer, Berlin 1902; cf. Gutman [*116: xiii–xvii]). There is also a brief reference to the impetus theory of Philoponus (cf. Gutman [*116: 192–193]), which would make this work, if it is indeed by Ḥunayn, the first appearance in Arabic of this theory (cf. Pines 1938 [*124]). The Latin translation of Ḥunayn's text has been recently edited and translated into English under the name of Pseudo-Avicenna (Gutman [*116]) because the editor failed to take into consideration or understand all the Arabic evidence which was discussed by Alonso Alonso and which justifies the identification (though cf. Glasner 1996 [*140: 92–93]).

The work contains the following chapters: 1. That the body is more perfect than every other quantity, and that the world is more perfect than every other body (*On the Heavens* I 1); 2. That the nature of heaven is outside the four natures, and that it is a simple body (*On the Heavens* I 2); 3. That the body of heaven does not increase (*On the Heavens* I 3, 270a23–26; *On Generation and Corruption* I 4–5); 4. That heaven is not susceptible to generation or decay in its nature (*On the Heavens* I 3, 270a13–23); 5. That heaven is finite (*On the Heavens* I 5); 6. That there is only one world (*On the Heavens* I 8); 7. That the motion of the circle of the fixed stars from east to west cannot be caused by a body (*On the Heavens* II 1); 8. That heaven is spherical in shape (*On the Heavens* II 4); 9. That the whole universe is spherical in shape (*On the Heavens* II 4); 10. That earth is spherical in shape (*On the Heavens* II 4); 11. That the motion of heaven is constant (*On the Heavens* II 6, including a discussion of the impetus theory taken from Philoponus); 12. The purpose of the diversity and multitude of the motions of heaven (excursus on *On the Heavens* II 6); 13. Concerning the nature of the planets (*On the Heavens* II 7); 14. Why heaven does not warm us while the sun and the other warming planets do (excursus on *On the Heavens* II 7); 15. That heaven moves with a motion which is visible to us, but not the stars (*On the Heavens* II 8); 16. Concerning the generation of the four elements and what need there was for them (discussion of the four elements and the four qualities, unrelated to *On the Heavens*).

°15 *Kitāb fī Masāʾilihi al-ʿarabiyya*
On his Questions Written in Arabic

Ibn Abī Uṣaybiʿa [*87: 199,29]. According to M. Steinschneider 1893 [*121: 229–232], the title is to be read *al-Masāʾil al-ṭabīʿiyya* (*On Questions on Physics*). If Steinschneider's emendation is correct, this work cannot be what has survived as the Arabic translation of Aristotelian and Pseudo-Aristotelian *Problemata Physica*, ed. and transl. by L. S. Filius 1999 [*144]. Despite the ascription of the translation in the manuscripts to Ḥunayn b. Isḥāq and the arguments by Filius (xiv and xxx–xxxv) in favour of this ascription, M. Ullmann has conclusively shown that it is erroneous (review of Filius in in ZDMG 153 [*151: 470–473]). The referent of Ibn Abī Uṣaybiʿa's entry, again if Steinschneider's correction is to be accepted, may be a work whose fragments are quoted by al-Masʿūdī, *Murūǧ* [*82: VII 182–186 (Pellat)]; cf. GAS [*3: VII 267 no. 2].

Astronomy/Astrology

°16 *Risāla fī Ḏawāt al-ḏawāʾib wa-mā ḏukira fīhā min al-ʿaǧāʾib*
On Comets and Their Reported Marvels

GAS [*3: VII 328 no. 2]; Ullmann 1972 [*131: 316]; Rosenfeld, İhsanoğlu [*150: 37 no. A1]. Not mentioned by the bibliographers, this astronomical or astrological treatise is ascribed to Ḥunayn in several manuscripts. Its authenticity and contents have yet to be studied. Also open is the question of the relationship that this treatise bears to another work in a Princeton manuscript on comets, ascribed to Aristotle, with a commentary by Ḥunayn (cf. GAS [*3: VII 372, regarding p. 134]).

Meteorology

°17 *Maqāla fī l-Madd wa-l-ǧazr, maqāla*
Essay on Tides, one book

Fihrist [*83: 294,27] = Ibn al-Qifṭī [*86: 173,20] = Ibn Abī Uṣaybiʿa [*87: 199,30]; GAS [*3: VII 267 no. 6; 328 no. 1]. The book is not extant in direct transmission, though Sezgin, who claims that it 'has astrometeorological contents,' says that it is quoted in the *Kitāb al-Dalāʾil* of al-Ḥasan b. Bahlūl.

°18 *Kitāb fī Afʿāl al-šams wa-l-qamar*
On the Effects of the Sun and the Moon

Ibn Abī Uṣaybiʿa [*87: 199,30]; GAS [*3: VII 134]. Not extant. Sezgin suggests that it might be an astrological work, though it seems more probable that it was dealing with the meteorological aspects of the question (of W °17), given the demonstrable interest of Ḥunayn in these matters.

°19 *Maqāla fī l-Sabab allaḏī min aǧlihī ṣārat miyāh al-baḥr māliḥa, maqāla*
Essay on the Reason for the Salinity of Sea Water, one book

Fihrist [*83: 294,27–28] = Ibn al-Qifṭī [*86: 173,21] = Ibn Abī Uṣaybiʿa [*87: 200,9]; GAS [*3: VII 267 no. 7]. Not extant. The attribution to Ḥunayn is probably inaccurate; a similarly entitled essay is attributed to Ṯābit b. Qurra who is the most likely author (see below. § 9.2.2, W °16).

°20 *Kalām fī l-Āṯār al-ʿulwiyya*
On Meteorology

Ibn Abī Uṣaybiʿa [*87: 200,15]; GAS [*3: VII 267 no. 1]. In all likelihood this piece is to be identified with the epitome (*Ǧawāmiʿ*) of the Meteorology published by Daiber in 1975, though Daiber says [*118: 2,-8] that it is not mentioned by bibliographers. This epitome appears to be based on a late Greek compendium of Aristotelian meteorology with the addition of later material, though the particular contribution of Ḥunayn remains to be established (cf. Daiber [*118: 1–17] and Lettinck 1999 [*146: 8–9]).

It contains the following thirteen chapters: 1. On the composition of the universe and the five elements (Arist. *Meteor.* I 1–3); 2. On the generation of rain, dew, hoar frost and snow (*Meteor.* I 9–11); 3. On hail (*Meteor.* I 12); 4. On rivers, springs, and wadis (*Meteor.* I 13–14); 5. On the oceans (*Meteor.* II 1–3); 6. On the winds (Meteor. II 4–6); 7. On earthquakes (*Meteor.* II 7–8); 8. On thunder and lightning (*Meteor.* II 9); 9. On the halo of the sun, the moon, and the stars (*Meteor.* III 2–3); 10. On the rainbow (*Meteor.* III 4–5); 11. On the pillars (of fire), shooting stars, and comets (*Meteor.* I 4–7); 12. On the redness which sometimes appears in the air on bright days (*Meteor.* III 6); 13. On the milky way (cf. *Meteor.* I 8, with additional material).

°21 *Maqāla fī Qaws quzaḥ*
On the Rainbow

Ibn Abī Uṣaybiʿa [*87: 200,15]; GAS [*3: VII 267 no. 3]. Not extant.

Mineralogy

°22 *Maqāla fī Tawallud al-nār bayna l-ḥaǧarayn, maqāla*
On the Generation of Fire Between Two Stones, one book

Fihrist [*83: 295,2–3] = Ibn al-Qifṭī [*86: 174,3] = Ibn Abī Uṣaybiʿa [*87: 200,3]. Not known to be extant. This essay also is probably spurious; an identically entitled essay is attributed to Ṯābit b. Qurra who is the most likely author (see below. § 9.2.2, W °19).

°23 *Kitāb Ḫawāṣṣ al-aḥǧār*
On the Properties of Stones

Ibn Abī Uṣaybiʿa [*87: 200,26] = GAL [*1: S I 368 no. 13]. Not known to be extant.

Optics

°24 *Fī anna l-ḍawʾ laysa bi-ǧism*
That Light Is Not a Body

GAS [*3: III 252 no. 4]. For editions and translations cf. the bibliography [*117].

°25 *Maqāla fī l-Alwān, maqāla*
On Colours, one book

Fihrist [*83: 294,28] = Ibn al-Qifṭī [*86: 173,21] = Ibn Abī Uṣaybiʿa [*87: 200,10]. Not known to be extant.

History

°26 *Kitāb Tāʾrīḫ al-ʿālam*
History of the Universe

Ibn Abī Uṣaybiʿa [*87: 200,15]. Not known to be extant. Ibn Abī Uṣaybiʿa gives the contents of the work as follows: 'The beginning (of the world), prophets, kings, nations, caliphs, kings in the Islamic period. He began the book with Adam and those who came after him, and mentioned the kings of the Israelites, the kings of the Greeks and Romans, the beginnings of Islam, the kings of the Umayyads, the kings of the Hāšimites (= Abbasids), up to his own time, which was the days of al-Mutawakkil' (regn. 232–247/847–861).

Theology and Religion

°27 *Kitāb fī Kaifiyyat idrāk al-diyāna*
On How to Understand Religion

Ibn Abī Uṣaybiʿa [*87: 199,20] = *Kitāb fī Idrāk ḥaqīqat al-adyān* (*On Understanding the Truth of* [*a*] *Religion*, Ibn Abī Uṣaybiʿa [*87: 200,26–27]). These two titles, which clearly refer to the same work, stand for a different recension of the answer Ḥunayn gave to ʿAlī b. Yaḥyā and which Ibn Abī Uṣaybiʿa [*87: 200,20–21] lists under the title *Kitāb ilā*

ʿAlī b. Yaḥyā, ǧawāb kitābihi fīmā daʿāhu ilayhi min dīn al-islām (*Letter to ʿAlī b. Yaḥyā, in Answer to the latter's Call to him to embrace Islam*). Edited and translated in the philosophical correspondence published by Samir and Nwyia [**109*].

°28 *Maqāla fī l-Āǧāl*
On the Terms of Life

Ibn Abī Uṣaybiʿa [**87*: 200,3] = *Fihrist* [*83: 295,2]. It survives as quoted by Ibn al-ʿAssāl in his work on the principles of religion, *Maǧmūʿ uṣūl al-dīn*, and was edited by Ḫ. Samīr (cf. GAS [*3: III 254 no. 32]).

°29 *Risāla fī Dalālat al-qadar ʿalā l-tawḥīd*
That Predestination Indicates the Oneness of God

Ibn Abī Uṣaybiʿa [**87*: 200,7]. Not known to be extant.

°30 *Maqāla fī Ḫalq al-insān wa-annahu min maṣlaḥatihi wa-l-tafaḍḍul ʿalayhi ǧuʿila muḥtāǧan*
On the Nature of Man, and That he has been Created not Self-sufficient for his Own Good and as a Favour to him

Ibn Abī Uṣaybiʿa [**87*: 200,1–2]. Samīr quotes [**132*: 413] al-Sāmarrāʾī and al-ʿAlūǧī as saying that this work is identical with the one known as *Tuḥfat al-alibbāʾ wa-ḏaḫīrat al-aṭibbāʾ* (*The Gift for the Sensible Ones and the Treasure of the Physicians*), a manuscript of which is preserved in Rabat (GAS [*3: III 254 no. 19]). If that is correct, the alternate title would make it a medical work, but Samīr lists it under the books on religion.

Popular Ethics

°31 *Ādāb al-falāsifa*
Anecdotes of the Philosophers

See above § 9.1 [**16*].

Grammar

°32 *Kitāb fī l-Naḥw*
On Grammar

Ibn Abī Uṣaybiʿa [**87*: 200,1]. Not known to be extant; presumably on Arabic grammar.

°33 *Kitāb fī Aḥkām al-iʿrāb ʿalā madhab al-yūnāniyyīn, maqālatān*
On the Rules of Inflection in Greek, two books

Ibn Abī Uṣaybiʿa [*87: 200,8] = *Fihrist* [*83: 294,21]. Not known to be extant. It can only be guessed that this work was intended as a teaching manual of Greek for the translators in Ḥunayn's circle. That the very title should have survived until the time of Ibn Abī Uṣaybiʿa for him to discover would mean that Ibn Abī Uṣaybiʿa was drawing upon a list of Ḥunayn's works that derived from Ḥunayn's successors. Cf. the evidence regarding Ṯābit b. Qurra's works.

2.1.3.2 *Translations*

In this listing only those works are mentioned of which eventually an Arabic translation was made – books that were translated only into Syriac are not included. For these books cf. Degen 1981 [*138: 131–166]. For information on the Arabic translations of Galen cf. the entries in Ullmann 1970 [*128] and in GAS [*3 III].

Aristotle
Introduction to Aristotle

°34 *Nikolaos [Damaskios], wa-lahu min al-taṣānīf Kitāb min ǧumal* (sic lege, *ḥumal*, ed.) *falsafat Arisṭūṭālīs , wa-lanā nusḫatuhu bi-l-suryānī naql Ḥunayn b. Isḥāq*
The Main Points of Aristotle's Philosophy, composed by Nicolaus, of which we have a copy in a Syriac translation by Ḥunayn b. Isḥāq

Barhebraeus, *Muḫtaṣar* [*88: 82].

Logic

°35 *al-Kalām ʿalā Qāṭīġūriyās bi-naql Ḥunayn*
Translation of the Categories

Fihrist [*83: 248,20] = Ibn al-Qifṭī [*86: 35,2].

°36 *al-Kalām ʿalā Bārī Armīniyās, naqala Ḥunayn ilā l-suryānī wa-Isḥāq ilā l-ʿarabī al-naṣṣ*
Translation of On Interpretation into Syriac, and into Arabic by Isḥāq

Fihrist [*83: 249,1] = Ibn al-Qifṭī [*86: 35,17].

°37 *al-Kalām ʿalā Anālūṭīqā al-ūlā, naqalahu Ṯiyādūrus ilā l-ʿarabī wa-yuqālu ʿaraḍahu ʿalā Ḥunayn fa-aṣlaḥahu wa-naqala Ḥunayn qiṭʿatan minhu ilā l-suryānī*
Correction of the Arabic Translation by Theodorus of the Prior Analytics

Fihrist [**83*: 249,6–7] = Ibn al-Qifṭī [**86*: 36,5].

°38 *al-Kalām ʿalā Abūdīqṭīqā … naqala Ḥunayn baʿḍahu ilā l-suryānī wa-naqala Isḥāq al-kull ilā l-suryānī wa-naqala Mattā naql Isḥāq ilā l-ʿarabī*
Partial Translation of the Posterior Analytics into Syriac

Fihrist [**83*: 249,11] = Ibn al-Qifṭī [**86*: 36,12]. Not extant.

Physics

°39 *al-Kalām ʿalā Kitāb al-Samāʿ al-ṭabīʿī … al-Maqāla al-ṯāniya min naṣṣ Kalām Arisṭālīs fī Maqāla wāḥida, wa-naqalahā min al-yūnānī ilā l-suryānī Ḥunayn wa-naqalahā min al-suryānī ilā l-ʿarabī Yaḥyā Ibn ʿAdī*
Translation into Syriac of Physics Book II

Fihrist [**83*: 250,10–11] = Ibn al-Qifṭī [**86*: 38,14]. Not extant.

°40 *al-Kalām ʿalā Kitāb al-Kawn wa-l-fasād, naqalahu Ḥunayn ilā l-suryānī wa-Isḥāq ilā l-ʿarabī*
Translation into Syriac of On Generation and Corruption

Fihrist [**83*: 251,3] = Ibn al-Qifṭī [**86*: 40,17]. Not extant.

°41 *al-Kalām ʿalā Kitāb al-Nafs … naqalahu Ḥunayn ilā l-suryānī tāmman wa-naqalahu Isḥāq illā šayʾan yasīran*
Complete Translation into Syriac of On the Soul

Fihrist [**83*: 251,11] = Ibn al-Qifṭī [**86*: 41,6]. Not extant.

Metaphysics

°42 *al-Kalām ʿalā Kitāb al-Ḥurūf … wa-naqala Ḥunayn b. Isḥāq hāḏihi l-Maqāla* [*ay Maqālat al-lām bi-Tafsīr al-Iskandar*] *ilā l-suryānī*
Translation into Syriac of Book XII of Aristotle's Metaphysics, with the Commentary by Alexander of Aphrodisias

Fihrist [**83*: 251,29 = Ibn al-Qifṭī [**86*: 42,3]. Not extant. Cf. Bertolacci 2005 [*152: 244–245 and n. 9].

Physiognomy

°43 *Šarḥ Kitāb al-Firāsa li-Arisṭāṭālīs*
Commentary on Aristotle's Physiognomy

Ibn Abī Uṣaybiʿa [*87: 200,25]. This is a commented translation of the Pseudo-Aristotelian text (Ullmann 1970 [*128: 96]), preserved in Istanbul MS Topkapı Sarayı 3207. There is a preliminary discussion of the work by Grignaschi 1974 [*132]; ed., transl. and study by Ghersetti 1999 [*145]; cf. also Swain 2007 [*153: 287–290. 294. 313].

Plato

°44 *Kitāb al-Siyāsa, fassarahu Ḥunayn b. Isḥāq*
Translation of the Republic

Fihrist [*83: 246,5] = Ibn al-Qifṭī [*86: 17,20]. Not extant in its entirety, though the preserved portions may well be Ḥunayn's translation.

°45 *Kitāb al-Nawāmīs, naqalahu Ḥunayn wa-naqalahu Yaḥyā Ibn ʿAdī*
Translation of Plato's Laws, probably as in Galen's epitome (see below W °55)

Fihrist [*83: 246,5] = Ibn al-Qifṭī [*86: 17,20].

°46 *Kitāb Ṭīmāwus ṯalāṯa maqālāt, naqalahu Ibn al-Biṭrīq wa-naqalahu Ḥunayn b. Isḥāq aw aṣlaḥa Ḥunayn mā naqalahu Ibn al-Biṭrīq*
Translation, or Correction of Ibn al-Biṭrīq's Translation, of the Timaeus

Fihrist [*83: 246,15]. Not extant.

Galen

°47 *Fī anna l-Ṭabīb al-fāḍil faylasūf*
That the Best Physician is also a Philosopher

Risāla no. 103, Bergsträsser [*105: 44,15].

°48 *Fī l-ḥaṯṯ ʿalā taʿallum al-ṭibb*
Exhortation to the Study of Medicine

Risāla no. 110, Bergsträsser [*105: 46,8].

°49 *Fī l-Burhān*
On Demonstration

Risāla no. 115, Bergsträsser [**105*: 47,10].

°50 *Fī l-Aḫlāq*
On Ethics

Risāla no. 119, Bergsträsser [**105*: 49,5].

°51 *Fī Ṣarf al-iġtimām*
On Averting Sorrow

Risāla no. 120, Bergsträsser [**105*: 49,15].

°52 *Fī anna l-aḫyār min al-nās qad yantafiʿūna bi-aʿdāʾihim*
That Virtuous People may Benefit from Their Enemies

Risāla no. 121, Bergsträsser [**105*: 49,20]. This treatise, whose title shows great similarity with that by Plutarch, is documented in the Arabic sources only. For references cf. Ullmann 1970 [*128: 65 no. 117].

°53 *Fī mā ḏakarahu Aflāṭūn fī kitābihi l-maʿrūf bi-Ṭīmāwus min ʿilm al-Ṭibb*
What Plato Mentions Concerning the Science of Medicine in his Book known as Timaeus

Risāla no. 122, Bergsträsser [**105*: 50,3].

°54 *Fī anna quwā l-nafs tābiʿatun li-mizāǧ al-badan*
That the Faculties of the Soul Follow the Temperament of the Body

Risāla no. 123, Bergsträsser [**105*: 50,8].

°55 *Ǧawāmiʿ kutub Aflāṭūn*
Epitomes of Plato's Books

Risāla no. 124, Bergsträsser [**105*: 50,13].

°56 *Fī anna l-muḥarrik al-awwal lā yataḥarraku*
That the First Mover is not in Motion

Risāla no. 125, Bergsträsser [**105*: 51,5].

°57 *Fī l-Madḫal ilā l-manṭiq*
Introduction to Logic

Risāla no. 126, Bergsträsser [**105*: 51,10].

(°58 *Fī ʿAdad al-maqāyīs*)
On the Number of Syllogisms

Risāla no. 127, Bergsträsser [**105*: 51,14].

°59 *Fī Ārāʾ Buqrāṭ wa-Aflāṭūn*
On the Opinions of Hippocrates and Plato

Risāla no. 46, Bergsträsser [**105*: 26,16].

Others

°60 *Qiṣṣat Salamān wa-Absāl*
The Story of Salamān and Absāl

The MSS attribute the translation to Ḥunayn who supposedly translated it from Greek. If the analysis of Pines 1996 [*141] is accurate, it is very likely that there is a Greek substrate to the story.

°61 *Translation of the Septuagint into Arabic*
Mentioned by al-Masʿūdī, *Tanbīh* [**81*: 112,13]. Many, al-Masʿūdī adds, regarded it as the most accurate version of the Pentateuch in Arabic. Not extant.

°62 (?) *Translation into Arabic of Artemidorus' Oneirocriticon*
The ascription in the manuscript to Ḥunayn has been disputed by Ullmann 1971 [*130: 204–211].

2.1.4 Doctrine

This is not the place to discuss Ḥunayn's strictly medical works. However, since in some of his medical works he touches upon medical theory, his arguments are significant for the history of natural philosophy (physics). This happens most explicitly in his theory of vision. The third treatise (or chapter) of his major ophthalmological and justly famous book, *Ten Treatises on the Eye*, is divided into three sections, the second and third of which discuss the 'visual spirit' (*al-rūḥ al-bāṣir*) and the theory of vision respectively (Meyerhof [**121*: 98–111 Arab. text, 27–39 Engl. transl.]). These sections follow Galen's *De Placitis*

Hippocratis et Platonis VII 3–7 and possibly, Meyerhof suggests, also Galen's *De Demonstratione* (Meyerhof [*121: xli–xlii and 27 n. 1]), both of which were translated by Ḥunayn. There is a German translation and discussion of precisely these two sections by M. Meyerhof and C. Prüfer [*121].

Closely related to this subject is another extant work on the nature of light and its incorporeality, *Fi anna l-ḍawʾ laysa bi-ǧism* (*That Light Is Not a Body*, W °24). The title in the unique manuscript that has preserved it mentions that it was a collection of passages on the subject of light from the works of Aristotle that were put together by Ḥunayn, and that the text preserved in the MS is an extract therefrom made by what appears to be a descendant of Ṯābit b. Qurra, a certain Ibn Hilāl al-Ṣābiʾ who bears the title 'al-Qayyim'. This person would appear to be either the great Buyid personality Abū Isḥāq Ibrāhīm b. Hilāl (d. 384/994) or his great-grandson, Muḥammad b. Hilāl (d. 480/1088; cf. de Blois 1995 [*196]), possibly the former: he was, among other things, a renowned administrator in Baghdad (and hence the title al-Qayyim, for which see Schaade 1978 [*136]) and a man whose many interests included the sciences as well as literature, a field in which he made a name for himself. As for the second person, Muḥammad b. Hilāl, although he was, for what appears to be a short time, also an administrative secretary, he was known by the byname of Ġarsanniʿma and perhaps one would have expected to see him called by that name in the title. The Muslim sources do not seem to know Abū Isḥāq Ibrāhīm by the title 'al-Qayyim', though if the manuscript in which the work is preserved derives from Christian Baghdadian and indeed Sabian sources – something clearly indicated by its contents – then the title 'al-Qayyim' in the manuscript, meaning 'the Manager', could well reflect how he was known in the Sabian community: the man who managed and protected their affairs with the Muslim authorities. L. Cheikho's attempts (1897 [*117: 128], 1899 [*117: 1106]) to identify him with another individual (with a different name) have remained unsuccessful. Bergsträsser (1913 [*122: 9]) is of the opinion that the expression *li-l-Qayyim* in the title refers to the dedicatee or sponsor of Ḥunayn's piece (i.e., 'Texts collected by Ḥunayn for al-Qayyim Ibn Hilāl al-Ṣābi"), which is eminently plausible, except for the fact that he knows (and we know) of no person in Ḥunayn's time who bore that name. Since Hilāl al-Ṣābiʾ in the literature of the 5th/11th-6th/12th centuries is a well established and easily recognizable name, it is difficult to avoid seeing the reference as being to him.

The essay on light (W °24, edited twice by Cheikho, 1897 and 1899 [*117]) consists of two parts. The first includes thirteen arguments taken from Aristotle that prove that light is not a body, and the second is an equally Aristotelian discussion of the nature of colour and its relation to light and the transparent.

Most of the arguments presented draw on a number of Aristotelian works: the German translation of the essay by Prüfer and Meyerhof [*117] identifies the Aristotelian passages from which Hunayn's arguments derive. However, the proximate source of a good number of these arguments is the Arabic epitome, apparently by Ibn al-Biṭrīq, of a late antique paraphrase of *On the Soul* (Arnzen 1998 [*143: 63–71]). Doubt has been cast on the authenticity of the attribution of this essay to Ḥunayn on the basis of its linguistic peculiarities which are divergent for the most part from those that have been normally taken to be those of Ḥunayn (Arnzen 1998 [*143: 708–717]), but this would seem to be hardly relevant here. If Ḥunayn were assembling a sourcebook from extant Arabic translations like that of the anonymous paraphrase of *On the Soul*, then the language of the translated texts would not be his. Rather, what would seem to favour the attribution of the essay to Ḥunayn is the subject matter, namely, vision and related subjects.

Ḥunayn's great contribution to medicine was in ophthalmology, and the physics of vision certainly interested him, as discussed above in connection with the theory of vision in his major book on the *Ten Treatises on the Eye*. The essay on light falls naturally within this subject, as does the other work mentioned by the bibliographers, *On Colours* (W °25). As far as we now know, this essay has not survived. However, as already mentioned, the second half of the essay on light is on colour, and it may not be implausible to suggest that this part is precisely what the bibliographers are referring to (as already timidly suggested by Bergsträsser 1913 [*122: 9]).

The fragmentation of Ḥunayn's work and the independent transmission of its parts that may have happened in this case are not unique; we meet them again in the case of Ḥunayn's philosophy of religion. Ḥunayn was on excellent terms with his patron ʿAlī b. Yaḥyā b. al-Munaǧǧim (d. 275/888–889). A man of his times, ʿAlī b. Yaḥyā expressed nothing but the rationalism of the Baghdad intellectuals when he wrote an epistle to Ḥunayn inviting him to convert to Islam on the grounds that he, ʿAlī, had provided demonstrative and geometrical proofs for the prophethood of Muḥammad: according to the beginning of the text as it has come down to us in a unique manuscript, he even entitled his epistle as *al-Burhān* ('The Demonstrative Proof', W °49). Apparently his son, Abū ʿĪsā Aḥmad, sent a similar letter a few decades later to the great translator and scientist Qusṭā b. Lūqā when the latter had already moved to Armenia; according to Ibn Abī Uṣaybiʿa, however, the title of this epistle was, *Fī nubuwwat Muḥammad* (*On the Prophethood of Muḥammad*, Ibn Abī Uṣaybiʿa [*87: 233,18]; cf. Nwyia's introduction in Samir, Nwyia [*109: 538–552]; for a different interpretation of the correspondents cf. Haddad 1974 [*134]; further literature cited in Samir, Nwyia [**109*: 532–533]). In reality, however, ʿAlī b. Yaḥyā's case for the prophethood of Muḥammad is but a variant of the standard arguments put forth by Muslim theologians of his time, derived from the doctrine of the inimitability of the Quran based on the inability of pre-Islamic Arabs to produce its like when challenged (*taḥaddī*) by the Prophet to do so. Similar arguments were put forth by ʿAlī b. Yaḥyā's contemporary, al-Ǧāḥiẓ.

The unique manuscript has preserved different parts of this debate: the original letter of ʿAlī b. Yaḥyā, Ḥunayn's response to him, and Qusṭā's response to Abū ʿĪsā Aḥmad's letter (edited and translated by Samir, Nwyia [**109*]), but not that letter itself. Ḥunayn's response has also been transmitted by itself as excerpted in the 7th/13th century Coptic theologian Ibn al-ʿAssāl and apparently in independent manuscript transmission, under the title *Kitāb fī Kayfiyyat idrāk al-diyāna* (*How to Grasp Religion*, Ibn Abī Uṣaybiʿa [**87*: 199,20]), or *Kitāb fī idrāk Ḥaqīqat al-adyān* (*How to Grasp the Truth of a Religion*, [**87*: 200,26–27], W °27). Samir has promised an edition, translation, and study of this branch of the transmission (Samir, Nwyia [**109*: 525]), but it has not yet appeared.

Ḥunayn's answer turns on epistemological arguments of a logical nature which, however, do not neglect what we would today call the anthropological or sociological and psychological dimensions of epistemology. He first denies that ʿAlī b. Yaḥyā has set up any 'demonstrative proofs' in support of his claim because, Ḥunayn says, such proofs are based on propositions admitted by everybody, whereas the propositions used by ʿAlī – i.e., the historical facts of Muḥammad's prophethood – are not such premises. He then proceeds to an analysis of the ways in which truth can be discriminated from falsehood. He says that there are six reasons for which people accept falsehood: (1) being forced against their will; (2) hope for improved circumstances when they happen to be in severe and intolerable difficulties; (3) abandoning one's religion in search of power, glory, and riches; (4) being misled by cunning interlocutors; (5) lack of social disapproval when one is a member of a very ignorant and uncultured society; (6) disinclination to break ethnic ties with one's people when the prophet (i.e., he who invites to a false religion) is a member of one's tribe. As for the reasons for which people accept truth, they are four: (1) miracles; (2) when the external aspects of a religion point to its internal and hidden truth; (3) when demonstration compels its acceptance; (4) and when historical developments in a religion are commensurate with its promise at its inception (i.e., historical vindication of its truth). Having said this, Ḥunayn concludes by pointing to the truth of Christianity on the basis of historical events that allegedly prove it. In this fashion the reader inevitably concludes that Ḥunayn has committed the same error for which he had rebuked ʿAlī b. Yaḥyā. If ʿAlī is responsible for the publication of this correspondence in the form that we have it, the point he thus scored is worthy of the elegant sophistication of the intellectuals of his day.

Ibn al-ʿAssāl has preserved another of Ḥunayn's essays by incorporating it in his theological encyclopedia on the principles of (the Christian) religion (*Uṣūl al-dīn*). The essay is on the appointed terms of life (W °28), a subject which Ḥunayn discusses by means of an interesting blend of philosophical and medical arguments, as one would expect. In the essay Ḥunayn is arguing against two interrelated positions: the first holds that God has appointed for each individual essentially two different terms of life, a general one, in the sense of the natural length of human life which ends in old age, and a particular one for the individual in question in the sense that he might die before he reaches old age either by violence or disease, etc. This position in turn is presented as being based on God's knowledge of the exact time when each individual will die, with the implication that God's knowledge of the time of death is also its cause. Ḥunayn rejects both positions, and starts his refutation by rejecting the claim that God's previous knowledge of the precise time of death of an individual also causes it. He says that if God's previous knowledge of an event also causes that event, then it must cause not only the good events but also the bad and the mixed, but this is clearly unacceptable because we cannot claim that God is the cause of any particular act of adultery or theft or murder, etc. In that case there remain only two alternatives: either God's previous knowledge causes only the good events but not the bad, or it does not cause any events at all. The first alternative also is rejected because it is impossible for man to distinguish which acts God's previous knowledge has caused and which it did not. There remains therefore the only possible alternative that God's previous knowledge does not cause events. Ḥunayn explains this by analogy to medicine: he says that a physician's knowledge that a particular illness will prove fatal for the patient concerned does not mean that it also causes that patient's death. Having thus shown that God's previous knowledge does not cause a man's death Ḥunayn next argues that God has accordingly appointed one term of life for humans, that which will end naturally in old age. This puts the burden of surviving to that ripe old age on each individual: he should live in such a fashion and take such precautions of hygiene as will enable him to avoid violent death or death by disease. God of course knows that a particular individual will die prematurely by either of these causes, but, the implication is (Ḥunayn never says this explicitly), God has not pre-ordained that that person will die prematurely and His knowledge certainly does not cause that death. This is an elegant discussion of the theological issue of free will and the question whether God's knowledge determines events or not. The medical context of much of this discussion and Ḥunayn's arguments in favour of prophylaxis bring it in relation to the wider issue of the attitude toward infection in Islamic societies, something that was much debated in medieval times and intensively studied in recent scholarship (cf. van Ess 2001 [*148: esp. 298–303 and his references there]). Thus it appears that the main purpose of the essay is the defense of medicine on theological grounds. In this respect it is related to the extensive treatment of the same subject by a philosopher that lived a century and a half after him, Ibn Hindū (cf. § 5.5), in his *Miftāḥ al-ṭibb* (*Key to Medicine*).

2.2 *Ṯābit b. Qurra*

2.2.1 Primary Sources – 2.2.2 Sources for Life and Works – 2.2.3 Life – 2.2.4 Works – 2.2.5 Doctrine

2.2.1 Primary Sources

2.2.1.1 Bio-bibliographical Testimonies [*151–*157] – 2.2.1.2 Works [*161–*163] – 2.2.1.3 Further Arabic Sources [*166–*167].

2.2.1.1 *Bio-bibliographical Testimonies*

151 al-Ṭabarī, Abū Ǧaʿfar Muḥammad b. Ǧarīr (d. 310/923). *Annales quos scripsit Abu Djafar Mohammed ibn Djarir at-Tabari cum aliis.* Ed. by M. J. de Goeje, 15 vols. Leiden, 1879–1901. – Partial Engl. transl. by Philip M. Fields, *The ʿAbbāsid Recovery.* The History of al-Ṭabarī, 37. Albany, 1987. – Partial Engl. transl. by Franz Rosenthal, *The Return of the Caliphate to Baghdad.* The History of al-Ṭabarī, 38. Albany, 1985.

152 al-Masʿūdī, Abū l-Ḥasan ʿAlī b. al-Ḥusayn (d. 345/956). *Murūǧ al-ḏahab wa-maʿādin al-ǧawhar.* Ed. by Charles Pellat, 7 vols. Beirut, 1966–1979.

153 Ibn al-Nadīm, Abū l-Faraǧ Muḥammad b. Isḥāq (d. 380/990). *Kitāb al-Fihrist.* Ed. by Gustav Flügel, August Müller and Johannes Roediger, vol. 1. Leipzig, 1871, 255–261 (ed. quoted below). – Repr. Beirut 1964, Frankfurt a.M., 2005. – Ed. by Riḍā Taǧaddud. Tehran, 1350 h.š./1971. – Ed. by Ayman Fuʾād Sayyid, 2 vols. London, 1430/2009. – Engl. transl. by Bayard Dodge, *The Fihrist of al-Nadīm*, 2 vols. New York, 1970.

154 Ibn Ǧulǧul, Sulaymān b. Ḥassān (d. around 384/994). *Ṭabaqāt al-aṭibbāʾ wa-l-ḥukamāʾ.* Ed. by Fuʾād Sayyid, *Les générations des médecins et des sages.* Cairo, 1955.

155 Ibn al-Qifṭī, Ǧamāl al-Dīn ʿAlī b. Yūsuf (d. 646/1248). *Taʾrīḫ al-Ḥukamāʾ* [*Iḫbār al-ʿulamāʾ bi-aḫbār al-Ḥukamāʾ*: epitome by Muḥammad b. ʿAlī al-Zawzanī]. Ed. by Julius Lippert, *Ibn al-Qifṭī's Taʾrīḫ al-Ḥukamāʾ.* Leipzig, 1903.

156 Ibn Abī Uṣaybiʿa, Muwaffaq al-Dīn Aḥmad b. al-Qāsim (d. 668/1270). *ʿUyūn al-anbāʾ fī ṭabaqāt al-aṭibbāʾ.* Ed. by August Müller, 2 vols. Cairo, 1299/1882; Königsberg, 1884. – Repr. Westmead, 1972.

157 Ibn al-ʿIbrī, Abū l-Farağ Gregorios [Barhebraeus] (d. 685/1286). *Tāʾrīḫ muḫtaṣar al-duwal*. Ed. by Anṭūn Ṣāliḥānī. Beirut, 1890, 1958 (2nd ed.).

2.2.1.2 *Works*

161 Pseudo-Aristotle. *De plantis: Kitāb Arisṭūṭālīs fī l-Nabāt, Tafsīr Nīqūlāwus, tarğamat Isḥāq b. Ḥunayn, bi-iṣlāḥ Ṯābit b. Qurra*. Ed. by Hendrik Joan Drossaart Lulofs and E. L. J. Poortman: *Nicolaus Damascenus, De plantis. Five Translations*. Amsterdam, 1989.
162 Sabra, Abdelhamid I. "Thābit ibn Qurra on the Infinite and Other Puzzles." *Zeitschrift für Geschichte der Arabisch-Islamischen Wissenschaften* 11 (1997): 1–33.
163 "Ğawāmiʿ Kitāb al-Ḥayawān li-Arisṭāṭālīs." In *The Problemata Physica Attributed to Aristotle*. Ed. by Lou S. Filius. Leiden, 1999.

2.2.1.3 *Further Arabic Sources*

166 Arisṭūṭālīs. *Fī l-Nafs*. Ed. by ʿAbd al-Raḥmān Badawī. Cairo, 1954.
167 Ibn Taymiyya. *Darʾ taʿāruḍ al-ʿaql wa-l-naql*, vol. 5. Beirut, 1997.

2.2.2 Sources for Life and Works

Information about Ṯābit's life and works comes to us from four different sources: (a) from the bibliographers who compiled them; (b) from the works of Ṯābit himself (many of which have yet to be edited and studied); (c) from the manuscripts of his works (some of which may yet be identified) and the scribal notes they contain; and (d) from the indirect transmission of his works as they were cited by later authors who provide information about them and their text.

The bibliographic sources which give us first hand information are actually five, all others being derived from them (for a partial list of these derivative sources cf. Rashed 1996 [*200: I 139–140 n. 4]):

(1) The first and most important of these is Abū ʿAlī al-Muḥassin b. Ibrāhīm b. Hilāl al-Ṣābiʾ (d. 401/1010), Ṯābit's great-great-grandson (cf. the brief notice and references by de Blois 1995 [*196: VIII 674b and the genealogical chart 673]), who compiled lists of the works of both his great-great-grandfather, Ṯābit, and his great-grandfather Sinān. Al-Muḥassin apparently prepared the list when he was relatively young. Toward the end of his list al-Muḥassin mentions that he had asked his grandmother's brother and Ṯābit's own grandson, Ṯābit b. Sinān b. Ṯābit (d. 365/976), about the authenticity of *al-Ḏaḫīra* and another work attributed to Ṯābit. If one assumes that al-Muḥassin asked this question when he was compiling the bibliography, and given that Ṯābit b. Sinān b. Ṯābit died in 365/976, al-Muḥassin must have compiled it before that date, say some time in the early 970s, when he must have been at most in his thirties (cf. also Richter-Bernburg 1983 [*186: 59]). Subsequently, the handwritten copy of al-Muḥassin's list fell into

the hands of Ibn al-Qifṭī, who copied it wholesale and thus preserved it for us. Al-Muḥassin's list is valuable because clearly he had access to Ṯābit's *Nachlass* as preserved in the family – material that perhaps had not been readied for publication – and also, it appears, to some sort of catalogue of Ṯābit's works.

(2) Second is al-Muḥassin's older contemporary, Ibn-al-Nadīm, who in his *Fihrist* (completed in 377/989) included various information on Ṯābit's works, apparently mostly derived from their manuscripts. For it appears that Ibn al-Nadīm did not know al-Muḥassin's list because he cites far fewer titles than are to be found in it. In the few cases where the information provided by Ibn-al-Nadīm is identical to that of al-Muḥassin, it is clear that Ibn al-Nadīm had access to and copied bibliographic information about Ṯābit's work from manuscripts which were related to those used by al-Muḥassin.

(3) The third source, Ibn al-Qifṭī, in addition to copying wholesale al-Muḥassin's list, adds a brief list of four titles at the very beginning of his bibliography. The text of Ibn al-Qifṭī that we have, however, is not his original text but al-Zawzanī's abridgment, compiled in 647/1249. It appears that al-Zawzanī omitted some minor phrases as he was copying Ibn al-Qifṭī, phrases that we can recover from Ibn Abī Uṣaybiʿa who copied from Ibn al-Qifṭī's original text and not al-Zawzanī's abridgment.

(4) Ibn al-Qifṭī's entry, both the initial four titles and al-Muḥassin's list, is copied without acknowledgment and almost verbatim, and in the same order, by Ibn Abī Uṣaybiʿa in his biographies of physicians (completed in 666/1268), in the second half of his own list of Ṯābit's works. The first half of his bibliography draws upon other sources, neither the number nor the origin of which is specified by Ibn Abī Uṣaybiʿa. If these other sources were lists of Ṯābit's works, then it is clear that he drew upon at least two of them, in addition to that of al-Muḥassin; this becomes apparent from the fact that one work, Ṯābit's piece on arthritis (*al-niqris*), is listed three times by Ibn Abī Uṣaybiʿa, once from al-Muḥassin's list (via Ibn al-Qifṭī), and twice from his two other lists. In copying Ibn al-Qifṭī's entire bibliography, Ibn Abī Uṣaybiʿa took pains to omit the items that he had mentioned already in the first part of his own list which he had taken from his two unknown sources; inadvertently, however, doublets and, in the case of the work on arthritis, triple mentions, remained.

(5) A fifth source is Barhebraeus (d. 685/1286) who gives us a list of the Syriac works of Ṯābit (Chwolsohn 1856 [*172: II ii–iii]). It is not clear, however, whether this list was compiled by Barhebraeus himself, who claims to have had in his possession some of these Syriac works, or, as I suspect, whether he was simply copying a list in Syriac that derived from al-Muḥassin's original bibliography, the last part of which contains the Syriac works. Barhebraeus' list has the works in the same

order as that of al-Muḥassin. Those additional works mentioned by Barhebraeus that are not to be found in the Ṯābit section of al-Muḥassin's list appear to be works by Ṯābit's son, Sinān, which were mistakenly ascribed also to Ṯābit. These additional titles are repeated, this time in Arabic, in Ibn al-Qifṭī's list of Sinān's works [*155: 195,10–13]. On the basis of these sources, Ṯābit's life and works can be reconstructed as follows.

2.2.3 Life

Although there is some slight discrepancy in the sources about Ṯābit's date of birth, it can be shown with relative accuracy that he was born in the year 209/824. This date is essentially based on the data given in the *Fihrist* [*153: 272,7–8], that Ṯābit died in 288/901 at the age of 77 solar years in Harran, the ancient city of Carrhae in South-East Asia Minor, which maintained its pagan character stubbornly and proudly well into the 4th/10th century.

We have no information whatsoever on Ṯābit's early years, though given his later proficiency with languages, one could safely guess that he received substantial training, apart from his native Syriac, in Greek and in Arabic. Some early facility with numbers would also seem to be indicated by the profession of money-changer (*ṣayrafī*) which he is said to have practiced (*Fihrist* [*153: 272,8]). It appears, though, that it was his proficiency in Arabic that attracted the attention of a Muslim mathematician and scientist, Muḥammad b. Mūsā b. Šākir, who met Ṯābit when Muḥammad was passing through Harran on his way back from an unidentified excursion into Byzantine territory: Muḥammad 'found Ṯābit speaking correct Arabic' (*raʾāhu faṣīḥan, Fihrist* [*153: 272,9]). This statement in our sources is doubtless to be interpreted as meaning that Ṯābit could converse in the high Arabic of the Abbasid elite in Baghdad, whereas at that time, speakers of Arabic in the Fertile Crescent, and especially non-Muslims, were not expected to be familiar with this idiom. In any case, it is this talent of Ṯābit's that is given in our sources as the reason for Muḥammad taking Ṯābit along with him to Baghdad and adopting him as student.

We are not informed about the date when this meeting took place. The sources mention next that Muḥammad b. Mūsā brought Ṯābit in contact with the caliph al-Muʿtaḍid (regn. 279–289/892–902). Already Chwolsohn (1856 [*172: I 548–549]), followed by Wiedemann (1920–1921 [*173: 193 n. 10]), pointed out the anachronism involved: Muḥammad died in 259/873 when al-Muʿtaḍid, as prince, was in his teens. The question is then during which caliph's reign Ṯābit came to Baghdad, where he was active all his life. Since the sources mention that Ṯābit studied with Muḥammad b. Mūsā, and that he had scientific correspondence with scholars active in the first half of the 3rd/9th century like Sanad b. ʿAlī who was active under al-Maʾmūn and participated in the astronomical observations of 214/829 and 217/832 (GAS [*3: V 242]), it is reasonable to suppose that he came to Baghdad early in his life, when he was still in his late teens and possibly during the caliphate of al-Muʿtaṣim (regn. 218–227/833–842). And thus, if Muḥammad b. Mūsā introduced him to any caliph, it was probably al-Muʿtaṣim, whose name could easily be misread in Arabic for 'al-Muʿtaḍid'. There is good reason why Muḥammad should have been on intimate terms with this caliph. According to our sources (Ibn al-Qifṭī [*155: 441]; cf. Hill 1993 [*195]) Muḥammad's father, Mūsā b. Šākir, who was from Khorasan, had become a close companion of al-Maʾmūn apparently already in Marw, before the latter's accession to the caliphate; so when Mūsā died al-Maʾmūn became the guardian of Mūsā's sons and ensured their proper and, as it turns out, very successful education. Al-Maʾmūn was succeeded in 218/833 by his brother, al-Muʿtaṣim, who supported with equal vigour the Graeco-Arabic sciences and philosophy and must have doubtless continued to have intimate relations with the Banū Šākir. This would explain Ṯābit's studies in Baghdad and his long and illustrious career there. It would also conform well with the conclusions, reached by a number of scholars, that Ṯābit's entire scientific education took place in Baghdad and not in Harran (cf. Rashed 1996 [*200: 142 and esp. n. 10]).

We can also guess that this was Ṯābit's motive for leaving his home town: access to higher education and the opportunity for social advancement in the empire's capital. A report in the late biographer Ibn Ḫallikān, however, suggests another motive: Ṯābit was supposed to have had liberal ideas about his religion, which he interpreted in a philosophical vein, and to have come into conflict with the traditional practices and rituals of the Sabians in Harran. He was thus allegedly excommunicated by his community and when the opportunity to leave presented itself with the advent of Muḥammad b. Mūsā, he is supposed to have seized it and left for Baghdad where he started a schismatic and philosophically oriented branch of Sabian beliefs. Much has been made of this alleged schism in secondary literature (Chwolsohn 1856 [*172: I 482], Hjärpe 1972 [*181]), but it appears to be based on flimsy evidence (cf. the criticisms of Tardieu 1986 [*190: 6–11], Strohmaier 1996 [*201]). Ibn Ḫallikān, a late writer (d. 681/1282), never mentions his source, and it is strange that such a report, had it been accurate, would not have appeared in an earlier and more reliable author. The fabrication of this story (by Ibn Ḫallikān or his source) may be based on some such statements like those made by al-Masʿūdī, who made a distinction between the beliefs of the 'commoner' Sabians (*ḥašwiyya, ʿawāmm*) and their 'elite philosophers' (*ḫawāṣṣ ḥukamāʾihim*) (*Murūǧ* [*152: IV 64 = § 1394]; Pellat translates, 'des philosophes de bas étage et vulgaires, dont les doctrines sont fort éloignées de celles de leurs sages de haut rang'). Such a distinction is natural in all religions – intellectuals always have more 'refined' beliefs – so the question is why the story of Ṯābit's break with his community would have been fabricated. There is an interesting parallel with Ḥunayn b. Isḥāq about whom also there is the curious story in Ibn Ǧulǧul [*154: 69–70], repeated in Ibn al-Qifṭī [*155: 172] and Ibn Abī Uṣaybiʿa [*156: I 190], of his 'unbelief' and excommunication (cf. Haddad 1974 [*134: 292]). Clearly the origin of such stories is to be sought in the intra- and inter-religious factionalism and competition in 9th century Baghdad, and just as clearly they do not deserve credence.

Ṯābit led a scholarly life in 3rd/9th century Baghdad in a climate which greatly appreciated his talents both as scientist and philosopher and as translator (cf. § 3.1 on the translations). His association, first of all, was with his teacher, Muḥammad b. Mūsā, and the latter's two brothers, Aḥmad and al-Ḥasan, for whom he continued to work throughout their lives. A report by Abū Sulaymān al-Siǧistānī preserved in the *Fihrist* [*153: 243,18–30] mentions that he, together with Ḥunayn b. Isḥāq and Ḥunayn's nephew, Ḥubayš, used to be paid by the Banū Mūsā a monthly salary of 500 dinars for translation and living expenses. (The Arabic says, *li-l-naql wa-l-mulāzama*, the second word of which, as M. Ullmann privately informed me (July 21, 1998), is to be understood as 'the expenses of residing (in the city)', cf. WKAS [*4: II 557a34–45]; cf. also Endress 1987 [*191: 427 n. 82]). Ṯābit also had professional relations with Ḥunayn and his family, for he collaborated with Isḥāq b. Ḥunayn on the translation of a number of scientific works, including Euclid's *Elements* and Ptolemy's *Almagest*. He doubtless met many of the leading intellectuals of his day, and there is good reason to believe that he collaborated with al-Kindī, who was his senior by about a quarter of a century, despite the enmity between Ṯābit's patrons, the Banū Mūsā, and al-Kindī; or at least it may be assumed that he provided source material for al-Kindī on at least two subjects which were treated by the philosopher, the Sabians and Plato's Socratic dialogues (cf. Gutas 1988 [*193: 42–47]). Toward the end of his life, at the court of al-Muʿtaḍid, he was acquainted with Aḥmad b. al-Ṭayyib al-Saraḫsī, al-Kindī's foremost student, with whom he also had a scholarly correspondence (*Fihrist* [*153: 262,19–20]; cf. Rosenthal 1943 [*175: 24]).

In his mature years Ṯābit became closely associated with the Abbasid prince Abū l-ʿAbbās, who was later to become the caliph al-Muʿtaḍid. According to a report by Ṯābit's grandson, Ṯābit b. Sinān b. Ṯābit, preserved by Ibn Abī Uṣaybiʿa [*156: I 216,5], Abū l-ʿAbbās, who had distinguished himself fighting against the Zanǧ with his father, the regent al-Muwaffaq (who was a brother of the caliph al-Muʿtamid), incurred his father's anger for reasons which are never spelled out, and was put by him under house arrest (275/888–889) in the house of the vizier Ismāʿīl Ibn Bulbul. To lessen the burden of the confinement of a prince who apparently was seen as the likely successor to the caliphate,

Ibn Bulbul commissioned Ṯābit to keep Abū l-ʿAbbās company. Ṯābit began to visit the prince every day and solace, entertain, and instruct him, talking of the sciences and philosophy. This lasted until the regent al-Muwaffaq's death on 19 Ṣafar 278/ 2 June 891, at which time Abū l-ʿAbbās succeeded in the offices of his father, supported by the troops (the events are described by al-Ṭabarī [*151: III 2115–2123; 157–168 Engl. transl. Fields]). The following year (279/892), upon the death of al-Muʿtamid, he became caliph (under the name al-Muʿtaḍid) and richly rewarded Ṯābit for his services during the imprisonment. He gave him a number of estates and had him in his court as his constant companion until Ṯābit's death.

In the autumn of 287/900, Ṯābit accompanied al-Muʿtaḍid on an expedition to Syria in search of a rebellious functionary. At the end of the mission, al-Muʿtaḍid proceeded to Antioch where he stayed from 2 to 10 Ḏū l-Ḥiǧǧa 287 / 28 November - 6 December 900 (al-Ṭabarī [*151: III 2200; 91 Engl. transl. Rosenthal]). It must have been during this week that Ṯābit seized the opportunity to visit the ancient temple in Antioch, which lay in ruins. For Ṯābit, a pagan, this was clearly an act of devotion. Always the scholar, he wrote a brief description of the temple and its history, which al-Masʿūdī later summarized (*Murūǧ* [*152: IV 56 = § 1382 Pellat]). The caliph with his retinue then left Antioch and eventually arrived in Baghdad on 7 Safar 288 / 31 January 901. The long trip, which lasted well over three months, must have tired Ṯābit severely; he may have even fallen sick. After the return to Baghdad at the very end of January, he did not have time to recuperate and died soon afterwards, on Thursday, 26 Safar 288 / 19 February 901.

Through the fame that he gained by means of his stupendous scientific work and the access to power he achieved in the last decades of his life through his close association with the caliph al-Muʿtaḍid, Ṯābit created an unassailable place for his family and his other co-religionists in the highest echelons of the Abbasid establishment. His descendants for many generations continued to play major roles both in government and the sciences. Modern scholarship acknowledges the unique contributions made by Ṯābit to mathematics and astronomy.

2.2.4 Works (W)

2.2.4.1 Introductions to the Study of Philosophy [°1–°3] – 2.2.4.2 Logic [°4–°12] – 2.2.4.3 Theoretical Sciences: Physics (Natural Science) [°13–°14]; Meteorology and Geology (Mineralogy) [°15–°20]; Theory of the Soul [°21–°23]; Zoology [°24]; Botany [°25]; – 2.2.4.4 Metaphysics [°26–°27] – 2.2.4.5 Practical Sciences: Ethics [°28–°31]; Politics [°32–°34] – 2.2.4.6 Philosophical Correspondence [°35]

In the following survey, individual works are referred to by W °1, W °2, W °3 etc.

Although Ṯābit has been valued as an original thinker, both in medieval and modern times, primarily in what we would today call the 'sciences', and in particular mathematics and astronomy, in his time and subsequently in the Islamic world he was known as a philosopher in the broad sense of the word; according to the classification of the sciences in effect at the time, philosophy included, after logic, the theoretical and practical sciences, the former consisting of physics, mathematics (the *quadrivium*) and metaphysics, and the latter of ethics, economics, and politics. The assessment of Ṯābit made by the 4th/10th century Andalusian scholar Ibn Ǧulǧul was valid, generally speaking, for most scholars in the medieval Islamic world: 'He was more concerned with philosophy than with medicine' (*wa-kāna l-ġālib ʿalayhi l-falsafa dūna l-ṭibb*; *Ṭabaqāt* [*154: 75]; cf. Sabra [*162: 2 n. 3]). Seen from this perspective, Ṯābit wrote on all subjects of philosophy works of different kinds, from translations, paraphrases and synopses, to commentaries and original works. Modern research has concentrated almost exclusively on his mathematical and astronomical treatises, perhaps rightly, for it is these works that have survived the best; his properly philosophical works have fared far worse, and although it is unfortunate that they are almost all lost, an evaluation of those that have survived as well as an analysis of the titles of those that have not shed important light on Ṯābit's qualities as a philosopher.

In what follows I will offer such an evaluation by discussing his works according to the classification of the sciences just mentioned, under each subject enumerating the individual works by genre.

2.2.4.1 *Introductions to the Study of Philosophy*

°1 *Kitāb ilā bnihi Sinān fī l-Ḥaṯṯ ʿalā taʿallum al-ṭibb wa-l-ḥikma*
Exhortation to the Study of Medicine and Philosophy, to his Son Sinān

Ibn al-Qifṭī [*155: 117,4] = Ibn Abī Uṣaybiʿa [*156: 219,29]; GAS [*3: III 263]. Not extant. In all probability Ṯābit drew his arguments from Galen's *Protrepticus*, *al-Ḥaṯṯ ʿalā taʿallum al-ṭibb* (GAS [*3: III 138 no. 151]), or *al-Ḥaṯṯ ʿalā ṣināʿat al-ṭibb* (Ullmann 1970 [*179: 53 no. 73]). A companion piece with similar content would appear to be his letter to the vizier Abū l-Qāsim ʿUbayd Allāh b. Sulaymān, on the nobility of medicine, *Kitāb fī Tašrīf ṣināʿat al-ṭibb* (Ibn Abī Uṣaybiʿa [*156: 219,20] = Ibn Abī Uṣaybiʿa [*156: 218,20]).

°2 *Kitāb fī l-Masāʾil al-mušawwiqa* [Ibn al-Qifṭī] = *al-Masāʾil al-mušawwiqa ilā l-ʿulūm* [Ibn Abī Uṣaybiʿa]
Problems Stimulating the Study of the Sciences

Ibn al-Qifṭī [*155: 117,6] = Ibn Abī Uṣaybiʿa [*156: 218,15]; GAS [*3: VII 269–270 no. 1]. This work appears to have survived in two manuscripts, Tehran, Malik 6188 and Rampur,

Riḍā 2367 [= Rampur II 808?]), but remains unpublished. The fuller title in the former manuscript gives an idea of its contents: *Problems collected by Ṯābit from the works of Aristotle and other philosophers, intending thereby to whet the appetite of those who taste a sampling of the sciences and to induce them to take up [scientific] investigation and research* (Arabic title cited by Kruk 1976 [*184: 255 n. 13]; translated into Russian from MS Tehran, Malik 6188 by Jamal ad-Dabbagh in Rosenfeld, Youshkevitch 1984 [*188: 243–247. 353–355]).

°3 *Kitāb fī Marātib qirāʾat al-ʿulūm = Kitāb fī Marātib al-ʿulūm*
On the Order of Reading, or Studying, the [Philosophical] Sciences

Ibn al-Qifṭī [**155*: 118,4] = Ibn Abī Uṣaybiʿa [**156*: 220,7] = Ibn Abī Uṣaybiʿa [**156*: 218,16]. Not extant. The book doubtless must have presented some form of the standard classification of the sciences as it was current in late antiquity in Alexandria and later in early Islam. If al-Kindī's essay on the number and order of Aristotle's books (*Fī Kammiyyat kutub Arisṭū*) is any indication, this work would have presented logic and, possibly, given Ṯābit's intense engagement with mathematics, also mathematics, as the preparatory sciences (as al-Kindī had done in the essay just mentioned), followed by the division of the rest into two, theoretical and practical. The theoretical sciences would then be further subdivided into physics (natural science), mathematics (the subjects of the *quadrivium* – arithmetic, geometry, astronomy, and music – this time studied at a higher level of sophistication than the introductory study of mathematics), and metaphysics. The practical sciences would be subdivided into ethics, household management (economics), and city management (politics). The sciences that are not included in this arrangement, like medicine, astrology, geography, etc., would come at the end as corollary sciences. The order in which these sciences are classified would also be the order in which they are to be studied.

2.2.4.2 *Logic*

°4 *Kitāb al-Mudḫal ilā l-manṭiq*
Introduction to Logic

Ibn al-Qifṭī [**155*: 115,13] = Ibn Abī Uṣaybiʿa [**156*: 219,27]. Not extant. The title of this work corresponds exactly with that by Galen (Ullmann 1970 [*179: 51]), and this led Chwolsohn (1856 [*172: I 560]) to suggest that it is a translation of Galen's book. It seems very doubtful that Ṯābit's work would be an actual translation of Galen's piece because Ḥunayn reports the following about the latter: 'This book consists of one part in which Galen explained the things that students need and from which they benefit in the study of demonstration. I translated it into Syriac and Ḥubayš translated it into

Arabic for Muḥammad b. Mūsā' (Bergsträsser [*105: 51 no. 126]). Given the close association of Ṯābit with Muḥammad, it would appear, if indeed Ṯābit's work is derived from that of Galen, that rather than a translation it is a revision (*iṣlāḥ*), an epitome (*ǧawāmiʿ*) or an abridgment (*iḫtiṣār*) of Ḥubayš's translation, most likely the former.

°5 *Iḫtiṣār Qaṭāġūriyās*
Abridgment of Aristotle's Categories

Ibn al-Qifṭī [*155: 120,7 = Ibn al-Qifṭī [*155: 118,17] = Ibn Abī Uṣaybiʿa [*156: 220,24]. Not extant.

°6 [*Iḫtiṣār*] *Bārīrmāniyās*
[*Abridgment of*] *On Interpretation*

Ibn al-Qifṭī [*155: 120,8] = Ibn al-Qifṭī [*155: 118,17] = *Fihrist* [*153: 249,4]. Not extant.

°7 *Ǧawāmiʿ Bārīrmīniyās*
Epitome of On Interpretation

Ibn al-Qifṭī [*155: 118,2] = Ibn Abī Uṣaybiʿa [*156: 218,13]. Not extant, though apparently it was distinct from the preceding abridgment.

°8 [*Iḫtiṣār*] *al-Qiyās*
[*Abridgment of the*] *Prior Analytics*

Ibn al-Qifṭī [*155: 120,8] = Ibn al-Qifṭī [*155: 118,17]. Not extant.

°9 *Kitāb fī Ǧawāmiʿ Anālūṭīqā al-ūlā*
Epitome of the Prior Analytics

Ibn al-Qifṭī [*155: 118,17] = Ibn Abī Uṣaybiʿa [*156: 218, 13]. Not extant, though apparently it was distinct from the preceding abridgment.

°10 *Kitāb fī l-Taṣarruf fī aškāl al-qiyās*
On Working with the Figures in Prior Analytics

Ibn al-Qifṭī [*155: 118,19] = Ibn Abī Uṣaybiʿa [*156: 219,7]. Not extant. Judging by its title, the work must have dealt with the figures of syllogisms, and as such it would appear to be based, in one way or another, on Galen's work on the number of syllogisms, *Kitāb fī ʿadad al-maqāyīs*, which was translated by Isḥāq b. Ḥunayn into Arabic (Bergsträsser

[*105: 51 no. 127]); Galen mentions this work, which is lost also in Greek, in his *On My Own Works* (Singer 1997 [*171: 20]). As such, it is ultimately based (like Galen's work) on Aristotle's *Prior Analytics*, where the different figures of the syllogisms are discussed.

°11 *Nawādir maḥfūẓa min Ṭūbiqā*
Precious [Rules] Preserved in the Topics [?]

Ibn Abī Uṣaybiʿa [*156: 218,13]. The authenticity of this work cannot be verified in the absence of any surviving copy. The title also is ambiguous. Since Aristotle's *Topics*, upon which this work draws, does not contain any anecdotes as such (the normal meaning of *nawādir*), the title most likely means 'Precious [rules] preserved in the Topics' and refers to the numerous rules for dialectical argumentation (the τόποι) included in that work. It would seem as if the work consisted of a listing, possibly with discussion and examples, of (some of?) the τόποι in Aristotle's Topics.

°12 *Kitāb fī Aġālīṭ al-sūfisṭāʾiyyīn*
On the Errors of the Sophists

Ibn Abī Uṣaybiʿa [*156: 218,15]. The authenticity of this work cannot be verified in the absence of any surviving copy. It would appear that this work, if authentic, was the counterpart of the preceding one. It apparently set out the different error-inducing arguments used in sophistic arguments, as discussed by Aristotle in his *Sophistical Refutations*.

2.2.4.3 *Theoretical Sciences*
Physics (Natural Science)

°13 *Kitāb fī Šarḥ al-Samāʿ al-Ṭabīʿī*
Commentary on Aristotle's Physics

Ibn al-Qifṭī [*155: 116,18] = Ibn Abī Uṣaybiʿa [*156: 219,27] = *Fihrist* [*153: 250,24]. Not extant. The commentary covered only a part of the first book, because Ṯābit died before completing it.

°14 *Ǧawābān ʿan Kitābay Muḥammad b. Mūsā b. Šākir ilayhi fī amr al-zamān*
Responses to two Letters Addressed to him by Muḥammad b. Mūsā b. Šākir on the Question of Time

Ibn al-Qifṭī [*155: 117,5] = Ibn Abī Uṣaybiʿa [*156: 219,30]. Not extant. Ṯābit would have drawn upon Aristotle's *Physics* to formulate these responses.

Meteorology and Geology (Mineralogy)

°15 Epaphroditus, *Kitāb Tafsīr Kalām Arisṭālīs fī l-hāla wa-qaws quzaḥ, naqalahu Ṯābit b. Qurra*
Translation of Epaphroditus' Commentary on Aristotle['s Meteorology Focusing] on the Halo and the Rainbow

Fihrist [*153: 254,16]; GAS [*3: VII 230 = 270 no. 4]. These two subjects were much discussed in Greek and Arabic meteorological writings; cf. Lettinck 1999 [*206: Index s.v. halo and rainbow]. Not extant.

°16 *Kitāb fī l-Sabab allaḏī lahu ǧuʿilat miyāh al-baḥr māliḥa*
On the Reason for the Salinity of the Sea

Ibn al-Qifṭī [*155: 116,19] = Ibn Abī Uṣaybiʿa [*156: 218,14] = *Fihrist* [*153: 272,15–16]; GAS [*3: VII 270 no. 5]. On this subject cf. also Lettinck 1999 [*206: Index, s.v. saltness]. The work is extant in MS Istanbul, Ahmet III, 3342 but remains unpublished. Transl. into Russian from this manuscript by Jamal ad-Dabbagh in Rosenfeld, Youshkevitch 1984 [188: 323–328. 380–381] An essay by the same title attributed to Ḥunayn b. Isḥāq (see above § 9.2.1, W °19) is in all probability spurious.

°17 *Ḏikr āṯār ẓaharat fī l-ǧaww wa-aḥwāl kānat fī l-hawāʾ mimmā raṣada Banū Mūsā wa-Abū l-Ḥasan Ṯābit b. Qurra*
On the Atmospheric Observations of the Banū Mūsā and Ṯābit

Ibn Abī Uṣaybiʿa [*156: 219,23]; GAS [*3: VII 270 no. 3]. This treatise, cited only by Ibn Abī Uṣaybiʿa, is not otherwise known.

°18 *Kitāb fī Sabab ḫalq al-ǧibāl*
On the Cause of the Formation of Mountains

Ibn al-Qifṭī [*155: 117,11] = Ibn Abī Uṣaybiʿa [*156: 218,11]. This treatise is otherwise unknown. For the subject cf. Lettinck 1999 [*206: 141–143].

°19 *Maqāla/Risāla fī Tawallud al-nār bayna ḥaǧarayn*
On Generating Fire Using Flint

Ibn al-Qifṭī [*155: 119,2] = Ibn Abī Uṣaybiʿa [*156: 220,14]. This treatise on kindling fire by striking flint is otherwise unknown. An essay by the same title attributed to Ḥunayn (cf. above § 9.2.1, WV °22) is in all probability spurious.

°20 *Kitāb fī l-Anwā'*
On Meteorological Lore

Ibn al-Qifṭī [*155: 119,1] = Ibn Abī Uṣaybiʿa [*156: 220,12]; GAS [*3: VII 270 no. 2]. This treatise is on the traditional Arab subject of the *anwā'*, the 'weather predictions according to weather stars' (see Pellat 1960 [*176]). It is best classified under Meteorology although it is not a part of the translated sciences. Not extant.

Theory of the Soul

°21 *Mā wuǧida min kitābihi Fī l-nafs*
The Extant Portions of his Book On the Soul

Ibn al-Qifṭī [*155: 118,18] = Ibn Abī Uṣaybiʿa [*156: 220,12]. Not extant. The title of the treatise, *On the Soul*, would indicate that it treated the entire subject, though it is uncertain which approach was taken by Ṯābit. He could have used the Neoplatonic version of the paraphrase of *On the Soul* (influenced by the theories of Philoponus) which must have already been available by the middle of the 9th century (cf. Arnzen 1998 [*203: 139], who suggests the quarter-century between 820–845 for its appearance) or, if Ṯābit's book was composed a bit later in his life, he could have used his collaborator Isḥāq b. Ḥunayn's own translation of Aristotle's *On the Soul*. As a matter of fact, bearing in mind the numerous revisions that Ṯābit did of Isḥāq's translations, it would not be far-fetched to suggest that what may lie hidden behind this title is precisely such a revision. Given the relative paucity of information that we have about the early history of the transmission of Aristotle's *On the Soul* in Arabic (cf. Gätje 1971 [*180]) and the loss of the Arabic original of Isḥāq's translation, it is deplorable that this work by Ṯābit has not survived.

°21a *Ǧawāmiʿ* [...] *sabʿ maqālāt fī l-nafs*
(the full title is, *Ǧawāmiʿ Kitāb al-Ḥayawān li-Arisṭāṭālīs, wa-baʿdahu sabʿ maqālāt fī l-nafs, lahu ayḍan, istaḫraǧahā Ṯābit b. Qurra li-Muḥammad b. Mūsā al-Munaǧǧim* [d. 259/873], *wa-huwa arbaʿa wa-sittūn bāban*)
Synopsis of [*Pseudo-Aristotle's*] *Seven Chapters on the Soul*

MS Yaḥyā Mahdawī, microfilm in Tehran University Library, no. 2234 (or 2443: cf. Arnzen [*203: 686 u. no. 19]), fols 88^{b}-94^{a}; cf. Kruk 1976 [*184: 251]. The syntax of the Arabic sentence in the MS attributing this work to Ṯābit implies that the pronoun *-hā* in *istaḫraǧahā* refers both to the *Ǧawāmiʿ* (synopsis) of the Zoology (see below, W °24) and to the *Seven Chapters on the Soul*. If that is correct, then this *istiḫrāǧ*, adaptation, would also be by Ṯābit, but it is not clear whether such a work exists in the MS. None of the scholars who have seen the Tehran manuscript discusses this issue; the answer to this problem must await the inspection of the manuscript.

The original *Seven Chapters on the Soul* is not by Aristotle but by Gregory Thaumatourgos (cf. Arnzen 1998 [*203: 681–689; 686 no. 19]) and survives in Arabic in two versions, a shorter and a longer one. The one allegedly done by Ṯābit is the longer one. If this is indeed by Ṯābit it could very well be identical with the preceding title, *On the Soul*.

°22 *Maqāla fī l-Naẓar fī amr al-nafs*
On the Investigation of the Nature (?) of the Soul

Ibn al-Qifṭī [*155: 119,3] = Ibn Abī Uṣaybiʿa [*156: 220,12]. This treatise, also not known to be extant, apparently studied one particular aspect of the soul (on this partitive use of *amr*, as in the title here, cf. GALex [*7: 390, no. 455), possibly even the subject mentioned in W °23.

°23 *Kitāb fī l-Radd ʿalā man qāla inna l-nafs mizāǧ*
Refutation of Those Who Claim that the Soul is a Mixture

Ibn Abī Uṣaybiʿa [*156: 218,16]. In all likelihood it dealt with the theories of the pre-Aristotelian philosophers, including Plato, who held different variants of such a position, as reported in Aristotle's *On the Soul* (404b7–405b30. 407b27, esp. 407b31; *mizāǧ* translates κράσιν ('mixture') in the Arabic translation of *On the Soul* 409b23 [*166: 18,9]). This title is mentioned only by Ibn Abī Uṣaybiʿa, however, and its authenticity cannot be assumed without further evidence or in the absence of the work itself. If authentic, it could easily be identical with the preceding work, the particular aspect (*amr*) of the soul referred to in the title being its composition.

Zoology

°24 *Ǧawāmiʿ Kitāb al-Ḥayawān li-Arisṭāṭālīs, wa-baʿdahu sabʿ maqālāt fī l-nafs, lahu ayḍan, istaḫraǧahā Ṯābit b. Qurra li-Muḥammad b. Mūsā al-Munaǧǧim, wa-huwa arbaʿa wa-sittūn bāban*
Synopsis of Aristotle's Zoology
[= Aristotle, *Problems* X], adaptation by Ṯābit

MS Yaḥyā Mahdawī, microfilm in Tehran University Library, no. 2234 (or 2443: cf. Arnzen [*203: 686 and no. 19]), fols 88^{b}-94^{a}; Filius 1999 [*205: lviii]; Kruk 1976 [*184:

251]; GAS [*3: III 351]; Ullmann 1972 [*182: 22]. The syntax of the Arabic sentence in the MS attributing this work to Ṯābit implies that the pronoun *-hā* in *istaḫraǧahā* refers both to the *Ǧawāmiʿ* (synopsis) of the Zoology and to the *Seven Chapters on the Soul* (see above, W °21a). If that is correct, then this *istiḫrāǧ*, adaptation, would also be by Ṯābit. However, though possibly correct, this attribution is not without its problems, for none of the medieval bibliographers mentions this work. What the Tehran manuscript contains is book XI only of the Arabic translation of the Greek *Problems* (book X of the Greek), which deals with zoology. The Greek text of book X, in fact, was described as 'a summary of Aristotle's *Historia, De Partibus* and *De Generatione Animalium*', which is precisely what the Arabic title in the Tehran manuscript says: *Ǧawāmiʿ Kitāb al-Ḥayawān li-Arisṭāṭālīs* (as noted by Kruk 1976 [*184: 252, citing H. Flashar]), i.e. *Synopsis of Aristotle's Book on Animals*. The title, therefore, is very apt, and clearly was given by someone who was knowledgeable – in this case, possibly Ṯābit himself (see below).

The Arabic translation of the *Problems*, which contains seventeen chapters or books, is extant complete and was recently edited (Filius 1999 [*205]). The Tehran manuscript, which contains only book XI (= Greek book X), does not have any significant variants from the Manisa MS which contains the entire text, the translation of which is attributed to Ḥunayn in the latter manuscript and in the medieval Hebrew version. Ullmann (2003 [*210]) has convincingly demonstrated that the translation cannot be by Ḥunayn, but regardless of its author, the question is, if the name of Ṯābit mentioned in the Tehran manuscript has some historical basis, what his relationship to this translation is. The descriptive title in the Tehran manuscript, if taken literally, may provide the solution. Filius is wrong to understand the title to mean that Ṯābit 'translated' book XI and then to try to disprove this (by using, in addition, irrelevant arguments: Filius 1999 [*205: xxx], and cf. Ullmann 2003 [*210: 470–471]). The manuscript simply says, *istaḫraǧahā*, i.e. the *Ǧawāmiʿ*, which in context can only mean that Ṯābit adapted Ḥunayn's translation, or even better, he (literally) extracted book XI from it as an independent treatise. The reason he did this is also given in the description following the title: he was commissioned to write a synopsis of zoology by his patron and benefactor, Muḥammad b. Mūsā (b. Šākir), and instead of doing it from scratch he simply copied book XI of the available translation of the *Problems* which, as mentioned above, is precisely such a text. To this Ṯābit must have added the title, *Ǧawāmiʿ Kitāb al-Ḥayawān li-Arisṭāṭālīs*. If this analysis is correct, then Filius' edition should have indicated that the edition of book XI is simultaneously the edition of Ṯābit's *Ǧawāmiʿ*.

Botany

°25 Pseudo-Aristotle: *Kitāb Arisṭūṭālīs fī l-Nabāt, Tafsīr Nīqūlāwus, tarǧamat Isḥāq b. Ḥunayn, bi-iṣlāḥ Ṯābit b. Qurra*
Correction of Isḥāq's Translation of Pseudo-Aristotle's On Plants in the version of Nicolaus of Damascus

GAS [*3: IV 312–313]; Ullmann 1972 [*182: 71]. Although absent from all the reports by the medieval bibliographers, the revision is mentioned by all the extant manuscripts of the work. Edited and translated by Drossaart Lulofs [*161: 127–215].

Metaphysics

°26 *Iḫtiṣār Kitāb mā baʿd al-ṭabīʿa*
Abridgment of [Aristotle's] Metaphysics

Ibn Abī Uṣaybiʿa [*156: 218,14]. Only Ibn Abī Uṣaybiʿa records this otherwise unknown abridgment of the *Metaphysics*. In all likelihood it is identical with W °26a.

°26a *Maqāla fī Talḫīṣ mā atā bihi Arisṭūṭālīs fī kitābihi fī Mā baʿd al-ṭabīʿa mimmā ǧarā l-amr fīhi ʿalā siyāqat al-burhān siwā mā ǧarā min ḏālika maǧrā l-iqnāʿ, katabahā li-l-wazīr Abī l-Ḥusayn al-Qāsim b. ʿUbayd Allāh*
Precise Exposition of what Aristotle presented in his book Metaphysics by way of demonstration, not persuasion; presented to the Vizier al-Qāsim b. ʿUbayd Allāh

Krause 1936 [*174: 456, no. 17b]; GAS [*3: V 80 and n. 4]. Not mentioned by any bibliographer in this form, the title of this treatise as it appears in the two extant manuscripts is hardly descriptive of its contents. In essence, the treatise is a precise analysis and exposition (*talḫīṣ*) of the main theses in the 'theological core of the *Metaphysics*, namely chapters 6–9 of its twelfth book' (Reisman, Bertolacci 2009 [*211: 719]), not the entire work. Although it is hard to imagine that Ṯābit would have misrepresented the extent of his coverage in this essay, the concern with methodology implicit in the title would tend to favour the assumption that it is by Ṯābit himself. Ibn Taymiyya also knew the treatise by this title [*167: 114], which would indicate that it was still circulating under this title at the end of the 7th/13th century. However, it appears that it may have circulated also under a different title, something like that given by Ibn Abī Uṣaybiʿa: *Iḫtiṣār K. Mā baʿd al-ṭabīʿa* (*Abridgment of [Aristotle's] Metaphysics*). It is possible that a later scribe or scholar, who saw the essay either without title or was loath to reproduce the very long actual one, concluded that it is an abridgment (*iḫtiṣār*) of the

Metaphysics from its opening and closing words: It begins, 'Aristotle entitled this book of his *Metaphysics*, both because ...,' and ends, 'This is the extent of what Aristotle says on this subject in a summary fashion' (*ʿalā ṭarīq al-ǧumla*; translation by Reisman, Bertolacci 2009 [*211]). In this case, this essay would be identical with the one mentioned by Ibn Abī Uṣaybiʿa (see W °26 above). It is much less likely that this essay would be a part of or an extract from a longer abridgment (*iḫtiṣār*) of the *Metaphysics*; it appears as self-contained and is addressed as such to a patron, the powerful Abbasid vizier al-Qāsim b. ʿUbayd Allāh (d. 291/904). For all information about this work see the edition, translation, and study by Reisman, Bertolacci 2009 [*211].

°27 *Revision of Isḥāq's translation of Themistius' Paraphrase of the Metaphysics*

This information comes from 'a note in manuscript Munich 108 of the Hebrew version' (from the Arabic) of Themistius' *Paraphrase*, done by Šemu'el Ibn Tibbon in 1255 (Peters 1968 [*178: 52]; cf. further Bertolacci 2001 [*208: 284 and n. 88]). This contradicts, however, the express testimony in the *Fihrist* [*153: 251,28–30] that the translation of Themistius' *Paraphrase* was done by Abū Bišr Mattā. It would seem that the formula 'translation by Isḥāq, revision by Ṯābit' had become a topos among scholars involved in the Graeco-Arabic transmission, and that it was (either indiscriminately or deliberately) misapplied to enhance the value of a translated piece, given the prestige of these two scholars. The French translator of Themistius' *Paraphrase* also finds this attribution suspect (Brague 1999 [*204: 17 top]). Unless there is more evidence to support the claim in the Munich manuscript, it should be considered as unverified.

2.2.4.4 *Practical Sciences*
Ethics

°28 Proclus: *Commentary on the Pythagorean Golden Verses*, partial translation

Fihrist [*153: 252,16–18] = Ibn al-Qifṭī [*155: 89,10]. The *Fihrist* informs us that Proclus Diadochus (the 'Successor', 411–485) wrote a commentary on the Pseudo-Pythagorean *Golden Verses* for his daughter, amounting to about one hundred folia in length; that there was a Syriac translation; and that Ṯābit translated three folia of it before his death. There is a number of problems with this report. In the first place, Ṯābit's translation attempt of a commentary on the *Golden Verses* attributed to Proclus is not recorded by al-Muḥassin, who should have known about it if the three or so folios of the translation were extant among Ṯābit's *Nachlass*; in a number of instances of similarly incomplete works al-Muḥassin is very meticulous in reporting the fact. If that is so, one wonders from where Ibn al-Nadīm could have received his information; in all probability from a note in some manuscript, but its authenticity is unverifiable for us. Secondly, the language from which Ṯābit started translating is not clear from Ibn al-Nadīm's report. The information that the text amounted to a hundred folia and that Ṯābit translated three folia of it must be assumed to refer to the Syriac translation rather than to any Greek manuscript; it is not at all clear that Ibn al-Nadīm would have had information about Greek manuscripts unless he had found it in the manuscript of the translation itself, but we have no way of knowing that. Finally, Ibn al-Nadīm does not mention who the translator into Syriac was. It could have been Ṯābit himself, but this work does not figure among the Syriac titles listed by Ibn al-Qifṭī and Barhebraeus.

Next, Proclus is not known in the Greek tradition to have written a commentary on the *Golden Verses*. However, such a commentary under his name was available in Arabic, and Abū l-Farağ Ibn al-Ṭayyib wrote a selective anthology (*istiṯmār*) of it, which is extant, though Ibn al-Ṭayyib's version does not mention the translator into Arabic (edited and translated by Linley 1984 [*187]; cf. also Endress 1973 [*183: 26–27]). Walzer tried to explain the discrepancy away by suggesting that the ascription to Proclus in Arabic, *Brqls*, is a mistake for [ʾ]*yrqls*, Hierocles the Neoplatonist, who did write an extant (and very famous) commentary on the *Golden Verses* [*177: 1340b]. There are two objections to this: first, as Linley observed, Ibn al-Ṭayyib's text and Hierocles' commentary have little in common. Second, Ibn al-Nadīm attributes the commentary to Diyadūḫus Buruqlus, the Diadochus, which was exclusively Proclus' honorific title. Furthermore, Ibn al-Ṭayyib's text is also distinct from the commentary which is attributed to Iamblichus and is also extant only in Arabic (Daiber 1995 [*197: 33–34]). It would thus appear that Ibn al-Nadīm's and Ibn al-Ṭayyib's attributions of the commentary to Proclus are correct. There is one slight problem, however, which will have to be resolved. Ibn al-Nadīm mentions that Proclus wrote the commentary for his daughter. Now it is certain that Proclus never married, and as far as is known he did not have a daughter otherwise. (See further W °29.)

°29 *Kitāb fī l-Ṭarīq ilā iktisāb al-faḍīla*
The Way to Acquiring Virtue

Ibn al-Qifṭī [**155*: 119,1] = Ibn Abī Uṣaybiʿa [**156*: 220,13]. If Ṯābit indeed started translating into Arabic Proclus' *Commentary on the Golden Verses* or even did the 100-folio Syriac translation of it known to Ibn al-Nadīm (cf. W °28), then his interest in the work is doubtless related to the interest in ethical texts in late antiquity as preliminary instruction to the study of logic and eventually of all philosophy (cf. D'Ancona 1996 [*198: 23–24] and the references there; further Gutas 1985 [*189]). It is in this context that this title mentioned by al-Muḥassin (in Ibn al-Qifṭī, and followed by Ibn Abī Uṣaybiʿa), otherwise lost, is to be seen. If Ṯābit's preoccupation with the *Golden Verses* indicates an interest in non-Aristotelian ethics, then in all likelihood *Kitāb fī l-Ṭarīq ilā iktisāb al-faḍīla* was an ethical exhortation to pre-philosophical morality as preparation for the study of logic, perhaps like the later, and similarly entitled, treatise by al-Fārābī, *Kitāb fī l-Tanbīh ʿalā sabīl al-saʿāda* (*Directing Attention to the Way to Happiness*), which depends heavily on Aristotle's *Nicomachean Ethics* (cf. Mallet 1987–1988 [*192] and Guerrero 1996 [*199]).

°30 *Kitāb fī l-Aḫlāq*
On Ethics

Ibn Abī Uṣaybiʿa [*156: 219,10]. This book on ethics, mentioned only by Ibn Abī Uṣaybiʿa from one of his undisclosed sources, is otherwise unknown. Its title would indicate a close affinity to Aristotle's *Nicomachean Ethics*, but its authenticity, let alone its contents, cannot be verified.

°31 *Muḫtaṣar fī l-Uṣūl min ʿilm al-aḫlāq*
Abridgment of the Principles Relating to Ethics

Ibn al-Qifṭī [*155: 117,10] = Ibn Abī Uṣaybiʿa [*156: 220,1]. The title of this work, listed by al-Muḥassin (in Ibn al-Qifṭī, followed by Ibn Abī Uṣaybiʿa), may indicate that it is an abridgment of a longer work on the principles of ethics, possibly entitled, *Fī l-uṣūl min ʿilm al-aḫlāq*, though such a conclusion is far from certain. A fragment in the Istanbul MS Köprülü 1608, fol. 65[a–b], in all likelihood belongs to (or is?) this work. It begins, *qāla Abū l-Ḥasan Ṯābit b. Qurra: min uṣūl al-ʿilm bi-amr al-aḫlāq an yuʿlama mā l-maʿnā l-musammā ḫayran wa-mā l-maʿnā l-musammā šarran* ('Abū l-Ḥasan Ṯābit b. Qurra says: Among the principles of ethics is to know what that which is called "good" and what which is called "bad" are'). This information on Ṯābit's ethical works, paltry as it is, is significant evidence for the early development of an ethical philosophical literature in Arabic, a field that has yet to be properly studied (cf. Gutas 1997 [*202]).

Politics

°32 *Risāla fī Ḥall rumūz Kitāb al-Siyāsa li-Aflāṭūn*
Analysis of the Allegories in Plato's Republic

Ibn al-Qifṭī [*155: 120,7] = Ibn Abī Uṣaybiʿa [*156: 220,24]. This treatise, not extant, appears to be a commentary explaining the allegories or parables in Plato's *Republic*. This can be expected from Ṯābit, insofar as the study of Plato was widespread among the Sabians of his time (cf. Gutas 1988 [*193: 44–47]).

°33 *Risāla fī l-Sabab allaḏī li-ağlihi alġaza l-nās fī kalāmihim*
The Reason Why People Speak Symbolically

Ibn al-Qifṭī [*155: 120,16] = Ibn Abī Uṣaybiʿa [*156: 220,27]. This treatise, also not extant, appears to be closely related to W °32, though most likely it is not identical with it. It is listed by al-Muḥassin (in Ibn al-Qifṭī, followed by Ibn Abī Uṣaybiʿa) under Ṯābit's Syriac works which were not translated into Arabic. It may be surmised that in this treatise Ṯābit would have touched upon some of the same subjects as in his interpretation of Platonic allegories and dealt with the familiar themes of the reasons for allegorical and symbolic expression in philosophy, viz., the need to shield philosophical truths, explicitly presented, from the ignorant masses lest they misunderstand them and cause harm to society; detecting which students have an aptitude for philosophy and training them, etc. (For a discussion of this subject, mainly in reference to Avicenna, see Gutas, 1988 and 2014 [*193: 225–234. 299–307]). On the other hand, since al-Muḥassin lists this work under the Syriac titles which were written for the Sabian community, it may well have treated issues of immediate concern to them, such as the ways in which they were to present their paganism to the Muslim authorities (cf. Gutas 1988 [*194: 46–47]).

°34 *Kalām fī l-Siyāsa*
On Governance

Ibn al-Qifṭī [*155: 120,4] = Ibn Abī Uṣaybiʿa [*156: 220,22]. A third treatise on politics, entitled simply *On Governance*, was written in Syriac and was translated into Arabic, according to al-Muḥassin (in Ibn al-Qifṭī: *Kalām fī l-Siyāsa, wuğida min taṣnīfihi fa-nuqila ilā l-ʿarabī*; Ibn Abī Uṣaybiʿa copies only the title and omits the mention of its original composition in Syriac). Since Ṯābit was acquainted with Plato's works, it may be surmised that this work had a Platonic orientation, though it can hardly be doubted that Ṯābit was also aware of Aristotle's *Politics*. Given the problems surrounding the transmission of Greek political texts and thoughts into Arabic, it is particularly regrettable that this treatise is not known to have survived.

2.2.4.5 *Philosophical Correspondence*

°35 *Masāʾil ʿĪsā b. Usayyid li-Ṯābit b. Qurra wa-ağwibatuhā li-Ṯābit*
Responses to Questions posed by ʿĪsā b. Usayyid

Fihrist [*153: 272,21] = Ibn Abī Uṣaybiʿa [*156: 219,25]. This is the title given by Ibn Abī Uṣaybiʿa in his list of Ṯābit's works; the *Fihrist* has a slightly different version: *Kitāb*

Ǧawābāt Ṯābit li-masāʾil ʿĪsā b. Usayyid, which Ibn Abī Uṣaybiʿa also reproduces in the section on Ṯābit's students (Ibn Abī Uṣaybiʿa [*156: 218,7–8]). The unique extant manuscript, London, British Library, Add. Or. 7473, has *Min al-masāʾil allatī saʾala ʿanhā Abū Mūsā ʿĪsā b. Usayyid Abā l-Ḥasan Ṯābit b. Qurra al-Ḥarrānī*, which would indicate that the extant portion of the text in the manuscript is only a selection from the larger original correspondence. Translated into Russian from the London manuscript by A. Y. Samsur, in Rosenfeld, Youshkevitch 1984 [*188: 278–284. 365–367]. Ed. and Engl. transl. by Sabra [*162]. Cf. below, 2.2.5. Doctrine.

2.2.5 Doctrine

The extensive list of Ṯābit's philosophical works makes it abundantly clear that he was a serious thinker in possession of detailed knowledge of the history of Greek philosophy, while what we have of his philosophical work 'reveals him as a philosopher in command of a wide range of philosophical problems much debated in late antiquity and subsequently in Islam and on which he held independent, indeed sometimes remarkably original opinions which he was able to support with skillful and effectively constructed arguments' (Sabra [*162: 2]). It is thus truly deplorable that there have survived only two of his philosophical works listed above, the brief essay on metaphysics (W °26a) and a set of responses to philosophical questions raised by a colleague (W °35).

The metaphysical piece, entitled *Precise Exposition of what Aristotle presented in his book Metaphysics by way of demonstration, not persuasion* (W °26a) consists, as its title indicates, of a close look – that is, a precise exposition, *talḫīṣ* – of the arguments presented by Aristotle in *Met.* XII, 6–9. The title is indicative of the preoccupation by the intellectuals of the generation of al-Kindī and those immediately following with precision in method in theoretical arguments, something which led, as argued above (§ 3.3), to the very resuscitation of philosophy in Arabic (cf. also the statement of concern about method in the correspondence of Ḥunayn b. Isḥāq on religious matters discussed above). Following the late Alexandrian tradition of the classification of all arguments on the basis of their reliability – apodeictic, dialectical, rhetorical, sophistic, and poetic, ranging from completely true to completely false (cf. Gutas 1983 [*185: 256–257]) – Ṯābit in this essay proposes to discuss only the apodeictic arguments in Aristotle and not the rhetorical (persuasive) ones. By this method he aims to establish the unassailable validity of those arguments he defends.

The essay is divided into nine sections (as analysed and discussed by Reisman, Bertolacci 2009 [*211]). In the introduction, which clearly corresponds to some of the preliminary questions to the study of Aristotle traditionally asked in the Alexandrian commentaries, Ṯābit explains the title of the *Metaphysics* and discusses some of the problems involved in the interpretation of the work, namely, the disagreement between Plato and Aristotle on the essence of the first principle, the difficulty of speaking directly about it (i.e., not by the *via negationis*), and the obscurity of Aristotle's writing. In the second section Ṯābit proves that the First Mover, because it causes the motion of corporeal substance, also causes its existence. This represents a Neoplatonic development of the main Aristotelian position in the *Metaphysics*. A possible objection to this position is that though the First Mover may be the cause of the motion of a corporeal substance and hence of its existence, it is not the cause of its matter if the matter is conceived as not having form, i.e., as being prime matter. This objection is disproved in the third section by arguing that matter devoid of form does not exist in actuality. In a further development of the Aristotelian position, Ṯābit proves in the fourth section that the first principle is the cause of the existence of the universe from eternity, not in time, in manifest repudiation of Philoponus' objections. The fifth section further supports the thesis stated in the fourth by arguing in favour of the compatibility between the eternity of the existence of the universe and its caused nature: creation in time would require both a further cause to prompt the First Cause into its creative action and imply a change in the First Cause from potency to actuality – both positions being impossible due to the immutability and absolute priority of the First Cause. A third argument in favour of the same position claims that just as nature does not delay the conferral of form to matter so too the first principle does not delay conferral of existence to the universe.

In the sixth section Ṯābit further develops the Aristotelian position by ascribing to the First Cause a will by means of which it brings corporeal substance into existence and denying that this is caused by its nature, since whatever acts by virtue of nature has desire and whatever has desire is caused. The seventh section, which contains four proofs of the fact that the First Cause is not a body, may be considered an expanded version of the arguments denying magnitude to the First Cause in *Met.* XII 7, 1073a5–11. In the eighth section Ṯābit offers a proof of the oneness of the First Cause, developing the ideas in *Met.* XII 8, 1074a 31–38, and further states that it is arrived at by way of negating (*salb*) for it the attributes of having a beginning, matter, and motion. In the ninth section, finally, which roughly corresponds to *Met.* XII 9, Ṯābit argues that the First Cause has the positive attribute of seeing itself and the other forms, and of being, in fact, the very act of seeing, and thus establishes that its essence is knowledge.

In his responses to ʿĪsā b. Usayyid's questions (W °35), Ṯābit displays the same kind of philosophical erudition and independent thinking. The title in the single extant manuscript of this work indicates that what has survived is only a selection from a larger whole; all in all 23 paragraphs have survived dealing with a number of issues (according to the presentation by Sabra [*162]). These can be grouped in three general categories: the question of infinity and the nature of numbers (§§ 1–3. 14. 20–22); the question of change in a substance and the status of statements about it (§§ 4–12); the nature of the categories, the five predicables, and related logical concepts (§§ 13. 15–19. 23).

The first question is about whether souls are finite in number or not. Ṯābit approaches the issue by discussing the problem of God's knowledge of particulars, which involves another question of philosophical significance, the existence of an actual infinite. Ṯābit argues, very much against the Aristotelian position but essentially on religious grounds, that God does know the particulars and that there is an actual infinite, and concludes that the number of souls is infinite. In the discussion of the mathematical infinite, Ṯābit asserts that an infinite can, in fact, be greater than another infinite by arguing that, since odd and even numbers are each one half of the totality of numbers, but both sets are infinite, the infinite totality of numbers is twice as great as the set of either the infinite odd or infinite even numbers. With regard to numbers, he held about their ontological status that they are real and that they are inherent forms in numbered objects that have them and are not accidental attributes, providing even a response to an objection against this position based on the third-man argument against Plato's theory of forms.

The second set of problems revolves around the question of change in a substance and the statements about it, centering around Aristotle's discussion in *Cat.* 4a10–4b19. The occasion for this set of questions is related to the first, namely the problem of God's knowledge of particulars. ʿĪsā b. Usayyid mentions the argument of those who claim that God cannot know the particulars because he would then suffer change. Ṯābit's position is essentially that statements about the change may change depending on the time when they are made but this does not also entail a change in the substance which knows the particulars.

The third set, finally, concerns the elucidation of various logical concepts relating to the categories and the five predicables, including the number of the former, genus and species, differentia, relation, accident, and homonymous names.

3 Philosophy and Natural Science

Eva Orthmann

3.1 Primary Sources – 3.2 Survey

3.1 *Primary Sources*

181 al-Kindī, Abū Yūsuf Yaʿqūb b. Isḥāq (d. between 247/861 and 252/866). *Rasāʾil al-Kindī al-falsafiyya*. Ed. by Muḥammad ʿAbd al-Hādī Abū Rīda. Vol. 1, Cairo, 1369/1950, vol. 2 [*al-Rasāʾil al-Ṭabīʿiyya*], Cairo, 1372/1953. – Repr. [rev. partial ed.] Cairo, 1978.

182 al-Kindī. *Risāla fī Kammiyyat kutub Arisṭū*. In *Rasāʾil al-Kindī al-falsafiyya*, vol. 1, 363–384.

183 Bos, Gerrit and Charles Burnett. *Scientific Weather Forecasting in the Middle Ages: The Writings of al-Kindī*. Studies, editions, and translations of the Arabic, Hebrew and Latin texts. London, 2000.

184 Abū Maʿšar al-Balḫī [Albumasar] (d. 272/886). *Kitāb al-Mudḫal al-kabīr ilā ʿilm aḥkām al-nuǧūm = Liber introductorii maioris ad scientiam judiciorum astrorum*. – Ed. by Richard Lemay, 9 vols. Naples, 1995.

185 al-Fārābī, Abū Naṣr Muḥammad b. Muḥammad (d. 339/950–951). *Fīmā yaṣiḥḥu wa-lā yaṣiḥḥu min aḥkām al-nuǧūm: Alfārābī's philosophische Abhandlungen aus Londoner, Leidener und Berliner Handschriften*. Ed. by Friedrich Dieterici. Leiden, 1890, 104–115. – German transl. by Friedrich Dieterici, *Über den Wert der Astrologie*. In *Alfārābī's philosophische Abhandlungen, aus dem Arabischen übers. von Friedrich Dieterici*. Leiden, 1892, 170–186.

186 al-Fārābī. *Iḥṣāʾ al-ʿulūm*. – Ed. by Angel González Palencia, *Catálogo de las ciencias*. Madrid, 1932, 1953 (2nd ed.).

187 al-Fārābī. *Mabādiʾ ārāʾ ahl al-madīna al-fāḍila: Al-Farabi on the Perfect State*. Revised text with introduction, translation, and commentary. Ed. by Richard Walzer. Oxford, 1985.

188 Iḫwān al-Ṣafāʾ (4th/10th cent.). *Rasāʾil Iḫwān al-Ṣafāʾ wa-ḫullān al-wafāʾ*, 4 vols. Beirut, 1376/1957.

189 Daiber, Hans. *Naturwissenschaft bei den Arabern im 10. Jahrhundert n. Chr. Briefe des Abū l-Faḍl Ibn al-ʿAmīd (gest. 360/970) an ʿAḍudaddaula*. With intro., annotated transl., and glossary. Leiden, New York, Cologne, 1993.

3.2 *Survey*

Among the scientific disciplines of the Greek tradition, the natural sciences (*ʿulūm al-ṭabīʿa*) aroused a particularly keen interest among Arabic-Islamic thinkers. Works on astronomy and astrology, on mathematics, medicine and other sciences were translated into Arabic early on, and soon formed the basis for original, autochthonous treatises that were composed on topics of natural science (Endress 1987 [*235: 418–429], Gutas 1998 [*248: 108–120]). While the scope of the sciences discussed was rather wide, the fundamental assumptions on the nature of the elements and their composition were generally the same. In what follows, I will therefore outline these basic assumptions first, before examining the question what kind of role they played for the individual sciences.

The philosophers developed various conceptions and classifications of the sciences. While al-Kindī, following Aristotle, divided the sciences into natural philosophy, mathematics, and metaphysics, al-Fārābī distinguished five different branches: (1) linguistics, (2) logic, (3) mathematics, (4) physics and metaphysics, and (5) politics, including law (*fiqh*) and theology (*kalām*). He considered the distinction between theoretical and practical disciplines to be fundamental (Schramm 1986 [*234: esp. 22]; cf. also Cortabarría Beitia 1972 [*228], Endress 1992 [*235: 47–52]).

Most systems of classification count medicine and alchemy, but also agriculture and navigation among the natural sciences, which are defined as concerned with changeable substance. The mathematical sciences, on the other hand, include arithmetic, geometry, music, and astronomy (Cortabarría Beitia 1972 [*228: 52–53. 57. 63], Schramm 1986 [*234: 22]). Astrology is mentioned either together with astronomy or with the natural sciences; in many cases, however, it is ignored entirely in the canon of the sciences (Nallino 1944 [*222: 2–4], Schramm 1986 [*234: 34–35]). Nevertheless astrology can be described as a supreme discipline, since it served to explain generation and corruption in the sublunar world. It connected the upper and the lower world and thus regarded the cosmos as a harmonic whole (*Mudḫal* [*184: 13–16]; Lemay 1962 [*223: 48–52], Lory 1992 [*240: 152–153], Adamson 2002 [*250a: 251–252]). This connection, which is explained in detail by Abū Maʿšar, was developed out of Peripatetic theories as they are found especially in Ptolemy and in Alexander of Aphrodisias (Lemay 1962 [*223: XXVI–XXVII. 41–48], Bos, Burnett [*183: 22], Barton 1994 [*243: 104–107]).

Central to these theories is a conception of the structure of the world, according to which the cosmos consists of several spheres of increasing size, with each sphere encompassing all the smaller spheres that come before it. How many spheres there are in total is a matter of dispute; the texts mention numbers between nine and fifteen. These differences in number can be accounted for by the fact that authors variously combine some spheres or assume yet further spheres beyond the sphere of the fixed stars. The sublunar world, in this system, consists of four spheres. Its very centre is where the heaviest element, earth, is located; it is surrounded by water, air, and fire, arranged in the order of their density. Above the sphere of fire we find the first planetary sphere, the sphere of the moon. Then follow the spheres of Mercury, Venus, the Sun, Mars, Jupiter, and Saturn, in their planetary order. Beyond the sphere of Saturn lies that of the fixed stars; in some authors this is again followed by the spheres of the zodiac, and of God's footstool (*kursī*) and throne (*ʿarš*), both mentioned in the Quran (e.g. Sura 2:13; 2:25; 23:86).

The extent to which spheres are combined or added appears to be determined, among other things, by the wish to place the sun in the middle of the order. This becomes evident when one compares al-Kindī's system with the much later one of Ibn ʿArabī: since al-Kindī's model ends with the sphere of the fixed stars, which means that there are only four spheres coming after the sun, he reduces the number of spheres beneath the sun to four as well. This he achieves by assigning a common sphere to each group of two elements, but also to Venus and Mercury (Bos, Burnett [*183: 245–246]). Where the zodiac gets its own sphere, however, Venus and Mercury can remain separate. Again, if each of the four elements receives its own sphere, two more spheres have to be added beyond the zodiacal sphere, in order for the sun to remain at the halfway point of the whole sequence (Burckhardt 1974 [*232: 13]). That it is indeed the position of the sun which determines the adopted model of the spheres can be observed clearly in the case of al-Kindī and the Iḫwān al-Ṣafāʾ. Having expounded his model of the spheres, al-Kindī goes on to emphasize the fact that the sun has an equal number of spheres below it and above it, and compares it to a king who stands in the middle of his people. The Iḫwān al-Ṣafāʾ liken it to a capital in the centre of an empire, and to a palace in the centre of a city (Bos, Burnett [*183: 246–247]; cf. *Rasāʾil* [*188: II 30]).

The lower or sublunar world is divided into the three realms of minerals, plants, and animals. All three realms are constituted by the four elements earth, water, fire and air. Each element combines two qualities within itself: earth is cold and dry, whereas water is cold and moist, air is warm and moist, and fire is warm and dry. Due to their respective affinities, the individual elements can be changed into each other: warm-dry fire, for instance, into warm-moist air or into cold-dry earth (on this, there is a particularly vivid account by Ibn al-ʿAmīd; cf. Daiber [*189: 106–115 and comm. 156–157]). The individual earthly bodies differ from each other not only in their form, but above all in their elemental mixture, which is responsible not only for the diversity of the various species, but also for that of the individuals within each species. Generation and corruption are effected by an alteration of the elements or rather, by the transformation of one element into another (Lemay 1962 [*223: 70–81]).

In order to explain how earthly bodies may realize their potentiality for such transformation, the planets are brought into play: their movements initiate the processes unfolding in the lower world (Bos, Burnett [*183: 247], Burnett 2002 [*250b: 206–207]; cf. *Mudḫal* [*184: ch. 1, section 3 and 4 = p. 19–29]). However, this leads to a problem: as the upper world is not subject to generation and corruption, it cannot be constituted by the four elements which make up the sublunar world. Instead it consists of a fifth element, aether (a different account is given by al-Fārābī, *Mabādiʾ* [*187: ch. 7, 3 and comm. 370. 375–376]). How, then, can the planets affect the lower world, if they are not built from the same elements? After all, according to Aristotle no effect can be elicited by an agent that is radically different from the object it acts on (*Mudḫal* [*184: 157]; cf. Lemay 1962 [*223: 65–66]). And how can one say that the planets consist of a fifth element, if they produce light and heat just as fire does? Again, how can one attribute individual properties and effects to each of the planets, if they all consist of the same element? (Lemay 1962 [*223: 95–97], Bos, Burnett [*183: 18–19].) Thus the Iḫwān al-Ṣafāʾ hold that the fifth element combines the properties of the other four elements (Nasr 1993 [*242: 62]).

Al-Kindī solves the problem by making the heat caused by the movement of the planets responsible for their effects on the lower world; moreover, he claims that both planets and elements emit rays which cause these effects (Bos, Burnett [*183: 163–164], Travaglia 1999 [*249: 20–25, 37–40]). Abū Maʿšar likewise assigns a central role to the heat that arises from the movement of the planets, explaining the different effects the planets have with reference to the differences in their movements. In addition he postulates the existence of a moving power that becomes effective from a distance, just like a magnet. Its effect depends on the disposition of the bodies on which it acts (*Mudḫal* [*184: 21–22]; cf. Lemay 1962 [*223: 60–65. 97–98. 105–109], Adamson 2002 [*250a: 254. 257–259]). Magnetism is also cited by Māšāʾ Allāh (Goldstein 1996 [*245: 15]).

The arguments developed by Abū Maʿšar and Māšāʾ Allāh are based on experience and analogical reasoning. Insights gained through the observation of sun and moon are used as bases for drawing inferences about the influence of the other planets (*Mudḫal* [*184: 7–14. 23. 39–41]; cf. Vadet 1963 [*224: 141–43], Bos, Burnett [*183: 336]). That they must have an effect is in addition inferred from the fact that the seasons vary each year rather than being uniform. As the course of the sun is always the same, these fluctuations must be attributable to the influence of the other planets, whose influence can furthermore be established empirically (Vadet 1963 [*224: 170–71], Lemay 1962 [*223: 51], Bos, Burnett [*183: 166–167]).

Such a view of the world, where planets have a direct influence on the events in the terrestrial world, will have encouraged people to believe in astrology and to try to assign an interpretation to the constellation of the stars (cf. the concise account in Freudenthal 1993 [*241: 77–84]). Of the authors mentioned above, al-Kindī, Abū Maʿšar and the Iḫwān al-Ṣafāʾ did this explicitly. However, even if it was possible to ground astrology on the very same foundations presupposed by the commonly accepted explanation of natural processes, it nevertheless met with numerous critics who questioned the efficacy of prognostication and scoffed at the tools of the astrologers. In his argument against astrology, al-Fārābī refers to a further dimension of the problem: chance or the existence of the possible [*185: 106–108]. Indeed, future contingents are hardly reconcilable with the notion of astral determinism. Would not all events have to be either necessary or impossible, if they could be read off the stars in advance? Abū Maʿšar solves this problem by declaring things happening in the future to be contingent up to the moment when they actually occur. Only then will they become either necessary or impossible. If several possibilities exist, it will be the elemental mixture as determined by the stars that decides which of the possibilities will be realized. For Abū Maʿšar the possible therefore constitutes the central focus of astrological interest (*Mudḫal* [*184: 32–38]; cf. Lemay 1962 [*223: 117–131], Adamson 2002 [*250a: 261–267], Burnett 2002 [*250b: 207–208]).

Elemental doctrine and cosmology left their marks on various areas of science. Their influence on meteorology is immediately obvious: meteorological observations formed the starting points for the analogical deductions that were supposed to demonstrate the influence of the planets. According to this understanding, the planets were directly responsible for heat and cold, drought and rain. The most important functions were hereby assigned to sun and moon: the former was essentially in charge of temperature, while the latter would determine humidity. The moon's connection with humidity was not least derived from people's observations of the tides, a phenomenon which is described in detail by Abū Maʿšar, who explains its complexities by referring to the varying positions that moon and sun take up towards each other (Bos, Burnett [*183: 178]; cf. *Mudḫal* [*184: 166–190]).

The different altitudes of the stars in the various regions of the world formed the basis for the division of the world into seven climes, each assigned to a planet (Nasr 1993 [*242: 87–89]). This division, which was fundamental for Arabic-Islamic geography, is first attested in Ptolemy (cf. Barton 1994 [*243: 182–183]). Starting from the observation that people of various cities and countries are different, these differences were explained with recourse to the positions of the stars, which were thus held responsible not only for temperature, flora and fauna, but also for the characters, customs and conventions of the human inhabitants of the earth, which again could be interpreted as consequences of the elemental mixtures (*Mudḫal* [*184: 163–165]).

A discipline closely linked to geography is geology. It was confronted with the fundamental problem that according to the model described above, the elements earth, water, air, and fire would have to form concentric spheres. This would leave earth at the very centre and entirely enclosed by water, something that not only contradicts all observation, but would also make any life on land impossible. Even if one were to postulate that God had just happened to create the continents (thus e.g. the Iḫwān al-Ṣafāʾ, *Rasāʾil* [*188: II 93–94]) it still would remain unclear why they were not gradually disappearing due to erosion. Mountains and stones therefore did not only have to erode, they needed to be generated anew. This process was explained with the existence of an oily liquid which did not evaporate and thus ensured the cohesion of stones (Freudenthal 1991 [*239: 49. 57–63], 1995 [*244: 161–172. 202]).

The notion of this oily liquid is also found in Arabic alchemy, a further branch of science based directly on the doctrine of the elements. In Ǧābir's works, the four elements are associated with four stages of distillation (Kraus 1942 [*221: 5–18], Freudenthal 1991 [*239: 61]). It is an essential assumption of alchemy that substances can be artificially transformed or created anew, by altering the proportions of their elements. In order to determine these proportions alchemy in turn relies on the use of numerology (Kraus 1942 [*221: 188–189], Hill 1990 [*238: 329–330. 335]). Stellar constellations again may influence the transformation processes. Alchemy is often regarded as younger sister science of astrology, not only because it is based on the latter's theoretical principles, but also because, like astrology, it has close ties to physics while at the same time belonging to magic (Marquet 1988 [*236: 16]).

Arabic medicine was decisively influenced by Hippocrates and, most importantly, by Galen. Galen's doctrine of the four humours which, in analogy to the four elements, combine two qualities each, was central to medicine in the Islamic world (Ullmann 1970 [*226: 97–100], Pormann, Savage-Smith 2007 [*252: 43–45]). The proportion of the four humours (black bile, yellow bile, blood and phlegm) in the body not only determined a person's state of health, but also their natural disposition and physiognomy. This proportion, on the other hand, was regarded as being influenced by the stellar constellation. As a result, a person's physical wellbeing was dependent on the clime in which they lived as well as to the actually prevailing stellar constellation (*Mudḫal* [*184: 27–28], Akasoy 2008 [*253: 129–134. 140]). This pertained especially to the development of the embryo, each month of which was supposed to be dominated by a particular planet (Burnett 1990 [*237], Baffioni 1997 [*247]). However, many physicians considered the stellar constellation as decisive also for the question whether someone would survive an illness or succumb to it (*Mudḫal* [*184: 45]; cf. Barton 1994 [*243: 187]). In yet another respect medicine found itself in close proximity to astrology: both were regarded as empirical sciences which were based not on logic but on experience and hence were not demonstrable (*Mudḫal* [*184: 13–15]; cf. Plessner 1972 [*230: 309]).

Human observation seems to confirm that the upper world is immune to generation and corruption (as is the case according to the worldview sketched above). This does not mean that Muslim thinkers did not contemplate the question whether the world as such was eternal, or finite and created: a problem that is intimately linked to the question of time and its limits. Following the example of the Greeks, time was associated with the movement of the planets; without movement there could not, therefore, be any time. Whether the movements of the planets are eternal or finite was, however, answered differently by various philosophers. While al-Kindī postulates that the movements have a beginning in time (Walzer 1962 [*225: 187–190. 200–201]), al-Fārābī considers the planetary movements to be eternal, explaining their existence within the framework of an emanationist model influenced by Neoplatonism (*Mabādiʾ* [*187: ch. 3]). The position of the Iḫwān al-Ṣafāʾ, finally, is characterized by cyclical notions of time, which correspond to their doctrine of prophecy and the imamate (Marquet 1972 [*229]). Here we see that concepts of time were closely linked to the religious commitments of the respective authors.

4 The Religious Application of Philosophical Ideas

Daniel De Smet

4.1 Ismaili Thinkers of the 4th/10th and the Early 5th/11th Century – 4.2 The Encyclopedia of the Iḫwān al-Ṣafāʾ

4.1 *Ismaili Thinkers of the 4th/10th and the Early 5th/11th Century*

4.1.1 Primary Sources – 4.1.2 Introduction – 4.1.3. Muḥammad al-Nasafī – 4.1.4 Abū Ḥātim al-Rāzī – 4.1.5 Abū Yaʿqūb al-Siǧistānī – 4.1.6 Ḥamīd al-Dīn al-Kirmānī

4.1.1 Primary Sources

4.1.1.1 Muḥammad al-Nasafī [*201–*203] – 4.1.1.2 Abū Ḥātim al-Rāzī [*211–*213] – 4.1.1.3 Abū Yaʿqūb al-Siǧistānī [*221–*228] – 4.1.1.4 Ḥamīd al-Dīn al-Kirmānī [*236–*255]

4.1.1.1 *Muḥammad al-Nasafī*

201 ʿAbdān. *Kitāb Šaǧarat al-yaqīn*. Ed. by ʿĀrif Tāmir. Beirut, 1982.

202 Abū Firās al-Maynaqī. *Kitāb al-Īḍāḥ*. Ed. by ʿĀrif Tāmir. Beirut, 1965.

203 al-Bustī. *Min Kašf asrār al-Bāṭiniyya*. Ed. by ʿĀdil Sālim al-ʿAbd al-Ǧādir. In *al-Ismāʿīliyyūn: Kašf al-asrār wa naqd al-afkār*. Silsilat al-buḥūṯ wa-l-dirāsāt al-islāmiyya, 2. Kuwait, 2002, 187–369.

4.1.1.2 *Abū Ḥātim al-Rāzī*

211 *Aʿlām al-nubuwwa*. – Ed. by Ṣalāḥ al-Ṣāwī and Ġulām Riḍā Aʿwānī. Engl. intro. by Seyyed Hossein Nasr. Tehran, 1397/1977. – *Aʿlām al-nubuwwa: al-radd ʿalā l-mulḥid Abī Bakr al-Rāzī*. No editor, Arab. intro. by Ǧūrǧ Ṭarābīšī. Beirut, 2003. – Ed. and Engl. transl. by Tarif Khalidi, *Abu Hatim al-Razi: The Proofs of Prophecy. A parallel English-Arabic text*. Provo, 2011. – Partial edition by Paul Kraus, "Raziana II: Extraits du *Kitāb Aʿlām al-nubuwwa* d'Abū Ḥātim al-Rāzī." *Orientalia*, N.S. 5 (1936): 35–56, 358–378. – Partial edition by Paul Kraus, in *Rasāʾil falsafiyya li-Abī Bakr Muḥammad b. Zakariyyāʾ al-Rāzī / Abi Bakr Mohammadi Filii Zachariae Raghensis Opera philosophica fragmentaque quae supersunt*. Cairo, 1939, 291–316. – Partial French transl. by Fabienne Brion, "Philosophie et révélation: Traduction annotée de six extraits du *Kitāb Aʿlām al-nubuwwa* d'Abū Ḥātim al-Rāzī." *Bulletin de philosophie médiévale* 28 (1987): 134–162. – Partial French transl. by F. Brion, "Le temps, l'espace et la genèse du monde selon Abū Bakr al-Rāzī: Présentation et traduction des chapitres I, 3–4 du *Kitāb Aʿlām al-nubuwwa* d'Abū Ḥātim al-Rāzī." *Revue philosophique de Louvain* 87 (1989): 139–164. – Partial Engl. transl. by Everett K. Rowson, "*Aʿlām al-nubuwwah*, Science of prophecy." In *An Anthology of Philosophy in Persia*, II: *Ismāʿīlī and Hermetico-Pythagorean Philosophy*. Ed by Seyyed Hossein Nasr and Mehdi Aminrazavi. Oxford, 2001, 140–171.

212 *Kitāb al-Iṣlāḥ*. – Ed. by Ḥasan Mīnūčihr and Mahdī Muḥaqqiq. Engl. intro. by Shin Nomoto. Tehran, 1377 h.š./1998. – Partial Engl. transl. by S. Nomoto, "An Ismāʿīlī Thinker on the Prophets in the Cosmic Correspondence: Translation of the *Kitāb al-Iṣlāḥ* by Abū Ḥātim al-Rāzī I." *Reports of the Keio Institute of Cultural and Linguistic Studies* 34 (2002): 97–152. – Partial Engl. transl. by S. Nomoto, "An

Ismāʿīlī Thinker on the Ethical Code of the Missionaries: Translation of the *Kitāb al-Iṣlāḥ* by Abū Ḥātim al-Rāzī 2." *Reports of the Keio Institute of Cultural and Linguistic Studies* 35 (2003): 105–131. – Partial Engl. transl. by S. Nomoto, "An Ismāʿīlī Thinker on Neoplatonist Cosmology: Translation of the *Kitāb al-Iṣlāḥ* by Abū Ḥātim al-Rāzī 3-(1)." *Reports of the Keio Institute of Cultural and Linguistic Studies* 36 (2004): 45–78.

213 *Kitāb al-Zīna fī l-kalimāt al-islāmiyya al-ʿarabiyya*. Ǧuzʾ 1–2. Ed. by Ḥusayn al-Hamdānī, 2 vols. Cairo 1956–1958. – Ǧuzʾ 3. Ed. by ʿAbd Allāh al-Sāmarrāʾī. In *al-Ġuluww wa-l-firaq al-ġāliya fī l-ḥaḍāra l-islāmiyya*. Baghdad, 1392/1972, 225–312.

4.1.1.3 *Abū Yaʿqūb al-Siǧistānī*

221 *Kitāb al-Yanābīʿ*. – Ed. and partial French transl. by Henry Corbin, in *Trilogie ismaélienne*. Tehran, Paris 1961, 1–97 (ed.), 5–127 (transl.). – Ed. by Muṣṭafā Ġālib. Beirut, 1965. – Partial French transl. by H. Corbin, in *Trilogie ismaélienne*. Lagrasse, 1994, 9–164. – Engl. transl. by Paul E. Walker, in *The Wellsprings of Wisdom: A Study of Abū Yaʿqūb al-Sijistānī's Kitāb al-Yanābīʿ*. Salt Lake City, 1994, 37–111. – Partial Engl. transl. by Latimah Parvin Peerwani, in *An Anthology of Philosophy in Persia*, vol. 2. Ed. by S. H. Nasr and M. Aminrazavi [cf. **211*], 124–137.

222 *Kašf al-maḥǧūb*. – Ed. by Henry Corbin. Tehran, Paris, 1949. – French transl. by H. Corbin, *Le dévoilement des choses cachées: Recherches de philosophie ismaélienne*. Lagrasse, 1988. – Engl. transl. by Hermann Landolt, in *An Anthology of Philosophy in Persia*, vol. 2. Ed. by S. H. Nasr and M. Aminrazavi [cf. **211*], 71–124.

223 *Iṯbāt al-nubūʾāt*. – Ed. by ʿĀrif Tāmir. Beirut, 1966.

224 *Kitāb al-Iftiḫār*. – Ed. by Muṣṭafā Ġālib. Beirut, 1980. – Ed. and Engl. intro. by Ismail K. Poonawala. Beirut, 2000.

225 *Sullam al-naǧāt*. – Ed. by Muhtadī Muṣṭafā Ġālib. Salamiyya, 2002.

226 *al-Risāla al-bāhira fī l-maʿād*. – Ed. by Bustān Hīrǧī, in *Taḥqīqāt-i islāmī* 7 (1371š./1992): 21–50.

227 *Tuḥfat al-mustaǧībīn*. – Ed. by ʿĀrif Tāmir, in *Ḫams rasāʾil ismāʿīliyya*. Salamiyya, 1956, 145–155. – Repr. in *Al-Mašriq* 61 (1967): 136–146. – Repr. in ʿĀ. Tāmir. *Ṯalāṯ rasāʾil ismāʿīliyya*. Beirut, 1983, 7–20.

228 *Kitāb al-Maqālīd*. – Ed. by Ismail K. Poonawala. Tunis, 2011.

4.1.1.4 *Ḥamīd al-Dīn al-Kirmānī*

236 *Kitāb Rāḥat al-ʿaql*. – Ed. by Muḥammad Kāmil Ḥusayn and Muḥammad Muṣṭafā Ḥilmī. Cairo, Leiden, 1953. – Ed. Muṣṭafā Ġālib. Beirut, 1967, 1983 (2nd ed.). – Russian transl. by Andrej V. Smirnov, *Uspokoenie razuma*. Moscow, 1995. – Partial Engl. transl. by Daniel Peterson, in *An Anthology of Philosophy in Persia*, vol. 2. Ed. by S. H. Nasr and M. Aminrazavi [cf. **211*], 175–192.

237 *Kitāb al-Riyāḍ*. – Ed. by ʿĀrif Tāmir. Beirut, 1960.
238 *al-Aqwāl al-ḏahabiyya*. – Ed. by Ṣalāḥ Ṣāwī. Engl. intro. by Seyyed Hossein Nasr. Tehran, 1397/1977. – Ed. by Muṣṭafā Ġālib. Beirut, 1977. – Ed. by ʿAbd al-Laṭīf al-ʿAbd, in *al-Ṭibb al-rūḥānī li-Abī Bakr al-Rāzī*. Cairo, 1978, 148–283.
239 *Maǧmūʿat Rasāʾil al-Kirmānī*. – Ed. by Muṣṭafā Ġālib. Beirut, 1403/1983.
240 *al-Risāla al-durriyya*. – Ed. by Muḥammad Kāmil Ḥusayn. Silsilat al-maḫṭūṭāt al-Fāṭimiyyīn, 7–8. Cairo, 1952, 13–34. – Ed. M. Ġālib [**239*: 19–26]. – Engl. transl. by Faquir M. Hunzai, in *An Anthology of Philosophy in Persia*, vol. 2. Ed. by S. H. Nasr and M. Aminrazavi [cf. **211*], 192–199.
241 *Risālat al-Nuẓum fī muqābalat al-ʿawālim*. Silsilat al-maḫṭūṭāt al-Fāṭimiyyīn, 7–8. Ed. by Muḥammad Kāmil Ḥusayn. Cairo, 1952, 35–59. – Ed. by M. Ġālib [**239*: 27–34].
242 *al-Risāla al-raḍiyya*. – Ed. by M. Ġālib [**239*: 35–42].
243 *al-Risāla al-muḍiyya fī l-amr wa-l-āmir wa-l-maʾmūr*. – Ed. by M. Ġālib [**239*: 43–60].
244 *al-Risāla al-lāzima fī ṣawm šahr Ramaḍān*. – Ed. by Muḥammad ʿAbd al-Qādir ʿAbd al-Nāṣir, in *Maǧallat Kulliyyat al-ādāb, Ǧāmiʿat al-Qāhira* 31 (1969): 1–52. – Ed. by M. Ġālib [**239*: 61–80].
245 *Risālat al-Rawḍa fī l-azal wa-l-azalī wa-l-azaliyya*. – Ed. by M. Ġālib [**239*: 81–91].
246 *al-Risāla al-zāhira*. – Ed. by M. Ġālib [**239*: 92–101].
247 *al-Risāla al-ḥāwiya fī l-layl wa-l-nahār*. – Ed. by M. Ġālib [**239*: 102–112].
248 *Risālat Mabāsim al-bišārāt*. – Ed. by Muḥammad Kāmil Ḥusayn, in *Ṭāʾifat al-Durūz*, Cairo, 1962, 55–74. – Ed. by M. Ġālib, in *al-Ḥarakāt al-bāṭiniyya fī l-islām*. Beirut, 1965, 205–233. – Ed. by M. Ġālib [**239*: 113–133].
249 *al-Risāla al-wāʿiẓa*. – Ed. by Muḥammad Kāmil Ḥusayn, in *Maǧallat Kulliyyat al-Ādāb, Ǧāmiʿat Fuʾād al-awwal* 14 (1952): 1–29. – Ed. by M. Ġālib [**239*: 134–147].
250 *al-Risala al-kāfiya fī l-radd ʿalā l-Hārūnī al-Ḥusaynī*. – Ed. by M. Ġālib [**239*: 148–182].
251 *al-Maṣābīḥ fī iṯbāt al-imāma*. – Ed. by Muṣṭafā Ġālib. Beirut, 1969. – Ed. and Engl. transl. by Paul E. Walker, *Master of the Age: An Islamic Treatise on the Necessity of the Imamate*. London, New York, 2007.
252 *al-Risāla al-waḍīʾa*. – Ed. by Muḥammad ʿĪsā al-Ḥarīrī. Kuwait, 1407/1987.
253 *al-Radd ʿalā man ankara al-ʿālam al-rūḥānī* (probably spurious). – Ed. by M. Ġālib [**239*: 183–189].
254 *Ḫazāʾin al-adilla* (probably spurious). – Ed. by M. Ġālib [**239*: 190–209].
255 *Usbūʿ dawr al-satr* (spurious). – Ed. by ʿĀrif Tāmir: *Arbaʿ rasāʾil ismāʿīliyya*. Salamiyya, 1952, 61–66.

4.1.2 Introduction

With its central focus on the doctrine of the imamate, Shiite Islam has always demonstrated a great openness for influences from very different directions: Greek philosophy, Christian gnosis, Jewish legends of the prophets, Iranian religious motifs. Understanding the text of the Quran as being subject to an interpretation that was continuously renewed under the authority of the Imam, Shiite authors resorted to conceptions and doctrines that were taken from ancient philosophy, with a view to placing the facts of revelation on a rational foundation. Beginning with the 4th/10th century, the Ismaili branch of Shiism in particular developed a specific form of Neoplatonism ('Ismaili Neoplatonism') aimed at establishing a harmony between the Quran and the late ancient interpretation of Plato and Aristotle (on the Ismāʿīliyya in general cf. Halm 2004 [*301: 160–201], Daftary 1990 [*309], 1998 [*319]). In their writings, we thus find complex cosmologies that were elaborated on the basis of the Plotinian hypostases – the ineffable One, Intellect, Soul, Nature (al-Nasafī, Abū Ḥātim al-Rāzī, Abū Yaʿqūb al-Siǧistānī), or the ten separate Intellects taken over from philosophy (*falsafa*) (al-Kirmānī). In the Ismaili thinkers' view of the soul and in their noetics one finds numerous analogies with the doctrines of contemporary philosophers, but also significant differences (on Ismaili philosophy in general cf. Nanji 1996 [*317], Walker 2005 [*328], De Smet 2011 [*335]). After the founding of Cairo in 358/969 the Ismaili dynasty of the Fatimids, in order to compete with the Abbasids, attracted philosophers, theologians and other scholars to its court. They built libraries, hospitals, and observatories in their capital, as well as a 'house of wisdom' (*dār al-ʿilm*) that was dedicated to the study of the profane sciences (Köhler 1994 [*313], Halm 1997 [*318]).

The oldest Ismaili texts, which go back to the mid 3rd/9th century, adhere to a cosmology of 'gnostic' character, which was to become the basis for the elaboration of Ismaili Neoplatonism. In its most complete form it is found in the *Risāla* by Abū ʿĪsā al-Muršid, a contemporary of the Fatimid caliph al-Muʿizz (regn. 341–365/953–975). The godhead, a brilliant light whose existence precedes both time and space, has formed the first creature from its light, by virtue of its will (*irāda, mašīʾa*). This creature is Kūnī, female hypostasis of the creative command *kun* ('be!'). As the godhead remains concealed from Kūnī, she regards herself as the only being in existence and thus feels a sense of pride. In order to show His omnipotence, God subsequently creates six further dignitaries (*ḥudūd*); hence it is Kūnī who has initiated cosmogony. Full of remorse, Kūnī pronounces the creed 'There is no Godhead but God, therefore I am not God.' Thereupon she is permitted to create a male aide from her own light: Qadar, the hypostasis of foreordination or predestination. Through Kūnī's mediation God creates (*kawwana*) all things, and through Qadar's mediation

He determines (*qaddara*) them. Seven cherubs (*karūbiyya*) who rule the seven heavenly spheres emerge from Kūnī's light, while Qadar creates twelve spiritual (*rūḥāniyya*) beings: the twelve signs of the zodiac. The Seven and the Twelve are the demiurges who form and govern the sublunar world (Halm 1978 [*290], Stern 1983 [*294: 3–29], Halm 1996 [*316: 75–83]).

In its original form this doctrine shares many features with the Christian gnostic systems of Late Antiquity. However, at the time when Abū ʿĪsā was writing his *Risāla* (probably in Egypt), Ismaili missionaries had already transformed the doctrine, using terminology borrowed from philosophy. The first Ismaili Neoplatonists, who were active mainly in Khorasan, Nishapur, and Rayy, established what Madelung has termed the 'Persian School' (Madelung 1961 [*278: 101–114]). Amongst its members were Muḥammad al-Nasafī (executed 332/943), his pupil Abū Tammām, Abū Ḥātim al-Rāzī (d. 322/934), and Abū Yaʿqūb al-Siǧistānī (d. around 361/971). The study of Ismaili Neoplatonism is still in its infancy; in addition, the identification of sources is hampered by the fact that Ismaili authors only rarely cite the ancient and Arabic-Islamic philosophers they refer to, since for them, all knowledge was, in principle, traced back to the Imams. The Ismailis therefore generally developed an ambivalent attitude towards philosophy: Ḥamīd al-Dīn al-Kirmānī (d. around 411/1020–1021) refuted the philosophers in his *Tanbīh al-hādī* (unpublished; cf. Walker 1999 [*406: 42–43. 52], De Smet 2016 [*412: 88–89]), while Abū Yaʿqūb al-Siǧistānī severely criticized the Abbasid caliph al-Maʾmūn for having sponsored the 'translation of books by the materialist and atheist Greek philosophers' (al-Siǧistānī, *Iftiḫār* [*224: 175]). Their own works are nevertheless strewn with philosophical terms and notions. The Iranian missionary (*dāʿī*) al-Naysābūrī (d. around 386/996) recorded that he and his colleagues were supposed to have mastered not only the Islamic sciences (*tafsīr, ḥadīṯ, fiqh*) but also the profane disciplines, i.e. logic, history, geography, astronomy, and philosophy (Klemm 1989 [*307: 239], Klemm, Walker 2011 [*339: 14–19 (ed.), 42–45 (transl.)]). Another missionary, Ibn al-Hayṯam (mid 4th/10th century), admitted to having studied Hippocrates, Plato, Aristotle, Socrates, Empedocles, and Dioscurides (Madelung, Walker 2000 [*324: 50. 52. 111. 137–140. 150–151. 154]). Abū Yaʿqūb al-Siǧistānī managed to avoid such incongruities by affirming that 'the best among the Greek philosophers' had successfully elevated their reflections to the 'spiritual realities' and had obtained valuable knowledge thanks to the instruction they had received from their predecessors, the prophets (al-Siǧistānī, *Iṯbāt* [*223: 158–159]; Walker 1993 [*381: 32–33]). In the same epoch, the prophetic origin of philosophy was emphasized also by Abū l-Ḥasan al-ʿĀmirī (§ 5.2.3) (Rowson 1988 [*304: 70–75], De Smet 1998 [*320: 38–45]).

Even though specific references are missing in the texts of the Ismaili Neoplatonists, the analysis of their doctrine shows that they had access to the

Arabic paraphrases of Plotinus, especially the 'long version' of the *Theology of Aristotle* (Pines 1954 [*274], Walker 1993 [*381: 41–44. 53. 60–61. 80. 86. 96–97. 177–180]; on the 'long version' cf. Aouad 1989 [*305: 564–570]); they furthermore made use of the Arabic Proclus (Walker 1993 [*381: 39. 82. 176 n. 3], De Smet 1995 [*401: 79–81. 264–270. 417–418]), the doxography of Pseudo-Ammonius (Rudolph 1989 [*308: 27–30], Walker 1993 [*381: 82. 85. 169 n. 58. 176 n. 3. 177–178], De Smet 2014 [*341: 491–518]), and the collection of texts that circulated in Arabic under the name of Empedocles (De Smet 1998 [*320]). The intellectual milieu within which these Neoplatonic Arabic texts originated is known only tentatively, and their exact relationship to the Ismāʿīliyya as yet awaits investigation. With regard to doctrine, we moreover find connections between the authors of the 'Persian school' and their non-Ismaili contemporaries in Iran, in particular the pupils of al-Kindī: Abū Zayd al-Balḫī, Ibn Farīġūn, Abū l-Ḥasan al-ʿĀmirī, and the circles centred around Abū Sulaymān al-Siǧistānī and Abū Ḥayyān al-Tawḥīdī (De Smet 2008 [*387]). Some scholars have surmised that al-Fārābī, too, was influenced by Ismaili thought; this, however, remains a matter of dispute (Daiber 1991 [*355], Steigerwald 1999 [*322]). Due to their use of common sources, Ismaili Neoplatonism finally exhibits numerous similarities to Jewish Neoplatonism, in particular to the philosophy of Isḥāq al-Isrāʾīlī (Pines 1947 [*272], Altmann, Stern 1958 [*275], Vajda 1958 [*276], Stern 1961 [*279], Vajda 1962 [*281: 172–173. 264–267. 396–403], Pines 1980 [*293], Kiener 1984 [*297]).

Even though Ismaili authors shared the intellectual milieu of the philosophers, they nevertheless followed their own paths. Adhering to the Ismaili distinction between 'worship through practice' (*al-ʿibāda al-ʿamaliyya*) and 'worship through knowledge' (*al-ʿibāda al-ʿilmiyya*), al-Kirmānī states that the 'first knowledge', i.e. the knowledge of the literary meaning of Quran and Sharia indispensable for religious practice, is a precondition for acquiring the 'second knowledge', through which the human soul will reach its second perfection (*al-kamāl al-ṯānī*) and will become an actual intellect able to subsist as a substance that is separate (*muǧarrada*) from the body (*Rāḥat al-ʿaql* [*236: 462], for the Ismaili concept of 'second perfection' cf. De Smet 1999 [*321]). Al-Kirmānī describes this 'second knowledge' (*ʿilm ṯānī*) as wisdom (*ḥikma*) that aims at the realities (*ḥaqāʾiq*), i.e. quiddities of things. It is obtained by interpreting (*taʾwīl*) the tenets that are mediated by the literal meaning of revelation and divine law (*Rāḥat al-ʿaql* [*236: 119. 462–463], De Smet 1995 [*401: 312. 354. 357–358. 361. 397]). As the literal text of Quran and Sharia consists in sensually perceptible symbols (*amṯila maḥsūsa*), it is in need of an interpretation which 'relates' (*awwala*) its external (*ẓāhir*) to its internal (*bāṭin*) meaning (al-Siǧistānī, *Iftiḫār* [*224: 154], al-Siǧistānī, *Iṯbāt* [*223: 3–4], al-Kirmānī, *Maṣābīḥ* [*251: 51. 55 Ġālib; 28–29. 31–32 Walker; 63–67 transl. Walker], De Smet

1994 [*312]). As practiced by the Imams, interpretation is a rational process which aims at showing that the verses of the Quran and the rules of the law are reconcilable with reason, even if their literal meaning often seems to contradict reason (al-Kirmānī, *Maṣābīḥ* [*251: 52–54 Ġālib; 29–31 Walker; 64–65 transl. Walker], al-Kirmānī, *al-Risāla al-ḥāwiya* [*247: 103. 106. 109]). A wisdom (*ḥikma*) that comprehends the inner meaning (*bāṭin*) of revelation therefore has nothing to do with irrational or occult knowledge. On the contrary, it concerns the essences (*maʿānī*) of things. Abū Yaʿqūb al-Siǧistānī thus sets the Islamic sciences, which relate to the external meaning (*ẓāhir*), in contrast to the profane sciences (metaphysics, mathematics, astronomy, medicine, politics, economics, and ethics), which he associates with the internal meaning (*bāṭin*). Between these two, perfect harmony obtains (al-Siǧistānī, *Iṯbāt* [*223: 119–122]; De Smet 2008 [*387]). Although al-Siǧistānī avoids using the term 'philosophy' (*falsafa*), it does transpire from his explications that wisdom (*ḥikma*), the subject of interpretation (*taʾwīl*), is nothing other than philosophy. The *ḥakīm* – the Imam and the 'inspired sage' – is defined by him as a 'pure human being' who is supported 'by the emanation of the spirit of holiness' (al-Siǧistānī, *Iṯbāt* [*223: 119]). However, if the philosophical disciplines contribute to understanding the deeper meaning of revelation, the strict parallelism obtaining between external and internal meaning also entitles one to invert the process and subject philosophical texts to an interpretation that will reveal their inner meaning (*bāṭin*). This inner meaning will relate to the 'world of religion' (*ʿālam al-dīn*). Al-Kirmānī calls this exegetical method, which is applicable in both directions, 'the balance of religion' (*mīzān al-diyāna*). It presupposes a view of the world which is characterized by continuity and perfect harmony obtaining between the two levels of being, which is what makes the transition from one level to the other possible (De Smet 1993 [*311], 1995 [*401: 27–31]). The Ismailis employ this method in order to explain the Quran with the help of philosophical concepts, and to understand its contents in the light of rational reflection (cf. e.g. al-Kirmānī, *Rāḥat al-ʿaql* [*236: 189–190. 203. 262. 288–289. 311. 328. 364–365. 451–452. 481–482]). No comparative study of philosophical exegesis of the Quran in Ismaili authors and in philosophers like Ibn Sīnā has yet been undertaken, but numerous similarities can be detected (De Smet, Sebti 2009 [*331]). In any case, it is clear that the Ismaili Shia appropriated part of the Arabic-Islamic philosophical tradition, with a view to providing rational foundations for its religious doctrine, in particular its imamology and its eschatology.

Despite their significance for the philosophical and religious history of medieval Islam, studies of the Ismailis are still in their infancy. Too many texts are yet to be made available in print, or are accessible in inadequate editions only. Philosophical reflection within the Ismāʿīliyya has not yet received the attention it deserves (cf. the bibliographies by Tajdin 1985 [*299] and Daftary 2004 [*326]). Access to the sources remains difficult. Arabic manuscripts that belong to the Pre-Fatimid and the Fatimid tradition and go back to the 4th/10th and the 5th/11th century were transmitted by the Ismaili Tayyibites, the Bohras. Since the 9th/15th century, the Bohras have mostly settled in India; however, due to the principle of secrecy (*taqiyya*) that surrounds their religious creed, their libraries have remained closed to anyone who is not a member of their sect (cf. the inventories by Ivanow 1933 [*271], 1963 [*282], Poonawala 1977 [*288]). For a few years now the Institute of Ismaili Studies in London has been compiling a collection of (mostly very recent) manuscripts as well as a portfolio of microfilms, which are made accessible to researchers (cf. the catalogues by Gacek 1984 [*296], Cortese 2000 [*323], 2003 [*325], de Blois 2011 [*334]). In addition they have initiated an ambitious project of editing and translating Ismaili texts ('Ismaili Texts and Translation Series'), whose aim it is to replace inadequate editions by critical editions, and to publish texts as yet unavailable in print.

4.1.3 Muḥammad al-Nasafī

Muḥammad b. Aḥmad al-Nasafī (or al-Naḫšabī) is usually considered to be the founding father of Neoplatonically inspired Ismaili philosophy (for different assessments see De Smet 2007 [*329], Hollenberg 2009 [*332], De Smet 2011 [*337]). Coming from the Nasaf area, today belonging to Uzbekistan, he was summoned to lead the Ismaili mission (*daʿwa*) in Nishapur. Later on he was sent to Bukhara, where he converted several Samanid dignitaries, including the emir Naṣr b. Aḥmad. His son and successor, Nūḥ, persecuted the Ismailis and in 332/943 had al-Nasafī executed (Stern 1960 [*277: 79–80], Poonawala 1977 [*288: 40–41], Halm 2004 [*301: 175–176], Daftary 1990 [*309: 122–123], Walker 1993 [*381: 15–16]).

His main work, *Kitāb al-Maḥṣūl* (*The Result* or *The Quintessence*), dated to 300/911 by Madelung (Madelung 1988 [*302: 96]), is lost, but lengthy excerpts from it have been preserved in both recensions of *Kitāb Šaǧarat al-yaqīn*, a work that Walker (1994 [*315]) ascribes to al-Nasafī's pupil Abū Tammām (ʿAbdān, *Šaǧarat al-yaqīn* [*201], Abū Firās al-Maynaqī, *al-Īḍāḥ* [*202]); further excerpts can be found in the work *Kašf asrār al-Bāṭiniyya* by the Zaydī Abū l-Qāsim al-Bustī (ca. 400/1010) [*203], in Abū Ḥātim al-Rāzī's *Kitāb al-Iṣlāḥ* [*212], and in al-Kirmānī's *Kitāb al-Riyāḍ* [*237]. Reconstructing *Kitāb al-Maḥṣūl* with the help of these fragments is one of the desiderata of Ismaili studies.

Due to the fragmentary transmission of his work al-Nasafī's philosophy is only partly known to us. Nevertheless it contains the most important metaphysical and cosmological doctrines of Ismaili Neoplatonism. God is conceived as an ineffable and incognizable reality beyond being and non-being.

He creates (*abdaʿa*) the Intellect, the first created being (*al-mubdaʿ al-awwal*), through His command or creative word (*amr, kalima*). The Intellect is a perfect and eternal entity which is perfectly at rest, and which contains within it the forms of all things that will come to be after it. Striving to separate the Creator (*al-mubdiʿ*) as far as possible from His creation (*al-mubdaʿ*), al-Nasafī introduces God's word or command, the principle of creation, as a kind of mediating hypostasis whose ontological status remains uncertain. He compares the word with the effect (*al-aṯar*) which is situated between cause (*al-muʾaṯṯir*) and result (*al-muʾaṯṯar*), or with the act (*al-fiʿl*) situated between the agent (*al-fāʿil*) and its result (*al-mafʿūl*). Effect and act do not, however, possess their own being outside of what they produce. The Intellect, bearer of forms, engenders (*tawallada*) the Universal Soul, which is incomplete at first, and can achieve perfection and rest only by turning towards the Intellect. Rest and motion within the essence of the Soul engender form (*ṣūra*) and matter (*hayūlā*) respectively, i.e. the principles of the bodily world. The Soul furthermore yields the spheres and the celestial bodies, which in turn generate the four elements, whose mixture yields minerals, plants, and animals. The last being to appear on the scene is man, whose soul constitutes a part (*ǧuzʾ*) of the Universal Soul enclosed in the body. It can only liberate itself from the body if, thanks to being instructed by prophets and imams, it manages to actualize its intellectual faculty. Having become an actual intellect, it will ascend through the celestial spheres and, as a luminous entity, will remain close to its origin, the Universal Soul, for ever (Walker 1993 [*381: 57–60], Netton 1994 [*314: 210–214], Walker 2005 [*328: 78–79]).

Kitāb al-Maḥṣūl, which is dependent on the doxography of Pseudo-Ammonius (Rudolph 1989 [*308: 27–30], Walker 1993 [*381: 39. 60]) and shows close proximity to Isḥāq al-Isrāʾīlī (Daftary 1990 [*309: 648 n. 228], Walker 1993 [*381: 35]), marks the origin of all later Ismaili philosophy – even though it in fact provoked many polemical reactions within the Ismāʿīliyya, reflecting varying interpretations of Arabic Neoplatonic texts as well as doctrinal differences. In the second part of his book, which is devoted to prophecy, al-Nasafī, an adherent of the Qarmaṭī movement, reveals a strong antinomism. Following Qarmaṭī messianism, he defends the view that the Mahdī Muḥammad b. Ismāʿīl abrogated all religious laws and would re-introduce the era of Adam, in which mankind is subject to no revealed law. The Fatimid Ismāʿīliyya therefore regarded the *Maḥṣūl* as heterodox, which is why it was not transmitted any further; moreover, al-Nasafī's antinomism became the subject of a refutation by Abū Ḥātim al-Rāzī (Stern 1983 [*295: 31–43], Daftary 1990 [*309: 167–168. 235–239], De Smet 2008 [*388], 2009 [*389], Poonawala 2012 [*340: 17–34]).

The only work by al-Nasafī that is extant in its entirety is a short cosmological treatise bearing the title *Kitāb Kawn al-ʿālam* (*The Generation of the World*).

The text is unpublished (a manuscript is extant in the Institute of Ismaili Studies in London; Gacek 1984 [*296: 35–36]; for a short survey of its contents and a preliminary account cf. Madelung 2010 [*345]).

4.1.4 Abū Ḥātim al-Rāzī

Born in the Rayy area, Abū Ḥātim Aḥmad b. Ḥamdān al-Layṯī al-Rāzī was in charge of the Ismaili propaganda in this city, and managed to convert its governor, Aḥmad b. ʿAlī. When Rayy was captured by the Sunni Samanids in 313/925–926, he had to flee to Daylam, where at first he enjoyed the protection of the emir Mardāwīǧ. Having fallen from the latter's grace, Abū Ḥātim al-Rāzī sought refuge in Azerbaijan, where he died in 322/934. Even though he does not seem to have recognized the authority of the Fatimids, his involvement with the Qarmaṭī movement remains a matter of dispute (Stern 1960 [*277: 61–67], Madelung 1961 [*278: 103–106], Poonawala 1977 [*288: 36–38], Halm 1982 [*353], De Smet 1992 [*356: 798–799], Nomoto [*212: 98–103]).

Abū Ḥātim al-Rāzī's erudition is on display in his *Kitāb al-Zīna* (*The Adornment*), a lexicographical study containing numerous quotations from Arabic poets and philologists, as well as ancient and Arabic-Islamic philosophers, which develops interesting ideas on the origin and structure of language (al-Hamdānī 1949 [*351], Vajda 1961 [*352]). Abū Ḥātim al-Rāzī's fame, however, rests mainly on a debate which he conducted with the philosopher Abū Bakr al-Rāzī (cf. § 6), and which is reflected in his *Kitāb Aʿlām al-nubuwwa* (*The Signs of Prophecy*). Here Abū Ḥātim al-Rāzī reproaches the philosophers for their arrogant belief of being able to reach certain knowledge by the power of reason alone, without the mediating help of revelation. In addition, he criticizes Abū Bakr al-Rāzī for upholding the existence of five eternal principles (God, Soul, time, space and matter) and the doctrine of the Soul's fall into matter (Goodman 1999 [*359], De Smet 2010 [*333: 113–119]). The work contains several quotations from the doxography of Pseudo-Ammonius (Rudolph 1989 [*308: 27–30], De Smet 2014 [*341]).

Abū Ḥātim al-Rāzī's philosophical views do not quite form a coherent whole. The main source for their reconstruction is his *Kitāb al-Iṣlāḥ* (*The Correction*), which is supposed to correct (*aṣlaḥa*) the errors contained in al-Nasafī's *Kitāb al-Maḥṣūl*. Despite his critical tone, al-Rāzī here turns out to be in fact dependent on his predecessor, from whom he inherits Neoplatonic metaphysics and cosmology. For just like al-Nasafī, Abū Ḥātim al-Rāzī considers God to be a transcendent reality which, through the word or command, creates (*abdaʿa*) the first being, Intellect, which encompasses all forms within it. Even though the act of creation (*ibdāʿ*), the word and the command represent an intermediate level between Creator and creation, they unite with the latter in order to form a single entity: the Intellect. In contrast to al-Nasafī, who regards

God and Intellect as eternal, Abū Ḥātim al-Rāzī lets time – and eternity – arise together with the Intellect. It is the source from which the Universal Soul emanates (*inbaʿaṯa*), in turn generating prime matter and form. Abū Ḥātim al-Rāzī distinguishes between three types of matter: (1) matter on the level of the Soul, which is 'imaginary' (*wahmiyya*), and which is tied to movement and rest as characteristics of its essence; (2) the matter of the four elemental qualities (*afrād*: dryness, moisture, heat and cold); (3) the matter of the four elements (*ummahāt*), whose mixture generates the four substances (*ǧawāhir*), i.e. minerals, plants, animals and humans. Abū Ḥātim al-Rāzī rejects al-Nasafī's thesis that the Soul is imperfect. According to him, Intellect and Soul form a primordial, male-female pair, a spiritual world (*ʿālam laṭīf*) which has no direct connection with the crude world (*ʿālam kaṯīf*) of sensually perceptible things, but which rules it by virtue of letting it benefit from its influence (*taʾṯīr*). Therefore human souls are not parts of the Universal Soul, but its effects (*āṯār*): not having emerged from the Universal Soul, they have no part in it. Thanks to the influence wielded by the Universal Soul via the instruction given by the prophets and imams, the thinking faculty of the human soul can, however, reach a level of perfection which approximates it to the Universal Soul, though without being able to unite with it. (Walker 1992 [*357], 1993 [*381: 51–55], 2005 [*328: 79–81], Nomoto [*212: 46–55]).

Apart from their possible influence on al-Fārābī's political philosophy (Daiber 1991 [*355]) and philosophy of language (Langhade 1994 [*358: 130–134]), Abū Ḥātim al-Rāzī's works have contributed importantly to philosophical reflection about the origin, the unity and the diversity of religions (Stern 1983 [*295: 30–46], Daiber 1989 [*354], Peerwani 2003 [*360]).

4.1.5 Abū Yaʿqūb al-Siǧistānī

Abū Yaʿqūb Isḥāq b. Aḥmad al-Siǧistānī (or al-Siǧzī), of whose extensive œuvre large parts have been preserved, is the most famous representative of the 'Persian School'. Concerning his life, however, we have little reliable information. He is said to have followed Abū Ḥātim al-Rāzī at the helm of the Ismaili mission in Rayy. Later on he was in charge of the Ismaili communities in Khorasan and Sīstān. In Sīstān he was executed by the Saffarid emir Ḫalaf b. Aḥmad (who ruled Khorasan from 353–393/964–1002), probably after 361/971, the year in which the redaction of his *Kitāb al-Iftiḫār* (*Pride*) is likely to have been carried out (Stern 1960 [*277: 68–70], Poonawala 1977 [*288: 82–89], De Smet 1992 [*380: 837–838], Walker 1982 [*375: 396–398], 1993 [*381: 16–24], 1996 [*384: 104–118], Daftary 2004 [*326: 153–155]). Abū Yaʿqūb al-Siǧistānī was close to al-Nasafī, whom he defended against Abū Ḥātim al-Rāzī's attacks in a work entitled *Kitāb al-Nuṣra* (*The Support*), which is lost today. At some point he seems to have been persuaded to join the Fatimid cause, though we do not know exactly when. He thus played an important role in the adoption of Neoplatonic philosophical speculation by the official Fatimid mission.

Abū Yaʿqūb al-Siǧistānī expounds his philosophical ideas in three of his main works: *Kitāb al-Yanābīʿ* (*The Wellsprings*) [*221], *Kašf al-maḥǧūb* (*The Revelation of the Veiled*) [*222] and *Kitāb al-Maqālīd* (*The Keys*) [*228]. The latter work contains quotations from the 'long version' of the *Theology of Aristotle* (on its contents cf. Poonawala 1976 [*371], Walker 1996 [*384: 112–115]). Each of the three works begins with a chapter on *tawḥīd*, God's unity. Compared with his predecessors al-Nasafī and Abū Ḥātim al-Rāzī, Abū Yaʿqūb al-Siǧistānī places even more emphasis on God's transcendence. The Highest is neither being nor substance, nor cause, nor essence; but neither is it non-being, non-substance, non-cause, non-essence. Each attribute of the Godhead is to be denied, while at the same time its denial is to be denied, too: the only way to approach God is that of double negation. Through the mediation of His word or command, the unreachable Highest creates (*abdaʿa*) the Intellect, from which the Universal Soul emanates (*inbaʿaṯa*), which in turn brings about (*kawwana*) the sense-perceptible world. This means that three modes of creation are sketched here: original creation (*ibdāʿ*), which lies outside time; emanation (*inbiʿāṯ*), which, through the movement of the Universal Soul, makes time appear; and the bringing about (*takwīn*) of things, which happens in time. While Intellect, as the first created being, is eternal, actually perfect and free of any movement, Soul, having emanated from it, is only potentially perfect. Its imperfection gives rise to a double movement within it: it strives towards the Intellect, whose effluence aids it in reaching actual perfection; at the same time, however, its imperfection pulls it downwards, towards the corporeal world. Abū Yaʿqūb al-Siǧistānī develops the Plotinian topic of the twofold orientation of the Soul in important ways, which seem to have influenced a number of philosophers, among them Ibn Sīnā (De Smet 2001 [*385]). The Soul's propensity towards matter sets off the generation of the sensually perceptible world, as well as the blending of innumerable particles of the Soul with matter: these are the human souls, parts of the Universal Soul, which have fallen into the corporeal world. In accordance with the Neoplatonic cycle of procession and return, this descent is juxtaposed to an ascent in which the human soul returns to its heavenly origin and, at the same time, the entire creation returns to its original source. This return occurs through the mediation of the prophets and imams, who are understood as earthly manifestations of the Intellect. Their teaching actualizes the potential human intellect, an actualization which is a necessary condition for the survival of the human soul outside the body, and for its return to the intelligible world (Kamada 1988 [*377], Netton

1994 [*314: 214–222], Walker 1993 [*381: 72–142], 2005 [*328: 81–84], De Smet 2010 [*333]). Abū Ya'qūb al-Siğistānī's philosophy is centred around four fundamental concepts: *ta'yīd, tarkīb, ta'līf* and *ta'wīl*. The Intellect supports (*ta'yīd*) the world in its existence thanks to the effluence emanating from it; the Soul shapes (*tarkīb*) the universe after the model of the forms that are contained in the Intellect; the prophet composes (*ta'līf*) the revealed texts; finally, the interpretation (*ta'wīl*) conducted by the Imam relates the outward meaning of the text to its archetype, the Intellect. Abū Ya'qūb al-Siğistānī recognizes these four methods in the four words which constitute the Islamic creed, as well as in the four arms of the Christian cross (*Yanābī'* [*221: 119–132 transl. Corbin; 91–95 transl. Walker], Walker 1996 [*384: 29–58]).

Some ambiguous passages of the *Kašf al-maḥğūb* have led to accusations that Abū Ya'qūb al-Siğistānī believed in the transmigration of souls (*tanāsuḫ*) (Madelung 1990 [*378], Walker 1991 [*379: 230–236], De Smet 2010 [*333: 125–130], De Smet 2014 [*342: 82–86, 95–103]). He seems to have looked favourably on astrology (Marquet 1994 [*382]) and has furthermore been credited with alchemical treatises, although these are certainly spurious (De Smet 2003 [*386]).

4.1.6 Ḥamīd al-Dīn al-Kirmānī

Ḥamīd al-Dīn al-Kirmānī, the most famous Ismaili philosopher from the Fatimid era, probably hailed from Kirmān in Eastern Iran. He was head of Ismaili mission in Baghdad and Basra, hence right in the centre of the Abbasid Empire. In 405/1014–1015 he was called to Cairo in order to fight against the extremist doctrine of certain missionaries (belonging to what was to become the sect of the Druze) who deified the Fatimid Imam-Caliph al-Ḥākim (De Smet 2007 [*330: 20–21]). There he remained until at least 408/1017, which is the date at which his *al-Risāla al-wā'iẓa* (*Epistle of Exhortation*) was completed. At an uncertain date and for undeterminable reasons, however, he had to return to Iraq, where he completed his *Kitāb Rāḥat al-'aql* (*Tranquillity of the Intellect*) in 411/1020–1021. After that, no further traces are left of him (Poonawala 1977 [*288: 94–102], De Smet 1992 [*399: 657–658], 1995 [*401: 3–16], Haji 1998 [*404: 9–21], Walker 1999 [*406: 1–46]).

There is no evidence to support the Ismaili tradition that makes al-Kirmānī a disciple of Abū Ya'qūb al-Siğistānī. In any case his philosophy is clearly distinct from that of his predecessor, whom he openly attacks in his *Kitāb al-Riyāḍ* (*The Gardens*). Al-Kirmānī here takes up the polemical dispute that had been waged between Abū Ḥātim al-Rāzī and Abū Ya'qūb al-Siğistānī, and gives his support to the view proclaimed in Abū Ḥātim al-Rāzī's *Iṣlāḥ*. He rejects his predecessors' speculations about the word or command mediating between the Creator (*mubdi'*) and the Intellect, as well as those about the nature of the Universal

Soul (Ivanow 1948 [*273: 130–153], Walker 1993 [*381: 60–63]). Though faithful to Ismaili Neoplatonism, his thought follows its own direction, as is manifest in particular in his most important work, *Kitāb Rāḥat al-ʿaql*.

Rāḥat al-ʿaql is designed according to the map of an imaginary city which is surrounded by seven 'walls' (*aswār*) and contains fifty-six 'crossroads' (*mašāriʿ*). The cosmology it presents uses decads as the principle according to which everything is ordered. A perfect harmony obtains between the three 'worlds' that constitute the universe: the ten separate Intellects, which are assigned to the intelligible world; the ten heavenly spheres, which rule over the world of nature, and the ten ranks of the Ismaili missionary organization (*daʿwa*), which constitute the world of religion. Outside this system we find the transcendent, ineffable and unknowable Creator (*mubdiʿ*). Al-Kirmānī describes Him in the same terms as Abū Yaʿqūb al-Siǧistānī, but emphasizes His transcendence even more than his predecessor did. Thus Intellect, after having been created, retains no connection to the Creator, who remains out of the reach of His creatures for ever. Even though al-Kirmānī's understanding of the Intellect agrees with the Ismaili Neoplatonism of his predecessors, he refines it further, employing concepts he finds in al-Fārābī's *Principles of the Opinions of the Inhabitants of the Excellent City* (*Mabādiʾ ārāʾ ahl al-madīna al-fāḍila*). He takes up al-Fārābī's description of the First Being as self-knowing intellect, but applies it to the Intellect, the first created being. He therefore effects an ontological shift in comparison with the philosophers' concept of the deity. Even though al-Kirmānī's Intellect is a created being, it furthermore takes on the features of the Quranic God, and is even called by His name, Allāh. As bearer of all forms and 'cause of causes' (*ʿillat al-ʿilal*) the Intellect is the origin for the emanation (*inbiʿāṯ*) of everything that is situated further below. However, this emanation does not give rise to the Plotinian hypostases (Soul, Nature) as envisaged by the earlier Ismailis, but to the separate Intellects familiar from al-Fārābī's *Principles of the Opinions of the Inhabitants of the Excellent City*. In this way al-Kirmānī introduced al-Fārābī's cosmology to the Ismāʿīliyya, around the same time that Ibn Sīnā was giving it its ultimate form in his *Kitāb al-Šifāʾ*. Although al-Kirmānī's system of emanation is directly dependent on al-Fārābī, it still bears the features of the old Plotinian triadic structure: in its property as knowing intellect (*ʿaql ʿāqil*), Intellect gives rise to an actual Intellect (the 'first emanated being', *al-munbaʿaṯ al-awwal*), from which a series of seven actual Intellects emanates. Insofar as it is an object of thought (*ʿaql maʿqūl*), on the other hand, Intellect brings about a potential intellect composed from matter and form. This is the tenth and last Intellect, the demiurge who shapes the sublunar world according to the models it obtains from the first Intellect, through the mediation of the eight actual Intellects. The first Intellect (or the first created being), the second actual Intellect (the first emanated being) and the tenth potential Intellect thus correspond to the three hypostases of earlier Ismaili Neoplatonism (and hence that of Plotinus): Intellect, Soul, and Nature.

In the field of noetics, al-Kirmānī is again indebted to al-Fārābī, to whom he owes its fundamental concepts: potential intellect (*al-ʿaql bi-l-quwwa*), material intellect (*al-ʿaql al-hayūlānī*), actual intellect (*al-ʿaql bi-l-fiʿl*), acquired intellect (*al-ʿaql al-mustafād*) and Agent Intellect (*al-ʿaql al-faʿʿāl*). Following in the footsteps of al-Fārābī, al-Kirmānī identifies the Agent Intellect with the tenth Intellect. Apart from its function as demiurge, he ascribes to it a noetic and eschatological role as the actualizing principle of the human capacity to think, in which man's happiness and eternal life reside. The description of the nature and activity of the Agent Intellect penned by the Ismaili al-Kirmānī is nevertheless clearly different from that by the philosopher al-Fārābī: according to al-Kirmānī, the Agent Intellect acts through the instruction (*taʿlīm*) of the prophets and imams. In contrast to the intellectual faculty of ordinary mortals, the intellect of the imams is perfect and always actual, without having to pass from potentiality to actuality. They may therefore be regarded as embodiments of the Agent Intellect – a somewhat precarious thesis, which al-Kirmānī developed with great circumspection in *Rāḥat al-ʿaql* (De Smet 1992 [*400], Netton 1994 [*314: 222–229], De Smet 1995 [*401], Walker 1999 [*406], 2005 [*328: 84–88]), De Smet 2008 [*409], 2008 [*410]).

The innovations introduced to the body of doctrines by al-Kirmānī were not taken over by his immediate successors responsible for the Fatimid mission (Nāṣir-i Ḫusraw, al-Mu'ayyad). Instead, they stuck to the path laid out by Abū Yaʿqūb al-Siǧistānī (De Smet 2010 [*333: 104–109]). However, al-Kirmānī's work had a remarkable impact upon the post-Fatimid Ismāʿīliyya of Ṭayyibī orientation, which was established towards the mid 6th/12th century in Yemen by al-Ḥāmidī; for al-Ḥāmidī was the first to attempt a harmonization between the contents of *Rāḥat al-ʿaql* and the *Rasāʾil Iḫwān al-Ṣafāʾ* (al-Hamdānī 1932 [*397], Netton 1994 [*314: 229–233]).

4.2 *The Encyclopedia of the Iḫwān al-Ṣafāʾ*

4.2.1 Primary Sources – 4.2.2 Authorship and Date of Composition – 4.2.3 Works – 4.2.4 Doctrine – 4.2.5 Impact

4.2.1 Primary Sources

4.2.1.1 *Rasāʾil Iḫwān al-Ṣafāʾ*: Complete Editions [*271]; Partial Editions [*273–*282]; Medieval Latin Translations [*285–*287]; Modern Translations [*291–*314] –

4.2.1.2 *Al-Risāla al-Ǧāmiʿa* [*321–*322] – 4.2.1.3 *Ǧāmiʿat al-Ǧāmiʿa* [*326] – 4.2.1.4 Testimonies Concerning Authorship and Work [*331]

4.2.1.1 *Rasāʾil Iḫwān al-Ṣafāʾ*

Complete Editions

A critical edition and annotated English translation of the *Rasāʾil Iḫwān al-Ṣafāʾ* is currently appearing with Oxford University Press, in collaboration with the Institute of Ismaili Studies, London, under the direction of Nader El-Bizri and Carmela Baffioni. For the list of manuscripts and the editorial principles cf. El-Bizri 2008 [*505: 20–23]. However, as this editing project has not yet been completed, the Beirut edition from 1376/1957 will be quoted in the following. A concordance of the Bombay, Cairo, and Beirut 1376/1957 editions was compiled by Blumenthal 1974 [*440].

271 *Kitāb Iḫwān al-Ṣafāʾ wa-Ḫullān al-Wafāʾ*, 4 vols. Bombay, 1305–1306/1887–1889. – *Rasāʾil Iḫwān al-Ṣafāʾ wa-Ḫullān al-Wafāʾ*. Ed. by Ḫayr al-Dīn al-Ziriklī. Intro. by Ṭāḥā Ḥusayn and Aḥmad Zakī Pāšā, 4 vols. Cairo, 1347/1928. – Ed. by Buṭrūs al-Bustānī. 4 vols. Beirut, 1376/1957. – Ed. by ʿĀrif Tāmir, 4 vols. Beirut/Paris, 1415/1995.

Partial Editions

273 Dieterici, Friedrich. *Thier und Mensch vor dem König der Genien: Ein arabisches Märchen aus den Schriften der lautern Brüder in Basra, im Urtext herausgegeben und mit einem Glossar versehen*. Leipzig, 1879. (Ep. 22). – F. Dieterici. *Die Abhandlungen der Ichwān es-Safā in Auswahl zum ersten Mal aus arabischen Handschriften herausgegeben*, 2 vols. Leipzig, 1883–1886.

274 Goodman, Lenn E. and Richard McGregor. *Epistles of the Brethren of Purity: The Case of the Animals versus Man Before the King of the Jinn*. An Arabic Critical Edition and English Translation of Epistle 22. Oxford, 2009.

275 Baffioni, Carmela. *Epistles of the Brethren of Purity: On Logic*. An Arabic Critical Edition and English Translation of Epistles 10–14. Oxford, 2010.

276 Wright, Owen. *Epistles of the Brethren of Purity: On Music*. An Arabic Critical Edition and English Translation of Epistle 5. Oxford, 2010.

277 de Callataÿ, Godefroid and Bruno Halflants. *Epistles of the Brethren of Purity: On Magic*. An Arabic Critical Edition and English Translation of Epistle 52, Part 1. Oxford, 2011.

278 El-Bizri, Nader. *Epistles of the Brethren of Purity: On Arithmetic and Geometry*. An Arabic Critical Edition and English Translation of Epistles 1–2. Oxford, 2013.

279 Baffioni, Carmela. *Epistles of the Brethren of Purity: On the Natural Sciences*. An Arabic Critical Edition and English Translation of Epistles 15–21. Oxford, 2013.

280 Sánchez, Ignacio and James Montgomery. *Epistles of the Brethren of Purity: On Geography*. An Arabic Critical Edition and English Translation of Epistle 4. Oxford, 2014.

281 Ragep, F. Jamil and Taro Mimura. *Epistles of the Brethren of Purity: On 'Astronomia'*. An Arabic Critical Edition and English Translation of Epistle 3. Oxford, 2015.

282 Walker, Paul E., David Simonowitz, Ismail K. Poonawala and Godefroid de Callataÿ. *Epistles of the Brethren of Purity: Sciences of the Soul and Intellect, Part I*. An Arabic Critical Edition and English Translation of Epistles 32–36. Oxford, 2016.

Medieval Latin Translations

285 Nagy, Albino. *Die philosophischen Abhandlungen des Jaʿqūb ben Isḥāq al-Kindī*. Münster, 1897, 41–64 (Ep. 14).

286 Gautier-Dalché, Patrick. "Epistola fratrum sincerorum in cosmographia: Une traduction latine inédite de la quatrième risāla des Iḫwān al-Ṣafāʾ." *Revue d'histoire des textes* 18 (1988): 137–167 (Ep. 4).

287 Sannino, Antonella. "Ermete mago e alchimista nelle biblioteche di Guglielmo d'Alvernia e Ruggero Bacone." Studi medievali 41 (2000): 185–189 (Ep. 52).

Modern Translations

No complete translation of the *Rasāʾil* has been published so far. The following list records translations of single epistles into Western languages. The 'translations' by Dieterici [*291–*296] are really paraphrases, sometimes of summary character, and often inexact and rather unreliable.

291 Dieterici, Friedrich. *Der Streit zwischen Mensch und Thier: Ein arabisches Mährchen aus den Schriften der lauteren Brüder übersetzt*. Berlin, 1858 (Ep. 22).

292 Dieterici, F. *Die Naturanschauung und Naturphilosophie der Araber im zehnten Jahrhundert: Aus den Schriften der lautern Brüder übersetzt*. Berlin 1861 (Ep. 14–21).

293 Dieterici, F. *Die Propaedeutik der Araber im zehnten Jahrhundert*. Berlin, 1865 (Ep. 1–6).

294 Dieterici, F. *Die Logik und Psychologie der Araber im zehnten Jahrhundert n. Chr.* Leipzig, 1868 (Ep. 7–13).

295 Dieterici, F. *Die Anthropologie der Araber im zehnten Jahrhundert n. Chr.* Leipzig, 1871 (Ep. 23–30).

296 Dieterici, F. *Die Lehre von der Weltseele bei den Arabern im X. Jahrhundert*. Leipzig, 1872 (Ep. 31–40).

297 Yusufji, D. H. "The Forty-Third Treatise of the Ikhwān al-Ṣafāʾ." *Muslim World* 33 (1943): 39–49 (Ep. 43).

298 Bauwens, Jan. “Zeventiende zendbrief van de *Rasāʾil Iḫwān aṣ-Ṣafāʾ*: Over de fysische lichamen.” *Orientalia Gandensia* 1 (1964): 171–185 (Ep. 17).

299 Goldstein, Bernard R. “A Treatise on Number Theory from a Tenth Century Arabic Source.” *Centaurus* 10 (1964): 129–160. – Repr. in: *An Anthology of Philosophy in Persia*, vol. 2. Ed by S. H. Nasr and M. Aminrazavi [cf. **211*], 225–245 (Ep. 1).

300 Shiloah, Amnon. “L'épître sur la musique des Ikhwān al-Ṣafāʾ.” *Revue des études islamiques* 32 (1964): 125–162; 34 (1966): 159–193 (Ep. 5).

301 Michot, Jean. “L'épître de la résurrection des Ikhwan as-Safa'.” *Bulletin de philosophie médiévale* 16/17 (1974/75): 114–148 (Ep. 37).

302 Diwald, Susanne. *Arabische Philosophie und Wissenschaft in der Enzyklopädie Kitāb Iḫwān aṣ-Ṣafāʾ*, vol. 3: *Die Lehre von Seele und Intellekt*. Wiesbaden, 1975, 31–556 (Ep. 32–41).

303 Bausani, Alessandro. *L'enciclopedia dei Fratelli della Purità*. Naples, 1978. – Summary of all epistles.

304 Goodman, Lenn E. *The Case of the Animals Versus Man Before the King of the Jinn: A Tenth-Century Ecological Fable of the Pure Brethren of Basra*. Boston, 1978 (Ep. 22).

305 Shiloah, Amnon. *The Epistle on Music of the Ikhwān al-Ṣafāʾ*. Tel-Aviv, 1978 (Ep. 5).

306 Poveda, Emilio Tornero. *La disputa de los animales contra el hombre*. Madrid, 1984 (Ep. 22).

307 Baffioni, Carmela. *L'epistola degli Iḫwān al-Ṣafāʾ 'Sulle opinioni e le religioni'*. Naples, 1989 (Ep. 42).

308 Giese, Alma. *Mensch und Tier vor dem König der Dschinnen: Aus den Schriften der Lauteren Brüder von Basra*. Aus dem Arabischen übersetzt, mit einer Einleitung und mit Anmerkungen herausgegeben. Hamburg, 1990 (Ep. 22).

309 van Reijn, Eric. *The Epistles of the Sincere Brethren* (*Rasāʾil Ikhwān al-Ṣafāʾ*). An annotated translation of epistles 43 to 47. Montreux, 1995 (Ep. 43–47).

310 Ricardo-Felipe, Albert R. “La *Risāla fī māhiyyat al-ʿišq* de las *Rasāʾil Ijwān al-Ṣafāʾ*.” *Anaquel de estudios árabes* 6 (1995): 185–207 (Ep. 37).

311 de Callataÿ, Godefroid. *Ikhwān al-Ṣafāʾ: Les révolutions et les cycles* (*Épîtres des Frères de la Pureté*, XXXVI). Traduction de l'arabe, introduction, notes et lexique. Beirut, Louvain-La-Neuve, 1996 (Ep. 36).

312 Peerwani, Latima Parvin. “Microcosm and Macrocosm.” In *An Anthology of Philosophy in Persia*, vol. 2. Ed. by S. H. Nasr and M. Aminrazavi [cf. **211*], 202–219 (Ep. 26); 219–225 (Ep. 43).

313 de Callataÿ, Godefroid. “Ikhwān al-Ṣafāʾ: Des arts scientifiques et de leur objectif: Présentation et traduction de l'épître VII des Frères de la Pureté.” *Le Muséon* 116 (2003): 231–258 (Ep. 7).

314 de Callataÿ, Godefroid. "Ikhwān al-Ṣafāʾ: Sur les limites du savoir humain (épître XXVIII des Frères de la Pureté)." *Le Muséon* 116 (2003): 479–503 (Ep. 28).

4.2.1.2 *al-Risāla al-Ǧāmiʿa*

321 *al-Risāla al-Ǧāmiʿa al-mansūba li l-ḥakīm al-Maǧrīṭī*. – Ed. by Ǧamīl Ṣalībā, 2 vols. Damascus, 1368–1370/1949–1951.

322 *al-Risāla al-Ǧāmiʿa. Tāǧ Rasāʾil Iḫwān al-Ṣafāʾ wa-Ḫullān al-Wafāʾ*. Taʾlīf Aḥmad b. ʿAbd Allāh b. Muḥammad b. Ismāʿīl b. Ǧaʿfar al-Ṣādiq. – Ed. by Muṣṭafā Ġālib. Beirut, 1394/1974.

4.2.1.3 *Ǧāmiʿat al-Ǧāmiʿa*

326 *Ǧāmiʿat al-Ǧāmiʿa*. – Ed. by ʿĀrif Tāmir. Beirut, 1378/1959.

4.2.1.4 *Testimonies Concerning Authorship and Work:*

331 al-Tawḥīdī, Abū Ḥayyān ʿAlī b. Muḥammad (d. 414/1023). *Kitāb al-Imtāʿ wa-l-muʾānasa*. – Ed. by Aḥmad Amīn and Aḥmad al-Zayn, 3 vols. Cairo, 1939–1944.

4.2.2 Authorship and Date of Composition

This oldest Arabic 'encyclopedia' of philosophy and the sciences proves to be a collective work that originated in a kind of brotherhood or secret circle whose anonymous members called themselves 'Brethren of Purity and Faithful Friends', Iḫwān al-Ṣafāʾ wa-Ḫullān al-Wafāʾ. Even though this name has been translated in several ways – *ṣafāʾ* can mean 'purity' but also 'integrity' or 'sincerity' – the common scholarly consensus, following Goldziher (1910 [*423]), assumes that it is borrowed from a fable from *Kalīla wa-Dimna* which focuses on the topic of solidarity among the animals, who may count on the support of their 'sincere brethren' (*Iḫwān al-Ṣafāʾ*). Apart from that, the word *Ṣafāʾ* is often linked to the Iḫwān al-Ṣafāʾ's assumed affiliation with Sufism (Tibawi 1955 [*429: 35. 37], Diwald [**302*: 16–22], Netton 1982 [*455: 4–6], Baffioni 2005 [*501: 449–450]).

More controversial is the question of the identity of the Iḫwān al-Ṣafāʾ. There are two main hypotheses competing with each other. The first one refers to the testimony of Abū Ḥayyān al-Tawḥīdī (d. 414/1023) (*Imtāʿ* [**331*: II 4–5]), according to which the redaction of the *Rasāʾil* was carried out by a group of official clerks in Basra, including, among others, the chancellery secretary Zayd b. Rifāʿa, the judge Abū l-Ḥasan ʿAlī b. Hārūn al-Zanǧānī, Abū Sulaymān Muḥammad b. Maʿšar al-Bustī al-Maqdisī, Abū Aḥmad al-Nahraǧūrī and al-ʿAwfī, all of them contemporaries of Abū Ḥayyān al-Tawḥīdī. It is corroborated by Abū Sulaymān al-Siǧistānī (d. ca. 374/985) and ʿAbd al-Ǧabbār (d. 415/1025), at least to some extent (Stern 1946 [*428], Diwald [**302*: 8–12], Hamdani 1978 [*446: 345–350], Stern 1983 [*456: 155–165], de Callataÿ 2005 [*502: 4–7]). The second hypothesis follows a rather late Ismaili tradition which appears at the beginning of the 6th/12th century and ascribes the *Rasāʾil* to one or several missionaries (*duʿāt*) of the second hidden Imam Aḥmad b. ʿAbd Allāh b. Muḥammad b. Ismāʿīl, or even to the Imam himself. This would point to a time shortly before the Fatimids' accession to the throne in Ifrīqiyya (297/909) (Stern 1983 [*456: 166–172], Hamdani 1979 [*449], Poonawala 2008 [*510]). Apart from these two, several further, rather fantastic attributions have been put forward in Arabic literature: to ʿAlī b. Abī Ṭālib, Ǧaʿfar al-Ṣādiq, Ǧābir b. Ḥayyān, al-Ḥallāǧ, al-Maǧrīṭī, Abū Sulaymān al-Siǧistānī and al-Ġazālī (Stern 1983 [*456: 173–174], de Callataÿ 2005 [*502: 9–10]).

The dating of the *Rasāʾil Iḫwān al-Ṣafāʾ* depends on the identification of their author or authors, as well as on the equally disputable question whether it is the work of a single author, or a collective work of several authors potentially belonging to different generations. If we can trust al-Tawḥīdī's testimony, the *Epistles* were composed between 360/970 and 370/980; in which case they would be the result of studies carried out within the group of the Iḫwān al-Ṣafāʾ of Basra and could well have been redacted by a secretary (Tibawi 1955 [*429: 37–38]). Internal evidence seems to confirm this dating: the mention of the Ašʿariyya (al-Ašʿarī died in 324/935–936), a passage which is probably loaned from al-Fārābī's (d. 339/950–951) *al-Madīna al-fāḍila*, and the appearance of verses by al-Mutanabbī (d. 354/965) (Baffioni 2005 [*501: 450], de Callataÿ 2005 [*502: 4]). By contrast, the 'Ismaili' hypothesis espoused by Hamdani is forced to interpret these pieces of internal evidence as interpolations and to regard al-Tawḥīdī's testimony as a forgery composed for the purpose of discrediting some of his contemporaries (Hamdani 1984 [*457]). Marquet (1973 [*439: 8], 1978 [*447]) suggests a compromise, according to which the majority of the *Rasāʾil* was written between 350/961 and 370/980, whereas some of them originated in the period before the Fatimid accession to the throne. Thus Marquet assumes that the *Rasāʾil* were composed during a long, drawn-out period of about eighty years. The late date of between 439/1047 and 443/1051, suggested by Casanova (1915 [*424]) on the basis of astronomical data, is no longer recognized as a valid option (Hamdani 1996 [*476]).

While the Shiite tendencies of the *Rasāʾil Iḫwān al-Ṣafāʾ* are obvious, their relation to the Ismāʿīliyya remains a point of contention. Corbin (1964 [*433: 190]) looked upon the *Rasāʾil* as an Ismaili work, as did Marquet (e.g. 1977 [*445], 1978 [*447], 1981 [*453]), who regarded the *Rasāʾil* as an instrument of Fatimid propaganda reflecting the official doctrine of the *daʿwa*. According to Hamdani (1999 [*489]), the Iḫwān al-Ṣafāʾ constituted a secret society which advocated the establishment of a Fatimid caliphate. However, neither pre-Fatimid nor Fatimid Ismaili literature seems to be aware of the Iḫwān al-Ṣafāʾ in any way, with the exception of Nāṣir-i Ḫusraw (d. after 462/1070) (De Smet 2010 [*333: 119–122]). It was only in the mid 6th/12th century that the *Rasāʾil* were read by the Ṭayyibite Ismailis of the Yemen (al-Hamdānī 1932 [*425], Stern 1983 [*456: 166–172]). Moreover, their concept of the imamate proves to be at odds with Ismaili imamology (Tibawi 1955 [*429: 34], Netton 1980 [*451]). This is not, however, to deny that the doctrine of the Iḫwān al-Ṣafāʾ shares numerous ideas with the Ismāʿīliyya (Netton 1981 [*454]) and seems to have originated in a similar intellectual milieu.

4.2.3 Works

4.2.3.1 *Rasāʾil Iḫwān al-Ṣafāʾ* – 4.2.3.2 *Al-Risāla al-Ǧāmiʿa* and *Ǧāmiʿat al-Ǧāmiʿa*

4.2.3.1 *Rasāʾil Iḫwān al-Ṣafāʾ*

The extant recension of the *Rasāʾil Iḫwān al-Ṣafāʾ* (*The Epistles of the Brethren of Purity*) comprises 52 epistles, whereas the text itself refers several times to their number as 51. This means that one epistle must have been added; most probably the 51st epistle, which merely takes up a part of the 21st epistle and does not blend in with the overall structure of the work (Marquet 1971 [*436: 1100], 1973 [*439: 10–11]). Doubts have also been raised concerning the authenticity of the last epistle, *On Magic* – though, it would appear, without justification (de Callataÿ 2005 [*502: 16]).

The structure and style of the *Rasāʾil* are very homogeneous, which suggests that the work was composed by a single author or at least redacted by a single editor. Most epistles present their doctrine in the name of the Iḫwān al-Ṣafāʾ, who address the readers (called 'Brethren') using the first person plural, occasionally the first person singular. The work is of encyclopedic character, covering all areas of profane and religious knowledge and communicating a universal view of the world which stretches from God to the lowliest creatures. The 52 epistles are divided in four classes: (1) propaedeutics (Epistle 1–14), in particular arithmetic, geometry, astronomy, geography, music, the theoretical and practical sciences, ethics, logic; (2) the natural sciences (Ep. 15–31) including the subject areas of physics, generation and corruption, meteorology, mineralogy, botany, biology, man as microcosm, the nature of the human soul, life and death, joy and sorrow, genesis and origin of language; (3) psychology and noetics (Ep. 32–41) according to the doctrine of the Pythagoreans and the Iḫwān al-Ṣafāʾ; further topics are: the macrocosm, the intellect, the cycles, love, and resurrection; (4) theological and religious sciences (Ep. 42–52), comprising the various religions, the creed of the Iḫwān al-Ṣafāʾ, the divine law, prophecy, politics, and finally, magic. At first sight, this structure appears rather strict; in part it takes up a division of sciences which loosely follows the order of Aristotle's logical and physical writings as established in the late Alexandrian tradition. Nevertheless several epistles seem to be out of place, and the work as a whole suffers from a lack of coherence which may have its roots in a faulty transmission, or in later revision efforts (Marquet 1973 [*439: 10–17], Baffioni 2005 [*501: 453–457], de Callataÿ 2005 [*502: 12–16], 2008 [*507], Baffioni 2008 [*506]).

In order to write this comprehensive work, the Iḫwān al-Ṣafāʾ exploited an impressive number of Arabic-Islamic, Persian, Indian, Christian, Jewish, and above all Greek sources. They possessed detailed knowledge of the Greek-Arabic translations, as is documented by the numerous pertinent quotations which permeate the *Rasāʾil* (collected and identified by Baffioni 1994 [*470], cf. also 1992 [*466], 1997 [*481], 1997 [*483]); quoted are in particular the Presocratics, Pythagoras (Baffioni 1994 [*469]), Socrates (Marquet 1998 [*486]), Plato (Baffioni 2001 [*493]), Aristotle (Marquet 1988 [*460], Baffioni 1991 [*462], 1991 [*463], 1995 [*475], 2002 [*495], 2002 [*496]), the Stoics, Plotinus, Archimedes (Baffioni 2001 [*492]), Euclid (Baffioni 1990 [*461]), Nicomachus of Gerasa (Baffioni 1995 [*474], 1997 [*480]), Ptolemy, and Galen.

4.2.3.2 *Al-Risāla al-Ǧāmiʿa* and *Ǧāmiʿat al-Ǧāmiʿa*

As we can see from its subtitle, *Tāǧ Rasāʾil Iḫwān al-Ṣafāʾ* (*The Crown of the Epistles of the Brethren of Purity*), the *Risāla al-Ǧāmiʿa* is presented as the quintessence of the doctrine of the Iḫwān al-Ṣafāʾ, whose esoteric meaning it is supposed to reveal. It would thus have been reserved for an initiated elite. In reality the text offers a rather incomplete summary of the *Rasāʾil*, which has been infiltrated by several remarks and doctrines (in particular concerning the transmigration of souls and the fall of the Soul into matter) that have no direct parallels in the writings of the Iḫwān al-Ṣafāʾ, or even contradict their ideas. The *Risāla al-Ǧāmiʿa* exists in two versions. One is attributed to the Andalusian mathematician and astronomer Maslama al-Maǧrīṭī (d. 398/1007) (*Ǧāmiʿa* [*321]), a man who was an adept of the occult sciences; the other to the second hidden Imam of the Fatimid Ismailis, Aḥmad b. ʿAbd Allāh b. Muḥammad b. Ismāʿīl (*Ǧāmiʿa* [*322]).

Even though the *Risāla al-Ǧāmiʿa* is mentioned occasionally in the *Rasāʾil* [*271: I 43; IV 250. 262. 340] (all these occurrences may well be interpolations, however), it is likely to have been composed in a later period by an Ismaili author (De Smet 1999 [*488: 46]). It was extensively quoted by the Ṭayyibite Ismailis of the Yemen, who ascribed it to the 'excellent person' (*al-šaḫṣ al-fāḍil*), i.e. the second hidden Imam Aḥmad, and played an important role in the adoption of the ideas of the Iḫwān al-Ṣafāʾ by the post-Fatimid Ismāʿīliyya.

Ǧāmiʿat al-Ǧāmiʿa is an abbreviated version of the *Risāla al-Ǧāmiʿa* as it was transmitted by the Ismāʿīliyya. It represents a yet further advanced phase of the Ismaili reception of the Iḫwān al-Ṣafāʾ. The study of these two works and their relation to the *Rasāʾil*, however, is still in its infancy (Baffioni 1997 [*484], 2000 [*490]).

4.2.4 Doctrine

According to Abū Ḥayyān al-Tawḥīdī, the Iḫwān al-Ṣafāʾ held the following view: 'The religious law (*šarīʿa*) has been besmirched by ignorance and mixed with all sorts of errors. Philosophy (*falsafa*) is the only instrument that can purge and cleanse it, because it unites within itself the wisdom of religious conviction and the benefit of investigation based on reason.' Al-Tawḥīdī concludes: 'They are of the opinion that perfection (*kamāl*) has been reached since Greek philosophy (*al-falsafa al-yūnāniyya*) and Arabic law (*al-šarīʿa al-ʿarabiyya*) have been brought into agreement. To this purpose they composed fifty epistles on all philosophical disciplines' (al-Tawḥīdī, *Imtāʿ* [*331: II 5]). This passage appositely describes the intellectual project of the Iḫwān al-Ṣafāʾ, which defines the structure and aim of the *Rasāʾil*.

According to the Iḫwān al-Ṣafāʾ, human beings indeed can reach happiness only if they simultaneously dedicate themselves to worship (of God) through the religious law (*al-ʿibāda al-šarʿiyya al-nāmūsiyya*) and through philosophy and metaphysics (*al-ʿibāda al-falsafiyya al-ilāhiyya*). While the former helps to cleanse body and soul, the latter helps the intellect to penetrate the realities of things (*ḥaqāʾiq al-mawǧūdāt*). A perfect harmony between these two has only ever been reached by an elite of prophets (including Muḥammad) and philosophers (including Aristotle). This is illustrated by a tradition (*ḥadīṯ*) ascribed to Muḥammad: 'I am the Aristotle of this community' (Iḫwān, *Rasāʾil* [*271: IV 262–263]; Marquet 1973 [*439: 333–334], 1988 [*460: 160]). Inspired prophets, Imams and philosophers have access to the same truths, which they express in different forms. The Quran, 'shaped' by Muḥammad and addressing a Bedouin society lacking any philosophical culture, contains imaginative symbols which are adapted to the limited intellectual capabilities of its readership (Marquet 1964 [*434: 279]). However, Muḥammad was, at the same time, a 'philosopher': he had mastered the divine philosophy (*al-falsafa al-ilāhiyya*), whose ancient representatives were none other than Pythagoras, Socrates, Plato and Aristotle. This philosophy has to be derived from the surface, literal meaning of the Quran by an exegesis conducted by sages who are 'deeply rooted in knowledge' (Quran, Sura 3:7). Only the 'divine sages and the scholars who dedicate themselves to philosophy' (*al-ḥukamāʾ al-rabbāniyyūn wa-l-ʿulamāʾ al-mutafalsifūn*) are able to comprehend the meaning of revelation in a philosophical manner (Iḫwān, *Rasāʾil* [*271: II 342–343; III 77–78. 345. 511–512; IV 132. 138. 263], Marquet 1973 [*439: 317–320. 461–476]). In their *Rasāʾil*, the Iḫwān al-Ṣafāʾ thus aim at cleansing religion and soul by means of 'worship through philosophy and metaphysics', attempting to establish a harmony between the religious sciences that emerged from revelation and the rational sciences inherited from the Greeks.

With their attitude of acquiring wisdom wherever it was to be found, i.e. without religious, cultural or ethnic prejudice towards their sources, the Iḫwān al-Ṣafāʾ developed a way of thinking that has been called 'syncretistic' or 'eclectic' (Netton 1996 [*478: 224–229], de Callataÿ 2005 [*502: 73–87]). In this way they united, in a more or less coherent manner, a (Neo-)Pythagorean arithmology, a Neoplatonically inspired system of emanation, an Aristotelian classification of the sciences, Aristotelian logic and physics, and Ptolemaic astronomy and geography, along with Hermetic astrology, enriched by Persian and Indian elements.

The universe of the Iḫwān al-Ṣafāʾ comprises nine levels which are generated from each other in successive emanation (*fayḍ, inbiǧās*): (1) the ineffable and unknowable Creator creates (*abdaʿa*), through emanation, (2) the Intellect, bearer of all forms. The Intellect, sole, perfect and unmoved, generates (3) the Universal Soul, which is perfect only potentially, and whose movement – a sign of its imperfection – generates (4) prime matter. Prime matter is 'spiritual', not corporeal matter and serves as a substrate for the influence of (5) Nature, which is a faculty of the Soul. Through this influence it receives three dimensions and becomes (6) second matter or absolute body, the first level of the corporeal world. Absolute body (7), which is moved by Nature in circular motion, enables the celestial spheres to appear; after that (8) the four elements are brought about, whose mixture constitutes (9) the three natural realms: minerals, plants, and animals (Farrukh 1963 [*432: 294–296], Nasr 1978 [*448: 51–66]). There is a close connection between the generation of these nine levels of being and the creation of the numbers 1 to 9: each level of being partakes in the qualities of the number to which it corresponds. This gives rise to an arithmological theology that is based on (Neo-)Pythagorean sources (Straface 1987 [*458], Marquet 2006 [*504], El-Bizri 2008 [*508]).

In its role as demiurge, the universal Soul holds a central place in this system. Taking up the Neoplatonic idea of a twofold orientation of the Soul, the Iḫwān al-Ṣafāʾ distinguish between its upper part, the 'head' (*raʾs*), which is joined to the Intellect, and its lower part, the 'tail' (*ḏanab*), which is turned towards the corporeal world. From the 'head' emanates a power (*quwwa*) which, with the help of the sun, descends and bestows life and movement on the corporeal things. These are the individual souls which ensoul animals, plants, and even minerals. The power that emerges from the 'tail', on the other hand, descends with the help of the moon. It attends to the world of generation and corruption in all its corporeality: it is the demiurge, organizing the bodies in this world (*tadbīr*) (*Rasāʾil* [*271: IV 214–215. 223–224], Marquet 1973 [*439: 115]). The actions of the sun, the 'queen of the heavens', and of the moon, which contribute to the generation of the corporeal world, are integrated within an astral theology which draws on Hermetic and Neoplatonic sources (De Smet 1999 [*488]).

Perfect continuity and harmony obtains between the various levels of the universe; this follows from the doctrine of emanation that determines the cosmology of the Iḫwān al-Ṣafāʾ. A continuous chain links the highest intelligible principles (Intellect and Soul) to the lowest corporeal beings, thus making it possible to proceed from one level to the other without interruption. Once the individual souls, the 'powers' of the Universal Soul, enter the bodies, the descending motion of emanation reverses its direction. In an ascending hierarchy, the mineral souls are followed by the souls of plants, animals and human beings; though only the latter possess a rational faculty. In this 'great chain of being', this *scala naturae* joining together minerals, plants and animals and finally culminating in man, Dieterici (1878 [*422]) wanted to detect a precursor of Darwin's evolutionary theory; an untenable thesis that nevertheless still has its supporters (Marquet 1992 [*468: 129–133. 138], 1999 [*439: VIII–IX]; cf. De Smet 2005 [*503: 85–89]).

Instead, the universe of the Iḫwān al-Ṣafāʾ, to whom evolution by natural selection would have been a rather alien idea, proves to be a living, organic universe enlivened by a multiplicity of souls which, each one on its own level, move the body in a quest to reunite themselves with the Universal Soul, the origin of all souls. Man is the most perfect creature of the sublunar world, the 'microcosm', whose essence is an image of the universe. He possesses the most perfect soul, which, on account of its rational faculty, is alone able to purify itself through asceticism and to actualize itself through knowledge, in order to release itself from its corporeal bonds. However, this purification is a lengthy process taking place in countless cycles which constitute the history of the world, and which are determined by stellar motions and conjunctions, in accordance with rather complicated astronomical and astrological laws (Marquet 1962 [*431], de Callataÿ [*311]).

While expecting the 'great resurrection', which will reunite all souls with the Universal Soul and bring about the end of our earthly world, the salvation of the individual soul consists in finding the perfect balance between a virtuous life and the acquisition of that knowledge which alone can liberate it. On the basis of this idea, the Iḫwān al-Ṣafāʾ developed the utopian concept of a 'spiritual ideal state' (*madīna fāḍila rūḥāniyya*) ruled by an imam-philosopher, a concept which exhibits parallels to al-Fārābī's 'ideal state' (Enayat 1977 [*444], Baffioni 2002 [*494]).

4.2.5 Impact

The Iḫwān al-Ṣafāʾ's project of uniting 'profane' and 'Islamic sciences' met with criticism among Sunni scholars, who were antagonistic towards their philosophy and also towards Shiism. Contemporaries like ʿAbd al-Ǧabbār, Abū Sulaymān al-Siǧistānī and Abū Ḥayyān al-Tawḥīdī expressed their scepticism with respect to the approach taken by the Iḫwān al-Ṣafāʾ. In 555/1160 the Abbasid caliph al-Mustanǧid had the *Rasāʾil* publicly burnt in Baghdad as a heretical work, together with Ibn Sīnā's *Kitāb al-Šifāʾ*; and Ibn Taymiyya's (d. 728/1328) famous *fatwā* against the Nuṣayrī sect contains numerous attacks against the Iḫwān al-Ṣafāʾ (Guyard 1871 [*421], Michot 2008 [*509]).

Nevertheless the *Rasāʾil* were widely disseminated in the Sunni world (up to the present day), being popular especially with the geographers (e.g. al-Idrīsī and al-Qazwīnī) and mystics (al-Ġazālī, Ibn ʿArabī; Diwald [*302: 6–7], 1981 [*452: 24]). Moreover, they were explicitly read and appropriated by the Ṭayyibite Ismailis (al-Hamdānī 1932 [*425]), and were also quoted as authoritative by the Twelver Shia. To mention but one example, Mullā Ṣadrā (d. 1050/1640) endeavoured to harmonize the thought of the Iḫwān al-Ṣafāʾ with that of Ibn Sīnā, al-Suhrawardī and Ibn ʿArabī (Nasr 1996 [*477: 643–644]). The *Rasāʾil* have furthermore left traces in Armenian literature (Dadoyan 1992 [*467]), and can thus claim influence on Oriental Christian circles as well.

Towards the end of the 4th/10th century, the *Rasāʾil* are said to have been introduced to Muslim Spain, either by Maslama al-Maǧrīṭī or by his pupil Abū l-Ḥakam al-Kirmānī. They were quoted by several Arabic-Andalusian poets (García Gómez 1939 [*426]) and, above all, were used extensively in *Ġāyat al-ḥakīm* (*The Goal of the Sage*), that famous handbook of magic, whose Latin translation, entitled *Picatrix*, was read throughout the Latin world (Plessner 1959 [*430], De Callataÿ 2013 [*514]). Traces of the 49th epistle are furthermore found in the Latin version of the *Secretum secretorum* ascribed to Aristotle (Gautier-Dalché [*286: 141]).

Several Jewish philosophers and encyclopedists, active in Muslim Spain and elsewhere, seem to have known the epistles (Zonta 1996 [*479: 269–270. 281–290], Krinis 2013 [*515]). However, the influence the *Rasāʾil* exerted on medieval Jewish thought has not yet been studied systematically.

A full Latin translation of the *Rasāʾil* is not documented, but translations of the 4th, 14th, and 52nd epistles are extant under the following titles: *Epistola fratrum sincerorum in cosmographia* (Gautier-Dalché [*286]), *Liber introductorius in artem logicae demonstrationis* (Nagy [*285: 41–64], Baffioni 1994 [*471]), *Liber de quattuor confectionibus* (Sannino [*287: 185–189], Baffioni 2003 [*497]). Apart from that, a Catalan adaptation of the 22nd epistle was composed in 1417 by Anselmo Turmeda (Nader 1994 [*473]). On the whole, however, the impact of the Iḫwān al-Ṣafāʾ on the Latin West is known to us only fragmentarily, as studies on the topic are yet to be conducted.

5 Secondary Literature

5.1 Works of Reference [*1–*7] – 5.2 Popular Ethics, Practical Politics [*11–*110] – 5.3 Scholars as Transmitters of Philosophical Thought [*121–*211] – 5.4 Philosophy and Science of Nature [*221–*253] – 5.5 Ismaili Thinkers of the 4th/10th and The Early

5th/11th Century [*271–*412] – 5.6 The Encyclopaedia of the Iḫwān al-Ṣafāʾ [*421–*515].

5.1 *Works of Reference*

1 GAL = Brockelmann, Carl. *Geschichte der arabischen Litteratur*, 2 vols; 3 suppl. vols. Leiden 1937–1949 (2nd ed.). – Edition adapted to the supplement volumes.

2 EI^2 = *The Encyclopaedia of Islam: New edition*. Ed. by Clifford Edmund Bosworth et al., 11 vols, 6 suppl. vols. Leiden, 1960–2005.

3 GAS = Sezgin, Fuat. *Geschichte des arabischen Schrifttums*, 17 vols. Leiden, Frankfurt a.M., 1967–2015.

4 WKAS = *Wörterbuch der Klassischen Arabischen Sprache*. Ed. by the Deutsche Morgenländische Gesellschaft, revised by Anton Spitaler and Manfred Ullmann, 2 vols. Wiesbaden, 1970–2009.

5 EIr = *Encyclopaedia Iranica*. Ed. by Ehsan Yarshater, vols 1 ff. London, 1982 ff.

6 GAP = *Grundriss der arabischen Philologie*, vol. 2: *Literaturwissenschaft*. Ed. by Helmut Gätje. Wiesbaden, 1987; vol. 3: *Supplement*. Ed. by Wolfdietrich Fischer. Wiesbaden, 1992.

7 GALex = *A Greek and Arabic Lexicon: Materials for a Dictionary of the Mediaeval Translations from Greek into Arabic*. Ed. by Gerhard Endress and Dimitri Gutas, vols 1 ff. Leiden, 2002 ff.

5.2 *Popular Ethics, Practical Politics*

5.2.1 Gnomologia, Doxographies, Mirrors for Princes [*11–*75] – 5.2.2 *Liber de Pomo* [*81–*110]

5.2.1 Gnomologia, Doxographies, Mirrors for Princes

11 Baumstark, Anton. "Griechische Philosophen und ihre Lehren in syrischer Überlieferung." *Oriens Christianus* 5 (1905): 1–25.

12 Merkle, Karl. *Die Sittensprüche der Philosophen. 'Kitâb Âdâb al-Falâsifa' von Ḥonein ibn Isḥâq in der Überarbeitung des Muḥammed ibn ʿAlî al-Anṣârî*. Leipzig, 1921 – Repr. in: F. Sezgin 1999 [*62: 261–321].

13 Gibb, Hamilton Alexander Rosskeen. "The Argument from Design: A Muʿtazilite Treatise Attributed to al-Jāḥiẓ." In *Ignace Goldziher Memorial Volume*. Ed. by Samuel Löwinger and Joseph Somogyi. Budapest, 1948, 150–162.

14 Barns, John. "A New Gnomologium: With Some Remarks on Gnomic Anthologies." *The Classical Quarterly* 44 (1950): 126–137; 45 (1951): 1–19.

15 Dunlop, Douglas Morton. “Biographical Material from the Ṣiwān al-ḥikmah.” *Journal of the Royal Asiatic Society* (1957): 82–89.
16 Ullmann, Manfred. *Griechische Spruchdichtung im Arabischen.* PhD Diss., University of Tübingen, 1959.
17 Rosenthal, Franz. “Al-Mubashshir ibn Fatik: Prolegomena to an Abortive Edition.” *Oriens* 13–14 (1960–1961): 132–158.
18 Rosenthal, Franz. Review of Ullmann 1961 [*6], in: *Orientalia* 32 (1963): 364–367.
19 Rosenthal, Franz. *Das Fortleben der Antike im Islam.* Zurich, 1965. – Engl. transl. by Emile and Jenny Marmorstein, *The Classical Heritage in Islam.* London, 1975, 1992, 2004 (2nd ed.).
20 Grignaschi, Mario. “Les Rasāʾil Arisṭāṭālisa ilā l-Iskandar de Sālim Abū l-ʿAlāʾ et l'activité culturelle à l'époque omayyade.” *Bulletin d'études orientales* 19 (1965–1966): 7–83.
21 Badawi, ʿAbdurraḥmān. *La transmission de la philosophie grecque au monde arabe.* Paris, 1968.
22 Brock, Sebastian. “The Laments of the Philosophers over Alexander in Syriac.” *Semitic Studies* 15 (1970): 205–218.
23 Stern, Samuel Miklos. *Aristotle on the World State.* Columbia, 1970.
24 Strohmaier, Gotthard. “Ethical Sentences and Anecdotes of Greek Philosophers in Arabic Tradition.” *Correspondance d'Orient* 11 (= Actes du Ve congrès international d'arabisants et d'islamisants, Bruxelles 1970) (1971): 463–471.
25 von Fritz, Kurt, ed. *Pseudepigrapha*, vol. 1. Vandœuvres-Genève, 1972.
26 Manzalaoui, Mahmoud. “The Pseudo-Aristotelian *Kitāb sirr al-asrār*.” *Oriens* 23–24 (1974): 147–257.
27 Grignaschi, Mario. “La as-Siyāsatu-l-ʿāmmīyah et l'influence iranienne sur la pensée politique islamique.” In *Monumentum H. S. Nyberg*, vol. 3. Leiden, 1975, 33–287.
28 Gutas, Dimitri. *Greek Wisdom Literature in Arabic Translation: A Study of the Graeco-Arabic Gnomologia.* New Haven, Conn., 1975.
29 Rosenthal, Franz. “The Symbolism of the *Tabula Cebetis* According to Abû l-Farağ ibn aṭ-Ṭayyib.” In *Recherches d'islamologie: Recueil d'articles offert à Georges C. Anawati et Louis Gardet.* Ed. by the Institut supérieur de philosophie. Louvain, 1977, 273–283. – Repr. in F. Rosenthal, *Greek Philosophy in the Arab World.* London, 1990, no. VI.
30 Brock, Sebastian. “Secundus the Silent Philosopher: Some Notes on the Syriac Tradition.” *Rheinisches Museum* 121 (1978): 94–100.
31 Brockelmann, Carl. “Kalīla wa-Dimna.” In EI² [*2: IV 503–506].
32 Zeegers-Vander Vorst, Nicole. “Une gnomologie d'auteurs grecs en traduction syriaque.” In *Symposium Syriacum 1976.* Rome, 1978, 163–177.

33 Gutas, Dimitri. "Classical Arabic Wisdom Literature: Nature and Scope." *Journal of the American Oriental Society* 101 (1981): 49–86.

34 Kindstrand, Jan Fredrik. *Anacharsis, the Legend and the Apophthegmata*. Uppsala, 1981.

35 al-Qāḍī, Wadād. "*Kitāb Ṣiwān al-ḥikma*: Structure, Composition, Authorship and Sources." *Der Islam* 58 (1981): 87–124.

36 Brock, Sebastian. "From Antagonism to Assimilation: Syriac Attitudes to Greek Learning." In *East of Byzantium: Syria and Armenia in the Formative Period, Dumbarton Oaks Symposium 1980*. Ed. by Nina Garsoïan, Thomas Mathews and Robert Thomson. Washington, D.C., 1982, 17–34. – Repr. in: S. Brock, *Syriac Perspectives on Late Antiquity*. Hampshire, London, 1984.

37 Gutas, Dimitri. "The Ṣiwān al-ḥikma Cycle of Texts." *Journal of the American Oriental Society* 102 (1982): 645–650.

38 Ryan, William Francis and Charles Bernard Schmitt, eds. *Pseudo-Aristotle, The Secret of Secrets: Sources and Influences*. London, 1982.

39 Daiber, Hans. "Der Ṣiwān al-ḥikma und Abū Sulaimān al-Manṭiqī as-Siǧistānī in der Forschung." *Arabica* 31 (1984): 36–68.

40 "Adab." In [*5: I 431–444]. – Djalal Khaleghi Motlagh, "Adab in Iran"; Charles Pellat, "Adab in Arabic Literature".

41 Gutas, Dimitri. "The Life, Works, and Sayings of Theophrastus in the Arabic Tradition." In *Theophrastus of Eresus: On His Life and Work*. Ed. by W. Fortenbaugh. New Brunswick, London 1985, 63–102. – Repr. in: D. Gutas 2000 [*63] no. VII.

42 van Esbroeck, Michel. "Les sentences morales des philosophes grecs dans les traditions orientales." In *L'eredità classica nelle lingue orientali*. Ed. by Massimiliano Pavan and Umberto Cozzoli. Rome, 1986, 11–23.

43 Gutas, Dimitri. "The Spurious and the Authentic in the Arabic Lives of Aristotle." In *Pseudo-Aristotle in the Middle Ages: The Theology and Other Texts*. Ed. by Jill Kraye, William Francis Ryan and Charles Bernard Schmitt. London, 1986, 15–36. – Repr. in: D. Gutas 2000 [*63], no. VI.

44 Samir, Khalil. "Les versions arabes de Némésius de Ḥomṣ." In *L'eredità classica nelle lingue orientali*. Ed. by Massimiliano Pavan and Umberto Cozzoli. Rome, 1986, 99–151.

45 "Andarz." In [*5: II 11–22]. – Shaul Shaked, "Andarz and Andarz Literature in Pre-Islamic Iran"; Zabihollah Safa, "Andarz literature in new Persian".

46 Crone, Patricia. "Did al-Ghazālī Write a Mirror for Princes? On the Authorship of Naṣīḥat al-Mulūk." *Jerusalem Studies in Arabic and Islam* 10 (1987): 167–191.

47 van Ess, Josef. "Al-Ārā' wa'l-Dīānāt." In [*5: II 200–201].

48 Gutas, Dimitri. "Plato's *Symposion* in the Arabic Tradition." *Oriens* 31 (1988): 36–60. – Repr. in: D. Gutas 2000 [*63], no. IV.

49 Baffioni, Carmela. *Sulle tracce di Sofia: Tre 'divini' nella Grecia classica*. Napoli, 1990.

50 Fähndrich, Hartmut. "Der Begriff 'adab' und sein literarischer Niederschlag." In *Orientalisches Mittelalter*. Ed. by Wolfhart Heinrichs. Wiesbaden, 1990, 326–345.

51 Gutas, Dimitri. "Ethische Schriften im Islam." In W. Heinrichs 1990 [cf. *50], 346–365.

52 Rosenthal, Franz. *Greek Philosophy in the Arab World: A Collection of Essays*. Aldershot, 1990.

53 Rudolph, Ulrich. "Christliche Theologie und vorsokratische Lehren in der Turba philosophorum." *Oriens* 32 (1990): 97–123.

54 al-Qāḍī, Wadād. "Early Islamic State Letters: The Question of Authenticity." In *The Byzantine and Early Islamic Near East*. Ed. by Averil Cameron and Lawrence I. Conrad. Princeton, 1992, 215–275.

55 Daiber, Hans. "Hellenistisch-kaiserzeitliche Doxographie und philosophischer Synkretismus in islamischer Zeit." In *Aufstieg und Niedergang der römischen Welt*, part II vol. 36/7. Ed. by Wolfgang Haase. Berlin, New York, 1994, 4974–4992.

56 Gutas, Dimitri. "Pre-Plotinian Philosophy in Arabic (other than Platonism and Aristotelianism): A Review of the Sources." In W. Haase 1994 [cf. *55], 4939–4973. – Repr. in: D. Gutas 2000 [*63], no. I.

57 Zakeri, Mohsen. "'Alī ibn 'Ubaida ar-Raiḥānī: A Forgotten Belletrist (*adīb*) and Pahlavi Translator." *Oriens* 34 (1994): 76–102.

58 Pohl, Stefan. "Die aristotelische Ethik im *Kitāb al-Sa'āda wa-l-is'ād*." In *The Ancient Tradition in Christian and Islamic Hellenism: Studies on the Transmission of Greek Philosophy and Sciences, Dedicated to H. J. Drossaart Lulofs on His Ninetieth Birthday*. Ed. by Gerhard Endress and Remke Kruk. Leiden, 1997, 201–238.

59 Latham, J. Derek. "Ebn al-Moqaffa'." In [*5: VIII 39–43].

60 Searby, Denis Michael. *Aristotle in the Greek Gnomological Tradition*. Uppsala, 1998.

61 Strohmaier, Gotthard. "Das Gnomologium als Forschungsaufgabe." In *Dissertatiunculae criticae*. Ed. by Christian-Friedrich Collatz et al. Würzburg, 1998. – Repr. in: G. Strohmaier, *Hellas im Islam*. Wiesbaden, 2003, 43–49.

62 Sezgin, Fuat et al., eds. *Ḥunain ibn Isḥāq (d. 260/873): Texts and Studies*. Frankfurt a.M., 1999.

63 Gutas, Dimitri. *Greek Philosophers in the Arabic Tradition*. Aldershot, 2000.

64 Zakeri, Mohsen. "Some Early Persian Apophthegmata (*tawqī'āt*) in Arabic Transmission." *Jerusalem Studies in Arabic and Islam* 27 (2002): 283–304.

65 Brock, Sebastian. "Syriac Translations of Greek Popular Philosophy." In *Von Athen nach Bagdad: Zur Rezeption griechischer Philosophie von der Spätantike bis zum Islam*. Ed. by Peter Bruns. Bonn, 2003, 9–28.

66 Overwien, Oliver. "Ḥunayn b. Isḥāq, *Ādāb al-falāsifa*: Griechische Inhalte in einer arabischen Spruchsammlung." In *Selecta colligere*, vol. 1. Ed. by Rosa Maria Piccione and Matthias Perkams. Alessandria, 2003, 95–115.

67 Bettiolo, Paolo. "'Gnomologia' siriaci: Un censimento." In M. S. Funghi 2003–2004 [*68: II 289–304].

68 Funghi, Maria Serena, ed. *Aspetti di letteratura gnomica nel mondo antico*, 2 vols. Florence, 2003–2004.

69 Hillenbrand, Carole. "A Little-Known Mirror for Princes by al-Ghazālī." In *Words, Texts and Concepts Cruising the Mediterranean Sea: Studies on the Sources, Contents and Influences of Islamic Civilization and Arabic Philosophy and Science: Dedicated to Gerhard Endress on His Sixty-Fifth Birthday*. Ed. by Rüdiger Arnzen and Jörn Thielmann. Leuven, Paris, Dudley, 2004, 592–601.

70 Reisman, David C. "The Pseudo-Avicennan Corpus, I. Methodological Considerations." In *Interpreting Avicenna: Science and Philosophy in Medieval Islam*. Ed. by Jon McGinnis and David C. Reisman. Leiden, 2004, 3–21.

71 Zakeri, Mohsen. "Ādāb al-falāsifa: The Persian Content of an Arabic Collection of Aphorisms." *Mélanges de l'Université Saint Joseph* 57 (2004): 173–190.

72 Overwien, Oliver. *Die Sprüche des Kynikers Diogenes in der griechischen und arabischen Überlieferung*. Stuttgart, 2005.

73 Forster, Regula. *Das Geheimnis der Geheimnisse*: *Die arabischen und deutschen Fassungen des pseudo-aristotelischen Sirr al-asrār/Secretum secretorum*. Wiesbaden, 2006. – PhD Diss., University of Zurich, 2005.

74 Gruendler, Beatrice. "In Aristotle's Words... al-Ḥātimī's (?) Epistle on al-Mutanabbī and Aristotle." In *Islamic Philosophy, Science, Culture, and Religion: Studies in Honor of Dimitri Gutas*. Ed. by Felicitas Opwis and David Reisman. Leiden, 2012, 89–129.

75 Griffel, Frank. "On the Character, Content, and Authorship of *Itmām Tatimmat Ṣiwān al-ḥikma* and the Identity of the Author of *Muntakhab Ṣiwān al-ḥikma*." *Journal of the American Oriental Society* 133 (2013): 1–20.

5.2.2 Liber de Pomo

81 Margoliouth, David Samuel. "The Book of the Apple: Ascribed to Aristotle" *Journal of the Royal Asiatic Society* (1892): 187–192. 230–252.

82 Steinschneider, Moritz. *Die hebraeischen Übersetzungen des Mittelalters und die Juden als Dolmetscher*. Berlin, 1893. – Repr. Graz, 1956.

83 Hertz, Wilhelm. "Die Sagen vom Tod des Aristoteles." In *Gesammelte Abhandlungen*. Ed. by Friedrich von der Leyen. Stuttgart, Berlin, 1905, 371–397.

84 Niese, Hans. "Zur Geschichte des geistigen Lebens am Hofe Kaiser Friedrichs II." *Historische Zeitschrift* 108 (1912): 473–540.

85 Massignon, Louis. *Recueil de texts inédits concernant l'histoire de la mystique en pays d'Islam*. Paris, 1929.

86 GAL [*1: S I 373].

87 Stauffer, Ethelbert. "Abschiedsreden." *Reallexicon für Antike und Christentum*, vol. 1. Stuttgart, 1941, 29–35.

88 Abel, Armand. *Aristote: La légende et l'histoire*. Brussels, 1944.

89 Kraemer, Jörg. "Das arabische Original des pseudo-aristotelischen *Liber de pomo*." In *Studi orientalistici in onore di Giorgio Levi Della Vida*, vol. 1. Rome, 1956, 493–506.

90 Plezia, Marian. "Neues zum ps.-aristotelischen Buch vom Apfel." In *Philologische Vorträge*. Ed. by Johannes Irmscher and Wiktor Steffen. Wrocław, 1959, 191–196.

91 Plezia, Marian. *Aristotelis qui ferebatur 'Liber de pomo': Versio Latina Manfredi*. Warsaw, 1960.

92 Mazzantini, Paolo. "Liber de pomo sive de morte Aristotilis." In *Il canto di Manfredi e il liber de pomo sive de morte Aristotilis*. Ed. by Bruno Nardi and Paolo Mazzantini. Turin, 1964, 25–51.

93 Ronconi, Alessandro. "Exitus illustrium virorum." *Reallexicon für Antike und Christentum*, vol. 6. Stuttgart, 1966, 1258–1264.

94 Rousseau, Mary F. *The Apple or Aristotle's Death* (*De pomo sive De morte Aristotilis*). Milwaukee, Wisconsin, 1968.

95 Bielawski, Józef. "Phédon en version arabe et le *Risālat al-Tuffāḥa*." In *Orientalia Hispanica sive studia F. M. Pareja octogenario dicata*, vol. 1 (arabica-islamica). Ed. by J. M. Barral. Leiden, 1974.

96 Wehrli, Fritz, ed. *Hermippos der Kallimacheer*. Basel, Stuttgart, 1974 [Die Schule des Aristoteles, Suppl. I].

97 Gutas, Dimitri. *Greek Wisdom Literature in Arabic Translation* [*28].

98 Döring, Klaus. *Exemplum Socratis: Studien zur Sokratesnachwirkung in der kynisch-stoischen Popularphilosophie der frühen Kaiserzeit und im frühen Christentum*. Wiesbaden, 1979.

99 Schmitt, Charles Bernard, and Dilwyn Knox. *Pseudo-Aristoteles Latinus: A Guide to Latin Works Falsely Attributed to Aristotle Before 1500*. London, 1985, 51–52.

100 Gutas, Dimitri. "The Spurious and the Authentic in the Arabic Lives of Aristotle" [*43].

101 Schmitt, Charles Bernard. "Pseudo-Aristotle in the Latin Middle Ages." In *Pseudo-Aristotle in the Middle Ages: The Theology and Other Texts*. Ed. by Jill Kraye, William Francis Ryan and Charles Bernard Schmitt. London, 1986, 3–14.

102 Gutas, Dimitri. "Plato's Symposion in the Arabic Tradition" [*48].

103 Aouad, Maroun. "Le De pomo." In *Dictionnaire des philosophes antiques*, vol. 1. Ed. by Richard Goulet. Paris, 1989, 537–541.

104 GAS [*3: III 50].

105 Acampora-Michel, Elsbeth. *Liber de pomo/Buch vom Apfel.* Frankfurt a.M., 2001.

106 Flashar, Hellmut. "Aristoteles." In *Grundriss der Geschichte der Philosophie: Die Philosophie der Antike*, vol. 3: *Ältere Akademie – Aristoteles – Peripatos*. Ed. by Hellmut Flashar. Basel, 2004 (2nd ed.), 276.

106a Ferrari, Cleophea. "Der Duft des Apfels. Abū l-Farağ ʿAbdallāh Ibn aṭ-Ṭayyib und sein Kommentar zu den *Kategorien* des Aristoteles." In *Aristotele e i suoi esegeti neoplatonici. Logica e ontologia nelle interpretazioni greche e arabe. Atti del convegno internazionale Roma 19–20 ottobre 2001*. Ed. by Vincenza Celluprica and Cristina D'Ancona. Rome, 2004, 85–106.

107 Ibn Sabʿīn. *Die Sizilianischen Fragen*. Arabisch-deutsch, übersetzt und eingeleitet von Anna Akasoy. Freiburg, Basel, Vienna, 2005.

108 Gerson, Lloyd P. *Aristotle and Other Platonists*. Ithaca, New York, London, 2005.

109 Karamanolis, George E. *Plato and Aristotle in Agreement? Platonists on Aristotle from Antiochus to Porphyry*. Oxford, 2006.

110 Kotzia, Paraskevi. *Περὶ τοῦ μήλου ἢ Περὶ τῆς Ἀριστοτέλους τελευτῆς: Liber de Pomo*. Thessaloniki, 2007.

5.3 *Scholars as Transmitters of Philosophical Thought*

5.3.1 Ḥunayn b. Isḥāq [*121–*153] – 5.3.2 Ṯābit b. Qurra [*171–*211]

5.3.1 Ḥunayn b. Isḥāq

121 Steinschneider, Moritz. *Die hebraeischen Übersetzungen* [*82].

122 Bergsträsser, Gotthelf. *Ḥunain ibn Isḥāḳ und seine Schule*. Leiden, 1913.

123 Ritter, Hellmut and Richard Walzer. "Arabische Übersetzungen griechischer Ärzte in Stambuler Bibliotheken." In *Sitzungsberichte der Preussischen Akademie der Wissenschaften*. Berlin, 1934, 801–846.

124 Pines, Shlomo. "Les précurseurs musulmans de la théorie de l'impetus." *Archeion* 21 (1938): 298–306. – Repr. in: *The Collected Works of Shlomo Pines*, vol. 2: *Studies in Arabic Versions of Greek Texts and in Mediaeval Science*. Jerusalem, Leiden, 1986, 409–417.

125 Graf, Georg. *Geschichte der christlichen arabischen Literatur*, vol. 2. Vatican City, 1947, 122–129.

126 Alonso Alonso, Manuel. "Ḥunayn traducido al latín por Ibn Dāwūd y Domingo Gundisalvo." *Al-Andalus* 16 (1951): 37–47. – Repr. in: F. Sezgin 1999 [*62: 323–333].

127 Strohmaier, Gotthard. "Ḥunayn ibn Isḥāq und die Bilder." *Klio* 43–45 (1965): 525–533. – Repr. in: G. Strohmaier, *Von Demokrit bis Dante*. Hildesheim, 1996, 207–215.

128 Ullmann, Manfred. *Die Medizin im Islam*, Leiden, 1970.
129 Strohmaier, Gotthard. "Ḥunayn b. Isḥāḳ." In EI² [*2: III 578].
130 Ullmann, Manfred. "War Ḥunain der Übersetzer von Artemidors Traumbuch?" *Die Welt des Islams* 13 (1971): 204–211.
131 Ullmann, Manfred. *Die Natur- und Geheimwissenschaften im Islam*. Leiden, 1972.
132 Grignaschi, Mario. "La 'Physiognomie' traduite par Ḥunayn ibn Isḥāq." *Arabica* 21 (1974): 285–291.
133 Ḥabbī, Yūsuf. *Ḥunayn b. Isḥāq*. Baghdad, 1974.
134 Haddad, Rachid. "Ḥunayn ibn Isḥāq, apologiste chrétien." *Arabica* 21 (1974): 292–302.
135 al-Sāmarrāʾī, ʿĀmir Rašīd and ʿAbd al-Ḥamīd al-ʿAlūǧī. *Āṯār Ḥunayn b. Isḥāq*. Baghdad, 1974.
136 Schaade, Arthur. "Ḳayyim." In EI² [*2: IV 847–848].
137 Klein-Franke, Felix. "The Arabic Version of Galen's Περὶ ἠθῶν." *Jerusalem Studies in Arabic and Islam* 1 (1979): 125–150.
138 Degen, Rainer. "Galen im Syrischen: Eine Übersicht über die syrische Überlieferung der Werke Galens." In *Galen: Problems and Prospects*. Ed. by Vivian Nutton. London, 1981, 131–166.
139 Fleischhammer, Manfred. "Munadjdjim, Banu'l." In EI² [*2: VII 558–561].
140 Glasner, Ruth. "The Hebrew Version of *De celo et mundo* Attributed to Ibn Sīnā." *Arabic Sciences and Philosophy* 6 (1996): 89–112.
141 Pines, Shlomo. "The Origin of the Tale of Salāmān and Absāl: A Possible Indian Influence." In *The Collected Works of Shlomo Pines*, vol. 3: *Studies in the History of Arabic Philosophy*. Ed. by Sarah Stroumsa. Jerusalem, 1996, 343–353.
142 Gutas, Dimitri. Review of Majid Fakhry, *Ethical Theories in Islam*. Leiden, 1994 (2nd ed.), in: *Journal of the American Oriental Society* 117 (1997): 171–175.
143 Arnzen, Rüdiger. *Aristoteles' De Anima: Eine verlorene spätantike Paraphrase in arabischer und persischer Überlieferung: Arabischer Text nebst Kommentar, quellengeschichtlichen Studien und Glossaren*. Leiden, 1998.
144 Filius, Lou S. *The Problemata Physica Attributed to Aristotle: The Arabic Version of Ḥunain ibn Isḥāq and the Hebrew Version of Moses ibn Tibbon*. Leiden, 1999.
145 Ghersetti, Antonella. *Il Kitāb Arisṭāṭālīs al-faylasūf fī l-firāsa nella traduzione di Ḥunayn b. Isḥāq*. Rome, 1999.
146 Lettinck, Paul. *Aristotle's Meteorology and Its Reception in the Arab World: With an Edition and Translation of Ibn Suwār's Treatise on Meteorological Phenomena and Ibn Bājja's Commentary on the Meteorology*. Leiden, Boston, Cologne, 1999.
147 Sezgin, Fuat et al., eds. *Ḥunain ibn Isḥāq* [*62], 323–333.
148 van Ess, Josef. *Der Fehltritt des Gelehrten: Die 'Pest von Emmaus' und ihre theologischen Nachspiele*. Heidelberg, 2001.

149 Reynolds, Dwight Fletcher. *Interpreting the Self: Autobiography in the Arabic Literary Tradition.* Berkeley, 2001.

150 Abramovič Rozenfel'd [Rosenfeld], Boris and Ekmeleddin İhsanoğlu. *Mathematicians, Astronomers, and Other Scholars of Islamic Civilization and Their Works (7th-19th c.).* [MAO] Istanbul, 2003.

151 Ullmann, Manfred. Review of Lou S. Filius, *The Problemata Physica Attributed to Aristotle*. Leiden, 1999, in: *Zeitschrift der Deutschen Morgenländischen Gesellschaft* 153 (2003): 470–473.

152 Bertolacci, Amos. "On the Arabic Translations of Aristotle's Metaphysics." *Arabic Sciences and Philosophy* 15 (2005): 241–275.

153 Swain, Simon. *Seeing the Face, Seeing the Soul: Polemon's Physiognomy from Classical Antiquity to Medieval Islam*. Oxford, 2007.

5.3.2 Ṯābit b. Qurra

171 Kühn, Carl G., ed. *Claudii Galeni opera omnia*. Leipzig, 1821–1833. – Partial Engl. transl. by Peter N. Singer, *Galen, Selected Works*. Translated with an Introduction and Notes. Oxford, 1997.

172 Avraamovič Chvol'son [Chwolsohn], Daniil. *Die Ssabier und der Ssabismus*. St. Petersburg, 1856.

173 Wiedemann, Eilhard. "Über Thabit ben Qurra, sein Leben und Wirken." *Sitzungsberichte der physikalisch-medizinischen Sozietät in Erlangen* 52–53 (1920–1921): 189–219.

174 Krause, Max. "Stambuler Handschriften islamischer Mathematiker." *Quellen und Studien zur Geschichte der Mathematik, Astronomie und Physik,* Abt. B, III (1936): 437–532.

175 Rosenthal, Franz. *Aḥmad b. aṭ-Ṭayyib as-Saraḫsī*. New Haven, Conn. 1943.

176 Pellat, Charles. "Anwāʾ." In EI^2 [*2: I 523–524].

177 Walzer, Richard. "Buruḳlus." In EI^2 [*2: I 1339–1340].

178 Peters, Francis E. *Aristoteles Arabus*. Leiden, 1968.

179 Ullmann, Manfred. *Die Medizin im Islam* [*128].

180 Gätje, Helmut. *Studien zur Überlieferung der aristotelischen Psychologie im Islam*. Heidelberg, 1971.

181 Hjärpe, Jan. *Analyse critique des traditions arabes sur les Sabéens Ḥarraniens*. PhD Diss., University of Uppsala, 1972.

182 Ullmann, Manfred. *Die Natur- und Geheimwissenschaften im Islam* [*131].

183 Endress, Gerhard. *Proclus Arabus: Zwanzig Abschnitte aus der Institutio theologica in arabischer Übersetzung, eingeleitet, herausgegeben und erklärt*. Beirut, Wiesbaden, 1973.

184 Kruk, Remke. "Pseudo-Aristotle: An Arabic Version of Problemata Physica X." *Isis* 67 (1976): 251–256.

185 Gutas, Dimitri. "Paul the Persian on the Classification of the Parts of Aristotle's Philosophy: A Milestone between Alexandria and Baġdād." *Der Islam* 60 (1983): 231–267. – Repr. in: D. Gutas 2000 [*63], no. IX.

186 Richter-Bernburg, Lutz. "Pseudo-Ṯābit, Pseudo-Rāzī, Yūḥannā b. Sarābiyūn." *Der Islam* 60 (1983): 48–77.

187 Linley, Neil. *Ibn aṭ-Ṭayyib, Proclus' Commentary on the Pythagorean Golden Verses: Arabic Text and Translation*. Buffalo, 1984.

188 Abramovič Rozenfel'd [Rosenfeld], Boris and Adol'f-Andrej Pavlovič Juškevič [Youshkevitch]. *Sabit ibn Korra: Matematičeskie traktaty*. Moscow, 1984.

189 Gutas, Dimitri. "The Starting Point of Philosophical Studies in Alexandrian and Arabic Aristotelianism." In W. Fortenbaugh 1985 [cf. *41], 115–123. – Repr. in: D. Gutas 2000 [*63], no. X.

190 Tardieu, Michel. "Ṣābiens coraniques et 'Ṣābiens' de Ḥarrān." *Journal asiatique* 274 (1986): 1–44.

191 Endress, Gerhard. "Die wissenschaftliche Literatur." In GAP [*6: II 400–506; III 3–152].

192 Mallet, Dominique. "Le rappel de la voie à suivre pour parvenir au bonheur de Abū Naṣr al-Fārābī." *Bulletin d'études orientales* 39–40 (1987–1988): 113–140.

193 Gutas, Dimitri. *Avicenna and the Aristotelian Tradition: Introduction to Reading Avicenna's Philosophical Works*. Leiden, 1988. – Second, revised and expanded edition, Leiden, 2014.

194 Gutas, Dimitri. "Plato's Symposion in the Arabic Tradition" [*48].

195 Hill, Donald Routledge. "Mūsā, Banū." In EI² [*2: VII *640–641*].

196 de Blois, François. " Ṣābiʾ." In EI² [*2: VIII 672–675].

197 Daiber, Hans. *Neuplatonische Pythagorica in arabischem Gewande: Der Kommentar des Iamblichus zu den Carmina Aurea*. Amsterdam, 1995.

198 D'Ancona, Cristina. *La casa della sapienza: La trasmissione della metafisica greca e la formazione della filosofia araba*. Milan, 1996.

199 Guerrero, Rafael Ramón. "La Etica Nicomaquea en el mundo arabe: El *Kitāb al-tanbīh ʿalā sabīl al-Saʿāda* de al-Fārābī." In *Actas del II congreso nacional de filosofía medieval*. Zaragoza, 1996, 417–430.

200 Rashed, Roshdi. *Les mathématiques infinitésimales du IXᵉ au XIᵉ siècle*, vol. 1. London, 1416/1996.

201 Strohmaier, Gotthard. "Die Ḥarrānischen Sabier bei Ibn an-Nadīm und al-Bīrūnī." In *Ibn-an-Nadīm und die mittelalterliche arabische Literatur*. Beiträge zum 1. Johann-Wilhelm-Fück-Kolloquium, Halle 1987. Wiesbaden, 1996, 51–56. – Repr. in: G. Strohmaier, *Hellas im Islam*. Wiesbaden, 2003, 167–169.

202 Gutas, Dimitri. Review of Majid Fakhry, *Ethical Theories in Islam*. Leiden, 1994 (2nd ed.), in: *Journal of the American Oriental Society* 117 (1997): 171–175.

203 Arnzen, Rüdiger. *Aristoteles' De Anima* [*143].

204 Brague, Rémi. *Thémistius: Paraphrase de la Métaphysique d'Aristote* (*livre lambda*). Traduit de l'hébreu et de l'arabe, introduction, notes et indices. Paris, 1999.

205 Filius, Lou S. *The Problemata Physica Attributed to Aristotle* [*144].

206 Lettinck, Paul. *Aristotle's Meteorology and Its Reception in the Arab World* [*146].

207 Gutas, Dimitri. *Greek Philosophers in the Arabic Tradition* [*63].

208 Bertolacci, Amos. "From al-Kindī to al-Fārābī: Avicenna's Progressive Knowledge of Aristotle's Metaphysics According to His Autobiography." *Arabic Sciences and Philosophy* 11 (2001): 257–295.

209 Abramovič Rozenfel'd [Rosenfeld], Boris and Ekmeleddin İhsanoğlu. *Mathematicians, Astronomers, and Other Scholars of Islamic Civilization* [*150].

210 Ullmann, Manfred. Review of Lou S. Filius, *The Problemata Physica Attributed to Aristotle* [*151].

211 Reisman, David C. and Amos Bertolacci. "Thābit ibn Qurra's Concise Exposition of Aristotle's Metaphysics: Text, Translation, and Commentary." In *Thābit ibn Qurra: Sciences and Philosophy in Ninth-Century Baghdad*. Ed. by Roshdi Rashed. Berlin, New York, 2009, 715–776.

5.4 *Philosophy and Science of Nature*

221 Kraus, Paul. *Jābir ibn Ḥayyān: Contribution à l'histoire des idées scientifiques dans l'Islam*, vol. 2. Cairo, 1942. – Repr. Paris, 1986.

222 Nallino, Carlo Alfonso. *Raccolta di scritti editi e inediti*, vol. 5: *Astrologia – astronomia – geografia*. Ed. by Maria Nallino. Rome, 1944.

223 Lemay, Richard. *Abu Maʿshar and Latin Aristotelianism in the Twelfth Century: The Recovery of Aristotle's Natural Philosophy through Arabic Astrology.* Beirut, 1962.

224 Vadet, Jean Claude. "Une défense de l'astrologie dans le *Madḫal* d'Abū Maʿšar al-Balḫī." *Annales islamologiques* 5 (1963): 131–180.

225 Walzer, Richard. "New studies on al-Kindī." In R. Walzer, *Greek into Arabic. Essays on Islamic Philosophy*. Oxford, Cambridge, Mass. (1962, 1963 (2nd ed.): 175–205).

226 Ullmann, Manfred. *Die Medizin im Islam* [*128].

227 GAS [*3] IV: "Alchimie – Chemie – Botanik – Agrikultur. Bis ca. 430 H." Leiden, 1971.

228 Cortabarría Beitia, Angel. "La classification des sciences chez al-Kindī." *Mélanges de l'Institut dominicain d'études orientales du Caire* 11 (1972): 49–76.

229 Marquet, Yves. "Les cycles de la souveraineté chez les Iḫwān aṣ-Ṣafāʾ." *Studia Islamica* 36 (1972): 47–69.

230 Plessner, Martin. "Al-Fārābī's Introduction to the Study of Medicine." In *Islamic Philosophy and the Classical Tradition. Essays presented to Richard Walzer on his seventieth birthday.* Ed. by Samuel Miklos Stern, Albert Hourani and Vivian Brown. Oxford, 1972, 307–314.

231 Ullmann, Manfred. *Die Natur- und Geheimwissenschaften im Islam* [*131].

232 Burckhardt, Titus. *Clé spirituelle de l'astrologie musulmane d'après Mohyiddîn Ibn Arabî.* Milan, 1974 (2nd ed.).

233 GAS [*3] VII: "Astrologie, Meteorologie und Verwandtes. Bis ca. 430 H." Leiden, 1979.

234 Schramm, Matthias. "Theoretische und praktische Disziplin bei al-Fārābī." *Zeitschrift für Geschichte der Arabisch-Islamischen Wissenschaften* 3 (1986): 1–55.

235 Endress, Gerhard. "Die wissenschaftliche Literatur." In GAP [*6: II 400–506; III 3–152].

236 Marquet, Yves. *La philosophie des alchimistes et l'alchimie des philosophes: Jābir ibn Ḥayyān et les Frères de la Pureté.* Paris, 1988.

237 Burnett, Charles. "The Planets and the Development of the Embryo." In *The Human Embryo: Aristotle and the Arabic and European Traditions.* Ed. by Gordon R. Dunstan. Exeter, 1990, 95–112.

238 Hill, Donald Routledge. "The Literature of Arabic Alchemy." In *Religion, Learning and Science in the 'Abbasid Period.* Ed. by M. J. L. Young, John D. Latham and Robert B. Serjeant. Cambridge, 1990, 328–341.

239 Freudenthal, Gad. "(Al-)chemical Foundations for Cosmological Ideas: Ibn Sīnā on the Geology of an Eternal World." In *Physics, Cosmology and Astronomy 1300–1700: Tension and Accomodation.* Ed. by Sabetai Uguru. Dordrecht, Boston, London, 1991, 47–73.

240 Lory, Pierre. "La magie chez les Iḫwān al-Ṣafā'." *Bulletin des études orientales* 44 (1992): 147–159.

241 Freudenthal, Gad. "Maimonides' Stance on Astrology in Context: Cosmology, Physics, Medicine, and Providence." In *Moses Maimonides: Physician, Scientist, and Philosopher.* Ed. by Fred Rosner and Samuel S. Kottek. London, 1993, 77–90 and 244–249.

242 Nasr, Seyyed Hossein. *An Introduction to Islamic Cosmological Doctrines: Conceptions of Nature and Methods Used for Its Study by the Ikhwān al-Ṣafā, al-Bīrūnī, and Ibn Sīnā.* Albany, 1993. – New ed.

243 Barton, Tamsyn. *Ancient Astrology.* London, New York, 1994.

244 Freudenthal, Gad. *Aristotle's Theory of Material Substance: Heat and Pneuma, Form and Soul.* Oxford, 1995.

245 Goldstein, Bernhard R. "Astronomy and Astrology in the Works of Abraham ibn Ezra." *Arabic Sciences and Philosophy* 6 (1996): 9–21.

246 Rashed, Roshdi and Régis Morelon, eds. *Encyclopedia of the History of Arabic Science,* 3 vols. London, New York, 1996.

247 Baffioni, Carmela. "L'influenza degli astri sul feto nell' Enciclopedia degli Iḫwān al-Ṣafā'." *Medioevo* 23 (1997): 409–439.

248 Gutas, Dimitri. *Greek Thought, Arabic Culture: The Graeco-Arabic Translation Movement in Baghdad and Early ʿAbbāsid Society (2nd–4th/8th–10th Centuries)*. London, 1998.

249 Travaglia, Pinella. *Magic, Causality and Intentionality: The Doctrine of Rays in al-Kindī*. Florence, 1999.

250 al-Hassan, Ahmad Y., Maqbul Ahmed and Albert Z. Iskandar, eds. *Science and Technology in Islam*, 2 vols. Paris, 2001.

250a Adamson, Peter. "Abū Maʿshar, al-Kindī and the Philosophical Defense of Astrology." *Recherches de théologie et philosophie médiévales* 69 (2002): 245–270.

250b Burnett, Charles. "The Certitude of Astrology: The Scientific Methodology of al-Qabīsī and Abū Maʿshar." *Early Science and Medicine* 7, no. 3: *Certainty, Doubt and Error. Practice of Pre- and Early Modern Science* (2002): 198–213.

251 Abramovič Rozenfel'd [Rosenfeld], Boris and Ekmeleddin İhsanoğlu. *Mathematicians, Astronomers, and Other Scholars of Islamic Civilization* [*150].

252 Pormann, Peter E. and Emilie Savage-Smith. *Medieval Islamic Medicine*. Edinburgh, 2007.

253 Anna Akasoy. "Arabic Physiognomy as a Link between Astrology and Medicine." In *Astro-Medicine. Astrology and Medicine, East and West*. Ed. by Anna Akasoy, Charles Burnett and Ronit Yoeli-Thalim. Florence, 2008, 119–141.

5.5 *Ismaili Thinkers of the 4th/10th and the Early 5th/11th Century*

5.5.1 General literature [*271–*342] – 5.5.2 Muḥammad al-Nasafī [*345] – 5.5.3 Abū Ḥātim al-Rāzī [*351–*361] – 5.5.4 Abū Yaʿqūb al-Siǧistānī [*371–*389] – 5.5.5 Ḥamīd al-Dīn al-Kirmānī [*395–*412]

5.5.1 General Literature

271 Ivanow, Wladimir. *A Guide to Ismaili Literature*. London, 1933.

272 Pines, Shlomo. "Nathanaël Ben al-Fayyūmī et la théologie ismaëlienne." *Bulletin des études historiques juives* 1 (1947): 5–22.

273 Ivanow, Wladimir. *Studies in Early Persian Ismailism*. Leiden, 1948.

274 Pines, Shlomo. "La longue recension de la *Théologie d'Aristote* dans ses rapports avec la doctrine ismaélienne." *Revue des études islamiques* 22 (1954): 7–20.

275 Altmann, Alexander and Samuel Miklos Stern. *Isaac Israeli, a Neoplatonic Philosopher of the Early Tenth Century*. Oxford, 1958.

276 Vajda, Georges. "Un opuscule ismaélien en transmission judéo-arabe (*Risālat al-Jawharayn*)." *Journal asiatique* (1958): 459–466.

277 Stern, Samuel Miklos. "The Early Ismāʿīlī Missionaries in North-West Persia and in Khurāsān and Transoxiana." *Bulletin of the School of Oriental and African Studies* 23 (1960): 56–90.

278 Madelung, Wilferd. "Das Imamat in der frühen ismailitischen Lehre." *Der Islam* 37 (1961): 43–135.

279 Stern, Samuel Miklos. "Abū'l-Qāsim al-Bustī and His Refutation of Ismāʿīlism." *Journal of the Royal Asiatic Society* (1961): 14–35.

280 Stern, Samuel Miklos. "Ibn Ḥasdāy's Neoplatonist: A Neoplatonic Treatise and Its Influence on Isaac Israeli and the Longer Version of the *Theology of Aristotle*." *Oriens* 13–14 (1961): 58–120.

281 Vajda, Georges. *Recherches sur la philosophie et la kabbale dans la pensée juive du moyen-âge*. Paris, 1962.

282 Ivanow, Wladimir. *Ismaili Literature: A Bibliographical Survey*. Tehran, 1963.

283 Makarem, Sami Nasib. *The Doctrine of the Ismailis*. Beirut, 1972.

284 Walker, Paul E. "An Ismāʿīli Answer to the Problem of Worshiping the Unknowable, Neoplatonic God." *The American Journal of Arabic Studies* 2 (1974): 7–21.

285 Walker, Paul E. "The Ismaili Vocabulary of Creation." *Studia Islamica* 40 (1974): 75–85.

286 Walker, Paul E. "An Early Ismaili Interpretation of Man, History, and Salvation." *Ohio Journal of Religious Studies* 3 (1975): 29–35.

287 Madelung, Wilferd. "Aspects of Ismāʿīlī Theology: The Prophetic Chain and the God Beyond Being." In *Ismāʿīlī Contributions to Islamic Culture*. Ed. by Seyyed Hossein Nasr. Tehran, 1977, 53–65.

288 Poonawala, Ismail K. *Biobibliography of Ismāʿīlī Literature*. Malibu, 1977.

289 Feki, Habib. *Les idées religieuses et philosophiques de l'ismaélisme fatimide (organisation & doctrine)*. Tunis, 1978.

290 Halm, Heinz. *Kosmologie und Heilslehre der frühen Ismāʿīlīya: Eine Studie zur islamischen Gnosis*. Wiesbaden, 1978.

291 Walker, Paul E. "Eternal Cosmos and the Womb of History: Time in Early Ismaili Thought." *International Journal of Middle East Studies* 9 (1978): 355–366.

292 Blumenthal, David R. "On the Theories of *ibdāʿ* and *ta'thīr*." *Die Welt des Islams* 20 (1980): 162–177.

293 Pines, Shlomo. "Shīʿite Terms and Conceptions in Judah Halevi's Kuzari." *Jerusalem Studies in Arabic and Islam* 2 (1980): 165–251.

294 Stern, Samuel Miklos. "The Earliest Cosmological Doctrines of Ismāʿīlism." In S. M. Stern 1983 [*295], 3–29.

295 Stern, Samuel Miklos. *Studies in Early Ismāʿīlism*. Jerusalem, Leiden, 1983.

296 Gacek, Adam. *Catalogue of Arabic Manuscripts in the Library of the Institute of Ismaili Studies*, vol. 1. London, 1984.

297 Kiener, Ronald. "Jewish Ismāʿīlism in Twelfth Century Yemen. R. Nethanel Ben al-Fayyūmī." *The Jewish Quarterly Review* 74 (1984): 249–266.

298 Makarem, Sami Nasib. "Isma'ili and Druze Cosmogony in Relation to Plotinus and Aristotle." In *Islamic Theology and Philosophy: Studies in Honor of George F. Hourani.* Ed. by Michael E. Marmura. Albany, 1984, 81–91; 294–295.

299 Tajdin, Najib. *A Bibliography of Ismailism.* Delmar, 1985.

300 Janusz Bilinski. "The Concept of Time in the Ismaelitic Gnosis." In *Folia Orientalia* 23 (1985–1986): 69–110.

301 Halm, Heinz. *Die Schia.* Darmstadt, 1988. – Engl. transl. by Janet Watson and Marian Hill: H. Halm, *Shiʿism*. New York, 1991, 2004 (2nd ed.).

302 Madelung, Wilferd. *Religious Trends in Early Islamic Iran.* Albany, 1988.

303 Poonawala, Ismail K. "Ismāʿīlī *Taʾwīl* of the Qurʾān." In *Approaches to the History of the Interpretation of the Qurʾān*. Ed. by Andrew Rippin. Oxford, 1988, 199–222.

304 Rowson, Everett K. *A Muslim Philosopher on the Soul and Its Fate: Al-ʿĀmirī's Kitāb al-Amad ʿalā l-abad.* New Haven, 1988.

305 Aouad, Maroun. "La Théologie d'Aristote et autres textes du Plotinus Arabus." In *Dictionnaire des philosophes antiques,* vol. 1. Ed. by Richard Goulet. Paris, 1989, 541–590.

306 De Smet, Daniel. "Le Verbe-impératif dans le système cosmologique de l'ismaélisme." *Revue des sciences philosophiques et théologiques* 73 (1989): 397–412.

307 Klemm, Verena. *Die Mission des fāṭimidischen Agenten al-Muʾayyad fī d-dīn in Šīrāz.* Frankfurt a.M., 1989.

308 Rudolph, Ulrich. *Die Doxographie des Pseudo-Ammonios: Ein Beitrag zur neuplatonischen Überlieferung im Islam.* Stuttgart, 1989.

309 Daftary, Farhad. *The Ismāʿīlīs: Their History and Doctrines.* Cambridge, 1990.

310 Alibhai, Mohamed A. "The Transformation of Spiritual Substance into Bodily Substance in Ismāʿīlī Neoplatonism." In *Neoplatonism and Islamic Thought.* Ed. by Parwiz Morewedge. New York, 1992, 167–177.

311 De Smet, Daniel. "*Mīzān ad-diyāna* ou l'équilibre entre science et religion dans la pensée ismaélienne." *Acta Orientalia Belgica* 8 (1993): 247–254.

312 De Smet, Daniel. "Au-delà de l'apparent: Les notions de *ẓāhir* et *bāṭin* dans l'ésotérisme musulman." *Orientalia Lovaniensia Periodica* 25 (1994): 197–220.

313 Köhler, Bärbel. *Die Wissenschaft unter den ägyptischen Fatimiden.* Hildesheim, 1994.

314 Netton, Ian Richard. *Allāh Transcendent: Studies in the Structure and Semiotics of Islamic Philosophy, Theology and Cosmology*. Richmond, 1994, 203–255.

315 Walker, Paul E. "Abū Tammām and his *Kitāb al-Shajara*: A New Ismaili Treatise from Tenth-Century Khurasan." *Journal of the American Oriental Society* 114 (1994): 343–352.

316 Halm, Heinz. "The Cosmology of the Pre-Fatimid Ismāʿīliyya." In *Mediaeval Ismaʿili History and Thought*. Ed. by Farhad Daftary. Cambridge, 1996, 75–83.

317 Nanji, Azim. "Ismāʿīlī Philosophy." In *History of Islamic Philosophy*, vol. 1. Ed. by Seyyed Hossein Nasr and Oliver Leaman. London, 1996, 144–154.

318 Halm, Heinz. *The Fatimids and Their Traditions of Learning*. London, 1997.

319 Daftary, Farhad. *A Short History of the Ismailis: Traditions of a Muslim Community*. Edinburgh, 1998.

320 De Smet, Daniel. *Empedocles Arabus: Une lecture néoplatonicienne tardive*. Brussels, 1998.

321 De Smet, Daniel. "Perfectio prima – perfectio secunda, ou les vicissitudes d'une notion, de S. Thomas aux Ismaéliens ṭayyibites du Yémen." *Recherches de théologie et de philosophie médiévales* 66 (1999): 254–288.

322 Steigerwald, Diane. "La pensée d'al-Fārābī" (259/872–339/950): Son rapport avec la philosophie ismaélienne." *Laval théologique et philosophique* 55 (1999): 455–476.

323 Cortese, Delia. *Ismaili and Other Arabic Manuscripts: A Descriptive Catalogue of Manuscripts in the Library of the Institute of Ismaili Studies*. London, 2000.

324 Madelung, Wilferd and Paul Walker. *The Advent of the Fatimids: A Contemporary Shi'i Witness: An Edition and English Translation of Ibn al-Haytham's Kitāb al-Munāẓarāt*. London, 2000.

325 Cortese, Delia. *Arabic Ismaili Manuscripts: The Zahid Ali Collection in the Library of the Institute of Ismaili Studies*. London, 2003.

326 Daftary, Farhad. *Ismaili Literature: A Bibliography of Sources and Studies*. London, 2004.

327 De Smet, Daniel. "The Sacredness of Nature in Shiʿi Ismaʿili Islam." In *The Book of Nature in Antiquity and the Middle Ages*. Ed. by Aryo Vanderjagt and Klaas Van Berkel. Leuven, 2005, 85–96.

328 Walker, Paul E. "The Ismāʿīlīs." In *The Cambridge Companion to Arabic Philosophy*. Ed. by Peter Adamson and Richard Taylor. Cambridge, 2005, 72–91.

329 De Smet, Daniel. "Les bibliothèques ismaéliennes et la question du néoplatonisme ismaélien." In *The Libraries of the Neoplatonists: Proceedings of the Meeting of the European Science Foundation Network 'Late Antiquity and Arabic Thought: Patterns in the Constitution of European Culture' Held in Strasbourg, March 12–14, 2004*. Ed. by Cristina D'Ancona. Leiden, Boston, 2007, 481–492.

330 De Smet, Daniel. *Les épîtres sacrées des Druzes: Rasāʾil al-ḥikma*, 2 vols: *Introduction, édition critique et traduction annotée des traités attribués à Ḥamza b. ʿAlī et à Ismāʿīl at-Tamīmī*. Leuven, 2007.

331 De Smet, Daniel and Meryem Sebti. "Avicenna's Philosophical Approach to the Qur'an in the Light of His *Tafsīr Sūrat al-Ikhlāṣ*." *Journal of Qur'anic Studies* 11 (2009): 134–148.

332 Hollenberg, David. "Neoplatonism in Pre-Kirmānīan Fāṭimid Doctrine: A Critical Edition and translation of the Prologue of the *Kitāb al-Fatarāt wa-l-qirānāt*." *Le Muséon* 122 (2009): 159–202.

333 De Smet, Daniel. "Was Nāṣir-e Ḫusraw a Great Poet and Only a Minor Philosopher? Some Critical Reflections on His Doctrine of the Soul." In *Ismaili and Fatimid Studies in Honor of Paul E. Walker*. Ed. by Bruce D. Craig. Chicago, 2010, 101–130.

334 de Blois, François. *Arabic, Persian and Gujarati Manuscripts: The Hamdani Collection in the Library of the Institute of Ismaili Studies*. London, New York, 2011.

335 De Smet, Daniel. "Ismaili Philosophical Tradition." In *Encyclopedia of Medieval Philosophy: Philosophy Between 500 and 1500*, vol. 1. Ed. by Henrik Lagerlund. Wiesbaden, 2011, 575–577.

336 De Smet, Daniel. "Philosophie grecque et religion musulmane: Aristote comme exégète du Coran selon la tradition shi'ite ismaélienne." *Ishrāq: Islamic Philosophy Yearbook* 2 (2011): 344–363.

337 De Smet, Daniel. "The *Risāla al-Mudhhiba* Attributed to al-Qāḍī al-Nuʿmān: Important Evidence for the Adoption of Neoplatonism by Fatimid Ismailism at the Time of al-Muʿizz?" In *Fortresses of the Intellect: Ismaili and other Islamic Studies in Honour of Farhad Daftary*. Ed. by Omar Ali-de-Unzaga. London, New York, 2011, 309–341.

338 Madelung, Wilferd and Paul E. Walker. "The *Kitāb al-Rusūm wa'l-izdiwāj wa'l-tartīb* Attributed to ʿAbdān (d. 286/899): Edition of the Arabic Text and Translation." In O. Ali-de-Unzaga 2011 [cf. *337], 103–165.

339 Klemm, Verena and Paul E. Walker. *A Code of Conduct. A Treatise on the Etiquette of the Fatimid Ismaili Mission. A critical edition of the Arabic text and English translation of Aḥmad b. Ibrāhīm al-Naysābūrī's al-Risāla al-mūjaza al-kāfiya fī ādāb al-duʿāt*. London, New York, 2011.

340 Poonawala, Ismail. "An Early Doctrinal Controversy in the Iranian School of Isma'ili Thought and its Implications." *Journal of Persianate Studies* 5 (2012): 17–34.

341 De Smet, Daniel. "La *Doxographie du Pseudo-Ammonius* dans ses rapports avec le néoplatonisme ismaélien." In *De l'Antiquité tardive au Moyen Âge. Études de logique aristotélicienne et de philosophie grecque, syriaque, arabe et latine offertes à Henri Hugonnard-Roche*. Ed. by Elisa Coda and Cecilia Martini Bonadeo. Paris, 2014, 491–518.

342 De Smet, Daniel. "La transmigration des âmes. Une notion problématique dans l'ismaélisme d'époque fatimide." In *Unity in Diversity. Mysticism, Messianism and the Construction of Religious Authority in Islam*. Ed. by Orkhan Mir-Kasimov. Leiden, Boston, 2014, 77–110.

5.5.2 Muḥammad al-Nasafī

345 Madelung, Wilferd. "*Kawn al-ʿĀlam*: The Cosmogony of the Ismāʿīlī dāʿī Muḥammad b. Aḥmad al-Nasafī." In B. Craig 2010 [cf. *333], 23–31.

5.5.3 Abū Ḥātim al-Rāzī

351 al-Hamdānī, Ḥusayn F.: "*Kitāb az-Zīnat* of Abū Ḥātim ar-Rāzī." In *Actes du XXIe congrès international des orientalistes (Paris, 23–31 juillet 1948)*. Paris, 1949, 291–295.
352 Vajda, Georges. "Les lettres et les sons de la langue arabe d'après Abū Ḥātim al-Rāzī." *Arabica* 8 (1961): 113–130.
353 Halm, Heinz. "Abū Ḥātem Rāzī." In EIr [*5: I 315].
354 Daiber, Hans. "Abū Ḥātim ar-Rāzī (10th century A.D.) on the Unity and Diversity of Religions." In *Dialogue and Syncretism*. Ed. by Jerald Gort et al. Amsterdam, 1989, 87–104.
355 Daiber, Hans. "The Ismaili Background of Fārābī's Political Philosophy." In *Gottes ist der Orient, Gottes ist der Okzident: Festschrift für Abdoljavad Falaturi zum 65. Geburtstag*. Ed. by Udo Tworuschka. Cologne, Vienna, 1991, 143–150.
356 De Smet, Daniel. "Rāzī, Abū Ḥātim." In *Encyclopédie philosophique universelle*, vol. 3: *Les œuvres philosophiques*, vol. 1. Ed. by Jean-François Mattéi, Paris, 1992, 798–799.
357 Walker, Paul E. "The Universal Soul and the Particular Soul in Ismāʿīlī Neoplatonism." In *Neoplatonism and Islamic Thought*. Ed. by Parwiz Morewedge. New York, 1992, 149–166.
358 Langhade, Jacques. *Du Coran à la philosophie: La langue arabe et la formation du vocabulaire philosophique de Farabi*. Damascus, 1994, 130–134.
359 Goodman, Lenn E. "Rāzī vs Rāzī – Philosophy in the Majlis." In *The Majlis: Interreligious Encounters in Medieval Islam*. Ed. by Hava Lazarus-Yafeh et al. Wiesbaden, 1999, 84–107.
360 Peerwani, Parvin. "Abū Ḥātim Rāzī on the Essential Unity of Religions." In *Beacon of Knowledge: Essays in Honor of Seyyed Hossein Nasr*. Ed. by Muḥammad H. Faghfoory. Louisville, 2003, 269–287.
361 Nomoto, Shin. "An Early Ismaili View of Other Religions: A Chapter From the *Kitāb al-Iṣlāḥ* by Abū Ḥātim al-Rāzī." In *Reason and Inspiration in Islam: Theology, Philosophy and Mysticism in Muslim Thought: Essays in Honour of Hermann Landolt*. Ed. by Todd Lawson. London, New York, 2005, 142–156.

5.5.4 Abū Yaʿqūb al-Siǧistānī

371 Poonawala, Ismail K. "Al-Sijistānī and His *Kitāb al-Maqālīd*." In *Essays on Islamic Civilization Presented to Niyazi Berkes*. Ed. by Donald Presgrave Little. Leiden, 1976, 274–283.

372 Walker, Paul E. "Cosmic Hierarchies in Early Ismāʿīlī Thought: The View of Abū Yaʿqūb al-Sijistānī." *Muslim World* 66 (1976): 14–28.

373 Heinen, Anton. "The Notion of *Taʾwīl* in Abū Yaʿqūb al-Sijistānī's *Book of the Sources* (*Kitāb al-Yanābīʿ*)." *Hamdard Islamicus* 2 (1979): 35–45.

374 Marquet, Yves. "La pensée d'Abū Yaʿqūb as-Sijistānī à travers l'*Iṯbāt an-nubuwwāt* et la *Tuḥfat al-mustajībīn*." *Studia Islamica* 54 (1981): 95–128.

375 Walker, Paul E. "Abū Yaʿqūb Sejestānī." In EIr [*5: I 396–398].

376 Arnaldez, Roger. "Influences néoplatoniciennes dans la pensée d'Abu Yaʿqub al-Siǧistani." In *Actes du colloque Pensée arabe et culture grecque*. Casablanca, 1985, 540–548.

377 Kamada, Shigeru. "The First Being: Intellect (*ʿaql/khiradh*) as the Link Between God's Command and Creation According to Abū Yaʿqūb al-Sijistānī." In *The Memoirs of the Institute of Oriental Culture, University of Tokyo* 106 (1988): 1–33.

378 Madelung, Wilferd. "Abū Yaʿqūb al-Sijistānī and Metempsychosis." In *Iranica Varia: Papers in Honor of Professor Ehsan Yarshater*. Leiden, 1990, *131–143*.

379 Walker, Paul E. "The Doctrine of Metempsychosis in Islam." In *Islamic Studies Presented to Charles J. Adams.* Ed. by Wael B. Hallaq and Donald P. Little. Leiden, 1991, 219–238.

380 De Smet, Daniel. "Sijistānī." In *Encyclopédie philosophique universelle,* vol. 3: *Les œuvres philosophiques,* vol. 1. Ed. by Jean-François Mattéi. Paris, 1992, 837–838.

381 Walker, Paul E. *Early Philosophical Shiism: The Ismaili Neoplatonism of Abū Yaʿqūb al-Sijistānī*. Cambridge, 1993.

382 Marquet, Yves. "La révélation par l'astrologie selon Abū Yaʿqūb as-Sijistānī et les Iḫwān aṣ-Ṣafāʾ." In *Studia Islamica* 80 (1994): 5–28.

383 Madelung, Wilferd. "Abū Yaʿqūb al-Siǧistānī and the Seven Faculties of the Intellect." In *Mediaeval Ismaʿili History and Thought*. Ed. by Farhad Daftary. Cambridge, 1996, 85–89.

384 Walker, Paul E. *Abu Yaʿqub al-Sijistani: Intellectual Missionary*. London, New York, 1996.

385 De Smet, Daniel. "La doctrine avicennienne des deux faces de l'âme et ses racines ismaéliennes." *Studia Islamica* 93 (2001): 77–89.

386 De Smet, Daniel. "L'élaboration de l'élixir selon Ps.-Siǧistānī: Alchimie et cosmogonie dans l'ismaélisme ṭayyibite." In *Proceedings of the 20th Congress of the Union européenne des arabisants et islamisants: Budapest, 10–17 September 2000*, vol. 2: *Islam, Popular Culture in Islam, Islamic Art and Architecture.* Ed. by Alexander Fodor. Budapest, 2003, 25–35.

387 De Smet, Daniel. "Loi rationnelle et loi imposée: Les deux aspects de la *šarīʿa* dans le chiisme ismaélien des Xe et XIe siècles." In *Mélanges de l'Université Saint-Joseph* 61 (2008): 515–544.

388 De Smet, Daniel. "Une classification ismaélienne des sciences: L'apport d'Abū Yaʿqūb al-Sijistānī à la 'tradition d'al-Kindī' et ses liens avec Abū l-Ḥasan al-ʿĀmirī." In *Islamic Thought in the Middle Ages: Studies in Text, Transmission and Translation, in Honour of Hans Daiber*. Ed. by Anna Akasoy and Wim Raven. Leiden, Boston 2008, 77–90.

389 De Smet, Daniel. "Adam, premier prophète et législateur? La doctrine chiite des *ulū al-ʿazm* et la controverse sur la pérennité de la *šarīʿa*." In *Le shīʿisme imāmite quarante ans après: Hommage à Etan Kohlberg*. Ed. by Mohammad Ali Amir-Moezzi, Meir M. Bar-Asher and Simon Hopkins. Turnhout, 2009, 187–202.

5.5.5 Ḥamīd al-Dīn al-Kirmānī

395 Kraus, Paul. "Hebräische und syrische Zitate in ismāʿīlitischen Schriften." *Der Islam* 19 (1930): 243–263.

396 Baumstark, Anton. "Zu den Schriftzitaten al-Kirmānīs." *Der Islam* 20 (1932): 308–313.

397 al-Hamdānī, Ḥusain F. "*Rasāʾil Ikhwān aṣ-Ṣafā* in the Literature of the Ismāʿīlī Ṭaiyibī *Daʿwat*." *Der Islam* 20 (1932): 281–300.

398 van Ess, Josef. "Zur Chronologie der Werke des Ḥamīdaddīn al-Kirmānī." *Die Welt des Orients* 9 (1977/78): 255–261.

399 De Smet, Daniel. "al-Kirmānī." In *Encyclopédie philosophique universelle*, vol. 3: *Les œuvres philosophiques*, vol. 1. Ed. by Jean-François Mattéi. Paris, 1992, 657–658.

400 De Smet, Daniel. "Le *Kitāb Rāḥat al-ʿaql* de Ḥamīd ad-Dīn al-Kirmānī et la cosmologie ismaélienne à l'époque fatimide." *Acta Orientalia Belgica* 7 (1992): 81–91.

401 De Smet, Daniel. *La quiétude de l'intellect: Néoplatonisme et gnose ismaélienne dans l'œuvre de Ḥamīd ad-Dīn al-Kirmānī*. Leuven, 1995.

402 Peterson, Daniel. "Ḥamīd al-Dīn al-Kirmānī on Creation." In *Perspectives arabes et médiévales sur la tradition scientifique et philosophique grecque. Actes du colloque de la SIHSPAI (Société internationale d'histoire des sciences et de la philosophie arabes et islamiques), Paris, 31 mars – 3 avril 1993*. Ed. by Ahmad Hasnawi, Abdelali Elamrani-Jamal and Maroun Aouad. Leuven, Paris, 1997, 555–567.

403 De Smet, Daniel and Jan M. F. Van Reeth. "Les citations bibliques dans l'œuvre du *dāʿī* ismaélien Ḥamīd ad-Dīn al-Kirmānī." In *Law, Christianity and Modernism in Islamic Society: Proceedings of the Eighteenth Congress of the Union européenne des arabisants et islamisants*. Ed. by Urbain Vermeulen and Jan M. F. Van Reeth. Leuven, 1998, 147–160.

404 Haji, Hamid. *A Distinguished dāʿī under the Shade of the Fāṭimids: Ḥamīd ad-Dīn al-Kirmānī (d. circa 411/1020) and his Epistles*. London, 1998.

405 Peterson, Daniel. "Al-Kirmani on the Divine *Tawḥīd*." In *Proceedings of the Third European Conference of Iranian Studies Held in Cambridge, 11th to 15th September 1995*, vol. 2. Ed. by Charles Melville. Wiesbaden, 1999, 179–194.

406 Walker, Paul E. *Ḥamīd al-Dīn al-Kirmānī: Ismaili Thought in the Age of al-Ḥākim*. London, New York, 1999.

407 Daftary, Farhad. "Ḥamīd ad-Dīn Kermānī." In EIr [*5: XI 639–641].

408 Hunzai, Faquir Muhammad. "The Concept of Knowledge According to al-Kirmānī (d. after 411/1021)." In *Reason and Inspiration in Islam: Theology, Philosophy and Mysticism in Muslim Thought: Essays in Honour of Hermann Landolt*. Ed. by Todd Lawson. London, New York, 2005, 127–141.

408a Baffioni, Carmela. "Contrariety and Similarity in God According to al-Fārābī and al-Kirmānī: a Comparison." In *Classical Arabic Philosophy. Sources and Reception*. Ed. by Peter Adamson. London, Turin 2007, 1–20.

409 De Smet, Daniel. "Al-Fārābī's Influence on Ḥamīd al-Dīn al-Kirmānī's Theory of Intellect and Soul." In *In the Age of al-Fārābī: Arabic Philosophy in the Fourth/Tenth Century*. Ed. by Peter Adamson. London, 2008, 131–150.

410 De Smet, Daniel. "Miroir, savoir et émanation dans l'ismaélisme fatimide." In *Miroir et savoir: La transmission d'un thème platonicien, des Alexandrins à la philosophie arabo-musulmane: Actes du colloque international tenu à Leuven et Louvain-la-Neuve, les 17 et 18 novembre 2005*. Ed. by Daniel De Smet, Meryem Sebti and Godefroid de Callataÿ. Leuven, 2008, 173–187.

411 Baffioni, Carmela. "L'influence des Ikhwān al-Ṣafā' sur la minéralogie de Ḥamīd al-Dīn al-Kirmānī." In *Une lumière venue d'ailleurs. Héritages et ouvertures dans les encyclopédies d'Orient et d'Occident au Moyen Âge*. Ed. by Godefroid de Callataÿ, Baudouin Van den Abeele. Louvain-la-Neuve, 2008, 31–47.

412 De Smet, Daniel. "*Kufr* et *takfīr* dans l'ismaélisme fatimide: le *Kitāb Tanbīh al-hādī* de Ḥamīd al-Dīn al-Kirmānī." In *Accusations of Unbelief in Islam. A Diachronic Perspective on Takfīr*. Ed. by Camilla Adang, Hassan Ansari, Maribel Fierro, and Sabine Schmidtke. Leiden, Boston, 2016, 82–102.

5.6 *The Encyclopaedia of the Iḫwān al-Ṣafā'*

There is a rich body of literature on the Iḫwān al-Ṣafā'. The following compilation only lists those titles that are cited in the article, or have a direct reference to philosophy. For a nearly complete bibliography cf. Daftary 2004 [*326].

421 Guyard, Stanislas. "Le Fetwa d'Ibn Taimiyyah sur les Nosairis." *Journal asiatique* 6/18 (1871): 158–198.

422 Dieterici, Friedrich. *Der Darwinismus im zehnten und neunzehnten Jahrhundert*. Leipzig, 1878.

423 Goldziher, Ignaz. “Über die Benennung der Ichwān al-Ṣafāʾ.” *Der Islam* 1 (1910): 22–26.

424 Casanova, Paul. “Une date astronomique dans les Épîtres des Ikhwān aṣ Ṣafāʾ.” *Journal asiatique* 11/5 (1915): 5–17.

425 al-Hamdānī, Ḥusain F. “*Rasāʾil Ikhwān aṣ-Ṣafā* in the Literature of the Ismāʿīlī Ṭaiyibī *Daʿwat*.” *Der Islam* 20 (1932): 281–300.

426 García Gómez, Emilio. “Alusiones a los Ijwān al-Ṣafāʾ en la poesía arábigo-andaluza.” *Al-Andalus* 4 (1939): 462–465.

427 Fackenheim, Emil L. “The Conception of Substance in the Philosophy of the Ikhwan as-Safaʾ (Brethren of Purity).” *Mediaeval Studies* 5 (1943): 115–122.

428 Stern, Samuel Miklos. “The Authorship of the *Epistles* of the Ikhwān al-Ṣafāʾ.” *Islamic Culture* 20 (1946): 367–372; 21 (1947): 403–404 (Additional notes).

429 Tibawi, Abdul-Latif. “Ikhwān aṣ-Ṣafā and Their *Rasāʾil*: A Critical Review of a Century and a Half of Research.” *Islamic Quarterly* 2 (1955): 28–46.

430 Plessner, Martin. “Die Stellung des *Picatrix* innerhalb der spanischen Kultur.” In *Actes du IXe congrès international d'histoire des sciences*. Barcelona, 1959, 312–324.

431 Marquet, Yves. “Imamat, résurrection et hiérarchie selon les Ikhwan as-Safa.” *Revue des études islamiques* 30 (1962): 49–142.

432 Farrukh, ʿUmar. “Ikhwān al-Ṣafa.” In *A History of Muslim Philosophy*, vol. 1. Ed. by M. M. Sharif. Wiesbaden, 1963, 289–310.

433 Corbin, Henri. *Histoire de la philosophie islamique*, vol. 1: *Des origines jusqu'à la mort d'Averroës (1198)*. Paris, 1964.

434 Marquet, Yves. “Coran et création: Traduction et commentaire de deux extraits des Iḫwān al-Ṣafāʾ.” *Arabica* 11 (1964): 279–285.

435 Stern, Samuel Miklos. “New Information about the Authors of the ‘Epistles of the Sincere Brethren’.” *Islamic Studies* 3 (1964): 405–428. – Repr. in: S. M. Stern 1983 [*456: 155–176].

436 Marquet, Yves. “Ikhwān al-Ṣafāʾ.” In EI^{2} [*2: III 1071–1076].

437 Widengren, Geo. “The Gnostic Technical Language in the *Rasāʾil Iḫwān al-Ṣafāʾ*.” In *IV congresso de estudos árabes e islâmicos, 1968: Actas*. Leiden, 1971, 181–203.

438 Diwald, Susanne. “Die Seele und ihre geistigen Kräfte: Darstellung und philosophiegeschichtlicher Hintergrund im K. Ikhwān aṣ-Ṣafā.” In S. M. Stern, A. Hourani, V. Brown 1972 [cf. *230], 49–61.

439 Marquet, Yves. *La philosophie des Iḫwān al-Ṣafāʾ*. Alger, 1973. – Repr. in: Y. Marquet, *La philosophie des Iḫwān al-Ṣafāʾ: Nouvelle édition augmentée*. Paris, Milan, 1999.

440 Blumenthal, David R. “A Comparative Table of the Bombay, Cairo, and Beirut Editions of the *Rasāʾil Iḫwān al-Ṣafāʾ*.” *Arabica* 21 (1974): 186–203.

441 Triki, Ahmed. *Néoplatonisme et aspect mystique de la création de l'univers dans la philosophie des Iḫwān*. Alger, 1974.

442 Nanji, Azim. "On the Acquisition of Knowledge: A Theory of Learning in the Rasāʾil Ikhwān al-Ṣafāʾ." *Muslim World* 66 (1976): 263–271.

443 Bausani, Alessandro. "Scientific Elements in Ismāʿīlī Thought: The *Epistles* of the Brethren of Purity (Ikhwān al-Ṣafāʾ)." In S. H. Nasr 1977 [*cf. 287], 123–140.

444 Enayat, Hamid. "An Outline of the Political Philosophy of the *Rasāʾil* of the Ikhwān al-Ṣafāʾ." In S. H. Nasr 1977 [*cf. 287], 25–49.

445 Marquet, Yves. "Iḫwān al-Ṣafāʾ, Ismaïliens et Qarmaṭes." *Arabica* 24 (1977): 233–257.

446 Hamdani, Abbas. "Abū Ḥayyān al-Tawḥīdī and the Brethren of Purity." *International Journal of Middle East Studies* 9 (1978): 345–353.

447 Marquet, Yves. "910 en Ifrīqiyā: Une épître des Iḫwān aṣ-Ṣafāʾ." *Bulletin d'études orientales* 30 (1978): 61–73.

448 Nasr, Seyyed Hossein. *An Introduction to Islamic Cosmological Doctrines: Conceptions of Nature and Methods Used for its Study by the Ikhwān al-Ṣafā, al-Bīrūnī, and Ibn Sīnā*. London, 1978 (2nd ed.), 23–104.

449 Hamdani, Abbas. "An Early Fāṭimid Source on the Time and Authorship of the *Rasāʾil Iḫwān al-Ṣafāʾ*." *Arabica* 26 (1979): 62–75.

450 Widengren, Geo. "The Pure Brethren and the Philosophical Structure of Their System." In *Islam: Past Influence and Present Challenge*. Ed. by Alford Welch and Pierre Cachia. Edinburgh, 1979, 57–69.

451 Netton, Ian R. "Brotherhood versus Imāmate: Ikhwān al-Ṣafāʾ and the Ismāʿīlīs." *Jerusalem Studies in Arabic and Islam* 2 (1980): 253–262.

452 Diwald, Susanne. "Die Bedeutung des Kitāb *Iḫwān aṣ-Ṣafāʾ* für das islamische Denken." In *Convegno sugli Ikhwān aṣ-Ṣafāʾ, Roma, 25–26 ottobre 1979*. Rome, 1981, 5–25.

453 Marquet, Yves. "Les Iḫwān aṣ-Ṣafāʾ et l'ismaïlisme." In *Convegno* [*452], 69–96.

454 Netton, Ian R. "Foreign Influences and Recurring Ismāʿīlī Motifs in the *Rasāʾil* of the Brethren of Purity." In *Convegno* [*452], 49–67.

455 Netton, Ian R. *Muslim Neoplatonists: An Introduction to the Thought of the Brethren of Purity*. Edinburgh 1982, 1991 (2nd ed.).

456 Stern, Samuel Miklos. *Studies in Early Ismāʿīlism*. Jerusalem, Leiden, 1983.

457 Hamdani, Abbas. "The Arrangement of the *Rasāʾil Ikhwān al-Ṣafāʾ* and the Problem of Interpolations." *Journal of Semitic Studies* 29 (1984): 97–110. – An updated version is published under the same title in: Nader El-Bizri, ed. *Epistles of the Brethren of Purity: The Ikhwān al-Ṣafāʾ and Their Rasāʾil: An Introduction*. Oxford, 2008, 83–100.

458 Straface, Antonella. "Testimonianze pitagoriche alla luce di una filosofia profetica: La numerologia pitagorica negli Iḫwān al-Ṣafāʾ." *Annali dell'Istituto Orientale di Napoli* 47 (1987): 225–241.

459 Marquet, Yves. *La philosophie des alchimistes et l'alchimie des philosophes: Jābir ibn Ḥayyān et les Frères de la Pureté*. Paris, 1988.

460 Marquet, Yves. "Les références à Aristote dans les Épîtres des Iḫwān aṣ-Ṣafā'." In *Individu et société: L'influence d'Aristote dans le monde méditerranéen*. Ed. by Thierry Zarcone. Istanbul, 1988, 159–164.

461 Baffioni, Carmela. "Euclides in the *Rasā'il* by Ikhwān al-Ṣafā'." *Études orientales* 5–6 (1990): 58–68.

462 Baffioni, Carmela. "Probable Syriac Influences in the Ikhwān al-Ṣafā's Logical Epistles?" *Aram* 3 (1991): 7–22.

463 Baffioni, Carmela. "Traces of Aristotelian Dialogues in the *Rasā'il* by Ikhwān al-Ṣafā'?" In *BRISMES: Proceedings of the 1991 International Conference on Middle Eastern Studies*. London, 1991, 439–448.

464 Meyer, Egbert. *Die Isagoge in der Wissenschaftsenzyklopädie der Lauteren Brüder von Baṣra*. In U. Tworuschka 1991 [cf. *355]: 182–206.

465 Rahman, A. Wahidur. "*Rasā'il Ikhwān al-Ṣafā'*: The Idea of Perfection of the Soul." *Hamdard Islamicus* 14 (1991): 25–48.

466 Baffioni, Carmela. "Greek Ideas and Vocabulary in Arabic Philosophy: The *Rasā'il* by Ikhwān al-Ṣafā'." In *Contacts between Cultures*, vol. 1. Ed. by Amir Harrak. Levinston, Queenston, Lampeter, 1992, 391–398.

467 Dadoyan, Seta B. "A Thirteenth Century Armenian Summary of the *Epistles* of the Brethren of Purity." *Al-Abḥāṯ* 40 (1992): 3–18.

468 Marquet, Yves. "La détermination astrale de l'évolution selon les Frères de la Pureté." *Bulletin d'études orientales* 44 (1992): 127–146.

469 Baffioni, Carmela. "'Detti aurei' di Pitagora in trasmissione araba." In *I moderni ausili all'ecdotica*. Ed. by Vincenzo Placella and Sebastiano Martelli. Naples, 1994, 107–131.

470 Baffioni, Carmela. *Frammenti e testimonianze di autori antichi nelle Rasā'il degli Iḫwān al-Ṣafā'*. Rome, 1994.

471 Baffioni, Carmela. "Il *Liber introductorius in artem logicae demonstrationis*. Problemi storici e filologici." *Studi filosofici* 17 (1994): 69–90.

472 Giese, Alma. "Zur Erlösungsfunktion des Traumes bei den Iḫwān aṣ-Ṣafā'." In *Gott ist schön und Er liebt die Schönheit: Festschrift für Annemarie Schimmel*. Ed. by Alma Giese and Johann Christoph Bürgel. Bern, Berlin, 1994, 191–207.

473 Nader, Albert. "Traces des Épîtres des Frères de la Pureté dans l'œuvre 'La disputation de l'âne' d'Anselme de Turmeda." In *Diálogo filósofico-religioso entre christianismo, judaismo e islamismo durante la edad media en la Península Ibérica*. Ed. by Horacio Santiago-Otero. Turnhout, 1994, 443–549.

474 Baffioni, Carmela and Claudio Baffioni. "Citazioni matematiche negli Iḫwān al-Ṣafā': Il caso di Nicomaco di Gerasa." In *La civiltà islamica e le scienze*. Ed. by Clelia Sarnelli Cerqua, Ornella Marra and Pier Giovanni Pelfer. Naples, 1995, 37–61.

475 Baffioni, Carmela. "Le 'testimonianze' sulla logica di Aristotele nelle *Epistole* degli Ikhwān al-Ṣafā'." In *Un ricordo che non si spegne: Scritti di docenti e collaboratori dell'Istituto Universitario Orientale di Napoli in memoria di Alessandro Bausani*. Naples, 1995, 1–10.

476 Hamdani, Abbas. "A critique of Paul Casanova's dating of the *Rasā'il Ikhwān al-Ṣafā'*." In *Mediaeval Isma'ili History and Thought*. Ed. by Farhad Daftary. Cambridge, 1996, 145–152.

477 Nasr, Seyyed Hossein. "Mullā Ṣadrā, His Teachings." In S. H. Nasr, O. Leaman 1996 [cf. *317], 643–662.

478 Netton, Ian R. "The Brethren of Purity (Ikhwān al-Ṣafā')." In S. H. Nasr, O. Leaman 1996 [cf. *317], 222–230.

479 Zonta, Mauro. "Mineralogy, Botany and Zoology in Hebrew Medieval Encyclopaedias." *Arabic Sciences and Philosophy* 6 (1996): 263–315.

480 Baffioni, Carmela. "Citazioni di autori antichi nelle *Rasā'il Ikhwān al-Ṣafā'*. Il caso di Nicomaco di Gerasa." In G. Endress, R. Kruk 1997 [cf. *58], 3–27.

481 Baffioni, Carmela. "Fragments et témoignages d'auteurs anciens dans les *Rasā'il* des Ikhwān al-Ṣafā'." In A. Hasnawi, A. Elamrani-Jamal and M. Aouad 1997 [cf. *402], 319–329.

482 Baffioni, Carmela. "Sulla ricezione di due luoghi di Platone e Aristotele negli Iḫwān al-Ṣafā'." *Documenti e studi sulla tradizione filosofica medievale* 8 (1997): 479–492.

483 Baffioni, Carmela. "Textual Problems in the Iḫwān al-Ṣafā''s Quotations of Ancient Authors." In *Proceedings of the 17th Congress of the Union européenne des arabisants et islamisants*. Ed. by Wilferd Madelung. St. Petersburg, 1997, 13–26.

484 Baffioni, Carmela. "Uso e rielaborazione degli autori classici nella *Risāla al-Ǧāmi'a*." In *La diffusione dell'eredità classica nell'età tardoantica e medievale: Forme e modi di trasmissione*. Ed. by Alfredo Valvo. Alessandria, 1997, 1–17.

485 Baffioni, Carmela. "From Sense Perception to the Vision of God: A Path Towards Knowledge According to the Ikhwān al-Ṣafā'." *Arabic Sciences and Philosophy* 8 (1998): 213–231.

486 Marquet, Yves. "Socrate et les Iḫwān aṣ-Ṣafā'." *Journal asiatique* 286 (1998): 409–449.

487 De Smet, Daniel. "Eléments chrétiens dans l'ismaélisme yéménite sous les derniers Fatimides: Le problème de la gnose ṭayyibite." In *L'Égypte fatimide, son art et son histoire: Actes du colloque organisé à Paris les 28, 29 et 30 mai 1998*. Ed. by Marianne Barrucand. Paris, 1999, 45–53.

488 De Smet, Daniel. "Le soleil, roi du ciel, dans la théologie astrale des Frères de la Pureté (Iḫwān aṣ-Ṣafā')." *Acta Orientalia Belgica* 12 (1999): 151–160.

489 Hamdani, Abbas. "Brethren of Purity, a Secret Society for the Establishment of the Fāṭimid Caliphate: New Evidence for the Early Dating of their Encyclopaedia." In M. Barrucand 1999 [cf. *487], 73–82.
490 Baffioni, Carmela. "Uso e rielaborazione degli autori classici nella Risāla *Ǧāmiʿa al-Ǧāmiʿa*." In *La diffusione dell'eredità classica nell'età tardoantica e medievale: Filologia, storia, dottrina.* Ed. by. Carmela Baffioni. Alessandria, 2000, 1–10.
491 Mohamed, Yasien. "The Cosmology of Ikhwān al-Ṣafāʾ, Miskawayh and al-Iṣfahānī." *Islamic Studies* 39 (2000): 657–679.
492 Baffioni, Carmela. "Aspetti della dottrina di Archimede nella tradizione araba: nuovi testi negli Ikhwān al-Ṣafāʾ." In *Autori classici in lingue del vicino e medio oriente.* Ed. by Gianfranco Fiaccadori. Rome, 2001, 327–339.
493 Baffioni, Carmela. "Frammenti e testimonianze platoniche nelle *Rasāʾil* degli Ikhwān al-Ṣafāʾ." In G. Fiaccadori 2001 [cf. *492], 163–178.
494 Baffioni, Carmela. "Al-Madīnah al-fāḍilah in al-Fārābī and in the Ikhwān al-Ṣafāʾ: A Comparison." In *Studies in Arabic and Islam: Proceedings of the 19th Congress of the Union européenne des arabisants et islamisants, Halle 1998.* Ed. by Stefan Leder. Leuven, 2002, 3–12.
495 Baffioni, Carmela. "Echi di *Meteorologica* IV nell'enciclopedia dei Fratelli della Purità." In *Aristoteles Chemicus: Il IV libro dei Meteorologica nella tradizione antica e medievale.* Ed. by Cristina Viano. Sankt Augustin, 2002, 113–131.
496 Baffioni, Carmela. "Les sens chez les Ikhwān al-Ṣafāʾ et l'héritage aristotélicien." *Micrologus* 10 (2002): 463–476.
497 Baffioni, Carmela. "Un esemplare arabo del *Liber de quattuor confectionibus.*" In *Hermetism from Late Antiquity to Humanism* Ed. by Paolo Lucentini, Ilaria Parri and Vittoria Perrone Compagni. Turnhout, 2003, 295–313.
498 Baffioni, Carmela. "The 'General Policy' of the Ikhwān al-Ṣafāʾ: Plato and Aristotle Restated." In R. Arnzen and J. Thielmann 2004 [cf. *69], 575–592.
499 de Callataÿ, Godefroid. "Sacredness and Esotericism in the *Rasāʾil Iḫwān aṣ-Ṣafāʾ*." In *Al-Kitāb: La sacralité du texte dans le monde de l'Islam: Actes du Symposium international tenu à Leuven et Louvain-la-Neuve du 29 mai au 1 juin 2002.* Ed. by Daniel De Smet, Godefroid de Callataÿ, and Jan M. F. Van Reeth. Brussels, Louvain-La-Neuve, Leuven, 2004, 389–401.
500 Baffioni, Carmela. *Appunti per un'epistemologia profetica: L'Epistola degli Iḫwān al-Ṣafāʾ sulle cause e gli effetti.* Naples, 2005.
501 Baffioni, Carmela. "Gli Iḫwān al-Ṣafāʾ e la loro enciclopedia." In *Storia della filosofia nell'Islam medievale,* vol. 1. Ed. by Cristina D'Ancona. Turin, 2005, 449–489.
502 de Callataÿ, Godefroid. *Ikhwan al-Safa': A Brotherhood of Idealists on the Fringe of Orthodox Islam.* Oxford, 2005.

503 De Smet, Daniel. "The Sacredness of Nature in Shi'i Isma'ili Islam" [*327].

504 Marquet, Yves. *Les Frères de la Pureté, pythagoriciens de l'Islam: La marque du pythagorisme dans la rédaction des Épîtres des Iḫwān aṣ-Ṣafāʾ*. Paris, 2006.

505 El-Bizri, Nader, ed. *Epistles of the Brethren of Purity: The Ikhwān al-Ṣafāʾ and their Rasāʾil: An Introduction*. Oxford, 2008.

506 Baffioni, Carmela. "The Scope of the Rasāʾil Ikhwān al-Ṣafāʾ." In N. El-Bizri 2008 [*505], 101–122.

507 de Callataÿ, Godefroid. "The Classification of Knowledge in the *Rasāʾil*." In N. El-Bizri 2008 [*505], 58–82.

508 El-Bizri, Nader. "Epistolary Prolegomena: On Arithmetic and Geometry." In N. El-Bizri 2008 [*505], 180–213.

509 Michot, Yahya. "Misled and Misleading... Yet Central in their Influence: Ibn Taymiyya's Views on the Ikhwān al-Ṣafāʾ." In N. El-Bizri 2008 [*505], 139–179.

510 Poonawala, Ismail K. "Why We Need an Arabic Critical Edition with an Annotated English Translation of the *Rasāʾil Ikhwān al-Ṣafāʾ*." In N. El-Bizri 2008 [*505], 33–57.

511 de Callataÿ, Godefroid. "Plato Ikhwanianus: Retour sur le récit platonicien de l'anneau de Gygès dans l'encyclopédie des Frères de la Pureté." *Res Antiquae* 7 (2010): 55–62.

512 Baffioni, Carmela. "Ibdāʿ, Divine Imperative and Prophecy in the *Rasāʾil Ikhwān al-Ṣafāʾ*." In O. Ali-de-Unzaga 2011 [cf. *337], 213–226.

513 Hamdani, Abbas. "The Ikhwān al-Ṣafāʾ: Between al-Kindī and al-Fārābī." In O. Ali-de-Unzaga 2011 [cf. *337], 189–212.

514 de Callataÿ, Godefroid. "Magia en al-Andalus. *Rasāʾil Ijwān al-Ṣafāʾ*, *Rutbat al-ḥakīm* y *Ġāyat al-ḥakīm (Picatrix)*." *Al-Qanṭara* 34 (2013): 297–344.

515 Krinis, Ehud. "*Al-Risāla al-jāmiʿa* and its Judeo-Arabic Manuscript." In *Islam: identité et altérité. Hommage au Père Guy Monnot*. Ed by Mohammad Ali Amir-Moezzi. Turnhout, 2013, 311–329.

Index of Arabic Words

This index lists Arabic words found in the Index of Subjects, where page numbers refer the reader to passages where the Arabic terms are mentioned.

abdaʿa ☞ creation
ʿāda, ʿādāt (ἔθος) ☞ habit(s)
adab ☞ literary culture, education
ʿadam ☞ non-being, non-existence
ʿadamī ☞ privative
aḏan ☞ pain(s)
adāt ☞ instrument
aḍdād ☞ contrary, contraries
ʿadl (δικαιοσύνη, δικαιότης) ☞ justice
iḫtiyārī ☞ justice – freely chosen
ṭabīʿī ☞ justice – natural
waḍʿī ☞ justice – conventional
afrād ☞ elemental qualities
ağnās ☞ genera (of musical metre)
ʿāliya ☞ category, categories, ☞ genus, genera – highest
ağyāl ☞ peoples
aḫbār ☞ anecdotes, historical
aḥkām al-nuğūm ☞ astrology, astrological
aḫlāq ☞ character – dispositions
ḥasana ☞ virtue(s)
aḥwāl ☞ states
ayna ☞ where
ayyun ☞ which
ʿālam
al-dīn ☞ world – of religion
kabīr ☞ macrocosm
kaṯīf ☞ world – crude
laṭīf ☞ world – spiritual
ṣağīr ☞ microcosm
alġāz ☞ riddle
allaḏī min ağlihi ☞ for-the-sake-of-which
ʿamal ☞ act, action, ☞ practice
ʿāmm ☞ common, general
amr ☞ command (of God)
amṯāl ☞ analogy, analogies
amṯila maḥsūsa ☞ symbol(s) – sensually perceptible
ʿan ☞ from/out of
anna ☞ that
anniyya ☞ essence (of God)
anwāʾ ☞ houses (of the moon), ☞ weather forecasting – according to stars
anwāʿ ☞ species
ʿāqil (νοῶν) ☞ intellecting
ʿaql (νοῦς) ☞ intellect, ☞ reason, ☞ investigation – semantic, of the word
ʿāqil ☞ intellect – intellecting
bi-l-fiʿl ☞ intellect – actual
bi-l-quwwa ☞ intellect – potential
faʿʿāl ☞ intellect – active/agent
hayūlānī ☞ intellect – material
maʿqūl ☞ intelligible, ☞ thought, – content(s) of thought
mustafād ☞ intellect – acquired
ʿaraḍ, aʿrāḍ ☞ accident(s)
al-arkān al-zağriyya ☞ prohibitions
ʿarš ☞ throne, God's
aṣḥāb al-kalām ☞ theologian(s)
aṣnāf ☞ class(es)
aṯar, āṯār ☞ effect(s)
awhām ☞ phantasms
awāʾil ☞ principle(s)
ʿawāmm ☞ commoners
azalī ☞ the eternal, ☞ substance(s), – eternal

badʾ ☞ beginning
baʿḍ ☞ part – equal and unequal
baʿd al-ṭabīʿa (μετὰ τὰ φυσικά) ☞ nature – what is beyond nature, ☞ metaphysics
al-badan al-tāmm al-ṣaḥīḥ ☞ body – intact and healthy
baḥṯ ☞ investigation
bayt al-ḥikma ☞ 'House of Wisdom'
baqāʾ al-nafs bi-l-šaḫṣ ☞ immortality – personal
bāriʾ ☞ Creator
baṣīra, baṣāʾir ☞ knowledge
basīṭ ☞ simple
bāṭin ☞ meaning(s), usage – internal
biḏr ☞ seed

buḫār (ἀτμίς) ☞ exhalation(s)
buḫl ☞ avarice
burhān, barāhīn ☞ proof(s), demonstration(s)

dahr (αἰών) ☞ eternity
ḏakāʾ ☞ acumen
dalīl ʿaqlī ☞ proof(s), demonstration(s) – rational
dāll ☞ signifying
ḍamīr ☞ enthymeme
ḏanab ☞ soul – downward orientation ('tail')
darrāk(a) ☞ perceptive
ḍarūrī ☞ necessary, necessity
ḏāt ☞ essence
  ilāhiyya ☞ essence – divine
  insāniyya ☞ essence – human
ḏawq ☞ taste
daʿwa ☞ mission (Ismaili)
dīn ☞ religion(s)
duʿāt ☞ missionaries, Ismaili

fāḍil ☞ excellent
faḍīla, faḍāʾil ☞ virtue(s)
  rūḥāniyya – virtue(s) – spiritual
faḍl (ἀγαθότης) ☞ benevolence, benevolent
fayḍ ☞ emanation
fāʾida ☞ information
fāʿil ☞ agent, ☞ cause – efficient
faylasūf, falāsifa ☞ philosopher(s)
falsafa ☞ philosophy
  ʿamaliyya ☞ philosophy – practical
  ilāhiyya ☞ philosophy – divine
  insāniyya ☞ philosophy – of humankind
  madaniyya ☞ philosophy – of the community
  siyāsiyya ☞ philosophy – of (political) governance
  yūnāniyya ☞ philosophy – Greek
faṣāḥa ☞ correctness of speech
faṣl (διορισμός) ☞ proof(s), demonstration(s) – Euclidean method
fazaʿ ☞ fear
fikr ☞ thought, thinking, – discursive
fiʿl, afʿāl ☞ act, action, ☞ verb
  al-afʿāl al-ǧamīla ☞ act, action – good
fiṭām ☞ gradual weaning
fiṭna ☞ prudence
fiṭra ṭabīʿiyya ☞ disposition, orientation, right direction – natural
fuǧūr ☞ profligacy

ǧabr ☞ determinism, determination
ġaḍab ☞ wrath, ☞ passion(s)
ġadr ☞ perfidy
ġayr munqasim (ἀδιαίπετον) ☞ being – indivisible
ǧamāʿāt ☞ scale(s)
ǧamīl ☞ good, the good
ġaraḍ (τέλος) ☞ goal(s), aim(s)
ǧawhar, ǧawāhir ☞ substance(s)
  azalī ☞ substance(s) – eternal
  mabsūṭ (ἁπλῆ οὐσία) ☞ substance(s) – simple
  qāʾim bi-ḏātihī (αὐθυπόστατος οὐσία) ☞ substance(s) – subsisting through itself
  rūḥānī laṭīf ☞ substance(s) – spiritual, subtle
ǧawhariyya ☞ substantiality
ǧawr ☞ injustice, ☞ violence
ǧawāmiʿ ☞ epitome
ǧazaʿ (λύπη) ☞ grief, ☞ sadness, sorrow
ǧihād ☞ war(s)
ǧihāt ☞ modes, ☞ aspect(s)
ǧūd (ἀγαθότης) ☞ benevolence, benevolent
ǧumhūr ☞ many, the
ǧuzʾ ☞ part – equal and unequal

ḫabar (πρόστασις) ☞ proof(s), demonstration(s) – Euclidean method
ḥadd ☞ definition(s)
ḥadīṯ ☞ *ḥadīṯ* (prophetic tradition)
ḥads ☞ inspiration
hayʾa ☞ disposition(s)
  fī mādda ☞ disposition(s) – in a body
al-ḫayr al-maḥḍ ☞ good, the good – the pure good
ḫayrāt (ἀγαθά) ☞ good, the good
ḥākim (ἡγεμονικόν) ☞ ruling force
ḥakīm ☞ sage, wise
hal ☞ yes-no question
ḫalāʾ ☞ vacuum
ḫalāṣ ☞ deliverance
ḫalf ☞ *reductio ad impossibile*
ḥaqāʾiq ☞ reality, realities
  al-umūr ☞ essence – true, of things
ḥaqq ☞ truth
ḥaraka ☞ motion
ḥarāra ☞ heat

ḥarf, ḥurūf ☞ particle(s)
ḥāss ☞ sense perception, sense(s)
muštarak ☞ sense perception, sense(s) – common
ḫāṣṣ ☞ specific
ḫāṣṣa, ḫawāṣṣ ☞ property, properties, proprium, propria, ☞ elite
ḥašwiyya ☞ commoners
ḫawf ☞ fear
hawā ☞ love, ☞ passion(s)
ḥawādiṯ ☞ affection – arising
ḫawālif ☞ pronouns
ḥawāšin ('fillers') ☞ utterance(s), linguistic expression(s), term(s)
ḫayāl ☞ imagination(s) – imaginary perceptions
ḥayāt ☞ life
aḫīra ☞ life – afterlife
hayūlā ☞ matter
muṭlaqa ☞ matter – absolute
hiǧā' ☞ comedy
ḥikma (γνῶσις) ☞ philosophy, ☞ wisdom
ʿalā l-iṭlāq ☞ wisdom – absolute
ilāhiyya ☞ theosophy
ḥilm ☞ prudence, ☞ knowledge
himma ☞ zeal
ḫiṣāl ☞ capacity, capacities – of intellect, human
ḥubb ☞ love
al-karāma ☞ love – of honour
al-zīna ☞ love – of pomp
ḥudūd ☞ dignitaries, ☞ definition(s)
ḫulq, ḫuluq (ἦθος) ☞ ethos, ☞ quality, qualities – moral, ☞ capacity, capacities – for ethical disposition, ☞ character
ḫuṭab ☞ speeches
ḥuzn (λύπη) ☞ grief, ☞ sadness, sorrow

iʿāda ☞ recreation, restoration (of actions)
ʿibāda ☞ worship (of God)
ʿamaliyya ☞ worship (of God) – through practice
falsafiyya ilāhiyya ☞ worship (of God) – through philosophy and metaphysics
ʿilmiyya ☞ worship (of God) – through knowledge
šarʿiyya nāmūsiyya worship (of God) – through the religious law
ibdāʿ ☞ creation
ibtidā' ☞ creation – initial
iḍāfa ☞ relation(s)
wa-l-muḍāf ☞ relation(s) – and the relative
ʿiffa (σωφροσύνη) ☞ chastity, ☞ moderation, ☞ temperance
ifrāṭ al-ḥubb ☞ love – excessive
īǧād ☞ being – bringing into being
iǧtahada ☞ effort, exertion – exerting oneself
iḫtiṣār ☞ abridgment (terminology, title of scholarly works)
iḫtiyār ☞ choice
iḫtiyārāt ☞ katarchic astrology
iktisāb ☞ acquisition – of deeds by human beings
ilāhiyyāt ☞ metaphysics
ilḥād ☞ heresy
ʿilla, ʿilal ☞ cause(s)
lam yazal ☞ cause(s) – eternal efficient
al-ʿilla al-ūlā ☞ cause(s) – First
ʿillat al-ʿilal ☞ cause(s) – of causes
ʿilm ☞ knowledge, ☞ science(s), ☞ theory
al-adab ☞ literary culture
al-aḫlāq ☞ character – study of character
al-fiqh ☞ jurisprudence
al-iksīr ☞ alchemy
ilāhī ☞ theology, ☞ metaphysics
insānī ☞ science(s) – of humankind
al-kalām ☞ theology, ☞ *kalām*
al-lisān ☞ linguistics, ☞ grammar
mā baʿd al-ṭabīʿiyyāt ☞ metaphysics
madanī ☞ science(s) – of the community
al-manṭiq ☞ logic
al-mawāzīn ☞ alchemy
al-nuǧūm ☞ astrology
al-rubūbiyya ☞ knowledge – of Lordship
ṭabīʿī ☞ physics
al-taʿālīm ☞ mathematics
ṯānī ☞ knowledge – second knowledge
al-ta'rīḫāt ☞ historiography
yaqīn ☞ knowledge – certain
iltiḏāḏ ☞ joy
imām ☞ Imam(s), ☞ leader of the religious community
ʿimāra ☞ well-being
imtidād ☞ extension
imtiḥān ☞ examination
ʿinād ☞ contradiction
inbaʿaṯa, inbiʿāṯ ☞ emanation

inbiğās ☞ emanation
inʿikās ☞ reflection
inkisār ☞ refraction (of visual rays)
inšāʾ ☞ prose, artistic
insān kāmil, insān tāmm ☞ human(s) – perfect
insāniyya ☞ humanity
inṭibāʿ ☞ impression (through a form)
īqāʿ ☞ rhythm
iqnāʿ ☞ persuasion
al-iqrār bi-rubūbiyyatihi ☞ God – confirmation of His rule
iʿrāb ☞ inflection
irāda ☞ will
išārāt ☞ pointers
iṣlāḥ ☞ revision
  al-aḫlāq ☞ character – its improvement
ism, asmāʾ ☞ name(s), ☞ noun(s)
  muštarak ☞ homonym
ʿišq ☞ love, ☞ passion(s)
al-istidlāl bi-l-šāhid ʿalā l-ġāʾib ☞ inference(s)
istiḫrāğ ☞ adaptation (terminology, titles of scholarly texts)
iṣṭilāḥ ☞ convention
istiqrāʾ ☞ induction
al-ištirāk fī l-istinbāṭ ☞ inference – dialectical
istiṣlāḥ ☞ well-being – of the community
iʿtidāl ☞ balance
  al-mizāğ (εὐκρασία) ☞ state – temperate, balanced
iʿtiqād ☞ convincing, conviction(s)
ittiḥād ☞ union, unification
ittiṣāl ☞ union, unification
ʿiyār al-ʿaql ('touchstone of intellect') ☞ logic
ʿiẓam al-himma ☞ high-mindedness

kaḏib ☞ falsehood
kāḏib ☞ untrue, ☞ assent – false
kahāna ☞ divination
kayfa ☞ how
kayfiyya ☞ quality, qualities
kalām ☞ theology – Islamic, ☞ *kalām*, ☞ physics – of *kalām*
kalima ☞ word(s), ☞ logos, ☞ creative word of God
kam, kammiyya ☞ quantity
kamāl ☞ perfection, ☞ entelechy
  awwal ☞ perfection – first
  ṯānī ☞ perfection – second (of the human soul)
kāmil ☞ perfect, complete
karūbiyya ☞ cherub(s)
kaṯīf ☞ crude
kawwana ☞ creation, ☞ bringing about
kibr ☞ arrogance
kudūra ☞ state – unhappy
kullī ☞ universal
kulliyyāt ☞ universals
kursī ☞ footstool, God's

laḏḏa ☞ pleasure
  ḥāḍira ☞ pleasure – immediate, present
lafẓ, alfāẓ (αἱ φωναί) ☞ utterance(s), linguistic expression(s), term(s), ☞ phonemes
  alfāẓ dālla ☞ utterance(s) – which indicate something
  al-alfāẓ al-dālla ʿalā l-maʿānī (φωναὶ σημαντικαί) ☞ utterance(s) – symbolic
lāḥiq ☞ consequence
lahu ☞ having
laṭīf ☞ subtle, ☞ world – spiritual, ☞ substance – spiritual, subtle
lawḥ ☞ tablet
lawāḥiq ☞ concomitants
lawāzim ☞ implications
luṭf ☞ grace, divine
luṯġa ☞ speech defect(s)

mā ☞ what
mā baʿd al-ṭabīʿiyyāt ☞ metaphysics
maʿād ☞ return – of the rational soul
mabdaʾ, mabādiʾ ☞ principle(s)
  awwal ☞ principle(s) – First
maḏāhib ☞ belief(s), opinion(s), view(s) – religious
mādda ☞ matter
madīḥ ☞ tragedy
madīna ☞ city, ☞ community
  ḍālla ☞ community – erring
  fāḍila ☞ city – excellent
  fāḍila rūḥāniyya ☞ state – ideal, spiritual
  fāsiqa ☞ community – immoral
  ğāhiliyya ☞ community – ignorant
madīnat al-ğamāʿiyya ☞ democracy
  al-karāma ☞ timocracy
  al-naḏala ☞ oligarchy
  al-taġallub ☞ tyranny
maʿdūl ☞ metathetical
mafʿūl ☞ result, ☞ product, ☞ substrate(s) – receptive

maḥabba ☞ love
muʿtadila ☞ love – well-balanced
maḥsūsāt ☞ sensation, sense perception(s)
mayl (ῥοπή) ☞ impetus, ☞ inclination
makān ☞ place, ☞ space
malak ☞ angel(s)
malaka ☞ habit
maʿmūra ☞ community – global
maʿnā, maʿānī (τὸ [σημανόμενον] πρᾶγμα) ☞ meaning(s), ☞ essence
al-maʿānī al-maʿqūla ☞ intelligibles
l-ubuwwa ☞ paternity (Trinity)
manāzil ☞ stations (of the moon)
manāẓir ☞ optics
manqūl ☞ transposed
manṭiq ☞ logic
maqāyīs fiqhiyya ☞ inferences, legal
maqbūlāt ☞ statement(s), declarative – adopted from trustworthy people
maqṣūd, maqāṣid ☞ goal(s), aim(s)
aʿẓam ☞ goal(s), aim(s) – highest, of logic
maqūl, maqūla, maqūlāt (κατηγορία) ☞ statement(s), declarative, ☞ utterance(s), – categorial, ☞ category, categories
maʿqūl ☞ thought – content(s) of thought, ☞ intelligible (νοούμενον)
ṯānī ☞ intelligible – second
maʿqūlāt ☞ intelligibles
bi-l-fiʿl ☞ thought – objects of thought, actual
uwal ☞ intelligibles – first, primary
maʿrifa ☞ knowledge
martaba ☞ class(es)
mašhūr(āt) ☞ opinions, commonly accepted, ☞ statement(s), declarative – universally recognized, commonly accepted, ☞ premise(s) – commonly accepted
mašīʾa ☞ will
maṣlaḥa ☞ well-being – of the community
al-maʿšūq al-awwal ☞ beloved, the first
matā ☞ when
maṭbūʿ ☞ nature – thing of
maṭlūbāt ☞ aims of argumentation
mawḍūʿ (τὸ ὑποκείμενον) ☞ subject
awwal ☞ subject – primary subject matter (of metaphysics)
mawǧūd ☞ being(s)
mawǧūdāt ☞ entity, entities
mawhūmāt ☞ imagination(s)
mawt irādī (θάνατος προαιρετικός) ☞ death – voluntary
mawadda ☞ affection
milla, milal ☞ religion(s)
miṯāl(āt) ☞ analogy, analogies, ☞ idea(s), ☞ proof, demonstration – Euclidean method
mizāǧ, amziǧa (κρᾶσις, κράσεις) ☞ mixture, ☞ temperament(s)
muʿtadil (εὐκρασία) ☞ mixture – balanced
mīzān al-diyāna ☞ balance of religion
muʿāmalāt ☞ social interaction in the community
muʿānāt ☞ effort, exertion
muʾaṯṯar ☞ result
muʾaṯṯir ☞ cause(s)
muʿāwana ☞ social interaction in the community
mubdaʿ ☞ creation
awwal ☞ created – first, ☞ intellect – as the first created being
mubdiʿ ☞ Creator
muḍāf ☞ relative
mudda ☞ duration
muġayyar ☞ altered
muǧarrad(a) ☞ separate
muǧassamāt ☞ polyhedra
al-muǧāzāt ʿalā l-madḥ ☞ paying for praise
muḥākāt ☞ imitation, ☞ mimesis
muḫāṭaba burhāniyya ☞ disputation
muḥdaṯ ☞ created, ☞ contingency, contingent
muḥiss ☞ sense perception, sense(s) – possessing sensation
mukawwan ☞ coming-to-be, generation – generated
mulk ☞ rule
multamas al-nafs ☞ soul – its aim
mumkin ☞ possibility
ʿalā l-akṯar ☞ possibility – possible for the most part
munāsaba ☞ analogy
al-munbaʿaṯ al-awwal ☞ emanated being, the first
muqayyad ☞ statement(s), declarative – qualified
mušaǧǧar ☞ tree-diagram
musālama ☞ cooperation, harmonious
mušār ilayhi ☞ object(s)
musāwāt ☞ equality, ☞ equality – of measure
mustaʿār ☞ metaphorical
muštaqq ☞ derivative

al-muštaqqa asmāʾuhā (παρώνυμα) ☞ paronym(s)
muštarak ☞ equivocal, ☞ ambiguous
mutabāyin ☞ distinct
mutakallimūn ☞ theologians
mutalāzimāt ☞ concomitants
mutaqābilāt ☞ contrary, contraries
mutarādif ☞ synonym(s)
mutawāṭiʾ ☞ univocal
al-mutawāṭiʾa asmāʾuhā (συνώνυμα) ☞ synonym(s)
muṭlaq ☞ absolute, ☞ statement(s), declarative – not specified
al-muttafiqa asmāʾuhā (ὁμώνυμα) ☞ homonym(s)
muttaṣil (συνεχές) ☞ being – continuous

nabiyy ☞ prophet(s)
  mursal ☞ prophet(s) – entrusted with a message
nāfiʿ ☞ useful
nafs ☞ soul
  ʿāqila, nāṭiqa ☞ rational soul
  ġaḍabiyya ☞ soul, part(s) of – irascible, spirited
  šahwāniyya ☞ soul, part(s) of – appetitive
naġam ☞ note(s)
naḥw ☞ grammar
naʿīm ☞ happiness
nāmūs (νόμος) ☞ law(s)
naql ☞ tradition, ☞ translation(s) – practice of
  qadīm ☞ translation(s) – 'ancient'
naqla ☞ transposition
naṯr ☞ prose
naẓar ☞ knowledge – theoretical, ☞ reflection, ☞ proof(s), demonstration(s) – Euclidean method, ☞ scenery, stage setting (ὄψις)
naẓm ☞ poetry
nihāyat al-kamāl al-insānī ☞ perfection – ultimate human
nisba ☞ relation(s), ☞ proportion(s)
nizāʿ ☞ inclination
nubuwwa ☞ prophethood, prophecy
nuqṭa ☞ point
nuṣra ☞ enforcement (of religious opinions, through the theologians)
nuṭq ☞ discourse, logical
  dāḫil ☞ language – inner
  ṭabīʿī ʿāmm ☞ language – common, natural

qabla ☞ priority
qaḍāyā ☞ judgement
qaddara ☞ predestination, divine
qadīm ☞ uncreated
qāʾim bi-ḏātihi (αὐθυπόστατος) ☞ soul – subsisting in itself, ☞ substance – subsisting through itself
qālab ☞ form
qanāʿa ☞ moderation
qasāwa ☞ mercilessness
qāṭīġūriyās ☞ category, categories
qawl (λόγος) ☞ logos, ☞ sentence(s), ☞ utterance(s), linguistic expression(s)
  šiʿrī ☞ statement(s), declarative – poetic
qawānīn kulliyya ☞ rules, general
qisma ☞ diaeresis
qiyās fiqhī ☞ inference – analogical
qiyās al-šāhid ʿalā l-ġāʾib ☞ inference(s) – from the visible to the invisible
qudra (δύναμις) ☞ power(s), ☞ faculty, faculties
qunūm al-ab ☞ hypostasis – of the Father (Trinity)
qunya ☞ acquisition – of the good
quwwa ☞ power(s), ☞ faculty, faculties
  ʿallāma ☞ faculty, faculties – theoretical
  ʿammāla ☞ faculty, faculties – practical
  bāṣira ☞ vision – visual power
  dāfiʿa ☞ faculty, faculties – expelling
  fikriyya ☞ thought, thinking – faculty of thought
  ġaḍabiyya (θυμοειδές) ☞ soul, part(s) of – irascible
  ǧāḏiba ☞ faculty, faculties – attractive
  ġāḏiya ☞ faculty, faculties – nutritive
  ḥāssa ☞ faculty, faculties – perceptive
  māsika, hāḍima ☞ faculty, faculties – retaining, digesting
  muġayyira, ṯāniya ☞ faculty, faculties – transforming, the second
  mutaḫayyila ☞ faculty, faculties – imaginative

nāṭiqa (λογιστικόν) ☞ rational faculty, ☞ faculty, faculties – rational, ☞ soul, part(s) of – rational
naẓariyya ☞ rational faculty
nuṭqiyya ☞ faculty, faculties – of articulation
nuzūʿiyya ☞ faculty, faculties – appetitive
šahw(ān)iyya (ἐπιθυμητικόν) ☞ faculty, faculties – appetitive, ☞ soul, part(s) of – appetitive

raʿāyā ☞ subjects, political
raḏāʾil ☞ vice
radd ☞ refutation
rāǧiʿ ilā ḏātihī (πρὸς ἑαυτὸ ἐπιστρεπτικόν) ☞ return – to oneself
rāḥa ☞ tranquillity
raḥma ☞ mercy, ☞ grace, divine
raʾs ☞ soul – upward orientation ('head')
rasm, rusūm ☞ description(s)
rawābiṭ ☞ conjunctions
rawiyya ☞ deliberation, ☞ reflection
raʾy, ārāʾ (δόξα) ☞ belief(s), opinion(s), view(s), ☞ judgement – personal
riʾāsa ☞ leadership, political
rubūbiyya ☞ rule – of God
rūḥ, arwāḥ ☞ spirit, ☞ spiritual beings, ☞ pneuma
bāṣir ☞ spirit – visual
rūḥāniyya, rūḥāniyyāt ☞ entity, entities – spiritual, ☞ substance(s) – spiritual, ☞ spiritual beings
rumūz ☞ allegories
rusul ☞ messenger(s)
ruʾūs ☞ headings
ruʾya ☞ beatific vision
al-ruʾyā al-ṣādiqa ☞ dream – veridical

saʿāda ☞ happiness
ʿāmma ☞ happiness – general
ḫāṣṣa ☞ happiness – specific
quṣwā ☞ happiness – highest, supreme
saʿādāt ☞ happiness – states of
sabab (αἴτιον) ☞ cause(s)
ʿadawī (ὀργανικόν) ☞ cause(s) – instrumental
awwal ☞ cause(s) – First
fāʿil (ποιητικόν) ☞ cause(s) – efficient
kamālī (τελικόν) ☞ cause(s) – final
miṯālī (παραδειγματικόν) ☞ cause(s) – paradigmatic
ṣūrī (εἰδικόν) ☞ cause(s) – formal
ʿunṣurī (ὑλικόν) ☞ cause(s) – material
ṣadāqa ☞ friendship
ṣafāʾ ☞ purity, ☞ sincerity, ☞ integrity
safah ☞ irascibility
šaǧāʿa (ἀνδρεία) ☞ courage
saḫāʾ ☞ generosity
šaḫṣ, ašḫāṣ (ἄτομον) ☞ individual(s)
fāḍil ☞ person(s) – excellent
šahwa ☞ passion(s), desire
šayʾ ☞ thing(s), object(s)
al-ašyāʾ al-ʿāmmiyya ☞ common things
ṣāʿiqa ☞ lightning bolt
sakīna ☞ rest – in God
salb ☞ negation
šarah ☞ greed
šarīʿa, šarāʾiʿ ☞ law(s), ☞ Sharia
ʿarabiyya ☞ law(s) – Arabic
ṣawāb ☞ correct
ṣifāt ☞ attribute(s)
al-ḏāt ☞ attribute(s) – essential
al-fiʿl ☞ attribute(s) – functional
ṣiġar al-himma ☞ faint-heartedness
ṣināʿa (τέχνη) ☞ art, arts
ḫuluqiyya ☞ ethics
fāʿila ☞ art, arts – practical, ☞ medicine
ṣināʿat al-aḫlāq ☞ character – art of building character
al-mūsīqī ☞ musical theory
siyāsa ☞ governance, ☞ leadership, political
šubha (ἀπάτη) ☞ sophism, sophismata, ☞ argument(s) – specious
sukūn al-nafs ☞ soul, rest of
sunna ☞ Sunna, ☞ custom, ☞ law(s)
ʿaqliyya ☞ law(s)– of reason
ṭabīʿiyya ☞ law(s) – natural
waḍʿiyya ☞ law(s) – positive
sunnat al-ʿadl ☞ law(s) – of justice
al-tafaḍḍul ☞ law(s) – of eminence
ṣūra, ṣuwar ☞ form(s), ☞ imagination(s)

taʾaḥḥud ☞ union, unification
taʿālīm ☞ mathematics, ☞ mathematical disciplines, ☞ chapters (πράξεις)
taʿālīq ☞ scholia, ☞ annotations
taʾannus ☞ incarnation (of God's word)
taʿaqqul ☞ prudence
ṭabʿ, ṭabīʿa, ṭabāʾiʿ ☞ nature
  al-ṭabīʿa al-faʿʿāla ☞ nature – as an immanent, creative force
al-ṭabīʿiyyūn ☞ naturalists
tabkīt ☞ objection
tabyīn ☞ exposition, explanation
taḍādd (ἐναντίον) ☞ contrary, contraries
tadarrub ☞ practice
tadbīr al-manzil ☞ economics
taʾdīb ☞ education
tafsīr kabīr ☞ commentaries – large
taǧawhur ☞ substantialization
taǧriba ☞ experience, observation
taǧsīm ☞ corporealization (of God)
taḫayyul (φαντασία) ☞ imagination
tahḏīb al-aḫlāq ☞ rational soul – its purification, ☞ character – its refinement
taḫlīṣ ☞ liberation from the body
taḥrīk ☞ ornamentation, musical
taḫyīl ☞ imagination(s) – imaginative evocation
takwīn ☞ bringing about
  ṭabīʿī ☞ coming-to-be, generation – natural
talḫīṣ ☞ precise exposition
taʾlīf ☞ composing (of texts), ☞ combination (of utterances) (συμπλοκή)
  al-alḥān ☞ composition, musical
taʿlīm ☞ instruction
tamām (συμπέρασμα) ☞ proof(s), demonstration(s) – Euclidean method
tamṯīl ☞ paradigm, ☞ analogy, ☞ representation
tamyīz ☞ discernment
  bi-l-ḏihn ☞ discernment – rational
tanāsuḫ ☞ transmigration
taqiyya ☞ secrecy (of religious creed)
taqlīd ☞ tradition – blind following of
taqwīm ☞ disposition, orientation, right direction
tarġīb ☞ incentives
tarhīb ☞ deterrents
tarkīb ☞ composition, ☞ classification
ṭarīqa ☞ system
tasāwin ☞ equality
taṣawwuf ☞ Sufism
taṣawwur ☞ term(s), concept(s), ☞ *formatio*, ☞ representation – divine, ☞ imagination
tašbīh ☞ anthropomorphism
  wa-muḥākāt ☞ mimesis, ☞ imitation
taṣdīq ☞ judgement, ☞ assent, ☞ certainty, ☞ *credulitas*, ☞ *assertio seu creditio*
  kāḏib ☞ assent – false
tašǧīr ☞ tree-diagram
taṭabbuʿ ☞ impression (through a form)
taʾṯīr ☞ influence
tatlīṯ ☞ Trinity, Christian
ṭawʿ wa-ḫtiyār ☞ decision, free
tawḥīd ☞ oneness – profession of God's
tawqīf ☞ law(s) – institution by the Creator
tawāḍuʿ ☞ humility
tawahhum (φαντασία) ☞ imagination(s)
tawallada ☞ engendering
taʾwīl ☞ interpretation(s), interpreting
tawassuṭ ☞ mean
taʾyīd ☞ support
ṭibb ☞ medicine
tuʾada ☞ thoughtfulness
ṭūl ☞ length

ʿūd ☞ lute, oud
al-ʿuḍw al-raʾīs ☞ ruling organ
ufuq ☞ ideal – ethical
ʿulūm ☞ science(s), ☞ knowledge
  al-ʿaǧam ☞ science(s) – foreign
  ʿaqliyya ☞ science(s) – rational
  ḥaqīqiyya ☞ science(s) – true
  ḥissiyya ☞ knowledge – based on sense perception
  muḥaṣṣala ☞ knowledge – exact, definite
  qadīma ☞ science(s) – ancient
  al-taʿālīm ☞ mathematical disciplines – *artes doctrinales*
  al-ṭabīʿa ☞ science(s) – natural
  wahmiyya ☞ science(s) – imaginary
umma ☞ nation(s), ☞ community
ummahāt ☞ element(s)
uns ☞ companionship
ʿunṣur, ʿanāṣir ☞ element(s), ☞ matter
uqnūm, aqānīm (πρόσωπον, πρόσωπα) ☞ person(s), ☞ hypostasis

uqnūmiyya ☞ hypostatization
uskūl ☞ school(s)
uṣūl ☞ principle(s)
al-dīn ☞ principle(s) – of religion
al-fiqh ☞ principle(s) – of jurisprudence
al-naḥw ☞ hermeneutics – of grammar
usṭuquss(āt) ☞ element(s)

waḍʿ ☞ position, ☞ positing
wāḍiʿ al-milla ☞ religion, founder of
lisān ☞ language – 'giver of language'
wafāʾ ☞ faithfulness
wāǧib ☞ necessary, necessity
al-wuǧūd ☞ God – as necessary of existence, ☞ being(s) – necessary of existence
waḥda ☞ oneness
al-wāḥid ☞ the One
wahm, awhām ☞ supposition, ☞ imagination(s), ☞ phantasms
wasāwis al-ṣadr wa-aḥādīṯ al-nafs ☞ obsessive thoughts
wāṣilāt ☞ connectives, articles
wāsiṭāt ☞ prepositions

wazn ☞ metre (musical)
wilād ☞ incarnation
wudd ☞ friendship
wuǧūd ☞ being, ☞ existence
ḏātī ☞ existence – essential
ilāhī ☞ existence – divine
manṭiqī ☞ existence – logical
muṭlaq ☞ being –absolute
ṭabīʿī ☞ existence – natural

yafʿal ☞ influence
yanfaʿil ☞ affection
yaqīn ☞ certainty
ʿalā l-iṭlāq ☞ certainty – absolute

ẓāhir ☞ meaning(s), usage – external
zamān ☞ time
muṭlaq ☞ time – absolute
maḥṣūr ☞ time – limited
ẓann ☞ belief(s), opinion(s), view(s), ☞ opinion, ☞ speculation, ☞ supposition
zuhd ☞ renunciation of the world, ☞ asceticism
ẓulm (ἀδικία) ☞ tyranny

Index of Subjects

Abbasid 98–104, 107, 113, 116–117, 120, 152, 181, 236, 249, 276, 279, 331, 424–425, 431, 538, 660, 665, 672–673, 683–684, 693, 707, 709–710, 720, 737, 738, 746, 758
abridgment (*iḫtiṣār*) (terminology, title of scholarly works) 713, 720
absolute (*muṭlaq*) 410, 411, 556, 561
accident(s) 164, 169–170, 268, 313, 319, 323–324, 333–334, 349–350, 444–447, 452, 455, 459–460, 479, 485–486, 488–490, 549, 552–555, 559–561, 567–568, 572, 574, 582, 589, 606, 678–679, 726
  and substance 490
  ʿaraḍ, aʿrāḍ 485, 490, 548
  essential 488
  essentially concomitant 479
  their contingency 490
acquisition
  of deeds by human beings (*iktisāb*) 455, 466
  of the good (*qunya*) 634
act, action 258, 267, 296, 310, 323, 347, 398, 466, 547, 550, 563, 568, 589, 613–614, 624, 635, 703
  ʿamal 160, 177
  creative act 163
  fiʿl, afʿāl 160, 304, 411, 455, 465, 547, 576, 742
  good (*al-afʿāl al-ǧamīla*) 634
  human 235, 325, 331, 344, 465, 466
  just, ethical, good 342, 403, 404, 406, 408–409
  of sun and moon 757
  rational 310
  relation between knowledge and action 263, 267
actuality 168, 198, 302, 311, 315–317, 574, 612, 725, 748
acumen (*ḏakāʾ*) 575
adaptation (*istiḫrāǧ*) (terminology, titles of scholarly texts) 716, 718
aequilitterae 85
aether 730
affection (cf. also ☞ passion) 589
  arising (*ḥawādiṯ*) 336
  being acted upon 447
  mawadda 342
  yanfaʿil 555
affirmation 320, 403, 461, 466, 556
agent (cf. also ☞ efficient cause) 244, 258, 318, 730
  fāʿil 196, 244, 304, 465–466, 742
agriculture 484, 552, 686, 728
aims of argumentation (*maṭlūbāt*) 560
air 173–174, 183–187, 199, 258, 316, 320, 339, 486, 570, 729, 732
  as mover 496
alchemy 42, 99, 290, 328, 387, 571, 728, 732
  according to al-Fārābī 571
  classification of the sciences 728
  ʿilm al-iksīr 387
  ʿilm al-mawāzīn 328
algebra 279
Allāh ☞ God
allegories (*rumūz*) 14, 161–162, 554, 722
Almagest 50, 114, 118–119, 155, 162, 176, 277, 565–567, 610, 709
altered (*muġayyar*) 561
ambiguous (*muštarak*) 561
analogy, analogies 177, 327–328, 475, 581, 583, 624, 703
  amṯāl 320, 337
  ἀναλογία, τὸ ἀνάλογον 327, 338
  between body and soul 575
  between cosmos/God and excellent community/ruler 576
  between physician and statesman 575
  miṯālāt 626
  munāsaba 626
  tamṯīl 557, 562, 564
analysis, Euclidian 426
anamnesis ☞ recollection, memory
anatomy 339
Andalus (cf. also ☞ Spain) 634
anecdotes, historical (*aḫbār*) 280–281
angel(s) 269, 271, 285, 287, 316, 324, 475, 589
  malak 344
anger ☞ wrath

animal(s) 229, 289, 317, 321–322, 324, 339, 397, 399, 402, 455, 565, 568, 579, 581, 584, 742, 744, 752, 757–758
annotations (*taʿālīq*) 430
anthropology 286, 327, 338, 592
 ethical 338
 Galen's 331
 Platonic, according to al-Tawḥīdī and Abū Sulaymān al-Siǧistānī 299–300
anthropomorphism (*tašbīh*) 476
antinomism 742
aphorism(s) (cf. also ☞ saying) 55, 59, 179, 248, 262, 285, 662–663, 665, 668–669, 673–674, 685
apple 661, 675–679
apodeictics, philosophical demonstration (cf. also ☞ proof[s]) 295, 434, 445, 458–459, 478, 549, 558–564, 588, 599, 604–605, 607, 724
apologetics 110, 117, 390, 439, 458, 460–461, 463–464, 487
 Christian, in Ibn ʿAdī 439, 461
 Christian, in Ibn al-Ḫammār 487
 Christian, in Ibn Zurʿa 474
aporia(s) 465, 501, 605, 678
Arabic, Arabic language 5, 10, 15, 17, 60–64, 104–108, 114–118, 121, 191, 249, 283–284, 289, 296, 330, 412, 561, 602, 660–662, 665, 670, 675–676, 679, 680, 683–685, 694, 707, 718
Aramean, Aramaic 77, 98, 104, 109, 152, 156
argument(s) 78, 117, 162–163, 170, 195, 197, 125, 334, 449, 453–454, 464, 466, 477, 485, 490, 502, 547, 571–572, 608, 700–703, 714, 724–726
 dubitable (*šubah*) 21
 geometrical 171
 of the third man 726
 specious (*šubha*) 454
argument for God's existence 85, 196, 255, 333, 591–3
 cosmological 80, 475
 e contingentia mundi 19
 knowledge of 255, 284, 313, 327, 333, 488
 teleological 86
argumentum ex gradibus 85
Aristotle, Arabic 679
Aristotelian corpus 30, 37, 41, 46–47, 56, 58, 63, 192, 249, 385, 429, 431, 625, 632, 677
Aristotelianism (cf. also ☞ Peripatetic[s]) 30, 103, 110, 120, 196, 282, 339, 424, 465, 489, 595, 620, 632
arithmetic 17, 20, 34, 42–43, 118–120, 153, 156, 177–178, 180, 183–184, 201, 231, 248, 277, 284, 295, 547, 574, 599, 618, 721, 728
 decadic 153
 in al-Kindī 174
 in the classification of *Rasāʾil Iḫwān al-Ṣafāʾ* 754
 in the classification of sciences 728
arithmology, number theory 156, 170, 178
 Neo-Pythagorean 156, 188, 756
 Pythagorean 188, 426
Armenian 42, 113, 759
arrangement (τάξις) 443
arrogance (*kibr*) 467
ars vitae 48
art, arts 160, 186, 310, 331, 348, 350, 597
 practical (*ṣināʿa fāʿila*) 572, 613
 ṣināʿa 244, 284, 444, 494
 τέχνη 444
Ašʿariyya 753
ascendant 187
asceticism 166, 194, 239, 278, 299, 311, 397–398, 401–404, 467–468, 484, 662, 758
 zuhd 311, 467
aspect(s)
 ǧihāt 479, 556
 of the planets 182–183
assent (*taṣdīq*) 605
 false (*taṣdīq kāḏib*) 605
assertio seu creditio (*taṣdīq*) 605
astrologer(s) 88, 102, 154, 183, 265, 329, 426, 611
astrology, astrological 41, 43, 50, 53, 100–101, 118, 155, 174, 180–182, 187–188, 200, 202, 229, 326, 264, 269, 281, 287, 426, 442, 547, 567–568, 610–611, 673, 691, 712, 728, 731–733, 746, 757–758
 aḥkām al-nuǧūm 287
 ʿilm al-nuǧūm 567
 in Abū Zayd al-Balḫī 240
 in Aḥmad b. al-Ṭayyib al-Saraḫsī 227–228
 in the classification of sciences 728

astrometeorology 182–184
astronomer 87, 153, 156, 347, 425, 482, 568, 755
astronomy 17, 20, 40, 42–43, 49–51, 53, 59, 78–79, 118, 173, 175, 181–182, 184, 236, 248, 284, 295, 424, 442, 476, 547, 567–568, 610–611, 616, 672, 691, 708, 710–712, 728, 738, 740, 754–756, 758
  in al-Saraḫsī 227–228
  in al-Kindī 176–177
  in the classification of sciences 728
  in the classification of *Rasāʾil Iḫwān al-Ṣafāʾ* 754
  in the curriculum 712
  Ptolemaic 756
atomism 117, 202, 410, 448–449, 451, 594, 612
attribute(s) 195, 261, 294, 446, 457, 461–462, 464, 476–478, 483, 490, 495, 625, 725
  accidental 726
  divine 403–404, 453, 458, 461–465, 475, 477–479, 578, 593, 616, 745
  essential (*ṣifāt al-ḏāt*) 475, 479
  essential, as a part of substance 490
  functional (*ṣifāt al-fiʿl*) 475, 479
  of the soul 474
authenticity (τὸ γνήσιον) 443
autobiography
  of Ḥunayn b. Isḥāq 684, 686
  of Ibn Sīnā 257, 542
  of al-Rāzī 390
avarice 400
  buḫl 467
Averroism 1
Avesta 98
axiom(s) 170, 190, 606

backgammon 245
bad, the bad, evil 19, 85, 255–256, 269, 347, 350, 455, 575
balance (*iʿtidāl*) 243, 337
  of the temperaments 327
balance between body and soul 405
balance of religion (*mīzān al-diyāna*) 740
Bardesanites 117
beatific vision 166, 324
  ruʾya 628
beginning (*badʾ*) 244
being(s) 302–303, 314, 451, 463, 494–495, 547, 574–575, 578, 581, 603
  divine 464
  eternal and unique 85
  first 302–303, 747
  its hierarchy 459
  mawǧūd 302, 548
  necessary of existence (*wāǧib al-wuǧūd*) 271, 313, 333, 588, 594
  τὰ ὄντα 483
  true 32, 321
being (cf. also ☞ existence) 14, 294, 303, 313, 333, 409, 453, 455, 460, 463, 466, 495, 574–575, 581, 603, 615, 618, 633, 742, 745
  absolute (*al-wuǧūd al-muṭlaq*) 618
  as part of the second hypostasis, in Proclus 463
  bringing into being (*īǧād*) 465
  classes of 451, 459
  continuous (*muttaṣil*, συνεχές) 453
  'in a subject' 679
  indivisible (*ġayr munqasim*, ἀδιαίρετον) 453
  its hierarchy 576
  levels of 757
  that subsists in itself (οὐσία ἀυθυπόστατος) 335
belief(s), opinion(s), view(s) (*raʾy*, *ārāʾ*, δόξα) 158, 160, 547, 561, 576, 585, 622
  at first sight, accepted by the general public 614
  personal 102, 234
  raʾy 160, 234
  religious (*maḏāhib*) 229
  ẓann 319, 559–561
beloved, the first (*al-maʿšūq al-awwal*) 578
benefit 325, 342, 389, 397, 402, 546, 554–555, 560, 562, 567, 575, 576
  as a heading (*kephalaia*) in Alexandrian commentary tradition 426, 473, 483
  χρῆσις 443
  physiognomy 673
benevolence, benevolent 457, 463
  ἀγαθότης 463
  faḍl 327
  God's 465, 475, 480
  ǧūd 463, 475
Bible 80, 671

biography
  of Abū Bakr al-Rāzī 386–389
  of Abū Sulaymān al-Siǧistānī 291–292
  of Abū Zayd al-Balḫī 236–238
  of al-ʿĀmirī 256–257
  of al-Fārābī 536–545
  of Ḥunayn b. Isḥāq 683–685
  of Ibn ʿAdī 440–442
  of Ibn al-Ḫammār 482
  of Ibn Hindū 346–347
  of Ibn al-Samḥ 491–492
  of Ibn al-Ṭayyib 499
  of Ibn Zurʿa 470–471
  of al-Kindī 152–155
  of Miskawayh 308–309
  of al-Saraḫsī 224–225
  of Ṯābit b. Qurra 705–710
  of al-Tawḥīdī 276–283
biology 263, 612, 686
  in the classification of *Rasāʾil Iḫwān al-Ṣafāʾ* 754
body 34, 166–167, 170, 172–173, 187, 190, 192, 194, 197–198, 242–243, 254, 259, 268–269, 285, 294, 300, 303, 317–318, 323, 325, 327, 329, 333–336, 399–400, 404–405, 409–411, 446, 448, 485, 495–496, 547, 555, 570, 575–576, 578–580, 584, 589, 594, 616, 630, 690, 742, 745, 758
  absolute 757
  as three-dimensional substance 485
  celestial/heavenly 164, 171, 182, 184, 186, 194, 199, 240, 259–260, 268, 270, 292, 303, 322, 327, 339, 485, 568, 570, 578–579, 581, 584, 594, 616–617, 621, 742
  consisting of matter and form 612
  earthly 568, 730
  finite, cannot have infinite power 489
  human 594
  intact and healthy (*al-badan al-tāmm al-ṣaḥīḥ*) 624
  its happiness 310
  its relation to the soul 83–84, 197–199, 260, 269–270, 311–314, 320–321, 330, 335, 339–341, 349–350, 402–403, 581, 676, 679
  natural 572
  of the cosmos 195
  outermost 153
  perceptible, three-dimensional 610
  Platonic solids 178, 202
Bohras 741
botany
  in Ibn al-Ṭayyib 503
  in the classification of *Rasāʾil Iḫwān al-Ṣafāʾ* 754
brain 323, 336, 339, 572, 579, 612
bringing about (*kawwana, takwīn*) 745
Buddhism 245
Buyid(s) 256, 265, 276, 279–280, 282, 293, 297, 308, 330, 346, 349, 471, 499, 700
Byzantium, Byzantine(s) 54, 59, 61, 99, 100–102, 106, 108, 110, 114, 116, 178, 181, 280, 471, 664, 667, 672–673, 683–684, 707

caliphate 117, 181, 753
capacity, capacities
  for ethical disposition (*ḫulq*) 550
  of intellect, human (*ḫiṣāl*) 315
cardinal virtues 178, 243, 266, 268, 323, 338, 356
Catalan 759
category, categories 31, 34, 83, 111, 160, 178, 191, 231, 338, 409, 459, 475, 560, 574, 584, 589, 603, 615, 618
  aǧnās ʿāliya 555
  definition 284
  doctrine of the categories 34, 50, 290, 427, 433, 456, 487
  linked to substance 312
  maqūla, maqūlāt, κατηγορία 163, 483, 548
  qāṭīġūriyās 284
  spatio-temporal 319
  their being ten in number 445
  their nature 726
Catoptrics 176
causality, causation 191, 553
  in Ibn ʿAdī 465
causation, doctrine of 496
cause(s) 163–164, 171, 181–188, 196, 199, 244–245, 258–259, 266, 284, 301–302, 319–320, 426, 478, 485–486, 547, 568, 581–582, 584, 617, 725, 745
  approximate 171, 319
  divine 409, 411, 603

cause(s) (cont.)
efficient (*sabab fāʿil*, ποιητικόν) 465, 489–490
eternal efficient (*ʿilla lam yazal*) 229
final (*sabab kamālī*, τελικόν) 465, 489
First 37, 80–81, 168–169, 195, 254, 292–294, 303–304, 319, 458, 462, 578, 580–582, 591, 619, 622, 624
First (*al-ʿilla al-ūlā*) 159
First (*al-sabab al-awwal*) 615–616
formal (*sabab ṣūrī*, εἰδικόν) 465
ʿilal 244, 486
instrumental (*sabab ʿadawī*, ὀργανικόν) 465
material (*sabab ʿunṣurī*, ὑλικόν) 465
muʾaṯṯir 742
of all things 249, 467
of causes (*ʿillat al-ʿilal*) 747
of natural bodies 572
paradigmatic (*sabab miṯālī*, παραδειγματικόν) 465
sabab, αἴτιον 465
six kinds 465
celestial body 568, 570
as proximate cause of generation and corruption 171, 199–200
made of a fifth element 195, 339
sphere(s) 178, 182–184, 186, 196, 199–200, 245, 263, 266, 268, 270–272, 292–293, 298, 303–304, 313, 316, 322, 332–333, 335, 448–449, 485, 578, 589, 594, 617, 619, 728–729, 738, 742, 747, 757
their motion 690
their nature 690
their substance 33
celestial sphere 268, 270, 448–449, 747
certainty 288, 317–9, 340, 495, 575, 584, 607–608
absolute (*al-yaqīn ʿalā l-iṭlāq*) 559, 606
as perfect *taṣdīq* 606
yaqīn 558, 561–2, 606
Chaldeans 583
chance 731
chapters (πράξεις, *taʿālīm*) 501
chapters, division into (ἡ εἰς κεφάλαια διαίρεσις) 443
character 288, 311, 326, 329, 332, 337, 341, 399, 401, 403, 495, 547, 550, 732
art of building character (*ṣināʿat al-aḫlāq*) 324
dispositions (*al-aḫlāq*) 289, 300, 634
good 467
ḫulq, *ḫuluq*, ἦθος 285, 300, 323, 331, 338, 456, 466–67, 478
its improvement (*iṣlāḥ al-aḫlāq*) 403
its refinement (*tahḏīb al-aḫlāq*) 465, 495
psychological 178
study of character (*ʿilm al-aḫlāq*) 281
chastity (*ʿiffa*) (cf. also ☞ moderation) 467
chemistry 386, 612
cherub(s) (*karūbiyya*) 738
chess 242, 245
choice 598
human 245
iḫtiyār 160, 580
Christian(s), Christianity, Christian faith 15, 17, 21, 33, 41–43, 45–46, 52, 55, 63, 77, 81–82, 98, 101, 104, 111, 112, 118, 121, 260, 277, 294–295, 398, 423–424, 432, 460, 476, 479, 551, 631–632, 662, 671, 702
Christology 50
Church Fathers 50, 85, 98, 463, 475, 478, 676
circle(s) 82, 174, 178
circular motion 254, 570, 579, 757
of heavenly bodies 177, 199, 230, 292, 303, 327
city
as a perfect community 580, 623
excellent (*al-madīna al-fāḍila*) 624
imaginary 747
madīna 623
clarification (γνήσιον, of the κεφάλαιον) 677
class(es)
aṣnāf (of musical metre) 569
martaba 580
classification
of communities, according to al-Fārābī 627
of the sciences ☞ science(s) – its division
tarkīb 606
clime(s) 243, 731, 733
cold 171, 182, 199, 201, 579, 731, 758
colour(s) 172–3, 179, 187, 200–2, 258, 318, 320, 589, 700–1

combination (of utterances) (*ta'līf*, συμπλοκή) 444
comedy 564
  hiǧā' 431
coming-to-be, generation
  and corruption 153, 165, 171, 181–182, 184, 196, 199–200, 229, 253, 268, 327, 342, 411, 449, 486, 503, 570, 579, 584, 586, 612, 615, 690, 728, 730, 733, 754, 757
  and Mars 184
  generated (*mukawwan*) 244
  natural (*takwīn ṭabīʿī*) 485
command (*amr*) (of God) 165, 191, 269, 271, 737, 742–743, 745–746
  as mediating hypostasis 742
commentaries
  Alexandrian 159, 248–249, 443, 458, 473, 477, 488, 725
  large (*al-tafsīr al-kabīr*) 503
  late ancient 63, 506
  lemmas (λέξις) 501
  lemmatized (long) 30, 35–36, 434, 440, 599–600, 604, 611
  Neoplatonic 679
  on Aristotle, by al-ʿĀmirī 258
  on Aristotle, by Ibn al-Samḥ 492–493
  on Aristotle, by Ibn al-Ṭayyib 500–504
  on Greek works, by Abū Bakr al-Rāzī 389
  on Plato's *Laws*, by Ibn al-Ṭayyib 505
common, general (*ʿāmm*) 556, 560, 615
common sense ☞ sense, common
common things (*al-ašyā' al-ʿāmmiyya*) 452, 460
commoners (*ḥašwiyya*, *ʿawāmm*) 708
community (*umma*) 244, 547, 581–584, 598, 619, 622–624, 632–635
  corrupted 580
  erring (*madīna ḍālla*) 581, 627
  excellent 575, 577, 580, 583, 625–628
  global (*maʿmūra*) 580, 623
  ignorant (*madīna ǧāhiliyya*) 575, 580–581, 627
  immoral (*madīna fāsiqa*) 627
  perfect (*kāmil*) 580
companionship (*uns*) 325
compendia (on Aristotle, by Ibn al-Ṭayyib) 500–504
composing (of texts) (*ta'līf*) 746
composite 553, 555, 574
composition
  from matter and form 578
  presupposes a cause 464
  tarkīb 560, 746
composition, musical 179, 569
  ta'līf al-alḥān 565
conclusions 547, 611
concomitants 315
  lawāḥiq 244, 259, 448
  mutalāzimāt 555
conduct (ethical, philosophical) 285, 300, 329, 633, 662
conjunction (of planets) 181–182
conjunctions (*rawābiṭ*) 553
connectives, articles (*wāṣilāt*) 553, 608
consensus (*iǧmāʿ*) 234
consequence (*lāḥiq*) 561
consolation of philosophy 160
consonance, musical 180
content, intelligible (νοητόν) 465
context theory 603
contingency, contingent 86, 465–466, 607
  muḥdaṯ 485
  of creation 489
continuum 574
contradiction (*ʿinād*) 558, 560
contrary, contraries 173, 199
  opposite(s), opposed 327, 330, 555–556, 562, 578–579, 589, 616
  mutaqābilāt 560
  taḍādd, ἐναντίον 447
  aḍdād 560
convention (*iṣṭilāḥ*) 549
convincing, conviction(s) 331, 626
  iʿtiqād 559, 606
cooperation, harmonious (*musālama*) 328
Corpus Hermeticum 126
correct (*ṣawāb*) 600
correctness of speech (*faṣāḥa*) 406
corruption, passing away (cf. also ☞ coming-to-be – and corruption) 489
corporealization (*taǧsīm*) (of God) 245
cosmogony 737
  according to the Iḫwān al-Ṣafā' 757–758
cosmography 78

cosmology, cosmological 49, 55–56, 117, 155, 165, 171–172, 182, 199–200, 293, 327, 423, 542, 671, 731, 737, 743
in Abū Bakr al-Rāzī 389
in Abū Maʿšar al-Balḫī 426
in Abū Sulaymān al-Siǧistānī 301–304
in al-Fārābī 51, 578–579, 582, 616–617, 747
in Ibn al-Ḫammār 489–490
in al-Kindī 170–173, 199–200, 202
in the curriculum 582
Neoplatonic 282, 293–294, 302–304, 332–333, 743
Platonic 300, 331
cosmos (cf. also ☞ world) 165, 171–172, 176, 184, 187, 195, 199, 576, 580, 624, 728
cosmic principle 338
courage 268, 325, 338
as cardinal virtue 268
šaǧāʿa, ἀνδρεία 325
cowardice 323
creatio ex nihilo 410, 463, 679
created
muḥdaṯ 409
first (*al-mubdaʿ al-awwal*) 742
creation 255, 299, 411, 460, 463, 466, 489–490, 743, 745
abdaʿa, ibdāʿ 160, 411, 742, 743, 745, 757
as product of a divine act of will 465
contingency of 489
creative act 411, 743
gap between it and the transcendent God 409
initial (*ibtidāʾ*) 455
kawwana 737
mubdaʿ 742
structure of created world 261
three modes, according to Abū Yaʿqūb al-Siǧistānī 745
creation, doctrine of 408, 489
in Ibn ʿAdī 465–466
creation myth 409–410
creative word of God 743, 745–746
as mediating hypostasis 742
kalima 742
Creator (cf. also ☞ God) 32, 168, 170, 199, 259, 268, 271, 294, 302–303, 313–315, 319, 409, 453, 465, 474–475, 485, 502, 574, 743, 747, 757
absolute unity of 338
as eternal principle, according to Abū Bakr al-Rāzī 392
as one and first cause 462
as topic of metaphysics 618
bāriʾ 451
fāʿil 244
mubdiʿ 320, 742, 747
rulership of 249
credulitas (*taṣdīq*) 562
creed 737, 746, 754
cross, Christian (as a symbol) 96, 746
crude (*kaṯīf*) 321, 744
cryptography 153
cube 172, 202
cultural history 598, 602
in Abū Zayd al-Balḫī 240
in al-Saraḫsī 227
cultural theory 626
curriculum 29, 31, 34, 37, 43, 46, 52–53, 57, 110–114, 116, 249, 278, 348, 350, 473, 540, 550, 552, 554, 555, 556, 582, 599–600, 615, 689
custom (*sunna*) 576
Cynics 62, 662

darkness 85
day of judgement 269
death 85, 160, 194, 197, 199, 265, 269, 288, 317–313, 340, 342, 400, 402, 475, 575, 580, 583–384, 628, 675–678, 703, 754
and life 584, 754
of the will and natural 326
twofold 285
voluntary (θάνατος προαιρετικός, *mawt irādī*) 285, 301, 314, 321, 330, 341
decision, free (*ṭawʿ wa-ḫtiyār*) 550
definition(s) 82–83, 85, 159, 284, 297, 332, 344, 553, 560, 564, 574, 593, 605, 606, 610
as perfect *taṣawwur* 606
ḥadd, ḥudūd 159, 453, 552, 558
in logic 120
musical theory 569
philosophical 56
of living beings 572
deliberation 160, 568
rawiyya 580
deliverance (*ḫalāṣ*) 402

demiurge(s) 738, 747–748, 757
 Platonic 30, 46, 463, 489
democracy (*madīnat al-ǧamāʿiyya*) 628
derivative (*muštaqq*) 556
description(s) 553, 560
 rasm, rusūm 159, 552
desire ☞ passion
determinism, determination 85, 290, 340
 according to Ibn ʿAdī 465–466
 ǧabr 245
deterrents (*tarhīb*) 244
devil 269
diaeresis 558, 560, 564, 586
 qisma 553, 606
dialectics 117, 549, 559–562, 576, 583, 598–599, 714
 in the development of the sciences 549
dialogue(s), Platonic 34, 37–38, 41–43, 46–47, 58, 401, 577, 677, 709
didactics, didactical 473
didactic method (ὁ διδασκαλικὸς τρόπος) 443
dietetics 506
difference (*differentia*) 192, 445, 552, 553, 560
 specific 432, 448, 589, 726
dignitaries (*ḥudūd*) 737
discernment (*tamyīz*) 310, 550
 rational (*bi-l-ḏihn*) 550
discourse, logical (*nuṭq*) 433
disease(s), illness(es) 188, 200, 287, 317, 572, 584, 613, 703, 733
 of ignorance 58
 of the soul 243, 326, 337, 405, 466, 584, 590, 594, 757
disposition, orientation, right direction
 natural (*fiṭra ṭabīʿiyya*) 623, 634
 of the lower faculties towards reason 476
 of the rational soul 467
 taqwīm 467, 476
 twofold, of the Universal Soul 745, 757
disposition(s) 288, 575, 580, 730
 as the topic of *kephalaia* of the Alexandrian Prolegomena 483
 ġarīza 160
 hayʾa 624
 in a body (*hayʾa fī mādda*) 579
 natural 733
disputation (*muḫāṭaba burhāniyya*) 558–559
dissonance, musical 180
distinct (*mutabāyin*) 556
distinctio 569
divination 580
 kahāna 288, 314, 319
divine names 313
division 448, 462
divisiones Aristoteleae 504
doctrine of reproduction 612
dodecahedron 202
dogmatics 20
 Christian, in Ibn Zurʿa 474–478
 Islamic 51, 458
doubts 288, 605
doxography 62, 131, 158, 260, 313, 315, 323, 334, 385, 569, 661, 669, 671–672, 739, 742–743
dream (cf. also ☞ divination) 169, 198, 231–322, 563, 584
 Ibn ʿAdī's, about the soul 452
 Ibn Zurʿa's 474
 of the caliph al-Maʾmūn 102
 prophetic 169, 198, 268, 286, 314, 336
 veridical (*al-ruʾyā al-ṣādiqa*) 230
drugs 189, 201, 572, 613
Druze 746
dryness 182–183, 201, 729, 744
dualism (of body and soul) 479, 676
duration (*mudda*) 410
dynasty, dynasties, their rise and fall 674
Dyophysites 78

earth
 as a part of cosmos 186, 486, 568, 611
 as element 171–172, 183–184, 199, 201–202, 339, 486, 570–571, 729, 732
 its sphericity 177, 690
economics 248, 347, 406, 711, 740
 in the classification of sciences 712
 tadbīr al-manzil 374
education 177, 289, 323–324, 329, 343, 456, 495, 576, 708
 ideal of 278, 284
 moral 177, 179
 paideia 662
 taʾdīb 467, 583
effect(s) 164, 183
 aṯar, āṯār 742, 744

efficient cause (see also ☞ cause[s] – efficient) 171, 254, 259, 490
effluence 745
effort, exertion
exerting oneself (*iǧtahada*) 407
muʿānāt 320
Egypt, Egyptian 4, 33–34, 78, 99, 110, 114, 185, 243, 299, 396, 538, 583, 738
Eleatics 561
element(s) 153, 165, 171–173, 178, 180, 183–184, 186, 195, 199, 201–202, 243, 259, 270, 292, 303, 327, 339, 349, 410, 486, 569–571, 579, 581, 584, 589, 612, 690, 729–732
ʿanāṣir 229
Aristotelian 570
fifth 173, 195, 292, 303, 327, 339, 594, 730
their nature and mixture 185–186, 728, 729, 732, 742, 757
ummahāt (in Abū Ḥātim al-Rāzī) 744
usṭuquss(āt) 160, 569
elemental qualities (*afrād*) 744
elite 245, 289, 467, 549, 755–756
ḫāṣṣa, ḫawāṣṣ 169, 708
emanated being, the first (*al-munbaʿaṯ al-awwal*) 747
emanation 244, 270, 294, 298, 302–303, 314–316, 408, 411, 463, 616–621, 625, 733, 747, 756–757
fayḍ 337, 578, 616, 757
inbiǧās 757
inbaʿaṯa, inbiʿāṯ 744, 745, 747
stepwise 196
emanative triad 333
embryology 339
embryo, the development of 733
empiricism 33
encyclopedic, encyclopedia(s) 155, 249, 295, 426, 673, 752
encyclopedism 118
enforcement (of religious opinions, through the theologians) (*nuṣra*) 547
engendering (*tawallada*) 752
English, English language 3, 6, 15
entelechy 302, 311, 326, 333, 344
first 335
kamāl 310
the perfection of practical reason 495
the perfection of the body (soul) 160, 335, 679
the perfection of the soul 166
enthymeme (*ḍamīr*) 561–562
entity, entities 177, 615–616, 743
mawǧūdāt 601
perfect, eternal 742
spiritual (*rūḥāniyyāt*) 591, 614, 619
envy 399
Epicureanism 30, 47–48, 62, 404, 662
epistemology (cf. also ☞ scientific theory) 19–20, 119, 266, 331–332, 423, 471, 559, 609–610, 619, 702
Abū Bakr al-Rāzī's 406–408
al-ʿĀmirī's 266, 270–272
epistle (*risāla*), as a literary form for scientific discourse 153
epitome (*ǧawāmiʿ*) 692
equality
musāwāt 480
between cause and effect (ἄνθρωπος ἄνθρωπον γεννᾷ) 412
of measure (*musāwāt*) 325, 342
tasāwin 327, 338
equivocal (*muštarak*) 556
eros 230, 583
eschatology 388, 740
essence 80, 193, 270, 294, 301, 303, 426, 448, 455, 462, 478, 559, 574, 591, 606, 745
absolute 451–452
ḏāt 477, 614
divine (*ḏāt ilāhiyya*) 313, 333, 462–463, 465, 474–478, 495
eternal 464
human (*ḏāt insāniyya*) 477
maʿānī 464, 740
of God (*anniyya*) 261
of the First Cause is knowledge 725
of the human being 331
of the soul 255, 314, 330
true, of things (*ḥaqāʾiq al-umūr*) 331, 484
essential attributes, inherent 446
the eternal (*azalī*) 160
eternal creation 463, 489
eternity 85, 161, 163–164, 167, 170–171, 182, 190, 193, 269–270, 302, 314, 319, 333, 409–410, 460, 464, 475, 485, 489, 495, 570, 578, 580, 606, 616, 725, 733, 742–743, 745

αἰών 302, 485
dahr 302, 333, 410, 451, 485
of the world 45, 171, 190, 195–196, 333, 385, 393–394, 410, 450, 489, 570, 586, 612, 679
ethics 10, 11, 18–19, 35, 43, 62, 160, 194, 197, 248–249, 286, 311, 347, 406, 546, 560, 589, 596, 711, 740
aḫlāq tradition 544
and the ideal of the perfect human being 467
and the tripartite soul 336
Aristotelian 324, 337, 408, 426
as philosophical propaedeutics 549, 596
al-Fārābī's lost ethical works 587
Hellenistic 338
in Abū Bakr al-Rāzī 389, 401–405
in al-ʿĀmirī 267–268
in al-Fārābī 575–577, 596, 622–636
in Ibn ʿAdī 441, 455–456, 466–468
in Ibn Zurʿa 472, 479–480
in al-Kindī 194
in Miskawayh 322–328, 337–344
in al-Tawḥīdī and Abū Sulaymān al-Siǧistānī 299–304
in the classification of *Rasāʾil Iḫwān al-Ṣafāʾ* 754
in the curriculum 582, 712, 721
is the noblest art 331
medical 506
philosophical 281, 295, 301, 404, 455
Platonic 282, 285
political 286
popular 18, 98, 661, 665
positive 331
rationalist 19
religious 389
al-ṣināʿa al-ḫuluqiyya 634
social 341
ethos 177, 179, 243
ḫuluq 331
musical 180
evil, bad 495
evolution 312, 758
examination (*imtiḥān*) 558, 560
example (cf. also ☞ paradigm) 554, 561–562
excellent (*fāḍil*) 624
exhalation(s) (*buḫār*) 185–186
existence (cf. also ☞ being) 167, 255, 270, 302, 320, 325, 412, 426, 463, 465, 476, 478, 485, 582, 591–594, 605
before birth 167
divine (*al-wuǧūd al-ilāhī*) 451–452, 459
essential (*al-wuǧūd al-ḏātī*) 451–452
human 319
independent 679
intelligible 197
logical (*al-wuǧūd al-manṭiqī*) 451–452, 459
natural (*al-wuǧūd al-ṭabīʿī*) 451–452, 459
of an actual infinite 726
of an intelligence 465
of the corporeal substance 725
of the godhead 737
of the heavens 199
of the natural bodies 572
of the soul 348, 679
experience, observation 167, 186, 191, 269, 283, 547, 568, 730, 733
taǧriba 565
exposition, explanation (*tabyīn*) 569
extension (*imtidād*) 565
extramission theory 175

fable 673, 752
faculty, faculties (cf. also ☞ power[s], ☞ soul, part[s] of) 315, 582, 590
appetitive, concupiscible 84, 301, 323, 338, 399, 400, 405, 456, 466, 468, 480, 579, 613
appetitive (*nuzūʿiyya*) 579, 613
appetitive (*šahwiyya*, ἐπιθυμητικόν) 323
attractive (*ǧāḏiba*) 505
δυνάμεις 505, 678
expelling (*dāfiʿa*) 505
imaginative (*mutaḫayyila*) 579, 613
intellectual, of the human soul 271
natural, of nutrition and growth 505
nutritive (*ġāḏiya*) 579, 613
of articulation (*al-quwwa al-nuṭqiyya*) 347
of the intellect 271
perceptive (*ḥāssa*) 579
practical (*ʿammāla*) 315
qudra 634
quwwa 550

faculty, faculties (cont.)
rational (*nāṭiqa*, λογιστικόν) (cf. also ☞ rational soul) 323
retaining, digesting (*al-quwwa al-māsika, al-hāḍima*) 505
sensitive (*al-quwwa al-ḥissiya*) 160, 613
theoretical (*ʿallāma*) 315
transforming, the second (*al-quwwa al-muġayyira al-ṯāniya*) 505
faint-heartedness (*ṣiġar al-himma*) 467
faith 117, 329, 674
faithfulness (*wafāʾ*) 467
falconry 100
fallacy, fallacies 296, 444, 473, 559, 561, 584
liar-paradox 444
linguistic and non-linguistic 561
of accident 444
falsehood 296, 349, 601, 702
kaḏib 160
Farabi Latinus 544
fate 30, 85, 329, 342, 348, 622
of the citizens of the various communities in the hereafter 628
Fatimid(s) 299, 737, 741–3, 745–6, 748, 753, 755
fear (*ḫawf, fazaʿ*) 243
female 579
fifth element ☞ element, fifth; nature, fifth
fifths (in music) 179–180
figure(s)
fourth, of the syllogism 87
in syllogistics 56, 79, 82, 395, 447, 458, 557, 713
of the categorial syllogism (*Prior Analytics* I 7) 52, 57, 551, 595
finiteness 170, 195, 490, 726, 733
fire 171–3, 184, 199, 318, 339, 486, 488, 570, 579, 692, 729–30, 732
'first teacher' (Aristotle) 426
fixed stars 184, 315, 578, 616, 690, 729
fog 200
footstool, God's (*kursī*) 272, 729
foreknowledge, divine 453, 703
formatio (*taṣawwur*) 605
form(s) 165–169, 198, 244, 258–259, 293–294, 301–303, 311–313, 317–322, 333–334, 340, 344, 410, 448, 485, 570, 578–579, 581, 584, 586, 589, 612, 614–616, 725, 730, 742–744, 746, 757
eternal 270
imagined in the soul 452, 460
immanent (εἴδη ἔνυλα) 336
in their true reality 484
Platonic 33
qālab 321
ṣūra, ṣuwar 160, 451–452, 484, 742
universal 270, 271
for-the-sake-of-which (*allaḏī min aǧlihi*) 549
fourths (in music) 179–180
France, French 15, 16
freedom (human agency) 465
friend (true friend is a second self) 286
friendship 287, 301, 325–326, 341
ṣadāqa 342
wudd 467
from/out of (*ʿan*) 549
future contingents 426, 453, 465–466, 609, 731

Galenic corpus 385
Galenism 427
generosity 268, 325
saḫāʾ 323, 338, 467
genus, genera 56, 316, 334, 445–6, 552–4, 560, 569 574, 578
highest (*aǧnās ʿāliya*) 555, 584
genera (*aǧnās*), of musical metre 569
genus 159, 164, 192, 316, 445, 448, 453, 462, 726
geodesy 174
geography 234–235, 241, 243, 247, 712, 732, 738
in Abū Zayd al-Balḫī 240
in al-Saraḫsī 226
in *Rasāʾil Iḫwān al-Ṣafāʾ* 754
Ptolemaic 757
geology 732
geomancy 587
geometry, geometric 17, 20, 40–1, 43, 118, 174–7, 184, 231, 248, 277, 284, 295, 328, 450, 547, 565–6, 574, 590, 609–11, 618
construction by Bryson 473
in al-Kindī 119, 174–5, 190, 192, 199, 201–2
in the classification of sciences 728
in the curriculum 712
in the introduction of *Rasāʾil Iḫwān al-Ṣafāʾ* 754

Georgian (language) 113
German 506
Ghaznavids 247, 347
gnomologia (cf. also ☞ wisdom sayings) 100, 162, 279, 281, 484, 661–670
  Christian 669
  development of Arabic 664
  Miskawayh 328–330
gnosis, Christian 737–8
goal(s), aim(s) 618
  ġaraḍ 444, 624, 634
  highest, of logic (*al-maqṣūd al-aʿẓam*) 605
  maqāṣid 626
  of human beings 635
  τέλος 444
  to know causes of things 467
God 19, 46, 80–2, 101, 160–161, 163–164, 171, 186, 199, 245, 258, 260, 284–285, 298–299, 314–316, 325, 331, 342–343, 399, 407, 409, 411–412, 494–495, 500, 619–621, 703, 732, 737, 754
  according to Ibn ʿAdī 457
  Allāh 747
  and man 403, 592
  as cause 269
  as cause of all truth 163
  as efficient cause of the universe 229, 489
  as final cause and efficient cause 32, 46
  as First Cause 195, 462, 581, 615–616
  as first mover 176–177, 225, 313, 333
  as necessary of existence (*wāǧib al-wuǧūd*) 270, 313, 333, 451, 459, 588, 591–593
  as object of desire 327
  as only creator 466
  as origin of all being 574
  assimilation to 104, 337, 349, 404–408, 412
  as thought thinking itself 477
  as transcendent, unmoved First Cause 293
  as True One 193, 196
  as uncreated, primordial being, according to Abū Bakr al-Rāzī 410–411, 743
  as unmoved mover 176–177, 196
  confirmation of His rule (*al-iqrār bi-rubūbiyyatihi*) 229
  gap between Him and creation 408
  His action 319, 494–495
  His activity 33
  His attributes ☞ attribute(s) – divine
  His command 269
  His eternity 193
  His existence 313
  His knowledge of particulars 726
  His omnipotence 454, 465–466, 737
  His omniscience 454, 465
  His Oneness 170, 460, 475
  His previous knowledge 703
  His providential care (cf. also ☞ providence) 575
  His thinking 575
  His unity 261, 264, 461–462, 477, 745
  His will ☞ will – God's
  His wisdom 82
  is omniscient and just 398
  is one only, eternal, and incorporeal 333
  objects to pain 397, 402
  πρώτη οὐσία 336
  self-thinking and self-identical 478
  the Creator 320, 732, 742
  the First One and Perfect Being 547
  transcendent reality 743
  Trinitarian 464
good, the good 14, 19, 85, 269, 323, 324–327, 331–332, 341–342, 344, 347, 350, 480, 495, 575, 583, 613, 627, 634, 635
  ǧamīl 550
  ḫayrāt, ἀγαθά 337
  the pure good (*al-ḫayr al-maḥḍ*) 161, 327, 332, 494
governance (cf. also ☞ rule) 242, 244, 266, 284, 627, 660
  city management 712
  siyāsa 244
government, craft of 673
grace, divine 293
  luṭf 403
  raḥma 298
gradual weaning (*fiṭām*) 320
grammar 20, 117, 232, 248, 277, 288, 295, 406, 539, 546–547, 549–554, 583, 597–598
  ʿilm al-lisān 596
  in Ḥunayn b. Isḥāq 489

grammar (cont.)
its relation to logic 296, 433, 444, 459, 601
naḥw 296
greed 323, 400, 500
šarah 467
Greek, Greek language 61, 98–99, 101, 103, 105–106, 109–111, 114–115, 117, 120, 540, 663–666, 675–676, 683–684, 707
grief 160–161, 243, 310, 326, 398–399
ḥuzn 160, 243
ǧazaʿ 330, 243
λύπη 330
growth 503

habit(s) 181, 328, 575, 580, 586, 589
ʿāda, ʿādāt 323, 467
ἔθος 323
malaka 550, 624–625
of the parts of the soul 467
of virtue 467
ḥadīṯ (prophetic tradition) 8, 284, 315, 494, 590, 738, 756
hail 185, 692
halo 486, 692, 715
happiness 161, 267, 285, 310–311, 314, 323–325, 340–343, 404, 410, 547, 549–550, 575, 582–583, 591, 629, 634–636, 748, 756
corporeal and spiritual 343
divine 320
general (*al-saʿāda al-ʿāmma*) 310
goal of thinking 580
highest 161, 300, 310, 325–6, 328, 331, 337, 340, 342–343, 493
highest, supreme (*al-saʿāda al-quṣwā*) 310, 630
human and divine 344
its attainment as the final goal of acting ethically 466
naʿīm 400
saʿāda 580, 624, 627–628, 634
specific (*al-saʿāda al-ḫāṣṣa*) 310
states of (*saʿādāt*) 630
true 468, 479, 494, 547
harmonics, science of harmony 156, 177
harmonization of Plato and Aristotle (συμφωνία τῶν φιλοσόφων) 678
harmony 401
between Islamic and profane sciences 740
between macrocosm and microcosm 233
between Plato and Aristotle 29, 32–34, 39, 46, 58, 64, 489, 585–586, 599, 628–629
between the 'three worlds' 747
between the Quran and a late ancient interpretation of Plato and Aristotle 737
between the various levels of the universe 757
constitutive of the cosmos 187
musical 177, 327
of colours and scents 179
of the parts of the soul 404
συμπάθεια 338
universal 187
Harran and late ancient philosophical tradition 53–54, 112–113, 541, 595, 631
having (category of possession) 447, 589
lahu 555
headings (*ruʾūs*) (cf. also ☞ *kephalaia*) 443
health 268–269, 325–326, 328, 342, 572, 584, 613, 625
physical and spiritual 673
heart 160, 266, 278, 339, 401, 572, 579–580, 612, 624
heat 171, 182–183, 199, 201, 318–319, 339, 446, 488, 568, 572, 579, 616, 690, 730–731, 744
ḥarāra 318
innate (σύμφυτον πνεῦμα) 339
heavens 165, 171, 173, 177–178, 181–182, 184, 187, 196, 202, 229–230, 292–293, 303, 322, 327, 568, 570, 611, 616–617, 690, 757
Hebrew 36, 80, 156, 289, 503, 543, 555, 578, 587, 591, 659, 661, 666, 675–676, 679–680, 690, 718, 720
hell 257, 260
Hellenism 64, 98, 101–102, 108–109, 113, 181, 338–339, 662
Hellenization 77
hereafter 260, 264, 285, 348–349, 397, 399, 402, 408, 580–582, 586, 593–594, 622, 628–630

heresy 225, 298
  ilḥād 237
hermeneutics 79, 277
  Aristotelian 423, 487
  juridical 424, 433, 458
  logical 156, 295
  of grammar (*uṣūl al-naḥw*) 433
  philosophical, in al-Tawḥīdī and Abū Sulaymān al-Siğistānī 296–297
Hermetism 50
hierarchy 201, 287, 324, 412, 549, 572, 576, 579–580, 582–583, 624, 627
  cosmic 578
  of being 313–314, 333, 459, 576, 621
  of emanative motion 758
  of knowledge 460, 549
  of the celestial intellects 578, 615
high-mindedness (*ʿiẓam al-himma*) 467
Hindus 397
history
  as discipline 738
  constituted through countless cycles 758
  in Ḥunayn b. Isḥāq 693
historiography (*ʿilm al-taʾrīḫāt*) 248
Holy Spirit 463–464, 474, 477–478
homonym 302, 555, 561, 726
  al-muttafiqa asmāʾuhā, ὁμώνυμα 483
  ism muštarak 445
homonymy 311, 318, 548
horoscope 153, 181–182
'House of Wisdom' (*bayt al-ḥikma*) 104
household 575
houses (of the moon) (*anwāʾ*) 184
how (*kayfa*) 549
human(s) 182, 243, 245, 259–261, 268, 271, 288, 293, 298, 300, 315–317, 321–322, 325–328, 331, 337–342, 344, 347–349, 396–400, 404, 407–410, 455, 458, 465–466, 477, 480, 484, 493–495, 504, 548–549, 568, 575–576, 579–584, 589, 597–598, 604–605, 614–615, 622, 633, 732, 742, 744, 748, 756
  and God 403, 592
  and the divinatory dream 286
  as a composite of body and soul 83, 166, 285–287, 302, 312, 331, 343
  as a mediator between the higher and the lower world 324
  as a microcosm 754, 758
  as a political animal 314, 325, 341, 343
  as God's representative in the lower world 269
  body parts 572–573
  composite nature 488
  goal 635
  human beings as dependent on each other 400
  people 565, 567
  perfect (*insān kāmil, insān tāmm*) 467–468
  perfection 324
  pure 740
  winged 169
humanism, Arabic 277, 281
humanity (*insāniyya*) 310, 331, 467, 472
humility (*tawāḍuʿ*) 467
humour(s) 178, 180, 201, 319, 339, 732
hygiene 242–243, 326, 506
hypostasis 80, 294, 464, 478, 479, 489
  aqānīm 457, 464, 478
  ὑπόστασις, ὑποστάσεις 80, 463, 478
  mediating, as God's word or command 742
  of divine predestination 737
  of the creative command 737
  of the Father (Trinity) (*qunūm al-ab*) 474, 479
  Plotinian 737, 747–748
  Plotinian system of hypostases 261, 270
  second, in Proclus 463
hypostatization (*uqnūmiyya*) 294
hypotheses 606

iatromathematics 188
Iblīs 455
Iconoclastic 108
idea(s)
  divine 337
  miṯāl 335
  Platonic 460, 585
  transcendent (εἴδη χωριστά) 336
ideal
  ethical (*ufuq*) 472
  Socratic 341, 396–397
idolatry 245

ignorance 323, 397, 755
    ἀμαθία 405
Iliad 87
illness ☞ disease
illumination, spiritual 7
Illuminationism 8–9
illusion 285
    optical 176
imagination(s) 169, 198, 262, 270, 314, 320, 336, 341, 410, 579–580, 583, 622, 625
    imaginary perceptions (*ḫayāl*) 486
    imaginative evocation (*taḫyīl*) 563, 584, 604
    mawhūmāt 320
    ṣuwar 459
    taḫayyul, φαντασία 317
    taṣawwur 169
    tawahhum, φαντασία 160, 285
    wahm 169, 288, 318
Imam(s) 6, 276, 299, 343, 407–408, 737–738, 740, 742, 744–746, 748, 753, 755–756
imamate, doctrine of the 541, 733, 737
imamology 754
imam-philosopher 758
imitation 564, 604
    muḥākāt 563, 580
    tašbīh wa-muḥākāt, μίμησις 431
immateriality 165
immortality 33, 282
    individual 629–630
    of human beings 628–630
    of the soul 192, 255, 260, 334, 342, 475, 676, 678
    personal (*baqāʾ al-nafs bi-l-šaḫṣ*) 330
imperfection of the (Universal) Soul 745
impetus (*mayl*, ῥοπή) 45, 496, 690
implications (*lawāzim*) 560
impossible 259, 731
    mumtaniʿ 160
impression (through a form) (*inṭibāʿ*, *taṭabbuʿ*) 322
incarnation 464
    wilād 457
incarnation (*taʾannus*) of God's word 475
incentives (*tarġīb*) 244
inclination
    mayl 403
    nizāʿ 326
India, Indian 10, 16–17, 59, 153, 178, 245, 283, 661, 665, 667, 741, 754, 757
individual(s) 33, 56, 80, 164, 316, 318, 327–328, 342, 389, 445, 449, 452–453, 457, 463–464, 555, 579, 598, 634, 703, 730
    ἄτομον 445
    šaḫṣ, *ašḫāṣ* 316, 445, 457, 555
individuation 169
indivisibility (as characteristic of unity) 574
induction 554, 557–558, 560
    istiqrāʾ 557
infection 704
inference(s) 607
    analogical (*qiyās fiqhī*) 607, 730–731
    dialectical (*al-ištirāk fī l-istinbāṭ*) 558
    from the visible to the invisible (*bi-l-šāhid ʿalā l-ġāʾib*) 488, 558, 607
    legal (*maqāyīs fiqhiyya*) 558
infinite, infinity 170, 186, 190, 195, 254, 448–450
    of numbers 726
    of God 82
    no actual 594
inflection (*iʿrāb*) 444
influence
    acting (as one of the categories) 447
    of God 495
    taʾṯīr 744
    yafʿal 555
information (*fāʾida*) 408
injustice 323, 342, 397
    ǧawr 467
inspiration 401
    ḥads 288
    ilhām 186
instruction (*taʿlīm*) 583, 748
    in the right way to live 479
instrument (*adāt*) 553
    in Ibn ʿAdī's conception of the Trinity 464–465
integrity (*ṣafāʾ*) 752
intellect (cf. also ☞ mind) 29, 82, 163, 167–169, 191, 196–198, 249, 254, 294, 302, 319–321, 325, 329, 331–337, 339–341, 412, 474, 479, 573–574, 578–579, 601, 610, 618, 628, 746–748, 754, 756–757
    absolute, substantial 462

acquired (*al-ʿaql al-mustafād*) 304, 315, 614, 625
active (*al-ʿaql al-faʿʿāl*) 315–316, 579–581, 594, 614–616, 625–626, 630, 633, 635
actual (*al-ʿaql bi-l-fiʿl*) 316–317, 578, 614, 616, 739, 742, 747–748
agent (*al-ʿaql al-faʿʿāl*) 304, 313, 333, 335, 748
and soul, as primordial pair 744
ʿaql 168, 314–315, 451, 457, 464, 590, 613–615
Aristotelian 30, 46
as bearer of all forms 742–743, 747, 757
as entity 743
as part of the second hypostasis, in Proclus 463
as specific property of the human soul 584, 594
as the first created being (*al-mubdaʿ al-awwal*) 742
as topic of metaphysics 618
created through mediation of God's word 745
divine 44, 293, 332, 344
first 168, 197–198, 313, 315–316, 332–334, 485, 489, 594
human 198, 261, 267, 315–316, 745
in actuality 311, 317
in habitu 594
in Ibn ʿAdī's conception of the Trinity 464–465
in Ibn Zurʿa's conception of the Trinity 474–475, 477
in potentiality 311
intellected (*ʿaql maʿqūl*) 747
intellecting (*ʿaql ʿāqil*) 747
is not imagination 318
its types 168, 197–198
material 304, 748
material (*al-ʿaql al-hayūlānī*) 748
νόησις 464
νοῦς 464–465
passive 625
perfect, as quality of the first ruler of a community 625
potential (*al-ʿaql bi-l-quwwa*) 168, 198, 311, 316–317, 579, 584, 614, 745, 747–748
pure 260, 479
substantial, knowing itself 457
tenth 748
theoretical and practical 575, 580, 584
universal 270–271
intellect, doctrine of the
Aristotle's 573
in al-ʿĀmirī 265, 269–271
in al-Kindī 165–169, 196–199
in Miskawayh 312–322
intellecting 294, 317, 479
in Ibn ʿAdī's conception of the Trinity 464
in Ibn Zurʿa's conception of the Trinity 474–475, 477
νοῶν, *ʿāqil* 457, 464
intellects
celestial 581, 591, 615, 619–620
cosmic 593, 617, 619–620
heavenly, being specific individuals (*ašḫāṣ*) 316
human 316, 614–615
ten 315–316, 578, 616–617, 619, 737, 747
their division 316
intellectualism 155, 267, 300
intellectualist ethics 349, 484
intelligible 294, 317, 334, 477, 479
in Ibn Zurʿa's conception of the Trinity 475, 477, 479
maʿqūl (νοούμενον) 457, 464
second (*maʿqūl ṯānī*) 603
intelligibles 49, 166–168, 184, 194, 311, 317–318, 320–321, 325, 331, 334, 547–548, 580, 584, 601, 625
al-maʿānī al-maʿqūla 320
first and second, no third 548
first, primary (*maʿqūlāt uwal*) 550, 553, 557, 559, 580, 584, 606, 635
their division 579
interpretation(s), interpreting (*taʾwīl*) 245, 739–740, 746
interrogative pronouns 549
interval 569
introduction (cf. also ☞ Prolegomena)
general (θεωρία) 501
to Aristotle's philosophy 59–60, 332, 347, 550, 596
investigation
baḥṯ 408
semantic, of the word *ʿaql* 573, 613–615

Iran 5–7, 10, 16–17, 60, 112, 256, 276, 279, 537, 674, 739, 746
Iraq 16, 279, 309, 538, 674, 683, 746
irascibility (*safah*) 467
Islam 2–3, 5–6, 16, 54, 63, 98, 100–103, 108, 117, 153, 230, 245, 259–260, 270–271, 277–279, 282, 298, 404, 407–408, 426–427, 460–461, 476, 631, 662, 673, 693, 712, 724, 740
Ismāʿīliyya, Ismailis 181, 412, 542, 737–744, 746–748, 752–753, 755, 759

Jacobites (also: West Syrians) 78–83, 104, 457–458, 463, 478
joy 350, 397, 399, 410, 578
 and sorrow 754
 iltiḏāḏ 627
 true 495
Judaism 1–2, 15, 21, 224, 260, 277, 477, 478, 480, 490, 503, 543, 680, 737, 739, 754, 759
judgement 322, 331, 403, 406, 559–560, 571, 584, 594, 607, 635
 about the existence of something 605
 aḥkām 611
 categorical and conditional 556
 equivocal use of the term 568
 necessary 559, 611
 personal (*raʾy*) 102
 qaḍāyā 554
 taṣdīq 493, 554, 558, 562, 605–606
Jupiter 181–182, 184, 266, 578, 616, 729
jurisprudence (cf. also ☞ law[s]) 4, 7–8, 20, 295, 488, 549, 557–558, 576, 607–608
 defends the claims of religion with dialectical arguments 598
 ʿilm al-fiqh 547, 596
 in al-Fārābī's system of the sciences 596
 in the development of the sciences 549
justice 268, 314, 325, 341, 397–8, 401–2, 404, 406, 575, 578, 625, 673
 ʿadl 234, 311, 323, 327, 338, 403, 406, 467
 cardinal virtue 268, 323, 342
 conventional (*al-ʿadl al-waḍʿī*) 328
 divine 328
 freely chosen (*al-ʿadl al-iḫtiyārī*) 328
 natural (*ʿadl ṭabīʿī*) 327–328, 338
 realized in three ways 327, 338
 voluntative, as purpose of ethics 327, 338

kalām (cf. also ☞ theology – Islamic) 19, 441, 455, 458, 461, 465–466, 479, 488, 609
katarchic astrology (*iḫtiyārāt*) 182
kephalaia (κεφάλαια) 426, 443, 473, 483
Khorasanians 178
king(s) (cf. also ☞ ruler) 398, 467–468, 673, 693, 729
knowledge, cognition, understanding, insight(s), discernment 20, 37, 82, 161, 166–167, 177, 191, 198, 262, 266, 299, 310, 315–323, 325, 327, 328–329, 331, 340, 397–398, 403–404, 410–412, 463, 480, 493, 575, 580–581, 604, 606–607, 614, 620, 625–627, 630, 634, 738, 743, 758
 as the essence of the first causes 725
 based on sense perception (*ʿulūm ḥissiyya*) 349
 baṣīra, baṣāʾir 285, 626
 certain (*al-ʿilm al-yaqīn*) 494–495, 552
 conceptual 597, 626
 due to the divine light 285
 exact, definite (*ʿulūm muḥaṣṣala*) 568, 611
 faculty of cognition 622
 first and second 738
 γνῶσις 453
 ḥilm 401
 ʿilm 160, 177, 248, 285, 288, 323, 402–403, 411, 494
 intellectual 265
 its hierarchy 460
 its relationship with action 263, 267
 maʿrifa 408
 of actual intellect, of its self-knowledge 271
 of divine and human matters 484
 of Lordship (*ʿilm al-rubūbiyya*) 186
 of the First Principle 494
 of the intellect 270
 of things as they really are = wisdom 484
 perfect 282
 philosophical 485, 635
 prophetic 5, 7
 revealed 269
 second knowledge (*ʿilm ṯānī*) 739
 substantial 583
 theoretical (*naẓar*) 582–583
 transmission of 583
 true 583
 universal 572, 612

'Kontroverstheologie' 117
Kūnī 737–738
lack of reason (ἄνοια) 405

Lakhmids 683
language 32, 247, 290, 475, 479, 540, 548–550, 552, 556, 563, 597–598, 663
  as tool for transmitting knowledge 79
  combines expressions 553
  common, natural (*nuṭq ṭabīʿī ʿāmm*) 565
  'giver of language' (*wāḍiʿ lisān*) 549, 597
  inner (*al-nuṭq al-dāḫil*) 552
  its conventionality 296
  its origin 743, 754
  its relation to thinking 601–602
  its structure 117, 743
  linguistics within the division of the sciences 728
  most perfect 412
language, philosophy of
  in al-Fārābī 744
  in Severus Sebokt 79
last judgement 260
Latin 1–3, 109, 158, 384, 403, 431, 472, 502–503, 531, 539, 543, 569, 587, 659–662, 675–676, 679–680, 685, 690
laughter 287
law(s) (cf. also ☞ jurisprudence) 295, 324–5, 343, 584, 627
  Arabic (*šarīʿa ʿarabiyya*) 756
  Christian 477, 479
  divine 299, 314, 739, 754
  institution by the Creator (*tawqīf*) 477, 479
  Islamic 284, 458, 477, 480
  Jewish 477, 480
  Mosaic 480
  nāmūs, νόμος 342
  natural (*sunna ṭabīʿiyya*) 477, 479
  of eminence (*sunnat al-tafaḍḍul*) 477, 480
  of justice (*sunnat al-ʿadl*) 477, 480
  of non-contradiction 465
  of reason (*sunna ʿaqliyya*) 477, 479–480
  of thought 601
  positive (*sunna waḍʿiyya*) 477, 479
  religious 242, 245, 298, 400, 433, 473, 546–7, 549, 576, 593, 740, 742
  šarīʿa, šarāʾiʿ 229–230, 314, 324–325, 343, 547
  schools of 277, 296
  threefold, according to Aristotle 342
leader of the religious community (*imām*) 343, 407–408
leadership, political (*siyāsa, riʾāsa*) 547
length 610
  ṭūl 566
letter(s) (of the alphabet) 82, 180, 548
lexicography 295, 549, 597
Liber de Pomo 661, 675–680
liberation from the body (*taḫlīṣ*) 402
library, libraries 104, 109, 153–154, 256–257, 309, 440, 675, 684, 737, 741
life 85, 160, 197, 288, 294, 300, 303, 313, 334, 342, 396–397, 405, 578, 581, 611, 675, 757
  afterlife (*al-ḥayāt al-aḫīra*) 628, 630
  and death 584, 754
  as a part of the second hypostasis, in Proclus 463
  earthly, compared to a temporary disembarkation from a ship 193
  eternal, man's 748
  eternal, spiritual 479–480
  ḥayāt 629
  its appointed terms 703
  philosophical 396–397, 401, 404
  ten concepts of 'life' 285
  way of (βίος) 467, 484, 488, 633
light 85, 184, 199, 271, 316, 318–319, 334, 342–343, 484, 580, 730
  divine 325, 341, 737–738
  its nature and incorporeality 700–701
  metaphysics of 6
lightning bolt (*ṣāʿiqa*) 185
line 565, 610
linguistics
  ʿilm al-lisān 546
  in Abū Zayd al-Balḫī 239
literary culture (*adab*) 242–243, 246, 248–249, 278–281, 283–284, 286, 300–301, 330, 346, 386, 661, 671
  ʿilm al-adab 386
liver 339, 572, 579
logic 9, 11, 19, 34, 37, 43, 47, 51–52, 59, 82, 84, 86–87, 109, 112, 119–120, 158–160, 178, 237, 249, 277, 282, 284, 288, 290,

logic (cont.)
295–297, 331, 348–350, 424, 426, 432, 471, 544–545, 550, 571, 577, 584, 589, 596, 671, 711, 733, 738
Aristotelian 17, 51, 57, 77, 84, 98, 115, 277, 299, 428–429, 458, 478, 538–539, 608, 756
Aristotelian, in relation to theology 608
as methodological foundation of philosophy 605
as part of the curriculum 313
as the touchstone of intellect (*ʿiyār al-ʿaql*) 552, 600
demonstrative, of Sabians 230
explaining the concept of *manṭiq* 347, 550
al-Fārābī's lost logical works 586
in Abū Bakr al-Rāzī 389
in al-ʿĀmirī 265
in al-Fārābī 552–565, 599–609
in al-Fārābī's system of sciences 596
in Ḥunayn b. Isḥāq 688
in Ibn ʿAdī 443–447, 459
in Ibn al-Ḫammār 482–483, 488–489
in Ibn al-Samḥ 493
in Ibn Zurʿa 473
in al-Kindī 159–160, 189–193
in Ṯābit b. Qurra 712–714
in the division of sciences 728, 754
indispensable for theologians, according to Abū Bakr al-Rāzī 386
its highest aim (*al-maqṣūd al-aʿẓam*) 605
its relation to grammar 288, 295–396, 432–434, 444, 459, 601
manṭiq, *ʿilm al-manṭiq* 433, 546, 596
restriction on study of logic 52, 57, 111, 192, 551, 595
serves to defend the truth 444
universal, in al-Saraḫsī 232
logos 462
kalima 321, 335
qawl, λόγος 453, 462, 483
love 342–343, 401, 583, 754
excessive (*ifrāṭ al-ḥubb*) 467
hawā 399
ʿišq 230, 342, 467
maḥabba 160, 325–326, 342
of God 343
of honour (*ḥubb al-karāma*) 467
of pomp (*ḥubb al-zīna*) 467
well-balanced (*maḥabba muʿtadila*) 467
lute, oud (*ʿūd*) 178–179, 198, 201, 569

macrocosm 314–318, 754
ʿālam kabīr 338
madness 583
μανία 405
magic 200, 260–261, 732, 754, 759
in al-Kindī 187
magnet(ism) 730
man 579
Manicheans 117, 398
many, the 549, 573, 583–584
ǧumhūr 613
Maronites 87
Mars 182–184, 266, 578, 729
materialism 335
mathematical disciplines (*taʿālīm*) 320
artes doctrinales (*ʿulūm al-taʿālīm*) 176
mathematics 34, 41, 43, 49, 51, 53, 78, 118–119, 160, 167, 174–175, 184, 188, 190–192, 328, 331, 336, 347, 403, 406, 424, 546–547, 549, 565, 571, 577, 598, 600, 660, 710–711, 728, 740
and physics 496
as a prerequisite for the study of philosophy 119
as a propaedeutic of philosophy 159, 183
ʿilm al-taʿālīm 547, 596
in al-Fārābī 565–569, 596–597, 609–615
in Ibn ʿAdī 448–451
in al-Kindī 173, 200–202
in al-Saraḫsī 228
in the classification of sciences 728
in the curriculum 313, 582, 712
mathematician-philosopher 51
matter 167, 169, 244, 259, 288, 298, 301–302, 313, 320–321, 333–335, 409–412, 448, 452, 460, 570, 574, 579, 581, 584, 589, 610, 612, 614, 616, 630, 745, 755
absolute (*hayūlā muṭlaqa*) 410
as intermediate entity, in Abū Bakr al-Rāzī 411
as uncreated principle, according to Abū Bakr al-Rāzī 392, 410–411
hayūlā 160, 322, 451, 742

mādda 322
prime 410, 474, 579, 612, 617, 725, 744, 757
second 757
three types, according to Abū Ḥātim al-Rāzī 744
ʿunṣur 160, 322
maxims ☞ aphorism(s)
mean 323, 325, 338, 342, 402, 404, 504, 575
tawassuṭ 550
meaning(s), usage 117, 165, 289, 296, 311, 332, 433, 459, 449, 553, 555, 597, 602
external (*ẓāhir*) 739–740
internal (*bāṭin*) 739
logical, of the linguistic expressions 608
maʿnā, maʿānī 248, 561, 605
maʿnā, τὸ [σημαινόμενον] πρᾶγμα 444
medicine 17, 20, 48–49, 51, 56, 59, 62, 82, 98, 110, 118, 236, 244, 249, 269, 284, 295, 317, 331, 338–340, 386–387, 424, 426–427, 482, 506, 547, 550–552, 572–576, 612–613, 618, 660, 683–686, 703, 711–712, 728, 732–733, 740
as practical art (*ṣināʿa fāʿila*) 572, 613
in Abū Zayd al-Balḫī 240
in Gundishapur 103
in Ḥunayn b. Isḥāq 701
in Ibn al-Ḫammār 487
in Ibn al-Ṭayyib 506
in Ibn Hindū 348–350
in al-Kindī 188–189
in al-Saraḫsī 228
in the classification of sciences 728
its defense 704
its division into seven sub-domains, according to al-Fārābī 572
spiritual 326, 398–399
theoretical 350
ṭibb 711
meditatio mortis 341
Megarians 444
Melkites 457, 478
melody 179–180, 569
memory (cf. also ☞ recollection) 198, 336, 340, 589
Meno's paradox 605
mercilessness (*qasāwa*) 467
Mercury 182, 184, 266, 578, 616, 729
mercy 403–404, 406, 408
raḥma 403, 467, 323
messenger(s) (cf. also ☞ prophet[s]) 314, 461
rusul 159, 229
messianism, Qarmatian 742
métahistoire 6
metaphor(s) 193, 461, 479, 602
metaphorical 164–165, 196, 561
mustaʿār 556
metaphysics 7, 9–10, 30, 43, 46–47, 50, 156, 159, 167, 177, 184, 190, 193, 248–249, 347, 385, 456, 473, 545, 603–604, 629, 633, 711, 740
Aristotelian 37, 425, 432, 460, 616
as primarily ontology 618
ilāhiyyāt 441
al-ʿilm al-ilāhī 547, 596
ʿilm mā baʿd al-ṭabīʿiyyāt 621
in Abū Bakr al-Rāzī 389
in Abū Sulaymān al-Siğistānī 301–304
in al-ʿĀmirī 260–261, 264, 270
in al-Fārābī 573–574, 577, 587, 597, 615–622
in Ibn ʿAdī 451–455, 460–465
in al-Kindī 157–158, 162–165, 195–196
in Miskawayh 332–337
in Ṯābit b. Qurra 719–720, 724–726
in the curriculum 313, 582, 712
in the division of sciences 728
Neoplatonic 295, 743
Platonic 337
metathetical (*maʿdūl*) 556
metempsychosis ☞ transmigration
meteorology 84, 183, 200, 287, 672, 685, 716, 731
in Ḥunayn b. Isḥāq 691–692
in al-Kindī 184–187
in the classification of *Rasāʾil Iḫwān al-Ṣafāʾ* 754
metre (musical) 179, 569
wazn 565
metre (poetic) 563
microcosm 314–318
ʿālam ṣaġīr 338
man as 754, 758
Middle Ages, medieval 1–2, 121, 339, 429, 662, 675, 685, 704, 711, 740
military manuals (*tactica*), Byzantine 100

mimesis (*tašbīh wa-muḥākāt*) 431
theory of 632
mind (cf. also ☞ intellect) 166, 169, 311, 452, 605
mineral(s) 321, 579, 581, 584, 729, 742, 744, 757
in Ḥunayn b. Isḥāq 692–693
in the classification of *Rasāʾil Iḫwan al-Ṣafāʾ* 754
miracle(s) 408, 473, 702
mirror 176, 200, 317–318, 349, 484
mirror(s) for princes 59, 99, 118, 228, 231, 279, 283, 389, 592, 625, 661, 672–675
misfortune 193, 310
misogyny 663
mission (Ismaili) (*daʿwa*) 741, 743–744, 746, 753
missionaries, Ismaili (*duʿāt*) 753, 783
mist 185
mixture (cf. also ☞ temperament) 186, 319, 505, 594
balanced (*mizāǧ muʿtadil*, εὐκρασία) 319
mizāǧ, κρᾶσις 323, 717
of the elements 171, 199, 349, 731–732, 742, 744, 757
modality 111, 556
moderation (cf. also ☞ chastity) 400
ʿiffa 323
qanāʿa 467
σωφροσύνη 325, 484, 488
modernity 11
modes
ǧihāt 556
musical 179, 181, 569
of being 575
of syllogisms 556–557
modus tollens 190
moisture, humidity 183–6, 201, 579, 731, 744
Monophysite(s) 78, 446, 462–463, 478, 489
monotheism 157, 302, 425
Christian 461, 489
Islamic 463
moon 182–184, 266, 578, 616, 729, 730–731, 757
its sphere 196
lunar cycle 188
morphology 247, 546, 561
mortality (of the individual) 33
motion (*ḥaraka*) 170–173, 177–178, 183–185, 187, 197, 253, 292, 302–303, 314, 322, 394, 411, 451, 465, 490, 496, 502, 578, 594, 617, 690, 742, 757–758
according to Ibn al-Ṭayyib 502
Aristotelian doctrine of 333, 489
circular and linear 253–254
double, of the Universal Soul 745
inanimate 496
its origin 464
of corporeal substance 725
of heaven 199–200, 690
of soul 333–334
of the elements and the spheres 196, 199, 255
of the planets 730, 733
six types of movement, according to Aristotle 478
within the essence of the Soul 742
mover 316, 496
the first 254–255, 292–293, 303–304, 313, 448, 464, 502, 725
multiplicity 85, 163, 193, 294, 314, 333, 460, 477, 495, 574, 579, 616, 618
music 118, 153, 160, 184, 188, 201, 248, 286, 327, 538, 544, 547, 563, 610–611
in al-Saraḫsī 228
in the curriculum 712
in the division of *Rasāʾil Iḫwān al-Ṣafāʾ* 754
in the division of the sciences 728
its effect on human beings 569, 611
legend of its discovery 231
listening to music 243
musical theory
in al-Fārābī 568–569, 611
in al-Kindī 177–181, 201
in al-Saraḫsī 230–231
ṣināʿat al-mūsīqī 569
Muʿtazila, Muʿtazilī 19, 225, 476, 571, 608
mysticism, Islamic ☞ Sufism

name(s) 284
of the hypostases 464
ism, asmāʾ 578, 605
name, title 311, 473, 548
nation(s) 582

as a perfect community 380, 623
umma 623, 626
naturalists (*al-ṭabīʿiyyūn*) 327
natural laws 184
natural philosophers 340, 672, 699
natural philosophy
in Ibn al-Ḫammār 489–490
in Ibn al-Samḥ 495–496
natural sciences 190, 236, 248–249, 290, 754
in al-ʿĀmirī 258
in al-Kindī 199–201
in the classification of sciences 728
their definition 728
nature 192, 268–269, 294, 303, 313, 322, 323–324, 327, 333, 397, 402, 404, 553, 578, 584, 586, 615, 621, 623, 626, 737
and divinatory dreams 286
as a source of motion 394
as an immanent, creative force (*al-ṭabīʿa al-faʿʿāla*) 433
as Plotinian hypostasis 747
caused, of the universe 725
corporeal 263, 343–344, 476
definition of 385
fifth 178, 229
human 285, 311, 472, 488
its influence 757
of Christ, the same essence as the Father (ὁμοούσιος) 463
of the Creator 409
φύσις 464
primordial natures 612
ṭabʿ 409
ṭabīʿa, ṭabāʾiʿ 160, 229, 297, 301, 402, 451, 464, 612
thing of (*maṭbūʿ*) 409
three realms (of minerals, plants, animals) 729, 742, 757
what is beyond nature (*baʿd al-ṭabīʿa*, μετὰ τὰ φυσικά) 320, 328
navigation 728
necessary, necessity 195, 259, 270, 333, 402, 404, 407, 453, 465–466, 475, 488, 558–559, 589, 591, 592, 594, 606, 611, 623, 731
ḍarūrī 556
wāǧib 160
negation 320, 465–466, 556
double 745
salb 725
Neoplatonism, Neoplatonic 36, 43, 45–47, 50, 61–63, 157, 159, 166–167, 194, 196–197, 199, 253–256, 292–294, 298, 302–303, 332, 337, 404, 408, 411–412, 430, 478, 484, 489, 500, 506, 595, 610, 616, 619, 631, 667, 725, 733, 742, 745, 757
Ismaili 737–739, 741, 747–748
Jewish 739
Neoplatonists 196, 293, 463–465, 679
Neopythagoreanism 49, 63
Nestorians (also: East Syrians) 78, 83–87, 102–104, 295, 457, 460, 463, 478
noetics 155, 633, 738
in al-Fārābī 542
in al-Kirmānī 748
in Miskawayh 332–337
in *Rasāʾil Iḫwān al-Ṣafāʾ* 754
non-being, non-existence 160, 453, 463, 465, 485, 489, 745
ʿadam 465
non-cause 745
non-essence 745
non-substance 745
notation, musical 181
note(s) 179, 569
naġam 180
noun(s) 555, 556, 589, 602
indefinite 589, 608
ism 553, 605
numbers(s) 160, 174, 178, 186, 224, 328, 447, 449–450, 547, 574, 599, 757
and the oneness of God 460
of souls 726
their infinity 726
theory of 156
Nuṣayrī 758

object(s) 167, 198, 201, 249, 258, 288, 313, 326–327, 486, 565, 568, 572, 589, 610, 613, 616, 726
first object of intellect 474
mušār ilayhi 602
of perfect love 578
objection (*tabkīt*) 560

obsessive thoughts (*wasāwis al-ṣadr wa-aḥādīṯ al-nafs*) 243
occult sciences 247, 249, 673, 755
octave(s) 179–180
Odyssey 87
oligarchy (*madīnat al-naḏala*) 628
the One 120, 163, 193, 294, 302, 314, 319, 412, 453, 460, 495, 737
  al-wāḥid 618
oneness 460
  God's 170, 460, 475
  of the First Cause 725
  profession of God's (*tawḥīd*) 302, 461–462, 746
  waḥda 289, 302
ontology 327, 427, 548, 593, 604, 618, 620
  Aristotelian 299
  in Ibn ʿAdī 451–453, 459–460
  in al-Kindī 162–163, 195–196
ophthalmology 684–685, 701
opinion (*ẓann*) 319
opinions, commonly accepted
  ἔνδοξα 493
  mašhūr 553
opposition (planets) 182, 184
optics 547
  in Ḥunayn b. Isḥāq 693
  in al-Kindī 175–176, 200–201
  manāẓir 176
Oracles, Chaldean 37, 41
Orientalism 2, 6
ornamentation, musical (*taḥrīk*) 230
Ottoman ☞ Turkish, Turkish language
Ottoman Empire 10
ousia 77, 80, 460, 463, 478, 483

Pahlavi (cf. also ☞ Persian, Middle) 79, 115
pain(s) 397–400, 402, 405
  aḏan 550
  and pleasure 405
  excessive (λύπαι) 405
parable(s) 722
paradigm 589, 608
  tamṯīl 557, 562
paradise 260
parallax, optical 176
paraphrase (as literary genre) 35
paronym(s) 555
  al-muštaqqa asmāʾuhā, παρώνυμα 484
paronymy 548
parrhesia 662
part (*ǧuzʾ*) 448–449, 742, 745
  equal and unequal (*ǧuzʾ, baʿḍ*) 566
participation (μέθεξις) 495
particle(s) 256, 548–549, 555, 602
  ḥarf, ḥurūf 547, 553
particular(s) 191, 316–318, 334–336, 397, 454, 460, 463, 576, 613, 625, 726
passion(s), affection(s), desire 161, 166, 268–269, 285, 300, 301, 314, 321, 329–330, 337, 340, 397, 399–400, 403–404, 407, 467, 479, 484, 500, 568, 575, 581
  ġaḍab 495
  hawā 402
  ʿišq 326, 342
  šahwa, šahwiyya 323, 466, 495
paternity (Trinity) (*maʿnā l-ubuwwa*) 474, 479
paying for praise (*al-muǧāzāt ʿalā l-madḥ*) 467
peace, inner 311
peoples 289, 328, 493
  aǧyāl 260
perceptive (*darrāk*[*a*]) 229
perfect, complete (*kāmil*) 580, 623
perfection 293–294, 300, 303, 313, 319, 325, 331, 335, 342, 344, 458, 479, 495, 583, 628, 630, 634, 742, 744
  absolute, of God 616
  of things 495
  ultimate human (*nihāyat al-kamāl al-insānī*) 550
  of the human being 467, 488, 493–494, 623, 634
  kamāl 310, 324, 624, 756
  final 630
  first (*al-kamāl al-awwal*) 285
  second (of the human soul) (*al-kamāl al-ṯānī*) 739
perfidy (*ġadr*) 467
Peripatetic(s) 36, 339, 452, 460, 463, 678
Persian 15, 659, 661, 674–676, 679–680
Persian, Middle 60, 98–99, 101, 112–116, 329, 332, 661, 665, 667, 672, 674
person(s) 80
  divine 475
  excellent (*al-šaḫṣ al-fāḍil*) 755

πρόσωπον, πρόσωπα (*uqnūm, aqānīm*) 80, 464, 478
of the Trinity 164, 192, 457, 464, 478–479
persuasion 563, 583–584, 604
iqnāʿ 561
petitio principii 561
phantasms (*awhām*) 318
pharmacology 348, 686
in al-Kindī 188–189
phenomena 32, 176, 201, 319, 731
archetypal, of the soul 6
contingent 485
meteorological 183, 186, 200, 229, 486
of the tides 731
optical 489
physical 486
philology, Arabic 277, 285–286, 295
philosopher(s)
attitude towards death 675
faylasūf, falāsifa 18, 288, 311, 625
form of life (βίος) 467
pre-Plotinian 668
signet rings of the 665–666
philosopher king 290, 299, 488, 541, 583, 635
philosophical circle (around Ibn ʿAdī and around al-Siǧistānī) 492
philosophical propaedeutics 471
in Ibn ʿAdī 443–447
in Ibn al-Ḫammār 483–484, 488
in Ibn al-Samḥ 492–495
in Ibn al-Ṭayyib 500
in Ibn Zurʿa 473
in al-Kindī 158–160, 189–193
in Miskawayh 309–312
in Ṯābit b. Qurra 711–712
philosophy
and religion 271–272, 288, 297–299, 581, 583, 599, 622, 625–626
and theology 12, 21
and the sciences 48–51
'Arabic' 1–2, 15
as a guide to political rule 118
as apodeictic science 434, 607
as *ars vitae* 48
as art of arts and wisdom of wisdoms 186
as theoretical (conceptual) knowledge 582
beginnings of philosophical literature in Arabic 108–121
Christian 337
concept of 13
development from 'poetry' 598
divine (*al-falsafa al-ilāhiyya*) 756
falsafa 4, 12, 18, 234, 241, 246, 465, 492, 711, 737, 740
First 440
Greek (*falsafa yūnāniyya*) 14, 756
Greek philosophical texts in Arabic translation 121–135
ḥikma 233, 242
in Abū Zayd al-Balḫī 239–240
in al-Saraḫsī 226
in the development of sciences 549
independence of Arabic 121
'Islamic' 5–9, 15
its branches (ἡ ὑπὸ τί μέρος τῆς φιλοσοφίας ἀναφορά) 443
its classification, division 19, 165, 189–190, 248, 347, 594–599, 634
its definition 14, 403, 406, 484, 494, 594–599
its emergence in Arabic 109
its 'exoteric' and 'esoteric' presentation 619
its history 666
its legitimation 153
its methodological foundation 605
its name 587
its necessity 271
its prophetic origin 738
its purpose 494
its resurrection in Arabic 113, 120
Neoplatonic, between al-Balḫī and al-ʿĀmirī 253–256
of humankind (*al-falsafa al-insāniyya*) 634
of (political) governance (*al-falsafa al-siyāsiyya*) 634
of the community (*al-falsafa al-madaniyya*) 634–635
of the modern Islamic world 10
'Oriental' 9
φιλοσοφία 13
political 7, 389–390, 541, 543, 632–633, 744
practical (*al falsafa al-ʿamaliyya*) 323, 337, 494, 624, 631–636, 660–661, 671

philosophy (cont.)
theoretical 609, 611, 635
theoretical and practical 324–325, 331, 347, 406, 550, 575, 635
throughout antiquity only in Greek 108, 120
true 583
'philosophy of compromise' 489
phonemes 230–231, 549, 597
al-alfāẓ, αἱ φωναί 444
physician(s) 48–49, 51–53, 58, 228, 249, 265, 277, 286, 289, 292, 316, 338, 340, 348, 350, 386, 401, 412, 426–427, 429–431, 441, 471, 482, 487, 492, 499, 572, 575, 577, 666, 668, 683–684, 703, 706, 733
comparison to 61
studying medicine 110
physician-philosopher, physician and philosopher 49, 51, 331, 431
physics 9–10, 19, 37, 39, 43, 45, 50, 118–119, 159, 165, 177, 184, 190, 193, 195, 229, 301, 331, 336, 348, 385, 403, 406, 471, 549, 565–566, 570–574, 589, 597–598, 618, 699, 711, 732
al-ʿilm al-ṭabīʿī 547
and mathematics 496
Aristotelian 277, 299, 340, 425–427, 456, 756
in Abū Bakr al-Rāzī 389
in Abū Bišr Mattā 433
in Abū Sulaymān al-Siğistānī 301–304
in al-ʿĀmirī 261, 268–269
in al-Fārābī 569–573, 578, 584, 596, 609–615
in Ḥunayn b. Isḥāq 689–691
in Ibn ʿAdī 448–451
in Ibn al-Ḫammār 485–487
in Ibn Zurʿa 474
in al-Kindī 170–173, 199–200
in al-Saraḫsī 226–227
in the division of the sciences 728
in the introduction of *Rasāʾil Iḫwān al-Ṣafāʾ* 754
in the syllabus 313, 582, 712
lost physical works by al-Fārābī 586
of *kalām* 490
physiognomy 673, 733
physiology 48, 319, 339
physis 80
pilgrimage 278
place (cf. also ☞ space) 165, 167, 184–185, 197, 571, 578, 594
makān 160
plane, surface 449, 565–566, 610
planet(s) 171, 181–184, 263, 266, 315, 690, 729–733
plant(s) 229, 321, 324, 339, 503, 568, 579, 581, 584, 729, 742, 744, 757
Plato Arabus 676
Platonic corpus 35, 677
Platonism 6, 30, 160, 460, 595, 631–632
Platonists 48, 332, 463
pleasure 397–400, 404–405, 410
and pain 399, 405
excessive (ἡδοναί) 405
highest, through knowledge of God 327
illusory 326
immediate, present (*ladda ḥāḍira*) 402, 404
ladda 550
of the body, bodily 320, 402
pure 325, 343
topic of a treatise by Abū Bakr al-Rāzī 388, 391
true and false 583
plurality ☞ multiplicity
pneuma (cf. also ☞ spirit) 339–340
rūḥ, arwāḥ 505, 590
Pneumatists 571
poetics 159, 554, 563, 575, 583, 588, 604, 611
poetry 179, 248, 296, 346–347, 386, 406, 549, 559, 563–565, 598, 599–600
development of philosophy from 598
its definition 564
naẓm 290
point 449, 475, 565–566, 574, 610
nuqṭa 302
pointers (*išārāt*) 320, 337
politics, political science 11, 35, 159, 243, 248–249, 290, 347, 389, 400–401, 406, 546, 549, 604, 609, 673, 711, 740, 754
as the knowledge of how to live 583
in Abū Zayd al-Balḫī 239–240
in al-Fārābī 575–577, 596, 622–636
in al-Saraḫsī 226

in Ṯābit b. Qurra 722–723
in the division of sciences 712, 728
in the philosophical curriculum 582
practical 661, 665, 675
polygon (cf. also ☞ polyhedra) 172
polyhedra (cf. also ☞ polygon) 178, 451, 474
muǧassamāt 178
polyphony 181
polytheism 260
popular philosophy 50, 55, 77, 284
positing (*waḍʿ*) 560
position 312, 447
waḍʿ 555, 560
possibility 86, 186, 594, 731
mumkin 160, 409, 556
possible for the most part (*mumkin ʿalā l-akṯar*) 611
the possible 259, 568, 594, 731
potentiality, potency 170, 198, 316–317, 454, 574, 612, 725, 748
quwwa 160
power(s) (cf. also ☞ faculty) 254, 294, 302–303, 319–320, 457, 475, 485, 579, 581
divine 288, 411, 466
δύναμις 453, 463
of the soul ☞ soul – its faculties
primary, of the macrocosm 318
psychological, in humans 263
qudra 411, 453
quwwa 757
practice (cf. also ☞ action) 406, 599, 739
ʿamal 248, 402
practice (*tadarrub*) 323
precise exposition (*talḫīṣ*) 719, 724
predestination, divine (cf. also ☞ foreknowledge, divine) 85, 259, 737–738
qaddara 738
predicables 192–193, 552, 560, 726
predicate(s), predication 159, 475, 552–556, 574, 589
pre-existence 167, 197
premise(s) 494, 557–560, 562, 405, 416, 420–421
commonly accepted (*mašhūr*) 560, 702
dialectical 560
universal, true, and necessary 614
prepositions (*wāsiṭāt*) 553
Presocratics 62, 158, 658, 755
princely virtues 283, 468
principle(s) 317, 335, 473, 494, 580, 606, 614, 621, 624, 627
awāʾil 186, 317, 335
First (*al-mabdaʾ al-awwal*) 332–333, 494, 593, 621, 725
five eternal, according to Abū Bakr al-Rāzī 392, 411, 743
intelligible 757
mabādiʾ 486, 622
metaphysical 619
of being 618
of categorial doctrine 461
of governance 627
of jurisprudence (*uṣūl al-fiqh*) 4, 427
of religion (*uṣūl al-dīn*) 19, 578, 622
of substance and the categories 442
of the bodily world 742
priority 442, 485
absolute 725
ontological, of the universal 460
qabla 442
privative (*ʿadamī*) 556
probable 568
product 303
mafʿūl 302
profligacy (*fuǧūr*) 467
prognostication (astrological) 182, 567–568, 611, 731
prohibitions (*al-arkān al-zaǧriyya*) 260
prolegomena 43–44, 60, 160, 332, 336, 433, 443, 459, 477, 483, 488–489, 501, 552, 596, 634, 424
three different types 44
pronouns (*ḫawālif*) 553
pronouns, indefinite 608
proof(s), demonstration(s) (cf. also ☞ apodeictics) 82, 183, 296, 319, 332, 434–444, 459, 495, 547, 558, 562, 581, 583–584, 589, 605–606
apodeictic 459
Aristotelian 427, 458, 461, 561, 605, 608
arithmetical 119
burhān, barāhīn 174, 230, 494, 610, 626
Euclidean method 174

proof(s), demonstration(s) (cont.)
for the incorporeality of the first causes 725
for the prophethood of Muḥammad 701–702
geometrical 118–119, 156
inductive 488
logical 47, 403, 406, 444
mathematical 170
rational (*qiyāsiyya ʿaqliyya, dalīl ʿaqlī*) 477, 480, 494
scriptural (*kitābiyya ṣaḥafiyya*) 477–478, 480
propaedeutics 49, 301, 467, 549
ethical 34, 193, 330–331, 337–338, 479, 484, 494
in Abū Sulaymān al-Siǧistānī 295–296
in al-Fārābī 549–552
in Ibn al-Ḫammār 488
in Ibn Hindū 347–349
in Ibn al-Samḥ 493–495
in al-Kindī 160–162, 193–194
in Miskawayh 310–312
philosophical 341, 596
property, properties; proprium, propria 159, 430, 445, 552–554, 560
ḫāṣṣa, ḫawāṣṣ 457, 464
prophet(s) 84, 186, 191, 225, 230, 271, 290, 299, 314–315, 320, 324, 336–337, 389, 407–408, 477, 493, 580, 590, 693, 702, 738, 742, 744–746, 748, 756
entrusted with a message (*al-nabī al-mursal*) 314
Jewish legends concerning 737
nabiyy 625
prophethood, prophecy 261, 300, 313, 319, 336, 407–408, 423, 473, 580, 592–593, 613, 622, 733, 742, 754
nubuwwa 314
of Muḥammad 118, 476, 701–702
prophetology (in al-Fārābī) 577
prophylaxis 703
proportion(s) 201, 231, 342, 565, 732
nisba 327–328, 338, 548
proposition (cf. also ☞ statement[s], declarative) 444, 586, 589
prose 297
naṯr 290
artistic (*inšāʾ*) 280
prostration 153, 165
providence, divine 171, 199, 320, 456, 463, 575, 585, 594
prudence 583
fiṭna 408
ḥilm 323, 401, 467
φρόνησις 635
σωφρασύνη (temperance) 488
taʿaqqul 575–576, 613–614
pseudepigraphy 663, 672, 676
psychology 159, 190, 192–194, 201, 335, 633
Aristotelian and Platonic 678
in Abū Bakr al-Rāzī 389, 409–410, 412
in al-ʿĀmirī 263, 265–266, 269–271
in al-Fārābī 577, 613–615
in al-Kindī 165–169, 196–199
in Miskawayh 312–322
in al-Saraḫsī 226
in the philosophical curriculum 582
in the introduction of *Rasāʾil Iḫwān al-Ṣafāʾ* 754
Neoplatonic 331, 335, 348
punishment 270
purity (*ṣafāʾ*) 752
purpose, aim 244, 258, 323–324, 327, 338, 554, 562
of studying philosophy 494
origins of things 468
pyramids 235
Pythagoreans 49, 322, 328, 440, 554, 754

qadar 737–738
Qarmatians 742
quadrivium 43, 159, 711–712
quality, qualities 184, 186, 191, 312, 327, 338, 426, 447, 478, 589, 678, 729, 732–733, 757
kayfiyya 160, 555
moral (*ḫuluq, aḫlāq*, ἦθος) ☞ character
quantity 191, 258, 312, 327, 338, 447–449, 462, 589, 690
kam 555
kammiyya 160
question(s) 549, 603
four scientific, following Aristotle 287, 312, 332, 426, 443, 451, 477–478
question and answer form 688
standardized (κεφάλαιον) 677

quiddity 553, 739
quinque voces (cf. also ☞ predicates) 445
Quran 2, 7–8, 20, 159, 163, 165, 191, 237, 242, 263, 271, 283–284, 288, 290, 295, 298, 300, 315, 320, 403, 408, 460–461, 590, 608, 729, 737, 739–740, 756
  its inimitability 408, 702
Quranic exegesis 20, 237, 261, 277
Quranic sciences (in Abū Zayd al-Balḫī) 238–239

rain 183–185, 200, 731
  indicators of 183
rainbow 486, 715
rational faculty 166, 579, 582–583, 613, 742, 744, 748
  νοῦς 465
  al-quwwa al-nāṭiqa 579, 613
  al-quwwa al-naẓariyya 580
rationalism 33, 64, 116, 282, 295, 462, 701
rationality 7, 14, 403, 605, 607
rational soul 161, 188, 282, 285, 323, 336, 340, 349, 400, 467, 479, 484, 488
  its purification (*tahḏīb al-aḫlāq*) 282
  al-nafs al-ʿāqila 334
  al-nafs al-nāṭiqa 456
ray(s) 187, 200, 568, 730
reality, realities 14, 166–167, 318
  of things 756
  spiritual 738
  ḥaqāʾiq 739, 756
  composite 488
recreation, restoration (of actions) (*iʿāda*) 455, 466
reason 80, 120, 165–166, 268, 288, 300, 310, 315, 318, 327, 334, 337, 343, 348, 397, 400, 404, 407, 456, 478, 488, 589, 740, 743, 755
  ʿaql 159, 289, 297, 315, 402–403, 406, 408, 573
  as coming from God 398
  as God's representative in this world 288, 298
  theoretical and practical 494–495
reception
  Arabic, of ancient philosophy and science 48, 60–64, 156–158, 243–244, 253, 423–434, 440, 506
  of Aristotle, in antiquity 677
  of al-Fārābī's doctrines and writings 541–545, 573
  of Greek popular philosophy, in late antiquity 77
  Syriac, of Aristotle 44, 54–60
recollection 157, 167, 197–198, 287, 312, 340, 401, 584–585
  ἀνάμνησις 197
Reconquista 2
reductio ad absurdum (cf. also ☞ *reductio ad impossibile*) 458
reductio ad impossibile (cf. also ☞ *reductio ad absurdum*) 558, 560
  ḫalf 557
refutation (*radd*) 21, 505
regress, infinite 466
reflection 176, 399, 407, 465, 580, 738
  and spontaneity 290
  divine 616
  inʿikās 486
  naẓar 408
  philosophical 14, 631, 740, 744
  rawiyya 160, 311
refraction (of visual rays) (*inkisār*) 486
relation(s) 46, 258, 430, 447, 453, 462, 485, 495, 578, 589, 615, 726
  and the relative (*al-iḍāfa wa-l-muḍāf*) 555
  iḍāfa 160, 548
  nisba 327, 338, 548, 566
  specific 566
relative (*muḍāf*) 160, 410
religion(s) 15, 33–34, 121, 271, 282, 288–289, 326, 389, 407–408, 412, 452, 473, 476, 478–479, 489, 570, 702, 708, 744, 754, 756
  and kingship 299, 343
  and philosophy 271, 290, 581, 583, 599, 622, 625–626
  and philosophy, according to Abū Zayd al-Balḫī 242–243
  and philosophy, according to al-ʿĀmirī 271–272
  and philosophy, according to al-Tawḥīdī and Abū Sulaymān al-Siǧistānī 297–299
  as symbolic representation of philosophy 544

religion(s) (cont.)
creates the God-given conditions for happiness 343
dīn 233, 246
founder of (*wāḍiʿ al-milla*) 547
history of (in al-Saraḫsī) 225, 229–230
in the development of the sciences 549
its definition, according to al-Fārābī 576
milla, milal 547, 549, 626
proclaims truth with the means of poetry and rhetoric 598
religion, philosophy of 715
in al-ʿĀmirī 258–260
religious community/communities 164, 343, 467, 493–494
religious studies (in Abū Zayd al-Balḫī) 239
renaissance 1, 7, 277
renunciation of the world (*zuhd*) ☞ asceticism
representation
divine (*taṣawwur*) 460
symbolic 626
tamṯīl 626
rest 160, 302, 485, 744
in God (*sakīna*) 285, 290, 300
perfect 742
within the essence of the soul 742
result (*muʾaṯṯar, mafʿūl*) 742
resurrection 260, 452, 477, 754
bodily 269
'great' 758
of the soul 271
return
of the human soul to its heavenly origin 745
of the rational soul (*maʿād*) 479
to God 82
to oneself (*rāǧiʿ ilā ḏātihi*, πρὸς ἑαυτὸ ἐπιστρεπτικόν) 335
revelation
according to Abū Bakr al-Rāzī 406–408
divine 34, 37, 268, 295, 298, 300, 314, 324, 576, 580, 592, 625
prophetic 191, 230, 336–337
religious 19–20, 423, 479–480, 604, 737, 739–740, 743, 756
revision (*iṣlāḥ*) 713
reward 270, 342, 350, 397, 402
rhetoric 50, 159, 278, 284, 295, 392, 406, 549, 554, 559–564, 575–576, 583, 588–589, 597–599, 604, 607–608, 611, 619
rhythm 179, 563, 569, 610
īqāʿ 160, 565
rhythmics 569, 611
riddle 289
alġāz 554
root (*ǧiḏr*) (in mathematics) 160
rule (cf. also ☞ governance) 200, 229, 343, 580
and religion 299, 343
mulk 260
of God (*rubūbiyya*) 229, 249
ruler (cf. also ☞ king) 242, 244, 248–249, 290, 299, 324, 326, 342, 484, 541, 576, 580–583, 624–627, 631, 673–674
rules, general (*qawānīn kulliyya*) 547
ruling force (*ḥākim*, ἡγεμονικόν) 328
ruling organ 339
ἡγεμονικόν 339
al-ʿuḍw al-raʾīs 624

Sabian(s) 155, 161, 222–223, 229–230, 260, 667, 700, 709–710, 722
sadness, sorrow (*ḥuzn, ǧazaʿ*) ☞ grief
Saffarid(s) 254, 291
sage, wise (*ḥakīm*) 403, 475, 625
Samanid(s) 237, 247, 257, 387, 741, 743
Sanskrit 661, 673
Sasanian(s) 98–101, 112, 249, 276, 283, 299, 343, 460, 665, 673–674, 683
Saturn 181–182, 266, 578, 616, 729
saying (*maṯal*) (cf. also ☞ aphorism[s]) 248, 281
scala naturae 758
scale(s) 179–180
ǧamāʿāt 569
modal 179
scapulomancy 187
scenery, stage setting (*naẓar*, ὄψις) 431
scent(s) 179, 675–676, 678
Sceptics, Scepticism 62, 335, 671
scholia (*taʿālīq*) 430, 432
school(s) 482
four Hellenistic 30, 48
of Abū Bišr Mattā and Ibn ʿAdī 429–434, 441–442, 471, 478, 505

of Alexandria 40–47, 77, 85, 331, 424, 595
of Antioch 55, 60
of Athens 36–39, 48, 53–54, 331
of Baghdad 55
of Edessa 60
of Gundishapur 60
of Harran 55, 60
of Nisibis 55, 60
philosophical, of late antiquity 29–31, 35, 39, 424, 467, 551, 662, 666, 668
uskūl 428
schoolmen, Latin 3
school tradition, fictitious 52
science(s), scientific discipline(s) 17–18, 260, 267–268, 287, 290, 295, 298, 310–311, 322–324, 331, 554, 583–584, 612, 618, 708
ancient (*al-ʿulūm al-qadīma*) 20
and philosophy 55, 98, 100
empirical 733
foreign (*ʿulūm al-ʿağam*) 20, 277
Greek 154
ʿilm 459, 494
imaginary (*al-ʿulūm al-wahmiyya*) 317
Islamic 20, 155, 427, 277, 738, 740, 758
its division, classification 20, 159, 239, 247–249, 311, 332, 406, 546, 550, 685, 711–712, 728, 754–755
its system, according to al-Fārābī 596
mathematical 35, 176
natural (*ʿulūm al-ṭabīʿa*) 18, 728
occult 247, 249, 673
of humankind (*al-ʿilm al-insānī*) 634
of the community (*al-ʿilm al-madanī*) 547, 576, 596–598, 634–635
of things human (πολιτική, according to Aristotle) 634–635
particular 574
practical 317, 614, 711–712, 218, 426
profane 737, 740
propaedeutics 754
rational (*al-ʿulūm al-ʿaqliyya*) 20, 286, 299, 349, 386, 433, 459, 467, 473, 756
religious 20, 260, 754, 756
theoretical 621
true (*al-ʿulūm al-ḥaqīqiyya*) 467
scientific theory 331–332, 348, 604
in al-Fārābī 546–549, 594–599
in Ibn ʿAdī 458–459
in Ibn al-Ḫammār 488
in al-Kindī 158–159, 189–193
seasons 171, 183–184, 201, 731
secrecy (of religious creed) (*taqiyya*) 741
Secretum secretorum 673
seed (*biḏr*) 335
self-awareness 37, 323
self-knowledge 160, 255, 271, 321, 578
self-reflection 334, 607
self-sufficiency 488
Seljuks 674
semantics 546
sensation, sense perception(s) 63, 163, 167–169, 191–192, 197, 230, 265, 270, 313–314, 316–319, 322, 333–334, 488, 557, 584, 586|
maḥsūsāt 553
sensible object 160, 194, 230, 565, 580, 584, 619, 744
maḥsūs 258, 553, 739
sense perception, sense(s) 165, 167, 169, 178, 192, 200, 285, 287–288, 312–314, 316–318, 320–321, 330, 335–337, 340, 349, 488, 579, 584, 589
common (*al-ḥāss al-muštarak*) 328, 336
ḥāss 160
ḥiss 160
internal 198, 336
possessing sensation (*muḥiss*) 402
theory of 339
sentence(s) 555–557
assertoric 557
qawl 553
types of 555
separate (*muğarrad[a]*) 739
seven 322, 738
Sharia 234, 241–242, 246, 288, 290, 300, 739
Shia, Shiism 6, 8, 225, 276, 298–299, 737, 758
Ismaili ☞ Ismāʿīliyya, Ismaili(s)
Twelver 5–6, 236, 541–542, 759
sign 562
linguistic 601–602
signifying (*dāll*) 564
simple (*basīṭ*) 556
sincerity (*ṣafāʾ*) 752
sky (cf. also ☞ heavens) 186–187
its blue colour 201

sleep 169, 198, 243, 287, 400, 410, 580, 584
snow 186
social interaction in the community
  muʿāmalāt 260
  muʿāwana 311
society, societies 20, 61, 99–100, 103, 105, 113, 116–118, 120, 290, 299–300, 311, 325–6, 328, 331, 341, 343, 389, 400, 402, 428, 484, 488, 495, 580–2, 611, 660–2, 704, 723, 756
Socratics 62
'Socratification' (of Aristotle) 677
Sogdian 540
solecisms 105
sophia perennis 5–7
sophism, sophismata 444
  šubha, ἀπάτη 454
sophist(s) 564, 583, 671
sophistics 549, 559–560, 562, 564, 583, 598
  in the development of the sciences 549
sorrow ☞ grief
soul 6, 29, 163, 165–169, 184, 196–199, 242–243, 253, 294, 302, 330, 333, 338, 397–398, 474–475, 500, 574–575, 580–581, 583, 589–590, 594, 601, 618, 672, 737
  affectible 339
  afterlife of 84, 340
  and divinatory dream 300
  and Intellect, as primordial pair 744
  and musical harmony 177
  animal 288, 349
  appetitive (*al-nafs al-šahwāniyya*) 323, 338, 456
  as eternal principle, according to Abū Bakr al-Rāzī 392, 411
  as form of the body 300
  as immaterial substance 196–197, 317–318, 330–331, 333–334
  as incorporeal substance 330, 349
  as intermediate entity, in Abū Bakr al-Rāzī 411
  as living substance 320
  as part (*ḥadd*) of the Universal Soul 742
  as perfection (ἐντελέχεια) of the body 160, 335, 679
  as Plotinian hypostasis 747
  as pure, substantial form 333
  as simple substance (*ǧawhar mabsūṭ*, ἁπλῆ οὐσία) 323, 335, 340
  as topic of metaphysics 618
  bestows life without being life itself 313, 320, 334
  combines meanings 553
  downward orientation ('tail', *ḏanab*) 757
  has five faculties, according to al-Fārābī 575, 579
  human 34, 161, 165, 167, 229, 259, 572, 737, 739, 742, 745, 754
  its afterlife 84
  its aim (*multamas al-nafs*) 285–286, 311
  its composition 717
  its definition 335
  its diseases 326, 405
  its divine origin 406, 408
  its education 575
  its essence 254, 290, 314, 742
  its faculties 84, 160, 178, 266, 268, 284, 301, 314, 324, 328, 337, 340, 399, 480, 613
  its fall into matter 743, 755
  its fate in the hereafter 348
  its guidance 633
  its happiness 310
  its healing 399
  its health 326
  its immortality 255, 260, 314, 334, 342, 676–678
  its liberation from the body 402–406, 675
  its movement 334–335
  its nature 678
  its perfection 456, 627
  its prior existence 198–199
  its purification 331, 494, 758
  its relation to the body 83, 260, 269–270, 311, 320–321, 330, 335, 339–341, 349–350, 399, 581, 676
  its relation to the human being 287
  its return to God 82
  its return to its original world 410
  its role in creation, according to Abū Bakr al-Rāzī 409–411
  its substance 495
  nafs 160, 290, 451, 590
  of the spheres 200

rational 84, 285, 301, 303, 314, 338, 399, 405, 473
reaches painless state after death 400
receives the gift of prophecy 288
rest of (*sukūn al-nafs*) 606, 609
subsisting in itself (*qāʾim bi-ḏātihi*) 320, 333
upward orientation ('head', *raʾs*) 757
soul, part(s) of 168, 194, 268–269, 287, 312, 322, 338, 343, 466–467, 614, 678
appetitive (ἐπιθυμητικόν, *al-quwwa al-šahwāniyya/al-šahwiyya, al-bahīmiyya*) 323, 466–467, 480
cognitive (ἐπιτημονικόν) 635
deliberative (βουλευτικόν) 635
irascible (*ġaḍabiyya*, θυμοειδές) 84, 301, 323, 338, 456, 466–467, 480
rational (λογιστικόν, *al-quwwa al-nāṭiqa*) 323, 466–467, 480
tripartite 336, 339, 399, 405, 456, 476, 480
Soul, Universal 166, 270, 272, 742, 744, 746–747, 757–758
as demiurge 757
emanated from the Intellect 745
its movement 745
soul-body dualism 479, 676
souls 758
celestial 591, 617
of human beings 591, 626
of the deceased 630
of the heavenly bodies 292
their number 726
sound(s) 200
space 165, 319, 333–334, 409, 462, 584, 594, 737
absolute and relative 410
as eternal principle, according to Abū Bakr al-Rāzī 392, 411, 743
as intermediate entity, in Abū Bakr al-Rāzī 411
makān 410, 451
Spain, Spanish 503, 536, 543, 666, 759
species 56, 159–160, 164–165, 168, 190, 192, 197, 313, 316, 327, 334, 445–446, 449–450, 452–453, 459, 462, 552–554, 560, 574, 578–579, 610, 726, 730
specific (*ḫāṣṣ*) 556, 560
speculation (*ẓann*) 288
speech defect(s) (*luṯġa*) 188
speeches (*ḫuṭab*) 279
sphere(s) 171, 178, 182–184, 186, 196, 199–200, 245, 263, 266, 268, 270–272, 292–293, 298, 303–304, 313, 315–316, 318–319, 321–322, 332–333, 335, 485, 578, 581, 589, 594, 616, 728–729, 732, 738, 742, 747, 757
nine 578, 616, 619
spirit (cf. also ☞ pneuma) 457, 500
of holiness 740
rūḥ 290, 321, 590
visual (*al-rūḥ al-bāṣir*) 699
spiritual beings 285
arwāḥ 321
rūḥāniyya 738
spontaneity (and reflection) 290
state
διάθεσις (of the soul) 323
temperate, balanced (*iʿtidāl al-mizāǧ*, εὐκρασία) 337
unhappy (*kudūra*) 407
states (*aḥwāl*) 289–290, 289, 300, 321, 466, 475–476, 478–479, 485
essential 476
of the divine substance 478–479
of the one essence 475
state (political) 299, 341, 575, 624, 627–628, 633
ideal, spiritual (*madīna fāḍila rūḥāniyya*) 758
statement(s), declarative (cf. also ☞ proposition)
adopted from trustworthy people (*maqbūlāt*) 553, 557
apodeictic and universally true 605
contrary, subcontrary, and contradictory 557
maqūl 602
not specified (*muṭlaq*) 387
not unequivocally quantified and modalized 608
poetic (*qawl šiʿrī*) 563
qualified (*muqayyad*) 561
universally recognized, commonly accepted (*mašhūrāt, mašhūr*) 553, 557, 559–560
stations (of the moon) (*manāzil*) 184

Stoic(s) 19, 29, 47–48, 55, 62, 325, 335, 338–340, 596, 662, 671, 678, 755
strings, string instruments 177–178, 180, 201, 569
students
of Ammonius 40–41, 45
of Ibn ʿAdī 441–442
of Ibn al-Ḫammār 482
of Iamblichus 36
of Olympiodorus 41
subject 474, 554, 574, 589, 678
from the Alexandrian *kephalaia* 473, 483
mawḍūʿ, τὸ ὑποκείμενον 444, 479
of perfect love 578
primary subject matter (*al-mawḍūʿ al-awwal*) (of metaphysics) 618
σκοπός 443
subjects, political (*raʿāyā*) 260
substance(s) 159, 165–166, 171–173, 177, 191, 199, 258, 261, 270, 293–294, 296, 300, 317–318, 320, 327–328, 333, 338, 340–341, 430, 445–448, 451, 466, 483, 485, 487, 503, 555, 579, 581, 584, 586, 589, 678, 745
and accidents 490
and essential attributes 490
Aristotelian doctrine of 479
becoming a substance 630
change in 726
changeable 728
classification of 322
corporeal 328, 725
corporeal and incorporeal 336
divine 457, 462, 464, 478–479
eternal (*ǧawhar azalī*) 474, 479
ǧawhar, ǧawāhir 302, 455, 548, 555, 603, 744
in Trinitarian theology 464
incorporeal 315
inherent in it, as inseparable accident (ἐν ὑποκειμένῳ) 446, 489
intelligible 313, 336
its essential attributes/essential properties (συμπληρωτικὰ τῆς οὐσίας) 308, 488
material 459
of an intelligence 465
of the soul 331, 334, 495
part of (μέρος τῆς οὐσίας) 446, 488–489
separate and motionless, of the First Mover 303
separate from the body (*muǧarrada*) 739
simple (*ǧawhar mabsūṭ*, ἁπλῆ οὐσία) 159, 166, 335, 343
spiritual (*rūḥāniyya*) 318
spiritual, subtle (*ǧawhar rūḥānī laṭīf*) 318
subsisting through itself (*ǧawhar qāʾim bi-ḏātihi*, αὐθυπόστατος οὐσία) 319
transformation of 732
two, of the human being 269
two kinds of incorporeal substances (ἀσώματα ἀχώριστα, χώριστα) 336
substantiality 335, 464
ǧawhariyya 294
substantialization (*taǧawhur*) 616
substrate(s) 166, 324, 339, 447, 452, 460, 475, 489, 505, 594, 757
bodily, corporeal 166, 319, 333, 485
imperishable 475
material 169, 313, 328
of the intellect 479
receptive (*mafʿūl*) 304
subtle (*laṭīf*) 321
succession (of accidents) 485
suffering 329, 495, 754
Sufism 6, 8, 256, 262, 269, 278–279, 284, 674, 752
taṣawwuf 4, 262, 278, 295
sun 166, 171, 182–185, 199, 266, 484, 568, 578, 580, 616, 690–691, 729–731, 757
compared to a king 729
its rays 153, 611
sphere of 268
Sunna (*sunna*) (cf. also ☞ custom, ☞ law[s]) 6, 229, 276, 283, 299
Sunni 758
support (*taʾyīd*) 746
supposition
wahm 160
ẓann 288
Šuʿūbiyya 181
syllogism, syllogistic 79, 82, 190, 295, 332, 395, 445, 554, 556–557, 560, 562–563, 584, 589, 604, 607–608, 714
Aristotelian 56, 59, 423
categorical 557–558

conditional 577
definition of 557
its division in five kinds 406, 552, 554, 603
logical form 111
poetical 563–565, 604
potential assertoric 564
significance for al-Fārābī 603
sophistic 565
syllogistic figures 87, 447, 458–459, 556–557, 713–714
theory of 156
transfer to the realm of noetics and ontology 604
symbol(s) 14, 295, 581, 599, 625–626, 756
sensually perceptible (*amṯila maḥsūsa*) 739
sympathy 404
synonym(s) 445, 555–556
mutarādif 556
al-mutawāṭi'a asmā'uhā, συνώνυμα 483
synonymy 311, 548
syntax 546, 602
synthesis 586, 610, 620
Syriac 17, 56, 60, 104–107, 109, 111–113, 117, 122, 332, 540, 662, 664, 683, 707, 720–721, 723
system
cosmic, of the intellects 616
ṭarīqa 440

tablet (*lawḥ*) 271
taste (*ḏawq*) 565
Ṭayyibites, Ismaili 741, 748, 753, 755, 759
temperament(s) (cf. also ☞ mixture) 178, 286, 320, 327–328, 337, 339–340
κρᾶσις, κράσεις 323, 337
mizāǧ, *amziǧa* 288, 300, 323, 337, 505
temperance, abstinence, abstemiousness 268, 323, 338, 398, 468, 484
as cardinal virtue 268
'iffa, σωφροσύνη 325, 488
term(s), concept(s) 191, 246, 285, 302, 338, 348, 431, 446, 462, 479, 571, 589, 594, 599, 601, 603, 610, 618, 738, 740, 746
general 574
intelligible 565
Quranic 271, 300
taṣawwur 554, 558, 605
terminology, Arabic technical 17
tetrachord 179, 569
that (*anna*) 548
theocracy 299
theologians 488, 490, 557, 547, 573
aṣḥāb al-kalām 459
Christian 201
mutakallimūn 258, 288, 297, 300, 450, 454, 461, 485
Syriac 671
theology 6–7, 50–51, 56, 118–119, 190, 193, 248, 286, 459, 471, 347, 349, 592, 607–608, 660
and philosophy 12, 20–21
and religion, in Ḥunayn b. Isḥāq 693–694
as dialectical 598, 604
astral 757
belongs to metaphysics according to al-Fārābī 621
Christian 41
Christian, in Ibn 'Adī 457–458, 460–465
Christian, in Ibn Zur'a 478
al-'ilm al-ilāhī 163, 403, 406, 574, 618
'ilm al-kalām 4, 19, 596
in Abū Bakr al-Rāzī 391
in Abū Zayd al-Balḫī 239
in al-Fārābī's system of sciences 596
is not a rational science 288
Islamic (*kalām*) 8, 12, 20, 63, 117, 249, 284, 295, 428, 440, 461, 557, 578, 622
negative, of the Sabians 230
philosophical 34, 176, 331, 349, 388–389, 424
philosophical, of Ibn Hindū 348
philosophical, of Miskawayh 312–322
Platonic 37–38, 331–332, 337, 424–425, 462
science of divinity 495
symbolic respresentation of philosophy 544
Trinitarian 463
Theology of Aristotle 63, 119, 157–158, 167, 385, 591, 739, 745
theory
'ilm, as opposed to practice (*'amal*) 248
of propulsion 496

theosophy 9, 19
ḥikma ilāhiyya 5
therapy 318, 326, 550
therapeutic use of music 243, 348
theurgy 33–34, 37, 42
thing(s), object(s) 160, 163, 167–170, 172, 175, 186–188, 190, 192, 196–198, 255, 269, 294, 302–303, 313–320, 322, 324, 327–328, 331, 333–334, 349, 400–401, 408–409, 411, 460, 465, 484, 495, 502, 555, 578, 593, 605–607, 614–615, 626–627, 630, 739–740, 742, 756
as the subject matter of the *Categories* 31–32, 34
corporeal 757
five uncreated 411
šay' 549
their essences 467
tout court (ἁλῶς, *'alā l-iṭlāq*) 466
third (*wusṭā*) (*in music*) 180
this world (as opposed to the hereafter) 193–194, 199, 286, 325, 340, 397, 400, 408, 581, 586
thought, thinking 62, 113, 120, 168, 225, 317, 329, 431, 459, 556, 562, 573, 578, 581, 589, 598, 603, 610, 625, 756, 759
conceptual 548–549
contemporary philosophical 10
content(s) of thought (*ma'qūl*) 602
discursive (*fikr*) 582
faculty of thought (*quwwa fikriyya*) 263
God's 575, 581, 594
human powers of, human thinking 322–323, 337, 349, 399–400, 575, 580, 614, 616
Islamic 4, 7–8
its relation to language 296, 433, 556, 601–602
its structures 14
νόησις 460
objects of thought, actual (*ma'qūlāt bi-l-fi'l*) 614
of Necessary Existent 594
philosophical xi, 4, 8, 10, 13, 18
scientific 547, 598
Shiite 6
Stoic 55, 77
thinking of thinking (νόησις νοήσεως) 464
thoughtfulness (*tu'ada*) 401
throne, God's (*'arš*) 272, 729
thunder 185
time 56, 165, 170, 195, 197, 244, 302, 319, 333, 409, 412, 462, 485, 502, 553, 584, 594, 725, 733, 737, 747
absolute (*zamān muṭlaq*) 410
arises together with the Intellect according to Abū Ḥātim al-Rāzī 744
as an eternal principle, according to Abū Bakr al-Rāzī 392, 410, 743
as the measure of motion 465, 490
first and second 466
limited (*zamān maḥṣūr*) 410
terms 703
χρόνος 302
zamān 160, 451
timocracy (*madīnat al-karāma*) 628
title of a work (ἡ ἐπιγραφή) 443
topography (in al-Saraḫsī) 226
topoi 559–561, 714
tradition
Aristotelian 63, 201, 600, 610, 635, 678
blind following of (*taqlīd*) 408
late Alexandrian 431, 754
naql 494
prophetic ☞ *ḥadīṯ*
tradition of teaching 55, 74, 551
tragedy 431, 564
madīḥ 431
tranquillity (*rāḥa*) 400
transcendence
of a third, higher world 314
of God 163, 745, 747
translation(s) 120, 155, 660, 664
'ancient' (*naql qadīm*) 106
Arabic, from Greek 17, 62, 253, 433, 602, 633, 754
Arabic, from Syriac 87–88
by Ibn Zur'a 471–472
difficulties of 289
from Abū Bišr Mattā's school 429–432
from Greek, into Syriac and Arabic 685–587
in the circle of al-Kindī 155–158
into Arabic, by Ḥunayn b. Isḥāq 695–699
its methods, phases, and significance 104–108
of Aristotle, by Ibn al-Samḥ 492–493
of medical texts 384–386

of the *Categories* 291
of the *Poetics* 431
of the *Rhetoric* 492
practice of (*naql*) 709
Syriac-Arabic, of the *Organon* 425, 428–429
Syriac-Greek 80–81, 87–88, 104, 431
translation movement
Graeco-Arabic 17, 56, 61, 64, 97–103, 107, 111–114, 118, 121, 424, 660, 664, 670
Persian-Arabic 98, 665
translators
circle of Ḥunayn b. Isḥāq 426–428
circle of al-Kindī 191, 193
school of Abū Bišr Mattā and Yaḥyā Ibn ʿAdī 429–432, 441–442, 471–472, 478
transmigration 402, 755
tanāsuḫ 746
transmission
of gnomologia 664
of Greek philosophy 'from Alexandria to Baghdad' 51–53
of Indian and Iranian heritage 59
oral (ἀπὸ φωνῆς) 40
transposed (*manqūl*) 556
transposition (*naqla*) 561, 597
tree diagram (*tašǧīr, mušaǧǧar*) 247, 249, 429
triad (of the syllogistic figures as a symbol for Trinity) 82
trigonometry 567
Trinity, Christian 46, 107, 126, 150, 201, 308, 315, 318, 320–321, 329–330, 332, 339
defence by Ibn ʿAdī 460–465
doctrine of 117, 164, 192, 224, 303, 462
taṯlīṯ 457
truth 159, 166, 176, 285, 296, 331, 340, 401, 405, 407–408, 444, 484, 488–489, 493, 598, 601, 625, 671, 702
demonstration of 473, 478
ḥaqq 600
of a proposition 466
quest for 609
ṣidq 160
Turkey 16
Turkish 15–16, 102–103, 276, 537, 539–540, 590, 661, 674
twelve 738
tyranny
madīnat al-taġallub 628
ẓulm, ἀδικία 311

Umayyad(s) 86, 98–99, 118, 672–673, 693
uncreated (*qadīm*) 410
unbelief 117, 271
unhappiness 314
unicity (cf. also ☞ Trinity) 85, 457
union, unification
ittiḥād 166, 457, 477
ittiṣāl 477
mystical 279
of the two essences in Christ 477
taʾaḥḥud 328
unity 163, 188, 196, 294, 314, 342, 475, 547, 619
God's ☞ God – His unity
of substance 462
universal (*kullī*) 555
universals 167, 191–192, 270, 316–319, 334–335, 445, 461, 463, 553–554, 576, 586, 589, 598, 635
kulliyyāt 452, 460
universe (cf. also ☞ world) 159, 327, 339, 448, 464, 489, 747
univocal (*mutawāṭiʾ*) 556
untrue (*kāḏib*) 564
Urdu 15
useful 584
nāfiʿ 550
utterance(s), linguistic expression(s), term(s)
categorial (*maqūlāt*) 163
'fillers' (*ḥawāšin*) 553
lafẓ, alfāẓ 248, 444, 548, 561, 601
qawl 565
symbolic (*al-alfāẓ al-dālla ʿalā l-maʿānī*, φοναὶ σημαντικαί) 444
which indicate something (*alfāẓ dālla*) 550, 553

vacuum 302, 318, 393, 496, 594, 612
ḫalāʾ 451
vapour ☞ exhalation
Venus 182, 184, 266, 578, 616, 729
verb 555–556
fiʿl 553
veterinary medicine 686

vice 178, 266, 268, 284, 288, 310, 323, 326, 330, 338, 343, 399, 456, 495
 raḏāʾil 467
violence (*ǧawr*) 401
virtue(s) 161, 178, 243, 248, 249, 263, 284, 310, 320–330, 337–338, 340–343, 353, 404, 456, 467–468, 480, 484, 493, 495, 504, 575–576, 582, 586, 589, 590, 613, 632, 725
 aḫlāq ḥasana 467
 apparent 325
 catalogue, canon of 301, 323, 456, 468, 550
 ethical and dianoetic 459–460, 575
 faḍīla, faḍāʾil 467, 624, 634
 human (*faḍāʾil insāniyya*) 160–161
 of the soul 268, 467, 484, 586
 perfect 484
 spiritual (*faḍīla rūḥāniyya*) 325
 their degrees 325
 true 493, 495
 true and alleged virtue 576
vision 173, 175, 200–201, 258, 316–317, 580, 586, 699, 701, 725
 visual power (*al-quwwa al-bāṣira*) 486
vital heat 318, 339, 572, 579
vocabulary, scientific 191

wakefulness 169, 580, 584
war(s) 575, 673
 ǧihād 633
warmth ☞ heat
water 183–187, 199, 201, 339, 486, 570, 729, 732
weather forecasting 182–183, 200
 according to stars (*anwāʾ*) 716
well-being (*ʿimāra*) 244
 of the community (*maṣlaḥa, istiṣlāḥ*) 244
what (*mā*) 549
when (*matā*) 548, 555
where (*ayna*) 555
which (*ayyun*) 549
will 584, 589, 624
 free 19–20, 245–246, 290, 730
 God's 160–161, 240, 398, 409, 411, 585, 737
 human 584, 634
 irāda 160, 580, 737
 mašīʾa 737
 of the First Cause 725
wind(s) 184
wind instrument 569
wisdom 5, 160, 186, 268, 325, 338, 341, 408, 457, 467, 475, 484, 488, 575, 756
 absolute (*al-ḥikma ʿalā l-iṭlāq*) 597
 as cardinal virtue 268
 foreign 191
 γνῶσις 453
 ḥikma 13, 178, 310, 323, 328, 332, 453, 484, 739–740
 political 661, 672
 practical (φρόνησις) 635
 σοφία 13, 325, 463
wisdom literature 59, 283, 593, 665, 672
wise sayings 329
word(s) 85, 296, 332, 549, 533, 555, 597, 602
 as the topic of the *Categories* 32
 kalima 553
world (cf. also ☞ this world) 166, 184, 282, 409
 corporeal 745, 757
 crude (*ʿālam kaṯīf*) 744
 intelligible 30, 32, 298, 745, 747
 is a body 485
 is non-eternal 195
 its beginning, causal or temporal 244, 485, 489–490
 its creation and generation 111, 170, 408–409, 622
 its division into seven climes 731
 its eternity ☞ eternity – of the world
 its existence 725
 its perfection 690
 its perishability 589
 its structure 19, 622, 728
 of (the) intellect(s) 166–167, 194, 197, 199
 of generation and corruption 181, 293, 342, 612, 615, 757
 of light 321
 of nature 529
 of religion (*ʿālam al-dīn*) 740, 747
 of sublime ideas (*al-miṯālāt al-šarīfa*) 300
 sensible 32, 34, 49, 167, 285, 488

spatio-temporal 465
spiritual (*ʿālam laṭīf*) 744
sublunar 165, 171, 199, 268, 315, 327, 339, 486, 578–579, 581, 584, 612, 616, 622, 728–730, 738, 747, 758
supralunar, superlunary, the upper, the higher 260, 268–269, 331, 410, 578–579, 581, 622, 730, 733
terrestrial 731
world map 231
world soul ☞ Soul, Universal
worship (of God)
through knowledge (*al-ʿibāda al-ʿilmiyya*) 739
through philosophy and metaphysics (*al-ʿibāda al-falsafiyya al-ilāhiyya*) 756
through practice (*al-ʿibāda al-ʿamaliyya*) 739
through the religious law (*al-ʿibāda al-šarʿiyya al-nāmūsiyya*) 756
wrath 268, 399, 500
ġaḍab 243

yes-no question (*hal*) 549

Zand 98
Zaydiyya 242
zeal (*himma*) 408
zodiac (signs of) 272, 729, 738
zodiacal sphere 266, 272, 729
zoology 717–718
Zoroastrian(s), Zoroastrianism 100, 112, 245, 260

Index of Names

Abā II (d. 751) of Kashkar 87, 222
ʿAbd al-Ǧabbār (b. Aḥmad al-Hamaḏānī al-Asad Ābādī, d. 415/1025) 230, 347, 490, 752, 758
ʿAbd al-Ḥamīd b. Yaḥyā (d. 132/750) 672–673
ʿAbd Allāh al-Ḏahabī ☞ al-Ḏahabī, ʿAbd Allāh
ʿAbd Allāh b. Ṭāhir, general to the caliph al-Maʾmūn 102
ʿAbd al-Laṭīf al-Baġdādī (Muwaffaq al-Dīn Abū Muḥammad b. Yūsuf, d. 629/1231) 254, 431
ʿAbd al-Malik (b. Marwān, regn. 65–86/685–705), Umayyad caliph 99
ʿAbdān 741
ʿAbd al-Rāziq, Muṣṭafā (d. 1947) 4, 5
ʿAbdīšōʿ bar Berīḵā 87
Abraham Ibn Ḥasday 675
Abū Aḥmad al-Nahraǧūrī ☞ al-Nahraǧūrī, Abū Aḥmad
Abū l-ʿAlāʾ al-Maʿarrī ☞ al-Maʿarrī, Abū l-ʿAlāʾ
Abū l-ʿAlāʾ Sālim, secretary to the Umayyad caliph Hišām b. ʿAbd al-Malik 99, 673
Abū ʿAlī ʿĪsā b. Isḥāq Ibn Zurʿa ☞ Ibn Zurʿa, Abū ʿAlī ʿĪsā b. Isḥāq
Abū ʿAmr al-Ṭabarī, pupil of Abū Bišr Mattā 429, 432
Abū Bakr al-Ādamī ☞ al-Ādamī al-ʿAṭṭār, Abū Bakr
Abū Bakr al-Ṣiddīq (d. 13/634) 280
Abū l-Barakāt al-Baġdādī (Hibat Allāh b. Malkā, d. after 560/1164–1165) 594
Abū Bišr Mattā (Matthaeus) b. Yūnus (Yūnān) al-Qunnāʾī (d. 328/940) 17, 104, 256, 289, 295–296, 332, 403, 421, 424–425, 428–432, 445, 458, 471, 492, 495–496, 507, 511, 539, 601–602, 606, 720
Abū l-Faḍl Ibn al-ʿAmīd ☞ Ibn al-ʿAmīd (Abū l-Faḍl Muḥammad b. al-Ḥusayn)
Abū l-Fatḥ Ibn al-ʿAmīd Ḏū l-Kifāyatayn ☞ Ibn al-ʿAmīd (Abū l-Fatḥ Ḏū l-Kifāyatayn)
Abū Ǧaʿfar b. Bānūya (Aḥmad b. Muḥammad b. Ḫalaf, regn. 311–352/923–963), Saffarid ruler 291
Abū Ǧaʿfar al-Ḫāzin ☞ al-Ḫāzin (Abū Ǧaʿfar Muḥammad b. Muḥammad)
Abū Ǧaʿfar Muḥammad b. al-Qāsim al-Karḫī ☞ al-Karḫī, Abū Ǧaʿfar Muḥammad b. al-Qāsim
Abū l-Ḥakam al-Kirmānī ☞ al-Kirmānī, Abū l-Ḥakam
Abū Ḥāmid al-Ġazālī ☞ al-Ġazālī, Abū Ḥāmid
Abū Ḥanīfa al-Dīnawarī ☞ al-Dīnawarī, Abū Ḥanīfa
Abū l-Ḥasan ʿAlī b. Hārūn al-Zanǧānī ☞ al-Zanǧānī, Abū l-Ḥasan ʿAlī b. Hārūn
Abū l-Ḥasan ʿAlī b. Razīn 231
Abū l-Ḥasan Ibn Abī Ḏarr ☞ Ibn Abī Ḏarr, Abū l-Ḥasan
Abū Ḥātim al-Rāzī ☞ al-Rāzī, Abū Ḥātim
Abū Ḥayyān al-Tawḥīdī ☞ al-Tawḥīdī, Abū Ḥayyān
Abū Hilāl al-ʿAskarī ☞ al-ʿAskarī (Abū Hilāl al-Ḥasan b. ʿAbd Allāh)
Abū l-Huḏayl (d. 235/849) 450, 490
Abū l-Ḥusayn Isḥāq b. Ibrāhīm al-Kātib 248
Abū ʿĪsā Aḥmad Ibn al-Munaǧǧim ☞ Ibn al-Munaǧǧim, Abū ʿĪsā Aḥmad
Abū ʿĪsā al-Muršid, contemporary of the Fatimid caliph al-Muʿizz 737
Abū ʿĪsā al-Warrāq (Muḥammad b. Hārūn, 3rd/9th cent.) 439, 457, 461
Abū Isḥāq Ibrāhīm Quwayrā (Cyrus), teacher of Abū Bišr Mattā 429
Abū Maʿšar al-Balḫī (d. 272/886) 51, 154–155, 200, 229, 426, 728, 730–731
Abū Naḍr Nafīs 266
Abū Naṣr al-Fārābī, Muḥammad ☞ al-Fārābī (Abū Naṣr Muḥammad b. Muḥammad)
Abū Naṣr al-Fārābī al-Ǧawharī 590
Abū Nūḥ al-Anbārī, secretary to the governor of Mosul 425
Abū l-Qāsim al-Kātib, pupil of Abū l-Ḥasan al-ʿĀmirī 430
Abū Sahl Aḥmad b. ʿUbayd Allāh b. Aḥmad 232
Abū Sahl ʿAlī b. Muḥammad 283
Abū Sahl b. Nawbaḫt, court astrologer of the Abbasid caliph al-Manṣūr 100
Abū Saʿīd al-Sīrāfī ☞ al-Sīrāfī, Abū Saʿīd
Abū l-Šaraf ʿImād, son of Ibn Hindū 346

Abū Sulaymān Muḥammad b. Maʿšar al-Bustī al-Maqdisī ☞ al-Bustī al-Maqdisī, Abū Sulaymān Muḥammad b. Maʿšar
Abū Tammām, pupil of Muḥammad al-Nasafī 738, 741
Abū Tammām al-Naysābūrī 242, 290
Abū ʿUbayda (ʿĀmir b. ʿAbd Allāh b. al-Ǧarrāḥ, d. 18/639) 280
Abū ʿUṯmān al-Dimašqī ☞ al-Dimašqī, Abū ʿUṯmān
Abū Yaḥyā Ibrāhīm al-Marwazī ☞ al-Marwazī, Abū Yaḥyā Ibrāhīm
Abū Yaʿqūb al-Siǧistānī ☞ al-Siǧistānī, Abū Yaʿqūb
Abū Zakariyyāʾ Yaḥyā Ibn ʿAdī b. Ḥamīd b. Zakariyyāʾ ☞ Ibn ʿAdī, Yaḥyā
Abū Zayd Aḥmad b. Sahl b. Hāšim, governor of Balkh 237
Abū Zayd al-Balḫī ☞ al-Balḫī, Abū Zayd Aḥmad b. Sahl
Adam 590, 670, 693, 742
al-Ādamī al-ʿAṭṭār, Abū Bakr (from the circle of Ibn ʿAdī) 442, 446, 454
Adamson, Peter 11, 162, 190–191, 200–201, 452
ʿAḍud al-Dawla (Abū Šuǧāʿ Fanāʾ Ḫusraw, d. 372/983), Buyid ruler 276, 282, 291, 293, 297, 309, 313, 346, 441, 471, 499
Aelian (ca. 170–235) 677
Aertsen, Jan A. 13
Aetius [Pseudo-Plutarch] (1st cent.) 62, 122, 132, 390, 394, 670–671
Aetius of Amida (6th cent.) 487
Afḍal al-Dīn-i Kāšānī ☞ Kāšānī, Afḍal al-Dīn
al-ʿAǧam, Rafīq 555, 557, 559, 560
Agathodaemon 229
Ahiqar 130
Aḥmad b. ʿAbd Allāh b. Muḥammad b. Ismāʿīl, second hidden Imam 742, 753, 755
Aḥmad b. Abī l-Naǧm 668
Aḥmad b. Abī Ṭāhir 222, 230
Aḥmad b. ʿAlī, governor of Rayy 743
Aḥmad b. Kāmil, Qāḍī (d. 350/961) 309
Aḥmad b. Mūsā b. Šākir 707, 708, 718
Aḥmad b. al-Muʿtaṣim 154, 164, 171, 179, 180
Aḥmad b. al-Sārī Ibn al-Ṣalāḥ, Abū l-Futūḥ ☞ Ibn al-Ṣalāḥ
Ahrun 99
Aḥūḏemmeh of Nisibis (d. 575) 83, 84, 86
Aitallahā/Aitilaha 79
Āl Yāsīn, Ǧaʿfar 567, 589
al-ʿAlawī al-ʿAqīqī (Abū Aḥmad), travel companion of Abū Ḥayyān al-Tawḥīdī 279
Albinus (2nd cent.) 37
Alexander the Great (356–323 BC) 98–99, 108–109, 112, 118, 124, 297, 329, 669–670
Alexander of Aphrodisias (around 200) 30–31, 35, 56, 64, 119, 123, 130, 132, 156, 168, 172, 254, 291, 303, 313, 333, 336, 373, 385, 427, 429, 432, 440, 443, 452, 460, 492, 495, 574, 614, 617, 670, 678, 696, 728
ʿAlī b. Abī Ṭālib (d. 40/661) 276, 280, 753
ʿAlī b. al-Ǧahm (d. 249/863) 154, 170
ʿAlī b. Hārūn al-Zanǧānī, Abū l-Ḥasan ☞ al-Zanǧānī, Abū l-Ḥasan ʿAlī b. Hārūn
ʿAlī b. ʿĪsā b. al-Ǧarrāḥ (d. 334/946), vizier 289, 427, 442
ʿAlī b. Rabban al-Ṭabarī ☞ al-Ṭabarī, ʿAlī b. Rabban
ʿAlī Ibn Riḍwān ☞ Ibn Riḍwān
ʿAlī b. ʿUbayda al-Rayḥānī ☞ al-Rayḥānī, ʿAlī b. ʿUbayda
ʿAlī b. Yaḥyā Ibn al-Munaǧǧim ☞ Ibn al-Munaǧǧim, ʿAlī b. Yaḥyā
Allīnūs 124, 483
Alon, Ilai 162
Alonso Alonso, Manuel 690
al-ʿAlūǧī, ʿAbd al-Ḥamīd 694
al-Amīn (regn. 193–198/809–813), Abbasid caliph 101
Amīn, Aḥmad (d. 1954) 4
al-ʿĀmirī, Abū l-Ḥasan (Muḥammad b. Yūsuf, d. 381/992) 13, 17, 132, 158, 233, 235–236, 238, 242, 244–245, 247–249, 252–253, 256–272, 277, 284, 286, 288, 298, 290, 300, 344, 346, 349, 353, 359, 430, 542, 672, 738–739
Ammonius Hermeiou (d. after 517) 32, 40–42, 44–47, 49–50, 56–57, 63, 77, 79, 81–82, 85, 124, 158, 488–489, 499, 501, 677–678
Anacharsis 124, 665
Anawati, Georges C. 16
Anaxagoras of Clazomenae (500/496–428 BC) 285, 670
al-Anbārī, Abū Nūḥ ☞ Abū Nūḥ al-Anbārī

al-Andalusī, Abū Ḥayyān (Muḥammad b. Yūsuf b. ʿAlī, d. 745/1344) 239
Andronicus of Rhodes (1st cent. BC) 552, 677
Anebo 33
Anqīlāʾus 110
al-Anṣārī, Muḥammad 666
Anselmo Turmeda 759
Anthemius of Tralles (d. around 534) 176
Antipater 678
Antony of Tagrit (9th cent.) 87
Anūširwān ☞ Ḫusraw I Anūširwān (regn. 531–578/9), Sasanian ruler
Apollonius of Perga (ca. 260–190 BC) 41
Arānī 229
Archigenes 162
Archimedes (ca. 287–212 BC) 41, 174, 755
Ardašīr I, founder of the Sasanian dynasty 98, 299, 343
Arius Didymus (1st cent. BC) 325
Arethas (9th–10th cent.) 108
Aristophanes (born ca. 450 BC) 106
Aristotle (384–322 BC) 9, 13, 17, 21, 29–40, 44–48, 50, 52, 55–60, 62–64, 74, 77, 79–88, 99, 102–103, 106–107, 109–111, 113–114, 117–119, 124–125, 131, 155–159, 163, 165–168, 170–172, 178, 183, 185–186, 189–199, 229, 248–249, 253–255, 258–260, 264–265, 267–268, 281, 286–293, 296, 301–303, 309–312, 316–317, 319, 321–322, 324–325, 327–344, 348–350, 385, 389–390, 394–395, 400, 404, 406, 410, 423–432, 434, 441, 443, 447–448, 450–453, 459–460, 462, 465–466, 471–473, 475, 478–479, 483–490, 492, 495–496, 501–507, 510, 511, 540, 543–544, 547–551, 554–556, 559, 561–565, 569–574, 577, 582–586, 589, 593–595, 598–599, 602–603, 606, 608, 610–616, 618, 620, 627–629, 632, 634–635, 658–659, 661, 665–666, 668–672, 674–679, 685, 689, 691, 695–697, 700, 712–720, 722–726, 728, 730, 737–738, 754, 756, 759
Aristoxenus of Tarent (born 376 BC) 43
Arkoun, Mohammed 4, 315
Arnzen, Rüdiger 716
al-ʿArūḍī (Abū Muḥammad), from the circle of Abū Sulaymān al-Siǧistānī 292
al-Asʿad Abū l-Faraǧ Hibat Allāh Ibn al-ʿAssāl ☞ Ibn al-ʿAssāl (al-Asʿad Abū l-Faraǧ Hibat Allāh)
al-Ašʿarī (Abū l-Ḥasan ʿAlī b. Ismāʿīl, d. 324/935–936) 21, 753
al-Ašʿaṯ b. Qays (d. ca. 40/661) 152
Asclepius (6th cent.) 32, 40, 669–670
al-ʿAskarī (Abū Hilāl al-Ḥasan b. ʿAbd Allāh, d. after 400/1010) 248
Athanasius II of Balad (d. 686) 57, 75, 78–81, 88, 111, 425, 471
Augustus (Octavian), Roman Emperor (63 BC to 14 AD) 551
Avempace ☞ Ibn Bāǧǧa
Averroes ☞ Ibn Rušd
Avicenna ☞ Ibn Sīnā
al-ʿAwfī 752

Badawī, ʿAbd al-Raḥmān 8, 19, 422, 571, 573, 592, 668
al-Badīhī, Abū l-Ḥasan ʿAlī b. Muḥammad (from the circle of Ibn ʿAdī) 442
Baḏōqā Michael 85
Baffioni, Carmela 202, 670, 749, 755
al-Baġdādī, ʿAbd al-Laṭīf ☞ ʿAbd al-Laṭīf al-Baġdādī
al-Baġdādī, Abū l-Barakāt ☞ Abū l-Barakāt al-Baġdādī
al-Baġdādī, Abū Isḥāq Ibrāhīm b. ʿAbd Allāh 531, 538, 567
Bahāʾ al-Dawla, son of ʿAḍud al-Dawla, emir of Fārs 346
al-Bāḫarzī (ʿAlī b. Ḥasan, d. 467/1075) 347
Bahmanyār b. al-Marzubān (d. around 430/1038–1039, or 458/1066–1067) 535, 591
al-Balḫī, Abū Maʿšar ☞ Abū Maʿšar al-Balḫī
al-Balḫī, Abū l-Qāsim al-Kaʿbī (ʿAbd Allāh b. Aḥmad b. Maḥmūd, d. 319/931) 237–238, 242, 391, 475, 571
al-Balḫī, Abū Zayd Aḥmad b. Sahl (d. 322/934) 17, 155, 224, 231–235, 236–238, 240–249, 256, 266, 278, 284, 287–290, 295, 298, 353–355, 388–389, 739
al-Balḫī, Šuhayd/Šahīd b. al-Ḥusayn 159, 163, 266, 268

Banū Mūsā (b. Šākir) 103–104, 154, 426, 684, 709, 715
Bardaiṣān (154–222) 55
Barhebraeus (d. 685/1286) 78, 87, 109, 221, 386–388, 695, 706, 721
Basil 463, 665, 669–670
Basil, priest from Cyprus 78
Basil of Caesarea (the Great, d. 379) 463, 665
al-Baṣrī, Abū l-Ḥusayn Muḥammad b. ʿAlī b. al-Ṭayyib (d. 436/1044) 432, 493, 495, 502
al-Baṣrī, Ḥasan ☞ Ḥasan al-Baṣrī
al-Bāqillānī (Abū Bakr Muḥammad b. al-Ṭayyib b. Muḥammad, d. 403/1013) 490
Bausani, Alessandro 396
al-Bayhaqī (Ẓahīr al-Dīn Abū l-Ḥasan ʿAlī b. Zayd Ibn Funduq, d. 565/1169–1170) 238, 386, 440, 473, 537, 546
Bergsträsser, Gotthelf 700–701
Bertolacci, Amos 719
Birkenmajer, Alexander 544, 569–570
al-Bīrūnī, Abū l-Rayḥān Muḥammad b. Aḥmad (362–ca. 442/973–ca.1050) 130, 181, 229–230, 347, 382, 386, 390–395, 482, 487
Bišr b. Bīšī ☞ Ibn ʿAnāyā al-Isrāʾīlī
Bišr b. al-Muʿtamir (d. 210/825) 403
Bišr b. Pinḥās b. Šuʿayb al-Ḥāsib 476
al-Biṭrīq (2nd half of the 2nd/8th cent.) 104
Blois, François de 705
Blumenthal, Henry J. 36, 39
Boer, Tjitze J. de 3–4
Boethius (d. 525) 109
Bolus Democritus (around 200, BC) 229
Bos, Gerrit 183
Brague, Rémi 15, 720
Brock, Sebastian 56–58, 61, 63, 79
Bruns, Ivo 466
Bryson, mathematician 473
Bryson (1st cent.?), Pythagorean 126, 324
al-Buḫārī (Abū l-ʿAbbās), pupil of Abū Sulaymān al-Siǧistānī 290, 475
al-Buḥayrī (Abū Ḥakīm Yūsuf), of Mayyāfāriqīn 475
Būlus (Paulus) 332
Burnett, Charles 182–183, 187
al-Bustī, Abū l-Qāsim (around 400/1010), Zaydī 741
al-Bustī al-Maqdisī, Abū Sulaymān Muḥammad b. Maʿšar 290, 752
al-Būzaǧānī (Abū l-Wafāʾ, d. 388/998) 279, 282
Buzurǧmihr b. Abī Manṣūr b. Farruḫānšāh al-Munaǧǧim 440

Carmody, Francis J. 182
Cassianus Bassus (6th cent.) 114
Cebes 126, 670
Celentano, Giuseppe 169
Cheikho, Louis 592, 700
Chrysippus of Soli (281/77–208/04 BC) 400, 662
Chwolsohn, Daniil Avraamovič 707, 712
Clearchus of Soli (born not later than 340 BC) 677
Cleopatra (d. 30 BC), Ptolemaic Queen 551
Colmo, Christopher A. 619
Constantine (the Great, d. 337), Roman Emperor 551
Corbin, Henry 5–9, 12, 14, 541–542, 630, 753
Critias 78
Crito 676
Crone, Patricia 623, 629, 633, 674

al-Dabbagh, Jamal 566
al-Ḏahabī, ʿAbd Allāh (4th/10th or 5th/11th cent.?) 555
Daiber, Hans 8, 15, 55, 121, 185, 542, 546, 590, 592, 692
al-Dalaǧī, Abū l-Qāsim, vizier in Shiraz 283
D'Alverny, Marie-Thérèse 187
Damascius (d. after 538) 37–40, 48
D'Ancona, Cristina 11, 30, 35–36, 38, 157–158
Dānišpažūh, Muḥammad Taqī 115, 557–560
Darwin, Charles Robert (d. 1882) 758
David (6th cent.) 32, 42, 47, 120, 501
David bar Paulus of Bēṯ Rabban (d. around 920) 83
David, King 178
al-Dawānī, Ǧalāl al-Dīn (Muḥammad b. Asʿad, d. 908/1502) 544, 628
Dāwūd b. Mūsaǧ, Abū l-Ḫayr 476–477
De Smet, Daniel 738
Degen, Rainer 695

Democritus of Abdera (ca. 460–380/370 BC) 665, 670, 676
Denḥā (Īhībā, Hībā) 86–87
Denḥā, Abū Zakariyyā' 87
Descartes, René (d. 1650) 620
Dhouib, Sarhan 11
Diebler, Stéphane 548
Dieterici, Friedrich 589, 592, 750, 758
al-Dimašqī, Abū ʿUṯmān (Saʿīd b. Yaʿqūb, 4th/10th cent.) 325, 343, 385, 405, 427, 432, 472
al-Dimašqī, Šams al-Dīn (Abū ʿAbd Allāh Muḥammad b. Abī Ṭālib al-Andalusī, d. 727/1327) 103
al-Dīnawarī, Abū Ḥanīfa (Aḥmad b. Dāwūd, 3th/9th cent.) 242, 284
Diocletian, Roman Emperor (regn. 284–305) 108
Diodorus of Tarsus (Alex. era) 670
Diogenes (of Sinope, 412/03–324/1 BC) 127, 299, 329, 484, 663, 669–670
Diogenes Laertius (end of 3rd cent.) 504, 677–678
Diophantus (around 250?) 43
Dioscurides (of Anazarbus, 1st cent.) 738
Dorotheus (of Sidon, 1st cent.) 183
Druart, Thérèse-Anne 194, 577, 615, 620
Dunlop, Douglas Morton 552, 554–555, 575, 668

Echecrates of Phleius (4th cent. BC) 177
Ehrig-Eggert, Carl 453, 460
Eichner, Heidrun 10
Elias (6th cent.) 41–42, 47, 115, 332, 433, 460, 501
El-Rouayheb, Khaled 10
Empedocles of Acragas (ca. 483/2–ca. 423 BC) 39, 260, 271, 554, 670, 738–739
Endress, Gerhard 8–10, 17, 20, 38, 52, 166, 181, 190, 443, 456, 543, 585, 709
Epaphroditus 715
Ephrem the Syrian (306–373) 55, 77
Epictetus (ca. 50, to ca. 138) 43, 193, 331
Epicurus (341–270 BC) 30, 662
Epiphanius (of Constantia/Salamis, 310/320–403/402) 671
Esʿad al-Yanyawī (ca. 1130–1143/1718–1730) 103
Escobar Gómez, Santiago 457
Ess, Josef van 19, 704
Euclid (4th/3rd cent. BC) 43, 49, 107, 118–119, 156, 174–176, 190, 201, 277, 426, 565–566, 609–610, 709, 755
Eudemus of Rhodes (born before 360 BC?) 127, 400, 670
Eumelus 677
Eunomius (d. 394) 50
Eusebius of Caesarea (260/4–337/40) 671
Eustathios (Usṭāṯ) 156
Eutocius (of Alexandria, 6th cent.) 41, 49

al-Faḍl b. Sahl Ibn Zāḏānfarrūḫ (d. 202/818), vizier to the Abbasid caliph al-Ma'mūn 329
Faḫr al-Dīn al-Rāzī (Abū ʿAbd Allāh Muḥammad b. ʿUmar, d. 607/1210) 3, 235, 245, 391
Faḫr al-Mulk, vizier to the Buyid emir Sulṭān al-Dawla 346
Fakhry, Majid (Faḫrī, Māǧid) 8, 11, 162, 539, 595
Falco, Vittorio de 177
al-Fārābī (Abū Naṣr Muḥammad b. Muḥammad, d. 339/950–951) XI, 13, 17–18, 20, 32–33, 51–54, 57, 128, 193, 197, 234, 246, 249, 291, 293, 299–300, 302, 313, 315, 329, 332–333, 336–337, 341, 377, 407, 423–424, 428–434, 440, 462, 465–466, 489, 505, 526–654, 722, 728, 730–731, 733, 739, 744, 747–748, 753, 758
Faraǧ b. Ǧirǧīs b. Afrām 293
Farmer, Henry George 180–181
Favorinus (ca. 80–150) 677
Filius, Lou S. 691, 718
Flashar, Hellmut 718
Frank, Tamar Zahara 159
Frede, Dorothea 466
Frederick II of Hohenstaufen (d. 1250), Holy Roman Emperor 675
Freudenthal, Gad 565, 591

Ǧābir b. Ḥayyān (b. ʿAbd Allāh al-Kūfī) 426, 732, 753
Gabriel b. Nūḥ (contemporary of the caliph al-Mutawakkil) 671

Ǧaʿfar al-Ṣādiq (d. 148/765), Shiite Imam 753
al-Ǧāḥiẓ (Abū ʿUṯmān ʿAmr b. Baḥr, d. 255/868–869) 86, 154, 225, 231, 242, 248, 279, 284, 290, 298, 329, 392, 456, 702
Ǧahm b. Ṣafwān (Abū Muḥriz, d. 128/746) 117
Ǧalāl al-Dīn al-Dawānī ☞ al-Dawānī, Ǧalāl al-Dīn
Ǧalāl al-Dīn al-Suyūṭī ☞ al-Suyūṭī, Ǧalāl al-Dīn
Galen (of Pergamon, 129, to ca. 216) 41, 48–49, 51, 56, 58, 62, 87, 105–107, 110, 127, 131, 188, 201, 243, 258, 308, 314, 316, 318, 323, 331–332, 334, 336, 338–340, 348, 350, 384–386, 390, 396, 399, 401, 404–405, 411–412, 426, 466, 472, 477, 487, 505–506, 562, 571–573, 577, 587, 596, 612, 669–670, 678, 683–688, 695, 697, 699–700, 711–714, 732, 755
Galston, Miriam 632–633
Garbers, Karl 189
Gardet, Louis 16
al-Ǧarīrī 234, 237, 241–242, 290
Gätje, Helmut 602
Gauthier, Léon 189
al-Ǧayhānī, Abū ʿAlī Muḥammad b. Aḥmad, minister to the Samanid Naṣr b. Aḥmad 237, 353
al-Ġazālī, Abū Ḥāmid (Muḥammad b. Muḥammad, d. 505/1111) 2–3, 298, 377, 379, 544, 674, 753, 759
Gellius (around 130) 677
Geminus (around 70 BC) 610
George, Bishop of the Arabs (d. 724) 57, 81–83
George Gemistus Plethon (ca. 1360–1452) 103, 129
Gerard of Cremona (ca. 1114–1187) 147, 169, 431, 529, 569
Gessius 110
Geyer, Bernhard 3
Ghersetti, Antonella 697
Ǧibrīl b. Baḫtīšūʿ (d. 211/827) 683
Gīlānšāh b. Kay Kāʾus, prince of Ṭabaristān 674
Gimaret, Daniel 19, 254, 670
Goldstein, Bernard R. 566
Goldziher, Ignaz 752
Goodman, Lenn E. 404
Graf, Georg 592
Gregory the Theologian 669–670
Gregorius Thaumatourgos (3rd cent.) 717
Gregory of Nazianz (d. 389/390) 464, 475
Gregory of Nyssa (d. after 394) 464
Griffith, Sidney Harrison 456
Grignaschi, Mario 540, 562, 673, 697
al-Ǧubbāʾī (Abū ʿAlī Muḥammad b. ʿAbd al-Wahhāb, d. 303/915–916) 571
al- Ǧubbāʾī (Abū Hāšim, d. 321/933) 609
al-Ǧunayd (Abū l-Qāsim b. Muḥammad b. al-Ǧunayd al-Ḫazzāz, d. 298/910) 278
Günther, Ursula 11, 597
Gutas, Dimitri 10, 52, 53, 61, 161, 536–537, 539, 551, 577, 632–633, 723

Haddad, Rachid 701
Hadot, Ilsetraut 32, 36, 43, 113, 331
Ḥāǧǧī Ḫalīfa 221
Hajatpour, Reza 11
al-Ḥākim (Abū ʿAlī al-Manṣūr), Fatimid caliph (regn. 386–411/996–1021) 746
al-Ḥakīm al-Tirmiḏī (d. 285/898) 18
Ḫalaf b. Aḥmad, Saffarid emir of Daylam 744
Ḫālid b. Yazīd b. Muʿāwiya, Umayyad prince 99
al-Ḥallāǧ (Abū l-Muġīṯ al-Ḥusayn b. Manṣūr, d. 309/922) 279, 753
Hamdani, Abbas 753
Ḥamīd al-Dīn al-Kirmānī ☞ al-Kirmānī, Ḥamīd al-Dīn
al-Ḥāmidī (Ibrāhīm b. al-Ḥusayn b. Abī l-Suʿūd al-Hamdānī, d. 557/1162) 748
Ḥammād b. Isḥāq b. Ibrāhīm al-Mawṣilī 225
Ḥamza (b. al-Ḥasan) al-Iṣfahānī (d. after 350/961) 232, 351
Hansberger, Rotraud 157, 198
al-Harawī, Abū Ǧaʿfar Aḥmad b. Muḥammad b. Sahl 346
al-Ḥarīzī (Ḥarizi), Yehuda ben Šelomo 666
Hartung, Jan-Peter 11
Hārūn al-Rašīd (regn. 170–193/786–809), Abbasid caliph 114, 152, 425
Harvey, Steven 577

al-Ḥasan b. Aḥmad b. ʿAlī al-Kātib 230
al-Ḥasan b. Bahlūl 691
Ḥasan al-Baṣrī (Abū Saʿīd b. Abī l-Ḥasan Yasār, d. 110/728) 329
al-Ḥasan b. Mūsā b. Šākir 708
al-Ḥasan b. Sahl b. Nawbaḫt 329
al-Ḥasan b. Sahl Ibn Zāḏānfarrūḫ (d. 236/850–851), secretary and governor to the Abbasid caliph al-Maʾmūn 329
al-Ḥasan b. Suwār ☞ Ibn al-Ḫammār
al-Ḥasan al-Ṭabarī 286
al-Ḫāzin (Abū Ǧaʿfar Muḥammad b. Muḥammad, d. between 350/961, and 360/971) 291
Heath, Th. L. 450–451
Heinrichs, Wolfhart 563–564
Heliodorus, brother of Ammonius 50
Hellenos 483
Hendrich, Geert 11
Heraclius (regn. 610–641), East Roman Emperor 108
Herman the German (d. 1272) 562
Hermes 126, 229, 329, 669–670
Hermippus of Smyrna (2nd half of 3rd cent. BC) 676–677
Heron of Alexandria (2nd half of 1st cent.) 43
Hesiod (around 700 BC) 665
al-Ḫiḍr b. ʿAlī 329
Hierocles (5th cent.) 43, 500, 721
Hilal, Aziz 548
Hīlyā the Melkite 114–116
Hippocrates (of Cos, 460–ca. 370 BC) 48, 110, 129, 188, 319, 350, 384, 505, 572–573, 669–670, 687, 732, 738
Hippolytus of Rome (d. 235) 130, 158, 670
Hišām b. ʿAbd al-Malik (regn. 105–125/724–743), Umayyad caliph 99, 673
Ḥnānīšōʿ I (d. 700) 86
Hobbes, Thomas (d. 1679) 620
Homer 47, 87, 285, 563, 598, 665, 669, 670, 683
Horten, Max 3–4
Hōšang (Ūshanǧ) 328–329
Hourani, Albert 10
Ḥubayš al-Aʿṣam 104–105, 684, 687, 709, 712–713
al-Ḫuḍayrī, Maḥmūd (d. 1960) 4
Hudry, Françoise 187
al-Ḫuldī (Abū Muḥammad Ǧaʿfar, d. 348/959), pupil of al-Ǧunayd 278
Ḫumārawayh b. Aḥmad b. Ṭūlūn 223, 227
Ḥunayn b. Isḥāq (Abū Zayd al-ʿIbādī, d. 260/873) 61, 104, 114, 118, 258, 384, 405, 426–428, 443, 503–504, 660, 665–666, 680–704, 709, 715, 724, 766
al-Ḫurāsānī, Aḥmad b. Muḥammad 155, 170
Ḫusraw I Anūširwān (regn. 531–578/9), Sasanian ruler 98, 112, 332, 432
Ḫusraw II Anūširwān, Sasanian ruler 116
al-Ḫwānsārī (Muḥammad Bāqir b. Zayn al-ʿĀbidīn, d. 1313/1895) 283
al-Ḫwārazmī (Abū ʿAbd Allāh Muḥammad b. Aḥmad b. Yūsuf al-Kātib, 4th/10th cent.) 249
Hypatia (of Alexandria, d. 415) 50
Hypsicles (lived around 175 BC in Alexandria) 177

Iamblichus (d. ca. 325) 33–37, 43, 49, 63, 130, 430, 721
Ibn ʿAbbād, al-Ṣāḥib (Abū l-Qāsim Ismāʿīl, d. 385/995), vizier to the Buyids 281, 285–286, 346
Ibn ʿAbd Rabbih (Aḥmad b. Muḥammad, d. 328/940) 163
Ibn ʿAbdūs, Abū Manṣūr Ṣāʿid b. Bišr 471
Ibn Abī ʿAwn (Ibrāhīm b. Muḥammad, d. 321/933) 667
Ibn Abī Ḏarr, Abū l-Ḥasan 262, 267
Ibn Abī Saʿīd al-Mawṣilī 490
Ibn Abī Uṣaybiʿa (Muwaffaq al-Dīn Aḥmad b. al-Qāsim, d. 668/1270) 18, 52, 104, 154, 170, 183, 185, 221, 223, 228, 236, 257, 386–387, 391–393, 395–396, 440, 455, 470, 472, 474, 476, 483, 486, 502–503, 506, 537–539, 546, 551, 565–566, 587–589, 591, 683–684, 687, 689, 691, 693, 695, 701, 706, 709, 715, 717, 719–724
Ibn ʿAdī, Ibrāhīm 440, 446, 538, 542, 585
Ibn ʿAdī, Yaḥyā (d. 363/974) 17, 88, 104, 164, 192, 211, 253, 282, 287–291, 293–297, 301–302, 309, 332, 364, 424, 427, 430–468, 471–472, 474–476, 478–479, 482–483, 486–492, 494, 505, 538, 541–542, 585

Ibn al-ʿAdīm (Kamāl al-Dīn Abū l-Qāsim ʿUmar b. Aḥmad, d. 660/1262) 224, 227–228
Ibn al-ʿAmīd (Abū l-Faḍl Muḥammad b. al-Ḥusayn, d. 360/970), vizier to the Buyids 256, 309–310, 330, 346, 729–730
Ibn al-ʿAmīd (Abū l-Fatḥ Ḏū l-Kifāyatayn, d. 366/976), vizier to the Buyids 256, 265, 281, 285–286
Ibn ʿAnāyā al-Isrāʾīlī 476
Ibn ʿArabī, Muḥyī l-Dīn (Abū ʿAbd Allāh Muḥammad b. ʿAlī, d. 638/1240) 6–7, 11, 18, 729, 759
Ibn ʿAsākir (Ṯiqat al-Dīn Abū l-Qāsim ʿAlī b. Abī Muḥammad al-Ḥasan, d. 571/1176) 221
Ibn al-ʿAssāl (al-Asʿad Abū l-Faraǧ Hibat Allāh, d. before 658/1260) 293
Ibn al-ʿAssāl (al-Muʾtaman Abū Isḥāq Ibrāhīm, d. around 658/1260) 293, 476, 694, 702–703
Ibn Bāǧǧa (Abū Bakr Muḥammad b. Yaḥyā b. al-Ṣāʾiġ al-Tuǧībī, d. 533/1139) 543, 586, 629
Ibn Bahrīz, Ḥabīb (ʿAbdīšūʿ) 120, 156, 183
Ibn Baḫtīšūʿ, Abū Saʿīd 161
Ibn Baḫtīšūʿ, Ǧibrīl (d. 211/827) 683
Ibn Bakkūs (Bakkūš?), Abū Isḥāq Ibrāhīm 441, 471, 486, 488
Ibn al-Biṭrīq, Yaḥyā (1st half of 3rd/9th cent.) 131, 156, 385, 425, 689, 697, 701
Ibn Bulbul, Ismāʿīl (Abū l-Ṣaqr, d. 278/892), vizier to the caliph al-Muʿtamid 709–710
Ibn Buṭlān (al-Muḫtār b. al-Ḥasan b. ʿAbdūn, d. 458/1066) 447, 500, 506
Ibn al-Dāya (Aḥmad b. Yūsuf, d. between 330/941, and 340/951) 154
Ibn Durayd (Abū Bakr Muḥammad b. al-Ḥasan al-Azdī, d. 321/933) 667
Ibn Faḍl Allāh al-ʿUmarī (d. 749/1349) 221, 386
Ibn Farīġūn 17, 238, 241, 246–249, 355–358, 456, 468, 739
Ibn al-Furāt, vizier 433
Ibn Ǧulǧul (Sulaymān b. Ḥassān, d. around 384/994) 386–387, 390, 676, 683, 688, 709, 711
Ibn Ǧumayʿ (d. 594/1198) 51, 53, 594
Ibn Ḫaldūn (Walī l-Dīn ʿAbd al-Raḥmān b. Muḥammad, d. 808/1406) 4, 100, 543, 633, 674–675
Ibn Ḫallikān (Abū l-ʿAbbās Šams al-Dīn Aḥmad b. Muḥammad, d. 681/1282) 277, 386–387, 537, 539–541, 708
Ibn al-Ḫammār (Abū l-Ḫayr al-Ḥasan b. Suwār b. Bābā b. Bihnām, d. after 407/1017) 17, 80, 88, 111, 285, 288–290, 309, 313, 346, 348–350, 427, 430, 434, 441, 446, 450, 476, 478, 480–490, 492, 670
Ibn Ḥawqal (Abū l-Qāsim b. ʿAlī, d. 2nd half of 4th/10th cent.) 243, 536
Ibn al-Hayṯam, Ismaili missionary (mid 4th/10th cent.) 738
Ibn al-Hayṯam (Abū ʿAlī al-Ḥasan, d. 430/1039) 456, 489
Ibn Ḥazm (Abū Muḥammad ʿAlī b. Aḥmad b. Saʿīd, d. 456/1064) 163, 411
Ibn Hilāl al-Ṣābiʾ, al-Qayyim 700
Ibn Hindū (Abū l-Faraǧ ʿAlī b. al-Ḥusayn, d. 423/1032, or 420/1029) 17, 162, 249, 257, 290, 344–350, 380, 434, 482, 487, 668, 704
Ibn Ḫurradāḏbih (Abū l-Qāsim ʿUbayd Allāh b. ʿAbd Allāh, d. 300/911) 231
Ibn al-ʿIbrī ☞ Barhebraeus
Ibn Kaškarāyā (Abū l-Ḥusayn), pupil of Sinān b. Ṯābit 471
Ibn Muḥtāǧ (Abū ʿAlī Aḥmad b. Muḥammad b. al-Muẓaffar, d. 344/955), ruler of Čaġāniyān 241, 247
Ibn al-Munaǧǧim, Abū ʿĪsā Aḥmad, son of ʿAlī b. Yaḥyā Ibn al-Munaǧǧim 598, 701
Ibn al-Munaǧǧim, ʿAlī b. Yaḥyā (d. 275/888–889) 118, 683, 686, 693, 701
Ibn al-Muqaffaʿ (ʿAbd Allāh [Rōzbih], d. 137/755, or 139/756) 116, 424, 509, 665, 673, 675
Ibn al-Muqaffaʿ, Muḥammad b. ʿAbd Allāh 114–115, 329
Ibn al-Muṭrān (Muwaffaq al-Dīn, d. 587/1191) 292, 301, 430, 507
Ibn al-Muẓaffar, Abū Bakr (Muḥtāǧid, ruler of Ḫurāsān) 241

Ibn al-Nadīm (Abū l-Farağ Muḥammad b. Isḥāq, d. 380/990) 18, 60, 88, 105, 122, 155–156, 162, 172, 174, 179, 184, 192, 221, 235–236, 241, 291, 293, 387–391, 424, 428–431, 441, 470, 472, 536–537, 545–546, 587, 706, 720–721
Ibn Nāʿima al-Ḥimṣī (ʿAbd al-Masīḥ) 88, 104, 111
Ibn Nubāta (b. Šams al-Dīn Ğamāl al-Dīn Muḥammad al-Miṣrī, d. 768/1366) 102
Ibn Qayyim al-Ğawziyya (Šams al-Dīn Abū Bakr Muḥammad b. Abī Bakr al-Zarʿī, d. 751/1350) 442
Ibn al-Qifṭī (Ğamāl al-Dīn ʿAlī b. Yūsuf, d. 646/1248) 18, 135, 185, 221, 390–391, 394, 429, 446, 454, 506, 537, 541, 546, 566, 587, 683, 689, 706–707, 709, 721–723
Ibn al-Rāwandī (Abū l-Ḥusayn Aḥmad b. Yaḥyā b. Isḥāq, 3rd/9th cent.) 407, 587
Ibn Riḍwān (Abū l-Ḥasan ʿAlī, d. 453/1061, or 460/1068) 51, 53, 447, 506, 594
Ibn Rušd (Abū l-Walīd Muḥammad b. Aḥmad, d. 595/1198) XI, 1–5, 7–9, 189, 193, 377, 431–432, 490, 502–503, 543, 555, 572, 586, 628–629
Ibn Rusta (Abū ʿAlī Aḥmad b. ʿUmar, 3rd–4th/9th–10th cent.) 230
Ibn Sabʿīn (ʿAbd al-Ḥaqq b. Ibrāhīm b. Muḥammad b. Naṣr, d. 668/1269, or 669/1271) 676, 679
Ibn Saʿdān, al-ʿĀriḍ 265, 282–283, 289–290
Ibn al-Ṣalāḥ (d. 548/1153) 87, 451, 474, 567
Ibn al-Samḥ (Abū ʿAlī Ḥasan b. Sahl b. Ġālib, d. 418/1027) XI, 17, 289, 364, 432, 434, 441, 465, 478, 488–496, 502
Ibn al-Sarrāğ (Abū Bakr Muḥammad b. al-Sarī, d. 316/928) 277, 295, 433, 539
Ibn Sīnā (Abū ʿAlī al-Ḥusayn b. ʿAbd Allāh, d. 428/1037) 5, 7, 9–10, 18, 45, 51, 159, 197–198, 211, 234, 249, 254–255, 257, 270, 293, 321, 326, 377, 412, 423, 427, 433, 496, 502–503, 505–506, 542–545, 565–566, 573, 588, 591–594, 617, 621, 690, 740, 745, 747, 758–759
Ibn Ṭawāba (Abū l-ʿAbbās Aḥmad b. Yaḥyā, d. 277/890–891, or 273/886–887) 227, 286
Ibn Ṭāwūs (d. 664/1266) 310
Ibn Taymiyya (Taqī l-Dīn Aḥmad, d. 728/1328) 719, 758
Ibn al-Ṭayyib (Abū l-Farağ ʿAbd Allāh al-ʿIrāqī, d. 435/1043) 17, 128, 492–493, 496–506, 523–524, 667–678, 721
Ibn Ṭufayl (Abū Bakr Muḥammad b. ʿAbd al-Malik, d. 581/1185) 9, 377, 543, 629
Ibn Yaʿīš 289
Ibn al-Yammān (or: Tammār) 392
Ibn Zurʿa (Abū ʿAlī ʿĪsā b. Isḥāq, d. 398/1008) XI, 17, 88, 285, 289–290, 364, 434, 441, 443, 451, 468–480, 483, 491–492, 520
Ibrāhīm b. Hilāl, Abū Isḥāq (d. 384/994) 700, 705
Ibrāhīm Ibn ʿAdī ☞ Ibn ʿAdī, Ibrāhīm
Ibycus 666
al-Idrīsī (Abū ʿAbd Allāh Muḥammad b. Muḥammad b. ʿAbd Allāh b. Idrīs, d. 560/1165) 243, 759
Iḫwān al-Ṣafāʾ 13, 63, 179, 242, 290, 298, 366–367, 377, 542, 588, 676, 729–733, 748–759
Imruʾ al-Qays 598
Īrānšahrī (3rd/9th cent.) 388, 411
Irenaeus (2nd cent.) 463
Isaac of Antioch 83–84
al-Iṣfahānī, al-Rāġib ☞ al-Rāġib al-Iṣfahānī
al-Isfizārī (Abū Ḥāmid Aḥmad b. Abī Isḥāq, 4th/10th cent.) 254–255, 294
Isḥāq b. Ḥunayn (d. 289/910–911) 385, 426–427, 431–432, 492, 665, 671, 684, 687, 709, 713, 716, 719, 720
Isḥāq b. Ibrāhīm al-Mawṣilī (d. 235/850) 225, 569
Isḥāq al-Isrāʾīlī (b. Sulaymān, d. around 338/950) 155, 159, 739, 742
Ismāʿīl Ibn Bulbul ☞ Ibn Bulbul, Ismāʿīl
Īšōʿ bar Nūn 87
Īšōʿbōḵt (9th cent.) of Rēwardašīr 86
Išōʿdnaḥ (8th cent.) of Baṣra 87
Isocrates (436/35–338 BC) 77, 130
al-Isrāʾīlī, Ibn ʿAnāyā ☞ Ibn ʿAnāyā al-Isrāʾīlī
al-Isrāʾīlī, Isḥāq ☞ Isḥāq al-Isrāʾīlī
al-Iṣṭaḫrī (Abū Isḥāq Ibrāhīm b. Muḥammad al-Fārisī, 4th/10th cent.) 243
Iwannīs of Dārā 84

Jacob of Edessa (d. 708) 57, 80–84
Jambet, Christian 12
Janos, Damien 566, 585, 589, 610–611, 617

Janssens, Jules 191
Jesus Christ 78, 459, 461, 463–464, 475, 477, 480
John of Alexandria 472
John the Grammarian ☞ John Philoponus
John Philoponus (d. 574) 32, 40, 45, 47–49, 56–57, 64, 81, 130, 166, 168, 195, 199, 333, 335, 385, 390, 412, 433, 440, 465, 473, 485, 489, 492–493, 495–496, 502, 570, 586–587, 612
John of Scythopolis (1st half of 6th cent.) 58, 110
Jonan, periodeutes 79
Justinian, Roman Emperor (482–565) 108, 112

al-Kaʿbī ☞ al-Balḫī, Abū l-Qāsim al-Kaʿbī
al-Kalābāḏī 267
Karam, Yūsuf (d. 1959) 4
al-Karḫī, Abū ʿĀʾiḏ Ṣāliḥ b. ʿAlī 290
al-Karḫī, Abū Ǧaʿfar Muḥammad b. al-Qāsim 538
Kāšānī, Afḍal al-Dīn 659
Kay Kāʾus (b. Iskandar, 5th/11th cent.), Ziyārid ruler of Ṭabaristān 674
Khatchadourian, Haig 171
al-Kindī (Abū Yūsuf Yaʿqūb b. Isḥāq b. al-Ṣabbāḥ, d. between 247/861 and 252/866) XI, 8, 17, 45, 51, 87, 103, 106, 113–114, 117–120, 131, 143–220, 222–224, 228–231, 236, 238, 243–244, 246–249, 254, 256, 267, 278, 284, 287, 289, 291, 295, 297, 300, 304, 326, 331–332, 335–338, 343, 349, 385, 389, 404, 424, 425, 439, 457, 461–462, 464–465, 468, 479, 488–489, 494, 542, 569, 573, 585, 586, 600, 612, 614, 618, 667, 679, 684, 709, 712, 724, 728, 729–731, 733, 739
al-Kirmānī, Abū l-Ḥakam, pupil of Maslama al-Maǧrīṭī 759
al-Kirmānī, Ḥamīd al-Dīn (Aḥmad b. ʿAbd Allāh, d. around 411/1020–1021) 390, 542, 737–741, 746–748
Klein-Franke, Felix 159, 188, 191
Kraemer, Jörg 87, 278, 291–293, 301–302, 675
Kraus, Paul 115, 386, 388–390, 392, 591
Krause, Max 177
Kruk, Remke 126, 712, 718
Kubesov, Audanbek 566
Kügelgen, Anke von XII, XIII, 11, 19

Lameer, Joep 53–54, 558, 585, 589, 594, 600, 627
Landolt, Hermann 5–6
Langermann, Y. Tzvi 189
Langhade, Jacques 540, 561
Larcher, Pierre 543, 548
Leaman, Oliver 8–9, 11
Lettinck, Paul 130, 385, 493, 496, 502
Levey, Martin 189
Lévy, Tony 120, 156, 183
Linley, Neil 721
Longinus (ca. 212–272) 109
Loth, Otto 150
Luckey, Paul 174
Luqmān 271, 329, 669–670
Lyco of Troas (ca. 300–ca. 226 BC) 678

al-Maʿarrī, Abū l-ʿAlāʾ (Aḥmad b. ʿAbd Allāh, d. 449/1058) 491
Madelung, Wilferd 738, 741–743
al-Maǧrīṭī, Maslama (Abū l-Qāsim b. Aḥmad al-Faraḍī, d. 398/1007) 432, 753, 755, 759
Mahadarǧis 669–670
Mahdawī, Yaḥyā 321, 390, 716–718
al-Mahdī (regn. 158–169/775–785), Abbasid caliph 87, 114, 117, 152, 425
Mahdi, Muhsin 130, 150, 533, 536, 540, 543, 548, 553, 568, 570, 574, 576, 577, 582, 587–588, 592, 619, 622, 632
Maḥfūẓ, Ḥusayn ʿAlī 536
Maḥmūd (b. Sebüktigin, d. 421/1030), Ghaznavid ruler 482
Maimonides (Mošeh ben Maimon, d. 601/1204) 412, 543, 572, 586
Malikšāh (I b. Alp Arslan, Ǧalāl al-Dawla Muʿizz al-Dīn, d. 485/1072), Seljuk ruler 674
Mallet, Dominique 550, 576, 585
al-Maʾmūn (regn. 198–218/813–833), Abbasid caliph 101–102, 154, 352, 425, 683–684, 686, 708, 738
Maʾmūn II b. Maʾmūn, Abū l-ʿAbbās (regn. 399–407/1009–1017), Ḫwārazmšāh of Gurgānǧ 482, 487
Manfred (regn. 1232–1266), King of Sicily 675

Mann, Thomas (1875–1955) 412
al-Manṣūr (regn. 136–158/754–775), Abbasid caliph 99–102, 114, 673
al-Manṣūr b. Ismāʿīl, governor of Rayy (290, to 296–297/902–903, to 908–909) 387, 399
Manṣūr al-Ṭāhirī 569
Manṣūr b. Ṭalḥa 396
al-Maqrīzī (Taqī l-Dīn Abū l-ʿAbbās Aḥmad b. ʿAlī, d. 845/1442) 243
Marcotte, Roxanne 314–315
Mardāwīğ b. Ziyār b. Wardānšāh (d. 323/935), founder of the Ziyārid dynasty 290, 743
Margoliouth, David Samuel 675
Marinus 110
Marmura, Michael 8
Marquet, Yves 357
Martini Bonadeo, Cecilia 585
Marwān (I, regn. 64–65/684–685), Umayyad caliph 99
Marwān (II b. Muḥammad b. Marwān b. al-Ḥakam, d. 132/750), last Umayyad caliph 276
al-Marwarrūḏī, Abū Ḥāmid 772
al-Marwarrūḏī, al-Ḥusayn b. ʿAlī, Qarmatī general 732
al-Marwazī, Abū Yaḥyā Ibrāhīm 429, 538
Mary 461, 477
Māsarğawayh 99
Māšāʾ Allāh (d. after 193/809) 181, 730
Maslama al-Mağrīṭī ☞ al-Mağrīṭī, Maslama
al-Masʿūdī (Abū l-Ḥasan ʿAlī b. al-Ḥusayn, d. 345/956) 51–53, 87, 99, 156, 393, 424, 428–429, 440, 594, 691, 699, 708, 710
al-Maʿṣūmī (Muḥammad b. ʿAbd Allāh, d. before 421/1030) 591
Mattā, Abū Bišr ☞ Abū Bišr Mattā
al-Māturīdī (Abū Manṣūr Muḥammad b. Muḥammad, d. 333/944) 21
al-Mawṣilī, Ibn Abī Saʿīd ☞ Ibn Abī Saʿīd al-Mawṣilī
al-Maynaqī, Abū Firās 741
Mazdak (d. 528, or 529) 432
McCarthy, Richard Joseph 147–192
McGinnis, Jon 171
Meḥmed II the Conqueror (regn. 848–850/1444–1446, and 855–886/1451–1481), Ottoman sultan 103
Melissus of Samos (5th cent. BC) 665
Menander of Kephisia (342/341–293/292 BC) 77, 669
Menn, Stephen 459, 543, 548
Metrodorus of Lampsacus (330–277 BC) 385
Meyerhof, Max 51–52, 700–701
Michael of Ephesus (12th cent.) 432
Mihr Āḏarğušnašp 669–670
Minovi, Mojtaba 266–267
Miskawayh (Abū ʿAlī Aḥmad b. Muḥammad b. Yaʿqūb, d. 421/1030) 17, 84, 155, 233, 255–256, 262, 265–267, 277, 280–282, 285–286, 289–290, 294–295, 300–301, 308–313, 316–318, 321, 325–326, 329–344, 349, 404, 430, 488, 494, 500, 504, 542, 590, 665, 667
al-Mismaʿī 392
Mohaghegh, Mehdi ☞ Muḥaqqiq, Mahdī
Mošeh ben Maimon ☞ Maimonides
Mošeh Ibn ʿEzra (d. 532/1138) 412
Mošeh Ibn Tibbon 565
Mošeh bar Kepha (d. 903) 80
al-Muʾaddib, Abū l-Qāsim 241
Muʿāwiya (I, regn. 41–60/661–680), Umayyad caliph 99
al-Muʾayyad (fī l-Dīn Abū Naṣr Hibat Allāh b. Abī ʿImrān Mūsā, d. 470/1077) 748
Muʾayyid al-Dawla (Abū Manṣūr Būya b. Rukn al-Dawla Ḥasan, regn. 366–373/976–984), Buyid ruler 281, 346
al-Mubaššir b. Fātik (Abū l-Wafāʾ, 5th/11th cent.) 162, 669
al-Muhallabī (Abū Muḥammad al-Ḥasan b. Muḥammad, d. 352/963), vizier to the Buyid Muʿizz al-Dawla 278, 308
Muḥammad, the Prophet (d. 11/632) 118, 152, 277, 407, 476, 590, 701–702, 756
Muḥammad b. ʿAbd Allāh Ibn al-Muqaffaʿ ☞ Ibn al-Muqaffaʿ, Muḥammad b. ʿAbd Allāh
Muḥammad b. al-Ğahm (contemporary of the caliph al-Maʾmūn) 147, 154, 170
Muḥammad b. Hilāl, Ġars al-Niʿma (d. 480/1088) 700
Muḥammad b. Ismāʿīl, the Mahdī 742
Muḥammad b. Malikšāh (Abū Šuğāʿ, regn. 498–511/1105–1118), Seljuk ruler 674
Muḥammad b. Maʿšar al-Bustī al-Maqdisī, Abū Sulaymān ☞ al-Bustī al-Maqdisī, Abū Sulaymān Muḥammad b. Maʿšar

Muḥammad b. Mūsā b. Šākir (d. 259/873) 153, 707–709, 713, 714, 718
Muḥammad b. Šabīb (3rd/9th cent.) 21
Muḥaqqiq, Mahdī (Mehdi Mohaghegh) 386, 390, 396
al-Muḥassin (b. Ibrāhīm b. Hilāl al-Ṣābi', Abū ʿAlī, d. 401/1010) 705–707, 720–723
Muḥyī l-Dīn Ibn ʿArabī ☞ Ibn ʿArabī, Muḥyī l-Dīn
al-Muʿizz (regn. 341–365/953–975), Fatimid caliph 737
Muʿizz al-Dawla (Abū l-Ḥusayn Aḥmad, d. 356/967), Buyid emir 278, 309
al-Muktafī bi-llāh (regn. 289–295/902–908), Abbasid caliph 387, 426
Mullā Ṣadrā Šīrāzī (Ṣadr al-Dīn Muḥammad, d. 1050/1640) 3, 5, 7–8, 11, 759
Munk, Salomon 2
al-Muqaddasī (Šams al-Dīn Abū ʿAbd Allāh Muḥammad b. Aḥmad, 4th/10th cent.) 230, 243
al-Muqri' (Abū Bakr Aḥmad b. al-Ḥusayn b. Mihrān, d. 381/992) 257
al-Muqtadir (regn. 295–320/908–932), Abbasid caliph 52, 429, 538
Mūsā b. Šākir 707–708
al-Mustanǧid bi-llāh (regn. 555–566/1160–1170), Abbasid caliph 758
al-Muʿtaḍid (regn. 279–289/892–902), Abbasid caliph 52, 223–227, 707–710
al-Muʿtamid (regn. 256–279/870–892), Abbasid caliph 710
al-Mutanabbī (Abū l-Ṭayyib Aḥmad b. al-Ḥusayn, d. 354/965) 753
Muṭarrif b. Muḥammad, vizier to the Ziyārid Mardāwīǧ 290
al-Muʿtaṣim (regn. 218–227/833–842), Abbasid caliph 146, 153, 162, 195, 708
al-Mutawakkil (regn. 232–247/847–861), Abbasid caliph 52, 102, 154, 428, 671, 693
al-Muwaffaq (Abū Aḥmad Ṭalḥa b. Ǧaʿfar, d. 278/891), son of the caliph al-Mutawakkil and Abbasid general 710

Nagy, Albino 189
al-Nahraǧūrī, Abū Aḥmad 752
Najjar, Fauzi M. (Fawzī M. Naǧǧār) 585, 630
al-Nasafī (Muḥammad b. Aḥmad, d. around 332/943) 737–738, 741–745
Naṣīr al-Dīn al-Ṭūsī ☞ al-Ṭūsī, Naṣīr al-Dīn
Nāṣir-i Ḫusraw (d. after 462/1070) 391, 393, 409–411, 748, 753
Nasr, Seyyed Hossein 6–11, 14
Naṣr b. Aḥmad (b. Ismāʿīl, al-Amīr al-saʿīd, regn. 301–331/914–943), Samanid ruler 237, 741
al-Nāṭiq bi-l-Ḥaqq Sayyid Abū Ṭālib Yaḥyā, Shiite Imam of Daylam 346
al-Nawbaḫtī (al-Ḥasan b. Mūsā, d. between 299/912, and 309/922) 671
al-Naysābūrī, Abū Tammām ☞ Abū Tammām al-Naysābūrī
al-Naysābūrī, Aḥmad b. Ibrāhīm (d. ca. 386/996) 738
Naẓīf b. Ayman al-Rūmī 289, 492
al-Naẓẓām (Abū Isḥāq Ibrāhīm b. Sayyār b. Hāni', d. before 232/847) 394, 449, 609
Negri, Salomon (d. 1728, or 1729) 392
Nemesius of Emesa 131, 671, 679
Nero (37–68), Roman Emperor 318
Neubauer, Eckhard 180, 569
Nicolaus of Damascus (born ca. 64 BC) 131, 472, 486, 503, 695, 719
Nicomachus of Gerasa (2nd cent.) 34, 119–120, 156, 159, 177, 183, 188, 231, 755
Niẓām al-Mulk (Abū ʿAlī al-Ḥasan b. ʿAlī, d. 485/1092), vizier to the Seljuk ruler Malikšāh 674
Nūḥ (I b. Naṣr b. Aḥmad, regn. 331–343/943–954), Samanid ruler 741
Numenius 34
al-Nūšǧānī (Abū l-Fatḥ), from the circle of Abū Sulaymān al-Siǧistānī 288, 292, 303
Nwyia, Paul 694, 701–702

O'Meara, Dominic J. 35, 627, 631
Olympias (born ca. 375 BC) 666
Olympiodorus (alchemist) 131
Olympiodorus (d. after 565) 32, 40, 41, 46–47, 50, 57, 63, 81, 131, 332, 336, 430, 440, 482, 486, 488, 501, 677
Origen (185–253) 677

Parens, Joshua 577, 619
Parmenides of Elea (6th/5th cent. BC) 47

Paul of Aegina (7th cent.) 487
Paul of Alexandria (4th cent.) 41
Paul the Persian (6th cent.) 59, 79, 82, 112, 115–116, 179, 311, 332, 336
Paul, St. 475
Pellat, Charles 708
Petrus Alfonsi (d. 1140) 214
Petrus Gallegus (d. 1267) 305
Philolaus of Croton (mid 5th cent. BC) 771
Phocas bar Sergius (8th cent.) 111
Photius (ca. 820–891) 108
Pines, Shlomo 8, 19, 388–392, 395, 480, 619, 632, 699
Plato (428/7–348/7 BC) 13, 29–35, 37–43, 45–49, 58, 62, 64, 77–78, 82, 113, 127–128, 131, 156–157, 161–162, 166, 168, 172–175, 177, 194, 197, 199, 202, 229, 236, 244, 254–256, 260, 281, 285, 301, 313–314, 319, 321–322, 325–326, 329–330, 332–334, 340–341, 385, 389, 391, 395, 399, 400, 404–406, 410, 426, 460, 466, 472, 475, 479, 484, 488–489, 504–505, 549, 554, 558, 562, 572, 577, 582–586, 592–593, 595, 598, 599, 623, 627–629, 631, 661, 663, 665, 668–670, 672, 675–678, 688, 697–699, 709, 717, 722–723, 725–726, 737–738, 756
Platti, Emilio 439, 457
Plessner, Martin 324, 573
Plotinus (ca. 205–270) 30–31, 36, 58, 63, 109, 111, 119–120, 132, 156, 157–158, 194, 196–197, 230, 287, 335, 404, 406, 591, 617, 670, 739, 748, 755
Plutarch of Athens (d. 432) 36
Plutarch of Chaeronea (ca. 45–ca. 125) 77, 132, 385, 394–395, 405, 670, 677, 698
Porphyry (d. ca. 305) 31–34, 36, 38, 63–64, 77, 79–81, 83–85, 109, 111, 113–114, 116, 120, 157, 163–164, 167, 192, 324–325, 332–333, 336–337, 341, 344, 349, 386, 422, 427, 430, 443–446, 483, 487–489, 501, 505, 552, 554, 670, 688–689
Posidonius of Apamea (ca. 135–51/0 BC) 339
Pourjavady, Reza 10
Praechter, Karl 43
Priam 342
Priscian (of Lydia, 6th cent.) 39
Prōbā (6th cent.) 56–57, 60
Proclus Diadochus (412–485) 32, 38, 40, 42, 45, 49, 63, 119–120, 132, 156–158, 194, 230, 244, 253–256, 261, 270–271, 314, 333–335, 385, 389, 394, 462–463, 465, 472, 485, 489, 500, 617, 631, 720–721, 739
Prüfer, Curt 700–701
Pseudo-Alexander 432
Pseudo-Ammonius 63, 119, 669–670, 739, 742–743
Pseudo-Archytas 34
Pseudo-Aristotle 80, 126, 312, 485, 719
Pseudo-Avicenna 690
Pseudo-Dionysius the Areopagite (end of the 5th cent.) 50, 56, 58, 110, 463, 475
Pseudo-Elias 501
Pseudo-Empedocles 63
Pseudo-Euclid 149, 180
Pseudo-Ǧāḥiẓ 670–671
Pseudo-Galen 129
Pseudo-Hippocrates 130
Pseudo-Ibn al-Muqaffaʿ 329
Pseudo-Maǧrīṭī 432
Pseudo-Maximus Confessor 664
Pseudo-Plato 84, 255, 294, 325, 337, 338, 359, 677
Pseudo-Plutarch ☞ Aetius
Pseudo-Polemon 132
Pseudo-Ptolemy 133
Ptolemy, Claudius (2nd cent.) 43, 49–50, 78, 103, 114, 118, 133, 155, 163, 175–176, 183, 201, 426, 610, 616, 669–670, 672, 709, 728, 732
Ptolemy al-Ġarīb 133
Pythagoras of Samos (ca. 570, to after 510 BC) 34, 37–38, 49, 55, 77, 133, 194, 197, 231, 260, 285, 329, 340, 500, 665, 668–670, 755, 756

Qābūs b. Wušmgīr, Šams al-Maʿālī (d. 403/1012), Ziyārid ruler of Ǧurǧān 279, 346, 347, 674
Qaḥṭān, legendary ancestor of the South Arabs 152
al-Qāsim b. ʿUbayd Allāh (d. 291/904), vizier to the caliph al-Muktafī 426, 719–720
al-Qazwīnī (Zakariyyāʾ b. Muḥammad, d. 682/1283) 540, 759

al-Qūmisī (Abū Bakr b. al-Ḥasan), from the circle of Abū Sulaymān al-Siǧistānī 289, 442, 492
Qusṭā b. Lūqā (d. ca. 300/912) 104–105, 118, 156, 177, 249, 385, 394, 406, 665, 701–702

al-Rāḍī (Abū l-ʿAbbās Aḥmad [Muḥammad] b. al-Muqtadir, regn. 322–329/934–940), Abbasid caliph 428
al-Rāġib al-Iṣfahānī (Abū l-Qāsim al-Ḥusayn b. Muḥammad b. al-Mufaḍḍal, 5th/11th cent.) 326, 404
Ramón Martí (d. 1285) 412
Ranking, George S. A. 392
Rashed, Marwan 452, 460, 585–586
Rashed, Roshdi 175, 201
al-Rayḥānī, ʿAlī b. ʿUbayda (d. 234/819) 329, 665
al-Rāzī, Abū Bakr (Muḥammad b. Zakariyyāʾ, d. 313/925) 17, 51, 62, 225, 236–237, 245, 331, 381–412, 440–441, 468, 479, 488, 571, 587, 743
al-Rāzī, Abū Ḥātim (Aḥmad b. Ḥamdān al-Layṯī, d. 322/934) 390, 392, 396, 407–408, 410–411, 737–738, 741–746
al-Rāzī, Faḫr al-Dīn ☞ Faḫr al-Dīn al-Rāzī
Reisman, David C. 254, 617, 620, 633, 720, 724
Renan, Ernest (1823–1892) 1–3, 5–6, 14–15
Rescher, Nicholas 131, 171
Ritter, Hellmut 160, 169
Rizvi, Sajjad 10
Robert of Ketton (d. after 1157) 182
Rosenfeld, Boris Abramovič 566, 590
Rosenthal, Franz 156, 223–225, 227–229, 231, 236, 248, 389, 405, 483, 630, 632, 667–669
Rowson, Everett K. 237, 242, 244, 264, 266, 278, 430
Rudolph, Ulrich 11, 15, 20, 158, 595, 672
Rufus of Ephesus (around 100?) 316–319, 340
al-Ruhāwī, Isḥāq b. ʿAlī 157
Rukn al-Dawla (Abū ʿAlī al-Ḥasan b. Būya, d. 366/976), Buyid emir 256, 309
al-Rūmī, Naẓīf b. Ayman ☞ Naẓīf b. Ayman al-Rūmī
al-Rummānī (Abū l-Ḥasan ʿAlī b. ʿĪsā, d. 384/994) 278–279, 295, 433, 454
Saʿadya (d. 330/942) 490
Saatchian, Firouzeh 10
Sab 669
Sabra, Abdelhamid I. 724, 726
Saʿd al-Dīn al-Taftāzānī ☞ al-Taftāzānī, Saʿd al-Dīn
al-Ṣafadī (Ṣalāḥ al-Dīn Ḫalīl b. Aybak, d. 764/1363) 103, 105, 152, 221, 232, 540, 546, 566, 587–588
al-Šāfiʿī, Abū Bakr 277
Šahīd b. al-Ḥusayn, Abū l-Ḥasan 388
al-Šahrastānī (Tāǧ al-Dīn Abū l-Fatḥ Muḥammad b. ʿAbd al-Karīm, d. 548/1153) 668–671
al-Šahrazūrī (Šams al-Dīn Muḥammad b. Maḥmūd, d. after 687/1288) 387–388, 668–670
Ṣāʿid b. Aḥmad al-Andalusī (Abū l-Qāsim, d. 462/1070) 18, 162–163, 386, 536–537, 539, 541, 545, 582, 689
Ṣalāḥ al-Dīn (al-Malik al-Nāṣir Abū l-Muẓaffar Yūsuf b. Ayyūb [Saladin], d. 589/1193), founder of the Ayyūbid dynasty 51
Salm of Harran, director of the *Bayt al-ḥikma* 114–115
Salmawayh b. Bunān 687
al-Sāmarrāʾī, ʿĀmir Rašīd 694
Samir, Khalil (Samīr, Ḫalīl) 694, 701–702
Ṣamṣām al-Dawla (Abū Kālīǧār Marzubān, d. 388/998), Buyid emir 291
Sanad b. ʿAlī (1st half of the 3rd/9th cent.) 708
al-Saraḫsī (Aḥmad b. al-Ṭayyib b. Marwān, d. 286/899) 17, 155, 181, 221–231, 236, 244, 246, 247, 249, 351–353, 684, 709
Sarǧūn b. Manṣūr al-Rūmī, secretary to the Umayyads from Muʿāwiya to ʿAbd al-Malik 89
Sayf al-Dawla (Abū l-Ḥasan ʿAlī b. Abī l-Hayǧāʾ ʿAbd Allāh, regn.333–356/945–967), Ḥamdānid emir 446, 538, 539, 541
al-Šayḫ al-Yūnānī 157, 591
al-Ṣaymarī, Abū Zakariyyāʾ, from the circle of Abū Sulaymān al-Siǧistānī 285, 292
Sbath, Paul 474, 487
Schaeder, Hans Heinrich 412–413
Schmidtke, Sabine XII, 10–11

Schöck, Cornelia 116, 596
Schoeler, Gregor 431
Schwarz, Michael 455
Secundus 133
Seleucus 385
Šem Ṭov Ibn Falaquera (d. 1295/694) 543, 587
Šemu'el Ibn Tibbon 720
Sergius, Mar 80
Sergius of Rēšʿainā (d. 536) 77, 80, 82, 109, 111
Sersen, William John 185
Seth 669
Severus of Antioch (d. 538) 464
Severus Sebōkt (d. 666/7) 78–81, 84
Sextus 77, 678
Sezgin, Fuat 387, 566, 691
Sharif, M. M. 8, 11
Shiloah, Amnon 179, 181
Sībawayh (d. ca. 180/796) 277
al-Siǧistānī, Abū Sulaymān (Muḥammad b. Ṭāhir b. Bahrām al-Manṭiqī, d. ca. 374/985) 13, 17, 104, 153, 223, 282, 285, 287–304, 309, 367, 430, 434, 441, 486, 488, 492, 494, 542, 668, 709, 739, 752–753, 758
al-Siǧistānī, Abū Yaʿqūb (Isḥāq b. Aḥmad, d. ca. 361/971) 249, 737–738, 740, 744–748
Silwānōs of Qardu (8th or 9th cent.) 84–85
Simmias 676
Simplicius (ca. 500, to after 533) 32, 39–40, 53–54, 134, 331, 336, 433, 485
Sinān b. Ṯābit 471, 705–706
al-Sīrāfī, Abū Saʿīd (al-Ḥasan b. ʿAbd Allāh, d. 368/979) 256, 277, 286, 289, 296–297, 433, 601
Sirǧīs b. Hilīyā al-Rūmī (3rd/9th cent.) 114
Socrates (ca. 470–399 BC) 55, 77–78, 134, 161, 162, 194, 226, 260, 285, 300, 321, 325, 329, 340, 341, 397–403, 405, 484, 500, 584, 593, 658, 665, 667–671, 675–677, 738, 755, 756
Solon (ca. 640–ca. 560 BC) 78, 229, 665, 669–670
Soranus (around 100) 350
Speer, Andreas 13
Spies, Otto 173
Steigerwald, Diane 542
Steinschneider, Moritz 546, 566, 569, 659, 690–691
Stephanus of Alexandria (6th/7th cent.) 42, 44, 108, 110, 134
Stern, Samuel Miklos 155, 278, 673
Stobaeus (ca. 5th cent.) 324, 504, 664
Strauss, Leo (d. 1973) 7, 619, 622
Strohmaier, Gotthard 52, 62, 708
Šuhayd/Šahīd al-Balḫī ☞ al-Balḫī, Šuhayd/Šahīd b. al-Ḥusayn
al-Suhrawardī, Šihāb al-Dīn (Abū l-Futūḥ Yaḥyā b. Ḥabaš b. Amīrak, d. 587/1191) 5–7, 9, 759
al-Ṣūlī (Abū Bakr Muḥammad b. Yaḥyā, d. 335/947) 154
Sulṭān al-Dawla (b. Bahāʾ al-Dawla Fīrūz, d. 415/1024), Buyid emir 346
Sunbāḏ (d. 137/755) 100
Šuštarī, Taqī al-Dīn Muḥammad 308
al-Suyūṭī, Ǧalāl al-Dīn (Abū l-Faḍl ʿAbd al-Raḥmān b. Abī Bakr b. Muḥammad, d. 911/1505) 548
Swain, Simon 697
Syrianus (d. ca. 437) 32, 37–38, 46, 134

al-Ṯaʿālibī (Abū Manṣūr ʿAbd al-Malik b. Muḥammad d. 429/1038) 242, 347
al-Ṭabarī (Abū Ǧaʿfar Muḥammad b. Ǧarīr, d. 310/923) 290, 309, 710
al-Ṭabarī, ʿAlī b. Rabban (3rd/9th cent.) 267
Ṯābit b. Qurra (209–288/824–901) 51, 104, 157, 225, 227, 230, 427, 432, 660, 680, 692, 692, 695, 700, 704–727
Ṯābit b. Sinān b. Ṯābit (d. 365/976) 705–706, 709–710
al-Taftāzānī, Saʿd al-Dīn (Masʿūd b. ʿUmar b. ʿAbd Allāh, d. 793/1390) 544
al-Taġlibī / al-Ṯaʿlabī, Muḥammad b. al-Ḥāriṯ 224
Ṭāhir b. al-Ḥusayn (b. Muṣʿab b. Ruzayq, d. 207/822), governor of Khorasan 156, 396
al-Takrītī, Nāǧī 390, 440
Ṭalḥa b. Ṭāhir (b. al-Ḥusayn, d. 213/828–829), governor of Khorasan 396
Tamer, Georges 7, 619
Tardieu, Michel 53–54, 59, 113, 156, 541, 595, 708

al-Tawḥīdī, Abū Ḥayyān (ʿAlī b. Muḥammad b. ʿAbbās, d. 414/1023) 17, 159, 221, 228, 231, 233, 242–243, 249, 256, 258, 262, 265–266, 268, 276–292, 294–302, 304, 309, 311, 329, 340, 428, 430, 433, 440–441, 442, 459, 470, 472, 476, 478–479, 488, 492, 542, 739, 752, 753, 755, 758
Ṭayfurī 103, 684
Taylor, Richard 11, 158
Tertullian (2nd/3rd cent.) 464
Thales of Milet (1st half of 6th cent. BC) 134, 665
Theano (around 600 BC) 77
Themistius (d. ca. 385) 35–36, 64, 77, 134, 293, 313, 317, 334, 336, 400, 427, 429–430, 440, 484, 489, 563, 574, 670, 689–690, 720
Theodore (Taḏārā) Abū Qurra (d. ca. 204/820) 425, 504
Theodore bar Konai (end of 8th cent.) 83–84, 87, 671
Theodoret of Cyrus (393–466) 671
Theodosius (2nd/1st cent. BC) 43
Theon (?) 135
Theon of Alexandria (ca. 335–ca. 405) 50, 175, 201
Theon of Smyrna (2nd cent.) 135, 176
Theophilus of Edessa (d. 785) 87–88, 425
Theophrastus of Eresus (372/69–288/5 BC) 77, 135, 186, 400, 441, 670
Thessalus of Tralles (around 60) 318
Thomann, Johannes XII, 566–567
Thoth 670
Thrasymachus (of Chalcedon), Sophistic rhetorician 584
Timaeus 572, 665
Timosthenes (of Rhodes, 3rd cent. BC) 81
Timothy I (d. 823), patriarch of the East Syrian church 80, 117, 425
Travaglia, Pinella 187, 200
al-Ṭurṭūšī (d. 520/1126, or 525/1131) 674–675
al-Ṭūsī, Naṣīr al-Dīn (Muḥammad b. Muḥammad, d. 672/1274) 3, 51, 177, 544, 628

Ueberweg, Friedrich (1826–1871) IX, 1–3
Ullmann, Manfred 105, 189, 504, 669, 691, 695, 698–699, 709, 718
al-ʿUmarī, Ibn Faḍl Allāh ☞ Ibn Faḍl Allāh al-ʿUmarī
al-ʿUtbī (Abū l-Ḥusayn ʿUbayd Allāh b. Aḥmad), vizier to the Samanids 257
al-ʿUtbī, Abū Naṣr 347

Vagelpohl, Uwe 106
Vallat, Philippe 391, 407, 539–541, 590, 595, 613, 631

al-Wāhibī (Abū Muḥammad ʿAbd Allāh b. Muḥammad) 258, 430
Walker, Paul E. 741
Walzer, Richard 125, 338, 536, 541–542, 563, 578, 588, 592, 616, 628, 630–631, 721
al-Warrāq, Abū ʿĪsā ☞ Abū ʿĪsā al-Warrāq
al-Wāṯiq (Abū Ǧaʿfar Hārūn b. al-Muʿtaṣim, regn. 227–232/842–847), Abbasid caliph 154
al-Wazīrī (Abū Muḥammad al-Ḥasan b. Muḥammad), pupil of Abū Zayd al-Balḫī 232
Weisser, Ursula 188
Wernst, Paul 7, 14
Wiedemann, Eilhard 187, 189, 707
Wisnovsky, Robert 9

Xenocrates of Chalcedon (396/5–314/3 BC) 558
Xenophon of Athens (ca. 430–ca. 354 BC) 484

Yaḥyā b. Abī Manṣūr al-Munaǧǧim 686
Yaḥyā Ibn ʿAdī ☞ Ibn ʿAdī, Yaḥyā
Yaḥyā Ibn al-Biṭrīq ☞ Ibn al-Biṭrīq, Yaḥyā
Yaḥyā b. Ḫālid (d. 190/805), vizier to the caliph Hārūn al-Rašīd 114–115
Yaḥyā al-Naḥwī ☞ John Philoponus
Yamamoto, Keiji 187, 200
Yano, Michio 187, 200
al-Yaʿqūbī (late 3rd/9th cent.) 598
Yāqūt (b. ʿAbd Allāh al-Ḥamawī al-Rūmī al-Baġdādī, d. 626/1229) 221, 223–225, 227, 232, 234–235, 238, 242, 283, 284, 286, 387–389
Yehuda ben Šelomo al-Ḥarīzī ☞ al-Ḥarīzī (Ḥarizi), Yehuda ben Šelomo

Yehuda ben Yiṣḥaq ben Mošeh Kohen (9th/15th cent.) 555
Yousef, May A. 667
Yūḥannā b. Ḥaylān 429, 538, 539–540
Yūḥannā b. Māsawayh (d. 243/857) 154, 683
Yūḥannā b. Nāzūk, Nestorian patriarch (regn. 1012–1022) 499

al-Zaǧǧāǧī (Abū l-Qāsim ʿAbd al-Raḥmān b. Isḥāq, d. 337/949) 277, 295
al-Zanǧānī, Abū l-Ḥasan ʿAlī b. Hārūn 752
al-Zawzanī (Muḥammad b. ʿAlī, 7th/13th cent.) 221, 706
Zayd b. Rifāʿa 752
Zeno 665, 669–670
Zeno of Elea (the Older) (ca. 495, to at least 445 BC) 593, 570
Zonta, Mauro 84, 543, 586
Zoroaster 670
Zurayk, Constantine K. 160